Text, Cases and Materials on Criminal Law

Third Edition

Text, Cases and Materials on Criminal Law

Stuart Macdonald

Pearson

Harlow, England • London • New York • Boston • San Francisco • Toronto • Sydney • Dubai • Singapore • Hong Kong
Tokyo • Seoul • Taipei • New Delhi • Cape Town • São Paulo • Mexico City • Madrid • Amsterdam • Munich • Paris • Milan

PEARSON EDUCATION LIMITED
KAO Two
KAO Park
Harlow CM17 9SR
United Kingdom
Tel: +44 (0)1279 623623
www.pearson.com/uk

First published 2015 (print and electronic)
Second edition published 2018 (print and electronic)
Third edition published 2026 (print and electronic)

ISBN: 978-1-292-49417-3 (print)
978-1-292-31824-0 (revel)
978-1-292-73796-6 (etext)
978-1-292-47731-2 (ePub)

British Library Cataloguing-in-Publication Data
A catalogue record for the print edition is available from the British Library

Library of Congress Cataloging-in-Publication Data
A catalogue record for the print edition is available from the British Library

10 9 8 7 6 5 4 3 2 1
29 28 27 26 25

Print edition typeset in 9.5/12 pt Charter ITC Std by Integra Software Services Pvt. Ltd.

NOTE THAT ANY PAGE CROSS REFERENCES REFER TO THE PRINT EDITION

Brief contents

Contents

About the author

Stuart Macdonald is Professor of Law at Swansea University. He has taught criminal law for over 20 years and has published widely on criminal justice issues, particularly counterterrorism and terrorist use of the internet.

Publisher's acknowledgements

At Pearson, we have a simple mission: to help people make more of their lives through learning. We combine innovative learning technology with trusted content and educational expertise to provide engaging and effective learning experiences that help people everywhere aim higher and fulfil their true potential. To learn more please visit us at www.pearson.com/uk.

The content in Revel for *Text, Cases and Materials on Criminal Law* has been checked to ensure that it has the right range of material, is pitched at the correct level and is of a standard that can be trusted by lecturers and students on the courses on which it is used.

We would like to thank **Professor Elwen Evans QC, Emily Finch and Stefan Fafinski, and Judge Paul Thomas QC** for participating in interviews with the author for this title.

We would also like to thank David Hemsley for his eagle-eyed proofreading in this Revel.

Table of cases

Note: Cases are listed under the names of the accused whenever the usual method of citation would cause them to appear as 'R v' signifying prosecution by the Crown. Page numbers followed by n represent foot notes.

1

Your criminal law toolkit

Learning Objectives

1.1 Discuss the principle of individual autonomy, the harm principle and the offence principle.

1.2 Discuss the social welfare principle, legal morality, legal paternalism and criminal law as the least restrictive appropriate intervention.

1.3 Discuss the principle of legality, the correspondence principle, the presumption of innocence, the ladder principle and the principle of fair labelling.

1.4 Explain the basic principles of criminal law.

1.5 Evaluate how these principles might apply in a specific situation.

1.6 Apply the law to a specific case scenario.

Introduction

As well as the standard academic texts, my collection of books on criminal law includes: *The World's Stupidest Laws*;[1] *The World's Funniest Laws*;[2] and *The Little Book of Loony Laws*.[3] According to these books,

1. In France, It is illegal to land a flying saucer in the vineyards of France.

2. In Madagascar, it is illegal for a pregnant woman to wear a hat.

3. In Alaska, it is illegal to push a live moose out of a moving aeroplane.

4. In Scotland, it is illegal to be drunk in possession of a cow.

5. In Thailand, you may not leave your house if you are not wearing underwear.

---

[1] Crombie, D. (2000) *The World's Stupidest Laws*. Michael O'Mara Books Ltd: London.
[2] Alexander, J. (2005) *The World's Funniest Laws*. Crombie Jardine Publishing Ltd: Cheam.
[3] Green, C. (2002) *The Little Book of Loony Laws*. Neil Wilson Publishing: Glasgow.

If these offences do indeed exist, they seem to be a strange use of the criminal sanction. That, after all, is why they appear in a book of loony laws! But why do they strike us as strange? Why is it inappropriate to use the criminal law in this way? How should the criminal sanction be used? That is the question that we will ask ourselves in this opening chapter. The chapter examines a range of important criminal law principles. The aim is to build a strong foundation for your study of this subject; these principles are the tools that we will use throughout the text to analyse and evaluate the criminal law. In the first half of the chapter we study the following principles:

- Individual autonomy
- The harm principle
- The offence principle
- Social welfare
- Legal moralism
- Legal paternalism
- Criminal law as the least restrictive appropriate intervention.

These are all concerned with the question: what conduct should the criminal law prohibit? In other words, they are relevant to criminalisation decisions, decisions as to what conduct should be criminal and what shouldn't.

In the second half of the chapter we study:

- The principle of legality
- The correspondence principle
- The presumption of innocence
- The ladder principle
- Fair labelling.

These are all concerned with the features of individual offences. They cover questions of definition, seriousness, proof and labels.

Before we turn to the individual principles, there are two preliminary points to bear in mind.

The first is that the 12 principles do not always pull in the same direction. Often the various principles will conflict. When this happens, a choice has to be made between the competing demands of different principles. One of the key skills that this chapter will help you to develop – and which you will need to use throughout the text – is the ability to recognise situations where the principles conflict, articulate the demands of the competing principles and explain which principles you believe should be given priority. Remember that not all of the principles we study are of equal importance. As we work through them, you should consider which ones you believe to be the most important.

The second point is that a number of the extracts in this chapter are taken from works of legal theory and legal philosophy. Some of these extracts use technical terms which you may not have come across before. You may find it helpful to refer back to these as you work through the chapter:

- **A priori:** To presume something without proof. So, an a priori assumption is one that has not been proved.
- **Censure:** Expression of disapproval or blame.
- **Discourse:** The language and terminology used in a particular field, such as legal discourse or moral discourse.

- **Empirical:** Based on experience or observation (as opposed to abstract reasoning or theorising). So, to test a claim empirically one must collect relevant information and evidence in order to determine whether or not the claim is justified.
- **Extra-legal:** Lying outside the boundaries of the legal system. So, an extra-legal example is one which does not involve laws or legal principles.
- **Majoritarianism:** To defer to the decisions of a majority within a society.
- **Normative:** Based on evaluative standards. A normative claim is based on a person's values or norms. By contrast, a 'positive' claim is a statement of fact that can be tested and verified.
- **Polity:** A society that has an organised system of politics and government.
- **Prima facie:** At first sight, or on the face of it.
- **Proscription:** Banning or outlawing. Proscribed conduct is conduct that has been prohibited.

Some of the extracts also use the letters D and V to refer to the defendant and the victim. You will find this convention in much writing on criminal law, and it will be used throughout this text.

Criminalisation principles (part 1)

1.1 Discuss the principle of individual autonomy, the harm principle and the offence principle.

Individual autonomy

We begin with the principle of individual autonomy. The premise of the principle of individual autonomy is that people have the freedom and the capacity to make their own decisions. The principle states that, since people have the ability to choose, we should respect their right to do so. Indeed, this is a person's most fundamental right: the right to decide how to live their own life. Of course, this cannot be an absolute right. Suppose that I decide that I really want to be a serial killer. By exercising my right to choose, I would be denying my victims the same right. The principle of individual autonomy therefore states that individuals should be given the right to choose how to live their lives as long as this does not involve denying the same right to others.

The principle of individual autonomy provides an answer to the question: why do we have the criminal law? The criminal law exists in order to protect the autonomy of individuals. By criminalising murder the criminal law prevents would-be killers from denying their victims the right to choose how to live their life. The same applies to other criminal offences. For example, the offence of rape protects individuals' right to choose whom to have sexual intercourse with. And the offence of theft protects individuals' right to choose what to do with their property.

Think about these questions and how you would respond to them.

Protection of individual autonomy is not the only potential justification for criminal laws. Can you think of any others? (By the end of the chapter you should be able to list several more!)

The principle of individual autonomy also helps us to answer another question: when should people be held criminally responsible? Since we each have the ability to make choices, the principle states that we should be held responsible for the choices that we make. So if I choose to become a serial killer and murder people, I should be held responsible for my victims' deaths. As well as being held responsible for results that I choose to bring about, the principle also states that I should be held responsible for results that I choose to risk bringing about. So if I choose to play football next to my neighbour's greenhouse, aware that the ball might smash the glass, the principle of individual autonomy states that I should be held responsible when the ball smashes the glass since I chose to take the risk that this would happen.

Conversely, the principle of individual autonomy tells us that individuals should not be held criminally responsible for conduct they did not freely choose. So, for example, a defendant should not be criminally liable for another person's death if they did not freely choose to either cause the death or to risk causing the death. This provides an explanation for why children under the age of ten and defendants who establish a defence of insanity are not found guilty of any crime: they lack sufficient capacity to be held responsible for their conduct.

Now, think about this scenario.

You are at a party. Knowing that you have to drive home later, you only drink fruit juice. Unbeknown to you, someone spikes your drink. You do not taste the alcohol and, when you drive home later in the evening, you have no idea that you are over the legal limit. You are stopped by police conducting random spot checks and subsequently convicted of drink-driving (a crime that does not require any proof of fault). According to the principle of individual autonomy, should you be criminally liable? Can you think of any arguments to support imposing criminal liability in a situation like this one?

The harm principle

Closely related to the principle of individual autonomy is the harm principle. The harm principle is the most common starting point for discussions of the scope of the criminal law. The nineteenth-century theorist John Stuart Mill famously described the harm principle as follows:[4]

> [T]he only purpose for which power can rightfully be exercised over any member of a civilised community against his will is to prevent harm to others. His own good, either physical or moral, is not a sufficient warrant.

As this extract illustrates, Mill's concern was to impose limits on the use of the criminal sanction. He emphasised that conduct should only be criminalised if it causes harm to others. Conduct which is not harmful should not be criminalised, even if the conduct is immoral or harmful to the person performing it. However, it does not follow from Mill's statement that all conduct that does cause harm to others should be criminalised. Take sports such as rugby or boxing as an example. Participants in these sports may well cause harm to their opponents (bruises, cuts, broken bones). Criminalising such sports may be compatible with Mill's version of the harm principle, but it does not follow that they should be criminalised. In other words, the harm principle expounded by Mill imposes a necessary, but not a sufficient, condition for criminalisation.

[4] Mill, J.S. (1874) *On Liberty*. Longmans: London.

One of the most thorough examinations of the harm principle is Joel Feinberg's four-volume work *The Moral Limits of the Criminal Law*. In it, Feinberg discusses how the word 'harm' should be understood in this context. He argues that a person causes harm to another when: (1) he sets back that other person's interests; *and* (2) he wrongs the other person. Having defined harm, Feinberg states the harm principle as follows:[5]

> It is always a good reason in support of penal legislation that it would probably be effective in preventing (eliminating, reducing) harm to persons other than the actor (the one prohibited from acting) and there is probably no other means that is equally effective at no greater cost to other values.

So in contrast to Mill's negative formulation, Feinberg's statement of the harm principle specifies a set of conditions which *do* justify criminalisation. These are:

- The conduct causes harm to another person, in that it sets back that other person's interests.
- The conduct is wrongful.
- There is no other way of preventing the harm that is equally effective and has no greater cost to other values.

If these conditions are satisfied, there is 'good reason' to criminalise the conduct. The next step is to balance the arguments in favour of criminalisation against any competing considerations. Feinberg explains that, when performing this balancing exercise, a range of considerations should be taken into account including: the gravity of the possible harm; the probability of it occurring; and the value and usefulness of the dangerous conduct.

Think about this question and how you would respond to it.

Can you use Feinberg's account of the harm principle to explain why it is not a criminal offence for a boxer to harm his opponent?

The offence principle

As well as the harm principle, Feinberg advocates another possible justification for criminalisation: the offence principle. He describes this as follows:[6]

> It is always a good reason in support of a proposed criminal prohibition that it is probably necessary to prevent serious offense to persons other than the actor and would probably be an effective means to that end if enacted.

So according to Feinberg's offence principle, conduct that is offensive to other people may potentially be criminalised even if it does not cause them any harm. Notice, however, that Feinberg insists that the offence must be 'serious'. He later expands on this:[7]

> Provided that very real and intense offense is taken predictably by virtually everyone, and the offending conduct has hardly any countervailing personal or social value of its own, prohibition seems reasonable even when the protected sensibilities are not.

[5] Feinberg, J. (1984) *The Moral Limits of the Criminal Law, Volume One: Harm to Others*. OUP: New York, p.26.
[6] Feinberg, J. (1984) *The Moral Limits of the Criminal Law, Volume One: Harm to Others*. OUP: New York, p.26.
[7] Feinberg, J. (1985) *The Moral Limits of the Criminal Law, Volume Two: Offence to Others*. OUP: New York, 35.

This is intended to impose a high threshold. So whilst a person who dribbles, scratches, farts and belches on a crowded bus might cause disgust, the level of offence would not be sufficiently 'real and intense' to satisfy the offence principle. By contrast, if a passenger on a crowded bus performs a sexual act on a dog this may very well satisfy Feinberg's test of offensiveness.

Although Feinberg's offence principle requires a high level of offence, it has been argued that it still casts the net of criminal liability too wide. In the following extract Simester and von Hirsch argue that, whilst the offence principle does provide a valid justification for criminalisation, some further constraints on the principle are necessary.

EXTRACT

In the following extract, Simester and von Hirsch argue that Feinberg's offence principle has too broad a scope. What reasons do they give for this?

According to Simester and von Hirsch, why does Feinberg's version of the offence principle dilute the requirement that only wrongful conduct should be criminalised? (Note that, in the extract, the Greek letter ϕ (phi) is used to denote an unspecified activity).

Simester, A.P. and von Hirsch, A. (2011) *Crimes, Harms, and Wrongs: On the Principles of Criminalisation*. Hart Publishing: Oxford, pp.95–97

The deficiency in Feinberg's analysis, in our view, lies in his equation of offence with affront to sensibility. If offence is defined in terms of displeasing activities (independent of any reasons why they are displeasing), its potential scope is vast. Anything you choose to do might irritate or exasperate me. A great deal depends, therefore, on how much weight is given to the various mediating principles Feinberg proposes.

As Feinberg acknowledges, this is not how offensiveness is understood in ordinary moral discourse. The mere fact that V dislikes what D is doing does not by itself make D's conduct offensive.

Ordinarily, when someone objects to behaviour as offensive, she can be expected to give reasons for objecting that are ulterior to the fact that she dislikes it.

By way of illustration, consider the following extra-legal example. Suppose that D meets V one day when D is wearing a garish Day-Glo orange tie. V objects. Were harmful conduct at issue, V might say, 'That's *my* tie, and you've taken it without permission'. But if the issue is offence, the mere fact that V's sensibilities are affronted does not imply any similar transgression. It is insufficient for V to say, 'Day-Glo ties get on my nerves', for the tie-wearer has no general obligation to spare the viewer's aesthetic sensibilities. The objector would normally be expected to supply a further normative reason why the conduct should be considered objectionable.

It is true, as Feinberg points out, that the objector may not be able to say why he finds luminescent orange ties irritating, or other conduct disgusting. What irritates or disgusts has its roots in social conventions, and V may dislike D's tie because he has accepted certain traditional notions of proper dress. But breach of such a convention does not necessarily show that there is anything wrong with the behaviour – and charging someone with being offensive involves charging him with a kind of misconduct. Were V to say, 'It's simply not done to wear Day-Glo orange', that would suggest merely that D is being unconventional, not that he has acted in an improper manner.

What is needed, therefore, is the provision of reasons why D's conduct is offensive: reasons going beyond the fact that it affronts V's sensibilities. Those reasons may be various. The objector may cite a personal relationship with the actor that demands special regard for the former's sensibilities in the circumstances ('It's my birthday party, and you know how I hate Day-Glo orange'). Or the reason may concern the insulting character of the conduct ('But this is the Hibernian Society Ball on St Patrick's Day!'). Or there might be reasons of enforced togetherness warranting special attention to others' sensibilities ('We're stuck together in this confounded submarine for the next three months, and many of us detest Day-Glo orange'). But if the actor is a stranger to the objector, and no such special reasons can be cited, the mere fact that the conduct causes displeasure or exasperation is insufficient.

While one must be careful when drawing parallels between extra-legal examples and criminal policy, similar reasoning holds when one is considering the legal proscription of purportedly offensive conduct. It is not affronting the sensibilities of other persons (even many of them) that should justify possible state intervention, but affront plus valid normative reasons for objecting to the conduct. Where state intervention is involved, the range of eligible reasons could well differ from those in everyday life: for example, our birthday-party example of a special personal relationship would not provide reasons for state action. But reasons there still should be.

Feinberg explicitly disavows the need to supply such reasons. Admittedly, he does restrict the scope of the Offence Principle to states of affront 'caused by the wrongful (rights-violating) conduct of others'. But he then sidelines this requirement with the assertion that 'there will always be a wrong whenever an offended state [i.e. a disliked mental state] is produced in another without justification and excuse'. This reasoning supposes a general, prima facie duty not to generate offended mental states in others: consequently, the separate requirement for a wrong disappears. Since people are taken to have a right not to be affronted, Feinberg slides effortlessly from affront to wrong, subsuming the latter criterion within the former. Thus it is no surprise to find that the wrongfulness requirement is disregarded in the rest of the book. Absent further considerations, 'we don't like it' suffices. If enough people find Day-Glo ties upsetting, there would be a case for prohibition.

By withdrawing the normative element from V's objection, the justification of prohibition rests, ultimately, merely on conventional sensibilities. As Feinberg intends, this avoids rendering the Offence Principle into one version of legal moralism – but only at the risk of permitting a type of aesthetic majoritarianism. Perhaps it is true that whenever D's φing causes displeasure to V, or affront to V's sensibilities, there is in every case a prima facie *reason* (as opposed to duty) for D not to φ. But, even if this be conceded, assuming D is a private citizen, her reasons not to φ are not quite the point. What matters is *whether the state has a prima facie reason to prohibit D from φing*. On the latter question, our objection, in short, is that Feinberg's portals to the Offence Principle are too wide. Affront to sensibility, by itself, should never suffice to invoke the Offence Principle and therefore qualify for the sort of weighing exercise that both Harm and Offence Principles must then conduct.

Simester and von Hirsch accordingly argue that the offence principle should require both: (1) an affront to people's sensibilities; and (2) an element of wrongdoing. They go on to list three examples of behaviour that would satisfy these criteria:

- **Insulting conduct that is grossly derogatory:** Such conduct is not only offensive. It is also wrongful because it undermines the victim's human dignity.
- **Exhibitionism (e.g. a couple having sexual intercourse on a crowded bus):** This is wrongful because privacy does not only require the exclusion of others from one's personal domain. It also involves not having the private matters of others being involuntarily forced upon you.
- **Infringements of anonymity in public spaces:** This is wrongful because individuals have the right to be left alone. So if a stranger follows you and repeatedly asks you to give him some money, this infringes your right to anonymity in public spaces.

Think about these questions and how you would respond to them.

- Do you agree that these three examples satisfy the two criteria set out by Simester and von Hirsch?
- Can you think of any other examples?

Quiz 1.1

1. What is the link between individual autonomy and the criminal law?
   a. There is no link between individual autonomy and the criminal law.
   b. Individual autonomy is the legal expression of moral culpability and blameworthiness.
   c. The criminal law exists to preserve the freedom to act as individual moral agents and to call people to account for their choices.
   d. The criminal law exists to restrict the individual autonomy of all people.
2. According to the harm principle, how should the criminal law be used?
   a. To prevent harm to all, including the individual against whom it is directed.
   b. To promote good rule and government.
   c. To uphold the moral standards of the community.
   d. To prevent harm to others.
3. How does Feinberg refine the harm principle?
   a. He clearly identifies how a person harms another.
   b. He clearly identifies positive conditions which justify the use of the criminal law.
   c. He fuses the concepts of harm, offence, legal paternalism and legal moralism into a fully coherent theory.
   d. He clearly identifies how a person harms another and deduces positive conditions which justify the use of the criminal law.
4. According to Feinberg, when can the use of the criminal law be justified by the offence principle?
   a. When just thinking about the behaviour in question makes a person feel offended.
   b. When there is justification and excuse for producing an offended state in another.
   c. When an offended state is produced in another without justification and excuse.
   d. When the harm principle is an insufficient basis for criminalisation.

Criminalisation principles (part 2)

1.2 Discuss the social welfare principle, legal morality, legal paternalism and criminal law as the least restrictive appropriate intervention.

Social welfare

The three principles that we have examined so far each focused on individuals. The principle of individual autonomy emphasised protecting the right of each individual to choose how to live their own life. The harm principle emphasised protecting individuals from harm. And the offence principle emphasised protecting individuals from offence. The principle of social welfare, by contrast, does not focus on individuals. Instead, it focuses on society as a whole. It focuses on collective goals.

There are some criminal offences which are easier to explain in terms of social welfare than in terms of individual autonomy, harm or offence. Take crimes against the environment as an example. In cases involving such things as litter or air or water pollution, it may not be possible to identify specific individuals who can be described as victims. The same applies to other offences such as tax evasion or driving without a licence. These crimes may instead be understood as protecting society's collective interest in protecting the environment, requiring people to pay taxes and ensuring that only licensed drivers use public roads.

A key question for the social welfare principle is: what collective goals should society pursue? This is a question on which people may hold widely differing views, yet the demands of this principle depend on how this question is answered. For example, one person might strongly believe that it is in the best interests of society to uphold a traditional view of marriage, whereas there are many others who would disagree with this. It is important, therefore, that claims about the collective good are grounded in empirical evidence. An activity should not be criminalised on the basis of vague assertions that it harms society. Any attempt to invoke the social welfare principle should explain how the activity in question harms social welfare and produce supporting evidence.

Legal moralism

If most members of a society regard a certain type of behaviour as immoral, is this a sufficient justification to criminalise it? Here we are not concerned with crimes like murder and rape. Whilst these are undoubtedly immoral, the existence of these crimes can be justified by reference to the harm principle. Our concern here is behaviour that does not cause harm to other people but is nonetheless regarded as immoral. Is it legitimate to criminalise such conduct? Take cruelty to animals as an example.[8] Most people would consider it wrong to cause an animal to suffer unnecessarily, notwithstanding the fact that other people are not harmed. Is this a sufficient reason to criminalise it?

The relationship between morality and the criminal law was debated in a famous exchange between Lord Devlin and Professor Hart. The context in which this exchange took place was the recommendation of the Wolfenden Report in 1957 that homosexual acts between consenting adult males in private should be decriminalised.[9] In the following extract Lord Devlin sets out the argument that criminal law may be used to prohibit immoral behaviour.

EXTRACT

In the extract Lord Devlin says that he aims to answer the following three questions:

1. Has society the right to pass judgement on matters of morals? Or are morals always a matter for private judgement?
2. If society has the right to pass judgement on matters of morals, may it use the law to enforce these judgements?
3. If so, should it resort to using the law in all cases or only some? And if only some, how should it distinguish those cases where it should from those where it shouldn't?

How does he answer each of these questions?

Devlin also addresses another issue: how are we to identify society's opinion on moral issues? How does Devlin answer this?

Can you think of any difficulties with, or objections to, Devlin's argument?

---

[8] See, for example, the Animal Welfare Act 2006.

[9] Wolfenden Committee (1957) *Report of the Committee on Homosexual Offences and Prostitution* (Cmnd 247).

Devlin, P. (1965) *The Enforcement of Morals*. OUP: London

The institution of marriage is a good example for my purpose because it bridges the division, if there is one, between politics and morals. Marriage is part of the structure of our society and it is also the basis of a moral code which condemns fornication and adultery. The institution of marriage would be gravely threatened if individual judgements were permitted about the morality of adultery, on these points there must be a public morality. But public morality is not to be confined to those moral principles which support institutions such as marriage. People do not think of monogamy as something which has to be supported because our society has chosen to organize itself upon it; they think of it as something that is good in itself and offering a good way of life and that it is for that reason that our society has adopted it. I return to the statement that I have already made, that society means a community of ideas; without shared ideas on politics, morals, and ethics no society can exist. Each one of us has ideas about what is good and what is evil; they cannot be kept private from the society in which we live. If men and women try to create a society in which there is no fundamental agreement about good and evil they will fail; if, having based it on common agreement, the agreement goes, the society will disintegrate. For society is not something that is kept together physically; it is held by the invisible bonds of common thought. If the bonds were too far relaxed the members would drift apart. A common morality is part of the bondage. The bondage is part of the price of society; and mankind, which needs society, must pay its price.

The answer to the first question determines the way in which the second should be approached and may indeed very nearly dictate the answer to the second question. If society has no right to make judgements on morals, the law must find some special justification for entering the field of morality: if homosexuality and prostitution are not in themselves wrong, then the onus is very clearly on the lawgiver who wants to frame a law against certain aspects of them to justify the exceptional treatment. But if society has the right to make a judgement and has it on the basis that a recognized morality is as necessary to society as, say, a recognized government, then society may use the law to preserve morality in the same way as it uses it to safeguard anything else that is essential to its existence. If therefore the first proposition is securely established with all its implications, society has a prima facie right to legislate against immorality as such.

[...]

[I]t is not possible to set theoretical limits to the power of the State to legislate against immorality. It is not possible to settle in advance exceptions to the general rule or to define inflexibly areas of morality into which the law is in no circumstances to be allowed to enter. Society is entitled by means of its laws to protect itself from dangers, whether from within or without. Here again I think that the political parallel is legitimate. The law of treason is directed against aiding the king's enemies and against sedition from within. The justification for this is that established government is necessary for the existence of society and therefore its safety against violent overthrow must be secured. But an established morality is as necessary as good government to the welfare of society. Societies disintegrate from within more frequently than they are broken up by external pressures. There is disintegration when no common morality is observed and history shows that the loosening of moral bonds is often the first stage of disintegration, so that society is justified in taking the same steps to preserve its moral code as it does to preserve its government and other essential institutions. The suppression of vice is as much the law's business as the suppression of subversive activities; it is no more possible to define a sphere of private morality than it is to define one of private subversive activity. It is wrong to talk of private morality or of the law not being concerned with immorality as such or to try to set rigid bounds to the part which the law may play in the suppression of vice. There are no theoretical limits to the power of the State to legislate against treason and sedition, and likewise I think there can be no theoretical limits to legislation against immorality. You may argue that if a man's sins affect only himself it cannot be the concern of society. If he chooses to get drunk every night in the privacy of his own home, is any one except himself the worse for it? But suppose a quarter or a half of the population got drunk every night, what sort of society would it be? You cannot set a theoretical limit to the number of people who can get drunk before society is entitled to legislate against drunkenness. The same may be said of gambling.

In what circumstances the State should exercise its power is the third of the interrogatories I have framed. But before I get to it I must raise a point which might have been brought up in any one of the three. How are the moral judgements of society to be ascertained? By leaving it until now, I can ask it in the more limited form that is now sufficient for my purpose. How is the law-maker to ascertain the moral judgements of society? It is surely not enough that they should be reached by the opinion of the majority; it would be too much to require the individual assent of every citizen. English law has evolved and regularly uses a standard which does not depend on the counting of heads. It is that of the reasonable man. He is not to be confused with the rational man. He is not expected to reason about anything and his judgement may be largely a matter of feeling. It is the viewpoint of the man in the street – or to use an archaism familiar to all lawyers – the man in the Clapham omnibus. He might also be called the right-minded man. For my purpose I should like to call him the man in the jury box, for the moral judgement of society must be something about which any twelve men or women drawn at random might after discussion be expected to be unanimous.

[…]

There must be toleration of the maximum individual freedom that is consistent with the integrity of society. It is not confined to thought and speech; it extends to action, as is shown by the recognition of the right to conscientious objection in war-time; this example shows also that conscience will be respected even in times of national danger. The principle appears to me to be peculiarly appropriate to all questions of morals. Nothing should be punished by the law that does not lie beyond the limits of tolerance. It is not nearly enough to say that a majority dislike a practice; there must be a real feeling of reprobation […] Not everything is to be tolerated. No society can do without intolerance, indignation, and disgust; they are the forces behind the moral law, and indeed it can be argued that if they or something like them are not present, the feelings of society cannot be weighty enough to deprive the individual of freedom of choice. I suppose that there is hardly anyone nowadays who would not be disgusted by the thought of deliberate cruelty to animals. No one proposes to relegate that or any other form of sadism to the realm of private morality or to allow it to be practised in public or in private. It would be possible no doubt to point out that until a comparatively short while ago nobody thought very much of cruelty to animals and also that pity and kindliness and the unwillingness to inflict pain are virtues more generally esteemed now than they have ever been in the past. But matters of this sort are not determined by rational argument. Every moral judgement, unless it claims a divine source, is simply a feeling that no right-minded man could behave in any other way without admitting that he was doing wrong. It is the power of a common sense and not the power of reason that is behind the judgements of society. But before a society can put a practice beyond the limits of tolerance there must be a deliberate judgement that the practice is injurious to society.

In the following extract Professor Hart responds to the arguments set out by Lord Devlin:

EXTRACT

What are Hart's criticisms of Devlin's argument? How do Hart's criticisms compare to your own?

Hart, H.L.A. (1963) *Law, Liberty and Morality*. OUP: London

[T]hough [Lord Devlin] says that society has the right to enforce a morality as such on the ground that a shared morality is essential to society's existence, it is not at all clear that for him the statement that immorality jeopardizes or weakens society is a statement of empirical fact. It seems sometimes to be an a priori assumption, and sometimes a necessary truth and a very odd one. The most important indication that this is so is that, apart from one vague reference to "history" showing that "the loosening of moral bonds is often the first state of disintegration", no evidence is produced to show that deviation from accepted sexual morality, even by adults in private, is something which, like treason, threatens the existence of society. No reputable historian has maintained this thesis, and there is indeed much evidence against it. As a proposition of fact it is entitled to no more respect than the Emperor Justinian's statement that homosexuality was the cause of earthquakes. Lord Devlin's belief in it, and his apparent indifference to the question of evidence, are at points traceable to an undiscussed assumption. This is that all morality - sexual morality together with the morality that forbids acts injurious to others such as killing, stealing, and dishonesty - forms a single seamless web, so that those who deviate from any part are likely or perhaps bound to deviate from the whole. It is of course clear (and one of the oldest insights of political theory) that society could not exist without a morality which mirrored and supplemented the law's proscription of conduct injurious to others. But there is again no evidence to support, and much to refute, the theory that those who deviate from conventional sexual morality are in other ways hostile to society.

There seems, however, to be central to Lord Devlin's thought something more interesting, though no more convincing, than the conception of social morality as a seamless web. For he appears to move from the acceptable proposition that some shared morality is essential to the existence of any society to the unacceptable proposition that a society is identical with its morality as that is at any given moment of its history, so that a change in its morality is tantamount to the destruction of a society. The former proposition might be even accepted as a necessary rather than an empirical truth depending on a quite plausible definition of society as a body of men who hold certain moral views in common. But the latter proposition is absurd. Taken strictly, it would prevent us saying that the morality of a given society had changed, and would compel us instead to say that one society had disappeared and another one taken its place. But it is only on this absurd criterion of what it is for the same society to continue to exist that it could be asserted without evidence that any deviation from a society's shared morality threatens its existence.

It is clear that only this tacit identification of a society with its shared morality supports Lord Devlin's denial that there could be such a thing as private immorality and his comparison of sexual immorality, even when it takes place "in private", with treason. No doubt it is true that if deviations from conventional sexual morality are tolerated by the law and come to be known, the conventional morality might change in a permissive direction, though this does not seem to be the case with homosexuality in those European countries where it is not punishable by law. But even if the conventional morality did so change, the society in question would not have been destroyed or "subverted". We should compare such a development not to the violent overthrow of government but to a peaceful constitutional change in its form, consistent not only with the preservation of a society but with its advance.

Whilst Devlin's account has been subjected to much criticism, in recent years there have been a number of other attempts to construct legal moralist accounts of the criminal law. These accounts emphasise that the criminal law speaks with a moral voice. A criminal conviction expresses disapproval and condemnation. It is hard to see why a person deserves moral condemnation unless his conduct was wrongful. A prominent example is Antony Duff. In the following extract Duff outlines his argument for a version of legal moralism that is 'positive' and 'modest'.

EXTRACT

Duff draws a distinction between positive and negative versions of legal moralism. What is the difference between these?

He also draws a distinction between ambitious and modest versions of legal moralism. What is the difference between these? Was Devlin's version of legal moralism modest or ambitious?

According to Duff, what kinds of wrongdoing may and may not be criminalised? Applying Duff's approach, may: (1) animal cruelty; and (2) homosexuality be criminalised?

Duff, R.A. (2014) 'Towards a Modest Legal Moralism' 8 *Criminal Law and Philosophy* 217

Negative Legal Moralism is, I believe, right, but it is also inadequately ambitious; it tells us when we may not criminalize a type of conduct (when that type of conduct is not wrong), but not when we should criminalize; it specifies a conclusive reason against criminalization, but does not tell us what could count as a good reason for criminalization. Although it is quite natural for theorists, faced by the apparently irresistible tendency of governments (at least in Britain and the United States) to reach for criminal law as a first rather than as a last resort, to look for negative principles that might constrain the tide of criminalization, we must also ask about the positive principles that should guide decisions about the scope of the criminal law; and positive Legal Moralism offers just such a principle.

However, a second distinction must now be drawn, between ambitious and modest versions of positive Legal Moralism. Moore's is an ambitious version, since he holds that every kind of moral wrongdoing is in principle worthy of criminalization, although other considerations, both principled and pragmatic, militate against criminalizing many kinds of wrongdoing, so that in the end the criminal law's scope might not be very different from that favoured by liberals who reject positive Legal Moralism. A modest Legal Moralism, by contrast, holds that only certain kinds of moral wrongdoing are even in principle worthy of criminalization; for many kinds of wrongdoing, the conduct's wrongness gives us no reason at all to criminalize it. A central task for a modest Legal Moralist is of course then to explain which kinds of wrongs are in principle criminalizable, and why.

The Legal Moralism that I favour is a modest one: the criminal law is, I believe, properly concerned not (even in principle) with every kind of moral wrongdoing, but only with wrongs that should count as 'public' rather than 'private' – which at once raises the question of how we are to distinguish public from private wrongs (see Marshall and Duff 1998, 2010). But it is a positive Legal Moralism, since I believe that the distinctive function of criminal law, the function that marks it off from other modes of legal regulation, is its focus on wrongdoing. It aims, in its substantive mode, to define the range of public wrongs that the polity is to mark and condemn as wrongs; and, in its procedural mode, to provide for those accused of committing such wrongs to be called to public account for them through the criminal trial. In a liberal republic of the kind in which we should aspire to live, the distinctive role of the criminal law is to define those wrongs for which we will be publicly called to answer by our fellow citizens, and to provide the formal, institutional mechanisms through which we can thus be called (see Duff 2007).

Legal paternalism

According to legal paternalism, the state is justified in placing restrictions on individuals' freedom of choice if doing so is in their best interests. A simple example is the criminal law duty to wear a seat belt. The law restricts individuals' choice whether to wear a seat belt in order to protect them from the risk of harm. But whilst being required to wear a seat belt is not particularly objectionable, legal paternalism has the potential to be very intrusive indeed. In the following extract Paul Roberts sets out three reasons why legal paternalism is not as attractive as it might at first appear.

EXTRACT

Roberts, P. (1995) 'Appendix C' in Law Commission *Consent in the Criminal Law* (Law Commission Consultation Paper No 139)

C.63 First, the paternalist argues from a philosophical slippery slope and is at constant risk of taking a tumble. The fact is that many of us make life-style choices which do not promote our immediate or long-term interests. Smoking certainly falls into this category of choices: for the paternalist it should be a clear target for criminalisation. But the point goes much further. If (as seems plausible) a balanced, healthy, diet and regular exercise would be in every person's interests the paternalist has a reason for criminalising fatty foods and sedentary life-styles. Risk-taking without good reason would also be ruled out. Sky-diving, mountaineering and most contact sports would have to be criminalised. In principle, the paternalist seems to be committed to using the criminal law to turn us all into super-fit, clean-living 'spartans', whether we like it or not. Paternalism seems less attractive when its implications are made apparent.

C.64 Secondly, some criminal prohibitions which have intuitive appeal and which are often justified by paternalist arguments are in fact best explained in terms of the harm principle and are therefore perfectly consistent with liberalism. Professor Glanville Williams gave an example of one such prohibition when he explained the rationale behind the criminalisation of duelling. At first sight this appears to be a paternalistic measure: (presumably) men who wanted to defend their honour in the traditional way were prevented from doing so for their own good. We are told, however, that many people were in fact hounded into duels against their will because prevailing social expectations effectively robbed them of any say in the matter. Once a man was slighted he was bound to offer a duel and his tormentor was bound to accept the challenge, even if neither wanted to fight. The duelling statute was therefore an exemplar of the harm principle. Far from interfering with people's choices in order to promote their welfare, by 'setting men free from the tyranny of custom' the statute gave effect to their authentic desires not to be injured at the hands of another. The liberal can and does support this type of statute without appealing to paternalistic arguments.

C.65 And thirdly, the liberal need not be as austere or uncompassionate as the paternalist paints her, because situations in which people might foolishly impair their own welfare do not present a straight choice between criminalisation and inaction. Modern-day liberals follow Mill in pointing out that the state can do a great deal to assist people to make the right choice without resorting to the coercion of criminal sanctions. The liberal state can educate, inform, remonstrate, persuade and exhort, and provided that it stops short of outright coercion it retains its liberal credentials. If, however, a man should freely and voluntarily consent to placing himself in permanent servitude, the consistent liberal will let him have his head. Although the paternalist's solution is apparently attractive in these extreme circumstances, it is purchased only with the sacrifice of autonomy, and that is too high a price for the liberal to pay.

To illustrate Roberts' final point – that liberals can assist people to make the 'right choice' without resorting to the criminal sanction – consider Thaler and Sunstein's nudge principle, which they describe as a combination of liberalism and paternalism:[10]

> Libertarian paternalism is a relatively weak, soft, and nonintrusive type of paternalism because choices are not blocked, fenced off, or significantly burdened. If people want to smoke cigarettes, to eat a lot of candy, to choose an unsuitable health care plan, or to fail to save for retirement, libertarian paternalists will not force them to do otherwise – or even make things hard for them. Still, the approach we recommend does count as paternalistic, because private and public choice architects are not merely trying to track or to implement people's anticipated choices. Rather, they are self-consciously attempting to move people in directions that will make their lives better. They nudge.

So if the state wishes to discourage people from eating unhealthily, it does not have to resort to criminalising fatty foods. It can 'nudge' people in this direction (by, for example, ensuring that unhealthy snacks are not placed at checkouts) whilst still maintaining their freedom to choose. This leads us neatly on to the next principle.

[10] Thaler, R.H. and Sunstein, C.R. (2009) *Nudge: Improving Decisions about Health, Wealth and Happiness*. Penguin Books: London, p.6.

Criminal law as the least restrictive appropriate intervention

You will often hear people say that the criminal law should only be employed as a last resort. The suggestion is that, if there are other methods for tackling a particular form of misconduct (such as civil law interventions or administrative regulation), these other methods should be used instead. Only where there is no other alternative form of intervention should we resort to using the criminal law. It is easy to understand why such a principle is attractive. Concern has repeatedly been expressed about the rate at which new criminal offences are created. One study found that, in the twelve months from May 2010 to May 2011, a total of 1760 new crimes were created![11] Encouraging the use of the criminal sanction as a last resort could lead to greater restraint.

However, there are difficulties with the last resort principle. First of all, in terms of punishment and moral condemnation, the criminal law is unique. As Douglas Husak explains in the following extract, some further elaboration is needed in order to explain the significance of the uniqueness of the criminal sanction.

EXTRACT

Husak, D. (2004) 'The Criminal Law as Last Resort' 24 *Oxford Journal of Legal Studies* 207

A superficial interpretation of the last resort principle is as follows: legislation has an objective. If non-criminal alternatives are preferable to the criminal law in attaining this objective, the former should be employed. I describe this interpretation as superficial because, as so construed, the principle says nothing distinctive about the criminal law, and seems equally applicable to *any* purposeful endeavour. In this respect, the principle is comparable to claims like 'the criminal law should not be used if it is not effective [in controlling conduct], or 'punishment ought not to be inflicted [where it] would produce more evil than the offence would'. Presumably, similar kinds of principles apply with equal force to all goal-directed activities; it is hard to see why any means should be employed that is known to be inferior to an alternative, ineffective, or counterproductive. These principles appear to be little more than requirements of practical reasoning. If a carpenter wants to turn a screw, why would he knowingly employ a means that will not succeed, would do more harm than good, or is worse than an alternative he rejects? I assume that the last resort principle is not simply a requirement of practical reasoning. A sensible interpretation of this principle must explain why it has a special (although not necessarily unique) application to the *criminal* law. This difficulty can be overcome by construing the last resort principle as a tie-breaker. The principle states that a criminal law should not be enacted unless other means are less effective in attaining the legislative objective.

[11] Chalmers, J. and Leverick, F. (2013) 'Tracking the Creation of Criminal Offences' *Criminal Law Review* 543. The Law Commission has also commented that: 'more than 2 and a half times as many pages were needed in Halsbury's Statutes to cover offences created in the 19 years between 1989 and 2008 than were needed to cover the offences created in the 637 years prior to that' (Law Commission (2010) *Consultation Paper on Criminal Law in Regulatory Contexts* (Consultation Paper No 195) para 1.17).

So it is not merely that the criminal sanction should not be used if there are other forms of intervention that are more effective; the criminal sanction should also not be used if there are other forms of intervention that are equally effective.

However, as Husak goes on to discuss, this merely raises questions about what effectiveness means in this context. Suppose that lawmakers are considering making it a crime to do X. One possible measure of effectiveness is whether the number of incidents of X will decrease after it becomes a criminal offence. But the criminal law does not exist solely to prevent crimes. It also has an expressive function. It communicates our disapproval and condemnation of certain forms of conduct. So if X is regarded as a really serious wrong, we might still want to criminalise it even if the new offence will not result in any drop in the number of times X occurs. Husak explains this point in the following extract.

EXTRACT

Husak, D. (2004) 'The Criminal Law as Last Resort' 24 *Oxford Journal of Legal Studies* 207

Expressive theories are incompatible with the preventive interpretation of the last resort principle. The [preventive] version of the principle states that non-criminal alternatives should be employed when they are as good or better at preventing given kinds of conduct. Once we understand that the criminal law has both preventive and expressive functions, we need to provide a new interpretation of the last resort principle. Even though alternative modes of social control may do a better job reducing the incidence of criminality, they may fail to achieve an indispensable objective of the criminal sanction: expressing censure. To decide whether alternatives to the criminal law are equally effective, we would have to evaluate not only their ability to reduce crime, but also their efficacy as expressions.

The following example may be helpful in recognizing this point. Suppose that criminal sanctions for domestic violence were ineffective in reducing the incidence of batteries that take place behind closed doors. Imagine that empirical research demonstrated that a criminal law against domestic violence led significant numbers of battered wives to be less inclined to notify the police because they did not want their husbands to be arrested and prosecuted. Suppose the state could adopt non-criminal means to prevent domestic violence that were just as successful as an approach that invoked the criminal sanction. This empirical finding, although important for many purposes, would not provide a decisive objection to criminalizing acts of domestic violence. The point of this law is not only to reduce the incidence of the proscribed conduct, but also to censure those who engage in it. If we used these empirical studies to conclude that laws against domestic violence should not have been enacted, we would frustrate an objective of the legislature by failing to retain our conventional methods of condemning persons who are guilty of spousal abuse.

In the following extract Andrew Ashworth and Lucia Zedner seek to restate the last resort principle in a way that respects both the preventive and expressive functions of the criminal law.

EXTRACT

Read the following extract from Ashworth and Zedner's article and then think back to the domestic violence example offered by Husak in the previous extract.

Would Ashworth and Zedner's approach support criminalisation?

Ashworth, A. and Zedner, L. (2012) 'Prevention and Criminalization: Justifications and Limits' 15 *New Criminal Law Review* 542

Like Bentham, Mill's view was that the criminal law should be used as a last resort, when it is clear that other methods of regulating behaviour will not succeed. However, this principle is concerned with the effectiveness of less censuring methods of regulation – an important element, but one that cannot be adopted without reference to the ser ousness of the wrong itself. Some wrongs are so egregious that they ought to be subject to the censure of the criminal law and state punishment. Other, lesser wrongs may properly, and without undermining significant social values, be dealt with in some kind of lesser system of administrative offenses or civil wrongs. Assigning offenses to one category or the other will not be straightforward, but the exercise is no more difficult than many other contested issues in criminal justice. The important point is that the principle must take account not merely of the effectiveness of different modes of regulation but also of the seriousness of the wrong involved, and that it should avoid treating different y wrongs that have the same level of seriousness. As the principle of the least restrictive appropriate intervention, it has much to commend it. Thus:

[. . .] Criminalization should only be resorted to if it is the least restrictive appropriate response.

Quiz 1.2

1. Which of the following is **not** a valid use of the social welfare basis for criminalisation?

a. The promotion of a free market economy.

b. The protection of public revenues.

c. The protection of the environment.

d. The promotion of road safety.

2. Which of the following is H.L.A. Hart's objection to Lord Devlin's view on the enforcement of morality by the criminal law?

a. Society means a community of ideas; without shared ideas on politics, morals, and ethics no society can exist, so attacks on those shared ideas including the shared morality can be understood as attacks on that society.

b. The criminal law can be used to enforce a moral principle where its breach is also a nuisance to the public or a part thereof.

c. The criminal law should only be used to enforce morality where its breach lies beyond the limit of tolerance as agreed by a group of people akin to a jury after discussion.

d. There is never a problem with using the criminal law to enforce public morality.

3. Which of the following groups of offences could be justified by the doctrine of legal paternalism?

a. Crimes relating to the failure to wear crash-helmets or car seat belts.

b. Crimes relating to euthanasia, suicide and self-mutilation.

c. Crimes relating to drunkenness and the possession/use of controlled drugs.

d. The other options are all examples of offences based on legal paternalism.

4. According to Ashworth and Zedner, in which of the following circumstances could intervention through the criminalisation of conduct be justified?

a. Where it censures those who engage in the proscribed conduct.

b. Where it reduces the incidence of the proscribed conduct, and also censures those who engage in it.

c. Where it reduces the incidence of the proscribed conduct, and also censures those who engage in it where neither aim can be achieved more effectively by less coercive means.

d. Where it reduces the incidence of the proscribed conduct.

Offence definition, seriousness, proof and labels

1.3 Discuss the principle of legality, the correspondence principle, the presumption of innocence, the ladder principle and the principle of fair labelling.

The principle of legality

The principle of legality is often referred to as the rule of law. In *R* v *Rimmington* [2005] UKHL 63 Lord Bingham described the principle as follows:

> 33 [. . .] There are two guiding principles: no one should be punished under a law unless it is sufficiently clear and certain to enable him to know what conduct is forbidden before he does it; and no one should be punished for any act which was not clearly and ascertainably punishable when the act was done.

We will look at each of these requirements in turn.

No one should be punished under a law unless it is sufficiently clear and certain to enable him to know what conduct is forbidden before he does it

This has been described as the 'principle of maximum certainty': the wording of criminal laws should be as clear and as certain as possible.[12] The reason for this is rooted in the principle of individual autonomy. If individuals are to be held responsible for their choices, criminal offences must be defined clearly enough for individuals to know what conduct is and isn't criminal. It would be unjust to hold a person criminally liable for their conduct if they had not been given fair warning that their conduct constituted a criminal offence.

Consider, for example, the statutory definition of 'anti-social behaviour'. This states that conduct is anti-social if it causes, or is likely to cause, harassment, alarm or distress to another person.[13] This definition has been applied to a very wide range of conduct, including: drunken disorder; threatening behaviour; drug abuse; noise nuisance; graffiti; fly-tipping; fly-posting; littering; abandoned vehicles; mini-moto misuse; dog fouling; prostitution; begging; high hedges; and young people hanging around.[14] Some of the items on this list may surprise you, but in fact the definition is capable of being applied even more broadly! The behaviour of the hypothetical bus passenger that we mentioned earlier – who dribbles, scratches, farts and belches in front of other passengers – is likely to cause other passengers harassment, alarm or distress. Even the person who has a barbeque in his back garden may satisfy the definition, if he happens to have a neighbour who does not like the smell of sausages.[15]

It is unsurprising, then, that critics of the definition of anti-social behaviour have argued that it is insufficiently clear and precise.[16] But in the eyes of supporters of the definition,

---

[12] Horder, J. (2016) *Ashworth's Principles of Criminal Law* (8th edn). OUP: Oxford, pp.85–87.

[13] Anti-Social Behaviour, Crime and Policing Act 2014, s.2(1).

[14] See Macdonald, S. (2006) 'A Suicidal Woman, Roaming Pigs and a Noisy Trampolinist: Refining the ASBO's Definition of "Anti-Social Behaviour"' 69 *Modern Law Review* 183 and the sources cited therein.

[15] This example was discussed during the Parliamentary debates on the Crime and Disorder Act 1998.

[16] In addition to Macdonald (n 3 above) see: Ashworth, A., Gardner, J., Morgan, R., Smith, A.T.H., von Hirsch, A. and Wasik, M. (1995) 'Overtaking on the Right' 145 *New Law Journal* 1501; and Ashworth, A., Gardner, J., Morgan, R., Smith, A.T.H., von Hirsch, A. and Wasik M. (1998) '*Clause* 1 – The Hybrid Law from Hell?' 31 *Criminal Justice Matters* 25.

this vagueness is beneficial since it ensures flexibility. This means that if new types of anti-social behaviour emerge which have not been foreseen, they will still fall within the scope of the legislation. One Government spokesman explained, '[W]idely drawn legislation with clarity of purpose, and with clear expectations placed on those who use it, can be a flexible method'.[17] But drafting deliberately far-reaching and imprecise laws in order to confer wide-ranging discretion on those using them is contrary to the principle of maximum certainty. It may not only fail to give individuals fair warning of what the law requires, it also creates the possibility that the discretion vested in officials will be applied in an inconsistent or discriminatory manner. Yet this legislative technique has also been applied in other contexts. For example, a number of the offences contained in the Terrorism Acts 2000 and 2006 have been criticised for being both overly broad and vague.[18]

So whilst the principle of maximum certainty is important, there are competing practical concerns that are sometimes given precedence by lawmakers. In fact, as we'll see in a moment, even though the principle of maximum certainty has been enshrined in Article 7 of the European Convention on Human Rights, the case law on Article 7 is weaker than one might expect. This leads us neatly to the second strand of the principle of legality.

No one should be punished for any act which was not clearly and ascertainably punishable when the act was done

Think about this scenario and how you would respond to it.

Imagine that tonight John has sexual intercourse with Christine, even though at the time he is married to Valerie. Then imagine that six months later Parliament creates a new law which states: 'It shall be a criminal offence to commit an act of adultery. This new offence shall apply retrospectively, starting from 12 months ago'. John is subsequently arrested and charged with the new crime of adultery.

What objections, if any, would you have to John being convicted of this crime?

In this example, the principal objection to John's conviction is that, at the time he committed adultery, he had no idea that his actions would subsequently be deemed to be a criminal offence. In other words, his conviction infringes the principle of individual autonomy because at no stage did he make a choice to break the criminal law. It is for this reason that the principle of legality insists that no one should be punished for an act which was not clearly punishable at the time it was done. This is known as the principle of non-retroactivity.[19] It is regarded as so important that it is enshrined in Article 7 of the European Convention on Human Rights as an absolute right (i.e. no exceptions are permitted, even in a time of war or other public emergency).

---

[17] Alun Michael (Home Office spokesman) HC Standing Committee B col 70 30 April 1998.

[18] A noteworthy example is the encouragement of terrorism offence (Terrorism Act 2006, s.1), on which see Marchand, S.A. (2010) 'An Ambiguous Response to a Real Threat: Criminalizing the Glorification of Terrorism in Britain' 42 *George Washington International Law Review* 123.

[19] Horder, J. (2016) *Ashworth's Principles of Criminal Law*. 8th edn. OUP: Oxford, pp.82–84.

EXTRACT

Article 7 of the European Convention on Human Rights

No punishment without law

(1) No one shall be held guilty of any criminal offence on account of any act or omission which did not constitute a criminal offence under national or international law at the time when it was committed. Nor shall a heavier penalty be imposed than the one that was applicable at the time the criminal offence was committed.

As indicated above, however, there are competing considerations at play here. What makes our example involving John so powerful is that it was completely unforeseeable that Parliament would make adultery a criminal offence. The weight that you attach to the principle of non-retroactivity might change if the new law was more predictable, or even to be expected. Take the case of *R* v *R* [1992] 1 AC 599 as an example. The issue for the House of Lords in this case was whether the defendant could be guilty of raping his wife. The alleged offence took place in 1989. According to the law as stated in 1736, a husband could not be convicted of raping his wife. This was known as the marital rape exception and was based on the view that a woman gave her consent upon marriage and could not later withdraw it. What made the case difficult was that at no stage between 1736 and 1989 had Parliament changed the law (in fact, the Law Commission urged Parliament to do so in 1990). The House of Lords handed down its judgment in 1991. It abolished the marital rape exception – stating that it was incompatible with the conditions of modern life – and upheld the defendant's conviction.

Think about these questions and how you would respond to them.

- Did the House of Lords' judgment infringe the principle of non-retroactivity?
- If so, was this justifiable?

Following the House of Lords' judgment the defendant in *R* v *R* pursued his case to the European Court of Human Rights. The European Court, in *SW* v *United Kingdom* (1995) 21 EHRR 363, held that the defendant's conviction did not violate Article 7. It explained the requirements of Article 7 as follows:

> 36. However clearly drafted a legal provision may be, in any system of law, including criminal law, there is an inevitable element of judicial interpretation. There will always be a need for elucidation of doubtful points and for adaptation to changing circumstances. Indeed, in the United Kingdom, as in the other Convention States, the progressive development of the criminal law through judicial law-making is a well entrenched and necessary part of legal tradition. Article 7 (art. 7) of the Convention cannot be read as outlawing the gradual clarification of the rules of criminal liability through judicial interpretation from case to case, provided that the resultant development is consistent with the essence of the offence and could reasonably be foreseen.

Applying this to the facts of the case, the Court stated that the abolition of the marital rape exception was 'consistent with the very essence of the offence' and that the evolution of the offence meant that the House of Lords' decision was 'a reasonably foreseeable development of the law'.[20] The Court added that:

> 44. [...] [T]he abandonment of the unacceptable idea of a husband being immune against prosecution for rape of his wife was in conformity not only with a civilised concept of marriage but also, and above all, with the fundamental objectives of the Convention, the very essence of which is respect for human dignity and human freedom.

So whilst the principle of non-retroactivity is important, it is clear from the decision in *SW* v *United Kingdom* that Article 7 leaves room for judges to develop the law, provided that these developments are reasonably foreseeable and consistent with the essence of the offence.

The correspondence principle

The correspondence principle also focuses on how offences are defined. More specifically, it is concerned with the relationship between the different requirements that must be proved in order to establish liability for an offence. Ashworth and Campbell offer the following definition:[21]

> [I]f the offence is defined in terms of certain consequences and certain circumstances, the mental element ought to correspond with that by referring to those consequences or circumstances. If a mental element as to a lesser consequence were acceptable, this would amount to constructive criminal liability.

Figure 1.1 illustrates this. The diagram focuses on offences against people. On the left are different 'consequences', that is different levels of injury that a victim might suffer. On the right are different 'mental elements', that is different states of mind that the prosecution might have to prove for a conviction. According to the correspondence principle, the state of mind that is required for a conviction should align with the specified consequence. So, for example, death is the specified consequence in homicide offences. So, according to the correspondence principle, the required state of mind should also refer to death. A homicide offence would therefore satisfy the correspondence principle if it required either proof of an intention to kill or recklessness as to whether the victim would be killed.

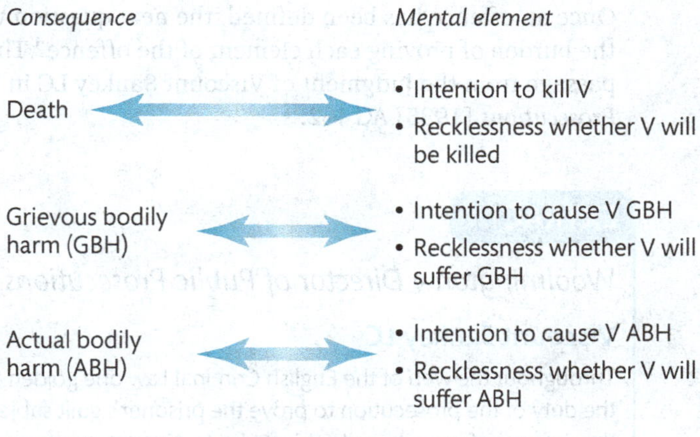

Figure 1.1

[20] Similar reasoning was employed by the Court of Appeal in *R* v *C* [2004] EWCA Crim 292. In this case the defendant was convicted in 2002 of having raped his wife in 1970.

[21] Ashworth, A. and Campbell, K. 'Recklessness in Assault – and in General?' (1991) 107 *Law Quarterly Review* 187.

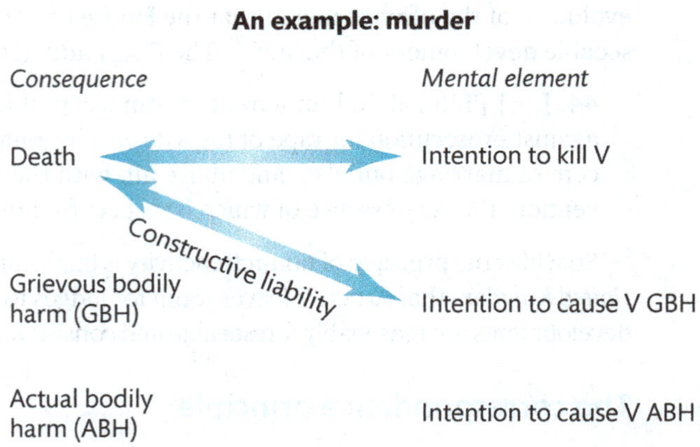

Figure 1.2

In order to understand why the correspondence principle is important, consider an example. In Chapter 5, we will study the offence of murder. We will learn that: (1) only intention will suffice for the offence of murder, recklessness is insufficient; and (2) the defendant need not have intended to kill, it is enough that he had an intention to cause grievous bodily harm. Figure 1.2 incorporates these two points.

So the definition of murder requires that the victim died, but to secure a conviction it is sufficient to show that the defendant had an intention to cause the victim grievous bodily harm. In other words, as long as the defendant intended to cause the victim serious harm he can be convicted of murder – even if the possibility of the victim dying never crossed his mind. This violates the correspondence principle and is an example of what criminal lawyers call 'constructive liability'. Constructive liability is controversial because it is difficult to reconcile with the principle of individual autonomy.[22] If the possibility of the victim dying never crossed the defendant's mind, then it cannot be said that the defendant at least chose to take a risk that the victim would be killed.

The presumption of innocence

The legality and correspondence principles each focus on how offences are defined. Once an offence has been defined, the next question which arises is: who should bear the burden of proving each element of the offence? The starting point here is a famous passage from the judgment of Viscount Sankey LC in *Woolmington* v *Director of Public Prosecutions* [1935] AC 462.

EXTRACT

Woolmington v *Director of Public Prosecutions* [1935] AC 462

Viscount Sankey LC

Throughout the web of the English Criminal Law one golden thread is always to be seen, that it is the duty of the prosecution to prove the prisoner's guilt subject to what I have already said as to the defence of insanity and subject also to any statutory exception. If, at the end of and on the whole of the case, there is a reasonable doubt, created by the evidence given by either the

[22] See: Horder, J. (1995) 'A Critique of the Correspondence Principle in Criminal Law' *Criminal Law Review* 759; and Mitchell, B. (1999) 'In Defence of a Principle of Correspondence' *Criminal Law Review* 195.

prosecution or the prisoner [...] the prosecution has not made out the case and the prisoner is entitled to an acquittal. No matter what the charge or where the trial, the principle that the prosecution must prove the guilt of the prisoner is part of the common law of England and no attempt to whittle it down can be entertained.

Being convicted of a crime has serious repercussions for an individual. Add to this the fact that the state has far greater resources with which to conduct prosecutions than individuals have to defend themselves, and it seems right that no one should be convicted unless the state has proven their guilt beyond reasonable doubt. This is known as the presumption of innocence. Or, to put it differently, it is the principle that the prosecution should bear the burden of proof.

As well as being important to criminal trials, the presumption of innocence also has a wider dimension – as the following extract emphasises.

EXTRACT

Read the following extract from Coleman's book.

What does she say are the procedural aspects of the presumption of innocence?

What are the non-procedural aspects?

Coleman, M. (2021) *The Presumption of Innocence in International Human Rights and Criminal Law.* Routledge: Abingdon, 170

[W]hile the presumption of innocence is relevant during trial there are specific parts which go beyond the limits of trial and the fact-finder's duty. The result is that the presumption of innocence has two aspects: the procedural and non-procedural. Both aspects are operative in the general context of criminal law, particularly once a person is 'charged' with a criminal offence. The procedural aspect is narrow in application as it applies only during trial. It protects accused people at trial and is a mandatory rebuttable legal presumption. As such, it is an instruction to the fact-finder because it tells the fact-finder to find the accused not guilty unless the standard of proof is met at trial. Further, it directs the burden of proof away from the accused, requiring someone else to prove guilt. As a result, the accused does not need to prove innocence nor disprove guilt. Through this aspect, the presumption of innocence works in conjunction with the burden of proof and the standard of proof but is not a restatement of either.

The non-procedural aspect is broad and extends the presumption of innocence beyond trial to all aspects of criminal procedure. This aspect protects legally innocent people from being treated as if they have been convicted of a crime. All public authorities and the media must uphold this aspect of the presumption of innocence by not engaging in pre-punishment and not presenting or otherwise treating people as if they are guilty when they have not been convicted. By requiring a guilty verdict before accused individuals can be treated the same as those who have been convicted, this aspect prevents shortcuts to punishment.

The presumption of innocence is enshrined in Article 6(2) of the European Convention on Human Rights.[23] In *Barberà, Messegué and Jabardo* v *Spain* (1988) 11 EHRR 360 the European Court of Human Rights explained the requirements of Article 6(2).

---

[23] Article 6(2) states: 'Everyone charged with a criminal offence shall be presumed innocent until proved guilty according to law.'

EXTRACT

Barberà, Messegué and Jabardo v Spain (1988) 11 EHRR 360 European Court of Human Rights

77. Paragraph 2 (art. 6-2) embodies the principle of the presumption of innocence. It requires, inter alia, that when carrying out their duties, the members of a court should not start with the preconceived idea that the accused has committed the offence charged; the burden of proof is on the prosecution, and any doubt should benefit the accused. It also follows that it is for the prosecution to inform the accused of the case that will be made against him, so that he may prepare and present his defence accordingly, and to adduce evidence sufficient to convict him.

At the same time, however, the European Court has accepted that states may reverse the burden of proof – as long as these reverse burden provisions are kept 'within reasonable limits' and 'take into account the importance of what is at stake and maintain the rights of the defence'.[24] You may also have noticed that, in spite of his grand-sounding rhetoric, Viscount Sankey LC also envisaged exceptions to the presumption of innocence. One of these was the defence of insanity, which we will study in Chapter 10. The other exception mentioned by Viscount Sankey LC was more open-ended. He accepted that Parliament could create statutory exceptions to the presumption of innocence. A study by Andrew Ashworth and Meredith Blake in 1996 found that this exception was being employed routinely.[25] Ashworth and Blake examined 540 offences triable in the Crown Court (i.e. 540 of the most serious offences) and found that 219 (40 per cent) placed the burden of proof for at least part of the offence on the defendant. Their study concluded by warning that the 'apparent casualness' with which Parliament was creating reverse burden provisions was undermining the presumption of innocence.

Since the introduction of the Human Rights Act 1998, there have been signs that the courts in this country are now taking a stricter approach to the presumption of innocence. To understand this case law, it is important to appreciate the distinction between an evidential and a persuasive burden:

- **An evidential burden:** this requires the party to produce sufficient relevant evidence of a matter to justify the jury being asked to consider it. For example, a defendant who wishes to claim that he acted in self-defence must discharge the evidential burden. He must produce sufficient evidence that he did indeed act in self-defence to justify leaving the defence to the jury.
- **A persuasive burden:** once the evidential burden has been discharged, the next question is who should bear the burden of persuading the jury. In other words, should the prosecution or the defence bear the burden of proof? In our self-defence example, once the defence has discharged the evidential burden the prosecution would bear the burden of proof. The prosecution would be required to convince the jury beyond reasonable doubt that the defendant did not in fact act in self-defence.

[24] *Salabiaku* v *France* (1988) 13 EHRR 379, [28].

[25] Ashworth, A. and Blake, B. (1996) 'The Presumption of Innocence in English Criminal Law' *Criminal Law Review* 306.

In *R* v *Lambert* [2001] UKHL 37 the defendant, Steven Lambert, had been convicted of possessing cocaine with intent to supply. The relevant statute provided that it was for the defendant to prove that he neither knew, nor suspected, nor had any reason to suspect that he was in possession of the cocaine.[26] By a majority of 4–1, the House of Lords held that the statute placed an evidential, not a persuasive, burden on the defendant. Notwithstanding the public interest in combating the illegal drug trade, the majority held that it would be disproportionate and a breach of Article 6(2) to impose a persuasive burden on defendants charged with this offence. Their Lordships then explained that the Human Rights Act imposes an obligation to interpret legislation compatibly with the European Convention whenever possible. Even though the natural interpretation of the statutory wording was that it imposed a persuasive burden, the wording was deemed sufficiently flexible to be interpreted as only requiring an evidential burden.

Since then this approach has been adopted in other cases.[27] When deciding whether a persuasive burden is disproportionate, issues for the court to consider include the seriousness of the misconduct the offence targets and the difficulties both prosecutors and the defence will face proving the matter in question. For example, in a licensing case it may be justifiable to impose a persuasive burden on the defendant, since it may be easier for them to prove that they have a licence than it is for the state to prove that they do not have one.

The ladder principle

The ladder principle is concerned with the relationship between different offences. In *R* v *Coutts* [2006] UKHL 39 Lord Bingham stated:

> 12 In any criminal prosecution for a serious offence there is an important public interest in the outcome (*R* v *Fairbanks* [1986] 1 WLR 1202, 1206). The public interest is that, following a fairly conducted trial, defendants should be convicted of offences which they are proved to have committed and should not be convicted of offences which they are not proved to have committed. The interests of justice are not served if a defendant who has committed a lesser offence is either convicted of a greater offence, exposing him to greater punishment than his crime deserves, or acquitted altogether, enabling him to escape the measure of punishment which his crime deserves. The objective must be that defendants are neither over-convicted nor under-convicted, nor acquitted when they have committed a lesser offence of the type charged.

As Lord Bingham explains, justice not only requires that the guilty are convicted and the innocent are acquitted. It also requires that the guilty are convicted of a crime that reflects the seriousness of their offence. They should not be 'over-convicted' or 'under-convicted'.

Building on this sentiment, the Law Commission has advanced the 'ladder principle'.[28] The ladder principle states that there should be a hierarchy – or ladder – of

[26] Misuse of Drugs Act 1971, s.28(2).

[27] See in particular: *Sheldrake* v *DPP; Attorney-General's Reference* (No 4 of 2002) [2004] UKHL 43.

[28] See: Law Commission (2005) *A New Homicide Act for England and Wales? A Consultation Paper* (Law Commission Consultation Paper No 177); and Law Commission (2006) *Murder, Manslaughter and Infanticide* (Law Commission Report No 304) HC 30.

criminal offences. This ladder should reflect the seriousness of the different offences, with the most serious ones at the top and the least serious at the bottom. In addition, the Law Commission explained that there should be minimal overlap between the different offences, and individual offences should not be so broad that they cover a large variety of conduct of widely differing levels of gravity. In short:[29]

> A ladder of offence seriousness is defensible so long as, by and large, the cases that fall within a particular tier are, other things being equal, more serious than the cases that, by and large, fall within the tier below.

Think about these scenarios and how you would respond to each.

1. When we study the law of homicide in Chapter 5, we will encounter the following three scenarios. In your opinion, should each defendant be: convicted of murder; convicted of manslaughter; or not convicted of any homicide offence?
   a. A woman suffering from an incurable, incapacitating disease repeatedly begs her husband to end her life. One night, after she keeps him awake for most of the night pleading to have her life ended, he gives into her requests. He puts a pillow over her face and asphyxiates her.
   b. A terrorist plants a bomb and then contacts the authorities and warns them. He plants a live bomb instead of a fake one – so that the authorities will fear him and listen to him – but he doesn't want the bomb to explode because he fears that he will lose public support if innocent people are killed. He gives the warning some time before the bomb is set to explode, so that the public can be evacuated and a bomb disposal expert can defuse the bomb. However, the bomb explodes and kills the bomb disposal expert.
   c. During an operation, an inexperienced and exhausted anaesthetist fails to notice that the tube supplying oxygen to the victim has become disconnected. Four-and-a-half minutes later, an alarm sounds on the blood pressure monitor. Still not noticing the disconnected tube, the anaesthetist administers some drugs to raise the patient's pulse. A few minutes later the patient suffers cardiac arrest and dies.
2. In Chapter 5 we will see that, under the current law of homicide, the outcomes of the three scenarios would be as follows:
   a. The husband would be convicted of a more serious offence (murder) than the other two defendants.
   b. The terrorist and the anaesthetist would be convicted of the same offence (manslaughter).

Are these outcomes what you expected? In your opinion, are these outcomes consistent with the ladder principle?

[29] Law Commission (2006) *Murder, Manslaughter and Infanticide* (Law Commission Report No 304) HC 30), para 2.47.

Fair labelling

Our final principle is fair labelling. This principle focuses on the names we give to criminal offences. It insists that the names that we attach to criminal offences should be fair. This immediately raises two questions: what does it mean for an offence label to be fair and why is it important? In their article on this topic, James Chalmers and Fiona Leverick discuss a number of potential justifications for fair labelling:[30]

- Fairness to offenders requires that offence labels represent their wrongdoing accurately (e.g. most would agree that it would be unfair to apply the label 'murder' to every case of unlawful killing).
- Offence labels have an educative function – they make clear to offenders exactly what it is they have done wrong.
- Offence labels have a deterrent effect – they dissuade potential offenders who do not wish to be stigmatised from committing the crime in question.
- Fairness to victims requires that offence labels reflect the nature of the defendant's wrongdoing accurately.
- Excessively broad offence labels confer too much discretion on sentencers.
- Offence labels need to be accurate since they communicate information to criminal justice agencies, for example, sentencing judges have regard to previous convictions.
- Offence labels should also be accurate because they communicate information to agencies operating outside the criminal justice process, for example, potential employers.
- Offence labels should be accurate since they have a symbolic function, communicating the nature of an offender's wrongdoing to society at large.

In addition, Gibson has identified two further justifications for fair labelling.[31]

- Offence labels communicate to citizens that specified conduct is wrong. Criminalising conduct that was not previously criminal can therefore be useful in changing public attitudes, as happened with drink driving. Similarly, creating tailored offences targeting wrongs that already fall under broader, generic offences can raise awareness of specific forms of wrongdoing (e.g., female genital mutilation).
- Offence labels aid criminal justice actors in applying offences at the investigation, prosecution and adjudication stages of the criminal process. For example, the name and elements of an offence may inform how the police investigate an alleged offence and the prosecutor's decision which offence to charge. At trial, they may also influence the deliberations of the jury.

Think about these questions.

- Which of these reasons do you believe are the most important?
- Are there any that you find unconvincing?

[30] Chalmers, J. and Leverick, F. (2008) 'Fair Labelling in Criminal Law' 71 *Modern Law Review* 217.
[31] Gibson, M. (2024) 'Three Justifications of Fair Labelling' 140 *Law Quarterly Review* 431.

EXTRACT

In the following extract Chalmers and Leverick explain which of the reasons they consider to be the most important. How closely does their assessment match your own?

Chalmers and Leverick draw a distinction between labelling in the sense of description and labelling in the sense of differentiation. What is the difference between these? Which form of labelling is most relevant to which groups of people?

Chalmers, J. and Leverick, F. (2008) 'Fair Labelling in Criminal Law' 71 *Modern Law Review* 217

Why, then, does labelling matter? The first thing that can be said is that, of the justifications examined above, some of them – the sentencing discretion argument, the educative argument and the deterrence argument – are unconvincing or tangential. Others, while not entirely unconvincing, are insufficiently developed. Clearly labelling raises issues of fairness to the offender but the precise nature of the unfairness concerned needs to be articulated. The interest in question is the offender's legitimate interest in protecting her reputation and on this basis the argument that insufficiently precise labels are unfair to the offender is one that has some force. At the very least, this is a convincing justification for labels that are not inaccurate or potentially misleading.

Another strong justification for fair labelling is that decision-makers rely on the offence name and the information it conveys in making decisions about the offender. These might be decisions within the criminal justice system – such as sentencing – or decisions made outside the criminal justice system, such as offers of employment. In both instances, the decision-maker uses the offence name to draw conclusions about the nature of the offender's previous criminal behaviour. Information on the length of sentence may or may not be available as an additional source of information (it would be for sentencing decisions, for employment decisions it may not), but while this can tell the decision-maker something about offence seriousness, it is not informative about the nature of the conduct. This does matter, for reasons of fairness both to the offender and for public protection, although the degree of information that is necessary to ensure fairness in this respect is another question.

Finally, it has been suggested that the victim (or her family) has a legitimate interest in fair labelling in that she deserves to have her suffering reflected by an offence of appropriate seriousness. But despite this legitimate interest, given that it would be unfair to the offender if the label over-represented her culpability and unfair to the public if it under-represented it, the victim's perspective appears to add little to those already considered.

Thus it can be said that the most convincing argument for fair labelling is that offence names communicate information about the offender to a number of different bodies – the public, agencies operating both within and outside the criminal justice system – and that members of these groups may form opinions or make decisions about the offender that turn on the information received. It is also clear, however, that what constitutes 'fair' labelling in each of these contexts may differ. Where information is being communicated to agencies and individuals operating outside the criminal justice system, no assumption of legal knowledge can be made. In addition, in the particular context of providing a signal to the public, information is likely to be filtered through media reports, which may distort the accuracy of the message. Fair labelling in this context is labelling that is fair in the descriptive sense – the use of simple, informative offence names that convey the essential nature of the wrongdoing and minimise the potential for misrepresentation or misunderstanding. To quote Ashworth's original formulation, 'the label applied to an offence ought fairly to represent the offender's wrongdoing'. What is important here is not so much the extent to which offences are differentiated but *the name itself*.

By contrast, in the context of decisions made by legal professionals, some reliance can be placed upon their legal knowledge, making the specific terms used to identify offences of less importance. What matters here is not so much the name itself but the differentiation of offences. Thus fair labelling in this context takes on a second meaning – labelling that fairly *differentiates* wrongdoing. For example, it was suggested earlier that the 'label' offered by section 20 of the Offences Against the Person Act 1861 may be unfair, in that it is liable to mislead the public as to the culpability of the defendant. But that is of little concern to a prosecutor who subsequently examines an individual's criminal record, as that prosecutor will be well aware of what is meant by section 20 of the 1861 Act. For her purposes, it is the fact that the individual has been deemed to have recklessly – rather than deliberately – caused grievous bodily harm to another that will be crucial. The wording of the 'label' which is used to communicate that fact is of little, if any, importance. For these purposes, the distinctions involved could just as validly be communicated by way of hieroglyphics, leaving aside the inefficiencies involved in such a system. It is differentiation rather than description which is crucial here.

Quiz 1.3

1. Which two ideas are central to the principle of legality?

a. Non-retroactivity and predictability.

b. Predictability and retroactivity.

c. Maximum certainty and non-retroactivity.

d. Minimum certainty and non-retroactivity.

2. Which of the following statements complies with the correspondence principle?

a. A defendant should only be convicted of a homicide offence if he had an intention to kill or was reckless as to whether the victim would be killed.

b. For offences involving grievous bodily harm, it should be sufficient for the prosecution to show that the defendant realised that there was a risk the victim would suffer some (non-serious) injury.

c. For assault occasioning actual bodily harm, it should not be necessary to show that the defendant realised that the victim might suffer injury.

d. It should sometimes be possible to convict a defendant of a homicide offence even if he did not realise there was a risk that the victim would be killed.

3. The presumption of innocence requires that 'the prosecution must prove the guilt of the prisoner… no attempt to whittle it down can be entertained'. What exceptions were recognised within that presumption?

a. Insanity and non-insane automatism.

b. Duress and statutory defences, which the defendant must prove.

c. Insanity and statutory defences, which the defendant must prove.

d. Self-defence and duress, which the defendant must prove.

4. Which of the following statements represents the ladder principle most effectively?

a. The Offences Against the Person Act 1861 is a beacon of the ladder principle, with its overlapping offences which are each broadly defined.

b. A burglar will escape liability under the ladder principle prescribing a hierarchy of offences with certain other characteristics if s/he uses a rope rather than a ladder to gain entry to premises.

c. There should be a hierarchy of narrowly defined offences of escalating levels of gravity with minimum overlap between the different offences.

d. It is as much a miscarriage of justice for a guilty person to go free as it is for an innocent person to be convicted.

5. What is the principle of fair labelling in criminal law?

a. A principle which insists that the names that are attached to criminal offences should be fair.

b. A survival from medieval law regarding the holding of markets.

c. Acts enforced by the Advertising Standards Authority in respect of misleading advertisements.

d. A principle which insists that judges should always speak to defendants politely and respectfully.

Conclusion

In this chapter we have looked at a number of principles that are important in the criminal law.[32] What may have struck you as you worked through the chapter is how malleable the different principles are. People may not only have very different views of which principles are the most important in particular contexts, they may also disagree over how to interpret the demands of particular principles. (We will see examples of each of these shortly in the "Evaluating the law" section). This demonstrates a simple fact that you should remember throughout the rest of this text: applying these principles is not a mathematical process which results in either a right or a wrong answer. The principles are tools for you to use when analysing and evaluating the law. It is important that you build the confidence and the ability to think critically and form your own opinions. As you do so you will develop your own view on the relative importance of each of the principles and what they require in specific contexts. This will enable you to write strong answers to exam essay and problem questions!

Self-test questions

1. Using the principles we have studied in this chapter, draw up a bullet point list of arguments for and against each of the following two statements:
   a. 'The ban on smoking cigarettes in public places should be repealed, so that people are free to smoke wherever they wish.'
   b. 'The ban on smoking cigarettes in public places should be extended, so that smoking is a criminal offence wherever it takes place.'
2. 'Any homeowner that has an unsightly or intrusive tree, hedge or other foliage which interferes with their neighbour's enjoyment of their garden should be convicted of a criminal offence.' With reference to the principles of criminal law, discuss the extent to which you agree with this statement.

[32] The chapter has not attempted to provide an exhaustive list of principles of criminal law. There are other principles that we could have studied. One example is necessitous over-inclusion. This is where it is deemed necessary for a criminal law to be over-inclusive. For example, in order to prevent the use of handguns in committing crimes a criminal offence might be enacted, which prevents all possession of handguns by members of the public.

Apply your learning: Your criminal law toolkit

1.4 Explain the basic principles of criminal law.

Quiz 1.4

1. According to Feinberg's statement of the harm principle, if three conditions are satisfied, criminalisation may be justified. Which of the following is not one of the three conditions?
   - **a.** The conduct is wrongful.
   - **b.** A majority of the populace support the criminalisation of the conduct in question.
   - **c.** The conduct causes harm to another person, in that it sets back that other person's interests.
   - **d.** There is no other way of preventing the harm in question that is equally effective and has no greater cost to other values.

2. Which of the following statements is correct?
   - **a.** The principle of individual autonomy focuses on protecting the individual from self-inflicted harm; the social welfare principle focuses on protecting society from the offensive conduct of others.
   - **b.** The principle of individual autonomy focuses on the right of the individual to choose how to live their life; the social welfare principle focuses on collective goals for society.
   - **c.** The principle of individual autonomy focuses on protecting the individual from self-inflicted harm; the social welfare principle focuses on collective goals for society as a whole.
   - **d.** The principle of individual autonomy focuses on the right of the individual to choose how to live their life; the social welfare principle focuses on protecting the individual from self-inflicted harm.

3. Antony Duff argues for which of the following versions of legal moralism?
   - **a.** Negative, ambitious legal moralism.
   - **b.** Positive, ambitious legal moralism.
   - **c.** Positive, modest legal moralism.
   - **d.** Negative, modest legal moralism.

4. According to Lord Bingham in *R* v *Rimmington*, the principle of legality encompasses which two guiding principles?
   - **a.** The criminal law should not be drafted so tightly and precisely as to result in inflexibility, and people must anticipate reasonably foreseeable developments in the law.
   - **b.** The criminal law should be sufficiently clear and certain to enable people to know what conduct is forbidden, and no one should be punished for any act that was not clearly punishable when the act was done.
   - **c.** The criminal law should be sufficiently clear and certain to enable people to know what conduct is forbidden, and people must anticipate reasonably foreseeable developments in the law.
   - **d.** The criminal law should not be drafted so tightly and precisely as to result in inflexibility, and no one should be punished for any act that was not clearly punishable when the act was done.

5. Which principle states that there should be a hierarchy of offences, in order of seriousness, with minimal overlap between the different offences?
   - **a.** The presumption of innocence.
   - **b.** The principle of fair labelling.
   - **c.** The correspondence principle.
   - **d.** The ladder principle.

Evaluating the law

1.5 Evaluate how these principles might apply in a specific situation.

A case study: *R* v *Brown*

Having studied these different principles, it is helpful to consider how they might be applied in a particular case. The case study that we will use is the House of Lords' decision in *R* v *Brown* [1994] 1 AC 212. This case involved a group of homosexual middle-aged men who committed acts of violence against each other for sexual pleasure. The acts included: whipping; caning; applying stinging nettles to the genitals; inserting fish hooks into the penis; nailing the scrotum or foreskin to pieces of board; and burning the penis with a candle. The activities were carried out in private and had been going on for a number of years. There was no evidence that any of the men had suffered permanent injury or ever sought medical treatment. The police discovered the group's activities by chance, when investigating other matters.

Five of the defendants were convicted of the offence of assault occasioning actual bodily harm. Three were convicted of the more serious offence of malicious wounding.[33] The prosecution accepted that the victims had consented to their injuries. The House of Lords had to decide whether consensually inflicting injury for the purpose of sexual gratification is a lawful or unlawful activity. By a majority of 3–2, the House of Lords held that it is an unlawful activity and upheld the men's convictions.

ACTIVITY

Each of the following sets of questions concerns one of the principles that we have studied in this chapter. Think through the questions and write down your answers. (You may find it helpful to look back at the relevant pages as you do this.)

- Did the House of Lords' decision infringe the principle of individual autonomy? If so, whose autonomy was infringed?
- Can the decision be justified using the harm principle? Did the defendants' conduct cause harm to the victims? If so, was their conduct wrongful?
- Can the decision be justified using the offence principle? Who (if anyone) was caused offence?
- Does the decision advance social welfare? If so, what collective goals does the decision advance? Is there supporting evidence that shows that the defendants' conduct harms social welfare?
- Were the defendants' activities immoral? If so, should the criminal law enforce this particular moral standard?
- Were the victims placing themselves at risk? If so, should the criminal law intervene in order to protect their best interests?
- Were other forms of intervention available to regulate the men's activities? If so, would these have been equally effective and appropriate?
- Was the conduct in question a crime prior to the House of Lords' decision? If not, did the decision infringe the principle of legality?
- Do the offence labels offer a fair indication of the nature of the defendants' offences? If not, does this matter, and to whom?

Now, having answered each of these questions, look back over your answers. Weighing up both sides of the argument, do you believe the conduct in *R* v *Brown* should constitute a criminal offence?

[33] Offences Against the Person Act 1861, sections 47 and 20 respectively. We will study these offences in Chapter 6.

EXTRACT

Read the following extracts from the judgments of Lord Templeman (majority) and Lord Mustill (minority).

These extracts address some of the above questions. What answers do they offer to these questions? How do their answers compare to your own? Who do you find yourself in agreement with?

R v Brown [1994] 1 AC 212

Lord Templeman

[I]t was said, every person has a right to deal with his body as he pleases. I do not consider that this slogan provides a sufficient guide to the policy decision which must now be made. It is an offence for a person to abuse his own body and mind by taking drugs. Although the law is often broken, the criminal law restrains a practice which is regarded as dangerous and injurious to individuals and which if allowed and extended is harmful to society generally. In any event the appellants in this case did not mutilate their own bodies. They inflicted bodily harm on willing victims.

[...]

A sadist draws pleasure from inflicting or watching cruelty. A masochist derives pleasure from his own pain or humiliation. The appellants are middle-aged men. The victims were youths some of whom were introduced to sado-masochism before they attained the age of 21. In his judgment in the Court of Appeal, Lord Lane C.J. said that two members of the group of which the appellants formed part, namely one Cadman and the appellant Laskey:

> "were responsible in part for the corruption of a youth K… It is some comfort at least to be told, as we were, that K. has now it seems settled into a normal heterosexual relationship. Cadman had befriended K. when the boy was 15 years old. He met him in a cafeteria and, so he says, found out that the boy was interested in homosexual activities. He introduced and encouraged K. in 'bondage affairs.' He was interested in viewing and recording on videotape K. and other teenage boys in homosexual scenes… One cannot overlook the danger that the gravity of the assaults and injuries in this type of case may escalate to even more unacceptable heights."

The evidence disclosed that drink and drugs were employed to obtain consent and increase enthusiasm. The victim was usually manacled so that the sadist could enjoy the thrill of power and the victim could enjoy the thrill of helplessness. The victim had no control over the harm which the sadist, also stimulated by drink and drugs might inflict. In one case a victim was branded twice on the thigh and there was some doubt as to whether he consented to or protested against the second branding. The dangers involved in administering violence must have been appreciated by the appellants because, so it was said by their counsel, each victim was given a code word which he could pronounce when excessive harm or pain was caused. The efficiency of this precaution, when taken, depends on the circumstances and on the personalities involved. No one can feel the pain of another. The charges against the appellants were based on genital torture and violence to the buttocks, anus, penis, testicles and nipples. The victims were degraded and humiliated sometimes beaten, sometimes wounded with instruments and sometimes branded. Bloodletting and the smearing of human blood produced excitement. There were obvious dangers of serious personal injury and blood infection. Prosecuting counsel informed the trial judge against the protests of defence counsel, that although the appellants had not contracted Aids, two members of the group had died from Aids and one other had contracted an H.I.V. infection although not necessarily from the practices of the group. Some activities involved excrement. The assertion that the instruments employed by the sadists were clean and sterilised could not have removed the danger of infection, and the assertion that care was taken demonstrates the possibility of infection.

[...]

Society is entitled and bound to protect itself against a cult of violence. Pleasure derived from the infliction of pain is an evil thing. Cruelty is uncivilised. I would answer the certified question in the negative and dismiss the appeals of the appellants against conviction.

Lord Mustill

Leaving aside repugnance and moral objection, both of which are entirely natural but neither of which are in my opinion grounds upon which the court could properly create a new crime, I can visualise only the following reasons.

(1) Some of the practices obviously created a risk of genito-urinary infection, and others of septicaemia. These might indeed have been grave in former times, but the risk of serious harm must surely have been greatly reduced by modern medical science.

(2) The possibility that matters might get out of hand, with grave results. It has been acknowledged throughout the present proceedings that the appellants' activities were performed as a pre-arranged ritual, which at the same time enhanced their excitement and minimised the risk that the infliction of injury would go too far. Of course things might go wrong and really serious injury or death might ensue. If this happened, those responsible would be punished according to the ordinary law, in the same way as those who kill or injure in the course of more ordinary sexual activities are regularly punished. But to penalise the appellants' conduct even if the extreme consequences do not ensue, just because they might have done so would require an assessment of the degree of risk, and the balancing of this risk against the interests of individual freedom. Such a balancing is in my opinion for Parliament, not the courts [. . .]

(3) I would give the same answer to the suggestion that these activities involved a risk of accelerating the spread of auto-immune deficiency syndrome [AIDS], and that they should be brought within the Act of 1861 in the interests of public health. The consequence would be strange, since what is currently the principal cause for the transmission of this scourge, namely consenting buggery between males, is now legal. Nevertheless, I would have been compelled to give this proposition the most anxious consideration if there had been any evidence to support it. But there is none, since the case for the respondent was advanced on an entirely different ground.

(4) There remains an argument to which I have given much greater weight. As the evidence in the present case has shown, there is a risk that strangers (and especially young strangers) may be drawn into these activities at an early age and will then become established in them for life. This is indeed a disturbing prospect, but I have come to the conclusion that it is not a sufficient ground for declaring these activities to be criminal under the Act of 1861. The element of the corruption of youth is already catered for by the existing legislation; and if there is a gap in it which needs to be filled the remedy surely lies in the hands of Parliament, not in the application of a statute which is aimed at other forms of wrongdoing. As regards proselytisation for adult sado-masochism the argument appears to me circular. For if the activity is not itself so much against the public interest that it ought to be declared criminal under the Act of 1861 then the risk that others will be induced to join in cannot be a ground for making it criminal.

We will return to *R* v *Brown* in Chapter 6, where we study it (the law, not the facts!) in more detail.

Applying the law

1.6 Apply the law to a specific case scenario.

Consider this scenario.

In *R* v *Gul* [2013] UKSC 64 the Supreme Court described the UK's statutory definition of "terrorism" as "concerningly wide" ([38]).

Now, think about this question. Which option would be the most suitable answer to this question?

From the perspective of the principle of fair labelling, which of the following best explains why a wide definition of terrorism is concerning?

a. An overly broad definition of terrorism may leave some citizens, such as protestors and activists, uncertain whether their actions fall within the scope of terrorism legislation.

b. Any definition of terrorism needs to be flexible, so that it can adapt to changes in society and technology.

c. Defining terrorism too widely will mean that terrorism offences overlap with other serious crimes.

d. It would not be right to prosecute a wrongdoer for a terrorism offence if this does not reflect the nature of their wrongdoing.

Your criminal law toolkit checklist

Having worked through this chapter, you should now have:

✓ An understanding of a range of the most important principles in the criminal law

✓ An awareness of the different opinions of what each of these principles require

✓ An ability to apply these principles to particular examples.

Further reading

Ashworth, A. and Zedner, L. (2012) 'Prevention and Criminalization: Justifications and Limits' 15 *New Criminal Law Review* 542.

Chalmers, J. and Leverick, F. (2008) 'Fair Labelling in Criminal Law' 71 *Modern Law Review* 217.

Cornford A. (2022) 'Beyond Fair Labelling: Offence Differentiation in Criminal Law' 42 *Oxford Journal of Legal Studies* 985.

Cornford, A. (2024) 'The Aims and Functions of Criminal Law' 87 *Modern Law Review* 398.

Dennis, I. (2005) 'Reverse Onuses and the Presumption of Innocence: In Search of Principle' *Criminal Law Review* 901.

Gibson, M. (2024) 'Three Justifications of Fair Labelling' 140 *Law Quarterly Review* 431.

Horder, J. (1995) 'A Critique of the Correspondence Principle in Criminal Law' *Criminal Law Review* 759.

Husak, D. (2004) 'The Criminal Law as Last Resort' 24 *Oxford Journal of Legal Studies* 207.

Mitchell, B. (1999) 'In Defence of a Principle of Correspondence' *Criminal Law Review* 195.

Murphy, C.C. (2010) 'The Principle of Legality in Criminal Law under the European Convention on Human Rights' *European Human Rights Law Review* 192.

Roberts, P. (1995) 'Taking the Burden of Proof Seriously' *Criminal Law Review* 783.

Simester, A.P. and von Hirsch, A. (2011) *Crimes, Harms, and Wrongs: On the Principles of Criminalisation*. Hart Publishing: Oxford.

Answers on the Companion Website

Please visit the companion website for the answers to Key Questions, Quizzes, Applying the Law scenarios as well as student support including glossaries. Please visit www.pearsoned.co.uk/Macdonald

2

The anatomy of a crime

Learning Objectives

2.1 Recall how criminal offences are structured.

2.2 Define the *actus reus* category.

2.3 Recall the *mens rea* category.

2.4 Recognise the requirement that the *actus reus* and *mens rea* of a crime must coincide in time.

2.5 Outline the substantive defences category.

2.6 Define key terms relating to the anatomy of a crime.

2.7 Apply the law on coincidence of *actus reus* and *mens rea* to hypothetical sets of facts.

Introduction

2.1 Recall how criminal offences are structured.

ACTIVITY

Imagine that I am reading this chapter in the library.

Once done, I leave on an unlocked cycle sitting outside.

What information could decide if I stole it or not?

Now, think about this question.

What information would you need in order to decide whether or not I stole the bike? Make a list of as many things as you can think of. Be as imaginative as you like!

There are lots of things you might want to know before deciding whether or not I committed theft of the bike. We can divide this information into three categories:

First Category

First, you would probably want to know who the owner of the bike was. Was the bike mine or someone else's? If it was someone else's had I been given permission to use it? Had the bike been abandoned, so that it was ownerless?

We can label this category:

actus reus (which is a Latin expression that means 'guilty act'). The *actus reus* of an offence specifies the conduct that must be proved for an offence to have occurred. So in our example, the *actus reus* of theft requires that the defendant appropriated an item of property that belonged to another person. We will study the offence of theft in detail in Chapter 8.

Second Category

Second, you probably would have several questions about what I was thinking when I took the bike. Was I aware that it wasn't my bike? If so, did I believe that I had the owner's permission to use it? Did I intend to return the bike or to keep it for myself?

We can label this category:

mens rea (which is a Latin expression that means 'guilty mind'). The *mens rea* of an offence specifies the state of mind the defendant must have possessed in order to be convicted of the offence. So in our example, the *mens rea* of theft requires that, when the defendant appropriated the property, he did so dishonestly and with an intention to permanently deprive the owner of the item.

Third Category

Third, if I knowingly took someone else's bike, you would want to know whether I had some good reason for doing so. Perhaps I was being chased by a knife-wielding student upset at the mark I gave him for his coursework, and I sped off on the bike in order to escape. Or perhaps the Law librarian pointed a gun at my head, marched me outside, and told me to 'steal the bike or else'. In other words, perhaps I acted in self-defence or under duress.

We can call this category:

substantive defences. When a defendant successfully pleads a substantive defence, he is found not guilty even though he perpetrated the *actus reus* of the offence with the necessary *mens rea*.

How crimes are structured

2.1 Recall how criminal offences are structured.

This simple example illustrates how crimes are structured. To establish criminal liability, the prosecution must establish: (1) the *actus reus* of the offence (the conduct element); (2) the *mens rea* of the offence (the mental element); and (3) the absence of a substantive defence. The expressions *actus reus* and *mens rea* come from the Latin maxim *actus non facit reum nisi mens sit rea* ('an act does not make a man guilty of a crime, unless his mind also be guilty'). We can sum this up as shown in Figure 2.1.

Actus reus **+** ***Mens rea*** **−** **Substantive defence** **=** **Criminal offence**

Figure 2.1

If the prosecution fails to establish either the *actus reus* or the *mens rea*, or if it fails to disprove any substantive defence raised by the defendant, there can be no conviction for the offence.

In this chapter we examine each of these three categories in turn. The objective is to give you a broad understanding of how criminal offences are structured. The chapter will also provide an overview of the rest of this text, to help you understand how the different chapters fit together and relate to one another.

As well as outlining the *actus reus*, *mens rea* and substantive defences categories, the chapter also looks in detail at one fundamental requirement for criminal liability: that the *actus reus* and *mens rea* of an offence coincide. Our discussion of this requirement will introduce us to two other important concepts: continuing acts and the transaction principle.

Quiz 2.1

1. To establish criminal liability, the prosecution must…
   - **a.** prove beyond reasonable doubt that the defendant committed the *actus reus* of the offence in question with any necessary *mens rea* specified in the definition of the offence, leaving it for the defendant to prove the existence of any substantive defence.
   - **b.** prove that the defendant committed the *actus reus* of the offence in question with any necessary *mens rea* specified in the definition of the offence.
   - **c.** prove the existence of *mens rea* in an offence of strict liability.
   - **d.** prove beyond reasonable doubt that the defendant committed the *actus reus* of the offence in question with any necessary *mens rea* specified in the definition of the offence and that any substantive defence raised by the defendant did not apply.
2. Which of the following statements is accurate?
   - **a.** If the prosecution fails to establish either the motive behind, or the planning of, any offence, then there can be no conviction for that offence.
   - **b.** If the prosecution establishes both the *actus reus* and mens rea set out in the definition of the offence, the defendant can be convicted of the offence irrespective of whether any substantive defence applies.
   - **c.** If the prosecution fails to establish either the *actus reus* or the *mens rea* set out in the definition of the offence, or if it fails to disprove any substantive defence raised by the defendant, there can be no conviction for the offence.
   - **d.** If the prosecution fails to establish either that the defendant was over the age of 16 or had a mischievous discretion, then there can be no conviction for the offence.
3. Which of the following could potentially form the basis of a substantive defence?
   - **a.** I was so drunk that I didn't know what I was doing and didn't intend to hurt anyone.
   - **b.** Yes, I intentionally pushed him, but only because he was about to attack me, and I needed to escape.
   - **c.** I was on holiday in another country when the victim was stabbed.
   - **d.** I thought I'd scanned everything at the self-service checkout. I didn't mean to leave the shop without paying for it.

Actus reus

2.2 Define the *actus reus* category.

The *actus reus* is the conduct element of an offence. The *actus reus* of every crime that we study in this book will consist of one or more of the following components:

- **Behaviour:** the behavioural part of the *actus reus* refers to some action that the defendant must have performed. On a charge of rape, for example, the defendant must have penetrated the victim's vagina, anus or mouth with his penis. For some crimes, no specific behaviour is required: it is enough simply to show that the defendant did something. For example, the *actus reus* of murder requires that the defendant did something that was a cause of the victim's death.
- **Circumstances:** this part of the *actus reus* specifies circumstances that must have existed at the time of the defendant's behaviour. For example, on a charge of rape the victim must not have been consenting. And on a charge of criminal damage, the property that was damaged must have belonged to someone else.

- **Consequences:** this part of the *actus reus* specifies consequences that must have occurred as a result of the defendant's behaviour. For example, the *actus reus* of murder requires proof that the victim died.

Section 3A of the Road Traffic Act 1988 (below) defines the offence of causing death by careless driving when under the influence of drink or drugs. Read the definition and identify the behavioural, circumstances and consequence components of the *actus reus* of the offence.

EXTRACT

Section 3A Road Traffic Act 1988

3A Causing death by careless driving when under influence of drink or drugs.

(1) If a person causes the death of another person by driving a mechanically propelled vehicle on a road or other public place without due care and attention, or without reasonable consideration for other persons using the road or place, and–

For this offence,

The required behaviour is:

must have been driving a mechanically propelled vehicle on a road or other public place without due care and attention or without reasonable consideration for other persons using the road or place.

The circumstances are:

unfit to drive through drink or drugs.

The consequence is:

the death of another person.

There are three other points to bear in mind:

- The *actus reus* of an offence will not necessarily have all three components: behaviour, circumstances and consequence. In fact, most offences will not contain one or more of these. For example, the *actus reus* of rape does not have a consequence component, and the *actus reus* of murder does not have a circumstances component.
- A distinction is often drawn between conduct crimes and result crimes:
  - A conduct crime is one whose *actus reus* consists of just a behavioural component. An example is the offence of fraud by false representation. As we'll see in Chapter 8, the *actus reus* of this offence only requires proof that the defendant made a false representation.
  - A result crime is one whose *actus reus* contains a consequence component. So murder is a result crime, since the *actus reus* of murder requires proof that the victim died. All result crimes require proof of causation: the defendant's behaviour must have been a factual and legal cause of the consequence.

- Sometimes, the *actus reus* of an offence will not include any behaviour requirement. Examples include crimes of possession (such as possession of weapons or illegal drugs) and so-called 'state of affairs' crimes (such as being in charge of a motor vehicle when under the influence of drink or drugs[1]).

In Chapter 3, we focus on some general *actus reus* concepts. The three that we study are:

- **Voluntariness:** if the defendant's conduct was involuntary, there can be no *actus reus*
- **Omissions:** a defendant cannot normally be held criminally liable for an omission, that is, a failure to act.
- **Causation:** a defendant can only be held criminally liable for a result crime if his conduct was a factual and legal cause of the specified consequence.

The reason that these three concepts have their own chapter is that they are overarching. One or more of these concepts will be relevant to every specific offence that we study.

Quiz 2.2

1. Assault requires proof that the defendant intentionally or recklessly committed an act which caused another person to apprehend the infliction of immediate, unlawful, force on his person. What is the *actus reus* of this offence?
   a. Committing an act which causes another person to apprehend the infliction of immediate, unlawful force on his person.
   b. Recklessly committing an act which causes another person to apprehend the infliction of immediate force on his person.
   c. Committing an act which causes another person to apprehend the infliction of immediate force on his person.
   d. Intentionally committing an act which causes another person to apprehend the infliction of immediate, unlawful, force on his person.
2. To establish the *actus reus* of assault, it must be shown that the defendant caused the victim to apprehend the infliction of immediate, unlawful force on his person. What are the circumstance and consequence components of this *actus reus*?
   a. The whole of the *actus reus* is a consequence.
   b. The circumstance is that the victim apprehended the infliction of immediate force on his person. The consequence is that the apprehended force was unlawful.
   c. The whole of the *actus reus* is a circumstance.
   d. The consequence is that the victim apprehended the infliction of immediate force on his person. The circumstance is that the apprehended force was unlawful.
3. What are the three overarching concepts, one or more of which relate to the *actus reus* of every criminal offence studied in this book?
   a. Complexity/clarity/causation.
   b. Voluntariness/causation/clarity.
   c. Voluntariness/omissions/causation.
   d. Acts/omissions/states of affairs.

Mens rea

2.3 Recall the *mens rea* category.

The *mens rea* of an offence specifies requirements which relate to the defendant's thought processes and state of mind at the moment he perpetrated the *actus reus*. For example, on a charge of rape, one of the *mens rea* requirements is lack of a reasonable belief that

[1] Road Traffic Act 1988, s.4.

the victim was consenting. And on a charge of criminal damage, one of the *mens rea* requirements is that the defendant destroyed or damaged the other person's property either intentionally or recklessly. There are a number of different *mens rea* concepts. In Chapter 4, we study two of these in detail – intention and recklessness – and also look more briefly at four others: knowledge; belief; negligence and strict liability. There are also other *mens rea* concepts that we encounter when studying specific offences, such as malice and dishonesty.[2]

For now, it is worth highlighting two general principles which are relevant when considering issues of *mens rea*: ignorance of the criminal law is no defence to a criminal charge; and a commendable motive does not negate *mens rea*. These principles demonstrate that the term *mens rea* – 'guilty mind' – is in fact misleading if taken literally. A defendant may be found to have had the *mens rea* of an offence even if he had no idea that he was committing a crime and even if he had a commendable motive for his actions. We will examine each of these general principles in turn.

1. Ignorance of the criminal law is no defence to a criminal charge

Think back to *R* v *Brown*, which we looked at in the last chapter. Suppose one of the defendants had said, 'I honestly thought that these activities are legal. I had no idea that I was committing a crime'. If the jury believed him, would this have provided him with a defence? The answer is no. The general principle is that ignorance of the criminal law is no defence to a criminal charge. A defendant cannot escape criminal liability by saying, 'I didn't know that what I was doing was an offence'.

A well-known example is *R* v *Esop* (1836) 7 C & P 456. The defendant was from Baghdad. He was accused of committing buggery whilst on board a ship docked in St Katharine Docks in London. The court stated that the fact Esop did not realise he was committing a crime was no defence, even though buggery was not a crime in his home country and Esop had no reason to think that he was breaking the law.

A more recent example is *R* v *Beard* [2007] EWCA Crim 3168. The defendant, Thomas Beard, was convicted of a firearms offence. Police had found 78 cartridges in Beard's caravan; 66 of these contained CS gas, and so they were prohibited ammunition under the Firearms Act 1968. Beard explained that a friend had left the gas cartridges in the caravan several years earlier. Beard thought they were blanks. The prosecution accepted that he did not know they were prohibited ammunition, and did not suggest that he should have known. Although there was a warning on the outside of the box, Beard was illiterate and could not read the label. He did not possess a weapon that could fire the cartridges. He had no intention of ever using them. He had no record of violent crime and expressed genuine remorse. A probation officer said that he posed little risk of reoffending. He was married with two children, one of which was just two weeks old. On appeal against sentence the Court of Appeal sentenced Beard to two years' imprisonment (reduced from the original sentence of five years imposed at trial).

Citing *R* v *Beard* – as well as several other cases – Andrew Ashworth has argued that the principle that ignorance of the criminal law is no defence is 'a preposterous doctrine, resting on insecure foundations within the criminal law and on questionable propositions about the political obligations of individuals and of the State'.

[2] The term 'malice' is used in some of the non-fatal offences against the person that we study in Chapter 6. The term 'dishonesty' is used in several of the property offences that we study in Chapter 8.

EXTRACT

Read the following extract from Ashworth's article.

He considers three alternatives to the existing law. What are these? Which is his preferred approach? Why?

Ashworth, A. (2011) 'Ignorance of the Criminal Law, and Duties to Avoid It' 74 *Modern Law Review* 1

[P]art of my argument is that it is fair and right to expect people to make a reasonable effort to find out what the law is; the other part of my argument [...] is that the State should also have an obligation to provide more information about the criminal law and about changes made to it, thus making the citizen's task easier. To impose this moderate duty on people is not inconsistent with the rule of law, so long as the State discharges its duty to make the criminal law sufficiently accessible.

My provisional conclusion, then, is that there is a fundamental problem of principle with the English ignorance-of-law doctrine. It subjects people to the censure of conviction when they may not have been culpable. It is not suited to protecting individuals from conviction in situations in which it would not be reasonable to expect them to have discovered the criminal prohibition, a failure that contravenes the rule of law and which cannot be justified by reference to any broader 'public interest.' Three ways of responding may be considered. *First*, ignorance of the criminal law could be allowed to negative liability, as part of or on a par with *mens rea*. That was rejected above, on the ground that it is fair and right to expect citizens to acquaint themselves with the criminal law and wrong to give them an incentive to remain ignorant. *Secondly*, ignorance of the law could be treated as a bar to trial, resulting in a stay of proceedings. This would recognise the State's role in the matter, and would of course avoid subjecting the defendant to trial. The Crown Prosecution Service would have guidance to the effect that a person who was reasonably ignorant of or mistaken about the law should not be prosecuted; to prosecute in spite of that guidance would be an abuse of process. However, the State's role would typically not have been so great as in cases of entrapment and of acting on official advice as to the law, and it is questionable whether reasonable ignorance of the law is not more appropriately dealt with by a lay tribunal (magistrates, jury) in the same way as duress and other excusing conditions.

My preference is therefore for a third approach: that of introducing a general but circumscribed defence of excusable ignorance of the law. This implies that citizens rightly have duties to try to find out about the criminal law, and these should be linked to the kind of duties of the State advocated by Fuller – notably the duty to give adequate publicity to laws, and particularly to criminal laws. Thus where a new piece of legislation introduces a whole raft of offences, the details of which receive little publicity (as a possible example, the Sexual Offences Act 2003), it may be understandable that an individual remains ignorant of some of the legislative changes, in the sense that there has been nothing to put her or him on notice. In those circumstances the law should recognise excusable ignorance of criminal law as a defence, supporting it by reference to (for example) Gardner's argument that the individual must have 'lived up to expectations in a normative sense.' Thus the defence should be based on an appropriate objective standard – what could reasonably be expected of an individual in the defendant's position – perhaps a little broader than the defence in Germany and Sweden. The grounds of excuse would be negligence-based, what could 'reasonably be expected,' and it would be proper for this to be subject to capacity-based exceptions for those unable to perform this citizen's duty.

On this model the rule of law cuts both ways, being part of the framework that constrains those in positions of public authority by imposing on them duties relating to the way in which they should carry out their legislative functions. There is room for debate about the degree of certainty that is required to fulfil the ideal of the rule of law: that ideal is sometimes expressed as if absolute certainty of definition is achievable and desirable, whereas in practice it is not and the law can be used to guide behaviour even if it does not achieve maximum certainty. Insofar as the criminal law employs both rules and standards, it should strive to ensure that terms such as 'reasonable' or 'dishonest' are supplemented by illustrations or sub-principles that enhance people's ability to use them as a gu de.

So the general principle is that ignorance of the criminal law is no defence to a criminal charge. However, Parliament has the ability to create exceptions to this. An example, which we will study further in Chapter 8, can be found in section 2(1)(a) of the Theft Act 1968. This states that a defendant is not guilty of theft if he genuinely believed that he had a legal right to appropriate the property in question – even if his belief was mistaken.

2. A commendable motive does not negate *mens rea*

A second general principle is that a defendant's *mens rea* is not negated by proof that he had a commendable motive. So, for example, if the defendant's wife has an incurable, incapacitating disease, and he eventually gives in to her repeated pleas to have her life ended, he has the *mens rea* of murder.[3] He intentionally killed his wife. His motive does not negate his *mens rea*.

A further illustration of this principle is *R* v *Smith* (John) [1960] 2 QB 423. The defendant, John Smith, was convinced that his local council was corrupt. Wanting to expose this corruption, Smith offered the town mayor a bribe. He was convicted of a corruption offence. He appealed against his conviction, saying that he simply wanted to expose the mayor. The Court of Appeal rejected his appeal. Smith had the necessary *mens rea* since his intention was to corrupt the mayor. His motive for so doing was irrelevant.

Again, though, whilst a commendable motive does not generally negate *mens rea*, there appear to be exceptions to this principle. In some circumstances it seems that a defendant's motive could be taken into account when determining his intention. We will examine this issue further in Chapter 4.

Quiz 2.3

1. The *mens rea* of an offence specifies requirements which relate to…

- **a.** the state of mind of the defendant when committing the *mens rea.*
- **b.** the state of mind of the defendant when committing the *actus reus* of an offence.
- **c.** the state of mind of the victim.
- **d.** the proof only of a guilty intention.

2. Ashworth levels a number of criticisms at the principle that ignorance of the law is no excuse. The following list contains three of these criticisms. Which item on the list is **not** one of the criticisms that Ashworth advances?

- **a.** The current application of the principle exposes people to condemnation when they may not have been blameworthy.
- **b.** A citizen should not be deemed to have knowledge of a criminal law if it is unreasonable to have expected individuals to have discovered that law.
- **c.** If citizens are to be deemed to have knowledge of a new criminal law, this should be linked to a requirement on the part of the state to publicise that law.
- **d.** It is not appropriate to apply the principle to those with specific legal training but to allow others without such training to plead ignorance as an excuse.

3. Which of the following statements about *R* v *Smith (John)* [1960] 2 QB 423 is accurate?

- **a.** Smith had not committed any offence because the town mayor should not have accepted the bribe.
- **b.** Smith had not committed any offence because he had a commendable motive.
- **c.** Since Smith's intention was to corrupt the mayor, his motive for wanting to do so was irrelevant.
- **d.** The Court of Appeal said that Smith had acted recklessly by taking matters into his own hands.

[3] See *R* v *Cocker* [1989] Crim LR 740, which we study in Chapter 5.

Coincidence of *actus reus* and *mens rea*

2.4 Recognise the requirement that the *actus reus* and *mens rea* of a crime must coincide in time.

Having studied general *actus reus* and *mens rea* concepts in Chapters 3 and 4, we then move on in Chapters 5–8 to study the *actus reus* and *mens rea* requirements of a number of specific criminal offences. We study the following four types of offence: homicide; non-fatal offences against the person; sexual offences; and property offences.

For a defendant to be convicted of any of the crimes that we study, all of the *actus reus* and *mens rea* requirements of the relevant offence must be established. Moreover, establishing the *actus reus* and *mens rea* requirements alone is not enough. The prosecution must also prove that they coincided in time. In other words, the defendant must have possessed the necessary *mens rea at the moment* he perpetrated the *actus reus*. So suppose that, as Andrew leaves a crowded lecture theatre, he inadvertently knocks someone's iPad onto the floor. The iPad breaks. When Andrew discovers that the iPad belonged to Robert he is secretly rather pleased, as he has always hated Robert and had been looking for an opportunity to upset him. On these facts Andrew is not guilty of criminal damage. At the moment he caused the damage to the iPad he lacked the necessary *mens rea*.[4] And by the time he subsequently discovered whose iPad it was the *actus reus* had already occurred.

Note that, if the crime in question is a result crime, the crucial point in time is not the moment the relevant consequence occurs but the moment of the defendant's behaviour that caused the consequence. Suppose that Andrew poisons Robert, intending to kill him. The poison is slow-working. A couple of hours after administering the poison Andrew has a change of heart. He tells Robert what he has done and rushes him to hospital, but it is too late. Robert dies and Andrew is charged with murder. The relevant moment in time is not when Robert died. It is the time of Andrew's behaviour that caused death, that is, the moment he administered the poison. At this moment he perpetrated the *actus reus* with the necessary *mens rea*. He would therefore be guilty of murder. His subsequent repentance came too late (just as his repentance would come too late if he stabbed Robert to death and then immediately regretted what he had done).[5]

1. Continuing acts

Having stated that the *actus reus* and *mens rea* must coincide in time, we now need to look at two specific types of case where this requirement is not so straightforward. The first concerns continuing acts. In *Fagan* v *Metropolitan Police Commissioner* [1969] 1 QB 439 the defendant, Vincent Fagan, was reverse parking his car. The victim, a police officer named David Morris, was directing him. Fagan reversed the car onto Morris' foot. Morris said, 'Get off, you are on my foot!' to which Fagan replied 'Fuck you, you can wait'. He then turned the ignition off. Several times Morris repeated, 'Get off my foot!' Eventually Fagan said 'okay, man, okay' and moved the car. At trial Fagan was convicted of

---

[4] Inadvertence is insufficient for the *mens rea* of criminal damage: see Chapter 8.

[5] Of course, if Andrew had managed to save Robert's life he would not have been guilty of murder, since there would have been no death and therefore no *actus reus*. On these facts, he would be guilty of attempted murder instead.

battery. He appealed against his conviction, arguing that there was no coincidence of *actus reus* and *mens rea*. He claimed: that when he drove onto Morris' foot there was an infliction of force (*actus reus*), but since this was accidental there was no *mens rea*; and when he subsequently refused to move the car there was *mens rea*, but the force had already been inflicted and so there was no *actus reus*. The Divisional Court dismissed his appeal and upheld the conviction.

EXTRACT

Read the following extract from the judgment of James J.

He draws a distinction between acts which are complete and acts which are continuing. How did he apply this distinction to the facts of Fagan's case?

Fagan v *Metropolitan Police Commissioner* [1969] 1 QB 439

James J

For our part we think the crucial question is whether in this case the act of the appellant can be said to be complete and spent at the moment of time when the car wheel came to rest on the foot or whether his act is to be regarded as a continuing act operating until the wheel was removed. In our judgment a distinction is to be drawn between acts which are complete – though results may continue to flow – and those acts which are continuing [...]

It is not necessary that *mens rea* should be present at the inception of the *actus reus*; it can be superimposed upon an existing act. On the other hand the subsequent inception of *mens rea* cannot convert an act which has been completed without *mens rea* into an assault.

[...]

There was an act constituting a battery which at its inception was not criminal because there was no element of intention but which became criminal from the moment the intention was formed to produce the apprehension which was flowing from the continuing act. The fallacy of the appellant's argument is that it seeks to equate the facts of this case with such a case as where a motorist has accidentally run over a person and, that action having been completed, fails to assist the victim with the intent that the victim should suffer.

So if an act is complete, any subsequent formulation of *mens rea* cannot convert the completed act into a crime. We saw this earlier in the example with Andrew and the iPad; by the time he discovered whose iPad it was the *actus reus* had already occurred.

But if a defendant forms the necessary *mens rea* whilst the act is still continuing, then he may be liable. Crucially, the Divisional Court held that the infliction of force onto Morris' foot was a continuing act, which began when Fagan drove onto it and continued until he drove off. Fagan thus formed the *mens rea* whilst the act was still continuing and so, as Figure 2.2 illustrates, *actus reus* and *mens rea* coincided in time.

Before moving on, it is worth noting that some commentators have questioned the reasoning in *Fagan* v *Metropolitan Police Commissioner*. They suggest that a better justification for Fagan's liability can be found in the law on omissions. We will examine this suggestion in the next chapter.

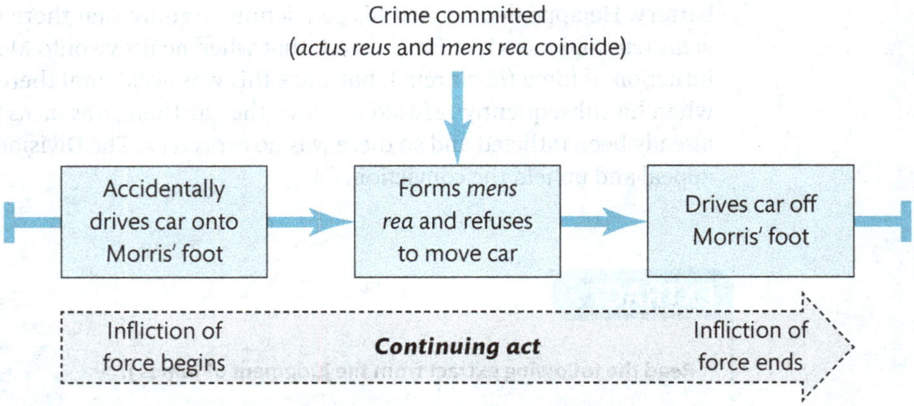

Figure 2.2

2. The transaction principle

Using the concept of a continuing act, it was possible in *Fagan* v *Metropolitan Police Commissioner* to find a moment in time at which *actus reus* and *mens rea* coincided. Things are different with the transaction principle. The leading case is *Thabo Meli* v *R* [1954] 1 WLR 228. The defendant was one of four men who formed a plan to kill the victim and make it look like an accident. They invited the victim to a hut and gave him some beer. The men then hit the victim over the head, knocking him unconscious. Mistakenly believing that he was dead, they rolled his body off a low cliff and left him there. The victim died, but medical evidence showed that the cause of death was not the injuries the men inflicted. He died from exposure as a result of being left at the foot of the cliff.

At trial the four men were convicted of murder. Meli appealed against his conviction. He argued that there was no coincidence of *actus reus* and *mens rea*: when he attacked the victim he had the *mens rea* of murder, but the attack was not the cause of death (so no *actus reus*); and there was the *actus reus* when he rolled the body off the cliff since this act caused death, but this act was not performed with an intention to kill since he believed the victim was already dead (so no *mens rea*). His appeal reached the Privy Council, who dismissed the appeal.

EXTRACT

Read the following extract from the judgment of Lord Reid.

Explain, in your own words, the transaction principle Lord Reid advances.

Thabo Meli v *R* [1954] 1 WLR 228

Lord Reid

It is said that two acts were necessary and were separable: first, the attack in the hut; and, secondly, the placing of the body outside afterwards. It is said that, while the first act was accompanied by *mens rea*, it was not the cause of death; but that the second act, while it was the cause of death, was not accompanied by *mens rea* [...]

> It appears to their Lordships impossible to divide up what was really one transaction in this way. There is no doubt that the accused set out to do all these acts in order to achieve their plan and as parts of their plan; and it is much too refined a ground of judgment to say that, because they were under a misapprehension at one stage and thought that their guilty purpose had been achieved before in fact it was achieved, therefore they are to escape the penalties of the law.

So the plan of the defendants in *Thabo Meli* v *R* formed one transaction. Since this transaction was carried out with the *mens rea* of murder, and it was a part of this transaction that caused death, the defendants were guilty of murder. Figure 2.3 illustrates this.

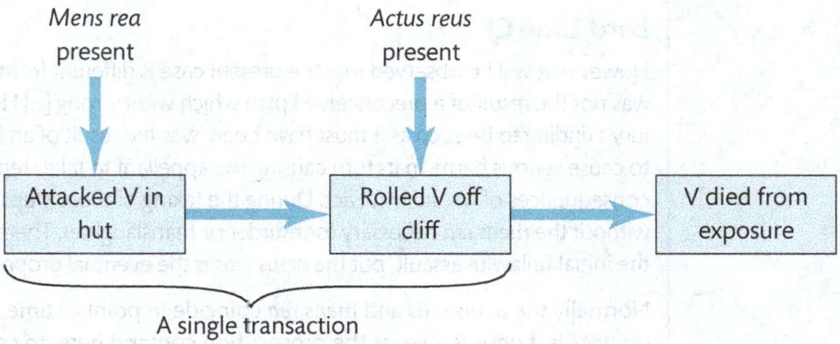

Figure 2.3

The transaction principle thus groups together a series of actions as one 'transaction'. As long as the *actus reus* is present at one stage of this transaction, and the transaction is carried out with the necessary *mens rea*, the defendant is liable – even if the *actus reus* and *mens rea* do not in fact coincide in time. The transaction principle is therefore an exception to the normal requirement that the *actus reus* and *mens rea* must coincide in time.

The transaction principle was also applied in *R* v *Le Brun* [1992] QB 61.[6] The defendant, John Le Brun, had an argument with his wife in the street outside their house. During the argument he struck her and knocked her unconscious. He then picked her up, in order to move her body inside and hide what he had done, but as he carried her he dropped her. She suffered a fractured skull and died. At trial Le Brun was convicted of manslaughter (since the jury found that he only intended to cause his wife non-serious harm when he struck her). He appealed against his conviction, arguing that there was no coincidence of *actus reus* and *mens rea*: when he struck his wife there was the *mens rea* of manslaughter but not the *actus reus*, since this act did not cause death and when he dropped his wife there was the *actus reus* of manslaughter but not the *mens rea* since it was an accident. The Court of Appeal dismissed his appeal and upheld the conviction.

---

[6] A further example is *R* v *Keane (David)* [2016] EWCA Crim 2018. In this case the defendant punched the victim repeatedly, then pushed him over and stamped on his head. The victim suffered a severe head injury and developed epilepsy. Two-and-a-half years later the epilepsy caused his death. On appeal, defence counsel suggested that the attack should be divided up into: (a) a series of punches; and, (b) the stamp, and that there might therefore not have been coincidence of *actus reus* and *mens rea*. Rejecting this as 'tenuous and artificial' ([27]), the Court of Appeal described the attack as a 'single incident' ([30]). Since the attack caused the victim's subsequent death, and was perpetrated with the necessary *mens rea*, the murder conviction was upheld.

EXTRACT

Read the following extract from the judgment of Lord Lane CJ.

In what ways does he say the facts of this case are different to *Thabo Meli* v *R*? Did the transaction principle still apply? Why/why not?

In your opinion, would the outcome in *R* v *Le Brun* have been different if Le Brun had dropped his wife whilst trying to carry her to hospital?

R v *Le Brun* [1992] QB 61

Lord Lane CJ

However, it will be observed that the present case is different from [*Thabo Meli* v R] in that death here was not the result of a preconceived plan which went wrong [...] Here the death, again assuming the jury's finding to be such as it must have been, was the result of an initial unlawful blow, not intended to cause serious harm, in its turn causing the appellant to take steps possibly to evade the consequences of his unlawful act. During the taking of those steps he commits the *actus reus* but without the *mens rea* necessary for murder or manslaughter. Therefore the *mens rea* is contained in the initial unlawful assault, but the *actus reus* is the eventual dropping of the head on to the ground.

Normally the *actus reus* and *mens rea* coincide in point of time. What is the situation when they do not? Is it permissible, as the prosecution contend here, to combine them to produce a conviction for manslaughter?

[...]

It seems to us that where the unlawful application of force and the eventual act causing death are parts of the same sequence of events, the same transaction, the fact that there is an appreciable interval of time between the two does not serve to exonerate the defendant from liability. That is certainly so where the appellant's subsequent actions which caused death, after the initial unlawful blow, are designed to conceal his commission of the original unlawful assault.

[...]

In short, in circumstances such as the present, which is the only concern of this court, the act which causes death, and the necessary mental state to constitute manslaughter, need not coincide in point of time.

There are two important points to note from Lord Lane CJ's judgment in *R* v *Le Brun*. First, the transaction principle applied even though there was no preconceived plan (as there was in *Thabo Meli* v *R*). Second, the judgment states that actions which are designed to conceal previous unlawful conduct form part of the same transaction. This suggests that subsequent actions which are lawful – such as trying to find medical help – will not be held to be part of the same transaction.

Quiz 2.4

1. What are the exceptions to the principle that the defendant must have possessed the necessary *mens rea* at the moment he perpetrated the *actus reus*?
   a. Where *mens rea* occurs at some point in a series of linked acts forming one overall transaction **and** where the *actus reus* will come into existence at some relatively distant point in the future from the point at which *mens rea* is formed.
   b. Where the *mens rea* occurs at some point in a continuing *actus reus* **and** where the offence is an offence of strict liability.

c. Where the *mens rea* occurs at some point in a continuing *actus reus* **and** where *mens rea* occurs at some point in a series of linked acts forming one overall transaction.

d. Where the *mens rea* will come into existence at some relatively distant point in the future from the point at which the *actus reus* occurs **and** where the *mens rea* occurs at some point in a continuing *actus reus*.

2. If the crime in question is a result crime, the crucial point in time for determining whether a defendant is guilty of that crime is…

a. at the moment of the act or omission which led to the prohibited result.

b. after the prohibited consequence occurs and not before.

c. when the prohibited result occurs and not before.

d. when the defendant first decided that he was going to commit the offence.

3. Which of the following is **not** a principle confirmed in, or derived from, *R* v *Le Brun* [1992] QB 61?

a. A defendant will be liable to conviction for a crime where *mens rea* occurs at some point in a series of linked acts forming one overall transaction.

b. The transaction principle applied even though there was no preconceived plan (as there was in *Thabo Meli* v *R*).

c. Subsequent actions which are lawful - such as trying to find medical help - will be held to be part of the same transaction.

d. Those actions which are designed to conceal previous unlawful conduct will be held to form part of the same transaction.

4. D attacks V so violently that he believes he has killed her. He throws her into the river to avoid detection. V was not dead when he did this, but she drowns. Which principle could be applied to establish D's liability for V's death?

a. The principle in *R* v *Beard*.

b. The principle in *Thabo Meli* v *R*.

c. The principle in *Fagan* v *MPC*.

d. The principle of correspondence.

Substantive defences

2.5 Outline the substantive defences category.

In a criminal trial there are two types of defences:

- First, the defendant may seek to defend himself by arguing that the prosecution has failed to prove the *actus reus* and *mens rea* of the offence. For example, a defendant charged with criminal damage might argue that the property was not in fact damaged. A defendant charged with rape might argue that the sexual intercourse was in fact consensual. And a defendant charged with attempted murder might argue that he lacked any intention to kill. Whilst these are all examples of defences, they are not 'substantive defences'. Rather, they are a denial of the *actus reus* or *mens rea*. In Chapters 9 and 10, we will look at some specific examples of 'denial of *actus reus*' and 'denial of *mens rea*' defences. In Chapter 9, we examine the law governing intoxicated defendants. It is common for defendants to argue that they were so drunk at the time of the alleged offence that they were incapable of forming the necessary *mens rea*. In Chapter 10, we examine the defences of sane automatism and insanity. Defendants who plead these defences are claiming that they acted involuntarily. These defences therefore constitute a denial of the *actus reus*.
- Substantive defences are different. We study five of these defences in total: necessity; duress by threats; duress of circumstances; prevention of crime; and private defence. Substantive defences only apply once the *actus reus* and the *mens rea* of the offence have been established. A defendant who seeks to plead a substantive defence is in effect saying, 'Yes, I perpetrated the *actus reus* with the necessary *mens rea*, but there is a good reason why I should nonetheless be found not guilty'. Perhaps there were circumstances which mean the defendant was justified to do as he did. For example, a surgeon

performing a life-saving operation would not be guilty of intentionally wounding his patient. Or perhaps there were circumstances which mean the defendant should be excused for acting as he did, such as where a person steals money because he has a gun pointed to his head. We study the substantive defences in Chapter 11.

Quiz 2.5

1. What are the two types of defence?
   a. Insanity **and** any statutory exception.
   b. Not guilty **and** not proven.
   c. Justifications **and** excuses.
   d. A denial that one or more of the component parts of the *actus reus* or *mens rea* existed **and** the existence of a substantive defence to the offence charged.
2. Which of the following defences does **not** amount to a denial of the *actus reus*?
   a. No causal link between D's behaviour and the specified consequence.
   b. Intoxication.
   c. Sane automatism.
   d. Insanity.
3. What do the following defences have in common: necessity; duress by threats; duress of circumstances; prevention of crime; and private defence?
   a. They are substantive defences which apply once the *actus reus* and the *mens rea* of the offence have been established.
   b. They apply to all offences.
   c. They are all statutory defences.
   d. They are all common law defences.

Conclusion

The offences that we will study in Chapters 5–8 all impose punishment on a defendant who has harmed another person or their property. But if the criminal law was limited to just offences like these it would be seriously defective. It needs a broader scope, in two respects:

- **Actions:** The criminal law should seek to prevent crimes as well as punish those who commit them. For this reason, there are a range of crimes – known as 'inchoate offences' – which penalise defendants who have embarked on preparations to commit an offence but not yet done so. We study the inchoate offences in Chapter 12.
- **Actors:** The criminal law should not only punish those who actually commit murders, rapes, thefts and so on. It should also punish those who provide assistance or encouragement to murderers, rapists, thieves and others who commit crimes. We refer to such people as 'accessories'. The final chapter of the text – Chapter 13 – examines the law which determines when a person may be held criminally liable as an accessory.

This completes our overview of how crimes are structured, and of how this text is structured. As you progress through the text, you may find it helpful to refer back to this chapter to remind yourself of how the different topics we study fit together.

Self-test questions

2.6 Define key terms relating to the anatomy of a crime.

Define each of the following terms: (a) *actus reus;* (b) *mens rea;* (c) substantive defence; (d) conduct crime; (e) result crime; (f) a continuing act; (g) the transaction principle and (h) a denial of *actus reus/mens rea* defence.

Applying the law

2.7 Apply the law on coincidence of *actus reus* and *mens rea* to hypothetical sets of facts.

Andrew and Robert

The following events involve the characters Andrew and Robert, who are work colleagues. Read the problem scenario carefully, then answer the multiple-choice questions below to apply your learning to the scenario.

Andrew and Robert are work colleagues. Andrew feels he is undervalued by his boss, David, and is very angry that Robert, whom he considers less capable and hardworking, has been promoted ahead of him. Andrew arranges to meet them both one evening and sets off in his car, planning to kill them when he arrives. On the way, and through no fault of his own, Andrew is involved in a road accident in which his car knocks over a pedestrian who is killed instantly. By sheer coincidence, the pedestrian happens to be Robert. Andrew is secretly rather pleased: opportunities at work improve, and all murderous thoughts as to David disappear from his mind.

a. Could Andrew be convicted of murdering Robert? Explain your reasoning.

b. How would your answer be different if, after the accident, Andrew had climbed out of his car, recognised Robert, pulled out a gun and shot him?

c. How would your answer be different if: Andrew had seen Robert and deliberately driven into him. Then, thinking that Robert was dead, Andrew had attempted to hide Robert's body but as he did so he dropped Robert on his head. Medical evidence later shows that Robert died from a fractured skull caused by his being dropped on his head.

1. For a defendant to be convicted of a crime, all of the *actus reus* and *mens rea* requirements of the relevant offence must be established. Moreover, as we saw in the chapter, establishing the *actus reus* and *mens rea* requirements alone is not enough. The prosecution must also prove that they coincided in time. Our starting point in analysing this scenario, therefore, is to identify the relevant moment in time at which all *actus reus* and *mens rea* requirements must coincide.

In Andrew's case, what is the relevant moment in time at which the prosecution would have to prove all *actus reus* and *mens rea* requirements coincided?

a. When Andrew set off in his car

b. When Andrew decided that he wanted to kill Robert

c. When Andrew's car collided with the pedestrian (who happened to be Robert)

d. When Andrew realised that the pedestrian was Robert

2. Having identified the relevant moment in time we now need to consider the key question: whether Andrew possessed the necessary *mens rea* at this moment.

The following four statements offer four different analyses of our scenario. Only one of the statements is correct. Which one?

a. Killing Robert was a continuing act. This act began when Andrew collided with him in his car, and was still continuing at the moment Andrew realised that the pedestrian was Robert.

b. The transaction principle applies. Andrew's course of conduct may be regarded as one transaction. This transaction caused Robert's death, and the transaction was perpetrated with the *mens rea* of murder.

c. At the moment Andrew collided with the pedestrian he had an intention to kill Robert. Therefore the *actus reus* and *mens rea* of murder coincided: Andrew performed an act that caused Robert's death and at the time he performed the act he had an intention to kill Robert.

d. At the moment of the collision Andrew did not intend to kill the pedestrian. The collision was an accident, and was not Andrew's fault. The fact Andrew was later secretly pleased that the pedestrian had been killed does not supply proof of *mens rea*, because by this time the act was already complete (Robert was killed instantly).

3. Turning to part (b), we need to identify the relevant moment in time at which all *actus reus* and *mens rea* requirements must coincide. On these facts, the key moment is when Andrew pulled the trigger. This was the moment at which Andrew performed an act with an intention to kill.

   Which of the following is not one of the principles expounded by the Divisional Court in *Fagan* v *Metropolitan Police Commissioner*?

   a. If the defendant formed *mens rea*, but only after the act was already complete, then he cannot be convicted of the offence.

   b. If the defendant did not possess the necessary *mens rea* at the inception of the act, but formed *mens rea* whilst the act was still continuing, then he may be convicted of the offence.

   c. A distinction must be drawn between acts which are complete and acts which are continuing.

   d. If the defendant's act was a continuing one, he may only be convicted of the offence if he possessed the necessary *mens rea* at the inception of the act.

4. We now turn to part (c). This scenario has obvious similarities with *Thabo Meli* v *R* and *R* v *Le Brun*. When Andrew drove into Robert there was the *mens rea* of murder but not the *actus reus* (since this act did not cause death), and when Andrew dropped Robert there was the *actus reus* of murder but not the *mens rea* (he thought Robert was already dead).

   Which of the following statements about the decision in *R* v *Le Brun* is incorrect?

   a. Actions which are designed to conceal previous unlawful conduct form part of the same transaction.

   b. Even when the transaction principle applies, for a defendant to be convicted it must still be possible to identify a moment in time when *actus reus* and *mens rea* coincided.

   c. The defendant attempting to move his wife's body formed part of the same transaction as the initial act of striking her.

   d. The transaction principle applied even though there was no preconceived plan.

The anatomy of a crime checklist

Having worked through this chapter, you should now have:

✔ An understanding of how crimes are structured

✔ An ability to identify the behaviour, circumstances and consequence components of a crime's *actus reus*

✔ An understanding of the general principles of *mens rea*

✔ An understanding of the requirement that *actus reus* and *mens rea* coincide in time

✔ An understanding of the concept of a continuing act and the transaction principle

✔ An understanding of the difference between denial of *actus reus*/*mens rea* defences and substantive defences.

Further reading

Arenson, K.J. (2013) '*Thabo Meli* Revisited: The Pernicious Effects of Result-driven Decisions' 77 *Journal of Criminal Law* 41.

Ashworth, A. (2011) 'Ignorance of the Criminal Law, and Duties to Avoid It' 74 *Modern Law Review* 1.

Chan, W. and Simester, A.P. (2011) 'Four Functions of *Mens Rea*' 70 *Cambridge Law Journal* 381.

Horder, J. (2000) 'The Irrelevance of Motive in Criminal Law' in J. Horder (ed.) *Oxford Essays in Jurisprudence: Fourth Series*. OUP: Oxford.

Answers on the Companion Website

Please visit the companion website for the answers to Key Questions, Quizzes, Applying the Law scenarios as well as student support including glossaries. Please visit www.pearsoned.co.uk/Macdonald

3

Key *actus reus* concepts

Learning Objectives

3.1 Explain the *actus reus* concept of voluntariness.

3.2 Explain the law governing criminal liability for omissions.

3.3 Construct arguments for or against extending the existing exceptions to the rule that there is no criminal liability for omissions.

3.4 Explain the tests used to determine causation.

3.5 Apply the law on voluntariness, omissions and causation to hypothetical sets of facts.

3.6 Evaluate the law on omissions liability.

3.7 Evaluate the case law on legal causation.

Introduction

In Chapter 2, we saw that the first step in proving criminal liability is to establish the *actus reus* of the crime in question. In this chapter we focus on three key *actus reus* concepts: voluntariness; omissions; and causation. What makes these concepts so important that they deserve their own chapter is that they will be relevant to most of the crimes we study in this text. In other words, they are general concepts. Having a firm understanding of these concepts will help you when you look at the *actus reus* of specific crimes in Chapters 5–8.

The importance of these three concepts is illustrated by the following three examples:[1]

Voluntariness

A "decent and devoted" husband who strangled his wife while he dreamt she was a intruder has been cleared of murder after the Crown Prosecution Service accepted he had not been in control of his actions but was not a danger to anyone else.

Father-of-two Brian Thomas killed his wife, Christine, as he was in the throes of a nightmare about a "boy racer" who had broken into the camper van they were sleeping in. Members of the jury at Swansea crown court wept after they were ordered to formally acquit Thomas, who had suffered "night terrors" for about 50 years without ever being treated.

Omissions

A grammar school pupil who left his date to drown without helping her after taking a cocktail of drink and drugs has been jailed for manslaughter.

Michael Bowditch, 21, admitted to killing 17-year-old student Becky Morgan by leaving her to drown after she fell into the sea off the Kent coast. He has been jailed for five-and-a-half years for manslaughter by gross negligence.

Causation

A woman has been jailed for life after being found guilty of a "sadistic and evil" acid attack that left her former partner with such terrible injuries that he was driven to euthanasia.

Berlinah Wallace threw sulphuric acid over Mark van Dongen in a fit of jealousy and rage after he began a relationship with another woman.

The chapter begins with the concept of **voluntariness**, which we deal with fairly briefly at this stage. We then turn to **omissions and causation**, which we examine in greater detail.

Voluntariness

3.1 Explain the *actus reus* concept of voluntariness.

If the defendant's conduct was involuntary, there can be no *actus reus*. The reason is simple: a defendant should not be held responsible for behaviour over which she had no control!

---

[1] Source Voluntariness: Steven Morris, Devoted husband who strangled wife in his sleep walks free from court, *The Guardian*, 20 Nov 2009. Source Omissions: "Nicola Harley, Former grammar school boy who did not help drowning teenager whilst high on drink on drugs is jailed for manslaughter, *Telegraph*, 26 May 2017. Source Causation: Steven Morris, Berlinah Wallace jailed for life for 'sadistic' acid attack on Mark van Dongen, *The Guardian*, 23 May 2018.

It is important to point out that there are different definitions of voluntariness. Later in the chapter we will see that, in the context of causation, voluntariness has been defined as 'free, deliberate and informed'. Here, however, we are talking about voluntariness in a different sense. There can be no *actus reus* when the defendant's conduct was involuntary, in the sense that she had no control over the movements of her body.

There are many reasons why someone's body might move involuntarily.

Suppose you are browsing in the Student Union shop.

Shutterstock

When I creep up behind you and push you into the wine display.

Shutterstock

Dozens of bottles of wine are smashed.

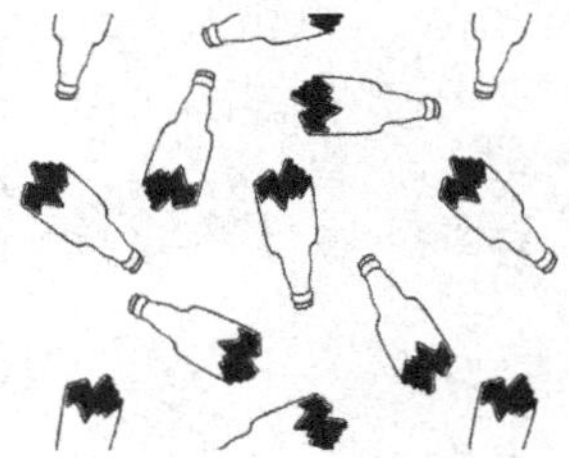

Shutterstock

You are not guilty of criminal damage because there is no actus reus. *Although it was your body which smashed the bottles, these movements were involuntary.*

Shutterstock

Another example would be if you are sitting on a sofa watching TV with your family

When you suffer a sudden, uncontrollable muscle spasm.

Your foot jerks outwards and hits the person sitting next to you.

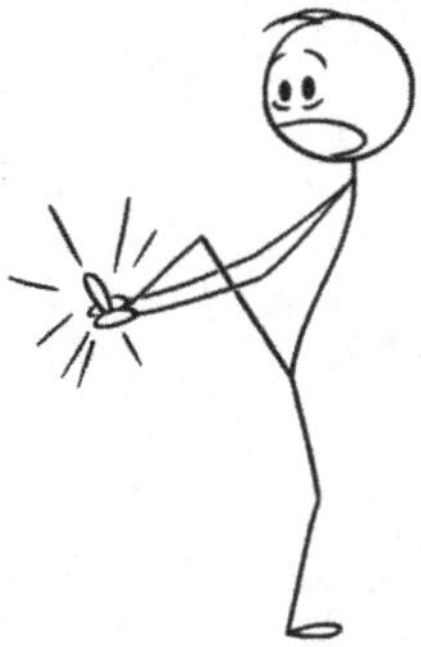

You are not guilty of battery because your bodily movements were involuntary. There is no actus reus.

One particularly important reason why someone might act involuntarily is known as automatism. What is 'automatism'? Its meaning was considered by the Court of Appeal in *Attorney-General's Reference (No 2 of 1992)* [1994] QB 91. The defendant in this case was a lorry driver. He had set off at 11 am. By 11 pm he had covered 343 miles (having taken regular breaks during the day), when he steered onto the hard shoulder and crashed into a white van that had broken down. Two people were killed. At his trial a psychologist gave evidence that the defendant had been in a condition known as 'driving without awareness'. This condition is caused by repetitive visual stimuli and results in a trance-like state. Although someone in this state will be largely unaware of what is happening, they are still able to steer the vehicle and are usually able to react and return to full awareness when confronted with strong visual stimuli.

At trial the trial judge gave the jury the option of finding that the defendant had been in a state of automatism. The jury acquitted the defendant. The Attorney-General subsequently referred the following question to the Court of Appeal: is the condition of driving without awareness capable of amounting to automatism? In his judgment Lord Taylor CJ stated:

> [T]he defence of automatism requires that there was a total destruction of voluntary control on the defendant's part. Impaired, reduced or partial control is not enough.

Since someone who is driving without awareness retains some awareness and some control over their actions, the condition is not capable of amounting to automatism. Automatism requires that the defendant suffered a 'total destruction of voluntary control'. This was confirmed by the Court of Appeal in *R* v *Coley* [2013] EWCA Crim 223, where Hughes LJ emphasised that acting irrationally is not the same as acting involuntarily:

> 22 [...] The essence of [automatism] is that the movements or actions of the defendant at the material time were wholly involuntary. The better expression is complete destruction of voluntary control [...] Examples which have been given in the past include the driver attacked by a swarm of bees or the man under hypnosis. 'Involuntary' is not the same as 'irrational'; indeed it needs sharply to be distinguished from it.

Applying this, the Court of Appeal held one of the defendants in the case, Colin McGhee, had not acted in a state of automatism. McGhee – who had become disinhibited and aggressive after taking prescription medication and drinking alcohol – had stabbed someone in an off-licence. Hughes LJ explained that someone who is disinhibited has not suffered a total destruction of voluntary control.

If the defendant acted in a state of automatism, the next question to ask is whether it was sane automatism or insane automatism. This distinction is crucial. Sane automatism results in a finding of not guilty, and the defendant is acquitted. But insane automatism results in a finding of not guilty by reason of insanity.

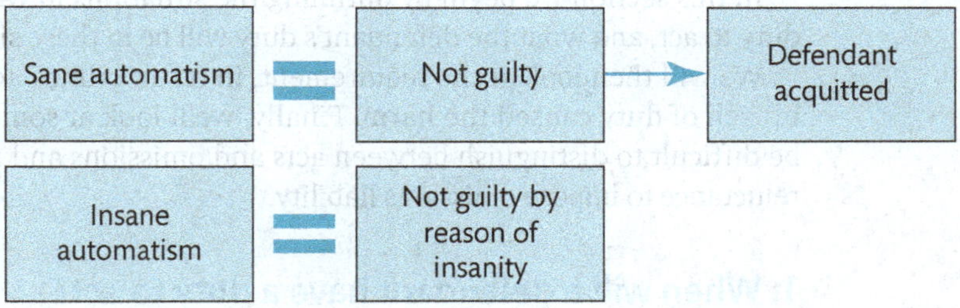

If the defendant is found not guilty by reason of insanity the trial judge can order hospitalisation, a supervision order or an absolute discharge.[2] We will look at the law which determines whether automatism was sane or insane in Chapter 10.

So our first *actus reus* concept is voluntariness. If the defendant acted involuntarily, in the sense that she had no control at all over her bodily movements, there can be no *actus reus*!

---

[2] Criminal Procedure (Insanity) Act 1964, s.5.

Quiz 3.1

1. The term *actus reus* refers to…
   a. the planning behind a crime.
   b. the combination of the physical act and the guilty mind coinciding in time.
   c. the process by which a crime is prosecuted.
   d. the behaviour, circumstances and/or consequences specified in the definition of the crime in issue.
2. Which of the following statements is true?
   a. The *actus reus* varies from crime to crime.
   b. It is not always necessary to prove all *actus reus* requirements in order to secure a conviction.
   c. The *actus reus* must be a positive act.
   d. The *actus reus* remains the same for all offences.
3. There can be no *actus reus* unless it is shown that the defendant acted…
   a. under coercion.
   b. voluntarily.
   c. when intoxicated.
   d. with a plan in mind.

Omissions

3.2 Explain the law governing criminal liability for omissions.

Our second *actus reus* concept is omissions. There are some crimes which can only be committed by doing an act. Of the offences we will study in this text, one example is (as its name suggests!) unlawful act manslaughter.[3] But many of the other offences that we will study can also be committed by omission, that is, by a failure to act.[4] Examples include murder,[5] gross negligence manslaughter,[6] offences involving bodily harm,[7] battery,[8] criminal damage[9] and fraud.[10]

Before a person can be found to have committed a crime by omission, two things must first be established: (1) that the defendant had a duty to act; and (2) that the defendant breached this duty.

In this section we begin by outlining the situations in which a defendant will have a duty to act, and what the defendant's duty will be in these situations.

We will then look at the requirement, in result crimes, to prove that the defendant's breach of duty caused the harm. Finally, we'll look at some situations in which it may be difficult to distinguish between acts and omissions and reflect on the criminal law's reluctance to impose omissions liability.

1. When will a defendant have a duty to act?

Generally, there is no criminal liability for omissions. This was made clear by the House of Lords in *R v Miller* [1983] 2 AC 161. So a defendant will not be criminally liable if he

[3] *R v Lowe* [1973] QB 702.

[4] It is also possible to be an accessory to a crime by omission (see Chapter 13).

[5] *R v Gibbins & Proctor* (1918) 13 Cr App R 134.

[6] *R v Adomako* [1995] 1 AC 171.

[7] *R v Gibbins & Proctor* (1918) 13 Cr App R 134.

[8] *DPP v Santana-Bermudez* [2003] EWHC 2908 (Admin) (though there is some uncertainty: see Chapter 6).

[9] *R v Miller* [1983] 2 AC 161.

[10] *R v Rai* [2000] 1 Cr App R 242.

stands and watches a stranger drown in the sea, nor if he refuses to call an ambulance for a stranger who has just been beaten up and instead walks off and leaves the victim lying injured on the ground.

However, there are a number of exceptions to the general rule that there is no criminal liability for omissions. In each of the following six situations a defendant may be criminally liable if he is under a duty to act and breaches this duty.

Six exceptions

i. Statutory duty
ii. Family relationships
iii. Voluntary assumption of responsibility
iv. Contractual duty
v. Creation of a dangerous situtaion
vi. Continuing acts

We will look at these in the subsequent text.

i. Statutory duty

Some statutes impose a duty to act in certain circumstances. If the defendant fails to act in the manner required by the statute he will breach his duty and may be criminally liable. There are many examples, which include:

- Failure to stop at or report a road traffic accident[11]
- Failure to provide a police officer with a specimen breath test when required to do so[12]
- Failure to disclose information which the defendant knows or believes might assist in the prevention of an act of terrorism.[13]

EXAMPLE

Aras Mohammed Hamid was found guilty of two counts of preparing for acts of terrorism. He had been planning for himself and another to travel to Iraq and engage in acts of terrorism.

Shivan Hayder Azeez Zangana was convicted of one offence of preparing for acts of terrorism. He had been in contact with Hamid about going to Iraq, before travelling from Sheffield to Birmingham, where he was arrested by officers from the West Midlands Counter Terrorism Unit.

The third man, Ahmad Ismail, was found guilty of failing to disclose information about the planned travel to the conflict zone.

- Allowing the death of a child or vulnerable adult who lives in the same household (also known as 'familial homicide').[14]

---

[11] Road Traffic Act 1988, s.170.

[12] Road Traffic Act 1988, s.6.

[13] Terrorism Act 2000, s.38B.

[14] Domestic Violence, Crime and Victims Act 2004, s.5.

EXAMPLE

A mother found guilty of the familial homicide of her 13-month-old baby in a landmark prosecution has been jailed for six years at Swansea Crown Court. Rebecca Lewis, 21, *failed to prevent baby Aaron Gilbert's murder* by her partner Andrew Lloyd, 23, in May 2005.

ii. Family relationships

The second exception is family relationships, though as we'll see this exception is actually quite limited in scope.

Parents–children

Parents have a duty to care for their children. In *R* v *Gibbins & Proctor* (1918) 13 Cr App R 134 the victim was a seven-year-old girl called Nelly. Nelly lived with Walter Gibbins (her father), Edith Proctor (Gibbins' girlfriend) and Gibbins and Proctor's other children. The other children were all healthy. But no one looked after Nelly. She was kept upstairs alone, away from the other children and starved to death. There was evidence that Proctor hated Nelly and had deliberately withheld food from her. Both Gibbins and Proctor were convicted of murder and sentenced to death. Their appeals were dismissed by the Court of Appeal. We will look at what the Court said about Edith Proctor shortly. For now our focus is Walter Gibbins. The Court stated that as Nelly's father Gibbins had a duty to care for her. He had breached this duty:

> [Gibbins] lived in the house and the child was his own, a little girl of seven, and he grossly neglected the child. He must have known what her condition was if he saw her, for she was little more than a skeleton. He is in this dilemma; if he did not see her the jury might well infer that he did not care if she died; if he did he must have known what was going on.

So parents have a duty to care for their children. How long does this duty last? For the whole of the child's life? Or until the child reaches independence? The general view, supported by the decision in *R* v *Shepherd* (1862) 9 Cox CC 123, is that the duty terminates once the child reaches independence.

A further question is whether the duty operates in both directions: do children have a duty to care for their parents? The answer to this question is unclear. Whilst some have argued that children do have a duty to care for their parents,[15] the better view is that children do not automatically have such a duty.[16] A duty would only arise if the child had voluntarily assumed responsibility for their parent (voluntary assumption of responsibility is the third exception to the general rule that there is no criminal liability for omissions, which we'll look at shortly).

Husband–wife

There will normally be a duty to act between spouses. However, the Court of Appeal's approach in *R* v *Smith* [1979] Crim LR 251 was to base this duty on a voluntary assumption of responsibility (the third exception to the general rule). In other words, spouses do not owe each other a duty to act simply because they are married. They owe each other the duty because they have voluntarily assumed responsibility for each other. This difference would

---

[15] See, for example, Ormerod, D. and Laird, K. (2015) *Smith and Hogan's Criminal Law* (14th edn). OUP: Oxford, p.78.

[16] See Simester, A.P., Spencer, J.R., Stark, F., Sullivan, G.R. and Virgo, G.J. (2016) *Simester and Sullivan's Criminal Law: Theory and Doctrine* (6th edn). Hart Publishing: Oxford, p.76.

be significant in a case involving a married couple who have separated. Although they are still married, the fact that they have chosen to separate shows that they are no longer assuming responsibility for one another, and so would no longer owe each other a duty to act.

Other family relationships

What about other family relationships? Brothers and sisters? Grandparents and grandchildren? Aunts/uncles and nephews/nieces? Cousins? Whatever the relationship, a duty to act will only arise if there has been a voluntary assumption of responsibility. The blood tie will not, in itself, generate a duty to act.

iii. Voluntary assumption of responsibility

The third exception is voluntary assumption of responsibility. A person may voluntarily assume a legal duty to act.

One obvious way in which a person might assume responsibility for others is through their choice of job. In *Airedale NHS Trust* v *Bland* [1993] AC 789 the House of Lords stated that doctors have a duty to act in the best interests of their patients. If they fail to act in their patients' best interests they breach their duty and may be criminally liable. Police officers may also be criminally liable for failing to perform their duties as a police officer.[17]

There are many other ways of assuming responsibility for someone, besides choosing a job. Think back to *R* v *Gibbins & Proctor*. We saw that the basis for Walter Gibbins' duty to look after Nelly was the parent–child relationship. But what about Edith Proctor? Nelly was not Proctor's daughter, so on what basis did the Court of Appeal conclude that Proctor owed Nelly a duty to act?

EXTRACT

Read the following extract from the judgment of Darling J.

What facts does he point to in support of the conclusion that Proctor had voluntarily assumed a duty to care for Nelly?

R v *Gibbins & Proctor* (1918) 13 Cr App R 134

Darling J

The case of Proctor is plainer. She had charge of the child. She was under no obligation to do so or to live with Gibbins, but she did so, and receiving money, as it is admitted she did, for the purpose of supplying food, her duty was to see that the child was properly fed and looked after, and to see that she had medical attention if necessary [...] Here Proctor took upon herself the moral obligation of looking after the children

For further insight into the factors the Courts will consider when deciding whether or not there has been a voluntary assumption of responsibility, we will look at two further cases. The first is *R* v *Stone & Dobinson* [1977] QB 354. The defendants in this case were John Stone – a 67-year-old man who was partially deaf, almost blind and had low average intelligence and no appreciable sense of smell – and Gwendoline Dobinson – a

[17] *R* v *Dytham* [1979] QB 722.

43-year-old woman who was Stone's housekeeper and mistress and who also had limited mental capacity. They lived with Stone's son, Cyril, who was 34 years old and mentally subnormal. In 1972 Stone's sister Fanny also came to live with them. Fanny was aged 61 and was anorexic. She was morbidly anxious about putting on weight and so went without proper meals. She would often stay in her room for days at a time.

In the Spring of 1975 the police found Fanny wandering the streets by herself, apparently not knowing where she was. Following this, Stone and Dobinson tried to find Fanny's doctor. But Fanny refused to tell them her doctor's name, and they were unable to find him. In the weeks that followed Fanny's condition deteriorated. By July she was unable to leave her bed. On 19 July a neighbour volunteered to help Dobinson wash Fanny. The neighbour described how Fanny was lying in her own excrement and how much of her body was 'raw'. The neighbour advised Dobinson to contact social services. A few days later Stone and Dobinson went to their local pub. Dobinson told the landlord about Fanny's condition, and the landlord advised her to contact a doctor. Whilst some efforts were made to arrange for a doctor to visit, these efforts were unsuccessful. By 2 August Fanny had died. Stone and Dobinson were convicted of manslaughter for their failure to care for Fanny and arrange medical assistance. They appealed against their convictions, arguing that there was no evidence that they had assumed responsibility for Fanny. The Court rejected their appeals.

EXTRACT

Read the following extract from the judgment of Geoffrey Lane LJ.

What facts does he point to in support of the conclusion that the jury were entitled to find that Stone and Dobinson had voluntarily assumed a duty to care for Fanny?

R v Stone & Dobinson [1977] QB 354

Geoffrey Lane LJ

The suggestion is that, heartless though it may seem, this is one of those situations where the appellants were entitled to do nothing; where no duty was cast upon them to help, any more than it is cast upon a man to rescue a stranger from drowning, however easy such a rescue might be.

This court rejects that proposition. Whether Fanny was a lodger or not she was a blood relation of the appellant Stone; she was occupying a room in his house; the appellant Dobinson had undertaken the duty of trying to wash her, of taking such food to her as she required. There was ample evidence that each appellant was aware of the poor condition she was in by mid-July. It was not disputed that no effort was made to summon an ambulance or the social services or the police despite the entreaties of Mrs. Wilson [the neighbour] and Mrs. West [the pub landlord]. A social worker used to visit Cyril. No word was spoken to him. All these were matters which the jury were entitled to take into account when considering whether the necessary assumption of a duty to care for Fanny had been proved.

This was not a situation analogous to the drowning stranger. They did make efforts to care. They tried to get a doctor; they tried to discover the previous doctor. The appellant Dobinson helped with the washing and the provision of food. All these matters were put before the jury in terms which we find it impossible to fault. The jury were entitled to find that the duty had been assumed. They were entitled to conclude that once Fanny became helplessly infirm, as she had by July 19, the appellants were, in the circumstances, obliged either to summon help or else to care for Fanny themselves.

As well as illustrating when a duty to act might arise, the judgment in *R* v *Stone & Dobinson* also reveals something about the standard of care that is expected. When deciding whether or not Stone and Dobinson breached the duty they owed to Fanny, the Court appears to have made no concession for their personal characteristics. Although they both had limited mental capacity, and Stone was partially deaf and almost blind, the Court nonetheless concluded that they had breached the duty they owed to Fanny.

The second case is *R* v *Sinclair, Johnson & Smith* (1998) 148 NLJ 1353. The three defendants – James Sinclair, Brian Johnson and Ian Smith – were all methadone addicts. Johnson and Smith lived together in a flat owned by Johnson. Johnson knew that Smith used the flat to sell methadone. One day Sinclair went to the flat with the victim – Darren Coleman – to buy some methadone from Smith. They bought the methadone and stayed at the flat to inject themselves. Ten minutes after injection, at about 2:30 pm, Coleman fell unconscious. He never regained consciousness. By 7 am the next morning Coleman was dead.

Sinclair remained with Coleman for the entire period that he was unconscious. But apart from pouring cold water over him and slapping him, he did nothing to help until he called an ambulance at 6:30 am the next morning. At some point between 7 pm and 8 pm Johnson had also injected Coleman with a saline solution in an effort to restore consciousness. At 11 pm he went to bed and slept until Sinclair woke him at 5 am concerned about Coleman's condition.

At trial Sinclair and Johnson were convicted of manslaughter for their failure to call medical assistance. They appealed, arguing that there was no evidence that they had voluntarily assumed responsibility for the victim. The Court of Appeal started by discussing Brian Johnson.

EXTRACT

Read the following extract from the judgment of Rose LJ.

According to the Court of Appeal, was there any evidence that Johnson had voluntarily assumed responsibility for Coleman? What facts does Rose LJ point to in support of this conclusion?

R v *Sinclair, Johnson & Smith* (1998) 148 NLJ 1353

Rose LJ

So far as Johnson is concerned, there is no English authority in which a duty of care has been held to arise, over a period of hours, on the part of a medically unqualified stranger [...] Johnson did not know the deceased. His only connection with him was that he had come to his house and there taken methadone and remained until he died. Others were coming and going in the meantime. The fact that Johnson had prepared and administered to the deceased saline solutions does not, as it seems to us, demonstrate on his part a voluntary assumption of a legal duty of care rather than a desultory attempt to be of assistance. In our judgment, the facts in relation to Johnson were not capable of giving rise to a legal duty of care and the judge should have withdrawn his case from the jury.

The Court of Appeal then turned to James Sinclair.

EXTRACT

Read the following extract from the judgment of Rose LJ.

According to the Court of Appeal, was there any evidence that Johnson had voluntarily assumed responsibility for Coleman? What facts does Rose LJ point to in support of this conclusion?

R v *Sinclair, Johnson & Smith* (1998) 148 NLJ 1353

Rose LJ

Sinclair was in a different position. The evidence was that he was a close friend of the deceased for many years and the two had lived together almost as brothers. It was Sinclair who paid for and supplied the deceased with the first dose of methadone and helped him to obtain the second dose. He knew that the deceased was not an addict. He remained with the deceased throughout the period of his unconsciousness and, for a substantial period, was the only person with him. In the light of this evidence, there was in our judgment material on which the jury properly directed, could have found that Sinclair owed the deceased a legal duty of care. The judge was therefore correct to leave Sinclair's case to the jury on this aspect.

In spite of this conclusion, Sinclair was not guilty of manslaughter. Although he had breached the duty he owed to his friend, there was insufficient evidence that the breach of duty caused Coleman's death. Even if Sinclair had called an ambulance, it might not have made any difference. The trial judge had misdirected the jury on the issue of causation, and so Sinclair's manslaughter conviction was quashed. (Both Sinclair and Johnson were, however, convicted of drugs offences.)

iv. Contractual duty

A defendant may have a contractual duty to act. Often this will be a contract of employment. The leading case on contractual duty is *R* v *Pittwood* (1902) 19 TLR 37. The defendant was a gatekeeper on a railway. He was employed to shut the gate at a level crossing whenever a train was passing, between the hours of 7 am and 7 pm. One day he left the gate open while he went for his lunch. As a result a haycart was struck by a train, and a man was killed. Pittwood was convicted of manslaughter for his failure to shut the gate.

When determining whether a defendant has breached a contractual duty, it is important to look closely at the terms of the contract. For example, Pittwood's contract of employment limited his duty to the hours of 7 am to 7 pm. So if someone else had carelessly left the gate open at 9 pm, and as a result there was an accident ten minutes later, Pittwood would not have been in breach of his contractual duty.

Remember too that:

- It is always necessary to establish that the defendant breached his duty. Suppose that an on-duty lifeguard notices that a swimmer is struggling. He reacts immediately and does his best to save the swimmer, but unfortunately the swimmer drowns. Although the swimmer died, the lifeguard is not criminally liable since he fulfilled his contractual duty to make all reasonable efforts to protect the safety of swimmers.
- The defendant's breach of duty must have caused the harm. Suppose that the lifeguard had noticed that the swimmer was struggling, but did nothing and sat and watched as the swimmer drowned. The lifeguard unquestionably breached his contractual duty.

But whether or not the lifeguard is guilty of a homicide offence will depend on whether it can be shown that his breach of duty was a cause of the swimmer's death. It might be that, even if the lifeguard had done everything he could, the swimmer would still have drowned. If this is the case then, as we'll see shortly, there would be no causal link between the lifeguard's failure to act and the swimmer's death.

v. Creation of a dangerous situation

The leading case here is *R* v *Miller* [1983] 2 AC 161. The defendant, James Miller, was homeless. He was squatting in an unoccupied house. One night Miller lit a cigarette and lay down on a mattress in the house. This is his account of what happened next:

> I went upstairs into the back bedroom where I've been sleeping. I lay on my mattress and lit a cigarette. I must have fell to sleep because I woke up to find the mattress on fire. I just got up and went into the next room and went back to sleep. Then the next thing I remember was the police and fire people arriving. I hadn't got anything to put the fire out with so I just left it.

Miller was convicted of arson. His conviction was based on his failure to take any steps to put the fire out once he had become aware of it. He appealed against his conviction, arguing that he could not be held criminally liable for his omission. The case reached the House of Lords, who unanimously dismissed the appeal and upheld the conviction. Lord Diplock explained:

> [T]he conduct of the accused that is causative of the result may consist not only of his doing physical acts which cause the fire to start or spread but also of his failing to take measures that lie within his power to counteract the danger that he has himself created [. . .] I see no rational ground for excluding from conduct capable of giving rise to criminal liability, conduct which consists of failing to take measures that lie within one's power to counteract a danger that one has oneself created, if at the time of such conduct one's state of mind is such as constitutes a necessary ingredient of the offence.

So if a defendant creates a dangerous situation, he has a duty to take steps to counteract the danger he has created.

Before moving on, notice that the duty imposed by *R* v *Miller* is to take such steps that 'lie within one's power'. So a defendant only breaches this duty if he fails to take steps that lie within his power.

R v *Miller* was applied in a different context by the Court of Appeal in *R* v *Evans* [2009] EWCA Crim 650. The victim in this case was a 16-year-old girl called Carly Townsend. She lived with her mother Andrea Townsend and her half-sister, 24-year-old Gemma Evans. Although all three women had a history of heroin addiction, Carly was trying to overcome her addiction and had not used heroin for at least three months. In May 2007 Evans bought some heroin from a drug dealer and gave it to Carly. Carly injected herself with it. Both her mother and half-sister were in the house when Carly injected herself with the drugs. Soon afterwards Carly developed symptoms which were consistent with a heroin overdose. But her mother and half-sister decided not to call an ambulance because they were worried that they would get into trouble. So instead they put Carly to bed, hoping that she would get better. By the next morning Carly had died.

At trial Andrea Townsend and Gemma Evans were both convicted of manslaughter for their failure to summon medical help. The trial judge told the jury that they could conclude that Evans had a duty to act since she supplied the heroin. On appeal Evans argued that this was a misdirection, and that supplying the drugs could not give rise to a duty to act. The Court of Appeal rejected this argument and applied the principle from *R* v *Miller*. Lord Judge CJ stated:

> When a person has created or contributed to the creation of a state of affairs which he knows, or ought reasonably to know, has become life threatening, a consequent duty on him to act by taking reasonable steps to save the other's life will normally arise.

So since Gemma Evans had contributed to the dangerous situation by giving Carly the heroin, she had a duty to take all reasonable steps to save Carly's life. By failing to call an ambulance she had breached this duty. Her breach of duty was a cause of Carly's death, and so her manslaughter conviction was upheld.

Notice two further points about the judgment in *R* v *Evans*. First, as the extract above indicates, if a defendant has a duty to act arising from the *R* v *Miller* principle, the duty only begins at the moment that the defendant realised, or ought to have realised, the danger. Second, in *R* v *Miller* Lord Diplock said that the *R* v *Miller* principle applies to defendants who created the dangerous situation. In *R* v *Evans* Lord Judge CJ went further than this, saying that the principle applies to defendants who created, *or contributed to*, the dangerous situation. This extension of the *R* v *Miller* principle was crucial in *R* v *Evans*. As we will see later in the chapter, in *R* v *Kennedy (No 2)* [2007] UKHL 38 the House of Lords held that voluntarily self-injecting drugs breaks the chain of causation. Therefore, Gemma Evans was not a (legal) cause of (i.e. she did not create) the dangerous situation that Carly found herself in, because Carly voluntarily self-injected the drugs.[18] Evans did, however, contribute to the dangerous situation by supplying the drugs in the first place. This extension of the *R* v *Miller* principle has been criticised by Ashworth, who argues that:

> Lord Judge's extension of the Miller principle dilutes it to too great a degree, not least because 'all kinds of background acts of facilitation' could now be found to support a duty sufficient for manslaughter liability, expanding both the potential ambit and the uncertainty of the duty-situations.[19]

Now, think about this scenario.

Johann is a cleaner in a supermarket. He washes the floor around the fish counter, then leaves the floor to dry while he goes to have his lunch. As he is eating his sandwich he realises that he has forgotten to put up the 'Caution: Wet Floor' sign. He decides to finish his sandwich quickly, and then go and put the sign up. When he returns to the fish counter with the sign he finds that Ludwig has already slipped on the wet floor and suffered a broken wrist. It is later discovered that Ludwig slipped after Johann had finished his sandwich, while he was collecting the sign from the cleaning cupboard.

- Apply the principle from R v Miller to this scenario. Does Johann fall within the 'creation of a dangerous situation' exception to the general rule that there is no criminal liability for omissions?
- Would your answer be any different if, upon realising that he had forgotten to put the sign up, Johann had immediately stopped eating his sandwich, collected the sign and returned to the fish counter only to find that Ludwig had already slipped and broken his wrist?
- Would any of the other exceptions that we have studied so far apply to Johann?

[18] To avoid confusion, remember to distinguish between the following: (1) the conduct that gave rise to the duty. In *R* v *Evans*, a duty arose because Evans gave Carly the heroin; and (2) the conduct that constituted a breach of the duty. In *R* v *Evans*, it was the failure to call an ambulance that amounted to a breach of the duty, and it was this failure that was held to be a factual and legal cause of Carly's death.

[19] Ashworth, A. (2015) 'Manslaughter by Omission and the Rule of Law' *Criminal Law Review* 563.

(Hint: In Johann's case, there are two omissions. The first is Johann's initial failure to put the sign up. The second is his failure to stop eating his sandwich and put the sign up. Consider each failure in turn.)

vi. Continuing acts

Strictly speaking, continuing acts are acts not omissions. So continuing acts are not really an exception to the general rule that there is no criminal liability for omissions, because they are not really omissions! But continuing acts can often seem very similar to omissions, so it is useful to mention them briefly here.

In Chapter 2 we looked at the case of *Fagan* v *Commissioner of Metropolitan Police* [1969] 1 QB 439, the case in which the defendant accidentally drove onto the policeman's foot and then refused to drive off. We saw that the Divisional Court upheld Fagan's battery conviction by applying the continuing acts doctrine. Remember, however, that *Fagan* was decided more than ten years before the House of Lords' decision in *R* v *Miller*. So at the time of the decision in *Fagan* the principle from *R* v *Miller* did not exist. If a case like *Fagan* occurred today, many commentators believe that the courts would apply the principle from *R* v *Miller*, not the continuing acts doctrine. The reasoning would go like this. When Fagan drove onto the policeman's foot he created a dangerous situation. From the moment he realised what he had done he was under a duty to counteract the danger he had created. By failing to drive off the policeman's foot he breached this duty.

If the continuing acts doctrine is not needed to explain the outcome of *Fagan*, does this mean that the doctrine is redundant? No! There are other situations in which the continuing acts doctrine would still apply. An example is *Kaitamaki* v *R* [1985] AC 147. In this case the defendant admitted having sexual intercourse with the victim. He said that when he penetrated her he genuinely believed that she was consenting. He only became aware that she was not consenting after penetration. But he admitted that once he realised she was not consenting he continued to have sexual intercourse with her and did not withdraw. At first this might look like an omission, a failure to withdraw. But it does not really make sense to talk of having sex by omission. It is more sensible to say that the defendant ignored the victim and continued the positive act of sexual intercourse. This was the reasoning the Privy Council used in upholding his rape conviction. Sexual intercourse is a continuing act, which begins at penetration and continues until withdrawal. The defendant formed the necessary *mens rea* whilst the guilty act was still continuing, and so the *actus reus* and *mens rea* of rape coincided.

2. Omissions and causation

Assessment advice

In exam problem questions, one mistake students commonly make is to write things like 'Johann would be guilty of an omission' or 'Johann would be guilty of a breach of his duty'. The problem here is that breach of duty is not, in itself, a crime. Establishing that the defendant may be criminally liable for his omission is only the first step. Once you have done this, you will then need to identify the relevant criminal offence (from the ones we will study in Chapters 5, 6, 7 and 8) and determine whether all the *actus reus* and *mens rea* elements of the offence are satisfied.

If the crime in question is a result crime (like murder or gross negligence manslaughter), you will need to discuss whether the defendant's breach of duty was a cause of the harm. As some of the examples we have looked at have illustrated, sometimes a defendant's breach of duty may not have made any difference. For example, suppose that the defendant sees his young daughter get run over by a car. The defendant does nothing to help, and does not call an ambulance. Medical evidence later shows that the girl died within minutes, and that doctors would not have been able to save her. On these facts the defendant breached his duty to his daughter, but the breach was not a cause of her death. Even if he had phoned an ambulance she would still have died. So he will not be guilty of a homicide offence.[20]

There are other offences which can be committed by omission which are not result crimes. Crimes like failing to stop at or report a road traffic accident, or failure to provide a police officer with a specimen breath test when required to do so, have no consequence element and so there is no requirement to prove causation. However, you still need to show that all the other *actus reus* and *mens rea* elements of the crime are satisfied before concluding that the defendant is criminally liable.

3. Distinguishing between acts and omissions

In most cases deciding whether the defendant's behaviour was an act or an omission will be straightforward. If the defendant points a gun at the victim and pulls the trigger, this is clearly an act. If the defendant stands on a pier and watches as a stranger drowns, this is clearly an omission. But sometimes there can be more difficult cases.

An example is *Airedale NHS Trust* v *Bland* [1993] AC 789. Tony Bland was a victim of the Hillsborough stadium disaster. Too many fans were allowed onto the terraces to watch an FA Cup semifinal between Liverpool and Nottingham Forest. Tony, who was aged 18 at the time, was crushed. His lungs were crushed and punctured, and as a result the supply of blood to his brain was interrupted. This caused him serious and irreversible brain damage. Tony was left in a persistent vegetative state (PVS). He could not see, hear or feel anything. He could not communicate in any way. And he would never regain consciousness. However, his brain stem, which controls heartbeat, digestion and breathing, continued to operate. In the eyes of the legal and medical world, a person is still alive as long as his brain stem is functioning. So although Tony was in a persistent vegetative state, for legal purposes he was still alive. But to keep him alive he had to be fed through a nasogastric tube.

By the time of this case Tony had been in this condition for three-and-a-half years. The undisputed medical consensus was that there was no prospect of Tony making any recovery from his condition. However, if he continued to receive the same medical care he could be kept alive in the same condition for many years to come. The hospital and Tony's parents decided that no useful purpose was to be served by continuing Tony's medical care. His father said that Tony would not have wanted 'to be left like that'. However, the doctors were concerned that ceasing Tony's medical treatment could constitute a criminal offence. So the hospital applied to the courts for a declaration that medical treatment could be ceased without any crime being committed. The case reached the House of Lords. The first question the House of Lords had to answer was whether ceasing Tony's treatment would be an act or an omission.

(Note: the doctors were not asking for permission to commit euthanasia. They were not seeking to actively bring Tony's life to an end. They were only applying for permission to cease treatment.)

At first this might seem straightforward. Not treating a patient looks like an omission. But it wasn't this easy! One of the things the doctors were asking for permission to do was remove the nasogastric tube that was feeding Tony, and removing a tube looks more like an act than an omission.

[20] *R* v *Broughton* [2020] EWCA Crim 1093.

EXTRACT

Read the following extracts from the judgments of Lord Goff and Lord Browne-Wilkinson.

Was ceasing Tony's treatment and removing the nasogastric tube an act or an omission? What reasons did they give for their conclusion?

Airedale NHS Trust v Bland [1993] AC 789

Lord Goff

I agree that the doctor's conduct in discontinuing life support can properly be categorised as an omission. It is true that it may be difficult to describe what the doctor actually does as an omission, for example where he takes some positive step to bring the life support to an end. But discontinuation of life support is, for present purposes, no different from not initiating life support in the first place. In each case, the doctor is simply allowing his patient to die in the sense that he is desisting from taking a step which might, in certain circumstances, prevent his patient from dying as a result of his pre-existing condition; and as a matter of general principle an omission such as this will not be unlawful unless it constitutes a breach of duty to the patient. I also agree that the doctor's conduct is to be differentiated from that of, for example, an interloper who maliciously switches off a life support machine because, although the interloper may perform exactly the same act as the doctor who discontinues life support, his doing so constitutes interference with the life-prolonging treatment then being administered by the doctor. Accordingly, whereas the doctor, in discontinuing life support, is simply allowing his patient to die of his pre-existing condition, the interloper is actively intervening to stop the doctor from prolonging the patient's life, and such conduct cannot possibly be categorised as an omission.

Lord Browne-Wilkinson

The positive act of removing the nasogastric tube presents more difficulty. It is undoubtedly a positive act, similar to switching off a ventilator in the case of a patient whose life is being sustained by artificial ventilation. But in my judgment in neither case should the act be classified as positive, since to do so would be to introduce intolerably fine distinctions. If, instead of removing the nasogastric tube, it was left in place but no further nutrients were provided for the tube to convey to the patient's stomach, that would not be an act of commission. Again, as has been pointed out (*Skegg, Law, Ethics and Medicine* (1984), pp. 169 et seq.) if the switching off of a ventilator were to be classified as a positive act, exactly the same result can be achieved by installing a time-clock which requires to be reset every 12 hours: the failure to reset the machine could not be classified as a positive act. In my judgment, essentially what is being done is to omit to feed or to ventilate: the removal of the nasogastric tube or the switching off of a ventilator are merely incidents of that omission: see *Glanville Williams, Textbook of Criminal Law*, p. 282; *Skegg*, pp. 169 et seq.

Think about this question.

- According to Lord Goff, if a stranger had crept into the hospital at night and removed the nasogastric tube that was feeding Tony, would this have been an act or an omission?

So the House of Lords decided that, when taken as a whole, what the doctors were doing was to cease Tony's treatment. Although this did involve some positive acts, like removing the nasogastric tube, ceasing treating is an omission. Having decided that ceasing Tony's treatment would be an omission, the next question was whether the doctors would be criminally liable for this omission. As we saw above, the House of Lords stated that doctors have a duty to act in their patients' best interests. Since Tony no longer had any interest in being kept alive, the House of Lords held that ceasing his treatment would not violate his best interests. Therefore the doctors would not be breaching their duty and so could not be held criminally liable.

The decision in *Bland* involves some difficult distinctions. It is an omission for a doctor to remove a patient's nasogastric tube in order to cease treatment, whereas if a stranger were to remove the tube it is an act. Is it right that the same action can be an act when performed by one person and an omission when performed by someone else? And whilst it was lawful to leave Tony Bland to starve to death in a hospital bed over a period of weeks,[21] it would have been unlawful to end his life immediately by lethal injection.

Quiz 3.2

1. A general principle of English Law is that…
   - **a.** an omission will never be considered a crime unless the defendant desired the outcome.
   - **b.** an omission does not usually lead to criminal liability.
   - **c.** an omission will always lead to criminal liability.
   - **d.** an omission will never be considered a crime when the defendant desired the outcome.

2. Which statement is false? For a defendant to be guilty by omission…
   - **a.** the circumstances must create a legal duty to act.
   - **b.** the crime must be capable of commission by omission.
   - **c.** his failure to act must have been involuntary.
   - **d.** he must have breached his duty to act.

3. In *R* v *Pittwood* (1902) 19 TLR 37, why was the defendant found guilty by omission?
   - **a.** He voluntarily assumed care for another.
   - **b.** He saw an immediate risk and failed to act.
   - **c.** He had a special relationship to the deceased.
   - **d.** He had a contractual obligation that he failed to carry out.

4. Why was the defendant in *R* v *Miller* convicted of arson?
   - **a.** He intended to start a fire.
   - **b.** He started a fire accidentally.
   - **c.** He intentionally started a fire but then failed to extinguish it.
   - **d.** He created a dangerous situation which he failed to rectify.

5. What is the concept of a continuing act, as explored in *Fagan* v *Metropolitan Police Commissioner*?
   - **a.** When there is a failure to desist from an initially innocent act, coupled with the formation of *mens rea*.
   - **b.** When a defendant commits a crime, but later changes his mind.
   - **c.** When a defendant has achieved his intention, but carries on with further crimes.
   - **d.** When a defendant has to commit a number of crimes in preparation for the planned *actus reus*.

6. In *Airedale NHS* v *Bland*, why did the NHS Trust seek a declaration to enable them to cease treatment?
   - **a.** There was a medical argument as to whether Bland would recover.
   - **b.** There were objections from many pro-life organisations.
   - **c.** The NHS Trust wanted to ensure that it would not be acting unlawfully if treatment was withdrawn.
   - **d.** Anthony Bland had relatives who objected.

7. In *Airedale NHS* v *Bland*, what reasons did the House of Lords give for allowing treatment to be withdrawn?
   - **a.** Discontinuing life-support was akin to an omission.
   - **b.** Objections from families were irrelevant.
   - **c.** Bland's treatment was a waste of NHS resources.
   - **d.** There was a breach of duty in withdrawing treatment as the treatment was futile.

[21] The House of Lords' judgment is dated 4 February 1993. Tony died on 3 March that year.

4. Is the scope of omissions liability too narrow?

3.3 Construct arguments for or against extending the existing exceptions to the rule that there is no criminal liability for omissions.

We have seen that there is normally no criminal liability for omissions. Whilst there are some exceptions to this general rule, they are quite limited in scope. It is worth pausing to consider whether these exceptions are *too* limited. In many European countries, for example, there is a duty of easy rescue.

In his article 'The Scope of Criminal Liability for Omissions' (below) Andrew Ashworth contrasts the 'conventional view' with the 'social responsibility view'. The conventional view insists 'that the criminal law should be reluctant to impose liability for omissions except in clear and serious cases'. Supporters of the conventional view 'tend to argue that there is moral distinction between acts and omissions'. Performing an act knowing that it will cause harm is morally worse, they argue, than a failure to prevent the same harm. The 'social responsibility view', by contrast, queries whether it is possible to draw such a hard-and-fast distinction[22]. It also emphasises the extent to which we, as citizens, rely and depend on one another. This means that sometimes 'it may be fair to place citizens under obligations to render assistance to other individuals in certain situations'.

EXTRACT

Read the following extract from Ashworth's article.

Summarise the arguments in favour of the 'conventional view'. Summarise the counter-arguments of the 'social responsibility view'. Can you think of any additional arguments for either viewpoint?

Ashworth, A. (1989) 'The Scope of Criminal Liability for Omissions' 105 *Law Quarterly Review* 424

The conventional view

The conventional view embodies a minimalist stance on criminal liability for omissions. It accepts that criminal law is the sharpest end of a legal structure which aims to ensure both that respect for social values is enforced and that essential social needs are provided for. It therefore accepts criminal liability for such omissions as non-payment of taxes. But it regards it as exceptional, and as requiring spec al justification, for the criminal law to impose duties to assist other individuals. Apart from spec al relationships (such as parent-child) and other voluntarily undertaken duties, there should be no criminally enforceable duties to assist others or to perform socially useful acts.

The main buttress is an argument from individual autonomy and liberty. Each person is regarded as an autonomous being, responsible for his or her own conduct. One aim of the law is to maximise individual liberty, so as to allow each individual to pursue a conception of the

[22] In his article 'Beyond acts and omissions: Remark-able criminal conduct', Mark Dsouza argues that, instead of distinguishing between acts and omissions, we should ask whether a defendant has belied a contextually salient expectation as to how he should, or routinely would, conduct himself. He calls this the 'Remark-able Conduct Requirement' and argues that it provides a better guide to what is really important to the criminal law than the distinction between acts and omissions (Dsouza, M. (2021) 'Beyond acts and omissions: Remarkable criminal conduct' 41 *Legal Studies* 1).

good life with as few constraints as possible. Constraints there must be, of course, in modern society: but freedom of action should be curtailed only so far as is necessary to restrain individuals from causing injury or loss to others. Setting these outer limits to freedom of action is, however, much more acceptable than requiring certain actions of a citizen, especially at times and in circumstances which may be inconvenient and may conflict with one's pursuit of one's personal goals. To impose a duty to do X at a certain time prevents the citizen from doing anything else at that time, whereas the conventional prohibitions of the criminal law leave the citizen free to do whatever else is wanted apart from the prohibited conduct. Moreover, the criminal law should recognise an individual's choices rather than allowing liability to be governed by chance, and the obligation to assist someone in peril may be thrust upon a chance passer-by, who may well prefer not to become involved at all. If I am driving to a concert 50 miles away which is to feature a soloist who is being heard for the last time in this country, should I be obliged to stop and render assistance to the victims of a road accident in which I was not involved, at the risk of missing part or the whole of the concert? It is no argument to say that such a journey is always open to the possibility of chance happenings, such as engine failure in the car, a road blocked by a fallen tree, and so on, because in the case of the accident victims I am physically free to drive on to my destination whereas the other happenings amount to physical prevention, and render me incapable of reaching my destination on time. Thus it is no argument to say that all arrangements are vulnerable to chance, since the law can strive to minimise its effect and to keep individual choice as wide as possible. There is a choice whether to stop and offer assistance or to continue on my way to the concert, but an offence requiring a citizen to stop and render assistance would effectively foreclose that choice, coercing me to sacrifice the pursuit of my own interests in favour of alleviating the misfortunes of others to whom I have not voluntarily assumed any duty. By its "chance" nature, the incidence of such a duty reduces the predictability of one's obligations and impinges on the liberty to pursue one's conception of the good life. On the conventional view, then, I deserve moral praise if I stop to assist the accident victims and thereby lose the opportunity to attend the (whole) concert, but it does not follow that I deserve blame if I do not stop. Praise may be appropriate for an act of "saintliness" going beyond duty, whereas the duties themselves require only the basic conditions of peaceful co-existence. Stopping to help is part of the morality of aspiration, not the morality of duty.

In thus equating individual autonomy with *negative* liberty (*i.e.* liberty not to do certain acts), the conventional view rejects broad duties to others as paternalistic, and as failing to respect each individual's right to self-determination. Any obligation to help others in peril begs the question of who is to decide what "peril" is. Individuals may choose to engage in amateur boxing or in motor cycle racing, knowing of the high risk of injury but deciding that it is worth the risk in order to enjoy the excitement of the sport. Are these boxers or motor cyclists "in peril"? Few would extend a citizen's obligation to intervene (where it exists) to these cases, probably because the individual's decision to engage in the sport may be assumed to be an informed and settled decision. Self-determination, a value closely entwined with individual autonomy, would be impaired by the intervention of others. But what about the person who decides to commit suicide and jumps from a bridge into the River Thames? Should the passing citizen be obliged to alert the emergency services or, if the conditions are favourable, to mount a rescue attempt? The passing citizen is unlikely to know about the potential suicide's state of mind. It is known that some attempts at suicide proceed from an unbalanced state of mind, and some are merely attempts to draw attention to the person's problems rather than to relinquish life. On the conventional view these possibilities for paternalistic intervention should not be made the basis of any legal duty. If a citizen sees what appears to be an attempted suicide, the citizen's freedom from non-voluntary obligations together with the potential suicide's right to self-determination are sufficient to conclude the case against a duty to intervene.

A third argument looks to the social consequences of the opposite, "social responsibility" view. Its effect in requiring each citizen to offer assistance to others in peril might on the one hand reduce the autonomy and privacy of others in pursuing their own objectives and enjoyment, however dangerous it may appear to others, and might on the other hand make citizens into busybodies who believe that they must be constantly advising others to avoid risk and danger. In other words, it might be too intrusive and too onerous – both tendencies which go against the maximisation of liberty which is the keynote of the conventional view.

Fourthly, there is the argument that the "social responsibility" view is unpractical because it would require each of us to avert or alleviate large numbers of situations which we know about. One strand of this argument calls attention to the problem of setting limits to the individuals duties on the social responsibility view: must I sell my car and my house, live at subsistence level and devote all my surplus earnings and time to preventing so many people from "sleeping rough" in London, or to provide towards the relief of starvation in Africa? In what way do perils of these kinds differ materially from the accident victims or the person who jumps into the River Thames? A second strand of the argument is that the "social responsibility" view may lead to the inculpation of large numbers of people, e.g. all the members of a crowd who witness someone being beaten up by others. It is excesses of this nature, in the depth and breadth of the obligations imposed, which are seen as sufficient to condemn the "social responsibility" view as an unworkable moral or legal standard.

A fifth argument draws strength from the principle of legality: it maintains that citizens are so unaccustomed to thinking in terms of legal duties to act (as distinct from the well-known prohibitions) that it is unfair to impose such burdens except in circumstances which are well-defined and well-publicised. Protagonists might add that few provisions on general liability for omissions attain these standards, and that the obligation to take reasonable steps to assist a person in peril is much too uncertain to meet these standards. The social consequence is likely to be that ignorance of the law is a frequent occurrence, which cannot be good either for society or for the individuals concerned. Wide conceptions of social responsibility must therefore be rejected as a basis for criminal legislation: the conventional view, with its few well-known and voluntarily assumed duties to others, is the preferable approach.

The individualism of the conventional view doubted

The arguments for the conventional view may appear strong and practical, but they depend on a narrow, individualistic conception of human life which should be rejected as a basis for morality and (although this raises further issues) as a basis for criminal liability. Let us look again at the arguments, in turn.

The first argument, based on individual autonomy and freedom, is altogether too pure. To the extent that the conventional view relies on "social fact" for some of its justifications, it is worth pointing out that rarely is individual autonomy promoted as a supreme value throughout a moral or legal system. For example, paternalistic considerations are taken to outweigh it when imposing a duty to wear a seat belt in the front seat of a car: this restricts individual liberty and self-determination, and it may be justified by reference to the known dangers of travelling without a seat-belt, combined with the relatively large benefit (in the social costs of health care) reaped from such a comparatively minor infringement of freedom of action. Systems of criminal law typically include a wide range of offences which impose duties to act, in relation to taxation, motoring and business activities. However, it is not necessary to turn "social fact" arguments against the conventional view, for its proclaimed principle of individual autonomy is itself unsatisfactory. If individual autonomy is truly a supreme value, then it requires social principles rather than this kind of isolationist individualism in order to secure its fulfilment. Individuals tend to place a high value on interpersonal contacts, relationships, mutual support and the fulfilment of obligations, and a society which values collective goals and collective goods may therefore provide a wider range of worthwhile opportunities for individual development. At the very least, then, there is no inherent logic in arguing from the ideal of individual autonomy to moral and legal principles which regard duties to other citizens *qua* fellow-citizens as prima facie objectionable and exceptional, for that neglects the importance of human interdependence to the realisation of individual autonomy. This is still a far cry from the utilitarian view, since that tends to aggregate people in its calculations and fails to respect each individual as an end in himself or herself. The counter-argument to the conventional view is thus that a duty to co-operate with or to assist others should not be ruled out *ab initio* by an asocial and falsely restricted view of individual automony. Moreover, the proposition is not that citizens should be permanently at the beck and call of one another, but that (at the very least) there is a strong case for going beyond the conventional view and, for example, creating a duty to assist a citizen whose life is in peril. This may not maximise the quantity of liberty left to individuals, but it increases the quality of social life.

The second and third arguments for the conventional view establish, however, that limits must be set to the obligations to others if the ideal of individual autonomy is not to be submerged beneath a welter of duties imposed on each person. The resolution of these conflicts of theory and practice is no easy matter, but the "social responsibility" view would at least start from the assumption that duties to others are not necessarily alien to individual autonomy, and would have to reconcile this with the desirability of individuals safeguarding their own interests too. This dilemma, which also underlies the fourth argument for the conventional view, demonstrates the need for principled debate about the extent of social co-operation necessary to realise individual autonomy. Those who advocate "social responsibility" bear the heavy burden of formulating defensible and workable criteria for the imposition of duties to act. Indeed, as the fifth argument showed, attention is also necessary to the promulgation of such rules. In so far as it is true that people do not consider that they have legal duties to assist others, any legislation to introduce such duties must be phrased as precisely as possible, and must be supported by a programme of education and information. These represent considerable challenges for the "social responsibility" view on criminal liability for omissions.

Think about this question.

- Look at your summary of the arguments for the 'conventional view' and the 'social responsibility view'. Which set of arguments do you find the most convincing?

Quiz 3.3

1. Which of the following is true?
   - **a.** Acts and omissions are considered equally culpable.
   - **b.** Homicide cannot be committed by an omission.
   - **c.** Omissions are considered less culpable than acts.
   - **d.** Acts are considered less culpable than omissions.
2. According to Ashworth, which of the following is an argument in favour of the conventional view that criminal liability for omissions should be strictly limited?
   - **a.** Other values, such as paternalism, should sometimes take priority over individual autonomy.
   - **b.** A duty to assist others in peril would be impractical since it would be unclear how far the duty extends.
   - **c.** A programme of education and information could explain to citizens the scope of a duty of easy rescue.
   - **d.** Society values collective goals and collective goods, so social principles should be prioritised over isolationist individualism.
3. According to Ashworth, which of the following is an argument in favour of the social responsibility view that the obligation to assist others should be extended?
   - **a.** Requiring individuals to intervene and assist others in peril would impede their autonomy and force them to sacrifice their own pursuits.
   - **b.** Requiring others to intervene would impede individuals' self-determination.
   - **c.** A duty of easy rescue would not meet the demands of the principle of maximum certainty.
   - **d.** A duty to assist others in peril should not be ruled out by an asocial and falsely restricted view of individual autonomy.

Causation

3.4 Explain the tests used to determine causation.

Our third *actus reus* concept is causation. In Chapter 2, we saw that crimes which have a consequence element as part of their *actus reus* are known as result crimes. Causation is an essential feature of all result crimes. Whenever a defendant is charged with a result crime a 'causal link' must be shown between the defendant's actions and the specified consequence. To establish a causal link it is necessary to prove both factual causation and legal causation. In this section we look first at factual causation, and then legal causation.

Assessment advice

This is the order in which you would discuss these issues in an exam problem question answer: begin with factual causation, and if this is present move on to consider legal causation.

1. Factual causation

To test for factual causation we use the 'but for' test. This simply asks: but for the defendant's actions, would the consequence have occurred in the same way? If the answer to this question is 'Yes, the consequence would have occurred in the same way without the defendant's actions' there is no factual causation. But if the answer is 'No, the consequence would not have occurred in the same way without the defendant's actions' there is factual causation, and you should move on to consider whether or not legal causation is also present.

The following two cases are helpful examples of the 'but for' test in action.

Case I

In *R* v *White* [1910] 2 KB 124 the defendant put poison in the victim's drink. The victim had a few sips, but suffered a fatal heart attack before she could drink any more. Medical evidence suggested that the heart attack was unrelated to the poison.

The poisoned drink was not a factual cause of the victim's death. But for the poison, the victim would still have suffered the heart attack and died in the same way. (Although this meant the defendant had not committed murder (he had not caused the victim's death), he was convicted of attempted murder.)

Case II

In *R* v *Dalloway* (1847) 2 Cox CC 273 the defendant was riding a horse-drawn cart. He was standing up, not holding the reins. A three-year-old child called Henry ran across the road in front of the horse. One of the wheels of the cart knocked Henry down and killed him. Dalloway was charged with manslaughter. The prosecution argued that his negligent driving had caused Henry's death.

The jury concluded that even if Dalloway had been driving carefully he would not have been able to avoid hitting Henry. So there was no factual causation. Dalloway's negligent driving was not a factual cause of Henry's death, because even if Dalloway had been driving carefully Henry would still have been knocked over and killed.

2. Legal causation

The 'but for' test sets a very low threshold. As a result, there can be many factual causes of a consequence which are not deserving of criminal liability.

Suppose that your lecturer overruns by ten minutes.

As a result, you miss your bus home and have to walk.

While you are walking home your housemate calls you on your mobile to find out where you are.

Preoccupied by the phone conversation, you step out in front of a car and are run over.

On these facts, both your lecturer and your housemate are factual causes of your death. **But for your lecturer overrunning**, you would have caught your bus and not been walking home. **And but for your housemate phoning you**, you would have not been distracted and not stepped out in front of the car.

The role of legal causation is to identify which factual causes should also be regarded as legal causes. In other words, the role of legal causation is to filter out those factual causes which are not deserving of criminal liability. This is what makes legal causation difficult. It is not a dispassionate exercise in logic. As we shall see, questions of legal causation involve difficult moral and policy considerations.

i. The basic test for legal causation: significant contribution

In *R* v *Cheshire* [1991] 1 WLR 844 Beldam LJ stated:

> It is not the function of the jury to evaluate competing causes or to choose which is dominant provided they are satisfied that the defendant's acts can fairly be said to have made a significant contribution to the victim's death. We think the word "significant" conveys the necessary substance of a contribution made to the death which is more than negligible.

So the starting point for determining questions of legal causation is to ask whether the defendant's actions made a significant contribution to the relevant consequence. If the contribution made by the defendant's actions was insignificant (in other words, negligible) there is no legal causation. So in our earlier example, the lecturer overrunning and the housemate phoning were not legal causes of your death because neither can be regarded as having made a significant contribution.

Notice one further point about this test: the question is simply whether the defendant's actions made a significant contribution. So you do not have to compare the defendant's actions to other factual causes of the consequence and ask which was the most significant. The question is simply whether the contribution made by the defendant's actions was significant or not. It is possible for more than one factual cause to make a significant contribution. This means that there might be several legal causes of the same consequence, as Beldam LJ explained in *R* v *Cheshire*:

> [W]e think it is sufficient for the judge to tell the jury that they must be satisfied that the Crown have proved that the acts of the defendant caused the death of the deceased adding that the defendant's acts need not be the sole cause or even the main cause of death it being sufficient that his acts contributed significantly to that result.

Deciding whether or not the defendant's contribution was significant can sometimes involve difficult moral and policy considerations. But questions of legal causation can become even more difficult if there was an intervening act (of a third party, of nature or of the victim herself) or if the victim had characteristics (physical or otherwise) that meant she was particularly susceptible. In *R* v *Hughes* [2013] UKSC 56 Lord Hughes and Lord Toulson explained that the approach to legal causation may vary depending on the context:

> 20 [. . .] It is trite law, and was common ground before us, that the meaning of causation is heavily context-specific and that Parliament (or in some cases the courts) may apply different legal rules of causation in different situations. Accordingly it is not always safe to suppose that there is a settled or "stable" concept of causation which can be applied in every case

In fact, as we work our way through the case law, we will see that the courts have developed and applied a total of five different principles of legal causation:

Five principles of Legal Causation:

- The voluntariness principle
- The fact of life principle
- The reasonable foreseeability principle
- The operative cause principle
- The thin skull principle

Source: Will Oliver/EPA/Shutterstock

These principles do not always pull in the same direction. In many situations some of these principles will conflict. Two questions for you to consider as we work our way through the relevant case law are: (1) Where there is conflict between these principles why did the courts choose to apply the principle(s) they did? and (2) Have the courts applied the principles in a coherent and consistent way?

ii. Intervening acts of a third party

The general principle is that voluntary intervening acts of a third party break the chain of causation. Suppose that Johann stabs Ludwig. As Ludwig lies on the ground, bleeding heavily, Hans walks up and shoots Ludwig dead. Medical evidence shows that, although Ludwig would probably have died from the stab wound, the fatal injury was the bullet wound. On these facts, the stabbing is not a legal cause of Ludwig's death. The chain of causation was broken by Hans' voluntary intervening act.[23]

The voluntariness principle is regarded as extremely important. As Glanville Williams explains in the following extract, the voluntariness principle is grounded in the principle of individual autonomy (which we studied in Chapter 1).

EXTRACT

Read the following extract.

What is the connection between the voluntariness principle and the principle of individual autonomy?

Williams, G. (1989) 'Finis for Novus Actus?' 48 *Cambridge Law Journal* 391

A person is primarily responsible for what he himself does. He is not responsible, not blameworthy, for what other people do. The fact that his own conduct, rightful or wrongful, provided the background for a subsequent voluntary and wrong act by another does not make him responsible for it. What he does may be a but-for cause of the injurious act, but he did not do it. His conduct is not an imputable cause of it. Only the later actor, the doer of the act that intervenes between the first act and the result, the final wielder of human autonomy in the matter, bears responsibility (along with his accomplices) for the result that ensues.

[…]

The autonomy doctrine, expressing itself through its corollary the doctrine of *novus actus interveniens*, teaches that the individual's will is the autonomous (self-regulating) prime cause of his behaviour. Although this may sound unbelievably metaphysical, the doctrine is supported because it accords with our ideas of moral responsibility and just punishment, and serves social objectives. The first actor who starts on a dangerous or criminal plan will often be responsible for what happens if no one else intervenes; but a subsequent actor who has reached responsible years, is of sound mind, has full knowledge of what he is doing, and is not acting under intimidation or other pressure or stress resulting from the defendant's conduct, replaces him as the responsible actor. Such an intervening act is thought to break the moral connection that would otherwise have been perceived between the defendant's acts and the forbidden consequence.

---

[23] Although Johann would not be guilty of murder, he would be guilty of other crimes: wounding with intent (Offences Against the Person Act 1861, s.18) and perhaps attempted murder.

In *R* v *Pagett* (1983) 76 Cr App R 279 the defendant, 31-year-old David Pagett, formed a relationship with the victim, 16-year-old Gail Kinchen. After several arguments, Gail, who was six months pregnant, left Pagett and moved back home with her mother and stepfather. Pagett armed himself with a shotgun, tracked Gail down, kidnapped her and took her to a block of flats. Police arrived at the scene and told Pagett to surrender and come out. Eventually Pagett came out, using Gail as a human shield. He fired at the police, and two officers instinctively fired back. Gail was hit three times and died. Pagett and the police officers were unharmed.

At trial Pagett was convicted of the manslaughter of Gail. He appealed, arguing that he was not a legal cause of Gail's death. The policemen's act of firing their guns was, he claimed, an intervening act which broke the chain of causation. The Court of Appeal rejected Pagett's appeal, saying that the policemen's actions were not voluntary and so did not break the chain of causation.

EXTRACT

Read the following extract from the judgment of Robert Goff LJ.

Why were the policemen's actions not voluntary?

What did Robert Goff LJ say the word 'voluntary' should normally be understood to mean in this context?

R v *Pagett* (1983) 76 Cr App R 279

Robert Goff LJ

Now the whole subject of causation in the law has been the subject of a well-known and most distinguished treatise by Professors Hart and Honorâ, *Causation in the Law*. Passages from this book were cited to the learned judge, and were plainly relied upon by him; we, too, wish to express our indebtedness to it. It would be quite wrong for us to consider in this judgment the wider issues discussed in that work. But, for present purposes, the passage which is of most immediate relevance is to be found in Chapter XII, in which the learned authors consider the circumstances in which the intervention of a third person, not acting in concert with the accused, may have the effect of relieving the accused of criminal responsibility. The criterion which they suggest should be applied in such circumstances is whether the intervention is voluntary, i.e. whether it is "free, deliberate and informed." We resist the temptation of expressing the judicial opinion whether we find ourselves in complete agreement with that definition; though we certainly consider it to be broadly correct and supported by authority. Among the examples which the authors give of non-voluntary conduct, which is not effective to relieve the accused of responsibility, are two which are germane to the present case, viz. a reasonable act performed for the purpose of self-preservation, and an act done in performance of a legal duty.

There can, we consider, be no doubt that a reasonable act performed for the purpose of self-preservation, being of course itself an act caused by the accused's own act, does not operate as a *novus actus interveniens* [...] Furthermore, in our judgment, if a reasonable act of self-defence against the act of the accused causes the death of a third party, we can see no reason in principle why the act of self-defence, being an involuntary act caused by the act of the accused, should relieve the accused from criminal responsibility for the death of the third party.

[...]

> No English authority was cited to us, nor we think to the learned judge, in support of the proposition that an act done in the execution of a legal duty, again of course being an act itself caused by the act of the accused, does not operate as a *novus actus interveniens* [...] Of course, it is inherent in the requirement that the police officer, or other person, must be acting in the execution of his duty that his act should be reasonable in all the circumstances: see section 3 of the Criminal Law Act 1967. Furthermore, once again we are only considering the issue of causation. If intervention by a third party in the execution of a legal duty, caused by the act of the accused, results in the death of the victim, the question whether the accused is guilty of the murder or manslaughter of the victim must depend on whether the necessary ingredients of the relevant offence have been proved against the accused, including in particular, in the case of murder, whether the accused had the necessary intent.

The definition of voluntary as 'free, deliberate and informed' provides a useful explanation for the decision in the old case of *R* v *Michael* (1840) 9 C & P 356. The defendant wanted to kill her illegitimate baby. She gave the baby's nurse a bottle of poison, telling her that it was the baby's medicine. The nurse decided that the baby did not need any medicine and left the bottle on the mantelpiece. Later, the nurse's five-year-old child took the bottle and gave some to the baby. The baby died and the defendant was convicted of murder. The five-year-old's actions did not break the chain of causation because they were not voluntary. They were not 'free, deliberate and informed'.

A more recent example of the voluntariness principle being applied is *R* v *Rafferty* [2007] EWCA Crim 1846. Joel Taylor, Joshua Thomas and Andrew Rafferty attacked the victim, 17-year-old Ben Bellamy. Taylor and Thomas punched, kicked and stamped on Ben. On a couple of occasions Ben tried to escape, but Rafferty knocked him over to stop him from running away. Rafferty then left the scene of the attack, taking Ben's debit card with him. After Rafferty had left, Taylor and Thomas carried Ben's unconscious body 100 metres to the sea in Swansea Bay, stripped him naked and drowned him in the water.

Rafferty pleaded guilty to robbery. At trial he was also convicted of the manslaughter of Ben. He appealed against the manslaughter conviction, arguing that the actions of Taylor and Thomas had broken the chain of causation. The Court of Appeal agreed. Quashing the manslaughter conviction the Court held that the actions of Taylor and Thomas were voluntary intervening acts which broke the chain of causation.

Although the principle that voluntary interventions of a third party break the chain of causation is well established, it has not been universally applied. In its controversial decision in *Environment Agency* v *Empress Car Co (Abertillery) Ltd* [1999] 2 AC 22 ('*Empress*') the House of Lords held that a third party had not broken the chain of causation even though the third party's actions were free, deliberate and informed. The defendant company in *Empress* had attached a tap to a diesel tank in its yard. The tap had no lock. One day a trespasser entered the yard, opened the tap and drained the entire contents of the tank. The contents poured out and flowed into a nearby river. At trial the company was convicted of causing polluting matter to enter controlled waters.[24] The company appealed against its conviction, arguing that its actions (fixing a tap with no lock) were not a legal cause of the pollution. It argued that the trespasser's actions had broken the chain of causation.

[24] Water Resources Act 1991, s.85(1).

EXTRACT

Read the following extract from the judgment of Lord Hoffmann.

What distinction does he draw? According to this distinction, when will the acts of a third party break the chain of causation? When will they not break the chain of causation?

Environment Agency v Empress Car Co (Abertillery) Ltd [1999] 2 AC 22

Lord Hoffmann

The true common sense distinction is, in my view, between acts and events which, although not necessarily foreseeable in the particular case, are in the generality a normal and familiar fact of life, and acts or events which are abnormal and extraordinary. Of course an act or event which is in general terms a normal fact of life may also have been foreseeable in the circumstances of the particular case, but the latter is not necessary for the purposes of liability. There is nothing extraordinary or abnormal about leaky pipes or lagoons as such: these things happen, even if the particular defendant could not reasonably have foreseen that it would happen to him. There is nothing unusual about people putting unlawful substances into the sewage system and the same, regrettably, is true about ordinary vandalism. So when these things happen, one does not say: that was an extraordinary coincidence, which negatived the causal connection between the original act of accumulating the polluting substance and its escape. In the context of [this offence], the defendant's accumulation has still caused the pollution. On the other hand, the example I gave of the terrorist attack would be something so unusual that one would not regard the defendant's conduct as having caused the escape at all.

So according to Lord Hoffmann's fact of life principle, the actions of a third party will not break the chain of causation if they were 'a normal and familiar fact of life' – even if the actions were free, deliberate and informed, and even if they were not 'foreseeable in the circumstances of the particular case'.

The outcome of *Empress* has been strongly criticised. The defendant company was lawfully storing oil on its own land. Perhaps the company should have taken greater care and locked the tap. But saying the company should have taken greater care to secure the tank is altogether different from saying that it was a legal cause of the pollution. Suppose a supermarket employee carelessly leaves an open till unattended, allowing a customer to steal £100 from the cash drawer. We might describe the employee as careless, but we would not describe the employee as a thief.[25] The customer's voluntary intervening act breaks the chain of causation. In *Empress* the trespasser made a free, deliberate and informed choice to drain the contents of the tank. The principle of individual autonomy tells us that the trespasser, not the company, should be held responsible for the consequences of the trespasser's voluntary choice.

It has been suggested that the House of Lords in *Empress* was influenced by the policy concern to protect the environment. Its strict approach encourages companies to take more stringent measures to safeguard potentially dangerous and hazardous materials. On this view, the fact of life principle set out by Lord Hoffmann should be confined to

[25] Even if the employee had deliberately left the till open so that someone else could steal from it, we would describe them as an accessory to theft, not as a principal (see Chapter 13).

cases involving environmental protection. This view has been confirmed by the House of Lords in *R* v *Kennedy (No 2)* [2007] UKHL 38.[26] Lord Bingham stated:

> 15 Questions of causation frequently arise in many areas of the law, but causation is not a single, unvarying concept to be mechanically applied without regard to the context in which the question arises. That was the point which Lord Hoffmann, with the express concurrence of three other members of the House, was at pains to make in *Environment Agency (formerly National Rivers Authority)* v *Empress Car Co (Abertillery) Ltd* [1999] 2 AC 22. The House was not in that decision purporting to lay down general rules governing causation in criminal law. It was construing, with reference to the facts of the case before it, a statutory provision imposing strict criminal liability on those who cause pollution of controlled waters.

Now, think about this scenario.

On 28 January 2013 footballer Paul Scholes had his top-of-the-range car stolen from his driveway. The car's windscreen was covered in ice, so Scholes left the engine running to melt the ice while he went back inside his house. While he was inside the thief got into the car and drove off in it.

(http://news.sky.com/story/1044488/paul-scholes-car-stolen-while-defrosting (accessed 1 March 2013).)

Were Scholes' actions a factual and legal cause of the theft?

iii. Intervening acts of a medical practitioner

Suppose the defendant injures the victim. The victim receives medical treatment, but the doctor treating her makes a mistake and as a result the victim suffers even greater harm or dies. May the defendant claim that the doctor's error broke the chain of causation?

In situations like this, bad medical treatment will only break the chain of causation in exceptional circumstances. The policy reason for this position is that the victim would not have needed medical treatment had the defendant not injured her. Since the defendant caused the victim to require medical treatment, he can hardly complain about the standard of care she received.

An example is *R* v *Smith* [1959] 2 QB 35. The defendant, Thomas Smith, was a soldier. He took part in a fight with soldiers from another regiment who were sharing the same barracks. During the fight he stabbed the victim twice. A fellow soldier attempted to carry the victim to the medical station, but tripped over a wire and dropped him. He picked him up, went a little further, then dropped him a second time. When the victim arrived at the medical station the medical officer was already trying to deal with some other serious cases and did not appreciate the seriousness of the victim's condition. Specifically, he did not realise that one of the stab wounds had pierced the victim's lung and caused haemorrhage. As a result he ordered treatment that was inappropriate (artificial respiration) and which might well have affected the victim's chances of recovery. An hour after arriving in the medical station the victim died. One of the issues on appeal was whether the chain of causation had been broken by the bad medical treatment and by the victim being dropped on his way to the medical station.

[26] See also Horder, J. (2024) 'Control over land and criminal pollution: *Empress Car* reconsidered' *Criminal Law Review* 230.

EXTRACT

Read the following extract from the judgment of Lord Parker CJ.

Did the bad medical treatment break the chain of causation?

Of the five principles we outlined earlier, which one did Lord Parker CJ apply? In what circumstances will bad medical treatment break the chain of causation?

R v *Smith* [1959] 2 QB 35

Lord Parker CJ

It seems to the court that if at the time of death the original wound is still an operating cause and a substantial cause, then the death can properly be said to be the result of the wound, albeit that some other cause of death is also operating. Only if it can be said that the original wounding is merely the setting in which another cause operates can it be said that the death does not result from the wound. Putting it in another way, only if the second cause is so overwhelming as to make the original wound merely part of the history can it be said that the death does not flow from the wound.

[...]

[I]n the opinion of the court, [the facts of the case] can only lead to one conclusion: a man is stabbed in the back, his lung is pierced and haemorrhage results; two hours later he dies of haemorrhage from that wound; in the interval there is no time for a careful examination, and the treatment given turns out in the light of subsequent knowledge to have been inappropriate and, indeed, harmful. In those circumstances no reasonable jury or court could, properly directed, in our view possibly come to any other conclusion than that the death resulted from the original wound. Accordingly, the court dismisses this appeal.

In *R* v *Smith* the victim died from injuries inflicted by the defendant. But what if the injuries the defendant inflicted were no longer life-threatening by the time of death? In this situation, will bad medical treatment break the chain of causation? This was the issue in *R* v *Cheshire* [1991] 1 WLR 844.

The defendant, David Cheshire, got into an argument with the victim, Trevor Jeffrey, late one night in a fish and chip shop. Cheshire produced a handgun and shot Jeffrey twice, once in the leg and once in the stomach. Jeffrey was taken to hospital and underwent surgery. Afterwards he developed problems breathing, and so a tracheotomy tube was placed in his windpipe. This tube remained in place for four weeks. A few weeks after the tube had been removed, Jeffrey complained of difficulty breathing. He was seen by a number of doctors, who concluded that the reason for his breathing problems was anxiety attacks. However, Jeffrey's condition deteriorated and (more than two months after the initial shooting) he died. At the time of death the original gunshot wounds were no longer life-threatening.

It was later discovered that Jeffrey's windpipe had narrowed near where the tracheotomy tube had been inserted. This was a rare, but not unknown, side effect of tracheotomies. Jeffrey's windpipe had become so narrow that even a small amount of mucus would block it and cause asphyxiation.

At trial Cheshire was convicted of murder. The issue for the Court of Appeal was whether the doctors' failure to diagnose the reason for Jeffrey's breathing problems broke the chain of causation.

EXTRACT

Read the following extract from the judgment of Beldam LJ.

Did the bad medical treatment break the chain of causation?

According to Beldam LJ, when will bad medical treatment break the chain of causation?

R v *Cheshire* [1991] 1 WLR 844

Beldam LJ

[W]hen the victim of a criminal attack is treated for wounds or injuries by doctors or other medical staff attempting to repair the harm done, it will only be in the most extraordinary and unusual case that such treatment can be said to be so independent of the acts of the defendant that it could be regarded in law as the cause of the victim's death to the exclusion of the defendant's acts.

[…]

In a case in which the jury have to consider whether negligence in the treatment of injuries inflicted by the defendant was the cause of death we think it is sufficient for the judge to tell the jury that they must be satisfied that the Crown have proved that the acts of the defendant caused the death of the deceased adding that the defendant's acts need not be the sole cause or even the main cause of death it being sufficient that his acts contributed significantly to that result. Even though negligence in the treatment of the victim was the immediate cause of his death, the jury should not regard it as excluding the responsibility of the defendant unless the negligent treatment was so independent of his acts, and in itself so potent in causing death, that they regard the contribution made by his acts as insignificant.

It is not the function of the jury to evaluate competing causes or to choose which is dominant provided they are satisfied that the defendant's acts can fairly be said to have made a significant contribution to the victim's death. We think the word "significant" conveys the necessary substance of a contribution made to the death which is more than negligible.

In the present case the passage in the summing up complained of has to be set in the context of the remainder of the direction given by the judge on the issue of causation. He directed the jury that they had to decide whether the two bullets fired into the deceased on 10 December caused his death on 15 February following. Or, he said, put in another way, did the injuries caused cease to operate as a cause of death because something else intervened? He told them that the prosecution did not have to prove that the bullets were the only cause of death but they had to prove that they were one operative and substantial cause of death. He was thus following the words used in *Reg. v. Smith [1959] 2 Q.B. 35*.

The judge then gave several examples for the jury to consider before reverting to a paraphrase of the alternative formulation used by Lord Parker C.J. in *Reg. v. Smith*. Finally, he reminded the jury of the evidence which they had heard on this issue. We would remark that on several occasions during this evidence the jury had passed notes to the judge asking for clarification of expressions used by the medical witnesses which showed that they were following closely the factual issues they had to consider. If the passage to which exception has been taken had not been included, no possible criticism could have been levelled at the summing up. Although for reasons we have stated we think that the judge erred when he invited the jury to consider the degree of fault in the medical treatment rather than its consequences, we consider that no miscarriage of justice has actually occurred. Even if more experienced doctors than those who attended the deceased would have recognised the rare complication in time to have prevented the deceased's death, that complication was a direct consequence of the appellant's acts which remained a significant cause of his death. We cannot conceive that, on the evidence given, any jury would have found otherwise.

There is an important difference between *R* v *Smith* and *R* v *Cheshire*. In *R* v *Smith* the physical cause of death was the haemorrhage the defendant inflicted. But in *R* v *Cheshire* the gunshot wounds were healing at the time of death and were no longer life-threatening. The Court of Appeal nonetheless concluded that the defendant's actions were still operative at the time of death. Simester and Sullivan explain that the doctors' error was an omission.[27] The defendant set in motion a chain of events that culminated in the victim's death. The doctors failed to step in and prevent this series of events, but the victim's death was the direct consequence of the defendant's actions: the shooting resulted in the tracheotomy and the tracheotomy resulted in the narrowing of the windpipe. So even if the gunshot wounds were not an operating cause of death, the defendant's actions were.

It is clear from *R* v *Cheshire* that bad medical treatment will rarely break the chain of causation. An example of a case in which the chain of causation was broken is *R* v *Jordan* (1956) 40 Cr App R 152. The defendant, James Jordan, stabbed the victim, Walter Beaumont. Beaumont was taken to hospital and the wound was stitched up. But a few days later Beaumont died. At trial Jordan was convicted of murder and sentenced to death.

Following the trial additional medical evidence became available, which showed that the stab wound had almost healed at the time of death. In order to prevent infection, Beaumont had been given an antibiotic called Terramycin™. After the initial doses Beaumont developed diarrhoea. The doctors concluded that Beaumont was allergic to Terramycin. However, the next day another doctor ordered that administration of the drug be recommenced. Moreover, the amount of the drug the doctor prescribed was 'wholly abnormal'. As a result of being given exceptionally high quantities of a drug he was allergic to, Beaumont contracted pneumonia and died. Quashing Jordan's conviction, the Court of Appeal said that the medical treatment in this case was so bad – the doctor made two errors which were both 'palpably wrong' – that the chain of causation had been broken.

iv. Intervening acts of the victim

To help us work our way through the case law on intervening acts of the victim, we will look at them in **three stages**. First, we will look at **'flight' cases**, then the **self-injection of drugs** and finally **cases involving suicide, assisted suicide or euthanasia**.

a. 'Flight' cases

Our starting point here is *R* v *Roberts* (1971) 56 Cr App R 95. The defendant, Kenneth Roberts, was giving the victim a lift in his car following a party. Here is the victim's account of what happened:

> He just jumped on me. He put his hands up my clothes and tried to take my tights off. I started to fight him off, but the door of the car was locked and I could not find the catch. Suddenly he grabbed me and then he drove off and I started to cry and asked him to take me home. He told me to take my clothes off and, if I did not take my clothes off, he would let me walk home, so I asked him to let me do that. He said, if he did, he would beat me up before he let me go. He said that he had done this before and had got away with it and he started to pull my coat off. He was using foul language [...] Again, he tried to get my coat off, so I got hold of my handbag and I jumped out of the car. When I opened the door he said something and revved the car up and I jumped out.

The victim suffered concussion and grazing.

[27] Simester, A.P., Spencer, J.R., Stark, F., Sullivan, G.R. and Virgo, G.J. (2016) *Simester and Sullivan's Criminal Law: Theory and Doctrine* (5th edn). Hart Publishing: Oxford, p.115.

At trial Roberts was convicted of assault occasioning actual bodily harm. He appealed against his conviction. The issue for the Court of Appeal was whether the victim's act of jumping from the car had broken the chain of causation.

EXTRACT

Read the following extract from the judgment of Stephenson LJ.

What test does he say must be applied to determine whether an intervening act of the victim breaks the chain of causation?

R v *Roberts* (1971) 56 Cr App R 95

Stephenson LJ

[Defence counsel] was wrong in submitting to this Court that the jury must be sure that a defendant, who is charged either with inflicting grievous bodily harm or assault occasioning actual bodily harm, must foresee the actions of the victim which result in the grievous bodily harm, or the actual bodily harm. That, in the view of this Court, is not the test. The test is: Was it the natural result of what the alleged assailant said and did, in the sense that it was something that could reasonably have been foreseen as the consequence of what he was saying or doing? As it was put in one of the old cases, it had got to be shown to be his act, and if of course the victim does something so "daft," in the words of the appellant in this case, or so unexpected, not that this particular assailant did not actually foresee it but that no reasonable man could be expected to foresee it, then it is only in a very remote and unreal sense a consequence of his assault, it is really occasioned by a voluntary act on the part of the victim which could not reasonably be foreseen and which breaks the chain of causation between the assault and the harm or injury.

The Court concluded that the trial judge had not misdirected the jury and so dismissed Roberts' appeal.

So according to *R* v *Roberts*, the reasonable foreseeability principle should be applied to determine whether or not an intervening act of the victim breaks the chain of causation. Only actions which are so daft or unexpected that no reasonable person could have been expected to foresee them will break the chain. A subsequent case, *R* v *Williams & Davis* [1992] 1 WLR 380, provided further guidance. The Court of Appeal in this case said that when applying the reasonable foreseeability test:

> The jury should bear in mind any particular characteristic of the victim and the fact that in the agony of the moment he may act without thought and deliberation.

In *R* v *Roberts* the victim's escape occurred when the defendant assaulted her.[28] What if there is a delay before the victim tries to escape, so that there is time for thought and deliberation? In *R* v *Tarasov* [2016] EWCA Crim 2278 the two defendants were brothers from Lithuania. They attacked the victim, a Polish man named Pawel Pacholak (PP), at around midnight. Pacholak sustained significant injuries and was bleeding heavily. He fled and locked himself in a first floor bathroom. Over an hour

[28] See also *R (on the application of Tracey John-Baptiste)* v *DPP* [2019] EWHC 1130 (Admin), in which the High Court held that, if V suffered fatal injuries after falling from a balcony whilst trying to escape unlawful violence from D, the facts would be capable of supporting a charge of manslaughter.

later, fearing a further attack, he climbed out of the bathroom window. The window was small (50 cm by 60 cm), and was 1.54 m off the bathroom floor. Pacholak fell head-first onto the ground below. Shortly afterwards he collapsed and died. At the Tarasov brothers' appeal against conviction, they argued that Pacholak's actions broke the chain of causation. This was rejected by the Court of Appeal. Citing *R* v *Roberts* and *R* v *Williams & Davis*, the Court held that the victim's actions were within the range of reasonable responses that might be expected from someone in his situation.

EXTRACT

Read the following extract from the judgment of Sharp LJ.

In 'flight' cases like this one, is there is a requirement that the victim feared immediate attack?

What reasons did Sharp LJ give for the Court's conclusion that Pacholak's actions were reasonably foreseeable?

R v *Tarasov* [2016] EWCA Crim 2278

Sharp LJ

35 […] Indeed, the very difficulty of this means of escape, given the size of the window, its height from the floor and the severity of his injuries, was potent evidence in support of the prosecution's case of his state of mind and fear at the time. In our judgment, the mere fact that there may have been a gap between the time when the beating occurred and PP's flight from further assaults through fear was not fatal to the prosecution's case either.

36 We accept that the cases on "flight" to which reference has been made involved "immediacy", in the sense that the assaults and the flight from them were close together in time. However, we can see no logical reason to make this a requirement, provided immediately before the victim sustained the fatal injuries he or she was in fear of being hurt […]. The length of time that a victim of an assault may hide from an attacker, may be relevant, depending on the facts, as to whether the fear of an immediate assault was still operative on the victim's mind when the attempt to escape was made. But the issue is fact specific: and in our judgment, mere length of time between assault and flight, cannot in and of itself fatally undermine a prosecution of this nature.

37 There was ample evidence to support the safe conclusion that the appellants were the perpetrators of the savage beating which PP had suffered before exiting the window. And it was open to the jury to find that his escape was within the range of reasonable responses to be expected from someone in his situation.

38 The [medical evidence], after all, was that PP had been subjected to a very serious assault which had resulted in very serious injury; multiple blows to the head, five areas of injury to the neck and multiple blows to the body, none of which were caused by the fall. There was scientific blood evidence coupled with CCTV evidence that the assault on PP had started outside [the property] and that it had continued inside in the living room. The fact that PP felt driven to escape through a tiny bathroom window on the first floor, notwithstanding the seriousness of his injuries, in the context of the other evidence in the case, entitled the jury to infer that he was in fear of further attack immediately before he exited the bathroom window, and had avoided going downstairs and out through the front door past "the lion's den" as [prosecuting counsel] put it, where he had already been seriously assaulted.

b. Self-injection of drugs

The approach taken in the 'flight' cases *R* v *Roberts* and *R* v *Tarasov* may be contrasted with the approach taken in cases involving self-injection of drugs. During the 2000s a line of cases involving drug abuse caused the Court of Appeal considerable difficulty.[29] All of these involved the same basic facts: the defendant helped the victim to self-inject drugs, the victim suffered an overdose and died. The issue in these cases was whether the defendant's acts of assistance were a factual and legal cause of death.

The issue eventually reached the House of Lords in *R* v *Kennedy (No 2)* [2007] UKHL 38. The defendant, Simon Kennedy, prepared a dose of heroin for his friend Marco Bosque. Bosque injected himself. Soon after Bosque stopped breathing and died. At trial Kennedy was convicted of the manslaughter of Bosque. He appealed, arguing that his acts of assistance were not a legal cause of death since Bosque's act of self-injection broke the chain of causation.

EXTRACT

Read the following extract from the judgment of Lord Bingham.

Did Bosque's act of self-injection break the chain of causation?

Of the five principles we outlined earlier, which one did Lord Bingham apply?

R v *Kennedy* (*No 2*) [2007] UKHL 38

Lord Bingham

14 The criminal law generally assumes the existence of free will. The law recognises certain exceptions, in the case of the young, those who for any reason are not fully responsible for their actions, and the vulnerable, and it acknowledges situations of duress and necessity, as also of deception and mistake. But, generally speaking, informed adults of sound mind are treated as autonomous beings able to make their own decisions how they will act, and none of the exceptions is relied on as possibly applicable in this case. Thus D is not to be treated as causing V to act in a certain way if V makes a voluntary and informed decision to act in that way rather than another.

[...]

18 [...] The finding that the deceased freely and voluntarily administered the injection to himself, knowing what it was, is fatal to any contention that the appellant caused the heroin to be administered to the deceased or taken by him.

So, in *R* v *Kennedy (No 2)*, the House of Lords applied the voluntariness principle, not the reasonable foreseeability principle. Had it applied the reasonable foreseeability principle the outcome may well have been different. It was reasonably foreseeable that Bosque would inject himself with the heroin (in fact, Bosque had asked Kennedy for the heroin saying he wanted it to help him sleep). The House of Lords' conclusion

[29] *R* v *Kennedy (No 1)* [1999] Crim. L.R. 65; *R* v *Richards* [2002] EWCA Crim 3175; *R* v *Dias* [2002] 2 Cr. App. R. 96; *R* v *Rodgers* [2003] EWCA Crim 945; *R* v *Finlay* [2003] EWCA Crim 3868.

that the chain of causation was broken is therefore difficult to reconcile with the insistence in *R* v *Roberts* that intervening acts of the victim only break the chain of causation if they are so daft or unexpected that no reasonable person could have foreseen them.

One way in which the cases might be reconciled would be to say that, in *R* v *Roberts*, the defendant placed the victim in a position where she was forced to react in some way or another, whereas in *R* v *Kennedy (No 2)* 'the victim could have decided not to self-inject; the defendant put no pressure whatsoever on him to do so'.[30] However, this merely raises the question to what extent Bosque's decision to self-inject was truly voluntary:

> [T]o find the victim in *Kennedy (no 2)* – a drug addict craving his next fix – held up as a prime specimen of "free, deliberate and informed" agency will appear no less strange to the ordinary person than to the philosopher, for whom the addict reaching for his drug constitutes a paradigm example of unfree agency (a "wanton" controlled by his desires who just cannot muster the willpower to resist the temptation to take the drug).[31]

The voluntariness-based approach taken in *R* v *Kennedy (No 2)* was followed in *R* v *Rebelo* [2021] EWCA Crim 306. The victim, Eloise Parry, suffered from a personality disorder, depression and the eating disorder bulimia. She went on an eating binge, after which she took four dinitrophenol (DNP) capsules, followed a few hours later by four more DNP capsules. Shortly afterwards, she suffered a cardiac arrest and died. DNP is a chemical that was originally used in the manufacturing of dyes, wood preservatives, explosives, insecticides and other industrial products, but which can act as a fat-burning drug. DNP has not undergone pharmaceutical development and has not been licensed as a medicinal drug. The toxic effects if consumed by a human can include kidney failure, liver failure and cardiac arrest. The defendant, Bernard Rebelo, was well aware of these risks, but nonetheless ran a business selling DNP as a food supplement that was claimed to promote weight loss. Eloise had purchased the capsules she took from Rebelo. At trial, the jury decided that Eloise's decision to take the DNP capsules was not voluntary (it was not free, deliberate and informed) and so Rebelo was convicted of gross negligence manslaughter. Rebelo's appeal against conviction was dismissed by the Court of Appeal. The Court explained that, when deciding whether a decision was free, deliberate and informed, there are a range of factors to be taken into account, including the capacity of the victim and their ability to assess the risk and understand the consequences.[32]

So the capacity of the victim to assess the risk and understand the consequences should be taken into account when deciding whether a decision was free, deliberate and

30 du Bois-Pedain, A. (2021) 'Novus Actus and Beyond: Attributing Causal Responsibility in the Criminal Courts' 80 Cambridge Law Journal S61, S66

31 du Bois-Pedain, A. (2021) 'Novus Actus and Beyond: Attributing Causal Responsibility in the Criminal Courts' 80 Cambridge Law Journal S61, S66. See also Jones, T.H. (2006) 'Causation, Homicide and the Supply of Drugs' 26 Legal Studies 139.

32 For criticism of *R* v *Rebelo*, see Baker, D. (2025) 'Commentary on *R* v *Bah*' *Criminal Law Review* 238, in which Baker argues that Eloise's decision to take the DNP capsules should have broken the chain of causation. Any involuntariness in Eloise's decision, he argues, was caused not by Rebelo but by Eloise's mental illness. Nor did Rebelo have any knowledge of Eloise's mental illness or her inability to resist taking the pills. On this basis, Baker argues that *R* v *Rebelo* should have been distinguished from *R* v *Roberts*, where the victim was compelled to jump from the moving car by Roberts' threat.

informed.[33] What about deceit? Suppose the defendant has an ulterior motive that they have kept hidden from the victim. Can this be taken into account? This was the issue in *R* v *Field* [2021] EWCA Crim 380.

The victim, Peter Farquhar, was a 69-year-old retired teacher. Although he was close to his family and had a wide circle of friends, he was described as lonely and lived alone. The defendant, Benjamin Field, was in his early twenties and was a university student. He set out to exploit Farquhar's vulnerability, seducing him and then moving in with him. Thinking that it was a loving relationship, Farquhar was persuaded to change his will so that Field would receive a large inheritance. Field then began a plan for Farquhar to 'die an alcoholic's death'. He began covertly drugging Farquhar, telling others that Farquhar was drinking too much and having suicidal thoughts. On 25 October 2015, Farquhar died. His body showed a high level of blood alcohol, as well as a small amount of Dalmane (a drug for insomnia, which should not be taken at the same time as alcohol). The prosecution case was that Field had given Farquhar the alcohol and/or Dalmane. At trial, Field was convicted of murder. He appealed, arguing that Farquhar had consumed the alcohol and Dalmane voluntarily and so there was a break in the chain of causation.

EXTRACT

Read the following extract from the judgment of Lord Justice Fulford VP.

When (if at all) can a defendant's undisclosed intention be taken into account when deciding whether an intervening act was free, deliberate and informed?

Lord Justice Fulford VP refers to the example of a weak swimmer. What similarities does he identify between the weak swimmer example and Farquhar's situation?According to Lord Justice Fulford VP, did Farquhar's consumption of the alcohol and Dalmane break the chain of causation?

R v *Field* [2021] EWCA Crim 380

Lord Justice Fulford VP

49. It is accepted by [defence counsel] that a defendant's intention can, in certain circumstances, be relevant to the risk attaching to a course of action. He gave this example. If an accused, for instance, encouraged a weak swimmer to take to the water having promised to provide assistance if the swimmer encountered difficulties, but privately had no intention of doing so and did not do so, the accused could be criminally liable for the

[33] In *R* v *Bah* [2024] EWCA Crim 1499, the defence argued that the voluntariness principle from *R* v *Kennedy (No 2)* and *R* v *Rebelo* should apply. The defendant was from Senegal and was travelling to the UK to seek asylum. He boarded an inflatable boat at Dunkirk that had been organised by traffickers. It had 45 asylum seekers on board. The defendant agreed to steer the boat. On its journey across the English Channel the boat sank. Four people died. Citing *R* v *Kennedy (No 2)* and *R* v *Rebelo*, the defence argued that the victims voluntarily chose to get onto the boat, and this voluntary decision broke the chain of causation between the defendant's actions and the victims' deaths. The Court of Appeal rejected this, distinguishing *R* v *Kennedy (No 2)* and *R* v *Rebelo*. The Court explained that the defendant and victims were 'acting in concert in the same, single episode which ended in the deaths … [T]here was no separate, voluntary act by any of the deceased that could be said to have broken the chain of causation' ([37]). In *R* v *Kennedy (No 2)* and *R* v *Rebelo*, by contrast, the victims' actions were 'entirely separate and distinct' from the acts of the defendant ([41]).

victim's death by drowning in these circumstances. The victim had volunteered to swim on the false assurance of rescue if the need arose. The victim's uninformed state as to the defendant's actual intention would have changed the nature of the act embarked upon and rendered it more dangerous.

[...]

59. The concession made by [defence counsel] in relation to the weak swimmer is both correct in our view and important. As he accepts, the victim's uninformed state of mind in this example as to the accused's real intention would have changed the nature of the undertaking on which the victim embarked, by rendering it more dangerous. The false friend was potentially liable to a conviction for homicide on account of his or her undisclosed intention that the victim should die by not providing assistance in the event of difficulty. This is highly pertinent in the present case. [Defence counsel's] concession also recognises that whether the victim's ignorance of the accused's real intention does relevantly change the nature of the undertaking on which the victim embarks, as in his example, will depend on the specific nature of the individual case. The concession acknowledges, moreover, the appropriateness of the trial judge addressing the nature of the individual case in deciding how to direct the jury. It follows that in situations exemplified by the weak swimmer example, it would be appropriate for the judge to give the jury a direction on causation referable to the victim's knowledge or ignorance of the accused's intentions.

60. The undisclosed murderous intention of the appellant, in our judgment, substantively changed the nature of the undertaking upon which PF [Peter Farquhar] embarked, in this particular case. The jury must have rejected the appellant's account that he was not present when the victim drank this large quantity of whisky which he had supplied. PF, therefore, would have believed that he was drinking 60% proof whisky in the company of someone who loved and would care for him, not someone who wished for his death. As a consequence, PF would not have had an informed appreciation of the truly perilous nature of what was occurring. Being provided with the whisky, he was being encouraged by the appellant to consume a significant quantity of a powerful alcoholic drink, which inevitably would have started to impair his judgment, most particularly as it interacted with the Dalmane. Engaging in this activity was not, as a consequence, the result of a free, voluntary and informed decision by PF. To the contrary, he was being deliberately led into a dangerous situation, as with the weak swimmer, by someone who pretended to be concerned about his safety: as was undisputed on the evidence in the case, the appellant posed as his lover and partner – someone who PF would undoubtedly have assumed would be solicitous of his wellbeing – whereas, in reality, the appellant simply desired PF's demise. The appellant, therefore, manipulated and encouraged PF into a position of grave danger, given the combination of the sedative effects of the substances risked decreasing the levels of the victim's consciousness, thereby fatally impairing his airway. The appellant's undisclosed homicidal purpose, in these circumstances, changed the nature of the act: PF was to a material extent unwittingly lured into a perilous drunken and drugged position by someone who feigned to be his loving partner. Once the effects of the substances started to affect PF's judgment and as he succumbed, the appellant would have been a mere bystander, or worse. He certainly would not have sought medical assistance, given he admitted he wanted to increase the risk of PF dying.

61. It follows we are of the view that the position of the appellant is to be likened to that of the deceived swimmer. It would be open to a jury in either case to conclude that the victims (real and fictional) had been lured into a false sense of security by the accused's undisclosed murderous purpose, embarking as a consequence on a fatal course of action uninformed as to or unaware of the true dangers of the undertaking, so that the deceit was a cause of death.

So, according to the Court of Appeal, since Farquhar was being deliberately led into a dangerous situation and – as a result of Field's deceit – was unaware of the true dangers of the undertaking, his consumption of the alcohol and Dalmane was not free, deliberate and informed and did not break the chain of causation. So, whilst Bosque's self-injection of heroin broke the chain of causation in *R* v *Kennedy* (*No 2*), neither the decision of Eloise to take DNP capsules in *R* v *Rebelo* nor the decision of Farquhar to consume alcohol and Dalmane in *R* v *Field* broke the chain of causation.

The decisions in *R* v *Rebelo* and *R* v *Field* suggest that 'the Court of Appeal is willing to explore the range of the evaluative concept of voluntariness and whether an act is free, deliberate and informed, in order to limit the exculpatory effect of the novus actus principle articulated by Lord Bingham in *Kennedy (No 2)*'.[34] Nonetheless, there are difficulties with the reasoning in *R* v *Field*, as the following extract highlights.

EXTRACT

Sullivan, G.R. & Simester A.P. (2022) 'Deadly Whisky' 138 Law Quarterly Review 11

V knew he was taking whisky from D and must have been aware of its intoxicating effect and the dangers of drinking too much of it. It was assumed, reasonably enough in the light of D's plans and ambitions, that he encouraged V to drink the large quantity of whisky that V consumed. But something encouraged remains something done voluntarily… The danger of drinking so much whisky remains the same irrespective of whether the appellant's purpose that V should die is hidden or revealed.

[…]

Fulford L.J. was very much influenced (see at [61]–[62]) by an example that the appellant had sought, unsuccessfully, to contrast with the present facts. The example was of a weak swimmer lured to her death by drowning, following an assurance from her companion that he would rescue her should she get into difficulty. For Fulford L.J., the undisclosed intention not to rescue demonstrated that the victim's choice to swim was something very different from what she took it to be. She was led to her death by deceit. That is certainly true. What is less clear is the finding that the weak swimmer example was closely analogous to the facts of *Field*. The weak swimmer example involves a positive act of deception with clear causal effect. But there was no comparative deception in *Field*. V agreed to drink the whisky he was given, knowing it was 60% proof. The danger of drinking so much whisky remains the same regardless of whether D encouraged V to drink intending that he should die from its effects or if he gave V that amount of whisky simply because V asked for it. *Kennedy* seemed to settle that, if a substance is taken without any duress and with knowledge of its properties, the taking of the substance is a voluntary intervention that is uncaused by the defendant.

[…]

None of this is to deny conclusively that D should have been convicted of murder. There was another possible route to distinguishing *Kennedy*. Rather than arguing that handing over the deadly whisky was a cause of death, the prosecution might have contended that D satisfied the *actus reus*

[34] Rasiah, N. (2021) 'Homicide: Novus Actus Interveniens' 80 Cambridge Law Journal 213.

when he refrained from helping V after V's life became endangered. That was an omission, done with intent that V should die. Moreover, on the facts of the case, it is plausible that D owed V a duty of care. If we think again about the weak swimmer example, surely the easiest route to convicting her deceptive companion would be by finding a duty to rescue, grounded in an explicit assumption of responsibility for the swimmer's welfare. Arguably, a similar duty of care arose in *Field*.

c. Suicide, assisted suicide and euthanasia

There is further confusion as a result of decisions in cases involving suicide, assisted suicide and euthanasia. Our starting point here is the decision in *R* v *Dear* [1996] Crim LR 595. The defendant, Dear, and the victim, McAuley, were drinking partners. When Dear's 12-year-old daughter claimed that McAuley had sexually assaulted her, Dear tracked McAuley down and slashed him repeatedly with a Stanley knife. McAuley refused to go to hospital. He wiped the wounds with a towel and put plasters on them, which seemed to stop the bleeding. But two days later he died. Medical evidence revealed that one of the cuts had severed a main artery and that McAuley had died from loss of blood from the multiple wounds. A medical expert said that McAuley would not have died if the wounds had been treated properly. A suicide note was found with McAuley's body and evidence was led that McAuley may have deliberately reopened his wounds.

At trial Dear was convicted of murder. Before the Court of Appeal, one of his grounds of appeal was that McAuley's actions had broken the chain of causation.

EXTRACT

Read the following extract from the judgment of Rose LJ.

Did McAuley's actions break the chain of causation?

Of the five principles we outlined earlier, which one did Rose LJ apply?

R v *Dear* [1996] Crim LR 595

Rose LJ

The real question in this case [. . .] was [. . .] whether the injuries inflicted by the defendant were an operating and significant cause of the death. It is immaterial whether some other cause was also operating. It would not, in our judgment, be helpful to juries if the law required them [. . .] to decide causation in a case such as the present by embarking on an analysis of whether a victim had treated himself with mere negligence or gross neglect, the latter breaking but the former not breaking the chain of causation between the defendant's wrongful act and the victim's death [. . .] The correct approach in the criminal law is [. . .]: were the injuries inflicted by the defendant an operating and significant cause of death? That question, in our judgment, is necessarily answered, not by philosophical analysis, but by common sense according to all the circumstances of the particular case . . . In the present case the cause of the deceased's death was bleeding from the artery which the defendant had severed. Whether or not the resumption or continuation of that bleeding was deliberately caused by the deceased, the jury were entitled to find that the defendant's conduct made an operative and significant contribution to the death.

So in *R* v *Dear* the Court of Appeal applied neither the reasonable foreseeability principle nor the voluntariness principle. Instead it applied the operating cause principle. This means that it is difficult to reconcile *R* v *Dear* with both *R* v *Roberts* (since it is arguable that McAuley's actions were not reasonably foreseeable and so broke the chain of causation) and *R* v *Kennedy (No 2)* (since it is arguable that McAuley's actions were voluntary and so broke the chain of causation).

In *R* v *Dear* the victim chose to commit suicide. The subsequent case *R* v *Wallace* [2018] EWCA Crim 690 (as you read in the Introduction) concerned a victim who was unable to commit suicide and so requested voluntary euthanasia. The issue for the Court of Appeal was whether the euthanasia broke the chain of causation. To determine this, the Court had to decide which of the three principles (operating cause, voluntariness, reasonable foreseeability) to apply.

The defendant, Berlinah Wallace, and the victim, Mark van Dongen, had lived together before their relationship broke down. Shortly after the breakdown of the relationship Wallace purchased a one litre bottle of sulphuric acid online. A few days later, at 3 a.m., Wallace woke van Dongen up, said 'If I can't have you, no-one else will', and threw acid in his face. van Dongen suffered terrible injuries. His face, chest and arms were grotesquely scarred. He lost the sight in his left eye and most of the sight in his right eye. His lower left leg had to be amputated. He was in a coma for four months and when he regained consciousness he was unable to move anything except for his tongue. He was in a permanent state of constant physical and psychological pain. After 14 months in hospital he was discharged to a care home with 24-hour support. The care home environment quickly proved unsustainable, so van Dongen's father took his son back to his home in Belgium, where he was admitted to hospital. After arriving in Belgium doctors told van Dongen that he would never regain the use of his arms. This was described by van Dongen's father as the straw that broke the camel's back. van Dongen applied for euthanasia (which is lawful in Belgium in certain circumstances). The application was granted and a month later the doctors in Belgium ended van Dongen's life.

Wallace was charged with murder and with the offence of applying a corrosive substance with intent.[35] At the end of the prosecution case defence counsel made a submission of no case to answer on the murder charge, on the basis that the euthanasia was a voluntary intervening act that broke the chain of causation between the original attack and van Dongen's death. This was accepted by the trial judge. The prosecution appealed against this ruling.

EXTRACT

Read the following extract from the judgment of Sharp LJ.

In the extract Sharp LJ considers whether the voluntariness principle applied to: (a) van Dongen's decision to request euthanasia; and (b) the Belgian doctors' commission of euthanasia. Did the voluntariness principle apply to either of these? Why/why not?

According to Sharp LJ, in what sense was the case: (a) distinguishable from *R* v *Kennedy (No 2)*; and (b) analogous to *R* v *Pagett*?

In [86] Sharp LJ set outs a suggested jury direction. Which principles of legal causation does the direction instruct the jury to apply?

[35] Offences Against the Person Act 1861, s.29.

R v *Wallace* [2018] EWCA Crim 690

Sharp LJ

75 It is undoubtedly the case that, generally speaking, informed adults of sound mind are treated by the law as autonomous beings able to make their own decisions about how they would act, and that a defendant may not be held responsible for the deliberate act of such a person [. . .] In *Kennedy* the accused prepared a syringe of heroin and handed it to B who injected himself, returned the syringe to the accused and died shortly afterwards from the effects of the drug. The House of Lords held that the accused had not "caused" the drug to be administered [. . .] This was because B had, knowing what he was doing, chosen (freely and voluntarily) whether to inject himself or not

76 However, it could be said that the position of the drug addict was not truly analogous to that of Mr van Dongen, any more than it would have been to that of the victims in *Dear, Roberts* and *Williams* or to that of the third party doctors in *Cheshire* and *Smith. Kennedy* was not concerned, as some of those cases were, and the jury could conclude this one is, with a response by a victim to (extreme) circumstances created by a defendant's unlawful act, which were persisting, and which had put the victim into a position where he made a "choice" that he would never otherwise have had to make or would have made (not therefore, as we have already said, the sort of free and unfettered volition presupposed by the *novus actus rule*). In the circumstances, in our view the fact that the Belgian doctors considered Mr van Dongen's decision/request to be "voluntary" for the purposes of the Belgian law on euthanasia does not determine whether his decision was voluntary for the purposes of the different legal issues arising here. To adapt the words used by Sedley LJ to describe the suicide of a worker in *Corr* v *IBC Transport* [2006] EWCA Civ. 331, [2007] QB 46 at para 69 (acknowledging as we do the different context in which they were used) the jury may conclude on the very special facts of this case, that there was nothing that could decently be described as voluntary either in the suffering or in the decision by Mr van Dongen to end his life, given the truly terrible situation he was in.

77 We are not persuaded either that the intervention of the doctors is determinative of the issue of legal causation in the defendant's favour. It is not contentious that it would have been unlawful in this jurisdiction to give Mr van Dongen a lethal injection to end his life [. . .] Keeping one's eye on first principles however, the focus of the inquiry in this case is the defendant's legal responsibility or otherwise for causing Mr van Dongen's death, not that of the doctors (she is charged with murder and they are not). The intervening act(s) occurred in Belgium where they were lawful. Mr van Dongen's father lived in Belgium; and he brought his son from England to Belgium when the care home which his son went to proved to be unsuitable. On the evidence, which we must assume to be established for present purposes, Mr van Dongen decided to ask for euthanasia after he had arrived in in Belgium and realised the overwhelming magnitude and permanence of his disability ("the straw that breaks the camel's back"). This case must be determined on its own particular facts, and not on a hypothetical basis.

78 It is true, as the judge pointed out, that the doctors were under no positive duty to agree to carry out euthanasia (because Article 14 of the Belgium 2002 Act gives scope for those doctors who did not wish to carry out euthanasia the right to refuse to do so). In this connection we should refer to the decision of the Court of Appeal in *Pagett*.

. . .

81 [T]he Court of Appeal held in *Pagett* that an act done in the execution of a legal duty (being an act caused by the act of the accused) does not operate as a *novus actus*

interveniens because as a matter of principle such an act cannot be regarded as a voluntary act, independent of the wrongful act of the accused. However *Pagett* described acts that were *not* to be treated as constituting a voluntary intervening act; the court was not defining the outer limits or boundaries of what *must* be treated as a *novus actus interveniens* in all circumstances. We think it is going too far therefore to say that the fact that the doctors in Belgium were not obliged to carry out Mr van Dongen's wishes, because of the existence of what amounted to a conscience clause in Article 14, precludes a finding by the jury that legal causation is established in this case. On the evidence, the doctors were doing no more than lawfully carrying out Mr van Dongen's wishes. They were acting in accordance with the law. In those circumstances, it seems to us there is little that is meaningful – on the duty issue at least – in the distinction between their conduct and that of the officers in *Pagett* who were surely not obliged to fire at the accused in that case, even if on the facts their conduct in doing so was lawful.

82 Foreseeability was not a feature of the court's decision in *Dear*. Nor was it in *Kennedy*, a point subsequently considered in *R* v *Dean Girdler* [2009] EWCA Crim 2666. In *Girdler* it was decided that there was a need for a test which places an outside limit on the culpability of a driver in circumstances where there is more than a trifling link between the dangerous (or careless) driving and a death in order to avoid consequences which are simply too remote from the driver's culpable conduct. This test where a defendant's case was that there was a new and supervening act or event, was an objective one of reasonable foreseeability (or as reworded for a jury "could [the supervening event] have been sensibly anticipated": see paras 35 and following).

83 We were told that foreseeability was not an issue raised by or before the judge in our case. The following summary by the learned editors of *Smith and Hogan's Criminal Law*, 14th edition, at para 4.5.6 however provides a helpful statement of the principles which may be applied in determining whether an intervening act by a third party or a victim may operate to "break the chain of causation" (see also the *Crown Court Compendium* at para 7.9):

> If despite the intervening event, D's conduct remains a "substantial and operative cause" of the result, D will remain responsible; and if the intervention is by another person, that actor may also become liable in such circumstances. Subject to this, and some exceptional cases the principles appear to be as follows:…(3) In relation to third party interventions, D will not be liable if a third party's intervening act is either: (a) One of a free, deliberate and informed nature (whether reasonably foreseeable or not); (b) If not a free, deliberate and informed act, one which was not reasonably foreseeable…(5) In relation to victims: (a) D will be liable if the victim has a pre-existing condition (which includes, after Blaue, a religious belief) rendering him unusually vulnerable to physical injury… (b) D will not be liable if the victim's subsequent conduct in response to D's act is not within a range of responses that could be regarded as reasonable in the circumstances. Was V's act so "daft" as to be wholly disproportionate to D's act? If so, it will break the chain.

85 It would, as the prosecution say, seem an odd result, if a defendant who paralysed one victim but not another in identical circumstances (so the second could take their own life, but the first could only do so through the intervention of a third party) would be legally responsible for the death of the second victim but not the first. In the event we consider that the jury could conclude on the facts as they were here that the acts of Mr van Dongen and the doctors were not sensibly divisible; that the doctors' (lawful) conduct in carrying out with their hands what he could not carry out with his own was but one link in the chain of events instigated by the defendant and, notwithstanding the intervening act of Mr van Dongen and/or the doctors, the defendant's conduct could fairly be said to have made a significant

contribution to Mr van Dongen's death. We have not lost sight of the issue of self-preservation and the fact that in none of the cases mentioned in *Pagett* was the victim's response one intended to bring about death (however grave the risk taken that it might do so). But in the light of the decision in *Dear* the seeking of death (suicide in that case) as a response to horrific injuries does not preclude the jury finding that the defendant's conduct made a significant contribution to Mr van Dongen's death.

86 The prosecution's appeal is accordingly allowed. A new trial will be ordered. It will be a matter for the trial judge to decide with the assistance of counsel the precise form of directions to give to the jury; and inevitably those directions will be tailored to the way the case has developed, by the end of the evidence. It may be helpful if we say however that we consider this wording or something similar may be appropriate:

Deliberate and unlawful act

1. Are you sure that the defendant deliberately threw acid over Mr van Dongen?

Intention

2. Are you sure that at the time of the attack the defendant intended to kill Mr van Dongen or at least cause him serious bodily harm?

Causation

3. In order to convict the defendant on count 1 you must be sure that the defendant's unlawful act of throwing acid over Mr van Dongen caused his death. This is a question of fact that you should answer using your collective common sense. It is common ground that but for the injuries caused by the acid attack, Mr van Dongen would not have undergone voluntary euthanasia. If you are sure this is the case, go on to ask yourself:

   (a) Are you sure that the defendant's unlawful act of throwing acid over Mr van Dongen was a significant and operating cause of death? The injuries do not need to be the only cause of death but they must play more than a minimal part in causing Mr van Dongen's death. Consider all the circumstances, including the nature and extent of Mr van Dongen's injuries, the passage of time, intervening events, the involvement of the doctors in carrying out the voluntary euthanasia at Mr van Dongen's request, what Mr van Dongen was told and what he said. If your answer is yes, proceed to question 3(b). If you are not sure, your verdict on count 1 will be not guilty.

   (b) Are you sure that at the time of the acid attack it was reasonably foreseeable that the defendant would commit suicide as a result of his injuries? In answering this question consider all the circumstances, including the nature of the attack, what the defendant did and said at the time and whether or not Mr van Dongen's decision to undergo voluntary euthanasia fell within the range of responses which might have been expected from a victim in his situation. If your answer is yes, your verdict on count 1 will be guilty. If your answer is no, your verdict on count 1 will be not guilty.

So according to the Court of Appeal, on the facts of *R* v *Wallace* the voluntariness principle did not apply. Neither van Dongen's decision to request euthanasia nor the Belgian doctors' (lawful) commission of euthanasia was voluntary in the relevant sense. Neither amounted to the exercise of what Sharp LJ described as 'free and unfettered volition' ([76]). Instead the Court held that both the operating cause and the reasonable foreseeability principles should be applied. So legal causation would only be established if the jury concluded that the acid attack made a significant contribution to van Dongen's death, was still operative at the time of death and that at the time of the attack it was reasonably foreseeable that van Dongen might choose to end his life as a result of his injuries.

Now, think about this question.

- Would the outcome of *R* v *Wallace* have been different if van Dongen had remained in England and a doctor had – at van Dongen's request – unlawfully ended his life?

Notice a further difference between *R* v *Dear* and *R* v *Wallace*. In *R* v *Dear* the wounds that Dear inflicted were an operating cause of death in a physical sense. As Rose LJ stated, 'the cause of the deceased's death was bleeding from the artery which the defendant had severed'. By contrast, in *R* v *Wallace* the physical cause of death was not the injuries inflicted by the defendant, but the fatal injection of drugs administered by the Belgian doctors. The prosecution's claim was that the injuries that Wallace inflicted were instead operating in a psychological sense: had it not been for the acid attack, van Dongen would not have suffered the terrible injuries that led him to request that his life be ended.[36] The Court of Appeal accepted that a jury could conclude that legal causation was established in such circumstances.

In the following extract, Simester and Sullivan discuss the Court of Appeal's conclusion in *R* v *Wallace* that the Belgian doctors' commission of euthanasia was not voluntary.

EXTRACT

In *R* v *Wallace* the Court of Appeal stated that there was little meaningful difference between the actions of the police officer in *R* v *Pagett* and the doctors in *R* v *Wallace*. Why do Simester and Sullivan disagree with this?

Why do Simester and Sullivan describe the model direction set out by the Court of Appeal in *R* v *Wallace* as 'quite extraordinary'?

---

36 See also *R* v *Dhaliwal* [2006] EWCA Crim 1139. In this case the defendant had abused his wife physically and mentally for a number of years. In February 2005 she committed suicide. Earlier that evening they had had an argument, during which he struck her on the forehead. Although it was this incident which triggered the suicide, psychiatric evidence suggested that the 'overwhelming primary cause' for the suicide 'was the experience of being physically abused by her husband in the context of experiencing many such episodes over a very prolonged period of time'. The defendant was charged with the manslaughter of his wife, and with inflicting grievous bodily harm on her. At trial the judge held that there was no case to answer. On appeal, the Court of Appeal said that the trial judge's ruling was correct and acquitted the defendant (because, as we shall see in Chapter 6, the psychological harm suffered by the victim fell short of a recognised psychiatric illness). For present purposes, the case is significant because of Sir Igor Judge P's *obiter* suggestion that 'subject to evidence and argument on the critical issue of causation, unlawful violence on an individual with a fragile and vulnerable personality, which is proved to be a material cause of death (even if the result of suicide) would at least arguably, be capable of amounting to manslaughter'.

Simester A.P. & Sullivan, G.R. (2019) 'Causing Euthanasia' 135 *Law Quarterly Review* 21

As Sharp L.J. emphasised at [76], T was responding to circumstances generated by D's unlawful act. The court's analysis in this paragraph introduces a novel qualification to the FDI [free, deliberate and informed] principle as hitherto understood. The intervention by T (or V) must, it seems, not only be free but also "unfettered" by the consequences of D's unlawful act. Of course, Kennedy's act of supplying the drug was unlawful too, but its effect was not to fetter V's choice to self-inject. By contrast, the very driver of V's request to die in Wallace was the ongoing pain and disfigurement caused by D. Nonetheless, the fact that V was driven to seek euthanasia from T does not make T's supervening act non-voluntary. If V had killed himself by, say, jumping from a cliff, the question whether the injuries inflicted by D caused him to do that might receive a different answer. In those circumstances D's moral responsibility for V's death may well align with her causal responsibility for his death. But, of course, V could not jump from a cliff; his injuries left him paralysed. In order to die, he needed to be killed by someone else. That changes everything in causal terms, even if it changes nothing in terms of D's moral responsibility for V's death.

But this novel qualification, that T's act must be unfettered as well as free, is accompanied by an unfortunate conflation. V did not commit suicide, as the court at one point suggests (at [86(3b)]). He was killed by T. The significance of that distinction is dismissed by the court (see especially at [81] and [85]), which assimilates the position of the doctors to that of the police officers under fire in *R.* v *Pagett* (1983) 76 Cr. App. R. 279. Yet the doctors were under no pressure of any kind, let alone the kind of pressure encountered in *Pagett*. Compassion can enable; it does not constrain. It was T's choice to give the injection: there was no obligation to do so. In that respect, the act of injection was a calm, considered, and deliberate act, by contrast to the pressurised and urgent responses demanded of the police in *Pagett*. Either way, however, the question whether T's intervention was free "and unfettered" is one for the jury to adjudicate. For the Court of Appeal to direct that, on the limited facts before it, the FDI possibility should be withdrawn from the jury therefore seems quite extraordinary. A model direction should have required the jury to consider whether T's intervention was free and unfettered; and further direct that if so, the jury should conclude it was T rather than D who caused V's death. Such guidance is entirely within the English tradition, provided it is made clear that the final decision is for the jury and the jury alone.

Following the judgment of the Court of Appeal in *R* v *Wallace* a new trial was held in May 2018. The jury convicted Wallace of applying a corrosive substance with intent but acquitted her of murder. She received a life sentence with a minimum term of 12 years' imprisonment.

v. Intervening acts of nature

Although there is little case law on this point in England and Wales, it is generally accepted that the reasonable foreseeability principle applies when determining whether an intervening act of nature broke the chain of causation.[37]

One case that illustrates this is *R* v *Israr Muhammed* [2021] EWCA Crim 802. The defendant, Israr Muhammed, was driving on the motorway with his wife and three children in the car with him. Muhammed was in the outside lane, racing another car and driving at over 100 m.p.h. when one of his rear tyres burst. The car veered across the carriageway and down an embankment, where it collided with a tree. Muhammed's three-year-old son was killed and his seven-year-old daughter suffered serious and

[37] See, for example, Simester, A.P., Spencer, J.R., Stark, F., Sullivan, G.R. and Virgo, G.J. (2016) *Simester and Sullivan's Criminal Law: Theory and Doctrine* (6th edn). Hart Publishing: Oxford, p.94.

life-changing facial injuries. At trial, Muhammed was convicted of causing death by dangerous driving. He appealed, arguing that the tyre blowout was an intervening act that broke the chain of causation between his dangerous driving and the death of his son. The Court of Appeal rejected this. The tyre that burst was 16 years old (manufacturers and experts recommend replacing tyres after ten years) and had had signs of cracking. Macur LJ explained that 'it may not matter that the specific manner in which the [harm] occurred was entirely unpredictable'. The key point was that 'the general form and risk of further harm was reasonably foreseeable' ([35]).

In a similar vein, if a defendant knocks someone unconscious, then leaves her body on the beach below the high tide mark, there will be no break in the chain of causation when the tide comes in and the victim drowns.[38]

vi. The thin skull principle

Suppose that the victim had some rare and unusual physical condition that made her particularly vulnerable. As a result of this condition, the defendant's actions cause the victim serious harm. Had the victim not had this condition the defendant's actions would not have caused her any harm at all, and the defendant had no way of knowing that the victim had the condition. In these circumstances, may the defendant argue that there is no legal causation?

It has long been accepted that the answer to this question is no. In terms of physical characteristics, the defendant must take his victim as he finds her. This is known as the thin skull principle. An example is *R* v *Hayward* (1908) 21 Cox CC 692. Witnesses heard a violent argument between Hayward and his wife. His wife ran out of the house with Hayward chasing her. She collapsed and died. It transpired that she had an abnormal heart condition. A person with this condition could die from a combination of fright, strong emotion and physical exertion. Ridley J held that Hayward was a factual and legal cause of his wife's death. His wife's rare condition did not negate legal causation; Hayward had to take his victim as he found her.

The question which arose in *R* v *Blaue* [1975] 1 WLR 1411 was whether the thin skull principle should be applied to other, non-physical, characteristics of the victim. The victim in *R* v *Blaue* was an 18-year-old girl named Jacolyn Woodhead. Jacolyn was a Jehovah's Witness. The defendant, Ronald Blaue, stabbed her four times. One of the stab wounds pierced her lung. An ambulance rushed her to hospital, where she was told that she would die unless she received a blood transfusion. In accordance with her religious beliefs, Jacolyn refused the blood transfusion. She died the next day. The issue for the Court of Appeal was whether Jacolyn's refusal broke the chain of causation.

EXTRACT

Read the following extract from the judgment of Lawton LJ.

On what basis did Blaue's counsel (Mr Comyn) argue that Jacolyn's refusal should break the chain of causation? Why did Lawton LJ reject this?

According to Lawton LJ, does the thin skull principle apply to physical and non-physical characteristics, or just physical ones?

[38] Cf. the New Zealand case *Hart* [1986] 2 NZLR 408.

R v *Blaue* [1975] 1 WLR 1411

Lawton LJ

The physical cause of death in this case was the bleeding into the pleural cavity arising from the penetration of the lung. This had not been brought about by any decision made by the deceased but by the stab wound.

Mr. Comyn tried to overcome this line of reasoning by submitting that the jury should have been directed that if they thought the deceased's decision not to have a blood transfusion was an unreasonable one, then the chain of causation would have been broken. At once the question arises – reasonable by whose standards? Those of Jehovah's Witnesses? Humanists? Roman Catholics? Protestants of Anglo-Saxon descent? The man on the Clapham omnibus? But he might well be an admirer of Eleazar who suffered death rather than eat the flesh of swine (2 Maccabees, ch. 6, vv. 18–31) or of Sir Thomas More who, unlike nearly all his contemporaries, was unwilling to accept Henry VIII as Head of the Church in England. Those brought up in the Hebraic and Christian traditions would probably be reluctant to accept that these martyrs caused their own deaths.

As was pointed out to Mr. Comyn in the course of argument, two cases, each raising the same issue of reasonableness because of religious beliefs, could produce different verdicts depending on where the cases were tried. A jury drawn from Preston, sometimes said to be the most Catholic town in England, might have different views about martyrdom to one drawn from the inner suburbs of London. Mr. Comyn accepted that this might be so: it was, he said, inherent in trial by jury. It is not inherent in the common law as expounded by Sir Matthew Hale and Maule J. It has long been the policy of the law that those who use violence on other people must take their victims as they find them. This in our judgment means the whole man, not just the physical man. It does not lie in the mouth of the assailant to say that his victim's religious beliefs which inhibited him from accepting certain kinds of treatment were unreasonable. The question for decision is what caused her death. The answer is the stab wound. The fact that the victim refused to stop this end coming about did not break the causal connection between the act and death.

The policy reasons for this judgment are clear enough: it would be offensive to allow a defendant to stab someone and then accuse them of having unreasonable religious beliefs. However, there are some concerns about the reasoning in *R* v *Blaue*:

- At first, it appears to be inconsistent with the decision in *R* v *Roberts*. Lawton LJ refused to assess the reasonableness of Jacolyn's decision not to have a blood transfusion. In *R* v *Roberts*, on the other hand, the Court of Appeal applied the reasonable foreseeability principle. Stephenson LJ said that if the victim's actions were so daft or unexpected that no reasonable man could have foreseen them they will break the chain of causation. On this approach, Blaue should have had the opportunity to argue that Jacolyn's refusal was so unexpected that it could not have reasonably been foreseen.
- It is possible, however, to reconcile *R* v *Blaue* and *R* v *Roberts*. In *R* v *Roberts* the victim's intervention was an act (jumping out of the car), whereas in *R* v *Blaue* it was an omission (refusal to have a blood transfusion). The cases can be reconciled by saying that the reasonable foreseeability principle applies to intervening acts of the victim, but not to intervening omissions.
- Although *R* v *Roberts* can be distinguished, another problem remains. The Court of Appeal in *R* v *Blaue* did not need to extend the thin skull principle to non-physical characteristics in order to reach the conclusion it did. It could have just applied the

operating cause principle. As we saw in the extract from Lawton LJ's judgment, the 'physical cause of death in this case was the bleeding into the pleural cavity arising from the penetration of the lung'. The stab wound was thus an operating cause of death. The case could have been decided on this basis alone without any mention of the thin skull principle.

- The extension of the thin skull principle to non-physical characteristics was not only unnecessary, it is also potentially far too broad. What about a victim who is irrational, neurotic, vindictive or spiteful? Would the thin skull principle still apply? Since the operating cause principle was sufficient to explain the outcome in *R* v *Blaue*, Lawton LJ's comments about the thin skull principle may be regarded as *obiter dictum* and not binding on future cases

In the following extract, Andrew Simester criticises the reasoning in *R* v *Blaue* for similar reasons.

EXTRACT

Simester A.P. (2017) 'Causation in (Criminal) Law' 133 *Law Quarterly Review* 416

Understanding omissions as non-interventions means their causal significance runs alongside the direct or indirect chains that they fail to prevent. Contra Hart and Honoré, it follows that an omission cannot constitute a *novus actus interveniens*, in the sense that it cannot break the relevant causal chain - precisely because it is the failure to break that chain which is our ground of complaint. To illustrate, consider another example:

Antidote: V is brought to hospital having been poisoned by P. D3, the on-duty doctor, correctly diagnoses V's condition but forgets to administer the standard antidote. V dies of the poison. Had the antidote been administered, V would have recovered.

Of what did V die? The poison. However egregious, D3's omission does not, indeed cannot, break the mechanical causal chain leading to V's death. It cannot break it as a conceptual matter, since it is that very failure to interrupt the causal chain which constitutes D3's omission; one cannot break causal chains by failing to break them. In this case, *both* P and D3 cause V's death. Their contributions are, in effect, concurrent causes.

This explanation is key to understanding the controversial case of *R. v Blaue*. In that case, V, a Jehovah's Witness, was brought to hospital after being stabbed four times by D. Despite having lost a large amount of blood, she refused a blood transfusion on the grounds of her religious beliefs. As she knew she would, V died of blood loss the next day. D appealed his conviction of manslaughter, on the ground that V's refusal to have a blood transfusion was a *novus actus interveniens* that broke the causal chain between the stabbing and V's death. Clearly, the non-transfusion was one cause of V's death. Nonetheless, the Court of Appeal ruled that the original wound inflicted by D remained an operating cause of death. Equally clearly, that ruling was correct. We can trace a straightforward, direct causal chain from the stabbing to V's death.

The court should have left the matter there. Alas, it did not. Counsel for D sought to argue that V's refusal of the blood transfusion was an unreasonable one. In effect, counsel sought to recharacterise the causal path to death as indirect, and thus subject to constraints of foreseeability. Misguidedly, the court met that submission on its own terms, responding that: "It has long been the policy of the law that those who use violence on other people must take their victims as they find them. This in our judgment means the whole man, not just the physical man. It does not lie in the mouth of the assailant to say that his victim's religious beliefs which inhibited him from accepting certain kinds of treatment were unreasonable."

That is not right. There is no legal requirement that we must take a victim's choices as we find them. As is well established by cases such as *R.* v *Roberts*, an intervening reaction by V does break the chain of causation where it is extraordinary (or, as was said in *Roberts*, "daft"). Responses by victims, just like other indirect causal interventions, are subject to reasonable foreseeability criteria. And this means that D does not have to bear responsibility for the consequences of V's choices whatever they may be. D must do so only in so far as V's reaction is a reasonably foreseeable possibility.

The truth of the matter is that *Blaue* did not turn at all on whether V's refusal of the transfusion was "daft" or unforeseeable, because the failure to transfuse blood was an omission. As such, the case presented a straightforward, unbroken mechanical chain from stabbing to death. We may wish that the causal chain had been severed. But an omission cannot, by itself, do that. The failure to transfuse, however unreasonable, could only be a concurrent cause of death.

Now, think about this scenario.

Johann stabs Ludwig. Although he is bleeding heavily, Ludwig refuses to go to hospital. He says, 'I've seen the news stories about hospital patients catching the MRSA infection. I'd rather go home and look after myself.' He staggers home and wraps towels around the stab wound. Two hours later he dies. Medical evidence shows that the cause of death was substantial loss of blood, and that if Ludwig had gone to hospital his life could have been saved. Is Johann a factual and legal cause of Ludwig's death? Which principle(s) of legal causation would you use to justify your conclusion?

Quiz 3.4

1. To prove the defendant was a legal cause of the result, the defendant…

- **a.** must have committed an omission of a substantial nature.
- **b.** must have committed an act of a substantial nature.
- **c.** must be the sole cause of the result.
- **d.** must have made a significant contribution to the result.

2. Why, in the case of *R* v *Pagett*, was the defendant held to be liable for another's death?

- **a.** The policemen's act of firing their guns was not voluntary.
- **b.** The police were not considered negligent.
- **c.** He used his ex-girlfriend as a human shield.
- **d.** He was acting in self-defence.

3. According to *R* v *Cheshire*, medical treatment will only be considered a *novus actus interveniens* if it is…

- **a.** independent and potent.
- **b.** completely independent of D's acts.
- **c.** so independent of D's acts and so potent in causing death as to render D's acts insignificant.
- **d.** a potent cause of death.

4. What were the victim's actions in the case of *R* v *Blaue*?

- **a.** She refused a blood transfusion.
- **b.** She refused to go to hospital.
- **c.** She agreed to undergo medical procedures which failed.
- **d.** She initiated her own attack.

5. The 'thin skull' rule means that…

- **a.** a defendant must take the victim as he or she finds them.
- **b.** a defendant needs to take more care with delicate victims.
- **c.** a defendant will not be held responsible for personal idiosyncrasies of the victim.
- **d.** the jury can decide on an objective basis whether a 'normal' victim would have suffered the level of injury.

Conclusion

When answering a problem question, it is sensible to begin by considering whether the *actus reus* of the crime in question can be established. In this chapter we have studied three important *actus reus* concepts. Figure 3.1 provides an overview.

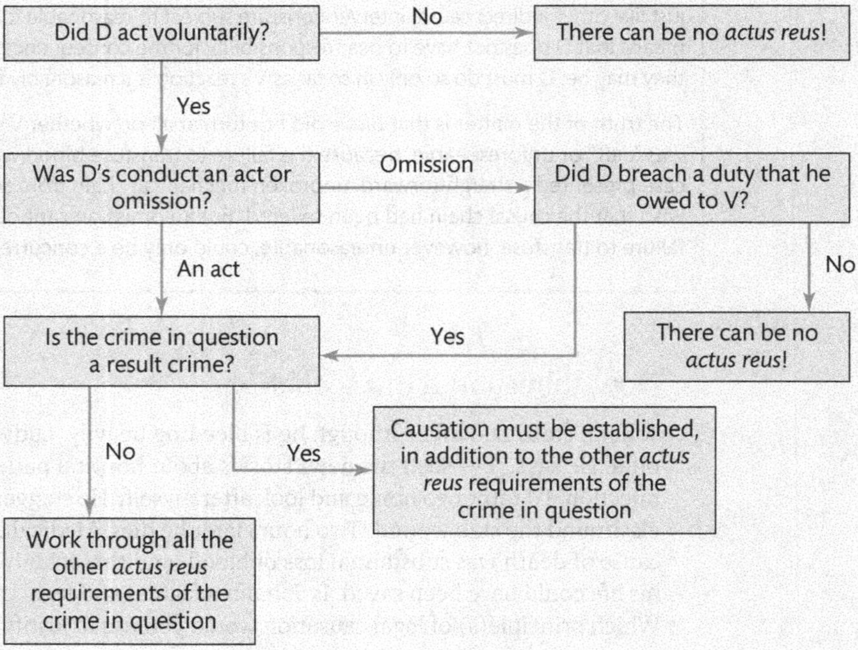

Figure 3.1

If the problem question you are answering raises the issue of the voluntariness of the defendant's behaviour it is logical to discuss this first, since if the defendant acted involuntarily there can be no *actus reus* and therefore the defendant cannot be guilty of the crime.

If the defendant did act voluntarily, next ask yourself whether the relevant conduct constituted an act or an omission. If it was an omission you will need to consider whether the defendant was under a duty to act and, if so, whether he breached this duty. If the defendant's conduct was an omission and he was not under a duty to act, or he did not breach his duty, there is no *actus reus* and the defendant cannot be guilty of the crime.

If the defendant's conduct was either: (1) an act; or (2) an omission which amounted to a breach of his duty to act, the next step is to work through the *actus reus* requirements of the crime in question. If the crime is a result crime, one of the *actus reus* requirements will be causation. To establish causation, you should begin with factual causation and, if this is established, then consider legal causation. For legal causation begin with the significant contribution test. If the defendant's actions did make a significant contribution then consider whether there was an intervening act or whether it is necessary to apply the thin skull principle. If there was an intervening act, determine which type of intervening act it was:

- Intervening acts of a third party: apply the voluntariness principle (*R* v *Pagett*), unless it is a case involving environmental protection where the fact of life principle is likely to apply (*Empress*).

- Intervening acts of a medical practitioner: apply the operating cause principle (*R* v *Cheshire*), unless the medical treatment was so 'palpably wrong' that it supersedes the defendant's actions (*R* v *Jordan*).
- Intervening acts of the victim: apply the reasonable foreseeability principle (*R* v *Roberts*), unless the case has factual similarities to *R* v *Kennedy (No 2)* (voluntariness principle), *R* v *Dear* (operating cause principle) or *R* v *Wallace* [2018] EWCA Crim 690 (operating cause and reasonable foreseeability principles).
- Intervening acts of nature: apply the reasonable foreseeability principle.

Legal causation might seem like a daunting topic, but in fact it offers a good opportunity to showcase your ability to construct legal arguments. For example, when you are considering whether the actions of the victim broke the chain of causation you could write something like: 'The prosecution would use [case name] to argue..., whereas the defence would use [case name] to argue... In my opinion the stronger argument is... because...' This displays the higher-level skills needed to achieve the best marks!

Applying the law

3.5 Apply the law on voluntariness, omissions and causation to hypothetical sets of facts.

Aref, Maryam and Eren

The following scenario takes place on a cliff top and involves the characters Aref, Maryam and Eren. Read the problem scenario carefully, then answer the multiple-choice questions below to apply your learning to the scenario.

Aref is out for an afternoon stroll along the cliff tops with his grown-up daughter Maryam. He is so preoccupied composing a text message on his mobile phone that he doesn't notice a rock in the path. He trips over the rock, falls into Maryam and knocks her off the path and over the cliff edge. At the last moment Maryam manages to grab hold of a branch to stop herself from falling. However, she cannot manage to pull herself up and dangles precariously over the edge. Maryam screams for help, but Aref is worried that he might slip and fall himself and so refuses to help.

Meanwhile Eren, a passer-by, hears Maryam's screams. He runs over, leans down and grabs hold of Maryam's sleeve. But just as Eren is about to pull Maryam to safety he recognises that she is his estranged wife (who had repeatedly cheated on him and made his life a misery). He decides not to help her after all, lets go of her sleeve and walks off. A few minutes later Maryam loses her grip and falls to her death.

a. Could Aref be criminally liable for his refusal to help Maryam? Was his refusal a factual and legal cause of Maryam's death?

b. Could Eren be criminally liable for his refusal to pull Maryam to safety? Was his refusal a factual and legal cause of Maryam's death?

c. How (if at all) would your answers to a and b be different if: Maryam had landed on a ledge unharmed; she was very prone to panic and anxiety and, after waiting for more than two hours, concluded that no one would rescue her and so chose to end her suffering by jumping to her death?

Quiz 3.5

1. The first question here is whether Aref could be criminally liable for his refusal to help Maryam. In *R v Miller* the House of Lords confirmed that generally there is no criminal liability for an omission. So the key issue is whether one of the exceptions to the general rule applies in Aref's case.

   Which of the following is not one of the exceptions to the general rule that there is no criminal liability for an omission?

   a. Easy rescue.
   b. Contractual duty.
   c. Voluntary assumption of responsibility.
   d. Creation of a dangerous situation.

2. Of the various exceptions, the most relevant one in Aref's case is the *R v Miller* principle.

   Which of the following statements summarises the *R v Miller* principle accurately?

   a. Don't go to sleep on a smouldering mattress.
   b. If you create a dangerous situation, you have a duty to counteract the danger you created.
   c. A duty to act may arise even if the defendant is asleep.
   d. If you spot a fire and could easily dial 999 you should do so.

3. Having established that Aref had a duty to help Maryam, the next question is whether he breached this duty. In Aref's case, there are two respects in which Aref may have breached his duty: first, by not pulling Maryam up to safety; and, second, by not calling 999. But remember that the *R v Miller* principle imposes a duty to take steps that 'lie within one's power'. Whilst it was clearly within Aref's power to call 999, whether it was within his power to pull Maryam to safety may be more debatable. It may depend on facts such as: whether he could reach her; whether he was strong enough to pull her up (we are not told Aref's age, for example); and whether he would have been endangering himself.

   Distinguishing between the two respects in which Aref may have breached his duty to act becomes crucial when we move onto the next part of the question: whether Aref's failure was a factual and legal cause of Maryam's death.

   Which of the following is the test that is used to establish factual causation?

   a. The 'operative cause' test: at the time the consequence occurred, were the defendant's actions still an operating cause?
   b. The 'but for' test: but for the defendant's actions, would the consequence have occurred in the same way?
   c. The 'predominant cause' test: were the defendant's actions the predominant cause of the relevant consequence?
   d. The 'culpability' test: was the defendant to blame for the occurrence of the relevant consequence?

4. If we apply the 'but for' test to Aref's failure to call 999, it would seem that this omission was not a factual cause of Maryam's death. Maryam lost her grip after only a few minutes. So even if Aref had called 999, it is unlikely the emergency services would have arrived before she fell. So, but for Aref's omission, Maryam would still have fallen to her death.

   This brings us back to Aref's other failure: his refusal to try and pull Maryam to safety. Some of the factors we have already identified - such as whether he could reach her and whether he had the necessary strength - would also be relevant to the 'but for' test for factual causation. If, for example, Aref could not reach Maryam then his refusal to try and pull her up would not be a factual cause of her death.

   Finally, suppose that: (1) it did lie within Aref's power to pull Maryam to safety; and (2) his refusal to do so was a factual cause of her death. The next step would be to decide whether Aref's failure was also a legal cause of Maryam's death. If Aref could have pulled Maryam to safety, it seems clear that his failure to do so made a 'significant contribution' to Maryam's death (*R v Cheshire*). But did Eren's intervention break the chain of causation?

   Which of the following principles of legal causation did the Court of Appeal apply in *R v Dear*?

   a. The 'operative cause' principle.
   b. The 'reasonable foreseeability' principle.
   c. The 'fact of life' principle.
   d. The 'voluntariness' principle.

5. Moving on to part (b), to decide whether Eren could be criminally liable for his omission, we must again begin by asking whether any of the exceptions to the general rule apply. Given that Maryam is Eren's estranged wife, the first possibility here is the family relationship.

Which one of the following relationships generates a duty to act?

- **a.** Parent–child.
- **b.** Married couples.
- **c.** Brothers/sisters.
- **d.** Grandparents–grandchildren.

6. Since the family relationship exception does not apply, we must instead ask whether Eren voluntarily assumed responsibility for Maryam.

Which of the following statements is incorrect?

- **a.** In *R* v *Sinclair, Johnson & Smith* the Court of Appeal held that Sinclair had voluntarily assumed responsibility for the victim because of their close relationship, the fact Sinclair purchased the drugs, and that Sinclair remained with the victim whilst he was unconscious.
- **b.** In *R* v *Sinclair, Johnson & Smith* the Court of Appeal held that Johnson had voluntarily assumed responsibility for the victim because he owned the flat and he injected the victim with a saline solution in an effort to restore consciousness.
- **c.** In *R* v *Gibbins & Proctor* the Court of Appeal held that Proctor had a legal duty to ensure Nelly was properly fed because she chose to accept money from Gibbins for the purpose of providing food.
- **d.** In *R* v *Stone & Dobinson* the Court of Appeal held that the defendants owed the victim a duty of care because they had allowed her to live in their house, had tried to wash her, had taken food to her and had tried to contact her doc.

7. So, the key issue in part (b) is whether, by leaning over and grabbing hold of Maryam's sleeve, Eren voluntarily assumed responsibility for her. The defence will argue that Eren's actions were insufficient to amount to an assumption of responsibility and draw an analogy with Brian Johnson in *R* v *Sinclair, Johnson & Smith*. The prosecution, on the other hand, will argue that Eren did assume responsibility for Maryam and draw an analogy with James Sinclair and/or the defendants in *R* v *Stone & Dobinson*. Looking at the facts of these cases, in your opinion did Eren voluntarily assume responsibility for Maryam?

If Eren did voluntarily assume responsibility for Maryam, it follows that he had a duty to help her. The two remaining issues will then be: (1) whether or not he breached this duty; and, if so, (2) whether this breach of duty was a factual and legal cause of Maryam's death. These issues are similar to the ones we considered in relation to Aref. If Eren owed Maryam a duty, the duty would have been to take reasonable steps. Whether trying to pull Maryam to safety could be considered as 'reasonable steps' would depend on the facts of the case, including how dangerous this would have been. And whilst failing to try and call for help would certainly amount to a breach of duty, it is doubtful whether the emergency services could have reached Maryam in time – so Eren's failure to call for help would not constitute a factual cause of her death.

Moving on to part (c), the key issue here is whether Maryam's actions broke the chain of causation. The prosecution and defence would each point to different cases and different principles of legal causation. One of the cases the prosecution would point to is *R* v *Dear*. As we saw above, the Court of Appeal in this case applied the operative cause principle. The prosecution would argue that Aref's initial act – knocking Maryam over the edge of the cliff – was still operative at the time of her death. Maryam jumped because she was stuck on the ledge, and she was stuck on the ledge because Aref knocked her over the cliff edge.

This brings us to another of the principles of legal causation.

Which principle did the Court of Appeal apply in *R* v *Blaue*?

- **a.** The 'reasonable foreseeability' principle.
- **b.** The 'voluntariness' principle.
- **c.** The 'operative cause' principle.
- **d.** The 'thin skull' principle.

8. Whilst the prosecution would point to *R* v *Dear* and *R* v *Blaue*, the defence would point instead to *R* v *Roberts* and *R* v *Tarasov*.

Which of the following principles did the Court of Appeal apply in *R* v *Roberts*?

- **a.** The 'reasonable foreseeability' principle.
- **b.** The 'voluntariness' principle.
- **c.** The 'operative cause' principle.
- **d.** The 'thin skull' principle.

Yeong, Voski and Gustav

Yeong, Voski and Gustav are members of a band. One day during rehearsals Yeong starts to argue with Voski. When Voski says, 'I quit', Yeong pushes him as hard as he can. Voski stumbles backwards and knocks over Gustav (who had been telling the pair to 'Calm down'). Gustav lands awkwardly and suffers a broken arm.

Gustav is taken to hospital. His doctor, Josef, fails to read Gustav's notes properly and as a result prescribes Gustav a painkiller to which he is allergic. Although the dose administered would not have harmed most people, Gustav suffers a violent allergic reaction and dies.

Now, think about these questions.

- Could Voski be criminally liable for knocking Gustav over and breaking his arm?
- Were Yeong's actions a factual and legal cause of Gustav's death?

Johann, Ludwig, Hans and Felix

Johann, Ludwig, Hans and Felix are housemates. One day Johann decides to play a practical joke on Ludwig (against whom he has a longstanding secret grudge). He says to Hans, 'I'm playing a joke on Ludwig. I've made him a cup of coffee and put salt in it. Could you take it to him?' Hans finds this very amusing and replies, 'Sure, I can't wait to see him drink it!' In fact, Johann has not put salt in Ludwig's coffee, but a large quantity of a potent laxative. To Hans's surprise, Ludwig drinks the entire cup without saying anything about the taste. Shortly afterwards Johann and Hans leave and go to the pub.

Unknown to his housemates, Ludwig suffers from a rare digestive disorder. An hour after drinking the coffee he starts having severe stomach cramps. Felix comes downstairs to find out what is happening. Ludwig asks him to call an ambulance, but Felix just tells him to stop being a wimp, goes back to his bedroom and shuts the door. Twenty minutes later Ludwig manages to call an ambulance himself. He is rushed to hospital, but soon after suffers cardiac arrest and dies.

Medical evidence later suggests that, if an ambulance had been called 20 minutes earlier, there would have been a slim chance that Ludwig could have been saved.

Now, think about these questions.

- Were Johann's actions a factual and legal cause of Ludwig's death?
- Could Felix be criminally liable for his failure to call an ambulance?

Evaluating the law: Part one

3.6 Evaluate the law on omissions liability.

'The criminal law is right to only impose liability for omissions in exceptional circumstances. Whilst it is possible to justify the existing exceptions to the general rule that there is no criminal liability for omissions, any further extension of these exceptions must be avoided.'

Step 1: Explanation

This question asks you to discuss whether the existing law on criminal liability for omissions is satisfactory. The statement asserts that the existing set of exceptions to the general rule that there is no criminal liability for omissions is sufficient, and that any extension of these exceptions would be unjustifiable. So your essay should consider whether the existing set of exceptions is sufficient, or whether they are too limited in scope.

- Discuss the extent to which you agree with this statement.

Step 2: Critical discussion

In the chapter, you read an extract from Ashworth's article, 'The Scope of Criminal Liability for Omissions', in which he outlined two competing perspectives on omissions liability: the 'conventional view'; and the 'social responsibility view'. The statement in this essay title reflects the 'conventional view'. It asserts that there should only be criminal liability for omissions in 'exceptional circumstances'. To help you consider this claim, look back at the notes you prepared in response to the following questions on Ashworth's article:

- Read the following extract from Ashworth's article. Summarise the arguments in favour of the 'conventional view'. Summarise the counter-arguments of the 'social responsibility view'. Can you think of any additional arguments for either viewpoint?
- Which set of arguments do you find the most convincing?

Once you have decided whether you support the conventional view or the social responsibility view, construct a set of arguments in support of your opinion and work out how you would respond to potential counter-arguments. Try to use case law to support and illustrate the points you wish to make. You may also wish to use other sources (including the piece by Alexander that can be found in the Further Reading list) to supplement your notes on Ashworth's article.You now have compiled all you need for the main body of your essay. The last task is to decide what to include in your introduction and conclusion.

- Construct a set of arguments in support of your views.

Step 3: Introduction and conclusion

The introduction should: (1) contextualise your discussion by briefly outlining the general rule (as stated in *R* v *Miller*) and the existing list of exceptions; and (2) give an indication of the argument you will present in your essay.

Write an introduction that

a. contextualises your discussion by briefly outlining the general rule (as stated in *R* v *Miller*) and the existing list of exceptions; and
b. gives an indication of the argument you will present in your essay.

The conclusion should round off your essay with a succinct statement of your argument and a summary of your supporting reasons.

- Write a conclusion that rounds off your essay with a succinct statement of your argument and a summary of your supporting reasons.

Evaluating the law: Part two

3.7 Evaluate the case law on legal causation.

'Questions of legal causation often involve difficult moral and policy assessments of responsibility. In spite of this, the Courts have managed to formulate a clear set of principles of legal causation which produce consistent and justifiable results.'

Discuss the extent to which you agree with this statement.

Key *actus reus* concepts checklist

Having worked through this chapter, you should now have:

- An understanding of the *actus reus* concept of voluntariness
- An understanding of the general rule that there is no criminal liability for omissions and the exceptions to this rule
- An ability to critically discuss the general rule that there is no criminal liability for omissions and the arguments for and against extending omissions liability
- An understanding of the law governing factual causation and legal causation
- An ability to critically discuss the case law governing legal causation.

Further reading

Alexander, L. (2002) 'Criminal Liability for Omissions: An Inventory of Issues' in S. Shute and A. Simester (eds) *Criminal Law Theory: Doctrines of the General Part*. OUP: Oxford.

Ashworth, A. (1989) 'The Scope of Criminal Liability for Omissions' 105 *Law Quarterly Review* 424.

Dsouza, M. (2021) 'Beyond acts and omissions: Remark-able criminal conduct' 41 *Legal Studies* 1

du Bois-Pedain, A. (2021) 'Novus Actus and Beyond: Attributing Causal Responsibility in the Criminal Courts' 80 *Cambridge Law Journal* S61

Horder, J. and McGowan, L. (2006) 'Manslaughter by Causing Another's Suicide' *Criminal Law Review* 1035.

Jones, T.H. (2006) 'Causation, Homicide and the Supply of Drugs' 26 *Legal Studies* 139.

Simester, A.P. (2017) 'Causation in (Criminal) Law' 133 *Law Quarterly Review* 416.

Answers on the Companion Website

Please visit the companion website for the answers to Key Questions, Quizzes, Applying the Law scenarios as well as student support including glossaries. Please visit www.pearsoned.co.uk/Macdonald

4

Key *mens rea* concepts

Learning Objectives

4.1 Recall the law on the concept of recklessness.

4.2 Analyse the *R* v *Cunningham* test.

4.3 Recall the law on the concept of intention.

4.4 Recall the *R* v *Woollin* direction and the issues surrounding it.

4.5 Formulate proposals for reform of the definition of intention.

4.6 Recall the law on the concepts of knowledge, belief, negligence and strict liability.

4.7 Recall the law on transferred *mens rea*.

4.8 Apply the law on recklessness and intention to hypothetical sets of facts.

4.9 Evaluate the *R* v *Cunningham* test.

4.10 Evaluate the law on the concept of intention.

Introduction: Key *mens rea* concepts

The dividing line between 'guilty' and 'innocent'

Mens rea ladder

Intention

Recklessness

Negligence

No guilty mind

Consider the minimum level of *mens rea* required for the following crimes: murder, attempted murder, wounding, assault occasioning actual bodily harm, and assault. Where would you place each of these on the *mens rea* ladder shown above to show the dividing line between guilt and innocence?

Quiz 4.1

1. Where would you place the dividing line between guilt and innocence, for murder?
   - **a.** Between negligence and no guilty mind.
   - **b.** Between intention and recklessness.
   - **c.** Between recklessness and negligence.
2. Where would you place the dividing line between guilt and innocence, for attempted murder?
   - **a.** Between intention and recklessness.
   - **b.** Between negligence and no guilty mind.
   - **c.** Between recklessness and negligence.
3. Where would you place the dividing line between guilt and innocence, for wounding?
   - **a.** Between recklessness and negligence.
   - **b.** Between intention and recklessness.
   - **c.** Between negligence and no guilty mind.
4. Where would you place the dividing line between guilt and innocence, for assault occasioning actual bodily harm?
   - **a.** Between intention and recklessness.
   - **b.** Between negligence and no guilty mind.
   - **c.** Between recklessness and negligence.
5. Where would you place the dividing line between guilt and innocence, for assault?
   - **a.** Between intention and recklessness.
   - **b.** Between negligence and no guilty mind.
   - **c.** Between recklessness and negligence.

Recklessness and intention

This chapter focuses on the two *mens rea* concepts that we will use most frequently in this text: recklessness and intention. The definitions of these two concepts are extremely important. For many of the crimes that we study in this text, recklessness is the minimum level of *mens rea* that is required. So for crimes like malicious wounding, assault occasioning actual bodily harm, assault and battery, the dividing line between recklessness and non-recklessness is also the dividing line between guilt and innocence. Similarly, liability for some of the most serious crimes turns on the absence or presence of intention. The obvious example is murder. To be guilty of murder, a defendant must have intended to kill or cause serious injury. Anything less than intention – even a high degree of recklessness – will not suffice. The same applies to attempted murder and to grievous bodily harm with intent.

So when we define terms like 'intention' or 'recklessness', what we are doing is drawing the boundaries between different offences and between guilt and innocence. This is what makes *mens rea* such an interesting and challenging topic.

We will examine the law on recklessness and intention in detail, evaluating whether there are ways in which the law might be changed and improved. The chapter then briefly outlines some other *mens rea* concepts – knowledge, belief, negligence and strict liability – before finishing by explaining the doctrine of transferred *mens rea*.

Table 4.1 *Mens rea* concepts

Most blameworthy	Intention	Knowledge
	Recklessness	Belief
	Negligence	
Least blameworthy	Strict liability	

Recklessness

4.1 Recall the law on the concept of recklessness.

There used to be two different tests for recklessness in the criminal law – the *R* v *Cunningham* test and the *R* v *Caldwell* test. But, as we will see, whilst the House of Lords' decision to overrule the *R* v *Caldwell* test was met with almost unanimous approval there remain some lingering doubts about the *R* v *Cunningham* test.

1. The *R* v *Cunningham* test for recklessness

Read the following text to understand the background of *R* v *Cunningham* [1957] 2 QB 396.

In *R* v *Cunningham* [1957] 2 QB 396 the defendant, Roy Cunningham, was engaged to be married. His future mother-in-law lived next door to an elderly couple called Mr and Mrs Wade. The two houses had originally been one house. When they were converted into two houses, a wall had been built in the cellar to divide it into two. The wall was poorly constructed and consisted of rubble loosely cemented together.

The poorly built wall, and the break-in

On the night of the offence, Cunningham broke into his soon-to-be mother-in-law's house.

r.classen/Shutterstock

Money is taken from the gas meter

In the cellar was a coin-operated gas meter. Cunningham ripped the meter off the wall, took some money out and then threw the meter away.

Stephen Barnes/Shutterstock

The gas stop tap is left on

Even though the gas stop tap was only two feet away, Cunningham did not turn it off. As a result a large volume of gas escaped.

Tatiana Kasatkina/Shutterstock

Gas seeps through the wall

Some of it seeped through the poorly built cellar wall into the Wades' cellar, up into the Wades' house and partially asphyxiated Mrs Wade, who was asleep in her bed.

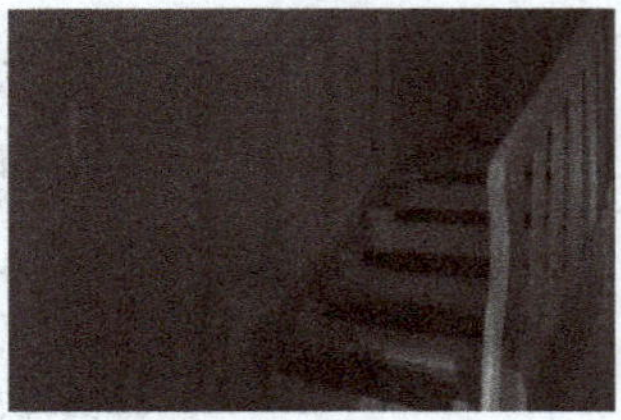

oleksandr biliy/Shutterstock

At trial Cunningham was convicted of an offence under the Offences Against the Person Act 1861.[1] The *mens rea* of this offence required that the defendant acted maliciously. On appeal, Cunningham argued that the trial judge had misdirected the jury on the meaning of maliciously. His appeal was successful and his conviction was quashed. In the course of his judgment Byrne J set out the meaning of recklessness, as well as the meaning of malice.

EXTRACT

In the following extract, how does Byrne J define malice? How does he define recklessness?

R v *Cunningham* [1957] 2 QB 396

Byrne J

[Counsel for the defence cited the following cases: *Reg.* v *Pembliton*, *Reg.* v *Latimer* and *Reg.* v *Faulkner*. In reply, Mr. Snowden, on behalf of the Crown, cited *Reg.* v *Martin*.]

We have considered those cases, and we have also considered, in the light of those cases, the following principle which was propounded by the late Professor C.S. Kenny in the first edition of his *Outlines of Criminal Law* published in 1902 and repeated at p. 186 of the 16th edition edited by Mr. J.W. Cecil Turner and published in 1952: "In any statutory definition of a crime, malice must be taken not in the old vague sense of wickedness in general but as requiring either (1) An actual intention to do the particular kind of harm that in fact was done; or (2) recklessness as to whether such harm should occur or not (i.e., the accused has foreseen that the particular kind of harm might be done and yet has gone on to take the risk of it). It is neither limited to nor does it indeed require any ill will towards the person injured." The same principle is repeated by Mr. Turner in his 10th edition of Russell on Crime at p. 1592.

We think that this is an accurate statement of the law

[1] He was convicted of the section 23 offence (maliciously causing Mrs Wade to take a noxious thing and thereby endangering her life).

Today this is known as the *R* v *Cunningham* test for recklessness. The test has two stages:

- First, did the defendant foresee the risk and choose to take it? The focus here is on what the defendant was thinking at the time. For this reason, you will sometimes see the *R* v *Cunningham* test referred to as subjective recklessness.
- Second, was the risk a justifiable one to take? Although this part of the test is not stated explicitly in Byrne J's judgment, it is widely accepted. Suppose that a surgeon carries out an operation which has a risk of some side effects. The surgeon satisfies the first stage of the *R* v *Cunningham* test because he foresaw the risks involved and went ahead and took them. But the potential benefits and the patient's consent mean that the risk was a justified one to take. Therefore, the doctor does not pass the second stage of the test and did not act recklessly.

An example of the *R* v *Cunningham* test being applied is *R* v *Stephenson* [1979] QB 695. The defendant, a tramp named Brian Stephenson, had a long history of schizophrenia. One day he went to a large straw stack in a field, made a hollow in the side of the stack, crept into the hollow and tried to go to sleep. He felt cold, so he lit a fire of twigs and straw inside the hollow. The stack caught fire. The fire then spread to a hut containing farming equipment and caused £3,500 worth of damage. Stephenson was charged with arson. At trial a psychiatrist gave evidence that, as a result of his schizophrenia, Stephenson may not have had the same ability to foresee risk as a mentally normal person. It was conceivable, the psychiatrist said, that Stephenson lit the fire to keep himself warm without having appreciated the risk of the straw stack catching fire. In spite of this evidence he was convicted. On appeal, the Court of Appeal quashed his conviction. The first stage of the *R* v *Cunningham* test requires that the defendant foresaw the relevant risk. Due to his schizophrenia, it was impossible to say beyond reasonable doubt that Stephenson had foreseen the risk of the fire spreading. Therefore he had not acted recklessly.

So the *R* v *Cunningham* test focuses on one state of mind. It encompasses the defendant who foresees a risk and unjustifiably chooses to take it. The key issue surrounding the *R* v *Cunningham* test is whether it is too narrow. Are there other states of mind which are also sufficiently culpable to be deemed reckless? This was addressed by the House of Lords in *R* v *Caldwell*.

2. The *R* v *Caldwell* test for recklessness

What was the *R* v *Caldwell* test?

In *R* v *Cunningham* the Court of Appeal explained the meaning of the word 'malice'. As we'll see in Chapter 6, this word is used in a number of offences in the Offences Against the Person Act 1861. It was also used in a number of offences in the Malicious Damage Act 1861, a statute which focused on offences against property. Unlike the Offences Against the Person Act 1861 (which is still in force today), the Malicious Damage Act 1861 was replaced in 1971 by the Criminal Damage Act. As we'll see in Chapter 8, instead of using the word 'malice' the Criminal Damage Act 1971 simply uses the words 'intention' and 'recklessness'. The issue for the House of Lords in *R* v *Caldwell* [1982] AC 341 was whether the word 'reckless' has the same meaning under the 1971 Act as it did under the 1861 Acts. By a majority of 3–2, the House of Lords held that it did not.[2] The following extract is taken from the leading judgment of Lord Diplock.

[2] In his dissenting judgment, Lord Edmund-Davies (with whom Lord Wilberforce agreed) stated that the *R* v *Cunningham* test should continue to apply to recklessness under the 1971 Act: 'recklessness involves foresight of consequences, combined with an objective judgment of the reasonableness of the risk taken'.

EXTRACT

According to Lord Diplock, recklessness covers a second state of mind in addition to the one encompassed by *R v Cunningham*. What is this second state of mind? What reasons does Lord Diplock give for saying that recklessness should also encompass this second state of mind?

R v Caldwell [1982] AC 341

Lord Diplock

My Lords, the restricted meaning that the Court of Appeal in *Reg. v. Cunningham* had placed upon the adverb maliciously in the Malicious Damage Act 1861 in cases where the prosecution did not rely upon an actual intention of the accused to cause the damage that was in fact done, called for a meticulous analysis by the jury of the thoughts that passed through the mind of the accused at or before the time he did the act that caused the damage, in order to see on which side of a narrow dividing line they fell. If it had crossed his mind that there was a risk that someone's property might be damaged but, because his mind was affected by rage or excitement or confused by drink, he did not appreciate the seriousness of the risk or trusted that good luck would prevent its happening, this state of mind would amount to malice in the restricted meaning placed upon that term by the Court of Appeal; whereas if, for any of these reasons, he did not even trouble to give his mind to the question whether there was any risk of damaging the property, this state of mind would not suffice to make him guilty of an offence under the Malicious Damage Act 1861.

Neither state of mind seems to me to be less blameworthy than the other; but if the difference between the two constituted the distinction between what does and what does not in legal theory amount to a guilty state of mind for the purposes of a statutory offence of damage to property, it would not be a practicable distinction for use in a trial by jury. The only person who knows what the accused's mental processes were is the accused himself – and probably not even he can recall them accurately when the rage or excitement under which he acted has passed, or he has sobered up if he were under the influence of drink at the relevant time. If the accused gives evidence that because of his rage, excitement or drunkenness the risk of particular harmful consequences of his acts simply did not occur to him, a jury would find it hard to be satisfied beyond reasonable doubt that his true mental process was not that, but was the slightly different mental process required if one applies the restricted meaning of "being reckless as to whether" something would happen, adopted by the Court of Appeal in *Reg. v. Cunningham*.

My Lords, I can see no reason why Parliament when it decided to revise the law as to offences of damage to property should go out of its way to perpetuate fine and impracticable distinctions such as these, between one mental state and another. One would think that the sooner they were got rid of, the better.

[...]

In my opinion, a person charged with an offence under section 1(1) of the Criminal Damage Act 1971 is "reckless as to whether any such property would be destroyed or damaged if" (1) he does an act which in fact creates an obvious risk that property will be destroyed or damaged and (2) when he does the act he either has not given any thought to the possibility of there being any such risk or has recognised that there was some risk involved and has nonetheless gone on to do it. That would be a proper direction to the jury; cases in the Court of Appeal which held otherwise should be regarded as overruled.

Note that the decision in *R* v *Caldwell* applied to the Criminal Damage Act 1971, but not to the Offences Against the Person Act 1861. In other words, following the House of Lords' decision we had one test for recklessness in cases involving offences against people,[3] and a different test for cases involving offences against property. This lacked coherence.

So following *R* v *Caldwell* the word 'reckless' in the Criminal Damage Act 1971 encompassed each of the two states of mind shown in Figure 4.1.

'I foresaw a risk and unjustifiably chose to take it'	'I failed to give any thought to an obvious risk'
Reckless under the *R* v *Cunningham* test and the *R* v *Caldwell* test	Reckless under the *R* v *Caldwell* test only

Figure 4.1

Why was the *R* v *Caldwell* test controversial?

In the previous extract Lord Diplock stated that neither of these two states of mind 'seems to me to be less blameworthy than the other'. He pointed out that there might be blameworthy reasons for a person's failure to give any thought to an obvious risk, such as rage or indifference. But a person might also fail to give any thought to an obvious risk for non-blameworthy reasons. *R* v *Stephenson* is an example. As we saw above, the reason Stephenson did not foresee the risk of the straw stack catching fire was his schizophrenia. Another example is *Elliott* v *C* [1983] 1 WLR 939. The defendant in this case was a 14-year-old schoolgirl. She was of low intelligence and in a remedial class at school. On the evening of the offence she had stayed out all night. At about 5 am she entered a garden shed belonging to the victim, Walter Davies. Inside the shed she found some white spirit, poured this onto the floor and then set fire to it with a match. The shed, which contained tools and paints worth a total of £3,206, was completely burnt down. The defendant was charged with criminal damage. At trial the justices found the following as fact:

- That while the defendant had realised that the contents of the bottle which contained white spirit were possibly inflammable, she had not handled it before and had not appreciated how explosively it would burn.
- That the defendant had given no thought at the time that she started the fire to the possibility of there being a risk that the shed and contents would be destroyed by her actions.
- That in the circumstances this risk would not have been obvious to her or been appreciated by her if she had given thought to the matter.

[3] A decade later the House of Lords in *R* v *Savage & Parmenter* [1992] 1 AC 699 confirmed that the *R* v *Cunningham* test still applied to the crimes contained in the Offences Against the Person Act 1861.

On the basis of these findings she was acquitted. The prosecutor then appealed to the Divisional Court. On appeal, the issue was the meaning of the word 'obvious' in the *R* v *Caldwell* test. Did it mean that the risk would have been obvious to the defendant if she had thought about it? Or did it mean obvious to the reasonable man? Allowing the prosecutor's appeal, the Divisional Court held that it meant obvious to the reasonable man. In his judgment Robert Goff LJ voiced his dissatisfaction with the *R* v *Caldwell* test:

> I [have reached this decision] simply because I believe myself constrained to do so by authority. I feel moreover that I would be lacking in candour if I were to conceal my unhappiness about the conclusion which I feel compelled to reach. In my opinion, although of course the courts of this country are bound by the doctrine of precedent, sensibly interpreted, nevertheless it would be irresponsible for judges to act as automata, rigidly applying authorities without regard to consequences. Where therefore it appears at first sight that authority compels a judge to reach a conclusion which he senses to be unjust or inappropriate, he is, I consider, under a positive duty to examine the relevant authorities with scrupulous care to ascertain whether he can, within the limits imposed by the doctrine of precedent (always sensibly interpreted), legitimately interpret or qualify the principle expressed in the authorities to achieve the result which he perceives to be just or appropriate in the particular case. I do not disguise the fact that I have sought to perform this function in the present case.

In spite of this criticism of the *R* v *Caldwell* test, the House of Lords expressed its approval of the decision by refusing the defendant leave to appeal against her conviction.[4]

The decision in *R* v *G & another*

So the *R* v *Caldwell* test classified as reckless all defendants who failed to give any thought to a risk which would have been obvious to the reasonable man – even if the reason for this failure was a non-blameworthy one such as age or mental incapacity. It was not until more than 20 years later, in *R* v *G & another* [2003] UKHL 50, that the House of Lords overruled *R* v *Caldwell*. The defendants in *R* v *G & another* were two boys, aged 11 and 12. They entered the backyard of a Co-op shop in the early hours of the morning. They found some bundles of newspapers, looked at them and then set fire to them using a lighter. Each of them threw some of the lit newspaper under a large plastic wheelie-bin. They then left the yard without putting out the fire. The wheelie-bin caught fire. The fire then spread to another wheelie-bin, then to the shop wall and guttering, then up into the roof space of the shop. Eventually the roof collapsed and the adjoining buildings all caught fire. Approximately £1m worth of damage was caused. The boys were charged with criminal damage of the buildings and with arson.

At trial the boys said they expected the newspapers to extinguish themselves on the concrete floor. It was accepted as a fact that neither of them appreciated that there was any risk whatsoever of the fire spreading in the way that it did. However, applying the *R* v *Caldwell* test they had acted recklessly. They had failed to give any thought to the risk that the shop would be damaged and this risk would have been obvious to the reasonable man. They were therefore convicted.

---

[4] A similar case is *R* v *Coles* [1995] 1 Cr App R 157, in which the Court of Appeal upheld the trial judge's refusal to admit evidence of the 15-year-old defendant's low mental capacity.

Their appeals against conviction reached the House of Lords. The House of Lords unanimously agreed that *R* v *Caldwell* should be overruled and that the *R* v *Cunningham* test should apply in all cases of criminal damage. The boys' convictions were accordingly quashed.

EXTRACT

In the following extract, Lord Bingham gives four reasons why he believed *R* v *Caldwell* should be overruled. Summarise each of these in your own words. Which of the reasons do you think is the most compelling? Do you disagree with any of Lord Bingham's reasons?

In [37] and [38] Lord Bingham considers the possibility of refining the *R* v *Caldwell* test instead of overruling it. What were the refinements that had been suggested? Why did Lord Bingham reject them?

R v *G & another* [2003] UKHL 50

Lord Bingham

32 First, it is a salutary principle that conviction of serious crime should depend on proof not simply that the defendant caused (by act or omission) an injurious result to another but that his state of mind when so acting was culpable. This, after all, is the meaning of the familiar rule *actus non facit reum nisi mens sit rea*. The most obviously culpable state of mind is no doubt an intention to cause the injurious result, but knowing disregard of an appreciated and unacceptable risk of causing an injurious result or a deliberate closing of the mind to such risk would be readily accepted as culpable also. It is clearly blameworthy to take an obvious and significant risk of causing injury to another. But it is not clearly blameworthy to do something involving a risk of injury to another if (for reasons other than self-induced intoxication: *R* v *Majewski* [1977] AC 443) one genuinely does not perceive the risk. Such a person may fairly be accused of stupidity or lack of imagination, but neither of those failings should expose him to conviction of serious crime or the risk of punishment.

33 Secondly, the present case shows, more clearly than any other reported case since *R* v *Caldwell*, that the model direction formulated by Lord Diplock (see paragraph 18 above) is capable of leading to obvious unfairness. As the excerpts quoted in paragraphs 6–7 reveal, the trial judge regretted the direction he (quite rightly) felt compelled to give, and it is evident that this direction offended the jury's sense of fairness. The sense of fairness of 12 representative citizens sitting as a jury (or of a smaller group of lay justices sitting as a bench of magistrates) is the bedrock on which the administration of criminal justice in this country is built. A law which runs counter to that sense must cause concern. Here, the appellants could have been charged under section 1(1) with recklessly damaging one or both of the wheelie-bins, and they would have had little defence. As it was, the jury might have inferred that boys of the appellants' age would have appreciated the risk to the building of what they did, but it seems clear that such was not their conclusion (nor, it would appear, the judge's either). On that basis the jury thought it unfair to convict them. I share their sense of unease. It is neither moral nor just to convict a defendant (least of all a child) on the strength of what someone else would have apprehended if the defendant himself had no such apprehension. Nor, the defendant having been convicted, is the problem cured by imposition of a nominal penalty.

34 Thirdly, I do not think the criticism of *R* v *Caldwell* [1982] AC 34 expressed by academics, judges and practitioners should be ignored. A decision is not, of course, to be overruled or

departed from simply because it meets with disfavour in the learned journals. But a decision which attracts reasoned and outspoken criticism by the leading scholars of the day, respected as authorities in the field, must command attention. One need only cite (among many other examples) the observations of Professor John Smith [1981] Crim LR 392, 393–396, and Professor Glanville Williams in "Recklessness Redefined" [1981] CLJ 252. This criticism carries greater weight when voiced also by judges as authoritative as Lord Edmund-Davies and Lord Wilberforce in *R* v *Caldwell* itself, Robert Goff LJ in *Elliott* v *C* [1983] 1 WLR 939 and Ackner LJ in *R* v *R (Stephen Malcolm)* 79 Cr App R 334. The reservations expressed by the trial judge in the present case are widely shared. The shopfloor response to *R* v *Caldwell* may be gauged from the editors' commentary, to be found in Archbold Pleading, Evidence and Practice in Criminal Cases, 41st ed (1982), pp 1009–1010, paras 17–25. The editors suggested that remedial legislation was urgently required.

35 Fourthly, the majority's interpretation of "reckless" in section 1 of the 1971 Act was, as already shown, a misinterpretation. If it were a misinterpretation that offended no principle and gave rise to no injustice there would be strong grounds for adhering to the misinterpretation and leaving Parliament to correct it if it chose. But this misinterpretation is offensive to principle and is apt to cause injustice. That being so, the need to correct the misinterpretation is compelling.

[...]

37 In the course of argument before the House it was suggested that the rule in *R* v *Caldwell* might be modified, in cases involving children, by requiring comparison not with normal reasonable adults but with normal reasonable children of the same age. This is a suggestion with some attractions but it is open to four compelling objections. First, even this modification would offend the principle that conviction should depend on proving the state of mind of the individual defendant to be culpable. Second, if the rule were modified in relation to children on grounds of their immaturity it would be anomalous if it were not also modified in relation to the mentally handicapped on grounds of their limited understanding. Third, any modification along these lines would open the door to difficult and contentious argument concerning the qualities and characteristics to be taken into account for purposes of the comparison. Fourth, to adopt this modification would be to substitute one misinterpretation of section 1 for another. There is no warrant in the Act or in the *travaux préparatoires* which preceded it for such an interpretation.

38 A further refinement, advanced by Professor Glanville Williams in his article "Recklessness Redefined" [1981] CLJ 252, 270–271, adopted by the justices in *Elliott* v *C* [1983] 1 WLR 939 and commented upon by Robert Goff LJ in that case is that a defendant should only be regarded as having acted recklessly by virtue of his failure to give any thought to an obvious risk that property would be destroyed or damaged, where such risk would have been obvious to him if he had given any thought to the matter. This refinement also has attractions, although it does not meet the objection of principle and does not represent a correct interpretation of the section. It is, in my opinion, open to the further objection of over-complicating the task of the jury (or bench of justices). It is one thing to decide whether a defendant can be believed when he says that the thought of a given risk never crossed his mind. It is another, and much more speculative, task to decide whether the risk would have been obvious to him if the thought had crossed his mind. The simpler the jury's task, the more likely is its verdict to be reliable. Robert Goff LJ's reason for rejecting this refinement was somewhat similar: *Elliott* v *C*, p 950.

> 39 I cannot accept that restoration of the law as understood before *R* v *Caldwell* [1982] AC 341 would lead to the acquittal of those whom public policy would require to be convicted. There is nothing to suggest that this was seen as a problem before *R* v *Caldwell*, or (as noted above in paragraphs 12 and 13) before the 1971 Act. There is no reason to doubt the common sense which tribunals of fact bring to their task. In a contested case based on intention, the defendant rarely admits intending the injurious result in question, but the tribunal of fact will readily infer such an intention, in a proper case, from all the circumstances and probabilities and evidence of what the defendant did and said at the time. Similarly with recklessness: it is not to be supposed that the tribunal of fact will accept a defendant's assertion that he never thought of a certain risk when all the circumstances and probabilities and evidence of what he did and said at the time show that he did or must have done.

Following the decision in *R* v *G & another,* whenever you come across the word 'reckless' in this text you know that you should apply the *R* v *Cunningham* test!

Now, think about these questions.

a. Lord Bingham gives four reasons why he believed *R* v *Caldwell* should be overruled. Summarise each of these in your own words. Which of the reasons do you think is the most compelling? Do you disagree with any of Lord Bingham's reasons?

b. In [37] and [38] of the extract, Lord Bingham considered the possibility of refining the *R* v *Caldwell* test instead of overruling it. What were the refinements that had been suggested? Why did Lord Bingham reject them?

Quiz 4.1

1. From which of the following cases is the current test of *recklessness* in offences against the person?

- **a.** *Elliott* v *C* [1983.]
- **b.** *R* v *Miller* [1983.]
- **c.** *R* v *Caldwell.*
- **d.** *R* v *Cunningham.*

2. What crime had the defendant in *R* v *Cunningham* committed?

- **a.** Section 24 Offences Against the Person Act 1861.
- **b.** Section 20 Offences Against the Person Act 1861.
- **c.** Section 23 Offences Against the Person Act 1861.
- **d.** Section 18 Offences Against the Person Act 1861.

3. In *Cunningham*, the Court of Appeal held that the term 'malice' covers which two types of *mens rea*?

- **a.** The word should be given its ordinary, everyday meaning.
- **b.** Recklessness and negligence.
- **c.** Recklessness and intention.
- **d.** Intention and negligence.

4. Which of the following statements regarding the case of *Elliott* v *C* [1983] 1 WLR 939 is true?

- **a.** The High Court found the defendant not guilty.
- **b.** *Elliott* v *C* [1983] 1 WLR 939 overruled *Caldwell*.
- **c.** This case was applauded as a good decision.
- **d.** This case highlights the harshness of the *Caldwell* test.

5. What reasons did the House of Lords state for overruling *Caldwell* in 2003?

- **a.** It did not command respect among practitioners and judges.
- **b.** The test was difficult for jurors to understand.
- **c.** Academic lawyers heavily criticised the judgment.
- **d.** All of the other options are correct.

Evaluation of the *R* v *Cunningham* test

4.2 Analyse the R v Cunningham test.

Is the *R* v *Cunningham* test under-inclusive?

Following the decision in *R* v *G & another*, David Ibbetson commented:[5]

> *Caldwell* was a terrible decision, and no lawyer will lament its consignment to the scrap-heap of legal history. It introduced into the criminal law an unprincipled distinction between criminal damage and offences against the person. Its mechanical application led to palpably unjust results, particularly where the defendant was young or educationally sub-normal. And as a piece of statutory interpretation it was shoddy, if not downright shocking. Whatever the threshold for the House of Lords to depart from its own previous decisions, it was comfortably satisfied here. Nonetheless, it would be premature simply to breathe a sigh of relief. For all its faults, *Caldwell* was a genuine response to problems which were perceived to exist in the criminal law in the late 1970s, and not all of these have simply disappeared through the effluxion of time.

The problems which Ibbetson refers to are illustrated by *R* v *Parker* [1977] 1 WLR 600. The defendant, Daryl Parker, had had a bad evening. He had been to a function in London and afterwards caught a train home from King's Cross station. However, he fell asleep on the train and by the time he woke up he had missed his station. He got off the train at the next opportunity, only to be charged the excess fare for travelling beyond his destination. Parker then went to a telephone box outside the station to call a taxi but couldn't get through to the taxi company. Frustrated and angry, Parker slammed the telephone handset down so hard that it smashed. It just so happened that at this moment two police officers were driving past the phone box and saw Parker smash the telephone handset. He was charged with criminal damage.

Importantly, when Parker gave evidence he said, 'It did not occur to me that what I was doing might damage [the telephone]. I was simply reacting to the frustration which I felt.' In other words, Parker claimed that he was so angry that he acted without thinking. He was so angry that the risk of damage to the telephone never crossed his mind.

At trial Parker was convicted of criminal damage. He appealed, arguing that under the *R* v *Cunningham* test he had not acted recklessly. The first stage of the *R* v *Cunningham* requires that the defendant foresaw the relevant risk. Parker claimed that, because he had acted in the heat of the moment and without thinking, he had not foreseen the risk of damage to the telephone. The Court of Appeal rejected this argument and upheld his conviction.

EXTRACT

Read the following extract from the judgment of Geoffrey Lane LJ.

How does he describe Parker's thought process at the moment he damaged the telephone?

---

[5] Ibbetsen, D. (2004) 'Recklessness Restored' 63 *Cambridge Law Journal* 13.

R v *Parker* [1977] 1 WLR 600

Geoffrey Lane LJ

[Parker] was fully aware that what he was handling was a telephone handset made of Bakelite or some such material. He was well aware that the cradle on to which he admittedly brought down the handset was made of similar material. He was well aware, of course, of the degree of force which he was using – a degree described by Mr. Tager [defence counsel] before us as slamming the receiver down and a demonstration by Mr. Tager, whether wittingly or not, was given of a hand brought down from head-height on to whatever the receiving object was.

In those circumstances, it seems to this court that if he did not know, as he said he did not, that there was some risk of damage, he was, in effect, deliberately closing his mind to the obvious – the obvious being that damage in these circumstances was inevitable. In the view of this court, that type of action, that type of deliberate closing of the mind, is the equivalent of knowledge and a man certainly cannot escape the consequences of his action in this particular set of circumstances by saying, "I never directed my mind to the obvious consequences because I was in a self-induced state of temper."

The key assertion here is that deliberately closing your mind to an obvious risk is equivalent to having foreseen the risk. The reasoning goes as follows: in order to be able to deliberately close your mind to an obvious risk, you must be aware that the risk exists; if you are aware that a risk exists, then you have foresight of it; if you have foresight of a risk and unjustifiably choose to take it, then you are reckless under the *R* v *Cunningham* test.

There are obvious policy reasons why it would be undesirable to allow a defendant like Parker to escape criminal liability on the basis that he acted angrily and without thinking. But the strained reasoning employed by the Court of Appeal in *R* v *Parker* suggests that the *R* v *Cunningham* test is too narrow. The test's insistence that the defendant must have foreseen the relevant risk means that, on a literal interpretation, it excludes defendants like Parker and so is under-inclusive. As Ibbetson has remarked:[6]

> At no time did Parker stop and decide not to think whether there was a risk of causing damage. He simply slammed down the receiver. If we believe that Parker should be convicted, and if we are honest in our use of language, we have no choice but to recognise that the purely subjective analysis of recklessness is not in itself enough.

The focus on foresight of risk

In the following extract from her article 'The Foresight Saga: The Biggest Mistake of All', Diane Birch evaluates the primacy that the *R* v *Cunningham* test attaches to a defendant's foresight of risk. She argues that the decision in *R* v *Parker* is at odds with the *R* v *Cunningham* test's insistence on foresight of risk, and that sometimes a defendant's attitude may be a better guide to his culpability than whether or not he had a fleeting awareness of risk.

---

[6] Ibbetson, D. (2004) 'Recklessness Restored' 63 *Cambridge Law Journal* 13.

EXTRACT

Read the extract and think about the following questions.

- Birch argues that the R v Cunningham test is based on the 'informed choice' theory. What is the informed choice theory?
- Why is it difficult to reconcile with the decision in R v Parker?
- What does Birch argue are the advantages of an attitude-based test for recklessness?
- What does she say are the obstacles to an attitude-based test?

Birch, D. (1988) 'The Foresight Saga: The Biggest Mistake of All?' *Criminal Law Review* 4

This takes us to [the assumption in the *R v Cunningham* test] that the presence of foresight is the only legally relevant consideration. In cases where foresight can be established, caring is irrelevant. What if foresight cannot be established, but a reprehensible attitude, such as that D "couldn't care less" what harm he does, is proved? Is that an adequate alternative to foresight?

Two examples suggest that the answer is a qualified "yes". The first concerns a result-crime where D knows all the relevant circumstances from which the reasonable man would have deduced the risk, but claims not to have put two and two together, perhaps in the heat of the moment.

A good example is the pre-*Caldwell* damage case of *Parker*. D, in a temper, banged down a telephone handset onto its cradle. He knew it was made of a lightweight material, and he knew the degree of force he employed, yet he claimed not to have thought about the possibility of damage until it was too late. He had not "chosen" to run the risk, yet he was convicted. The justifications for this outcome vary subtly on appeal from:

1. "if he did not know that there was some risk of damage he was deliberately closing his mind to the obvious." to:
2. "the knowledge or appreciation of risk of some damage must have entered the defendant's mind, even though he may have suppressed it or driven it out."

Both justifications require a re-appraisal of the "choice" model of recklessness, and both appear to accord primacy to the reprehensible attitude of D in refusing to think through the possible consequences of his actions. The difference is that in (1) this refusal appears to be a substitute for foresight, whereas in (2) it is coupled with the notion that, while D may not have calculated the odds and made a cold-blooded choice, nevertheless he must have experienced at least a flash of awareness.

Those who support the view that foresight alone is the test for [*R v Cunningham*] recklessness have attempted to square both (1) and (2) with their thesis; the former more half-heartedly than the latter. (1) is explained in terms of foresight not having to be a matter of instantaneous awareness at the time the act is done; it is enough if D has all the relevant knowledge and could easily bring it to the forefront of his mind if he chose to do so. (2) is explained on the ground that the suppression of the appreciation of risk by D is not an operative part of the fault element which must be proved. Rather it is the case that in [*R v Cunningham*] recklessness generally the flash of awareness is sufficient, whether it is followed by hasty suppression or a more leisurely contemplation of the odds.

Reading these explanations together we conclude that the goalposts have shifted somewhat from the "informed choice" theory, for the information in question may not need to be in the forefront of D's mind at the time, nor need the choice be a meaningful one in the common situation where D acts on the spur of the moment. Indeed in such cases the flash of awareness, if it comes at all, may occur too late, in that he may already be too committed to the action to withdraw from it. To apportion blame in such cases using the detached and reflective language of knowledge of risk and determinat on to run it rings false, and it is preferable to seek a more appropriate formula. But is it better to express it in terms of awareness (actual or potential) or attitude? Let us look at the second example before answering the question.

The second case is the extreme one where D's attitude was such that he would not have been put off by the risk had it occurred to him. The strong moral ground for convicting once led Professor Williams to suggest that attitude alone might, in such a case, prove recklessness, and in *Kimber* the Court of Appeal appears to have adopted the same stance. D was convicted of indecent assault on a mental patient, having raised the defence of honest belief in consent. He conceded that he could see that the woman was mentally unstable because "she kept mumbling", but nevertheless insisted that he thought she was a willing partner. However he admitted "I was not really interested in her feelings at all." His conviction was upheld, notwithstanding the absence of any proper direction on the defence, because:

> "His own evidence showed that h s attitude to her was one of indifference to her feelings and wishes. This state of mind is aptly described in the colloquial expression 'couldn't care less'. In law this is recklessness."

It is possible to explain this statement away on the ground that the point was that D's attitude was relevant only because it was inconsistent with the conclusion he claimed to have reached that his victim was consenting: a view which is supported by the Court's insistence that a direction should have been given tc acquit if D was genuinely mistaken. However it is submitted that the truth which surfaces in *Kimber* is more profound, and is one with which many trial judges would, I believe, associate themselves. If the jury believe that D would have done exactly as he did had he been aware of the risk, what does it matter if, at the time of acting, he did not experience the flash of awareness which would have sealed his fate beyond doubt?

A similar situation may arise regarding recklessness as to a result. Suppose that D, to impress his friends, vaults over a seaside breakwater without looking before he leaps. The seashore is crowded with holiday makers and their possessions, and it is entirely predictable that he will land on something or someone and cause damage or injury. He lands on a sunbather and causes painful bruising. A jury might well find it plausible that the thought of causing such harm never entered D's head, but insofar as his conduct suggests the indifference to others of one who "couldn't care less," and who would have jumped even if he had been fully apprised of the risk, they might well itch to convict him. By what moral principle should they be prevented from doing so?

If the answer is none, then we should have a second means of proving recklessness with an equal claim to recognition along with foresight, and perhaps a superior one, because the attitude of D, if it can be proved, may be a more reliable guide to moral fault than a momentary awareness of risk. The difficulty with preferring a test based on attitude alone is the practical one that the English rules of evidence are not geared to such an inquiry, and would stand in the way of using previous instances of D's off-hand or selfish behaviour in order to demonstrate his indifference to others. Awareness as an indicator, though it may be no easier to prove, has at least the virtue of confining itself to the occasion in question. However it cannot be claimed that for this reason alone it must oust all other considerations and stand in the way of a test in which attitude might also play an active role, although one would not think so judging by the majority of textbooks, cases, and even some statutes on criminal law. It may be that the search for a simple formula for this kind of recklessness has triumphed over the need for a comprehensive one. The extension of recklessness in *Caldwell* can be seen as in part an understandable attempt to bridge this gap.

Antony Duff has also argued that we should move away from a test based on foresight of risk (what Duff calls an 'orthodox subjectivist' test) and instead use a test based on attitude. Duff proposes a test based on 'practical indifference'.

EXTRACT

Read the extract and think about these questions.

- In the following extract, Duff gives an example involving a bridegroom who forgets his wedding. What does he say this example illustrates?
- What does Duff argue is the truth in orthodox subjectivist tests like R v Cunningham? What error does he say these tests make?
- What does Duff argue is the truth in the R v Caldwell test? What error does he say this test made?

Duff, A. (1990) *Intention, Agency & Criminal Liability*. Blackwell: Oxford, pp.163, 165–166

A bridegroom has missed his wedding; he explains to his (ex-)bride that he was in the pub with his friends at the time, and that the wedding just slipped his mind. On the orthodox subjectivist account that explanation should reduce the moral charge against him to one of mere negligence or forgetfulness; his fault is categorically less serious than it would have been had he realized that he was missing his wedding. But his bride would surely (and rightly) be unimpressed by this story: for to forget his wedding (when there was no sudden emergency which might have made even a 'reasonable man' forget his wedding) itself manifests an utter lack of concern for his bride and their marriage. Had he cared at all for her, he could not have forgotten their wedding. The fact that he forgot it shows that he did not care; and that lack of concern, as manifested in his conduct, is the fault for which she rightly condemns him.

This shows how I can be indifferent to what I do not notice. What I notice or attend to reflects what I care about; and my very failure to notice something can display my utter indifference to it. Orthodox subjectivist objections to defining recklessness as indifference may reflect the dualist conception of indifference as an occurrent mental state which is quite distinct from conduct, and therefore irrelevant to criminal liability. But once we reject this dualist distinction between attitude and action, and recognize that an agent's actions can manifest her attitudes as well as her intentions, we can explain criminal recklessness in terms of the practical indifference which the agent's actions display; and we can also see that such practical indifference can be displayed both in conscious risk-taking and in her very failure to notice a risk.

[...]

The truth in orthodox subjectivism is that an agent most clearly display her reckless indifference to a risk in consciously creating it, and that her unawareness of a risk often precludes the ascription of such reckless indifference: its error lies in the claim that only one who consciously creates a risk can be said to be reckless of that risk – that unawareness of risk must always preclude the ascription of recklessness. The truth in *Caldwell* [...] on the other hand, is that the indifference which constitutes recklessness can sometimes be shown in an agent's very failure to notice a risk which her action creates, as well as in her conscious risk-taking. [Its] error lies in [its] suggestion that *any* failure to notice an obvious (and serious) risk created by one's action displays a reckless indifference to that risk: for what matters is not just *that*, but *why*, the agent fails to notice an obvious risk; she is reckless only if she fails to notice it *because* she does not care about it.

So Duff's practical indifference test seeks to rectify both the narrowness of the *R* v *Cunningham* test (by also encompassing those who fail to notice a risk) and the breadth of the *R* v *Caldwell* test (by only encompassing those who fail to notice a risk as a result of reckless indifference).[7]

Now, think about this question.

Should the test for recklessness be changed to one based on attitude, like Duff's practical indifference test? Can you think of any possible objections to Duff's proposal?

In his book *Culpable Carelessness*, Findlay Stark also criticizes the view that culpability should be limited to a choice to take a risk.

EXTRACT

Stark, F. (2016) *Culpable Carelessness: Recklessness and Negligence in the Criminal Law*. Cambridge University Press: Cambridge, p.9

The Exclusive Thesis [the argument that only choices can ground culpability], if accepted, has profound implications for the criminal condemnation of inadvertent, unjustified risk-taking, typically understood as the mark of negligence. If choice is essential to culpability, culpability cannot exist in the absence of a belief that the relevant risk exists, and inadvertent risk-taking seems beyond the criminal law's grasp.

It will be argued that choices are important when it comes to culpability but are not the be-all and end-all of culpability. What is required for culpability is a *suitably* clear demonstration of the defendant's insufficient concern for the interests of others, and the work done so far by theorists to support the Exclusive Thesis does not do enough to show that *only* choices draw a sufficiently clear link between defendants and wrongdoing. The Exclusive Thesis presents an unduly narrow conception of culpability, and what can legitimately be expected of citizens in terms of the formation of beliefs about the risks attendant upon their behaviour.

Stark proposes a belief-centred account of recklessness. Importantly, he states that 'beliefs can *sometimes* be ascribed even when conscious attention is focussed elsewhere'.[8] He offers the example of a parent whose children are having a bath near a plugged-in radio. If the parent moves the radio without thinking, he 'might be ascribed the belief that there is a risk of electrocution if [the radio] is left there even if his conscious attention is focussed on other household tasks'.[9] With this in mind, Stark offers the following definition of recklessness:

---

[7] For critique, see Greenberg, A. (2024) 'Awareness and the Recklessness/Negligence Distinction' 18 *Criminal Law and Philosophy* 351

[8] Stark, F. (2016) *Culpable Carelessness: Recklessness and Negligence in the Criminal Law*. Cambridge University Press: Cambridge, p.8.

[9] Stark, F. (2016) *Culpable Carelessness: Recklessness and Negligence in the Criminal Law*. Cambridge University Press: Cambridge, p.8.

Recklessness: A person is reckless with regard to a risk that a particular piece of conduct will be engaged in, consequence will occur or circumstance will exist (the relevant risk) where he: (i) believed that the relevant risk was connected with his behaviour and (ii) failed to alter his behaviour, in circumstances where this demonstrated insufficient concern for the interests of others. The belief that the relevant risk existed need not be at the forefront of the defendant's mind at the time of acting.

Now, think about this question.

How does Stark's proposal differ from Duff's? If you identified any objections to Duff's proposal, do these objections also apply to Stark's proposal?

Quiz 4.2

1. Which of the following summarises the reasoning in *R* v *Parker* [1977] 1 WLR 600 accurately?
   - **a.** Parker had not acted recklessly under the *R* v *Cunningham* test because he was so angry the risk of the phone breaking never crossed his mind.
   - **b.** A defendant who fails to give any thought to a risk that would have been obvious to the reasonable man should be found to have acted recklessly.
   - **c.** Parker deliberately closed his mind to an obvious risk. This was equivalent to having foreseen the risk.
   - **d.** The value of the damage caused was so minimal that Parker's conviction was quashed.
2. Which of the following is **not** one of the points made by Birch in her article 'The Foresight Saga'?
   - **a.** The rules of precedent meant that the *R* v *Caldwell* test should be favoured over the *R* v *Cunningham* test.
   - **b.** The rules of criminal evidence are not well-suited to a test based on attitude.
   - **c.** A defendant's attitude may be a more reliable guide to culpability than foresight of risk.
   - **d.** It is difficult to reconcile the informed choice theory underpinning *R* v *Cunningham* with the decision in *R* v *Parker*.
3. Which of the following tests for recklessness was proposed by Antony Duff?
   - **a.** A test based on 'gross negligence'.
   - **b.** A test based on 'culpable choice'.
   - **c.** A test based on 'selfish disregard'.
   - **d.** A test based on 'practical indifference'.

Intention

4.3 Recall the law on the concept of intention.

In this section we examine the concept of intention. We begin by distinguishing two types of intention: direct intention and oblique intention (sometimes referred to as indirect intention). We then focus on oblique intention, considering: whether the courts' approach differentiates adequately between oblique intention and recklessness; whether it vests too much discretion in the jury; and options for reform.

First, though, a preliminary point. Many students often ask, 'How can we ever know what someone intended? We're lawyers, not mind-readers!' The answer is found in section 8 of the Criminal Justice Act 1967.

EXTRACT

Section 8 of the Criminal Justice Act 1967

8 Proof of criminal intent

A court or jury, in determining whether a person has committed an offence,

(a) shall not be bound in law to infer that he intended or foresaw a result of his actions by reasons only of its being a natural and probable consequence of those actions; but

(b) shall decide whether he did intend or foresee that result by reference to all the evidence, drawing such inferences from the evidence as appear proper in the circumstances

As paragraph (b) explains, we infer a defendant's intentions 'by reference to all the evidence'. Sometimes this will be straightforward. If Dwayne points a gun at Saalim's head, says 'Say goodbye' and then pulls the trigger, we will have no hesitation in inferring from Dwayne's actions that he intended to kill Saalim. Or, if you spend ten hours a day, seven days a week, revising for your criminal law exam I will have no hesitation in inferring from your actions that your intention is to achieve a good mark in the exam. Of course, there will sometimes be difficult cases. In these cases the jury's job is to look at all the evidence and decide whether they are sure, beyond reasonable doubt, that the intention required for the crime can be inferred.

Two types of intention: direct intention and oblique intention

We have seen that a defendant acts recklessly when he foresees a risk and unjustifiably chooses to take it. Intention also involves a choice: a choice to bring about a result. So, in the previous example, Dwayne intended to kill Saalim because he chose to bring about Saalim's death.

A defendant's choice to bring about a result may take one of two forms:

- The first is where he chooses to bring about a result because he wants it to occur. This is known as direct intention.
- The second is where the defendant may not want the result to occur but acts in the knowledge that it is a virtually certain side effect of his action. This is known as oblique intention.

We will look at each type of intention in turn.

i. Direct intention

Your direct intention is your aim or objective. In our previous example, Dwayne's objective was to kill Saalim. He hated Saalim and he wanted Saalim to die. So killing Saalim was Dwayne's direct intention.

A useful way of testing whether or not a result was a defendant's direct intention is Antony Duff's 'test of failure'.[10] This test simply asks whether the defendant would have regarded himself as having failed if the result did not occur. If Dwayne had pulled the trigger but Saalim had somehow managed to dodge the bullet, Dwayne would not have killed Saalim and would have regarded this as a failure. We can therefore conclude that killing Saalim was indeed his direct intention.

[10] Duff, A. (1990) *Intention, Agency & Criminal Liability*. Blackwell: Oxford, p.61.

Duff's success/failure test is helpful in analysing another example. This time Dwayne wants to give Saalim a shock. He sees Saalim sitting in an armchair in his lounge, near to the window. Dwayne picks up a brick and throws it through the window as hard as he can. On these facts, Dwayne had two objectives which were inextricably linked. First, his ultimate objective was to frighten Saalim. If the brick had smashed the window but Saalim had been totally unfazed, Dwayne would have regarded this as a failure. Second, it was also his objective to smash the window. This objective was purely instrumental – Dwayne only wanted to smash the window in order to frighten Saalim – but it was nonetheless his direct intention. Had the brick simply bounced off the window without smashing it, Dwayne would have regarded this as a failure. So smashing the window was also his direct intention.

So a person may directly intend a result either because it is his ultimate objective or for purely instrumental reasons.

Notice one further point, which is illustrated by the following example.

EXAMPLE

Armed with a sniper rifle, Dwayne is lying in wait for his enemy Saalim (whom he has hated for a long time). Dwayne has never fired a gun before, let alone practised with a sniper rifle. Plus Saalim is a kilometre away, it is windy and Dwayne is so nervous that he cannot hold the rifle steady. He pulls the trigger, doing all he can to try and hit Saalim and kill him.

Was it Dwayne's direct intention to kill Saalim? (Hint: remember to apply Duff's success/failure test.)

Yes, it was Dwayne's direct intention to kill Saalim. If Saalim was not killed, Dwayne would have considered this a failure.

As this example illustrates a person may directly intend a result even if he realises he is very unlikely to succeed.

ii. Oblique intention

Sometimes you may act not wanting a particular result to occur but knowing that it is virtually certain to do so. Suppose you go to the Student Union bar tonight and spend five hours drinking lager, then wine and then vodka. Your direct intention is not to give yourself a terrible hangover tomorrow. You do not want a hangover, and you will actually be pleasantly surprised if you wake up tomorrow feeling fine. But at the same time you realise that a hangover is the virtually certain consequence of your actions. On these facts, you obliquely intend to have a hangover tomorrow since you realise it is the virtually certain consequence of your actions.

A key point to grasp here is the difference between this example and the earlier one involving Dwayne smashing Saalim's window. The two examples are similar, in that both involve consequences which are inextricably linked. In Dwayne's example smashing the window was inextricably linked to his ultimate objective, frightening Saalim. In the Student Union bar example, tomorrow's hangover is inextricably linked to tonight's heavy alcohol consumption. The difference between them is that Dwayne wanted the window to smash (so smashing the window was his direct intention), whereas you did not want tomorrow's hangover (so having the hangover was your oblique intention).

With this distinction in mind, consider the following example.

Dwayne is about to stand trial fcr terrorism offences. A world-renowned lawyer, Saalim, is flying to London to act as prosecutor in Dwayne's case. Saalim has spent months examining the evidence and preparing the case aWgainst Dwayne. Dwayne puts a bomb on board the plane that is bringing Saalim to London. Dwayne wants Saalim to die but hopes that, by some miracle, the pilot Tariq will survive.

Is killing Saalim Dwayne's direct or oblique intention? Is killing Tariq Dwayne's direct or oblique intention?

Whilst killing Saalim was Dwayne's direct intention (he would have regarded it as a failure had Saalim not been killed), killing Tariq was his oblique intention (he did not want Tariq to die but realised that this was a virtually certain consequence of his actions).

This example illustrates why we need a category of oblique intention as well as direct intention. If we only had a category of direct intention Dwayne would be guilty of murdering Saalim, but not Tariq. This would be unacceptable. Even though Dwayne did not desire Tariq's death, he still *chose* to kill Tariq, just as he *chose* to kill Saalim.

In cases involving oblique intention we do not use Duff's success/failure test. Instead we use the following direction, which was set out by the House of Lords in R v *Woollin* [1999] 1 AC 82:

> Where the charge is murder and in the rare cases where the simple direction is not enough, the jury should be directed that they are not entitled to find the necessary intention, unless they feel sure that death or serious bodily harm was a virtual certainty (barring some unforeseen intervention) as a result of the defendant's actions and that the defendant appreciated that such was the case

So a jury are 'entitled to find' oblique intention if two conditions are satisfied: **(i) the result in question was a 'virtual certainty' (barring some unforeseen intervention); and (ii) the defendant realised this.**

Note the following four points about this direction:

- If either of the two conditions is not satisfied, the jury may *not* find oblique intention.
- If both conditions are satisfied, the jury are *entitled* to find oblique intention but are not obliged to do so. In other words, the jury has some discretion and may decide that, even though both conditions are satisfied, there was no oblique intention. This was confirmed by the Court of Appeal in *R* v *Matthews & Alleyne* [2003] EWCA Crim 192.
- The jury should only be given the *R* v *Woollin* direction if it is necessary to do so, on the basis of the facts of the particular case before them. So in a problem question always begin with direct intention, and only consider oblique intention if it is necessary to do so.
- *R* v *Woollin* was a murder case, and so the extract above refers to 'death or serious bodily harm'. In cases involving other offences the wording should be adapted accordingly.

ACTIVITY

Dwayne hides a bomb on a busy high street. Two hours before the bomb is set to explode, he gives a telephone warning to enable the surrounding area to be evacuated. He knows that a bomb disposal squad will attempt to defuse the bomb, and he expects them to succeed. In fact, however, the bomb explodes and a member of the bomb disposal squad is killed.

Afterwards Dwayne states that he expected the publicity generated by the bomb to draw attention to his cause. He explains that he gave the warning because he did not want anyone to suffer injury, since he feared that if this were to happen he would lose public support.

Did Dwayne intend (either directly or obliquely) to kill? How would your answer be different if he had given a deliberately unclear warning just 90 seconds before the bomb was due to explode?

It was not Dwayne's direct intention to kill. He did not want anyone to suffer injury, and so would not have regarded it as a failure if no one had been killed.

Nor was it Dwayne's oblique intention to kill. There was a chance that the bomb would be defused successfully, and so it was not a virtual certainty that people would be killed. If the warning had been unclear, and given only 90 seconds before the bomb was due to explode, then we might doubt the truth of Dwayne's assertion that he did not want to injure anyone and conclude that it was his direct intention to kill.

Quiz 4.3

1. What level of certainty must a defendant have if it is said that he or she has oblique intention to commit a crime?
   - **a.** Totally certain.
   - **b.** Highly certain.
   - **c.** Fairly certain.
   - **d.** Virtually certain.
2. When should a trial judge give the *R* v *Woollin* direction to a jury?
   - **a.** In any case in which the defendant may not have desired the result of his act.
   - **b.** At the trial judge's absolute discretion.
   - **c.** In every case where proof of dishonesty is in issue.
   - **d.** In every case where proof of an intention to bring about a prohibited result is in issue.
3. What is the difference between direct intention and oblique intention?
   - **a.** Direct intention is a choice to take an unjustified risk; oblique intention is a choice to bring about a result.
   - **b.** Your direct intention is your purpose; you obliquely intend results that you realise are a virtually certain consequence of your actions.
   - **c.** Direct intention is a choice to bring about a result; oblique intention is a choice to take an unjustified risk.
   - **d.** Direct intention is virtually certain consequences of your action; oblique intention is your purpose.

The distinction between oblique intention and recklessness

4.4 Recall the *R* v *Woollin* direction and the issues surrounding it.

In the remainder of this section we are going to examine the *R* v *Woollin* direction more carefully. There are two key issues for us to consider: first, whether the *R* v *Woollin* direction succeeds in drawing a clear dividing line between oblique intention and recklessness; and, second, whether the *R* v *Woollin* direction is correct to vest some discretion in the jury. Finally, we will look at proposals for reform.

So far we have seen that there is an important conceptual distinction between intention and recklessness. A defendant acts intentionally when he chooses to bring about a result, whereas he acts recklessly when he foresees a risk that the result will occur and unjustifiably chooses to take that risk. As we will see in the next chapter, this distinction is particularly important in the law of homicide. Only intention suffices for the *mens rea* of murder. A defendant who recklessly caused death will be convicted of manslaughter, not murder. So the dividing line between intention and recklessness is important because it is also the dividing line between murder and manslaughter. However, devising a definition of oblique intention that clearly distinguishes it from recklessness is far from easy. This is demonstrated by the following example.

EXAMPLE

Dwayne owns a two-bedroom house, which he shares with his lodger Saalim. Dwayne is behind with his mortgage payments and so decides to set fire to the house and then make an insurance claim. Even though Dwayne does not want Saalim to suffer any harm, he sets fire to the house knowing that Saalim is inside. Saalim is killed in the fire.

Did Dwayne: (a) have an oblique intention to kill Saalim; or (b) kill Saalim recklessly if, when he set fire to the house, Dwayne realised:

- **there was a 100 per cent chance Saalim would be killed?**
- **there was a 50 per cent chance Saalim would be killed?**
- **there was a 90 per cent chance Saalim would be killed?**

The first of these three alternatives is straightforward. Dwayne may not have wanted Saalim to die (so killing Saalim was not his direct intention), but he chose to set fire to the house knowing that Saalim's death was an inevitable consequence of his actions. The two conditions in the R v Woollin direction are satisfied and a jury would be entitled to find that Dwayne had an oblique intention to kill Saalim.

In the second alternative, by contrast, Saalim's death was far from inevitable. Although there was a 50 per cent chance Saalim would be killed, there was an equal chance he would survive. So what Dwayne did was take an unjustified risk that Saalim would be killed. In other words, he acted recklessly.

So somewhere between the first and second alternatives lies the dividing line between oblique intention and recklessness. The question is, where? The R v Woollin direction says that recklessness becomes oblique intention when the risk stops being merely a risk and becomes a virtual certainty. But how likely must a consequence be for it to stop being just a risk and become a virtual certainty? In the third alternative, there was a 90 per cent chance Saalim would be killed. Is something that is 90 per cent likely a virtual certainty, or a grave risk? This is a difficult question, but the answer will determine whether Dwayne is guilty of murder or manslaughter.

This example helps us to understand why some have suggested that the *R* v *Woollin* direction blurs the dividing line between oblique intention and recklessness. As Sir John

Smith explains in the following extract, the cause of this uncertainty is the qualification of the word 'certainty' with the word 'virtual'.

EXTRACT

Smith, J.C. (1990) 'A Note on Intention' *Criminal Law Review* 85

[Oblique intention] is intended to apply only to a person [...] who, though [it] is not his purpose [to cause the result in question], knows that he is going to cause that result. He is not merely taking a risk of causing that result. He is going to cause it and he knows it. But because nothing is certain in human affairs successive draftsmen and courts have felt obliged to qualify the [...] definition – he has *no substantial doubt* that the result will happen, he knows that it is *almost* certain, or *virtually* certain, or morally certain, to happen, or that it will happen *in the ordinary course of events*. There is a danger that any of these qualifications will be so interpreted as to blur the distinction between intention and recklessness. Once it is conceded that something less than certainty is required, it may be argued that we are into degrees of probability.

The obvious solution, therefore, would be to remove the word 'virtual' from the *R* v *Woollin* direction. This would produce a clear dividing line between oblique intention (where the consequence was 100 per cent certain to ensue) and recklessness (where the consequence was less than 100 per cent certain). But this clarity could have damaging effects in practice. In his article, Sir John Smith goes on to say that 'My friend, Brian Hogan, quotes *the Guinness Book of World Records* to show that, very occasionally, people have fallen out of planes from great heights and survived'. So think back to our example of Dwayne putting a bomb on board the plane carrying Saalim (the prosecutor) and Tariq (the pilot). We saw earlier that, under the *R* v *Woollin* direction, Dwayne obliquely intended to kill Tariq. But suppose that the word 'virtual' was removed from the *R* v *Woollin* direction and that Dwayne had read the Guinness Book of Records and was aware that there have been instances of people falling from planes and surviving. Smith explains that Dwayne would then have to be acquitted of murder:

> What of the case where the defendant gives evidence and says that *he did* contemplate the remote possibility, e.g. he, a devotee of *the Guinness Book of Records*, was aware of the remote chance that the crew of the doomed aircraft might escape and indeed hoped that they would? It would seem that the judge [...] must direct that jury that, if they thought the defendant might be speaking the truth, they must acquit him of an offence requiring proof of intention.

So, whilst the word 'virtual' in the *R* v *Woollin* direction might involve some sacrifice of clarity, it can be argued that this is necessary for practical reasons.

The element of discretion in the *R* v *Woollin* direction

We saw earlier that the *R* v *Woollin* direction vests some discretion in the jury. Even if the two conditions in the *R* v *Woollin* direction are both satisfied, the jury is not obliged to find oblique intention. It is 'entitled' to do so. There are conflicting opinions on whether this element of discretion is appropriate.

i. Arguments for an element of discretion

In June 2017 a fire broke out at Grenfell Tower, a 24-storey residential block in west London. In the days following the blaze stories emerged of parents being forced to throw their young children from the building to the crowds below. These included the mother of a four-year-old girl who was trapped on the fifth floor, and the mother of a baby who was trapped on the tenth floor. Both children were caught by those on the ground.[11]

Almost 20 years earlier, in a Parliamentary debate on the meaning of intention, Lord Goff had considered a similar, hypothetical, example:[12]

> Let us take this example. A house is on fire. A father is trapped in the attic floor with his two little girls. He comes to the conclusion that unless they jump they will all be burned alive. But he also realises that if they jump they are all likely to suffer serious personal harm. The children are too frightened to jump and so in an attempt to save their lives he throws one out of the window to the crowd waiting below and jumps with the other one in his arms. All are seriously injured, and the little girl he threw out of the window dies of her injuries.

Suppose that it was virtually certain that the girl that the father threw from the window would suffer serious injury, and that the father realised this. The two conditions in the *R* v *Woollin* direction would then be satisfied. Without an element of discretion, it follows that a jury would have to conclude that the father obliquely intended to seriously injure his daughter. But this would be nonsensical. He did not intend for her to suffer serious harm. Serious harm was the very thing that he was trying to save her from!

Another example is the case *R* v *Steane* [1947] KB 997. The defendant, Anthony Steane, was an English actor (alias: Jack Trevor). He was awarded the Military Cross for his service during World War I. But when World War II broke out he was working in

[11] White, C. (2017) 'The man who caught a 4-year-old girl from the Grenfell Tower blaze pictured' *Metro* 16 June 2017; 'Baby dropped from 10th floor of Grenfell Tower "caught by man on ground"' *The Telegraph* 14 June 2017. Other, similar, examples have also been reported. For example, in February 2008 a fire broke out in a four-storey building in Ludwigshafen in south-western Germany. A family found themselves trapped at a third-floor window. They threw their nine-month-old daughter out of the window, to a policeman on the ground 40 feet below. Thankfully he managed to catch the girl and she was unharmed. The girl's parents also survived.

[12] Hansard, HL Deb, vol 512, cols 469–470, 6 November 1989.

Germany and was immediately arrested. He was asked to broadcast for the Nazis. Initially he refused, but eventually agreed after Gestapo officers beat him badly (one of his ears was partly torn off) and threatened to send his wife and children (who were living in Germany) to a concentration camp. Following the end of the war, Steane was charged with doing acts likely to assist the enemy. At trial he was convicted. He appealed to the Court of Appeal, arguing that he lacked *mens rea*. He said that he had never intended to assist the enemy; he only broadcast in order to save his family. The Court of Appeal allowed his appeal and quashed his conviction. Lord Goddard CJ explained that, because Steane had been under pressure from the enemy, his actions were potentially consistent with either an 'innocent intent' to save his family or a 'guilty intent' to assist the enemy. Unless it could be shown, beyond reasonable doubt, that Steane had acted with a guilty intent to assist the enemy he was entitled to be acquitted.

R v *Steane* was decided many years before the House of Lords formulated the *R* v *Woollin* direction. But suppose that the *R* v *Woollin* direction had been in existence at the time *R* v *Steane* was decided. What would the outcome have been? Steane's actions were virtually certain to provide assistance to the enemy, and he realised this. The two conditions in the *R* v *Woollin* direction would therefore have been satisfied. Without an element of discretion, a jury would therefore have had to conclude that Steane intended to assist the enemy.

The burning building example and *R* v *Steane* demonstrate the principal benefit of the element of discretion in the *R* v *Woollin* direction. As Alan Norrie explains in the following extract, the element of discretion allows juries to make a moral assessment of the defendant's intention. The element of discretion thus acts as a moral safety valve, allowing juries to ensure that non-blameworthy defendants are not inappropriately convicted.

EXTRACT

Norrie, A. (1999) 'After Woollin' *Criminal Law Review* 532

These are cases where there is a "moral threshold" such that even though the accused could foresee a result as virtually certain, it is so at odds with his moral conception of what he was doing that it could not be conceived as a result that he intended. While a number of interpretations of *Steane* are possible, it is plausible to argue that at the nub of the case lies a moral gap between what Steane did, broadcasting to assist the enemy, and his purpose, to save his family. In that context, the judges declined to find that he had anything other than an intention to save his family. Yet this was clearly a case where they might have thought that it could be foreseen as virtually certain that assistance to the enemy would either result from the broadcasting, or was a necessary means to Steane's saving his family. It is therefore plausible to see this as a case where [oblique] intent could be established but was not found.

ii. Arguments against an element of discretion

There is another way of analysing the facts of *R* v *Steane*. Commenting on the Court of Appeal's reasoning, Glanville Williams wrote:[13]

> [A] more satisfactory way of deciding the case would have been to say that the accused did in law intend to assist the enemy but that duress was a defence.

[13] Williams, G. (1961) *Criminal Law: The General Part* (2nd edn). Stevens & Sons: London, section 18.

The argument here is not just that the availability of substantive defences renders the discretionary element in the *R* v *Woollin* direction unnecessary. It is that issues of justification and excuse are more appropriately addressed in the realm of the substantive defences. As we will see in Chapter 11, the courts have developed tests for defences like duress and self-defence. Each defence also has an accompanying body of case law which provides guidance on how the tests should be applied. By contrast, a jury applying the *R* v *Woollin* direction is given little guidance on how to exercise its discretion. William Wilson has written:[14]

> Even if the judge chooses to give the [*R* v *Woollin*] direction, moreover, it should be remembered that this does not foreclose the possibility of a linguistically sophisticated jury saying to themselves "OK, we are entitled to find intention here but we prefer not to. People intend what they set out to achieve. They do not intend the undesired side effects of what they are in business to achieve, particularly where these are inconsistent with the point of the defendant's action". Neither, more importantly, does it foreclose the possibility of a similar jury embarrassing the trial judge by asking for a further direction on this very point. How should a judge respond to such an inquiry? The real weakness of *Woollin* lies in its resounding silence on this issue.

Vesting this discretion in juries, but offering little or no guidance on how the discretion should be exercised, creates uncertainty. It also creates a risk of different juries reaching different verdicts in similar cases. This would infringe the rule of law.

Significantly, in *Re A (Children)(Conjoined Twins: Surgical Separation)* [2001] Fam 147 the Court of Appeal chose not to exercise its discretion under the *R* v *Woollin* direction.

Re A (Children)(Conjoined Twins: Surgical Separation) [2001] Fam 147

This case involved conjoined twins, Jodie and Mary. The twins were joined at the pelvis. Each had her own brain, heart, lungs and other vital organs, but Mary's heart and lungs were too deficient to oxygenate blood and pump it through her own body. However, the twins shared a common artery, which enabled Jodie's heart to pump the blood she oxygenated through Mary's body. Without an operation separating them it was expected that Jodie's heart would fail within a few months and both would die. On the other hand, if the twins were separated Jodie would have a good chance of survival but Mary would die within minutes. The Court of Appeal had to decide whether it would be lawful for doctors to separate the twins.

One of the questions the Court faced was whether, by separating the twins, the doctors would be murdering Mary. This in turn involved the question whether the doctors would be killing Mary intentionally.

By a majority of 2–1, the Court of Appeal held that the doctors would be killing Mary intentionally. The dissenting judge, Robert Walker LJ, acknowledged that the two conditions in the *R* v *Woollin* direction would be satisfied, but nonetheless concluded that the doctors would lack any intention to kill Mary:

> The proposed operation would not be unlawful. It would involve the positive act of invasive surgery and Mary's death would be foreseen as an inevitable consequence of

[14] Wilson, W. (1999) 'Doctrinal Rationality After *Woollin*' 62 *Modern Law Review* 448.

an operation which is intended, and is necessary, to save Jodie's life. But Mary's death would not be the purpose or intention of the surgery, and she would die because tragically her body, on its own, is not and never has been viable.

By contrast, the majority held that, because the two conditions in the *R* v *Woollin* direction would be satisfied, the doctors would have an oblique intention to kill Mary. Ward LJ stated:

> The test I have to set myself is that established by [*R* v *Woollin*]. I have to ask myself whether I am satisfied that the doctors recognise that death or serious harm will be virtually certain, barring some unforeseen intervention, to result from carrying out this operation. If so, the doctors intend to kill or to do that serious harm even though they may not have any desire to achieve that result. It is common ground that they appreciate that death to Mary would result from the severance of the common aorta. Unpalatable though it may be – and Mr Whitfield contends it is – to stigmatise the doctors with "murderous intent", that is what in law they will have if they perform the operation and Mary dies as a result.

Similarly, Brooke LJ said:

> Now that the House of Lords [in *R* v *Woollin*] has set out the law authoritatively in these terms, an English court would inevitably find that the surgeons intended to kill Mary, however little they desired that end, because her death would be the virtually certain consequence of their acts, and they would realise that for all practical purposes her death would invariably follow the clamping of the common aorta.

Both Ward and Brooke LJJ nonetheless concluded that the doctors would not be guilty of murdering Mary. As we will see in Chapter 11, both held that the doctors would be able to rely on a substantive defence.

Finally, it is worth considering how this approach of Glanville Williams and the majority of the Court of Appeal in *Re A* would apply in the earlier example of the father throwing his daughter from a burning building. Since the father's act of throwing the girl from the window was a factual and legal cause of her death there is the *actus reus* of murder. Moreover, if we remove the discretionary element from the *R* v *Woollin* direction, the father would have the *mens rea* of murder. He realised that serious injury to his daughter was a virtual certainty, and an oblique intention to cause serious injury is sufficient for the *mens rea* of murder. To avoid being guilty of murdering his daughter, he would therefore need to be able to plead a substantive defence. Two comments can be offered about this:

- As we will see in Chapter 11, the courts have taken quite a restrictive approach to the availability of the substantive defences on murder charges. The father's most obvious defence – duress of circumstances – would be unavailable, since the House of Lords has held that duress is not available as a defence to murder.[15] An alternative might be the defence of necessity, but there is uncertainty as to whether necessity is available as a defence to murder either. So the moral safety valve offered by

[15] *R* v *Howe* [1987] AC 417.

the discretionary element in the *R* v *Woollin* direction might be necessary after all, at least until changes have been made to the law governing the substantive defences.

- Even if the father could plead a substantive defence, and so be not guilty of murder, there remains the basic fact that it is nonsensical to say that he intended to cause his daughter serious harm when this was the very thing he was trying to save her from!

The second of these points leads us to consider whether there are other respects in which the *R* v *Woollin* direction might be improved.

Quiz 4.4

1. Which of the following is an argument for retaining the element of discretion in the *Woollin direction?*
   - **a.** By giving the jury the final say as to whether the necessary intention has been proved increases legal certainty.
   - **b.** By giving the jury the final say as to whether the necessary intention has been proved, they can give the benefit of the doubt to a defendant with an immoral purpose.
   - **c.** By giving the jury the final say as to whether the necessary intention has been proved, justice can be done in hard cases like *Steane* and practical examples.
   - **d.** By giving the jury the final say as to whether the necessary intention has been proved, justice can be done in hard cases like *R* v *Woollin* [1999] 1 AC 82 itself.
2. Which of the following is **not** an argument against allowing the jury an element of discretion in the application of the *Woollin* direction?
   - **a.** The Woollin test simply does not apply in cases like *Re A (Children)(Conjoined Twins: Surgical Separation)*.
   - **b.** Vesting a discretion in juries, but offering little or no guidance on how the discretion should be exercised, creates uncertainty.
   - **c.** Even judges are wary of exercising a discretion based on the *R* v *Woollin* example.
   - **d.** Issues of justification and excuse are more appropriately addressed in the realm of the substantive defences.
3. Which of the following is **not** a criticism of the *Woollin* direction?
   - **a.** The term virtually certain is ambiguous.
   - **b.** Its discretionary element is unnecessary.
   - **c.** It gives juries an unstructured discretion.
   - **d.** Its discretionary element provides a moral safety valve.

Proposals for reform

4.5 Formulate proposals for reform of the definition of intention.

The Law Commission considered the definition of intention in the 1990s and again in the 2000s. Here are three of the options it considered – have a think about which you think is best!

i. Option one: 'in the ordinary course of events'

The first option is found in clause 1(a) of the Law Commission's 1993 Draft Criminal Law Bill. The first limb (i) deals with direct intention. The second limb (ii) deals with oblique intention.

EXTRACT

Law Commission (1993) No 218 *Legislating the Criminal Code: Offences Against the Person and General Principles* Cm 2370 (1993)

Clause 1(a)

[A] person acts –

(a) "intentionally" with respect to a result when –

(i) it is his purpose to cause it, or

(ii) although it is not his purpose to cause it, he knows that it would occur in the ordinary course of events, if he were to succeed in his purpose of causing some other result;

The key points to note about this definition are:

- It used the phrase 'in the ordinary course of events' instead of the phrase 'virtual certainty' because it believed that this wording would be clearer.
- It does not contain a discretionary element. If the conditions in limb (ii) are satisfied the jury must find oblique intention.
- It adds the phrase '[...] if he were to succeed in his purpose of causing some other result'. This was designed to prevent the nonsensical conclusion in the burning building example. If the father succeeds in his purpose of saving his daughter from serious harm, then his daughter will not suffer serious harm in the ordinary course of events. So under this definition the father would not have an oblique intention to cause serious harm to his daughter.

Now, think about these questions.

Under this definition, would

a. Steane have had an oblique intention to assist the enemy; and

b. the doc have had an oblique intention to kill Mary?

ii. Option two: remove the discretionary element

The second and third options are both found in the Law Commission's consultation paper and final report on the law of homicide.[16] The second option is set out in the consultation paper as follows (limb (1) deals with direct intention and limbs (2) and (3) deal with oblique intention).

[16] See: Law Commission Consultation Paper No 177 (2005) *A New Homicide Act for England and Wales? Part 4*; and Law Commission No 304 (2006) *Murder, Manslaughter and Infanticide* HC 30, paras 3.9–3.27.

EXTRACT

Law Commission (2005) *A New Homicide Act for England and Wales?* (Law Commission Consultation Paper No 177)

4.62 [...] Subject to the proviso set out below:

a person acts "intentionally" with respect to a result when he or she acts either:

(1) in order to bring it about, or

(2) knowing that it will be virtually certain to occur; or

(3) knowing that it would be virtually certain to occur if he or she were to succeed in his or her purpose of causing some other result.

Proviso: a person is not to be deemed to have intended any result, which it was his or her specific purpose to avoid.

4.63 In directing a jury on the meaning of intention, the judge would be required only to refer the jury to the appropriate clause of this definition. There would be no need for a judge to refer jurors to the proviso, except in cases where the particular facts raise the possibility of it being applicable. A Practice Direction to this effect may be sufficient to ensure that this definition will provide a workable, clear, simple definition of intention.

The key points to note about this definition are:

- In *R* v *Woollin* Lord Steyn stated that 'over a period of 12 years [...] the test of foresight of virtual certainty has apparently caused no practical difficulties. It is simple and clear'. In the light of this, the Law Commission reverted to the phrase 'virtual certainty' instead of 'in the ordinary course of events'.
- It does not contain a discretionary element. If the conditions in limb (2) or (3) are satisfied the jury must find oblique intention.
- The proviso is designed to deal with the nonsensical conclusion in the burning building example.
- Unlike the 1993 proposal that we just looked at, this proposal splits the definition of oblique intention into two strands:

  Limb (3) mirrors the definition of oblique intention found in the 1993 proposal. Limb (3) was felt to be necessary in order to deal with cases of 'conditional oblique intention'. Think back to our example of Dwayne placing a bomb on board the plane carrying Saalim (the prosecutor) and Tariq (the pilot). We saw earlier that Dwayne had an oblique intention to kill Tariq. But suppose that Dwayne knew that the bomb he planted was defective, and only had a 50 per cent chance of exploding. Under the *R* v *Woollin* direction as it stands today, Dwayne would lack an oblique intention to kill Tariq because Tariq's death is not a virtual certainty. The phrase '[...] if he or she were to succeed in his or her purpose of causing some other result' corrects this. Dwayne knows that, if he succeeds in his purpose of killing Saalim, it is a virtual certainty that Tariq will die too.

However, sometimes defendants do not have 'some other result' that they hope to achieve.[17] An example is *R* v *Woollin* itself. Stephen Woollin lost his temper with his three-month-old son, and threw him onto a hard surface. The child suffered a fractured skull and died. Woollin would fall outside limb (3) because it was not his purpose to cause some other result. For this reason, limb (2) does not contain these extra words. A defendant like Woollin would therefore fall under limb (2).

Would Stephen Woollin be found to have had an intention to kill or cause serious harm to his son under the 1993 proposal?

Limb (ii) of the 1993 proposal referred only to defendant knowing that a result would occur in the ordinary course of events if he succeeded 'in his purpose of causing some other result'. Since it was not Woollin's purpose to cause some other result, (ii) did not seem to fit a situation like Woollin's.

iii. Option three: retain the *status quo*

The third option is to codify the existing law. The Law Commission set out this option in its consultation paper.

EXTRACT

Law Commission (2005) *A New Homicide Act for England and Wales?* (Law Commission Consultation Paper No 177)

4.69 A codification of the common law would need, first, to refer to the ordinary situation in which a person is to be regarded as acting intentionally. Then it should replicate the [Woollin] direction. Finally, the clause relating to the chances of the defendant succeeding in some other purpose should be introduced. The resulting formulation would be as follows:

(1) A person is to be regarded as acting intentionally with respect to a result when he or she acts in order to bring it about.

(2) In the rare case where the simple direction in clause (1) is not enough, the jury should be directed that:

they are not entitled to find the necessary intention with regard to a result unless they are sure that the result was a virtual certainty (barring some unforeseen intervention) as a result of the defendant's actions and that the defendant appreciated that such was the case.

(3) In any case where the defendant's chance of success in his or her purpose of causing some other result is relevant, the direction in clause (2) may be expanded by the addition of the following phrase at the end of the clause (2) direction:

'or that it would be *if he or she were to succeed in his or her purpose of causing some other result*, and that the defendant appreciated that such was the case.'

The key difference between this option and the previous one is that this option retains the discretionary element.

[17] A point made by Sir John Smith [1998] Crim LR 318.

The Law Commission's final report, in 2006, recommended the third option. It argued, first, that the phrase 'virtual certainty' should be retained since it has not caused any significant problems in practice:[18]

> 4.60 In 1998, Lord Steyn pointed out in *Woollin*, that "over a period of 12 years since *Nedrick*, the test of foresight of virtual certainty has apparently caused no practical difficulties. It is simple and clear…". This raises the question of whether it would be better to use the expression "virtually certain" in a new statutory definition of "intentionally", rather than "in the ordinary course of events". In our view, in light of the observations of Lord Steyn in *Woollin*, it would be preferable to use the tried and tested phrase "knowing that it is virtually certain to occur". The phrase has the advantage of simplicity and it has proved to be workable.

It then argued that the element of discretion should be retained:[19]

> 3.21 We acknowledge that this approach gives the jury an element of discretion in deciding whether, […] a verdict of […] murder can and should be returned. The result in such cases will not be wholly determined by legal rules governing the meaning of intention. We believe that it is sometimes necessary and desirable that juries should have that element of discretion if the alternative is a more complex set of legal rules that they must apply. It is the price of avoiding complexity.

Now, think about these questions.

- Do you agree with the Law Commission's recommendation?
- Or would you favour one of the other two proposals?
- Or can you construct a better proposal of your own?

Quiz 4.5

1. The Law Commission's 1993 Draft Criminal Law Bill proposed replacing the phrase 'virtual certainty' with what?
   a. In the ordinary course of events.
   b. More likely than not.
   c. Highly likely.
   d. Definitely.

2. Why did the Law Commission's 2006 report *Murder, Manslaughter and Infanticide* recommend retaining the phrase 'virtual certainty'?
   a. The Government instructed the Law Commission to retain the wording from *R* v *Woollin*.
   b. The Law Commission recommended replacing the phrase 'virtual certainty', not retaining it.
   c. Finding a better alternative was taking too long.
   d. It has not caused any significant problems in practice.

3. What did the Law Commission's 2006 report *Murder, Manslaughter and Infanticide* say about the discretionary element in the *R* v *Woollin* direction?
   a. The discretionary element should be retained in order to increase the conviction rate for murder.
   b. The discretionary element should be retained in order to avoid the need for a more complex set of rules governing the meaning of intention.
   c. The discretionary element should be removed as it causes inconsistency.
   d. The discretionary element should be removed as it causes too much uncertainty.

---

[18] Law Commission (2005) *A New Homicide Act for England and Wales?* (Consultation Paper No 177).

[19] Law Commission (2006) *Murder, Manslaughter and Infanticide* (No 304) HC 30.

Other *mens rea* terms

4.6 Recall the law on the concepts of knowledge, belief, negligence and strict liability.

So far in this chapter we have examined recklessness and intention – the two *mens rea* concepts that we will use most frequently in this text – in detail. We will now briefly introduce some other concepts that you will encounter as you study criminal law.

1. Knowledge

The *mens rea* concept of knowledge is used in some of the property offences that we will study in Chapter 8 (burglary and fraud) and in the law on accessories (Chapter 13). The word is normally used in relation to circumstances (so we might say, for example, that the defendant knew that his representation was false).

There are two types of knowledge. The first is actual knowledge. This is where someone has formed a belief, and that belief is correct. As the House of Lords stated in *R* v *Saik* [2006] UKHL 18, 'knowledge means true belief'.

The second type of knowledge is known as wilful blindness. This is where the only reason that the defendant has not yet formed a (correct) belief is because he has deliberately failed to investigate his suspicions. In *Westminster CC* v *Croyalgrange Ltd* [1986] 1 WLR 674 Lord Bridge explained wilful blindness as follows:

> it is always open to the tribunal of fact, when knowledge on the part of a defendant is required to be proved, to base a finding of knowledge on evidence that the defendant had deliberately shut his eyes to the obvious or refrained from enquiry because he suspected the truth but did not want to have his suspicion confirmed.

2. Belief

We will encounter the *mens rea* concept of belief in Chapter 6 (non-fatal offences against the person), Chapter 7 (sexual offences) and Chapter 8 (property offences). Like knowledge, the concept of belief is used primarily in relation to circumstances (so we might say, for example, that the defendant genuinely believed that he had a legal right to the property).

The difference between knowledge and belief is that knowledge cannot be mistaken but a belief can be. Belief must also be distinguished from suspicion. As Beldam LJ explained in *R* v *Forsyth* [1997] 2 Cr App R 299, a person who believes something has concluded that it is true whereas someone who suspects something has not:

> It is beyond question that even great suspicion is not to be equated with belief [...] The ordinary meaning of belief is the mental acceptance of a fact as true or existing.

3. Negligence

A defendant acts negligently if his behaviour falls short of the standard that we would expect of a reasonable person in the same situation. This is an objective test. So unlike intention, knowledge, belief and recklessness, which as we have seen focus on the defendant's state of mind, negligence simply requires an assessment of whether the defendant's conduct lived up to the objective standard of reasonableness.

Although negligence is used in the *mens rea* of a large number of regulatory offences, it is not used in any of the crimes that we study in this text. However, we will study one offence which requires proof of gross negligence: namely, gross negligence manslaughter.

4. Strict liability

The term 'strict liability' is used to describe crimes which have one or more *actus reus* requirements that do not have any corresponding mens rea requirement. An example is the offence of rape of a child under the age of 13.[20] This crime has two *actus reus* requirements, but only one of these has a corresponding *mens rea* requirement:

- The defendant penetrated the vagina, anus or mouth of the other person. This *actus reus* requirement has a corresponding *mens rea* requirement: the penetration must have been intentional.
- The other person was aged under 13. This requirement does not have a corresponding *mens rea* requirement.[21] A defendant can therefore be convicted of this offence even if he honestly believed the victim was aged 16 and the possibility that she was aged under 13 never crossed his mind.

It is important to understand the difference between crimes of strict liability and crimes of constructive liability. As shown in Figure 4.2, in crimes of constructive liability every *actus reus* requirement does have a corresponding *mens rea* requirement. However, as we saw in Chapter 1, in crimes of constructive liability one or more of the *mens rea* requirements will specify a lesser consequence or circumstance than the corresponding *actus reus* requirement. The example we looked at in Chapter 1 was murder. The *actus reus* of murder requires that the victim died, but the corresponding *mens rea* requirement states that it is enough that the defendant intended to cause serious harm.

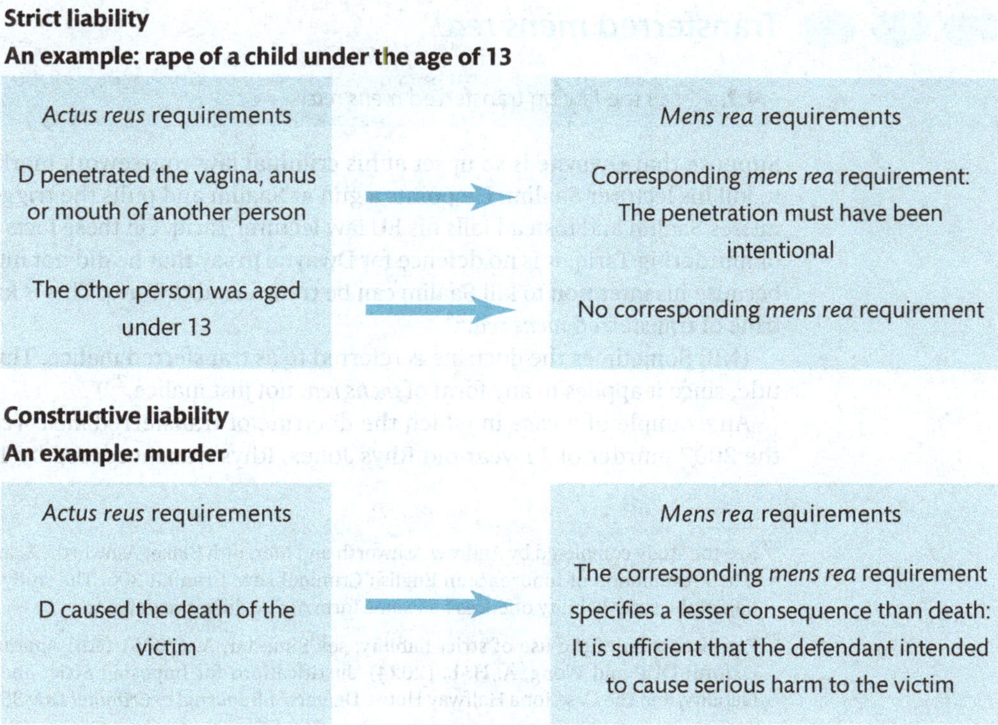

Figure 4.2

[20] Sexual Offences Act 2003, s.5.

[21] *R* v *G* [2008] UKHL 37.

In *Criminal Law* we will study several offences which impose constructive liability, but none which impose strict liability. This does not mean that offences of strict liability are rare. On the contrary, roughly 45 per cent of all criminal offences are crimes of strict liability.[22] For many regulatory offences, such as drink driving and parking tickets, strict liability is commonplace.[23]

Quiz 4.6

1. Which of the following words best describes an offence of strict liability?
   a. Possession.
   b. Recklessness.
   c. Knowledge.
   d. Intention.

2. Strict liability offences can be considered unjust because…
   a. prosecution will always lead to a conviction.
   b. the lack of *mens rea* requirement often makes a potentially successful prosecution fail in court.
   c. the lack of *mens rea* requirement often makes a potentially successful prosecution morally doubtful.
   d. prosecution will never lead to a conviction.

3. Which one of the following IS a justification for having strict liability in the criminal law?
   a. Law enforcement is easier if *mens rea* need not be proved.
   b. Strict liability shows greater respect for individual autonomy.
   c. Morality demands that if citizens break the law then they should be punished for it.
   d. Only the intentional criminal or reckless person is liable to commit a strict liability offence and so the careful citizen will not be subject to prosecution.

Transferred *mens rea*

4.7 Recall the law on transferred *mens rea*.

Suppose that Dwayne is so upset at his criminal law coursework mark that he decides to kill his lecturer Saalim. He points a gun at Saalim and pulls the trigger, but somehow misses Saalim and instead kills his EU law lecturer Tariq. On these facts Dwayne is guilty of murdering Tariq. It is no defence for Dwayne to say that he did not intend to kill Tariq, because his intention to kill Saalim can be transferred to Tariq. This is known as the doctrine of transferred *mens rea*.[24]

(NB: Sometimes the doctrine is referred to as transferred malice. This is a misleading title, since it applies to any form of *mens rea*, not just malice.[25])

An example of a case in which the doctrine of transferred *mens rea* was applied is the 2007 murder of 11-year-old Rhys Jones. Rhys was murdered by 16-year-old Sean

---

[22] See the study completed by Andrew Ashworth and Meredith Blake: Ashworth, A. and Blake, M. (1996) 'The Presumption of Innocence in English Criminal Law' Crim LR 306. The study found that roughly half of the strict liability offences had some form of due diligence defence.

[23] For discussion of the use of strict liability, see Simester, A. (2005) (ed.) *Appraising Strict Liability* Oxford: OUP and Wong, A. H. L. (2024) 'Justifications for Imposing Strict and Absolute Criminal Liability, and the Case for a Halfway House Defence' 88 *Journal of Criminal Law* 358.

[24] See: *R* v *Latimer* (1886) 17 QBD 359; *R* v *Pembliton* (1874) LR 2 CCR 119. For criticism of the doctrine, see Stark, F. (2023) 'Recycled Malice' 82 *Cambridge Law Journal* 509.

[25] Child, J. J., Simester, A. P., Spencer, J. R., Stark, F. & Virgo, G. J. (2022) *Simester and Sullivan's Criminal Law: Theory and Doctrine* (8th edn) Oxford: Hart Publishing, p222. For a contrary view, see Bohlander, M. (2025) 'Transferred Recklessness?' 89 *Journal of Criminal Law* 244.

Mercer. Mercer was a member of a gang in Liverpool called the Croxteth Crew. The killing occurred when Mercer fired three gunshots at the members of a rival gang – the Norris Green gang – across a pub car park. Rhys, who was walking home from football practice, was hit by the second shot and killed. Mercer's intention to kill one of the members of the Norris Green gang was transferred to the actual victim, Rhys.

Note the following three points about the doctrine of transferred *mens rea*:

- It does not only apply to cases of murder. If I throw a stone at your bedroom window intending to smash it, but miss and smash your neighbour's window instead, my intention to smash your window can be transferred to your neighbour's window. So I would be guilty of criminal damage. However, an intention to injure a person cannot be transferred to an intention to damage property (and vice versa). So if I throw a brick at you, but miss and hit your neighbour's window instead, my intention to injure you cannot be transferred to your neighbour's window. Where the doctrine does not apply, you should consider other offences instead. Often it will be possible to charge the defendant with a criminal attempt (e.g. I could be charged with attempted battery of you) and with another full offence which involves recklessness (e.g. I could also be charged with reckless criminal damage of your neighbour's window).
- Be careful to distinguish cases of transferred *mens rea* from two slightly different types of scenario. First, suppose Dwayne wants to kill Saalim. He sees a man across the street and, believing that the man is Saalim, shoots him dead. In fact, it turns out that the man was not Saalim, but Tariq. Here there is no need to apply the doctrine of transferred *mens rea*. Dwayne did not fire his gun at one person and mistakenly hit someone else. He shot the person he intended to shoot: the man on the other side of the street. Dwayne's mistake as to the person's identity does not negate his intention to kill this person. Second, suppose Dwayne plants a bomb on a busy high street. The bomb explodes and kills several people. Here there is no need to apply the doctrine of transferred *mens rea* either. Dwayne did not target the bomb at anyone in particular: he had an indiscriminate intention to kill passers-by.
- In *Attorney-General's Ref (No 3 of 1994)* [1998] AC 245 the defendant stabbed a woman even though he knew that she was (between 22 and 24 weeks) pregnant. Seventeen days later the baby was born premature. The baby lived for 121 days before dying due to the effects of the premature birth. The defendant could not be charged with murder of the foetus, since a foetus is not a 'person in being' for the purposes of the offence of murder (see Chapter 5). Nor was the defendant guilty of murder of the baby, since the doctrine of transferred *mens rea* could not be used to transfer the defendant's intention to seriously injure the woman to the baby. Lord Mustill in the House of Lords explained that this would require 'a double "transfer" of intent: first from the mother to the foetus and then from the foetus to the child as yet unborn'.[26]

---

[26] Before the baby died the defendant had already pleaded guilty to wounding with intent (section 18 of the Offences Against the Person Act 1861: see Chapter 6) and been sentenced to four years' imprisonment. Following the child's death he was charged with murder. The trial judge ruled that the facts could not support a charge of either murder or manslaughter and directed the jury to acquit the defendant. The Attorney-General then referred a point of law of general importance to the appeal courts. The House of Lords held that the defendant had not committed murder, but that the facts were capable of supporting a manslaughter conviction.

Quiz 4.7

1. Which doctrine of the criminal law is illustrated in the case of Sean Mercer?
   - **a.** That ignorance of the law is no excuse.
   - **b.** That if A acts intending to kill B but in fact kills C, A is as guilty of the murder of C as s/he would have been had s/he killed the intended victim.
   - **c.** That the voluntary intervention of a third party will discharge the liability of the defendant.
   - **d.** That a defendant should only be liable if he acted involuntarily.
2. Why does the doctrine of transferred *mens rea* not apply in a situation where D throws a stone intending to injure V, but misses and breaks a window instead?
   - **a.** This is an example of the principle of non-retroactivity.
   - **b.** Breaking the window was an unintended consequence of D's act, which was of a different type from which he intended.
   - **c.** the doctrine of transferred *mens rea* would apply in such circumstances.
   - **d.** Breaking the window was a pure accident.
3. Which of the following is **not** part of the reasoning of House of Lords in *Attorney-General's Ref (No 3 of 1994)*?
   - **a.** The defendant could not be charged with murder of the foetus, since a foetus is not a 'person in being' for the purposes of the offence of murder.
   - **b.** The doctrine of transferred malice is an arbitrary exception to general principles.
   - **c.** The doctrine should have noticed the injury to the child at the time of the attack.
   - **d.** The doctrine of transferred *mens rea* did not apply, since it would have involved a double transfer: first from the mother to the foetus and then from the foetus to the child as yet unborn.

Three steps to addressing issues of *mens rea*

When answering problem questions, there are three basic steps to addressing issues of *mens rea*. These are set out in the following table, along with some practical advice:

Three steps	Pointers
• **First**, identify all of the *mens rea* requirements of the relevant offence. So, for example, the offence of murder has one *mens rea* requirement (an intention to kill or cause serious injury) and the offence of criminal damage has two *mens rea* requirements (the defendant intentionally or recklessly destroyed or damaged the property and the defendant knew that the property belonged to another person or was reckless as to whether it did).	• Use Chapters 5–8 of this text to identify the *mens rea* requirements of the relevant offence.
• **Second**, identify the meaning and any applicable legal tests for each of the *mens rea* concepts that are used in the offence definition.	• In this chapter we have examined the meaning and legal tests for the *mens rea* concepts that we will encounter most frequently in this text.
• **Third**, use the facts of the problem question to assess whether the defendant satisfies each of the *mens rea* requirements.	One of the key skills that problem questions test is the ability to apply the law to factual scenarios. So don't just write something like 'Dwayne acted recklessly on an application of the *R v Cunningham* test'. Make sure that you use the facts of the question to explain your reasoning and justify your conclusion.

The material that we have covered in this chapter will help you with the second of these three steps. We have examined the meaning of recklessness and the *R* v *Cunningham* test and the two types of intention and how to test for each of these. We have also looked briefly at the concepts of knowledge, belief, negligence and strict liability, as well as the doctrine of transferred *mens rea*.

That is the end of the first part of the text! In these first four chapters we have looked at the basic principles of criminal law and at the key general *actus reus* and *mens rea* concepts. In part two we move onto specific offences, beginning in Chapter 5 with the law of homicide.

Applying the law

4.8 Apply the law on recklessness and intention to hypothetical sets of facts.

Alessandro and Fabio

The following scenario takes place in a TV studio. Read the problem scenario carefully, then answer the multiple-choice questions below to apply your learning to the scenario.

Alessandro is a famous magician. He plans an illusion in which he will appear to play Russian roulette live on television. The illusion will involve a member of the studio audience spinning the barrel of a six-barrel pistol which will appear to contain one live bullet. Alessandro will then proceed to point the gun at his head and pull the trigger. Alessandro will do this a total of five times, with an additional bullet added before each spin. Alessandro is confident that he can use the power of his incredible mind to prevent his untimely death but, just in case he has an 'off night', the 'bullets' will in fact be duds.

On the evening of the performance Alessandro's manager Fabio tells Alessandro that the press have been inquiring as to whether he will use real bullets, and adds, 'Wouldn't it be more exciting, and a better story, if we did it for real?' Thinking Fabio is joking, Alessandro says 'No problem'. Unbeknown to Alessandro, Fabio was serious and replaces the duds with real bullets.During the performance the barrel is spun for the first time, Alessandro pulls the trigger and he survives. This also happens on the second occasion, the third and the fourth. However, tragedy strikes following the final spin of the barrel (which now contains five live bullets and only one empty barrel). Alessandro is killed.

Did Fabio intend to kill Alessandro?

Quiz 4.8

1. As we saw in the chapter, there are two types of intention: direct intention and oblique intention. The courts have stated that juries should only be given the *R* v *Woollin* direction on oblique intention if it is necessary on the basis of the facts of the particular case before them. So we should begin by asking whether it was Fabio's direct intention to kill Alessandro. What test has Antony Duff suggested using to decide whether a defendant had a direct intention to cause a particular result?

a. The 'test of failure': would the defendant have regarded himself as having failed if the result did not occur?

b. The 'test of foresight': did the defendant foresee a risk that the result might occur and choose to take it?

c. The 'test of inevitability': did the defendant realise that the result was virtually certain to occur (barring some unforeseen intervention)?

d. The 'test of flippancy': could the defendant have cared less whether the result occurred or not?

2. We can use Duff's failure test to determine whether it was Fabio's direct intention (i.e. his purpose) to kill Alessandro. Had Alessandro not been killed, would Fabio have regarded this as a failure? The answer is obviously no. Fabio was Alessandro's manager. They worked together and they both wanted the illusion to be a great success. He did not directly intend to kill Alessandro. We must therefore turn instead to oblique intention. Which of the following statements paraphrases the *R* v *Woollin* direction correctly?

a. If a result was virtually certain to occur as a result of D's actions, and D realised this, then the jury may find that D obliquely intended that result.

b. If a result was virtually certain to occur as a result of D's actions, and D realised this, then the jury must conclude that D obliquely intended that result.

c. If a result was virtually certain to occur as a result of D's actions, then the jury must conclude that he obliquely intended that result.

d. If D thought that a result was virtually certain to occur as a result of his actions, then the jury may find that he obliquely intended that result.

So when deciding whether it was Fabio's oblique intention to kill Alessandro, the first step for the jury is to decide whether the two conditions in the *R* v *Woollin* direction are satisfied.

First condition:

The first condition is that Alessandro's death was a virtual certainty. Using the facts of the question, it is possible to calculate the probability that Alessandro would be killed. He pulled the trigger a total of five times:

1. On the first occasion he pulled the trigger there was one bullet in the gun. The chance of being killed on this occasion was therefore one-in-six (16.7%).
2. On the second occasion he pulled the trigger there were two bullets in the gun. The chance of being killed on this occasion was therefore two-in-six (33.3%).
3. On the third occasion he pulled the trigger there were three bullets in the gun. The chance of being killed on this occasion was therefore three-in-six (50%).
4. On the fourth occasion he pulled the trigger there were four bullets in the gun. The chance of being killed on this occasion was therefore four-in-six (66.7%).
5. On the fifth occasion he pulled the trigger there were five bullets in the gun. The chance of being killed on this occasion was therefore five-in-six (83.3%).

The chance of surviving all five occasions was therefore 1.5% (83.3% × 66.7% × 50% × 33.3% × 16.7%). In other words, there was a 98.5% likelihood that Alessandro would be killed. The jury would have to decide, therefore, whether a result that has a 98.5% chance of occurring is a virtual certainty. Or, does the fact that Alessandro had a 1.5% chance of surviving mean that his death was not virtually certain?

Second condition:

Moving on to the second condition in the *R* v *Woollin* direction, the jury would have to decide whether Fabio thought that Alessandro's death was a virtual certainty. If you were Fabio's defence counsel, how would you argue that Fabio did not regard Alessandro's death as a virtual certainty? If you were the prosecutor, how would you respond to these arguments? If you were a juror, which of these arguments would you find the most persuasive?

If both of the conditions in the *R* v *Woollin* direction are satisfied, then the jury may find that Fabio had an oblique intention to kill Alessandro. But if both conditions are not satisfied, there can be no finding of oblique intention.

Dwayne and Judy

Dwayne, on his motorcycle on a busy Saturday afternoon, decides it would be fun to speed along a pedestrian precinct. He skilfully avoids many shoppers, but as he speeds round a corner he hits Judy, a small child who had wandered out of a shop. Judy suffers serious injuries. At trial, expert evidence is admitted that Dwayne suffers from a psychiatric condition, one effect of which could be to deprive him of the ability of a normal person to foresee or appreciate the risk of harm inherent in driving as he did. In his evidence Dwayne says that he had not thought about the risk of hurting anyone but that he didn't really care.

Now, think about this question.

Consider whether Dwayne caused Judy's injuries recklessly. (Hint: try constructing the arguments that the prosecutor would use, and then the arguments that defence counsel would use. Looking at both sets of arguments would you feel sure beyond reasonable doubt that Dwayne acted recklessly?)

Alice, Beth and Charles

Alice wants to kill Beth, who has stolen her boyfriend Charles. She breaks into Beth's house and waits for her. The front door opens. Alice shoots at Beth but misses. Instead, the bullet hits Charles who has followed Beth into the house and is the last person Alice would want to harm. Charles dies.

Now, think about these questions.

- Does Alice have the *mens rea* of murder?
- Suppose that, instead of hitting Charles, the bullet smashed a window. Could Alice's intention to shoot Beth be transferred to the window?

Alessandro and Fabio

Moving on to the second condition in the *R* v *Woollin* direction, the jury would have to decide whether Fabio thought that Alessandro's death was a virtual certainty.

Now, think about these questions.

- If you were Fabio's defence counsel, how would you argue that Fabio did not regard Alessandro's death as a virtual certainty?
- If you were the prosecutor, how would you respond to these arguments?
- If you were a juror, which of these arguments would you find the most persuasive?

Evaluating the law: Part one

4.9 Evaluate the R v Cunningham test.

Think about this question.

In *R* v *G & another* [2003] UKHL 50, Lord Bingham stated: 'I cannot accept that restoration of the law as understood before *R* v *Caldwell* [1982] AC 341 would lead to the acquittal of those whom public policy would require to be convicted' ([39]).

Explain and critically discuss Lord Bingham's assertion.

Step 1: Explanation

As we saw in the chapter, in *R* v *G & another* the House of Lords overruled *R* v *Caldwell* and reinstated the *R* v *Cunningham* test for recklessness. Lord Bingham's statement in the essay title is therefore asserting that the *R* v *Cunningham* test will not result in 'the acquittal of those whom public policy would require to be convicted'. In other words, the assertion is that the *R* v *Cunningham* test is not under-inclusive. Explain this in your own words.

- Explain Lord Bingham's assertion.

Step 2: Critical discussion

Having explained Lord Bingham's assertion the next task is to critically discuss it. In your opinion, is the *R* v *Cunningham* test under-inclusive? A useful case to consider here is *R* v *Parker* [1977] 1 WLR 600. For some (including Ibbetson, as we saw in the chapter), the reasoning in this case was strained and illustrates the problems with the *R* v *Cunningham* test. For others, the reasoning in *R* v *Parker* was logical and the fact that Parker's conviction was upheld shows that the existing law is not under-inclusive. You should evaluate these contrasting perspectives and decide which you agree with.

To help with this, look back at your reading and the notes you prepared in response to the following questions.

On Birch's article 'The Foresight Saga: The Biggest Mistake of All':

- Birch argues that the *R* v *Cunningham* test is based on the 'informed choice' theory. What is the informed choice theory? Why is it difficult to reconcile with the decision in *R* v *Parker*?
- What does Birch argue are the advantages of an attitude-based test for recklessness? What does she say are the obstacles to an attitude-based test?

On Duff's proposal for a test based on practical indifference:

- Duff gives an example involving a bridegroom who forgets his wedding. What does he say the example illustrates?
- What does Duff argue is the truth in orthodox subjectivist tests like *R* v *Cunningham*? What error does he say these tests make?

- What does Duff argue is the truth in the *R* v *Caldwell* test? What error does he say this test made?
- Should the test for recklessness be changed to one based on attitude, like Duff's practical indifference test? Can you think of any possible objections to Duff's proposal?

On Stark's proposal for a belief-centred account of recklessness:

- How does Stark's proposal differ from Duff's? If you identified any objections to Duff's proposal, do these objections also apply to Stark's proposal?

Once you have formed an opinion on Lord Bingham's assertion, construct a set of arguments in support of your views.

- Construct a set of arguments in support of your views.

You now have compiled all you need for the main body of your essay. The last task is to decide what to include in your introduction and conclusion.

Step 3: Introduction and conclusion

The introduction should contextualise your discussion by briefly outlining the judgment in *R* v *G & another*, and give an indication of the argument you will present in your essay

- Write an introduction that contextualises your discussion by briefly outlining the judgment in *R* v *G & another*, and give an indication of the argument you will present in your essay.

The conclusion should round off your essay with a succinct statement of your argument and a summary of your supporting reasons.

- Write a conclusion that rounds off your essay with a succinct statement of your argument and a summary of your supporting reasons.

Evaluating the law: Part two

4.10 Evaluate the law on the concept of intention.

In its report (No 304) *Murder, Manslaughter and Infanticide* the Law Commission argued that the *R* v *Woollin* direction should be retained and codified. The Commission explained that the phrase 'virtual certainty' is simple and has been tried and tested, and that the element of discretion is necessary and desirable.

Do you agree with the Law Commission's recommendation? Or do you prefer one of the other suggested reform options?

Key *mens rea* concepts checklist

Having worked through this chapter, you should now have:

- An understanding of the concept of recklessness
- An ability to critically discuss the *R* v *Cunningham* test

- An understanding of the concept of intention
- An ability to critically discuss the *R* v *Woollin* direction and proposals for reform
- A basic understanding of the concepts of knowledge, belief, negligence and strict liability
- An understanding of the doctrine of transferred *mens rea*.

Further reading

Birch, D.J. (1988) 'The Foresight Saga: The Biggest Mistake of All?' *Criminal Law Review* 4.

Chan, W. and Simester, A.P. (2011) 'Four Functions of *Mens Rea*' 70 *Cambridge Law Journal* 381.

Duff, A. (1990) *Intention, Agency & Criminal Liability*. Blackwell: Oxford.

Greenberg, A. (2024) 'Awareness and the Recklessness/Negligence Distinction' 18 *Criminal Law and Philosophy* 351.

Halpin, A. (1998) 'Definitions and Directions: Recklessness Unheeded' 18 *Legal Studies* 294.

Horder, J. (2006) 'Transferred Malice and the Remoteness of Unexpected Outcomes from Intentions' *Criminal Law Review* 383.

Ibbetson, D. (2004) 'Recklessness Restored' 63 *Cambridge Law Journal* 13.

Kugler, I. (2004) 'Conditional Oblique Intention' *Criminal Law Review* 284.

Law Commission (2005) *A New Homicide Act for England and Wales?* (Consultation Paper No 177) Part 4.

Law Commission (2006) *Murder, Manslaughter and Infanticide* (No 304) HC 30, paras 3.9–3.27.

Norrie, A. (1999) 'After *Woollin*' *Criminal Law Review* 532.

Pedain, A. (2003) 'Intention and the Terrorist Example' *Criminal Law Review* 579.

Smith, J.C. (1990) 'A Note on Intention' Criminal Law Review 85.

Stark, F. (2016) *Culpable Carelessness: Recklessness and Negligence in the Criminal Law*. Cambridge University Press: Cambridge.

Wilson, W. (1999) 'Doctrinal Rationality after *Woollin*' 62 *Modern Law Review* 448.

Answers on the Companion Website

Please visit the companion website for the answers to Key Questions, Quizzes, Applying the Law scenarios as well as student support including glossaries. Please visit www.pearsoned.co.uk/Macdonald

5

Homicide

Learning Objectives

5.1 Explain the requirements for establishing criminal liability for murder.

5.2 Explain the requirements for establishing the partial defence of loss of control.

5.3 Recall the requirements for establishing criminal liability for unlawful act manslaughter.

5.4 Explain the requirements for establishing criminal liability for gross negligence manslaughter.

5.5 Explain the requirements for establishing criminal liability for corporate manslaughter.

5.6 Describe the Law Commission's proposals for reform of the law of homicide.

5.7 Apply the law of homicide to a hypothetical set of facts.

5.8 Evaluate the loss of control defence.

5.9 Formulate proposals for the reform of the law of homicide, based on evaluation of its existing two-tier structure and the *mens rea* of murder.

Introduction: Homicide

Read each of these five scenarios and decide whether you think the defendants are **guilty of murder**, **guilty of manslaughter**, or **not guilty of a homicide offence**. As we explore each of these in more detail over the chapter, think back on your responses here and whether you'd change any of them.

Scenario 1: The one-punch killer

Studio Romantic/Shutterstock

The defendant intentionally punches the victim in the face. The punch breaks the victim's nose and causes the victim to fall to the ground. In falling, the victim hits his head on the kerb, causing a massive and fatal brain haemorrhage.

Is the defendant guilty of murder, guilty of manslaughter, or not guilty of a homicide offence?

Scenario 2: The abused spouse

ostill/123RF

For many years, the defendant suffers physical and emotional abuse from her husband, the victim. One evening the victim threatens to beat the defendant the following morning. During the night, the cefendant kills the victm while he is asleep.

Is the defendant guilty of murder, guilty of manslaughter, or not guilty of a homicide offence?

Scenario 3: The terrorist

carl ballou/Shutterstock

The defendant hides a bomb on a busy high street. He wants to draw attention to his cause, but doesn't want anyone to be harmed because he thinks this will cost him public support. So two hours before the bomb is due to explode, he gives a telephone warning. The area is evacuated. A bcmb disposal squad attempts to defuse the bomb, but the bomb explodes and a member of the disposal squad is killed.

Is the defendant guilty of murder, guilty of manslaughter, or not guilty of a homicide offence?

Scenario 4: The mercy killer

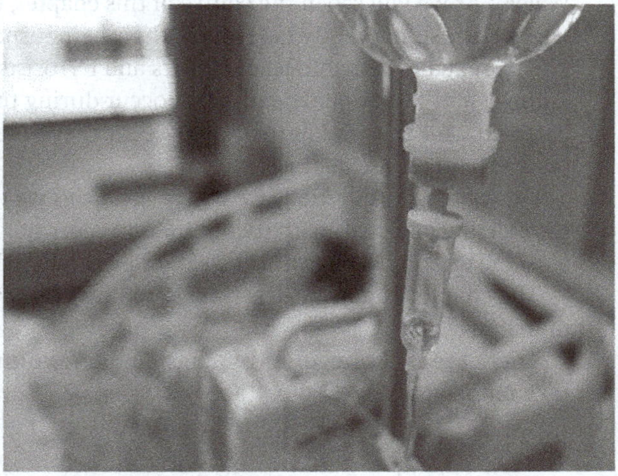

Be Panya/Shutterstock

The defendant's wife suffers from an incurable, incapacitating disease. She says that her life is not worth living and repeatedly asks the defendant to end her suffering. Eventually, the defendant agrees and suffocates her with a pillow.

Is the defendant guilty of murder, guilty of manslaughter, or not guilty of a homicide offence?

Scenario 5: The hapless surgeon

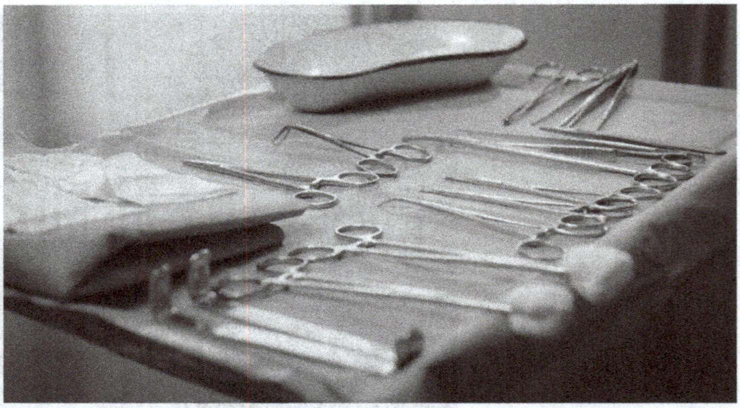

Aleksandrs Tihonovs/123RF

The defendant is performing a routine surgical procedure on the victim. Having worked a 16-hour shift the day before, and only had three hours' sleep, the defendant makes a careless error that no reasonable surgeon would have made. As a result of the error, the victim dies.

Is the defendant guilty of murder, guilty of manslaughter, or not guilty of a homicide offence?

Topics in this chapter

In the year ending September 2024, there were a total of 550 homicides in England and Wales.[1] As we will see in the course of this chapter, there are a wide range of homicides which vary significantly in terms of their heinousness and culpability. There are serial killers, sexually motivated child killers and terrorists. But we will also encounter honour killings, non-intentional deaths that occur during the commission of some other crime, battered women who kill their abusive partners, mercy killers and hapless medics who inadvertently cause death.

One of the key questions we will be asking as we work through the chapter is whether the existing law deals with these different types of killing appropriately. In other words, does the existing law respect the ladder principle (which we studied in Chapter 1)?

The chapter begins by describing the **law of murder**. It then moves on to the **law of manslaughter**.

There are two categories of manslaughter: **voluntary manslaughter** and **involuntary manslaughter**.

---

[1] Office for National Statistics, *Crime in England and Wales: Year Ending September 2024*. This figure covers the offences of murder, manslaughter, corporate manslaughter and infanticide.

Voluntary manslaughter is where the defendant satisfies the *actus reus* and *mens rea* of murder but is able to plead a partial defence. There are three partial defences in total. We study two of them in this text.[2] The first is loss of control, which we examine in this chapter. The other is diminished responsibility, which we will introduce here but go on to study in more detail in Chapter 10.

Involuntary manslaughter is where the defendant caused the victim's death without the *mens rea* of murder but is nonetheless sufficiently blameworthy to deserve being held criminally liable for the death. There are two forms of involuntary manslaughter: unlawful act manslaughter (sometimes referred to as constructive manslaughter); and gross negligence manslaughter.[3] We study both of these in this chapter, as well as the offence of corporate manslaughter.

The chapter finishes by outlining the **Law Commission's proposals for restructuring the law of homicide**.

Murder

5.1 Explain the requirements for establishing criminal liability for murder.

Before examining the definition of murder, it is important to first understand how those convicted of murder are sentenced.

EXTRACT

Murder (Abolition of Death Penalty) Act 1965

1 Abolition of death penalty for murder

(1) No person shall suffer death for murder, and a person convicted of murder shall be sentenced to imprisonment for life.

Notice the word 'shall'. The sentencing court has no discretion; a sentence of life imprisonment must be imposed. It is mandatory.

When a sentencing court imposes a sentence of life imprisonment, it must state how many years the defendant must spend in prison before he can be considered for parole. Here the courts must apply Schedule 21 of the Sentencing Code.[4]

Categories of murder

This Act creates different categories of murder. For each category the statute states a starting point, which is a presumption of how long a defendant should spend in prison

[2] The third partial defence is suicide pact. This is governed by the Homicide Act 1957, s.4.

[3] In his article 'Reckless Manslaughter', Findlay Stark rebuts the suggestion that there exists a third category of involuntary manslaughter called reckless manslaughter but argues that such a category should be created (Stark, F. (2017) 'Reckless Manslaughter' *Criminal Law Review* 763).

[4] The current regime for sentencing those receiving a life sentence was first introduced by the Criminal Justice Act 2003. The Sentencing Code – which came into effect on 1 December 2020 – consolidated all existing sentencing law into a single Act, the Sentencing Act 2020.

before he is eligible for release on parole. This starting point can be adjusted by the sentencing court if there are any aggravating or mitigating features. The following list explains the starting points for the different categories.

- For the most serious category, the starting point is a whole life order (i.e. the defendant should never be released).[5] This category applies if the defendant was aged 21 or over at the time of the murder and includes cases where: he killed two or more persons and the killings involved a substantial degree of premeditation or planning, the abduction of the victim or sexual or sadistic conduct; he killed a child and the killing involved either abduction or a sexual or sadistic motive; and he killed to advance a political, religious, racial or ideological cause.
- For the next category the starting point is 30 years. This category applies if the defendant was aged 18 or over at the time of the murder and includes cases where: he killed a police officer in the course of his duty; the killing involved a firearm or explosives; the killing was done for financial gain (such as during a robbery or in return for payment); and the killing was racially or religiously aggravated.
- For the next category the starting point is 25 years. This category applies if the defendant was aged 18 or over at the time of the murder and covers cases where the defendant took a knife or other weapon to the scene of the crime and used it to murder the victim.
- For the final category the starting point is 15 years. This category applies to all killings where the defendant was aged 18 or over at the time of the murder which do not fall into one of the previous categories.[6]

Remember, too, that if a defendant serves his minimum term and is released, his release is not unconditional. He is released on a life licence. If he subsequently breaks the conditions of his release or is found to pose a danger to the public, he can be immediately returned to prison.

Minimum terms and the broad scope of murder

It is important to understand the sentencing framework for murder in order to be able to evaluate the definition of the offence. As we will see, the offence of murder has a broad scope. At one end of the spectrum are serial killers, sexually motivated sadistic murderers and terrorist killings. But at the other end of the spectrum are mercy killers and battered women who kill their abusive spouse. Everyone convicted of murder receives the mandatory life sentence. And for adults, the starting point for the least serious category of murder is 15 years. Many commentators believe that the sentencing framework for murder is too rigid and unjustifiably harsh on some defendants who are convicted of murder. This has resulted in many calls for the mandatory life sentence to be replaced with a discretionary life sentence – or, failing that, a greater range of partial defences to murder.

---

[5] In *Vinter* v *UK* (app no. 66069/09) the Grand Chamber of the European Court of Human Rights held that, for a life sentence to be compatible with Article 3 of the Convention, there has to be both a possibility of review and a prospect of release. In *R* v *McLoughlin and another* [2014] EWCA Crim 188 the Court of Appeal subsequently held that the judgment in *Vinter* did not mean that the imposition of whole life orders violates Article 3, since domestic law provides for the possibility of release in exceptional circumstances which render the whole life order no longer justifiable.

[6] The rules governing those aged under 18 at the time of the killing can be found in paragraphs 5A and 6 of Schedule 21 of the Sentencing Act 2020.

Definitions and requirements of murder

With the introduction out of the way, we can now examine how murder has been defined. You may be surprised to discover that there is, in fact, no statutory definition of the offence. However, case law has established that it has the following four requirements:

1. The victim was a person
2. The victim died
3. The defendant caused the victim's death
4. The defendant intended to kill the victim or cause the victim grievous bodily harm.

Some definitions of murder also contain the following two requirements:

- The killing must have occurred during the 'King's peace'. This simply means that it is not murder to kill an enemy alien during a war.[7]
- The killing must have been 'unlawful'. This simply means that the defendant is unable to plead any of the substantive defences (which we study in Chapter 11).

Assessment advice

In an exam problem question you can safely assume that the events took place during the King's peace, so it will not be necessary to mention this particular requirement. When answering an exam problem question it is best to establish whether the *actus reus* and *mens rea* of murder are satisfied first, and if they are, to then go on to consider possible defences.

Numbers 1, 2 and 3 on the list above are *actus reus* requirements. Number 4 is a *mens rea* requirement. We will work through them in turn.

The four requirements of murder

1. The victim was a person (*actus reus* requirement)

The key question here is when does life begin?

For the purposes of the criminal law, the courts have held that a foetus becomes a person once it has emerged into the world and has an existence independent of its mother.[8] This means that a defendant who destroys a viable foetus is not guilty of murder or manslaughter. However, there are other offences which might apply, including procuring a miscarriage[9] and child destruction.[10]

[7] In *R* v *Adebolajo & another* [2014] EWCA Crim 2779 one of the men who killed Fusilier Lee Rigby in the Woolwich terrorist attack argued that the killing had not taken place under the King's peace since it was part of a war with the British Government. Rejecting this argument, the Court explained that the term 'King's peace' is concerned with the status of the victim as an enemy alien, and has 'nothing whatsoever' to do with the status of the killer ([33]).

[8] *R* v *Poulton* (1832) 5 C & P 329.

[9] Offences Against the Person Act 1861, s.58.

[10] Infant Life (Preservation) Act 1929.

It is also important to note that a defendant may be guilty of murder or manslaughter if he attacks a foetus pre-birth, and the foetus is born alive but later dies as a result of the injuries sustained in the attack. This was confirmed by the House of Lords in *Attorney-General's Ref (No 3 of 1994)* [1998] AC 245 (which we studied at the end of the previous chapter, in the section on transferred *mens rea*).

2. The victim died (*actus reus* requirement)

The key question here is when does life end?

In *Airedale NHS Trust* v *Bland* [1993] AC 789 (the case involving Tony Bland, a victim of the Hillsborough disaster, which we studied in Chapter 3) the House of Lords held that legally a person is dead once their brain stem is dead (i.e. once they are brain dead).

3. The defendant caused the victim's death (*actus reus* requirement)

Was the defendant's conduct a factual and legal cause of the victim's death?

Here you apply the law governing causation that we studied in Chapter 3.
Note that it is possible to commit murder by act or by omission.[11]

Assessment advice

If you are answering an exam question which involves an omission, remember the following:

- Before considering whether or not the defendant satisfies the *actus reus* of murder, you must first of all show that the defendant breached a duty of care which he/she owed the victim (see Chapter 3).
- When applying the test for factual causation, you must ask whether, but for the defendant's omission, the victim would have died. In other words, the prosecution must show, beyond reasonable doubt, that the victim would not have died had the defendant not breached his duty. If there is a realistic possibility that the victim would still have died even if the defendant had not breached their duty of care, then factual causation is not established.[12]

4. The defendant intended to kill the victim or cause the victim grievous bodily harm (*mens rea* requirement)

To establish the ***mens rea*** of murder the prosecution must show either that the defendant intended to kill the victim or that the defendant intended to cause the victim grievous bodily harm. This was confirmed by the House of Lords in *R* v *Cunningham* [1982] AC 566.[13]

[11] An example of murder by omission is *R* v *Gibbins & Proctor* (1918) 13 Cr App R 134, which we studied in Chapter 3.

[12] *R* v *Broughton* [2020] EWCA Crim 1093.

[13] A different case to the one we studied in the last chapter on recklessness!

There are two points to note here:

- The prosecution may establish either **direct intention** or **oblique intention** (see Chapter 4 for the distinction between these two types of intention).
- As we will see in the next chapter, the House of Lords has held that **grievous bodily harm ('GBH')** simply means 'really serious' harm.[14] Examples of GBH include broken bones, injuries causing substantial loss of blood and injuries resulting in lengthy treatment or incapacity.

The *mens rea* of murder

There has been much discussion of the *mens rea* of murder. This has focused on two important issues:

i. It is sufficient to show that the defendant intended to cause the victim GBH.
Some have argued that in this respect the *mens rea* of murder is too wide. Someone may satisfy the *mens rea* of murder even though they did not intend to kill and the possibility of the victim dying never crossed their mind.

Think back to the example of the 'one punch killer' at the beginning of the chapter. Did D intend to kill his friend? If not, did he intend to cause his friend GBH?

ii. Only intention will suffice.
Some have argued that in this respect the *mens rea* of murder is too narrow. A defendant who recklessly kills another person lacks the *mens rea* of murder even if he displayed a high degree of recklessness.

Think back to the example of the terrorist planting a bomb at the beginning of the chapter. Was it the terrorist's direct intention to kill or cause GBH to anyone? If not, was it his oblique intention?

Let's consider each of these issues in turn.

Mens rea requirement i: Intention to cause GBH will suffice for the *mens rea* of murder: is this too wide?

The rule that an intention to cause GBH will suffice for the *mens rea* of murder is known as the **'GBH rule'**. Although the GBH rule was reaffirmed by the House of Lords in *R* v *Cunningham*, there have been cases since then in which it has been criticised. For example, in *Attorney-General's Ref (No 3 of 1994)* [1998] AC 245 Lord Mustill stated:

> My Lords, murder is widely thought to be the gravest of crimes. One could expect a developed system to embody a law of murder clear enough to yield an unequivocal result on a given set of facts, a result which conforms with apparent justice and has a sound intellectual base. This is not so in England, where the law of homicide is permeated by anomaly, fiction, misnomer and obsolete reasoning. One conspicuous anomaly is the [GBH] rule which identifies the [*mens rea* of murder] not only with a conscious intention to kill but also with an intention to cause grievous bodily harm. It is, therefore, possible to commit a murder not only without wishing the death of the victim but without the least thought that this might be the result of the assault. Many would doubt the justice of this rule, which is not the popular conception of murder and (as I shall suggest) no longer rests on any intellectual foundation.

---

[14] *DPP* v *Smith* [1961] AC 290.

The GBH rule was also criticised by Lord Steyn in *R v Powell & English* [1999] 1 AC 1.

EXTRACT

Read the extract below from Lord Steyn's judgment and think about these questions.

a. What does Lord Stein identify as the principal justification for the GBH rule? Why does he reject this justification?

b. What criticisms does Lord Steyn make of the GBH rule?

c. What amendment does Lord Steyn suggest to the *mens rea* of murder? Do you agree with his proposal?

R v Powell & English [1999] 1 AC 1

Lord Steyn

In English law a defendant may be convicted of murder who is in no ordinary sense a murderer. It is sufficient if it is established that the defendant had an intent to cause really serious bodily injury. This rule turns murder into a constructive crime. The fault element does not correspond to the conduct leading to the charge, i.e. the causing of death. A person is liable to conviction for a more serious crime than he foresaw or contemplated [...] This is a point of considerable importance. The Home Office records show that in the last three years for which statistics are available mandatory life sentences for murder were imposed in 192 cases in 1994; in 214 cases in 1995; and in 257 cases in 1996. Lord Windlesham, writing with great Home Office experience, has said that *a minority* of defendants convicted of murder have been convicted on the basis that they had an intent to kill: "Responses to Crime," vol. 3 (1996), at 342, n.29. That assessment does not surprise me. What is the justification for this position? There is an argument that, given the unpredictability whether a serious injury will result in death, an offender who intended to cause serious bodily injury cannot complain of a conviction of murder in the event of a death. But this argument is outweighed by the practical consideration that immediately below murder there is the crime of manslaughter for which the court may impose a discretionary life sentence or a very long period of imprisonment. Accepting the need for a mandatory life sentence for murder, the problem is one of classification. The present definition of the mental element of murder results in defendants being classified as murderers who are not in truth murderers. It happens both in cases where only one offender is involved and in cases resulting from joint criminal enterprises. It results in the imposition of mandatory life sentences when neither justice nor the needs of society require the classification of the case as murder and the imposition of a mandatory life sentence.

[...] There is available a precise and sensible solution, namely that a killing should be classified as murder if there is an intention to kill or an intention to cause really serious bodily harm coupled with awareness of the risk of death; 14th Report of the Law Revision Committee on Offences against the Person (1980) (Cmnd. 7844), p.14, para. 31, adopted in the Criminal Code for England and Wales (Law Com. No. 177) (1989), clause 54(1). This solution was supported by the House of Lords Select Committee on Murder and Life Imprisonment, H.L. Paper (1988–1989) No. 78-1, p.25, para.68.

Mens rea requirement i continued: Murder as a crime of constructive liability

In the previous extract, Lord Steyn describes murder as a **constructive crime** – in other words, a **crime of constructive liability.**[15] One of the principles we examined in Chapter 1 was the **principle of correspondence**. Explore Figure 5.1 to find out more about this.

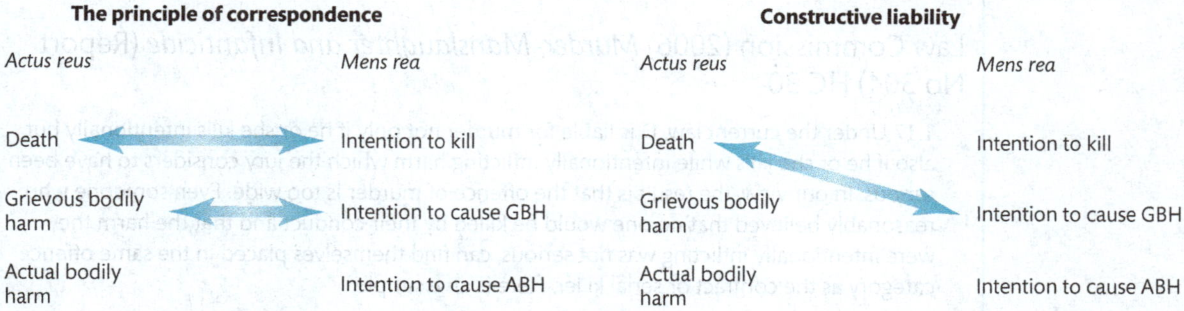

As this shows, according to this principle the *mens rea* of a crime should correspond with its *actus reus*. So, applying this to murder, the principle states that the defendant should be shown to have had *mens rea* in relation to death, not merely GBH.

The GBH rule violates this, and therefore means that murder is a crime of constructive liability. As Lord Steyn explains, the practical upshot of this is that a defendant may be guilty of murder even though the possibility of the victim dying never occurred to him.

Figure 5.1 Murder as a crime of constructive liability

The Law Commission's criticism of the GBH rule

In the following extract the Law Commission also criticises the GBH rule. It goes on to argue that the **two-tier structure** of our existing law of homicide (murder and manslaughter) is inadequate. As we will see later in the chapter, the Commission proposes a new, **three-tier structure.**

EXTRACT

Read the extract and think about these questions.

a. Why does the Law Commission criticise the GBH rule?

The Law Commission suggests that cases that involve a defendant who intended to cause GBH but not kill should be subdivided into two categories: those where the defendant realised that his conduct posed a serious risk of death and those where he did not.

[15] In their study of individuals serving life sentences, Hulley, Crewe and Wright found that, of those convicted of murder who regarded their conviction as lacking legitimacy, the most common reason for this perceived illegitimacy was the GBH rule. These individuals believed that, since they had not intended to kill, they should have been convicted of manslaughter, not murder. See Hulley, S., Crewe, B. and Wright, S. (2019) 'Making Sense of "Joint Enterprise" for Murder: Legal Legitimacy or Instrumental Acquiescence?' 59 *British Journal of Criminology* 1328.

b. According to the Law Commission, where should each of these two subcategories fit in their proposed three-tier structure (top, middle or bottom tier)?

c. What reasons does the Commission give?

d. Do you agree?

Law Commission (2006) *Murder, Manslaughter and Infanticide* (Report No 304) HC 30

1.17 Under the current law, D is liable for murder not only if he or she kills intentionally but also if he or she kills while intentionally inflicting harm which the jury considers to have been serious. In our view, the result is that the offence of murder is too wide. Even someone who reasonably believed that no one would be killed by their conduct and that the harm they were intentionally inflicting was not serious, can find themselves placed in the same offence category as the contract or serial killer. Here is an example:

D intentionally punches V in the face. The punch breaks V's nose and causes V to fall to the ground. In falling, V hits his or her head on the curb causing a massive and fatal brain haemorrhage.

1.18 This would be murder if the jury decided that the harm that D intended the punch to cause (the broken nose) can be described as 'serious'. Whilst it is clear that a person who kills in these circumstances should be guilty of a serious homicide offence, it is equally clear to the great majority of our consultees that the offence should not be the top tier or highest category offence.

[…]

1.20 The inclusion of all intent-to-do-serious-harm cases within murder distorts the sentencing process for murder. The fact that an offender only intended to do serious harm, rather than kill, is currently regarded as a mitigating factor that justifies the setting of a shorter initial custodial period as part of the mandatory life sentence. On the face of it, this seems perfectly reasonable. However, there is a strong case for saying that when an offence carries a *mandatory* sentence, there should be no scope for finding mitigation in the way in which the basic or essential fault elements come to be fulfilled.

1.21 We have been informed by research, carried out by Professor Barry Mitchell, into public opinion about murder. This shows that the public assumes that murder involves an intention to kill or its moral equivalent, namely a total disregard for human life. The latter may not be evident in a case where someone has intentionally inflicted harm the jury regards as serious, as when D intentionally breaks someone's nose. Indeed, some members of the public regarded deaths caused by intentionally inflicted harm that was not inherently life threatening as being in some sense "accidental".

1.22 Having said that, we do not recommend that killing through an intention to do serious injury should simply be regarded as manslaughter. Manslaughter is an inadequate label for a killing committed with that degree of culpability. In any event, to expand the law of manslaughter still further would be wrong because manslaughter is already an over-broad offence.

1.23 We will be recommending that the intent-to-do-serious-injury cases should be divided into two. Cases where D not only intended to do serious injury but also was aware that his or her conduct posed a serious risk of death should continue to fall within the highest category or top tier offence. This is warranted by the kind of total disregard for human life that such Ds show. They are morally equivalent to cases of intentional killing. Cases where D intended to do serious injury but was unaware of a serious risk of killing should fall (along with some instances of reckless killing) into a new middle tier homicide offence.

Assessment advice

Although the GBH rule is not difficult to understand, in the pressure of a timed exam it is common for students to forget it and write that to establish the *mens rea* of murder an intention to kill must be shown.

Before moving on to the second requirement for *mens rea*, consider the following scenario:

ACTIVITY

D believes that V knows where a large stash of money is hidden. To force V to tell him where the money is, D kidnaps V and tortures him. V suffers awful injuries. These injuries cause his death before he divulges the money's whereabouts.

In your opinion, in which tier of the Law Commission's proposed three-tier structure would this killing fall (top, middle or bottom tier)?

Mens rea *requirement ii: Recklessness will not suffice for the* mens rea *of murder: is this too narrow?*

If a defendant lacked any intention to kill or cause GBH, he is not guilty of murder – even if he was reckless as to the possibility of killing the victim.

Consider the following example that we introduced at the beginning of the chapter:

> A terrorist plants a bomb and then contacts the authorities and warns them. He plants a live bomb instead of a fake one – so that the authorities will fear him and listen to him – but he doesn't want the bomb to explode because he fears that he will lose public support if innocent people are killed. He gives the warning some time before the bomb is set to explode, so that the public can be evacuated and a bomb disposal expert can defuse the bomb. However, the bomb explodes and kills the bomb disposal expert.

On these facts it was not the defendant's direct intention to kill anyone or cause anyone GBH (he would not have regarded it as a failure if the bomb had been defused and no one had been harmed). Nor was it his oblique intention (serious harm to others was not a virtual certainty since the bomb might have been defused successfully). So notwithstanding the terrorist's disregard for human life, he would be not guilty of murder. His crime would be **unlawful act manslaughter** (which we study below).

Examples like this well-known 'terrorist example' have led some (including Lord Goff[16]) to suggest that the *mens rea* of murder is too narrow, and should be widened to include those who kill with a high degree of recklessness.[17] In the following extract Andrew Ashworth discusses this proposal.

---

[16] The Mental Element in the Crime of Murder' (1988) 104 *Law Quarterly Review* 30.

[17] For an alternative approach – which asks whether the defendant knew that death or GBH was likely and was reconciled to this since it would make a useful contribution to his purpose – see Leigh, G. (2022) 'Murderous Intent? The Attitude of a Murderer' 86 *Journal of Criminal Law* 18.

As you read the article, consider the following question and compile a list of arguments, adding in any arguments of your own.

According to Ashworth, what are the arguments for and against widening the *mens rea* of murder to include a high degree of recklessness?

EXTRACT

Ashworth, A. (1990) 'Reforming the Law of Murder' *Criminal Law Review* 75

It may be argued, however, that there are some reckless killings which ought to be classified as murder, since they show such a high disregard for human life as to be socially and morally equivalent to many intentional killings. It is not difficult to accept the latter proposition, but it is difficult to identify with precision the characteristics of these cases. Perhaps the most frequent example is the terrorist bomber who places a bomb and then gives a warning, despite which death is caused by the ensuing explosion. It was this example and a number of actual cases which led Lord Goff to advocate the adoption in English law of the Scots definition of murder, which goes beyond an intention to kill and labels as murder a killing which displays "such wicked recklessness as to imply a disposition depraved enough to be regardless of the consequences." Glanville Williams has disputed whether all the cases used by Lord Goff would be regarded as "wickedly reckless." A further objection is that its vagueness is such as to transfer too much power to the jury. It is less a rule of law than a rule permitting juries to respond to what they see as the equity of the case. As Sheriff Gordon has written in relation to Scots law: "to say that 'A is guilty of murder when he kills with wicked recklessness' means only 'A is guilty of murder when he kills with such recklessness that he deserves to be treated as a murderer.'

The question whether to widen the *mens rea* of murder was considered by a House of Lords Select Committee in 1989.[18]

EXTRACT

In the following extract Ashworth explains why he agreed with the Committee's recommendation that the *mens rea* of murder not be extended to include wicked recklessness.

As you read the extract, think about this question.

In light of your list of arguments for and against extending the *mens rea* of murder, do you agree with Ashworth and the Committee that the *mens rea* of murder should not be extended to include wicked recklessness?

Ashworth, A. (1990) 'Reforming the Law of Murder' *Criminal Law Review* 75

The Committee decided that "it is neither satisfactory nor desirable to distort [the principle that only intention will suffice for the *mens rea* of murder] in order to deal with the reckless terrorist

[18] *Report of the Select Committee on Murder and Life Imprisonment* (Session 1988–89, HL Paper 78).

and other 'wickedly' reckless killers, who will, in any event, be [guilty of manslaughter and] liable to imprisonment for life." This may be seen as a victory for the "rule of law" values of certainty and predictability over the merits of a vague test which would not only allow juries to reflect the subtler shades of moral and social culpability but also invite juries to return verdicts based on a distaste for the defendant's background, allegiance or general activities. Critics were quick to point out this gap between the Committee's proposals and the alleged public view that terrorist killings, even where a warning is given, should be murder. The reply to this is that the definition of the highest crime should not be broadened and loosened when there are many other offences (e.g. manslaughter, causing an explosion) to deal condignly with terrorist cases.

Two-tier vs three-tier

Whilst it is true that the terrorist in our example would be guilty of manslaughter and liable to life imprisonment, the Law Commission has argued that a manslaughter conviction would be insufficient. 'A manslaughter verdict', the Commission states, 'is an inadequate label for the offence'[19] (we studied the principle of fair labelling in Chapter 1). The Commission also offers the following two examples of cases where the defendant would be not guilty of murder but a manslaughter conviction would be inadequate.

EXTRACT

Read these cases and think about these questions.

a. Why would the defendants in the Law Commission's two examples below be not guilty of murder?

b. Do you agree that a manslaughter conviction would be inadequate in these two examples?

Law Commission (2005) A *New Homicide Act for England and Wales*? A *Consultation Paper* (Consultation Paper No 177)

EXAMPLE 2: In the small hours of the morning, D, knowing that a dwelling house is occupied by a rival in love, pours petrol through the letter box and sets light to it. The house burns down killing one or more of the sleeping occupants.

EXAMPLE 3: D lifts a large piece of concrete on to the parapet of a bridge over a busy road. He or she waits until a car is just about pass underneath the bridge and then pushes the piece of concrete off the parapet. It crushes to death one of the occupants of the car.

3.45 Suppose that, in both of these examples, the defendant says that his or her intention was simply to give the victims a severe fright but also admits that he or she went ahead despite knowing that it was likely that someone would be killed as a result of his or her action. The defendant says that he or she was not sure this would be the result, however, because (in example 1) the defendant knew the property had an exit at the back and (in example 2) the defendant thought the concrete might miss the car.

19 Law Commission (2006) *Murder, Manslaughter and Infanticide* (Report No 304) HC 30, para 1.31.

> 3.46 In both examples the defendant's admission is an admission of an exceptionally high degree of fault. At present, if the prosecution wishes to convict the defendant of murder they must at the very least show that the defendant foresaw death as the virtually certain consequence of his or her action. Even then, this only provides the basis for a possible inference by the jury that the defendant intended to kill or to do serious harm. Yet if one puts on one side this process of inference, there may sometimes be no significant moral difference between foresight of virtual certainty and foresight of high probability as such. So, justice is not served by putting the prosecution to this extra burden of proof.

The Law Commission goes on to argue that cases like these demonstrate a further reason why we need a new three-tier structure for the law of homicide. Under our existing two-tier structure, the terrorist and the defendants in these other two examples fall in the bottom tier (manslaughter). But under the Commission's proposed scheme they would fall in the middle tier, and so would be convicted of a more serious offence than manslaughter.

Now, think about this question.

Reflecting on all the extracts you have read in the last section, list the arguments for and against the *mens rea* of murder being expanded in order to ensure that the terrorist in the example is convicted of murder, not manslaughter.

Quiz 5.1

1. Which of the following examples would not give rise to a charge of murder?

- **a.** Killing a baby who was in the process of being delivered from the mother.
- **b.** All of these scenarios.
- **c.** Killing a baby who was detached from the placenta and breathing normally.
- **d.** Killing a baby who was born, but not yet detached from the placenta.

2. What sentence would a convicted murderer expect to receive?

- **a.** Depends on the judge's discretion.
- **b.** Fifteen years.
- **c.** Life imprisonment.
- **d.** The death penalty.

3. The *actus* reus of murder is the 'unlawful' killing of a human being. Which of the scenarios below would be considered murder?

- **a.** Killing by a citizen effecting a lawful arrest and using reasonable force.
- **b.** Killing by an officer of the law in the execution of his duty, using unreasonable force.
- **c.** Execution carried out by the person who is appointed for the task.
- **d.** Killing as a result of a lawful, but negligently performed, operation.

4. In which of the following scenarios is D likely to be guilty of murder?

- **a.** D is asleep one night when he hears burglars breaking into his house. D, although frightened, creeps out of his bedroom and into the main part of the house and retrieves his gun, which he normally uses to shoot rats on his farm, from the gun cabinet. D shouts a warning to the burglars and, on hearing them make more noise, he fires into the room where they are located. The following day the police find one of the burglars dead in that room.
- **b.** D is a sprightly 85-year-old. She is driving into town one morning when she sees a pair of robbers holding up a cash-transit vehicle and beating the driver in the cab. Incensed at this she drives her car into the side of the cab in order to prevent the robbery being completed or the robbers from escaping. As she does this one of the robbers was getting out of the cab and the impact of D's car kills him.

c. D is a police officer engaged in the act of arresting a very uncooperative V, who is putting up a fierce resistance. D resorts to spraying V with his CS spray in order to subdue him. V has an allergic reaction to this and dies immediately.

d. D is a hospital surgeon and operates to separate conjoined twins. A set of twins is presented to him that consists of a twin who will be capable of living if separate from her sister, and a twin who will certainly die if separate from the first because the second twin lacks a necessary vital organ and is only living while conjoined by virtue of the first twin's organ support. D knows that if he operates to separate the two girls, the second will die because of his act. D also knows that if he does nothing then both girls will die in a matter of months as they become too large to sustain life while conjoined. D decides to save the one by removing the second (V) from her. V dies.

5. In which of the following scenarios is D likely to be guilty of murder?

   a. D is the spouse of V, a terminally ill person in a great deal of pain and for whom D has great affection and whose needs he spends his life looking after. V intends to commit suicide but is too weak and D agrees, at V's request, to smother V with a pillow in order to provide her with an ending to her suffering. D does this with V's consent.

   b. D intends to rob a bank. Holding a customer hostage, he compels the bank clerk to give him access to the cash side of the counter area. Wanting only to restrain them he then ties up the clerk and the customer and gags them while he fills his bag with money; then he makes good his escape. The clerk survives until rescue arrives but the customer, who is asthmatic, suffocates and dies.

   c. D is a police marksman who attends a report of a man threatening others with a shotgun. D, at a distance, confronts the suspect V and orders him to put down his weapon. V spins round towards D at hearing D shouting at him. V is holding the weapon level at D. D immediately fires his own weapon at V and kills him. The weapon that V was wielding turns out to be an antique gun, deactivated and completely incapable of firing anything.

   d. D is a doctor treating a patient who has an incurable and very painful cancer. The patient begs D to give her a sufficient amount of painkillers to end her life and therefore allow her an exit from her suffering. D refuses the request but he does administer to the patient a dose of painkillers that he considers sufficient to numb her pain. D knows that the patient, V, is likely to die from the effect of the powerful painkillers although that is not his desire. V dies shortly after D administers the painkillers to her.

6. The *mens rea* requirement for a murder charge is malice aforethought. How is malice aforethought currently interpreted?

   a. Intention to kill or to cause grievous bodily harm.

   b. Intention to cause grievous bodily harm.

   c. Recklessness to death occurring.

   d. Intention to kill.

7. Where D kills V, and does so with the *mens rea* for murder, which one of the following circumstances will NOT apply to support a verdict by the jury in convicting D only of (voluntary) manslaughter and not murder?

   a. D was acting as part of a suicide pact.

   b. D acted out of loss of control.

   c. D acted while suffering from insanity.

   d. D was suffering from diminished responsibility.

8. Where D does an act from which the death of V is caused, but he does so without the *mens rea* for murder, which one of the following circumstances will NOT apply to support a conviction of D for (involuntary) manslaughter?

   a. D acted with negligence.

   b. D acted with extreme negligence.

   c. D acted recklessly.

   d. D caused death during the commission of another crime.

Loss of control

5.2 Explain the requirements for establishing the partial defence of loss of control.

The **partial defence of loss of control** was introduced by the Coroners and Justice Act 2009, replacing the partial defence of provocation. It is called a partial defence because, if successful, it does not result in the defendant being found not guilty of any crime. Instead it reduces the defendant's liability from murder to manslaughter.

Note, too, that loss of control is a **special defence.** It is only available on a charge of murder or being an accessory to murder. For all other crimes the fact that the defendant lost his self-control is not a defence (although it may be taken into account when sentencing).

Assessment advice

A common error in exam problem questions is that students often make the mistake of discussing the loss of control defence even though the alleged offence is one of the non-fatal offences that we will study in the next chapter.

The requirements for the loss of control defence are set out in section 54 of the Act.

EXTRACT

Coroners and Justice Act 2009

54 Partial defence to murder: loss of control

(1) Where a person ("D") kills or is a party to the killing of another ("V"), D is not to be convicted of murder if _____

(a) D's acts and omissions in doing or being a party to the killing resulted from D's loss of self-control,

(b) the loss of self-control had a qualifying trigger, and

(c) a person of D's sex and age, with a normal degree of tolerance and self-restraint and in the circumstances of D, might have reacted in the same or in a similar way to D.

[...]

(7) A person who, but for this section, would be liable to be convicted of murder is liable instead to be convicted of manslaughter.

(8) The fact that one party to a killing is by virtue of this section not liable to be convicted of murder does not affect the question whether the killing amounted to murder in the case of any other party to it.

This tells us that the defence has three requirements:

1. The defendant's conduct was the result of a loss of self-control.
2. The loss of self-control had a qualifying trigger.
3. A person of the defendant's age and sex, with a normal degree of tolerance and self-restraint and in the circumstances of the defendant, might have reacted in the same or in a similar way to the defendant.

Under the old law, the trial judge had to leave the defence of provocation to the jury if there was *any* evidence that the defendant was provoked to lose his self-control, however unlikely the defence was to succeed. This was regarded as unsatisfactory, not least because it created the possibility that an unmeritorious claim might succeed. The 2009 Act therefore requires the trial judge to 'undertake a much more rigorous evaluation of the evidence before the defence [can] be left to the jury'.[20] Section 54(5) states that 'sufficient evidence' must be adduced, which is defined in section 54(6) as evidence on which a jury could reasonably conclude that the defence *might* apply.[21] However, the trial judge must not usurp the role of the jury. His role remains a 'gatekeeping' one.[22] The focus is not 'his own assessment of the evidence' but rather 'the findings which it would properly be open to the jury to make'.[23] In essence, the question the trial judge should ask himself is whether a jury might be persuaded by the defence's evidence.[24]

Note also that section 54(5) requires sufficient evidence to be adduced for all three of the requirements listed above.[25] Each requirement should be considered in turn. For the first requirement, the nature of the attack is relevant, but not determinative. A frenzied attack might be the result of a loss of self-control, but might equally be due to a desire for revenge.[26] Equally, the fact that a defendant claims that he lost his self-control, or cannot remember what happened, does not in itself amount to sufficient evidence.[27] Such claims must be assessed in the context of the other evidence of the case.[28]

If there is not sufficient evidence that the defendant's conduct was the result of a loss of self-control, there is no need to consider the other two requirements. Similarly, if there is not sufficient evidence that the defendant's loss of self-control had a qualifying trigger, then there is no need to consider the final requirement. The defence will only be left to the jury if there is sufficient evidence of all three requirements. If this evidential threshold is met, then the onus passes to the prosecution to disprove the defence beyond reasonable doubt (s.54(5)).

We will work through the three requirements for the defence in turn.

Requirement 1: The defendant's conduct was the result of a loss of self-control

The first requirement is that the defendant had **lost his self-control** at the time of the killing. Note three points here:

[20] *R* v *Gurpinar* [2015] EWCA Crim 178, [14].

[21] An analysis of the first 110 loss of control appeal cases concluded that the 'sufficient evidence' test has been applied haphazardly, and that it has not succeeded in filtering out unmeritorious cases: Carline, A., Gibson, M., Singh, S. and Soubise, L. (2024) 'Civilising loss of control? The role of criminal justice gatekeepers' 44 *Legal Studies* 612.

[22] *R* v *Turner* [2023] EWCA Crim 1626, [39].

[23] *R* v *Turner* [2023] EWCA Crim 1626, [45]. Though in practice this distinction can be a difficult one to draw: see Manwaring, J. (2024) 'Homicide: Losing Control' 83 *Cambridge Law Journal* 210.

[24] Hungerford-Welch, P. (2024) 'Commentary on *R* v *Turner*' *Criminal Law Review* 339.

[25] *R* v *Gurpinar* [2015] EWCA Crim 178, [22]. For the argument that it is inappropriate to require the defendant to adduce 'sufficient evidence' of the last of the three requirements of the defence (the response of the normal person), see Storey, T. (2015) 'Loss of Control: "Sufficient Evidence" (Again)' 79 *Journal of Criminal Law* 154.

[26] *R* v *Drake* [2023] EWCA Crim 1454, [56]. See also *R* v *Cheng* [2024] EWCA Crim 1400, [39].

[27] *R* v *Drake* [2023] EWCA Crim 1454, [54]-[55].

[28] *R* v *Myles* [2023] EWCA Crim 943.

- The Coroners and Justice Act 2009 does not define the term 'loss of self-control', leaving the courts with the 'unenviable task' of interpreting and applying it.[29] In *R* v *Jewell* [2014] EWCA Crim 414 the Court of Appeal accepted as correct David Ormerod's definition of the term as 'a loss of the ability to act in accordance with considered judgment or a loss of normal powers of reasoning'. However, in the later case *R* v *Gurpinar* [2015] EWCA Crim 178, the prosecution criticised this definition, arguing that it is potentially too broad. In particular, it could include someone who merely loses their temper. Yet, as the Court of Appeal subsequently stated in *R* v *Tabarhosseini* [2022] EWCA Crim 850, it is clear that 'not every loss of temper will be a loss of control' ([32]). Since the issue was not raised by the facts of the case, in *R* v *Gurpinar*, the Court in that case opted to leave the question whether or not to define the term 'loss of self-control' to a future case, where the issue arose on the facts.
- Later in the chapter we will see that fear of serious violence may trigger a loss of self-control. However, it does not follow from this that feelings of shock, fear or panic necessarily involve a loss of self-control. As Davis LJ stated in *R* v *Martin (Jovan)* [2017] EWCA Crim 1359, 'a panicky or scared response to aggressive conduct of another person is not of itself indicative of the existence of an issue of loss of control' ([50]). In *R* v *Drake* [2023] EWCA Crim 1454 the Court of Appeal held that there was insufficient evidence of a loss of control where the defendant 'acted instinctively, in the heat of the moment to protect himself' and the picking up of the knife was 'a deliberate and rational act' ([64]).[30] The Court therefore upheld the trial judge's decision not to leave the defence to the jury.
- The question for this part of the defence is *not* whether it was reasonable for the defendant to lose his self-control. Rather, it is a subjective test: did the defendant lose his self-control or not? If so, then the first requirement for the defence is satisfied. If not, then the defence fails.

The question of whether the defendant lost his self-control assumes that the defendant possessed powers of self-control to begin with.

EXTRACT

As Richard Holton and Stephen Shute explain in the following extract, some defendants will not be able to plead loss of control because they lacked the ability to exercise self-control in the first place. What examples do Holton and Shute give of defendants who cannot plead loss of control because they lacked an ability to exercise self-control to begin with? Can you think of any other examples?

[29] Sullivan, G.R., Crombag, H.S. & Child, J.J. (2021) 'Loss of control in the appeal courts' 72 *Northern Ireland Legal Quarterly* 200.

[30] This reasoning has been criticised, on the basis that a defendant who loses self-control out of fear may nonetheless act deliberately and with at least some degree of rationality: see Benn, A. (2024) 'Commentary on *R* v *Drake*' *Criminal Law Review* 265.

Holton, R. and Shute, S. (2007) 'Self-Control in the Modern Provocation Defence' 27 *Oxford Journal of Legal Studies* 49

The subjective test is far more complex, and far more demanding, than has been generally realized. It requires not simply that agents must kill in response to provocation, but that they must kill *as a result of losing self-control* in response to provocation. We aim to take seriously the idea of loss of self-control. Once we do so, we find that the subjective test provides a substantial hurdle, for the simple reason that only an agent who antecedently possessed self-control can lose it as a result of provocation. To borrow Muddy Waters' words, you can't lose what you ain't never had; nor, we might add, can you lose what you have already lost.

Irascibility and drunkenness plausibly fall into the class of characteristics that should result in the defendant failing the subjective test. Irascible agents have never gained self-control, drunks have already lost it.

In order to decide whether the defendant lost his self-control, the jury may take into account any past events that are relevant.[31] So they are not limited to looking just at the events that occurred at the time of the killing; the cumulative impact of past events may also be taken into account.

Section 54 of the Coroners and Justice Act 2009 also offers the following guidance for juries trying to decide whether or not the defendant lost his self-control.

EXTRACT

Coroners and Justice Act 2009

54 Partial defence to murder: loss of control

[…]

(2) For the purposes of subsection (1)(a), it does not matter whether or not the loss of control was sudden.

[…]

(4) Subsection (1) does not apply if, in doing or being a party to the killing, D acted in a considered desire for revenge.

So the loss of self-control need not have been sudden, but the defendant must not have formed a considered desire for revenge.

Before moving on to the next part of the defence, it is important to consider how the loss of self-control requirement applies in three specific contexts: **mercy killings**, **revenge killings** and cases involving **domestic abuse**.

[31] *R* v *Dawes* [2013] EWCA Crim 322.

Requirement 1: i. Mercy killings

R v *Cocker* [1989]

In *R* v *Cocker* [1989] Crim LR 740 the defendant's wife suffered from an incurable disease. She had become severely incapacitated and repeatedly begged Cocker to kill her. One morning, after deliberately keeping Cocker awake for most of the night, she woke him by clawing his back and demanded that he kill her. Cocker put a pillow over her face and asphyxiated her. He later explained that her pleas to have her life ended had become too much for him. At trial, the trial judge ruled that there was no evidence of provocation and so Cocker pleaded guilty to murder. He then appealed against the trial judge's ruling. The Court of Appeal upheld his murder conviction. The Court explained that Cocker had not suffered a loss of self-control. He was not out of control at the time he killed his wife. He was in full control of himself and had acted calmly and deliberately.

Although *R* v *Cocker* was a case under the old law, the same principle would apply today. A mercy killer will not be able to plead loss of control unless he suffered a loss of self-control at the time of the killing. This is unlikely to be the case, as the notion of a mercy killing suggests a conscious decision to relieve the victim's suffering. If a mercy killer is to avoid a murder conviction and the mandatory life sentence, the only possible partial defence is therefore **diminished responsibility** (which also may well not be available, as we'll see in Chapter 10). Some, including Keating and Bridgeman, have accordingly argued for the creation of a partial defence specifically for mercy killers.[32]

Requirement 1: ii. Revenge killings

As we have seen, section 54(4) states that the loss of control defence is unavailable if the defendant 'acted in a considered desire for revenge'. The word 'considered' is important here. The Court of Appeal in *R* v *Clinton, Parker & Evans* [2012] EWCA Crim 2 approved the following explanation of when section 54(4) applies:

> 129 [. . .] An act of retribution as a result of a deliberate and considered decision to get your own back, that is one that has been thought about. If you are sure that what the defendant did was to reflect on what had happened and the circumstances in which he found himself and decided to take his revenge [. . .] that would not have been a loss of self-control as the law requires

So section 54(4) would *not* apply to a defendant who momentarily loses his self-control and acts vengefully, because on these facts the desire for revenge was not 'considered'.

An example (from the old law) of when section 54(4) would apply is *R* v *Ibrams & Gregory* (1981) 74 Cr App R 154.

If a case like this occurred under the new loss of control defence, the outcome would be the same: section 54(4) would apply. The defendants acted in a considered desire for revenge, so the defence would be unavailable.

[32] Keating, H. and Bridgeman, J. (2012) 'Compassionate Killings: The Case for a Partial Defence' 75 *Modern Law Review* 697.

R v Ibrams & Gregory (1981) 74 Cr App R 154

Ibrams had been bullied and terrorised by his fiancée's former boyfriend – the victim – for some time. Ibrams' friend Gregory had also been targeted. They had contacted the police twice but no effective action had been taken, so they formed a plan. Ibrams' fiancée would get the victim drunk and take him to his bed. She would leave the front door open for Ibrams and Gregory, who would then burst in, attack the victim and break both his legs. They carried out the plan. Following the attack the victim died. Ibrams and Gregory were convicted of murder. The Court of Appeal upheld their murder convictions, ruling that there was no evidence that the defendants had lost their self-control. On the contrary, they had taken time to construct a plan and then carried it out.

Requirement 1: iii. Loss of control in the context of slow-burn reactions and domestic abuse cases

Under the old law, a defendant could only plead the defence of provocation if his loss of self-control was 'sudden and temporary'.[33] As we have seen, things are different under the new defence. Section 54(2) states that it does not matter whether or not the loss of control was sudden. The reason for this change was to make allowance for **slow-burn reactions** (where a person's anger and resentment fester and then some time later explode). The Government explained that slow-burn reactions are associated particularly with domestic abuse cases.[34] The old law's requirement for a 'sudden and temporary' loss of self-control therefore presented an obstacle to battered women who seek to plead this defence after killing their abusive partners.

An important case under the old law which illustrates a slow-burn reaction is *R* v *Ahluwalia* [1992] 4 All ER 889.[35]

R v Ahluwalia [1992] 4 All ER 889

The defendant in this case was Kiranjit Ahluwalia. Her family arranged for her to marry the victim, Deepak Ahluwalia, whom she had never previously met. She suffered violence and abuse from the outset of the marriage. After suffering for many years, her husband's violence intensified in January 1989. For example, at Easter that year Ahluwalia was knocked unconscious, suffered a broken tooth, swollen lip and was off work for five days. In addition to this Ahluwalia discovered in March 1989 that her husband was having an affair with a woman he worked with. He would taunt her with this relationship. Despite all of this Ahluwalia wished to hold the marriage together, partly for the sake of their children and partly out of a sense of duty. In fact, in April 1989 her husband left her and Ahluwalia wrote a grovelling letter begging that he come back. On the evening of 8 May 1989 Ahluwalia tried to talk to her husband about their relationship, but he refused and said it was over. He demanded money from her for a telephone bill, and said he

---

33 *R* v *Duffy* [1949] 1 All ER 932.

34 *Murder, Manslaughter and Infanticide: Proposals for Reform of the Law* (Consultation Paper CP 19/08, 2008).

35 See also *R* v *Thornton* [1992] 1 All ER 306.

would beat her if she did not give him the money the next morning. Ahluwalia went to bed but couldn't sleep, thinking about his threat to beat her the next morning and his insistence that their relationship was over.

A few days earlier Ahluwalia had bought a can of petrol, which she had left outside. At 2:30am she got up, went downstairs, poured two pints of petrol into a bucket (to make it easier to throw), lit a candle on the gas cooker and carried these things upstairs. She also took an oven glove and a stick. She went into her husband's bedroom, threw in some petrol, lit the stick from the candle and threw it into the room. She then went to her son's bedroom, dressed him and went downstairs. Neighbours who saw her said she looked calm. Her husband died from his injuries.

At trial Ahluwalia was convicted of murder. On appeal, defence counsel produced fresh medical evidence, which showed that Ahluwalia had been suffering from a depressive illness. Since this evidence could potentially form the basis of a defence of diminished responsibility, a retrial was ordered. Before the retrial took place the prosecution accepted a plea of guilty to manslaughter on the grounds of diminished responsibility. Ahluwalia was sentenced to 40 months' imprisonment (the time she had already served) and was released immediately.[36]

Importantly, at Ahluwalia's appeal the Court of Appeal also discussed the defence of provocation. Lord Taylor CJ confirmed that the defence would only apply if the defendant's loss of self-control was 'sudden and temporary', but did add that as long as the loss of control was sudden and temporary it didn't matter if it didn't immediately follow the provocative event:

> We accept that the subjective element in the defence of provocation would not as a matter of law be negatived simply because of the delayed reaction in such cases, provided that there was at the time of the killing a "sudden and temporary loss of self-control" caused by the alleged provocation. However, the longer the delay and the stronger the evidence of deliberation on the part of the defendant, the more likely it will be that the prosecution will negative provocation.

In spite of Lord Taylor CJ's judgment, it remained unlikely that women like Ahluwalia would be able to plead provocation. It was difficult to regard Ahluwalia's actions as a 'sudden and temporary' loss of self-control. She had been lying awake thinking what to do. She went and collected the petrol and other items, lit a candle and then took the items upstairs. All of this suggested thought and planning, which are the antithesis of a 'sudden and temporary' loss of self-control. The Government believed that removing the requirement that the loss of self-control was 'sudden and temporary' would enable more victims of domestic abuse to plead the new loss of control defence.

Now, think about these questions.

Imagine that a case like *R* v. *Ahluwalia* occurred today. In your opinion, would the defendant satisfy this first requirement for the loss of control defence? In other words, did Ahluwalia suffer a loss of self-control?

NB: When answering this question, you may find it helpful to bear in mind the following statement from the Court of Appeal in *R* v. *Clinton, Parker & Evans:* 10 [...] In reality, the greater the level of deliberation, the less likely it will be that the killing followed a true loss of self-control.

---

36 Her story has since been made into a film, *Provoked* (2006).

Before moving on, it is worth noting that some do not believe that there should be a loss of self-control requirement at all. In fact, prior to the introduction of the Coroners and Justice Act 2009, the Law Commission described the loss of self-control requirement as 'unnecessary and undesirable' and recommended that it be removed altogether.[37] One of the reasons for this was that:

> The requirement of a loss of self-control has been widely criticised as privileging men's typical reactions to provocation over women's typical reactions. Women's reactions to provocation are less likely to involve a 'loss of self-control', as such, and more likely to be comprised of a combination of anger, fear, frustration and a sense of desperation. This can make it difficult or impossible for women to satisfy the loss of self-control requirement, even where they otherwise deserve at least a partial defence.[38]

In her survey of research from the fields of philosophy and social psychology, Sarah Sorial argues that emotions, including anger, 'are not simply forces that take us by surprise, and over which we have no control'.[39] The notion that anger may so overwhelm a person that they are deprived of their ability to reason is therefore both inaccurate and misleading:

> [W]hile we may have no control over feeling emotions, we have significant control over how we express them. Moreover, expressing anger using violence is only one way among many other ways we can express anger, suggesting that we cannot explain violence by reference to the loss of self-control. The fact that we have some choice in how we express emotions suggests that using violence is also a choice, based on assessment of the situations and on one's chances of success. It is therefore misleading to claim that the provoked, angry defendant lost his self-control, causing him to kill his victim.[40]

Sorial accordingly argues that the loss of self-control requirement should be removed and that the focus should instead be an assessment of the defendant's reasons for acting.

Requirement 2: The loss of self-control had a qualifying trigger

Under the old law, the subjective limb of the defence of provocation simply required that the defendant lost his self-control in response to things said or done.[41] This was criticised for being both too wide and too narrow:

- It was regarded as **too wide** because it meant that defendants could seek to plead provocation in cases where the victim's conduct was trivial or blameless. In *R v Doughty* [1986] 83 Cr App R 319, for example, the defendant killed his baby son. He said he lost his self-control because he was fatigued and the baby had cried persistently despite being fed, changed and other attempts made to settle him. The Court of Appeal reduced his conviction from murder to manslaughter on the basis of provocation.

[37] Law Commission (2006) *Murder, Manslaughter and Infanticide* (Report No 304) HC 30, para 5.17.

[38] Law Commission (2006) *Murder, Manslaughter and Infanticide* (Report No 304) HC 30, para 5.18.

[39] Sorial, S. (2019) 'Anger, Provocation and Loss of Self-Control: What Does 'Losing It' Really Mean?' 13 *Criminal Law & Philosophy* 247, 257.

[40] Sorial, S. (2019) 'Anger, Provocation and Loss of Self-Control: What Does 'Losing It' Really Mean?' 13 *Criminal Law & Philosophy* 247, 265.

[41] Homicide Act 1957, s.3.

- It was regarded as **too narrow** because it focused exclusively on one emotion: anger. This was widely regarded as problematic on the basis that it was gender-biased. Men are more likely to lash out in anger than women. Psychiatrists explain that a person is more likely to lose his self-control in response to provocation if the provoker is physically smaller and weaker. If the provoker is stronger the person is less likely to lose his self-control. This is why abused women tend to attack their abusers when they are off-guard.

The Coroners and Justice Act 2009 sought to address each of these criticisms of the old law by introducing the requirement that the defendant's loss of control was caused by a qualifying trigger. The qualifying triggers are defined in section 55.

EXTRACT

Coroners and Justice Act 2009

55 Meaning of "qualifying trigger"

(1) This section applies for the purposes of section 54.

(2) A loss of self-control had a qualifying trigger if subsection (3), (4) or (5) applies.

(3) This subsection applies if D's loss of self-control was attributable to D's fear of serious violence from V against D or another identified person.

(4) This subsection applies if D's loss of self-control was attributable to a thing or things done or said (or both) which –

(a) constituted circumstances of an extremely grave character, and

(b) caused D to have a justifiable sense of being seriously wronged.

(5) This subsection applies if D's loss of self-control was attributable to a combination of the matters mentioned in subsections (3) and (4).

The **first qualifying trigger** (in s.55(3)) responds to the concern that the old law was too narrow by creating a qualifying trigger based on fear. It applies where the defendant's loss of self-control was attributable to the defendant's fear of serious violence from the victim.

The **second qualifying trigger** (in s.55(4)) responds to the concern that the old law was too wide by limiting the availability of the defence in cases where the defendant acted in anger. It only applies if the defendant had a justifiable sense of being seriously wronged as a result of things done or said (or both) which constituted circumstances of an extremely grave character.

We will look at each of these qualifying triggers in turn. (Note that there is also a third qualifying trigger (in s.55(5)), which applies where the defendant's loss of self-control was attributable to a combination of the other two qualifying triggers.)

Requirement 2: i. First qualifying trigger: D feared serious violence from V against D or another identified person

A defendant who fears serious violence and uses force to defend himself will normally plead the **defence of prevention of crime** or **private defence** (which we study in

Chapter 11). Defendants will prefer to plead these defences because if successful they result in a complete acquittal, whereas loss of control is only a partial defence. However, as we will see later in the book, prevention of crime and private defence are only available if the amount of force used by the defendant was reasonable. A defendant who is charged with murder and found to have used an excessive amount of force to defend himself will therefore be unable to plead prevention of crime or private defence. Under the old law, such a defendant had no other defence and so would have been guilty of murder.

There were many who believed this to be too harsh. They argued that a defendant who genuinely feared serious violence but used excessive force to defend himself only deserves to be convicted of manslaughter, not murder. Following the changes made by the Coroners and Justice Act 2009, such defendants may now plead loss of control.[42]

Note the following four points about this qualifying trigger:

Four points about the first qualifying trigger

The defendant must have feared *serious* violence.

Helder Almeida/123RF

There only has to be *fear* of serious violence. There is no requirement that violence was actually used.

Curioso/Shutterstock

[42] In *R* v *Goodwin* [2018] EWCA Crim 2287, the Court of Appeal confirmed that this qualifying trigger may still apply even if the defendant cannot plead prevention of crime or private defence because he used excessive force to defend himself.

The threat of violence need not necessarily have been directed at the defendant. It may have been directed at another identified person. So, for example, the qualifying trigger applies where the defendant fears that his child will suffer serious violence from the victim.

Dennis Steen/Shutterstock

The threat of violence must emanate from the victim. The defence is unavailable if the defendant fears serious violence from one person (T) but kills someone else (V).

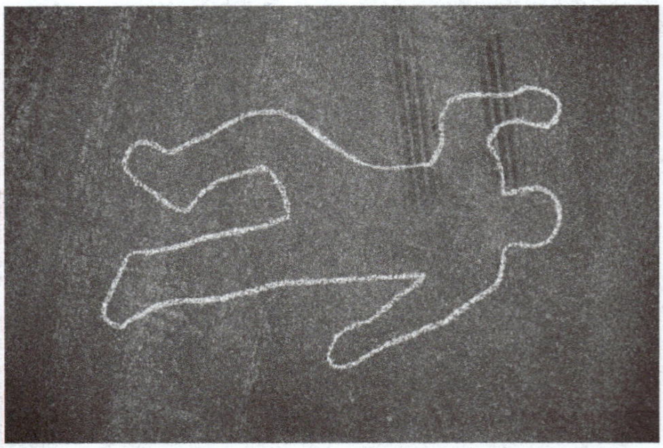

Joseph Belanger/123RF

The concept of fear in relation to cases of domestic abuse

As we have already seen, in practice it was very difficult for women like Kiranjit Ahluwalia to successfully plead the old defence of provocation. The provocation defence not only required that the defendant suffered a 'sudden and temporary' loss of self-control. It also focused exclusively on anger. The Government believed that adding this new qualifying trigger based on fear of serious violence would make the loss of control defence available to victims of domestic abuse. It stated that the defence would apply:[43]

> where a victim of sustained abuse kills his or her abuser in order to thwart an attack which is anticipated but not immediately imminent.

---

[43] Ministry of Justice (2008) *Murder, Manslaughter and Infanticide: Proposals for Reform of the Law* (Consultation Paper CP 19/08).

This is all the more important given that research has found that it is rare for victims of domestic abuse who kill their abuser to be acquitted on the basis of prevention of crime or private defence.[44] However, commentators have pointed out that a qualifying trigger based on fear of serious violence sits uneasily alongside the partial defence's requirement that the defendant suffered a loss of self-control.

In the following extract, Susan Edwards explains that there is a tension between the kind of fear suffered by victims of domestic abuse and the law's requirement of a momentary eruption in which the battered woman experiences a loss of self-control.

EXTRACT

Read the extract and think about these questions.

- What characterises the kind of fear that victims of domestic abuse suffer?
- Why is such fear hard to reconcile with the requirement of a loss of self-control?
- According to Edwards, how is this tension likely to be resolved? In your opinion, is this satisfactory?

Edwards, S. (2010) 'Anger and Fear as Justifiable Preludes for Loss of Self-Control', *Journal of Criminal Law* 74(3), 223–241

Instead of an eruptive moment, as is anger, fear is an enduring underlying state. For the abused woman living with and in domestic violence, the state of fear is in the continuous present. Victims of domestic violence do not suffer from general anticipatory fear, i.e. the fear we all might experience when walking unaccompanied at night in a deserted place that we might fall prey to attack. Instead they suffer from an extreme and continuous fear or state of continuous terror. Fear, therefore does not sit comfortably with loss of self-control as an eruptive moment. Fear is a breakdown in control; it is an inability to control circumstances because of an outside force rather than an inner eruptive response. It may be accompanied by a state of despair, a feeling of powerlessness and frustration of being robbed of effective agency, but it by no means follows that a person who lives in a state of fear is passive. As Burke noted, 'No passion so effectively robs the mind of all power of acting and reasoning as fear'. In the tenth book of *The Iliad*, the two Greek leaders aimed a spear at the head of a Trojan, 'He stood still and fell into a gibbering terror-his teeth began to chatter in his mouth and he went white with fear… He burst into tears… His body was trembling'. Yet the new definition of provocation requires fear, like anger, to result in a loss of self-control which is predicated on a roused state. So, what exactly will that fear-loss of self-control look like? Under the previous defence of provocation, the battered woman's fear was constructed around an habituated toleration of male violence which saps and undermines her will until the victim snaps. As Helena Kennedy once expressed it, 'the final surrender of frayed elastic'. But 'snapping' or 'last straw' articulations of cumulative provocation, and the loss of self-control of battered women, were so expressed as a means

---

[44] Howes, S.K., Swaine Williams, K. and Wistrich, H. (2021) 'Women who kill: why self-defence rarely works for women who kill their abuser' *Criminal Law Review* 945.

of bringing the battered woman within the ambit of anger-provocation-loss of self-control, which hitherto required an immediate response to an act done by the deceased. And to further bolster such an ill-fitting defence the battered woman syndrome typology was developed to emphasise that her fragile mental state was of relevance to capacity arguments.

Such expressions may now be formulated under the defence of fear-loss of self-control, s. 55(3), or anger-loss of self-control under s. 55(4), or both (s. 55(5)). The predicament of Pauline Wyatt sums up this dualism of fear and snapping or breaking, 'I was frightened to death of him . . . I couldn't take any more.' It must also be understood that expressions of anger and fear are linguistic devices, and represent attempts by the defendant to negotiate the legal outcome, rather than a true reflection of an underlying inner state. Joanna Bourke writes, 'Fear acquires meaning through cultural language and rites . . . Emotions enter the historical archive only to the extent to which they transcend the insularity of individual psychological experience and present the self in the public realm.' A new set of fear descriptors is therefore destined to enter the legal arena and it will be for the courts to identify the evidence that can bear upon it.

In fact, in her subsequent study of 40 homicide cases involving female defendants who killed intimate current or former partners, Edwards concluded that the 'fear of serious violence' qualifying trigger had had 'little impact'. It is 'likely little used and when used likely unsuccessful'.[45]

Requirement 2: ii. D had a justifiable sense of being seriously wronged as a result of things done or said (or both) which constituted circumstances of an extremely grave character

The **second qualifying trigger** applies where the defendant had a justifiable sense of being seriously wronged as a result of things done or said (or both) which constituted circumstances of an extremely grave character. As we saw above, the aim of this trigger was to impose some limitations on when defendants who lash out in anger may plead the defence. However, the wording used in section 55(4) has been criticised for being vague.[46] When will a sense of being seriously wronged be justifiable? And what constitutes circumstances of an extremely grave character?

As Figure 5.2 illustrates, there are four steps to work through to decide whether or not this qualifying trigger applies.

[45] Edwards, S. (2021) 'Women who kill abusive partners: reviewing the impact of section 55(3) 'fear of serious violence' manslaughter – some empirical findings' 72 *Northern Ireland Legal Quarterly* 245. Similarly, Carline et al's study of the first 110 loss of control appeals found an ongoing tendency to mitigate male violence and a 'failure to recognise and respond adequately to domestic abuse that women suffer, whether as a victim or an offender' (Carline, A., Gibson, M., Singh, S. and Soubise, L. (2024) 'Civilising loss of control? The role of criminal justice gatekeepers' 44 *Legal Studies* 612, 630).

[46] See, for example, Simester, A.P., Spencer, J.R., Stark, F., Sullivan, G.R. and Virgo, G.J. (2016) *Simester and Sullivan's Criminal Law: Theory and Doctrine* (6th edn). Hart Publishing: Oxford, p.401.

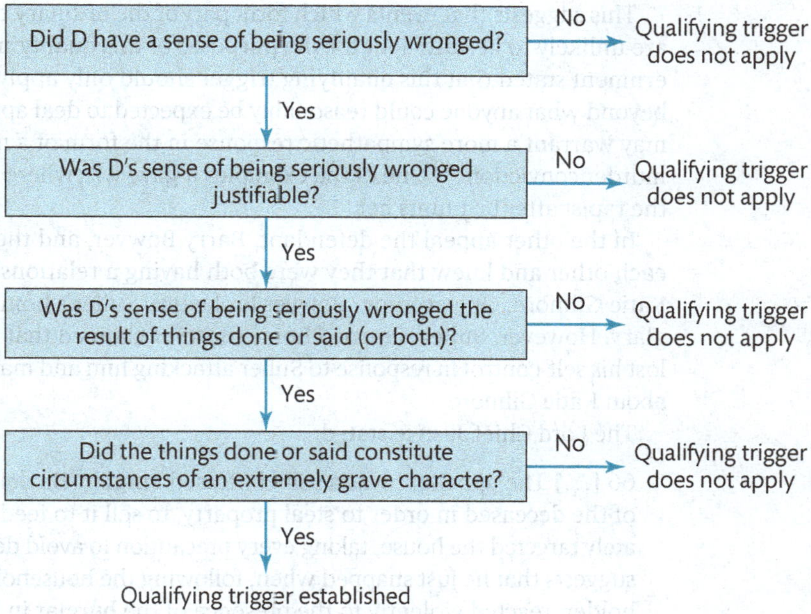

Figure 5.2 An overview of the section 55(4) qualifying trigger

Assessment advice

Remember to work through the four steps when answering an exam problem question to decide whether or not this qualifying trigger applies.

The first step is to determine whether the defendant had a sense of being seriously wronged. The Court of Appeal in *R* v *Clinton, Parker & Evans* explained that this is a subjective test based on the defendant's own perception. So the question is whether the defendant himself believed he had been seriously wronged.

The second step is to determine whether the defendant's sense that he had been seriously wronged was justifiable. The Court of Appeal in *R* v *Clinton, Parker & Evans* explained that this must be assessed objectively.

In *R* v *Dawes* [2013] EWCA Crim 322 the Court of Appeal considered three separate appeals against conviction. Two of these involved the question whether the defendant's sense of being seriously wronged was justifiable. In the first the defendant, Mark Hatter, fatally stabbed his girlfriend following the break-up of their relationship. The Lord Chief Justice stated:

> 65 [. . .] Dealing with it generally, we agree that the fact of the break-up of a relationship, of itself, will not normally constitute circumstances of an extremely grave character and entitle the aggrieved party to feel a justifiable sense of being seriously wronged.[47]

[47] To similar effect, in *R* v *Jacob* [2021] EWCA Crim 1401 the Court stated 'We understood the appellant effectively to concede that being told that his wife no longer loved him and was leaving him did not in itself give rise to a justifiable sense of being seriously wronged' ([28]).

This suggests that events which form part of the ordinary trials and tribulations of life are unlikely to be sufficient for the purposes of this qualifying trigger. Indeed, the Government stated that this qualifying trigger should only apply in 'situations which go far beyond what anyone could reasonably be expected to deal appropriately with and which may warrant a more sympathetic response in the form of a manslaughter rather than a murder conviction'.[48] One of the examples it gave was where a woman who is raped kills the rapist after he taunts her.

In the other appeal the defendant, Barry Bowyer, and the victim, Gary Suller, knew each other and knew that they were both having a relationship with the same woman, Katie Gilmore. One evening, Bowyer broke into Suller's home in order to commit a burglary. However, Suller returned home. Bowyer claimed that he killed Suller because he lost his self-control in response to Suller attacking him and making provocative comments about Katie Gilmore.

The Lord Chief Justice stated:

> 66 [...] The appellant was a self-confessed burglar. He deliberately entered the home of the deceased in order to steal property, to sell it to feed his drug habit. He deliberately targeted the house, taking every precaution to avoid detection. At the very best, he suggests that he just snapped when, following the householder's return, he, the householder, reacted violently to the presence of the burglar in his home and used deliberately insulting remarks about the appellant's girlfriend. To that the somewhat colloquial answer is, "So what"? If either of these men was justified in losing his self-control, it was the deceased. The deceased was entitled to say and do anything reasonable, including the use of force, to eject the burglar from his home. Even taking the appellant's evidence at face value (and we bear in mind that the jury must have rejected it) it is absurd to suggest that the entirely understandable response of the deceased to finding a burglar in his home provided the appellant with the remotest beginnings of a basis for suggesting that he had any justifiable sense of being wronged, let alone seriously wronged.

So whether or not the defendant's sense that he had been seriously wronged was justifiable must be assessed objectively. What is uncertain, however, is whether the defendant's particular circumstances can be taken into account.

Imagine the following example (which is based on a case decided under the old law[49]).

> One evening the defendant, who has strongly held religious beliefs, finds his teenage daughter in her bedroom with a young man. This is in spite of warnings he has given her previously. The defendant is so angry that he lashes out and kills his daughter.

On these facts it would seem that the defendant had a sense that he had been seriously wronged. But was this objectively justifiable? The answer to this question may vary depending on whether or not the defendant's strongly held religious beliefs may be taken into account.[50] Yet at present it is unclear whether these beliefs would be considered.

The third step in Figure 5.2 is to ask whether the defendant's sense of being seriously wronged was the result of things done or said (or both). In other words, the defendant's grievance must have been due to some human activity. So if the defendant was extremely upset because his house had been flooded in a freak rainstorm, this qualifying trigger would not apply.

48 Ministry of Justice (2008) *Murder, Manslaughter and Infanticide: Proposals for Reform of the Law* (Consultation Paper CP 19/08) para 33.

49 *R v Mohammed* [2005] EWCA Crim 1880.

50 Of course, the loss of control defence will only apply if the defendant also satisfies the third requirement for the defence, which we study below.

The final step is to ask whether the things that were said or done constituted circumstances of an extremely grave character. The Court of Appeal in *R* v *Clinton, Parker & Evans* confirmed that whether or not the circumstances were extremely grave must be assessed objectively. As with the second step, it would seem that circumstances will only qualify as extremely grave if they go beyond the ordinary ups and downs of everyday life.

Requirement 2: iii. Restrictions on what may constitute a qualifying trigger

So far we have studied what the qualifying triggers are. But the statute goes on to list three specific things which may *not* amount to a qualifying trigger. These can be found in section 55(6).

EXTRACT

Section 55(6) of the Coroners and Justice Act 2009

(6) In determining whether a loss of self-control had a qualifying trigger –

(a) D's fear of serious violence is to be disregarded to the extent that it was caused by a thing which D incited to be done or said for the purpose of providing an excuse to use violence;

(b) a sense of being seriously wronged by a thing done or said is not justifiable if D incited the thing to be done or said for the purpose of providing an excuse to use violence;

(c) the fact that a thing done or said constituted sexual infidelity is to be disregarded.

The first two exclusions are relatively straightforward. A defendant may not rely on the fear of serious violence qualifying trigger if he:

1. incited the victim to cause him fear; and
2. did this *in order* to provide himself with an excuse to use violence.

So suppose Harold forms a plan. He persistently provokes Peter until Peter reacts violently. Harold then attacks Peter, kills him and says, 'Peter attacked me and I feared for my life.' On these facts, section 55(6)(a) states that Harold may not rely on the fear of serious violence qualifying trigger.

Similarly, a defendant may not rely on the justifiable sense of being seriously wronged qualifying trigger if he: (1) incited the victim to provoke him; and (2) did this *in order* to provide an excuse to use violence.

So suppose Harold forms a plan. He persistently irritates Peter until Peter starts shouting gravely provocative comments back. Harold then attacks Peter, kills him and says, 'Peter insulted me so gravely that I lost my temper and lashed out.' On these facts, section 55(6)(b) states that Harold may not rely on the justifiable sense of being seriously wronged qualifying trigger.

Whilst these two exclusions are straightforward, it is questionable whether they are in fact necessary. In *R* v *Dawes* the Lord Chief Justice commented:

> 58 [. . .] One may wonder (and the judge would have to consider) how often a defendant who is out to incite violence could be said to "fear" serious violence; often he may be welcoming it. Similarly, one may wonder how such a defendant may have a justifiable sense of being seriously wronged if he successfully incites someone else to use violence towards him.

The third exclusion, found in section 55(6)(c), has generated much comment and we will go on to consider this in more depth.

The third exclusion: sexual infidelity

The third exclusion found in section 55(6)(c) states that, where a defendant claims to have had a justifiable sense of being seriously wronged, anything said or done that 'constituted sexual infidelity' must be disregarded. The aim of this provision is to ensure that the loss of control defence is unavailable to men who kill their partners after discovering that they have been unfaithful. The Government explained:

> It is quite unacceptable for a defendant who has killed an unfaithful partner to seek to blame the victim for what occurred. We want to make it absolutely clear that sexual infidelity on the part of the victim can never justify reducing a murder charge to manslaughter.

However, there are several issues regarding the wording of section 55(6)(c):

- Not all cases involving infidelity fall within section 55(6)(c), only those which involve 'sexual' infidelity.

> So if Harold kills his wife after discovering that she has been having a sexual relationship with another man, section 55(6)(c) would apply. But if Harold kills his wife after discovering that she has been dating another man, but the relationship was not yet a sexual one, it seems that section 55(6)(c) would not apply.

- **The word 'infidelity' suggests an ongoing relationship**. The relationship need not be a marriage or a civil partnership. It is sufficient that the parties have a mutual understanding.[51] However, the word 'infidelity' means that section 55(6)(c) would not apply if there never was a relationship or if the relationship has already ended.

> So if a jealous stalker kills the victim when he finds her having sex with another man,[52] section 55(6)(c) would not apply because there was no infidelity: the stalker was not in a relationship with the victim. Or suppose Harold's wife tells him that their marriage is over. The next day Harold returns home to collect some of his belongings and discovers his wife having sex with another man. Section 55(6)(c) would not apply because there was no infidelity: the relationship was over.

These are fine and arguably tenuous distinctions.

- Whilst it is clear how a thing that is 'done' can constitute sexual infidelity, it is less obvious how a thing that is 'said' can.

---

[51] R v *Clinton, Parker & Evans* [2012] EWCA Crim 2, [19].

[52] This example is based on the Australian case R v Stingel [1990] 171 CLR 312.

> If a husband hears his wife say 'I love you' to another man this may be evidence of sexual infidelity, but it does not necessarily 'constitute' it. Moreover, suppose that in the heat of an argument the victim falsely boasts to her spouse that she has had sex with other men simply in order to hurt his feelings. The statement cannot 'constitute' sexual infidelity since it is false, but the fact it is untrue does not mean it will be any less hurtful and provocative.

The Court of Appeal in *R* v *Clinton, Parker & Evans* stated, 'We are required to make sense of this provision.' Saying that it would be illogical for section 55(6)(c) to apply to statements of sexual infidelity that are true but not ones that are false, the Court held that admissions of sexual infidelity (even if untrue) cannot amount to a qualifying trigger. Nor do reports (by others) of sexual infidelity.[53]

These interpretative difficulties have led Andrew Ashworth to describe section 55(6)(c) as having 'more than [its] fair share of obscurities' and as 'little more than a crass attempt to level the playing field'.[54]

In a series of interviews conducted by Kate Fitz-Gibbon, professionals working within the criminal justice system also criticised the provision.

EXTRACT

Fitz-Gibbon, K. (2013) 'Replacing Provocation in England and Wales: Examining the Partial Defence of Loss of Control' 40 *Journal of Law and Society* 280

Interestingly, however, rather than welcoming the exclusion of such cases from the new partial defence, respondents across all samples interviewed were overwhelmingly critical of this provision in the formulation of the new defence. Legal counsel respondents described the exclusion as 'incredibly convoluted' (UKCounselE) and 'barmy' (UKCounselQ), while one judicial respondent posed that it was 'ill-advised' and 'bad law' (UKJudgeB). Similarly, policy respondents described the sexual infidelity provision as 'very problematic' (UKPolicyA), 'dire' (UKPolicyB), and 'really unnecessary' (UKPolicyC). These criticisms were often based upon respondents' belief that the exclusion of a particular situation was not conducive to good law-making and that it would lead to significant questions surrounding the situations in which the new partial defence would and would not apply. In explaining this perceived problem, a senior member of the English judiciary commented that:

> to try to produce specific subcategories of conduct that couldn't amount to a defence was not good law-making, it was better to lay down the general principles and provide the judicial check mechanism rather than try and carve out an additional specific exception. (UKJudgeA)

This judicial respondent further stated that the exclusion was 'unwise' for two key reasons: it was 'unnecessary' given that traditional sexual infidelity defences had lost favour with juror members in recent years, and that one should 'never say never' because 'there may be cases of which sexual infidelity forms a part, where a properly directed jury might say on the particular facts of this case we do think there is' an argument for a partial defence to succeed (UKJudgeA).

In agreement, other respondents also considered that there was no need to overtly exclude sexual infidelity, because, where unreasonably used, juries could discount it themselves. As one

[53] *R* v *Clinton, Parker & Evans* [2012] EWCA Crim 2.

[54] Ashworth, A. (2012) Commentary on *R* v *Clinton, Parker & Evans* Crim LR 543.

counsel respondent noted, 'it should be left completely to a jury with the usual directions' (UKCounselQ). In supporting the ability of the jury to adequately assess the individual circumstances of such cases, a policy respondent argued that:

> you have to trust the jury to use its common sense and I think what has happened here is that there has been an over-engineering of the law to try and make sure that juries can't consider certain things (UKPolicyA).

These viewpoints reflect a shared view amongst several respondents interviewed that juries inject an important community value judgement into the evaluation and categorization of differing culpabilities in homicide cases, a judgement that respondents believed should not be overridden by legislation.

R v Clinton, Parker & Evans and section 55(6)(c)

The central issue in *R* v *Clinton, Parker & Evans* was whether section 55(6)(c) applies not only where sexual infidelity is the only element relied on to establish a qualifying trigger, but also where it forms part of the context for another, admissible, qualifying trigger.

R v *Clinton, Parker & Evans*

The defendant in this case was Jon-Jacques Clinton. He and the victim, his wife Dawn Clinton, had been married for almost 10 years and had two children together. Two weeks before her death, they separated. Dawn went to live with her parents, but they continued to spend time together with the children as a family. On the day of the killing Clinton, who had been on medication for depression, looked at several websites containing material on suicide. He also logged in to Dawn's Facebook account and found photos of her with another man, including some that were sexually explicit. That afternoon Clinton confronted Dawn. She told him that she had had sex with five different men, going into graphic detail. She also noticed that he had been looking at suicide websites and taunted him about this, saying he didn't have the nerve and 'it would have been easier if you had, for all of us'. Clinton then attacked her, striking her with a piece of wood and strangling her. At trial he was convicted of murder. The trial judge ruled that the jury should not be asked to consider the possibility of a defence of loss of control. She explained that, according to section 55(6)(c), Dawn's description of having sex with other men had to be disregarded. Once these remarks were disregarded, all that was left were Dawn's remarks about Clinton not having the nerve to commit suicide. The trial judge held that these remarks alone provided insufficient evidence of circumstances of an extremely grave character and a justifiable sense of being seriously wronged. On appeal, Clinton challenged the trial judge's ruling.

The Court of Appeal held that the trial judge had been wrong not to ask the jury to consider a possible defence of loss of control. It accordingly allowed Clinton's appeal and ordered a retrial. The Court stated that the section 55(6)(c) exclusion only applies where sexual infidelity *on its own* is claimed to constitute a qualifying trigger. Where sexual infidelity arises for consideration in the context of other matters which may constitute a qualifying trigger, the section 55(6)(c) exclusion does not apply. Applying this, the Lord Chief Justice explained that Dawn's remarks about Clinton not having the nerve to commit suicide had to be evaluated in the context of the evidence of Dawn's sexual infidelity.

EXTRACT

Read the following extract from the judgment of the Lord Chief Justice and think about these questions.

What reasons does he give for saying that the section 55(6)(c) exclusion does not apply when the sexual infidelity forms part of the context for another, admissible, qualifying trigger?

R v Clinton, Parker & Evans [2012] EWCA Crim 2

Lord Judge CJ

23. [. . .] A much more formidable and difficult example would be the defendant who kills her husband when she suddenly finds him having enthusiastic, consensual sexual intercourse with her sister. Taken on its own, the effect of the legislation is that any loss of control consequent on such a gross betrayal would be totally excluded from consideration as a qualifying trigger. Let us for the purposes of argument take the same example a little further. The defendant returns home unexpectedly and finds her spouse or partner having consensual sexual intercourse with her sister (or indeed with anyone else), and entirely reasonably, but vehemently, complains about what has suddenly confronted her. The response by the unfaithful spouse or partner, and/or his or her new sexual companion, is to justify what he had been do ng, by shouting and screaming, mercilessly taunting and deliberately using hurtful language which implies that she, not he, is responsible for his infidelity. The taunts and distressing words, which do not themselves constitute sexual infidelity, would fall to be considered as a possible qualifying trigger. The idea that, in the search for a qualifying trigger, the context in which such words are used should be ignored represents an artificiality which the administration of criminal justice should do without. And if the taunts by the unfaithful partner suggested that the sexual activity which had just been taking place was infinitely more gratifying than any earlier sexual relationship with the defendant, are those insults – in effect using sexual infidelity to cause deliberate distress – to be ignored? On the view of the legislation advanced for our consideration by [counsel for the prosecution], they must be. Yet, in most criminal cases, as our recent judgment in the context of the riots and public order demonstrates, context is critical.

24. We considered the example of the wife who has been physically abused over a long period, and whose loss of self-control was attributable to yet another beating by her husband, but also, for the first time, during the final beating, taunts of his sexual activities with another woman or other women. And so, after putting up with years of violent ill-treatment, what in reality finally caused the defendant's loss of control was hurtful language boasting of his sexual infidelity. Those words were the final straw. [Counsel for the prosecution] invited us to consider (he did not support the contention) whether, on a narrow interpretation of the statutory structure, if evidence to that effect were elicited (as it might, in cross-examination), there would then be no sufficient qualifying trigger at all. Although the persistent beating might in a different case fall within the provisions for qualifying triggers in section 55(4)(a)(b), in the case we are considering, the wife had endured the violence and would have continued to endure it but for the sudden discovery of her husband's infidelity. On this basis the earlier history of violence, as well as the violence on the instant occasion, would not, without reference to the claims of sexual infidelity, carry sufficient weight to constitute a qualifying trigger. Yet in the real world the husband's conduct over the years, and the impact of what he said on the particular occasion when he was killed, should surely be considered as a whole

[...]

39. [...] It may not be unduly burdensome to compartmentalise sexual infidelity where it is the only element relied on in support of a qualifying trigger, and, having compartmentalised it in this way, to disregard it. Whether this is so or not, the legislation imposes that exclusionary obligation on the court. However, to seek to compartmentalise sexual infidelity and exclude it when it is integral to the facts as a whole is not only much more difficult, but is unrealistic and carries with it the potential for injustice. In the examples we have given earlier in this judgment, we do not see how any sensible evaluation of the gravity of the circumstances or their impact on the defendant could be made if the jury, having, in accordance with the legislation, heard the evidence, were then to be directed to excise from their evaluation of the qualifying trigger the matters said to constitute sexual infidelity, and to put them into distinct compartments to be disregarded. In our judgment, where sexual infidelity is integral to and forms an essential part of the context in which to make a just evaluation whether a qualifying trigger properly falls within the ambit of subsections 55(3) and 55(4), the prohibition in section 55(6)(c) does not operate to exclude it.

So according to *R* v *Clinton, Parker & Evans,* the section 55(6)(c) exclusion does not apply where sexual infidelity arises for consideration in the context of other matters which may constitute a qualifying trigger. This greatly limits the scope of the sexual infidelity exclusion. As Clough-Ricci observes, sexual infidelity 'rarely occurs without other issues within a relationship' and so 'it is hard to see how it would ever be excluded from being heard by the court'[55].

Is section 55(6)(c) actually necessary?

Before moving on, it is worth noting **four further points.**

First, commentators have questioned whether section 55(6)(c) is actually necessary.[56] Even if a jealous husband did suffer a loss of self-control in response to discovering his wife's sexual infidelity, he will only be convicted of manslaughter instead of murder on the basis of loss of control if he also passes the final part of the defence: **the objective test** (which we will study in a moment). In many cases, jealous husbands will not pass this test. In fact, Withey notes that the evidence gathered by the Government showed that under the old law jealous men were *not* avoiding murder convictions by claiming provocation.[57]

Second, there has been criticism of the failure of the sexual infidelity exclusion to differentiate between the rationales behind the sexual infidelity or reaction to it. Clough-Ricci explains that, 'Whilst we want to exclude some killings, especially those involving jealousy, we may want to preserve the defence in others, that involve

[55] Clough-Ricci, A. (2025) 'Sexual Infidelity and a Justifiable Sense of Being Seriously Wronged: What Next for the Loss of Control Defence?' 89 *Journal of Criminal Law* 155, 163.

[56] Alternatively, Wake and Reed argue that the sexual infidelity exclusion attempts to address gender disparity without getting to the nub of the issue. They advance reform proposals aimed at 'the broader issue of the dire risk victims of coercive control are in from the point at which their partner suspects they may leave or be unfaithful' (Wake, N. & Reed, A. (2024) 'Reconceptualising Sexual Infidelity Provocation: New Anglo-Scottish Reform Proposals' 88 *Journal of Criminal Law* 17, 30).

[57] Withey, C. (2011) 'Loss of Control, Loss of Opportunity?' *Criminal Law Review* 263.

abusive relationships, gross breach of trust and humiliation'.[58] She illustrates this using the case of Sally Challen:

> Initially looked upon as a jealous woman, in particular because she had uttered the words 'if I can't have him, no one can' before she was arrested. However, the note she had left after taking a hammer to her husband's head explained that he had tricked her into thinking they were reconciling and tried to have her sign over all of her financial assets in doing so. The things she said in her police interview, that everything had to be on her husband's terms, that she constantly tried to please him whilst he was always critical of her, insinuated what we would now deem to be coercing and controlling behaviour. Even their own children attested to this in her defence. There is nothing to be gained in respect of justice by removing his numerous affairs from the equation. Speaking on Challen's case, Stark said that what was unbearable for her was not that her husband often wanted someone else, but that he had made her into 'nothing' in the process. The first time she questioned his infidelity, he threw her down the stairs. Again, an example of how difficult it would be to disentangle the infidelity from the other actions.

Third, some have questioned why there is a specific statutory exclusion for cases of sexual infidelity but not for other types of case such as honour killings.[59] Withey discusses this point in the following extract.

EXTRACT

As you read the extract, reflect on the following questions:

Do you agree that honour killings are a 'more worthy' candidate for exclusion than killings in response to sexual infidelity? What moral message do you think section 55(6)(c) sends out?

Withey, C. (2011) 'Loss of Control, Loss of Opportunity?' *Criminal Law Review* 263

The public might question why sexual infidelity has been singled out for exclusion. Some might sympathise with a person who receives the mandatory life sentence because they killed their partner upon discovering their adultery. Recent media reports involving celebrity affairs have shown how the public frown on those who cheat on their loved ones. There are perhaps more worthy candidates for exclusion. Few sympathise with those who commit honour killings. In *Mohammed (Faqir)* a Muslim father stabbed his daughter to death having discovered a young man in her bedroom. The defence of provocation could be considered by the jury. There is no express restriction in the new law for such cases, as there is with sexual infidelity. This does not mean that D who commits an honour killing will be able to rely upon the partial defence; the thing done, the conduct of a daughter, will have to be seriously grave and give a justifiable sense of being seriously wronged. In addition, the objective test will have to be met, which is highly unlikely. By not excluding situations like this from the ambit of the partial defence, Parliament has indirectly sent out a moral message regarding those who resort to killing having discovered sexual infidelity.

---

58 Clough-Ricci, A. (2025) 'Sexual Infidelity and a Justifiable Sense of Being Seriously Wronged: What Next for the Loss of Control Defence?' 89 *Journal of Criminal Law* 155, 161.

59 See also Clough, A. (2016) 'Honour Killings, Partial Defences and the Exclusionary Conduct Model' 80 *Journal of Criminal Law* 177.

Lastly, Horder and Fitz-Gibbon have shown that, when sentencing for murder, the courts have continued to regard evidence of sexual infidelity as capable of amounting to grave provocation that may justify a significantly lower minimum term of imprisonment. They argue that this ignores the spirit of the sexual infidelity exclusion and threatens the integrity of the moral message that section 55(6)(c) was intended to communicate.[60]

Requirement 3: A person of the defendant's age and sex, with a normal degree of tolerance and self-restraint and in the circumstances of the defendant, might have reacted in the same or in a similar way to the defendant

The third requirement for the defence is that a person of the defendant's age and sex, with a normal degree of tolerance and self-restraint and in the circumstances of the defendant, might have reacted in the same or in a similar way to the defendant. This is an **objective test**. It is designed to stop defendants from pleading loss of control when they have failed to show the level of self-restraint that society is entitled to expect from its members.

We can break the wording of the objective test down into the following four parts as follows.

i. '... might have reacted in the same or in a similar way to the defendant'

First, note that section 54(1)(c) uses the word 'might'. The question is whether a normal person might have reacted in the same or a similar way to the defendant, not whether a normal person would have done so. Remember too that the burden of proof rests on the prosecution: the prosecution must establish beyond reasonable doubt that a normal person would not have reacted as the defendant did. So if a jury is unsure whether a normal person might have reacted as the defendant did or not, this part of the loss of control defence is satisfied.

Second, note that it is not enough that a normal person might also have lost their self-control in the same situation. The test is whether a normal person might have reacted 'in the same or in a similar way to the defendant'. In other words, might a normal person not only have lost their self-control, but also killed the victim in the same or in a similar way to the defendant?

ii. 'A person of the defendant's age and sex...'

The wording of section 54(1)(c) makes it clear that the hypothetical normal person is the same age and gender as the defendant. This is the same as under the old law, as set out by the House of Lords in *R* v *Camplin* [1978] AC 705. In this case the defendant was a 15-year-old boy. He killed the victim, a middle-aged man named Mohammed Lal Khan, by splitting his skull with a chapati pan. Camplin said that Khan had sexually assaulted him and that he lost his self-control and lashed out when Khan later laughed at him. The House of Lords held that Camplin should be judged according to the standards of a normal 15-year-old boy, not a normal adult. Lord Diplock explained that 'to require old heads upon young shoulders' would be inconsistent with the rationale of the defence: to make some concession for human frailty.

[60] Horder, J. and Fitz-Gibbon, K. (2015) 'When Sexual Infidelity Triggers Murder: Examining the Impact of Homicide Law Reform on Judicial Attitudes in Sentencing' 74 *Cambridge Law Journal* 307.

Why the statute explicitly refers to the defendant's gender is less clear. There is no obvious reason why the level of self-restraint society is entitled to expect should differ according to whether the defendant is male or female. One possible explanation might be that adolescent girls mature more quickly than adolescent boys. If this is correct (and it would require scientific validation), a 15-year-old girl might be expected to show more self-restraint than a 15-year-old boy.

iii. '... in the circumstances of the defendant...'

When applying the objective test, the jury should consider the reaction of a normal person 'in the circumstances of the defendant'. There are two types of situation where this will be particularly important:

- Cases which involve a cumulative impact. In such a case the jury may take into account any past events that are relevant. This will be important in order to appreciate the significance of the events at the time of the killing. So, for example, in a case like *R* v *Ahluwalia* a jury would not only take into account the threats that occurred in the hours before the killing. They would be able to take into account the full history of violence and abuse.
- Cases where the defendant is taunted about a particular characteristic. Where the defendant is taunted about a particular characteristic, the jury should consider the impact on someone with that characteristic. For example, if the victim shouts racist abuse at the defendant, the jury should take into account the defendant's ethnicity. Or if the victim taunts the defendant about his recent release from prison, calling him a jailbird, the jury should take into account the fact that the defendant is an ex-offender.[61] This was confirmed by the Court of Appeal in *R* v *Asmelash* [2013] EWCA Crim 157. The Court stated that if 'a defendant with a severe problem with alcohol or drugs was mercilessly taunted about the condition, to the extent that it constituted a qualifying trigger, the alcohol or drug problem would then form part of the circumstances for consideration'.[62]

Note also that the Court of Appeal in *R* v *Clinton, Parker & Evans* held that sexual infidelity may be taken into account when applying the objective test. The statutory exclusion contained in section 55(6)(c) only applies to the second limb of the defence (i.e. whether or not there was a qualifying trigger). In his judgment the Lord Chief Justice commented on the difficulties this may present to juries:

> 32 We must reflect briefly on the directions to be given by the judge to the jury. On one view they would require the jury to disregard any evidence relating to sexual infidelity when they are considering the second component of the defence, yet, notwithstanding this prohibition, would also require the same evidence to be addressed if the third component arises for consideration. In short, there will be occasions when the jury would be both disregarding and considering the same evidence. That is, to put it neutrally, counter intuitive

[61] Sir John Smith wrote: 'Suppose that an old lag, now trying to go straight, is taunted with being "a jailbird". This might be extremely provoking, especially if it reveals his murky past to new friends or employers unaware of it. It really would not make much sense to ask the jury to consider the effect of such provocation on a man of good character' (Smith, J.C. (1993) Commentary on R v Morhall Crim LR 957).

[62] This mirrors the position under the old law. In R v Morhall [1996] AC 90 the victim taunted the defendant about his glue-sniffing addiction. The House of Lords held that the jury should have been told to consider the effect of the taunts on a person with such an addiction.

iv. '... with a normal degree of tolerance and self-restraint...'

Whilst the general rule is that the jury may take the defendant's circumstances into account, there is one exception. This can be found in section 54(3).

Section 54(3)

EXTRACT

Section 54(3) of the Coroners and Justice Act 2009

54 Partial defence to murder: loss of control

[...]

(3) In subsection (1)(c) the reference to "*the circumstances of D*" is a reference to all of D's circumstances other than those whose only relevance to D's conduct is that they bear on D's general capacity for tolerance or self-restraint.

So suppose the defendant is particularly hot-headed or short-tempered. The jury should not be instructed to consider whether a normal hot-headed or short-tempered person would have reacted in the same or in a similar way. Individuals who are hot-headed or short-tempered are expected to show a normal level of tolerance and self-restraint. To hold otherwise would dilute the objectivity of the test and undermine its rationale.

Section 54(3) and mental abnormalities

Importantly, section 54(3) applies not only to characteristics like hot-headedness and short-temperedness. It also applies to mental abnormalities which impair an individual's capacity for tolerance and self-restraint.[63] So a defendant who has a depressive illness which affects his powers of self-control will still be expected to show a normal level of tolerance and self-restraint notwithstanding his illness. This was confirmed by the Court of Appeal in *R* v *Rejmanski* [2017] EWCA Crim 2061:

> 25 ... [T]he wording of s. 54(1)(c) is clear: in assessing the third component, the defendant is to be judged against the standard of a person with a normal degree, and not an abnormal degree, of tolerance and self-restraint. If, and in so far as, a personality disorder reduced the defendant's general capacity for tolerance or self-restraint, that would not be a relevant consideration.

Imagine a case in which the defendant had a personality disorder that reduced his powers of self-control. The defendant lost his self-control and killed the victim after the victim had taunted him about his personality disorder. According to *R* v *Rejmanski*, the defendant's condition:

> 25 [...] would not be a relevant consideration even if the personality disorder was one of the "circumstances" of the defendant because it was relevant to the gravity of the trigger... Expert evidence about the impact of the disorder would be irrelevant and inadmissible on the issue of whether it would have reduced the capacity for tolerance and self-restraint of the hypothetical "person of D's sex and age, with a normal degree of tolerance and self-restraint"

[63] This was also the position under the old law: see *Attorney-General for Jersey* v *Holley* [2005] UKPC 23.

Such a case would therefore be another example of an occasion where the jury would be expected to both disregard and consider the same evidence: the jury should consider the personality disorder when assessing the gravity of the qualifying trigger but then disregard it when deciding whether the defendant showed a normal level of tolerance and self-restraint.

Sections 54(1)(c) and 54(3) and R v Ahluwalia

Kiranjit Ahluwalia suffered from a depressive illness and from battered woman syndrome. Both of these conditions reduced her ability to exercise self-control. So, in a case like *R* v *Ahluwalia*, section 54(1)(c) and section 54(3) tell us that when applying the objective test, the long history of violence may be considered but the defendant's reduced powers of self-control may not.

Now, think about these questions.

a. Do you think a normal person might have reacted in the same or in a similar way to Ahluwalia?

b. Considering your answer to the previous question, and the other two requirements for the loss of control defence, do you think that if a case like *R* v *Ahluwalia* occurred today the defendant would be able to plead loss of control?

(Your answers will be important in assessing whether the new defence achieves one of its key objectives.[64]) Finally, note that the Court of Appeal has also held that a defendant's voluntary intoxication may not be taken into account when applying the objective test.[65]

Quiz 5.2

1. Which partial defence has been replaced by the defence of loss of control?
   a. Provocation.
   b. Infanticide.
   c. Diminished responsibility.
   d. Suicide pact.

2. Which section of the Coroners and Justice Act 2009 sets out the criteria for the defence of loss of control?
   a. Section 52.
   b. Section 53.
   c. Section 54.
   d. Section 56.

3. Which of the following is not a 'qualifying trigger' for the defence of loss of control?
   a. A thing said of an extremely grave character.
   b. Sexual infidelity.
   c. A thing done of an extremely grave character.
   d. A fear of serious violence.

4. To meet the requirements for the defence of loss of control, a defendant…
   a. Must have a sudden loss of control.
   b. Must have a sudden and temporary loss of control.
   c. Need not experience a loss of control.
   d. Must experience a loss of control.

[64] It is also important to point out that there is a 'very real possibility' that, if a case like *R* v *Ahluwalia* occurred today and the defendant was convicted of murder, the minimum term that would be imposed would be around 20 years' imprisonment. This is nearly double the tariff period of twelve years that Ahluwalia originally received, before the Court of Appeal heard her appeal and ordered a retrial. See Horder, J. and Fitz-Gibbon, K. (2015) 'When Sexual Infidelity Triggers Murder: Examining the Impact of Homicide Law Reform on Judicial Attitudes in Sentencing' 74 *Cambridge Law Journal* 307.

[65] *R* v *Asmelash* [2013] EWCA Crim 157.

Diminished responsibility: An introduction

The second of the two partial defences to murder that we study in this text is **diminished responsibility**. The defence of diminished responsibility is defined by section 2 of the Homicide Act 1957 (as amended by the Coroners and Justice Act 2009). Section 2(1) tells us that the defence has four requirements:

1. The defendant was suffering from an abnormality of mental functioning.
2. The defendant's abnormality of mental functioning arose from a recognised medical condition.
3. The defendant's abnormality of mental functioning substantially impaired his ability to do one of the things listed in subsection (1A).
4. The defendant's abnormality of mental functioning provides an explanation for the defendant's participation in the killing.

We will examine these four requirements in detail in Chapter 10, in order to compare the diminished responsibility defence to the defence of insanity (though if you'd like to read about them now, you should do so!).

The reason for introducing the diminished responsibility defence in this chapter is to explain the thinking behind section 54(3) of the Coroners and Justice Act 2009. As we have just seen, section 54(3) states that when applying the final, objective requirement for the defence of loss of control, the jury may not take into account any circumstances 'whose only relevance is that they bear on D's general capacity for tolerance or self-restraint'. This includes defendants with a mental abnormality that impairs their capacity for tolerance or self-restraint. The reason for this apparently strict approach to defendants with mental abnormalities is to preserve a distinction between the defence of loss of control and the defence of diminished responsibility, as the following example illustrates.

> Harold has a mental abnormality which impairs his capacity for tolerance and self-restraint. One day, in response to Peter gently teasing him, Harold lashes out violently and kills Peter.

In such circumstances, the predominant cause of Harold's loss of self-control was not Peter's gentle teasing. Rather it was Harold's mental abnormality, which caused Harold to react disproportionately and lash out.

The approach of the existing law is effectively to say that, if the predominant cause of a defendant's loss of self-control was his mental abnormality, then he should plead diminished responsibility, not loss of control.[66] So in our example, since the predominant cause of Harold's loss of self-control was his mental abnormality he should plead diminished responsibility. To take Harold's mental abnormality into account in the objective test for loss of control would blur the distinction between the two defences by encouraging him to plead loss of control.

You may be reading this thinking, why is the distinction between the two defences so important? After all, both are partial defences which lead to the same result – a manslaughter conviction instead of a murder conviction. The reason the distinction matters is the burden of proof. As we saw earlier, for the loss of control defence, the burden of proof rests on the prosecution. The prosecution must disprove the defence beyond reasonable doubt.

---

[66] For criticism of this distinction see Mitchell, B.J., Mackay, R.D. and Brookbanks, W. J. (2008) 'Pleading for Provoked Killers: In Defence of *Morgan Smith*' 124 *Law Quarterly Review* 675.

But for diminished responsibility it is the defendant who bears the burden of proof. The defendant must show, on the balance of probabilities, that he is entitled to the defence. If mental abnormalities which reduce a defendant's powers of self-control could be taken into account in the objective test for loss of control, a defendant like Harold in our example would be able to circumvent the more onerous burden of proof which applies to diminished responsibility by pleading loss of control instead.

We will return to diminished responsibility in Chapter 10 on mental condition defences.

Unlawful act manslaughter

5.3 Recall the requirements for establishing criminal liability for unlawful act manslaughter.

There is no statutory definition of **unlawful act manslaughter**. So instead we must look at how it was defined by the House of Lords in *DPP* v *Newbury & Jones* [1977] AC 500. In this case Lord Salmon stated that a person is guilty of unlawful act manslaughter if:

> he intentionally did an act which was unlawful and dangerous and that act inadvertently caused death.

This tells us that the offence has the following five requirements:

1. The defendant did an act
2. The act was unlawful
3. The act was dangerous
4. The act caused the victim's death
5. The defendant intended to do the act.

(In *R* v *Dalby* [1982] 1 WLR 425 Waller LJ suggested that there is a further requirement, namely that the unlawful and dangerous act was 'directed at the victim'. However, this is inconsistent with other decisions[67] and was rejected by the House of Lords in *Attorney-General's Reference (No 3 of 1994)* [1998] AC 245.)

We will now work through each requirement in turn.

Requirement 1: The defendant did an act

In other words, a defendant cannot commit unlawful act manslaughter by omission.[68]

Assessment advice

If you are answering an exam problem question on **involuntary manslaughter** and the defendant's conduct constituted an **omission**, not an act, this offence will not apply. You should consider **gross negligence manslaughter** instead.

---

67 Such as *R* v *Mitchell* [1983] QB 741.

68 *R* v *Lowe* [1973] QB 702. For an argument that *R* v *Lowe* can be interpreted differently, so as not to preclude liability for unlawful act manslaughter by omission, see Taylor, R. (2019) 'The Contours of Involuntary Manslaughter – A Place for Unlawful Act by Omission' *Criminal Law Review* 205.

Requirement 2: The act was unlawful

The second requirement is that the defendant's act was unlawful. Here, the word 'unlawful' has been understood to mean criminal. So it is not enough to show that the defendant's act was a civil wrong. It must have been a criminal offence. An example which illustrates this is *R* v *Franklin* (1883) 15 Cox CC 163.

R v *Franklin*

The defendant was walking along Brighton Pier on a bank holiday Monday when he picked up a 'good sized box' from a refreshments stall and threw it into the sea. The box landed on a swimmer who was swimming underneath the pier and killed him. At trial, the prosecution's case was that the defendant's actions amounted to the tort of trespass to goods. Field J stated that proof of a tort was insufficient to establish liability for unlawful act manslaughter:

> the mere fact of a civil wrong committed by one person against another ought not to be used as an incident which is a necessary step in a criminal case

Two more recent examples are *R* v *Lamb* [1967] 2 QB 981 and *R* v *Grey* [2024] EWCA Crim 487.

R v *Lamb*

The defendant, Terence Lamb, had acquired a revolver. The revolver had a five-chambered cylinder which rotated when the trigger was pulled. One day the defendant was joking around with his best friend, the victim Timothy O'Donaghue. He pointed the revolver at O'Donaghue and pulled the trigger. Although there were two bullets in the chambers, neither Lamb nor O'Donaghue expected the gun to fire because neither bullet was in the chamber opposite the barrel. Neither realised that when the trigger was pulled the cylinder would rotate and place a bullet opposite the barrel. O'Donaghue was killed. At trial it was accepted that Lamb had not realised that the gun would fire. Three experts testified that Lamb's mistake was a natural one for somebody who was unfamiliar with firearms. Lamb was nonetheless convicted. Importantly, the trial judge told the jury that it was unnecessary for them to decide whether or not Lamb had committed the crime of assault. Lamb appealed against his conviction, arguing that the judge had misdirected the jury. In the Court of Appeal Sachs LJ held that the act in question must have been a crime:

> It is long settled that it is not in point to consider whether an act is unlawful merely from the angle of civil liabilities.

Lamb's appeal was therefore successful. Without proof that he had committed an assault he could not be convicted of unlawful act manslaughter.

R v *Grey*

The defendant – a 46 year-old woman who suffered from cerebral palsy, impaired vision and cognitive impairment – was walking on a pavement. The 77 year-old victim was cycling along the pavement in the opposite direction. It was a shared access path, and there was ample space for both of them. But the defendant waved her arm at the victim and said 'Get off the fucking pavement'. The victim fell off her bike and into the road, in the path of an oncoming car. She was killed. At the defendant's trial for unlawful act manslaughter, no-one identified the crime alleged to constitute the unlawful act. As it was not clear whether there had in fact been any contact between the two of them (which, as we'll see in chapter 6, is required for battery), the most relevant offence would have been assault. But the jury had not been required to consider whether the defendant had in fact formed the *mens rea* of this offence. Since an unlawful act had not been proved, the conviction was unsafe and was quashed.

Before moving on, it is important to note two further points:

- Whilst the unlawful act must be a crime, it does not have to be a crime of violence. For example, in a few pages' time we will look at *R* v *Watson* [1989] 1 WLR 684. In this case the relevant crime was burglary. Another example is *R* v *Goodfellow* (1986) 83 Cr App R 23, where the relevant crime was criminal damage.[69]
- The prosecution must prove both the *actus reus* and the *mens rea* of the crime in question. So if the relevant offence is battery, the prosecution must establish both the *actus reus* and *mens rea* of battery.

Requirement 3: The act was dangerous

The third requirement is that the act was dangerous. Here we need to consider two issues:

i. What test is used to assess dangerousness?

ii. What information may the jury take into account when applying this test?

i. The test for dangerousness

The courts have developed a legal test which must be applied when deciding whether or not the defendant's unlawful act was dangerousness.

Assessment advice

One of the most common mistakes students make when answering exam problem questions on unlawful act manslaughter is to apply their own understanding of the word 'dangerous' instead of applying the test the courts have set out.

The first point to note about the test for dangerousness is that it is an objective test. Lord Salmon in *DPP* v *Newbury Jones* stated:

> In judging whether the act was dangerous, the test is not did the accused recognise that it was dangerous but would all sober and reasonable people recognise its danger?

So, when applying the dangerousness test, you must focus on what the reasonable person would have foreseen, not on what the defendant himself foresaw. No concession is made for individual characteristics, such as age or mental capacity.[70]

---

[69] Whether or not a crime of strict liability may form the unlawful act in unlawful act manslaughter is unclear: see Freer, E. (2018) 'We Need to Talk About Charlie: Putting the Brakes on Unlawful Act Manslaughter' *Criminal Law Review* 612.

[70] This is illustrated by *R* v *JF & NE* [2015] EWCA Crim 351. JF and NE were both young people (aged 14 and 16 respectively), and JF had an exceptionally low IQ (such that a psychologist said that JF's answers in police interviews should be judged as if he were a six-year-old). The Court of Appeal rejected defence counsel's suggestion that the objective test for dangerousness should be reconsidered, stating that 'the law is clear and well established' and that it is 'for Parliament to determine' whether reform is needed ([33]).

Second, in *R* v *Church* [1966] 1 QB 59 Edmund Davies J explained that, for the act to qualify as dangerous, the prosecution must show that the reasonable man would have foreseen a risk that the victim would suffer some harm. Importantly, he explained that the reasonable man need not have foreseen a risk of serious harm:

> The unlawful act must be such as all sober and reasonable people would inevitably recognise must subject the other person to, at least, the risk of some harm resulting therefrom, albeit not serious harm.

The scope of the *R* v *Church* test was considered in *R* v *JM & SM* [2012] EWCA Crim 2293. In this case the Court of Appeal had to consider whether it is necessary to show that the reasonable man would have foreseen the type of harm that the victim suffered.

R v *JM & SM*

The victim in *R* v *JM & SM* was 40-year-old Peter Jopling. He worked at a nightclub as a doorman and was believed to be in good health. One evening the two defendants were ejected from the club and then tried to force their way back in. Jopling was one of the doormen who dealt with them. Shortly after the disturbance Jopling collapsed and died. It was later discovered that he had been suffering from a renal artery aneurysm. The shock and surge in blood pressure triggered by the disturbance had caused the aneurysm to rupture. The two defendants were charged with affray and unlawful act manslaughter.

At trial the judge ruled that, even if the jury decided that the defendants had committed an unlawful act (the offence of affray[71]), there was no evidence on which they could convict the defendants of unlawful act manslaughter. The judge stated that the *R* v *Church* test for dangerousness is only satisfied if the reasonable man would have foreseen the *type* of harm that the victim suffered. The prosecution appealed against this, arguing that it placed an unwarranted restriction on the scope of the *R* v *Church* test.

EXTRACT

Read the following extract from the judgment of Lord Judge CJ.

For the dangerousness test, must the prosecution prove: (1) that the reasonable man would have foreseen a risk that the victim would suffer the type of injury the victim suffered; or (2) that the reasonable man would have foreseen a risk of some injury (not necessarily the sort of injury the victim actually suffered)?

R v *JM & SM* [2012] EWCA Crim 2293

Lord Judge CJ

18. [T]he judge misdirected himself when he required the Crown to establish [...] that the reasonable and sober person envisaged in *R* v *Church* must realise that there was a risk that the unlawful act would cause the sort of physical harm as a result of which the victim died. We agree that such a requirement provided a gloss on the ingredients of this offence which is

[71] Public Order Act 1986, s.3.

not justified by the authorities [...] Indeed, the observations at the end of the judgment appear to elevate the requisite risk from an appreciation that some harm will inevitably occur into foresight of the type of harm which actually ensued and indeed the mechanism by which death occurred. Of course, unless the Crown can prove that death resulted from the defendant's unlawful and dangerous act, the case of manslaughter would fail on causation grounds. However a requirement that the bystander must appreciate the "sort" of injury which might occur undermines the "some" harm principle explained in *R* v *Church*

[...]

20. In our judgment, certainly since *R* v *Church* [1966] 1 QB 59 and *Director of Public Prosecutions* v *Newbury* [1977] AC 500, it has never been a requirement that the defendant personally should foresee any specific harm at all, or that the reasonable bystander should recognise the precise form or "sort" of harm which did ensue. What matters is whether reasonable and sober people would recognise that the unlawful activities of the defendant inevitably subjected the deceased to the risk of some harm resulting from them.

[...]

22. In our judgment there is evidence from which a jury properly directed could conclude that sober and reasonable people observing events on 12 December 2012 would readily have recognised that all the doormen involved in the effort to control the defendants were at the risk of some harm, and that the fatal injury incurred while it was in progress or in its immediate aftermath while Mr Jopling was still subject to its effects.

23. Accordingly this appeal will be allowed.

The Court also stated that, whilst general stress and anxiety do not amount to harm for the purposes of the *R* v *Church* test, emotional shock does. This followed the decision in *R* v *Watson*, which we will look at shortly.

So, to summarise, the test for dangerousness is an objective one. The prosecution must show that the reasonable man would have foreseen a risk that the victim would suffer some harm. No concession is made for an individual's characteristics, such as age or mental capacity, and it is not necessary to show that the reasonable man would have foreseen the precise type of harm that the victim actually suffered.

Criticism of the test for dangerousness

This test has been widely criticised for setting the bar too low, particularly given that unlawful act manslaughter is a homicide offence. The Law Commission, for example, has stated:[72]

> 1.15 At the less serious end of the involuntary manslaughter spectrum, the law may be too harsh on defendants who kill as a result of an unlawful and dangerous act. The risk of harshness arises when defendants do not realise that the act may cause harm:
>
> EXAMPLE 1: D is seeking to steal a large book from the fourth floor of a library whose windows face on to a busy street. Seeing the librarian coming towards him, D quickly drops the book out of the window. It lands on V's head as she walks underneath the window, killing her.
>
> 1.16 D's theft of the book should not be sufficient to convict D of the manslaughter of V even though, in the circumstances, there was an obvious risk of some harm arising from D's action.

[72] Law Commission (2005) *A New Homicide Act for England and Wales? A Consultation Paper* (Consultation Paper No 177).

Do you agree that the defendant in the Law Commission's example should not be convicted of manslaughter?

Do you agree with the Law Commission that the *R v Church* test for dangerousness is too harsh on defendants who do not realise that their unlawful act may cause harm?

Requirement 3: ii. What information may the jury take into account when applying the dangerousness test?

In some situations there may be particular facts or circumstances which affect the dangerousness of the defendant's act. For a number of cases, the courts set out guidance on when such facts or circumstances may be taken into account.

In the next section, we are going to look at five cases in detail. For each case, determine which of the following four situations the court was addressing and identify the principle that the court said should be applied:

- The information was available to D before the crime was committed.
- The information became available to D during the commission of the crime.
- The information only became available to D after the crime had been committed.
- The defendant possessed a mistaken belief at the time the crime was committed.

CASE 1: R v Bristow [2013] EWCA Crim 1540

R v *Bristow*

The victim, Julian Gardner, ran an off-road vehicle repair business from premises on a secluded farm. The four defendants committed a night-time burglary of the business. Gardner interrupted the burglary and attempted to intervene. As the defendants escaped, they drove into Gardner and killed him. At trial the defendants were convicted of unlawful act manslaughter (the unlawful act being the burglary). They appealed against their convictions, arguing that the burglary did not satisfy the *R* v *Church* test for dangerousness (at least not until one of the defendants started to drive dangerously, which they argued was too late as the prosecution had not proved who ran Gardner over). The Court of Appeal dismissed their appeal.

EXTRACT

Read the following extract from the judgment of Treacy LJ.

At what point in time does he say the dangerousness of the burglary should be assessed: before the defendants embarked on the burglary; when Gardner intervened; or when the defendants started to drive dangerously?

Note the reasons Treacy LJ gives for saying that the burglary satisfied the *R* v *Church* test for dangerousness.

R v *Bristow* [2013] EWCA Crim 1540

Treacy LJ

16. The prosecution case [...] was one of unlawful act manslaughter. The unlawful act was alleged to be the burglary of the farm, which was committed as a joint enterprise. Although

the Crown could not say who was driving the vehicle or vehicles that had struck Mr Gardner, they asserted that each appellant took part in the burglary and in doing so, in the particular circumstances, foresaw a real possibility that somebody intervening at the scene might suffer harm as a result of the carrying out of the burglary, including harm caused during their escape from the scene. The presence of residential farm buildings would have alerted the appellants to the risk of being caught in the act of burglary, which would result in the need to escape promptly from the scene in vehicles along the single track.

17. In those circumstances a reasonable bystander would, the Crown submitted, recognise the risk of some harm being caused to a person intervening at night, in the dark, in a relatively confined space, where powerful vehicles were involved, and there was only one route of escape from the workshops. In this context, it is worth recording that the jury went on a view of the scene as well as having many still images provided.

[…]

34. This is not a case […] where the circumstances demonstrating the risk of harm to the occupier of property did not arise until a point during the burglary or at all. Whilst burglary of itself is not a dangerous crime, a particular burglary may be dangerous because of the circumstances surrounding its commission. We consider that the features identified by the Crown, as set out earlier in this judgment, were capable of making this burglary dangerous when coupled with foresight of the risk of intervention to prevent escape.

35. In those circumstances we consider that the features of this crime were sufficient for the burglary to be capable of being an unlawful act which a reasonable bystander would inevitably realise must subject any person intervening to the risk of some harm resulting.

[…]

37. Since the crime to be focussed on was the burglary, we reject Mr Nelson's submission as to the point at which foresight and danger were to be assessed. We consider that on the facts of this case the judge was correct to focus the jury's attention on the period up to the inception of the burglary. It is that question which lies at the very heart of the submissions made on behalf of the appellants, namely the point in time at which foresight and recognition of danger arose. What needed to be considered was the foresight of the participants as they embarked upon the crime, and what, if anything a reasonable bystander would inevitably have recognised as a risk of physical harm to any person intervening.

So in *R* v *Bristow* the information which demonstrated the dangerousness of the act was available to the defendants **before** they committed the burglary. The application of the *R* v *Church* test was therefore based on what the reasonable person would have foreseen at the moment the defendants embarked on the crime. But what if there are special facts or circumstances which only become evident **whilst the crime is being committed**? This was the issue in *R* v *Watson* [1989] 1 WLR 684.

CASE 2: *R* v *Watson* [1989] 1 WLR 684

R v *Watson*

The defendant, Clarence Watson, broke into the home of an 87-year-old man named Harold Moyler, who had a weak heart. Moyler woke up whilst Watson was in the house. Watson verbally abused him and then escaped. Shortly afterwards Moyler suffered a fatal heart attack.

At trial the judge told the jury that, when applying the *R* v *Church* test, they could take into account information which became available to Watson during the course of the burglary (including the fact that Moyler was frail and elderly). Watson was convicted of unlawful act manslaughter. He appealed against his conviction, arguing that the trial judge had misdirected the jury.

EXTRACT

According to the following extract from Lord Lane CJ's judgment, had the trial judge misdirected the jury? When applying the *R* v *Church* test, may the jury take into account facts and circumstances which become evident to the defendant?

R v *Watson* [1989] 1 WLR 684

Lord Lane CJ

The judge clearly took the view that the jury were entitled to ascribe to the bystander the knowledge which the appellant gained during the whole of his stay in the house and so directed them. Was this a misdirection? In our judgment it was not. The unlawful act in the present circumstances comprised the whole of the burglarious intrusion and did not come to an end upon the appellant's foot crossing the threshold or windowsill. That being so, the appellant (and therefore the bystander) during the course of the unlawful act must have become aware of Mr. Moyler's frailty and approximate age, and the judge's directions were accordingly correct.

So any relevant facts or circumstances can be taken into account when applying the *R* v *Church* test if they were available to the defendant **before** he embarked on the unlawful act or if they became available to him **during** the unlawful act. But what about facts which only transpire **afterwards**? This was the issue in *R* v *Dawson* (1985) 81 Cr App R 150 which we will consider next.

CASE 3: R v Dawson (1985) 81 Cr App R 150

R v *Dawson*

The victim in this case was a 60-year-old petrol station attendant named Robert Black. Black suffered from heart disease. He was at work one evening when the defendant, Brian Dawson, and two other men attempted to rob the petrol station. They were armed with a replica gun and a pickaxe handle. As they demanded money they saw Black press an alarm button and fled. Shortly afterwards Black suffered a heart attack and died. At trial the three men were convicted of unlawful act manslaughter. They appealed against their convictions. The key issue on appeal was whether the trial judge was right to tell the jury to take into account Black's heart condition when applying the test for dangerousness.

EXTRACT

Read the following extract from the judgment of Watkins LJ.

Was the trial judge correct to tell the jury to take into account Black's heart condition? Why/why not?

R v *Dawson* (1985) 81 Cr App R 150

Watkins LJ

[The dangerousness] test can only be undertaken upon the basis of the knowledge gained by a sober and reasonable man as though he were present at the scene of and watched the unlawful act being performed and who knows that, as in the present case, an unloaded replica gun was in use, but that the victim may have thought it was a loaded gun in working order. In other words, he has the same knowledge as the man attempting to rob and no more. It was never suggested that any of these appellants knew that their victim had a bad heart. They knew nothing about him.

A jury must be informed by the judge when trying the offence of manslaughter what facts they may and those which they may not use for the purpose of performing the [dangerousness] test. The judge's direction here, unlike the bulk of an admirable summing up, lacked that necessary precision and in the form it was given may, in our view, have given the jury an erroneous impression of what knowledge they could ascribe to the sober and reasonable man.

For these reasons we see no alternative to quashing the convictions for manslaughter as unsafe and unsatisfactory. The appeal against the convictions for manslaughter is therefore allowed.

A similar case to *R* v *Dawson* is *R* v *Carey* [2006] EWCA Crim 17.

CASE 4: R v Carey [2006] EWCA Crim 17

R v *Carey*

The victim, 15-year-old Aimee Wellock, was out with her friends. They were approached by the three defendants, who started acting aggressively. One of the defendants punched Aimee, while one of the other defendants punched one of Aimee's friends. Aimee managed to run away, but then collapsed and died later that night. Unknown to Aimee, she had a severely diseased heart. Her running had caused her heart to stop pumping blood.

At trial the defendants were convicted of affray and unlawful act manslaughter (the unlawful act being the affray). They appealed, arguing that the *R* v *Church* test for dangerousness was not satisfied. The Court of Appeal agreed and quashed the manslaughter convictions (but upheld the convictions for affray). Dyson LJ stated:

> 37 [...] Even if the affray had caused Aimee to suffer shock as opposed to emotional upset, the affray lacked the quality of dangerousness in the relevant sense. This is because it would not have been recognised by a sober and reasonable bystander that an apparently healthy 15-year-old (or indeed anyone else present) was at risk of suffering shock as a result of this affray. In our view, this affray was less dangerous in the relevant sense than the attempted robbery of the 60-year-old petrol station attendant in *Dawson*. The risk of that victim suffering shock leading to a heart attack would have been recognised by a sober and reasonable person as more likely than the risk of Aimee suffering shock leading to a heart attack as a result of the affray.

So in both *R* v *Dawson* and *R* v *Carey* the victims' heart conditions were not taken into account when applying the *R* v *Church* test because a reasonable bystander would not have been aware of them.

The final question is whether the jury should take into account any **mistaken beliefs** held by the defendant. This was the issue in our fifth case *R* v *Ball* [1989] Crim LR 730.

CASE 5: R v Ball [1989] Crim LR 730

R v *Ball*

The defendant allowed the victim, Mrs Green, to store her Land Rover™ on his land. Then one day he sold the vehicle without Mrs Green's consent. When Mrs Green went to Ball's house to ask him to return the Land Rover, the two started to argue. Mrs Green then ran away and, as she was trying to climb over the garden wall, Ball raised his shotgun and shot her. Ball's defence was that he kept live and blank shotgun cartridges together in the pocket of his overalls in his house. When he picked up the gun he also grabbed a handful of cartridges. He believed he had only loaded blank cartridges into the gun (the blanks were lighter than the live ones). He said he only fired the gun in order to frighten Mrs Green and had not intended to kill her. The jury accepted Ball's account (which is why he was acquitted of murder). However, the trial judge told the jury that they should not take Ball's mistaken belief into account when applying the *R* v *Church* test for dangerousness. Ball was accordingly convicted of unlawful act manslaughter. He appealed, arguing that the trial judge had misdirected the jury.

EXTRACT

Read the following extract from the judgement of Stuart Smith LJ.

Was the trial judge correct to tell the jury not to take into account Ball's mistaken belief? Why/why not?

R v *Ball* [1989] Crim LR 730

Stuart Smith LJ

[Counsel for the defendant] submits that the reference to the sober and reasonable man having the same knowledge as the [defendant] and no more, involves the proposition that if that person has a mistaken belief, albeit brought about by his own carelessness, the sober and reasonable man must share that mistaken belief. But in our judgment *Dawson's* case goes no further than showing that the sober and reasonable man must look at the unlawful act to see if it is dangerous and not at peculiarities of the victim.

[...]

Once these matters are established, namely, that the act was both unlawful and that he intended to commit the assaults, the question whether the act is a dangerous one is to be judged not by the appellant's appreciation but by that of the sober and reasonable man, and it is impossible to impute into his appreciation the mistaken belief of the appellant that what he was doing was not dangerous because he thought he had a blank cartridge in the chamber. At that stage the appellant's intention, foresight or knowledge is irrelevant.

So according to *R* v *Ball* any mistaken beliefs held by the defendant should be disregarded when applying the *R* v *Church* test. This principle has been criticised on the basis that it could potentially lead to harsh results.[73] The judgment suggests that any mistaken belief held by the defendant should be disregarded, however reasonable the mistake might have been. Suppose Ball had instead purchased a box of blank cartridges, but owing to a mishap at the factory the box also contained some live ones. Ball's mistaken belief that he was firing a blank cartridge would have been entirely justified. Yet following the Court of Appeal's judgment the dangerousness test would be applied on the basis that the reasonable man knew that the cartridge was in fact live.

Late one night, to annoy his elderly neighbour Peter, Harold puts a smoke bomb through the letterbox of Peter's front door. Unbeknownst to Harold, Peter suffers from asthma. Peter begins to suffer breathing difficulties and dies. When applying the dangerousness test, may (1) Peter's age and (2) Peter's asthma be taken into account?

Options: (a) Neither Peter's age nor his asthma may be taken into account; (b) Peter's age may be taken into account, but not his asthma; (c) Peter's asthma may be taken into account, but not his age; (d) both Peter's age and his asthma may be taken into account

Having explored the third requirement that the act was dangerous, we continue with the fourth and fifth requirements.

Requirement 4: The act caused the victim's death

The defendant's unlawful act must have been a factual and legal cause of the victim's death. Here you apply the law governing causation that we studied in Chapter 3.

Harold breaks into Peter's house whilst Peter is asleep upstairs. Peter wakes up, hears sounds from downstairs and realises that there is an intruder. Terrified, he runs out of the house and straight into the road in front of a car that is being driven in excess of the speed limit by Fred. Peter is killed.

Was the burglary a factual and legal cause of Peter's death?

Requirement 5: The defendant intended to do the act

The second requirement for this offence was that the act in question was a criminal offence. As we saw earlier, this means that the defendant must satisfy both the *actus reus* and *mens rea* requirements of the relevant crime. Beyond this, the only other *mens rea* requirement of unlawful act manslaughter is that the defendant intended to do the relevant act. In *DPP* v *Newbury & Jones* Lord Salmon confirmed that it is unnecessary to prove that the defendant knew that the act was unlawful and it is unnecessary to prove that the defendant knew that the act was dangerous. This is why this offence is sometimes

[73] Simester, A.P., Spencer, J.R., Stark, F., Sullivan, G.R. and Virgo, G J. (2016) *Simester and Sullivan's Criminal Law: Theory and Doctrine* (6th edn). Hart Publishing: Oxford, p.413.

referred to as **'constructive manslaughter'**. It is possible that a defendant may be guilty of this offence even if he was unaware of any risk that the victim would suffer physical harm (let alone death).

It is also important to note that in *Andrews* v *DPP* [1937] AC 576 HL Lord Atkin attempted to draw a distinction between two types of act. He said:

> There is an obvious difference in the law of manslaughter between doing an unlawful act and doing a lawful act with a degree of carelessness which the Legislature makes criminal.

He explained that a defendant can only be convicted of **unlawful act manslaughter** if he commits the first type of act (an unlawful act). If a defendant commits the second type of act (a careless lawful act), you should consider **gross negligence manslaughter** instead.

This distinction is not an easy one. It has been criticised for being unclear and unsustainable (the second type of act is really a subcategory of the first type of act, since a lawful act which is performed so carelessly as to become criminal is an unlawful act!). Lord Atkin may be understood as saying that where the allegation is of carelessness the defendant should be charged with gross negligence manslaughter, not unlawful act manslaughter.

> Suppose that Harold is driving his car. He is looking out of the window at the view, fails to notice Peter (a frail old man) crossing the road at a zebra crossing and knocks him over. Peter dies. Since the allegation is that Harold drove carelessly he should be charged with gross negligence manslaughter, not unlawful act manslaughter. On the other hand, suppose Harold had seen Peter and decided it would be fun to scare him by accelerating and driving as close to him as possible without hitting him. Peter is so frightened that he suffers a heart attack and dies.

On these facts Harold intentionally committed an unlawful act (assault: see Chapter 6) and so the appropriate offence is unlawful act manslaughter.

Quiz 5.3

1. In the offence of unlawful act manslaughter, what the does the phrase *unlawful* act mean?

- **a.** Any act that is criminal and dangerous.
- **b.** Any act (or omission if D has a duty to act) that is criminal and dangerous.
- **c.** Any reckless act that is criminal.
- **d.** Any act that is criminal or tortious that is dangerous.

2. Which case formulated the test for objective dangerousness of the unlawful act?

- **a.** *Dawson* (1985) 81 Cr App R 150.
- **b.** *Carey* [2006] EWCACrim 17.
- **c.** *Watson* [1989] 1 WLR 684.
- **d.** *Church* [1966] 1 QB 59.

3. In the case of *Carey* [2006] EWCA Crim 17, why was the defendant found not guilty of manslaughter?

- **a.** The victim was not a 'human being'.
- **b.** The unlawful act was not dangerous.
- **c.** There was insufficient evidence of *mens rea*.
- **d.** There was no unlawful act.

4. In the case of *Watson* [1989] 1 WLR 684, which unlawful act formed the basis of the charge of constructive manslaughter?

- **a.** Burglary.
- **b.** Kidnapping.
- **c.** Robbery.
- **d.** Theft.

Gross negligence manslaughter

5.4 Explain the requirements for establishing criminal liability for gross negligence manslaughter.

There is no statutory definition of gross negligence manslaughter. The original definition of the offence was set out by the House of Lords in *R* v *Adomako* [1995] 1 AC 171. Over the years the definition evolved, such that in *R* v *Broughton* [2020] EWCA Crim 1093 (confirmed in *R* v *Bah* [2024] EWCA Crim 1499), the Court of Appeal stated that the offence has a total of six requirements:

1. The defendant owed the victim a duty of care.
2. The defendant breached his duty of care.
3. There must have been a serious and obvious risk of death.
4. The serious and obvious risk of death must have been reasonably foreseeable.
5. The breach of duty caused the death of the victim.
6. The breach of duty should be characterised as gross negligence and therefore as a crime.

Numbers 1 to 5 are *actus reus* requirements. Number 6 is a *mens rea* requirement. We will work through each requirement in turn.

Requirement 1: The defendant owed the victim a duty of care

The first requirement is that the defendant owed the victim a duty of care. Whether such a duty exists is a question of law which the judge must answer; it is not a question of fact for the jury.[74] In general terms, to determine whether or not there is a duty of care you must apply the ordinary principles of the law of tort, specifically, the law of negligence.[75]

There are many situations in which a duty of care will arise. Some examples are:

- A doctor owes a duty of care to his patients[76]
- A driver owes a duty of care to other road users[77]
- An employer owes a duty of care to his employees[78]
- A teacher owes a duty of care to his pupils[79]
- A restaurant owner owes a duty of care to his customers (including a duty to take reasonable steps to avoid injury to customers who declare a food allergy)[80]
- A gatekeeper at a railway crossing owes a duty of care to those who use the crossing[81]
- A prison officer owes a duty to prisoners who are a known suicide risk.[82]

---

[74] This was confirmed by the Court of Appeal in *R* v *Evans* [2009] EWCA Crim 650.

[75] *R* v *Adomako* [1995] 1 AC 171.

[76] *R* v *Adomako* [1995] 1 AC 171.

[77] *Page* v *Smith* [1996] AC 155.

[78] *Wilson and Clyde Coal Co* v *English* [1938] AC 57.

[79] *Wilkin-Shaw* v *Fuller* [2013] EWCA Civ 410.

[80] *R* v *Zaman* [2017] EWCA Crim 1783.

[81] *R* v *Pittwood* (1902) 19 TLR 37.

[82] *R (on the application of the Justice Secretary)* v *HM Deputy Coroner for the Eastern District of West Yorkshire* [2012] EWHC 1634 (Admin).

A duty of care was also held to exist in *R* v *Evans* [2009] EWCA Crim 650, which we studied in Chapter 3. This was the case in which the defendant bought some heroin and gave it to the victim (her half-sister, who was a recovering addict). The defendant owed the victim a duty of care because she had contributed to the dangerous situation the victim was in, and she breached this duty by failing to call for medical assistance.

Similar reasoning was also applied in *R* v *Bowler* [2015] EWCA Crim 849.[83]

R v *Bowler*

In this case the victim, W, was interested in masochistic sexual experiences, particularly mummification. The defendant wrapped W in cling film and PVC, had sex with him, then left him. He checked on W half an hour later. W was moving. The defendant left again and didn't return for some time. When he did return, W was lifeless. The defendant was convicted of gross negligence manslaughter. A duty of care arose because W 'was left helpless and in a situation which was obviously dangerous' ([20]), and the defendant breached this duty by failing to monitor and check on W properly.

The *ex turpi causa* principle applied to gross negligence manslaughter?

One question which the courts have had to address is whether a duty of care can exist in cases where the defendant and victim were jointly embarked on an unlawful enterprise. This issue arose in *R* v *Wacker* [2002] EWCA Crim 1944.

R v *Wacker*

The defendant, Perry Wacker, was a lorry driver. He had agreed to help 60 Chinese immigrants enter the UK illegally by hiding them in his lorry. The immigrants got onto the lorry in Holland. They were hidden in a concealed container behind crates of tomatoes. The only ventilation came from a small vent at the front of the container. Before boarding the ferry at Zeebrugge, Wacker closed the air vent in order to reduce the likelihood of detection. The immigrants had been warned that this would happen, but were told the vent would only be closed for a short time. However, Wacker failed to reopen the vent during the ferry crossing. By the time the ferry arrived at Dover more than five hours later, 58 of the immigrants had died of suffocation. At trial, Wacker was convicted on 58 counts of gross negligence manslaughter.

Wacker's appeal focused on whether or not he owed the immigrants a duty of care. In the law of tort there is a principle known as *ex turpi causa*. This principle states that no action can be based on a disreputable cause. It prevents one party from suing another in the law of tort where both were jointly engaged in an unlawful enterprise. The issue for the Court of Appeal was whether the *ex turpi causa* principle also applies to the crime of gross negligence manslaughter. If so, Wacker would not have owed the immigrants a duty of care and so could not be found guilty of gross negligence manslaughter.

---

[83] See also *R* v *S* [2015] EWCA Crim 558, in which the defendant S, a gang member, had been given a gun to look after by another member of the gang. S removed the magazine from the handle of the gun, but did not realise that there was still a bullet in the chamber. Whilst showing off, he pointed the gun at his girlfriend and pulled the trigger. The gun fired and his girlfriend was killed. S was acquitted of murder but convicted of gross negligence manslaughter. The duty of care S owed to his girlfriend appeared to be based on the dangerous situation he created by pointing the gun and pulling the trigger without ensuring that it was safe to do so (see [10] of Cranston J's judgment).

EXTRACT

Read the following extract from the judgment of Kay LJ.

What reasons does he give for saying that Wacker owed the immigrants a duty of care? Does the *ex turpi causa* principle apply to the crime of gross negligence manslaughter? Why/why not?

R v *Wacker* [2002] EWCA Crim 1944

Kay LJ

38. The next question which is posed is whether it is right to say in this case that no duty of care can arise because it is impossible or inappropriate to determine the extent of that duty. We do not accept this proposition. If at the moment when the vent was shut one of the Chinese had said, "You will make sure that we have enough air to survive", the defendant would have had no difficulty understanding the proposition and clearly, by continuing with the unlawful enterprise in the way that he did, he would have been shouldering the duty to take care for their safety in this regard. The question was such an obvious one that it did not need to be posed and we have no difficulty in concluding that in these circumstances the defendant did voluntarily assume the duty of care for the Chinese in this regard. He was aware that no one's actions other than his own could realistically prevent the Chinese from suffocating to death and if he failed to act reasonably in fulfilling this duty to an extent that could be characterised as criminal, he was guilty of manslaughter if death resulted.

39. One further issue merits consideration, namely is it any answer to a charge of manslaughter for a defendant to say, "We were jointly engaged in a criminal enterprise and, weighing the risk of injury or death against our joint desire to achieve our unlawful objective, we collectively thought that it was a risk worth taking"? In our judgment it is not. The duty to take care cannot, as a matter of public policy, be permitted to be affected by the countervailing demands of the criminal enterprise. Thus, in this case, the fact that keeping the vent shut increased the chances of the Chinese succeeding in entering the United Kingdom without detection was not a factor to be taken into account in deciding whether the defendant had acted reasonably or not.

In *R* v *Willoughby* [2004] EWCA Crim 3365 the Court of Appeal confirmed that the *ex turpi causa* principle does not apply to gross negligence manslaughter.

R v *Willoughby*

The defendant, Keith Willoughby, owned a pub in Canterbury but had run into financial trouble. He decided to set fire to the pub and asked his friend Derek Drury to help him. One evening the two men went to the pub together, poured petrol inside and ignited it. There was then an explosion, which injured Willoughby and killed Drury. At trial Willoughby was convicted of gross negligence manslaughter. On appeal, Willoughby's counsel argued that Willoughby had not owed Drury a duty of care. He tried to distinguish *R* v *Wacker* by arguing that in that case the immigrants were in a vulnerable position and Wacker had chosen to assume responsibility for them. By contrast, Willoughby and Drury took part in the unlawful plan as equals.

In the following extract note the reasons Rose LJ gives for holding that Willoughby did owe Drury a duty of care.

EXTRACT

R v *Willoughby* [2004] EWCA Crim 3365

Rose LJ

20. In the present case, we accept that there could not be a duty in law to look after the deceased's health and welfare arising merely from the fact that the defendant was the owner of the premises. But the fact that the defendant was the owner, that his public house was to be destroyed for his financial benefit, that he enlisted the deceased to take part in this enterprise, and that the deceased's role was to spread petrol inside were, in conjunction, factors which were capable, in law, of giving rise to a duty to the deceased on the part of the defendant. In a very different situation the lorry driver in *R* v *Wacker* [2003] QB 1207 was held to owe a duty of care to the illegal immigrants he was carrying. The civil law doctrine of *ex turpi causa* was held not to apply in the criminal law.

Lastly, it should be noted that it is possible to commit gross negligence manslaughter by omission. We have already seen three examples: *R* v *Evans*, *R* v *Bowler* and *R* v *Wacker*. In cases that involve an omission it must be shown that the defendant had both: (1) a duty to act (see Chapter 3); and (2) a duty of care under the law of tort (which we have worked through here).

Assessment advice

In an exam problem question, you should begin by discussing whether the defendant had a duty to act which he breached. Once you've done this you can then focus on gross negligence manslaughter and discuss whether the defendant owed the victim a duty of care. (In practice, if there was a duty to act there will almost certainly be a duty of care too.)

Requirement 2: The defendant breached his duty of care

The second requirement is that the defendant breached the duty of care he owed to the victim. The standard of care is an objective one: the defendant will breach his duty if he fails to live up to the standard of the reasonable person. If the defendant is performing a skilled activity he will be required to live up to the standard of the reasonable person with that skill. So a driver must live up to the standard of the reasonable motorist, and a doctor must live up to the standard of a reasonable doctor.These points are illustrated by *R* v *Adomako*.

R v Adomako

The defendant in this case, John Adomako, was an anaesthetist. He was part of a team carrying out an eye operation on the victim. During the operation the tube that was supplying oxygen to the victim became disconnected. An expert witness said that Adomako should have noticed this within 15 seconds. But Adomako did not notice the disconnection. Four-and-a-half minutes later an alarm sounded on the blood pressure monitor. Adomako administered some drugs to raise the victim's pulse, but still didn't notice the disconnection. Approximately nine minutes after the original disconnection the victim suffered cardiac arrest and died. Only then did Adomako discover the disconnection. Another expert witness described the standard of care Adomako provided as 'abysmal'.

In his defence, Adomako explained that he was exhausted. The day before he had worked a long shift and had not got to bed until 3:30am. He was then back on the wards at 7am. He also said that, although he had some experience of eye operations, he had never acted as the sole anaesthetist in such an operation before. The House of Lords nonetheless upheld his conviction for gross negligence manslaughter. The standard of care for this offence is determined objectively. Adomako therefore had to be judged by the standard of a reasonably competent anaesthetist. If he did not achieve the standard of a reasonably skilled anaesthetist he breached his duty of care to the patient.[84]

Requirement 3: There must have been a serious and obvious risk of death

In *R* v *Singh (Gurphal)* [1999] Crim LR 582, Schiemann LJ said that the trial judge had been correct to tell the jury that they could only convict the defendant of gross negligence manslaughter if:

> A reasonably prudent person in the position of the appellant would have foreseen a serious and obvious risk of death.

This has since been confirmed in numerous cases, including *R* v *Rudling* [2016] EWCA Crim 741, *R* v *Rose (Honey Maria)* [2017] EWCA Crim 1168 and *R* v *Kuddus* [2019] EWCA Crim 837.

The direction from *R* v *Singh (Gurphal)* involves two questions. The first question is whether there was a serious and obvious risk of death. The second question is whether a reasonable person would have foreseen this. Although these questions are closely related, they are distinct. You must first determine whether something existed, before asking whether it could reasonably have been foreseen!

So this requirement of gross negligence manslaughter asks whether there was a serious and obvious risk of death. Further guidance on this requirement was provided in *R* v *Rudling* [2016] EWCA Crim 741.

84 For discussion from a clinical perspective, including the argument that in the medical context gross negligence manslaughter focuses too much on the individual defendant and pays insufficient regard to the influence of wider factors, see Samanta, A. & Samanta, J. (2021) 'Death caused by negligent medical care: Reconsidering the role of gross negligence manslaughter in the aftermath of Bawa-Garba' 21 *Medical Law Internationcl* 293.

R v *Rudling*

The victim was a 12-year-old boy named Ryan Morse. On Thursday 6 December 2012 Ryan was sent home from school unwell. The following morning he was still ill. He was feeling dizzy, his head was aching, and he had vomited twice and had diarrhoea. That afternoon he had diarrhoea again. As his mother was cleaning him up, she noticed that his genitalia were black. She phoned the doctor's surgery and spoke to Dr Rudling. She asked Dr Rudling to come and see Ryan. Her reply was, 'No, it's to do with his hormones. Ring up on Monday, we'll fit him in to be seen by a male doctor.' The next day Ryan died of Addison's disease. Dr Rudling was charged with gross negligence manslaughter. The prosecution's case was that Dr Rudling's failure to either immediately visit Ryan at home or call an ambulance was a grossly negligent breach of duty. However, the trial judge accepted defence counsel's submission of no case to answer. The prosecution applied for leave to appeal against the trial judge's decision, arguing that it was not reasonable to conclude that there was no case to answer.

EXTRACT

Read the following extract from the judgement of Sir Brian Leveson P and consider the following questions.

According to the Court of Appeal, was it reasonable for the trial judge to conclude that, at the time of the phone call, there was no evidence of an obvious and serious risk of death? What did the Court say must be distinguished from an obvious and serious risk of death?

R v *Rudling* [2016] EWCA Crim 741

Sir Brian Leveson P

38. The nub of [the prosecution's] argument was that if it is necessary to have a face to face assessment in order to risk manage a patient and assess what might potentially be a life-threatening condition, it is necessarily implicit that there is an obvious and serious risk of death at that time. As he put it, the thrust of [the prosecution's expert witness] Dr Peter's evidence was that a reasonably competent GP would have said to himself/herself "I cannot eliminate the possibility that this child may be suffering from a rare risk to life without the child being seen urgently" and that that equates to an obvious and serious risk of death.

39. In our judgment, that proposition simply does not follow, as is apparent when one focuses on each of the three aspects of this ingredient of the offence of gross negligence manslaughter. At the time of the breach of duty, there must be a risk of death, not merely serious illness; the risk must be serious; and the risk must be obvious. A GP faced with an unusual presentation which is worrying and undiagnosed may need to ensure a face to face assessment urgently in order to investigate further. That may be in order to assess whether it is something serious, to use Dr Peter's expression, which may or may not be so serious as to be life-threatening. A recognisable risk of something serious is not the same as a recognisable risk of death.

40. What does not follow is that if a reasonably competent GP requires an urgent assessment of a worrying and undiagnosed condition, it is necessarily reasonably foreseeable that there is a risk of death. Still less does it demonstrate a serious risk of death, which is not to be equated with an "inability to eliminate a possibility". There may be numerous remote possibilities of very rare conditions which cannot be eliminated but which do not present a

serious risk of death. Further, and perhaps most importantly, a mere possibility that an assessment might reveal something life-threatening is not the same as an obvious risk of death. An obvious risk is a present risk which is clear and unambiguous, not one which might become apparent on further investigation.

41. These distinctions are not a matter of semantics but represent real differences in the practical assessments which fall to be made by doctors. It is clearly of significance that Dr Peter did not in his evidence suggest that the need for a face to face assessment was because of an obvious and serious risk of death at the time of the phone call, either in chief or on any of the three occasions in cross examination when the opportunity to do so arose.

42. Accordingly the Judge's conclusion that there was no evidence upon which a jury could safely find an obvious and serious risk of death at the time of the phone call with Dr Rudling was not only a reasonable one, but in our view obviously correct.

So the prosecution must prove that there was a risk of death, and that this risk was both serious and obvious. It is insufficient to prove a risk of something serious, or that the defendant failed to eliminate the possibility of something life-threatening.

This raises a further question: what information may the jury take into account when deciding whether there was a serious and obvious risk of death? To answer this, we need to look at the judgment in *R* v *Kuddus* [2019] EWCA Crim 837.

The defendant, Mohammed Abdul Kuddus, was the owner of the takeaway business Royal Spice. He also worked there as a tandoori chef. The business was managed by Harun Rashid. In December 2016, the victim, Megan Lee, and a friend ordered a meal from Royal Spice via a website. Megan was allergic to nuts and prawns, so they entered 'nuts, prawns' in the comments section of the webpage. In spite of this, the food that was provided contained peanuts. Although Megan's allergy was believed to only be a mild one, she suffered a severe allergic reaction and died in hospital two days later.

At trial, Rashid was convicted of gross negligence manslaughter. Kuddus was also convicted of gross negligence manslaughter. He appealed against his conviction, on two grounds. The second ground – which we will return to shortly – concerned the fact that it was Rashid, not Kuddus, who read the order containing the warning about nuts and prawns. The first ground of appeal concerned the fact that, at the time the order was placed, Megan was believed to have only a mild allergy. Here the defendant pointed to expert evidence that there was nothing in Megan's previous history that would have suggested such a severe reaction. The question for the Court of Appeal was whether the fact that Megan's allergy was believed to be a mild one could be taken into account when asking whether there was a serious and obvious risk of death.

EXTRACT

Read the following extract from the judgement of Sir Brian Leveson P and consider the following questions.

According to the Court of Appeal, is the correct question in a case like this one whether a breach of duty would give rise to a serious and obvious risk of death to (a) a nut allergy sufferer or (b) the specific victim who died? In [72], the Court stated that its answer to the previous question was based on a specific assumption: what was this assumption?

R v Kuddus [2019] EWCA Crim 837

Sir Brian Leveson P

69. In our judgment, to focus on the particular circumstances of this specific victim is to misunderstand what has to be established to prove gross negligence manslaughter. There is no requirement that there must be proved to be a serious and obvious risk of death for the specific victim who dies. If it is in issue, the question to be answered is whether the defendants' breach gave rise (as an objective fact) to a serious and obvious risk of death to the class of people to whom the defendant owed a duty. Thus, in the present case, where the duty was to take reasonable steps not to injure members of the class of nut allergy sufferers (of whom Megan was one), the question to be answered would be whether any proved breach by the appellant would give rise to a serious and obvious risk of death for members of that class.

[...]

71. The fact that the doctors did not think that the risk for Megan was such that she required an EpiPen is not to the point. In the absence of special circumstances, none of which arise in the present case, the relevant question in this case would be whether the appellant's breach gave rise to (a) a risk of death that was (b) serious and (c) obvious for nut allergy sufferers of the class to whom the relevant duty was owed and of which Megan was a member. That question, if asked, should be answered by reference to all relevant and admissible evidence.

72. For these reasons we consider that the submission advanced by [defence counsel] before the trial judge was mistaken because it over-personalised the question of fact that he submitted should be left to the jury. We therefore endorse the Judge's decision not to direct the jury in accordance with his submission. There was no separate and independent requirement that the Crown prove that the particular victim, in this case Megan, was at serious and obvious risk of death. The individual idiosyncrasies of individuals at potential risk, on the assumption that they will be unknown to the defendant, cannot determine the question whether there is in fact a serious and obvious risk of death. We leave open the different issue, which does not fall for decision in this case, whether and if so when personal knowledge on the part of a defendant of the characteristics of the specific person to whom a duty is owed may affect the answer to that question.

So the fact that Megan's allergy was believed to be mild – and that there was nothing in her previous history that would have suggested she would suffer a severe reaction – should not be taken into account: the question was whether a breach of duty would give rise to a serious and obvious risk of death to a nut allergy sufferer. This was because the defendant did not know the details of Megan's allergy. The Court left open the question whether a victim's personal characteristics should be taken into account if the defendant was aware of these characteristics.

Requirement 4: The serious and obvious risk of death must have been reasonably foreseeable

Having established that there was a serious and obvious risk of death, the next requirement is that this risk was reasonably foreseeable when the duty was breached. Here we need to look at three cases that offer guidance on what can be taken into account when applying this test.

The first case is *R* v *Rose (Honey Maria)* [2017] EWCA Crim 1168. The question in this case was whether personal characteristics of the victim, of which the defendant was unaware, can be taken into account if the reason that the defendant was unaware of them was the defendant's own breach of duty.

R v Rose (Honey Maria)

The defendant, Honey Maria Rose, was a registered optometrist. In February 2012 Joanne Barker took her two children, Vincent (aged 7) and Amber (aged 4), for routine eye tests and examinations. Rose was on duty. After retinal images had been taken by an optical consultant/assistant, Rose carried out Vincent's sight test and recorded no issues of concern.

Five months later Vincent was taken ill. His condition deteriorated rapidly, and he was rushed to hospital. By the time he arrived he was in cardiac arrest. He died a short time later. The cause of death was acute hydrocephalus (acute build-up of fluid within the brain). It was agreed that this had been a longstanding problem and would have been treatable (by draining the fluid), but Vincent had not shown any symptoms of hydrocephalus (such as repeated headaches and vomiting).

It was subsequently found that the retinal images taken during Vincent's eye examination in February 2012 showed significant swelling of the optic nerve (known as papilloedema). This would have been a cause for concern for a competent optometrist and would have led to an immediate referral to hospital. The prosecution's case was that Rose had breached the duty of care she owed to Vincent to examine his eyes properly, and that had she not breached this duty Vincent could have been successfully treated in hospital and would not have died.

An important issue in the case was what facts the jury could take into account when deciding whether a reasonably competent optometrist would have foreseen a serious and obvious risk of death. Defence counsel argued that the jury should only take into account facts that were known to Rose at the time of her breach of duty (i.e., Vincent's papilloedema should not be taken into account since Rose had no knowledge of it at this point in time). The trial judge rejected this, stating that the test should instead be decided "by reference to the knowledge that the Defendant either had or would have had but for the breaches of duty that are alleged against her". In other words, the trial judge said they jury should take the papilloedema into account when deciding whether a reasonably competent optometrist would have foreseen a serious and obvious risk of death because Rose would have been aware of this condition had she not breached the duty of care she owed to Vincent. Rose was subsequently convicted of gross negligence manslaughter. She appealed against her conviction, arguing that the trial judge had misdirected the jury. The Court of Appeal upheld her appeal and quashed her conviction.

EXTRACT

Read the following extract from the judgment of Sir Brian Leveson P.

a. Was the trial judge correct to tell the jury to take Vincent's papilloedema into account when deciding whether the serious and obvious risk of death was reasonably foreseeable? Why/why not?

b. Reflect on the reasons Sir Brian Leveson P gave for his ruling. Do you agree with him?

R v *Rose (Honey Maria)* [2017] EWCA Crim 1168

Sir Brian Leveson P

84 … The test of reasonable foreseeability simply requires the notional objective exercise of putting a reasonably prudent professional in the shoes of the person whose conduct is under scrutiny and asking whether, at the moment of breach of the duty on which the prosecution rely, that person ought reasonably (i.e. objectively) to have foreseen an obvious and serious risk of death.

85 In that regard, the factual matrix is critical. In this case, the purpose of an examination of the back of a person's eyes with an ophthalmoscope or a 'slit lamp' is to fulfil an optometrist's statutory duty under s.26(1) of the 1989 Act to detect "…signs of injury, disease or abnormality in the eye or elsewhere". The fact that an intra-ocular examination *might* reveal a serious abnormality, or even in some cases serious life-threatening problems, does not mean that there is a "serious and obvious risk of death" if such an examination is not carried out. It might be different if the patient presented with symptoms which themselves either pointed to the risk of a potentially life threatening condition or provided a flag that alerted a competent optometrist to that risk but that was not this case (this being an entirely routine examination with no material pre-existing history).

86 Put at its highest, what a reasonably prudent optometrist would or should have known at the time of the breach was that, if he or she did not carry out a proper examination of the back of Vincent's eyes, there remained the possibility that signs of potentially life-threatening disease or abnormality might be missed. This is not enough to found a case of gross negligence manslaughter since there must be a "serious and obvious risk of death" at the time of breach. This was conceded by the prosecution at the trial, who recognised that for the matter to proceed beyond half time, the Crown need to rely upon the knowledge of the clear signs of papilloedema which Ms Rose "…would have had if she had conducted an internal investigation or looked at the retinal images."

87 Consistently with this approach, the factual matrix of the other cases mentioned above reveals the existence of such circumstances. By way of example, in *Adomako*, the court was concerned with an anaesthetist who, as would have been clear at the time, was required to monitor breathing during the course of an operation: failure to do so created an obvious risk of death. In *Singh (Gurpal)*, the landlord did not merely fail to maintain or service the gas fire (aware that such failure could create a risk) but failed to do so notwithstanding complaints by the tenants of the smell of gas and resulting illnesses. In *Misra*, there were obvious post-operative symptoms and information which generated the obvious risk of death. These cases contrast with *Rudling*, discussed above, in which the court made clear (at [40]):

> "[A] mere possibility that an assessment might reveal something life-threatening is not the same as an obvious risk of death. An obvious risk is a present risk which is clear and unambiguous, not one which might become apparent on further investigation."

…

91 So that the matter is not in doubt, the fact that the cause of the defendant's lack of knowledge of a serious and obvious risk of death to the victim was the defendant's own breach of duty to carry out a requisite examination or inspection is not to point. This fact may often be the case and, indeed, given that death will always have resulted in cases of gross negligence manslaughter, it is difficult to visualise how a serious risk of death would not

have been obvious if the test is premised on what would have been known had there been no breach of duty. In that event, the requirement of serious and obvious risk of death adds nothing. There is no legitimate basis for altering what is a prospective test of foresight into one which judges with hindsight.

92 Further, the fact also that the purpose of the duty in the present case is to detect signs of injury, disease or abnormality is also not to point. As explained above, all a reasonably prudent optometrist would have known is that, if he or she did not carry out a proper examination, signs of potentially life-threatening conditions might be missed. But this is a very different matter from knowledge that such signs in fact existed and that there was a "serious and obvious risk of death". In some cases, there might be 'wilful blindness' to a serious and obvious risk of death, but that is not the present case.

. . .

Conclusion

94 Reverting to the question posed at the commencement of this judgment, we conclude that, in assessing reasonable foreseeability of serious and obvious risk of death in cases of gross negligence manslaughter, it is not appropriate to take into account what the defendant would have known but for his or her breach of duty. Were the answer otherwise, this would fundamentally undermine the established legal test of foreseeability in gross negligence manslaughter which requires proof of a "serious and obvious risk of death" at the time of breach. The implications for medical and other professions would be serious because people would be guilty of gross negligence manslaughter by reason of negligent omissions to carry out routine eye, blood and other tests which in fact would have revealed fatal conditions notwithstanding that the circumstances were such that it was not reasonably foreseeable that failure to carry out such tests would carry an obvious and serious risk of death. For these reasons, this appeal is allowed and the conviction is quashed.

95 We add that this decision does not, in any sense, condone the negligence that the jury must have found to have been established at a high level in relation to the way that Ms Rose examined Vincent and failed to identify the defect which ultimately led to his death. That serious breach of duty is a matter for her regulator; in the context of this case, however, it does not constitute the crime of gross negligence manslaughter.

So the fact that Vincent had not shown any symptoms that pointed to the risk of a life-threatening condition was crucial and was what distinguished this case from *R* v *Adomako*, *R* v *Singh (Gurpal)* and *R* v *Misra*. It was simply a routine eye examination, and whilst a reasonably prudent optometrist would have known that a failure to perform the examination competently might result in signs of a potentially life-threatening condition being missed this is not the same as saying that a reasonably prudent optometrist would have foreseen a serious and obvious risk of death. Moreover, facts that would have been discovered had the examination been performed competently – such as Vincent's papilloedema – cannot be taken into account when making this assessment. To do so would turn 'a prospective test of foresight into one which judges with hindsight' ([91]).

In the following extract Karl Laird criticises the Court of Appeal's reasoning in *R* v *Rose (Honey Maria)*, arguing that it dilutes the objectivity of the assessment whether the serious and obvious risk of death was reasonably foreseeable. **According to Laird, how does the decision in *R* v *Rose (Honey Maria)* dilute the objectivity of this test?**

EXTRACT

Laird, K. (2018) 'Commentary on *R* v *Rose (Honey Maria)* *Criminal Law Review* 78

The problem with this reasoning, however, is that although the court makes reference to the reasonably prudent professional, its approach endows that notional figure with D's shortcomings. If the reasonably prudent professional would have checked the back of V's eyes, then why should that notional figure not be endowed with the knowledge that would have been gleaned had the eye examination been conducted in accordance with the duty of care? If the expert evidence had suggested that the signs of papilloedema were so subtle that a reasonably prudent optometrist, even after having conducted a proper eye examination, would not have noticed the condition and therefore would not have referred V for urgent medical treatment, then D should not be guilty. If, on the other hand, the signs of papilloedema would have been obvious to the reasonably prudent professional, why should D benefit from the fact that, even though the reasonably prudent professional would have checked the back of V's eyes, she did not? ... There is no principled distinction between the case of the optometrist who conducts an internal investigation negligently and the optometrist who is so negligent that he or she does not even attempt an internal investigation. If anything, the latter seems more culpable than the former. For this reason, it is irrational that he or she is at less risk of being held criminally liable. The most worrying aspect of the Court of Appeal's judgment, however, is that in endowing the reasonably competent GP/optometrist/surgeon, etc. with D's shortcomings, it has undermined the objective nature of the test set out in *Adomako*. For that reason, it is hoped the Court of Appeal has the opportunity to revisit this issue in the near future.

Having examined the judgment in *R* v *Rose (Honey Maria)*, we can now turn to the second ground of appeal in *R* v *Kuddus*. As we saw above, it was Rashid (the takeaway manager) who read the order, including the details of Megan's allergy. Although Kuddus owned the business and was working there, Rashid did not notify him of Megan's allergy. Yet at trial, the trial judge said that, since it was Kuddus' responsibility, as owner, to ensure that appropriate systems were in place to safeguard customers with declared allergies, the jury should treat him as having been aware of Megan's allergy. Kuddus' counsel argued that this was incorrect.

EXTRACT

Read the following extract from the judgment of Sir Brian Leveson P and consider the following questions.

a. According to the Court of Appeal, should Kuddus have been treated as having been aware of Megan's allergy? Why/why not?

b. In his judgment, Sir Brian Leveson P draws an analogy between this case and *R* v *Rose (Honey Maria)*. What does he say is the similarity between the two cases?

c. In your opinion, could Laird's criticism of the judgment in *R* v *Rose (Honey Maria)* (that the defendant benefitted from her own breach of duty) also be applied to the judgment in *R* v *Kuddus*?

R v *Kuddus* [2019] EWCA Crim 837

Sir Brian Leveson P

78. There is no doubt that the scope of any defendant's duty is fact-sensitive. The Judge rightly directed the jury that they should consider the charge of manslaughter against each defendant separately and return separate verdicts against each. However, in relation to manslaughter, the summing up treated giving notice of allergy to "Royal Spice" as sufficient to demonstrate notice to both Mr Rashid and to the appellant. No difficulty arises in relation to Mr Rashid because it was common ground that he received the form of order with the words "nuts prawns" clearly marked on it. However, the position with the appellant was different as there was no evidence that he was notified about the terms of the order: indeed, it seems to have been common ground that he was not.

79. In our judgment, the fact that the appellant was the sole director of the Company placed upon him the duty of ensuring that appropriate systems were in place to avoid the risk that a customer with a declared allergy was not served food which contained the allergen. That is the same as the duty placed in *Honey Rose* of conducting an appropriate examination to accord with the requirements of the legislation. In both cases, the risk, however, was the risk that a customer or patient respectively might present with the underlying condition which the system should have been designed to prevent, rather than the obvious and serious risk of death. To put it more generally, if a reasonable person possessed of the knowledge available to the defendant would have foreseen only a chance that the risk of death might arise, that is not enough to justify a conviction for gross negligence manslaughter. What is required is that the reasonable person would have foreseen an obvious and serious risk of death.

80. Using the same two examples of this case and *Honey Rose*, the foreseeable risk for the purposes of gross negligence manslaughter is that, armed with notice that a particular customer or patient falls into the category which the system (or statute) was designed to deal with, a reasonable person in the position of the restaurateur or optometrist would, at the time of breach of duty, have foreseen an obvious and serious risk of death. It is in those circumstances that the jury would have to go on to consider whether the negligent breach of duty was 'gross' within the meaning of that term defined by the authorities.

81. The difficulty with the approach in this case was that it was not suggested that the appellant was armed with notice that Megan fell into the category of those in respect of whom a reasonable person in the position of the appellant could have foreseen an obvious and serious risk of death by serving the food that he did. He knew nothing of the allergy which she had declared. In those circumstances, the conviction for gross negligence manslaughter cannot stand.

So Kuddus' breach of duty – his failure to ensure that appropriate systems were in place to safeguard customers with declared allergies – created a risk that the takeaway might serve such a customer with food containing the allergen. But this must be distinguished from serving a customer knowing that appropriate systems were not in place *and* knowing that that customer had the allergy in question. Only in the latter situation could it be held that a reasonable person would foresee an obvious and serious risk of death.

R v *Rose (Honey Maria)* and *R* v *Kuddus* may be contrasted with *R* v *Winterton* [2018] EWCA Crim 2435. In this case the defendant, Andrew Winterton, was the manager of a construction site. The victim, Shane Wilkinson, was a labourer on the site, where nine new houses were being built. An L-shaped trench had been dug in front and to the side of one of the houses, in order to lay drainage pipes. The trench was 2 metres deep, but its sides were vertical, not battered (slanted), and were unsupported. Shane Wilkinson was working in the trench when it collapsed. He was buried in earth and rubble, and died as a result of a fractured skull.

At trial, Winterton was convicted of gross negligence manslaughter. Winterton had breached the duty of care he owed to Wilkinson by allowing him to work in an unsafe trench. On appeal, Winterton claimed that he had been unaware that the trench was unsafe. The issue for the Court of Appeal was whether Winterton could be guilty if he had not in fact known that the trench was unsafe (even though he should have known).

EXTRACT

Read the following extract from the judgment of Macur LJ and consider the following questions.

a. According to the Court of Appeal, *R* v *Rose (Honey Maria)* and *R* v *Rudling* were both distinguishable. Why?

b. According to the Court, why could Winterton be convicted of gross negligence manslaughter even if he had not known that the trench was dangerous?

R v *Winterton* [2018] EWCA Crim 2435

Macur LJ

27. We regard the evidence in this case regarding the excavation of the trench, depicted so starkly in a photograph handed to us during the appeal and which had been in the jury bundle, clearly demonstrated the dangerous workmanship that posed a real and significant risk of death. Further, there was evidence from which the jury could have concluded that the Appellant had actual knowledge of the same, or otherwise adopted a wilful blindness/ ignorance of the excavation of what would necessarily be a deep drainage trench in unstable ground and therefore intrinsically dangerous. The Appellant's duty of care to those on site would be continuous throughout the excavation. The breach of duty was ongoing from the time that excavation of the trench had reached a stage which required battering or other means of support and required a workman to enter into it to lay the pipes, or else allowed them to encroach on the area next to it.

28. The factual matrix in this case was that it was a question of 'when' not 'if' the trench would collapse, and this was or should have been apparent to anybody. Consequently, there was reasonable foreseeability of serious and obvious risk of death to anyone in or near the trench. The Appellant's breach of duty is not able to be cast as that in the case of the optometrist in *R* v *Honey Rose*, and the GP in *R* v *Rudling*. They were not sufficiently alerted - and had no cause to be - to the risk of death on the facts available to them at the time of the breach of their respective duties of care, and which when objectively assessed should have alerted them to the serious and obvious risk of death. For example, in *R* v *Honey Rose*, the deceased little boy did not present with symptoms which should have put the optometrist on notice that there might be increased pressure in his brain, so alerting her to the positive need to examine the back of his eyes. In both cases, the prosecution was inviting the jury to a retrospective scrutiny of foreseeability of death on the basis of the ultimate and fatal outcome of the progress of a disease that could have been detected sooner but for

> breach of their duty of care, not that this risk should have been apparent to them prospectively at the moment they failed to investigate further.
>
> 29. The evidence in this case simply does not permit [defence counsel] to argue that 'but for the trench collapse, no objective observer would have been aware from the facts available to the Appellant at the time that there was a significant risk of death arising from his breach of duty.' We agree with [prosecuting counsel] that this Appellant is in the position of the anaesthetist in *Adomako* and the doctors in *Misra* and *Strivastata*, the warning signs and serious and obvious risk of death were there for them to see. They either did see them and ignored them, or failed to do so in circumstances that would provoke an objective observer to say, 'but on the facts and in their position they should have done'.

So in both *R* v *Rose (Honey Maria)* and *R* v *Rudling* an objective assessment of the situation at the time of the breach of duty would not have alerted a reasonable person to a serious and obvious risk of death. Things were different in *R* v *Winterton*. The warning signs were there for all to see. So whether Winterton was aware of the danger or not, a reasonable observer would have foreseen a serious and obvious risk of death. Winterton's appeal was therefore dismissed and his conviction upheld.

Lastly, note one final point. In a case involving a victim whose condition deteriorates, the key moment in time is the moment at which the victim's condition reaches the threshold of a serious and obvious risk of death.[85] You should focus on this point in time and ask whether the *actus reus* and *mens rea* requirements were satisfied at this moment.

Requirement 5: The breach of duty caused the death of the victim

The fifth requirement is that the breach of duty was a factual and legal cause of the victim's death. Here you apply the law governing causation that we studied in Chapter 3. Remember that the correct test for factual causation is: but for the defendant's breach of duty, would the victim have died? The prosecution must prove, beyond reasonable doubt, that the answer to this question is 'No'. In *R* v *Broughton* [2020] EWCA Crim 1093 the defendant, Ceon Broughton, was at a music festival with the victim, Louella. He provided her with the Class A drug 2-CP and 'bumped' it up (either by giving her an increased dose or mixing it with ecstasy or ketamine). Louella suffered a bad reaction to the drugs. Broughton remained with her, but did not secure medical assistance. She died and at trial Broughton was convicted of gross negligence manslaughter. On appeal, his conviction was quashed. According to expert evidence there was a 'realistic possibility' ([100]) that Louella would have died even if she had received timely medical assistance. So it could not be said, beyond reasonable doubt, that, but for Broughton's omission, Louella would not have died.

Note also one other point. In Chapter 3 we saw that the basic test for legal causation is the 'significant contribution' test from *R* v *Cheshire*. In cases involving medical negligence, the significant contribution test will be satisfied if the defendant's negligence caused the victim to die significantly sooner. In other words, in such cases the question is whether competent treatment would have saved or significantly prolonged the victim's life.[86]

---

85 *R* v *Broughton* [2020] EWCA Crim 1093.

86 *R* v *Bawa-Garba* [2016] EWCA Crim 1841.

Requirement 6: The breach of duty should be characterised as gross negligence and therefore as a crime

The final requirement is that the defendant's breach of duty was **grossly negligent**. Whether or not the breach of duty amounted to gross negligence is a question of fact for the jury to decide. The role of an expert witness is to provide material for juries to evaluate when considering this question. Expert witnesses may also express an opinion on whether the negligence was gross, but if they do the trial judge must make it clear to the jury that they are not bound by the expert's opinion.[87]

The test for gross negligence

In *R* v *Adomako* Lord Mackay offered the following guidance on how to distinguish gross negligence from mere negligence:

> This will depend on the seriousness of the breach of duty committed by the defendant in all the circumstances in which the defendant was placed when it occurred. The jury will have to consider whether the extent to which the defendant's conduct departed from the proper standard of care incumbent upon him, involving as it must have done a risk of death to the patient, was such that it should be judged criminal [. . .] The essence of the matter which is supremely a jury question is whether having regard to the risk of death involved, the conduct of the defendant was so bad in all the circumstances as to amount in their judgment to a criminal act or omission.

Lord Mackay conceded that this test involves 'an element of circularity': the defendant's conduct is criminal if it was grossly negligent, and it was grossly negligent if it deserves to be criminal. The test has also been criticised for being too vague and vesting too much discretion in juries. This, it has been argued, violates the principle of maximum certainty (which we studied in Chapter 1). In fact, in *R* v *Misra* [2004] EWCA Crim 2375 defence counsel argued that the test is so vague that it violates Article 7 ECHR. Counsel's submissions emphasised the ambiguity and circularity of the test, and claimed that the offence definition fails to give citizens fair warning on what conduct is and isn't prohibited.

EXTRACT

Read the following extract from the judgement of Judge LJ.

- Did he agree that the definition of gross negligence manslaughter is vague? Why/why not?
- Who do you think is correct: defence counsel or Judge LJ?

R v *Misra* [2004] EWCA Crim 2375

Judge LJ

64. In our judgment the law is clear. The ingredients of the offence have been clearly defined, and the principles decided in the House of Lords in *Adomako*. They involve no

---

[87] *R* v *Sellu* [2016] EWCA Crim 1716.

uncertainty. The hypothetical citizen, seeking to know his position, would be advised that, assuming he owed a duty of care to the deceased which he had negligently broken, and that death resulted, he would be liable to conviction for manslaughter if, on the available evidence, the jury was satisfied that his negligence was gross. A doctor would be told that grossly negligent treatment of a patient which exposed him or her to the risk of death, and caused it, would constitute manslaughter.

65. After Lord Williams' sustained criticism of the offence of manslaughter by gross negligence, the House of Lords in *Adomako* clarified the relevant principles and the ingredients of this offence. Although, to a limited extent, Lord Mackay accepted that there was an element of circularity in the process by which the jury would arrive at its verdict, the element of circularity which he identified did not then and does not now result in uncertainty which offends against Article 7, nor if we may say so, any principle of common law. Gross negligence manslaughter is not incompatible with the ECHR.

One thing that a jury might wish to consider when applying this requirement is whether or not the defendant foresaw the risk of death. If the defendant did foresee the risk of death, a jury might be more inclined to decide that his negligence was gross. But remember that a jury can find that the defendant's negligence was gross even if the risk of death never occurred to the defendant. Some people feel that this stretches the bounds of homicide liability too far. They argue that manslaughter liability should only be imposed on those who foresaw a risk of death and unjustifiably chose to take it (i.e. those who were reckless according to the *R* v *Cunningham* test). They argue that manslaughter liability should not be imposed on someone (like Adomako) who never chose to take a risk that the victim would be killed.

Quiz 5.4

1. Which of the following is NOT a requirement for gross negligence manslaughter?
   a. The defendant realised that there was a serious and obvious risk of death.
   b. The defendant breached a duty of care that he owed to the victim.
   c. The breach of duty caused the death of the victim.
   d. The breach of duty was grossly negligent.

2. Which of the following defendants was NOT guilty of gross negligence manslaughter?
   a. John Adomako.
   b. Perry Wacker.
   c. Gemma Evans.
   d. Joanne Ruling.

3. Which of the following statements about *R* v *Rose (Honey Maria)* is accurate?
   a. The Court of Appeal stated that in gross negligence manslaughter cases a jury should apply a test based on hindsight, not a prospective test of foresight.
   b. The defendant did not owe the victim a duty of care.
   c. At the time of the eye examination, a reasonably prudent optometrist would not have foreseen a serious and obvious risk of death.
   d. When applying the reasonable foreseeability test, the jury may take into account facts that the defendant would have known had it not been for the breach of duty.

Corporate manslaughter

5.5 Explain the requirements for establishing criminal liability for corporate manslaughter.

The offence of corporate manslaughter was a long time in the making. Prior to the creation of the offence in 2007, prosecutors seeking to hold a company criminally responsible for a death had to rely on the offence of gross negligence manslaughter. One of the major difficulties with this was the identification principle. To establish liability, there had to be an individual within the company who not only was sufficiently senior to be identified as the company's directing mind and will, but who also satisfied the *actus reus* and *mens rea* requirements of gross negligence manslaughter. While this was sometimes possible with smaller companies, in practice it proved impossible for larger ones where senior management were not involved in day-to-day operations. There were numerous calls for reform of the law, especially given the failure to secure convictions for large-scale disasters such as the Zeebrugge ferry disaster and the rail crashes at Hatfield, Potter's Bar and Southall.

Following a Law Commission report in 1996 and a Home Office consultation paper in 2000[88], the offence of corporate manslaughter was finally created by the Corporate Manslaughter and Corporate Homicide Act 2007. The definition of the offence is found in section 1.

EXTRACT

Section 1 of the Corporate Manslaughter and Corporate Homicide Act 2007

(1) An organisation to which this section applies is guilty of an offence if the way in which its activities are managed or organised –

a. causes a person's death, and

b. amounts to a gross breach of a relevant duty of care owed by the organisation to the deceased.

[…]

(3) An organisation is guilty of an offence under this section only if the way in which its activities are managed or organised by its senior management is a substantial element in the breach referred to in subsection (1).

This tells us that corporate manslaughter has the following five requirements:

1. The defendant organisation owed the victim a duty of care.
2. The organisation breached its duty of care due to the way in which its activities were managed or organised.
3. The breach of duty caused the death of the victim.
4. The way in which the organisation's activities were managed or organised by its senior management was a substantial element in the breach.
5. The breach of duty was gross.

[88] Law Commission (1996) *Legislating the Criminal Code: Involuntary Manslaughter* (Law Commission Report No 237); Home Office (2000) *Reforming the Law on Involuntary Manslaughter: The Government's Proposals.*

Numbers 1 to 4 are *actus reus* requirements. Number 5 is a *mens rea* requirement.

Before working through each of these requirements, it is important to first consider who may be guilty of the offence. According to section 1(1), the offence applies to organisations. As section 1(2) explains, this is broader than just companies.

EXTRACT

Section 1(2) of the Corporate Manslaughter and Corporate Homicide Act 2007

(2) The organisations to which this section applies are –

a. a corporation;

b. a department or other body listed in Schedule 1;

c. a police force;

d. a partnership, or a trade union or employers' association, that is an employer.

So it is not just corporations that can be liable for the offence. Partnerships and the police can be liable, as can trade unions and employer associations that are employing people. So too can the entities listed in Schedule 1 of the Act. This list contains more than 40 different departments and other bodies, including the Department for Health, Department for Transport, Home Office and Ministry of Defence.

The punishment for those convicted of the offence is a fine (of up to any amount) (s1(6)). The sentencing court also has the power to issue an order requiring the organisation to remedy the breach (s9) and an order requiring the organisation to publicise the fact it has been convicted, along with the details of the offence (s10).

Requirement 1: The defendant organisation owed the victim a duty of care

Whether or not there is a duty of care is a question of civil law. Section 2 of the Corporate Manslaughter and Corporate Homicide Act 2007 lists the different types of duty that may apply.

EXTRACT

Section 2 of the Corporate Manslaughter and Corporate Homicide Act 2007

(1) A "relevant duty of care", in relation to an organisation, means any of the following duties owed by it under the law of negligence –

a. a duty owed to its employees or to other persons working for the organisation or performing services for it;

b. a duty owed as occupier of premises;

c. a duty owed in connection with –

(i) the supply by the organisation of goods or services (whether for consideration or not),

(ii) the carrying on by the organisation of any construction or maintenance operations,

(iii) the carrying on by the organisation of any other activity on a commercial basis, or

(iv) the use or keeping by the organisation of any plant, vehicle or other thing;

d. a duty owed to a person who, by reason of being a person within subsection (2), is someone for whose safety the organisation is responsible.

(2) A person is within this subsection if –

a. he is detained at a custodial institution or in a custody area at a court, a police station or customs premises;

aa. he is detained in service custody premises;

b. he is detained at a removal centre, a short-term holding facility or in pre-departure accommodation;

c. he is being transported in a vehicle, or being held in any premises, in pursuance of prison escort arrangements or immigration escort arrangements;

d. he is living in secure accommodation in which he has been placed;

e. he is a detained patient.

In total, section 2 lists seven different types of duty of care:

- Duties as an employer (s2(1)(a))
- Duties as an occupier or premises (s2(1)(b))
- Duties arising from the supply of goods or services (s2(1)(c)(i))
- Duties arising from undertaking construction or maintenance work (s2(1)(c)(ii))
- Duties arising from other commercial activities (s2(1)(c)(iii))
- Duties arising from the use or keeping of any plant, vehicle or other thing (s2(1)(c)(iv))
- A duty for the safety of those individuals listed in subsection (2) (s2(1)(d))

Whether or not a duty of care exists is a question of law for the judge (s2(5)). Note that the *ex turpi causa* principle does not apply (s2(6)(a)). So the fact that individuals were jointly engaged in unlawful conduct does not prevent a duty of care from applying. This is the same as for gross negligence manslaughter, as we saw earlier in the Chapter. The *volenti non fit injuria* principle also does not apply (s2(6)(b)). So the fact that the victim had accepted the risk of harm does not prevent a duty of care from applying.

However, there are some types of duty that are excluded from the offence. These are detailed in sections 3 to 7. They relate to decisions on matters of public policy (section 3), military operations, activities and training (section 4), the policing of terrorism, civil unrest or serious disorder (section 5), the emergency services responding to an emergency (section 6) and child protection and probation (section 7).

Requirement 2: The organisation breached its duty of care due to the way in which its activities were managed or organised

Whether or not the organisation breached its duty of care is a question of fact for the jury. But notice that it is not enough that the duty was breached. The breach must also have been due to the way in which the organisation managed or organised its activities. Note that the focus here is on the organisation as a whole, as opposed to just senior management. So the jury should consider how the organisation's activities were managed or organised across all levels of management, and decide whether this amounted to a breach of its duty of care.

Requirement 3: The breach of duty caused the death of the victim

The third requirement is that the breach of duty caused the death of the victim. Here you apply the law governing causation that we studied in Chapter 3.

One question that may arise is whether the actions of an employee constituted an intervening act that broke the chain of causation. To determine this, you should apply the principles of legal causation – although remember that, as we saw in Chapter 3, these principles do not always pull in the same direction. Remember too that there can be multiple causes of a result. This is emphasised by the Explanatory Notes that accompanied the 2007 Act, which state: 'the management failure need not have been the sole cause of death; it need only be a cause' (para. 15). So it is possible that both the organisation and an individual employee were factual and legal causes of death.

Requirement 4: The way in which the organisation's activities were managed or organised by its senior management was a substantial element in the breach

This requirement asks whether the way in which the organisation's activities were managed or organised by its senior management was a substantial element in the breach of duty. Here we see a crucial difference to the previous law. While the old focused on specific individuals, the 2007 Act is concerned with gross negligence in how the activities of the organisation are run. The focus is on a failure of management at an organisational level.

However, the Act adds an important qualification. The way in which *senior* management managed or organised the organisation's activities must have been a substantial element in the breach. The meaning of 'senior management' is found in section 1(4)(c).

EXTRACT

Section 1(4)(c) of the Corporate Manslaughter and Corporate Homicide Act 2007

(4)(c) "senior management", in relation to an organisation, means the persons who play significant roles in –

(i) the making of decisions about how the whole or a substantial part of its activities are to be managed or organised, or

(ii) the actual managing or organising of the whole or a substantial part of those activities.

Remember that multiple individuals can make a substantial contribution to a result. So as long as the way in which senior management managed or organised the organisation's activities made a substantial contribution to the breach of duty, it does not matter if the actions of other, non-senior individuals also made a substantial contribution.

In the following extract, Celia Wells discusses this requirement of the offence.

EXTRACT

Read the extract from Wells' article. What concerns does she express about this requirement of the offence? Has the 2007 Act succeeded in addressing the problems under the old law?

Wells, C. (2014) 'Corporate criminal liability: a ten year review' *Criminal Law Review* 849

The offence is only committed if the way senior management have managed or organised activities has played a substantial role in the breach of a relevant duty. This in turn means we need to know to whom or what "senior management" refers. "Senior management" means the persons who play "*significant roles*" in making decisions about, or in actually managing, the "*whole or a substantial part*" of the organisation's activities. It might appear that the more definitions we are given the better except that the adjectives "significant" and "substantial" leave much room for debate. What does "substantial" mean? It is used both to define the extent to which senior management is involved in the breach and to define those within an organisation who might be regarded as "senior" management. Often in criminal law the word "substantial" has a broad meaning, something more than de minimis. In common usage it can mean something much more restrictive, more like "a large part of". In relation to its use to define those within an organisation who might be regarded as part of the *senior* management, it could well be interpreted as including only a narrow range of people whose responsibilities are central to the organisation's decision-making. The reasoning here is that "substantial" supplements "the whole", suggesting that it means something close to the whole if not the whole itself. And this still leaves the question of "significant" role. Far from addressing the difficulties in capturing organisational fault, the [Corporate Manslaughter and Corporate Homicide] Act slips between two grammatical uses of the word management. "Management" can mean either "the action or manner of managing", or the "power of managing", or it could function as a collective noun for "a governing body". Again the Explanatory Notes do not shed much light: "... [senior management] covers both those in the direct chain of management as well as those in, for example, strategic or regulatory compliance roles". The CPS also hedges its bets: senior management is "likely to be limited to those whose involvement is influential and will not include those who simply carry out the activity" and recommends prosecutors to obtain an organogram to determine whether the breach is at senior management level.

"... [the test] is wider than the former 'controlling mind' which effectively restricted the offence to actions of directors. A regional manager would probably count but this may itself depend on the number of regions, the number of higher tiers of management, the diversity of the organisation's activities and his own job description."

[...]

By requiring the "substantial" involvement of "senior management" and then defining this body as "those persons who play significant roles" the Act gives the lie to the Government's claimed commitment to an organisational version of fault that is not dependent on the actions of specified individuals.

Requirement 5: The breach of duty was gross

The final requirement of the offence is that the breach of duty was gross. The test for whether or not a breach of duty was gross is set out in section 1(4)(b).

EXTRACT

Section 1(4)(b) of the Corporate Manslaughter and Corporate Homicide Act 2007

(4)(b) a breach of a duty of care by an organisation is a "gross" breach if the conduct alleged to amount to a breach of that duty falls far below what can reasonably be expected of the organisation in the circumstances;

Section 8 provides some guidance on the factors a jury should take into account when asking whether the organisation's breach of duty fell far below what could reasonably have been expected of it in the circumstances.

EXTRACT

Read section 8 of the Act and make a list of the factors that a jury should consider. Which factors 'must' a jury consider? And which factors 'may' a jury consider? Can you think of any other things that a jury might want to consider?

Section 8 of the Corporate Manslaughter and Corporate Homicide Act 2007

(1) This section applies where –

a. it is established that an organisation owed a relevant duty of care to a person, and;

b. it falls to the jury to decide whether there was a gross breach of that duty.

(2) The jury must consider whether the evidence shows that the organisation failed to comply with any health and safety legislation that relates to the alleged breach, and if so –

a. how serious that failure was;

b. how much of a risk of death it posed.

(3) The jury may also –

a. consider the extent to which the evidence shows that there were attitudes, policies, systems or accepted practices within the organisation that were likely to have encouraged any such failure as is mentioned in subsection (2), or to have produced tolerance of it;

b. have regard to any health and safety guidance that relates to the alleged breach.

(4) This section does not prevent the jury from having regard to any other matters they consider relevant.

(5) In this section "health and safety guidance" means any code, guidance, manual or similar publication that is concerned with health and safety matters and is made or issued (under a statutory provision or otherwise) by an authority responsible for the enforcement of any health and safety legislation.

Quiz 5.5

1. Which of the following is NOT one of the requirements of corporate manslaughter?
   - **a.** The organisation owed the victim a duty of care.
   - **b.** The breach of duty caused the victim's death.
   - **c.** The breach of duty was committed by an individual who was the company's directing mind and will.
   - **d.** The breach of duty was gross.
2. Which of the following could NOT be a relevant duty of care for the purposes of corporate manslaughter?
   - **a.** A duty owed in respect of a policy decision concerning the allocation of resources.
   - **b.** A duty owed as an occupier of premises.
   - **c.** A duty arising from the provision of a service.
   - **d.** A duty owed as an employer.
3. Which of the following statements in the most accurate?
   - **a.** Under the 2007 Act, there is no need to prove that senior management bore any responsibility for the breach of duty.
   - **b.** Health and safety legislation is a separate area of the law that has no bearing on whether an organisation is guilty of corporate manslaughter.
   - **c.** It is for the jury to determine whether a duty of care existed and, if so, whether it had been breached.
   - **d.** A duty of care may exist even though the relevant individuals were jointly engaged in unlawful activity.

Proposals for reform: The Law Commission's homicide ladder

5.6 Describe the Law Commission's proposals for reform of the law of homicide.

In its report on the existing law of homicide, the Law Commission stated that it had been guided by the ladder principle. The meaning of this principle is set out in the extract below.

EXTRACT

Read the extract and in your own words, explain the relevance of the ladder principle to:

1. The existing two-tier structure of the law of homicide
2. The mandatory life sentence
3. The partial defences.

Law Commission (2006) *Murder, Manslaughter and Infanticide* (Law Commission Report No 304) HC 30

1.64 In structuring the general homicide offences we have been guided by a key principle: the 'ladder' principle. Individual offences of homicide should exist within a graduated system or hierarchy of offences. This system or hierarchy should reflect the offence's degree of seriousness, without too much overlap between individual offences. The main reason for adopting the 'ladder' principle is, as Lord Bingham has recently put it (in a slightly different context):

The interests of justice are not served if a defendant who has committed a lesser offence is either convicted of a greater offence, exposing him to greater punishment than his crime deserves, or acquitted altogether, enabling him to escape the measure of punishment which his crime deserves. The objective must be that defendants are neither over-convicted nor under-convicted…

1.65 The 'ladder' principle also applies to sentencing. The mandatory life sentence should be confined to the most serious kinds of killing. A discretionary life sentence should be available for less serious (but still highly blameworthy) killings.

1.66 Partial defences currently only affect the verdict of murder. This is because a verdict of murder carries a mandatory sentence. That sentence is not appropriate where there are exceptional mitigating circumstances of the kind involved in the partial defences. These mitigating circumstances necessitate a greater degree of judicial discretion in sentencing. The law creates this discretion by means of the partial defences which reduce what would otherwise be a verdict of murder, which carries a mandatory sentence, to manslaughter, which does not. Therefore, our recommended scheme does not extend the application of the partial defences to second degree murder or manslaughter. These offences would permit the trial judge discretion in sentencing and they therefore lack the primary justification for having partial defences.

Now, think about these questions.

1. Think back to the five cases and examples introduced right at the beginning of the chapter in the engagement activity:
   - The one-punch killer
   - The terrorist bomber
   - *R* v *Cocker*
   - *R* v *Ahluwalia*
   - *R* v *Adomako*

   Applying what you have learned in this chapter, under the existing law, would the defendant in each scenario be convicted of murder or manslaughter?

2. Comparing your five answers to the activity above, to what extent do you think the existing law respects the ladder principle?

The Law Commission's proposed three-tier structure

The Law Commission has proposed replacing the existing two-tier law of homicide with a three-tier structure.[89]

As Figure 5.3 shows, the Law Commission's proposed scheme would have first-degree murder at the top, with second-degree murder in the middle and manslaughter at the bottom.

[89] *Murder, Manslaughter and Infanticide* (Report No 304, 2006) HC 30.

Current law	Law Commission's proposal
Murder • Intention to kill or to cause GBH *(Mandatory sentence of life imprisonment)*	**First degree murder** • D intended to kill • D intended to do serious injury *and* was aware there was a serious risk of causing death *(Mandatory sentence of life imprisonment)*
Manslaughter • Voluntary manslaughter (killing with *mens rea* of murder where partial defence applies) • Involuntary manslaughter (culpable killing where D lacked the *mens rea* of murder) *(Discretionary maximum of life imprisonment)*	**Second degree murder** • D intended to do serious injury • D intended to cause some injury or a fear or risk of injury *and* was aware of a serious risk of causing death • Where a partial defence applies to what would have been first degree murder *(Discretionary maximum of life imprisonment)*
	Manslaughter • Killing by gross negligence • Killing through a criminal act intending to cause injury or aware of a serious risk of causing injury *(Discretionary maximum of life imprisonment)*

Figure 5.3 The Law Commission's proposed homicide ladder

Now, think about these questions.

Look back once again at the five cases and examples referred to on the previous page.

a. Which offence would the defendant in each scenario be convicted of under the Law Commission's proposed scheme?

b. To what extent does the Law Commission's proposal respect the ladder principle?

c. To what extent does the Law Commission's proposal rectify the problems with the existing law?

Definitions of first- and second-degree murder under the Law Commission's proposals

EXTRACT

In the following extract, Andrew Ashworth discusses the Law Commission's proposals, focusing particularly on the definitions of first-degree and second-degree murder.

Read the extract and then think about these questions.

- In his discussion of first-degree murder, what concerns does Ashworth raise regarding the terms 'serious injury' and 'serious risk'?
- What concerns does Ashworth express regarding the killings that fall within second-degree murder?

Ashworth, A. (2007) 'Principles, Pragmatism and the Law Commission's Recommendations on Homicide Law Reform' *Criminal Law Review* 333

1. Defining first degree murder

The Law Commission is right to support a "ladder principle" in recommending reform of the law of homicide, although any process of categorising or "stratifying" homicides for this purpose is bound to be controversial. In its consultation paper it advanced strong arguments in favour of confining first-degree murder to cases of intention to kill – a close connection with public opinion, a clear dividing line, and consistency with the correspondence principle (by dropping the "grievous bodily harm rule", which allows people to be convicted of murder when they merely intend to do serious harm). This reasoning has now been discarded in favour of a "moral equivalence" argument supported by quotations from Sir James Fitzjames Stephen – that first-degree murder (hereinafter murder 1) should include both cases of intent to kill and cases of intent to cause serious injury where that is coupled with awareness of a serious risk of killing…

(b) Serious injury.…[T]he Commission decides against recommending that "serious injury" should be defined. This decision is not discussed in relation to murder 1, perhaps because it is assumed that the question whether or not an intended injury was "serious" will be overshadowed, in murder 1, by the question whether D was aware of the serious risk of causing death… Under existing law, the minimum task for the prosecution is to prove an intent to cause really serious harm. Under the recommended law, the minimum task for the prosecution would be to prove an intent to do "serious injury" combined with awareness of a serious risk of causing death. It is likely that many cases will turn on this head of liability, and, if so, this suggests some need for precision in the law. After all, where the prosecution prove that D intended only non-serious injury, coupled with awareness of a serious risk of causing death, that is a form of murder 2. So the difference between that category of murder 2 and the second head of murder 1 lies only in the distinction between injury and serious injury. It may well be concluded that any definition of "serious injury" would have to be so complex as to be counter-productive, since it would confuse juries and give rise to frequent appeals. But, given the vital boundary that it marks, one might have expected more exploration of the possibilities of a definition or partial definition.

(c) Serious risk.… What is a "serious risk" of causing death? Risks may be ranged, theoretically, on a probability scale from 0 to 100. Nobody expects a criminal statute to specify a particular degree of probability, but it ought to indicate the approximate level of risk required. The Commission asserts that "serious risk" is one of those concepts that juries "can safely be left to apply to the facts of a case with a minimum amount of embellishment", and that minimum is found in the recommendation "that a risk is to be regarded as serious if it is more than insignificant or remote." There are two weaknesses in this approach. The first is that the word "serious" is already used in a different sense in the same clause – intent to cause *serious* injury coupled with awareness of a *serious* risk of causing death. It is surely best to avoid that, especially when there are other statutes that use a phrase such as "a *significant* risk of serious harm", thereby avoiding the use of "serious" as indicating a degree of risk. If the Commission really wants to have "serious" rather than "significant", it needs to say much more about the difference. The second weakness is the Commission's suggestion that the term "serious" is preferred because it is not just a question of probability, but also one of "whether the risk ought to be taken seriously." Degree of risk is merely "one factor" in the assessment. Does this indicate a further evaluative element? Does it suggest that juries should be free to evaluate whether taking this degree of risk with someone's life might render the offence unworthy of the murder 2 label and sufficient only for manslaughter? If so, the Commission must explain

the proper parameters of such crucial judgements. If not, the use of the word "serious" here should be reconsidered.

[...]

2. The second rung on the ladder

... The recommendation is that murder 2 should include 5 separate heads of liability – intent to do serious injury; awareness of the serious risk of causing death coupled with an intent to cause injury or fear or risk of injury; murder 1 with [loss of control]; murder 1 with diminished responsibility; and murder 1 in the context of a suicide pact. The brief comments here will focus on the first two heads of liability, with additional reflections on the structure.

(a) Killing through an intention to do serious injury. It could be said that this is the only part of the Law Commission's package that involves any down-grading. Killing in these circumstances is currently murder and attracts the mandatory sentence of life imprisonment. Many believe this is inappropriate, since there are forms of intent to do serious injury that do not make death a foreseeable consequence (e.g. knee-capping, breaking a limb). Moving this form of killing away from murder 1 and its mandatory penalty is therefore justified. However, it creates boundaries that will inevitably become the site of intense forensic argument. It will be necessary to distinguish injury from serious injury (see 1(b) above), which the Commission admits may be a "fine distinction"; and it will be necessary to distinguish those cases where the intent to cause serious injury is and is not accompanied with awareness of a serious/significant risk of causing death (see 1(c) above).

(b) Reckless killing.... The recommended formula for reckless killings falling within murder 2 is therefore those cases "where the defendant intended to cause injury or fear or risk of injury aware that his or her conduct involved a serious risk of causing death." It is necessary to place this on a spectrum of four forms or levels of reckless (or "undesired") killing: those where D knew the risk of death was so high as to be virtually certain are murder 1; those where D was aware of taking a serious risk of causing death and intended serious injury also fall within murder 1; the present group falls within murder 2; and then there are reckless killings where D may realise the risk of death but is not intending to cause fear or risk of injury, which will fall into manslaughter in the third tier. Common to the second and third forms of reckless killing is an awareness of a significant/serious risk of causing death, already discussed critically at 1(c) above. The distinguishing element of the murder 2 variety of reckless killing is that D must have one of three attitudes towards injury (not necessarily serious injury). D may intend to cause injury, even if that is not a serious injury. It is sufficient if D intends to cause *fear* of injury, as by driving straight at a police officer hoping to be able to swerve away at the last moment (although that would be a case of fear of serious injury, but such cases fall within this category because murder 1 includes only an intent to *cause* serious injury). It is also sufficient if D intentionally creates a *risk* of injury (or, for the reason just given, of serious injury), which would presumably capture the driver who overtakes on a blind bend and causes the death of someone in an oncoming vehicle. There is no reference here to the magnitude of the risk created – certainly no reference to "serious/significant risk". Could it not be argued that to include an intent to cause (any degree of) risk of injury over-extends this head of murder 2?

(c) Labels and sentences. One of the objections to the present law of homicide is that the mandatory penalty of life imprisonment applies to too large a number of cases, on

account of the wide definition of murder. We have seen that the Commission provisionally proposed to resolve this by confining the mandatory sentence to murder 1 and defining that offence narrowly in terms of an intent to kill. The Report now recommends a broader form of murder 1 that encompasses cases of killing with intent to do serious injury coupled with awareness of a significant/serious risk of causing death. Probably that will not greatly reduce the number of killings to which the mandatory penalty applies, since it will exclude chiefly cases where the serious injury intended would not normally be life-threatening. This raises the question why the second rung on the ladder should still be labelled "murder", albeit in the second degree, since four of its five heads are killings that are currently classified as manslaughter. Suggestions of a different label for the middle tier, such as grave or culpable homicide, have not moved the Commiss on. One may grant the Commission its argument that the current law is too generous to some reckless killings, and that such cases should be placed one tier below the highest category; but the argument put forward is that the culpability in these cases is so high that manslaughter is an inadequate label, not that they justify classification as "murder". If indeed the culpability in these cases is so high, is it right that killings under [loss of control] or diminished responsibility should be given the same label? Is the Commission confident that juries will be prepared to apply the label "murder", as in murder 2, to killings under [loss of control] or diminished responsibility? There is a strong argument that this is not an appropriate label, not least for killings that are often sentenced in the five to seven-year range. The Commission's view is that the sentence mitigation principle is more important here than the use of the label "murder": partial defences operate solely in murder cases, because it is the only offence with a mandatory penalty. Whatever the historical merits of that assertion, it is not persuasive at the level of principle, since there is a cogent argument that the mitigating force of [loss of control] (well explained by the Law Commission itself) and of diminished responsibility ("substantial impairment" resulting from mental abnormality) is such that a label other than murder is called for. Moreover, in practice it may not accord with popular conceptions of what should and should not be called "murder", and thus jurors may expect provoked killings to have a different and lesser label. These reservations point towards a different label for the second tier, and may also raise an argument for a different tier for the three killings with partial defences--a move that may or may not reduce the practical problems caused by having 5 different heads of murder 2 with a single verdict. The Commission concedes that the labelling issue should be revisited at the next stage of the review.

Now, think about these questions.

Having read Ashworth's critique, do you believe

a. a different label should be used for the middle rung of the Law Commission's proposed homicide ladder; and/or

b. an additional rung is needed for those cases in which a defendant successfully pleads a partial defence to first-degree murder?

Answering exam problem questions

We have covered a lot of material in this chapter. The flow chart in Figure 5.4 shows how you should structure this material when answering an exam problem question.

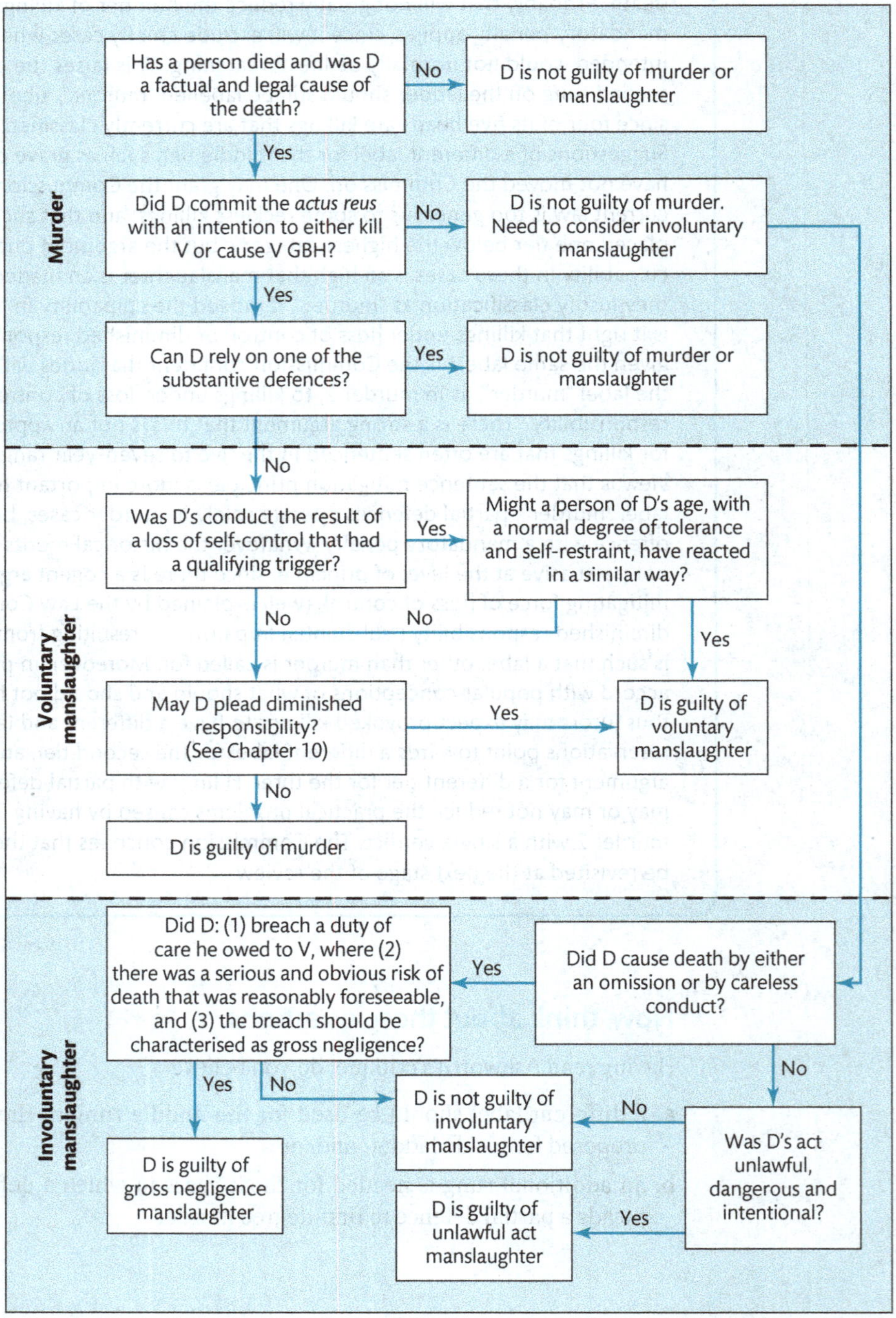

Figure 5.4 Answering exam problem questions

The first question to ask is whether a person has died and the defendant was a factual and legal cause of death. In other words, are all of the *actus reus* requirements of murder satisfied? If not, then the defendant cannot be guilty of murder or manslaughter. When this is the case in an exam problem question, you need to consider other possible offences instead, such as whether the defendant was an accessory to murder (see Chapter 13), whether the defendant is guilty of conspiracy to murder or attempted murder (see Chapter 12) or whether the defendant is guilty of a non-fatal offence (see Chapter 6).

If a person has died and the defendant was a factual and legal cause of death, the next question is whether the defendant had the *mens rea* of murder. If the defendant lacked the *mens rea* of murder you should consider involuntary manslaughter instead. The first issue here will be to decide whether to discuss unlawful act manslaughter or gross negligence manslaughter. To help you decide you should use the distinction Lord Atkin drew in *Andrews* v *DPP* between unlawful acts and careless lawful acts.

If the defendant had the *mens rea* of murder then, on the face of it, he is guilty of murder. However, before reaching a conclusion you need to consider possible defences. It is best to begin with the substantive defences (see Chapter 11). Since these result in a complete acquittal, defendants will prefer to plead a substantive defence rather than a partial defence. If no substantive defence is available, you should then consider the partial defences instead.

Assessment advice

In some exam questions it will not be possible to answer some of the questions in this flow chart with certainty. For example, it might be debatable whether the defendant had the *mens rea* of murder or not. In this case, your answer should discuss all possible eventualities. So you should write something like, 'If the jury concluded that Harold had the *mens rea* of murder, he would seek to plead the partial defence of loss of control.' After discussing whether Harold's defence of loss of control would succeed or not, you should then write something like, 'On the other hand, if the jury concluded that Harold lacked the *mens rea* of murder, involuntary manslaughter would need to be considered instead.' You should then discuss whether Harold satisfies the requirements of the relevant type of involuntary manslaughter.

Quiz 5.6

1. Which of the following principles has provided an overarching framework for the Law Commission's proposals for the reform of the law of homicide?

a. The thin skull principle.

b. The ladder principle.

c. The correspondence principle.

d. The sentence mitigation principle.

2. In the context of the Law Commission's three-tier law of homicide, in which of the following scenarios is Jeffrey likely to be charged with second-degree murder?

a. Jeffrey is driving at high speed on a deserted main road at 3am. Due to the high speed, he is unable to see an old man crossing the road and hits him with his car. He takes the man to the hospital, but the doctor declares him dead on arrival.

b. Jeffrey's wife was killed in a hit-and-run accident by a young man. Jeffrey asks to meet the man on the terrace of a 30-storey hotel and avenges his wife's death by pushing him off the terrace. The man dies.

c. Jeffrey and his brother have an ongoing feud regarding ancestral property. To be able to inherit the entire property, Jeffrey plans to kill his brother. After a week of planning, he shoots his brother dead.

d. When Jeffrey walks out of his kitchen, he sees a burglar in the living room. He becomes furious and runs towards the man with a knife to scare him away. As the burglar trips on the sofa and falls down, the knife slips from Jeffrey's hand and cuts the man's neck. The man dies from the injury.

3. Which of the following would fall within second-degree murder?
   a. The perpetrator of the killing intended to cause serious injury to the victim and was aware that there was a serious risk of causing death.
   b. The perpetrator of the killing intended to create a risk of injury to the victim and was aware that there was a serious risk of causing death.
   c. The perpetrator of the killing intended to create a fear of injury but did not believe that there was any risk of causing death.
   d. The perpetrator of the killing intended to cause the death of the victim.
4. Rohan, a businessman, has a longstanding rivalry with his competitor Karim. Both Rohan and Karim apply for a government contract, but when Karim wins the contract through an underhand deal, Rohan, who is facing bankruptcy, becomes furious and decides to do something about it. He breaks into Karim's home and shoots Karim three times with a gun. Karim dies as a result of the injuries sustained. If Rohan was being tried for first-degree murder under the proposed three-tier law of homicide, which of the following would most likely be the minimum task for the prosecution?
   a. Proving Rohan's intent to cause a risk of injury regardless of whether there was an awareness of a serious risk of causing death.
   b. Proving Rohan's intent to cause really serious harm.
   c. Proving Rohan's intent to do serious injury combined with an awareness of a serious risk of causing death.
   d. Proving Rohan's intent to cause fear of injury with an awareness of a serious risk of causing substantial disability.
5. The Law Commission has proposed a reform to move killing through an intention to do serious injury away from first degree murder and its mandatory penalty of life imprisonment. Which of the following statements helps justify this reform?
   a. In most cases, the terms 'injury' and 'serious injury' mean the same and are difficult to distinguish.
   b. The wide definition of manslaughter means that the mandatory penalty of life imprisonment applies to too many cases of homicide.
   c. There are forms of intent to do serious injury that do not make death a foreseeable consequence.
   d. In almost all cases, an intent to cause serious injury is accompanied by an awareness of a serious risk of causing death.

Applying the law

5.7 Apply the law of homicide to a hypothetical set of facts.

Now that you have an understanding of the law of homicide, the next step is to learn how to apply this knowledge to factual scenarios. The following scenario takes place at the airport and involves the characters Maeve, Rory, Andreas and Eleni. Read the facts carefully, then answer the multiple-choice questions below to apply your learning to the scenario.

Maeve has worked at the airport check-in desk for many years, and has grown tired of dealing with customer complaints. Rory arrives at the check-in desk 10 minutes before his scheduled take-off time. He had left home four hours earlier to catch a train to the airport, but had been held up, first, by a traffic jam and, second, by his train being delayed due to signal problems on the train line. Out of breath and agitated, he insists, 'I need to check in, my flight leaves in 10 minutes.' Maeve replies, 'Sorry sir, you're too late. You'll have to wait for the next available flight.' Annoyed, Rory asks, 'When is the next available flight?' 'Tomorrow morning,' Maeve answers, 'and it will cost an extra £150.' 'What?' shouts Rory, 'I am booked on a flight that takes off in 10 minutes and I demand that you let me on it.' Frustrated, Maeve responds, 'Don't shout at me. It's your own stupid fault for being late.' At this Rory snaps. He climbs over the check-in desk and attacks Maeve, hitting her repeatedly. Unknown to Rory, Maeve has a weak heart. She suffers a heart attack and dies.

Elsewhere at the airport there is a long queue at the check-in desk for the flight to Athens. Andreas, who has been queuing for almost one-and-a-half hours, is incensed when he sees Thanos arrive and push in at the front of the queue. He immediately marches up behind Thanos and shoves him out of the queue. Thanos stumbles and collides with an elderly passenger named Eleni. Eleni falls over and cracks her head on the hard floor. She later dies in hospital.

Discuss the criminal liability of Rory and Andreas. How (if at all) would your answer be different if, when Eleni arrived at hospital, a junior doctor failed to check her medical records properly and prescribed her a drug to which she was allergic? She died as a result of an allergic reaction to the drug. Had this mistake not been made, she would have made a full recovery.

Quiz 5.7

Now answer the following questions which apply the law to this scenario.

1. The first defendant to consider is Rory. The starting point is the offence of murder. The victim in Rory's case, Maeve, was a person, and Maeve died, so the first two *actus reus* requirements of the offence are satisfied. The remaining *actus reus* requirement is whether Rory was a factual and legal cause of Maeve's death.

   Which of the following is the test that is used to establish factual causation?

   a. The 'culpability' test: was the defendant to blame for the occurrence of the relevant consequence?

   b. The 'operative cause' test: at the time the consequence occurred, were the defendant's actions still an operating cause?

   c. The 'but for' test: but for the defendant's actions, would the consequence have occurred in the same way?

   d. The 'predominant cause' test: were the defendant's actions the predominant cause of the relevant consequence?

2. In Rory's case it is obvious that, but for his actions, Maeve would not have died in the same way. Factual causation is therefore established. Turning next to legal causation, we must begin by asking whether Rory's actions made a significant contribution to Maeve's death (*R* v *Cheshire*). Again, the answer is self-evident. Rory climbed over the check-in desk and hit Maeve repeatedly. This led to the fatal heart attack. However, unbeknown to Rory, Maeve suffered from a weak heart. Could Rory argue that this pre-existing vulnerability negates legal causation?

   In *R* v *Hayward* the victim had an abnormal heart condition. Which of the following principles did the Court apply?

   a. The unawareness principle: if the victim had an unusual characteristic of which the defendant was unaware, and the relevant consequence occurred as a result of this characteristic, then the defendant was not a legal cause of the result.

   b. The significant contribution principle: if the victim had an unusual characteristic of which the defendant was unaware, and that characteristic made a significant contribution to the occurrence of the relevant consequence, then the defendant was not a legal cause of the result.

   c. The thin skull principle: the defendant must take his victim as he finds her, even if the relevant characteristic was unusual and the defendant was unaware of it.

   d. The reasonable bystander principle: if the victim had an unusual characteristic which would not have been apparent to the reasonable bystander, and the relevant consequence occurred as a result of that characteristic, then the defendant was not a legal cause of the result.

3. Applying the thin skull principle to Rory's case, Rory must take his victim as he finds her. So Maeve's weak heart does not negate legal causation. Rory was therefore both a factual and legal cause of Maeve's death, and so the *actus reus* of murder is established.

   The next question is whether Rory caused Maeve's death with the *mens rea* of murder.

   Which of the following states the *mens rea* of murder correctly?

   a. An intention to kill the victim or recklessness as to whether the victim will be killed.

   b. An intention to kill the victim.

   c. An intention to kill the victim or an intention to cause the victim grievous bodily harm coupled with an awareness of a serious risk of death.

   d. An intention to kill the victim or an intention to cause the victim grievous bodily harm.

4. Rory attacked Maeve and hit her repeatedly. On these facts, it seems inevitable that a jury would conclude that Rory's direct intention (i.e. his purpose) was to at least cause Maeve grievous bodily harm. Moreover, even if Rory were to try and argue that his purpose was not to harm Maeve but merely to vent his frustration (which seems strained at best), he would still be found to have had an oblique intention to cause Maeve grievous bodily harm since this was the virtually certain consequence of his actions and he would have been aware of this (*R v Woollin*).

Having established the *actus reus* and *mens rea* of murder, we can now consider possible defences. In Rory's case the most relevant defence would be the partial defence of loss of control (Coroners and Justice Act 2009, section 54). This defence has three requirements.

Which of the following is not one of the requirements for the loss of control defence?

a. A person of the defendant's age and sex, with a normal degree of tolerance and self-restraint and in the circumstances of the defendant, might have reacted in the same or in a similar way to the defendant.

b. The defendant's loss of self-control had a qualifying trigger.

c. The defendant's loss of self-control was sudden.

d. The defendant's conduct was the result of a loss of self-control.

5. We will work through the three requirements for the defence in turn. The first requirement is that the defendant lost his self-control.

Which of the following statements is incorrect?

a. This part of the defence is subjective: the test is whether the defendant lost his self-control; it is not whether it was reasonable for the defendant to have lost his self-control.

b. The defendant cannot claim that he suffered a loss of self-control if he acted in a considered desire for revenge.

c. In order to plead the defence the defendant must prove, on the balance of probabilities, that he lost his self-control.

d. When deciding whether the defendant's conduct was the result of a loss of self-control, the jury may take into account any past events that are relevant.

6. So when deciding whether or not Rory satisfies the first requirement of this defence, the jury would not be limited to looking at the immediate trigger for the claimed loss of self-control (Maeve's statement 'It's your own stupid fault'); it could also look at relevant events from earlier that day (the traffic jam, the train delay, the wait until the next morning and the extra £150). The combination of these events makes it more plausible that Rory did, in fact, lose his self-control, and indeed the facts of the question itself state that he snapped.

The second requirement for the defence is that Rory's loss of self-control had a qualifying trigger.

Which of the following is **not** a qualifying trigger for the loss of control defence?

a. D's loss of self-control was attributable to things done or said which constituted circumstances of an extremely grave character and caused D to have a justifiable sense of being seriously wronged.

b. D's loss of self-control was attributable to an overwhelming sense of desperation caused by circumstances of an extremely tragic nature.

c. D's loss of self-control was attributable to D's fear of serious violence from V against D or another identified person.

d. D's loss of self-control was attributable to a combination of a fear of serious violence from V and a justifiable sense of being seriously wronged.

7. In Rory's case the relevant qualifying trigger would be the one contained in section 55(4): things done or said which constituted circumstances of an extremely grave character and caused D to have a justifiable sense of being seriously wronged.

As we saw in the chapter, there are four steps to work through to decide whether or not this qualifying trigger applies. First, the jury must decide whether Rory had a sense of being seriously wronged. Second, the jury must decide whether Rory's sense of being seriously wronged was justifiable. Third, the jury must decide whether Rory's sense of being seriously wronged was the result of things done or said (or both). And, fourth, the jury must decide whether the things done or said constitute circumstances of an extremely grave character.

In *R v Clinton, Parker & Evans* the Court of Appeal offered guidance on how to apply section 55(4). Which of the following statements summarises this guidance correctly?

a. The first step involves a subjective test. The second and fourth steps involve an objective assessment. The third step is a factual enquiry.

b. The third step is a factual enquiry. The other three steps are all assessed objectively.

c. The first two steps are tested subjectively. The third step involves a factual enquiry. The fourth step is assessed objectively.

d. The third step is a factual enquiry. The other three steps are all assessed subjectively.

8. If you were a juror applying these four steps to Rory, would you decide that the qualifying trigger is established or not? If, in your opinion, the qualifying trigger would not be established, which of the four steps would not be satisfied? Why?

The third requirement for the defence is that a person of the defendant's age and sex, with a normal degree of tolerance and self-restraint and in the circumstances of the defendant, might have reacted in the same or in a similar way to the defendant.

Which of the following statements about this part of the defence is incorrect?

a. When applying this part of the defence, the jury are not limited to considering events that took place at the time of the killing. Any past events which are relevant may also be considered.

b. If the jury concludes that a person of the defendant's age and sex, with a normal degree of tolerance and self-restraint and in the circumstances of the defendant, might also have lost their self-control, this part of the defence is satisfied.

c. If the defendant had been taunted about a particular characteristic, then when applying this part of the defence, the jury should consider the impact of the taunts on someone with that characteristic.

d. When applying this part of the defence, the jury may not take into account any characteristics (including mental abnormalities) whose only relevance is that they affected the defendant's capacity for tolerance or self-restraint.

9. The next defendant is Andreas. Again, our starting point is the offence of murder. Eleni was a person, and she died, so the first two *actus reus* requirements of murder are satisfied. The third *actus reus* requirement is that Andreas' actions were a factual and legal cause of her death. As we saw above, we apply the 'but for' test to determine questions of factual causation. It is clear that, but for Andreas' actions, Eleni would not have died in the same way. Turning to legal causation, it is also clear that Andreas' actions made a significant contribution to Eleni's death (*R* v *Cheshire*). But there are two other issues that also need to be considered in relation to legal causation.

First, Eleni was elderly and so may have been more frail and vulnerable than other bystanders. However, as in Rory's case, the thin skull rule would apply and Andreas must take his victim as he finds her (*R* v *Hayward*). Second, it was Thanos who collided with Eleni and knocked her over, not Andreas. So did Thanos' actions break the chain of causation?

The general principle is that voluntary intervening acts of a third part break the chain of causation. In *R* v *Pagett* how did the Court of Appeal define 'voluntary'?

a. A defendant's actions are voluntary unless he was acting in a state of automatism.

b. A defendant's actions are voluntary as long as he had control over his bodily movements.

c. A defendant's actions are voluntary when they are free, deliberate and informed.

d. A defendant's actions are voluntary only when he had time to think and reflect before deciding what to do.

10. Applying this definition of voluntary as 'free, deliberate and informed', Thanos' actions would be held to have been involuntary. As Andreas pushed him, Thanos' actions were neither free nor deliberate. Therefore Thanos' actions would not break the chain of causation.

Having established the *actus reus* of murder, we can now turn to the *mens rea*. Here we need to begin by addressing the fact that Andreas shoved Thanos, not Eleni, and apparently had no intention to harm Eleni at all.

Which of the following principles would apply in Andreas's case?

a. The principle of transferred *mens rea*.

b. The ladder principle.

c. The offence principle.

d. The correspondence principle.

11. Since the principle of transferred *mens rea* applies, we must next ask the question, what *mens rea* did Andreas have in respect of Thanos? Specifically, did he have the *mens rea* of murder, i.e. did he intend to kill Thanos or cause him grievous bodily harm? It seems clear that Andreas did not intend to kill Thanos, but did he intend to cause him grievous bodily harm? If you were the prosecutor in Andreas' case, how would you argue that Andreas did intend to cause Thanos grievous bodily harm? If you were Andreas' defence counsel, how would you respond to these arguments? Which arguments do you find the most persuasive?

It seems unlikely that a jury would conclude that Andreas intended to cause Thanos grievous bodily harm. It is arguable that Andreas' direct intention (i.e. his purpose) was to force Thanos out of the queue, not to harm him. And even if Andreas' direct intention was to harm Thanos, it seems unlikely that he hoped to cause such a serious level of harm as grievous bodily harm. Similarly, it is difficult to say that grievous bodily harm was a virtual certainty as a result of Andreas' actions, so the *R* v *Woollin* direction would not be satisfied and there could be no finding of an oblique intention to cause grievous bodily harm.

So Andreas would not be guilty of the murder of Eleni. Although the doctrine of transferred *mens rea* could apply in theory, no such transfer was possible since Andreas did not have the necessary *mens rea* in respect of Thanos. We must therefore consider involuntary manslaughter instead. Here, the first step is to decide which type of involuntary manslaughter applies. The allegation is not that Andreas acted carelessly. Rather it is that he intentionally committed an unlawful act. Therefore we should apply unlawful act manslaughter.

Unlawful act manslaughter has a total of five requirements. But which of the following is not a requirement of the offence?

a. The act was directed at the victim.

b. The act caused the victim's death.

c. The act was dangerous.

d. The act was unlawful.

12. Of the five requirements for unlawful act manslaughter, two are self-evident in Andreas' case (Andreas obviously did an act – he pushed Thanos – and he performed the act intentionally) and we established earlier that Andreas' act was a factual and legal cause of Eleni's death. So that leaves the following two issues: (1) was Andreas' act unlawful; and (2) was Andreas' act dangerous? The first of these issues is straightforward. Andreas unlawfully and intentionally inflicted force on Thanos. In other words, he committed the offence of battery. So liability hinges on whether Andreas' act was dangerous.

What is the test for dangerousness that was set out in *R* v *Church*?

a. Did the defendant foresee a risk that his act would result in some harm to the victim (not necessarily serious harm)?

b. Would the reasonable man have foreseen a risk that the defendant's act would result in serious harm to the victim?

c. Did the defendant foresee a risk that his act would result in serious harm to the victim?

d. Would the reasonable man have foreseen a risk that the defendant's act would result in some harm to the victim (not necessarily serious harm)?

13. If you were a juror applying the *R* v *Church* test to Andreas' actions, what would you decide? If his act was dangerous according to *R* v *Church*, he is guilty of unlawful act manslaughter.

In the alternative scenario the key issue is whether the junior doctor's mistake broke the chain of causation. If so, Andreas would not be guilty of any homicide offence as he would not be a legal cause of Eleni's death. It is clear from cases such as *R* v *Smith* and *R* v *Cheshire* that bad medical treatment will not normally break the chain of causation. An example of a case in which the chain of causation was broken by bad medical treatment is *R* v *Jordan*.

In *R* v *Jordan* what reason did the Court of Appeal give for deciding that the medical treatment the victim received broke the chain of causation?

a. The doctor in the case had made not one but two errors, which were both palpably wrong.

b. The stab wound had almost healed at the time of death, so had it not been for the treatment the victim received he would have made a full recovery.

c. A failure to diagnose a condition is an omission, and so does not break the chain of causation, whereas the negligent administration of treatment is a positive act and so does break the chain of causation.

d. The actions of the doctors were voluntary – in the sense of free, deliberate and informed – and so broke the chain of causation.

Applying the law II

Consider this scenario.

Suppose that, elsewhere in the airport, Jia went to a café and ordered a chicken sandwich. She was served by Omar and told him that she was allergic to peanuts. Omar was not paying attention. When he made Jia's sandwich, he added some pesto that contained peanuts. Jia ate the sandwich, suffered a severe allergic reaction, and died.

Now, think about this question. Which option would be the most suitable answer to this question?

Which of the following best explains why the airport café would not be found guilty of corporate manslaughter?

a. The café did not owe Jia a duty of care.
b. There was no causal link between the breach of duty and the death, because most customers do not have a peanut allergy and so would not have suffered any harm.
c. Omar's breach of duty was not gross.
d. The way in which the café was managed or organised by its senior management was not a substantial element in the breach.

Evaluating the law: Part one

5.8 Evaluate the loss of control defence.

Think about this question.

'The loss of control defence successfully addresses a number of problems with the old defence of provocation. The new law not only ensures that those who are hot-headed, short-tempered, jealous or possessive no longer escape a murder conviction, it also achieves justice for those who fear serious violence, suffer a slow-burn reaction and endure years of abuse.'

Discuss the extent to which you agree with this statement.

Step 1: Deconstruct the essay title

To prepare an essay plan for this question, you should begin by **deconstructing the essay title** and identifying the key points you need to address. This essay title suggests that the loss of control defence remedies certain problems with the old defence of provocation. Specifically, it makes two key claims:

1. that those who are hot-headed, short-tempered, jealous or possessive could use the provocation defence to escape a murder conviction, but cannot use the loss of control defence to do so;
2. that the provocation defence risked injustice for those who feared serious violence suffered a slow-burn reaction and endured years of abuse, but the loss of control defence now achieves justice for such defendants.

Step 2: Work through each claim, form an opinion and construct a set of arguments in support of your views

The first claim focuses on the fact that the subjective limb of the **defence of provocation** simply required that the defendant lost his self-control in response to things said or done. There was no requirement that the loss of self-control was caused by a qualifying trigger. The effect of this is illustrated by cases such as *R* v *Doughty*. By contrast, **the loss of control defence** requires that the loss of self-control was caused by a **qualifying trigger**. You should identify the relevant qualifying trigger and consider whether outcomes like the one in *R* v *Doughty* would be possible today.

Your discussion of the first of the essay title's claims should also consider **section 55(6)(c),** which states that sexual infidelity may not constitute a qualifying trigger. This is relevant to jealousy and possessiveness, two of the characteristics identified in the essay title.

You should consider the judgment in *R* v *Clinton, Parker & Evans*, in order to discuss: (a) the scope of the sexual infidelity exclusion and whether it does in fact prevent jealous and possessive men from pleading loss of control; and (b) if so, whether it is an appropriate method for achieving this goal.

The second claim focuses on whether individuals such as **Kiranjit Ahluwalia** will be able to plead the loss of control defence. To help with this, look back at the journal notes you prepared in response to the following questions:

i. **Did Ahluwalia suffer a loss of self-control?**

ii. **Fear and the requirement for loss of self-control in cases of domestic violence.**

iii. **Sections 54(1)(c) and 54(3) and R v Ahluwalia.**

You will also find it helpful to look at the relevant items in the further reading list.

Step 3: Planning your introduction and conclusion

The last task is to decide what to include in your introduction and conclusion.

- Form an opinion and construct a set of arguments in support of your views about the first claim, which focuses on the fact that the subjective limb of the defence of provocation simply required that the defendant lost his self-control in response to things said or done.
- Form an opinion and construct a set of arguments in support of your views about the second claim, which focuses on whether individuals such as Kiranjit Ahluwalia will be able to plead the loss of control defence.
- Write an introduction that contextualises your discussion by briefly outlining the loss of control defence and how it differs from the old provocation defence, and gives an indication of the argument you will present in your essay.
- Write a conclusion that rounds off your essay with a succinct statement of your argument and a summary of your supporting reasons.

Evaluating the law: Part two

5.9 Formulate proposals for the reform of the law of homicide, based on evaluation of its existing two-tier structure and the *mens rea* of murder.

Think about this question.

'Under the existing law of homicide, some defendants may only be convicted of manslaughter when a murder conviction would be more appropriate, whilst some other defendants who do not deserve the label "murderer" may be convicted of this offence.

Enacting the Law Commission's proposed homicide ladder would rectify this situation.'

Discuss the extent to which you agree with this statement.

Step 1: Deconstruct the essay title

To prepare an essay plan for this question, you should begin by **deconstructing the essay title** and identifying the key points you need to address. This essay title makes three key claims:

1. that under the current law, some defendants may only be convicted of manslaughter when a murder conviction would be more appropriate;
2. that under the current law, some defendants may be convicted of murder who do not deserve the label 'murderer';
3. that each of these two problems would be rectified by the Law Commission's proposed homicide ladder.

Step 2: Work through each of the three claims, form an opinion and construct a set of arguments in support of your views

For all three parts of the essay title, you will also find it helpful to look at the relevant items in the Further Reading list. Once you have formed an opinion of each of the claims made by the essay title, construct a set of arguments in support of your views. Ensure that your essay includes reference to the principle of correspondence and the notion of constructive liability.

(1) The focus of the first claim is the fact that recklessness will not suffice for the *mens rea* of murder. To help you evaluate this aspect of the existing law, look back at the notes you prepared in the following questions:

 i. Not guilty of murder, but is a manslaughter conviction inadequate?

 ii. Should the *mens rea* of murder be extended to include wicked recklessness?

 iii. Andrew Ashworth's arguments for and against widening the *mens rea* of murder in 'Reforming the Law of Murder'.

- Form an opinion and construct a set of arguments in support of your views about the first claim, which focuses on the fact that recklessness will not suffice for the *mens rea* of murder: that under the current law, some defendants may only be convicted of manslaughter when a murder conviction would be more appropriate.

(2) The focus of the second claim is the **GBH rule**. Your essay will need to explain what the GBH rule is, and then go on to evaluate this rule. To help with this, look back at the notes you prepared in the following questions:

 i. Lord Steyn's judgment in *R* v *Powell & English*.

 ii. The Law Commission's criticism of the GBH rule.

- Form an opinion and construct a set of arguments in support of your views about the second claim, which focuses on the GBH rule: that under the current law, some defendants may be convicted of murder who do not deserve the label 'murderer'.

(3) The focus of the third claim is the Law Commission's proposed homicide ladder. To help with this, look back at the notes you prepared in response to the following questions:

i. The Law Commission's criticism of the GBH rule.

ii. The relevance of the ladder principle?

iii. Does the existing law respect the ladder principle?

iv. The Law Commission's proposed scheme.

v. Ashworth's critique and first-degree murder.

vi. Ashworth's critique and second-degree murder.

vii. Ashworth's critique and the homicide ladder.

- Form an opinion and construct a set of arguments in support of your views about the third claim, that each of the other two problems would be rectified by the Law Commission's proposed homicide ladder.

You now have all the material you need for the main body of your essay.

Step 3: Plan your introduction and conclusion

The last task is to decide what to include in your introduction and conclusion.

- Write an introduction that contextualises your discussion by briefly outlining the structure of the existing law of homicide, and gives an indication of the argument you will present in your essay.
- Write a conclusion that rounds off your essay with a succinct statement of your argument and a summary of your supporting reasons.

Homicide checklist

Having worked through this chapter, you should now have achieved the following Learning Objectives:

- Explain the requirements for establishing criminal liability for murder
- Explain the requirements for establishing the partial defence of loss of control
- Explain the requirements for establishing criminal liability for unlawful act manslaughter
- Explain the requirements for establishing criminal liability for gross negligence manslaughter
- Explain the requirements for establishing criminal liability for corporate manslaughter
- Describe the Law Commission's proposals for reform of the law of homicide

- Apply the law of homicide to hypothetical sets of facts
- Evaluate the loss of control defence
- Formulate proposals for the reform of the law of homicide, based on evaluation of its existing two-tier structure and the *mens rea* of murder.

Further reading

Ashworth, A. (2007) 'Principles, Pragmatism and the Law Commission's Recommendations on Homicide Law Reform' *Criminal Law Review* 333.

Ashworth, A. (2015) 'Manslaughter by Omission and the Rule of Law' *Criminal Law Review* 563.

Ashworth, A. and Mitchell, B. (eds) (2004) *Rethinking English Homicide Law*. OUP: Oxford.

Baker, D.J. and Zhao, L.X. (2012) 'Contributory Qualifying and Non-Qualifying Triggers in the Loss of Control Defence: A Wrong Turn on Sexual Infidelity' 76 *Journal of Criminal Law* 254.

Carline, A., Gibson, M., Singh, S. and Soubise, L. (2025) 'Civilising loss of control? The role of criminal justice gatekeepers' 44 *Legal Studies* 612.

Clough-Ricci, A. (2025) 'Sexual Infidelity and a Justifiable Sense of Being Seriously Wronged: What Next for the Loss of Control Defence?' 89 *Journal of Criminal Law* 155

Cornford, A. (2016) 'Mitigating Murder' 10 *Criminal Law and Philosophy* 31.

Edwards, S. (2010) 'Anger and Fear as Justifiable Preludes for Loss of Self-Control' 74 *Journal of Criminal Law* 223.

Edwards, S. (2021) 'Women who kill abusive partners: reviewing the impact of section 55(3) 'fear of serious violence' manslaughter – some empirical findings' 72 *Northern Ireland Legal Quarterly* 245

Fitz-Gibbon, K. (2013) 'Replacing Provocation in England and Wales: Examining the Partial Defence of Loss of Control' 40 *Journal of Law and Society* 280.

Herring, J. and Palser, E. (2007) 'The Duty of Care in Gross Negligence Manslaughter' *Criminal Law Review* 24.

Keating, H. and Bridgeman, J. (2012) 'Compassionate Killings: The Case for a Partial Defence' 75 *Modern Law Review* 697.

Law Commission (2005) *A New Homicide Act for England and Wales? A Consultation Paper* (Consultation Paper No 177).

Law Commission (2006) *Murder, Manslaughter and Infanticide* (Report No 304) HC 30.

Lodge, A. (2017) 'Gross Negligence Manslaughter on the Cusp: The Unprincipled Privileging of Harm over Culpability' 81 *Journal of Criminal Law* 125.

Mitchell, B.J., Mackay, R.D. and Brookbanks, W.J. (2008) 'Pleading for Provoked Killers: In Defence of *Morgan Smith*' 124 *Law Quarterly Review* 675.

Norrie, A. (2010) 'The Coroners and Justice Act 2009 – Partial Defences to Murder (1) Loss of Control' *Criminal Law Review* 275.

Nourse, V. (1997) 'Passion's Progress: Modern Law Reform and the Provocation Defense' 106 *Yale Law Journal* 1331.

Reed, A. and Bohlander, M. (eds) (2011) *Loss of Control and Diminished Responsibility: Domestic, Comparative and International Perspectives*. Ashgate Publishing.

Sorial, S. (2019) 'Anger, Provocation and Loss of Self-Control: What Does 'Losing It' Really Mean?' 13 *Criminal Law & Philosophy* 247.

Tadros, V. (2006) 'The Homicide Ladder' 69 *Modern Law Review* 601.

Taylor, R. (2007) 'The Nature of "Partial Defences" and the Coherence of (Second Degree) Murder' *Criminal Law Review* 345.

Wake, N. & Reed, A. (2024) 'Reconceptualising Sexual Infidelity Provocation: New Anglo-Scottish Reform Proposals' 88 *Journal of Criminal Law* 17.

Wilson, W. (2006) 'The Structure of Criminal Homicide' *Criminal Law Review* 471.

Withey, C. (2011) 'Loss of Control, Loss of Opportunity?' *Criminal Law Review* 263.

Answers on the Companion Website

Please visit the companion website for the answers to Key Questions, Quizzes, Applying the Law scenarios as well as student support including glossaries. Please visit www.pearsoned.co.uk/Macdonald

6

Non-fatal offences against the person

Learning Objectives

6.1 Define the requirements for establishing criminal liability for assault.

6.2 Define the requirements for establishing criminal liability for battery.

6.3 Define the requirements for establishing criminal liability for assault occasioning actual bodily harm.

6.4 Explain the requirements for establishing criminal liability for malicious wounding or infliction of grievous bodily harm.

6.5 Explain the requirements for establishing criminal liability for wounding or grievous bodily harm with intent.

6.6 Explain the case law governing consent obtained by fraud and consent to injury.

6.7 Explain the Law Commission's proposed reforms of the non-fatal offences against the person.

6.8 Apply the law on non-fatal offences to hypothetical sets of facts.

6.9 Evaluate the case law on consent to injury.

6.10 Evaluate the Law Commission's proposed reforms of the non-fatal offences against the person.

Introduction

There are a large number of non-fatal offences against the person. Many of these are contained in the Offences Against the Person Act 1861 (OAPA). If you flick through the sections of this Act you'll find some offences which you've probably heard of before (like assault with intent to resist arrest (s.38) and solicitation to murder (s.4)), and others which now seem very dated (like not providing apprentices or servants with food whereby life is endangered (s.26) and drivers of carriages injuring persons by furious driving (s.35)).

The following account contains details some may find upsetting.

Marius Gustavson: the "Eunuch Maker"

Gustavson was the leader of an extreme body modification network. From 2017 to 2021 he carried out at least 22 procedures. These included penis amputations, the removal of testicles, the use of clamps to crush testicles and the freezing of limbs. There was evidence of cannibalism, and that Gustavson kept some body parts as trophies and sold others online.

Gustavson was not medically trained, and the procedures were carried out in non-sterile conditions. His victims suffered irreversible and life-changing injuries.

Gustavson filmed the explicit surgeries and streamed them to more than 22,000 paying subscribers on his Eunuchmaker.com website. He had earned over £300,000 from the website.

Gustavson pleaded guilty to a number of offences, including causing grievous bodily harm with intent. In May 2024, he was sentenced to life imprisonment with a minimum term of 22 years.

Although this is an extreme example, it does raise an important question: when should the criminal law prohibit consensual injury? Think back to Chapter 1, where we examined the case *R* v *Brown* and considered the House of Lords' decision that the infliction of injury in the course of sado-masochistic sexual encounters is an unlawful activity. Other examples of consensual injuries that we will study in this chapter include:

- Body modification procedures, such as splitting the tongue
- Bodily adornments, such as tattooing, ear piercing and even branding
- Dangerous sports, such as boxing
- Rough horseplay.

In your opinion, which (if any) of these activities should be lawful? We will return to this question later in the chapter.

The first part of this chapter focuses on five of the most significant **non-fatal offences**. As Figure 6.1 illustrates, these offences are meant to form a ladder with the least serious at the bottom and the most serious at the top. But, as we'll see, it is questionable whether the offences adequately respect the ladder principle.

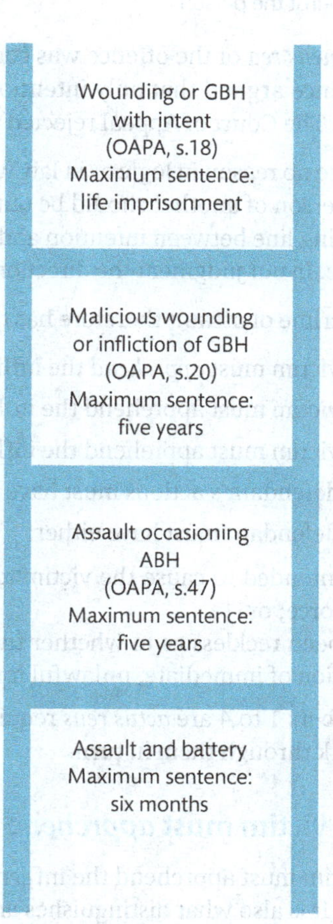

Figure 6.1

We're going to start at the bottom of the ladder, with the crimes of assault and battery, and work our way up, finishing with the most serious of the five offences: wounding or GBH with intent.

In the second part of the chapter we explore some difficult **issues relating to consent**. These are: first, what happens if the defendant fraudulently tricks the victim into consenting to an activity; and, second, when does the criminal law allow individuals to consent to injury? The final part of the chapter examines the Law Commission's proposals for reform of the non-fatal offences against the person.

Assault

6.1 Define the requirements for establishing criminal liability for assault.

There is no statutory definition of assault, so instead we must turn to case law. The *actus reus* of the offence was set out by Robert Goff LJ in *Collins* v *Wilcock* [1984] 1 WLR 1172:

> An assault is an act which causes another person to apprehend the infliction of immediate, unlawful, force on his person

The *mens rea* of the offence was considered in *R* v *Venna* [1976] QB 421. In this case, the defence argued that only intention will suffice; recklessness, it was claimed, is not enough. The Court of Appeal rejected this, stating:

> We see no reason in logic or in law why a person who recklessly applies physical force to the person of another should be outside the criminal law of assault. In many cases the dividing line between intention and recklessness is barely distinguishable. This is such a case. In our judgment the direction was right in law and this ground of appeal fails.

The crime of assault therefore has the following five requirements:

1. The victim must *apprehend* the infliction of force on his person
2. The victim must apprehend the infliction of *immediate* force
3. The victim must apprehend the infliction of *unlawful* force
4. The defendant's actions must have been the *cause* of the victim's apprehension
5. The defendant must have either:
   a. intended to cause the victim to apprehend the infliction of immediate, unlawful force; or
   b. been reckless as to whether the victim would be caused to apprehend the infliction of immediate, unlawful force.

Numbers 1 to 4 are *actus reus* requirements. Number 5 is a *mens rea* requirement. We will work through them in turn.

1. The victim must *apprehend* the infliction of force on his person

The victim must apprehend the infliction of force on his person. This is the essence of an assault. It is also what distinguishes an assault from a battery. As we shall see shortly, for a battery there must have been contact with the victim's body. But no contact is required for an assault. It is sufficient to show that the victim apprehended the infliction of force.

Think about this question.

In which two of the following scenarios is there the *actus reus* of an assault?

a. **Scenario 1**: I pull a gun out of my pocket and point it at you. You fear that I am going to shoot you and are terrified.
b. **Scenario 2**: I pull a gun out of my pocket and point it at you. Knowing that I am joking, you laugh then turn around and walk away.
c. **Scenario 3**: I take my gun out of my pocket and show it to you, saying, 'Don't worry, it isn't loaded'. You think that I am lying and believe that I am going to shoot you.
d. **Scenario 4**: I creep up behind you, pull a gun out of my pocket and point it at the back of your head. You are completely unaware of my presence.

2. The victim must apprehend the infliction of *immediate* force

In *Collins* v *Wilcock* Robert Goff LJ stated that the victim must apprehend the infliction of *immediate* force. The *Merriam-Webster* definition for 'immediate' is 'occurring, acting, or accomplished without loss or interval of time'. So this appears to place a strict limitation on the scope of the offence. Taken literally, the victim must believe that the apprehended force will follow instantly, without any delay.

In fact, however, the courts have not applied the immediacy requirement strictly. There are several cases in which the immediacy requirement has been diluted. Take *R* v *Lewis* [1970] Crim LR 647 as an example. V, Lewis' wife, said that Lewis treated her violently. So she locked their home – a third floor flat – and would not let him in. Lewis shouted threats to her and said he would kill her. V then heard the sound of breaking glass from one of the other rooms in the flat. Thinking that he was breaking into the flat, and fearing what would happen if she stayed in the flat, V then jumped out of the window. The fall broke both her legs. Lewis was charged with maliciously inflicting GBH (OAPA, s.20). Even though Lewis was locked outside the flat, the Court of Appeal held that V had apprehended the infliction of immediate force. This obviously stretches the meaning of immediate.

Similar issues were examined by the House of Lords in *R* v *Ireland & Burstow* [1998] AC 147. In this judgment the House of Lords considered two cases. The first case concerned Robert Ireland. During a three-month period in 1994 he harassed three women by repeatedly making silent telephone calls to them. Most of the calls were at night. The women suffered psychiatric illness as a result. At trial Ireland was convicted of assault occasioning ABH. His appeal against conviction was dismissed by the Court of Appeal, and reached the House of Lords.

The second case concerned Anthony Burstow. He had had a relationship with the victim, Tracey Sant. When she ended the relationship Burstow refused to accept it and began to harass her. During an eight-month period in 1995 he made both silent and abusive telephone calls to her, he distributed offensive cards in the street where she lived, he frequently turned up at her home and her place of work, he secretly photographed her and her family and he sent a menacing note. As a result of his actions Sant suffered a severe depressive illness. The Court of Appeal dismissed Burstow's appeal against his conviction for malicious infliction of GBH (OAPA, s.20), and he appealed to the House of Lords.

One of the issues the House of Lords had to consider was whether it is possible to commit assault by making silent telephone calls. In the leading judgment, Lord Steyn examined this question in three steps. First, he considered whether it is possible to commit an assault simply by speaking.

EXTRACT

Read the following extract.

According to Lord Steyn, is it possible to commit assault by words alone?

R v *Ireland & Burstow* [1998] AC 147

Lord Steyn

Counsel argued that as a matter of law an assault can never be committed by words alone and therefore it cannot be committed by silence. The premise depends on the slenderest authority, namely, an observation by Holroyd J. to a jury that "no words or singing are equivalent to an assault:" *Rex v. Meade and Belt* (1823) 1 Lew. 184. The proposition that a gesture may amount to an assault, but that words can never suffice, is unrealistic and

> indefensible. A thing said is also a thing done. There is no reason why something said should be incapable of causing an apprehension of immediate personal violence, e.g. a man accosting a woman in a dark alley saying, "Come with me or I will stab you." I would, therefore, reject the proposition that an assault can never be committed by words.

Second, Lord Steyn said that if it is possible to commit an assault by words alone, then it is possible to commit an assault by speaking on a telephone. He commented:

> [T]here is no reason why a telephone caller who says to a woman in a menacing way "I will be at your door in a minute or two" may not be guilty of an assault if he causes his victim to apprehend immediate personal violence.

So, third, is it possible to commit an assault by making a silent telephone call? Here is Lord Steyn's answer:

> That brings me to the critical question whether a silent caller may be guilty of an assault. The answer to this question seems to me to be "Yes, depending on the facts." It involves questions of fact within the province of the jury.
>
> [...]
>
> Take now the case of the silent caller. He intends by his silence to cause fear and he is so understood. The victim is assailed by uncertainty about his intentions. Fear may dominate her emotions, and it may be the fear that the caller's arrival at her door may be imminent. She may fear the *possibility* of immediate personal violence. As a matter of law the caller may be guilty of an assault: whether he is or not will depend on the circumstance and in particular on the impact of the caller's potentially menacing call or calls on the victim.

So whether there is the *actus reus* of assault in cases like these all depends on the response of the victim. If the victim is caused to apprehend the possibility of immediate, unlawful force, there will be the *actus reus* of assault.

Think about this question.

In the light of Lord Steyn's judgment, decide whether there is the *actus reus* of an assault in each of the following two scenarios.

a. As a prank, a student decides to make a silent telephone call to his Contract Law lecturer. When the lecturer answers the phone, the student says nothing for a few seconds, then starts breathing heavily down the phone line. Thinking it is a wrong number, the lecturer hangs up and quickly forgets about it.

b. As a prank, a student decides to make a silent telephone call to his Criminal Law lecturer. Having just finished reading a particularly gruesome case, the lecturer is already feeling edgy. When he answers the phone and hears nothing but heavy breathing he begins screaming hysterically, 'Who's there?' He quickly locks all the windows and doors, draws the curtains and hides behind the sofa.

Before moving on, there are two further points to note about Lord Steyn's judgment:

- Notice how the judgment stretches the meaning of immediacy. Lord Steyn said that the caller who says 'I will be at your door *in a minute or two*' causes the victim to apprehend immediate force. He also said that a victim might react to a silent telephone call with fear that 'the caller's arrival at her door may be *imminent*'. So according to *R v Ireland & Burstow*, for the crime of assault 'immediate' has a broader meaning than the one found in a dictionary. It means something more like imminent.
- It is not necessary for the victim to have believed that the defendant would inflict immediate, unlawful force. It is enough that the victim believed that the defendant *might* do so. For example, in the extract above, Lord Steyn said that it is sufficient if the victim feared the *possibility* of immediate personal force. Similarly, in R v Constanza [1997] 2 Cr App R 492 the Court of Appeal stated that 'it is enough if the Crown have proved a fear of violence at some time not excluding the immediate future'. *R v Ireland & Burstow* and *R v Constanza* were applied by the Court of Appeal in *RN v CICA* [2023] EWCA Civ 882. This case involved a victim of sexual abuse, RN, who was aged 12 when he met his abuser. The abuser initially posed online as a 14-year-old girl, and embarked on a campaign of online sexual grooming and abuse. When RN realised the identity was false, he became scared. The abuser knew where RN lived, knew where he went to school, and suggested that he could be hiding in a bush near RN's house. The Court held that it is sufficient for the crime of assault that the victim feared violence at some time not excluding the immediate future. The victim's evidence confirmed he feared violence – 'namely that the abuser would take him behind a building and have his way with him'– and 'did not exclude such violence materialising in the immediate future' ([47]).

Lastly, note that the *Ireland* and *Burstow* cases occurred before Parliament enacted the Protection from Harassment Act 1997. This legislation was introduced specifically to deal with the problem of stalking. So if similar cases occurred today prosecutions could be brought under this Act instead.

3. The victim must apprehend the infliction of *unlawful* force

There are a number of reasons why the apprehended force might not be unlawful. First, it might be consensual. For example, suppose Valentina asks her boyfriend Romeo for a hug. When she sees him putting his arms around her she apprehends the infliction of force, but the force is lawful. We consider issues relating to consent in more detail later in the chapter.

Second, the force might be lawful because it is used in self-defence. Suppose I attack you, and you have no choice but to push me backwards and run away. As I see your hands coming towards me I apprehend the infliction of force, but the force is lawful. We study self-defence in Chapter 11.

Third, a lawful occupier may use reasonable force to remove an unwanted trespasser[1] Suppose Romeo is standing in the doorway of Valentina's flat. Valentina asks him to leave several times, but he refuses, so Valentina pushes him out of the door. As Romeo sees Valentina's hands coming towards him, he apprehends the infliction of force, but the force is lawful.

[1] *R v Day* [2015] EWCA Crim 1646.

Fourth, the force might be lawful because it is legally authorised. Suppose a policeman is about to arrest Romeo. When Romeo sees the policeman make a grab for him he apprehends the infliction of force, but the force is lawful.

In all four of these examples there is not the *actus reus* of assault, because in each case the victim does not apprehend the infliction of *unlawful* force.

4. The defendant's actions must have been the *cause* of the victim's apprehension

The defendant's actions must have been a factual and legal cause of the victim's apprehension. Here you apply the law governing causation, which we studied in Chapter 3.

5. The defendant must have either: (a) intended to cause the victim to apprehend the infliction of immediate, unlawful force; or (b) been reckless as to whether the victim would be caused to apprehend the infliction of immediate, unlawful force

As we saw above, the *mens rea* of assault was set out by the Court of Appeal in *R* v *Venna* [1976] QB 421. One question which emerged in the years that followed was whether the *Cunningham* definition of recklessness applies here. In *R* v *Savage & Parmenter* [1992] 1 AC 699 the House of Lords confirmed that *Cunningham* recklessness applies.

Quiz 6.1

1. According to the House of Lords in *R* v *Ireland & Burstow* [1998] AC 147, which of the following statements is inaccurate?

- **a.** Assault can be committed by deeds, but not by words.
- **b.** It is possible to commit assault by a silent phone call.
- **c.** It is possible to commit assault by words spoken over the phone.
- **d.** It is possible to commit an assault by words alone.

2. What is the *mens rea* of assault?

- **a.** Intentionally or negligently causing V to apprehend force.
- **b.** Intentionally causing V to apprehend force.
- **c.** Strict liability.
- **d.** Intentionally or recklessly causing V to apprehend force.

3. Which of the following situations could amount to an assault?

- **a.** Unbeknown to V, D creeps up behind him and points a gun at him.
- **b.** V hands D an unloaded gun. Thinking it is loaded, D points it at V.
- **c.** D points a replica gun at V. Afterwards he tells V it was not a real gun.
- **d.** D points a gun at V and says 'Give me £20 or I'll send my Dad round'.

Battery

6.2 Define the requirements for establishing criminal liability for battery.

There is also no statutory definition of battery, so again we must turn to case law. The *actus reus* of the offence was set out by Robert Goff LJ in *Collins* v *Wilcock* [1984] 1 WLR 1172:

> [A] battery is the actual infliction of unlawful force on another person.

As we saw above, the argument that only intention should be sufficient for the *mens rea* was rejected by the Court of Appeal in *R* v *Venna*. Recklessness will also suffice.

The offence of battery therefore has the following three requirements:

1. The defendant must have inflicted force on the victim
2. The force must have been unlawful
3. The defendant must have either: (a) intended to inflict unlawful force on the victim; or (b) been reckless as to whether unlawful force would be inflicted on the victim.

Numbers 1 and 2 are *actus reus* requirements. Number 3 is a *mens rea* requirement.

1. The defendant must have inflicted force on the victim

As we have seen, no contact is required for an assault. But contact is necessary for a battery. This is the essence of a battery. The defendant must have inflicted force on the victim. There are four issues we need to consider on this limb of the *actus reus*, which we are going to discuss in the following pages.

i. How much force is necessary?

First, how much force is necessary? This question was answered by Robert Goff LJ in *Collins* v *Wilcock*.

EXTRACT

Read the following extract from Robert Goff LJ's judgment.

Which of the following statements is correct?

a. The force used must have been overpowering.
b. The amount of force must have been significant.
c. Any contact, however slight, is sufficient.

Collins v *Wilcock* [1984] 1 WLR 1172

Robert Goff LJ

The fundamental principle, plain and incontestable, is that every person's body is inviolate. It has long been established that any touching of another person, however slight, may amount to a battery. So Hold C.J. held in *Cole v. Turner* (1704) 6 Mod. 149 that "the least touching of another in anger is a battery." The breadth of the principle reflects the fundamental nature of the interest so protected. As Blackstone wrote in his *Commentaries*, 17th ed. (1830), vol. 3, p. 120:

> "the law cannot draw the line between different degrees of violence, and therefore totally prohibits the first and lowest stage of it; every man's person being sacred, and no other having a right to meddle with it, in any the slightest manner."

The effect is that everybody is protected not only against physical injury but against any form of physical molestation.

Robert Goff LJ went on to say that such a broad rule must be subject to exceptions. These exceptions are set out in the following extract.

EXTRACT

Read the extract and compile a list of all the exceptions stated by Robert Goff LJ.

Looking at your list, decide whether there is the *actus reus* of battery in each of the following scenarios:

- It is rush hour on the London Underground. You are waiting on the platform. When a tube train arrives, it is packed full of people. The only way you can squeeze onto the train is by pushing those already onboard backwards.
- Halfway through a lecture your pen runs out. You don't have a spare pen with you, so you tap the person sitting in front of you on the shoulder to ask whether you can borrow one. They ignore you, so you keep tapping them until they eventually turn around.

Collins v *Wilcock* [1984] 1 WLR 1172

Robert Goff LJ

But so widely drawn a principle must inevitably be subject to exceptions. For example, children may be subject to reasonable punishment; people may be subjected to the lawful exercise of the power of arrest; and reasonable force may be used in self-defence or for the prevention of crime. But, apart from these special instances where the control or constraint is lawful, a broader exception has been created to allow for the exigencies of everyday life. Generally speaking consent is a defence to battery; and most of the physical contacts of ordinary life are not actionable because they are impliedly consented to by all who move in society and so expose themselves to the risk of bodily contact. So nobody can complain of the jostling which is inevitable from his presence in, for example, a supermarket, an underground station or a busy street; nor can a person who attends a party complain if his hand is seized in friendship, or even if his back is, within reason, slapped: see *Tuberville v. Savage* (1669) 1 Mod. 3. Although such cases are regarded as examples of implied consent, it is more common nowadays to treat them as falling within a general exception embracing all physical contact which is generally acceptable in the ordinary conduct of daily life [...]

Among such forms of conduct, long held to be acceptable, is touching a person for the purpose of engaging his attention, though of course using no greater degree of physical contact than is reasonably necessary in the circumstances for that purpose [...] But a distinction is drawn between a touch to draw a man's attention, which is generally acceptable, and a physical restraint, which is not. So we find Parke B. observing in *Rawlings v. Till* (1837) 3 M. & W. 28, 29, with reference to *Wiffen v. Kincard*, that "There the touch was merely to engage [a man's] attention, not to put a restraint upon his person." Furthermore, persistent touching to gain attention in the face of obvious disregard may transcend the norms of acceptable behaviour and so be outside the exception. We do not say that more than one touch is never permitted; for example, the lost or distressed may surely be permitted a second touch, or possibly even more, on a reluctant or impervious sleeve or shoulder, as may a person who is acting reasonably in the exercise of a duty. In each case, the test must be whether the physical contact so persisted in has in the circumstances gone beyond generally acceptable standards of conduct; and the answer to that question will depend upon the facts of the particular case.

In *Collins* v *Wilcock* Alexis Collins was accused of assaulting policewoman WPC Wilcock in the execution of her duty.[2] Wilcock was in her police car when she saw Collins walking along a street with another woman who was a known prostitute. They appeared to be soliciting men in the street. Wilcock asked the two women to get into the car so that she could have a word with them. Collins refused to do so, and walked away. Wilcock got out of the car and asked for Collins' name and address. Collins said she didn't want to talk to the police and started to walk away again. Wilcock took hold of Collins' left arm to restrain her. Collins responded by scratching Wilcock's forearm with her fingernails.

At trial Collins was convicted. She appealed to the High Court. The issue in the case was whether Wilcock committed a battery when she took hold of Collins to stop her from walking away. If so, then Wilcock's actions were unlawful and outside the course of her duties as a police officer – which in turn would mean that Collins could not be convicted of assaulting Wilcock *in the execution of her duties*. (It is important to note that Wilcock was not exercising her power of arrest.)

EXTRACT

In your opinion, did Wilcock's actions fall within any of the exceptions to the rule that any touching is sufficient for a battery? So did Wilcock commit a battery when she took hold of Collins to stop her from walking away?

Now read the following extract to see the conclusion of the High Court!

Collins v *Wilcock* [1984] 1 WLR 1172

Robert Goff LJ

But if a police officer, not exercising his power of arrest, nevertheless reinforces his request with the actual use of force [...] then his act in thereby detaining the other person will be unlawful. [H]is action will constitute a battery.

Having regard to the facts of the present case, we have no doubt that the magistrate framed his question having in mind the act of the woman police officer in taking hold of the defendant's arm to restrain her, which we have held to be a battery and so unlawful.

[2] A similar case is *Marland* v *DPP* [2023] EWHC 1046 (Admin), in which the defendant held the intoxicated victim's shoulders and guided her to his car against her will. The High Court held that this amounted to physical restraint, so there was no implied consent. These cases may be contrasted with *Pegram* v *DPP* [2019] EWHC 2673 (Admin), in which the police officer was held not to have physically restrained the defendant, even though he held the defendant's arm for longer than would normally be consistent with merely attracting someone's attention, because 'There was a need to gain [D's] attention not just to make him aware of the officer's presence, but also to keep [D's] attention for long enough to receive the warning it was the officer's role to give him, for his own benefit as well as the public's' ([36]). Note also the decisions in *Dixon* v *Crown* Prosecution Service [2018] EWHC 3154 (Admin), in which it was held that a police officer who 'acts reasonably to protect a fellow officer from unjustified assault is acting lawfully and in the execution of his duty' ([30]), and *McMillan* v *CPS* [2008] EWHC 1457 (Admin). In this case a police officer led a woman from a property to the street before speaking to her because she was drunk and unsteady on her feet and the garden was on a steep slope. It was held that the force used fell within generally acceptable standards of conduct.

ii. Is there an infliction of force if the defendant touches the victim's clothes, not the victim's body?

The short answer is yes. In *R* v *Thomas* [1985] 81 Cr App R 331 a school caretaker rubbed the bottom of an 11-year-old pupil's skirt, lifted the skirt, then dropped it again. At no stage did the caretaker touch the girl's body, or try to do so. The Court of Appeal held that a defendant does inflict force on a person by touching the clothes she is wearing.[3] Ackner LJ stated:

> There could be no dispute that if you touch a person's clothes whilst he is wearing them that is equivalent to touching him.

iii. Can force be inflicted indirectly or using an object?

In Chapter 2, we looked at the case *Fagan* v *Metropolitan Police Commissioner* [1969] 1 QB 439, the case in which a motorist accidentally drove onto a policeman's foot and then refused to move his car. One of the issues in this case was whether there is a battery when the force is inflicted using an object. In *Fagan*, for example, the force was inflicted through the medium of the defendant's car.

EXTRACT

Read the following extract from the judgment of James J.

Can there be a battery when the force is inflicted using an object?

Fagan v *Metropolitan Police Commissioner* [1969] 1 QB 439

James J

Where an assault involves a battery, it matters not, in our judgment, whether the battery is inflicted directly by the body of the offender or through the medium of some weapon or instrument controlled by the action of the offender. An assault may be committed by the laying of a hand upon another, and the action does not cease to be an assault if it is a stick held in the hand and not the hand itself which is laid on the person of the victim. So for our part we see no difference in principle between the action of stepping on to a person's toe and maintaining that position and the action of driving a car on to a person's foot and sitting in the car whilst its position on the foot is maintained.

In *DPP* v *K* [1990] 1 WLR 1067 D, a 15-year-old schoolboy, took a boiling tube of sulphuric acid out of a chemistry lesson, without permission, to the school toilets. He said that he wanted to pour some of the acid onto toilet paper to test the reaction. While he was in the toilet cubicle he heard footsteps outside and panicked. He went to one of the hot air hand driers, turned the nozzle upwards and poured the acid into the nozzle. He then went back to his lesson, intending to return and clean the drier later. In the meantime, however, another pupil V went to the toilets to wash his hands. When V turned the drier on the acid was blown onto his face, leaving a permanent scar.

D was charged with assault occasioning ABH (OAPA, s.47). At trial the case was dismissed. The prosecutor appealed, and the case reached the High Court. The Court held

[3] Although his conviction for indecent assault was quashed due to lack of corroborative evidence.

that D had inflicted force on V, and so would be guilty of battery if he had acted with the necessary *mens rea*. The key points for our purposes are:

1. The infliction of force can be through a medium. In this case the force was inflicted via the acid. Similarly, I would commit a battery if I throw my pint of beer over you. And I would commit a battery if I am driving on a rainy day, see you walking on the pavement, and deliberately splash you by driving through a puddle.[4]
2. The infliction of force can be indirect. In *DPP* v *K* the defendant did not directly inflict force on the victim. The victim turned the hand drier on himself. The Court said that this was immaterial.

Another example of force being applied indirectly is *Haystead* v *Chief Constable of Derbyshire* [2000] 3 All ER 890. In this case John Haystead punched his ex-partner Angela in the face whilst she was holding her 12-month-old son Matthew. As a result she dropped Matthew, and he hit his head on the floor. Haystead was not only charged with battery of Angela, but also battery of baby Matthew. At trial he was convicted. He subsequently appealed against his conviction for battery of Matthew. The High Court dismissed his appeal. Haystead had committed battery of Matthew. He indirectly applied force to him by causing Angela to drop him.

iv. Can you inflict force by doing nothing?

Think back to *Fagan* again. In this case the three members of the Divisional Court unanimously agreed that it is not possible to commit the offence of battery by omission. The majority of the Court nonetheless upheld Fagan's conviction, applying the doctrine of continuing acts.

As we saw in Chapter 3, however, the reasoning in *Fagan* has been questioned. Some have argued that it is possible to commit battery by omission. There is now case law which supports this viewpoint.

In *DPP* v *Santana-Bermudez* [2003] EWHC 2908 (Admin) policewoman PC Hill approached D in a tube station. She suspected that he was a ticket tout. She informed D that she intended to search him, took him to a supervisor's office and asked him to turn out his pockets. D did so, and placed a number of items on the table, including some syringes without needles. PC Hill then asked, 'Is that everything?' D replied, 'Yes.' She then asked, 'Are you sure?' He said, 'Yes'; She then asked, 'Are you sure that you don't have any needles or sharps on you?' D answered, 'No.' PC Hill then commenced her search. She put two fingers of her left hand into a breast pocket on D's jacket and felt a stinging sensation. She took her fingers out of the pocket and found that her finger had been pierced by a hypodermic needle, which was still hanging from her fingertip. She noticed D smirking. D then took another needle from a pocket on his trousers. PC Hill then said, 'I thought you didn't have any sharps on you', at which D shrugged his shoulders and smirked. Fortunately, although D was HIV positive and had hepatitis C, PC Hill was not infected.

D was charged with assault occasioning ABH. At trial the defence argued that he had not performed a positive act – all he had done was fail to tell the truth. The trial judge agreed, and dismissed the prosecution's case on the basis that battery cannot be

[4] In May 2020, a woman who claimed she had the coronavirus and deliberately coughed on police officers was imprisoned for assaulting a police officer. So coughing on someone also appears to be an infliction of force. See 'Two years' imprisonment for coronavirus police assault': https://www.cps.gov.uk/east-midlands/news/two-years-imprisonment-coronavirus-police-assault.

committed by omission. The prosecutor appealed against this finding. The issue for Maurice Kay J in the High Court was whether there was any evidential basis for the charge of assault occasioning ABH.

EXTRACT

Read the following extract from the judgment.

When (if at all) may a defendant commit a battery by doing nothing?

DPP v *Santana-Bermudez* [2003] EWHC 2908 (Admin)

Maurice Kay J

10. A great deal of undesirable complexity has bedevilled our criminal law as a result of quasi theological distinctions between acts and omissions. Some of the illogicality is identified in Smith and Hogan, *Criminal Law*, 10th Edition, pages 46 to 52. In my judgment, and without the need to express oneself in the language of universal principle, the authorities of *Roberts*, *K* and *Miller* support the following proposition: where someone (by act or word or a combination of the two) creates a danger and thereby exposes another to a reasonably foreseeable risk of injury which materialises, there is an evidential basis for the *actus reus* of an assault occasioning actual bodily harm. It remains necessary for the prosecution to prove an intention to assault or appropriate recklessness.

11. In the present case, if (as the court implicitly found) the respondent, by giving PC Hill a dishonest assurance about the contents of his pockets, thereby exposed her to a reasonably foreseeable risk of an injury which materialised, it was erroneous of the court to conclude that there was no evidential basis for the *actus reus* of assault occasioning actual bodily harm [...]

2. The force must have been unlawful

As noted above, many applications of force will be lawful. They might have been consensual. They might have been in justifiable self-defence. They might have been a reasonable attempt to remove an unwanted trespasser. They might have been legally authorised (e.g. the police's power of arrest). In all of these situations there is not the *actus reus* of battery because there is not an infliction of *unlawful* force.

3. The defendant must have either: (a) intended to inflict unlawful force on the victim; or (b) been reckless as to whether unlawful force would be inflicted on the victim

The *mens rea* of battery was set out by the Court of Appeal in *R* v *Venna* [1976] QB 421. As was the case with assault, the *Cunningham* definition of recklessness applies here. This was confirmed by the House of Lords in *R* v *Savage & Parmenter* [1992] 1 AC 699.

Quiz 6.2

1. For a charge of assault the prosecution must prove that the defendant…
   a. Intentionally or recklessly caused the victim to apprehend the infliction of immediate unlawful force on his person.
   b. Intentionally or recklessly caused the victim to apprehend the infliction of instantaneous unlawful force on his person.
   c. Negligently caused the victim to apprehend the infliction of immediate unlawful force on his person.
   d. Intentionally or recklessly inflicted unlawful force on his person.
2. For a charge of battery, the prosecution must prove that the defendant had the *mens rea* of…
   a. recklessness to some physical harm.
   b. intention or recklessness to make the victim apprehend unlawful physical harm.
   c. intention to cause actual bodily harm.
   d. intention or recklessness to the infliction of some unlawful force.
3. In which of the following scenarios is the defendant not guilty of battery?
   a. A passenger on a crowded underground train deliberately touches the buttocks of another passenger (without their consent).
   b. A man lifts the hem of his victim's skirt (without her consent) without actually touching her body.
   c. A tourist asks a passer-by for directions, and, when the man refuses to help, grabs hold of his arm to stop him from walking off.
   d. At a party, a man sees an old friend he has not seen for years, walks up to him, and slaps him on the back.

Assault occasioning ABH (actual bodily harm)

6.3 Define the requirements for establishing criminal liability for assault occasioning actual bodily harm.

Section 47 of the Offences Against the Person Act 1861 states:

> Whosoever shall be convicted upon an indictment of any assault occasioning actual bodily harm shall be liable [...] to be imprisoned for any term not exceeding five years.

This tells us that the offence has three requirements:

1. The defendant must have committed an assault
2. The victim must have suffered ABH (actual bodily harm)
3. The assault must have occasioned the ABH.

We will work through these in turn.

1. The defendant must have committed an assault

Here the word 'assault' has a different meaning. It is not being used to refer specifically to the crime we studied a few pages ago. Instead, it is being used as a collective term to refer to *both* assault *and* battery. In other words, the first step in establishing liability for this offence is to prove that the defendant committed either an assault or a battery.

Assessment advice

If you are answering a problem question and trying to decide whether to establish an assault or a battery, begin by asking yourself whether there was an actual infliction of force or just an apprehension that force would be applied. If there was an infliction of force you should focus on battery. If there was an apprehension of force you should focus on assault. Remember that you need to establish both *actus reus* and *mens rea* of the relevant offence.

2. The victim must have suffered ABH (actual bodily harm)

The victim must have suffered ABH. There are two issues we need to consider here.

i. Is ABH limited to physical injuries?

Although the OAPA uses the words 'bodily harm', and although the statute was enacted in 1861 long before the emergence of psychiatry as we know it today, the courts have held that ABH is not limited to physical injuries. In *R* v *Ireland & Burstow* the House of Lords held that recognised psychiatric illnesses may also amount to ABH.

EXTRACT

The following extract is taken from Lord Steyn's judgment in *R* v *Ireland & Burstow*.

What reasons does he give for interpreting 'bodily harm' to include psychiatric illness?

R v *Ireland & Burstow* [1998] AC 147

Lord Steyn

[T]he correct approach is simply to consider whether the words of the Act of 1861 considered in the light of contemporary knowledge cover a recognisable psychiatric injury [...] Bearing in mind that statutes are usually intended to operate for many years it would be most inconvenient if courts could never rely in difficult cases on the current meaning of statutes. Recognising the problem Lord Thring, the great Victorian draftsman of the second half of the last century, exhorted draftsmen to draft so that 'An Act of Parliament should be deemed to be always speaking:' *Practical Legislation* (1902), p. 83; see also Cross, *Statutory Interpretation*, 3rd ed. (1995), p. 51; Pearce and Geddes, *Statutory Interpretation in Australia*, 4th ed. (1996), pp. 90–93. In cases where the problem arises it is a matter of interpretation whether a court must search for the historical or original meaning of a statute or whether it is free to apply the current meaning of the statute to present day conditions. Statutes dealing with a particular grievance or problem may sometimes require to be historically interpreted. But the drafting technique of Lord Thring and his successors have brought about the situation that statutes will generally be found to be of the 'always speaking' variety: see *Royal College of Nursing of the United Kingdom v. Department of Health and Social Security* [1981] A.C. 800 for an example of an 'always speaking' construction in the House of Lords.

The proposition that the Victorian legislator when enacting sections 18, 20 and 47 of the Act of 1861, would not have had in mind psychiatric illness is no doubt correct. Psychiatry was in its infancy in 1861. But the subjective intention of the draftsman is immaterial. The only relevant inquiry is as to the sense of the words in the context in which they are used. Moreover the Act of 1861 is a statute of the 'always speaking' type: the statute must be interpreted in the light of the best current scientific appreciation of the link between the body and psychiatric injury.

[...]

I would hold that 'bodily harm' in sections 18, 20 and 47 must be interpreted so as to include recognisable psychiatric illness.

A question that arose following *R* v *Ireland & Burstow* was whether only recognised psychiatric illness may amount to ABH, or whether psychological harm may also qualify. This was addressed in *R* v *Dhaliwal* [2006] EWCA Crim 1139. Mrs Dhaliwal committed suicide as a result of the psychological and physical abuse she suffered from her husband over a number of years. Her husband was charged with manslaughter and inflicting GBH, but Judge Roberts at the Central Criminal Court ruled that the case could not proceed to trial because there was no evidence on which a reasonable jury could be satisfied that Mrs Dhaliwal had suffered GBH. The prosecution appealed against this ruling. Medical evidence suggested that the years of abuse had caused Mrs Dhaliwal psychological harm, but not recognised psychiatric illness. So the issue for the Court of Appeal was whether, in the light of *R* v *Ireland & Burstow*, psychological harm not amounting to recognised psychiatric illness could constitute bodily harm.

EXTRACT

According to the Court of Appeal, can psychological harm that does not amount to recognised psychiatric illness constitute bodily harm? What reasons did the Court give for its conclusion?

R v *Dhaliwal* [2006] EWCA Crim 1139

Sir Igor Judge

31 Our conclusion can be briefly expressed. The problem which we have to address is whether psychological injury, not amounting to recognisable psychiatric illness, falls within the ambit of bodily harm for the purposes of the 1861 Act [...] [T]he extension sought by the prosecution would introduce a significant element of uncertainty about the true ambit of the relevant legal principles to which the concept of "bodily harm" in the 1861 Act applies, which would be compounded by the inevitable problems of conflicting medical opinion in this constantly developing area of expertise. By adhering to the principle of recognisable psychiatric illness, although some medical experts may be concerned with the way in which the definitions are arrived at, the issue which requires to be addressed can be clearly understood and those responsible for advising the prosecution and defendants can approach their cases with an appropriate degree of certainty.

In the following extract, Emily Finch criticises the decision in *R v Dhaliwal*.

EXTRACT

Finch, E. (2022) 'Psychological injury: where's the harm in it?' *Criminal Law Review* 358

In setting the highest possible threshold for liability in relation to non-physical injuries, the Court of Appeal in *Dhaliwal* has departed from the hierarchical structure of non-fatal offences that exists in relation to non-physical injuries and has created an either/or approach in which any non-physical consequences that do not satisfy the diagnostic requirements for psychiatric illness are relegated to the status of mere emotions thereby falling outside the scope of the criminal law. This reliance on medical diagnosis is ill-founded given the widespread qualms about accuracy of diagnosis and the use of classification systems designed for clinical use in a forensic setting that are prevalent within the medical profession. *Dhaliwal* advocates a need for diagnosis in the interests of certainty but the diagnostic system itself is replete with uncertainties and offers immense scope for a different diagnosis in relation to the same symptoms. This problem is evident in *Dhaliwal* where all three experts agreed on the victim's symptoms but not on diagnosis and so the prosecution failed.

Far better and far more consistent with the approach taken in relation to physical injuries would be to take expert evidence about the victim's symptoms and leave it to the jury to determine whether these symptoms satisfy the requirements of harm. Not only would this restore the jury's role as finders of fact, but it would be consistent with the stance taken in relation to psychological injuries in relation to sentencing. On the basis of this argument, this article expresses a fervent wish to see the issue in *Dhaliwal* revisited by the courts and a more appropriate approach formulated based upon more nuanced interpretation of the previous authorities. This would create parity in the protection offered by the law in relation to physical and non-physical harm and it would also pave the way for prosecutions for manslaughter in cases such as *Dhaliwal* where the defendant's mistreatment of the victim has led to their suicide. Of course, there are questions to be answered here regarding issues of *mens rea*, dangerousness and causation as well as the more general issue about the desirability of easing the path towards liability for manslaughter in suicide cases. There may also be concerns about the possibility of over-criminalisation that need to be explored and debated but these questions do not even fall to be asked unless this important preliminary step of affording legal recognition to emotional harm short of recognised psychiatric injury is taken.

However, even if the criticisms made of *Dhaliwal* are entirely baseless and the Court of Appeal was correct to adopt the interpretation of the previous law that it did, then the alternative conclusion of this article is simply that the law on criminal liability for non-physical harm is wrong. It must be wrong. It is impossible to look at the facts of the case and think that Gurprit Dhaliwal did not suffer harm. She had been harmed by years of abuse and ill-treatment within her marriage. All the experts were agreed on this point. She was not experiencing mere emotions. She did not shed a few tears following a matrimonial argument. By that point in time, her state of mind was so harmed by the treatment meted out to her by her husband that she walked out of the house and hanged herself. If the criminal law does not categorise causing a person's mind and mental state that degree of disruption and damage as harm, then it is wrong and in urgent need of change.

ii. How bad must the injuries have been to amount to ABH?

Whether or not a victim's injuries in a particular case amount to ABH is a question of fact to be answered by the jury. The trial judge may offer the jury some guidance on how to approach this task. In *R v Chan-Fook* [1994] 1 WLR 689 Hobhouse LJ explained what trial judges should (and shouldn't!) say to the jury:

> ['Actual', 'bodily' and 'harm'] are three words of the English language which require no elaboration and in the ordinary course should not receive any. The word "harm" is a synonym for injury. The word "actual" indicates that the injury (although there is no need for it to be permanent) should not be so trivial as to be wholly insignificant.

Similarly, in *R* v *Donovan* [1934] 2 KB 498 the Court of Appeal stated that to constitute ABH the harm 'need not be permanent, but must, no doubt, be more than merely transient and trifling'. So bruising, grazing and scratches may all potentially be found to amount to ABH.

In *T* v *DPP* [2003] EWHC 266 Admin the defendant kicked the victim, causing him to temporarily lose consciousness. The defendant was convicted of assault occasioning ABH. The defendant appealed against his conviction, arguing that the victim's loss of consciousness was too short-lived to be able to amount to ABH. The High Court rejected this. It said that a loss of consciousness can amount to ABH since it involves 'an injurious impairment to the victim's sensory functions'.

If a loss of consciousness can amount to ABH, what about cutting off someone's ponytail? This was the issue in *DPP* v *Smith* [2006] EWHC 94 (Admin). The victim, Michelle Tether, was the ex-partner of the defendant, Michael Smith. Smith and Tether had had an on-off relationship for five years. In April 2005 Tether went to Smith's house. She went to his bedroom, where he was asleep, and woke him up. He pushed her onto the bed, produced some kitchen scissors, and cut off her ponytail. Smith was charged with assault occasioning ABH, but when the case went to the Magistrates' Court the justices held that there was no case to answer since cutting someone's hair cannot amount to ABH. The prosecution appealed against this finding. The issue for the High Court was whether cutting off someone's ponytail can constitute ABH.

Notice, first of all, that any upset or distress that Tether may have felt was irrelevant. As we saw above, psychological harm cannot amount to ABH unless it is a recognised psychiatric illness – and there was no suggestion that Smith's actions had caused Tether psychiatric illness. The focus was simply on the physical act of cutting off the ponytail.

EXTRACT

Read the following extract from the Court's judgment.

Is cutting off someone's hair capable of constituting ABH? How did the Court justify its conclusion?

DPP v *Smith* [2006] EWHC 94 (Admin)

Sir Igor Judge

In my judgment, whether it is alive beneath the surface of the skin or dead tissue above the surface of the skin, the hair is an attribute and part of the human body. It is intrinsic to each individual and to the identity of each individual. Although it is not essential to my decision, I note that an individual's hair is relevant to his or her autonomy. Some regard it as their crowning glory. Admirers may so regard it in the object of their affections. Even if, medically and scientifically speaking, the hair above the surface of the scalp is no more than dead tissue, it remains part of the body and is attached to it. While it is so attached, in my judgment it falls within the meaning of "bodily" in the phrase "actual bodily harm". It is concerned with the body of the individual victim.

> In my judgment, the defendant's actions in cutting off a substantial part of the victim's hair in the course of an assault on her – like putting paint on it or some unpleasant substance which marked or damaged it without causing injury elsewhere – is capable of amounting to an assault which occasions actual bodily harm.

3. The assault must have occasioned the ABH

The word 'occasioned' simply means caused. So the assault or battery must have been the factual and legal cause of the actual bodily harm suffered by the victim.

NB: Must the prosecution prove that the defendant intended to cause/recklessly caused the ABH?

In Chapter 1 we looked at the correspondence principle. According to this principle a defendant should only be convicted of assault occasioning ABH if he at least realised that there was a possibility that his actions would cause ABH. It is an infringement of a defendant's autonomy to hold him responsible for an outcome which he did not foresee.

This issue was examined by the House of Lords in *R* v *Savage & Parmenter*. The House of Lords had to decide whether the section 47 offence contains a *mens rea* element which corresponds to the *actus reus* requirement that the victim suffered ABH. Lord Ackner stated:

> The verdict of assault occasioning actual bodily harm may be returned upon proof of an assault together with proof of the fact that actual bodily harm was occasioned by the assault. The prosecution are not obliged to prove that the defendant intended to cause some actual bodily harm or was reckless as to whether such harm would be caused

Think about this scenario.

In the light of *R* v *Savage & Parmenter*, decide whether the defendant in the following scenario is guilty of assault occasioning ABH:

Romeo is trying to enjoy a quiet drink at his local pub, but his evening is being spoilt by the raucous behaviour of Vincenzo. Romeo gets so frustrated that he throws his pint of beer over Vincenzo. As he does so, the glass slips out of his hand. It hits Vincenzo and smashes, causing a painful bruise and graze. The possibility of the glass slipping out of his hand never crossed Romeo's mind.

The decision in *R* v *Savage & Parmenter* means that assault occasioning ABH is a crime of constructive liability (see Chapter 1). The only *mens rea* which has to be proved is the *mens rea* necessary to establish an assault (requirement Number 1: The defendant must have committed an assault). This means that someone like Romeo can be convicted of assault occasioning ABH even though the possibility of the victim suffering ABH never crossed his mind.

Now, think about this question.

Can you think of any possible justifications for this example of constructive liability? (Hint: think back to some of the other principles we studied in Chapter 1.)

Quiz 6.3

1. For a charge of actual bodily harm, the victim must suffer from what level of injury?
   a. Trivial bruising.
   b. Serious harm.
   c. An injury that is more than transient or trifling.
   d. Really serious harm.

2. Which of the following is a true statement regarding the section 47 Offences Against the Person Act offence of assault occasioning actual bodily harm?
   a. A s.47 offence must be caused by a direct physical attack.
   b. There is no need to prove causation for a s.47 offence.
   c. A recognised psychiatric illness may amount to actual bodily harm.
   d. The *mens rea* of a s.47 offence is intention or recklessness as to the occasioning of actual bodily harm.

3. Which of the following is incapable of amounting to ABH?
   a. A momentary loss of consciousness.
   b. Cutting off a ponytail.
   c. Depressive illness.
   d. Psychological distress.

Malicious wounding or infliction of GBH (grievous bodily harm)

6.4 Explain the requirements for establishing criminal liability for malicious wounding or infliction of grievous bodily harm.

Section 20 of the Offences Against the Person Act 1861 states:

> Whosoever shall unlawfully and maliciously wound or inflict any grievous bodily harm upon any other person, either with or without any weapon or instrument, shall be guilty of an offence, and being convicted thereof shall be liable [. . .] to imprisonment for a term not exceeding five years.

This tells us that the offence has three requirements:

1. The defendant must have *either* wounded the victim *or* inflicted GBH (grievous bodily harm) on her
2. The wounding or infliction of GBH must have been unlawful
3. The defendant must have acted maliciously.

Numbers 1 and 2 are *actus reus* requirements. Number 3 is a *mens rea* requirement. We will work through them in turn.

1. The defendant must have either wounded the victim or inflicted GBH (grievous bodily harm) on her

'Wound' and 'GBH' are two separate terms with different meanings. It only has to be shown that the defendant *either* wounded the victim *or* that he inflicted GBH on her.

The meaning of 'wound' was considered in *C* v *Eisenhower* [1984] QB 331. The Court held that a wound requires 'a break in the continuity of the whole skin'. So a cut would constitute a wound, but a scratch would not.

Turning next to 'GBH'. This can include broken bones, injuries causing substantial loss of blood and injuries resulting in lengthy treatment or incapacity. As we saw previously, the House of Lords in *R* v *Ireland & Burstow* held that it can also include recognised psychiatric illness. Sexually transmitted diseases may also amount to GBH. In *R* v *Dica* [2004] EWCA Crim 1103 the defendant had unprotected sexual intercourse with two women even though he knew he was HIV positive. We'll be looking at this case more closely shortly. For now, the important point to note is that the Court of Appeal held that contracting HIV (or another sexually transmitted disease[5]) can amount to GBH.

Now, think about these questions.

a. If a sexually transmitted disease can amount to GBH, should non-sexually transmitted diseases (such as the coronavirus) also be capable of amounting to GBH?

b. Even though he is suffering from tuberculosis, Romeo attends his criminal law lecture. Throughout the lecture he coughs and sneezes repeatedly. Fellow student Valentina subsequently contracts the disease from Romeo.

- Should Romeo face criminal liability for infecting Valentina?
- Why/why not?

Whether or not the victim suffered GBH is a question of fact for the jury. The House of Lords in *DPP* v *Smith* [1961] AC 290 said that a trial judge giving guidance to a jury should tell them to give the words their ordinary meaning:

> I can find no warrant for giving the words "grievous bodily harm" a meaning other than that which the words convey in their ordinary and natural meaning. "Bodily harm" needs no explanation, and "grievous" means no more and no less than "really serious."[6]

When deciding whether a victim's injuries were grievous, may the jury take into account the characteristics of the particular victim? This was the issue in *R* v *Bollom* [2003] EWCA Crim 2846. The victim in this case was a 17-month-old baby called Alex. She had suffered bruising and abrasions to her body, arms and legs. The injuries were inflicted by Alex's mother's boyfriend, Stephen Bollom. At Bollom's trial the trial judge told the jury that, when deciding whether the harm Alex suffered was grievous, they could take into account Alex's young age. Bollom was subsequently convicted of the section 18 offence of

[5] For example, in *R* v *Golding* [2014] EWCA Crim 889 the Court of Appeal held that genital herpes can amount to GBH. In his commentary on this case, Laird criticises the Court of Appeal for relying on intuition and argues that greater use of expert evidence is needed when deciding whether a disease constitutes a harm for the purposes of the Offences Against the Person Act 1861 ([2014] Crim LR 687).

[6] In *R* v *O'Casey* [2021] EWCA Crim 1581 the trial judge told the jury that the words 'really serious bodily harm' should be given 'their ordinary and natural meaning'. He added, 'it is not necessary that such harm should be either permanent or dangerous or that such harm would have lasting consequences, but bear in mind that you are deciding that in the context of intent in this case'. Defence counsel argued that this further direction was unnecessary and was likely to have had the effect of reducing the level of intended harm that the prosecution had to prove. The Court of Appeal rejected the appeal. The Court said that, whilst 'it will not normally be necessary or helpful for the judge in summing-up the law to go beyond directing the jury that the words "grievous bodily harm" or "really serious bodily harm" should be given their ordinary and natural meaning', a further direction 'may be justified depending upon the facts of the particular case and where, as here, the judge repeats the overarching requirement that the words should be given their ordinary and natural meaning' ([20]).

GBH with intent. One of his grounds of appeal was that the trial judge was wrong to tell the jury to take the victim's age into account.

EXTRACT

Read the following extract from the judgment of Fulford J.

What factors may the jury take into account when deciding whether the harm the victim suffered is grievous?

R v *Bollom* [2003] EWCA Crim 2846

Fulford J

52. Mr Davies, on behalf of the appellant, at paragraph 9 of his Advice and orally before us, submits that the injuries should be assessed without reference to the particular victim. He suggests the age, health or any other particular factors relating to the person harmed should be ignored when deciding whether the injuries amounted to really serious harm. We are unable to accept that proposition. To use this case as an example, these injuries on a 6 foot adult in the fullness of health would be less serious than on, for instance, an elderly or unwell person, on someone who was physically or psychiatrically vulnerable or, as here, on a very young child. In deciding whether injuries are grievous, an assessment has to be made of, amongst other things, the effect of the harm on the particular individual. We have no doubt that in determining the gravity of these injuries, it was necessary to consider them in their real context.

We also need to consider the meaning of the word 'inflict'. There is some confusion here, stemming from the fact that both Lord Mackay in *R* v *Mandair* [1995] 1 AC 208 and Lord Steyn in *R* v *Ireland & Burstow* said that 'inflict' does not have the same meaning as 'cause'.[7] What is unclear is how the meaning of the two words differs:

- For both 'cause' and 'inflict' it is not necessary to prove that there was an assault (see *R* v *Wilson* (Clarence) [1984] AC 242).
- For both 'cause' and 'inflict' it is not necessary to prove that there was a direct application of force. In *R* v *Ireland & Burstow* Anthony Burstow was held to have inflicted GBH on Tracey Sant even though he had not directly applied force to her.
- In *R* v *Ireland & Burstow* Lord Hope suggested that the difference between 'cause' and 'inflict' is that 'the word "inflicts" implies that the consequence of the act is something which the victim is likely to find unpleasant or harmful.' But this is problematic. Think back to *R* v *Brown* [1994] 1 AC 212, which we looked at in Chapter 1 (and will be looking at again shortly). Three of the defendants in this case were convicted of malicious wounding. Suppose that some of the others had been charged with maliciously inflicting GBH. On Lord Hope's interpretation of 'inflict', these other defendants would have been acquitted because their victims did not find the injuries unpleasant (on the contrary, in fact). This seems implausible.

[7] Lord Mackay stated, 'In my opinion, as I have said, the word "cause" is wider or at least not narrower than the word "inflict"', whilst Lord Steyn stated, 'I am not saying that the words "cause" and "inflict" are exactly synonymous. They are not.'

So where does this leave us? Until we have some clear explanation of what (if any) difference there is between the terms 'inflict' and 'cause' the most sensible approach is to treat them as synonymous. So to establish an infliction you should simply apply the law governing factual and legal causation.

Think about this scenario.

Decide whether Valentina inflicts GBH on Romeo in the following example:After several months Romeo finally builds up the courage to ask out Valentina. Valentina replies that she wants to be 'just good friends'. She knows that Romeo is a fragile and sensitive individual who will take this very badly. In fact, he is so crushed that he suffers clinical depression as a result.

2. The wounding or infliction of GBH must have been unlawful

It is not always unlawful for a person to inflict GBH or wound another person. A person acting in reasonable self-defence would not be acting unlawfully. And as we shall see later in the chapter, a person may lawfully inflict GBH or wound another person in the course of certain lawful activities like surgery, tattooing and sports such as boxing.

3. The defendant must have acted maliciously

In the early part of this chapter we saw that, for the purposes of assault, the courts have given the word 'immediate' a very different meaning to the standard dictionary definition. It is a similar story with the word 'malicious'. Ordinarily, malice would be understood to mean ill-feeling or hatred. For the purposes of the section 20 offence, however, the word has a quite different meaning, which was given to it by the Court of Appeal in *R* v *Cunningham* [1957] 2 QB 396.

EXTRACT

Read the following extract from Byrne J in R v Cunningham.

What test does he set out to establish malice? Must it be shown that the defendant had ill-feeling or hatred towards the victim?

R v *Cunningham* [1957] 2 Q.B. 396

Byrne J

We have considered [the cases cited by counsel], and we have also considered, in the light of those cases, the following principle which was propounded by the late Professor C. S. Kenny in the first edition of his *Outlines of Criminal Law* published in 1902 and repeated at p. 186 of the 16th edition edited by Mr. J. W. Cecil Turner and published in 1952: "In any statutory definition of a crime, malice must be taken not in the old vague sense of wickedness in general but as requiring either (1) An actual intention to do the particular kind of harm that in fact was done; or (2) recklessness as to whether such harm should occur or not (i.e., the accused has foreseen that the particular kind of harm might be done and yet has gone on to take the risk of it). It is neither limited to nor does it indeed require any ill will towards the person injured." The same principle is repeated by Mr. Turner in his 10th edition of *Russell on Crime* at p. 1592. We think that this is an accurate statement of the law.

A simple example will illustrate how different the *Cunningham* definition of malice is to the dictionary definition. Imagine a surgeon delivering a baby by Caesarian section. To deliver the baby the surgeon must cut through the mother's abdomen. As we've just seen, the cut would be classified as a wound since all layers of the skin are broken. Does the surgeon wound the mother maliciously? If we apply the test from Cunningham the answer is yes, since the doctor wounded the mother intentionally. Of course, in everyday conversation we would not use the word 'malice' in this way.

Assessment advice

When answering a problem question, it is important to remember that your job is not to apply the word in its everyday sense. You must apply the technical, legal meaning given to it by the Court of Appeal in *R* v *Cunningham*.

(And don't worry, the doctor would not be guilty of the section 20 offence! The mother's consent to the operation means that the wound was not unlawful.) If you look back at the test from *R* v *Cunningham* you'll see that it refers to the 'particular kind of harm'.

Malice requires either: (1) An actual intention to do the particular kind of harm that in fact was done; or (2) That the defendant foresaw that the particular kind of harm might be done and yet has gone on to take the risk of it. It is unclear from this what is meant by the 'particular kind of harm'.

You might think that, since the *actus reus* of the section 20 offence requires either GBH or wounding, the defendant should only be convicted if he intended or foresaw GBH or wounding. This would be consistent with the correspondence principle. But it is not the position the courts have adopted. Lord Ackner in *R* v *Savage & Parmenter* stated:

> My Lords, I am satisfied that [. . .] it is quite unnecessary that the accused should either have intended or have foreseen that his unlawful act might cause physical harm of the gravity described in section 20, i.e. a wound or serious physical injury. It is enough that he should have foreseen that some physical harm to some person, albeit of a minor character, might result

In other words, the section 20 offence is a crime of constructive liability (in the same way as assault occasioning ABH). The only *mens rea* requirement is 'malice', and this is satisfied if the defendant either: (1) intended to cause the victim some harm; or (2) was reckless as to whether the victim would suffer some harm.

Think about this scenario.

After several months, Romeo finally builds up the courage to ask Valentina out on a date. But she replies 'No chance' and laughs at him. Romeo is so upset that he pushes her. She stumbles backwards, falls and lands awkwardly, breaking her arm. Is Romeo guilty of the section 20 offence?

Quiz 6.4

1. According to *R v Cunningham* [1957] 2 QB 396 and *R v Savage & Parmenter* [1992] 1 AC 699, what is the meaning of malice for the purposes of the section 20 offence?
   - **a.** D intended to cause V some harm or was reckless as to this possibility.
   - **b.** There was bad feeling between D and V.
   - **c.** D intended to cause V serious harm.
   - **d.** D caused V serious harm either intentionally or recklessly.
2. What is the maximum sentence for the section 20 offence of maliciously inflicting grievous bodily harm or wounding?
   - **a.** Ten years.
   - **b.** Five years.
   - **c.** Life imprisonment.
   - **d.** Three years.
3. What is the most usual interpretation for the term 'grievous' bodily harm?
   - **a.** Really serious bodily harm.
   - **b.** Some bodily harm.
   - **c.** Reasonably serious bodily harm.
   - **d.** Life threatening harm.

Wounding or GBH with intent

6.5 Define the requirements for establishing criminal liability for wounding or grievous bodily harm with intent.

Section 18 of the Offences Against the Person Act 1861 states:

> Whosoever shall unlawfully and maliciously by any means whatsoever wound or cause any grievous bodily harm to any person... with intent... to do some... grievous bodily harm to any person, or with intent to resist or prevent the lawful apprehension or detainer of any person, shall be guilty of an offence, and being convicted thereof shall be liable,... to imprisonment for life...

This tells us that the offence has four requirements:

1. The defendant must have *either* wounded the victim *or* caused her GBH (grievous bodily harm)
2. The wounding or causing of GBH must have been unlawful
3. The defendant must have acted maliciously
4. The defendant must have *either* intended to cause the victim GBH *or* intended to resist or prevent a lawful arrest.

The first three requirements on this list are identical to the section 20 offence (the only difference is that section 18 uses the word 'cause' instead of 'inflict', but as we've seen this is of no practical significance). The sole difference between the two offences is that section 18 has an additional *mens rea* requirement: the defendant must have either intended to cause the victim GBH or intended to resist or prevent a lawful arrest.

In other words, section 18 is an aggravated version of the section 20 offence. The extra *mens rea* requirement makes a very big difference to sentencing. The maximum sentence for the section 20 offence is five years' imprisonment, whereas the maximum sentence for the section 18 offence is life imprisonment.

Assessment advice

When answering a problem question, the best approach is therefore to begin with the section 20 offence. If the requirements of this offence are satisfied, you should then ask whether the additional *mens rea* requirement of the section 18 offence is satisfied. If it is, the defendant will be guilty of the aggravated offence (and liable to up to life imprisonment!).

Quiz 6.5

1. Sending countless letters to a victim with the intention of causing some minor harm, and actually causing a severe depressive illness, would best be charged as…
   a. section 18 OAPA (grievous bodily harm with intent).
   b. section 47 of the Offences Against the Person Act (OAPA) (assault occasioning actual bodily harm).
   c. section 20 OAPA (malicious infliction of grievous bodily harm).
   d. assault.
2. The difference between a section 18 and a section 20 offence of grievous bodily harm contrary to the Offences Against the Person Act 1861 is…
   a. there is no difference, only to the sentence.
   b. there is no need to prove causation for a section 20 offence.
   c. the section 18 offence has an additional *mens rea* requirement.
   d. the level of physical harm required is less for a section 20 offence.
3. What is the *mens rea* requirement that is contained in the section 18, but not the section 20, offence?
   a. Intention to endanger the life of the victim.
   b. Intention to cause the victim GBH.
   c. Intention to (a) cause the victim GBH **or** (b) resist or prevent a lawful arrest.
   d. Intention to (a) cause the victim GBH **and** (b) resist or prevent a lawful arrest.

Issues relating to consent

6.6 Explain the case law governing consent obtained by fraud and consent to injury.

For each of the offences we have looked at, one of the requirements is that the defendant acted unlawfully. As we have seen, there are various reasons why a defendant's actions may not have been unlawful. One possible reason is that the victim consented to the defendant's actions. We now need to look more closely at this concept of consent.

First of all we need to understand an important point. Sometimes a victim might agree to something without having consented. For example, the victim might have lacked mental capacity. So although she agreed to the defendant's actions, she did not consent because she lacked the capacity to do so. Alternatively, the victim might have been pressurised by threats. So although she submitted to the defendant's actions she did not consent because her choice was not a free one.[8] In cases like these there is no *effective* consent.

[8] This distinction is discussed further in Chapter 7 when we look at the definition of consent found in the Sexual Offences Act 2003.

In this part of the chapter we are going to look at two other types of case in which the victim's consent may not have been effective. First, we will look at cases in which the victim only agreed to the defendant's actions because the defendant deceived her. Second, we will look at how the criminal law regulates when individuals may choose to consent to injury.

1. Consent obtained by fraud

i. The general rule

For more than a century the courts held that a victim's consent will only be vitiated (i.e. invalidated) by fraud if the victim was deceived about the nature of the act or the identity of the person. So as long as the deception did not relate to either the nature of the act or the defendant's identity the victim's consent will be deemed effective.

An example is *R* v *Richardson* [1999] QB 444. The defendant in this case was a dentist named Diana Richardson. On 30 August 1996 she was suspended from practice by the General Dental Council. In spite of this, she continued to treat a number of patients. The mother of two of these patients complained to the police, because she thought Richardson had been under the influence of drink and drugs. The police subsequently discovered that Richardson had been practising whilst disqualified, and she was charged with assault occasioning ABH. The key issue in the case was whether Richardson had committed a battery. This depended on whether the force she had inflicted on her patients had been unlawful, which in turn depended on whether her deception had vitiated her patients' consent.

The prosecution conceded that Richardson had not deceived the patients about the nature of the act. At first you might find this quite surprising. Isn't there an important difference between treatment by a registered dentist and treatment by a suspended dentist? Arguably there is. But the criminal law draws a distinction between the nature of an act and the quality of an act. Whether or not the dentist treating you is registered or suspended is relevant only to the quality of the act. As long as the patients understood that they were receiving dental treatment they understood the nature of the act. There was no suggestion that Richardson had tricked them into believing they were not receiving dental treatment, and so there was no deception as to the nature of the act.

Instead, the prosecution argued that Richardson had deceived the patients about her identity. The prosecution's argument was that a person's identity covers not only their name and who they are, but also their attributes and qualifications. So when Richardson fraudulently failed to tell the patients that she had been suspended, she deceived them as to her identity.

EXTRACT

Read the following extract from the Court of Appeals' judgment in *R* v *Richardson*.

Did the Court accept the prosecution's argument? Had Richardson deceived the patients as to her identity?

R v *Richardson* [1999] QB 444

Otton LJ

In essence the Crown contended that the concept of the "identity of the person" should be extended to cover the qualifications or attributes of the dentist on the basis that the patients consented to treatment by a qualified dentist and not a suspended one. We must reject that submission. In all the charges brought against the defendant the complainants were fully aware of the identity of the defendant. To accede to the submission would be to strain or distort the everyday meaning of the word identity, the dictionary defin tion of which is "the condition of being the same."

It was suggested in argument that we might be assisted by the civil law of consent, where such expressions as "real" or "informed" consent prevail. In this regard the criminal and the civil law do not run along the same track. The concept of informed consent has no place in the criminal law. It would also be a mistake, in our view, to introduce the concept of a duty to communicate information to a patient about the risk of an activity before consent to an act can be treated as valid. The gravamen of the defendant's conduct in the instant case was that the complainants consented to treatment from her although their consent had been procured by her failure to inform them that she was no longer qualified to practise. This was clearly reprehensible and may well found the basis of a civil claim for damages. But we are quite satisfied that it is not a basis for finding criminal liability in the field of offences against the person.

So the Court of Appeal drew a distinction between, on the one hand, a person's identity and, on the other hand, a person's attributes and qualifications. Richardson did not inform the patients that she had been suspended, so she deceived them as to her attributes, but she did not deceive them as to her identity. Therefore, their consent was not vitiated.

To some, the distinction drawn in *R* v *Richardson* seems dubious. Suppose that you had been one of Richardson's patients. You may well have been more concerned to know that you were being treated by a licensed dentist than to know that you were being treated by Diana Richardson herself. Indeed, in the subsequent case *R* v *Melin* [2019] EWCA Crim 557 the prosecution argued that, sometimes, a person's identity is inextricably linked to their qualifications. The defendant, Ozan Melin, administered botox injections to two women, Marcelle King and Carol Kingscott. Melin held no medical qualifications. He offered both women a free top-up injection two weeks after the first. After the second injection, both women suffered really serious harm. The prosecution's case was that King and Kingscott only consented to the treatment because they believed that Melin was medically qualified. At trial he was convicted on two counts of malicious infliction of GBH. One of the issues at his appeal against conviction was whether a deception as to one's qualifications is capable of vitiating consent.

EXTRACT

According to the Court of Appeal, may deception as to whether someone is medically qualified constitute deception as to that person's identity? How did the Court distinguish *R* v *Richardson*?

R v *Melin* [2019] EWCA Crim 557

Simler J

29 … [W]e have no doubt that [the judgment in *R* v *Richardson*] is correct. Plainly it would be undesirable for the law to treat all false or fraudulent representations as vitiating consent because that would lead to, at least potentially, trivial lies about the person or the conduct, treatment or activity as giving rise to criminal liability.

30 However, it seems to us that there may be cases where a person's identity is inextricably linked to his or her professional status. As the authors of *Smith and Hogan's Criminal Law* (15th edition) argue (at 672):

> "It could be argued that there are some situations in which the status or attribute of the individual is inextricably bound up with his identity for the purposes of the specific activity he is performing. Indeed, it could be that the attribute is actually *more* important than the identity. For example, would a patient visiting a general practitioner and being told that a new doctor is taking the surgery be more concerned as to the "status" of the person or his "identity"? The same argument might apply to the attribute of being a police officer."
>
> 31 We agree with that as a general principle… The word 'identity' is an ordinary English word, defined as "the fact of being who or what a person is". Depending on the facts, it seems to us that deception as to a person's identity as a doctor where that is integral to his or her identity, can as a matter of law vitiate consent. That is different to what happened in *R* v *Richardson* and does not amount to including qualifications within this definition in the sense referred to in *R* v *Richardson*.
>
> 32 [Defence counsel] maintained that this general principle cannot apply as a matter of law in the circumstances of this case because Botox is not required to be administered by a doctor and so being a doctor cannot be integral to the identity of the person administering the injection.
>
> 33 We disagree that this raises an argument of law. Rather, it seems to us that this is a challenge to the application of the principles to the facts of this case. Here, unlike in *R* v *Richardson*, where the fraud was not as to whether the defendant was a qualified dentist but as to whether she remained licensed by her regulatory body, the treatment was said to have been given by a person impersonating a medically qualified practitioner. Whether the fact of being medically qualified was operative in the minds of the complainants in giving consent cannot be determined solely by reference to the regulatory requirements for the administration of Botox injections, though that might play a part in the factual matrix depending on what was known and understood by the complainants concerned. If as a matter of fact, administration of the injection by a medically qualified practitioner was for each complainant a condition of giving her consent and without it, consent would not have been given or would have been withdrawn, it seems to us that this would go to the question of the appellant's identity and the legal validity of their consent. Accordingly, in our judgment there was at least potentially a deception as to identity rather than merely qualifications or attributes in this case. We also consider… that whereas in *R* v *Richardson* there was a failure to inform, here there were, on the Crown's case, positive false representations that the Appellant was a doctor.

So Melin's misrepresentation that he was medically qualified was not merely a deception as to his qualifications or attributes. It was a deception as to his identity.[9] This was different from *R* v *Richardson*, because Richardson did not deceive her patients as to whether she was medically *qualified*. Rather, she deceived them as to whether she was *licensed* to practice dentistry. According to the Court of Appeal in *R* v *Melin*, misleading a patient into believing that you are properly licensed does not constitute deception as to identity. As Pegg and Thomas note, this distinction between being medically qualified and being properly licensed is a 'rather subtle' one. It also leaves open the question whether there are other factors, besides being medically qualified, that may be considered integral to an individual's identity. For example, Pegg and Thomas ask, 'What of a hairdresser who professes to be skillful in the art but lacks any sort of experience or technique – would consent be vitiated there also?[10]

---

[9] Melin's conviction in respect of Carol Kingscott was accordingly upheld. However, his conviction in respect of Marcelle King was quashed, since there was insufficient evidence that any false statement he made about being medically qualified had had an operative effect on King's decision to take up the treatment.

[10] Pegg, S. and Thomas, M. (2019) 'Deception and Qualifications: Revisiting the Ruling in *R* v *Richardson*?' 83 *Journal of Criminal Law* 298.

Now, think about this scenario.

Romeo looks a lot like the footballer Wayne Rooney. Although Valentina does not find Wayne Rooney attractive, she has always dreamt of enjoying the wealthy lifestyle of a footballer's wife and so begins to flirt with Romeo. Although Romeo realises her mistake he does not correct her and, after a few minutes, they kiss. When Valentina realises her mistake she is horrified. She says she would never have kissed Romeo had she known that he was not a wealthy footballer and accuses him of battery. Did Romeo's deception vitiate Valentina's consent?

ii. Sexually-transmitted diseases

An early example of the application of the rule that only fraud as to the nature of the act or the identity of the person vitiates consent is the 19th-century case *R* v *Clarence* (1888) 22 QBD 23. Charles Clarence was suffering from the sexually transmitted disease gonorrhoea. Although he knew of his condition, he did not tell his wife Selina. They had sexual intercourse, and shortly afterwards Selina contracted the disease. She said she would not have had sex with her husband had she known of his condition. Clarence was charged with malicious infliction of GBH. At trial he was convicted. On appeal, the conviction was quashed by a majority of nine to four. In response to the suggestion that Selina's consent had been vitiated by fraud, one of the majority, Stephen J, stated:

> The woman's consent here was as full and conscious as consent could be. It was not obtained by any fraud either as to the nature of the act or as to the identity of the agent.

One of the problems with this assertion is that it fails to distinguish between: (1) consent to sexual intercourse; and (2) consent to the risk of infection. As far as (1) is concerned, Stephen J was correct. Selina was not deceived as to the nature of sexual intercourse. Her consent to sexual intercourse was effective. But the prosecution had not alleged non-consensual sex! They had not charged Clarence with rape. They had charged him with malicious infliction of GBH. For this offence, it is (2) that is crucial. Had Selina consented to the risk of harm? Or was her consent to the risk of harm vitiated because her husband had deceived her as to the nature of the harmful act?

In *R* v *Dica* [2004] EWCA Crim 1103 the Court of Appeal had the opportunity to revisit the decision in *R* v *Clarence*. The facts of *R* v *Dica* were similar to *R* v *Clarence*. Although he knew that he was HIV positive, Mohammed Dica had unprotected sexual intercourse with two women. Both women subsequently contracted HIV. At trial Dica was convicted on two counts of maliciously inflicting GBH. He appealed, arguing that his conviction was inconsistent with the decision in *R* v *Clarence*.

The Court of Appeal drew the distinction outlined above between consent to sexual intercourse and consent to the risk of infection. The key question, it said, was whether the two women had consented to the risk of infection.

EXTRACT

Read the following extract from the judgment of Judge LJ.

Had the two women consented to the risk of infection? So was the infliction of GBH lawful or unlawful?

R v *Dica* [2004] EWCA Crim 1103

Judge LJ

39. In our view, on the assumed fact now being considered, the answer is entirely straightforward. These victims consented to sexual intercourse. Accordingly, the defendant was not guilty of rape. Given the long-term nature of the relationships, if the defendant concealed the truth about his condition from them, and therefore kept them in ignorance of it, there was no reason for them to think that they were running any risk of infection, and they were not consenting to it. On this basis, there would be no consent sufficient in law to provide the defendant with a defence to the charge under section 20.

Having reached this conclusion, Judge LJ held that *R* v *Clarence* should be overruled:

> 31. In our judgment, the reasoning which led the majority in *Clarence* to decide that the conviction under section 20 should be quashed has no continuing application. If that case were decided today, the conviction under section 20 would be upheld.

Shortly after *R* v *Dica* came the case *R* v *Konzani* [2005] EWCA Crim 706. Konzani, who was HIV positive, had had unprotected sexual intercourse with three women without telling them that he was HIV positive. Each of them subsequently contracted the virus. At trial he was convicted of malicious infliction of GBH. He appealed against his conviction on two grounds:

1. At trial Konzani's counsel had argued that, by consenting to unprotected sexual intercourse, each of the women had consented to all of the risks associated with unprotected sex, including the risk of contracting HIV. The trial judge rejected this, telling the jury that Konzani could only rely on the women's consent as a defence if their consent had been 'informed and willing'. On appeal, Konzani argued that this was wrong.
2. Konzani's counsel also argued that, even if the three women had not consented to the risk of infection, Konzani genuinely believed that they had. Counsel argued that Konzani's claimed belief in consent should have resulted in an acquittal, even if the belief was unreasonable. The Court of Appeal examined each of these grounds of appeal.

EXTRACT

Read the following extract from the judgment of Judge LJ.

On the first ground of appeal, did the Court agree that a distinction must be drawn between giving a general consent to the risks of unprotected sexual intercourse and giving an informed consent to the specific risk of contracting HIV? According to the Court, had the three women consented to the risk of contracting HIV from Konzani? Why/why not?

On the second ground of appeal, the Court accepted that a defendant should be acquitted if he genuinely believed the victim had consented to the risk of contracting HIV. According to the Court, did Konzani genuinely believe the three women had consented to the risk of contracting HIV? Why/why not?

R v *Konzani* [2005] EWCA Crim 706

Judge LJ

41. [. . .] There is a critical distinction between taking a risk of the various, potentially adverse and possibly problematic consequences of sexual intercourse, and giving an informed consent to the risk of infection with a fatal disease. For the complainant's consent to the risks of contracting the HIV virus to provide a defence [. . .] her consent must be an informed consent. If that proposition is in doubt, we take this opportunity to emphasise it. We must therefore examine its implications for this appeal.

42. The recognition in *R* v *Dica* of informed consent as a defence was based on but limited by potentially conflicting public policy considerations. In the public interest, so far as possible, the spread of catastrophic illness must be avoided or prevented. On the other hand, the public interest also requires that the principle of personal autonomy in the context of adult non-violent sexual relationships should be maintained. If an individual who knows that he is suffering from the HIV virus conceals this stark fact from his sexual partner, the principle of her personal autonomy is not enhanced if he is exculpated when he recklessly transmits the HIV virus to her through consensual sexual intercourse. On any view, the concealment of this fact from her almost inevitably means that she is deceived. Her consent is not properly informed, and she cannot give an informed consent to something of which she is ignorant. Equally, her personal autonomy is not normally protected by allowing a defendant who knows that he is suffering from the HIV virus which he deliberately conceals, to assert an honest belief in his partner's informed consent to the risk of the transmission of the HIV virus. Silence in these circumstances is incongruous with honesty, or with a genuine belief that there is an informed consent. Accordingly, in such circumstances the issue either of informed consent, or honest belief in it will only rarely arise: in reality, in most cases, the contention would be wholly artificial.

[...]

44. In deference to Mr Roberts' submission, we accept that there may be circumstances in which it would be open to the jury to infer that, notwithstanding that the defendant was reckless and concealed his condition from the complainant, she may nevertheless have given an informed consent to the risk of contracting the HIV virus. By way of example, an individual with HIV may develop a sexual relationship with someone who knew him while he was in hospital, receiving treatment for the condition. If so, her informed consent, if it were indeed informed, would remain a defence, to be disproved by the prosecution, even if the defendant had not personally informed her of his condition. Even if she did not in fact consent, this example would illustrate the basis for an argument that he honestly believed in her informed consent. Alternatively, he may honestly believe that his new sexual partner was told of his condition by someone known to them both. Cases like these, not too remote to be fanciful, may arise. If they do, no doubt they will be explored with the complainant in cross-examination. Her answers may demonstrate an informed consent. Nothing remotely like that was suggested here. In a different case, perhaps supported by the defendant's own evidence, material like this may provide a basis for suggesting that he honestly believed that she was giving an informed consent. He may provide an account of the incident, or the affair, which leads the jury to conclude that even if she did not give an informed consent, he may honestly have believed that she did. Acknowledging these possibilities in different cases does not, we believe, conflict with the public policy considerations identified in *R* v *Dica*. That said, they did not arise in the present case.

45. Why not? In essence because the jury found that the complainants did not give a willing or informed consent to the risks of contracting the HIV virus from the appellant. We recognise that where consent does provide a defence to an offence against the person, it is generally speaking correct that the defendant's honest belief in the alleged victim's consent would also

provide a defence. However for this purpose, the defendant's honest belief must be concomitant with the consent which provides a defence. Unless the consent would provide a defence, an honest belief in it would not assist the defendant. This follows logically from *R v Brown*. For it to do so here, what was required was some evidence of an honest belief that the complainants, or any one of them, were consenting to the risk that they might be infected with the HIV virus by him. There is not the slightest evidence, direct or indirect, from which a jury could begin to infer that the appellant honestly believed that any complainant consented to that specific risk. As there was no such evidence, the judge's ruling about "honest belief" was correct. In fact, the honest truth was that the appellant deceived them.

In a case like *R v Dica* or *R v Konzani* the defendant can only be convicted if he acted maliciously – which, as we saw above, means that he inflicted the harm intentionally or recklessly. As we saw in Chapter 4, the *Cunningham* test for recklessness asks whether the defendant foresaw the relevant risk and unjustifiably chose to take it. In both *R v Dica* and *R v Konzani* this issue was straightforward, since both defendants were aware of the risk of transmitting the virus and yet chose not to use any protection.

Consider this scenario.

Romeo is HIV positive but has not yet told Valentina, whom he has been dating for almost a month. When they have sexual intercourse for the first time, Romeo uses a condom. He does not believe it is necessary to tell her that he is HIV positive because he knows that the condom will greatly reduce the risk of transmitting the virus to Valentina. Unfortunately Valentina contracts the virus. Applying the *Cunningham* test, did Romeo act recklessly? In other words, did he foresee the risk of Valentina contracting the virus and did he *unjustifiably* choose to take this risk?

Some commentators have criticised the reasoning in *R v Dica* and *R v Konzani*. Ryan argues that the reasoning in *R v Konzani:*

> 'rests upon the assumption that the person infected is the sole source of knowledge regarding risk of HIV transmission. It overlooks the fact that the sexual partner may be fully aware of the various risks associated with different types of sexual activity even without disclosure by the infected partner. It improperly gives full responsibility for transmission to the infected individual, ignoring the role the sexual partner plays in acquiring the disease by willingly engaging in high-risk activity'.

She goes on to say that the reasoning also 'fails to give sufficient weight to the autonomy and privacy interests of the HIV+ individual which are clearly infringed by a requirement to disclose their HIV status. In light of the potential for stigma and discrimination, an infected individual has strong reasons for seeking to protect the confidentiality of their medical diagnosis. Furthermore, whilst it may be argued that it is the infected person's actual knowledge of their status that tips the balance in favour of placing greater responsibility on them, it is questionable whether this responsibility can only be met through disclosure (as opposed to using precautions or engaging in low-risk activity)'.[11]

---

[11] Ryan, S. (2019) '"Active Deception" v Non-Disclosure: HIV Transmission, Non-Fatal Offences and Criminal Responsibility' *Criminal Law Review* 4.

Meanwhile, Weait points out that, if a person must have known he was HIV positive in order to be found to have acted recklessly, the effect of the decisions could be to dissuade people from having an HIV test and accessing available medical care and treatment. More fundamentally, he argues that the transmission of HIV should be seen first and foremost as a public health issue:[12]

> Some commentators, including the present author, have argued that where a person is aware of the risks associated with unprotected sex and has not satisfied him- or herself that a partner is HIV negative (or free from other serious sexually transmitted infections (STIs)) the defence of consent should, in principle, be available. The reason for taking such a position is, primarily, that the transmission of HIV should be seen first and foremost as a public health issue and that everyone, not just those who are HIV positive, has a responsibility for minimising the spread of the virus. To impose criminal liability on those who recklessly transmit HIV or STIs to people who are in a position to protect themselves against infection, and elect not to, sends a message that people are, and should be, entitled to assume that their partners will ensure that transmission does not occur. The very fact that the virus has spread so dramatically in recent years among the sexually active demonstrates that this is simply not the case.

These issues were considered by the Law Commission in its 2015 scoping report on the non-fatal offences against the person.[13] The Commission commented that it 'seems unlikely that anyone, while conscious of a significant risk that he or she is indeed infected with HIV or a serious disease, would deliberately refrain from being tested in order to avoid satisfying the recklessness requirement of the offence under section 20. Such an attitude would combine exceptional legal knowledge with exceptional indifference to one's own health and safety' (para 6.70). As for the argument that the law places responsibility exclusively on those with HIV or STIs to ensure that transmission does not occur, the Commission expressed doubts. For a start, a person would 'have to be naïve in the extreme' to take no responsibility themselves in reliance on the deterrent effect of the criminal law: 'people rely on the existence of the offence of burglary to discourage break-ins and punish them when they occur, but still lock the door to their homes' (para 6.77). More fundamentally, the Commission stated that decriminalising the transmission of disease would be unfair: 'If two people are confronting the same danger, and one of them is aware of it and the other is not, the primary blame for failing to avoid it must be that of the person who was aware. This must be all the more true when the danger is only to the party who was not aware' (para 6.78). So, whilst stating that there needs to be a wider review of the law governing the transmission of disease, the Commission provisionally recommended preserving the current position.

2. Consent to injury

At the beginning of the chapter we considered the question: when should the criminal law prohibit consensual injury? Figure 6.2 shows the ladder of offences against the person. It is the same as the one at the start of the chapter, except it has an extra rung at the top for murder and manslaughter. As you can see, in England and Wales a defendant who is charged with murder or manslaughter may never rely on the fact the victim consented as a defence.

[12] Weait, M. (2005) 'Knowledge, Autonomy and Consent: R v Konzani' *Criminal Law Review* 763.

[13] We examine the report in detail later in the chapter.

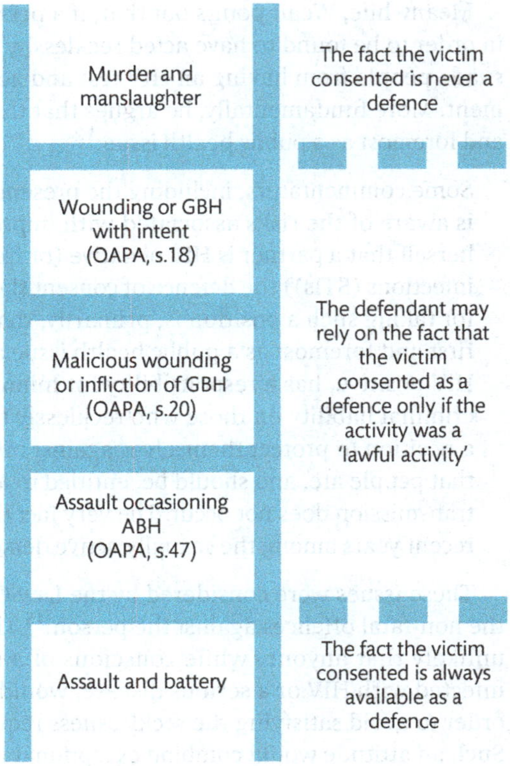

Figure 6.2

At the bottom of the ladder are the offences of assault and battery. The House of Lords in *R* v *Brown* [1994] 1 AC 212 held that a defendant charged with either of these offences may always rely on the fact the victim consented as a defence.

In the middle of the ladder are the section 47, 20 and 18 offences. For these offences, the House of Lords in *R* v *Brown* held that the consent of the victim is only available as a defence if the injury (ABH/GBH/wounding) occurred in the course of a 'lawful activity'. What we need to do is to examine which activities are lawful activities and which are unlawful activities. We will also consider the approach the courts have taken to deciding whether an activity should be classified as lawful or unlawful.

i. Unlawful activities

a. Fighting and brawling

The first unlawful activity is fighting and brawling. In *Attorney-General's Reference (No. 6 of 1980)* [1981] QB 715 the defendant and victim began arguing in the street, and then agreed to have a fist fight. The victim suffered bruises on his face and a bleeding nose. The defendant was charged with assault occasioning ABH. The trial judge told the jury that if both parties consented to the fight then the fight may well be lawful. The defendant was subsequently acquitted. The Attorney-General referred a point of law of general importance to the Court of Appeal: if two people agree to a fight, can one of them rely on the consent of the other as a defence to a charge of ABH/GBH/wounding? The Court of Appeal answered no, stating that 'it is not in the public interest that people should try to cause, or should cause, each other bodily harm for no good reason'. In *R* v *Brown* the House of Lords agreed with this and confirmed that fighting and brawling is an unlawful activity.

b. Sado-masochism: R v Brown

The activity that was in question in *R v Brown* was sado-masochism. A group of homosexual middle-aged men committed acts of violence against each other for sexual pleasure. The acts included: whipping; caning; applying stinging nettles to the genitals; inserting fish hooks into the penis; nailing the scrotum or foreskin to pieces of board; and burning the penis with a candle. The activities were carried out in private and had been going on for a number of years. The activities were videoed and the tapes were distributed amongst the members of the group. There was no evidence that any of the men had suffered permanent injury or ever sought medical treatment. The police discovered the group's activities by chance, when investigating other matters. At trial the defendants were convicted of assault occasioning ABH. Three were also convicted of malicious wounding. The case reached the House of Lords. By a majority of 3–2 the Lords decided that sado-masochism (i.e. deliberately causing ABH/GBH/wounding for sexual pleasure) is an unlawful activity and upheld the convictions.

It is important to understand the approach the majority took when deciding whether sado-masochism is a lawful or unlawful activity. They started from the assumption that deliberately causing ABH/GBH/wounding is unlawful, and asked whether there are good policy and public interest reasons for classifying the activity as lawful. For example, Lord Templeman stated:

> [T]he courts have accepted that consent is a defence to the infliction of bodily harm in the course of some lawful activities. The question is whether the defence should be extended to the infliction of bodily harm in the course of sado-masochistic encounters
>
> [...]
>
> The question whether the defence of consent should be extended to the consequences of sado-masochistic encounters can only be decided by consideration of policy and public interest.

And Lord Lowry stated:

> [T]here are prima facie offences against sections 20 and 47 and the next question is whether there is good reason to add sado-masochistic acts to the list of exceptions.

The underlying assumption is that sado-masochism is an unlawful activity. Should the defence of consent be *extended* to sado-masochism? Are there good reasons to *add* sado-masochism to the list of exceptions? This has been described as a 'social utility' model: an activity that deliberately causes ABH/GBH/wounding will only be lawful if it has social utility.

Having set out this approach, the majority then considered whether policy and public interest considerations required sado-masochism to be a lawful activity.

EXTRACT

Read the following extracts from the judgments of Lord Templeman and Lord Jauncey and make a list of the reasons they gave for deciding that policy and public interest considerations did not require sado-masochism to be a lawful activity.

Look back at the principles we studied in Chapter 1. Try and match each of the reasons given by Lord Templeman and Lord Jauncey to at least one of the principles from Chapter 1.

R v *Brown* [1994] 1 AC 212

Lord Templeman

Counsel for the appellants argued that consent should provide a defence to charges under both section 20 and section 47 because, it was said, every person has a right to deal with his body as he pleases. I do not consider that this slogan provides a sufficient guide to the policy decision which must now be made. It is an offence for a person to abuse his own body and mind by taking drugs. Although the law is often broken, the criminal law restrains a practice which is regarded as dangerous and injurious to individuals and which if allowed and extended is harmful to society generally. In any event the appellants in this case did not mutilate their own bodies. They inflicted bodily harm on willing victims [...]

The assertion was made on behalf of the appellants that the sexual appetites of sadists and masochists can only be satisfied by the infliction of bodily harm and that the law should not punish the consensual achievement of sexual satisfaction. There was no evidence to support the assertion that sado-masochist activities are essential to the happiness of the appellants or any other participants but the argument would be acceptable if sado-masochism were only concerned with sex, as the appellants contend. In my opinion sado-masochism is not only concerned with sex. Sado-masochism is also concerned with violence. The evidence discloses that the practices of the appellants were unpredictably dangerous and degrading to body and mind and were developed with increasing barbarity and taught to persons whose consents were dubious or worthless.

A sadist draws pleasure from inflicting or watching cruelty. A masochist derives pleasure from his own pain or humiliation. The appellants are middle-aged men. The victims were youths some of whom were introduced to sado-masochism before they attained the age of 21. In his judgment in the Court of Appeal, Lord Lane C.J. said that two members of the group of which the appellants formed part, namely one Cadman and the appellant Laskey:

> "were responsible in part for the corruption of a youth K... It is some comfort at least to be told, as we were, that K. has now it seems settled into a normal heterosexual relationship. Cadman had befriended K. when the boy was 15 years old. He met him in a cafeteria and, so he says, found out that the boy was interested in homosexual activities. He introduced and encouraged K. in 'bondage affairs.' He was interested in viewing and recording on videotape K. and other teenage boys in homosexual scenes... One cannot overlook the danger that the gravity of the assaults and injuries in this type of case may escalate to even more unacceptable heights."

The evidence disclosed that drink and drugs were employed to obtain consent and increase enthusiasm. The victim was usually manacled so that the sadist could enjoy the thrill of power and the victim could enjoy the thrill of helplessness. The victim had no control over the harm which the sadist, also stimulated by drink and drugs might inflict. In one case a victim was branded twice on the thigh and there was some doubt as to whether he consented to or protested against the second branding. The dangers involved in administering violence must have been appreciated by the appellants because, so it was said by their counsel, each victim was given a code word which he could pronounce when excessive harm or pain was caused. The efficiency of this precaution, when taken, depends on the circumstances and on the personalities involved. No one can feel the pain of another. The charges against the appellants were based on genital torture and violence to the buttocks, anus, penis, testicles and nipples. The victims were degraded and humiliated sometimes beaten, sometimes wounded with instruments and sometimes branded. Bloodletting and the smearing of human blood produced excitement. There were obvious dangers of serious personal injury and blood infection. Prosecuting counsel informed the trial judge against the protests of defence counsel, that although the appellants had not contracted Aids, two members of the group had died from Aids and one other had contracted an H.I.V. infection although not necessarily from the practices of the group. Some activities involved excrement. The assertion that the instruments employed by the sadists were clean and sterilised could not have removed the danger of infection, and the assertion that care was taken demonstrates the possibility of infection. Cruelty to human beings was on occasions supplemented by cruelty to animals in the form of bestiality. It is fortunate that there were no permanent injuries to a victim though no one knows the extent of harm inflicted in other cases. It is not surprising that a victim does not complain to the police when the complaint would involve him in giving details of acts in which he participated. Doctors of course are subject to a code of confidentiality.

In principle there is a difference between violence which is incidental and violence which is inflicted for the indulgence of crue ty. The violence of sado-masochistic encounters involves the indulgence of cruelty by sadists and the degradation of victims. Such violence is injurious to the participants and unpredictably dangerous. I am not prepared to invent a defence of consent for sado-masochistic encounters which breed and glorify cruelty and result in offences under sections 47 and 20 of the Act of 1861 [...] Society is entitled and bound to protect itself against a cult of violence. Pleasure derived from the infliction of pain is an evil thing. Cruelty is uncivilised. I would answer the certified question in the negative and dismiss the appeals of the appellants against conviction [...]

Lord Jauncey

[I]n considering the public interest it would be wrong to look only at the activities of the appellants alone, there being no suggestion that they and their associates are the only practitioners of homosexual sado-masochism in England and Wales. This House must therefore consider the possibility that these activities are practised by others and by others who are not so controlled or responsible as the appellants are claimed to be. Without going into details of all the rather curious activities in which the appellants engaged it would appear to be good luck rather than good judgment which has prevented serious injury from occurring. Wounds can easily become septic if not properly treated, the free flow of blood from a person who is H.I.V. positive or who has Aids can infect another and an inflicter who is carried away by sexual excitement or by drink or drugs could very easily inflict pain and injury beyond the level to which the receiver had consented. Your Lordships have no information as to whether such situations have occurred in relation to other sado-masochistic practitioners. It was no doubt these dangers which caused Lady Mallalieu to restrict her propositions in relation to the public interest to the actual rather than the potential result of the activity. In my view such a restriction is quite unjustified. When considering the public interest potential for harm is just as relevant as actual harm. As Mathew J. said in *Reg. v. Coney*, 8 Q.B.D. 534, 547: "There is, however, abundant authority for saying that no consent can render that innocent which is in fact dangerous." Furthermore, the possibility of proselytisation and corruption of young men is a real danger even in the case of these appellants and the taking of video recordings of such activities suggests that secrecy may not be as strict as the appellants claimed to your Lordships. If the only purpose of the activity is the sexual gratification of one or both of the participants what then is the need of a video recording?

In his dissenting judgment, Lord Mustill took a quite different approach. His starting point was as follows:

> I ask myself, not whether as a result of the decision in this appeal, activities such as those of the appellants should *cease* to be criminal, but rather whether the Act of 1861 (a statute which I venture to repeat once again was clearly intended to penalise conduct of a quite different nature) should in this new situation be interpreted so as to *make* it criminal [...]

In other words, Lord Mustill started from the assumption that sado-masochism is a lawful activity and asked whether there are policy and public interest reasons to make it unlawful. This is the opposite of the majority's approach. It has been described as a 'social disutility' model: deliberately causing ABH/GBH/wounding will only be unlawful if it causes social disutility. We will soon consider which is best: the majority's social utility model or Lord Mustill's social disutility model.

Having set out his starting point, Lord Mustill then explained why he felt policy and public interest reasons did not require sado-masochism to be an unlawful activity.

EXTRACT

Read the following extract from Lord Mustill's judgment and make a list of the reasons he gave for deciding that policy and public interest considerations did not require sado-masochism to be an unlawful activity.

Look back at the principles we studied in Chapter 1. Try and match each of the reasons given by Lord Mustill to at least one of the principles from Chapter 1.

R v *Brown* [1994] 1 AC 212

Lord Mustill

Leaving aside repugnance and moral objection, both of which are entirely natural but neither of which are in my opinion grounds upon which the court could properly create a new crime, I can visualise only the following reasons.

1. Some of the practices obviously created a risk of genito-urinary infection, and others of septicaemia. These might indeed have been grave in former times, but the risk of serious harm must surely have been greatly reduced by modern medical science.
2. The possibility that matters might get out of hand, with grave results. It has been acknowledged throughout the present proceedings that the appellants' activities were performed as a pre-arranged ritual, which at the same time enhanced their excitement and minimised the risk that the infliction of injury would go too far. Of course things might go wrong and really serious injury or death might ensue. If this happened, those responsible would be punished according to the ordinary law, in the same way as those who kill or injure in the course of more ordinary sexual activities are regularly punished. But to penalise the appellants' conduct even if the extreme consequences do not ensue, just because they might have done so would require an assessment of the degree of risk, and the balancing of this risk against the interests of individual freedom. Such a balancing is in my opinion for Parliament, not the courts […]
3. I would give the same answer to the suggestion that these activities involved a risk of accelerating the spread of auto-immune deficiency syndrome [AIDS], and that they should be brought within the Act of 1861 in the interests of public health. The consequence would be strange, since what is currently the principal cause for the transmission of this scourge, namely consenting buggery between males, is now legal. Nevertheless, I would have been compelled to give this proposition the most anxious consideration if there had been any evidence to support it. But there is none, since the case for the respondent was advanced on an entirely different ground.
4. There remains an argument to which I have given much greater weight. As the evidence in the present case has shown, there is a risk that strangers (and especially young strangers) may be drawn into these activities at an early age and will then become established in them for life. This is indeed a disturbing prospect, but I have come to the conclusion that it is not a sufficient

ground for declaring these activities to be criminal under the Act of 1861. The element of the corruption of youth is already catered for by the existing legislation; and if there is a gap in it which needs to be filled the remedy surely lies in the hands of Parliament, not in the application of a statute which is aimed at other forms of wrongdoing. As regards proselytisation for adult sado-masochism the argument appears to me circular. For if the activity is not itself so much against the public interest that it ought to be declared criminal under the Act of 1861 then the risk that others will be induced to join in cannot be a ground for making it criminal.

Leaving aside the logic of this answer, which seems to me impregnable, plain humanity demands that a court addressing the criminality of conduct such as that of the present should recognise and respond to the profound dismay which all members of the community share about the apparent increase of cruel and senseless crimes against the defenceless. Whilst doing so I must repeat for the last time that in the answer which I propose I do not advocate the decriminalisation of conduct which has hitherto been a crime; nor do I rebut a submission that a new crime should be created, penalising this conduct, for Mr. Purnell has rightly not invited the House to take this course. The only question is whether these consensual private acts are offences against the existing law of violence. To this question I return a negative response.

[The defendants in *R* v *Brown* pursued their case to the European Court of Human Rights. The Court unanimously held that there had been no violation of the men's Article 8 right to respect for their private lives: see *Laskey* v *UK* (1997) 24 EHRR 39.]

As your list of reasons and principles should illustrate, *R* v *Brown* is a stark example of how people can hold very different views on the role and function of the criminal law. Principles like social welfare, legal paternalism and legal moralism can sometimes conflict very sharply with principles like individual autonomy.

The case also raises questions about the principle of legality: more specifically, whether the decision operated retrospectively.

Now, think about these questions.

A. Imagine that on the day before the defendants in *R* v *Brown* were arrested someone had asked you whether their activities were criminal. What would you have said? To put the previous question slightly differently, which of the following statements would you agree with?

1. The defendants' activities were criminal from the day the Offences Against the Person Act 1861 became law. The House of Lords in *R* v *Brown* were simply explaining and applying the meaning that the statute had had for over 100 years.
2. Before the House of Lords' decision in *R* v *Brown* it was uncertain whether the defendants' activities were criminal or not. The House of Lords decided that it should be a crime to deliberately inflict ABH/GBH/wounding in the course of sado-masochism and then applied this decision to the defendants.

B. If you thought statement 2 was more plausible than statement 1, this suggests that the House of Lords effectively criminalised the defendants' conduct and applied this decision retrospectively.

1. Is this defensible?
2. Could it be justified on the basis that it was a reasonably foreseeable development of the law (see Chapter 1)?

c. Sado-masochism: other case law

It is immaterial that the defendants in *R* v *Brown* were homosexual; heterosexual sado-masochism that deliberately causes ABH/GBH/wounding is also an unlawful activity. In *R* v *Emmett* (*The Times* 15 October 1999) the defendant, Stephen Emmett, and his girlfriend, the victim, cohabited. During sexual activity Emmett tied his girlfriend up, put a plastic bag over her head and tied it around her neck, and then performed oral sex on her. When he became aware that she was distressed he pulled the bag off her head. It is probable that she lost consciousness. Her eyes became bloodshot, so she went to see her doctor. The doctor found haemorrhages in both her eyes and bruising around her neck. No treatment was prescribed, and after a week her eyes returned to normal. A few weeks later, again during sexual activity, Emmett poured lighter fuel on his girlfriend's breasts and set light to it. She suffered a burn measuring 6 cm by 4 cm. The burn became infected, so she went to see her doctor again. In fact the burn healed fully without any scarring, but the doctor was so alarmed by these two visits that he contacted the police. Emmett was arrested and charged with assault occasioning ABH. At trial Emmett was convicted following a ruling by the trial judge that the pair were engaged in an unlawful activity and so his girlfriend's consent was not available as a defence. Emmett's appeal against conviction was dismissed by the Court of Appeal. Pointing to the degree of harm Emmett's girlfriend suffered, and the degree of unpredictability and potential harm, the Court held that the pair had been engaged in an unlawful activity.

So, *R* v *Brown* and *R* v *Emmett* make it clear that if a defendant deliberately causes a victim ABH/GBH/wounding during sado-masochistic sexual activity he will not be able to rely on the victim's consent as a defence. This has now been codified by section 71 of the Domestic Abuse Act 2021, which states that the consent of the victim is not available as a defence to the offences in section 18, 20 and 47 of the OAPA if the harm was inflicted 'for the purposes of obtaining sexual gratification'. This applies whether the harm was inflicted for the sexual gratification of the defendant, victim or some other person.

Before moving on, let's consider two more, slightly different, scenarios.

1. Valentina consents to Romeo spanking her for sexual pleasure. Valentina suffers some bruising which is serious enough to amount to ABH, but the prosecution decides to only charge Romeo with battery.[14]

   - Can Romeo rely on Valentina's consent as a defence?

Although there is a case *R* v *Donovan* [1934] 2 KB 496 which suggests Romeo could not rely on Valentina's consent as a defence, it must now be read in the light of the judgments in *R* v *Brown*. In *R* v *Brown* the House of Lords stated quite clearly that a victim's consent is always available as a defence on a charge of assault or battery. So Romeo would be able to rely on Valentina's consent as a defence to a charge of battery. Had he been charged with assault occasioning ABH he would not have been able to rely on Valentina's consent as a defence, since deliberately injuring someone for sexual pleasure is an unlawful activity.

[14] This situation is based on the case *R* v *Donovan* [1934] 2 KB 498. Donovan consensually caned a 17-year-old for sexual gratification.

2. Romeo and Valentina engage in sexual activity with no intention of causing ABH/GBH/wounding, and no idea that ABH/GBH/wounding might result. Unfortunately, however, Valentina does suffer ABH and Romeo is charged with assault occasioning ABH.[15]

- Can Romeo rely on Valentina's consent as a defence?

In this scenario, the harm was not inflicted for the purpose of sexual gratification. This means that section 71 of the Domestic Abuse Act 2021 would not apply, and that the activities were not sado-masochistic. So, Romeo and Valentina were engaged in sexual intercourse, not sado-masochism. Since sexual intercourse is a lawful activity, the consent of the victim is available as a defence and so Romeo would not be guilty of assault occasioning ABH.

d. Body modification

A further unlawful activity is body modification. This is to be distinguished from tattooing and ear piercing. As we'll see shortly, tattooing and ear piercing are lawful activities that are subject to a regulatory regime (meaning that they can only be conducted in registered premises by registered practitioners). But body modification is unregulated, meaning that those who practice it need no particular training or qualification.

In *R* v *BM* [2018] EWCA Crim 560 the defendant was a tattooist and body piercer who also offered body modification services. The case concerned procedures performed on three customers. The first customer was Ezechiel Lott. The defendant removed Ezechiel Lott's left ear. The second customer had a nipple removed. And the third customer had her tongue split so that it looked reptile-like. All three procedures were consensual and all three were performed without anaesthetic. The defendant, who had attended some short courses on body modification but had no medical qualifications, was charged with three counts of wounding with intent to cause GBH. A preparatory hearing was held before the start of the trial, at which the trial judge said (in reliance on *R* v *Brown*) that the consent of the customers was not available as a defence. The defendant appealed against this ruling.

At the preparatory hearing two experts had described the risks involved in these procedures. Removal of the ear can cause the ear canal to close, which is difficult to correct surgically. Since the facial nerve is located close to the ear there is also a risk of facial paralysis. Splitting the tongue also carries particular risks. The mouth is a dirty environment and hard to keep sterile, so there is a risk of infection. A forked tongue also has an adverse impact on speech and feeding. The experts stated that a plastic surgeon would not perform any of these three procedures for purely aesthetic reasons. A surgeon whose patient requested extreme cosmetic surgery would also be alert to the possibility of Body Dysmorphic Disorder and consider a referral to a psychiatrist or psychologist.

At the appeal defence counsel argued that the personal autonomy of the customers should be respected. He also argued that the procedures in this case should be regarded as akin to body adornment. Tattooing and ear piercing are both regarded as lawful activities and body modification is a natural extension of these. In contrast, the prosecutor argued that these procedures were, in truth, cosmetic surgery, carrying adverse physiological consequences and involving significant risk. There was, he argued, no public interest in making them lawful.

[15] This situation is based on the case *R* v *Meachen* [2006] EWCA Crim 2414. In this case the victim suffered serious anal injuries. The defendant claimed that the cause of the injuries was him inserting his fingers into the victim's anus with her consent.

The Court of Appeal examined the House of Lords' judgment in *R* v *Brown*. Burnett LCJ stated that neither Lord Mustill nor Lord Slynn (the two dissenting Law Lords in *R* v *Brown*) 'accepted that consent could provide a defence for consensual violence causing really serious bodily harm. Each would have allowed the appeal because the charges were for causing actual bodily harm or wounding, not for causing grievous bodily harm' ([32]). He then discussed the arguments of the prosecution and defence in this case.

EXTRACT

Read the following extract from the judgment of Burnett LCJ.

What are the two features that Burnett LCJ said underpin almost all of the existing lawful activities? In his view, may the Courts add new activities to the existing list of lawful activities?

What was the Court of Appeal's response to defence counsel's argument that: (a) the personal autonomy of the customers should be respected; and (b) the procedures were akin to body adornment?

According to the Court of Appeal, what were the public interest reasons against making body modification a lawful activity?

R v *BM* [2018] EWCA Crim 560

Burnett LCJ

39 [T]he most that might be said about the [lawful activities] is that they represent a balance struck by the judges to reflect a series of different interests. There is a general interest of society in limiting the approbation of the law for significant violence, albeit inflicted with consent. There is some need to protect from themselves those who have consented, most particularly because they may be vulnerable or even mentally unwell. Moreover, serious injury, even consented to, brings with it risk of unwanted injury, disease or even death and may impose on society as a whole substantial cost. Yet there is a need to reflect the general values of society which have long accepted tattooing and piercing (not just of ears) as acceptable, along with such things as ritual circumcision, sports and the other sub-categories identified in the cases. That is not to say that each receives universal support from all sections of society, but the exceptions are so deeply embedded in our law and general culture that it would require Parliament to render such activities subject to the ordinary criminal law of assault. We have seen that Parliament has indeed intervened to provide for the regulation of activities such as tattooing, piercing and the like, and had earlier done so as regards children: Tattooing of Minors Act 1969.

40 Whilst the exceptions are incapable of being accommodated within any universally stated test, there are two features which may be thought to underpin almost all of them. First, they may produce discernible social benefit. That is true of the sporting exceptions and may even be true of boxing or "dangerous exhibitions" as entertainment. It is possible that those with a religious hue might also be considered as conferring a social benefit, at least at the time they were recognised. But the second is that it would simply be regarded as unreasonable for the common law to criminalise the activity if engaged in with consent by (on behalf of) the injured party. That would apply to tattooing and piercing and, again, perhaps to those with a religious hue, including ritual male circumcision.

41 New exceptions should not be recognised on a case by case basis, save perhaps where there is a close analogy with an existing exception to the general rule established in the *Brown* case. The recognition of an entirely new exception would involve a value judgement which is policy laden, and on which there may be powerful conflicting views in society. The criminal

trial process is inapt to enable a wide-ranging inquiry into the underlying policy issues, which are much better explored in the political environment.

42 That said, there is, to our minds, no proper analogy between body modification, which involves the removal of parts of the body or mutilation as seen in tongue splitting, and tattooing, piercing or other body adornment. What the defendant undertook for reward in this case was a series of medical procedures performed for no medical reason. When Lord Lane referred to "reasonable surgical interference" in the *Attorney General's Reference* case (quoted in [23] above) it carried with the implication that elective surgery would only be reasonable if carried out by someone qualified to perform it. The professional and regulatory superstructure which governs how doctors and other medical professionals practice is there to protect the public. The protections provided to patients, some of which are referred to in the medical evidence before the judge, were not available to the appellant's customers or more widely to the customers of those who set themselves up as body modifiers. It is immaterial that this appellant took some trouble to ensure a sterile environment when he operated, or that his work was in some respects tidy and clean. Consent as a defence could not turn on the quality of the work then performed.

43 The protection of the public in this context extends beyond the risks of infection, bungled or poor surgery or an inability to deal with immediate complications. Those seeking body modification of the sort we are concerned with in this appeal invited the appellant to perform irreversible surgery without anaesthetic with profound long-term consequences. The fact that a desire to have an ear or nipple removed or tongue split is incomprehensible to most, may not be sufficient in itself to raise the question whether those who seek to do so might be in need of a mental health assessment. Yet the first response in almost every other context to those who seek to harm themselves would be to suggest medical assistance. That is not to say that all who seek body modification are suffering from any identifiable mental illness but it is difficult to avoid the conclusion that some will be, and that within the cohort will be many who are vulnerable. There are good reasons why reputable medical practitioners will not remove parts of the body simply when asked by a patient. One only has to reflect on the care, degree of inquiry and support given to a patient before gender reassignment surgery can be performed to appreciate the extensive nature of the protections provided in the medical context.

44 The personal autonomy of his customers does not provide the appellant with a justification for removing body modification from the ambit of the law of assault. It is true that Mr Lott could have cut his own left ear off and in doing so would have committed no criminal offence. So too the other customers. But the personal autonomy of one individual does not extend to involving another in what would otherwise be a crime. We note that the European Court of Human Rights rejected the arguments advanced under article 8 of the Convention by the appellants in the *Brown case*, (1997) 24 EHRR 39, and remind ourselves that the level of harm engaged in that case was below really serious injury.

45 In short, we can see no good reason why body modification should be placed in a special category of exemption from the general rule that the consent of an individual to injury provides no defence to the person who inflicts that injury if the violence causes actual bodily harm or more serious injury. Even were the general rule to be revisited by Parliament or the Supreme Court and a different line drawn which allows consent to act as a defence to causing actual bodily harm and wounding, body modification causes really serious harm. Neither of the dissentient voices in the *Brown* case would have been willing to allow consent to act as a defence to causing grievous (serious) bodily harm and we note that the proposals of the Law Commission, whilst suggesting some loosening of the constraints found in *Brown*, would also not have gone that far. The appellant's argument envisages consent to surgical treatment providing a defence to the person performing the surgery whether or not that person is a suitably qualified as a doctor, and whether or not there is a medical (including psychological) justification for the surgery. Even were we attracted by the argument, which we are not, such a bold step is one that could only be taken by Parliament.

So the Court of Appeal followed the majority in *R* v *Brown* and applied the social utility model. They asked whether there was 'good reason' to place body modification in 'a special category of exemption' from the general rule that consent is not available as a defence on a charge involving ABH/GBH/wounding ([45]). Burnett LCJ rejected defence counsel's argument that the personal autonomy of the customers should be respected and that body modification of the type in this case was analogous to body adornment such as tattooing and ear piercing. Instead, he emphasised the risk of infection and the possibility that those requesting such procedures may be vulnerable and in need of medical support. He also stated that the courts should only recognise new forms of lawful activity if there is a 'close analogy' to an existing lawful activity; it is for Parliament to create 'entirely new' forms of lawful activity ([41]).

The distinction between body modification and body adornment may sometimes prove difficult to draw, as may the distinction between entirely new forms of lawful activity and activities that are closely analogous to an existing one. For example, other procedures that the defendant in *R* v *BM* offered included subdermal and transdermal implants. These involve placing an implant under or between the layers of the skin to create a raised design. Should these be regarded as body modification and an entirely new form of activity, or as a form of body adornment that is closely analogous to tattooing (which involves the insertion of ink into the skin)? Furthermore, as Laird explains in the following extract, the relationship between body modification and cosmetic surgery is also uncertain.

EXTRACT

Laird, K. (2018) 'Commentary on *R* v *BM*' *Criminal Law Review* 848

The instant case reveals yet another problem with the law as it relates to the limits of consent. It is unclear whether the body modification performed by the defendant was unlawful because he was not qualified to perform it, or whether it was inherently unlawful because of its grave nature (i.e. it was irreversible and effected significant physical changes to the body). The court's description of the potentially debilitating consequences of the procedures performed by the defendant would suggest the latter, whereas its description of the professional and regulatory superstructure which governs how doctors and other medical professionals practise suggests the former. This question has practical implications. To take an example, it is now unclear whether a cosmetic surgeon who removed one of his or her patient's nipples for purely aesthetic reasons would commit a criminal offence. Even though the surgeon may have been qualified to perform the procedure, the Court of Appeal's reasoning does not reveal whether the patient's consent would be valid or whether such "body modification", by its very nature, cannot be consented to in the absence of legislative intervention . . . The potential for uncertainty is exacerbated by the fact the Court of Appeal did not engage with the meaning of the term "body modification" and how it differs from cosmetic surgery. If the court understood this term to mean medical procedures that are performed without any therapeutic benefit, then it should have made this clear. As has already been pointed out, however, the same description could apply to more mainstream forms of cosmetic surgery. As a result of the Court of Appeal's judgment, a broad spectrum of what had hitherto been considered lawful conduct may now be criminal. Responsibility for this state of affairs lies not necessarily with the court, however, but with the policymakers who have made little effort to regulate body modification. As the Lord Chief Justice recognised, body modification, unlike tattooing and piercing, is unregulated and those who practice it require no particular training or qualifications.

In the following extract, Samantha Pegg discusses the Court of Appeal's statement that there was 'no good reason' ([45]) why body modification should be classified as a lawful activity.

EXTRACT

According to Pegg, why might the judgment in *R* v *BM* fail to protect those seeking body modification services?

Pegg offers two objections to the link Burnett LCJ appeared to draw between undergoing body modification procedures and mental illness. What are these objections? What questions does Pegg say the judgment in *R* v *BM* leaves unanswered?

Pegg, S. (2019) 'Not So Clear Cut: The Lawfulness of Body Modifications' *Criminal Law Review* 579

As noted, tattooists and piercers are required to submit to regulation and monitoring to ensure that the requisite standards of hygiene and safety are maintained, and procedures performed in these premises benefit from this licensing regime. The Law Commission, considering this issue in its 1995 Consultation Paper, noted that the respondents to that consultation had warned that if procedures were to take place otherwise than in licenced premises they may be performed in unhygienic conditions, that inappropriate and dangerous equipment may be used and there would, resultantly, be a risk of HIV infection. If the court in *BM* was seeking to protect putative victims of body modifications from injury, disease and death then declaring these practices unlawful is likely to do little other than, as those same respondents to the Law Commission had advised, drive these practices underground. The physical dangers that so occupied the court could perhaps be more effectively countered by following those models established for tattooing and piercing, where local governance provides a framework within which practitioners effectively self-regulate.

[. . .]

Characterising body modification procedures as surgical procedures also led Lord Burnett CJ to an a priori assumption that additional safeguards—not available to the clients of body modifiers—should be in place to protect those seeking out body modifications . . . As part of pre-operative assessment, surgeons undertaking cosmetic procedures may require patients to undergo a psychological assessment to identify conditions such as body dysmorphic disorder but, as the court recognised, a psychiatric assessment is not mandated for all cosmetic procedures. Adults who are mentally ill are also free to have tattoos and piercings without inquiries being made into their state of mind, however ill-advised those procedures may be. Many people may question the wisdom of having a large facial tattoo but, if a customer requests such, a tattooist is not obliged to refer that client for psychological assessment. There is no sound rationale for protecting individuals from the harm a tongue split may cause when the law tolerates the lawful application of a facial tattoo which poses a risk of not only physical harm, but social stigma.

Several references were made to mental illness in this relatively short decision. In one portion, the court appeared to equate the desire to undergo body modification procedures with—at least in some incidences—mental illness . . . Two objections can be made to this line of reasoning. First, his Lordship assumes that those seeking body modifications are looking to "harm themselves". This reasoning axiomatically distances body modification procedures from piercing and tattooing—procedures which are viewed, in law, as decorative rather than intrinsically harmful. On the face of it this is an odd distinction to make; tattoos and piercings cause bodily harm and are no more medically warranted than a tongue split or a nipple removal. The real crux of the court's argument was that these modification procedures would be "incomprehensible to most"—that there were no strong public policy arguments for exempting them from the general rule.

Yet, there was no real consideration by Lord Burnett CJ of how prevalent or well-practised body modification procedures are; the court took for granted that these were marginal activities. When *Brown* was decided, body piercing was considered a subcultural practice, yet in 2008 Bone et al put the prevalence of body piercing at 10 per cent of the population. More specifically the proportion of 16 to 24 year olds with a tongue piercing was 6.5 per cent and a lip piercing 2.7 per cent and it is likely these percentages have now increased. It is of course difficult to say how widespread more extreme body modifications are in the current population, many modifications will be hidden from public view and there are no figures on their prevalence in England and Wales. It is reasonable to assume that modifiers offer these services as there is a market for them, and that they are more widespread than the court had appreciated.

Secondly—and of more importance in any legal analysis—Lord Burnett CJ appeared to be putting the cart before the horse in his examination of capacity. The ability to give valid consent should not be a decisive matter in any consideration of whether an activity should be exempted from the general rule. Instead it should go to the quite separate question of whether a particular individual, on a particular day has the capacity to give consent. Mental illness may mean that an individual is not capable of giving valid consent, and their professed consent would not then negate liability. Inferring that those who seek out bodily modifications may be mentally ill is, however, not a sound rationale on which to exclude modifications from the class of activities to which one may consent. The law does not typically take such a broad-brush approach to limiting autonomy. Activities have not previously been excluded on the basis that, if we do not exclude them, then those who are mentally ill or otherwise vulnerable may participate in that activity. Dangerous sports and cosmetic surgery are activities that those who are mentally ill and/or vulnerable can engage in to their physical detriment, but we trust that their governing bodies will self-regulate.

[…]

The judgment in *BM* also leaves a number of questions unanswered. The court was tasked with addressing whether consent provided a defence against charges of causing grievous bodily harm with intent, yet it gave no indication that it was restricting its comments solely to procedures intended to cause serious harm. Due to the nature of the procedures performed by the appellant the court's discussion was necessarily focussed on injuries which were serious and irreversible, those which involved the removal or mutilation of body parts and, in light of that analysis, it is unsurprising Lord Burnett CJ concluded "body modification causes really serious harm". However, this is a sweeping generalisation which does not take into account that several popular modification procedures—including transdermal and subdermal implants, scarification and branding—may result in less serious harm. Are these procedures then unlawful to perform even with client consent?

The severity and irreversibility of the injuries in *BM* may have prompted the decision to prosecute, but the majority of the House in *Brown* drew no distinction between how the defence of consent operates for injuries which amount to actual bodily harm and those which amount to grievous bodily harm, relying instead on the category-based exceptions to supply the necessary defence. In *BM*, Lord Burnett CJ gave thoughtful consideration to the opinions of the minority in *Brown*, noting that Lords Mustill and Slynn would have accepted a defence in *Brown* for actual bodily harm or wounding, but not for more serious injury. His appraisal suggests that the courts may be more accommodating of those body modification procedures that result in less serious harm, but it fails to provide any definitive statement of the law.

Now, think about this question.

How would you argue that the following are: (a) lawful activities; and (b) unlawful activities?

- Subdermal and transdermal implants
- The removal of a nipple, by a qualified cosmetic surgeon, for purely aesthetic reasons

e. Scarification

The final activity that we need to look at is scarification, including branding and carving. As we will see, the legal position on scarification is not entirely clear. As Pegg explained in the extract above, scarification typically involves a lesser degree of harm than the modification procedures in *R* v *BM*. It has been considered in two Court of Appeal cases. The first of these – *R* v *Wilson* [1997] QB 47 – involved branding.

One day the victim, a woman of 'mature years' named Julie Wilson, went to her husband Alan and asked him to tattoo his name on her breasts. Alan explained that he 'didn't know how to do a tattoo'. Julie replied, 'Well, there must be some way. If you can't do a tattoo, there must be some way [...] I'm not scared of anybody knowing that I love you enough to have your name on my body.' They talked about it some more, and then 'hit on this idea of using a hot knife on her bum'. So Alan heated up a knife and branded a 'W' on Julie's right buttock. A few days later he finished the job and branded an 'A' on her left buttock. He told police, 'It wasn't life threatening, it wasn't anything, it was done for love. She loved me. She wanted me to [...] put my name on her body.' Alan was convicted at trial of assault occasioning ABH. He appealed against his conviction, arguing that Julie's consent should be available to him as a defence.

This case came a couple of years after *R* v *Brown*. Since Julie suffered ABH the fact that she consented was only available as a defence if the injuries occurred in the course of a lawful activity. Applying the approach of the majority in *R* v *Brown*, the activity should be presumed to be unlawful and good policy and public interest reasons should be shown for the activity to be classified as lawful. This was the difficulty facing Alan Wilson. What were the good policy and public interest reasons that required branding to be lawful?

In spite of this difficulty, the Court of Appeal allowed Alan Wilson's appeal and quashed the conviction. A number of commentators have questioned whether the Court's reasoning can be reconciled with the House of Lords' judgment in *R* v *Brown*.

ACTIVITY

Earlier we saw the different underlying approaches of the majority and Lord Mustill in *R* v *Brown* (the social utility and social disutility models).

According to the doctrine of precedent, should the Court of Appeal in *R* v *Wilson* have applied the social utility model or the social disutility model?

EXTRACT

Read the following extract from the judgment of Russell LJ in *R* v *Wilson*.

- Did he apply the social utility or social disutility model? (Hint: the clearest indication can be found in the final paragraph.)
- Make a list of the reasons Russell LJ gave for saying that *R* v *Brown* and *R* v *Wilson* are distinguishable.

R v *Wilson* [1997] QB 47

Russell LJ

We are abundantly satisfied that there is no factual comparison to be made between the instant case and the facts of either *Rex v. Donovan* [1934] 2 K.B. 498 or *Reg. v. Brown* [1994] 1 A.C. 212: Mrs. Wilson not only consented to that which the appellant did, she instigated it. There was no aggressive intent on the part of the appellant. On the contrary, far from wishing to cause injury to his wife, the appellant's desire was to assist her in what she regarded as the acquisition of a desirable piece of personal adornment, perhaps in this day and age no less understandable than the piercing of nostrils or even tongues for the purposes of inserting decorative jewellery.

In our judgment *Reg. v. Brown* is not authority for the proposition that consent is no defence to a charge under section 47 of the Act of 1861, in all circumstances where actual bodily harm is deliberately inflicted. It is to be observed that the question certified for their Lordships in *Reg. v. Brown* related only to a "sado-masochistic encounter." However, their Lordships recognised in the course of their speeches, that it is necessary that there must be exceptions to what is no more than a general proposition. The speeches of Lord Templeman, at p. 231, Lord Jauncey of Tullichettle, at p. 245, and the dissenting speech of Lord Slynn of Hadley, at p. 277, all refer to tattooing as being an activity which, if carried out with the consent of an adult, does not involve an offence under section 47, albeit that actual bodily harm is deliberately inflicted.

For our part, we cannot detect any logical difference between what the appellant did and what he might have done in the way of tattooing [...] The latter activity apparently requires no state authorisation, and the appellant was as free to engage in it as anyone else. We do not think that we are entitled to assume that the method adopted by the appellant and his wife was any more dangerous or painful than tattooing. There was simply no evidence to assist the court on this aspect of the matter.

Does public policy or the public interest demand that the appellant's activity should be visited by the sanctions of the criminal law? The majority in *Reg. v. Brown* clearly took the view that such considerations were relevant. If that is so, then we are firmly of the opinion that it is not in the public interest that activities such as the appellant's in this appeal should amount to criminal behaviour. Consensual activity between husband and wife, in the privacy of the matrimonial home, is not, in our judgment, normally a proper matter for criminal investigation, let alone criminal prosecution [...]

Each of the reasons Russell LJ gave for distinguishing *R* v *Brown* has been carefully scrutinised by Paul Roberts in his case note 'Consent To Injury: How Far Can You Go?' (1997) 113 *Law Quarterly Review* 27. First, Roberts discusses the significance of the fact that Julie Wilson instigated the branding and Russell LJ's statement that Alan Wilson lacked any 'aggressive intent'.

EXTRACT

Roberts, P. (1997) 'Consent to Injury: How far can you go?' 113 *Law Quarterly Review* 27

That "an aggressive element" or "hostility" is in law an essential ingredient of an assault was an argument pressed by the appellants in *Brown*, and, in substance, unequivocally rejected by the House (Lord Jauncey of Tullichettle at p. 244; Lord Lowry at p. 254; Lord Mustill at pp. 260–261; Lord Slynn of Hadley at p. 280). Russell L.J.'s assertion that the facts of *Brown* were "truly extreme" is also problematic. Although the *Brown* appellants' idea of recreation might strike many people as bizarre or disgusting, the agreed facts, as they appear from the judgment of Lord Jauncey, were that "the receivers ["victims"] had neither complained to the police nor suffered any permanent injury as a result of the activities of the appellants" (p. 238). Mrs Wilson's scar tissue was, if anything, greater and more permanent disfigurement than any of the excruciating but temporary discomforts inflicted and suffered by the *Brown* defendants; although none of the injuries in either case could properly be described as "serious". What of Russell L.J.'s reliance on the fact that Mrs Wilson herself asked to be branded rather than merely agreeing to it? The question of which participants actually instigated the acts causing injury was not explored in *Brown*, but it is difficult to see how a distinction between instigation and consent could form the basis of a defensible or even workable boundary between lawful and criminal conduct. Victim-precipitation is usually irrelevant to criminal liability, which turns on whether or not the conduct in question is prohibited, not on whether the victim "asked for it". If the "victim's" consent is no answer to criminal liability for causing injury, his or her "instigation" is no answer either; except to expose the victim to possible prosecution for incitement or as an accomplice. Moreover it seems that the facts as well as the law are against [the instigation argument]. Responses to the Law Commission's consultation paper *Consent and Offences Against the Person* (1994) suggest that the sadomasochistic encounters in the *Brown* litigation were more than likely instigated and controlled by the apparently submissive partner, much as Mrs Wilson invited her husband to sign his name on her body (see Law Com. C.P. No. 139, *Consent in the Criminal Law* (1995) para. 10.32). There are no grounds to distinguish *Wilson* from *Brown* here.

Next, Roberts considers Russell LJ's comment that Alan Wilson's motive was to help his wife acquire what she regarded as 'a desirable piece of personal adornment':

EXTRACT

Roberts, P. (1997) 'Consent to Injury: How far can you go?' 113 *Law Quarterly Review* 27

Nor do Russell L.J.'s references to the defendant's "wishes" and "desires" [. . .], although faithful to the agreed facts, appear to take the Court of Appeal's argument much further. It is well established that "desire" is not to be equated with the "intent" required to prove *mens rea* (*R. v. Moloney* [1985] 1 A.C. 905, at p. 926), and, as the House of Lords recently and emphatically reaffirmed in *R. v. Kingston* [1995] 2 A.C. 355, the defendant's motive is usually irrelevant to his criminal liability. If the defendant did the prohibited act in one of the specified mental states and without a recognised defence, that is enough to establish legal guilt, no matter how innocuous or even laudable his motivation. Mr Wilson, on his own admission, intentionally burned his initials into his wife's flesh with a hot knife. In the absence of a valid "defence" of consent (either a true "defence" or a negation of liability), that admission is sufficient proof that Mr Wilson committed assault occasioning actual bodily harm.

Roberts then examines the analogy Russell LJ drew between Alan Wilson's actions and tattooing.

EXTRACT

Roberts, P. (1997) 'Consent to Injury: How far can you go?' 113 *Law Quarterly Review* 27

It is true that [in *R* v *Brown*] Lord Templeman and Lord Slynn accepted the legality of tattooing, although without argument and without citing any authority [. . .] It also seems reasonable to speculate that the pains and dangers incident to amateur branding are not too dissimilar to those inflicted by the amateur tattooist, although, as Russell L.J. himself observed, "there was simply no evidence to assist the court on this aspect of the matter" (p. 128b) [. . .] But even this narrow point fails to establish a truly satisfactory foundation for the court's decision in *Wilson* [. . .]

Two points need to be emphasised. First, by setting up a general proposition, hinting at an open list of exceptions, yet failing to specify what they are, *Brown* left the law in a state of considerable uncertainty. At a stroke, an extremely diverse range of injury-causing activities became presumptively unlawful, at least until the courts should determine otherwise. But many of these activities had hitherto been conducted beyond the law's gaze and it is far from easy to predict how the courts will judge them when they fall to be scrutinised. As the Law Commission has recently observed, "The less common minority practices of branding and scarification, which carry considerable risks if not carried out by skilled people in proper safe and hygienic conditions, fall into a grey area which the common law and statute have hardly touched" (*Consent in the Criminal Law*, para. 9.1). The second point to note is that, when it came to creating new exceptions to the general liability rule, the House of Lords in *Brown* declined to make "logical" connections between the defendants' behaviour and lawful forms of body decoration. For although the activities of the *Brown* defendants could arguably be described as "tattooing" and "piercing", or at least as close analogies to these lawful practices, the House recoiled from creating any exception for the particular forms of consensual injury confronting them on that occasion. Lord Jauncey sardonically remarked at p. 246f-g that:

> "If it is to be decided that such activities as the nailing by A of B's foreskin or scrotum to a board or the insertion of hot wax into C's urethra followed by the burning of his penis with a candle or the incising of D's scrotum with a scalpel to the effusion of blood are injurious neither to B, C and D nor to the public interest then it is for Parliament with its accumulated wisdom and sources of information to declare them to be lawful."

It therefore seems pertinent to ask whether their Lordships would have looked any more favourably on the activities of amateur branders such as Mr Wilson; and this must be open to doubt. The majority in *Brown* took the view, most clearly expressed by Lord Lowry, that "[a] proposed *general* exemption is to be tested by considering the likely *general* effect" (p. 255h). In deciding against creating an exception to the general liability rule their Lordships consequently took into account the possibility that sadomasochistic encounters might get out of hand, that serious injuries might result, that disease and infection might spread, and that practitioners might corrupt the young and impressionable. Lord Jauncey candidly admitted that "your Lordships have no information as to whether such situations have occurred in relation to other sado-masochistic practitioners" (p. 246b), but the majority preferred to err on the side of caution: "[w]hen considering the public interest potential for harm is just as relevant as actual harm" (p. 246c).

Now these arguments could equally well apply to Mr Wilson's exploits.

Lastly, Roberts examines Russell LJ's underlying approach:

EXTRACT

Roberts, P. (1997) 'Consent to Injury: How far can you go?' 113 *Law Quarterly Review* 27

Russell L.J. correctly observed that in *Brown* their Lordships had regard to "public policy" and to "the public interest" in order to determine the legal status of consensually inflicted injury. From this, the Court of Appeal deduced that the crucial question is: "Does public policy or the public interest demand that the appellant's activity should be visited by the sanctions of the criminal law?" In other words, the court began with a presumption of legality and looked for reasons to extend the criminal law to the appellant's activities. In view of the appellant's and his wife's weighty interests in keeping their private lives private, and in the absence of any evidence to suggest that Mrs Wilson actually objected to being branded, Russell L.J. could find no such reasons. The court refused to speculate about the potential for amateur branding to be excessively painful or unpredictably dangerous, since such contingencies did not arise on the facts.

[...]

But this proposition, invoking a presumption of legality in favour of consensual injury, directly contradicts the majority's decision in *Brown* and must therefore be considered *per incuriam*. It propounds the same approach to the relationship between consent and criminal liability that animates Lord Mustill's dissent in *Brown*. Lord Mustill embraced a minimalist principle of criminalization according to which "the state should interfere with the rights of an individual to live his or her life as he or she may choose no more than is necessary to ensure a proper balance between the special interests of the individual and the general interests of the individuals who together comprise the populace at large" (p. 273e-f). His Lordship explicitly observed that his dissenting conclusion flowed from his fundamental disagreement with the majority's approach to determining the proper shape and content of the criminal law: "... if the question were differently stated it might well yield a different answer.... Thus, if I had begun from the same point of departure as my noble and learned friend, Lord Jauncey of Tullichettle, I would have arrived at a similar conclusion; but differing from him on the present state of the law, I venture to differ" (pp. 273, 274). The *Brown* majority rejected Lord Mustill's approach, founded on the value of individual autonomy, preferring instead to adopt a general rule that "the infliction of actual or more serious bodily harm is an unlawful activity to which consent is no answer" (*per* Lord Jauncey, at p. 245), subject, as we have observed, to an open and ill-defined list of exceptions. Russell L.J.'s [approach] would therefore have placed him in the dissenting minority in *Brown*.

[...]

None of the above is intended to cast any doubt on the good sense of Russell L.J.'s judgment, nor on its strong foundation in principle; only its legality is denied. Beyond its ephemeral voyeuristic and entertainment value, *Wilson* is an unremarkable case, but it does valuable service by demonstrating that *Brown* was a regrettable decision that has become an unsatisfactory precedent. In an area of the criminal law which bears upon such controversial subjects as surgical intervention, contact sports (-including boxing), dangerous exhibitions, and traditional religious practices such as circumcision, as well as the minority sexual practices and tattooing and scarification which arose respectively in *Brown* and *Wilson*, it is inconceivable that the Court of Appeal, much less prosecutors and first instance judges, will be able to turn a blind eye to the leading case indefinitely. Nor should they have to. The criminal law is seriously defective when the Court of Appeal feels obliged to go as far as it did in *Wilson* in taking liberties with their Lordships' decisions so that common sense and justice can prevail. The House of Lords will surely have to reconsider *Brown* before too long, and one suspects that Russell L.J. will be amongst those hoping that Lord Mustill gets to write the majority judgment next time.

ACTIVITY

Look back at your list of the reasons Russell LJ gave in *R* v *Wilson* for distinguishing *R* v *Brown*. In the light of Roberts' comments, do you believe the two cases are distinguishable?

The judgment in *R* v *Wilson* was discussed in the second of our scarification cases. This case – *R* v *Hobday* [2025] EWCA Crim 46 – involved cutting. The defendant, Martin Hobday, met the 17-year-old victim outside a bar. She asked him for some speed. Shortly afterwards, they went to Hobday's home and engaged in sexual activity. The victim then started to carve Hobday's initial into her own buttock, using a Stanley knife she found on the windowsill. She asked him to finish it, which he did. Then she asked him to make it bleed more, which he refused.

At trial, the trial judge distinguished *R* v *Wilson* and ruled that Hobday and the victim had been engaged in an unlawful activity. Hobday was therefore convicted of assault occasioning ABH. He appealed against his conviction, saying that the trial judge's ruling had been incorrect.

EXTRACT

Read the following extract from the judgment of Edis LJ in R v Hobday.

The trial judge in Hobday's case distinguished *R* v *Wilson*, saying that Hobday and the victim were not married, nor were they in a loving relationship. According to Edis LJ, was this a valid basis on which to distinguish *R* v *Wilson*?

In the earlier extract from Lord Templeman's judgment in *R* v *Brown*, you may have noticed that one of the victims in that case had been branded on two occasions. Edis LJ refers to this in [40]. What principle does he derive from it?

According to Edis LJ, should the Courts take into account the public interest when deciding whether a consensual activity should be lawful or unlawful? If not, when might judges consider the public interest?

In the light of *R* v *Hobday*, does *R* v *Wilson* still have any precedential value? If so, what principle(s) can we derive from *R* v *Wilson*?

R v *Hobday* [2025] EWCA Crim 46

Edis LJ

32. It is quite correct that the majority in the House of Lords in *Brown* clearly took the view that there was a role for public policy in deciding whether sado-masochistic sexual activity in which actual bodily harm was intended should thereafter be recognised as one of the exceptions to the general rule. However, the House did not attach any relevance to the nature of the relationship between the alleged offender and the proposed victim, going beyond their part in the conduct. The proposition that conduct which would be criminal in other circumstances is not so where the alleged offender and the proposed victim are married to each other is not one which can be sustained as a rule of the criminal law.

33. We suggest that nearly 30 years after *Wilson* there would now be much less enthusiasm for deterring police investigation of possible criminal activity on the ground that the parties were in a domestic relationship with each other. The new offence of coercive and controlling behaviour and modern approaches to domestic abuse would be significantly undermined were the police to adopt the approach suggested by the court in *Wilson*. [...] *Wilson* is no doubt correct is in its assertion that a prosecutor must consider not only whether there is a realistic prospect of conviction but also whether a prosecution is in the public interest. It is also correct in its implied proposition that, although consent is not a defence to an offence contrary to section 47 of the Offences Against the Person Act 1861 except where the conduct is a recognised exception to the rule, it is plainly highly relevant to sentence.

[...]

39. The real basis of this appeal is that the judge ought to have applied the decision in *Wilson* to the facts of this case and should have directed the jury that consent was a defence. In our judgment he was quite right not to do so.

40. First, we consider that *Wilson* should be treated as a case where the court decided that, on its particular facts, the conduct of Mr. Wilson should have been treated as closely analogous to tattooing. Tattooing is the infiltration of ink into the surface of the skin and is required by law to be carried out in registered premises if done in the course of a business. It does not involve branding. Branding was referred to in *Brown* as one of the activities of the defendants which the decision in *Brown* rendered unlawful: see [25] and [26] above. The

decision in *Wilson* is, therefore, hard to justify as an application of the rule in *Brown*. It would, therefore, be even harder to describe a further extension of the decision in *Wilson* as a close analogy with an exception in *Brown*.

41. Secondly, the approach in *Wilson* was, by implication, not followed in BM. The court in *Wilson* considered that the law should develop on a case by case basis "in our changing times" and no doubt understood that that is what it was doing. *BM* at [41] rejects this approach, "save perhaps where there is a close analogy with an existing exception to the general rule established in *R* v *Brown (Anthony)*." In this respect *BM* is plainly to be preferred. The suggestions in *Boyea* and *Wilson* that judges in the Court of Appeal Criminal Division are able to assess the relevant considerations would, if followed, lead to uncertainty in the law. The law as established in Brown and explained in *BM* is clear in most respects and, if it requires changing, that is a matter for Parliament.

42. The present case is not a close analogy with an exception in Brown and, although the harm is far less grave than the harms in BM, the case is within the principle explained in BM. It follows that we are bound by those decisions to dismiss this appeal.

43. Thirdly, in any event, if we considered that we were free to decide whether cutting the skin of a young person with an unsterile Stanley knife should be a lawful activity if she consented to it, we would decide that it should not be. In BM at [43] the court said:-

"Yet the first response in almost every other context to those who seek to harm themselves would be to suggest medical assistance. That is not to say that all who seek body modification are suffering from any identifiable mental illness but it is difficult to avoid the conclusion that some will be, and that within the cohort will be many who are vulnerable."

44. Cutting the skin is a commonly encountered form of self-harm to which the young and vulnerable are particularly prone. There are good reasons why people should not be permitted to do this to others and no good reason, outside the recognised *Brown* exception of medical intervention, why they should be.

Conclusion

45. For these reasons this appeal is dismissed.

[...]

47. As we have said at [33] above, consent may not be a defence to a charge of assault but it may (on proper investigation) amount to a reason why a prosecution should not be brought in the public interest and it is very relevant to sentencing, especially in cases where the harm is not really serious.

The judgment in *R* v *Hobday* raises some important questions. The first is: where does it leave *R* v *Wilson*? Is it possible to distinguish *R v Hobday* on the basis that it involved scarification by carving, whereas *R* v *Wilson* involved scarification by branding? This seems unlikely. In *R v Wilson*, Edis LJ states that the decision in *R* v *Wilson* was based on a flawed analogy with tattooing. Tattooing, he says, 'does not involve branding' and, in any event, the House of Lords in *R* v *Brown* had listed branding as an unlawful activity ([40]). As a result, *R* v *Wilson* is 'hard to justify as an application of the rule in Brown' ([40]). This means that 'the exception for branding as personal adornment – thought to have existed since Wilson – is now in serious doubt'.[16]

The next set of questions concerns the underlying approach taken by the Court of Appeal in *R* v *Hobday*. In the following extract, Murray argues that the judgment represents a movement away from a policy-based approach to one focused on reasoning by analogy. He questions whether this succeeds in achieving its objective of making the law more certain.

[16] Murray, K. L. (2025) 'Commentary on *R* v *Hobday*' *Criminal Law Review* 349, 351.

EXTRACT

Murray, K. L. (2025) 'Commentary on *R* v *Hobday*' *Criminal Law Review* 349

Doubling down on Brown: the strict analogy approach. [*R* v *Wilson*] also sees the Court of Appeal doubling down on the *Brown* categories. We see this both in the reasoning summarised above—requiring a convincing chain of analogy going back to one of the exceptions as expressed in *Brown*—and in some more explicit comments made.

Building on its comments in *BM* that "[n]ew exceptions should not be recognised on a case-by-case, save perhaps where there is a close analogy with an existing exception", the Court of Appeal emphasised its limited freedom to develop this area from the position in *Brown*. If a change is needed, "that is a matter for Parliament" ([41]). The list is, essentially, closed.

The alternative—that the Court of Appeal can expand *Brown*'s exceptions based on its own assessment of the "relevant considerations"—would "lead to uncertainty in the law" (at [41]). As warned in *BM*, a looser approach would also involve the courts in "value judgement[s] which [are] policy laden" and subject to "conflicting views in society".

This is a step away from earlier comments, such as those from Lord Woolf CJ, effectively leaning into a policy-based, ad hoc approach. Evidently concerned with ensuring clarity, and distancing itself from controversial policy choices, the Court of Appeal's solution is to anchor itself firmly to the *Brown* categories.

This explains why the court framed the question not as whether, in its judgement, "cutting the skin of a young person with an unsterile Stanley knife should be a lawful activity if she consented to it", but only whether it can be convincingly placed under an existing *Brown* category (at [43]).

In doubling down on *Brown*, however, this judgment will not do much to alleviate concerns that this approach, and these categories, are already lacking in principle and coherence.

It is also worth recalling—as the courts occasionally have—that the Brown categories were themselves based on policy. What logic can be found for the existing categories, we were told in *BM*, is based on the courts' recognition of a "discernible public benefit" from the activity, and the assessment that it would be "regarded as unreasonable for the common law to criminalise the activity if engaged in with consent".

Thus, the court's solution to the risk of making controversial policy-driven decisions on an ad hoc basis appears to be to fix the law to the ad hoc policy decisions and values recognised by the courts of the 1990s. Whether this is a step forwards or backwards is open to debate.

The clarity of the analogy approach. How much clarity the analogy approach brings in practice is also questionable. The elephant in the room is that analogies—and their persuasiveness—depend on how the nature of the act is characterised in the first place, as well as how the exception is described. The problem is that the same activity can be described in various ways, emphasising different details, or at different levels of abstraction.

To see this, we can look more closely at the basis on which the court rejected the analogy between tattooing and branding (and, by extension, carving). It took a narrow, seemingly technical, approach: "Tattooing is the infiltration of ink into the surface of the skin … It does not involve branding" (at [40]).

Some may see the court's definition of tattooing as missing some rather important details. It makes no mention of the fact that this "infiltration" occurs through the repeated and painful insertion of a *sharp instrument* through *both layers* of the skin, to leave a *lasting* —often *permanent* —mark. Described *this* way, a direct analogy between carving and tattooing would be

> more straightforward: carving also involves the *painful* insertion of a *sharp instrument* through *both layers of the skin* with the aim of leaving a *lasting mark* (although notably in this case it was not clear how permanent the mark would be (at [6])).
>
> [...]
>
> This illustrates that even a seemingly technical "nature of the act" approach will involve discretion over how to characterise the activities being compared in the first place. These descriptions are not self-evident. They involve choices as to which feature(s) to emphasise as essential parts of that activity. We can therefore still expect arguments over how convincing an analogy is, and more fundamentally, over what the essential features of an activity are. This approach to analogising with *Brown* brings considerably less certainty than the court appears to realise.
>
> [...]
>
> Clarity aside, there is also a risk that the malleability of analogies, or what we might call the definitional discretion involved, also leaves room for value judgements to creep back in. Indeed, despite rejecting the idea that the court's own assessment of the relevant considerations is relevant to deciding cases in this area, the court nonetheless ends the judgment by providing just that:
>
> "Cutting the skin is a commonly encountered form of self-harm to which the young and vulnerable are particularly prone. There are good reasons why people should not be permitted to do this to others and no good reason, outside the recognised *Brown* exception of medical intervention, why they should be." (at [44])
>
> Given that the decision was based on the technical distinguishing of branding and tattooing, as well as the applicability of *Wilson*, these comments are *obiter*. Nonetheless, the references to "good" reasons do not sit easily in a judgment otherwise concerned with moving the court away from relying on its own evaluations of particular activities.

So Edis LJ said that Court of Appeal judges should not develop the law on consent to injury on a case-by-case basis. For judges to develop the law in this way would, he said, 'lead to uncertainty' ([41]). He agreed with the Court in *R* v *BM* that such changes should instead be made by Parliament. At the same time, it is also worth noting that Edis LJ said that the fact that a victim consented to the carving or branding may mean that the bringing of a prosecution is not in the public interest. It may be argued, however, that the demands of legal certainty are no better served by this reliance on the discretion of prosecutors in individual cases.

ACTIVITY

A registered tattooist is considering also offering scarification services, including branding. They ask for your legal advice whether scarifying their customers would constitute a criminal offence. How would you advise them?

ii. Lawful activities

In *R* v *Brown* the House of Lords listed a number of lawful activities. These included: surgery; sports (such as boxing); tattooing; and ear-piercing.[17] So, for example, a surgeon who cuts open his patient in order to perform an operation is not guilty of malicious

[17] Lord Mustill also listed religious mortification. For discussion of this, and religious exorcism, see Hall, H. (2016) 'Exorcism, Religious Freedom and Consent: The Devil in the Detail' 80 *Journal of Criminal Law* 241.

wounding because the consent of the patient is available as a defence. Following the case *DPP* v *Smith* we can also add having your hair cut to the list of lawful activities. The hairdresser who cuts off your ponytail would not be guilty of assault occasioning ABH because he could rely on your consent as a defence.

a. Non-deliberate transmission of disease

Earlier we looked at the case *R* v *Dica*, in which the defendant had unprotected sexual intercourse with two women without telling them that he was HIV positive. In its judgment the Court of Appeal also discussed the situation where the defendant *does* tell the victim that he is HIV positive, the victim consents to unprotected sexual intercourse and subsequently contracts the virus. The Court of Appeal said that this is a lawful activity as long as the couple were not having sex in order to deliberately spread the disease.

EXTRACT

Read the following extract from the Court's judgment.

What reasons did the Court give for saying that sexual intercourse where there is a risk of infection but no desire to pass on the disease is a lawful activity?

R v *Dica* [2004] EWCA Crim 1103

Lord Justice Judge

49 [Suppose] one of a couple suffers from HIV. It may be the man: it may be the woman. The circumstances in which HIV was contracted are irrelevant. They could result from a contaminated blood transfusion, or an earlier relationship with a previous sexual partner, who unknown to the sufferer with whom we are concerned, was himself or herself infected with HIV. The parties are Roman Catholics. They are conscientiously unable to use artificial contraception. They both know of the risk that the healthy partner may become infected with HIV. Our second example is that of a young couple, desperate for a family, who are advised that if the wife were to become pregnant and give birth, her long-term health, indeed her life itself, would be at risk. Together the couple decide to run that risk, and she becomes pregnant. She may be advised that the foetus should be aborted, on the grounds of her health, yet, nevertheless, decide to bring her baby to term. If she does, and suffers ill health, is the male partner to be criminally liable for having sexual intercourse with her, notwithstanding that he knew of the risk to her health? If he is liable to be prosecuted, was she not a party to whatever crime was committed? And should the law interfere with the Roman Catholic couple, and require them, at the peril of criminal sanctions, to choose between bringing their sexual relationship to an end or violating their consciences by using contraception?

50 These, and similar risks, have always been taken by adults consenting to sexual intercourse. Different situations, no less potentially fraught, have to be addressed by them. Modern society has not thought to criminalise those who have willingly accepted the risks, and we know of no cases where one or other of the consenting adults has been prosecuted, let alone convicted, for the consequences of doing so.

51 The problems of *criminalising* the consensual taking of risks like these include the sheer impracticability of enforcement and the haphazard nature of its impact. The process would undermine the general understanding of the community that sexual relationships are pre-eminently private and essentially personal to the individuals involved in them. And if adults were to be liable to prosecution for the consequences of taking known risks with their health, it

would seem odd that this should be confined to risks taken in the context of sexual intercourse, while they are nevertheless permitted to take the risks inherent in so many other aspects of everyday life, including, again for example, the mother or father of a child suffering a serious contagious illness, who holds the child's hand, and comforts or kisses him or her goodnight.

52 In our judgment, interference of this kind with personal autonomy, and its level and extent, may only be made by Parliament.

b. Horseplay (where there is no intention to cause injury)

The final lawful activity is horseplay (where there is no intention to cause injury). There are three examples of this lawful activity in case law.

EXAMPLE

The first example is *R* v *Jones (Terence)* (1986) 83 Cr App R 375. The defendants in this case were six schoolboys aged 14 to 17. They grabbed hold of the first victim, a 14-year-old pupil, threw him about nine to ten feet in the air, and didn't catch him. The victim suffered a ruptured spleen, which had to be removed. The second victim was a 15-year-old pupil. They threw him in the air, didn't catch him, and the victim suffered a broken arm. The defendants were convicted of the section 20 offence of maliciously inflicting GBH. On appeal the Court of Appeal quashed their convictions.

The second example is *R* v *Aitken* [1992] 1 WLR 1006. The three defendants in this case were RAF Officers. They were at a party with a number of other officers. Everyone was wearing their fire resistant flying suits. Two of the men fell asleep. As a joke, the others decided to set light to the trouser leg of their fire resistant suits. Both men woke up with a start. Shortly afterwards the party broke up and the defendants left. On their way home, they noticed the victim, Flying Officer Gibson, staggering around drunk. Gibson had been at the party earlier when the two other men had had their trouser legs set alight, so the three defendants decided to set light to Gibson's suit. They did so. Gibson was engulfed in flames. He suffered extremely severe burning; 35 per cent of his body was covered in life-threatening burns. The defendants were convicted of the section 20 offence of maliciously inflicting GBH. On appeal, their convictions were quashed.

The third example is *R* v *Richardson & Irwin* [1999] 1 Cr App R 392. The two defendants, Richardson and Irwin, and the victim, Simon Rose, were university students. One night they were at Irwin's student accommodation and started 'bundling'. Irwin then suggested that they hold Rose over the edge of the balcony. There was a tussle, they lifted Rose over the balcony, then accidentally dropped him. He fell approximately 12 feet and suffered serious injuries. The defendants were convicted of the section 20 offence of maliciously inflicting GBH. On appeal the convictions were quashed.

These three cases establish two important points. First, they establish that horseplay is a lawful activity as long as there was no intention to cause injury. This is difficult to justify. The social utility model set out by the majority in *R* v *Brown* states that activities which cause ABH/GBH/wounding must be presumed to be unlawful, and good policy and public interest reasons are required for them to be classified as lawful. What are the policy and public interest reasons which require that horseplay be classified as a lawful activity? Suggestions that rough and undisciplined play is commonplace in environments like the playground and the locker room, and that it helps people bond and develop camaraderie, seem inadequate. Moreover, to say that horseplay is a lawful activity, but the activities in *R* v *Brown* were unlawful, might be perceived as discriminatory.

You may be thinking to yourself, surely the victims in these cases didn't consent? Surely the schoolboys in *R* v *Jones (Terence)* didn't consent to being thrown in the air? Surely Flying Officer Gibson didn't consent to being set alight? Surely Simon Rose didn't consent to being held over the balcony? This leads us to the second important point from these three cases. Even if the victim did not consent, the defendant still has a defence if he *genuinely believed* that the victim was consenting. Notice the word 'genuinely'. The belief need not have been a reasonable one; it is sufficient that it was honestly held. In *R* v *Jones (Terence)* the defendants said that they genuinely believed that the victims were consenting. They thought the victims were taking it as a joke. In *R* v *Aitken* the defendants said that since Gibson had joined in with setting the other men's trouser legs alight earlier in the evening they genuinely thought that he was consenting to being set alight himself. And in *R* v *Richardson & Irwin* the defendants said that since tussles were a regular occurrence amongst the group they genuinely believed Rose was consenting to being lifted over the balcony. So in a case involving a lawful activity, the defendant will have a defence to a charge of ABH/GBH/wounding if he genuinely believed that the victim was consenting to the activity, even if that belief was unreasonable and even if the victim was in fact not consenting.

Now, think about this question.

In your opinion, can the case law on horseplay be reconciled with *R* v *Brown*?

iii. The social utility or social disutility model?

Earlier we saw that the majority and minority in *R* v *Brown* took quite different approaches to determining whether an activity which causes injury should be classified as lawful or unlawful. The majority adopted a social utility approach, whereas Lord Mustill's dissenting judgment took a social disutility approach. An important question to consider is which approach is the most appropriate.

EXTRACT

Read the following extract from David Kell's article 'Social Disutility and the Law of Consent' (1994) 14 *Oxford Journal of Legal Studies* 121.

In your own words, summarise the three reasons he gives for favouring the social disutility approach. Do you agree or disagree with David Kell? Try and use the principles that we studied in Chapter 1 to explain your reasoning.

Kell D. (1994) 'Social Disutility and the Law of Consent' 14 *Oxford Journal of Legal Studies* 121

[The majority of the House of Lords in *R* v *Brown*] espoused a social utility model whereby, once injury reached the level of bodily harm, the accused was required to demonstrate that the particular activity was needed in the public interest (social utility), rather than the prosecution having to prove that good reason exists for prohibiting the conduct (social disutility). Yet the public interest underpinning most listed exceptions is yet to be articulated.

While at one end of the spectrum are those exceptions clearly serving a valuable social purpose, including reasonable surgical (and dental) interference, necessary for the preservation of life and good health, at the other end are to be found tattooing, ear-piercing, and dangerous sports, such as boxing, where the social purpose served is perhaps less clear

[...]

The social disutility model has a number of attractive advantages. First, by refusing to prohibit conduct unless the State provides cogent reasons, the model is better suited to a modern democratic society which places significant value on individual autonomy. Although autonomy cannot be the only value which the law seeks to enhance and must be balanced against what the Supreme Court of Canada termed 'some larger societal interest', the overriding question should always be 'what justifies the intervention?' The present social utility model often allows this question to be completely evaded. Thus although the House of Lords majority were quite thorough in rejecting the case for an exception for sado-masochistic conduct, the Court of Appeal, in language closer to assertion than reason, was able almost summarily to reject the defendants' appeals, stating: 'What may be "good reason" [i.e. justifying an exception] it is not necessary for us to decide. It is sufficient to say... that the satisfying of sado-masochistic libido does not come within the category of good reason...'.

Second, although it is not suggested that it was a motivating force in shaping the present law, the model may actually provide a better explanation for many of the proffered exceptions to the general rule, than does the social utility model that currently holds sway. It may, for instance, be difficult to state why tattooing or ear-piercing are needed in the public interest, but it may be equally difficult to state why the public interest would require their prohibition. And even in the case of the daredevil stuntmen referred to above in [the judgment of the Supreme Court of Canada in *R* v *Jobidon* [1991) 2 SCR 714], a social disutility approach might be more persuasive than talk of 'socially valuable cultural products'. Of course, for some forms of conduct, for instance public brawling, the choice of model would make no difference. *Jobidon* itself involved an allegedly consensual fight in the parking lot of an Ontario public bar, and the court, employing the language of social utility, was quick to note the social uselessness of such fights. But not only are such consensual fights not required in the public interest (in social utility terms), there are persuasive public policy reasons for prohibiting the conduct (social disutility). Such fights can often lead to injury more serious than intended by the combatants, and to larger, disorderly brawls as supporters join in. Moreover, such combatants if permitted to fight consensually may, on some future occasion, 'too readily find their fists raised against a person whose consent they forgot to ascertain with full certitude'; and, though often not amounting to a legal vitiation of consent, those drawn into such fights often do so more out of fear of being branded a coward than out of a genuine desire to face the aggressor. And one should note also that a social disutility model should not be too radical a change for the judiciary to bear, as evidenced perhaps by occasional judicial slippage into the language of social disutility.

Third, arguably one unfortunate consequence of the social utility model, as advocated by the courts, is an unreasonable distortion of the criterion of 'bodily harm'. In *R* v *Boyea* [(1992) 156 J.P. 505] in a well-intentioned attempt to liberate the law on consensual, unorthodox sexual conduct from the strictures placed on it in 1934 by the Court of Appeal in *Donovan*, the Court of Appeal sought to refine the definition of bodily harm. After noting that the court ought to take into account changing social attitudes to sexual activities between consenting adults, the court stated:

> As a generality, the level of vigour in sexual congress which is generally acceptable, and therefore the voluntarily accepted risk of incurring some injury, is probably higher now than it was in 1934. It follows... that the phrase 'transient or trifling' [in the *Donovan* definition] must be understood in the light of conditions in 1992 rather than those of nearly 60 years ago.

The bodily harm criterion represents the level at which the effectiveness of consent is brought into question, under the present law by the accused facing the often difficult task of demonstrating why a particular activity is needed in the public interest. By manipulating the bodily harm criterion the court in *Boyea*, albeit obiter, foreshadowed an approach whereby, in an attempt to avoid such difficulty, injuries (resulting from particular conduct) once considered to fall within the definition are now classified as outside it, thus permitting consent to operate effectively. While any attempt at liberation may be considered a welcome advance on the current state of the law, it is arguable that the bodily harm criterion, perhaps more comfortably positioned as a rigid, rather than a normative, concept, is being asked to bear too much of the weight of reform.

A social disutility model, on the other hand, with greater weight being given to individual autonomy and possessing sufficient flexibility to re-examine, in an appropriate case, the merits of prohibiting (previously-outlawed) conduct in the light of changed social conditions, would remove the need for reform of the law by the more cumbersome, and indirect, means of manipulating the bodily harm criterion.

Quiz 6.6

1. In which of the following circumstances will a mistake induced by the defendant's fraud not vitiate the consent of the victim?

a. The victim is deceived into believing that the extraction of a tooth is necessary whereas in fact the dentist wants to cause the victim pain and discomfort and the tooth is perfectly healthy.

b. The defendant has sexual intercourse with the victim without telling her that he is HIV positive.

c. The defendant claims to be a fully qualified dentist when she has in fact been suspended from practice.

d. The victim agrees to be spanked by the defendant because the victim believes him to be a famous film actor.

2. Why was the decision in *R* v *Clarence* [1888] 22 QBD 23 subject to much critical comment before it was overruled?

a. The law should not intervene in the sexual relations of a married couple.

b. The consent of the victim was not obtained by fraud as to the sexual health or identity of the defendant.

c. The victim's consent to unprotected sexual intercourse implied consent as to the risk of infection.

d. It failed to distinguish between consent given to sexual intercourse and consent given to the risk of infection.

3. Why have the decisions in *R* v *Dica* and *R* v *Konzani* been subject to some academic criticism?

a. They will encourage those who suspect that they might have contracted HIV to seek medical treatment promptly.

b. They suggest that everyone, and not just those who are HIV positive, has a responsibility for maximising the spread of the virus.

c. They undermine the principle that everyone, and not just those who are HIV positive, has a responsibility for minimising the spread of the virus.

d. They have insufficient respect for the autonomy of victims.

4. A defendant may always rely on the fact that the victim consented to harm as a defence in cases involving what level of injury?

a. Any level of harm injury, including death.

b. Any level of injury up to and including grievous bodily harm.

c. Only injuries that are transient or trifling.

d. Any level of injury up to and including actual bodily harm.

5. Following the decision in *R* v *Brown*, which of the following statements sums up most accurately the lawfulness of causing another person consensual injury?

a. Heterosexual sado-masochistic behaviour that causes ABH, GBH or wounding is lawful, whereas same-sex sado-masochistic behaviour that causes such injuries is unlawful.

b. It is never lawful to cause ABH, GBH or wounding, whether or not the victim consents.

c. It is lawful to cause ABH, GBH or wounding provided that the victim consents and the activity in question is lawful.

d. The consent of the victim always provides a defence if the harm in issue is at GBH level or below.

6. Which of the following activities is not on the list of lawful activities even if engaged in consensually?

a. Tattooing.

b. Body-piercing.

c. Non-fatal sado-masochistic activities engaged in for sexual pleasure.

d. Sports involving physical contact and a risk of injury.

7. What is the social utility model for determining the legality of an activity that causes ABH, GBH or wounding?

a. All activities that involve a risk of ABH, GBH or wounding should be presumed to be lawful unless good policy and public interest reasons can be shown for making them unlawful.

b. A defendant should only be liable for ABH/GBH/wounding which he intends or foresees.

c. The social utility model dictates that an activity that deliberately causes harm at ABH/GBH/wounding level will only be lawful if it serves some useful social purpose.

d. The most socially beneficial approach is to proceed on a case-by-case basis, with no general rules and each case being determined on its merits.

8. Which of the following is **not** an advantage that David Kell ('Social disutility and the law of consent') sees in applying the social disutility model to the law of consent?

a. The social disutility model requires the defendant to show why an activity has social utility rather than requiring the state to prove that it does not.

b. The social disutility model provides a better explanation of the reason for treating certain activities as exceptions to the 'no valid consent to harm at ABH level or above' rule.

c. The social disutility model reflects the tendency of modern democratic society to place significant value on individual autonomy.

d. The social disutility model avoids distortions of the criteria of bodily harm.

The Law Commission's proposals for reform

6.7 Define the Law Commission's proposed reforms of the non-fatal offences against the person.

As part of its 11th programme of Law Reform, the Law Commission was asked by the Ministry of Justice to carry out a scoping exercise as a first step towards reform of the Offences Against the Person Act 1861. The Commission published a scoping consultation paper in November 2014,[18] followed one year later by a scoping report containing its recommendations.[19]

1. Rationale for reform

Before examining the Law Commission's proposals, it is useful to begin by looking at the reasons why the Commission felt that reform of the OAPA 1861 is necessary.

EXTRACT

Read the following extract from the final report. In your own words, list the Commission's criticisms of the OAPA 1861.

(Note: in this extract, and the ones that follow below, the acronym 'SCP' refers to the scoping consultation paper that preceded the final report.)

---

[18] Law Commission (2014) *Reform of Offences Against the Person: A Scoping Consultation Paper* (Consultation Paper No 217).

[19] Law Commission (2015) *Reform of Offences Against the Person* (Law Commission No 361) HC 555.

Law Commission (2015) *Reform of Offences Against the Person* (No 361) HC 555

Definitions of offences

3.3 In the SCP we argued that the drafting of the offences in the 1861 Act is unnecessarily complex, in particular in two respects: there are too many divisions between the offences, and too many divisions within the offences.

1. There are often several narrowly defined and highly detailed offences relating to the same subject matter, which could be covered by a single broader offence with fewer elements. For example, there are four offences relating to the misuse of explosives and similar substances (and three more under the Explosives Substances Act 1883).
2. In other cases, the same section of the 1861 Act contains a list of different but related detailed situations, leaving doubt about whether the section creates one offence or several. One example is section 18, which arguably creates four offences, covering ten different factual situations. We argue in the SCP that "if there is a common theme to the scenarios listed, the offence should be defined by that common theme. If there is not, the scenarios should be separate offences set out in separate sections."

3.4 We also argued that there is no clear hierarchy among the main offences. At first sight there does appear to be a hierarchy: the offence under section 18 (wounding or grievous bodily harm with intent) is the most serious, the offence under section 20 (malicious wounding or grievous bodily harm) is the middle-ranking offence and the offence under section 47 (assault occasioning actual bodily harm) is the least serious. However, this apparent hierarchy is marred by two facts:

1. the maximum sentence for the offences under sections 20 and 47 is the same (5 years);
2. the special status given to "wounding" means that the offences are not clearly distinguished by the seriousness of the injury caused: a wound can be quite minor and nevertheless constitute the offence under section 20 or even section 18.

Unnecessary offences

3.5 There are several offences which are seldom or never encountered in modern conditions and could be considered for abolition. Examples include:

1. assaulting a magistrate or other person in the exercise of his duty preserving a wreck;
2. impeding a person escaping from a shipwreck;
3. not providing apprentices or servants with food;
4. exposing children to danger; and
5. setting a spring gun, man trap or other engine calculated to destroy life or cause grievous bodily harm.

Language and style

3.6 Further criticisms of the 1861 Act are that:

1. it uses archaic vocabulary, such as "grievous" (to describe a serious injury) and "detainer" (to mean detention);
2. it uses words without a clear meaning, such as "maliciously", that have required extensive interpretation by the courts and are sometimes redundant;
3. it refers to specific devices and chemicals, such as laudanum, as means of committing offences and is therefore liable to obsolescence as these means fall out of use or further inventions are made;

4. it refers to obsolete legal concepts, such as felony, misdemeanour and penal servitude, which have to be re-interpreted by provisions in other statutes; and
5. it does not state the penalties for major offences, such as those under sections 47 and 20: these have to be deduced from a chain of interlocking provisions in other statutes.

Having set out these criticisms of the OAPA 1861, the Commission then listed three options:

1. To say that most ambiguities have been resolved by judicial interpretation and the 1861 Act works well in practice, so there is no pressing practical need for reform;
2. To retain the 1861 Act, but amend it to update its language and abolish any obsolete offences; or
3. To replace the 1861 Act with a comprehensive new statute.

During the consultation phase, the vast majority of consultees favoured the third option. The main arguments advanced by the minority who favoured option one or two were that 'the present system works in practice and that a new statute would be difficult to draft and probably result in further mistakes' (para 3.15). The Law Commission rejected each of these concerns. First, there remain some unresolved ambiguities, and unforeseen ones still sometimes emerge. In addition:

> 3.18 [. . .] [E]ven assuming that the meaning of the 1861 Act is now settled by judicial decision, it is not apparent on the face of the statute. In effect, the law in this area is the product of 'judicial legislation', accessible only to those lawyers and officials who are experts in the field. From the point of view of that class the law may be clear and the system may work without problems. That however is not good enough. One basic function of law is to inform the public clearly about what conduct is permitted or forbidden, and if it is forbidden what the consequences are. This is not achieved by a statute which is in effect written in code.

As for the argument that a new statute would generate further problems, the Commission pointed out that over the past few decades there have been several drafts of replacement legislation, and none of these generated 'any suggestion of "problems or mistakes" at all comparable to those in the existing Act' (para 3.19).

2. The Law Commission's proposals

Having recommended that the 1861 Act should be replaced by a comprehensive, modern statute, the Law Commission then set out its proposed new scheme of offences. In developing this new scheme, the Commission used as its starting point the draft Bill contained in the 1998 Home Office Consultation Paper *Violence: Reforming the Offences Against the Person Act 1861*. Building on this, the 2015 report proposed amending the five offences we have studied in this chapter as set out in Table 6.1.

Table 6.1 Proposed reform of offences against the person

Existing offences			Proposed offences	
	Description	**Maximum sentence**	**Description**	**Maximum sentence**
OAPA 1861, s18	Wounding or causing grievous bodily harm with intent to cause grievous bodily harm	Life	Intentionally causing serious injury Note: wounding is not included unless the wound is a serious injury	Life
OAPA 1861, s20	Malicious wounding or infliction of grievous bodily harm Note: the defendant must intend or be reckless about some harm; not necessarily about a wound or grievous bodily harm	5 years	Recklessly causing serious injury Note: D must be reckless about the risk of serious injury; wounding is not included unless the wound is a serious injury	7 years
OAPA 1861, s47	Assault occasioning actual bodily harm Note: this includes every assault or battery which in fact causes injury, whether or not the defendant intended or was reckless about injury	5 years	Intentionally or recklessly causing injury (whether or not by assault) Note: D must intend or be reckless about the risk of some injury	5 years
			Aggravated assault Note: includes every physical or threatened assault which in fact causes injury, whether or not D intended or was reckless about injury	12 months
Common law	Battery Note: this means actual physical violence, including any unlawful touching however slight. At present, this offence is sometimes used for cases of low-level injuries	6 months	Physical assault Note: should not be used for cases of low-level injury, as these may be charged as aggravated assault	6 months
Common law	Assault Note: this means causing a person to apprehend physical violence, in the same sense as for battery above	6 months	Threatened assault	6 months

Source: Adapted from table at pp200–204 of Law Commission (2015) *Reform of Offences Against the Person* (No 361) HC 555.

In its exposition of the proposed offences, the Law Commission addressed a number of issues, including:

- Whether to distinguish between different types of injury, such as shooting, poisoning and stabbing;
- The appropriate hierarchy of offences, having regard to the level of injury suffered and the *mens rea* of the defendant;

- Whether a definition of injury is necessary and, if so, which kinds of mental harm it should include;
- Whether assault and battery should be merged into a single offence; and
- The rationale for creating an additional offence, called aggravated assault.

(Note that the report did not consider issues relating to consent. The Commission did state, however, that the principle from *R* v *Brown* that consent is only available as a defence in cases involving a lawful activity would apply to the top three offences in its hierarchy. For aggravated assault, physical assault and threatened assault, the consent of the victim would always be available as a defence.)

EXTRACT

Read the following extract from the Law Commission's report. In respect of each of the five issues listed above, what did the Law Commission recommend and why?

(Note: in the extracts that follow, the term 'draft Bill' refers to the 1998 draft Bill that the Law Commission took as its starting point.)

Law Commission (2015) *Reform of Offences Against the Person* (No 361) HC 555

4.15 If we were devising a law of offences of violence from scratch, there would, in very general terms, be a choice between two different approaches.

(1) In approach 1, the main offences would have external elements defined as the causing of "injury", without distinguishing the type of injury or the means by which it was caused.

(2) In approach 2, there would be separate offences in which the external elements consisted of causing injuries of different types or by different means: for example, offences of "wounding" and "poisoning".

4.16 Both these approaches are found in other areas of the criminal law.

(1) Approach 1 is found in the law of homicide. Both murder and manslaughter can consist of causing death by any means: shooting, strangling, drowning, poisoning etc.

(2) Approach 2 is found in property offences. Theft, robbery and handling stolen goods are all distinct offences, though all involve dishonest interference with another's property interests. In addition, there are offences of fraud and cheat, each describing a particular means of dishonest property interference.

4.17 The 1861 Act does not consistently follow either approach.

(1) The offence under section 18 was based on an older offence covering only wounding and shooting. It can now consist of either wounding or causing grievous bodily harm by any means.

(2) Some forms of the section 18 offence involve causing grievous bodily harm "with intent to resist or prevent the lawful apprehension or detainer of any person". This does not restrict the kind of harm or the means by which it is caused, but does require highly specific circumstances.

(3) The offence under section 20 can consist of either wounding or "inflicting" grievous bodily harm. Infliction was once thought to mean a direct forcible injury such as an assault. It is now

recognised as being wider than this, and can cover indirect injuries such as the transmission of infection. There now seems to be little if any distinction between "inflict" in section 20 and "cause" in section 18. This offence, like that under section 18, would therefore appear to cover injuries of any kind (provided they are serious enough) caused by any means.

(4) In the offence under section 47, the actual bodily harm must be occasioned by an assault (or a battery).

4.25 The options for reform are broadly as follows:

(1) adopt the scheme of the draft Bill (approach 1): general injury offences only;

(2) create particularised offences of causing injury by wounding, poisoning, maiming etc, but have no general injury offence (approach 2); or

(3) retain a mixture, as at present: some detailed offences – wounding, choking, etc – and one or more residual general offences.

4.26 The first option has the advantage of being a clear, streamlined and readily understandable scheme. As argued in the SCP, there is just one offence of murder and one of manslaughter, which do not distinguish between different means of causing death. These offences are readily understood by the public and would not be improved or made more accessible by being divided into separate offences of causing death by stabbing, shooting, poisoning and so on. Exactly the same reasoning is applicable to causing non-fatal injuries.

4.27 The second option did not have any support from consultees. It would also be impractical, as human inventiveness will always extend to new ways of causing injury.

4.28 The main argument for the third option is that some means of causing injury, such as poisoning and the use of explosives, rightly attract an especially high level of public disapproval. It is therefore just that people who are guilty of them are labelled appropriately, and where necessary given a higher sentence. This argument needs to be considered separately under the head of labelling and that of appropriate punishment.

4.29 In our view the scheme of the draft Bill meets the requirement for appropriate labelling, because it is possible to charge an offence of administering substances capable of causing injury or causing danger by explosives together with one of the general injury offences.

4.30 The draft Bill also meets the sentencing needs in the most serious cases. The need for punishment is strongest when there is either an intention to cause death or an intention to cause serious injury. In a case involving poisoning or explosives the current offence of attempted murder (which would be unaltered by the recommendations), and the proposed offence of intentionally causing serious injury under the draft Bill (and therefore the offence of attempting to do so), all carry a maximum life sentence. These charges, with or without a charge of causing danger by drugs or explosives, fully meet the need for adequate punishment.

4.31 When there is no intention to cause death or serious injury, the main reason for public disapproval of the acts involving poisons or explosives is that the defendant was acting in a dangerously irresponsible way. Adequate punishment for this is achieved by charging an offence of causing danger by drugs or explosives together with that of recklessly causing serious injury, or intentionally or recklessly causing injury, as the case may be.

4.32 For these reasons, we favour the first option, which is to follow the scheme of the draft Bill.

4.33 We recommend that any new statute governing crimes of violence should follow the scheme of the draft Bill by providing for one or more general offences of causing injury, rather than offences of causing injury of particular types or by particular means.

[…]

4.35 The levels of harm distinguished by the present law and practice are as follows:

(1) "Grievous bodily harm" – the 1861 Act contains two offences of "grievous bodily harm" (sections 18 and 20), and variants of this phrase are found in some other offences such as those relating
to explosives and poisons. The offences under sections 18 and 20 can also consist of "wounding".

(2) "Actual bodily harm" – section 47 distinguishes those assaults that occasion "actual bodily harm". However, the maximum sentence is five years, the same as for section 20.

(3) Low level harm – in practice, and following CPS charging standards, assaults causing low level harms are usually charged as [assault or battery] though technically they fall within the scope of the section 47 offence.

4.36 In the SCP we criticised this as not providing a clear hierarchy of seriousness. That is, in principle there is a distinction between serious harm (sections 18 and 20) and less serious harm (section 47). However, this distinction is blurred because:

(1) the offences under sections 18 and 20 can be committed by wounding, without causing serious harm; and

(2) the distinction is not reflected in sentencing, as the maximum sentences for sections 20 and 47 are the same.

4.43 The main distinction in the present law is between "grievous bodily harm" and "actual bodily harm". The draft Bill preserves this distinction, modernising the language to read "serious injury" and "injury".

4.44 Assuming that some distinction of degrees of injury is desirable, the next question is whether distinguishing between "serious injury" and "injury" is sufficiently precise. As pointed out in the SCP, the word "serious" is ambiguous, as it can mean either "really serious", that is to say of exceptional gravity, or "sufficient to be taken seriously", that is to say more than minor. To avoid ambiguity, it might be best for the offences under clauses 1 and 2 to be defined using wording making clear that the offences must involve an exceptionally grave injury. This would have the effect of preserving the test in the present law, which describes grievous bodily harm as being "really serious".

4.45 We recommend using the hierarchy of injury offences in the draft Bill, distinguishing between serious or severe injuries and injury in general.

Grading by level of injury intended or foreseen

4.46 An important question discussed in the SCP is whether offences should generally require that the defendant intended or foresaw the same level of injury as that described in the external elements of the offence. For example, if an offence involves causing serious injury, should the requirement be that the defendant intended or foresaw serious injury, or only that the defendant intended or foresaw any injury?

4.47 In Chapter 3 of the SCP we discussed the general principle and explained the differences between the possible positions:

(1) Some offences conform to the "correspondence principle". In these offences, the level of harm that D must intend or foresee in any given offence is the same as the level of harm defined in the external element of the offence. This is the position in battery: D must intend or be reckless about the possible touching of the victim, and that touching must occur.

(2) Others are offences of "constructive liability". In these, it is accepted that, once D intends or foresees a basic level of harm, he or she may also be held to blame for any greater degree of harm that results. An example is murder, where D is guilty if he or she kills, despite only intending to cause grievous bodily harm.

(3) There are also offences of "ulterior intent", where D must intend a consequence that need not occur in fact: for example, assault with intent to rob, where no actual robbery need take place. Following that discussion, we addressed the choice between these approaches as applied to the injury offences under the 1861 Act and the draft Bill.

Current law

4.48 In the 1861 Act:

(1) the section 18 offence requires

(a) grievous bodily harm or wounding

(b) with intent either to cause grievous bodily harm or "to resist or prevent the lawful apprehension or detainer of any person";

(2) the section 20 offence requires

(a) grievous bodily harm or wounding;

(b) with intent or recklessness as to some harm;

(3) the section 47 offence requires

(a) assault (or battery) occasioning actual bodily harm;

(b) with the necessary intent or recklessness for assault or battery.

4.49 The second and third offences are offences of "constructive liability" in the sense defined above. The first offence is more complicated, and combines elements from all three approaches:

(1) It can consist of causing grievous bodily harm, with intent to do grievous bodily harm. In this form, it conforms to the correspondence principle.

(2) It can consist of wounding, with intent to do grievous bodily harm. This is an offence of both constructive liability (the defendant need not intend or foresee a wound) and ulterior intent (the wound that actually occurs need not amount to grievous bodily harm).

(3) It can consist of wounding or grievous bodily harm, with intent to resist or prevent arrest or detention. Again this is an offence of both constructive liability (the word "maliciously" implies that the defendant must intend or foresee some harm, but no more) and ulterior intent (the attempt to resist or prevent arrest or detention may be unsuccessful).

[…]

4.97 In conclusion, the arguments [in favour of constructive liability] do not shake our belief that the correspondence principle is correct in principle and should be the default position, though there may be reasons for departing from it in particular instances. In a previous report, we mentioned the argument that, if any factor is important enough to make the difference between guilt and innocence, awareness of that factor or of the possibility of it should in principle be an element of the offence. Otherwise potential defendants will not know whether they are committing the offence, and the requirement of fair warning is not met. The alternative, namely constructive liability, accepts the fault element for a lower level but related offence on the argument that D knew that he or she was doing "something wrong". This is in effect a reversion to the Victorian concept of malice in "the old vague sense of wickedness in general".

4.98 As concerns the injury offences that we are considering, the scheme of the draft Bill, which reflects the correspondence principle, will enable prosecutors to choose levels of offence that more effectively reflect the wrong that occurred. At the same time, it will not weaken the protection given by the current law, as the disputed cases [where serious injury occurs, but is not intended or foreseen], will continue to carry a maximum sentence of five years.

4.99 We recommend using the hierarchy of offences in the draft Bill, in which the offence of recklessly causing serious injury is only committed if the defendant is aware of the risk that his or her conduct will cause serious injury.

[…]

4.123 We agree with the conclusion of a majority of consultees that a definition [of injury] is required. The terms "grievous bodily harm" and "actual bodily harm", vague though they are in themselves, are hallowed by usage and the boundaries have been clarified judicially. The word "injury" is comparatively straightforward, but is not generally understood as including mental harm of any kind (other than perhaps harm resulting from brain damage). Clarification of the kind of mental harm covered is certainly required, whatever boundary is decided upon.

4.124 On the substantive question of what kinds of mental harm to include, the main problem is one of drawing clear boundaries. There may be some merit in extending injury beyond the boundaries of recognised psychiatric harm. However, in medical practice the distinction between psychiatric harm and other undesirable psychological conditions is reasonably clear, and the courts do not appear to have experienced difficulty in applying it. There is far less clarity in distinguishing treatable psychological conditions from unpleasant but normal states of mind such as shock, distress and feelings of depression, as the difference is often one of degree rather than kind.

4.125 Another point is that the new offences do not require any kind of physical attack, but include every possible means of causing injury. This is a further reason for caution. There is a case for criminalising a physical attack which causes any kind of harm, however remote from physical injury. There is also a case for criminalising any act that causes a physical or related injury. But allowing the offence to cover purely psychological means of causing purely psychological harm goes too far. A statutory code primarily concerned with offences of violence should not cover examples such as causing depression by dismissing a person from employment or ending a relationship, and we have not been able to devise a test for distinguishing these from more deserving examples such as inducing depression by systematic domestic abuse. This last example will however often be caught by section 76 of the Serious Crime Act 2015, which makes it an offence to engage in controlling or coercive behaviour towards a person in an intimate or family relationship which "causes [V] serious alarm or distress which has a substantial adverse effect on [V]'s usual day-to-day activities".

4.126 We recommend that the definition of mental injury should have the same limits as the existing law, namely recognised psychiatric conditions.

[…]

5.16 Though the offences of assault and battery are distinct, in many (possibly most) cases they occur together. That is, where D makes a frontal attack on V, V will see the attack coming (so D has committed assault), and D in fact hits V (so D has committed battery). The two exceptional cases are:

(1) assault without battery: D threatens V, or swings a fist at V but misses;

(2) battery without assault: D hits V from behind, or while V is asleep.

5.17 Nevertheless we adhere to the view in the SCP that assault and battery are fundamentally different wrongs, particularly since assault includes threatening behaviour such as telephone calls that need not form the opening stage of an intended attack: it is enough that V apprehends that an attack will take place in the near future. The complexity of the draft clauses in both the

1998 draft Bill and its predecessors, and the wide variations among them, testify to the difficulty of embodying both forms of behaviour in a single concept.

[...]

5.46... Section 47 [assault occasioning ABH] performs two different functions.

(1) In its original context, it did not create a separate offence: it was simply a provision about the sentencing powers for assault, to the effect that a somewhat higher sentence (originally three years) was available if the assault caused bodily harm than if it did not. That is why the offence still does not require any intention to cause bodily harm, or foresight of bodily harm.

(2) In current practice, it is the offence of choice for some quite significant injuries. This is consistent with the fact that the sentencing powers extend to five years, the same as for the section 20 offence.

It is because there is significant strain between these two functions that the first function has in current practice been largely removed from section 47 and taken over by [assault and battery].

Offence of aggravated assault?

5.47 One solution would be to separate these two functions. The [intentionally or recklessly causing injury offence], triable either way, would continue to cover the causing of injury of any level by any means, provided that it was intentional or reckless. There would also be a separate offence triable only in a magistrates' court, covering cases where D causes injury by assault or battery, whether the injury was foreseen or not. We suggest that it should be called "aggravated assault".

Advantages

5.48 This would have the advantages that the lesser offence is not wholly covered by the greater and that there is a clear distinction between the two: one offence is confined to intentional or reckless injuries, while the other includes inadvertent injuries. The new offence of aggravated assault would also provide an adequate label for D's conduct and avoid alienating victims by telling them that their injuries are minor.

5.49 As explained, the formal distinction between the two injury offences is that the [intentionally or recklessly causing injury offence] requires intention or recklessness as to the causing of injury, while aggravated assault would not (though it would require intention or recklessness as to the underlying assault or battery). In practice, aggravated assault would be used for three types of cases:

(1) cases involving low level injuries – black eyes, split lips, bruising, abrasions – which are currently charged as [assault or battery] following the charging standard; the charging standard would accordingly be amended to refer to aggravated assault...

(2) cases where, currently, the prosecution brings a charge under section 47 but seeks to keep the case in the magistrates' court, because the facts are at the lower end of the range for that offence and the expected sentence is within the power of that court (up to 12 months, if our recommendation below is accepted); and

(3) cases involving injuries of any level where it is impossible to prove intention or recklessness as to causing injury.

In the first two types of case, D will often in fact have intended or been reckless about the risk of some injury; but if aggravated assault is charged there will be no need to prove this.

5.50 In short, the new offence would be used to cover both the more serious cases now prosecuted as [assault or battery] and the less serious offences now prosecuted under section 47 (assault occasioning actual bodily harm). As argued above, this would have the advantage of keeping these cases in the magistrates' courts: at present a considerable proportion of cases under section 47 are tried in the Crown Court but receive sentences which would have been within the power of a magistrates' court...

Disadvantages

5.51 In the SCP we criticised the offence under section 47 for its failure to respect the correspondence principle:

In short, here is an offence popularly known as "ABH", of which the main distinguishing feature is the causing of bodily harm. Yet, for the purpose of assessing how far D is to blame, D's state of mind about bodily harm is ignored. Juries may find this confusing, and the offence appears both lopsided and misdescribed.

5.52 The proposed offence of aggravated assault would be open to the same theoretical criticism. However, the main injustice involved in the section 47 offence is that a purely accidental consequence, of which D need have no awareness at all, appears to be the central feature of the offence and increases the possible sentence from six months to five years. In the proposed offence of aggravated assault, the assault would be the central feature of the offence and the injury caused would be mainly relevant as an aggravating factor, with limited consequences for sentencing. Significantly, some consultees who in general favoured following the correspondence principle thought that a limited degree of constructive liability was acceptable at the lower end of the scale of offences.

3. Critique of proposals

In the following extract, Matthew Gibson discusses the Law Commission's proposals.

EXTRACT

Which aspects of the proposals does Gibson support, and why? Which does he express concern about, and why?

(Note: in this extract Gibson refers to the Law Commission's proposed offences of intentionally causing serious injury, recklessly causing serious injury and intentionally or recklessly causing injury as offences 1, 2 and 3 respectively.)

Gibson, M. [2016] 'Getting Their "Act" Together? Implementing Statutory Reform of Offences Against the Person' *Criminal Law Review* 597

Reflecting wrongdoing #1: offences 1, 2 and 3

[…]

The modernisation of language in the form of "serious injury" and "injury", along with the removal of words like "inflict", "bodily" and "occasioning", represents an important updating of relevant terms.

To be sure, "serious injury" and "injury" are readily understandable to the public as descriptions of harm. Like "wounding", "grievous bodily harm" and "actual bodily harm", they are condemnatory in tone, conveying the idea that it is wrong – and illegal – to cause such outcomes. This recognition of the actual harm caused is particularly important for the victims of these offences. Nonetheless, some might lament the loss of the current harm descriptions for the moral resonance they create in the public imagination. There is no denying that "wounding", "grievous bodily harm" and "actual bodily harm" (along with the abbreviations "GBH" and "ABH") are distinctly evocative. As Gardner states, they contain a "moral clarity which makes them accessible to the ordinary people who must be guided by them." Consequently, it must be wondered whether the pursuit of textual certainty justifies the removal of all morally loaded harm-phrasing from offences against the person. These debates also have fair labelling implications on conviction. The descriptions "serious injury" and "injury" may not sufficiently distinguish the harmful outcome caused. For instance, Horder remarks that:

> "Someone who deliberately breaks another's nose in punching him hard is lumped together in the same offence category—intentionally causing serious injury – as someone who deliberately saws another's leg off, puts out a victim's eyes, severs his spine or castrates him."

Has the scoping report missed an opportunity to variegate outcomes in these more detailed ways? Ultimately, there is the concern that particularism in offence outcomes encourages technical arguments over whether D's conduct falls within the relevant crime. The desire to avoid these strategies by describing more general – if morally sterilised – harms is understandable. Similarly, the absence in offences 1, 2 and 3 of any mention of how D has brought about the harmful outcome alludes to the practical difficulties of discerning between different modes of responsibility – for example, stabbing, cutting or piercing. This is a continuation of the status quo: ss.18, 20 and 47 are also silent on this matter.

[…]

Overall, in defining conduct, the new hierarchy presents a simple and logical ladder of harms across offences 1, 2 and 3. It is therefore more intelligible to practitioners and the public.

However, in some respects, the revised scheme of harms perpetuates existing problems. In particular, the scoping report is vague about the boundary between "serious injury" and "injury". Of course, some degree of overlap in classifying harms is inevitable. However, the scoping report could have been clearer on this distinction. For example, it notes that the word "serious" remains ambiguous, before debating – without resolving – whether it might be preferable for offences 1 and 2 to require "exceptionally grave injury". That extra layer of definition would have better delimited the severity of physical or mental suffering that isolates offences 1 and 2 from offence 3. It is therefore regrettable that the scoping report does not provide more precision on how "serious" should be understood, especially given that demand for precision on this issue is longstanding. At the moment, assuming the split between "serious injury" and "injury" mimics the actus rei divide between ss.18/20 and 47, the problems of overlap, fair warning and fair labelling that have long stalked the law may well persist. The uncertainty created by this gap would need addressing by CPS guidance, keeping in mind the point in *Bollom* that assessment of an injury's seriousness must take into account the effect of the harm on the particular individual.

Notwithstanding these criticisms, offences 1 and 2 should be welcomed for containing requirements of fault (intention or recklessness, respectively, as to causing serious injury) which directly track the harm proscribed by those crimes (serious injury). This satisfies the correspondence principle: there is no constructive liability. This is surely good for fair warning. Moreover, fault corresponds with punishment. Offence 1 – which can only be committed intentionally – contains a higher sentence (life imprisonment) than that in offence 2 (seven years) which can only be committed recklessly. Such sentencing features are a vast improvement on those in ss.18 and 20 where neither necessarily accorded with D's conduct or culpability. Unfortunately, that rule is not adhered to in offence 3. Here, the sentence (five years) is the same irrespective of D's mens rea (intention or recklessness as to causing injury). As Eriera comments:

> "This is not obviously rational. The greater seriousness of intentionally caused injury as compared with recklessly caused injury ought to be reflected in a difference in the maximum sentence available."

Consequently, it might be doubted whether convicting intentional and reckless wrongdoers under the same offence amounts to fair labelling. Offence 3 now also houses those individuals who cause serious harm which is neither intended nor foreseen - under the OAPA such situations are governed by s.20 due to the imposition of constructive liability. The scoping report reveals that the CPS argued in its response to the SCP that serious injuries, however caused, ought to be labelled as such under offence 2 - and not offence 3. However, the Commission submits that this view presupposes that offence 3 is the "new" s.47 - effectively, a minor provision which theoretically deals with all injuries, however insignificant. In fact, as explained in the scoping report, offence 3 will only cover the more serious injuries falling within s.47 due to the proposed creation of a new assault-based crime ("aggravated assault") which will deal with s.47's less serious injury cases.

Reflecting wrongdoing #2: aggravated assault, physical assault and threatened assault

The scoping report maintains assault and battery as separate offences, albeit relabelled as "threatened assault" and "physical assault", respectively. The actus rei of these crimes reflect their common law roots: applying force to, or causing an impact on, the body or another (physical assault); and causing another to think that any such force or impact is or may be imminent (threatened assault). Interestingly, "assault" conjures up a particular mode of responsibility which, when combined with the adjectives "physical" or "threatened", implies the harmful outcome with which these offences are concerned. This sharpens understanding of the requisite outcomes more clearly than the singular labels "assault" and "battery". Moreover, continued use of "assault" retains a moral as well as factual sense of the harms involved in these revised crimes. These references to mode of responsibility and moral character stand in stark contrast to their absences in offences 1, 2 and 3. Such observations confirm that the different harms prohibited by assault and battery will now be more accurately conveyed to the public as matters of fair warning. They will also be more fully captured on conviction. Both crimes can be committed intentionally or recklessly, with conviction for either resulting in a maximum sentence of six months' imprisonment. Whilst these sentencing arrangements are the same as under current law, the fairness of drawing parity of punishment between physical and threatened assault has been questioned.

Meanwhile, above the two assault offences, but below offence 3, the scoping report introduces a brand new crime: aggravated assault. Unlike the continuation of the blurred boundary between "serious injury" and "injury", this substantially minimises any overlap between "injury" and "physical assault" - a problem which affects the parallel offences of s.47 and battery. The offence requires intention or recklessness as to an initial physical or threatened assault which goes onto cause "some injury". In existing law, harm amounting to "some injury" - that is, minor injury - is often mis-labelled: it can be under-charged as common assault (which does not recognise that any injury has been caused) or over-charged as ABH (which technically includes all minor injuries). If minor harms were to be charged under a crime of "aggravated assault", the offence description would more precisely criminalise D according to the harm caused - there would be no under- or over-charging. One type of harm that will be difficult to fit under aggravated assault is disease transmission. As with s.47, this difficulty arises because of the need for a base offence of physical or threatened assault. Infection is not normally passed on via these forms of conduct.

A particularly noteworthy feature of aggravated assault is its imposition of constructive liability: *mens rea* is not needed in relation to causing "some injury". Nonetheless, the scoping report defends this breach of the correspondence principle. Unlike ss.47 and 20, the base offence remains the central focus of D's conduct, with the subsequent injury acting only as an aggravating characteristic. That characteristic is labelled on conviction and represented through a proportionate rise in maximum sentence – from six months for the base crime to twelve months in its aggravated form. The offence is triable summarily only, a factor which would save inordinate time and money. This is because many of the minor harms currently charged under s.47 would instead be tried in the magistrates' courts. At present, such cases are often tried in the Crown Court despite the eventual punishment being one which would have come within the powers of the magistrates' courts.

Others have suggested that the Law Commission's proposals place too much emphasis on the correspondence principle. For example, Jackson and Storey argue for a 'moderate' form of constructive liability so that a defendant's liability reflects the level of harm he caused the victim.[20] They give the example of a domestic argument, in which D1 aims to slap his partner, X, hard across the face, intending to injure her. However, X ducks out of the way and D1 instead slaps their 3-year-old child, V, who was sitting behind X on the kitchen table. V is knocked to the floor and suffers a broken arm. Under the current law, D1 could be charged with maliciously inflicting GBH, since he had an intention to cause X some harm (which can be transferred to V[21]). Under the Law Commission's proposals, if D1 did not intend or foresee serious injury, the relevant offence would be intentionally or recklessly causing injury. Jackson and Storey argue that convicting D1 of this offence 'would fail to reflect the fact that serious injury (a broken arm) had been caused to the victim'. In a similar vein, Demetriou writes:[22]

> '[I]t has to be acknowledged that the criminal law is not solely concerned with D's culpability and fault. The criminal law is also concerned with the harm suffered by V. Recent developments, such as the introduction of the Criminal Injuries Compensation Scheme and of the Victim's Impact Statement, pay particular attention to V's harm and highlight his enhanced role within the criminal justice system (CJS). Allowing D to 'get away' with a lesser crime because he did not foresee the full extent of the injuries that he in fact caused, runs counter to the growing victim focus approach adopted by the CJS.'

Now, think about this question.

For the Law Commission's response to the concerns expressed by Jackson and Storey, and Demetriou, refer back to paragraphs 4.97–4.98 in the earlier extract from its report. In your opinion, do the Law Commission's proposals place too much emphasis on the correspondence principle?

[20] Jackson, A. and Storey, T. (2015) 'Reforming Offences Against the Person: In Defence of 'Moderate' Constructivism' 79 *Journal of Criminal Law* 437.

[21] See the discussion of transferred *mens rea* in Chapter 4.

[22] Demetriou, S. (2016) 'Not Giving Up the Fight: A Review of the Law Commission's Scoping Report on Non-fatal Offences Against the Person' 80 *Journal of Criminal Law* 188.

Quiz 6.7

1. Which of the following is not one of the offences found in the Law Commission's proposed new scheme of non-fatal offences against the person?
   a. Intentionally or recklessly causing injury.
   b. Aggravated assault.
   c. Threatened assault.
   d. Intentionally or recklessly causing serious injury.
2. Which of the following is **not** one of the situations in which the proposed new offence of aggravated assault would apply?
   a. Cases in which it is impossible to prove that the defendant intended or foresaw any injury.
   b. Cases which involve the consensual infliction of injury.
   c. Cases which are currently charged as assault occasioning ABH, but are expected to be heard in the magistrates' court because they are of a lower level of seriousness.
   d. Cases involving low-level injuries and which are currently charged as assault or battery following the charging standards.
3. Which of the following is **not** one of the points made by Gibson in his discussion of the Law Commission's proposals?
   a. The terms 'wounding', 'grievous bodily harm' and 'actual bodily harm' are old-fashioned, unclear and their replacement is welcome.
   b. The proposed ladder of offences is more intelligible to practitioners and the public.
   c. The offences of intentionally causing serious injury and recklessly causing serious injury should be welcomed for satisfying the correspondence principle.
   d. The proposed offence of aggravated assault addresses the existing problem of minor injuries being either under- or over-charged.

Conclusion

In the first part of this chapter we looked at five of the most significant non-fatal offences against the person. In the second and third parts of the chapter we analysed these offences from two perspectives. We examined the case law that governs consent to injury, considering the coherence and consistency of these cases and evaluating the majority (social utility) and minority (social disutility) approaches in *R* v *Brown*. We then examined the Law Commission's proposals for reform, including why the Commission concluded that reform is necessary and the thinking behind its proposed new scheme. For each of these two topics there is a corresponding essay title in the 'Evaluating the Law' section that follows below.

Turning to problem questions, something that some students find difficult is integrating the material from the first two parts of the chapter. To help with this, Figure 6.3 sets out a four-step guide. The first step is to determine the level of injury the victim suffered: this will allow you to identify the relevant offence. Next, putting any issues related to consent to one side, you should work through all the other requirements of the offence. If these are satisfied, the third step is to ask whether the victim consented to the activity and, if so, whether the victim's consent is available as a defence. If the victim did not consent, then the final step is to ask whether the defendant genuinely believed the victim was consenting to the activity and, if so, whether his belief in consent is available as a defence.

Step one: Determine the level of injury the victim suffered in order to identify the relevant offence

The victim suffered no injuries, or only trivial or insignificant injuries:
The relevant offence will be either assault or battery. This depends on whether there was an actual infliction of force (battery) or force was only apprehended (assault)

The victim suffered ABH:
The relevant offence will be assault occasioning ABH

The victim suffered GBH or wounding:
Begin with the s.20 offence of malicious wounding or infliction of GBH. If this is established then consider whether the aggravating *mens rea* requirement needed for the s.18 offence of wounding or GBH with intent is present

Step two: Putting any possible defence of consent or belief in consent to one side for a moment, decide whether all of the other requirements of the relevant offence are established

If all the other requirements of the relevant offence are established, go to step three

If all of the other requirements of the relevant offence are not established, the defendant is not guilty of the offence.
[Consider whether there are other offences that might be applicable]

Step three: Did the victim consent to the activity?

Consent here means effective consent (Did the victim have the capacity to consent? Was the victim pressurised by threats? Was the consent vitiated by fraud?)

If there was not effective consent, go to step four.

If there was effective consent, decide whether the victim's consent is available as a defence:
- Assault and battery: Victim's consent always available as a defence
- ABH/GBH/wounding: Victim's consent only available as a defence if injury occurred during a lawful activity

If victim's consent is available as a defence, the defendant is not guilty.
If it is not available, the defendant is guilty.

Step four: Did the defendant genuinely believe the victim was consenting to the activity?

If not, the defendant is guilty of the offence.

If the defendant did genuinely believe the victim was consenting, decide whether his belief in consent is available as a defence:
- Assault and battery: Genuine belief in consent always available as a defence.
- ABH/GBH/wounding: Genuine belief in consent only available as a defence if injury occurred during a lawful activity.

If the genuine belief in consent is available as a defence, the defendant is not guilty.
If it is not available, the defendant is guilty.

Figure 6.3 Non-fatal offences against the person: how to approach problem questions

Applying the law

6.8 Apply the law on non-fatal offences to hypothetical sets of facts.

Romeo, Valentina, Dr Dario and Vincenzo

The following scenario takes place between the characters Romeo, Valentina, Dr Dario and Vincenzo. Read the problem scenario carefully, then answer the multiple-choice questions below to apply your learning to the scenario.

Romeo and Valentina have been dating for a month when Valentina declares, 'I love you'. In fact, she says she loves Romeo so much that she asks him to give her a love bite as a sign of his affection. Romeo obliges and gives Valentina a love bite on her neck. The next day Romeo posts a picture of the love bite on Facebook with the message 'Look what I did LOL'. When Valentina sees it she feels so humiliated that she reports the love bite to the police.

(1) Discuss Romeo's criminal liability.

After a couple of days Valentina's love bite becomes infected and very painful. She goes to her local doctors' surgery. Her normal doctor is fully booked, so reluctantly she agrees to see Dr Dario instead. When she is called, Valentina is surprised at how young Dr Dario is. She explains that she had been hoping to see a more experienced doctor, but he reassures her by saying, 'Don't worry, I have several years' experience. I just look younger than I am'. On hearing this, Valentina relaxes and lets Dr Dario examine her. In fact, Dr Dario has only just qualified and this is his first week in his first job. When Valentina discovers this, she is outraged. She says she would never have let Dr Dario examine her had she known how inexperienced he was.

(2) Discuss Dr Dario's criminal liability.

Later that year Romeo and Valentina are reconciled, get back together, and after a few months get engaged. On the night before the wedding it is Romeo's stag party. Romeo's best man, Vincenzo, decides that he should mark the occasion by playing a joke on Romeo. He waits until Romeo has had a few drinks, then asks some of the other partygoers to hold Romeo down while he shaves off Romeo's eyebrows.

The next morning Vincenzo is surprised at how angry Romeo is. When Valentina discovers what has happened she is so distraught that she telephones the police.

(3) Discuss Vincenzo's criminal liability.

When Vincenzo arrives home from picking up his best man's suit on the morning of the wedding, he is shocked to find two policemen waiting for him by his front door. When they explain that Valentina has filed a complaint, Vincenzo panics. He pushes one of the policemen out of the way and begins to run away. The policeman falls backwards and cracks his head on the pavement. His colleague chases Vincenzo and arrests him. The policeman's head injury requires stitches.

(4) Discuss Vincenzo's criminal liability.

At no point during their relationship has Romeo told Valentina that he is HIV positive. On their wedding night they have sexual intercourse together for the first time. Romeo does not wear a condom, and Valentina contracts the virus. Romeo subsequently claims that Valentina consented to the risk of contracting the virus by agreeing to have unprotected sex and by promising in her wedding vows to love Romeo 'for better, for worse, for richer, for poorer, in sickness and in health'.

(5) Discuss Romeo's criminal liability.

Quiz 6.8

1. The first incident involves a non-fatal injury: a love bite. The first step is therefore to determine what level of injury Valentina suffered, if any, in order to identify the relevant offence. What guidance did Hobhouse LJ offer on the meaning of ABH in *R* v *Chan-Fook?*
   - **a.** Anyone who suffers pain or discomfort - however short-lived - has suffered ABH.
   - **b.** To constitute ABH an injury need not be permanent, but it should not be so trivial as to be wholly insignificant.
   - **c.** Psychiatric harm cannot amount to ABH; physical injury is required.
   - **d.** An injury only constitutes ABH if it is serious enough to require hospital treatment.

2. Whilst it is ultimately a question of fact for the jury, there is good reason to think that the love bite Romeo gave Valentina would be held to amount to ABH. It was not a permanent injury, but presumably it did cause bruising or swelling and so cannot be described as wholly insignificant. The relevant offence in this case would therefore be assault occasioning ABH (section 47 of the Offences Against the Person Act 1861).

   As we have seen in the chapter, the offence of assault occasioning ABH has three requirements. We have already stated that Valentina's injury is likely to constitute ABH. The other two requirements are: (1) that the defendant committed either an assault or a battery; and, (2) that the assault/battery occasioned the ABH. The causal link between Romeo's actions and Valentina's injury is self-evident. So the key requirement in this case is whether or not Romeo committed an assault or battery. In Romeo's case the relevant offence would be battery.

   Which of the following statements defines battery correctly?
   - **a.** The defendant inflicted unlawful force on the victim either intentionally or recklessly.
   - **b.** The defendant inflicted significant, unlawful force on the victim either intentionally or recklessly.
   - **c.** The defendant intentionally inflicted significant, unlawful force on the victim.
   - **d.** The defendant intentionally inflicted unlawful force on the victim.

3. We saw earlier in the chapter that any contact, however slight, is sufficient for the *actus reus* of battery. In Romeo's case it is therefore clear that there was an infliction of force (he obviously made contact with Valentina's body), and that this infliction of force was intentional. So the key issue is whether the force that Romeo inflicted was unlawful. This brings us to the issue of consent. More specifically, it raises the question whether giving a love bite is a lawful or an unlawful activity.

   According to the majority of the House of Lords in *R* v *Brown*, in a case involving ABH/GBH/wounding the consent of the victim is only available as a defence if the injury occurred in the course of a lawful activity. Which approach did the majority take to determining whether an activity which causes injury is lawful?
   - **a.** Wherever possible the criminal law should not concern itself with activities which involve the deliberate but consensual infliction of ABH/GBH/wounding, since these are matters of private morality.
   - **b.** An activity which involves deliberately causing ABH/GBH/wounding is assumed to be lawful, unless there are good policy and public interest reasons for classifying it as unlawful.
   - **c.** An activity which involves deliberately causing ABH/GBH/wounding is assumed to be unlawful, unless there are good policy and public interest reasons for classifying it as lawful.
   - **d.** Whether or not an activity which involves deliberately causing ABH/GBH/wounding is lawful or unlawful should be decided on a case-by-case basis.

4. If we apply the majority's approach to the facts of the question, the prosecution would argue that Romeo giving Valentina a love bite should be assumed to be an unlawful activity. So unless the defence could show good policy and public interest reasons why giving love bites should be classified as a lawful activity, the fact that Valentina consented to the love bite would be unavailable as a defence. Can you think of any good policy and public interest reasons why giving love bites should be classified as a lawful activity? Were these arguments considered by the House of Lords in *R* v *Brown*? If so, what did the majority say about them?

   The defence might also argue that giving a love bite is analogous to some of the other accepted lawful activities.

   Which one of the following statements is correct?
   - **a.** Tattooing and surgery are both lawful activities.
   - **b.** Horseplay (where there is no intention to cause injury) and brawling are both lawful activities.
   - **c.** Ear-piercing and heterosexual sado-masochism are both lawful activities.
   - **d.** Homosexual sado-masochism and boxing are both lawful activities.

One of the reasons the Court of Appeal in *R* v *Wilson* offered in support of its conclusion that Mr and Mrs Wilson were engaged in a lawful activity was that it was analogous to tattooing. Could the defence employ similar reasoning in Romeo's case, and argue that giving a love bite is analogous to tattooing? Alternatively, could the prosecution argue that giving a love bite is analogous to one of the existing unlawful activities (such as sado-masochism in *R* v *Brown* or cutting in *R* v *Hobday*)?

When writing your answer, you should work through the issues in the order we have here, explaining that Romeo's liability for assault occasioning ABH will hinge on whether giving the love bite was a lawful or an unlawful activity (since this will determine whether or not Valentina's consent is available to him as a defence). You should explain how the prosecution would argue that giving a love bite is an unlawful activity, and how the defence would argue that it is a lawful activity. Finally, you should explain which line of reasoning you consider to be strongest in order to assess the likelihood of Romeo being convicted.

5. Moving on to (2), and the criminal liability of Dr Dario: the starting point is to decide whether to focus on the offence of assault or the offence of battery. Which of the following statements correctly describes the *actus reus* of assault and battery?

a. For battery, the defendant must have actually inflicted unlawful force on the victim. For assault it is sufficient that the victim apprehended the infliction of immediate, unlawful force.

b. For assault, the defendant must have inflicted force on the victim without consent. For battery there must also have been an infliction of force, but there is no requirement that this was non-consensual.

c. For assault, the victim must have apprehended the infliction of immediate, unlawful force. For battery the victim must also have apprehended the infliction of unlawful force, but there is no requirement that the force apprehended was immediate.

d. For assault, the victim must have apprehended the infliction of immediate, unlawful force. For battery, the victim must not only have apprehended the infliction of force, force must also have actually been inflicted.

6. In this case, it is safe to assume that Dr Dario would have touched Valentina as part of the examination. Therefore the relevant offence is battery. This offence has three requirements: (1) the defendant inflicted force on the victim; (2) the force was unlawful; and (3) the defendant inflicted the force either intentionally or recklessly.

According to *Collins* v *Wilcock*, how much force must the defendant have inflicted for the *actus reus* of battery?

a. Any contact, however slight, is sufficient.

b. The level of force required by the offence of battery is determined by the jury on a case-by-case basis.

c. The amount of force must have been significant.

d. The force used must have been overpowering.

7. Since Dr Dario touched Valentina, and the touching was intentional, the key issue in the case is whether the force inflicted was unlawful. This will in turn depend on whether the force was consensual. The defence would argue that Valentina agreed to the examination, whereas the prosecution would argue that Valentina's consent was vitiated by Dr Dario's deception.

According to *R* v *Richardson*, when is a victim's consent vitiated by deception?

a. Any deception as to the nature or quality of the act, or as to the identity or attributes of the person, vitiates consent.

b. Any deception as to the nature of the act, or as to the identity of the person, vitiates consent. Deception as to the quality of the act, or the attributes of the person, does not.

c. Any deception as to the nature of the act, or as to the identity or attributes of the person, vitiates consent. Deception as to the quality of the act does not.

d. Any deception as to the nature or quality of the act, or as to the identity of the person, vitiates consent. Deception as to the attributes of the person does not.

Whether or not Valentina's consent to the examination was vitiated by deception would therefore depend on whether Dr Dario deceived her about his identity or his attributes. If his level of experience goes to his identity, Valentina's consent would be vitiated, whereas if it goes to his attributes, Valentina's consent would be valid. Based on the facts and decision in *R* v *Richardson* and *R* v *Melin*, in your opinion would Dr Dario's level of experience be held to go to his identity or his attributes?

8. We now move on to (3), and the aftermath of the stag party. Again, the initial question here is what level of injury the victim – Romeo – has suffered, if any.

Which of the following statements accurately summarises the judgment in *DPP* v *Smith*?

a. Cutting off a substantial part of a victim's hair always constitutes ABH.

b. Cutting off someone's hair will never amount to ABH.

c. Cutting off a substantial part of a victim's hair only constitutes ABH if the victim suffers significant upset or distress.

d. Cutting off a substantial part of a victim's hair is capable of constituting ABH. Whether or not it does so in a particular case is a question of fact for the jury.

9. So whether or not Romeo's shaved eyebrows constitute ABH is a question of fact for the jury. One of the issues the jurors will have to consider is whether the harm Romeo suffered is 'actual', i.e., whether it is 'more than merely transient and trifling' (*R* v *Donovan*). When deciding this, may the jury take into account the fact that Romeo is getting married the next day? Or should the harm be assessed objectively?

In *R* v *Bollom* the Court of Appeal had to decide what factors a jury may take into account when deciding whether a victim has suffered GBH. What did the Court decide?

a. It is up to the trial judge whether or not the jury should be told to consider any factors relating to the particular victim.

b. The context of the harm should be considered, in order to assess its effect on the particular victim.

c. The age, health and other particular factors relating to the victim should be ignored.

d. The jury may decide whether or not to consider any factors relating to the particular victim.

Let's assume for now that a jury would decide that Romeo's injuries constitute ABH. To establish liability for assault occasioning ABH, the prosecution would have to show that Vincenzo committed either an assault or a battery. In Vincenzo's case, battery would apply since Vincenzo made contact with Romeo's body (through the medium of the shaver: Fagan v Metropolitan Police Commissioner [1969] 1 QB 439). Vincenzo did so intentionally. Whether or not there was a battery therefore depends on whether the force inflicted was unlawful, which brings us to the issue of consent. Here three points need to be considered.

First, there is the question whether Romeo did in fact consent to having his eyebrows shaved off. The defence might argue that any groom who arranges and attends a stag-do impliedly consents to some kind of rough horseplay. By contrast, the prosecution would argue that Romeo had had several alcoholic drinks (and so may have lacked the capacity to consent) and point out that Romeo had to be physically restrained.

Second, even if Romeo did consent to having his eyebrows shaved off, there is the question whether his consent is available to Vincenzo as a defence. According to the House of Lords in R v Brown [1994] 1 AC 212, the consent of the victim is only available as a defence if the injury occurred in the course of a lawful activity.

And third, if Romeo did not in fact consent, Vincenzo will still have a defence if he genuinely believed that Romeo was consenting provided that the injury occurred in the course of a lawful activity (R v Jones (Terence) (1986) 83 Cr App R 375; R v Aitken [1992] 1 WLR 1006). The defence would no doubt argue that Vincenzo genuinely believed that Romeo was impliedly consenting, on the basis that Romeo must have expected some sort of prank and still attended the stag-do. By contrast, the prosecution would point out that Vincenzo deliberately waited until Romeo had had a few drinks and asked other partygoers to hold Romeo down.

10. Putting these three points together, which of the following statements is incorrect?

a. Vincenzo will be guilty of assault occasioning ABH if the prank was an unlawful activity.

b. Vincenzo will not be guilty of assault occasioning ABH if Romeo consented and the prank was an unlawful activity.

c. Vincenzo will not be guilty of assault occasioning ABH if the prank was a lawful activity and Vincenzo genuinely believed that Romeo was consenting.

d. Vincenzo will not be guilty of assault occasioning ABH if the prank was a lawful activity and Romeo consented.

Finally, how would the analysis differ if the jury decided that Romeo had not suffered ABH? In cases that do not involve injury, the courts do not draw a distinction between lawful and unlawful activities (R v Brown [1994] 1 AC 212). So if Romeo consented to having his eyebrows shaved off or if Vincenzo genuinely believed that Romeo was consenting, Vincenzo will be not guilty of battery.

11. In (4) the starting point is to determine the level of injury the policeman has suffered.

How did the Court in C v *Eisenhower* define a 'wound'?

a. An injury that results in the loss of a limb

b. A break in the continuity of the whole skin

c. An injury that results in substantial loss of blood

d. Any injury which damages the outer layers of the skin

12. The relevant offences are therefore the ones found in section 20 and section 18 of the Offences Against the Person Act 1861. Since the section 18 offence is an aggravated version of the section 20 offence, it is sensible to discuss the section 20 offence first.

The section 20 offence has three requirements: (1) that the defendant either wounded the victim or inflicted GBH; (2) the wounding/infliction of GBH was unlawful; and (3) the defendant acted maliciously. We have already established that Vincenzo wounded the policeman. This was self-evidently unlawful (there is no suggestion that the injury was consensual or that Vincenzo was acting in self-defence). So the key question is whether Vincenzo acted maliciously.

Based on the decisions in *R* v *Cunningham* and *R* v *Savage & Parmenter*, what is the meaning of 'malicious' in this context?

a. The defendant acted with ill will or hatred towards the victim.

b. The defendant either intended to cause the victim some harm or foresaw that the victim might suffer some harm.

c. The defendant either intended to cause the victim serious harm or foresaw that the victim might suffer serious harm.

d. The defendant either intended to kill the victim or foresaw that the victim might be killed.

13. One way in which Vincenzo might claim that he divvvd not foresee the risk that the policeman might suffer some harm is by claiming that he acted without thinking.

In *R* v *Parker* (which we studied in Chapter 4) the defendant claimed that he was so angry that he acted without thinking and that as a result the risk of damaging the telephone never crossted his mind. Which of the following statements accurately describes the Court of Appeal's reasoning in this case?

a. Parker's actions demonstrated a 'couldn't care less' attitude. A defendant who displays such an attitude acts recklessly.

b. Parker's failure to consider the risk of damaging the phone was the result of his attitude of indifference. A defendant who displays such indifference acts recklessly.

c. Parker had foreseen the risk of damaging the phone. He had deliberately closed his mind to this obvious risk and deliberately closing your mind to an obvious risk is equivalent to having foreseen it.

d. Parker's actions were completely thoughtless and showed lack of consideration. A defendant who displays such an attitude acts recklessly.

14. Having established liability for the section 20 offence, the final question is whether Vincenzo could be held liable for the more serious section 18 offence.

Which of the following four statements about the section 20 and section 18 offences is correct?

a. Self-defence is available as a defence to the section 20 offence, but is not available as a defence to the section 18 offence.

b. To establish liability for the section 18 offence it must be proved that the victim's injuries were life-threatening. This is not the case for the section 20 offence.

c. The section 18 offence requires proof that the defendant displayed a grave level of recklessness. The section 20 offence does not.

d. The section 18 offence requires proof that the defendant either intended to cause the victim GBH or intended to resist or prevent a lawful arrest. The section 20 offence does not.

15. Moving on to (5), the Court of Appeal has held that HIV can amount to GBH (*R* v *Dica*), so the starting point here is the malicious wounding or infliction of the GBH offence (section 20 of the Offences Against the Person Act 1861). This offence has three requirements: (1) that the defendant either wounded the victim or inflicted GBH; (2) the wounding/infliction of GBH was unlawful; and (3) the defendant acted maliciously. We have already stated that Romeo inflicted GBH on Valentina by causing her to contract HIV. In respect of malice, a defendant acts maliciously if he either intended to cause the victim some harm or foresaw that the victim might suffer some harm. It seems clear that Romeo foresaw a risk that Valentina might suffer some harm (the facts indicate that he was aware that he had the virus). So the key question is whether the infliction of GBH was unlawful. This brings us to the issue of consent.

Which of the following statements accurately summarises the reasoning in *R* v *Dica*?

a. The decision in *R* v *Clarence* should be overruled. The victim in *R* v *Dica* had been deceived as to the identity of the person, and so had not consented to either sexual intercourse or the risk of infection.

b. The decision in *R* v *Clarence* should be followed. Only fraud as to the nature of the act or the identity of the person vitiates consent – and being HIV positive is relevant only to the quality of an act (not its nature) and a person's attributes (not their identity).

c. The decision in *R* v *Clarence* should be overruled. The victim in *R* v *Dica* had been deceived as to the nature of the act, and so had not consented to either sexual intercourse or the risk of infection.

d. The decision in *R* v *Clarence* should be overruled. A distinction should be drawn between consent to sexual intercourse and consent to the risk of infection. The victim in *R* v *Dica* consented to sexual intercourse, but did not consent to the risk of infection.

16. In the light of the reasoning in *R* v *Dica*, the prosecution would argue that – whilst Valentina may have consented to sexual intercourse – she did not consent to the risk of contracting HIV. In response, the defence would argue that Valentina did consent to the risk of contracting the virus by agreeing to have unprotected sex and by promising in her wedding vows to love Romeo 'for better, for worse, for richer, for poorer, in sickness or in health'. This is similar to the argument advanced by the defendant in *R* v *Konzani*.

What did the Court of Appeal decide in *R* v *Konzani*?

a. That if a victim is aware of the risks associated with unprotected sexual intercourse and has not taken reasonable steps to determine whether his/her sexual partner is HIV negative, the defence of consent should be available to the defendant

b. That since HIV had not been discovered at the time the Offences Against the Person Act 1861 was introduced, contracting the virus does not constitute grievous bodily harm for the purposes of the Act

c. That if a defendant conceals the fact he is HIV positive from the victim, it almost inevitably follows that the victim cannot give an informed consent to the risk of contracting the virus

d. That someone who consents to unprotected sexual intercourse consents to all of the risks associated with unprotected sex, including the risk of contracting HIV

Finally, Romeo might argue that, even if Valentina did not give an informed consent to the risk of infection, he had a genuine belief that she had consented to this risk (*R* v *Konzani*). Whether Romeo had such a belief or not is a question of fact for the jury to decide. In your opinion, what would a jury decide? If a jury decided that Romeo did not have such a belief, the section 20 offence would be established. You should then go on and consider whether Romeo also committed the section 18 offence. This would depend on whether or not he had an intention to cause Valentina GBH.

In your opinion, would a jury conclude that Romeo intended to cause Valentina GBH?

Applying the law II

Now, consider this scenario.

Suppose that, some years later, Romeo and Valentina break up. Romeo is distraught. He decides he would like to change his appearance. He goes online and finds someone who offers body modification services. Romeo asks them to split his tongue, so that it looks reptile-like.

Now, think about this question. Which option would be the most suitable answer to this question?

Which of the following statements best summarises the decision in *R* v *BM* [2018] EWCA Crim 560?

a. The Court concluded that there was no good reason why body modification should be a lawful activity. If it were to be legalised, this decision would need to be made by Parliament.

b. The Court of Appeal applied the social disutility model.

c. The Court held that new forms of lawful activity may be recognised if they are closely analogous to an existing lawful activity, and concluded that body modification is closely analogous to other forms of bodily adornment such as ear piercing.
d. Respect for individual autonomy should be prioritised over concerns that those seeking body modification procedures may be vulnerable or in need of medical support.

Evaluating the law: Part one

6.9 Evaluate the case law on consent to injury.

Think about this question.

'The case law on consent to injury is completely unsatisfactory. It is impossible to reconcile a number of the leading decisions, and the social utility model advocated by the majority in *R* v *Brown* [1994] 1 AC 212 is inappropriate.'

How far (if at all) do you agree with this statement?

Step 1: Deconstruct the essay title

To prepare an essay plan for this question, you should begin by **deconstructing the essay title** and **identifying the key points** you need to address. Here, the statement in the essay title makes two key claims:

1. that a number of the leading decisions on consent to injury are irreconcilable; and
2. that the social utility model advocated by the majority in *R* v *Brown* is inappropriate.

Step 2: Work through each claim, form an opinion and construct a set of arguments in support of your views

To address the first of these claims, there are a number of possible inconsistencies that could be discussed. These include (1) whether the decision in *R* v *Wilson* can be reconciled with the decision in *R* v *Brown*; (2) whether the decisions in *R* v *BM* and *R* v *Hobday* can be reconciled with the decision in *R* v *Wilson*; and, (3) whether the decisions in *R* v *Jones (Terence)*, *R* v *Aitken* and *R* v *Richardson & Irwin* can be reconciled with *R* v *Brown*. To help you think about this, look back at the sections earlier in this chapter on '**Unlawful activities**' and '**Lawful activities**' and the notes you prepared in response to the following questions:

On *R* v *Brown*:

- Read the following extracts from the judgments of Lord Templeman and Lord Jauncey and make a list of the reasons they gave for deciding that policy and public interest considerations did not require sado-masochism to be a lawful activity.
- Look back at the principles we studied in Chapter 1. Try and match each of the reasons given by Lord Templeman and Lord Jauncey to at least one of the principles from Chapter 1.

- Read the following extract from Lord Mustill's judgment and make a list of the reasons he gave for deciding that policy and public interest considerations did not require sado-masochism to be an unlawful activity.
- Look back at the principles we studied in Chapter 1. Try and match each of the reasons given by Lord Mustill to at least one of the principles from Chapter 1.

On *R* v *BM*:

- Read the following extract from the judgment of Burnett LCJ. Did the Court of Appeal apply the social utility model or the social disutility model?
- What are the two features that Burnett LCJ said underpin almost all of the existing lawful activities? In his view, may the Courts add new activities to the existing list of lawful activities?
- What was the Court of Appeal's response to defence counsel's argument that: (a) the personal autonomy of the customers should be respected; and, (b) the procedures were akin to body adornment?
- According to the Court of Appeal, what were the public interest reasons against making body modification a lawful activity?
- According to Pegg, why might the judgment in *R* v *BM* fail to protect those seeking body modification services?
- Pegg offers two objections to the link Burnett LCJ appeared to draw between undergoing body modification procedures and mental illness. What are these objections?
- What questions does Pegg say the judgment in *R* v *BM* leaves unanswered?

On *R* v *Wilson*:

- Earlier we saw the different underlying approaches of the majority and Lord Mustill in *R* v *Brown* (the social utility and social disutility models). According to the doctrine of precedent, should the Court of Appeal in *R* v *Wilson* have applied the social utility model or the social disutility model?
- Read the following extract from the judgment of Russell LJ in *R* v *Wilson*. Did he apply the social utility or social disutility model? (Hint: the clearest indication can be found in the final paragraph.)
- Make a list of the reasons Russell LJ gave for saying that *R* v *Brown* and *R* v *Wilson* are distinguishable.
- Look back at your list of the reasons Russell LJ gave in *R* v *Wilson* for distinguishing *R* v *Brown*. In the light of Roberts' comments, do you believe the two cases are distinguishable?

On *R* v *Hobday*:

- Read the following extract from the judgment of Edis LJ in *R* v *Hobday*. The trial judge in Hobday's case distinguished *R v Wilson*, saying that Hobday and the victim were not married, nor were they in a loving relationship. According to Edis LJ, was this a valid basis on which to distinguish *R v Wilson*?
- In the earlier extract from Lord Templeman's judgment in R v Brown, you may have noticed that one of the victims in that case had been branded on two occasions. Edis LJ refers to this in [40]. What principle does he derive from it?

- According to Edis LJ, should the Courts take into account the public interest when deciding whether a consensual activity should be lawful or unlawful? If not, when might judges consider the public interest?
- In the light of *R* v *Hobday*, does *R* v *Wilson* still have any precedential value? If so, what principle(s) can we derive from *R* v *Wilson*?

On *R* v *Jones (Terence)*, *R* v *Aitken* and *R* v *Richardson & Irwin*:

- In your opinion, can the case law on horseplay be reconciled with *R* v *Brown*?

Once you have formed an opinion on whether or not the different decisions are reconcilable, use your answers to these questions to form a set of arguments in support of your point of view.

The second of the claims made in the essay title is that the social utility model advocated by the majority in *R* v *Brown* is inappropriate. The implication is that the social disutility model adopted by Lord Mustill in his dissenting judgment is preferable. To form a view on this, look back at the section earlier in the chapter on **'The social utility or social disutility model?'** and the notes you prepared in response to the following questions:

- Read the following extract from David Kell's article 'Social Disutility and the Law of Consent' (1994) 14 Oxford Journal of Legal Studies 121. In your own words, summarise the three reasons he gives for favouring the social disutility approach.
- Do you agree or disagree with David Kell? Try and use the principles that we studied in Chapter 1 to explain your reasoning.

You may also find it helpful to look at your list of the principles underlying the judgments of Lords Templeman, Jauncey and Mustill in *R* v *Brown*. Which of these principles should be prioritised and take precedence over the others?

Once you have decided whether to argue for the social utility or social disutility model, use your notes to construct a set of arguments in support of your opinion.

Step 3: Planning your introduction and conclusion

You now have all the material you need for the main body of your essay. The last task is to decide what to include in your introduction and conclusion. The introduction should contextualise your discussion by briefly outlining the key legal principles which govern cases involving consent to injury, and give an indication of the argument you will present in your essay. The conclusion should round off your essay with a succinct statement of your argument and a summary of your supporting reasons.

Evaluating the law: Part two

6.10 Evaluate the Law Commission's proposed reforms of the non-fatal offences against the person.

Think about this question.

'There is no need to amend the law governing non-fatal offences against the person. Whilst some of the language used in the Offences Against the Person Act 1861 is admittedly archaic, its meaning has been clarified through judicial interpretation. Moreover, the Law Commission's proposals for reform would merely create a new set of difficulties, including an undue emphasis on the correspondence principle.'

How far (if at all) do you agree with this statement?

Step 1: Deconstruct the essay title

To prepare an essay plan for this question, you should begin by **deconstructing the essay title** and **identifying the key points** you need to address. Here, the statement in the essay title makes three key claims:

1. that there is no need to amend the law governing non-fatal offences against the person;
2. that the archaic language used in the 1861 Offences Against the Person Act (OAPA) has been clarified through judicial interpretation; and
3. that the Law Commission's proposals for reform would create a new set of difficulties, including an undue emphasis on the correspondence principle.

Step 2: Work through each claim, form an opinion and construct a set of arguments in support of your views

The first and second claims focus on whether **reform of the 1861 Act** is in fact necessary. The first claim simply states that reform is not needed, with the second claim adding an argument in support of this view. You therefore need to evaluate: (1) the Law Commission's reasons for concluding that reform is necessary; and (2) the claim that it is not necessary to update the language used in the 1861 Act since the courts have clarified its meaning through case law. To help with the first of these, look back at the notes you prepared in response to the following question:

- Read the following extract from the final report. In your own words, list the Commission's criticisms of the OAPA 1861.

To help with the second, look back at the **three options the Law Commission set out** (no reform; retain the 1861 Act but update its language; replace the 1861 Act with a new statute). What did the Law Commission conclude? Do you agree with its reasoning?The third of the essay title's claims focuses on the **Law Commission's proposed reforms**. It argues that these proposals would merely create a new set of problems. To help you think about this, look back at the notes you prepared in response to the following questions:

- Read the following extract from the Law Commission's report. In respect of each of the five issues listed above, what did the Law Commission recommend and why?
- Which aspects of the proposals does Gibson support, and why? Which does he express concern about, and why?
- For the Law Commission's response to the concerns expressed by Jackson and Storey, and Demetriou, refer back to paragraphs 4.97–4.98 in the extract from its report. In your opinion, do the Law Commission's proposals place too much emphasis on the correspondence principle?

You should now have formed an opinion on whether reform of the 1861 Act is in fact necessary, and whether the Law Commission's proposed scheme would be an improvement on the current law. The next step is to organise your notes into a series of arguments in support of your opinion.

Step 3: Planning your introduction and conclusion

You now have all the material you need for the main body of your essay. The last task is to decide what to include in your introduction and conclusion. The introduction should contextualise your discussion by briefly outlining the relevant offences contained in the Offences Against the Person Act 1861, and give an indication of the argument you will present in your essay. The conclusion should round off your essay with a succinct statement of your argument and a summary of your supporting reasons.

Non-fatal offences against the person checklist

Having worked through this chapter, you should now have:

- An understanding of the requirements of the crimes of assault and battery
- An understanding of the requirements of the crime of assault occasioning ABH
- An understanding of the requirements of the crimes of malicious wounding or infliction of GBH and wounding or GBH with intent
- An understanding of when a victim's consent will be vitiated by fraud
- An understanding that on a charge involving ABH/GBH/wounding the consent of the victim will only be available as a defence if the injury occurred in the course of a lawful activity and the ability to state which activities are lawful and which are unlawful
- An ability to critically discuss the existing case law on which activities are lawful and which are unlawful
- An ability to compare the social utility and social disutility models and discuss which is the most appropriate
- An ability to critically discuss the Law Commission's proposed reforms of the non-fatal offences against the person.

Further reading

Anderson, J. (2014) 'The Right to a Fair Fight: Sporting Lessons on Consensual Harm' 17 *New Criminal Law Review* 55.

Cooper, S. and James, M. (2012) 'Entertainment – The Painful Process of Rethinking Consent' *Criminal Law Review* 188.

Cowan, S. (2014) 'Offenses of Sex or Violence? Consent, Fraud, and HIV Transmission' 17 *New Criminal Law Review* 135.

Demetriou, S. (2016) 'Not Giving Up the Fight: A Review of the Law Commission's Scoping Report on Non-Fatal Offences Against the Person' 80 *Journal of Criminal Law* 188.

Finch, E. (2022) 'Psychological injury: where's the harm in it?' *Criminal Law Review* 358.

Gibson, M. (2016) 'Getting Their "Act" Together? Implementing Statutory Reform of Offences Against the Person' *Criminal Law Review* 597.

Hall, H. (2016) 'Exorcism, Religious Freedom and Consent: The Devil in the Detail' 80 *Journal of Criminal Law* 241.

Jackson, A. and Storey, T. (2015) 'Reforming Offences Against the Person: In Defence of "Moderate" Constructivism' 79 *Journal of Criminal Law* 437.

Kell, D. (1994) 'Social Disutility and the Law of Consent' 14 *Oxford Journal of Legal Studies* 121.

Law Commission (2015) *Reform of Offences Against the Person* (Law Commission No 361) HC 555.

Pegg, S. (2019) 'Not so Clear Cut: The Lawfulness of Body Modifications' *Criminal Law Review* 579.

Roberts, P. (1997) 'Consent to Injury: How Far Can You Go?' 113 *Law Quarterly Review* 27.

Ryan, S. (2019) '"Active Deception" v Non-Disclosure: HIV Transmission, Non-Fatal Offences and Criminal Responsibility' *Criminal Law Review 4*

Spencer, J. (2004) 'Liability for Reckless Infection: Part One' 154 *New Law Journal* 384.

Spencer, J. (2004) 'Liability for Reckless Infection: Part Two' 154 *New Law Journal* 448.

Spencer, J. (2004) 'Retrial for Reckless Infection' 154 *New Law Journal* 762.

Tolmie, J. (2012) 'Consent to Harmful Assaults: The Case for Moving Away from Category Based Decision Making' *Criminal Law Review* 656.

Walker, S. (2019) '*R* v *BM*: Errors in the Judicial Interpretation of Body Modification' 83 *Journal of Criminal Law* 245.

Weait, M. (2004) 'Dica: Knowledge, Consent and the Transmission of HIV' 154 *New Law Journal* 826.

Weait, M. (2005) 'Knowledge, Autonomy and Consent: *R* v *Konzani*' *Criminal Law Review* 763.

Weait, M. (2005) 'Criminal Law and the Sexual Transmission of HIV: *R* v *Dica*' 68 *Modern Law Review* 121.

Answers on the Companion Website

Please visit the companion website for the answers to Key Questions, Quizzes, Applying the Law scenarios as well as student support including glossaries. Please visit www.pearsoned.co.uk/Macdonald

7

Sexual offences

Learning Objectives

7.1 Define the actus reus requirements for establishing criminal liability for rape.

7.2 Explain the conclusive presumptions contained in section 76 of the Sexual Offences Act 2003.

7.3 Explain the evidential presumptions contained in section 75 of the Sexual Offences Act 2003.

7.4 Explain the general definition of consent contained in section 74 of the Sexual Offences Act 2003.

7.5 Define the mens rea requirements for establishing criminal liability for rape.

7.6 Define the requirements for establishing criminal liability for assault by penetration.

7.7 Define the requirements for establishing criminal liability for sexual assault.

7.8 Define the requirements for establishing criminal liability for causing a person to engage in sexual activity without consent.

7.9 Apply the law on sexual offences to hypothetical sets of facts.

7.10 Evaluate the section 74 definition of consent, the conclusive and evidential presumptions contained in sections 76 and 75 and the change to the mens rea of rape introduced by the Sexual Offences Act 2003.

Introduction

Evidential difficulties and the burden of proof (many cases are often one person's word against another's).

Shutterstock

Rules on the admission of evidence relating to the complainant's previous behaviour.

Shutterstock

Complainants not telling the police or withdrawing from the process. Reasons for withdrawal from the process can include the length of time it takes (which prolongs the trauma and prevents victims from moving forwards with their lives), the intrusiveness of the investigation (which may heavily scrutinize the victim's personal life and make them feel disbelieved), a poor relationship between the victim and the police, and a lack of available victim support.

Shutterstock

Public attitudes towards sexual violence (e.g. research published in 2005 by Amnesty International reported that a third of people in the UK believe that a woman is partially or totally responsible for being raped if she has behaved in a flirtatious manner).

Shutterstock

So-called 'rape myths', such as the perception that 'true rapes' involve rape by a stranger, occur outdoors, involve violence or threats of violence and normally result in physical injuries, and the belief that a woman can always withhold consent however drunk she is. Research has found that, whilst few jurors believe the obvious rape myths, a significant minority reported being unsure whether many rape myths are true or false. This indicates the potential for these myths to influence juries' decision-making.

Shutterstock

It has also been suggested that concern about the number of convictions could itself become counter-productive if it leads to other important priorities being neglected, particularly the support and care of victims.

Shutterstock

In the ending June 2024, the police recorded a total of 69,184 rapes year.[1] However, the actual number of rapes that occurred is much higher, as data has shown that less than one in six victims reports the offence to the police.[2] Moreover, only a small proportion of police recorded rapes result in a prosecution. In 2023/24, the Crown Prosecution Service charged a total of 2,572 suspects and brought a total of 2,283 prosecutions. Convictions were secured in 53.4 percent of these cases.[3]

Many factors have been identified as contributing to this large disparity between the prevalence of rape and the number of rape convictions. These include:

- Evidential difficulties and the burden of proof (many cases are often one person's word against another's)
- Rules on the admission of evidence relating to the complainant's previous behaviour
- Complainants not telling the police,[4] or withdrawing from the process.[5] Reasons for withdrawal from the process can include the length of time it takes (which prolongs the trauma and prevents victims from moving forwards with their lives), the intrusiveness of the investigation (which may heavily scrutinize the victim's personal life and make them feel disbelieved), a poor relationship between the victim and the police, and a lack of available victim support.[6]
- Public attitudes towards sexual violence (e.g. research published in 2005 by Amnesty International reported that a third of people in the UK believe that a woman is partially or totally responsible for being raped if she has behaved in a flirtatious manner).[7]
- So-called 'rape-myths'[8], such as the perception that 'true rapes' involve rape by a stranger, occur outdoors, involve violence or threats of violence and normally result in physical injuries, and the belief that a woman can always withhold consent

[1] Office for National Statistics (2024) *Crime in England and Wales: Year ending June 2024*.

[2] 'Rape: Levels of Prosecutions' (2025) *House of Lords Library* https://lordslibrary.parliament.uk/rape-levels-of-prosecutions.

[3] George, R. & Ferguson, S. (2021) *Review into the Criminal Justice System response to adult rape and serious sexual offences across England and Wales.*

[4] Gillen, J. (2019) Gillen Review: R*eport into the law and procedures in serious sexual offences in Northern Ireland*.

[5] One of the most distressing parts of complainants' experiences within the criminal justice system is cross-examination. An empirical study of the questions asked during cross-examination of rape complainants suggests that, in spite of the reforms that have been implemented in recent decades to improve the criminal justice response for rape complainants, when it comes to cross-examination little has changed in the past 50 years. The study concludes that complainants still find cross-examination to be distressing and demeaning, and this is understandable given the tactics employed by defence lawyers (Zydervelt, S., Zajac, R., Kaladelfos, A. & Westera, N. (2017) 'Lawyers' Strategies for Cross-examining Rape Complainants: Have We Moved Beyond the 1950s?' 57 *British Journal of Criminology* 551).[1] George, R. & Ferguson, S. (2021) *Review into the Criminal Justice System response to adult rape and serious sexual offences across England and Wales.* On attempts to address these issues, see King, A., Munro, V. E. & Young Andrade, L. (2025) 'Increasing partnership, progression and procedural justice? Reflecting on lessons learned about rape prosecution under "Operation Soteria"' *Criminal Law Review* 198.

[6] George, R. & Ferguson, S. (2021) *Review into the Criminal Justice System response to adult rape and serious sexual offences across England and Wales.*

[7] Office for Criminal Justice Reform (2006) *Convicting Rapists and Protecting Victims – Justice for Victims of Rape: A Consultation Paper.*

[8] Drawing on the field of mythological studies, Hayes argues that the use of myth as a medium is not necessarily bad. In the context of rape, the problem is the content of rape myths, i.e., they 'are bad not because they are myths, but because they are patriarchal' (171, emphasis original). Myth could also be used, he argues, to contest this patriarchal orthodoxy: Hayes, D. J. (2024) 'Are Rape Myths "Myths"?' 44 Oxford Journal of Legal Studies 156.

however drunk she is.[9] Research has found that, whilst few jurors believe the obvious rape myths, a significant minority reported being unsure whether many rape myths are true or false. This indicates the potential for these myths to influence juries' decision-making.[10]

- During trials, narratives constructed by the defence responsibilise the victim – scrutinising and dissecting their behaviour – while there is a lack of attention to the responsibility of the defendant to ascertain the victim's consent.[11]

At the same time, concern has been expressed that criticism of the proportion of rapes that result in a criminal conviction could have counter-productive knock-on effects. It could result in criminal justice agencies focusing on attrition rates at the expense of other important priorities, particularly the support and care of victims.[12] It could also lead to some victims choosing to withdraw from investigations and prosecutions because they believe a conviction is unlikely. Indeed, the proportion of victims in rape cases who withdraw their support for police action is notably higher than for other types of crimes.[13] Yet as noted above, in 2023/24 convictions were secured in 53.4 percent of cases in which a prosecution was brought. In other words, when a rape charge is pursued to trial by jury, juries are more likely to convict than acquit.[14]

Rape cases and convictions from 2017–2020

2017/18-2019/20

In the three-year period from 2017/18 to 2019/20, there were an estimated 128,000 victims of rape and attempted rape each year.

Yet the total number of adult rapes recorded by the police in 2019/20 was significantly lower, at 43,187.

Moreover, only 3 percent of the adult rape offences assigned a police outcome in 2019/20 were given an outcome of charged/summonsed.

The total number of defendants prosecuted for rape of an adult in 2019/20 was 885; the number convicted was just 344.

---

[9] Temkin, J. (2010) '"And Always Keep A-Hold of Nurse, for Fear of Finding Something Worse": Challenging Rape Myths in the Courtroom' 13 *New Criminal Law Review* 710; Smith, O. & Skinner, T. (2017) 'How Rape Myths Are Used and Challenged in Rape and Sexual Assault Trials' 26 *Social & Legal Studies* 441. For a contrasting view, see Reece, H. (2013) 'Rape Myths: Is Elite Opinion Right and Popular Opinion Wrong?' 33 *Oxford Journal of Legal Studies* 445 and Gurnham, D. (2016) 'Victim-Blame as a Symptom of Rape Myth Acceptance? Another Look at How Young People in England Understand Sexual Consent' 36 *Legal Studies* 258.

[10] Gillen, J. (2019) Gillen Review: *Report into the law and procedures in serious sexual offences in Northern Ireland.*

[11] Dowds, E. (2022) '"I presume she wanted it to happen": rape, reasonable belief in consent, and law reform in Northern Ireland' 73 *Northern Ireland Legal Quarterly 501*.

[12] A point made by *The Stern Review* (Home Office (2010) *The Stern Review: A report by Baroness Vivien Stern CBE of an independent review into how rape complaints are handled by public authorities in England and Wales)*. See also Carline, A. & Gunby, C. (2017) 'Rape Politics, Policies and Practice: Exploring the Tensions and Unanticipated Consequences of Well-Intended Victim Focused Measures' 56 *Howard Journal of Crime and Justice 34.*

[13] 'Rape: Levels of Prosecutions' (2025) *House of Lords Library* https://lordslibrary.parliament.uk/rape-levels-of-prosecutions.

[14] In her empirical study of rape and serious sexual offence trials, Candida Saunders urges the importance of ensuring that victims and the wider public understand that, in cases that go to trial, juries convict more often than they acquit. She also highlights other rape trial "myths", pointing out that when victims testify special measures are routinely employed and cross-examination – while undoubtedly difficult – is considerably shorter than often portrayed: Saunders, C. (2025) 'Myths and reality: an empirical challenge to false beliefs about courtroom practice in rape and serious sexual offence cases' *Criminal Law Review* 396.

In this chapter we focus primarily on the **offence of rape**. The definition of this offence was given an overhaul by the Sexual Offences Act 2003. A new, statutory definition of consent was introduced, presumptions were created to structure and guide juries' decision-making and the *mens rea* of the offence was changed. At the time the Act was passed, one of its key objectives was to increase the number of rape convictions. We will examine the Act's definition of rape and evaluate the changes it made and its impact on the number of rape convictions.

Once we have worked through the offence of rape we will then look at three other serious sexual offences: **assault by penetration**; **sexual assault**; and causing a person to engage in **sexual activity without consent**. Like the offence of rape, these three offences all target forms of non-consensual sexual activity.

Actus reus of rape

7.1 Define the actus reus requirements for establishing criminal liability for rape.

The offence of rape is defined by section 1 of the Sexual Offences Act 2003:

EXTRACT

Section 1 of the Sexual Offences Act 2003

1 Rape

(1) A person (A) commits an offence if –

(a) he intentionally penetrates the vagina, anus or mouth of another person (B) with his penis,

(b) B does not consent to the penetration, and

(c) A does not reasonably believe that B consents.

(2) Whether a belief is reasonable is to be determined having regard to all the circumstances, including any steps A has taken to ascertain whether B consents.

(3) Sections 75 and 76 apply to an offence under this section.

(4) A person guilty of an offence under this section is liable, on conviction on indictment, to imprisonment for life.

This tells us that the offence has four requirements:

1. The defendant penetrated the vagina, anus or mouth of the victim with his penis
2. The victim did not consent to the penetration
3. The defendant intentionally penetrated the victim's vagina, anus or mouth with his penis
4. The defendant lacked a reasonable belief that the victim was consenting to the penetration.

Numbers 1 and 2 are *actus reus* requirements. Numbers 3 and 4 are *mens rea* requirements. We will work through them in turn.

1. The defendant penetrated the vagina, anus or mouth of the victim with his penis

The first requirement for the offence of rape is that the defendant penetrated the vagina, anus or mouth of the victim with his penis. It follows from this requirement that:

- Only men can commit rape, since the offence is limited to penetration with a penis. But whilst women cannot commit rape as principals, they can be convicted of being accessories to rape. They can also commit the other sexual offences we will study later in this chapter.
- Both men and women can be the victims of rape, since the offence includes anal and oral penetration as well as vaginal penetration.

Section 79 of the Sexual Offences Act 2003 also tells us the following:

EXTRACT

Section 79 of the Sexual Offences Act 2003

79 Part 1: general interpretation

(1) The following apply for the purposes of this Part.

(2) Penetration is a continuing act from entry to withdrawal.

(3) References to a part of the body include references to a part surgically constructed (in particular, through gender reassignment surgery).

[...]

Subsection (3) means that female-to-male transsexuals can be convicted of rape, since the offence covers penetration with a surgically constructed penis. It also means that male-to-female transsexuals can be vaginally raped.

Subsection (2) tells us that penetration is a continuing act, which begins on entry and does not end until withdrawal. So suppose the victim consents to the initial penetration, but during sexual intercourse she withdraws her consent and asks the defendant to stop. If the defendant chooses to ignore her and fails to withdraw he commits rape. At the moment he refuses to withdraw there is coincidence of *actus reus* (non-consensual penetration) and *mens rea* (no belief that the victim is consenting).

For centuries the criminal law stated that a husband could not be convicted of raping his wife. This was based on the outdated notion that, by entering into a marriage, a wife consented to sexual intercourse for the duration of the marriage. Shockingly, it was not until the 1990s that this notion was firmly rejected.[15] Today, a husband can be convicted of raping his wife.

2. The victim did not consent to the penetration

The second *actus reus* requirement is that the penetration was non-consensual.

It is important to begin by stating that whether or not the victim consented is a question that must be answered by looking at the victim's state of mind. In *R* v *Malone* [1998] 2 Cr App R. 447 CA the victim was a 16-year-old girl. At the time the defendant had sexual intercourse with her she was very drunk. She said that, although she had

[15] *R* v *R* [1992] 1 AC 599 HL.

not attempted to resist, the sex was non-consensual. She said she had been too drunk to resist. At trial the defendant was convicted of rape. On appeal his counsel argued that a defendant should not be convicted of rape if the victim failed to demonstrate or communicate her lack of consent. The Court of Appeal rejected this argument. Roch LJ explained that the issue is whether or not the victim was consenting, not whether or not the victim demonstrated her lack of consent:

> The *actus reus* of rape is an act of sexual intercourse with a woman who at the time of the act of sexual intercourse does not consent to that act of sexual intercourse. There is no requirement that the absence of consent has to be demonstrated or that it has to be communicated to the defendant for the *actus reus* of rape to exist.

However, this does not mean that the victim not communicating her lack of consent is completely irrelevant. Although it is not relevant to the *actus reus* of rape[16], it might be one of the factors a jury takes into account when applying the *mens rea* requirement that the defendant lacked a reasonable belief in consent. We'll look at the *mens rea* in detail below.

The concept of consent is central to all of the offences we will study in this chapter. But whilst it is an extremely important concept, it is also very difficult to define.

In 2000 the Home Office published a review of the old law on sexual offences,[17] in which it emphasised how important it is to define consent clearly.

EXTRACT

Read the following extract from the review.

Why did the Home Office say it is important to define consent clearly? These reasons are based on which of the principles we studied in Chapter 1?

Home Office (2000) *Setting the Boundaries: Reforming the law on sex offences*

2.7.3 It is vitally important that in this most private and difficult area of sexual relationships the law should be as clear as possible so that the boundaries of what is acceptable, and of criminally culpable behaviour, are well understood. This understanding is essential for all those involved in the criminal justice system in practicing and interpreting the law (and we had evidence that it was not always well understood even by professionals). It is important for society as a whole for sexual relationships to be based on mutual respect and understanding.

2.7.4 This led us to the inescapable conclusion that it was vital for the law on rape and sexual assault to be, as far as possible, set out in statute so that it was accessible and available to all. The complexity of the common law on consent, and the uncertainty caused by differing decisions, were not helpful to the criminal justice system or to the wider community. There will always be a continuing role for the common law to develop as cases raise new issues over time, but the key principles of the meaning of consent should be set out clearly in the law for all to see.

---

16 For the argument for an 'affirmative consent' requirement – that is, that the law should require that the victim was positively consenting in her mind *and* communicated this approval to the defendant – see McCormack, S. & Herring, J. (2025) 'Is Affirmative Consent the Answer? Yes, Sort of, Maybe' 89 *Journal of Criminal Law* 16.

17 Home Office (2000) *Setting the Boundaries: Reforming the law on sex offences*.

The review went on to state that:

> 2.10.3 [...] Clarifying the meaning of consent in statute would enable judges to be able to explain what the law said and for juries to understand just what is meant by consent. It would also enable Parliament to consider and recommend what should and should not form acceptable standards of behaviour in a modern society [...]

As we examine the provisions which resulted from these recommendations (sections 74 to 76 of the Sexual Offences Act 2003), ask yourselves whether they achieve these objectives. Have they clarified the meaning of consent so that judges can explain the law and juries understand it? In these sections has Parliament clearly specified what behaviour is acceptable and distinguished it from behaviour that is unacceptable and prohibited?

Sections 74 to 76 of the 2003 Act contain a definition of consent (section 74) and two sets of presumptions (sections 75 and 76). We will work through these three sections in reverse order, because this is the order in which you would consider them when answering a problem question.

Quiz 7.1

1. Which of the following statements is true?
   - **a.** Only females can be a victim of rape.
   - **b.** A woman cannot commit rape as either a principal or an accessory.
   - **c.** Only a man can perform the *actus reus* of rape.
   - **d.** In the majority of cases, victims are raped by someone they had never previously met.
2. How might the *actus reus* of rape be performed?
   - **a.** Penetration by fingers of the vagina of another without consent.
   - **b.** Penetration by penis of another's vagina with consent.
   - **c.** Penetration by penis of the mouth of another without consent.
   - **d.** Penetration by penis of the anus of another with consent.
3. Penetration with a penis, begun with consent, becomes rape in which **one** of the following circumstances?
   - **a.** If V ceases to consent.
   - **b.** When D exceeds a reasonable time for negotiating the continuance of the intercourse with V.
   - **c.** If the man, upon realising V no longer consents, does not immediately withdraw his penis completely from V.
   - **d.** If D asks V whether he can record them on his mobile phone.
4. In which one of the following circumstances would the prosecution not be able to prove a lack of consent?
   - **a.** Where V has not communicated any disagreement to D.
   - **b.** Where V was very drunk and submitted to the penetration.
   - **c.** Where D has obtained the free agreement of V and V is of sufficient capacity to give that agreement.
   - **d.** Where D has an honest belief in V's consent.
5. Which section of the Sexual Offences Act 2003 defines the meaning of consent?
   - **a.** Section 75.
   - **b.** Section 74.
   - **c.** Section 76.
   - **d.** Section 1.

i. Section 76: Conclusive presumptions

7.2 Explain the conclusive presumptions contained in section 76 of the Sexual Offences Act 2003.

In a problem question, you should begin by asking yourself whether section 76 applies. Section 76 states:

EXTRACT

Section 76 Sexual Offences Act 2003

76 Conclusive presumptions about consent

(1) If in proceedings for an offence to which this section applies it is proved that the defendant did the relevant act and that any of the circumstances specified in subsection (2) existed, it is to be conclusively presumed–

(a) that the complainant did not consent to the relevant act, and

(b) that the defendant did not believe that the complainant consented to the relevant act.

(2) The circumstances are that–

(a) the defendant intentionally deceived the complainant as to the nature or purpose of the relevant act;

(b) the defendant intentionally induced the complainant to consent to the relevant act by impersonating a person known personally to the complainant.

The word 'conclusive' means that these presumptions cannot be rebutted by the defendant. So if *either* of the two circumstances listed in subsection (2) existed, the conclusion must be that the victim did not consent to the penetration *and* that the defendant lacked a reasonable belief in consent. In other words, if the defendant intentionally penetrated the vagina, anus or mouth of the victim with his penis and either of the circumstances listed in subsection (2) existed, he is guilty of rape.

So what are the two circumstances in which section 76 applies?

The defendant intentionally deceived the victim as to the nature or purpose of the relevant act

The first is that the defendant intentionally deceived the victim as to the nature or purpose of the relevant act. The leading case here is *R* v *Jheeta* [2007] EWCA Crim 1699. As this case illustrates, it is not enough that the defendant intentionally deceived the victim. The defendant must have intentionally deceived the victim as to the nature or purpose of vaginal, anal or oral penetration.

The victim met the defendant, Harvinder Singh Jheeta, at college. They became friends and started a sexual relationship. Consensual sex took place, usually in hotel rooms booked by Jheeta. After a few months the victim started receiving threatening text messages and phone calls, containing comments like 'We are going to kidnap you', 'We are going to convert you', 'We are going to kill you'. She thought that the messages were from other Muslim students at the college and confided in Jheeta. He reassured her and said he would protect her. In fact, he was the one responsible for the messages. Eventually, the victim said she wanted to tell the police. Jheeta said that he would go to the police and make a complaint on her behalf. She agreed. Soon afterwards the victim received a text message from a PC Ken, who said he was in charge of her case. She received regular text messages from PC Ken. But PC Ken did not exist; Jheeta was the one sending the messages. PC Ken was later replaced by PC Bob and then by PC Thomas. Again, both of these figures were fictitious and Jheeta was the one sending the messages.

During this time the victim never suspected Jheeta. But she had grown tired of their relationship, and on several occasions tried to break it off. Each time she did so, she would receive a text message from one of the police officers telling her that Jheeta had tried to kill himself and that she should take care of him. She was even told that if she did not sleep with Jheeta she would be fined for causing him distress. Each time she complied and had sex with the defendant in a hotel room.

In March 2006 the victim went to the police, and Jheeta was arrested. When interviewed, he said that the reason for his scheme was that he had been worried that the victim was going off him. He also made an important concession. He said that, although the victim had been willing to have sexual intercourse with him for the entire period of their relationship, the text messages ensured that the intercourse was more frequent than would otherwise have been the case.

Jheeta was charged with rape. He accepted his lawyer's advice to plead guilty, but subsequently appealed claiming that his lawyer had explained the law to him incorrectly. In its judgment the Court of Appeal considered how section 76 should be interpreted.

EXTRACT

Read the following extract from the judgment of Sir Igor Judge.

When will section 76(2)(a) apply?

Did section 76(2)(a) apply in *R* v *Jheeta*? Why/why not?

R v *Jheeta* [2007] EWCA Crim 1699

Sir Igor Judge

23 [...] [S]ection 76 raises presumptions conclusive of the issue of consent, and thus where intercourse is proved, conclusive of guilt. They therefore require the most stringent scrutiny.

24 In our judgment the ambit of section 76 is limited to the "act" to which it is said to apply. In rape cases the "act" is vaginal, anal or oral intercourse. Provided this consideration is constantly borne in mind, it will be seen that section 76 (2)(a) is relevant only to the comparatively rare cases where the defendant deliberately deceives the complainant about the *nature or purpose* of one or other form of intercourse. No conclusive presumptions arise merely because the complainant was deceived in some way or other by disingenuous blandishments of or common or garden lies by the defendant. These may well be deceptive and persuasive, but they will rarely go to the nature or purpose of intercourse. Beyond this limited type of case, and assuming that, as here, section 75 has no application, the issue of consent must be addressed in the context of section 74.

[...]

28 With these considerations in mind, we must return to the present case. On the written basis of plea the appellant undoubtedly deceived the complainant. He created a bizarre and fictitious fantasy which, because it was real enough to her, pressurised her to have intercourse with him more frequently than she otherwise would have done. She was not deceived as to the nature or purpose of intercourse, but deceived as to the situation in which she found herself. In our judgment the conclusive presumption in section 76 (2)(a) had no application, and counsel for the appellant below were wrong to advise on the basis that it did.

As these paragraphs explain, this was not the end of the story in *R* v *Jheeta*. Where the conclusive presumptions don't apply you must go on to consider whether the evidential presumptions apply. And where (as in *R* v *Jheeta*) the evidential presumptions don't apply either you must go on and apply section 74's definition of consent. So we will be returning to *R* v *Jheeta* when we examine section 74.

The Court of Appeal in *R* v *Jheeta* also discussed the facts of another case called *R* v *Linekar* [1995] QB 250. Linekar promised to pay a prostitute £25 if she had sexual intercourse with him. He never intended to pay her. Clearly Linekar deceived the prostitute, but did he deceive her as to the nature or purpose of sexual intercourse? The Court of Appeal in *R* v *Jheeta* said that he did not:

> 27 [...] Linekar deceived the prostitute about his intentions. He undoubtedly lied to her. However she was undeceived about either the nature or the purpose of the act, that is intercourse. Accordingly the conclusive presumptions in section 76 would have no application.

So if a case like *R* v *Linekar* occurred today, whether or not the prostitute consented to sexual intercourse would have to be decided by applying the section 74 definition of consent.

Case law has also established that section 76(2)(a) would *not* apply in the following six situations:

1. **Where the defendant deceives the victim as to their gender.**
   In *R* v *McNally* [2013] EWCA Crim 1051 the female defendant pretended to be male. Believing the defendant was male, the victim consented to oral sex. The Court of Appeal stated that 76(2)(a) did not apply (although, as we'll see shortly, the defendant's conviction for the section 2 offence of assault by penetration was upheld, applying section 74).

2. **Where the victim has stated that she will only consent to sexual intercourse if the defendant uses a condom, but he does not use one.**

   In *Assange* v *Swedish Prosecution Authority* [2011] EWHC 2849 (Admin) the High Court held that, whilst such conduct is deceptive, the deception does not relate to the nature of sexual intercourse. Again, section 74 should be applied instead.

3. **Where the victim has stated that she will only consent to sexual intercourse if the defendant withdraws before ejaculating, but after penetration he refuses to withdraw and ejaculates inside her.**

   In *R (F)* v *Director of Public Prosecutions* [2013] EWHC 945 (Admin) the High Court assumed that such a case would fall outside section 76(2)(a) and instead applied section 74.

4. **Where the victim has stated that she will only consent to unprotected sexual intercourse if the defendant has had a vasectomy, and the defendant falsely states that he has had one.**

   In *R* v *Lawrance* [2020] EWCA Crim 971 the Court of Appeal stated that section 76(2)(a) does not apply in such a situation.

5. Where the victim has sexual intercourse with the defendant believing that he is a fellow environmental activist, when in fact he is an undercover police officer.

It was implicit in the judgment in *R (Monica)* v *Director of Public Prosecutions ex parte Boyling* [2018] EWHC 3508 (Admin) that section 76(2)(a) would not apply on these facts.

6. Where the defendant has unprotected sex with the victim without telling her that he is HIV positive.

In the previous chapter we studied the decision in *R* v *Dica* [2004] EWCA Crim 1103. We saw that in a situation like this there is no consent to the risk of infection, but there is consent to sexual intercourse. So whilst the defendant might be guilty of maliciously inflicting GBH, he is not guilty of rape (Confirmed in *R* v *B* [2006] EWCA Crim 2945).

(We will look at the first five of these cases in greater detail later in the chapter, under **cases involving deception**.)

So far we have seen eight situations in which section 76(2)(a) would not apply. Our next case, *R* v *Williams* [1923] 1 KB 340, is an example of when it would apply. The defendant in this case, Owen Williams, was a choirmaster. He was giving the 16-year-old victim singing lessons. During their second lesson Williams told her that her breathing was not right. He told her to lie down, removed some of her clothes and climbed on top of her. He said: 'It is quite all right; do not worry. I am going to make an air passage. This is my method of training. Your breathing is not quite right and I have to make an air passage to make it right'. The victim believed him and made no attempt to resist. She did not know that he was having sexual intercourse with her. Williams was convicted of rape and his conviction was upheld by the Court of Appeal. The Court held that the sexual intercourse was non-consensual. The victim had given her consent to a medical procedure, but had not given her consent to sexual intercourse.

These events took place in 1922, long before the Sexual Offences Act 2003. But they are a useful illustration of the rare and unusual circumstances in which section 76(2)(a) would apply. Williams intentionally deceived the victim as to the nature of the act. He tricked her into believing that it was a medical procedure when in fact it was sexual intercourse.

In *R* v *Williams* there was deception as to the 'nature' of sexual intercourse. Our next three cases focus instead on 'purpose'. Before we turn to them, note first of all that none of these cases was actually a rape case (the defendant and victim did not have sexual intercourse in any of them). In spite of this, all three are still relevant since they give us further guidance on when section 76(2)(a) will apply.

THE FIRST CASE is *R* v *Green* [2002] EWCA Crim 1501.

The defendant in this case was a doctor. He misled a number of male teenage patients into believing that they had potential impotency or infertility problems, and carried out bogus investigations which involved touching the victims' genitals and requiring them to masturbate so that he could take a sample. The case itself occurred before the Sexual Offences Act 2003, but if a similar case occurred today section 76(2)(a) would apply (confirmed in *R* v *Jheeta* [2007] EWCA Crim 1699). The victims were deceived as to the purpose of the activities. They believed the activities were for a medical purpose, when in fact they were for the defendant's sexual gratification.

THE SECOND CASE is *R* v *Devonald* [2008] EWCA Crim 527.

The defendant, 37-year-old Stephen Devonald, had a 16-year-old daughter. His daughter had been dating a 16-year-old boy. When the boy decided to end the relationship, Devonald decided to seek revenge. He went onto the Internet, pretended to be a 20-year-old female named 'Cassey', and struck up an online relationship with his daughter's ex-boyfriend. Pretending to be Cassey, he convinced the boy to masturbate twice in front of a web cam. His plan was to embarrass and humiliate the boy. It seems that he intended to place a video of the boy masturbating on the Internet.

After the trial judge ruled that section 76(2)(a) could apply to the facts of this case, Devonald pleaded guilty to the section 4 offence of causing a person to engage in sexual activity without consent (which we'll study more closely below). He subsequently applied to the Court of Appeal for leave to appeal against his conviction, arguing that the trial judge had been wrong to rule that section 76(2)(a) might apply.

EXTRACT

Read the following extract from the judgment of Leveson LJ.

According to the Court of Appeal, was the trial judge right to rule that section 76(2)(a) might apply? Had the victim been deceived as to the purpose of the act of masturbation?

R v *Devonald* [2008] EWCA Crim 527

Leveson LJ

7 [...] The learned judge ruled that it was open to the jury to conclude that the complainant was deceived as to the purpose of the act of masturbation. We agree. On the facts, as we have described them, it is difficult to see how the jury could have concluded otherwise that the complainant was deceived into believing that he was indulging in sexual acts with, and for the sexual gratification of, a 20-year-old girl with whom he was having an on line relationship. That is why he agreed to masturbate over the sex cam. In fact, he was doing so for the father of his ex girlfriend who was anxious to teach him a lesson doubtless by later embarrassing him or exposing what he had done. It is an inevitable inference that it is for that reason that the applicant changed his plea to guilty when the judge so ruled. Miss Howell has over focussed on the phrase "nature of the act", which undoubtedly was sexual but not on its purpose, which encompasses rather more than the specific purpose of sexual gratification by the defendant in the Act of masturbation. In our judgment, this ruling was correct and there is no grounds for challenging the basis on which the applicant changed his plea. This application is therefore refused.

The Court of Appeal in *R* v *Devonald* also confirmed that section 76(2)(a) applies in cases like *R* v *Green*, but does not apply in cases like *R* v *Linekar*.

EXTRACT

In the following extract from Leveson LJ's judgment, how does he distinguish *R* v *Linekar* from *R* v *Green* and *R* v *Devonald*?

In your opinion, is this distinction satisfactory?

R v *Devonald* [2008] EWCA Crim 527

Leveson LJ

7 [...] In relation to those charges in *Green* in which the victim masturbated himself, it was not suggested that he was unaware what he was doing: he believed, however, that the purpose of the act was linked to a medical examination. The distinction with cases such as *Linekar* is that the purpose of "the act" was consensual sexual intercourse between complainant and defendant. The fact that agreement was obtained by promise of money (or any other blandishment) merely identifies a secondary motive for that agreement.

THE THIRD CASE – which also has quite extraordinary facts – is *R* v *B* [2013] EWCA Crim 823.

The defendant, B, had been in a sexual relationship with the victim for five years. In 2009 he created a false profile on Facebook, calling himself Grant. 'Grant' then contacted the victim, developed a relationship with her and persuaded her to send him topless photos of herself. Having received the photos, 'Grant' threatened to send the photos to the victim's employer and to publish them online unless she performed sexual acts over the Internet. The victim told the defendant what had happened (not realising that the defendant was in fact Grant).

The defendant said she should lure Grant to a meeting and that he would go in her place to confront Grant. After the supposed meeting, the defendant told the victim that he had killed Grant. The defendant then created a second false Facebook profile, this time calling himself Chad. 'Chad' contacted the victim, said that he was Grant's friend, knew what Grant had done, and that he had the topless photos and would send them to her employer if she did not perform further sexual acts over the Internet. Reluctantly, she complied.

EXTRACT

Read the following extract from the judgment of Hallett LJ.

Did the facts of *R* v *B* fall within section 76(2)(a)? Why/why not?

According to Hallett LJ, what was the defendant's purpose for forcing the victim into performing the relevant acts? What did the victim believe to be the purpose of the acts? Is the case distinguishable from *R* v *Devonald*?

R v B [2013] EWCA Crim 823

Hallett LJ

19 There is no definition of the word *purpose* in the Act. It is a perfectly ordinary English word and one might have hoped it would not be necessary to provide a definition. It has been left to the courts and academics to struggle with its meaning in the context of a sexual act. We say 'struggle' advisedly because it may not be straightforward to ascertain the *purpose* of a sexual act. Those engaging in a sexual act may have a number of reasons or objectives and each party may have a different objective or reason. The Act does not specify whose *purpose* is under consideration. There is, therefore, a great danger in attempting any definition of the word *purpose* and in defining it too widely. A wide definition could bring within the remit of section 76 situations never contemplated by Parliament.

20 We shall, therefore, simply apply the normal rules of statutory construction and echo what was said in *Jheeta*. Where, as here, a statutory provision effectively removes from an accused his only line of defence to a serious criminal charge it must be strictly construed. We respectfully adopt the approach of the court in *Jheeta*. If there is any conflict between the decisions in *Jheeta* and *Devonald*, we would unhesitatingly follow *Jheeta*. Thus, it will be a rare case in which section 76 should be applied.

21 Is this one of those rare cases? [Counsel for the prosecution] reminded the court of the extent of the deception and the affect upon the complainant. It was not unlike the extent and effect of the deception in *Jheeta*. Just as in *Jheeta*, this appellant undoubtedly deceived his girlfriend in a cruel and despicable way. However, the fact that there was a catalogue of deception of an unpleasant kind begs the question as to whether it was deception as to *purpose* so as to trigger the operation of section 76. We have our doubts.

22 The complainant was never asked what her purpose or understanding of the purpose of the act was and the appellant's purpose seems far from clear. His accounts varied but the most likely explanation, as the prosecution argued, was some kind of perverted sexual gratification. The complainant knew full well what she was being asked to do and what she did in fact do, namely perform a sexual act for the benefit of the camera. She could have been in no doubt that the motive was at least in part sexual gratification. If so, on one view, even if one were to extend the definition of *purpose* to include the appellant's intention, as has been suggested, there is here no evidence going to the issue of deceit as to his purpose.

23 Further, we see force in [counsel for the defence's] submission that if reliance was to be placed on section 76, which effectively withdrew the accused's only line of defence, it was incumbent upon the judge to identify the evidence which went to the issue of "deceit as to purpose". Here there was no such analysis, and the jury were never directed that the word had a restricted meaning – see *Jheeta*. They were not informed that deceit as to what some commentators have called "peripheral matters" was not enough.

24 For those reasons we are troubled by the way in which the prosecution put their case and by the way in which it was left to the jury. We understand how prosecuting counsel and the judge may have thought that the decision in *Devonald* applied and appeared to support reliance on section 76. However, as we have indicated, reliance upon section 76 in this case, on these facts and this evidence, was misplaced. The prosecution needed to look no further than the provisions of Section 74. It provides that "a person consents if he agrees by choice and has the freedom and capacity to make that choice". If the complainant only complied because she was being blackmailed, the prosecution might argue forcefully she did not agree by choice.

ACTIVITY

In this section we have looked at twelve cases on the scope of section 76(2)(a): *R v Jheeta; R v Linekar; R v McNally; Assange v Swedish Prosecution Authority; R (F) v Director of Public Prosecutions; R v Lawrance; R (Monica) v Director of Public Prosecutions ex parte Boyling; R v Dica; R v Williams; R v Green; R v Devonald;* and *R v B.*

Place each case in the correct column of the following table.

Cases where section 76(2)(a) would apply	Cases where section 76(2)(a) would not apply

Now, think about these questions.

a. For each case, include a one-sentence summary of why section 76(2)(a) would or wouldn't apply.

b. Using the table you have just completed, decide whether section 76(2)(a) would apply in the following two scenarios:

- Lawrence says to his secretary, a single mother named Mandy: 'I'm going to fire you unless you have sex with me.' Mandy does not want to have sex with Lawrence but reluctantly agrees. In fact, Lawrence had intended all along to fire Mandy whether or not she had sex with him. The next day he fires her.
- Lawrence, who is unemployed, has a celebrity girlfriend named Mandy. One day he initiates sexual intercourse with Mandy without telling her that he is filming it. The next day he says to her: 'Pay me £10,000 or I'll put the video on the Internet.'

In November 2017 Daryll Rowe became the first person in the UK to be convicted of deliberately transmitting HIV.[18] During a four-month campaign in the Brighton area he tried to infect as many men as possible (using sabotaged condoms). He mocked his victims, texting one 'I have HIV. Lol. Whoops!' He was convicted on five counts of causing GBH with intent and a further five counts of attempting to do so.

c. Would section 76(2)(a) have applied to Rowe's case (so that he was also guilty of rape)?

The defendant intentionally induced the victim to consent to the relevant act by impersonating a person known personally to the victim

The second situation in which the conclusive presumptions apply is set out in section 76(2)(b). It is where the defendant intentionally induced the victim to consent to the relevant act by impersonating a person known personally to the victim.

---

[18] Watt, H., 'Man found guilty of trying to infect 10 Grindr dates with HIV' *The Guardian* 15 November 2017.

Before discussing section 76(2)(b), it is helpful to first look at an important case from the 1990s: *R* v *Elbekkay* [1995] Crim LR 163. Elbekkay was staying the night with the victim and her boyfriend (who had been living together for 18 months). Elbekkay and the victim's boyfriend had fallen asleep in the lounge, while the victim was sleeping in the bedroom. During the night the victim was woken up by someone moving on her bed. Assuming it was her boyfriend, she said, 'I love you'. She then felt herself being penetrated. Twenty seconds later they kissed. At this point the victim realised that something was not quite right. She opened her eyes and, seeing that it was Elbekkay not her boyfriend, punched him and ran into the lounge. Elbekkay was charged with rape.

At the time of this case it was accepted that a man committed rape if he had sex with a woman by impersonating her husband. The issue in *R* v *Elbekkay* was whether this should be extended to include impersonation of a long-term partner. The trial judge issued the following ruling:

> I now have to consider whether in 1994 at a time when a wife is no longer under a duty to submit to intercourse with her husband, whether there is such a fundamental difference between a wife agreeing to sexual intercourse with her husband and a fiancé or girlfriend agreeing to sexual intercourse with their regular partner that the law should hold that the consent of the wife, if obtained by fraud, is no consent but the consent of the others is still consent in law. I am bound to say, after careful consideration I can find no justification for so finding. It would be wholly contrary to modern attitudes and values at which the law should seek to reflect where possible. It would also very seriously curtail or interfere with the right of women to choose, understanding the true facts, whether to participate or not in the act of sexual intercourse.

Following this ruling Elbekkay was convicted of rape. He appealed against his conviction to the Court of Appeal, arguing that the trial judge's ruling was wrong.

EXTRACT

Read the following extract from the judgment of McCowan LJ.

Did the Court of Appeal decide that the trial judge's ruling was right or wrong? What reasons did McCowan LJ give for his decision?

R v *Elbekkay* [1995] Crim LR 163

McCowan LJ

We wholly agree [with the trial judge's ruling]. Indeed, we think it would be extraordinary for us to come to any other conclusion in 1994. How could we conscientiously hold that it is rape to impersonate a husband in the act of sexual intercourse, but not if the person impersonated is merely, say, the long-term, live-in lover, or in the even more modern idiom, the "partner" of the woman concerned?

The vital point about rape is that it involves the absence of consent. That absence is equally crucial whether the woman believes that the man she is having sexual intercourse with is her husband or another.

Importantly, the final sentence of this extract appears to be open-ended. It refers to 'another', and so does not seem to be limited to impersonation of a husband or long-term partner. It therefore supports the following principle: if the victim is having sex with X, but believes she is having sex with Y, then she is not consenting to sex with X. We can refer to this as the *R* v *Elbekkay* principle.

There are three points to note about the *R* v *Elbekkay* principle:

1. If the principle applies you must then go on and consider whether the defendant had the necessary *mens rea*.

In other words, the *R* v *Elbekkay* principle alone does not determine guilt. It only determines whether or not the victim consented to sexual intercourse with the defendant.

2. The *R* v *Elbekkay* principle applies to the defendant's identity, not to the defendant's attributes and qualifications.

In the previous chapter we looked at the case *R* v *Richardson* [1999] QB 444 (the case of the suspended dentist) and saw that fraud as to attributes does not generally vitiate consent. However, we also saw that, in *R* v *Melin* [2019] EWCA Crim 557 (the case of the non-medically qualified defendant administering botox injections), the Court of Appeal recognized that in some cases a person's identity may be inextricably linked to their professional status. Similarly, in *R (Monica)* v *Director of Public Prosecutions ex parte Boyling* [2018] EWHC 3508 (Admin), the Court stated that if a defendant engages in sexual activity with the victim, having deceived the victim as to their gender, then this 'could be analysed as an identity or impersonation case, given the centrality of an individual's sexuality to his or her identity' ([77]).

3. McCowan LJ's judgment used the word 'believes'. So the *R* v *Elbekkay* principle only applies if the victim believes she is having sexual intercourse with Y but in fact is having sex with X.

It would not apply if the victim has a lower degree of certainty than 'belief'. For example, it would not apply if the victim is unsure whether she is having sex with X or Y, or if the victim hopes she is having sex with Y but suspects that she is actually having sex with X.

ACTIVITY

A. Miles is attracted to wealthy men. One evening he meets Lawrence at a nightclub. Lawrence tells Miles that he is a successful businessman. Miles is impressed and begins to flirt with Lawrence. Later that evening they have sexual intercourse. In fact, Lawrence is a poorly paid cleaner.

Decide whether the *R* v *Elbekkay* principle would apply in this situation.

B. Lawrence looks a lot like the famous actor Brad Pitt. He goes to a nightclub and meets Mandy, who is a massive Brad Pitt fan. They begin chatting and, after a while, go to Lawrence's hotel room and have sexual intercourse. Mandy says that she thought it was unlikely that the man she had sex with was Brad Pitt, but had desperately hoped that it was.

Decide whether the *R* v *Elbekkay* principle applies here.

Now that we have a firm understanding of the *R* v *Elbekkay* principle we can turn to section 76(2)(b). At first sight, it might appear that section 76(2)(b) simply enshrines the *R* v *Elbekkay* principle in statute. But in fact section 76(2)(b) is narrower than the *R* v *Elbekkay* principle in two important respects:

- **The statute refers specifically to impersonation.** The *R* v *Elbekkay* principle, on the other hand, does not require any impersonation. In fact, Elbekkay did not impersonate his victim's boyfriend. He did not dress up like the victim's boyfriend, or try to sound like the victim's boyfriend. What he did was exploit the situation. The victim assumed it was her boyfriend on the bed, and Elbekkay took advantage of this. So the *R* v *Elbekkay* principle is broader than section 76(2)(b) in that it is not limited to cases involving impersonation; it also applies where the victim has made a mistake and the defendant has taken advantage of this.
- **The statute refers specifically to impersonation of a person known personally to the victim.** So if the defendant deceives the victim by intentionally impersonating Brad Pitt, the case will fall outside section 76(2)(b) (assuming, of course, that the victim does not know Brad Pitt personally!). The *R* v *Elbekkay* principle, on the other hand, is not limited in this way. As we saw above, McCowan LJ said that the principle applies if the victim mistakenly believes that she is having sexual intercourse with 'her husband *or another*'.

So where does this leave us? In a problem question you should begin by asking whether section 76(2)(b) applies. If it does, then you should use the conclusive presumptions. If it does not apply, this does not mean that *R* v *Elbekkay* is irrelevant. You may still use the judgment from *R* v *Elbekkay* when interpreting the general definition of consent in section 74 (which we will look at shortly).

We have now looked at each of the circumstances in which the conclusive presumptions apply. As we have seen, section 76 has quite a narrow scope. In the following extract Karl Laird suggests that this should be welcomed.

EXTRACT

What reasons does Laird give for welcoming the narrow scope of the conclusive presumptions? Do you agree that this is welcome?

Laird, K. (2014) 'Rapist or Rogue? Deception, Consent and the Sexual Offences Act 2003' *Criminal Law Review* 492

[T]he applicability of s.76 has been reduced to vanishing point. This, it is submitted, is to be welcomed. No injustice will be done to C [the victim] given that the issue of her consent can still be considered under s.74 and it is fairer to D, as the conclusive presumptions will not apply. Given the now limited scope of s.76, prosecuting counsel have no option but to place reliance upon s.74 in circumstances where D has deceived C. This is an advantage from the prosecution's perspective, given that s.76 is only applicable in cases where D *intentionally* deceived C. Section 74 does not, prima facie, contain the same restriction. It is not surprising that the judiciary have evinced a preference for reliance upon s.74 over s.76. The presumptions in s.76 are conclusive and so once established all but ensure D will be convicted (provided it is proven that he performed the relevant act). Given that this is the case, reliance upon s.74 at least permits D to mount a defence and so avoids the issue of whether any subsequent conviction violates the presumption of innocence enshrined in art.6 of the ECHR.

Quiz 7.2

1. Which one of the following is a complete list of conditions that are relevant in giving rise to a conclusive presumption?
   - **a.** Deceiving V as to the nature or purpose of the sexual act; deceiving V into believing that D is a person known personally to her.
   - **b.** Deceptions as to the nature or purpose of the sexual act; deceptions as to the identity or attributes of D.
   - **c.** Using or creating a fear of violence against V; using or creating a fear of violence against another person.
   - **d.** Using or creating a fear of violence against V; using or creating a fear of violence against another person; deceiving V as to the nature or purpose of the sexual act; deceiving V into believing that D is a person known personally to her.
2. Why did section 76 not apply in *Jheeta* [2007] EWCA Crim 1699?
   - **a.** The deception did not relate to the nature or purpose of sexual intercourse.
   - **b.** The victim had not been tricked by the defendant's efforts to deceive her.
   - **c.** Section 76 did apply in *Jheeta*.
   - **d.** The prosecution had not proved there had been deception beyond reasonable doubt.
3. In which of the following situations would section 76 apply?
   - **a.** D tricks V into agreeing to sex by impersonating a movie star that V idolises.
   - **b.** D tricks V into agreeing to sex by falsely telling her that he will wear a condom.
   - **c.** D tricks V into thinking that he is performing a medical procedure when it is in fact sex.
   - **d.** D tricks V into agreeing to oral sex by pretending that she is male.

ii. Section 75: Evidential presumptions

7.3 Explain the evidential presumptions contained in section 75 of the Sexual Offences Act 2003.

An evidential presumption is one which the defendant has the opportunity to rebut. The evidential presumptions are governed by section 75.

EXTRACT

Section 75 Sexual Offences Act 2003

75 Evidential presumptions about consent

(1) If in proceedings for an offence to which this section applies it is proved–

(a) that the defendant did the relevant act,

(b) that any of the circumstances specified in subsection (2) existed, and

(c) that the defendant knew that those circumstances existed,

the complainant is to be taken not to have consented to the relevant act unless sufficient evidence is adduced to raise an issue as to whether he consented, and the defendant is to be taken not to have reasonably believed that the complainant consented unless sufficient evidence is adduced to raise an issue as to whether he reasonably believed it.

(2) The circumstances are that–

(a) any person was, at the time of the relevant act or immediately before it began, using violence against the complainant or causing the complainant to fear that immediate violence would be used against him;

(b) any person was, at the time of the relevant act or immediately before it began, causing the complainant to fear that violence was being used, or that immediate violence would be used, against another person;

(c) the complainant was, and the defendant was not, unlawfully detained at the time of the relevant act;

(d) the complainant was asleep or otherwise unconscious at the time of the relevant act;

(e) because of the complainant's physical disability, the complainant would not have been able at the time of the relevant act to communicate to the defendant whether the complainant consented;

(f) any person had administered to or caused to be taken by the complainant, without the complainant's consent, a substance which, having regard to when it was administered or taken, was capable of causing or enabling the complainant to be stupefied or overpowered at the time of the relevant act.

(3) In subsection (2)(a) and (b), the reference to the time immediately before the relevant act began is, in the case of an act which is one of a continuous series of sexual activities, a reference to the time immediately before the first sexual activity began.

So if the prosecution proves, beyond reasonable doubt, that one of the six circumstances listed in subsection (2) existed, *and* the defendant knew that it existed, then it will be presumed that:

- The victim did not consent, and
- The defendant lacked a reasonable belief in consent.

The defendant can rebut the first presumption by producing some evidence that the victim did in fact consent. And he can rebut the second presumption by producing some evidence that he did in fact have a reasonable belief that the victim was consenting. Whether or not the defendant has produced sufficient evidence is a matter for the trial judge. It seems that relatively little evidence needs to be produced in order to rebut the presumptions.[19] Often, the defendant's own testimony will be sufficient.

If the defendant rebuts the first presumption the prosecution must then prove, beyond reasonable doubt, that the victim did not consent. And if he rebuts the second presumption the prosecution must then prove, beyond reasonable doubt, that the defendant lacked a reasonable belief in consent.

Figure 7.1 presents an overview of this, quite complicated, process.

So what are the six circumstances in which the evidential presumptions might apply?

The first three situations, found in paragraphs (a)–(c) of section 75, deal with the use or threat of immediate violence and unlawful detention. We studied the meaning of the word 'immediate' in the previous chapter, and saw that the courts have interpreted it to mean 'imminent'. Although this is a fairly broad interpretation, the word 'immediate' means that the evidential presumptions would not apply where, for example, the defendant says something like, 'Have sex with me or I'll beat you up tomorrow'.

Paragraph (a) applies where violence, or the threat of violence, is used against the victim. Notice that it needn't be the defendant himself who uses or threatens violence. It is enough that the defendant knew that another person was using or threatening violence. So if Lawrence is a member of a gang which attacks the victim, and during the attack Lawrence has sexual intercourse with the victim, the evidential presumptions will apply even if it was the other gang members that used violence, not Lawrence.

---

[19] See the extract below from Gunby, Carline and Beynon's article 'Alcohol-related Rape Cases: Barristers' Perspectives on the Sexual Offences Act 2003 and Its Impact on Practice'.

Prosecution	Defence
For the evidential presumptions to apply the prosecution must prove, beyond reasonable doubt, that: (1) one of the circumstances listed in subsection (2) existed; and (2) that the defendant knew this	
	If the prosecution manage to do this, the defendant can rebut the presumptions: • To rebut the presumption that V did not consent, he must produce some evidence that V did in fact consent • To rebut the presumption that he lacked a reasonable belief in consent, D must produce some evidence that he did have a reasonable belief in consent
The trial judge decides whether or not D has successfully rebutted the presumptions: • If D rebuts the presumption that V did not consent the prosecution must then prove, beyond reasonable doubt, that V did not consent • If D rebuts the presumption that he lacked a reasonable belief in consent the prosecution must then prove, beyond reasonable doubt, that D lacked a reasonable belief in consent	

Figure 7.1 The process for determining whether the evidential presumptions apply

Paragraph (b) applies where violence, or the threat of violence, is not used against the victim, but against someone else. For example, paragraph (b) would apply if Lawrence, armed with a gun, says to the victim, 'Have sex with me or I'll shoot your friend'. And again, paragraph (b) will apply even if it is someone else that uses or threatens violence, not the defendant. So if Lawrence's fellow gang member grabs hold of the victim's friend and says 'Have sex with Lawrence or I'll shoot your friend', the evidential presumptions will apply.

Paragraph (c) applies where the victim was unlawfully detained (and the defendant was not). So it would apply where the defendant kidnaps the victim and has sexual intercourse with her whilst she is being held hostage.

At this point you might be wondering whether evidential presumptions are really necessary in these sorts of situations. Surely if the defendant was using or threatening violence against the victim or one of the victim's friends or family members, or if the victim was being unlawfully detained, a jury would readily conclude that the victim was not freely consenting to sexual intercourse and that the defendant lacked a reasonable belief in consent? Is the extra complexity created by the evidential presumptions really justified?

Much the same applies to the fourth situation, found in paragraph (d). This deals with victims who were asleep or unconscious at the relevant time. A sleeping or unconscious person is unable to consent to sexual intercourse. They lack the capacity to do so. So surely in a situation like this a jury would readily conclude that the victim was not consenting and that the defendant lacked a reasonable belief in consent. In fact, as Temkin and Ashworth state in the following extract, it is difficult to see why a defendant who has sexual intercourse with a sleeping or unconscious victim should be given the opportunity to rebut the presumptions at all:

> [I]t has always been the law that consent must be present at the time of the sexual act. This means that consent is necessarily regarded as absent once it is proved beyond doubt that C was asleep or unconscious at the time sexual intercourse

took place. If the absence of consent is not conclusively presumed in these situations, as it was at common law, then the law is being taken backwards rather than forwards.[20]

The fifth situation, found in paragraph (e), is where the victim is unable to communicate whether or not she is consenting as a result of physical disability.

The sixth situation, found in paragraph (f), is where the victim was given a substance, without her consent, which was capable of causing or enabling her to be stupefied or overpowered. There are a number of points to note about this paragraph:

- The substance must have been given to the victim without her consent. So if the victim consumed the substance voluntarily, paragraph (f) will not apply.
- It need not be the defendant that gives the substance to the victim. But remember, the defendant must have known that the circumstance existed. So the defendant must at least have known that the victim had been given the substance.
- It is not enough that the substance is capable of causing the victim to become disinhibited. The substance must have been capable of causing the victim to be overpowered or stupefied.
- Strangely, the statute does not require that the victim was actually overpowered or stupefied. Instead, it focuses on the potential effect of the substance. It is enough that the substance was *capable* of causing or enabling the victim to be stupefied or overpowered. So the evidential presumptions will apply if the substance was capable of having this effect, even if it did not in fact do so.
- To assess whether the substance was capable of having this effect, you must have regard to 'when it was administered or taken'. Suppose the defendant buys the victim a glass of wine and falsely tells her it is non-alcoholic. If this is the victim's first drink of the night the wine is unlikely to be capable of causing the victim to be overpowered or stupefied. But if the defendant knows that the victim has already drunk several shots of vodka and is feeling quite drunk, then the wine may well be capable of causing her to be overpowered or stupefied.

As with the previous paragraphs you might wonder why paragraph (f) only results in evidential presumptions, not conclusive ones. If the defendant knew that the victim had been given an overpowering or stupefying substance against her will, and consent is about freedom to choose, why should he have an opportunity to argue that the victim did in fact consent to sexual intercourse and that he did in fact have a reasonable belief in consent? Temkin and Ashworth state:

> [I]f the stupefying effect is established, it is questionable whether D should be able to argue that C nevertheless consented to the subsequent sexual act and that the drug or alcohol did not in fact prevent her from consenting. Can freedom and capacity to make a choice really exist in any meaningful sense in this situation?

[20] Temkin, J. and Ashworth, A. (2004) 'The Sexual Offences Act 2003 – (1) Rape, Sexual Assaults and the Problems of Consent' *Criminal Law Review* 328 at 337. The fact that the presumptions are rebuttable in such cases implies that Parliament believed that there could be situations in which a person consents to sexual activity even though they are asleep. An example might be where express consent is indicated in advance of the sexual activity, such as where a person agrees in advance to their partner waking them up later by touching them in an intimate way. For discussion, see Jarvis, P. (2019) 'The Timing of Consent' *Criminal Law Review* 394.

Lawrence, Mandy and Miles are at a bar. Lawrence has liked Mandy for some time, but she has never shown any interest in him. Mandy has already had several glasses of wine when Lawrence says to Miles, 'I dare you to spike her drink'. Miles does so. Later that evening Mandy has sexual intercourse with Lawrence. The next day Mandy says that she only had sex with Lawrence because she was really drunk, and would never have done it if she'd been sober.

- Decide whether the evidential presumptions would apply in this situation.
- Would your answer be any different if Lawrence had only mentioned the 'dare' as a joke, did not realise that Miles had taken it seriously and spiked Mandy's drink and by the time he had sexual intercourse with Mandy had completely forgotten all about it?

We have now worked through the conclusive and evidential presumptions. Before moving on to look at the general definition of consent, it is worth pausing for a moment to reflect. Earlier we saw that the Sexual Offences Act 2003 was intended to escape the complexity of the old law, set out clear principles governing consent and explain in an accessible manner what should and should not form acceptable standards of behaviour. Do sections 75 and 76 achieve these objectives?

In their article 'Alcohol-related Rape Cases: Barristers' Perspectives on the Sexual Offences Act 2003 and Its Impact on Practice' (2010) 74 *Journal of Criminal Law* 579, Clare Gunby, Anna Carline and Caryl Beynon report the findings of their interviews with a total of 14 barristers with experience of prosecuting and defending rape cases. One of the things they asked the barristers about was how the evidential presumptions operate in practice and whether they feel they have been successful.

EXTRACT

Read the following extract and produce a bullet point list of the key findings from the study.

Looking at your list of findings, assess whether sections 75 and 76 achieve their identified objectives.

Gunby, C., Carline, A. and Beynon, C. (2010) 'Alcohol-related Rape Cases: Barristers' Perspectives on the Sexual Offences Act 2003 and Its Impact on Practice' 74 *Journal of Criminal Law* 579

3. Barristers' perspectives on the 'consent presumptions'

As previously noted, the consent presumptions were introduced in an attempt to 'strike the right balance' between the complainant and the defendant and to '... send a clear signal to the public about the circumstances in which sexual activity is likely to be wrong' and will therefore 'encourage genuine victims to bring cases to court'. Academic opinion, however, has been far less positive about the introduction of the presumptions, and the decision to construct s. 75 as an exhaustive list has been subject to criticism. Barristers were therefore asked to comment on the frequency of presumption use at trial [...]

Presumption frequency and rebuttal evidence

Considering the heavy workload of the barristers interviewed, one would perhaps assume that the majority of advocates would have had experience with cases in which the presumptions had arisen. In fact, very few had worked on cases in which either the evidential or conclusive presumptions had been incorporated into a trial. Indeed, when asked about the application of the presumptions there was unanimous agreement that they were 'rarely' (barrister 9) used and that they may intentionally be 'side-tracked' (barrister 10) and 'circumvented' (barrister 14) in cases. Indeed, one barrister talked about physical violence having been a feature of a rape they defended but commented that the judge had intentionally avoided using the violence presumption (s. 75(2)(a) and (b)). There was a general consensus that those involved in rape cases – the prosecutor, barrister and judge alike – would try to avoid using the presumptions as much as possible. Barrister 1 argued that 'judges try very hard now to keep their presumptions to a minimum ... [and] tend to have broadly similar view [to the barristers] which is don't overload the jury with either too many counts or too much law'. It was argued that judges did not like the presumptions due to the perception that they amounted to the judge 'trespassing into the jury's ... domain' (barrister 2). Furthermore, it was argued that the presumptions complicated the trial process and overloaded the jury with additional, and complicated, legal concepts. Again, in light of jurors' perceived difficulties with applying and following legal directions and definitions, this is perhaps unsurprising: '... I think judges shy away from them [the presumptions] ... because they want ... I think they're reaching for clarity and making things straightforward for the jury' (barrister 10). These findings again reflect the conclusions of the Home Office stocktake that suggested the conclusive and evidential presumptions had infrequently been utilised thus far, and have consequently had little impact on the prosecution of rape cases.

When asked their opinions on the presumptions, certain barristers argued that they were patronising and that it was not necessary for them to have been specifically written into the law. Indeed, barrister 3 stated, 'I think all the presumptions do is state the ... obvious ... I don't see sometimes how all these very clever amendments to very good old-fashioned laws make the system any better'. Whilst several advocates disagreed with this viewpoint and felt that it was useful to have a set list of circumstances in which consent was likely to have been absent, these barristers still suggested that jurors would be intelligent enough to realise that if someone was detained, asleep or threatened with violence, they would be unlikely to have consented to the intercourse. For example, barrister 4 argued:

> You know, do people need to have pointed out to them that ... she's not really giving consent ... that if he's spiked her drink ... that she's not really consenting? I don't think people are that daft really, you know, that they have to be given a definitive list ... did they really need it pointing out to them?

Certain advocates also felt the presumptions swung the balance too far in favour of the prosecution and had been specifically included for the purpose of increasing the conviction rate. However, when asked about the amount of evidence necessary to rebut the evidential presumptions barristers generally agreed it was 'not a lot' (barrister 9) and that 'I can't think of a case in which ... an evidential burden wouldn't be discharged by a defendant' (barrister 8). The defendant's own testimony or ability to 'float the contrary possibility' (barrister 10) and suggest that sex was consensual, was often perceived sufficient. This finding provides empirical support for Finch and Munro's speculation that the amount of evidence necessary to rebut the evidential presumptions may not be substantial.

[...]

Overall, there was a general consensus, especially amongst the more experienced barristers, that the presumptions have not only been overwhelmingly unsuccessful: 'I don't think they've helped in the slightest' (barrister 3) and 'I don't think that presumptions really have that much impact on the whole thing' (barrister 12); but also that they are considered to be somewhat of an obstacle and something to be avoided, as opposed to a measure which has helped to achieve justice.

Quiz 7.3

1. Which one of the following is a complete list of conditions that are relevant in giving rise to an evidential presumption?
   a. Using or creating a fear of violence against V; using or creating a fear of violence against another person; using or creating a fear of violence against V's property; deceiving V as to the nature or purpose of the sexual act; performing the sexual act on V who is unlawfully detained; performing the sexual act on V who is asleep; performing the sexual act on V who is disabled and unable to communicate consent or the lack of it; administering to V a substance capable of stupefying her.
   b. Using or creating a fear of violence against V; using or creating a fear of violence against another person.
   c. Using or creating a fear of violence against V; using or creating a fear of violence against another person; performing the sexual act on V who is unlawfully detained; performing the sexual act on V who is asleep; performing the sexual act on V who is intoxicated; performing the sexual act on V who is disabled and unable to communicate consent or the lack of it; administering to V a substance capable of stupefying her.
   d. Using or creating a fear of violence against V; using or creating a fear of violence against another person; performing the sexual act on V who is unlawfully detained; performing the sexual act on V who is asleep; performing the sexual act on V who is disabled and unable to communicate consent or the lack of it; surreptitiously administering to V a substance capable of stupefying or overpowering her.
2. Which of the following is false? Section 75 of the Sexual Offences Act 2003 creates a rebuttable presumption that V did not consent and D lacked a reasonable belief in consent if…
   a. V had a physical disability that prevented her from communicating whether or not she was consenting.
   b. V was unlawfully detained.
   c. V had voluntarily taken stupefying or overpowering drugs.
   d. V was asleep.
3. In which of the following situations will section 75 (evidential presumptions) apply?
   a. D engages in sexual activity with V whilst V is sleeping.
   b. D bought V lots of alcoholic drinks so that she would become disinhibited and agree to sex.
   c. D grooms a 12-year-old girl and engages in sexual activity with her.
   d. D tricked V into agreeing to sex by impersonating V's boyfriend.

iii. Section 74: The general definition of consent

7.4 Explain the general definition of consent contained in section 74 of the Sexual Offences Act 2003.

In situations where:

- neither the conclusive nor the evidential presumptions apply or
- the evidential presumptions apply, but the defendant has rebutted them

you will need to apply section 74's definition of consent in order to determine whether or not the victim consented. Section 74 states the following.

EXTRACT

Section 74 Sexual Offences Act 2003

74 "Consent"

For the purposes of this Part, a person consents if he agrees by choice, and has the freedom and capacity to make that choice.

This is a very abstract definition. What is clear, however, is that sometimes a victim might agree to sexual intercourse but not be consenting. There is only consent if the victim agreed by choice, had the *capacity* to be able to choose, and had sufficient *freedom* to make that choice.

There is case law which gives us some guidance on how section 74 should be interpreted. These cases address the following three themes: **the distinction between 'real consent' and 'mere submission'**; **deception**; and **capacity to consent**.

The distinction between 'real consent' and 'mere submission'

Even before the 2003 Sexual Offences Act the courts had made it clear that there is a distinction between 'real consent' and 'mere submission'. In *R* v *Olugboja* [1982] QB 320 the defendant Olugboja and his friend Lawal met the victim Jayne (aged 16) and her friend Karen (aged 17) at a disco. The men offered the girls a lift home, but instead of taking them home drove in the opposite direction and took them to a bungalow. Olugboja entered the bungalow but both girls refused to go inside and started to walk off. Lawal followed them in the car. After an argument the girls got back in. There was another argument, Karen got out of the car, but Lawal drove off with Jayne, parked the car and raped her.

Lawal then drove Jayne back to the bungalow, picking Karen up on the way. The defendant was asleep on the sofa. It was obvious that Jayne had been crying. Lawal dragged Karen into a bedroom, leaving Olugboja and Jayne alone in the living room. Olugboja told Jayne that he was going to have sex with her. Jayne told him what Lawal had done and asked him to leave her alone, but he told her to take off her trousers. Afraid, she did as he said. He then pushed her onto the sofa and had sex with her. She did not struggle or resist. She did not scream or cry for help.

At trial Olugboja was convicted of rape. He appealed against his conviction, arguing that for rape there must have been violence, or a threat of violence, or fraud. He claimed that he had not used violence or threatened violence, and so his conviction should be quashed. This argument was rejected by the Court of Appeal and Olugboja's rape conviction was upheld.

EXTRACT

In the following extract from the judgment of the Court, Dunn LJ makes several important statements about the concept of 'consent'. Make a list of these statements.

R v *Olugboja* [1982] QB 320

Dunn LJ

Although 'consent' is an equally common word it covers a wide range of states of mind in the context of intercourse between a man and a woman, ranging from actual desire on the one hand to reluctant acquiescence on the other. We do not think that the issue of consent should be left to a jury without some further direction. What this should be will depend on the circumstances of each case. The jury will have been reminded of the burden and standard of proof required to establish each ingredient, including lack of consent, of the offence. They should be directed that consent, or the absence of it, is to be given its ordinary meaning and if need be, by way of example, that there is a difference between consent and submission; every consent involves a submission, but it by no means follows that a mere submission involves consent: *per* Coleridge J. in Reg. v. Day, 9 C. & p. 722, 724 [...] In addition to the general direction about consent which we have outlined, the jury will probably be helped in such cases by being reminded that in this context consent does comprehend the wide spectrum of states of mind to which we earlier referred, and that the dividing line in such circumstances between real consent on the one hand and mere submission on the other may not be easy to draw. Where it is to be drawn in a given case is for the jury to decide, applying their combined good sense, experience and knowledge of human nature and modern behaviour to all the relevant facts of that case.

ACTIVITY

Lawrence and Mandy have been married for 13 years. One Friday night Lawrence suggests that they have sexual intercourse. Although Mandy does not want to have sex, she does so because she knows from experience that Lawrence will sulk for the entire weekend if she does not.

Looking at the guidance provided by Dunn LJ, does Mandy consent to sexual intercourse or merely submit?

The distinction between 'real consent' and 'mere submission' was applied in *R* v *Kirk* [2008] EWCA Crim 434.[21] The victim in this case was a 13-year-old girl who had run away from home. Hungry, she went for help to the minicab office where the defendant (a family member) worked, even though the defendant had abused her in the past. He offered to give her £3.25 in exchange for sexual intercourse. She agreed. She later explained, 'I was very hungry and needed to eat so I went to [the defendant's place of work] [...] All I can say is that I ended up having sex with [him] for £3.25. I used the money to buy food'. The defendant was convicted of rape, and on appeal the conviction was upheld by the Court of Appeal. The Court explained that the victim had submitted to sexual intercourse, but not consented to it.

Sometimes applying the distinction between 'real consent' and 'mere submission' could be difficult.

[21] See also *R* v *Doyle* [2010] EWCA Crim 119, in which the Court of Appeal referred to the distinction between 'reluctant but free exercise of choice on the one hand, especially in the context of a long term and loving relationship, and unwilling submission to demand in fear of more adverse consequences from refusal on the other' ([21]).

Now, think about this scenario.

A woman has committed a serious crime. She has been arrested. The police officer in charge of her case says he will drop all charges if she has sexual intercourse with him. She agrees.

- Does she consent to sexual intercourse? Or merely submit?
- Would your answer be any different if the woman had not committed the crime and had been wrongly accused?
- Would your answer be any different if the woman had been arrested for a minor motoring offence, not a serious crime?

At the end of the extract from Dunn LJ's judgment in *R* v *Olugboja* above, he said that questions like these should be answered by juries employing 'their combined good sense, experience and knowledge of human nature and modern behaviour'. Is it satisfactory to vest this much discretion in juries, or should juries be given more guidance on the distinction between 'real consent' and 'mere submission'? There are concerns here regarding the principle of maximum certainty. There are also concerns about consistency. Will different juries reach the same verdict in cases with similar facts?[22]

Cases involving deception

Some cases involving deception will fall under the conclusive presumptions set out in section 76. But as we saw above, the circumstances listed in section 76 are quite limited in scope. There are many instances of deception which will fall outside of the conclusive presumptions. In these cases, whether or not the victim consented must be determined using section 74's definition of consent.

We have already seen some examples of cases involving deception which fell outside the scope of section 76. The first was *R* v *Jheeta*: the case involving the defendant who deceived the victim by sending a series of threatening text messages. As the conclusive presumptions did not apply, the Court of Appeal used the section 74 definition of consent to determine whether the victim consented to sexual intercourse.

EXTRACT

Read the following extract from the judgment of Sir Igor Judge.

Was the sexual intercourse consensual? Why/why not?

R v *Jheeta* [2007] EWCA Crim 1699

Sir Igor Judge

29 We are being asked to examine the safety of convictions for rape where the appellant pleaded guilty. He did so on the basis of plea which accepted the accuracy of his admissions in interview with the police, and in particular did not question his unequivocal admission that

[22] For an alternative, categories-based, approach see Williams, R. (2008) 'Deception, Mistake and Vitiation of the Victim's Consent' 124 *Law Quarterly Review* 132.

> there were occasions when sexual intercourse took place when the complainant was not truly consenting. This is entirely consistent with his acknowledgement that he persuaded the complainant to have intercourse with him more frequently than otherwise, and the persuasion took the form of the pressures imposed on her by the complicated and unpleasant scheme which he had fabricated. This was not a free choice, or consent for the purposes of the 2003 Act. In these circumstances we entertain no reservations that on some occasions at least the complainant was not consenting to intercourse for the purposes of section 74, and that the appellant was perfectly well aware of it. His guilty plea reflected these undisputed facts. Accordingly the appeal against conviction is dismissed.

In terms of the wording used in section 74, the reasoning in this extract focuses on the victim's freedom to choose. This approach is rooted in the principle of individual autonomy (see Chapter 1). Individuals have the right to choose how to live their lives. In *R* v *Jheeta* the victim's autonomy – her freedom to choose – had been so undermined by the defendant's 'complicated and unpleasant scheme' that it could not be said that she had consented to sexual intercourse. On many occasions she had not agreed to sex by choice.

This emphasis on autonomy and freedom to choose has also been seen in some subsequent cases. In *R* v *McNally* [2013] EWCA Crim 1051 the defendant, 17-year-old Justine McNally, met the 16-year-old victim through the social networking game Habbo. At the time they were aged 13 and 12 respectively. McNally used a male avatar named Scott. Over the next three-and-a-half years the victim's friendship with 'Scott' developed. McNally arranged to travel to London to visit the victim shortly after the victim's 16th birthday. When she arrived McNally was wearing gothic clothing and a strap-on dildo under her trousers. During the visit the victim consented to oral sex. Over the following months McNally visited again, and the victim again consented to oral sex and to digital penetration. After the victim discovered that McNally was not in fact 'Scott', McNally was charged with the section 2 offence of assault by penetration (which we study below). At trial McNally was convicted. She appealed, arguing that a deception as to gender cannot vitiate consent. The Court of Appeal rejected her appeal. Leveson LJ explained:

> 26 Thus while, in a physical sense, the acts of assault by penetration of the vagina are the same whether perpetrated by a male or a female, the sexual nature of the acts is, on any common sense view, different where the complainant is deliberately deceived by a defendant into believing that the latter is a male. Assuming the facts to be proved as alleged, M chose to have sexual encounters with a boy and her preference (her freedom to choose whether or not to have a sexual encounter with a girl) was removed by the defendant's deception.[23]

[23] In her article 'Queering Judgment: The Case of Gender Identity Fraud', Alex Sharpe questions whether McNally did in fact deceive the victim. She argues that if McNally genuinely identified as male at the time of the penetrative acts – or if McNally chose to identify as a masculine woman with no intention to deceive – then there was no deception as a matter of law. To conclude otherwise would be to 'give the imprimatur of law to the idea that gender non-conforming people are, by definition, duplicitous and/or that other people have a right to know intimate details about their personal and private lives ... Ultimately, law, and especially criminal law, ought to respect the self-determination that is implicit in gender identity claims unless it can be clearly established that they are fabricated' (Sharpe, A. (2017) 'Queering Judgment: The Case of Gender Identity Fraud' 81 *Journal of Criminal Law* 417). See also Brooks, V. and Clayton Thompson, J. (2019) 'Dude Looks Like a Lady: Gender Deception, Consent and Ethics' 83 *Journal of Criminal Law* 258 and Gibson, M. (2020) 'Deceptive Sexual Relations: A Theory of Criminal Liability' 40 *Oxford Journal of Legal Studies* 82, 89–92; and, Sharpe, A. (2024) 'European human rights law and the legality of sex offence prosecutions based on deception as to gender history' 44 *Legal Studies* 631; and, Sharpe, A. (2025) 'Deceptive Sex: Rethinking Consent from the Gender Margins' 88 *Modern Law Review* 689.

Our next case, *Assange* v *Swedish Prosecution Authority* [2011] EWHC 2849 (Admin), concerned an incident involving WikiLeaks co-founder Julian Assange. Assange was accused of committing four offences whilst he was in Sweden to give a lecture. He left Sweden, unaware that an arrest warrant had been issued against him. A European Arrest Warrant was subsequently issued. After a district judge ruled that he should be extradited from England to Sweden, Assange appealed to the High Court against the extradition order. One of the issues the Court had to address was whether the alleged incidents in Sweden also amounted to criminal offences under English law. The relevant incident for our purposes involved a victim, AA, who only consented to sexual intercourse with Assange on the basis that he would use a condom. It was alleged that Assange had either not used a condom, or used a condom but had torn it. Applying the section 74 definition of consent, the Court held that, if proved, Assange's conduct would amount to rape.

A further example of the application of section 74 is *R (F)* v *Director of Public Prosecutions* [2013] EWHC 945 (Admin). The victim in this case married the defendant in an Islamic ceremony. He was abusive from the outset of the marriage. The victim was adamant that she did not want to become pregnant. She was unable to take the contraceptive pill, for medical reasons, and the defendant did not like using a condom, so their agreed method of contraception was withdrawal. On one occasion, the defendant penetrated the victim with consent but shortly afterwards told her that he would be coming inside her 'because you are my wife and I'll do it if I want'. He ejaculated before she could do anything to stop him. She later became pregnant. The victim made a formal complaint to the police, but the Director of Public Prosecutions (DPP) decided not to prosecute on the basis that, even if the victim's account could be proved, there was no realistic prospect of conviction. The victim sought judicial review of the DPP's decision. The High Court held that the defendant's actions, if proved, amounted to rape and therefore ordered that the DPP's decision should be reviewed.

EXTRACT

According to the following extract from the judgment of Lord Judge CJ, why was the sexual intercourse not consensual?

R (F) v *Director of Public Prosecutions* [2013] EWHC 945 (Admin)

Lord Judge CJ

26 In law, the question which arises is whether this factual structure can give rise to a conviction for rape. Did the claimant consent to this penetration? She did so, provided, in the language of section 74 of the 2003 Act, she agreed by choice, when she had the freedom and capacity to make the choice. What the *Assange* case 108(44) LSG 17 underlines is that "choice" is crucial to the issue of "consent", and indeed we underline that the statutory definition of consent provided in section 74 of the 2003 Act applies equally to section 1(1)(c) as it does to section 1(1)(b). The evidence relating to "choice" and the "freedom" to make any particular choice must be approached in a broad common sense way. If before penetration began the interested party had made up his mind that he would penetrate and ejaculate within the claimant's vagina, or even, because "penetration is a continuing act from entry to withdrawal" (see section 79(2) of the 2003 Act) he decided that he would not withdraw at all, just because he deemed the claimant subservient to his control, she was deprived of choice relating to the crucial feature on which her original consent to sexual intercourse was based. Accordingly her consent was negated. Contrary to her wishes, and knowing that she would not have consented, and did not consent to penetration or the continuation of penetration if she had any inkling of his intention, he deliberately ejaculated within her vagina. In law, this combination of circumstances falls within the statutory definition of rape.

In contrast to *R* v *McNally*, *Assange* v *Swedish Prosecution Authority and R (F)* v *Director of Public Prosecutions*, a more restrictive approach was adopted by the High Court in *R (Monica)* v *Director of Public Prosecutions ex parte Boyling* [2018] EWHC 3508 (Admin). The victim in this case, known as 'Monica' to protect her anonymity, was an environmental activist. The defendant, Andrew Boyling, was an undercover police officer who had infiltrated the movement. He befriended Monica and their relationship developed into a sexual one. The sexual relationship lasted for six months. Nearly 14 years later, following media reports, Monica discovered that Boyling had been an undercover police officer. She said she would not have entered into any sort of relationship with Boyling had she known the truth. The Director of Public Prosecutions decided not to prosecute Boyling for rape. Monica applied for judicial review of the decision not to prosecute. The High Court dismissed the application. It stated that in both *Assange* v *Swedish Prosecution Authority* and *R (F)* v *Director of Public Prosecutions* the deception was 'closely connected' with the sexual act ([74]), whilst in *R* v *McNally* the deception struck 'at the heart of the complainant's sexuality' and so 'could be analysed as an identity or impersonation case, given the centrality of an individual's sexuality to her or his identity' ([77]). The Court stated that the principle that consent may be vitiated by deception 'has never been applied to deceptions which are not closely connected to the performance of the sexual act, or are intrinsically so fundamental, owing to that connection, that they can be treated as cases of impersonation' ([80]). To hold that consent was vitiated by deception in a case such as Boyling's would constitute a 'fundamental change in the understanding of consent' ([85]). Such a change would 'inevitably result in the criminalisation of much conduct which, hitherto, has fallen outside the embrace of the criminal law' ([86]) and so should only be made by Parliament, not the courts.

In *R* v *Lawrance* [2020] EWCA Crim 971, the Court of Appeal applied the distinction drawn in *R (Monica)* v *Director of Public Prosecutions ex parte Boyling* between, on the one hand, deceptions that are closely connected with the nature or purpose of sexual intercourse and, on the other hand, deceptions that concern the broad circumstances surrounding the sexual act. Lawrance met the victim on a dating website. During a conversation between them, Lawrance told the victim that he had had a vasectomy. When they met, they went to the victim's house and – before having sexual intercourse – the victim told Lawrance she did not want to become pregnant and asked him again whether he had had a vasectomy. He said that he had. The following morning he sent her a message saying, 'I have a confession. I'm still fertile. Sorry'. She fell pregnant and underwent a termination. At trial, Lawrance was convicted of rape. On appeal, Lawrance argued that the facts of the case were incapable of supporting a rape conviction and so the trial judge should have accepted the defence's submission of no case to answer.

EXTRACT

Read the following extract from the judgment of Lord Burnett CJ.

According to the Court of Appeal, was the defendant's deception closely connected with the nature or purpose of sexual intercourse? Or did it concern the broad circumstances surrounding the sexual act?

How did the Court of Appeal distinguish *Assange* v *Swedish Prosecution Authority* and *R (F)* v *Director of Public Prosecutions?*

R v *Lawrance* [2020] EWCA Crim 971

Lord Burnett CJ

34 Returning to the facts of this case, the jury concluded that the complainant relied on the appellant's deception regarding a vasectomy and that she would not have consented to unprotected sexual intercourse had she thought him to be fertile. However, the "but for" test is insufficient of itself to vitiate consent. There may be many circumstances in which a complainant is deceived about a matter which is central to her choice to have sexual intercourse. *Monica* was an example, but they can be multiplied: lies concerning marital status or being in a committed relationship; lies about political or religious views; lies about status, employment or wealth are such examples. A bigamist does not commit rape or sexual assault upon his or her spouse despite the fundamental deception involved. The consent of the deceived second spouse, even if it would not have been forthcoming had the truth been known, does not vitiate consent for the purposes of sexual offending. Neither is the consent of a sex worker vitiated if the client never intends to pay.

35 The question is whether a lie as to fertility is so closely connected to the nature or purpose of sexual intercourse rather than the broad circumstances surrounding it that it is capable of negating consent. Is it closely connected to the performance of the sexual act?

In our opinion, a lie about fertility is different from a lie about whether a condom is being worn during sex, different from engaging in intercourse not intending to withdraw having promised to do so and different from engaging in sexual activity having misrepresented one's gender.

37 Unlike the woman in Assange, or in R(F), the complainant agreed to sexual intercourse with the appellant without imposing any physical restrictions. She agreed both to penetration of her vagina and to ejaculation without the protection of a condom. In so doing she was deceived about the nature or quality of the ejaculate and therefore of the risks and possible consequences of unprotected intercourse. The deception was one which related not to the physical performance of the sexual act but to risks or consequences associated with it. We should add that the question of consent could not be affected by whether pregnancy followed or not; and neither could it be affected by the gender of the person who was guilty of deceit. On the prosecution case, a woman who lied about her fertility in circumstances where the man would not otherwise have consented to sexual intercourse would be in the same position, albeit guilty of a different sexual offence.

38 In terms of section 74 of the 2003 Act, the complainant was not deprived by the appellant's lie of the freedom to choose whether to have the sexual intercourse which occurred.

So, according to *R* v *Lawrance*, wearing a condom and withdrawal before ejaculation both relate to the 'physical performance of the sexual act' (since they both impose 'physical restrictions'), whereas a vasectomy does not affect the physical performance of the sexual act, only the 'nature or quality of the ejaculate' and the 'risks or consequences associated with [unprotected sexual intercourse]'.

The reasoning in *R* v *Lawrance* has been described as 'superficial' because it 'does not reflect the fact that the complainant did impose a physical restriction, namely that the defendant's ejaculate did not contain sperm'.[24] In the following extract, David Ormerod also criticises the judgment.

[24] Laird, K. (2021) 'Commentary on *R* v *Lawrance*' *Criminal Law Review* 610, 612 (emphasis original).

EXTRACT

In the opening paragraph, Ormerod outlines three possible perspectives on the judgment. What are they? Which do you agree with? Why?

Ormerod says that the judgment in *R* v *Lawrance* has 'broader consequences'. What are these?

Ormerod, D. (2020) 'Rape and Deception (Again)' *Criminal Law Review* 877

Some may welcome the decision, agreeing with the Court that the complainant did consent to the physical acts (i.e. unprotected "sexual intercourse" which the court treats as the relevant "act"). They might adopt the argument of Jonathan Rogers that these offences "are designed to protect a person's sexual autonomy, not her health or her desire not to carry a baby". Others may accept the Court's distinction based on whether the deception relates to the "physical acts", but challenge its application on the facts. They might argue that V did not agree to all the physical acts—she agreed to unprotected intercourse but not the deposit of sperm (but nor did the complainants in F or Assange). Yet others will reject any attempt to draw such "artificial distinctions" (as the trial judge called them) based on "physical acts" given that they become difficult to articulate and apply consistently. Critics might ask how resolutely the Court of Appeal will be able to maintain a clear distinction between: unprotected intercourse with a deception as to withdrawal resulting in A ejaculating in B (F —rape); unprotected intercourse with a deception as to use of a condom resulting in A ejaculating into A (*Assange* —rape) and unprotected intercourse with deception that the ejaculate will not contain sperm because of a vasectomy (*Lawrance* —not rape)? In each case there is an active deception by the defendant as to a factor known by the defendant to be a condition precedent of the complainant's consent.

The decision has broader consequences than exposing apparent inconsistencies in the jurisprudence. In practical terms it does not render any easier the prosecutor's task in determining which deceptive conduct reported by complainants constitutes rape. Nor, in policy terms, is the message one that maximises the protection of sexual autonomy. Applying the reasoning in [37] [of *R* v *Lawrance*], a complainant's autonomy is afforded less protection in law where she is deceived about her partner's need to use a condom (leading her to impose no "physical restrictions") than about whether he was actually wearing a condom.

...

The decision of the Court of Appeal in *R* v *BVA* [2025] EWCA Crim 1359 raises further questions about the consistency of the case law. The defendant and the victim had met on Tinder and had a sexual relationship. One night, while the victim was asleep, the defendant filmed himself touching the victim's breasts and resting his penis on her hand. He was charged with sexual assault (which we study below). The defendant claimed that he had the victim's express consent to touch her while she was asleep. However, she said that she would not have agreed to this if she had known it would be filmed. The defendant was convicted and appealed, arguing that the filming of the touching was incapable of negating consent. The Court of Appeal rejected the appeal. Lady Carr CJ agreed with the distinction drawn in *R* v *Lawrance* between deceptions that are closely connected to the sexual activity as opposed to the broad surrounding circumstances. Applying this, she said that the deception in this case was 'far more closely connected to the sexual activity in question' than the deception in *R* v *Lawrance* ([50]). The filming started when the touching began and ended when the touching stopped. The filming was a central, if not the sole, purpose of the touching. The defendant was creating a pornographic video. The filming thus 'transformed what might otherwise have been a transient sexual touching into a permanent medium which could be watched in the future' ([49]). The victim had been deprived of her freedom to choose.

ACTIVITY

Do you agree with Lady Hale CJ that the deception in *R* v *BVA* was 'far more closely connected to the sexual activity in question' ([50]) than the deception in *R* v *Lawrance*?

In *R* v *Lawrance* Lord Burnett CJ said that the deception in that case 'related not to the physical performance of the sexual act but to risks or consequences associated with it' ([37]). In your opinion, did the deception in *R* v *BVA* relate to the physical performance of the sexual act or the risks or consequences associated with it?

In their discussion of *R* v *Lawrance*, Murray and Beattie argue that the apparent inconsistencies in the case law reflect two different underlying approaches. They evaluate these two approaches in the following extract.

EXTRACT

In the following extract, Murray and Beattie contrast a 'restrictive' approach to choice with an 'expansive' approach. What are the key features of each approach? Which approach do Murray and Beattie say took hold in *R* v *Lawrance*?

Which cases do Murray and Beattie say exemplify the expansive approach? What reasons do Murray and Beattie give for favouring the expansive approach? Do you agree?

Murray, K. L. and Beattie, T. (2021) 'Conditional Consent and Sexual Offences: Revisiting the Sexual Offences Act 2003 After Lawrance' *Criminal Law Review* 556

[I]t is worth reflecting briefly on the broad approaches which may be taken to consent-vitiation...

a. A restrictive approach to "choice"

On what we call the "restrictive" approach, the law limits, by content, which premises are capable of undermining choice. Various standards may be suggested for drawing these lines. The pre-2003 common law approach is one example: only deceptions which altered the "nature" of the act, or amount to specific impersonations, would do. Another way may be to look at the relevance of the matter to the sexual acts in question from a "common sense" view (namely, what most people might think): for example, it might be suggested that someone's wealth is not, on any "common sense" view, relevant to sexual activity, and, accordingly, lying about one's fortunes to obtain sex would not vitiate consent in the eyes of the law. As will be seen, Leveson LJ's references to "common sense" [in *R* v *McNally*] have indeed been widely taken in this restrictive way.

For this approach, it is crucial to note that the actual choices of the complainant are not wholly decisive as to whether they have consented in law. There will be some false premises which can never suffice to legally negate sexual consent, regardless of their importance to the complainant.

b. An expansive approach to "choice"

A second—"expansive"—approach focusses on the premises actually operative in the choice of the complainant. In principle, what this specific premise may be is left open: the law concerns itself with the choices in fact made by the complainant. If the complainant has in fact based their consent on a premise which turns out to be false, their consent is negated in law. Subject to the other elements being satisfied—including, importantly, a defendant's lack of reasonable belief—a sexual offence will thereby be committed.

The only general restriction would arise from what the evidence can reasonably be taken to establish. On this line, the direction from Lord Judge CJ that the "evidence" must be "approached in a broad common sense way" is merely a reminder of the usual evidential tests which apply in bringing a criminal charge, and directing a jury. Of course, the more obscure the basis of an individual's choice, the more difficult it may be to convince a jury of its factual relevance. "Common sense" may also be used in assessing whether the defendant had a reasonable belief in consent. For example, it might be thought that the more obscure the condition, the less reasonable it is to expect the defendant to have realised its importance to the complainant.

In practice, therefore, "common sense"—what a jury believes most people would find relevant—may already be a significant limiting factor, in the absence of some particularly compelling evidence. However, what is crucial to note about this approach is that it leaves the door open for idiosyncratic, perhaps even counter-intuitive, claims about someone's consent—if the evidential threshold can be met.

[...]

It can now be seen that, through the closely connected test, it is the legally restrictive approach that has taken hold in *Lawrance*.

[...]

[T]his section argues that it is an expansive approach to conditional consent, of the kind set out earlier, that can be properly grounded in the SOA 2003.

a. Statutory interpretation

It is noteworthy that s.74 mentions no limitation as to which specific premises can be taken as relevant to consent. It states only that the issue of consent is to be determined through the idea of agreement to sexual contact "by choice". The focus is squarely on the choice of the complainant, with no prerequisites mentioned regarding the substance of that choice. Taken at face value, therefore, reading in such limits would run contrary to this section, and the enacted intention that an individual's "choice" be central to consent.

Further support for this interpretation can be found by looking to the policy intention behind the 2003 reforms. In the consultation paper leading to those reforms, the Government set out its view that sexual offences are "primarily crimes against the sexual autonomy of others". "Sexual autonomy"—in their view—means that "[e]very adult has the right and responsibility to make decisions about their sexual conduct". The reference to "choice" should be read in this light: the concern for the freedom of an individual to make decisions about their sexual conduct would suggest that it is the individual's choices which should be decisive. This is required to fully respect their sexual autonomy. Setting substantive limits on these choices—external to the individual engaging in the sexual activity—does not sit well with the concern for sexual autonomy and the primacy of personal choice behind the 2003 Act, because it dictates the scope of that choice, and diminishes the individual's preferences.

The immediate consequence is that, contrary to what was suggested in *Lawrance*, it is not an *expansive* approach to the conditions which can vitiate consent that conflicts with Parliamentary intention, but, rather, restrictive approaches of the kind deployed in that case.

b. An expansive approach to conditional consent

The wider consequences of our argument rejecting the restrictive approach would be as follows: where an individual chooses to engage in a sexual act, guided by a particular premise, and this premise turns out not to be the case, there is no consent under s.74.

Their freedom of choice has been violated. Where the other party knowingly and deliberately violates this premise, there is an argument that they do not have a reasonable belief in consent. "Common sense", or other external standards, would be relevant, at most, to assessing whether the evidence suggests these facts exist. If there is sufficient evidence, then a sexual offence can be charged, and, at trial, the issue must be left to the jury.

In principle, therefore, this leaves the range of unfulfilled premises which can vitiate sexual consent under s.74 unlimited. The key is whether an individual's consent was, in fact, premised on that factor. Provided the other elements of a sexual offence are made out, any unfulfilled condition could give rise to a sexual offence.

This approach is exemplified by the pre-*Monica* 2003 Act case law–*Assange*, *F*, and *McNally*, interpreted in the way we have indicated. As noted, these cases depended on the principle that the complainant had consented on the basis of a premise which was false, and the defendant knew this. We argue that this was, and is, the correct approach.

Others have disagreed with Murray and Beattie. Dyer, for example, argues that there is an urgent need to reform the law as set out in *R* v *Lawrance*. But he says that there is no clear indication that, when Parliament passed the Sexual Offences Act 2003, it intended to radically change the previous law – and so the Court's interpretation of the 2003 Act in *R* v *Lawrance* was correct as a matter of statutory interpretation.[25]

In *R* v *Lawrance*, the Court of Appeal also considered a further issue, namely, whether a distinction should be drawn between 'express deception' (which is capable of vitiating consent) and 'failure to disclose' (which is not capable of doing so). Burnett LCJ rejected this, stating that such a distinction would be a difficult one to draw:

> 40 … deceit and deception are very slippery concepts which, at one end of the spectrum, may result from a clear short lie, through more obscure utterances, obfuscation or evasion, to conduct designed to convey an unspoken false impression. In this area it is difficult to draw clear principled lines which could distinguish a deceit resulting from one course from another

In her discussion of *R* v *McNally*, *Assange* v *Swedish Prosecution Authority* and *R (F)* v *Director of Public Prosecutions*, Alex Sharpe also argues that this distinction 'lacks a convincing basis for setting the parameters of criminal liability'.

EXTRACT

In the following extract Sharpe sets out four hypothetical scenarios, which she uses to illustrate her argument that the distinction between 'active deception' and 'non-disclosure of information' is flawed. In Sharpe's opinion, what flaws do these scenarios expose? Do you agree?

Sharpe, A. (2016) 'Expanding Liability for Sexual Fraud Through the Concept of "Active Deception": A Flawed Approach' 80 *Journal of Criminal Law 28*

Hypothetical scenarios (A–D)

(1) D, aware V would not have consented to sex had D disclosed his HIV+ status, had sex with V.

(2) D, aware V would not have consented to sex had D disclosed his HIV+ status, lied when asked and then had sex with V.

(3) D, aware V would not have consented to sex had D disclosed his HIV+ status, had sex with V. Sexual intercourse was unprotected and D was not on ART (anti-retroviral treatment).

(4) D, aware V would not have consented to sex had D disclosed his HIV+ status, lied when asked and then had sex with V. D was on ART, had a very low viral load, and used a condom.

[25] Dyer, A. (2024) 'How should English law deal with deceptive sex?' 53 *Common Law World Review* 3.

Justifications for the distinction

[...]

[A]pplication of the [active deception – non-disclosure of information] distinction would lead to convictions in scenarios B and D, but not A and C. I would argue that such outcomes, ones that follow the line of reasoning exhibited in the cases discussed, contradict any claim that the distinction satisfactorily distributes defendants in terms of moral culpability. In all four scenarios, the defendant was unwilling to disclose his HIV+ status and was aware that sex was conditional on his not being HIV+. In this regard, the scenarios are not distinguished by an intent/recklessness divide. That is, none of the scenarios involve only risk-taking. Two differences between scenarios B and D, and scenarios A and C, are that in scenarios B and D the victim is proactive in asking about the defendant's HIV status and the defendant lies. However, in relation to the culpability question, only lying is relevant. Of course, lying is a more active form of deception than non-disclosure. But this does not, of itself, demonstrate greater culpability. Indeed, I would suggest that while the defendant in scenario B may be more morally culpable than the defendant in scenario A, it is certainly not the case that active deception in scenario D is more morally culpable than non-disclosure in scenario C. This is because in scenario D lying needs to be considered in relation to other features of the scenario.

The specific features that ought to be valued here are that the defendant is (i) on anti-retroviral drugs and has a low viral load and (ii) used a condom. While the defendant's actions might be viewed as unethical, they do demonstrate a quite different relation to risk and harm, one that might be viewed as lessening culpability. Certainly, in scenario C, the defendant exposes the victim to a significant risk of serious harm, whereas in scenario D, though the defendant lies, the risk of harm to which the victim is exposed is minimal. Moreover, while the defendant in scenario C is highly likely to be aware of a serious risk of harm to the victim, the defendant in scenario D is likely to be aware of the exceptionally low risk of transmission of the virus. It is true in scenario D, that while lying might not be motivated by a desire to have sex, the defendant is aware of the absence of consent. However, this is true in all four scenarios. What is problematic is the fact that the defendant who took responsibility for his own sexual health, practised safe sex and who accordingly exhibited some degree of care and concern toward the 'victim', is more likely to be convicted of a sexual offence under the judicial distinction under consideration. This appears to me to be intuitively wrong. Reasoning by analogy in this way suggests that the assumption that active deception necessarily involves a greater breach of trust than non-disclosure is misplaced, at least in some plausible cases. As Ashworth has reminded us, 'the act-omission distinction should not be used as a cloak for avoiding the moral issues.'

We have one final case involving a deception left to consider: *R* v *Linekar* (the case involving the defendant who had no intention to pay the prostitute). This case occurred under the old law and so the section 74 definition of consent was not yet in existence. According to the case law we have studied in this section, if a case like *R* v *Linekar* happened today, how would section 74 apply?

In his article 'Mistaken Sex', Jonathan Herring argues that a defendant like the one in *R* v *Linekar* should be convicted of rape.[26]

[26] See also McCormack, S. and Herring, J. (2024) 'The Duties of the Penetrator and the Limits of Consent' *Criminal Law Review* 94.

EXTRACT

Herring, J. (2005) 'Mistaken Sex' *Criminal Law Review* 511

The main point to note [about section 74's definition of consent] is the emphasis on the notion of agreement. The focus is not just on the victim and whether she said yes or no; but rather on both parties and seeking to ascertain whether there had been an agreement, a meeting of the minds between them. The complainant's version of what happened will not be restricted legally to her either saying yes or no to sexual intercourse, but the jury will be required to take a broader view of how the parties understood their sexual activity and reach a conclusion as to whether there was a sufficient co-operation to amount to an agreement. I would suggest that the use of agreement enables the court to develop an approach in line with the arguments made in this article. In particular it makes it easier to argue that if one party knows the other is mistaken over an issue which is an essential prerequisite to their consent then the parties do not agree.

[...]

[Some] argue that as the prostitute agreed to have sexual intercourse for £25 the harm to her when the defendant ran off after sex without paying can be valued at £25. In other words, if a deception over such a 'small' sum is sufficient to induce her to consent the wrong done to her is very minor. The error here is to see the only loss in *Linekar* as to the money she was not paid and to ignore the fact that here sexual autonomy had been infringed. A victim of theft or obtaining property by deception is not harmed in the same way as a person who accidentally loses property of the same value. The harm in *Linekar* was the interference of her right to choose with whom and under what conditions to have sexual intercourse and not just the loss of £25.

Conclusion

In the past it was said:

> [A] male [may] make promises that will not be kept, ... indulge in exaggeration and hyperbole, or ... assure any trusting female that ... the ugly frog is really the handsome prince. Every man is free, under the law, to be a gentleman or a cad.

But we should no longer be in an age when the "gentle art of seduction" is revered and praised; when women or men are sexual objects to be prised open by whatever means comes to hand. It should no longer be enough just to ask did the complainant say "yes" in relation to the proposed sexual activity. Now the values that should underpin our sexual offences law are those of mutual respect, reciprocity, connection and honesty. If we respect sexual integrity and the importance of being able to choose with whom to have sexual partners then the choice must be one that is free from coercion and fraud. A man who has sexual intercourse with another knowing that that person would not be agreeing to the activity if s/he knew the truth is using that person for his own ends. It is the "sheer use of another person". It should be rape.

Others have advanced slightly less ambitious reform proposals. Dyer says that, as a matter of principle, he agrees with Herring's position. But, he argues, most people would disagree with some of the outcomes that result from Herring's approach. It is necessary, therefore, to consider the legitimacy of the law: 'to achieve its purposes, the law must retain its authority – and, to retain its authority, the law cannot stray too far beyond what the public will accept'.[27] He accordingly states that deceptive sex should amount to

[27] Dyer, A. (2024) 'How should English law deal with deceptive sex?' 53 *Common Law World Review* 3, 28.

rape, except in two situations: (1) where the victim was deceived as to a trivial matter, and (2) where the issue on which the victim was deceived only exerted great influence because of the victim's irrational prejudice.[28] Meanwhile Yean has argued that the criminal law should draw upon the contract law doctrine of misrepresentation, so that a lack of consent should be found where a misrepresentation by D to V causatively induced V to engage in the sexual act with D, D's misrepresentation was a positive statement or act, the misrepresentation was a false statement of fact and not opinion or mere puff, and D knew that V would not have consented but for his misrepresentation.[29] This approach, he argues, addresses 'the most common and most powerful objections' against Herring's proposal and has the added benefit of providing 'a coherent framework built on over a century of case law that can be applied by analogy'.[30]

Now, think about these questions.

1. Imagine that a case with identical facts to *R* v *Linekar* occurred today. You are the prosecutor. Looking back at the case law on consent obtained by deception, construct the outline of your argument that the victim did not consent to sexual intercourse.
2. Now imagine you are defence counsel. Looking back at the case law on consent obtained by deception, construct the outline of your argument that the victim did consent to sexual intercourse.
3. Looking at the arguments for the prosecution and defence, would your conclusion be that the victim did or did not consent?

Now, consider the following scenario.

Lawrence and Mandy have been seeing each other for six months. Lawrence has decided to end the relationship tonight, but decides not to tell Mandy until after they have had sexual intercourse. They have dinner together at Mandy's flat. At the end of the meal Lawrence takes Mandy's hand, looks into her eyes and says 'I love you'. They kiss, and then go to the bedroom and have sexual intercourse. Afterwards Lawrence gets dressed, says 'Sorry Mandy, I don't want to see you anymore', and leaves. Mandy is devastated. She says she would never have had sex with Lawrence if she had known he was going to break up with her.

According to Herring's proposal, should Lawrence be convicted of rape? Do you agree with Herring? Would it amount to rape under the proposals advanced by Dyer and Yean?

[28] See also the proposals advanced by Mark Dsouza. He labels Herring's approach the 'subjective dealbreakers' view and argues that it spreads 'the net of criminal liability too widely to be plausible or practical'. Instead, Dsouza advances an approach that criminalises 'more conservatively' whilst also seeking to respect what V considers important to her consent. On this approach, it is 'possible (though not inevitable)' that a defendant like the one in *R* v *Linekar* committed rape. See further Dsouza, M. (2022) 'False Beliefs and Consent to Sex' 85 *Modern Law Review* 1191.

[29] Yean, A. (2025) 'Misrepresentation and Sexual Consent: Lessons from the Law of Contract' 89 *Journal of Criminal Law* 78.

[30] ibid, 90.

What makes situations like *R* v *Linekar* particularly difficult is the all-or-nothing nature of the decision. As we saw in the extract from Ormerod above, under the old law there was an offence of procuring sexual intercourse with a woman by false representations (maximum sentence: two years' imprisonment).[31] A situation like the one in *R* v *Linekar* was a straightforward example of this offence.[32] But the 2003 Act abolished this offence and did not replace it.[33] So today the defendant in *R* v *Linekar* has either committed rape or he has committed no sexual offence at all. Temkin and Ashworth observe:[34]

> [I]t appears that, when a court is deciding whether a particular deception or threat is sufficient to negative ostensible consent, it is effectively deciding between conviction of a serious offence and a complete acquittal. There is no lesser offence, no middle way [... so] the vague terms of s74 now assume a heightened importance.

Before moving on, remember that the principle from *R* v *Elbekkay* may be used when interpreting section 74's definition of consent. We examined this principle in detail above. So if the case involved impersonation of someone the victim did not know personally, or if it involved the defendant taking advantage of a case of mistaken identity, the *R* v *Elbekkay* principle can be applied.

Capacity to consent

As well as freedom to choose, section 74 also states that the victim must have had the capacity to be able to choose. We are going to examine three reasons why a victim might have lacked the capacity to be able to choose: mental disorder; age and intoxication.

The first reason is mental disorder. In *R* v *Cooper* [2009] UKHL 42 the defendant, Gary Cooper, befriended the victim – a 28-year-old woman with a history of serious mental disorders – gave her crack cocaine and then made her perform oral sex on him. The victim said she did as he asked because she feared violence. Cooper was convicted of an offence under the Sexual Offences Act 2003. He appealed against his conviction, arguing that the woman understood what oral sex was and so did not lack the capacity to consent. The House of Lords rejected this. Baroness Hale explained:

> [T]he case law on capacity has for some time recognised that, to be able to make a decision, the person concerned must not only be able to understand the information relevant to making it but also be able to "weigh [that information] in the balance to arrive at [a] choice".

So when deciding whether a victim had the capacity to consent, a jury should not only consider whether she was able to understand the relevant information but also whether she was capable of weighing up this information in order to make a decision. The jury in Cooper's case decided that, although the victim knew what oral sex was, the fear that she had experienced as a result of her mental disorder meant that she had lacked the capacity to agree by choice.

[31] Sexual Offences Act 1956, s.3. The maximum sentence was set out in Part II of the Second Schedule to the Act.

[32] This offence was not left to the jury in *R* v *Linekar*, but when quashing the defendant's rape conviction the Court of Appeal stated that, 'If anything, the appellant was guilty of an offence under section 3 of the Act of 1956'.

[33] For an argument that a similar offence should be created today, see: Laird, K. (2014) 'Rapist or Rogue? Deception, Consent and the Sexual Offences Act 2003' *Criminal Law Review* 492.

[34] Temkin, J. and Ashworth, A. (2004) 'The Sexual Offences Act 2003 – (1) Rape, Sexual Assaults and the Problems of Consent' *Criminal Law Review* 328 at 346.

The second reason a victim might have lacked the capacity to consent is age. For the offence of rape, the law does not specify a particular age at which individuals acquire the capacity to consent to sexual intercourse. Whether a child had the capacity to be able to agree to sexual intercourse by choice is instead a question of fact, to be answered in a particular case by assessing the child's level of maturity and understanding. This is illustrated by *R* v *Robinson* [2011] EWCA Crim 916. The events in this case took place in the 1990s, and did not come to light until years later. The defendant, Sean Robinson, was charged with the rape of his girlfriend's daughter, ZK. Over time Robinson had formed a close relationship with ZK. At the age of 11 or 12 she would go round to his flat and play computer games with him. On one occasion ZK got into bed with her mother and Robinson and he touched her legs under the cover. When they were in the car together Robinson would kiss and stroke her leg. He began showing her pornographic films when they were at his flat. Gradually, this developed into a fuller sexual relationship. They first had sexual intercourse when ZK was aged 12. The relationship continued for three years. When ZK was asked whether or not she consented on the first occasion they had sexual intercourse, she replied: 'I did not ask the defendant not to, I did not move to stop him. He reassured me that it was okay. I did not make it plain to him that I didn't want to. There was no occasion when I said that I didn't want him to do it.'

At trial Robinson was convicted of rape. He appealed against his conviction, arguing that the trial judge should not have allowed the rape charge to go to the jury since there was no evidence of rape. The evidence, he claimed, showed that the sexual intercourse was consensual and ZK was a willing participant. The Court of Appeal rejected Robinson's appeal and upheld the conviction.

EXTRACT

Read the following extract from the judgment of Elias LJ.

For the purposes of rape, could a 12-year-old child consent to sexual intercourse?

What reasons did Elias LJ give for saying that there was evidence that ZK had not consented?

R v *Robinson* [2011] EWCA Crim 916

Elias LJ

21 Grooming is not a term of art, but it suggests cynical and manipulative behaviour designed to achieve a particular sexual objective. Not all relationships with underage children can fairly be characterised as involving grooming, although many will. But even where they can, the fact of grooming plainly does not necessarily vitiate consent. Many a seducer achieves his objectives with the liberal and cynical employment of gifts, insincere compliments and false promises. But such manipulative and deceitful methods could not be relied upon to establish a lack of consent whenever the seduction was successful. The situation will often be no different where the complainant is under age. But where the exploitation is of a girl who is of an age where she does not, or may not, have the capacity to understand the full significance of what she is doing, and in particular, where, as here, there was evidence of acquiescence or acceptance rather than positive consent, we think that, as the judge found, it would be open to the jury to conclude that the complainant, perhaps out of embarrassment or some other reason, had in reality unwillingly gone along with the acts which she did not in fact wish to engage in.

[...]

23 The only question we have to decide is whether, in view of this girl's age, and having regard to the passages in her interview and when she gave evidence, there was sufficient evidence from which the jury could infer a lack of consent. We are satisfied that the judge was right to say that there was. As Galbraith emphasises, the judge should not usurp the jury's functions by withdrawing the case from them. Some 12-year-olds plainly do not have the capacity to consent. Whilst this young girl did not fall into that category, in our judgment there was evidence on which a jury was entitled to find that her immaturity, coupled with the evidence of acquiescence rather than enthusiastic consent, particularly in the context of what could be perceived as grooming, meant that there was no proper consent.

R v Robinson was followed by the Court of Appeal in *R v Ali* (Yasir Ifran) [2015] EWCA Crim 1279. The defendants in this case targeted young girls, often from troubled backgrounds, whom they befriended and groomed for sexual purposes. One of the 29 counts concerned the defendant Ali's sexual relationship with a 15-year-old girl, SS. At trial, the defence submitted that there no was evidence on which a reasonable jury could convict because SS did not at any stage assert that she had not consented. The trial judge rejected this submission, stating that 'it seems to me that there is evidence on which a jury would be entitled to find that her immaturity, coupled with the evidence of acquiescence rather than enthusiastic consent, particularly in the context of what could be perceived as grooming, meant that there was no proper consent on her part' ([39]). Ali was subsequently convicted of rape, and appealed against his conviction. The Court of Appeal rejected the appeal, holding that since there were 'credible competing submissions as to whether there had been true consent' the issue of consent had properly been left to the jury ([65])[35].

EXTRACT

Read the following extract from the judgment of Fulford LJ.

In cases involving grooming, why might a victim's apparent consent not in fact have been real consent?

R v *Ali (Yasir Ifran)* [2015] EWCA Crim 1279

Fulford LJ

57 One of the consequences when vulnerable people are groomed for sexual exploitation is that compliance can mask the lack of true consent on the part of the victim. As the judge directed the jury in the summing up in this case, where there is evidence of exploitation of a young and immature person who may not understand the full significance of what he or she is doing, that is a factor the jury can take into account in deciding whether or not there was genuine consent

[...]

58 Although, as Elias LJ observed [in *R v Robinson*], grooming does not necessarily vitiate consent, it starkly raises the possibility that a vulnerable or immature individual may have been placed in a position in which he or she is led merely to acquiesce rather than to give proper or real consent. One of the consequences of grooming is that it has a tendency to limit or subvert the alleged victim's capacity to make free decisions, and it creates the risk that he or she simply submitted because of the environment of dependency created by those responsible for treating the alleged victim in this way. Indeed, the individual may have been manipulated to the extent that he or she is unaware of, or confused about, the distinction between acquiescence and genuine agreement at the time the incident occurred.

[35] *R v Ali (Yasir Ifran) was subsequently followed in R v Gray [2025] EWCA Crim 1042.*

Before moving on, it is worth pointing out that, even if a defendant is not guilty of rape, there are other crimes which might apply if he had sexual intercourse with a child. For example, sections 5 to 8 of the Sexual Offences Act 2003 contain crimes which apply to sexual activity with children aged under 13, and sections 9 and 10 contain crimes which apply where the child was aged under 16.

The third reason a victim might lack the capacity to be able to choose to agree to sexual intercourse is intoxication. If the victim was so drunk that she passed out, and the defendant was aware of this, then there will be an evidential presumption that she did not consent (section 75(2)(d)). Similarly, if the defendant is aware that the victim was involuntarily given an overpowering or stupefying substance there will be an evidential presumption that she did not consent (section 75(2)(f)). But what about cases where the presumptions don't apply? And cases where the defendant manages to rebut the presumptions?

The leading case is *R* v *Bree* [2007] EWCA Crim 804. Benjamin Bree, aged 25, was visiting his brother Michael, who was a student at Bournemouth University. Benjamin and Michael went out for the evening with Michael's girlfriend, Holly, and Michael's flatmate M, the eventual victim. They each consumed a lot of alcohol. M drank two pints of cider and between four and six drinks of vodka and Red Bull. Benjamin drank two pints of lager before he too moved on to vodka and Red Bull. Michael and Holly left first. Benjamin and M left soon after. CCTV footage showed them returning to her flat arm-in-arm. Once inside, M vomited in the shower in her room. Benjamin looked after her. He washed her hair. M could not remember having her hair washed, but did remember someone asking her where she kept her shampoo.

There were different accounts of what happened next.

- Here is M's account. She said that she must have become unconscious. After being asked for shampoo, her next memory was of lying on her bed. Benjamin was on top of her, with his mouth and tongue on and in her vagina. In her statement she said: 'I did nothing or said anything in response. I felt as if I wasn't in my body. I hadn't recovered significantly from how I felt in the bathroom, and I didn't know how long his mouth was in my vagina. I remember his fingers in my vagina. I could just feel this. I don't know where his head was. The next thing I recall is his coming close by my face and asking if I had a condom. I said no.' She didn't want to have sex, but said that she had not said this to Benjamin. In her statement she said: 'I knew I didn't want this but I didn't know how to go about stopping it.' To try and avoid sexual intercourse she turned over and curled up in a ball facing the wall. Although his penis was withdrawn for a while, he penetrated her again. She had no idea how long intercourse lasted. When it ended she was still facing the wall. Afterwards Benjamin asked if she wanted him to stay, and she said 'no'. In her mind she thought 'get out of my room', although she did not actually say it.
- Here is Benjamin's account. Benjamin said that M was in a much better state after being sick. He gave her her pyjamas. He said that he left the room and had a cigarette while she put them on. CCTV footage confirmed that he did leave the building for five minutes. When he returned, she was sitting on the edge of her bed. He started to stroke her. M seemed to welcome this, and it went from being stroking of a comforting nature to sexual touching. She did nothing to stop him. He put the top of his fingers inside the waistband of her pyjama trousers, and she did nothing to discourage him. He pulled the trousers down slightly, and then she removed them altogether. He said that they then had 'brief sex'. While they were having sex she asked whether he had a condom. He said no and asked whether she had one. She replied no. She was concerned about having unprotected sex, and so he stopped. He did not ejaculate. He went to the

bathroom, washed his face, and asked M whether she wanted him to stay the night. She said no, and he left.

Importantly, during the trial the prosecution accepted that M had not lost consciousness. The gaps in her memory were not because she was unconscious; they were due to an alcohol-induced 'blackout' (excessive alcohol consumption can result in impaired memory and recollection).[36]

The key issue in the case was whether or not M consented to sexual intercourse. The prosecution argued that, even though M never lost consciousness, she had not consented to sexual intercourse. By contrast, Benjamin insisted that, although M may have become less inhibited because she was intoxicated, she was lucid enough to be able to consent to sexual intercourse and she did in fact consent.

At trial Benjamin was convicted of rape. The Court of Appeal subsequently quashed the conviction because of a number of defects in how the trial judge directed the jury. In its judgment the Court sought to clarify the meaning of 'capacity' in cases like this one.

EXTRACT

Read the following extract from the judgment of Sir Igor Judge.

Does a disinhibited person still have the capacity to consent?

Can a conscious person ever lack the capacity to consent?

R v *Bree* [2007] EWCA Crim 804

Sir Igor Judge

26 In cases which are said to arise after voluntary consumption of alcohol the question is not whether the alcohol made either or both less inhibited than they would have been if sober, nor whether either or both might afterwards have regretted what had happened, and indeed wished that it had not. If the complainant consents, her consent cannot be revoked. Moreover it is not a question whether either or both may have had very poor recollection of precisely what had happened. That may be relevant as to the reliability of their evidence. Finally, and certainly, it is not a question whether either or both was behaving irresponsibly. As they were both autonomous adults, the essential question for decision is, as it always is, whether the evidence proved that the defendant had sexual intercourse with the complainant without her consent.

[...]

34 In our judgment, the proper construction of section 74 of the 2003 Act, as applied to the problem now under discussion, leads to clear conclusions. If, through drink (or for any other reason) the complainant has temporarily lost her capacity to choose whether to have intercourse on the relevant occasion, she is not consenting, and subject to questions about the defendant's state of mind, if intercourse takes place, this would be rape. However, where

---

36 The fact that excessive alcohol consumption can cause impaired memory and recollection means that it is important to distinguish between absence of memory and absence of consent. This was emphasised in *R* v *Tambedou* [2014] EWCA Crim 954, in which the Court of Appeal held that the fact that the victim could not recall whether or not she consented was not, in itself, sufficient reason to withdraw the case from the jury. There was ample evidence relevant to the question whether she had had the capacity to consent to go before a jury.

the complainant has voluntarily consumed even substantial quantities of alcohol, but nevertheless remains capable of choosing whether or not to have intercourse, and in drink agrees to do so, this would not be rape. We should perhaps underline that, as a matter of practical reality, capacity to consent may evaporate well before a complainant becomes unconscious. Whether this is so or not, however, is fact-specific, or more accurately, depends on the actual state of mind of the individuals involved on the particular occasion.

35 Considerations like these underline the fact that it would be unrealistic to endeavour to create some kind of grid system which would enable the answer to these questions to be related to some prescribed level of alcohol consumption. Experience shows that different individuals have a greater or lesser capacity to cope with alcohol than others, and indeed the ability of a single individual to do so may vary from day to day. The practical reality is that there are some areas of human behaviour which are inapt for detailed legislative structures. In this context, provisions intended to protect women from sexual assaults might very well be conflated into a system which would provide patronising interference with the right of autonomous adults to make personal decisions for themselves.

36 For these reasons, notwithstanding criticisms of the statutory provisions, in our view the 2003 Act provides a clear definition of "consent" for the purposes of the law of rape, and by defining it with reference to "capacity to make that choice", sufficiently addresses the issue of consent in the context of voluntary consumption of alcohol by the complainant. The problems do not arise from the legal principles. They lie with infinite circumstances of human behaviour, usually taking place in private without independent evidence, and the consequent difficulties of proving this very serious offence.

One of the criticisms of the judgment in *R* v *Bree* is that it gives insufficient guidance on the meaning of 'capacity'. The reason that juries need more detailed guidance is because different people have very different understandings of what capacity means. This is illustrated by research done by Emily Finch and Vanessa Munro. They conducted a number of mock rape trials, and recorded each jury's deliberations in order to gain an insight into the reasoning employed by the (mock) jurors. The facts were similar to those in *R* v *Bree*. The following extract reports Finch and Munro's findings on the different understandings of 'capacity'.

EXTRACT

Finch, E. and Munro, V. (2006) 'Breaking Boundaries? Sexual Consent in the Jury Room' 26 *Legal Studies* 303

Given that the complainant experienced a high level of intoxication across all the trials in this study – while conscious and able to communicate, she was confused, having trouble walking, slurring her words, and the defendant admitted that she was largely unresponsive as he undressed her – it is perhaps not surprising to find that most jurors concluded that she did not consent to intercourse, since she lacked the capacity to do so under s 74. As one juror expressed this view, 'when he was undressing her, she was a floppy doll. There's no sign of consent there at all, it's, you know, just a lifeless thing' (Jury M). It is important to point out, however, that even in this situation, that view was not shared by everyone. A number of participants indicated that the complainant, so long as she remained conscious, retained the capacity to exercise a choice. Coupling this with a view that the non-consenting complainant had a responsibility to express her dissent to intercourse, such jurors commented, 'why could she not say no, I mean hang on a minute, my arms aren't moving, fine, but why can't you say no, keep on saying no' (Jury G), or similarly 'even though her whole body was slumped, she was still slurring. She could still speak. Even if she was slumped, she could still have said no' (Jury N).

These minority views testify to the way in which the concept of capacity under s 74, when applied to concrete cases, can lead to disparate results, depending on the extent to which jurors adopt a minimalist understanding of it as requiring little more than mere consciousness. Equally, however, the fact that there was a general consensus of outcome on the question of capacity, such that consent was not found, should not be thought to suggest too much interpretive unanimity amongst those jurors who supported this majority conclusion. Indeed, it was apparent from the deliberations that such jurors did not in fact share any common standard by which to judge this issue, whether across the different trials, across different juries or even within the same jury. Some participants, for example, adopted an approach to determining capacity to consent that compelled them to examine the complainant's state during the entire evening. By contrast, others invoked a broader perspective, taking into account factors such as the complainant's normal drinking habits and her likely level of alcohol tolerance. At the same time, other jurors adopted a far narrower time frame, focusing only on her responsiveness to the defendant at the time of intercourse, and attributing different emphases to factors such as her ability to communicate, her ability to weigh up options or her ability to make a decision reflecting her sober preferences.

While in the specific context of the present study, these differential tests rarely led to divergent conclusions, it is clear that this may not have been the case had the scenario involved a less intoxicated complainant. Some jurors, who adopted a highly rationalist understanding, for example, expressed the view that any intoxication would necessarily vitiate capacity under s 74. As one juror explained: 'When it's consent by choice and when you've got freedom and capacity to make consent, surely when you're drunk it eliminates that? How can you give consent when you're drunk?' (Jury A). By contrast, other jurors, who focused on communicative or cognitive ability, suggested that someone who was heavily intoxicated (albeit to a lesser extent than the present complainant) could retain a relevant capacity.

In addition, it was suggested that the issue of capacity would become more complex in these less extreme situations because the complainant may be deemed to have capacity for some acts but not for others, and so the significance of the decision to consent to intercourse would itself need to be considered. As one juror put it, 'it's not as simple ... to be able to decide because maybe she was enjoying the physical sensation, the physical act, but not emotionally' (Jury B). This is significant, of course, because it highlights the extent to which including the requirement that the complainant has capacity to make a choice, in the absence of guidance as to what level of consciousness, communication or self-awareness this requires, creates a malleable and unpredictable legal test. What's more, it suggests that in such situations, jurors' views about the level of responsibility an individual ought to take for his/her social and sexual behaviour may prove to be determinative.

Despite this marked divergence in the jurors' interpretations of s 74, what was also clear in the present study was the extent to which participants themselves seemed (paradoxically) confident in their understanding of the law. During their deliberations, mock jurors frequently seized on the statutory language and deployed it in support of their conclusions. Thus, for example, one juror commented, 'the thing that struck me was that in order for her to have consented, it meant that she had the choice and she had to be ... she had to have made her choice and had the freedom to make that choice. I don't think that she was in a situation to have done that' (Jury I). Likewise, another noted, 'the whole thing is her capacity to make any sort of judgement. I mean, that's, from my point of view, where it all hangs because she didn't have the freedom and capacity to make any sort of rational judgement whatsoever' (Jury U). This suggests that participants found the terms used in the s 74 definition to be familiar ones that they could work with. But while we generally applaud law that is user-friendly in this way, in this context, it is submitted that there is cause for caution. After all, as discussed, the fact that freedom, choice and capacity are terms whose meaning is within everyone's understanding does not entail that everyone understands those terms to mean the same thing, either in the abstract or in specific cases. Thus, the familiarity of the terms may itself be problematic since it presents the illusion of greater consensus in the jury room, and in the legal tests that are applied therein, than in fact exists.

Alongside these findings about the way in which participants responded to, interpreted and applied the s 74 provision, there is one further insight into the operation of the 2003 Act that emerged from this study. Across the different jury deliberations, it was apparent that the introduction of the requirement that the complainant agree by choice in circumstances of capacity and freedom, while predicted to promote a more proactive and communicative understanding of sexuality, did little to prevent some jurors from continuing to presume consent in the absence of positive dissent. The statements cited above from jurors who concluded that the complainant retained the capacity to consent, despite intoxication, testify to this, since these jurors moved on to assert that failing to dissent in a context in which the complainant was capable of so doing constituted agreement to intercourse. Significantly, moreover, these jurors were far from isolated in taking this approach. Indeed, while some jurors read the terms of s 74 as requiring something 'active rather than passive' (Jury S), as 'saying that consent isn't just being there and not saying no' (Jury Q), many others did not concur, or at least did not allow this to prevent them from taking a different line. Thus, a number of jurors operated from the opposite direction, commenting, for example: 'I think maybe that's why she consented, because she didn't say anything' (Jury B), or 'in order to not consent you have to ... she has to actually make it clear that she has not consented' (Jury I).

Although the jurors who took this latter approach did not all require evidence of dissent to take the form of physical resistance, there were some participants who insisted that, even in the case of a heavily intoxicated complainant, they would expect to find some evidence of struggle to establish non-consent. As one juror put it, 'a woman's got to cooperate with a man to be able to do it, to have intercourse, unless he thumps her or what, and he didn't – there was no bruising on her body anywhere. I would say she was probably drunk but at the same time she more or less consented' (Jury I). These comments testify to the tenacity of the force requirement in the popular understanding of rape, but their existence is particularly disconcerting here, since the jurors were specifically advised during medical evidence in the trial that lack of complainant injury does not necessarily contra-indicate rape. And while it is true that such comments, when voiced, were sometimes met with stark rebukes from fellow jurors, it is significant that the basis for this did not appear to lie in anything provided by the s 74 definition itself.

Overall, then, while the limitations of the study's method, and the fact that it involved a relatively small sample (168 mock jurors), must be borne in mind, the deliberations undertaken in response to the rape scenarios do indicate considerable support for the concerns raised above by critics of the 2003 Act. Of course, it might be argued that the new legislation has brought some improvements – in the absence of a specific direction to consider capacity and freedom, for example, jurors may have been more inclined to consider that a heavily intoxicated complainant had consented. That said, what is clear is that the s 74 definition did not do all that might have been hoped, either for the complainant or the juror, in the present study, partly as a result of stereotypical views about 'appropriate' gender roles, but partly also because of the vagueness of its central definitional terms.

This extract raises concerns about both the clarity of the law and consistency of its application. The lack of guidance given by the Court of Appeal in *R* v *Bree* does little to ease these concerns.

Quiz 7.4

1. The authority of *R* v *Bree* states that ...
   a. absence of complaint is equivalent to consent.
   b. consent by force is not valid consent.
   c. consent when involuntarily intoxicated is not consent.
   d. drunken consent is still consent.
2. How does section 74 define consent?
   a. A person consents if he agrees willingly, without being subjected to deceit or manipulation.
   b. A person consents if he agrees freely, without being subjected to undue pressure or threats.
   c. A person consents if he agrees by choice, and has the freedom and capacity to make that choice.
   d. A person consents if he agrees unconditionally, without any doubts or second thoughts.
3. What distinction did the Court of Appeal draw in *Olugboja* [1982] QB 320?
   a. Real consent – reluctant acquiescence.
   b. Real consent – mere submission.
   c. Real consent – erroneous agreement.
   d. Real consent – apparent consent.

Mens rea of rape

7.5 Define the mens rea requirements for establishing criminal liability for rape.

1. The defendant intentionally penetrated the victim's vagina, anus or mouth with his penis

The first of the two *mens rea* requirements is that the penetration was intentional. In cases where the *actus reus* of rape has been established this *mens rea* requirement will almost inevitably be satisfied too. It is very difficult, if not impossible, to imagine how a defendant could penetrate the victim's vagina, anus or mouth with his penis through carelessness or by accident!

2. The defendant lacked a reasonable belief that the victim was consenting to the penetration

Under the old law the *mens rea* of rape was lack of a genuine belief in consent.[37] So if the defendant genuinely believed the victim was consenting he could not be convicted of rape, however unreasonable his belief in consent. This was heavily criticised. When the Government introduced the Sexual Offences Act 2003 it changed the *mens rea* to lack of a reasonable belief in consent. As the following extract from the 2002 Home Office document *Protecting the Public* explains, it was hoped that this change would increase the conviction rate.

[37] *DPP* v *Morgan* [1976] AC 182 (HL).

EXTRACT

Home Office (2002) *Protecting the Public: Strengthening Protection Against Sex Offenders and Reforming the Law on Sexual Offences* (Cm 5668)

33 We will also be modifying the test of mistaken belief in relation to non-consensual offences. The current defence of an "honest" belief in consent means that no crime is committed when a person is forced against their will to have sexual intercourse with a person who can convince the court that they "honestly" interpreted their protestations or actions as consent to sex, however unreasonable such a belief might be. We believe the difficulty in proving that some defendants did not truly have an "honest" belief in consent contributes in some part to the low rate of convictions for rape. This in turn leads many victims, who feel that the system will not give them justice, not to report incidents or press for them to be brought to trial.

34 We will therefore alter the test to include one of reasonableness under the law. This will make it clear that, where the prosecution can prove that there is reasonable room for uncertainty about whether someone was consenting and that the defendant did not take reasonable action in the circumstances to ensure that the other person was willing to take part in the sexual acts, he will commit an offence. "Reasonable" will be judged by reference to what an objective third party would think in the circumstances. The jury would however have to take into account the actions of both parties, the circumstances in which they have placed themselves and the level of responsibility exercised by both. The jury would also expect, where relevant, to take account of the circumstances in which the accusation or revelation is delivered (including any media involvement) and the time that has elapsed.

Assessment advice

When answering an exam problem question, it is important to remember that the conclusive and evidential presumptions set out in sections 76 and 75 also apply here. If the conclusive presumptions apply, the defendant will automatically be held to satisfy this mens rea requirement. If the evidential presumptions apply, you will need to consider whether the defendant can rebut the presumption by producing some evidence that he had a reasonable belief in consent.

Where the presumptions don't apply (or have been rebutted), you should work through this *mens rea* requirement in two steps:

First, you should ask, 'Did the defendant believe that the victim was consenting?' In Chapter 4 we saw that to believe something you must have mentally accepted it as being true. So a defendant does not believe the victim is consenting if he isn't sure whether she is consenting or not and decides to carry on anyway.

- First, you should ask, 'Did the defendant believe that the victim was consenting?' In Chapter 4 we saw that to believe something you must have mentally accepted it as being true. So a defendant does not believe the victim is consenting if he isn't sure whether she is consenting or not and decides to carry on anyway.
- If so, you should ask, 'Was the defendant's belief in consent reasonable?' When answering this question, remember that section 1(2) of the Act states, 'Whether a belief is reasonable is to be determined having regard to all the circumstances, including any steps A has taken to ascertain whether B consents'.

If the answer to either of these questions is no, the defendant lacked a reasonable belief in consent.

One issue the courts have had to address is whether mental illness may be taken into account when assessing whether a defendant's belief in consent was reasonable.[38] In *R* v *B* [2013] EWCA Crim 3 the defendant was a paranoid schizophrenic. His condition caused him to hold delusional beliefs. A psychiatrist stated that the defendant thought he had sexual healing powers and that the reason he had sexual intercourse with the victim (his partner) in spite of her objections might have been because he thought it would be good for her. At trial the defendant was convicted of rape. The Court of Appeal dismissed his appeal against his conviction. Hughes LJ explained that a delusional belief in consent is, by definition, not a reasonable belief:

> 35 If [...] the defendant's delusional beliefs could have led him to believe that his partner consented when she did not, we take the clear view that such delusional beliefs cannot in law render reasonable a belief that his partner was consenting when in fact she was not. The Act does not ask whether it was reasonable (in the sense of being understandable or not his fault) for the defendant to suffer from the mental condition which he did. Normally no doubt, absent at least fault such as self-induced intoxication by drink or drugs, the answer to that in the case of acute illness such as this defendant seems to have suffered will be that it is reasonable. What the answer would be if the condition were an anti-social, borderline or psychopathic personality disorder may be more problematic. But the Act asks a different question: whether the belief in consent was a reasonable one. A delusional belief in consent, if entertained, would be by definition irrational and thus unreasonable, not reasonable.

Hughes LJ went on to say that defendants like the one in *R* v *B* should instead seek to plead insanity (which we study in Chapter 10) – and if the defence of insanity is unavailable then the defendant's mental illness should be taken into account when sentencing. He also emphasised that he was not saying that a defendant's mental illness should never be taken into account when assessing whether a defendant's belief in consent was reasonable. He explained that evidence of mental illness could be relevant in some, limited, circumstances:

> 41 It does not follow that there will not be cases in which the personality or abilities of the defendant may be relevant to whether his positive belief in consent was reasonable. It may be that cases could arise in which the reasonableness of such belief depends on the reading by the defendant of subtle social signals, and in which his impaired ability to do so is relevant to the reasonableness of his belief. We do not attempt exhaustively to foresee the circumstances which might arise in which a belief might be held which is not in any sense irrational, even though most people would not have held it. Whether (for example) a particular defendant of less than ordinary intelligence or with demonstrated inability to recognise behavioural cues might be such a case, or whether his belief ought properly to be characterised as unreasonable, must await a decision on specific facts. It is possible, we think, that beliefs generated by such factors may not properly be described as irrational and might be judged by a jury not to be unreasonable on their particular facts. But once a belief could be judged reasonable only by a process which labelled a plainly irrational belief as reasonable, it is clear that it cannot be open to the jury so to determine without stepping outside the Act.

Citing this passage from Hughes LJ's judgment, the Court of Appeal in *R* v *Jacobs* [2023] EWCA Crim 1503 stated that in some cases a defendant's autism may be relevant to

[38] Another issue is whether a defendant's intoxication should be taken into account. For discussion of this, see Cann, W. (2024) '"Having regard" to intoxication in the Sexual Offences Act 2003 – an analysis of the *mens rea* in the Sexual Offences Act, and the measuring of circumstances' *Criminal Law Review* 778.

whether he had a reasonable belief in consent. This will depend on the facts of the specific case. For example, if the autism impairs the defendant's ability to read behavioural cues or subtle social signals, then it may be relevant to whether the defendant's belief in consent was reasonable. However, on the facts of *R v Jacobs*, the Court held that the defendant's autism was not relevant to the issue of reasonable belief in consent.

As we have seen, the change to the mens rea introduced by the 2003 Act was designed to increase the conviction rate. But from the outset critics doubted whether it was capable of having this effect.[39] Of particular concern is the invitation, in section 1(2), to have regard to 'all the circumstances' when assessing the reasonableness of the defendant's belief.

EXTRACT

The following extract is from an article written by Temkin and Ashworth.

What sorts of things do they think a jury might take into account when having regard to 'all the circumstances'. Why does this worry them?

Temkin, J. and Ashworth, A. (2004) 'The Sexual Offences Act 2003 – (1) Rape, Sexual Assaults and the Problems of Consent' *Criminal Law Review* 328

The broad reference to "all the circumstances" is an invitation to the jury to scrutinise the complainant's behaviour to determine whether there was anything about it which could have induced a reasonable belief in consent. In this respect the Act contains no real challenge to society's norms and stereotypes about either the relationship between men and women or other sexual situations, and leaves open the possibility that those stereotypes will determine assessments of reasonableness. Is B's sexual history to be taken to be a relevant part of the circumstances? In answer to a question raised in Committee, the Minister agreed that the section "should focus the court's attention on what is happening at the time of the offence" and "should make the previous sexual history of the complainant far less relevant." But this does not seem to reflect the natural meaning of the words "all the circumstances," which contain no limitation to circumstances existing at the time of the event in question. Further, it is true that s.1(2) requires consideration of "any steps A has taken to ascertain whether B consents," however, if A enquires about consent; B says no, but A concludes that B's "no" is tantamount to "yes," is his culturally engendered belief to be regarded as reasonable or not? In deciding what it is "relevant" to consider, what is to prevent the influence of stereotypes about B's dress, B's frequenting of a particular place, an invitation to have a drink, and so forth?

These concerns were reiterated by the Gillen Review in 2019, which stated that the failure to 'clearly delineate what should and should not be considered reasonable [leaves] the door open for stereotypes to determine assessments of reasonableness'.[40] The mock trials conducted by Finch and Munro allow us to assess the extent to which these concerns are justified.

[39] In 2006, the Home Office reported that there was little evidence that the 2003 Act had resulted in a greater number of convictions for rape: see Home Office (2006) Sexual Offences Act 2003: *A stocktake of the effectiveness of the Act since its implementation.*

[40] Gillen, J. (2019) *Gillen Review: Report into the law and procedures in serious sexual offences in Northern Ireland*, para 11.16.

EXTRACT

Finch, E. and Munro, V. (2006) 'Breaking Boundaries? Sexual Consent in the Jury Room' 26 *Legal Studies* 303

[I]n the absence of specific guidance to the contrary, jurors often interpreted the notion of 'reasonable in all the circumstances' extremely broadly, taking into account not only factors about the defendant, about 'the way he thought' (Jury E) and about whether he felt remorse (Jury T), but also about 'the whole situation, the party, the drinking and so on' (Jury R). As one juror put it: 'you might think yeah, that is very unreasonable but from his point of view you might think it's not as unreasonable and the fact that she is at a party, she does look and appear to be drunk, she hasn't told him no and from the other person's point of view it might look like he's not being unreasonable' (Jury E). These statements are significant because they illustrate the extent to which, on the invitation to consider 'all the circumstances', jurors effectively deduced sexual consent (or at least the defendant's reasonable belief therein) from other, often unrelated, events that lacked any temporal correspondence with intercourse.

The introduction of these wider circumstantial factors is problematic because it allows scope for juror reliance on inferences extrapolated from surrounding circumstances, even when those circumstances bore no necessary relevance to the evaluation of consent between the parties themselves. In addition, moreover, it generates an opportunity for the introduction into the jury room of a range of (ill-founded) views about 'appropriate' socio-sexual interaction, either on the basis that they are shared by jurors who are assessing the signals sent out by the complainant's conduct, or on the basis that the jurors, while not sharing these views themselves, nonetheless consider that they may have been harboured by the defendant and so may be relevant to the question of his reasonableness. The references made in the previous quotes to 'the party and the drinking' clearly allude to these background social conventions, but in a number of the jurors' comments this linkage is made far more explicit. Thus, for example, one juror argued that had the complainant 'gone upstairs' with the defendant at the party (rather than on her own), the defendant could have reasonably taken from this that she was consenting to intercourse (Jury Q), while another suggested that this belief would have been reasonable if the complainant had 'been drinking all night, and flirting with him' (Jury E). In both these contexts, of course, jurors have tapped into highly dubious, but widely supported, social conventions which indicate that women who drink or flirt with men, or who take steps to initiate some intimacy, cannot complain when men take this behaviour to imply a willingness to engage in intercourse thereafter.

The extent to which jurors relied on these questionable stereotypes to afford leniency to the defendant within the confines of the present study was noteworthy. Indeed, even the fact that the complainant had been passive during intercourse was deemed, by some jurors, to be sufficient to support the defendant's claim to reasonable belief. As one juror put it, 'I don't think him having made all the advances and having to undress her is as important an issue ... because it's not unusual for one party to be more into it than the other, it's never 50:50% I would have thought and women are often sort of coy in these circumstances ... and he might have thought that as well' (Jury E). Similarly, another juror commented, 'her lack of showing consent, I think on that alone, you know, you could understand him reasonably thinking it was a sign of consent' (Jury C); and another added: 'I think from the fact that she was able to speak, albeit incoherently ... that it was reasonable for him to think that if she'd wanted to say no, she could have done' (Jury E).

It should be noted that in some juries, when these views were raised, they were challenged by other jurors, often through reliance on the wording of the statute. Thus, as one juror commented, 'I don't think the defendant ascertained sufficiently whether she was willing to consent, he didn't ask, he took some potentially token gestures as consent' (Jury M). This supports the claim alluded to in previous discussion that the requirement under the 2003 Act to consider the steps taken by the defendant to ascertain consent will counter these questionable interpretations, both of consent and of reasonableness. However, as noted above, the overall tenor of the jury deliberations in the present study did not bear this out. Indeed, it was apparent that jurors who adopted this line of thinking were rarely moved by the counters of their peers. The following exchange in Jury P reflects this most clearly:

'1: Why ... how do you think if you were in that event or just in the situation that he saw ... how do you think he saw consent? How do you think he ascertained that she was giving consent?

3: Well she didn't say no.

1: Because she didn't say no?

7: She wasn't paralytically unconscious was she?'

This suggests that the positive impact of requiring a defendant to take proactive steps to ascertain consent may be substantially undermined by a permission under the 2003 Act to take account of all the circumstances, especially where the 'good sense' of the jury is relied upon to determine the relevance of dubious social conventions indicating that passivity can reasonably be equated with consent.

The findings of Finch and Munro's study were echoed by an Australian study conducted by Larcombe *et al*. In this study, the researchers held eleven focus group discussions with three sets of participants: professionals working in the sexual assault sector; legally trained professionals; and community members. These participants expressed dissatisfaction with legal definitions of rape that require proof that the defendant lacked a reasonable belief in consent.

EXTRACT

Larcombe, W., Fileborn, B., Powell, A., Hanley, N. and Henry, N. (2016) '"I Think it's Rape and I Think He Would be Found Not Guilty": Focus Group Perceptions of (un)Reasonable Belief in Consent in Rape Law' 25 *Social & Legal Studies* 611

Across [sexual assault professionals, legal professionals and general community members], we found that a definition of rape that turns on whether the accused may have had a reasonable belief in consent is perceived as biased in favour of the defendant. Reasonable belief in consent was also perceived to enable jury members to apply assumptions and expectations about reasonable sexual conduct and inferred or continuing consent that many of our participants personally rejected. Whilst there was no agreement among our participants about what sexual consent is or how it can be inferred or established, it was expected that at least some jury members would think that it was reasonable for a person to believe that consent was present when a former sexual partner does not protest or resist. This was perceived to impose an unreasonable expectation on the victim of a sexual assault to unequivocally communicate non-consent. As a result, the law was perceived to lag behind these participants' own understandings of rape and to undermine conceptions of affirmative consent. Further law reform was suggested to restrict or abolish the reasonable belief defence or to ensure that a person accused of rape who claimed that they believed in consent should have to testify to their actions and submit to questioning about the grounds for any such belief.

Quiz 7.5

1. What is the *mens rea* of rape?
   - **a.** Intention to penetrate with reasonable belief of the victim's consent.
   - **b.** Intention to penetrate and recklessness to obtaining consent.
   - **c.** Intention to penetrate with a lack of reasonable belief of the victim's consent.
   - **d.** Recklessness to penetration and consent.
2. In relation to an accused's lack of reasonable belief, the accused will not have the necessary *mens rea* if…
   - **a.** he gives no thought to whether the other is consenting.
   - **b.** he has made reasonable efforts to ascertain that the other is consenting.
   - **c.** he knows the victim is not consenting.
   - **d.** he has no reasonable grounds for believing that the other is consenting.
3. The authority of *R v B* states that…
   - **a.** belief in consent for the purposes of section 1(1) of the Sexual Offences Act 2003 has not only to be genuinely held, it also has to be reasonable in the circumstances.
   - **b.** a belief in consent should be deemed reasonable even if it was delusional, as long as the defendant was not at fault for the delusion.
   - **c.** a delusional belief short of insanity was by definition reasonable.
   - **d.** an intoxicated complainant may lack the capacity to consent even if she is still conscious.

Assault by penetration

7.6 Define the requirements for establishing criminal liability for assault by penetration.

The offence of assault by penetration is defined by section 2 of the Sexual Offences Act 2003.

EXTRACT

Section 2 of the Sexual Offences Act 2003

2 Assault by penetration

(1) A person (A) commits an offence if –

(a) he intentionally penetrates the vagina or anus of another person (B) with a part of his body or anything else,

(b) the penetration is sexual,

(c) B does not consent to the penetration, and

(d) A does not reasonably believe that B consents.

(2) Whether a belief is reasonable is to be determined having regard to all the circumstances, including any steps A has taken to ascertain whether B consents.

(3) Sections 75 and 76 apply to an offence under this section.

(4) A person guilty of an offence under this section is liable, on conviction on indictment, to imprisonment for life.

This tells us that the offence has five requirements:

1. The defendant penetrated the vagina or anus of the victim with a part of his body or anything else
2. The penetration was sexual
3. The victim did not consent to the penetration
4. The defendant intentionally penetrated the vagina or anus of the victim
5. The defendant lacked a reasonable belief that the victim was consenting to the penetration.

Numbers 1 to 3 are *actus reus* requirements. Numbers 4 and 5 are *mens rea* requirements. We will work through them in turn.

1. The defendant penetrated the vagina or anus of the victim with a part of his body or anything else

Rape was limited to penetration with a penis. This offence is broader. It covers penetration of the vagina or anus (but not the mouth) with other parts of the body (like a finger) or anything else (like a bottle). The offence can be committed by both men and women.

The offence might also be used where the evidence shows that the victim's vagina or anus was penetrated, but it is uncertain whether or not the penetration was with a penis (perhaps because the victim was unconscious).

2. The penetration was sexual

The term 'sexual' is an important one. It is used not only in the definition of this offence, but also the section 3 definition of sexual assault and the section 4 definition of causing a person to engage in sexual activity without consent, which we will study shortly.

The term is defined in section 78 of the Sexual Offences Act 2003.

EXTRACT

Section 78 of the Sexual Offences Act 2003

78 'Sexual'

For the purposes of this Part (except section 71), penetration, touching or any other activity is sexual if a reasonable person would consider that—

(a) whatever its circumstances or any person's purpose in relation to it, it is because of its nature sexual, or

(b) because of its nature it may be sexual and because of its circumstances or the purpose of any person in relation to it (or both) it is sexual.

A jury deciding whether a particular activity was sexual or not should begin with section 78(a). Section 78(a) states that if an activity was, 'because of its nature', sexual the defendant's purpose is irrelevant. In other words, some activities are intrinsically sexual, even if the defendant's purpose was not a sexual one. An example of an activity which is intrinsically sexual is oral sex.

More problematic is the reasoning in *R* v *Abdulahi* [2022] EWCA Crim 412. In this case, a nurse was performing a medical examination when the defendant touched her breast. The Court of Appeal held that section 78(a) applied since 'the deliberate touching of a woman's breast in the manner described, was obviously and inevitably sexual' ([35]). However, as Thomas and Pegg observe,

> The question to ask is whether the touching of a woman's breast is inevitably sexual, as opposed to the touching of this particular woman's breast in these particular circumstances ... Section 78(a) requires the court to consider the nature of the activity divorced from its circumstances, and divorced from any person's purpose in respect of it. In light of this, it cannot be the case that s 78(a) is brought into play in the context of the touching of a woman's breast'. They continue:

> To treat the act of touching a woman's breast as inevitably sexual is problematic in a number of circumstances. For instance, it renders any touching by a doctor conducting a bona fide medical examination as sexual. It treats the piercing/ tattoo artist, applying their trade to an adult woman's breast, as having touched another sexually. Whilst these individuals would not be liable for criminal offences, due to the presence of consent in these examples, it remains troubling that the effect of the instant case appears to treat any touching of a woman's breast as being inevitably sexual.[41]

If the activity in question was not intrinsically sexual the jury must turn instead to section 78(b). The correct approach to this paragraph was set out by the Court of Appeal in *R* v *H* [2005] EWCA Crim 732:

- First, the jury must consider whether, 'because of its nature', the activity may be sexual. An activity which is incapable of being regarded as sexual by reasonable people cannot be made sexual because of the defendant's purpose.
- If the activity may be sexual the jury must consider the surrounding circumstances and the defendant's purpose and decide whether, in this particular instance, it was in fact sexual.

So, for example, suppose that the defendant spanked a 12-year-old girl on the buttocks. Spanking is not intrinsically sexual. Some parents spank their children to tell them off. So section 78(a) does not apply. Turning to section 78(b), spanking may be sexual (as some of the cases studied in the previous chapter illustrated!). So the surrounding circumstances and the defendant's purpose would need to be considered. In *R* v *Court* [1989] AC 28 (HL) the defendant worked in a shop. Whilst working in the shop he pulled a 12-year-old girl onto his lap and spanked her. He later blamed his actions on a 'buttock fetish'. Taking this into account, it is clear that his actions would be deemed 'sexual' for the purposes of section 78.

Think about these questions.

A. It is a Saturday afternoon on a busy high street. Lawrence is armed with a knife. He walks up to a young woman named Mandy, points the knife at her, and says, 'Strip naked or else'. Terrified, Mandy strips naked. Lawrence later says that he did it to humiliate Mandy.

Applying the test set out in section 78, were Lawrence's actions sexual?

---

[41] Thomas, M. & Pegg, S. (2022) '"Whatever its Circumstances": Odd Behaviour and Sexual Touchings' 86 *Journal of Criminal Law* 216.

B. How (if at all) would your answer be different in each of the two following situations?

- Lawrence forced Mandy to strip naked in private and took photos of her. He sold the photos to an adult website, and kept a copy of one of the pictures for himself.
- Mandy was not a young woman, but an 86-year-old pensioner.

3. The victim did not consent to the penetration

This part of the offence is the same as for the offence of rape. So sections 74–76 which we looked at previously also apply here.

4. The defendant intentionally penetrated the vagina or anus of the victim

As for the offence of rape, it is difficult to imagine how the penetrative act could be anything other than intentional. So this *mens rea* requirement will always be straightforward.

5. The defendant lacked a reasonable belief that the victim was consenting to the penetration

Like the offence of rape, the second *mens rea* requirement for this offence is lack of a reasonable belief in consent. Everything we said about the lack of reasonable belief test when examining rape also applies here.

Quiz 7.6

1. Assault by penetration is an offence that occurs in which **one** of the following sets of facts?
   a. When D intentionally and sexually penetrates the anus or vagina of V, who does not consent, with any part of his body or any other object.
   b. When D intentionally and sexually penetrates the mouth, anus or vagina of V, who does not consent, with any part of his body or any other object.
   c. When D intentionally and violently penetrates the anus or vagina of V, who does not consent, with any part of his body or any other object.
   d. When D intentionally and sexually penetrates the anus or vagina of V, who does not consent, with an inanimate object.
2. 'Sexual' is defined by section 78 of the Sexual Offences Act 2003. Which one of the following statements about this definition is **incorrect**?
   a. Activities which are intrinsically sexual should be regarded as sexual irrespective of the defendant's purpose.
   b. Activities which are incapable of being regarded as sexual by reasonable people cannot be made sexual by the defendant's purpose.
   c. Whether or not an activity is sexual depends wholly on the defendant's purpose.
   d. If, because of its nature, an activity may or may not be sexual, whether or not it was in fact sexual should be determined by reference to the circumstances and the defendant's purpose.
3. Which of the following is not an *actus reus* requirement of assault by penetration?
   a. The victim did not consent to the penetration.
   b. The defendant lacked a reasonable belief that the victim was consenting to the penetration.
   c. The penetration was sexual.
   d. The defendant penetrated the vagina or anus of the victim with a part of his body or anything else.

Sexual assault

7.7 Define the requirements for establishing criminal liability for sexual assault.

The offence of sexual assault is defined by section 3 of the Sexual Offences Act 2003.

EXTRACT

Section 3 of the Sexual Offences Act 2003

3 Sexual assault

(1) A person (A) commits an offence if –

(a) he intentionally touches another person (B),

(b) the touching is sexual,

(c) B does not consent to the touching, and

(d) A does not reasonably believe that B consents.

(2) Whether a belief is reasonable is to be determined having regard to all the circumstances, including any steps A has taken to ascertain whether B consents.

(3) Sections 75 and 76 apply to an offence under this section.

(4) A person guilty of an offence under this section is liable –

(a) on summary conviction, to imprisonment for a term not exceeding 6 months or a fine not exceeding the statutory maximum or both;

(b) on conviction on indictment, to imprisonment for a term not exceeding 10 years.

This tells us that the offence has five requirements:

1. The defendant touched the victim
2. The touching was sexual
3. The victim did not consent to the touching
4. The defendant intentionally touched the victim
5. The defendant lacked a reasonable belief that the victim was consenting to the touching.

Numbers 1 to 3 are *actus reus* requirements. Numbers 4 and 5 are *mens rea* requirements. We will work through them in turn.

1. The defendant touched the victim

The two previous offences both involved penetration. Sexual assault is much broader. It only requires sexual touching. So, for example, it would apply where the defendant fondled the victim. It is also the offence that would apply in a situation like the famous 'Mormon sex in chains case' (which was the subject of the 2010 movie *Tabloid*). In this case the alleged victim – a male Mormon missionary – claimed that the female perpetrator had chained him to a bed and had non-consensual sexual intercourse with him. On these facts the woman could not be convicted of rape (only men can commit rape) or assault by penetration (she did not penetrate the man's anus), so the relevant offence would be sexual assault.[42]

Some guidance on the meaning of 'touching' can be found in section 79(8). This gives a non-exhaustive list of actions which amount to a 'touching'.

EXTRACT

Section 79(8) of the Sexual Offences Act 2003

(8) Touching includes touching–

(a) with any part of the body,

(b) with anything else,

(c) through anything,

and in particular includes touching amounting to penetration.

So 'touching' includes touching someone with an object (paragraph (b)) and touching someone through their clothes (paragraph (c)). The Court of Appeal has also held, in *R* v *H* [2005] EWCA Crim 732, that touching the clothes someone is wearing (without any contact with the person's body) constitutes a touching for the purposes of this offence.

2. The touching was sexual

We studied the meaning of sexual when looking at the offence of assault by penetration. Everything we said there also applies here.

If there was touching of a non-sexual nature you should instead consider the offences against the person (which we studied in the previous chapter).

3. The victim did not consent to the touching

This part of the offence is the same as for the offence of rape. So sections 74–76 which we looked at previously also apply here.

---

[42] For arguments that such a situation should be regarded as rape, see Weare, S. (2018) '"Oh You're a Guy, How Could You be Raped by a Woman, That Makes No Sense": Towards a Case for Legally Recognising and Labelling "Forced-to-Penetrate" Cases as Rape' 14 *International Journal of Law in Context* 110; and McKeever, N. (2019) 'Can a Woman Rape a Man and Why Does it Matter?' 13 *Criminal Law and Philosophy* 599.

4. The defendant intentionally touched the victim

The touching must have been intentional. We studied the meaning of intention in Chapter 4. Reckless, negligent or accidental touching falls outside the offence of sexual assault.

Note that there is no requirement to prove that the defendant intended the touching to be sexual. It is sufficient to prove that the defendant intended to touch the victim and that the touching was sexual. This was confirmed by the Court of Appeal in *Attorney-General's Reference (Section 36 of the CJA 1972) (No 1 of 2020)* [2020] EWCA Crim 1665. In this case, the defendant kissed the victim on her lips without her consent. The Court of Appeal explained that a defendant's purpose may be relevant when determining whether or not the touching was sexual (see above), but there is no separate requirement to prove that the defendant intended the touching to be sexual.

5. The defendant lacked a reasonable belief that the victim was consenting to the touching

Like the offence of rape, the second *mens rea* requirement for this offence is lack of a reasonable belief in consent. Everything we said about the lack of reasonable belief test when examining rape also applies here.

Quiz 7.7

1. On indictment what is the maximum sentence for sexual assault (section 3 of the Sexual Offences Act 2003)?
   - **a.** Ten years.
   - **b.** Seven years.
   - **c.** Life imprisonment.
   - **d.** Five years.
2. Which of the following would **not** be 'touching' for the purposes of the Sexual Offences Act 2003?
   - **a.** Taking hold of the victim's clothing rather than her/his body.
   - **b.** Using a finger to prod the victim.
   - **c.** Using an implement to prod the victim.
   - **d.** Taking an intimate photograph of the victim using a telephoto lens without consent.
3. In which one of the following circumstances will D be guilty of having committed a sexual assault?
   - **a.** D pulls V's shoe off her foot whilst she is sitting on an underground train. D later explains that the reason he did so was because he has a shoe fetish.
   - **b.** D grabs V's outer clothing and gives it a pull whilst saying to V, 'Do you fancy a shag?' D does not make contact with V's skin at all and V does not apprehend any personal violence or feel threatened at all.
   - **c.** D, a participant in a rugby scrum, reaches forwards and intentionally squeezes the testicles of another player, V, whom he dislikes. V does not consent to the touching and D knows this.
   - **d.** D falls forward on a moving train and places the palm of his hand fully on V's breast as he stops himself from falling over. Later he thinks about it and derives sexual gratification from having touched her.

Causing a person to engage in sexual activity without consent

7.8 Define the requirements for establishing criminal liability for causing a person to engage in sexual activity without consent.

The offence of causing a person to engage in sexual activity without consent is defined by section 4 of the Sexual Offences Act 2003.

EXTRACT

Section 4 of the Sexual Offences Act 2003

4 Causing a person to engage in sexual activity without consent

(1) A person (A) commits an offence if–

a. he intentionally causes another person (B) to engage in an activity,

b. the activity is sexual,

c. B does not consent to engaging in the activity, and

d. A does not reasonably believe that B consents.

(2) Whether a belief is reasonable is to be determined having regard to all the circumstances, including any steps A has taken to ascertain whether B consents.

(3) Sections 75 and 76 apply to an offence under this section.

(4) A person guilty of an offence under this section, if the activity caused involved–

a. penetration of B's anus or vagina,

b. penetration of B's mouth with a person's penis,

c. penetration of a person's anus or vagina with a part of B's body or by B with anything else, or

d. penetration of a person's mouth with B's penis. is liable, on conviction on indictment, to imprisonment for life

(5) Unless subsection (4) applies, a person guilty of an offence under this section is liable–

a. on summary conviction, to imprisonment for a term not exceeding 6 months or to a fine not exceeding the statutory maximum or both;

b. on conviction on indictment, to imprisonment for a term not exceeding 10 years.

This tells us that the offence has five requirements:

1. The defendant caused the victim to engage in an activity
2. The activity was sexual
3. The victim was not consenting to the activity

4. The defendant intentionally caused the victim to engage in the activity
5. The defendant lacked a reasonable belief that the victim was consenting to the activity.

Numbers 1 to 3 are *actus reus* requirements. Numbers 4 and 5 are *mens rea* requirements. We will work through them in turn.

1. The defendant caused the victim to engage in an activity

This offence may be used where the defendant did not penetrate or touch the victim. Examples include where the defendant forces the victim to masturbate and where a female defendant forces the victim to penetrate her.

For this first requirement, a causal link must be established between the defendant's actions and the victim's participation in the activity. As we saw in Chapter 3, to establish a causal link it is necessary to show both factual and legal causation.

It is possible to commit this offence by words alone. There is also no requirement that the defendant was present when the victim engaged in the activity. For example, in *R* v *Devonald* [2008] EWCA Crim 527 (the case we studied earlier in which the defendant tricked his daughter's ex-boyfriend into masturbating in front of a web cam) the defendant was convicted of causing the victim to engage in sexual activity without consent, even though he was not in the room when the victim masturbated.

2. The activity was sexual

We studied the meaning of sexual when looking at the offence of assault by penetration. Everything we said there also applies here.

3. The victim was not consenting to the activity

This part of the offence is the same as for the offence of rape. So sections 74–76 which we looked at previously also apply here.

4. The defendant intentionally caused the victim to engage in the activity

We studied the meaning of intention in Chapter 4. Both direct and oblique intention will suffice.

5. The defendant lacked a reasonable belief that the victim was consenting to the activity

Like the offence of rape, the second *mens rea* requirement for this offence is lack of a reasonable belief in consent. Everything we said about the lack of reasonable belief test when examining rape also applies here.

Quiz 7.8

1. Which of the following statements regarding section 4 of the Sexual Offences Act 2003 (causing a person to engage in sexual activity without consent) is false?
   - **a.** This offence would occur where a woman forces a man to have sexual intercourse with her.
   - **b.** This offence can be performed both by males and females.
   - **c.** This offence has two levels, and offences contrary to section 4(4) have a higher level of sentencing to reflect the seriousness of the offence.
   - **d.** To be charged with this offence the defendant must touch the victim either with his body or with an object.
2. What is the maximum prison sentence for section 4 of the Sexual Offences Act 2003 (causing a person to engage in sexual activity without consent)?
   - **a.** Section 4(1): 10 years; section 4(4): life imprisonment.
   - **b.** For any section: 10 years.
   - **c.** Section 4(1): seven years; section 4(4): life imprisonment.
   - **d.** For any section: life imprisonment.
3. In which one of the following circumstances will D be guilty of having committed an offence of causing a person to engage in sexual activity without consent?
   - **a.** D threatens V, via chatroom messaging, that he will destroy her computer hard drive using remote access unless she masturbates for him across a webcam link. V knows that D is unable to carry out his threat and she refuses his demands.
   - **b.** D visits T who, for money, supplies him with a 17-year-old girl, V, to have sexual activity with. V speaks no English and looks forlorn at her predicament but she submits to D's gentle touching. D does not have sexual intercourse with her but he does massage her breasts and her vagina before changing his mind and leaving.
   - **c.** D offers a lift to V, a hitchhiker. Many miles from where D picked up V, V suggests that she 'pay for her fare' by allowing D to take nude photos of her. D agrees. V does not know that D, who is not attracted to her because he is homosexual, merely wants the photos in order to sell them to an internet pornographic publisher.
   - **d.** D tells V, falsely, that he is a religious leader of the religion to which she subscribes and that she must perform ritual sexual acts in front of him as part of their worship. D does not know that V secretly knows these claims to be false but that she derives sexual pleasure from acting out her part as if she were deceived. V performs the acts.

Conclusion

As we have seen, the conclusive and evidential presumptions introduced by the Sexual Offences Act 2003 have made the process for assessing a defendant's guilt quite complex. The flow chart is designed for you to use when attempting the self-test questions below. It focuses on the offence of rape, and is designed to help you structure your answers correctly. It begins by asking whether the defendant intentionally penetrated the victim's vagina, anus or mouth with his penis (combining the first of the offence's *actus reus* and *mens rea* requirements). It then works through the remaining *actus reus* requirement (absence of consent) and the remaining *mens rea* requirement (lack of a reasonable belief in consent).

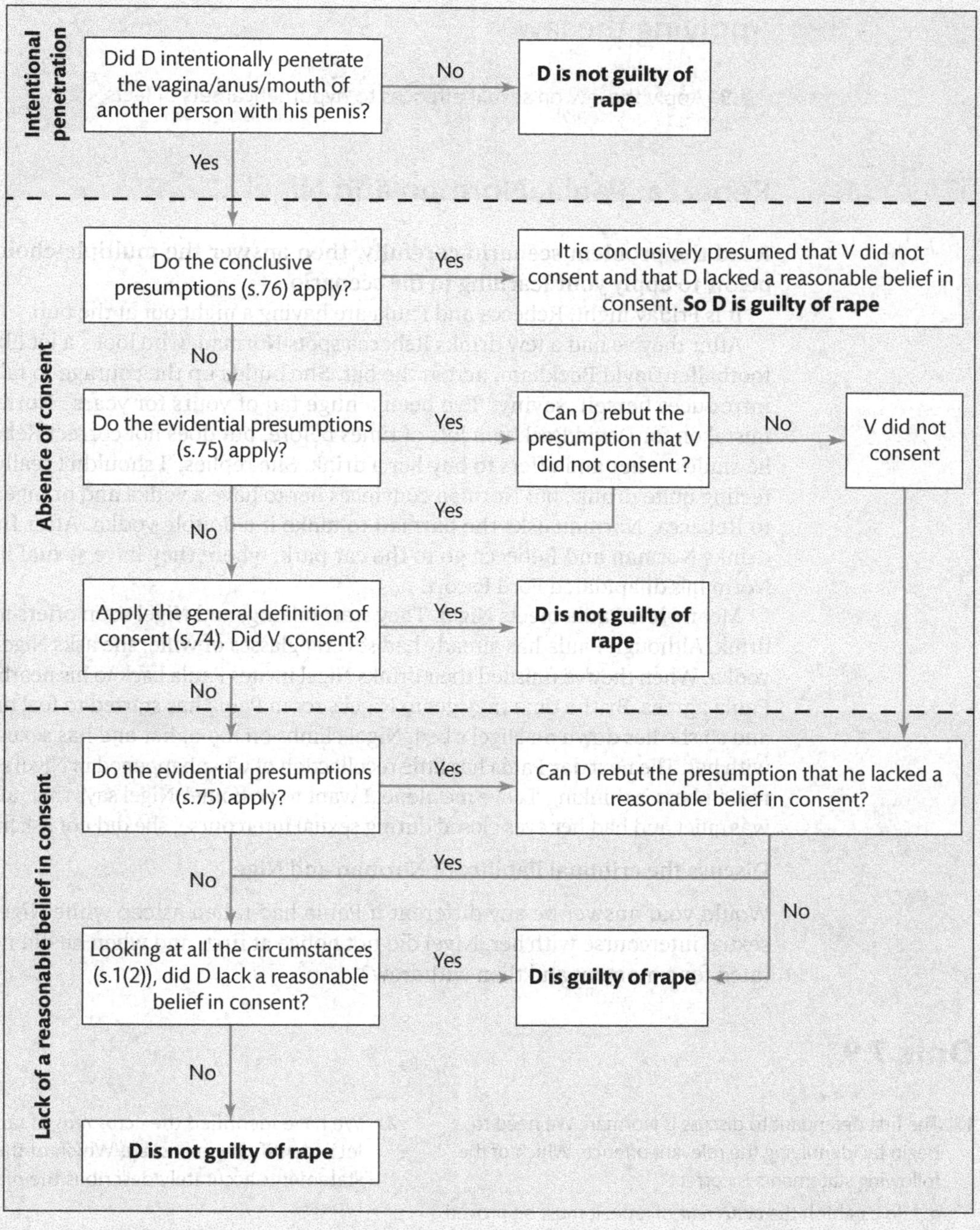

Now, using this flow chart as your starting point, can you adapt it to create similar charts for the other three offences we have studied?

Applying the law

7.9 Apply the law on sexual offences to hypothetical sets of facts.

Rebecca, Paula, Norman and Nigel

Read the problem scenario carefully, then answer the multiple-choice questions below to apply your learning to the scenario.

It is Friday night. Rebecca and Paula are having a night out at the pub.

After they've had a few drinks Rebecca spots Norman, who looks a lot like the famous footballer David Beckham, across the bar. She builds up the courage to talk to him and introduces herself, saying, 'I've been a huge fan of yours for years'. Norman has been mistaken for David Beckham lots of times before, but does not correct Rebecca. Instead he smiles at her and offers to buy her a drink. She replies, 'I shouldn't really, I'm already feeling quite drunk', but Norman convinces her to have a vodka and orange. Unbeknown to Rebecca, Norman asks the barman to make it a double vodka. After finishing their drinks Norman and Rebecca go to the car park, where they have sexual intercourse in Norman's dilapidated Ford Escort.

Meanwhile Paula meets Nigel. They start talking, and Nigel soon offers to buy Paula a drink. Although Paula has already had several glasses of wine, she asks Nigel for a double vodka. When they've finished their drinks Nigel invites Paula back to his nearby hotel room. Paula agrees. By the time they get to Nigel's room Paula has started to feel dizzy and sick, and so she lies down on Nigel's bed. Nigel climbs on top of her and has sexual intercourse with her. The next day Paula has little recollection of what happened in Nigel's room. All she remembers is thinking 'Leave me alone, I want to go home'. Nigel says that, although Paula was quiet and had her eyes closed during sexual intercourse, she did not ask him to stop.

Discuss the criminal liability of Norman and Nigel.

Would your answer be any different if Paula had fallen asleep while Nigel was having sexual intercourse with her, Nigel did not notice at first, and when he did notice he hesitated for a moment and then withdrew?

Quiz 7.9

1. The first defendant to discuss is Norman. We need to begin by identifying the relevant offence. Which of the following statements is correct?
   a. To establish the *actus reus* of rape, it must be proved that the defendant penetrated the victim's vagina, anus or mouth with his penis without consent.
   b. To establish the *actus reus* of rape, it must be proved that the defendant penetrated the victim's vagina or anus with any part of his own body without consent.
   c. To establish the *actus reus* of rape, it must be proved that the defendant penetrated the victim's vagina with his penis without consent.
   d. To establish the *actus reus* of rape, it must be proved that the defendant penetrated the victim's vagina or anus with his penis without consent.

2. We have identified the *actus reus* of rape. Now let's identify the *mens rea*. Which of the following statements accurately describes the *mens rea* of rape?
   a. D intentionally penetrated V's vagina, anus or mouth with his penis, and he lacked a reasonable belief that V was consenting to the penetration.
   b. D intentionally penetrated V's vagina, anus or mouth with his penis, and knew that V was not consenting to the penetration.
   c. D intentionally penetrated V's vagina, anus or mouth with his penis, and hoped that V was not consenting to the penetration.
   d. D intentionally penetrated V's vagina, anus or mouth with his penis, and he lacked a genuine belief that V was consenting to the penetration.

3. So far we have established that the first *actus reus* requirement (penile penetration) and the first *mens rea* requirement (intentional penetration) are both satisfied. Whether or not Norman is guilty of rape therefore hinges on: (1) whether Rebecca consented to the penetration; and (2) whether Norman lacked a reasonable belief that Rebecca was consenting to the penetration.

   We will consider each of these in turn. When considering whether or not the victim consented, you should begin by asking whether the conclusive presumptions apply. According to section 76 of the Sexual Offences Act 2003, the conclusive presumptions apply in two situations.

   In which of the following four circumstances would the conclusive presumptions **not** apply?

   a. Where D intentionally deceived V as to the nature of penetration.

   b. Where D intentionally administered to V, or caused V to take, without V's consent, a substance which, having regard to when it was administered or taken, was capable of causing or enabling V to be stupefied or overpowered at the time of the penetration.

   c. Where D intentionally deceived V as to the purpose of penetration.

   d. Where D intentionally induced V to consent to penetration by impersonating a person known personally to V.

4. Since the conclusive presumptions do not apply, we must next consider whether the evidential presumptions apply. According to section 75 of the Sexual Offences Act 2003, the evidential presumptions apply in six circumstances.

   Which of the following is **not** one of the circumstances in which the evidential presumptions apply?

   a. Where D intentionally penetrated V knowing that V was asleep or otherwise unconscious.

   b. Where V was unlawfully detained at the time of the penetration, and D was not.

   c. Where V chose to consume a substance which, having regard to when it was consumed, was capable of causing or enabling V to be stupefied or overpowered at the time of the penetration.

   d. Where, at the time of the penetration or immediately beforehand, D caused V to fear that immediate violence would be used against her.

5. Of the six circumstances listed in section 75, the one which is relevant in Norman's case is found in s75(2)(f) (involuntary intoxication). Rebecca asked for a vodka and orange but, unbeknown to her, Norman asked the barman for a double vodka and orange. The extra shot of vodka was therefore administered by Norman without Rebecca's consent. The key issue is whether, having regard to when the extra shot was taken, it was capable of causing or enabling Rebecca to be stupefied or overpowered when Norman penetrated her. If the prosecution can prove, beyond reasonable doubt, that the extra shot was capable of having this effect there will be an evidential presumption that Rebecca did not consent to the penetration. Norman will then have the opportunity to try and rebut this presumption. To do so, he will need to produce some evidence that Rebecca did in fact consent. Experience to date suggests that not much evidence is needed to discharge this evidential burden.

   If either: (1) the prosecution fails to prove that the extra shot was capable of causing or enabling Rebecca to be stupefied or overpowered; or (2) Norman rebuts the presumption that Rebecca did not consent, then it will be necessary to turn instead to the general definition of consent in section 74. How does section 74 define consent?

   a. A person consents whenever he agrees freely or is persuaded to submit by non-violent means.

   b. A person consents if he agrees by choice, and has the freedom and capacity to make that choice.

   c. A person consents to an activity if he has physical control over his body at the time he participates.

   d. A person consents to an activity only if that activity is one he actively wishes to participate in.

6. If neither the conclusive nor the evidential presumptions apply, a jury would have to apply the section 74 definition to the facts of Norman's case in order to decide whether or not Rebecca consented. When applying section 74, there are two issues in particular that should be considered. First, did Rebecca have the capacity to consent? And, second, did Rebecca have the freedom to consent? We will consider Rebecca's capacity to consent first.

   In *R* v *Bree* the Court of Appeal set out a number of important principles. Which one of the following is **not** one of the principles the Courts expounded?

   a. If a person was intoxicated at the time of the alleged offence, and would not have agreed to sexual intercourse had they been sober, then they did not consent for the purposes of section 74.

   b. An intoxicated person who consents to sexual intercourse cannot later withdraw their consent because they regret what happened.

   c. A person's capacity to consent to sexual intercourse may evaporate well before they become unconscious.

   d. An intoxicated person can still consent to sexual intercourse for the purposes of section 74 even if they were disinhibited as a result of the intoxication and they would not have agreed to sexual intercourse had they been sober.

7. The second issue related to consent that we need to consider is whether Rebecca had the freedom to consent. The starting point here is the judgment in *R* v *Elbekkay*.

Which of the following correctly states the *R* v *Elbekkay* principle?

a. If V is having sex with X, but believes she is having sex with Y, then she is not consenting to sex with X.

b. If V chooses to have sex with X even though she has not met X before and is unsure who he is, then V is not consenting to sex with X.

c. If V is having sex with X, but suspects she might actually be having sex with Y, then she is not consenting to sex with X.

d. If V is having sex with X because X possesses a particular attribute, but in fact X does not possess that attribute, then V is not consenting to sex with X.

If the prosecution were to prove, beyond reasonable doubt, that Rebecca believed she was having sex with David Beckham then the *R* v *Elbekkay* principle would apply. Rebecca would therefore not have consented to sex with Norman. On the other hand, Norman might argue that, even if Rebecca thought he was David Beckham at first, she did not still hold this belief at the time of the alleged offence.

The other point to consider when discussing whether Rebecca had the freedom to consent is the fact that Norman asked the barman to add an extra shot of vodka to her drink. In the chapter we studied several cases involving deception, including *R* v *Jheeta; R* v *McNally; Assange* v *Swedish Prosecution Authority; R (F)* v *Director of Public Prosecutions; R (Monica)* v *Director of Public Prosecutions ex parte Boyling; and, R* v *Lawrance*. How do you think these cases would apply in Norman's case?

Having discussed whether or not Rebecca consented to the penetration, we must now turn to the remaining mens rea requirement: whether Norman lacked a reasonable belief that Rebecca was consenting. Remember that sections 76 (conclusive presumptions) and 75 (evidential presumptions) also apply to this mens rea requirement. We saw above that section 76 would not apply in Norman's case, but section 75 might (if the prosecution could prove, beyond reasonable doubt, that the extra shot of vodka was capable of causing or enabling Rebecca to be stupefied or overpowered when Norman penetrated her). If section 75 were to apply, there would be an evidential presumption that Norman lacked a reasonable belief in consent. In order to rebut this presumption, Norman would therefore have to produce some evidence that he did in fact believe that Rebecca was consenting to sexual intercourse and that this belief was reasonable.

If either: (1) the prosecution fails to prove that the extra shot was capable of causing or enabling Rebecca to be stupefied or overpowered; or, (2) Norman rebuts the presumption that he lacked a reasonable belief in consent, then it will be necessary to decide whether or not he satisfies this mens rea requirement without the aid of presumptions. As we saw in the chapter, it is best to work through this mens rea requirement in two steps. First, ask whether the defendant believed the victim was consenting. And, if so, next ask whether the defendant's belief was reasonable.

In Norman's case, for the first of these two steps it is important to remember the *R* v *Elbekkay* principle. In other words, the jury should ask themselves whether Norman believed Rebecca was consenting to sexual intercourse with him (as opposed to David Beckham). The prosecution might argue that Norman thought Rebecca was consenting to sexual intercourse with David Beckham, and so did not believe she was consenting to sex with him. Remember that the prosecution bear the burden of proof, so they would have to prove, beyond reasonable doubt, that Norman lacked a belief that Rebecca was consenting to sex with him. If the prosecution fails to do so, then at the next stage it could argue that Norman's belief that Rebecca was consenting to sex with him was not reasonable. If you were the prosecutor, how would you argue this? If you were Norman's defence counsel, how would you respond to these arguments?

8. Turning now to Nigel's liability, which of the following accurately summarises the judgment in *R* v *Malone?*

a. To establish the *actus reus* of rape, there is no requirement that the victim demonstrated or communicated to the defendant the fact that she was not consenting.

b. To establish the *actus reus* of rape, the prosecution must prove that an ordinary person in the position of the victim would have attempted to communicate the fact that she was not consenting.

c. To establish the *actus reus* of rape, the prosecution must prove that the victim clearly demonstrated to the defendant that she was not consenting.

d. To establish the *actus reus* of rape, the prosecution must prove that the victim attempted to physically resist sexual intercourse.

9. Following *R* v *Malone*, the jury should focus on Paula's state of mind and consider whether (in the words of section 74) she was agreeing to sex by choice. What distinction did the Court of Appeal draw in *R* v *Olugboja?*

a. The Court drew a distinction between 'overpowering a victim using violence' and 'persuading a victim using non-violent means'.

b. The Court drew a distinction between 'physical coercion' and 'non-physical coercion'.

c. The Court drew a distinction between 'real consent' and 'reluctant acquiescence'.

d. The Court drew a distinction between 'real consent' and 'mere submission'.

The prosecution in Nigel's case might use the reasoning in *R* v *Olugboja* to argue that Paula submitted to sexual intercourse, but did not consent to it. In addition, the prosecution might also argue that Paula lacked the capacity to consent. As we saw above, in *R* v *Bree* [2007] EWCA Crim 804 the Court of Appeal held that a person's capacity to consent to sexual intercourse may evaporate well before they become unconscious. The prosecution might therefore point to the fact that Paula was intoxicated and had started to feel dizzy and sick to argue that she lacked the capacity to consent.

If the jury decide that Paula had not consented to the sexual intercourse, Nigel's liability will hinge on whether or not he lacked a reasonable belief in consent. For this requirement the jury will have to consider, first, whether or not Nigel believed Paula was consenting and – if he did – whether the belief was reasonable.

10. If the jury decide that Paula had not consented to the sexual intercourse, Nigel's liability will hinge on whether or not he lacked a reasonable belief in consent. For this requirement the jury will have to consider, first, whether or not Nigel believed Paula was consenting and – if he did – whether the belief was reasonable. According to section 1(2) of the Sexual Offences Act 2003, what should a jury do when deciding whether or not D's belief that V consented was reasonable?

a. Form their own opinion, based on what they would have done in the same situation.

b. Have regard to all the circumstances, including any steps the defendant took to ascertain whether the victim was consenting.

c. Disregard rape myths and other popular stereotypes which have no factual basis.

d. Only take into account things that were said or done at the time of the alleged offence, and not things which occurred prior to this.

Rose, Dr Jones and Dr Jekyll

Over the years Rose has made a lot of money by seducing celebrities, having sexual intercourse with them and then selling her story to the press.

When Rose discovers that members of the local Premier League football team are having a night out at a nearby nightclub she decides to go along. At the nightclub she begins chatting to Wayne, a married man who is also one of the team's star players. After flirting with him for some time she says, 'Let's go somewhere more private'. They go to Wayne's hotel room and have sexual intercourse. The next day Rose contacts several national tabloid newspapers and sells her story for £5,000.Wayne is horrified, and says that he would never have had sex with Rose had he known that she would sell her story. Rose says that she only had sex with Wayne for the money. She adds that she despises men who cheat on their partners and hopes that the tabloid headlines embarrass and humiliate Wayne.

a. Discuss Rose's criminal liability.

Suppose, instead, that Rose had been a prostitute. She only sold her story because Wayne had offered to pay her £1,000 if she had sexual intercourse with him, but afterwards Wayne refused to pay her, saying 'I never had any intention of paying you'. How would your answer be different in this situation?

Dr Jones works as a gynaecologist in a hospital. When Vera, one of her patients, arrives for her appointment Dr Jones tells Vera that she needs to take a sample from her to order to diagnose her condition. Dr Jones explains that to take the sample she has to insert a smear brush into Vera's vagina. Vera gives her permission. In fact, Dr Jones did not need to take the sample to diagnose Vera's condition. She collected the sample for her own personal sexual gratification. One of the other doctors at the hospital, Dr Jekyll, discovers that Dr Jones has been misleading her patients. Dr Jekyll threatens to report Dr Jones to the hospital management unless she has sexual intercourse with him. Terrified at the possibility of losing her job, Dr Jones reluctantly agrees and they have sexual intercourse.

b. Discuss the criminal liability of Dr Jones and Dr Jekyll.

c. How (if at all) would your answer be different if Dr Jones had taken the sample from Vera not for sexual gratification, but for some private research she was conducting into cervical cancer?

Applying the law II

Now, read this scenario involving Norman, Nigel, Rebecca and Paula

In the alternative scenario, the first *actus reus* requirement of rape (penile penetration) is satisfied (since section 79(2) states that penetration is a continuing act from entry to withdrawal), as is the first *mens rea* requirement (intention to penetrate). So, as in the original scenario, liability hinges on: (1) whether Paula consented to the penetration; and (2) whether Nigel lacked a reasonable belief that Paula was consenting to the penetration.

Now, think about this question. Which option would be the most suitable answer to this question?

Which of the following statements best summarises the relevance of section 75 in this situation?

a. Section 75(2)(d) would not apply because Paula was awake at the moment Nigel penetrated her.

b. Section 75(2)(d) would not apply because Nigel did not know that the relevant circumstance existed.

c. Section 75(2)(d) would apply since Nigel realised that Paula had fallen asleep before he withdrew.

d. Although section 75(2)(d) does not apply in this situation, section 75(2)(f) may be applied instead.

Evaluating the law

7.10 Evaluate the section 74 definition of consent, the conclusive and evidential presumptions contained in sections 76 and 75 and the change to the mens rea of rape introduced by the Sexual Offences Act 2003.

Think about this question.

'The Sexual Offences Act 2003 successfully modernises the offence of rape. It contains a clear and unambiguous definition of consent. The introduction of conclusive and evidential presumptions not only provide a simple and straightforward mechanism for structuring jury's decision-making, but also clearly communicate forms of unacceptable sexual behaviour. And the change in the *mens rea* helps secure convictions by preventing defendants from being able to rely on dubious social conventions and stereotypes.'

Discuss the extent to which you agree with this statement.

Step 1: Deconstruct the essay title

To prepare an essay plan for this question, you should begin by **deconstructing the essay title** and **identifying the key points** you need to address. Here, the statement in the essay title covers three sets of issues:

- whether section 74's general definition of consent is clear and unambiguous;

- whether the conclusive and evidential presumptions set out in sections 76 and 75 provide a simple and straightforward mechanism for structuring jury decision-making and clearly communicate forms of unacceptable sexual behaviour; and
- whether the change to the mens rea of the offence helps secure convictions by preventing reliance on dubious social conventions and stereotypes.

Step 2: Work through each issue, form an opinion and construct a set of arguments in support of your views

To discuss the first set of issues, you should consider the key terms used in section 74. These are:

- Agrees by choice
- Freedom to make that choice
- Capacity to make that choice.

Look back over the case law and commentary we studied on section 74, and use this to evaluate whether the terms used are indeed clear and unambiguous:

- **On 'agrees by choice'**, consider the distinction drawn in *R* v *Olugboja* between 'real consent' and 'mere submission'. How did Dunn LJ explain this distinction? When will a person be found to have submitted to sexual intercourse, but not to have consented to it?
- **On 'freedom'**, consider the various cases which involved deception. When will a deception be deemed to have so undermined a victim's autonomy that it cannot be said that she consented? Which forms of deception (if any) will not negate a victim's consent? Do you agree with Sharpe's argument that the courts have drawn a flawed distinction between active deception and non-disclosure of information?
- **On 'capacity'**, consider the different reasons a victim may lack capacity to consent. In particular, consider cases involving intoxicated victims. Do the principles in *R* v *Bree* give juries sufficient guidance for deciding such cases? What insights can we gain from the study conducted by Finch and Munro?

To discuss the second set of issues, look back at your answers to the following questions:

- What reasons does Laird give for welcoming the narrow scope of the conclusive presumptions? Do you agree that this is welcome?
- Read the following extract [from the article by Gunby, Carline and Beynon] and produce a bullet point list of the key findings from the study.
- Looking at your list of findings, assess whether sections 75 and 76 achieve their identified objectives.

To discuss the third set of issues, look back at your answer to the following question, and at the relevant extracts from the articles by Finch and Munro and Larcombe et al.

- The following extract is from an article written by Temkin and Ashworth. What sorts of things do they think a jury might take into account when having regard to 'all the circumstances'? Why does this worry them?

Having completed these tasks, you may also find it helpful to read some of the items on the further reading list. This will allow you to explore these issues in greater depth.

Now that you have formed an opinion on each of the sets of issues raised by the essay title, construct a set of arguments in support of your point of view.

Step 3: Planning your introduction and conclusion

You now have all the material you need for the main body of your essay. The last task is to decide what to include in your introduction and conclusion. The introduction should contextualise your discussion by briefly outlining the objectives of the relevant parts of the Sexual Offences Act 2003, and give an indication of the argument you will present in your essay. The conclusion should round off your essay with a succinct statement of your argument and a summary of your supporting reasons.

Sexual offences checklist

Having worked through this chapter, you should now have:

- An understanding of the requirements of the crime of rape
- An understanding of the requirements of the crime of assault by penetration
- An understanding of the requirements of the crime of sexual assault
- An understanding of the requirements of the crime of causing a person to engage in sexual activity without consent
- An understanding of the conclusive and evidential presumptions and the general definition of consent contained in sections 74 to 76 of the Sexual Offences Act 2003 and an ability to critically discuss whether these provisions achieve their stated objectives
- An understanding of the change to the *mens rea* of rape introduced by the 2003 Act and an ability to critically discuss whether this change has helped secure an increase in the conviction rate for rape.

Further reading

Conaghan, J. (2019) 'The Essence of Rape' 39 *Oxford Journal of Legal Studies* 151.

Dowds, E. (2020) 'Towards a Contextual Definition of Rape: Consent, Coercion and Constructive Force' 83 *Modern Law Review* 35.

Dsouza, M. (2022) 'False Beliefs and Consent to Sex' 85 *Modern Law Review* 1191

Dyer, A. (2024) 'How should English law deal with deceptive sex?' 53 *Common Law World Review* 3

Finch, E. and Munro, V. (2006) 'Breaking Boundaries? Sexual Consent in the Jury Room' 26 *Legal Studies* 303.

Firth, G. (2011) 'Not an Invitation to Rape: The Sexual Offences Act 2003, Consent and the Case of the "Drunken" Victim' 62 *Northern Ireland Legal Quarterly* 99.

Gardner, J. (2018) 'The Opposite of Rape' 38 *Oxford Journal of Legal Studies* 48.

Gibson, M. (2020) 'Deceptive Sexual Relations: A Theory of Criminal Liability' 40 *Oxford Journal of Legal Studies* 82

Gunby, C., Carline, A. and Beynon, C. (2010) 'Alcohol-related Rape Cases: Barristers' Perspectives on the Sexual Offences Act 2003 and Its Impact on Practice' 74 *Journal of Criminal Law* 579.

Herring, J. (2005) 'Mistaken Sex' *Criminal Law Review* 511.

Home Office (2010) *The Stern Review: A report by Baroness Vivien Stern CBE of an independent review into how rape complaints are handled by public authorities in England and Wales.*

Laird, K. (2014) 'Rapist or Rogue? Deception, Consent and the Sexual Offences Act 2003' *Criminal Law Review* 492.

Larcombe, W., Fileborn, B., Powell, A., Hanley, N. and Henry, N. (2016) '"I Think it's Rape and I Think He Would be Found Not Guilty": Focus Group Perceptions of (un)Reasonable Belief in Consent in Rape Law' 25 *Social & Legal Studies* 611.

McCormack, S. and Herring, J. (2024) 'The Duties of the Penetrator and the Limits of Consent' *Criminal Law Review* 94

McCormack, S. & Herring, J. (2025) 'Is Affirmative Consent the Answer? Yes, Sort of, Maybe' 89 *Journal of Criminal Law* 16

Murray, K. L. and Beattie, T. (2021) 'Conditional Consent and Sexual Offences: Revisiting the Sexual Offences Act 2003 After Lawrance' Criminal Law Review 556.

Ormerod, D. (2020) 'Rape and Deception (Again)' *Criminal Law Review* 877.

Rumney, P.N.S. and Fenton, R.A. (2008) 'Intoxicated Consent in Rape: *Bree* and Juror Decision-making' 71 *Modern Law Review* 279.

Sharpe, A. (2016) 'Expanding Liability for Sexual Fraud through the Concept of 'Active Deception': A Flawed Approach' 80 *Journal of Criminal Law* 28.

Sharpe, A. (2025) 'Deceptive Sex: Rethinking Consent from the Gender Margins' 88 *Modern Law Review* 689

Tadros, V. (2006) 'Rape Without Consent' 26 *Oxford Journal of Legal Studies* 515.

Temkin, J. and Ashworth, A. (2004) 'The Sexual Offences Act 2003 – (1) Rape, Sexual Assaults and the Problems of Consent' *Criminal Law Review* 328.

Wallerstein, S. (2009) '"A Drunken Consent Is Still Consent" – Or Is It? A Critical Analysis of the Law on a Drunken Consent to Sex Following Bree' 73 *Journal of Criminal Law* 318.

Williams, R. (2008) 'Deception, Mistake and Vitiation of the Victim's Consent' 124 *Law Quarterly Review* 132.

Yean, A. (2025) 'Misrepresentation and Sexual Consent: Lessons from the Law of Contract' 89 *Journal of Criminal Law* 78.

Answers on the Companion Website

Please visit the companion website for the answers to Key Questions, Quizzes, Applying the Law scenarios as well as student support including glossaries. Please visit www.pearsoned.co.uk/Macdonald

8

Property offences

Learning Objectives

- **8.1** Define the actus reus requirements for establishing criminal liability for theft.
- **8.2** Evaluate the case law on appropriation within the law of theft.
- **8.3** Define the mens rea requirements for establishing criminal liability for theft.
- **8.4** Evaluate the case law on dishonesty within the law of theft.
- **8.5** Define the requirements for establishing criminal liability for robbery.
- **8.6** Define the requirements for establishing criminal liability for burglary.
- **8.7** Define the requirements for establishing criminal liability for fraud.
- **8.8** Define the requirements for establishing criminal liability for criminal damage.
- **8.9** Apply the law on property offences to hypothetical sets of facts.
- **8.10** Evaluate the case law on appropriation and dishonesty.

Introduction

The concept of dishonesty is central to the property offences that we study in this chapter. In your opinion, which of the following individuals[1] acted dishonestly?

1. Couple who found winning lottery ticket ordered to pay back money

A couple who found a winning lottery ticket and cashed it in were today ordered by a court to pay back half of the prize money to the woman who bought it.

Dorothy McDonagh, 61, dropped the £1 ticket on the floor of her local Co-op store in Swindon on 20 October last year.

Michael and Amanda Stacey found the ticket, cashed it and then spent half of the £30,000 prize money clearing their debts.

The couple were each given an 11-month suspended sentence for fraud in April this year. Today a judge at Swindon crown court ordered Michael Stacey, 43, to pay McDonagh £15,111 – the £111 being interest on the payment.

2. If you go down to the beach today ... you're bound to find something to steal

Jane and Mary huffed and puffed as they rolled the oak wine cask across the shingle towards the Sea Shanty car park. "Honestly, we just came for a walk and a chat", said Mary, a retired teacher, "but then we saw all this stuff here and the police told us we could help ourselves. So we did."

They were not the only ones.

Branscombe Beach, usually deserted at this time of year, was heaving yesterday with hundreds of - depending on your point of view - looters, salvagers or beachcombers. While a desperate rescue operation was under way to try to prevent ecological disaster a mile off the Devon coast, a scramble of a different kind was taking place, one unlikely to have cheered the insurers of the 62,000 tonne cargo ship that was stricken in last week's storm.

3. Warrant for Bermondsey man's arrest after stealing free newspapers at London Bridge

Two men have been convicted for stealing free newspapers from London Bridge station in a 'landmark' ruling – while a warrant has been issued for one of their arrests.

Marcel Javier Larez-Serrano, of Camilla Road, Bermondsey and Jhon Mejia, of Hampson Way, Lambeth, were spotted loading batches of free papers into a van on the evening of Thursday, 6 April 2017.

The pair are believed to have stolen more than a thousand copies of the free papers.

When questioned by officers, the pair admitted to planning to sell the papers to a recycling plant, claiming they were being paid £30 each by an undisclosed boss to do it.

Larez-Serrano, 37, was convicted in his absence for theft and fraud and sentenced to eight weeks in prison – and now a warrant has been issued for his arrest.

---

[1] Sources: 1. Tom Roberts, Couple who found winning lottery ticket ordered to pay back mone, 24 Jul 2009, Guardian News & Media Limited; 2. Steven Morris, If you go down to the beach today ... you're bound to find something to steal, 23 Jan 2007, Guardian News & Media Limited; 3. Josh Salisbury, Warrant for Bermondsey man's arrest after stealing free newspapers at London Bridge, 15 February, 2019, Southwark News Limited; 4. Ed Beavan, Protester goes out for a date, 28 January 2009; Stop the sale of 'West Bank' produce, 14 Dec 2009, Guardian News & Media Limited.

Mejia pleaded guilty to counts of theft and fraud committed in April 2017, December 2017 and January 2018, all relating to the excessive theft of newspapers at London Bridge station.

4. Protester goes out for a date

A PENSIONER from Swansea, Greg Wilkinson, has been stealing dates from Tesco as a protest against Israeli settlements in the West Bank.

Mr Wilkinson, aged 72, has regularly taken King Solomon-brand dates from the supermarket. A former observer for the Quakers in the Middle East, and describing himself as a "Christian atheist", he was arrested and charged with theft for his latest stunt on Tuesday, when he and another protester stole a trolley packed with dates and herbs. He was arrested and charged with theft, before police dropped charges against him for lack of evidence.

Mr Wilkinson sells the stolen dates for £1 a box to raise money for Islamic Relief and the Oxfam Gaza appeal. He says that the dates are the produce of "illegal settlements" in the Jordan Valley, and that their labelling as "West Bank" is ambiguous to the consumer.

Stop the sale of 'West Bank' produce

Under new labelling rules, customers will be able to distinguish between Israeli settlement products and Palestinian goods from the occupied West Bank (Report, 11 December). It should also be made clear that those settlements are illegal under international law.

But since when has the implementation of law been a matter of individual choice? It was the government, not shoppers, who signed up to the Geneva conventions and security council resolutions that made the settlements illegal. It's up to the government to enforce its own commitment and ban the import and sale of what amount to stolen goods.

Meanwhile, in the absence of proper enforcement, I have been conducting my own "citizen's seizures", removing "West Bank" dates from supermarket shelves. I have offered Tesco and Sainsbury's repayment if they can show the dates are not the produce of illegal settlements.

Some dates I have "sold" in aid of Gaza charities, and some I have sent to UK lawmakers and enforcers with an invitation to consider who stole them. A recent consignment is on its way "home" to Gaza with the Viva Palestina convoy.

Now, think about this question.

What criteria did you apply to determine the difference between honest and dishonest conduct?

In this chapter we study five property offences: theft; robbery; burglary; fraud; and criminal damage. Of the different types of offences that we study in this text, these offences are by far the most prevalent. According to police-recorded crime figures, these five offences were committed a total of more than 3.8 million times during 2023.[2] That is more than 400 times every hour! This compares to a total of 2 million offences of violence against the person and 191, 052 sexual offences.

[2] Office for National Statistics (2024) *Crime in England and Wales, Year Ending December 2023.*

The chapter begins by examining the law governing theft. Of the five property offences listed above, theft is the most common.

The police recorded a total of 1.8 million thefts during 2023.[3]

The definition of theft is therefore very important, because it is applied many times every day. Yet as we will see, the way in which the offence has been defined by the courts has been heavily criticised. This criticism has focused on two concepts in particular – **appropriation** and **dishonesty**. We will explore these criticisms so that you can evaluate whether or not they are justified.

After examining theft in detail, we will then work through the offences of **robbery**, **burglary, fraud** and **criminal damage**.

Theft

8.1 Define the actus reus requirements for establishing criminal liability for theft.

The offence of theft is defined by section 1 of the Theft Act 1968:

EXTRACT

Section 1 of the Theft Act 1968

1 Basic definition of theft

(1) A person is guilty of theft if he dishonestly appropriates property belonging to another with the intention of permanently depriving the other of it; and "thief" and "steal" shall be construed accordingly

This tells us that the offence has five requirements:

1. The item in question was property
2. The property belonged to another person
3. The defendant appropriated the property
4. The defendant had an intention to permanently deprive the other person of the property
5. The defendant acted dishonestly.

Numbers 1, 2 and 3 are *actus reus* requirements. Numbers 4 and 5 are *mens rea* requirements. We will work through them in turn.

[3] Compared to 81,094 robberies, 271,449 burglaries, 1.2 million fraud offences and 484,720 criminal damage offences.

1. The item in question was property

The first requirement is that the item was property. Property is defined in section 4(1):

> **EXTRACT**
>
> **Section 4(1) of the Theft Act 1968**
>
> **4 "Property"**
>
> (1) "Property" includes money and all other property, real or personal, including things in action and other intangible property.

Some of the terms used in this definition require some explanation:

- The first is real property. Put simply, real property means buildings and land. Note, however, that section 4(2) goes on to state that land can only be stolen in certain circumstances. These include: where the defendant is a trustee and commits a breach of confidence by appropriating the land (s.4(2)(a)); where the defendant is a trespasser and appropriates an item by severing it from the land (e.g. a garden shed or fence) (s.4(2)(b)); and where a tenant removes a fixture or structure from the place he is renting (e.g. wall panelling) (s.4(2)(c)).
- The second term which requires some explanation is personal property. Any property that is not real property is personal property. So banknotes, furniture and a flat-screen TV are all examples of personal property.
- The third term is intangible property. Most property – like banknotes, furniture and a flat-screen TV – is tangible. It has a physical existence, so you can touch it and pick it up (if it isn't too big or too heavy!). But some property does not have a physical existence (e.g. a copyright). It is intangible.
- The fourth term – things in action – is an example of intangible property. A thing in action is a property right that cannot be asserted physically (since the property has no physical existence) but which can be enforced by legal action. An example is a debt. Suppose Derek owes Aubrey £50. Aubrey's right to the money is an item of property. It is a thing in action which can be enforced in the courts. Other examples of things in action are patents, copyrights and shares in a company.

It should be clear from this that the section 4(1) definition of property has a broad scope. It encompasses real property and personal property. It encompasses tangible property and intangible property. It includes things in action.

The definition also includes illegal drugs. In *R* v *Smith* [2011] EWCA Crim 66 the Court of Appeal held that the fact that property is possessed unlawfully does not mean that it falls outside the definition. The defendant, Michael Smith, arranged to meet a man called Chesterfield Jordan to buy £50 worth of heroin from him. When they met Smith beat Jordan up and took the heroin without paying for it. Smith was charged with theft of the heroin. He argued that the heroin did not fall within the section 4 definition because Jordan's possession of the drug was illegal. The Court of Appeal rejected this argument. It explained that to decide otherwise would result in anarchy:

> Carried to its logical conclusion, the argument would suggest that the drug-misusing community is permitted to conduct itself in the context of what would otherwise be theft from each other with impunity. The public interest would hardly be secured by the inevitable public warfare which would ensue.

However, despite the breadth of section 4, there are some things which are not included in the definition of property:

- The first is electricity. A person cannot be charged with stealing electricity. Instead, section 13 of the Theft Act 1968 creates a specific offence of dishonestly using electricity. Note also that, whilst electricity is not property for the purposes of theft, gas and water are. So a person can be guilty of stealing gas or water.
- The second is services. Things like a bus ride or a train journey are not property for the purposes of theft. So if Derek goes to a hairdresser's and has his haircut, but never has any intention of paying, he cannot be guilty of stealing the haircut. In a situation like this another property offence should be used instead.[4]
- The third is confidential information. In *Oxford* v *Moss* (1978) 68 Cr App R 183 the defendant was a university student named Paul Moss. Before his exams took place Moss somehow managed to get hold of one of the exam papers. He read it, and then put it back where it belonged. Moss was charged with theft of confidential information. The issue for the Divisional Court was whether confidential information constitutes property for the purposes of theft. The Court held that it does not.

In the vast majority of problem questions deciding whether or not the item was property will be straightforward. Occasionally, however, there are borderline cases. In these instances you will need to consider whether or not the case involves property in greater detail.

The first borderline case involves wild mushrooms, flowers, fruit and foliage. These cases are governed by section 4(3).

EXTRACT

According to this subsection, a person can only be guilty of stealing wild mushrooms, flowers, fruit or foliage in what circumstances?

[4] In Derek's case the offence of fraud by false representation could apply. By asking the hairdresser to cut his hair Derek impliedly represented that he would pay for the service and this was a false representation of his intentions (see the discussion of this offence later in the chapter). Another possible offence is making off without payment (which can be found in section 3 of the Theft Act 1978).

Section 4(3) of the Theft Act 1968

(3) A person who picks mushrooms growing wild on any land, or who picks flowers, fruit or foliage from a plant growing wild on any land, does not (although not in possession of the land) steal what he picks, unless he does it for reward or for sale or other commercial purpose.

For purposes of this subsection "mushroom" includes any fungus, and "plant" includes any shrub or tree.

The second borderline case involves wild creatures. These cases are governed by section 4(4).

EXTRACT

According to this subsection, when can a person be found guilty of stealing a wild creature? Can you think of an example of when section 4(4) might apply?

Section 4(4) of the Theft Act 1968

(4) Wild creatures, tamed or untamed, shall be regarded as property; but a person cannot steal a wild creature not tamed nor ordinarily kept in captivity, or the carcase of any such creature, unless either it has been reduced into possession by or on behalf of another person and possession of it has not since been lost or abandoned, or another person is in course of reducing it into possession.

The third borderline case is human body parts. In *R* v *Kelly* [1999] QB 621 the defendant, Anthony Kelly, was an artist. He asked another man named Neil Lindsay, who worked as a junior technician at the Royal College of Surgeons, to give him a number of body parts from the college. These included three heads, six arms (or parts of an arm) and ten legs (or parts of a leg). Kelly used these to make casts, some of which were exhibited in an art gallery. Kelly and Lindsay were convicted of theft of the body parts. On appeal, one of the issues for the Court of Appeal was whether the body parts were property under the section 4 definition.

EXTRACT

Read the following extract from the judgment of Rose LJ.

Is the general rule: that a corpse (or apart of a corpse) is property or that a corpse (or a part of a corpse) is not property? What are the exceptions to this general rule?

Were the body parts that Kelly and Lindsay took property or not?

R v *Kelly* [1999] QB 621

Rose LJ

We return to the first question, that is to say whether or not a corpse or part of a corpse is property. We accept that, however questionable the historical origins of the principle, it has now been the common law for 150 years at least that neither a corpse nor parts of a corpse are in themselves and without more capable of being property protected by rights [...]

If that principle is now to be changed, in our view, it must be by Parliament, because it has been express or implicit in all the subsequent authorities and writings to which we have been referred that a corpse or part of it cannot be stolen.

To address the point as it was addressed before the trial judge and to which his certificate relates, in our judgment, parts of a corpse are capable of being property within section 4 of the Theft Act 1968 if they have acquired different attributes by virtue of the application of skill, such as dissection or preservation techniques, for exhibition or teaching purposes [...]

Furthermore, the common law does not stand still. It may be that if, on some future occasion, the question arises, the courts will hold that human body parts are capable of being property for the purposes of section 4, even without the acquisition of different attributes, if they have a use or significance beyond their mere existence. This may be so if, for example, they are intended for use in an organ transplant operation, for the extraction of DNA or, for that matter, as an exhibit in a trial

Since the decision in *R* v *Kelly* the Court of Appeal has held, in *Yearworth and others* v *North Bristol NHS Trust* [2010] QB 1, that frozen sperm stored in a sperm bank constitutes property. In this case, six men who had been diagnosed with cancer provided samples of semen before starting chemotherapy in case they wanted to father children in the future. However, as a result of the defendant's negligence, the semen perished. The men brought a civil action for negligence. One of the issues for the Court of Appeal was whether the sperm was property which belonged to the men. The Court held that it was. Importantly, the Court queried the traditional common law approach that was applied in *R* v *Kelly*. Instead of applying the principles outlined in *R* v *Kelly*, the Court emphasised that the sperm was the product of the men's bodies and that the sole purpose for which they had ejaculated it was so that it could be stored and later used for their benefit. The Court thus concluded that 'for the purposes of their claims in negligence, the men had ownership of the sperm which they ejaculated'. This suggests that in future cases the courts will be more willing to decide that people have property rights in their bodily parts and products.

2. The property belonged to another person

The second requirement for the offence of theft is that the property belonged to another person. The word 'belong' is defined in section 5(1) of the Theft Act 1968:

EXTRACT

Section 5(1) of the Theft Act 1968

5 "Belonging to another"

(1) Property shall be regarded as belonging to any person having possession or control of it, or having in it any proprietary right or interest (not being an equitable interest arising only from an agreement to transfer or grant an interest).

To fully grasp the significance of this definition, it is important to understand the following two points:

- Section 5(1) gives the word belong a far broader meaning than ownership. For the purposes of the offence of theft, property can belong to someone other than the actual owner. Section 5(1) says that property belongs to anyone who has 'possession or control' of the property and to anyone that has 'any proprietary right or interest' in it. As we saw earlier in *R* v *Smith*, the person's possession of the property does not have to be lawful. Smith was guilty of stealing the heroin from Jordan even though Jordan's possession of the drug was unlawful.

  (Notice that there is one exception contained in the brackets at the end of section 5(1): property does not belong to somebody who only has an equitable interest arising only from an agreement to transfer or grant an interest. This is quite a specific exception which is best explained using an illustration. Suppose that Derek agrees to sell his car to Aubrey. Under the contract of sale Derek is due to transfer the car to Aubrey in one week's time. But a few days later, before ownership is transferred, Derek sells the car to somebody else. Although Aubrey had an equitable interest in Derek's car, arising from the contract of sale, the car did not belong to Aubrey for the purposes of theft.)

- Since the section 5(1) definition is broader than ownership, it follows that property can belong to more than one person at a time. Suppose Derek lends Rodney his iPad. Rodney takes it to the pub with him, and is showing Mickey a video on YouTube when someone snatches the iPad from Mickey's hands and runs off with it. In this scenario the iPad belonged to Mickey (he had control of it), Rodney (he had possession of it) and Derek (as owner, he had proprietary rights in it).

One question which the courts have had to address is whether property can belong to someone even though they are unaware that the property exists! This question arose in *R* v *Woodman* [1974] QB 754. A company called English China Clays owned a factory. In 1970 the business closed down and the factory shut. At this time there was a large quantity of scrap metal on the factory site, so English China Clays sold this scrap metal to the Bird Group of companies. People from the Bird Group came to the factory site and removed most of the scrap metal. They left some of the scrap metal behind because it was difficult to access, and they decided that it was not worth the cost of recovering it. After this English China Clays put a barbed wire fence around the site and put up a number of signs saying things like 'Private Property', 'Keep out' and 'Trespassers will be prosecuted'. The site then wound down and remained disused for two years.

In 1973 the defendant, George Woodman, turned up at the site in a van. He helped himself to all of the scrap metal that had been left behind (weighing more than one tonne). At trial he was convicted of stealing the scrap metal from English China Clays. He appealed, arguing that the scrap metal did not belong to English China Clays. The Court of Appeal agreed that English China Clays no longer had *ownership* of the scrap metal. The key question, in terms of the section 5(1) definition, was whether they had *possession or control of it*.

EXTRACT

Read the following extract from the judgment of Lord Widgery CJ.

Did English China Clays have possession or control of the scrap metal? What reasons does Lord Widgery CJ give for the decision?

R v *Woodman* [1974] QB 754

Lord Widgery CJ

We have formed the view without difficulty that [...] there was ample evidence that English China Clays were in control of the site and had taken considerable steps to exclude trespassers as demonstrating the fact that they were in control of the site, and we think that in ordinary and straightforward cases if it is once established that a particular person is in control of a site such as this, then prima facie he is in control of articles which are on that site.

[...]

So far as this case is concerned, arising as it does under the Theft Act 1968, we are content to say that there was evidence of English China Clays being in control of the site and prima facie in control of articles upon the site as well. The fact that it could not be shown that they were conscious of the existence of this or any particular scrap iron does not destroy the general principle that control of a site by excluding others from it is prima facie control of articles on the site as well.

Following *R* v *Woodman* another question has arisen: when will property be regarded as abandoned and ownerless? The issue of abandonment was considered in *Ricketts* v *Basildon Magistrates' Court* [2010] EWHC 2358 (Admin). In the early hours of the morning Robert Ricketts went to two charity shops. At the first shop, which belonged to the British Heart Foundation, he took some bags that had been left outside by donors. At the second shop, which belonged to Oxfam, he took some bags of items which had been placed in bins at the rear of the shop. Ricketts said that he had planned to sell the items he had taken at a car boot sale. He was charged with theft. At Ricketts' committal hearing he argued that there was no evidence that was capable of supporting a charge of theft. The Magistrates' Court rejected this claim and committed Ricketts to the Crown Court to stand trial. Ricketts then sought judicial review of the Magistrates' decision. The issue for the court was whether there was any evidence that the bags that Ricketts took belonged to another person.

EXTRACT

In the following extract from the Court's judgment, Wyn Williams J looks at each charge of theft in turn. First, he considers the alleged theft of the bags from outside the British Heart Foundation shop. Had these bags been abandoned? If not, whom did they belong to for the purposes of the offence of theft?

He then considers the alleged theft of the bags from the rear of the Oxfam shop. Had these bags been abandoned? If not, whom did they belong to for the purposes of the offence of theft?

Ricketts v *Basildon Magistrates' Court* [2010] EWHC 2358 (Admin)

Wyn Williams J

12 In my judgment it cannot be said that the British Heart Foundation acquired possession of the items or assumed control of them or even acquired a proprietary interest in them simply by virtue of the fact that they were left in close proximity to the shop.

13 However, it is clearly the case, in my judgment, that it was open to the court to infer that the items had not been abandoned. The obvious inference on the bare facts before the justices was that persons unknown had intended the goods to be a gift to the British Heart Foundation. Those persons had an intention to give; they had also attempted to effect delivery. Delivery would be complete, however, only when the British Heart Foundation took possession of the items. Until that time, although the unknown would-be donor had divested himself of possession of the items, he had not given up his ownership of the items [...]

14 In my judgment the above analysis shows that it was open to the court to conclude that there was evidence from which a court could properly determine that the property belonged to another at the time of appropriation by the claimant. That being the case, in my judgment, the claimant was properly committed on that charge for trial. It will obviously be a matter for the prosecution to consider how best to frame the indictment when the claimant is actually indicted in the Crown Court.

15 I turn to the charge alleging theft from Oxfam since it is somewhat different on the facts. The claimant admits that the items taken from Oxfam were items which had been placed in bins in close proximity to the rear of the shop. In my judgment, it would be open to a court to infer either that would-be donors had placed the items in the bins for receipt by Oxfam or that employees of Oxfam had placed the items in the bins for onward disposal by the local authority. This analysis assumes of course that the bins belonged to or were controlled by Oxfam, which is not presently disputed.

16 Upon that assumption it would be open to a court to infer that Oxfam had taken delivery of the items once placed within the bins. Alternatively, it could infer that Oxfam had taken possession of the items and had then placed them in the bins for disposal. Either way, Oxfam were in possession of the items at the time of the appropriation by the claimant.

17 I am also of the view that it would be open to the court to conclude that the bins were controlled by Oxfam even if this is disputed. The bins were in close proximity to the rear of the premises. That of itself, in my judgment, raises a permissible inference, in the absence of any other evidence, that the bins were under the control of Oxfam. In any event, if the prosecutor so chooses he or she can allege in the indictment in the Crown Court that the property belongs to a person unknown. That cannot be objectionable for the reasons I have given earlier in this judgment.

So in Ricketts' case none of the bags had been abandoned. Similarly, when you put your bin bags full of rubbish outside your house on collection day you do not abandon them. You put them outside your house so that an authorised refuse collector can come and collect them. By placing them outside, you are not inviting all-comers to rummage through your rubbish and help themselves to anything they like. In other words, until your bin bags are collected you continue to exercise some rights over them. You have not abandoned the bin bags, because you have not relinquished all of your rights over them. This is the test for whether property has been abandoned: has the owner intentionally relinquished all of her rights over the property?

There is also an important distinction between property that is lost and property that has been abandoned. Suppose that Derek drops his wallet in the high street while he is out shopping. Later that day, when he realises, he goes back to the high street and searches for his wallet but cannot find it. Reluctantly, he admits defeat and gives up the search. In this scenario Derek has lost his wallet but has not abandoned it because he did not intentionally relinquish all of his rights over it.

The next question to consider is whether the owner of an item of property can be guilty of stealing his own property. This was the issue in *R* v *Turner* (No 2) [1971] 1 WLR 901. The defendant, Frank Turner, took his car to Arthur Brown's garage for repairs. When Brown told Turner that the car was ready to be collected Turner said that he would pick the car up and pay for the repairs the following day. That evening Brown parked the car on a street outside the garage but kept the key in his office. The next day the key was still there but the car had disappeared. Turner had taken the car away using a spare key. He was charged with theft of the car and was convicted at trial. He subsequently appealed, arguing that he could not be guilty of theft since the car belonged to him and not to Brown. The Court of Appeal dismissed Turner's appeal and upheld his conviction.

Whilst most commentators agree that the outcome in *R* v *Turner* (No 2) was the correct one, the reasoning has been strongly criticised.[5] In order to understand this criticism, it is helpful to compare *R* v *Turner* (No 2) with another case, *R* v *Meredith* [1973] Crim LR 253. Meredith left his car parked in a street while he went to watch a football match. The car was causing an obstruction, so the police removed it and took it to a police pound. After the match had finished Meredith sneaked into the police pound and surreptitiously removed the car. Two days later the police caught up with him and charged him with theft of the car from the police. In the Crown Court Judge Da Cunha held that Meredith could not be convicted of theft, since the police had no right to retain possession of the car. Had Meredith reported to the police station as he should have done he would have had to choose whether to pay the fine or face prosecution. However, whichever of these he chose, the police would have had to return the car to him. Since the police had no right to retain possession of the car, Meredith could not be guilty of stealing the car from them.

So Turner was guilty of stealing his car from Arthur Brown, but Meredith was not guilty of stealing his car from the police. The key to reconciling these cases is a right known as a lien. A lien is a right to retain possession of an item of property until payment has been received. In Turner's case Arthur Brown had a lien. He had a right to retain possession of Turner's car until Turner paid for the repairs. By contrast, in Meredith's

[5] See, for example, Simester, A.P., Spencer, J.R., Stark, F., Sullivan, G.R. and Virgo, G.J. (2016) *Simester and Sullivan's Criminal Law: Theory and Doctrine* (6th edn). Hart Publishing: Oxford, pp.515–516, and Ormerod, D. and Laird, K. (2015) *Smith and Hogan's Criminal Law* (14th edn). OUP: Oxford, pp.919–920.

case the police had no lien. They had no right to retain possession of Meredith's car. The crucial difference between the cases is thus that in *R* v *Turner* (No 2) there was a lien whereas in *R* v *Meredith* there was not. Unfortunately, however, the trial judge in *R* v *Turner* (No 2) told the jury that it was irrelevant whether Brown had had a lien or not. Yet in spite of this the Court of Appeal upheld Turner's conviction.

One further point to note from the decisions in *R* v *Turner* (No 2) and *R* v *Meredith*: whether or not an item of property belongs to someone for the purposes of theft can depend on who it was that appropriated the property! We have seen that in *R* v *Meredith* when Meredith was charged with theft the car was held not to belong to the police. But suppose that a stranger had crept into the police pound and taken the car, not Meredith. On these facts the stranger would be guilty of stealing the car from the police, because the police would have a right to retain possession against the stranger. So whether or not the car belonged to the police for the purposes of theft depends on who the alleged thief is! This highlights how important it is in problem questions to clearly identify the particulars of the alleged offence before embarking on your analysis.

Finally, note that sections 5(3) and 5(4) deal with two specific scenarios:[6]

EXTRACT

Sections 5(3) and 5(4) of the Theft Act 1968

(3) Where a person receives property from or on account of another, and is under an obligation to the other to retain and deal with that property or its proceeds in a particular way, the property or proceeds shall be regarded (as against him) as belonging to the other.

(4) Where a person gets property by another's mistake, and is under an obligation to make restoration (in whole or in part) of the property or its proceeds or of the value thereof, then to the extent of that obligation the property or proceeds shall be regarded (as against him) as belonging to the person entitled to restoration, and an intention not to make restoration shall be regarded accordingly as an intention to deprive that person of the property or proceeds.

For section 5(3) to apply the obligation to deal with the property in a particular way must be a legal, not merely a moral, obligation.[7] An example would be where Rodney gives his housemate Derek money to pay the gas bill, but instead Derek goes to the pub and spends the money on expensive drinks. On these facts Derek had a legal obligation to deal with the money or its proceeds 'in a particular way', and so for the purposes of theft the money is regarded as belonging to Rodney.[8]

Section 5(4) deals with property received by mistake. Like section 5(3), the obligation to return the property must be a legal, not merely a moral, obligation.[9] An example of when section 5(4) would apply is where Derek receives his wages and realises that he

[6] Section 5(2) also deals with a specific scenario: cases involving trusts with no individual beneficiary with an equitable interest in the trust (e.g. a charitable trust).

[7] *R* v *Foster* [2011] EWCA Crim 1192.

[8] *Davidge* v *Bunnett* [1984] Crim LR 297. Whether or not the parties intended to create a legal obligation is a question of fact. So, for example, if our example involved members of the same family section 5(3) may well not apply since family members would presumably not intend to create a legally binding arrangement: see *R* v *Cullen* (1974, unreported, no 968/c/74).

[9] *R* v *Gilks* [1972] 1 WLR 1341.

has been overpaid by £100. Although the money is now in Derek's bank account he has an obligation to repay his employers and so if he dishonestly decides to keep the money he commits theft.[10]

3. The defendant appropriated the property

The third requirement for the offence of theft is that the defendant appropriated the property. The word 'appropriates' is defined in section 3(1):

EXTRACT

Section 3(1) of the Theft Act 1968

3 "Appropriates"

(1) Any assumption by a person of the rights of an owner amounts to an appropriation, and this includes, where he has come by the property (innocently or not) without stealing it, any later assumption of a right to it by keeping or dealing with it as owner.

The key words are the opening ones: an appropriation is 'any assumption by a person of the rights of an owner'. These words have generated a series of four important House of Lords cases, which focus on two questions: Is it enough to show an assumption of any of the rights of an owner, or is it necessary to show an assumption of all of the rights of an owner? And, can there be an appropriation if the owner consented to the assumption of the rights? We will look at each of these questions in turn.

i. Is it enough to show an assumption of any of the rights of an owner, or is it necessary to show an assumption of all of the rights of an owner?

The owner of an item has numerous rights. For example, an owner has the right to use the item, the right to sell the item and the right to destroy it. For this reason ownership is often described as a bundle of rights. The first question which the House of Lords has had to consider is whether, in order to establish an appropriation, it is necessary to show that the defendant assumed *all* of these rights or whether it is sufficient that he assumed *any* of these rights.

This question was first considered in *R* v *Morris* [1984] AC 320. This case involved two separate appeals, one from David Morris and the other from James Burnside. The case involved the switching of price labels in supermarkets (the case occurred in the days before barcodes!). Morris had entered a supermarket and swapped the price labels on two products so that he would be charged a lower price for the item he wished to buy. At the checkout he paid the lower price, and was then arrested. The only difference in Burnside's case was that he was arrested at the checkout but before he had paid for the item. Both men were convicted of theft and both appealed, arguing that there was no appropriation. The case reached the House of Lords.

---

[10] See *Attorney-General's Reference (No 1 of 1983)* [1985] QB 182.

EXTRACT

Read the following extract from the judgment of Lord Roskill.

For an appropriation, is it enough to show an assumption of any of the rights of an owner? Or is it necessary to show an assumption of all of the rights of an owner?

R v *Morris* [1984] AC 320

Lord Roskill

Mr. Denison [counsel for the defendants] submitted that the phrase in section 3(1) "any assumption by a person of *the rights*" (my emphasis) "of an owner amounts to an appropriation" must mean any assumption of "*all the rights of an owner*." Since neither respondent had at the time of the removal of the goods from the shelves and of the label switching assumed *all* the rights of the owner, there was no appropriation and therefore no theft. Mr. Jeffreys for the prosecution, on the other hand, contended that *the* rights in this context only meant *any* of the rights. An owner of goods has many rights – they have been described as "a bundle or package of rights." Mr. Jeffreys contended that on a fair reading of the subsection it cannot have been the intention that every one of an owner's rights had to be assumed by the alleged thief before an appropriation was proved and that essential ingredient of the offence of theft established.

My Lords, if one reads the words "the rights" at the opening of section 3(1) literally and in isolation from the rest of the section, Mr. Denison's submission undoubtedly has force. But the later words "any later assumption of a right" in subsection (1) and the words in subsection (2) "no later assumption by him of rights" seem to me to militate strongly against the correctness of the submission. Moreover the provisions of section 2(1)(a) also seem to point in the same direction. It follows therefore that it is enough for the prosecution if they have proved in these cases the assumption by the respondents of any of the rights of the owner of the goods in question

This decision means that the concept of appropriation has a wide scope. It was not necessary for the prosecution to show that Morris and Burnside had assumed all of the rights of an owner. It was enough that they had assumed any of the rights of an owner. It is an owner's right to fix a price label to a supermarket item, so by switching the price labels Morris and Burnside assumed this right. Switching the labels therefore amounted to the *actus reus* of theft. Moreover, since Morris and Burnside had the *mens rea* of theft when they switched the labels the offence was complete at this moment. It did not matter that they had not left the shop with the items. Nor did it matter that Burnside had not yet paid the lower price at the checkout. Both men were guilty of theft as soon as they switched the labels.

The decision in *R* v *Morris* was controversial. It has been described as 'depressing',[11] 'obviously wrong'[12] and 'at variance with the plain words of the statute'.[13] Yet in the subsequent case *DPP* v *Gomez* [1993] AC 442 a majority of the House of Lords held that the

---

[11] Spencer, J. (1984) 'Theft – Appropriation and Consent' 43 *Cambridge Law Journal* 7, 10.

[12] Ormerod, D. and Laird, K. (2015) *Smith and Hogan's Criminal Law* (14th edn). OUP: Oxford, p.893.

[13] Simester, A.P., Spencer, J.R., Stark, F., Sullivan, G.R. and Virgo, G.J. (2016) *Simester and Sullivan's Criminal Law: Theory and Doctrine* (6th edn). Hart Publishing: Oxford, p.534.

decision in *R* v *Morris* was correct on this point.[14] On behalf of the majority, Lord Keith stated:

> In my opinion Lord Roskill was undoubtedly right when he said [...] that the assumption by the defendant of any of the rights of an owner could amount to an appropriation within the meaning of section 3(1), and that the removal of an article from the shelf and the changing of the price label on it constituted the assumption of one of the rights of the owner and hence an appropriation within the meaning of the subsection

We will examine the implications of this in more detail shortly.

ii. Can there be an appropriation if the owner consented to the assumption of the rights?

The second question the House of Lords has had to consider is whether an action can amount to an appropriation if the owner consented to it. The first case in which this was addressed was *Lawrence* v *MPC* [1972] AC 626. An Italian man named Eugenio Occhi arrived at Victoria Station on his first visit to England. He spoke little English. The defendant, Alan Lawrence, was a taxi driver. Occhi showed Lawrence a piece of paper with an address written on it. Lawrence said it was very far away and very expensive. Occhi got into the taxi, gave Lawrence £1 and then held his wallet open while Lawrence took another £6 from it. Lawrence then drove Occhi to the address. The correct fare was less than £1. At trial Lawrence was convicted of theft of the £6. He appealed, arguing that he had not appropriated the £6 because Occhi had allowed him to take it. The issue for the House of Lords was whether an action can amount to an appropriation if it was consensual.

EXTRACT

According to the following extract from the judgment of Viscount Dilhorne, can there be an appropriation if the owner consented to the assumption of the rights?

Lawrence v *MPC* [1972] AC 626

Viscount Dilhorne

Prior to the passage of the Theft Act 1968, which made radical changes in and greatly simplified the law relating to theft and some other offences, it was necessary to prove that the property alleged to have been stolen was taken "without the consent of the owner" (Larceny Act 1916, section 1 (1)).

These words are not included in section 1 (1) of the Theft Act, but the appellant contended that the subsection should be construed as if they were, as if they appeared after the word "appropriates." Section 1 (1) reads as follows:

> "A person is guilty of theft if he dishonestly appropriates property belonging to an other with the intention of permanently depriving the other of it; and 'thief' and 'steal' shall be construed accordingly."

[14] In his dissenting judgment Lord Lowry stated: '"the rights" may mean "*all* the rights," which would be the normal grammatical meaning, or (less probably, in my opinion) "any rights" [...] Still looking at section 3(1), I point out that "any later assumption of a right to it" (that is, a right to the property) amounts to an appropriation of a right to it and that normally "a right to it" means a right *to* the property and not a right *in* it' (emphasis original).

> I see no ground for concluding that the omission of the words "without the consent of the owner" was inadvertent and not deliberate, and to read the subsection as if they were included is, in my opinion, wholly unwarranted. Parliament by the omission of these words has relieved the prosecution of the burden of establishing that the taking was without the owner's consent. That is no longer an ingredient of the offence.
>
> [...]
>
> That there was appropriation in this case is clear. Section 3 (1) states that any assumption by a person of the rights of an owner amounts to an appropriation. Here there was clearly such an assumption

Following the judgment in *Lawrence* v *MPC* the position was clear. Just over a decade later, however, things were complicated by the House of Lords' decision in *R* v *Morris*. In his judgment in this case Lord Roskill discussed whether or not the honest shopper appropriates items when she takes them off the supermarket shelf and places them in her trolley. The prosecutor in the case argued that this does amount to an appropriation. In response Lord Roskill stated:

> With the utmost respect, I cannot accept this statement as correct. If one postulates an honest customer taking goods from a shelf to put in his or her trolley to take to the checkpoint there to pay the proper price, I am unable to see that any of these actions involves any assumption by the shopper of the rights of the supermarket. In the context of section 3(1), the concept of appropriation in my view involves not an act expressly or impliedly authorised by the owner but an act by way of adverse interference with or usurpation of those rights. When the honest shopper acts as I have just described, he or she is acting with the implied authority of the owner of the supermarket to take the goods from the shelf, put them in the trolley, take them to the checkpoint and there pay the correct price, at which moment the property in the goods will pass to the shopper for the first time. It is with the consent of the owners of the supermarket, be that consent express or implied, that the shopper does these acts and thus obtains at least control if not actual possession of the goods preparatory, at a later stage, to obtaining the property in them upon payment of the proper amount at the checkpoint. I do not think that section 3(1) envisages any such act as an "appropriation," whatever may be the meaning of that word in other fields such as contract or sale of goods law.

Lord Roskill's comments contradicted the decision in *Lawrence* v *MPC*. In *Lawrence* v *MPC* the House of Lords had said that it is irrelevant whether or not the owner consented to the action. The sole question is whether the defendant assumed the rights of an owner. But in the passage from *R* v *Morris* above Lord Roskill says that an action cannot amount to an appropriation if it was 'expressly or impliedly authorised by the owner'. Importantly, however, Lord Roskill's comments were *obiter dicta* since the owner of the property in *R* v *Morris* had not consented to the act in question (swapping price labels). In *Lawrence* v *MPC*, by contrast, Viscount Dilhorne's comments were part of the *ratio decidendi* of the case, since Occhi had consented to Lawrence taking the money from his wallet.

This conflict between *Lawrence* v *MPC* and *R* v *Morris* was resolved by the House of Lords in *DPP* v *Gomez* [1993] AC 442. The defendant in this case, Edwin Gomez, was assistant manager of an electrical goods shop. He formed a plan with his friend Jit Ballay. Ballay placed an order for £7,950 worth of goods and paid using a stolen building society cheque. When Gomez went to his manager to ask him to authorise the transaction he told his manager that he had checked with the bank that the cheque was acceptable and that the cheque was 'as good as cash'. A few days later Ballay collected the goods and Gomez helped him load them into his car. Shortly afterwards Ballay placed a second order – this time for £9,250 worth of goods – and Gomez did the same thing again. Later the bank returned the two cheques and informed the shop manager that they were stolen. At trial Gomez was convicted on two counts of theft. He appealed, arguing that there had been no appropriation since the shop manager had consented to the goods being handed over. The case reached the House of Lords. The majority judgment was delivered by Lord Keith (Lord Lowry dissented).

EXTRACT

Read the following extract from the judgment of Lord Keith.

Did he follow *Lawrence* v *MPC* or *R* v *Morris*?

DPP v *Gomez* [1993] AC 442

Lord Keith

The actual decision in *Morris* was correct, but it was erroneous, in addition to being unnecessary for the decision, to indicate that an act expressly or impliedly authorised by the owner could never amount to an appropriation [...] *Lawrence* makes it clear that consent to or authorisation by the owner of the taking by the rogue is irrelevant. The taking amounted to an appropriation within the meaning of section 1(1) of the Act of 1968. *Lawrence* also makes it clear that it is no less irrelevant that what happened may also have constituted the offence of obtaining property by deception under section 15(1) of the Act.

The decision in *Lawrence* was a clear decision of this House upon the construction of the word "appropriate" in section 1(1) of the Act, which had stood for 12 years when doubt was thrown upon it by obiter dicta in *Morris*. *Lawrence* must be regarded as authoritative and correct, and there is no question of it now being right to depart from it.

Now, think about this question.

Following *DPP* v *Gomez*, can there be an appropriation if the owner consented to the assumption of the rights?

In his dissenting judgment, Lord Lowry argued that the majority's decision was at odds with the basic meaning of 'appropriate':

> The ordinary and natural meaning of "appropriate" is to take for oneself, or to treat as one's own, property which belongs to someone else. The primary dictionary meaning is "take possession of, take to oneself, especially without authority," and that is in my opinion the meaning which the word bears in section 1(1). The act of appropriating property is a one-sided act, done without the consent or authority of the owner. And, if the owner consents to transfer property to the offender or to a third party, the offender does not appropriate the property, even if the owner's consent has been obtained by fraud

Lord Lowry then went on to examine the 1966 report of the Criminal Law Revision Committee (CLRC),[15] on which the Theft Act 1968 was based. He explained that the

[15] *Theft and Related Offences* (1966) Cmnd 2977.

Committee had intended the word 'appropriation' to mean an unauthorised usurpation of another's property rights. This was designed to maintain a distinction between the offence of theft and the offence of obtaining property by deception (which, as we'll see later in the chapter, has since been replaced by the offence of fraud – but the point still applies). The majority, however, declined to consider the CLRC's report. Lord Keith stated that to do so would serve 'no useful purpose'.

So following *DPP* v *Gomez* the answers to our two questions are clear. It is not necessary to show that the defendant assumed all of the rights of an owner. Nor is it necessary to show that the assumption of the rights was non-consensual. This means that the legal test for an appropriation is quite straightforward. The question is simply: did the defendant assume any of the rights of an owner (regardless of consent)?

iii. Summary: examples of appropriations

In our discussion so far we have seen a number of examples of appropriations:

- Taking money from someone
- Swapping price labels
- Picking an item up
- Taking delivery of goods.

Offering to sell an item of property is also an appropriation: *R* v *Pitham & Hehl* (1976) 65 Cr App R 45. So too is accepting a gift, as we'll see shortly in *R* v *Hinks* [2001] 2 AC 241.

A further example of an appropriation is found in the second half of section 3(1):

EXTRACT

Section 3(1) of the Theft Act 1968

3 "Appropriates"

(1) Any assumption by a person of the rights of an owner amounts to an appropriation, and this includes, where he has come by the property (innocently or not) without stealing it, any later assumption of a right to it by keeping or dealing with it as owner.

So keeping or dealing with an item as its owner amounts to an appropriation, including where you came by the property innocently. So suppose Derek borrows Aubrey's lawn mower. Aubrey says to 'bring it back tomorrow'. After cutting his grass Derek decides that he would like to keep the mower. The next day he doesn't return the mower as promised. Instead he leaves the mower in his garden shed and hopes that Aubrey will forget having lent it to him. On these facts Derek has appropriated the mower since he kept it 'as owner'.[16]

[16] Compare the decision in *Broom* v *Crowther* (1984) 148 JP 592. The defendant purchased a stolen theodolite. When he discovered it was stolen he kept the theodolite for another week until it was seized by the police. He told the police that once he had discovered it was stolen he had merely left the theodolite sitting in his bedroom whilst he decided what to do with it. The Divisional Court held that there had been no appropriation and quashed his theft conviction. Although he had kept the theodolite, the Court said he had not kept it 'as owner' since he had only had it for a few days while he pondered what to do.

Although appropriation is very broadly defined, section 3 does set out two restrictions on the concept's scope. The first is found in the words 'without stealing it' in section 3(1). A person can appropriate the same item multiple times until he steals it. But once he has stolen it there can be no further appropriations. You cannot keep restealing the same item again and again! So suppose Derek finds an iPhone on the pavement. He is in a rush to catch a train, so decides to pick the phone up and try and discover its owner later that day. While he is on the train he takes the phone out of his pocket and looks through the address book to try and discover the owner. But by the time he gets home Derek has decided to keep the phone for himself. That evening he uses the phone to make a call and to read the news online. On these facts Derek steals the phone when he decides to keep it for himself. There were multiple appropriations prior to this: picking the phone up off the pavement; putting it in his pocket; looking through the address book. But using the phone to make a call and to read the news were not appropriations because by then Derek had already stolen the phone.

The second restriction on the scope of appropriation is found in section 3(2):

EXTRACT

Section 3(2) of the Theft Act 1968

(2) Where property or a right or interest in property is or purports to be transferred for value to a person acting in good faith, no later assumption by him of rights which he believed himself to be acquiring shall, by reason of any defect in the transferor's title, amount to theft of the property

So suppose Derek has stolen Aubrey's lawn mower and then sells the stolen mower to Mike. When he buys the mower, Mike has no idea that it is stolen. A week later, however, Mike discovers that the mower is stolen. Section 3(2) states that any subsequent assumption by Mike of the rights of an owner will not amount to theft since Mike purchased the mower in good faith. However, note that: (i) section 3(2) only applies where the item was 'transferred for value' – it would not apply if Derek gave Mike the lawn mower as a gift; and (ii) the section 3(2) exemption would not apply if Mike sold the mower on to someone else without telling them that it was stolen – on these facts he could be convicted of fraud (which we study below).

Quiz 8.1

1. For theft contrary to section 1 of the Theft Act 1968, the *actus reus* is ...
   - **a.** a dishonest intention to permanently deprive.
   - **b.** an appropriation of property belonging to another.
   - **c.** an appropriation of property with intention to permanently deprive.
   - **d.** a dishonest appropriation of property.
2. What is the *mens rea* of theft?
   - **a.** An appropriation of property with intention to permanently deprive.
   - **b.** An appropriation of property belonging to another.
   - **c.** A dishonest appropriation of property.
   - **d.** A dishonest intention to permanently deprive.
3. Which of the following is considered to be property for the purposes of section 4 of the Theft Act 1968?
   - **a.** Confidential information.
   - **b.** Shares in a company.
   - **c.** Electricity.
   - **d.** A manicure.

4. What issue was decided by the case of *Oxford* v *Moss*?
   a. Electricity is not property.
   b. Parts of a human corpse are not property.
   c. Wild mushrooms are not property.
   d. Information is not property.

5. Which of the actions below might result in a charge of theft contrary to section 1 of the Theft Act 1968?
   a. Allowing a neighbour's cat into your house.
   b. Taming a stray cat to keep as a pet.
   c. Inviting a stray cat into your house.
   d. Taming your neighbour's cat to keep as a pet.

6. Which of the actions below would result in a charge of theft contrary to section 1 of the Theft Act 1968?
   a. Picking mushrooms from a forest floor.
   b. Collecting berries from a wild-growing hedgerow.
   c. Picking apples from a wild-growing tree.
   d. Picking apples from a neighbour's orchard.

7. Which of the following statements is incorrect?
   a. Property can belong to someone for the purposes of theft even if they have no idea that the property exists.
   b. For the purposes of theft, property can belong to more than one person at a time.
   c. The owner of an item of property cannot be guilty of stealing it.
   d. Property is only regarded as abandoned if the owner has intentionally relinquished all rights over it.

Appropriation within the law of theft

8.2 Evaluate the case law on appropriation within the law of theft.

Earlier we saw that the decision in *DPP* v *Gomez* clarified that there can be an appropriation even if the owner consented to it. However, the decision has been heavily criticised for a number of other reasons. The first reason is that it defines the concept of appropriation too broadly. The second is that it collapses the distinction between theft and deception/fraud offences. The third is that theft now encompasses many situations which should be regarded as criminal attempts. And finally, it produces a conflict between the civil and criminal laws. We will look at each of these criticisms of *DPP* v *Gomez* in turn.

The breadth of the definition of an appropriation

Following the House of Lords' decision in *DPP* v *Gomez* Sir John Smith commented that the decision 'reduces the *actus reus* of theft almost to vanishing point'.[17] Suppose that Aubrey decides to buy an expensive bottle of champagne to impress the guests at his dinner party. He goes to the supermarket, finds the alcohol aisle and picks up the most expensive bottle he can find. Meanwhile another shopper, Derek, has decided to steal a bottle of champagne from the same supermarket. Derek enters the store, walks to the alcohol aisle and picks up the most expensive bottle of champagne he can find. On these facts, both Aubrey and Derek have committed an appropriation. By picking the bottle up they assumed a right of an owner. Following *DPP* v *Gomez*, it is not necessary to assume *all* of the rights of an owner, and it is irrelevant that the supermarket gives its consent to shoppers picking items up. So in both Aubrey's case and Derek's case there is the *actus reus* of theft. They both appropriated property belonging to another.

The fact that there is the *actus reus* of theft in Aubrey's case illustrates just how broad the definition of appropriation is. Aubrey had not done anything that was wrongful or that caused harm to the supermarket. In fact, he was going to pay for the champagne! For his conduct to amount to the *actus reus* of theft is very difficult to reconcile with the harm principle (see Chapter 1), which states that only harmful wrongdoing should be criminalised.

[17] Smith, J.C. (1993) 'Commentary on *R* v *Gomez*' *Criminal Law Review* 305, 306.

In fact, if we focus solely on their conduct, Derek did nothing different to Aubrey. He picked a bottle of champagne up off the shelf, just as Aubrey did. Yet Derek is guilty of theft, because at the moment he picked the bottle up he had the *mens rea* of theft. In this sense, the decision in *DPP* v *Gomez* renders theft little more than a thought crime. A defendant like Derek can be guilty of theft, even though his conduct is no different from that of other citizens, simply on the basis of his guilty mind at the time.

The distinction between the offence of theft and the offence of fraud

Think back to the facts of *DPP* v *Gomez*. At first, it looks like a straightforward example of a deception/fraud offence. Gomez lied to the shop manager in order to trick him into handing over the goods. Yet Gomez was convicted not of a deception offence but theft, and the House of Lords upheld this conviction. The Lords acknowledged that the result of this was a significant overlap between the offences of theft and obtaining property by deception (note that the offence of obtaining property by deception has now been replaced by the offence of fraud – but the same point still applies).[18] This overlap between theft and the deception/fraud offences has been criticised by a number of commentators. One example is Christopher Clarkson's piece 'Theft and Fair Labelling'.

EXTRACT

As you read the following extract from Clarkson's commentary, bear in mind the principles we studied in Chapter 1.

Clarkson, C. (1993) 'Theft and Fair Labelling' 56 *Modern Law Review* 554

The House of Lords in *DPP* v *Gomez* has largely collapsed the distinction between theft and obtaining property by deception by holding that an authorised act can amount to an appropriation. Lord Keith (with whom three other Lords agreed) makes no argument for this extraordinary conclusion other than to say that Lawrence is a "clear decision" which has "stood for 12 years" and that "there is no question of it now being right to depart from it." [...]

Criminal offences should accurately describe the prohibited conduct as far as possible. English law has chosen to reject the plea for a single offence of homicide. Even those arguing for the abolition of the mandatory life sentence for murder would retain the separate offences of murder and manslaughter. Similarly, arguments for abandoning the distinction between rape

[18] Whilst there may now be a significant overlap between theft and fraud, there is not complete overlap. There are some situations in which only fraud would apply. An example is *R* v *Darroux* [2018] EWCA Crim 1009. In this case the defendant worked for a Housing Association. Each month she submitted claims for overtime using a claim form. These were processed by a payroll company that managed the Housing Association's bank account. Over a three-year period, the defendant submitted a number of inflated claims for overtime pay. At trial she was convicted of theft. This was quashed on appeal. The Court of Appeal explained that the defendant's conduct could not amount to theft because she had not appropriated the funds. She had not had control over the Housing Association's bank account and had not been the one that instructed the bank to make payments from the account. What she had done was to dishonestly cause the payroll company to transfer money to her. As Davis LJ stated, the appropriate charge on these facts would have been fraud by false representation.

and indecent assault and replacing them with a broad offence of sexual assault have been resisted. The reasons for this are clear. Offences should be structured, labelled and punished to reflect the extent of wrongdoing and/or harm involved. Criminal offences are categorised for symbolic reasons. It is to communicate the differing degrees of rejection or unacceptability of different types of conduct. Such symbolic messages are not conveyed by the creation of broad morally uninformative labels such as "unlawful homicide." Further, such broadly defined offences increase the discretionary powers of the law enforcement agencies and the judges in sentencing, and infringe what Ashworth has called "the principle of maximum certainty." Increased efforts to control or structure such discretionary powers would be thwarted by the introduction of over-broad substantive offences.

Turning to the property offences, all of which share the same concern, namely, the protection of a variety of interests in property, English law has sought to maintain clear distinctions between the various offences in an effort to mark the different wrongs and harms involved therein. For example, robbery, burglary and handling stolen goods are clearly differentiated for obvious reasons. The various offences of deception are perhaps most clearly related to theft. In both theft and obtaining property by deception, the owner has lost property to another – but it is the method of losing such property that marks the moral distinction between the two.

[...]

The paradigmatic theft involves a surreptitious or forcible taking, while deception offences involve a confrontation and a participation by the victim in the loss of the property. With theft, the owner is generally helpless against such a taking. If interrupted there is a risk of violence. With the typical obtaining, the victim has a real opportunity to prevent the commission of the crime. With greater alertness he or she might not have been deceived. He or she has agreed to part with the property. In our society, where mutual transactions based on trust are valued and encouraged, the wrong of *deceiving* another into parting with property is a distinctive wrong – quite different in quality from the paradigmatic theft. Shute and Horder are right to conclude that whereas "the thief makes war on a social practice from the outside, the deceiver is the traitor within."

[...]

Parliament has enacted separate penalties for theft (seven years) and obtaining by deception (ten years), underlining the moral distinction between the two [the penalty for fraud is also ten years]. It is lamentable that the majority in *Gomez* should have brazenly ignored this [...] Urgent statutory reform is imperative. A new definition of theft or appropriation is called for. In devising a new formula, the legislature needs to keep firmly in mind the necessity for clear differentiation between morally distinguishable offences and a definition of theft should be devised that is consistent with the theft paradigm

Now, think about these questions.

a. Keeping in mind Criminal Law principles we studied in Chapter 1, which of these principles is Clarkson's argument based on?

b. What reasons does Clarkson give for the importance of this principle?

c. According to Clarkson, what are the key differences between theft and deception/fraud offences? Why does fair labelling require this distinction?

On this view, the House of Lords in *DPP* v *Gomez* should have held that there can only be an appropriation if the assumption of the owner's rights took place without the owner's consent. Cases in which the owner was tricked into consenting should be prosecuted using the deception (or, today, fraud) offences.

However, not all commentators agree with this criticism of the decision in *DPP* v *Gomez*. In the following extract from his provocatively titled note 'Thief or Swindler: Who Cares?' Peter Glazebrook argues that it is mistaken to try and draw a 'trivial and morally irrelevant' distinction between theft and deception/fraud offences.

EXTRACT

Glazebrook, P. (1991) 'Thief or Swindler: Who Cares?' 50 *Cambridge Law Journal* 389

[In *Lawrence* v *MPC* the House of Lords] held that though property had been, or might have been, obtained by deception the crook could still be convicted of theft for there was nothing in the definition of stealing in section 1 of the 1968 Act that required the courts to make the trivial and morally irrelevant distinction between someone who dishonestly appropriated another's property by stealth, and one who did so by deceit. The crook is as dishonest in the one case as the other, and the gain to him, and the loss to his victim, is exactly the same. In plain English, a person who obtains another's property by deception appropriates property belonging to another – indeed he plainly misappropriates it – and in *Lawrence* the House of Lords ruled emphatically that the courts should not write into the Theft Act restrictive or qualifying words that are not there. It would certainly be bizarre if a defendant who appropriated property he had received because the transferor had made a mistake to which the defendant had not contributed were guilty of theft (as he is: s. 5(4)), but was not guilty if the property had come to him because of a mistake which he had deliberately induced.

What is more, it may be either difficult to decide, or the merest matter of chance, whether the crook had resorted to deception in order to get his sticky mits on to the property he coveted. In *Lawrence* it would have been as difficult as it would have been pointless to set about deciding whether the travel-weary and English-less Signor Occhi had been deceived by taxi-driver Lawrence into believing that it was so very much more than a Sabbath day's journey from Victoria Station, SW1, to Ladbroke Grove, W10, that the authorised fare was more than £6 rather than less than £1 (1969 money), or whether Signor Occhi was just too bemused to know what exactly was happening as Lawrence helped himself to the notes in his wallet.

Now, think about these questions.

- What reasons does Glazebrook give for rejecting the argument that a distinction should be drawn between theft and the deception/fraud offences?
- Whose argument do you find most compelling: Clarkson's or Glazebrook's?
- Was the House of Lords in *DPP* v *Gomez* right to say that cases involving consensual appropriations may be prosecuted as theft?

The distinction between theft and criminal attempts

Not only does the offence of theft overlap with the deception/fraud offences. It also now encompasses much conduct that you might expect would be regarded as a criminal attempt. Think back to the earlier example involving Derek. He decides to steal a bottle of champagne from a supermarket. He walks into the store, goes to the alcohol aisle, picks the most expensive bottle he can find off the shelf, then turns around and starts walking to the exit. But before he reaches the exit Derek is stopped by a store detective. As we saw earlier, on these facts Derek committed theft as soon as he picked the bottle up. As soon as he picked the bottle up he appropriated property belonging to another, and at the moment he did so he had the *mens rea* of theft.

In the eyes of many commentators this outcome is counter-intuitive. Following the decision in *DPP* v *Gomez,* for example, Sir John Smith commented, 'Acts which common sense would regard as attempts or merely preparatory acts are the full offence of theft'.[19] On this view, Derek should at most be convicted of attempted theft (whether he is guilty of attempted theft would depend on whether he had gone beyond mere preparation – see Chapter 12). A conviction for the full offence of theft is not a fair reflection of what actually happened. In fact, suppose that Derek had not been stopped by a store detective but instead had simply changed his mind before leaving the shop and put the bottle back on the shelf. Since his change of heart occurred after he picked the bottle up (i.e. after the offence was already complete), he would still be guilty of the full offence of theft even though he never got so far as to try and leave the shop without paying!

Sometimes this criticism (the theft–criminal attempts distinction) and the previous one (the theft–deception/fraud offences distinction) apply simultaneously. An example is *R* v *Morris*. James Burnside switched the price labels on two items. His plan was to deceive the checkout operator into charging him a lower price for the item he wanted. But the plan was unsuccessful.

He was arrested at the checkout before he was able to pay the lower price for the item. Intuitively, this looks like an (unsuccessful) attempt to obtain property by deception (or, today, an attempt to commit fraud). Yet he was not convicted of attempting to obtain property by deception. He was convicted of the full offence of theft!

The relationship between the criminal law and the civil law

So far we have studied three of the four major House of Lords cases on the meaning of appropriation. There is one final one for us to consider: *R* v *Hinks* [2001] 2 AC 241. This case also involved a consensual appropriation, but there was one significant difference to the earlier cases of *Lawrence* v *MPC* and *DPP* v *Gomez*. In *DPP* v *Gomez* the shop manager was deceived into selling the goods. This deception meant that the contract of sale was voidable. In other words, Gomez and Ballay only acquired *defeasible* title. Similarly in *Lawrence* v *MPC* the contract between Lawrence and Occhi was voidable, and so Lawrence only acquired defeasible title. So in both *Lawrence* v *MPC* and *DPP* v *Gomez* the victims could recover the property that had been stolen from them. But things were different in *R* v *Hinks*. In this case the defendant, Karen Hinks, acquired *indefeasible* title. In other words, the property that she was alleged to have stolen was hers to keep. The question for the House of Lords was whether someone can be convicted of theft when, under the civil law, the property is theirs to keep.

Karen Hinks was a 38-year-old woman who was friendly with a 53-year-old man named John Dolphin. Dolphin was of limited intelligence, with a below-average IQ. A psychiatrist described him as naïve and trusting with no idea of the value of his assets or the ability to calculate their value. In the words of Lord Steyn, the prosecution case was that Hinks 'had taken Mr Dolphin for as much as she could get'. Between April and November 1996 Dolphin withdrew a total of £60,000 and deposited it in Hinks' bank

[19] Smith, J.C. (1993) 'Commentary on *R* v *Gomez*' *Criminal Law Review* 305, 306.

account. During the summer Dolphin was going to his building society almost every day, making the maximum daily withdrawal of £300. Employees of the building society said that during these visits Hinks would do most of the talking and would interrupt if Dolphin tried to say anything. By the end of November Dolphin had lost most of his savings, and his inheritance from his father.

At trial, Hinks was convicted of theft of the £60,000, and of a TV that Dolphin had given her. Importantly, however, the psychiatrist accepted that although Dolphin was naïve and trusting he understood the concept of ownership and was capable of making a gift. So under the civil law Dolphin's transfer of property to Hinks was a valid gift. Hinks therefore appealed, arguing that since she had acquired indefeasible title to the property she had not appropriated it. By a majority of 3–2, the House of Lords dismissed her appeal.[20] Lord Steyn delivered the judgment on behalf of the majority.

EXTRACT

In the following extract from Lord Steyn's judgment he responds to some of the arguments Hinks' counsel gave for saying that she had not appropriated the property. What were these arguments?

R v *Hinks* [2001] 2 AC 241

Lord Steyn

Counsel for the appellant submitted in the first place that the law as expounded in *Gomez* and *Lawrence* must be qualified to say that there can be no appropriation unless the other party (the owner) retains some proprietary interest, or the right to resume or recover some proprietary interest, in the property. Alternatively, counsel argued that "appropriates" should be interpreted as if the word "unlawfully" preceded it. Counsel said that the effect of the decisions in *Lawrence* and *Gomez* is to reduce the *actus reus* of theft to "vanishing point" (see *Smith & Hogan, Criminal Law*, 9th ed (1999), p 505). He argued that the result is to bring the criminal law "into conflict" with the civil law. Moreover, he argued that the decisions in *Lawrence* and *Gomez* may produce absurd and grotesque results. He argued that the mental requirements of dishonesty and intention of permanently depriving the owner of property are insufficient to filter out some cases of conduct which should not sensibly be regarded as theft. He did not suggest that the appellant's dishonest and repellent conduct came within such a category. Instead he deployed four examples for this purpose, namely:

1. S makes a handsome gift to D because he believes that D has obtained a First. D has not and knows that S is acting under that misapprehension. He makes the gift. There is here a motivational mistake which, it is submitted, does not avoid the transaction. (*Glanville Williams, Textbook of Criminal Law*, 1st ed (1978), p 788.)
2. P sees D's painting and, thinking he is getting a bargain, offers D £100,000 for it. D realises that P thinks the painting is a Constable, but knows that it was painted by his sister and is worth no more than £100. He accepts P's offer. D has made an enforceable contract and is entitled to recover and retain the purchase price. (*Smith & Hogan, Criminal Law*, pp 507–508.)
3. A buys a roadside garage business from B, abutting on a public thoroughfare; unknown to A but known to B, it has already been decided to construct a bypass road which will

[20] Lords Hutton and Hobhouse dissented.

divert substantially the whole of the traffic from passing A's garage. There is an enforceable contract and A is entitled to recover and retain the purchase price. The same would be true if B *knew* that A was unaware of the intended plan to construct a bypass road. (Compare Lord Atkin in *Bell v Lever Bros Ltd* [1932] AC 161, 224.)

4. An employee agrees to retire before the end of his contract of employment, receiving a sum of money by way of compensation from his employer. Unknown to the employer, the employee has committed serious breaches of contract which would have enabled the employer to dismiss him without compensation. Assuming that the employee's failure to reveal his defaults does not affect the validity of the contract, so that the employee is entitled to sue for the promised compensation, is the employee liable to be arrested for the theft the moment he receives the money? (Glanville Williams, "Theft and Voidable Title" [1981] Crim LR 666, 672.)

My Lords, at first glance these are rather telling examples. They may conceivably have justified a more restricted meaning of section 3(1) than prevailed in *Lawrence* [1972] AC 626 and *Gomez* [1993] AC 442. The House ruled otherwise and I am quite unpersuaded that the House overlooked the consequences of its decision. On the facts set out in the examples a jury could possibly find that the acceptance of the transfer took place in the belief that the transferee had the right in law to deprive the other of it within the meaning of section 2(1)(a) of the Act. Moreover, in such cases a prosecution is hardly likely and if mounted, is likely to founder on the basis that the jury will not be persuaded that there was dishonesty in the required sense. And one must retain a sense of perspective. At the extremity of the application of legal rules there are sometimes results which may seem strange. A matter of judgment is then involved. The rule may have to be recast. Sir John Smith has eloquently argued that the rule in question ought to be recast. I am unpersuaded. If the law is restated by adopting a narrower definition of appropriation, the outcome is likely to place beyond the reach of the criminal law dishonest persons who should be found guilty of theft. The suggested revisions would unwarrantably restrict the scope of the law of theft and complicate the fair and effective prosecution of theft. In my view the law as settled in *Lawrence* and *Gomez* does not demand the suggested revision. Those decisions can be applied by judges and juries in a way which, absent human error, does not result in injustice.

Counsel for the appellant further pointed out that the law as stated in *Lawrence* [1972] AC 626 and *Gomez* [1993] AC 442 creates a tension between the civil and the criminal law. In other words, conduct which is not wrongful in a civil law sense may constitute the crime of theft. Undoubtedly, this is so. The question whether the civil claim to title by a convicted thief, who committed no civil wrong, may be defeated by the principle that nobody may benefit from his own civil or criminal wrong does not arise for decision. Nevertheless there is a more general point, namely that the interaction between criminal law and civil law can cause problems: compare J Beatson and A P Simester, "Stealing One's Own Property" (1999) 115 LQR 372. The purposes of the civil law and the criminal law are somewhat different. In theory the two systems should be in perfect harmony. In a practical world there will sometimes be some disharmony between the two systems. In any event, it would be wrong to assume on a priori grounds that the criminal law rather than the civil law is defective. Given the jury's conclusions, one is entitled to observe that the appellant's conduct should constitute theft, the only available charge. The tension between the civil and the criminal law is therefore not in my view a factor which justifies a departure from the law as stated in *Lawrence* and *Gomez*. Moreover, these decisions of the House have a marked beneficial consequence. While in some contexts of the law of theft a judge cannot avoid explaining civil law concepts to a jury (e.g. in respect of section 2(1)(a)), the decisions of the House of Lords eliminate the need for such explanations in respect of appropriation. That is a great advantage in an overly complex corner of the law.

Think about this question.

What reasons did Lord Steyn give for rejecting these arguments?

The decision in *R* v *Hinks* is very controversial. Sir John Smith reacted to the decision by saying that it 'is contrary to common sense. It is absurd that a person should be guilty of stealing property which is his and in which no one else has any legal interest whatsoever'.[21] Similarly, Beatson and Simester commented:[22]

> Property offences are designed to protect property rights. Unlike crimes such as assault, the rights being protected are necessarily rooted in the civil law. Remove dependence on the law of property, and property offences have no rationale. To hold otherwise is not merely to put the cart before the horse, but to motorise it

However, there were others who defended the decision. In the following extract Stephen Shute responds to the criticisms advanced by Beatson and Simester.

EXTRACT

Shute, S. (2002) 'Appropriation and the Law of Theft' *Criminal Law Review* 445

Beatson and Simester argue, in other words, that *Hinks* forces us to choose between abandoning a well-founded principle of civil law and divorcing property offences from their underlying rationale. Since each alternative is highly unattractive *Hinks* must, they conclude, have been wrongly decided. But, despite its ingenuity, this argument is mistaken. It is, as we have already seen, false to assume that, if the law allows a property offence to be committed without a property right having been infringed, then the link between property offences and property rights will necessarily have been broken. Beatson and Simester's error arises because they fail to see that even without breaching a recognised proprietary right the criminalised act may nonetheless have had a *tendency* to undermine property rights, either directly by attacking the interests that they protect, or indirectly by weakening an established system of property rights and so threatening the public good that that system represents. In either case the justification for criminalising the act may still be the protection of property rights, even though in this instance no property right has been violated.

For this reason there is no necessary threat to the underlying rationale of property offences if the law of theft is extended to cover otherwise unimpeachable transfers. Nor is there a threat to that rationale if a crime committed in these circumstances is able to "trump" the normal civil law rules thus rendering an otherwise valid transfer voidable. In fact, the law of property has long since acknowledged such a possibility. It does so by giving legal effect to the principle that "no-one may benefit from his own wrong". The principle is both limited in its application and relatively weak: first, it applies only where there has been a "wrong"; second, even where there has been a wrong, the principle is often redundant because the wrong itself will generate a cause of action that is, on its own, sufficient to strip the wrongdoer of his benefit; third, the principle is of limited weight and hence may easily be overridden or excluded by other considerations; fourth, even where operative, the principle usually works by estopping a wrongdoer from relying on the wrongful transaction

---

[21] Smith, J.C. (2001) 'Commentary on *R* v *Hinks*' *Criminal Law Review* 163, 164.

[22] Beatson, J. and Simester A.P. (1999) 'Stealing One's Own Property' 115 *Law Quarterly Review* 372.

rather than by creating a new cause of action in some other party; and, fifth, even when not outweighed, the principle need not require that the wrongdoer be stripped of all the benefits he obtained from his wrongdoing: a partial restitution may be all that is required to meet its demands. That said, however, the "no benefit principle" comes into its own when a criminal wrong has been committed which is not based on a civil law wrong. In these circumstances, driven by a criminal law wrong but not by a civil law wrong, the principle can result in a thief such as Hinks being stripped of (at least some of) the benefits obtained through her wrongdoing. When this happens the civil law is, in a sense, required to "yield" to the criminal law: if it had not been for the criminal wrong no restitution would have been possible. But this is not an indication of an unacceptable conflict between the civil and the criminal law. Nor is it an indication that there has been a "serious distortion" of the law of property. Rather, it is an indication that both the criminal law and the law of property have (wisely) chosen to give legal effect to an important moral proposition.

Now, think about these questions.

- According to Shute, what is the flaw in Beatson and Simester's argument?
- Why, in Shute's opinion, does *R* v *Hinks* not result in an 'unacceptable' conflict between the civil and criminal laws?

The next extract is taken from an essay that Simester co-authored with Sullivan a few years after Shute's article was published. In it, they again criticise the decision in *R* v *Hinks* and respond to the arguments advanced by Shute.

EXTRACT

Simester, A.P. and Sullivan, G.R. (2005) 'On the Nature and Rationale of Property Offences' in R.A. Duff and Stuart P. Green (eds) *Defining Crimes: Essays on the Special Part of the Criminal Law*. OUP: Oxford, pp.168–195

[In *Hinks*] the House of Lords was prepared to put the criminal law directly at odds with the civil law concerning the rules of ownership. D was convicted of stealing cheques and money from V. It was accepted that the property passed from V to D by way of gifts valid at civil law; so that, in civil law, D owned the money she stole. How, then, had she stolen it? Because, apparently, within the domain of criminal law, title to the money remained with V at the point of the theft. One may concede that, in the circumstances, it was dishonest of D to solicit and accept the gifts. (V was said to be a gullible man of somewhat limited intelligence.) Yet even if we acknowledge D's dishonesty, how, at one and the same time, could title to the money be vested in D under civil law yet remain with V for the purposes of the criminal law? One might defend this possibility by arguing that the policies and protected interests of the civil and criminal laws can diverge: the civil law may be concerned primarily with certainty and the security of transactions, whereas the criminal law may be more concerned with the protection of the vulnerable and the punishment of dishonesty. Hence, in the civil law, property could be vested in D while still belonging to V, for the purposes of the criminal law, in order to convict D of theft. *Hinks*, in effect, invents a new category of property that can be owned solely by one person at civil law and owned simultaneously by another person at criminal law. The criminal law property right will trump the civil law right, at least in criminal proceedings held to determine whether D stole from V when acquiring a valid title to the property.

The disruptive potential of this possibility may be illustrated by an example discussed in *Hinks* itself. Suppose D sells his roadside petrol station to V, without disclosing that planning permission has been granted for the building of a bypass road – which, when built, will divert most of the traffic. The contract would be valid under English law; there was no special relationship between the parties, no duress or undue influence, no misrepresentation. Yet a majority of the House of Lords was prepared to accept that, if dishonest, D could have stolen the consideration he receives.

The argument has so far been made that it is in the nature and rationale of the law of theft to protect the proprietary status quo, a status quo consisting of the proprietary rights recognised by civil law. *Hinks* turns this on its head, placing the criminal law in opposition to the civil law where acquisitions of property through indefeasible civil law transaction contravene community standards of honesty. While the academic response to *Hinks* has been predominantly hostile, the decision has its defenders. In the eyes of its supporters, its major merit is the very lack of subjugation of the criminal law to the civil law that has been argued for here. The decision has been perceived as a wedge whereby communitarian and public values of the criminal law (as assumed) can militate against the private and commercial concerns of the civil law. Which, of course, they can, in specified targeted contexts such as consumer protection legislation. But not by the law of theft. If the behaviour in *Hinks* was wrong, it was a wrong of exploitation. It was not the wrong of stealing.

For those who criticise the decision, one ground of complaint is the deployment of the concept of dishonesty to segregate non-criminal from criminal transactions. And it is, we think, undesirable for rule of law reasons that this amorphous and vague concept should bear very significant weight.

Now, consider these questions.

- Make a list of Simester et al.'s criticisms of the decision in *R* v *Hinks*.
- What reasons do Simester et al. give for rejecting the arguments of those who (like Shute) have defended the decision in *R* v *Hinks*?

In the final two sentences of this extract Simester and Sullivan highlight the important role that the concept of dishonesty now plays in the offence of theft. Since appropriation has been defined so broadly – reducing the *actus reus* of theft almost to vanishing point – in most theft cases the defendant's liability will hinge on whether or not he acted dishonestly. As we shall see shortly, however, many are concerned about giving the concept of dishonesty such a pivotal role.

Quiz 8.2

1. What is the rule still to be derived from the case of *R* v *Morris* [1984] AC 320?
   - **a.** That an appropriation has to be adverse to the interests of the owner.
   - **b.** That an appropriation of any of the rights of the owner of property amounts to an appropriation of that property.
   - **c.** That a shoplifter cannot be arrested before he leaves the shop.
   - **d.** That there must be a physical taking of property before it can be said to have been appropriated.

2. Which of the following propositions is **incorrect** following the decision in *DPP* v *Gomez*?
   - **a.** It is not necessary to prove that an appropriation occurred without the consent of the owner.
   - **b.** If the owner of property makes a valid gift of that property to D, D cannot be said to have appropriated it.
   - **c.** The decision in *Lawrence* v *MPC* remains good law.
   - **d.** It is not necessary to prove that the defendant assumed all the rights of the owner before s/he can be said to have appropriated property.

3. Which of the following is **not** a criticism of the case law on the meaning of appropriation?

a. It causes a conflict between the criminal law and the civil law.

b. There is no need to distinguish between a thief and a fraudster.

c. The definition of appropriation gives the *actus reus* of theft an extremely wide scope.

d. The offence of theft now applies to situations that would be better regarded as attempted crimes.

Mens rea of theft

8.3 Define the mens rea requirements for establishing criminal liability for theft.

1. The defendant had an intention to permanently deprive the other person of the property

We can now turn to the *mens rea* of theft. The first of the two *mens rea* requirements is that the defendant had an intention to permanently deprive the other person of the property. When applying this *mens rea* requirement to the facts of a problem question, remember the following points:

- It is a *mens rea* requirement, not an *actus reus* one. The question is whether the defendant intended to permanently deprive the other person of the property, not whether the other person was in fact permanently deprived of the property. This means that a defendant may satisfy this *mens rea* requirement even if the owner recovers the property.
- Intention here means direct or oblique intention (see Chapter 4).
- The test is whether the defendant intended to permanently deprive the other person of the property, not whether the defendant intended to gain personally. Section 1(2) states, 'It is immaterial whether the appropriation is made with a view to gain, or is made for the thief's own benefit'. So if Derek takes Rodney's lecture notes and throws them on a camp fire, Derek satisfies this *mens rea* requirement even though he made no personal gain. It is enough that he intended to permanently deprive Rodney of the lecture notes.
- The test is whether the defendant intended to permanently deprive the other person of the property, not whether the defendant intended to cause the other person permanent deprivation. Suppose Derek goes to his local supermarket to buy a tin of baked beans. When he picks them off the shelf he does not intend to cause the supermarket permanent deprivation since he intends to pay for the beans. But he does intend to permanently deprive the supermarket of the beans, since he intends to take them home and eat them. The fact that he intended to pay for them does not negate this part of the *mens rea*. It is taken into account when assessing whether the defendant acted dishonestly.
- The test is item specific: did the defendant intend to permanently deprive the other person of that specific item of property? If the defendant took an item, the fact that he intended to replace it with an equivalent item does not negate this part of the *mens rea*. Rather, it is taken into account when assessing whether the defendant acted dishonestly. This is illustrated by *R* v *Velumyl* [1989] Crim LR 299. The defendant borrowed over £1,000 from a safe at work. He did so without authority and in breach of company rules. He said that he had intended to return the same amount the following week. The Court of Appeal nonetheless held that he satisfied this *mens rea* requirement since

he did not intend to return the same notes and coins that he took. The fact that he intended to repay the money was relevant to dishonesty, but not to whether he intended to permanently deprive his employer of the money. The test is item specific. Another example would be if you drink a bottle of your housemate's milk, intending to buy him a replacement bottle later in the day.

Now, consider this question.

With these points in mind, decide whether Derek satisfies this part of the *mens rea* in each of the following three scenarios:

a. Derek is on a train journey with Rodney. Derek is bored, so to amuse himself he picks up Rodney's wallet and throws it out of the train window. Derek does not expect the wallet to ever be found, but to his astonishment Rodney gets it back a few days later after a dog-walker finds it and posts it to him.

b. Derek notices that Rodney rarely uses his iPod, so decides to sell it on eBay (figuring that Rodney will never even notice that it has gone). He places the item on eBay, but a few hours before the sale is due to close he changes his mind and withdraws the iPod from sale.

c. Derek borrows Rodney's van. He tells Rodney that he only needs to drive 'a few miles', but in fact he travels over one hundred miles in it. Before returning the keys to Rodney Derek goes to the petrol station and replaces the petrol he used.

Occasionally a defendant may have what is known as a conditional intention. In other words, he intends to permanently deprive the other person of an item only if some condition is satisfied (often the condition will be that the item turns out to be valuable!). In such cases it is especially important to take care when wording the particulars of the alleged offence. This is illustrated by *R* v *Easom* [1971] 2 QB 315. In this case the defendant, John Easom, picked up a handbag in a cinema, looked through it, decided that there was nothing worth stealing inside and put the handbag back. At trial he was convicted of theft of 'one handbag, one purse, one notebook, a quantity of tissues, a quantity of cosmetics and one pen'. On appeal the Court of Appeal quashed the conviction. At no point had Easom intended to permanently deprive the owner of her handbag. His plan had been to look through the handbag and put it back. Nor had Easom intended to permanently deprive the owner of a purse, or a notebook, or any of the other items listed. Whatever he had intended to take (presumably, money), he hadn't found. If the charge had been worded slightly differently, however, Easom's conviction would not have been quashed. It is sufficient for the offence of theft to establish a conditional intention, and when Easom first picked up the handbag he had a conditional intention to steal its contents (the condition being that the contents turned out to be desirable to him).[23] So if Easom had been charged with 'theft of the contents of the handbag' the conviction would have stood.

Now imagine a slightly different scenario. This time the defendant picks up a handbag intending to steal anything that he can find inside that is valuable. But it turns out that the handbag is empty. On these facts the defendant cannot be charged with theft of the contents of the handbag, since there were no contents inside for him to appropriate!

[23] The use of the term conditional intention in this context is not unproblematic: see Child, J. (2017) 'Understanding Ulterior Mens Rea Future Conduct Intention *Is* Conditional Intention' 76 *Cambridge Law Journal* 311.

Instead he would be guilty of attempted theft (we will study attempts and impossibility in Chapter 12).

So the test for this *mens rea* requirement is whether the defendant intended to permanently deprive the other person of the property. If the answer is yes, this requirement is satisfied. But if the answer is no, this is not the end of the matter. Section 6(1) states that, even if the defendant lacked such an intention, he will still satisfy this *mens rea* requirement in two situations:

EXTRACT

Section 6(1) of the Theft Act 1968

6 "With the intention of permanently depriving the other of it"

(1) A person appropriating property belonging to another without meaning the other permanently to lose the thing itself is nevertheless to be regarded as having the intention of permanently depriving the other of it if his intention is to treat the thing as his own to dispose of regardless of the other's rights; and a borrowing or lending of it may amount to so treating it if, but only if, the borrowing or lending is for a period and in circumstances making it equivalent to an outright taking or disposal.

The wording of section 6(1) is not terribly clear. In fact, John Spencer commented that it 'sprouts obscurities at every phrase'![24] Figure 8.1 sets out the structure of section 6(1).

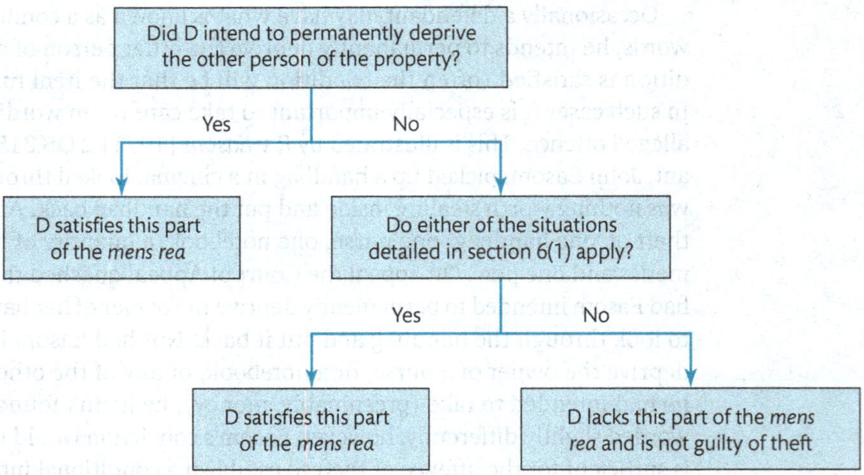

Figure 8.1 The structure of section 6(1)

The two situations which are described in section 6(1) are: the defendant intended to treat the thing as his own to dispose of regardless of the other's rights and the defendant intended to borrow the item, but the borrowing was equivalent to an outright taking or disposal. We will consider each in turn.

[24] Spencer, J. (1977) 'The Metamorphosis of Section 6 of the Theft Act' *Criminal Law Review* 653.

i. The defendant intended to treat the thing as his own to dispose of regardless of the other's rights

As a result of its unclear wording, there is some uncertainty over the breadth of the first limb of section 6(1). But before looking at this uncertainty, let's begin with some examples of when this limb would definitely apply.

The first example is set out in section 6(2), which states:

EXTRACT

Section 6(2) of the Theft Act 1968

(2) Without prejudice to the generality of subsection (1) above, where a person, having possession or control (lawfully or not) of property belonging to another, parts with the property under a condition as to its return which he may not be able to perform, this (if done for purposes of his own and without the other's authority) amounts to treating the property as his own to dispose of regardless of the other's rights.

Suppose Derek takes Rodney's expensive watch and pawns it for £500. Derek plans to use the money to buy some shares on the Stock Exchange. He is confident that in just one month he will make £1,000 profit, and plans to then buy the watch back and return it to Rodney. On these facts Derek does not intend to permanently deprive Rodney of the watch, and so we need to determine whether section 6(1) applies. Section 6(2) states that section 6(1) will apply if the defendant parts with property under a condition as to its return which he may not be able to perform. So, since there was no guarantee that Rodney's watch would still be available or that Derek would be able to make enough money to buy the watch back, he must be deemed to have had an intention to treat the watch as his own to dispose of regardless of Rodney's rights. Derek therefore satisfies this part of the *mens rea* of theft.

The second example is *R* v *Raphael* [2008] EWCA Crim 1014. The victim, Gbemi Adeosun, wanted to sell his car. Pretending to be interested in buying the car the defendant, Jermaine Raphael, arranged a meeting with Adeosun. At the meeting Adeosun was attacked and Raphael drove off in the car. He later phoned Adeosun and offered to sell the car back to him for £500. At trial Raphael was convicted of robbery. As we'll see later in the chapter, to establish robbery the prosecution must prove that there was a theft. Raphael appealed against his robbery conviction, arguing that there had been no theft since he had not intended to permanently deprive Adeosun of the car. The Court of Appeal rejected the appeal. The Court held that the case fell within the first limb of section 6(1):

> [47] The express language of s 6 specifies that the subjective element necessary to establish the mens rea for theft includes an intention on the part of the taker "to treat the thing as his own to dispose of regardless of the other's rights". In our judgment it is hard to find a better example of such an intention than an offer, not to return Adeosun's car to him in exactly the same condition it was when it was removed from his possession and control, but to sell his own property back to him,

and to make its return subject to a condition or conditions inconsistent with his right to possession of his own property

So pawning an item and demanding a ransom for the return of an item both fall within the first limb of section 6(1).[25] The judgment in *R* v *Fernandes* [1996] 1 Cr App R 175 suggests that other situations may also fall within the first limb of section 6(1). The defendant, Roland Fernandes, was a solicitor. He was experiencing severe financial difficulties, so he took £20,000 out of the bank account which contained his clients' money and invested it in a firm of licensed backstreet money-lenders. He intended to return the money, but before he could do so it disappeared. At his trial the judge directed the jury to consider whether the first limb of section 6(1) applied. The jury found Fernandes guilty of the theft of his clients' money. Fernandes appealed, arguing that section 6(1) did not apply to the facts of the case and that the trial judge should not have mentioned it to the jury. This was rejected by the Court of Appeal. Auld LJ stated:

> We consider that section 6 may apply to a person in possession or control of another's property who, dishonestly and for his own purpose, deals with that property in such a manner that he knows he is risking its loss.
>
> In the circumstances alleged here, an alleged dishonest disposal of someone else's money on an obviously insecure investment, we consider that the judge was justified in referring to section 6.

So, according to *R* v *Fernandes*, the first limb of section 6(1) is not limited to situations where an item has been pawned or a ransom demanded for an item's return.[26] Its scope is broader than this.

The breadth of section 6(1) was also considered in *R* v *Mitchell* [2008] EWCA Crim 850. This case involved a carjacking. The defendant, Walter Mitchell, was one of five men in a car being chased by police. Mitchell's car, a Subaru, crashed. The men got out of the crashed car and went to a BMW that was parked nearby. The victim, Mrs Davis, was sitting in the BMW talking on her phone. The men used metal bars to smash the car windows, then dragged Mrs Davis out of the car and drove off in it. A couple of hours later the BMW was discovered a few miles away with the engine running, doors open and hazard lights flashing. The men had abandoned the BMW and taken another car. At trial Mitchell was convicted of robbery of the BMW. As we noted earlier, to establish robbery it is necessary to first prove that there was a theft. Mitchell appealed against his robbery conviction, arguing that he had not stolen the

[25] *R* v *Raphael* may be contrasted with *R* v *Waters* [2015] EWCA Crim 402, in which the defendants (Sian Waters and Kareem Wasiu) took a mobile phone from the alleged victims (Saskia Voigt and Rhys Faoud) and said they would only return it if the victims first persuaded another person (Dale Holloway) to come and speak to them. At trial the defendants were convicted of robbery. On appeal, Jackson LJ stated that '... if the condition attached to the return of the item ... can readily be fulfilled and may be fulfilled in the near future, the jury may well conclude that intention to deprive has not been made out' ([18]). Since the jury might have thought Dale Holloway could be found in the near future, and therefore it was likely that the phone would be rapidly returned to its owner, the convictions were quashed.

[26] In *DPP* v *SJ* [2002] EWHC 291 (Admin) the High Court held that a defendant who snatched the victim's headphones from him, snapped them and then gave them back fell within the first limb of section 6(1), citing *R* v *Fernandes* in support of this conclusion.

BMW since he had not had an intention to permanently deprive Mrs Davis of the BMW. The issue for the Court of Appeal was whether the case fell within the first limb of section 6(1).

EXTRACT

Read the following extract from the judgment of Rix LJ.

Did Mitchell's case fall within section 6(1)? Why/why not?

R v *Mitchell* [2008] EWCA Crim 850

Rix LJ

[28] In our judgment the facts of this case simply do not support a case to go before a jury of theft and therefore robbery of the BMW. The BMW was plainly taken for the purposes of a getaway. There was nothing about its use or subsequent abandonment to suggest otherwise. Indeed, its brief use and subsequent abandonment show very clearly what was the obvious *prima facie* inference to be drawn from its taking which was that the occupants of the Subaru needed another conveyance that evening. We therefore consider that the judge erred in being beguiled by s 6 into leaving this count of robbery to the jury.

[29] [... T]he purpose of s 6 is not greatly to widen the requirement of s 1's intention permanently to deprive. A slightly broader definition of that intention is there provided in order to deal with a small number of difficult cases which had either arisen in the past under the common law or might arise in the future where, although it might be hard to put the matter strictly in terms of an intention permanently to deprive, in the sense of meaning the owner permanently to lose the thing itself, nevertheless something equivalent to that could be obtained through the intention to treat the thing as his own to dispose of, regardless of the other's rights, remembering Professor Smith's Oxford English dictionary use of the words "to dispose of". Thus, the newspaper taken but only returned on the next day when it is out of date, or a ticket which had been used, or a cheque which is paid, or something which has been substantially used up or destroyed, or something which would only be returned to its owner subject to a condition, all these are the sorts of examples to be found in the jurisprudence which discusses s 6. All of these cases are of ready equivalence to an intention permanently to deprive. None of them go any way towards extending the scope of s 6 to a case, however violent, of the taking of a car for the purposes of its brief use before being abandoned with its lights on. It must be remembered of course that a car with its licence plates on, left on the road, is utterly unlike a bundle of newspapers which have disappeared from a newsagents shop to a place where they would not be found.

So while Mitchell may have intended the treat the BMW as his own, he did not intend to treat the BMW as his own *to dispose of*.[27] The car was only driven a short distance, and

[27] Note that section 12 of the Theft Act 1968 creates an offence of taking a motor vehicle without authority, which is designed for situations like joyriding where the perpetrators lack an intention to permanently deprive the owner of the car.

when Mitchell abandoned it he did nothing to prevent it being returned to its owner (e.g. he did not hide the car or remove the number plates).[28]

Given the reasoning in *R* v *Mitchell*, the broad interpretation of section 6(1) in *DPP* v *Lavender* [1994] Crim LR 297 must now be doubted. Melvyn Lavender took two doors from one council property and used them to replace damaged doors at another council property. The High Court held that he had stolen the two doors. The Court said that the case fell within the first limb of section 6(1) since Lavender had shown an intention to treat the doors as his own. It is impossible to reconcile this with the Court of Appeal's insistence in *R* v *Mitchell* that section 6(1) should only apply in situations which are equivalent to the owner permanently losing the property. The council did not lose the two doors in *DPP* v *Lavender* – the doors were simply moved from one council property to another!

ii. The defendant intended to borrow the item, but the borrowing was equivalent to an outright taking or disposal

The second situation in section 6(1) is where the defendant intended to borrow the item and the borrowing was equivalent to an outright taking or disposal.

The leading case is *R* v *Lloyd* [1985] QB 829. The defendant, Sidney Lloyd, worked as chief projectionist in a cinema. For a number of months Lloyd secretly removed films from the cinema and, with the help of two co-conspirators, made large numbers of pirate copies. The process was rapid, so that the films were never out of the cinema for more than a few hours. Lloyd and his co-conspirators then sold the pirate copies. At trial Lloyd was convicted of conspiracy to steal. Lloyd appealed against his conviction, arguing that the case did not involve theft since he only borrowed the films from the cinema. The issue for the Court of Appeal was whether the case fell within the second limb of section 6(1).

EXTRACT

Read the following extract from the judgment of Lord Lane CJ.

What test does he set out for whether a borrowing falls within the second limb of section 6(1)?

Did Lloyd's actions fall within the second limb of section 6(1)? Why/why not?

Lord Lane CJ gives two examples of situations which would fall within the second limb of section 6(1). What are these?

---

[28] See also *R* v *Vinall* [2011] EWCA Crim 2652, in which the defendants attacked the victim and took his bike. The bike was later found abandoned at a bus stop half a mile away. The Court of Appeal emphasised that the *actus reus* and *mens rea* must coincide in time. On the facts, the case against the defendant could be constructed in one of two ways: the defendants could have been said to have appropriated the bike either when they took it or when they abandoned it. If the alleged theft occurred when the bike was abandoned, the defendants must be shown to have had the necessary intention at this moment. If the alleged theft occurred when the bike was taken, the fact that the defendants later abandoned the bike may be used *as evidence* to prove that they intended to treat the bike as their own to dispose of at the moment they took it. Since the defendants in this case had been charged with robbery, it was important to identify the precise moment at which the alleged theft occurred in order to decide whether force was used before or at the time of the theft (see the discussion of robbery below).

R v Lloyd [1985] QB 829

Lord Lane CJ

Borrowing is ex hypothesi not something which is done with an intention permanently to deprive. This half of the subsection, we believe, is intended to make it clear that a mere borrowing is never enough to constitute the necessary guilty mind unless the intention is to return the "thing" in such a changed state that it can truly be said that all its goodness or virtue has gone: for example *Reg. v. Beecham* (1851) 5 Cox C.C. 181, where the defendant stole railway tickets intending that they should be returned to the railway company in the usual way only after the journeys had been completed. He was convicted of larceny. The judge in the present case gave another example, namely, the taking of a torch battery with the intention of returning it only when its power is exhausted.

That being the case, we turn to inquire whether the feature films in this case can fall within that category. Our view is that they cannot. The goodness, the virtue, the practical value of the films to the owners has not gone out of the article. The film could still be projected to paying audiences, and, had everything gone according to the conspirators' plans, would have been projected in the ordinary way to audiences at the Odeon Cinema, Barking, who would have paid for their seats. Our view is that those particular films which were the subject of this alleged conspiracy had not themselves diminished in value at all. What had happened was that the borrowed film had been used or was going to be used to perpetrate a copyright swindle on the owners whereby their commercial interests were grossly and adversely affected in the way that we have endeavoured to describe at the outset of this judgment. That borrowing, it seems to us, was not for a period, or in such circumstances, as made it equivalent to an outright taking or disposal. There was still virtue in the film.

Think about this question.

In *R* v *Mitchell* Rix LJ stated that a defendant who borrows a newspaper and then returns it the following day when it is out of date falls within section 6(1) ([29]). Do you agree?

There is one issue regarding the *R* v *Lloyd* test that is unclear. Suppose that the owner of the property had the item for a specific purpose. When deciding whether all the goodness or virtue has gone from the item, may the jury take this purpose into account? For example, if the defendant takes someone's wedding dress the day before the wedding and then returns it the day after, has all the goodness or virtue gone from the dress?[29]

Now, think back to Oxford* v *Moss (the case involving the student who read his exam paper before the exam).

Imagine that you were the prosecutor in the case and that, instead of charging Moss with theft of confidential information (which, as we saw earlier, is not property), you charged him with theft of the exam paper.

- Using section 6(1), can you construct an argument that he should be convicted?

  Now imagine that you are Moss' defence counsel.

- How would you argue that Moss should be acquitted of the charge of theft of the exam paper?

---

[29] Herring, J. (2016) *Criminal Law: Text, Cases, and Materials* (7th edn). OUP: Oxford, p.516.

5. The defendant acted dishonestly

The second *mens rea* requirement is dishonesty. A partial definition of dishonesty can be found in section 2. It is a partial definition because it does not tell us what dishonesty *is*. Rather, it lists three mind-sets which are *not* dishonest. These three beliefs are listed in subsection (1):

EXTRACT

Section 2 of the Theft Act 1968

2 "Dishonestly"

(1) A person's appropriation of property belonging to another is not to be regarded as dishonest-

(a) if he appropriates the property in the belief that he has in law the right to deprive the other of it, on behalf of himself or of a third person; or

(b) if he appropriates the property in the belief that he would have the other's consent if the other knew of the appropriation and the circumstances of it; or

(c) (except where the property came to him as trustee or personal representative) if he appropriates the property in the belief that the person to whom the property belongs cannot be discovered by taking reasonable steps.

(2) A person's appropriation of property belonging to another may be dishonest notwithstanding that he is willing to pay for the property

When answering a problem question you should begin with section 2. If the defendant held one of the three beliefs listed in section 2(1) he was not dishonest and is not guilty of theft. The three beliefs are: D believed he had a legal (not merely a moral) right to the property (paragraph (a))[30]; D believed the owner of the property would have consented to the appropriation, had they known about it (paragraph (b)); and, D believed the owner of the property could not be discovered taking reasonable steps (paragraph (c)).

If section 2 does not apply then you need to apply the objective standards of ordinary decent people to determine whether or not the defendant was dishonest.[31] We will look at this test in a moment. But first, notice two other points about section 2:

- When applying section 2(1), the question is whether the defendant genuinely held the belief, not whether the belief was a reasonable one. If the belief was genuine section 2(1) applies even if the belief was unreasonable.
- Section 2(2) states that a defendant may be found to have acted dishonestly even if he was willing to pay for the property. Suppose that Derek owns a signed photo of John Lennon. Aubrey wants to buy it from Derek, but Derek refuses to sell. Aubrey knows that it is worth £500. One day, when Aubrey is at Derek's flat having dinner, Aubrey sneaks into Derek's bedroom and finds the photo. He pockets the photo and replaces it with a cheque for £500. Section 2(2) makes it clear that Aubrey could be found to have acted dishonestly even though he was willing to pay for the photo.

[30] An example is *R* v *Mahmud* [2024] EWCA Crim 130, in which D took a mobile phone from V because he genuinely believed the phone belonged to him (in fact, it did not).

[31] See *Ivey* v *Genting Casinos* [2017] UKSC 67, which we examine further ahead.

ACTIVITY

The defendant in each of the following three scenarios is not dishonest under section 2(1). One defendant falls under section 2(1)(a), one falls under section 2(1)(b) and the other falls under section 2(1)(c). Match the defendants to the correct subsection:

- Derek finds a £20 note on the floor in the middle of the market. He looks around to see if anyone is searching for it, but no one is. Concluding that it will be impossible to discover the owner he decides to keep it for himself.
- Mike works in a fast-food restaurant. Every now and then during the day he helps himself to some chips from the fryer. Mike's understanding is that employees are entitled to do this, but in fact they are not.
- When Rodney goes to the kitchen to have his breakfast he finds that there is no milk for his cereal and cup of tea. Rather than go to the shop, he helps himself to some of Albert's milk thinking that Albert will not mind.

Quiz 8.3

1. Which of the following statements about 'the intention to permanently deprive the other person of the property' requirement is **inaccurate**?
   a. The defendant must have intended to cause the other person permanent deprivation.
   b. The defendant need not have intended to make any personal gain.
   c. It does not matter whether or not the person was in fact permanently deprived of the property.
   d. The test is whether the defendant intended to permanently deprive the other person of that specific item of property.
2. According to *R* v *Lloyd*, when will an intended borrowing be deemed equivalent to an outright taking or disposal?
   a. When the defendant never actually intends to return the item at all.
   b. When the returned item has suffered a reduction in its financial value.
   c. When the intention is to return the item in such a changed state that all its goodness or virtue is gone.
   d. When the defendant intends to keep the item and replace it with an equivalent item.
3. Section 2 of the Theft Act 1968 sets out three mindsets that are not dishonest. Which of the following is **not** one of the mindsets listed in section 2?
   a. D believed the owner of the property could not be discovered by taking reasonable steps.
   b. D believed the owner of the property would have consented to the appropriation, had she known about it.
   c. D believed he had a legal right to deprive the other person of the property.
   d. D believed that the appropriation of the property was morally justified.

Dishonesty within the law of theft

8.4 Evaluate the case law on dishonesty within the law of theft.

If section 2 does not apply, the jury must apply the common law test for dishonesty instead. From 1982 until 2017, the test that was used was the one from *R* v *Ghosh* [1982] QB 1053. The following extract, from the judgment of Lord Lane CJ, explains the thinking that lay behind the *R* v *Ghosh* test.

EXTRACT

Lord Lane CJ began by rejecting a 'purely objective' test for dishonesty. What reasons did he give for rejecting such a test? What example did he use to illustrate the problems with a purely objective test?

Lord Lane CJ then rejected one type of subjective test for dishonesty. What reasons did he give for this? What examples did he use to illustrate the problems with such a test? Having rejected these two alternatives, Lord Lane CJ then set out the *R* v *Ghosh* test. What was this test?

R v *Ghosh* [1982] QB 1053

Lord Lane CJ

This brings us to the heart of the problem. Is "dishonestly" in section 1 of the Theft Act 1968 intended to characterise a course of conduct? Or is it intended to describe a state of mind? If the former, then we can well understand that it could be established independently of the knowledge or belief of the accused. But if, as we think, it is the latter, then the knowledge and belief of the accused are at the root of the problem.

Take for example a man who comes from a country where public transport is free. On his first day here he travels on a bus. He gets off without paying. He never had any intention of paying. His mind is clearly honest; but his conduct, judged objectively by what he has done, is dishonest. It seems to us that in using the word "dishonestly" in the Theft Act 1968, Parliament cannot have intended to catch dishonest conduct in that sense, that is to say conduct to which no moral obloquy could possibly attach. This is sufficiently established by the partial definition in section 2 of the Theft Act itself. All the matters covered by section 2 (1) relate to the belief of the accused. Section 2 (2) relates to his willingness to pay. A man's belief and his willingness to pay are things which can only be established subjectively. It is difficult to see how a partially subjective definition can be made to work in harness with the test which in all other respects is wholly objective.

If we are right that dishonesty is something in the mind of the accused (what Professor Glanville Williams calls "a special mental state"), then if the mind of the accused is honest, it cannot be deemed dishonest merely because members of the jury would have regarded it as dishonest to embark on that course of conduct.

So we would reject the simple uncomplicated approach that the test is purely objective, however attractive from the practical point of view that solution may be.

There remains the objection that to adopt a subjective test is to abandon all standards but that of the accused himself, and to bring about a state of affairs in which "Robin Hood would be no robber": *Reg. v. Greenstein* [1975] 1 W.L.R. 1353. This objection misunderstands the nature of the subjective test. It is no defence for a man to say "I knew that what I was doing is generally regarded as dishonest; but I do not regard it as dishonest myself. Therefore I am not guilty." What he is however entitled to say is" I did not know that anybody would regard what I was doing as dishonest." He may not be believed; just as he may not be believed if he sets up "a claim of right" under section 2 (1) of the Theft Act 1968, or asserts that he believed in the truth of a misrepresentation under section 15 of the Act of 1968. But if he is believed, or raises a real doubt about the matter, the jury cannot be sure that he was dishonest.

In determining whether the prosecution has proved that the defendant was acting dishonestly, a jury must first of all decide whether according to the ordinary standards of reasonable and honest people what was done was dishonest. If it was not dishonest by those standards, that is the end of the matter and the prosecution fails.

If it was dishonest by those standards, then the jury must consider whether the defendant himself must have realised that what he was doing was by those standards dishonest. In most cases, where the actions are obviously dishonest by ordinary standards, there will be no doubt about it. It will be obvious that the defendant himself knew that he was acting dishonestly. It is dishonest for a defendant to act in a way which he knows ordinary people consider to be dishonest, even if he asserts or genuinely believes that he is morally justified in acting as he did. For example, Robin Hood or those ardent anti-vivisectionists who remove animals from vivisection laboratories are acting dishonestly, even though they may consider themselves to be morally justified in doing what they do, because they know that ordinary people would consider these actions to be dishonest.

So the *R* v *Ghosh* test had two stages. First, having regard to the defendant's conduct and his state of mind, was he dishonest according to the standards of reasonable and honest people? If so, did he realise that what he was doing was dishonest by those standards?

The *R* v *Ghosh* test was heavily criticised, for a number of reasons. John Spencer argued that the test was too convoluted: a claim encapsulated by the title of his commentary, 'What the Jury Thinks the Defendant Thought the Jury Would Have Thought'. He also argued that the effect of the *R* v *Ghosh* test was to allow defendants to set standards of behaviour.

EXTRACT

Spencer, J. 'Dishonesty: What the Jury Thinks the Defendant Thought the Jury Would Have Thought' (1982) 41 *Cambridge Law Journal* 222

In other words, the jury must first decide what they think of the defendant's behaviour, and then decide what the defendant would have thought the jury would think of it, had the matter crossed his mind. Clearly, intelligence tests for juries will soon be needed.

At the root of all this confusion is a failure to recognise an elementary fact: that the concept of dishonesty involves not one question, but two. First, there is the question what the accused thought and intended. Did he really intend to repay the money? Did he really believe that a cheque was coming from Canada to enable him to do so? This is a question of primary fact, properly within the province of the jury, and to this extent dishonesty is obviously a question of the defendant's state of mind. Secondly, there is an evaluative question: given that he so thought and intended, was it honest to do as he did? Here, by contrast, dishonesty is a qualification of the defendant's conduct. This question, surely, must be for the court to decide, applying its own and not the defendant's standards. Such evaluative questions are in essence questions of law, for all we call them questions of 'secondary fact' when, as here, juries are made to answer them. It is a case of setting standards of behaviour, and we cannot possibly allow the defendant to set his own, even to the attenuated extent the Court of Appeal in *Ghosh* allows. By letting him say 'I'm sorry, I thought society tolerated till-dipping, or cheating bookmakers, or fiddling the N.H.S.,' we are letting him advance what is in effect a mistake of law as a defence. For the courts to take their criminal law from the man on the Clapham omnibus is one thing; to take it from the man accused of stealing it is quite another.

Think about these questions.

- Spencer drew a distinction between two types of question. What was this distinction?
- Why did Spencer argue that it was inappropriate to answer the second type of question by reference to what the defendant believed?

Suppose, for example, that at the first stage of the *R* v *Ghosh* test a jury decided that there were three different views of what honesty required in a given situation, all of which are commonly held by ordinary and honest members of society (views X, Y and Z). It followed that, at the second stage, a defendant might claim that he was aware of view X, but not views Y and Z.[32] Perhaps the defendant believed so strongly that his own view (view X) was correct that he was oblivious to the fact that other members of society hold different views. It followed that, contrary to the assertion of Lord Lane CJ, the *R* v *Ghosh* test could have resulted in Robin Hood being found to have not acted dishonestly. As Edward Griew argued:

> A person may defend his attack on another's property by reference to a moral or political conviction so passionately held that he believed (so he claims) that 'ordinary' decent members of society would regard his conduct as proper, even laudable. If the asserted belief is treated as a claim to have been ignorant that the conduct was 'dishonest' by ordinary standards (and it has been assumed that it might be so treated), and if the jury think (as exceptionally they might) that the belief may have been held, *Ghosh* produces an acquittal. The result is remarkable. Robin Hood must be a thief even if he thinks the whole of the right-thinking world is on his side.[33]

The decision in *R* v *Ghosh* also meant that there were different legal tests for dishonesty in civil and criminal law. In the civil law, the test is whether the defendant's conduct is dishonest according to the standards of ordinary, decent people.[34] There is no requirement that the defendant realised that his conduct was dishonest according to those standards. In *Ivey* v *Genting Casinos* [2017] UKSC 67 the Supreme Court queried why the word 'dishonesty' should mean different things in different types of legal proceedings:

> 63 ... [T]here can be no logical or principled basis for the meaning of dishonesty (as distinct from the standards of proof by which it must be established) to differ according to whether it arises in a civil action or a criminal prosecution. Dishonesty is a simple, if occasionally imprecise, English word. It would be an affront to the law if its meaning differed according to the kind of proceedings in which it arose. It is easy enough to envisage cases where precisely the same behaviour, by the same person, falls to be examined in both kinds of proceeding.

The Supreme Court's judgment in this case therefore considered whether *R* v *Ghosh* should be overruled.[35] The claimant, Phil Ivey, was a professional gambler. He won £7.7m at Crockfords Club casino playing the card game Punto Banco. Ivey used a technique called edge-sorting, which involves identifying tiny differences in the patterns on the back of playing cards to increase the chances of winning. To enable him to deploy this technique, Ivey had deceived the croupier into rotating playing cards of a certain value before putting them back into the dealing shoe, so that he could identify them the next time they were dealt. After reviewing the CCTV footage, Crockfords refused to pay the winnings. Ivey sued. It was accepted that Ivey genuinely believed that what he had done was not cheating but 'legitimate gamesmanship'. The case reached the Supreme Court. One of the issues the Court addressed was whether Ivey had acted dishonestly.

---

32 Halpin, A. (1996) 'The Test for Dishonesty' *Criminal Law Review* 283.

33 Griew, E. (1985) 'Dishonesty: The Objections to *Feely* and *Ghosh*', *Criminal Law Review* 341.

34 See the judgments of Lord Nicholls in *Royal Brunei Airlines Sdn Bhd* v *Tan* [1995] 2 AC 378 and Lord Hoffmann in *Barlow Clowes International Ltd* v *Eurotrust International Ltd* [2005] UKPC 37.

35 Although technically the discussion of the *R* v *Ghosh* test in *Ivey* was *obiter*, it is clear that the Supreme Court intended for its judgment to be binding. This view of *Ivey* was confirmed in *DPP* v *Patterson* [2017] EWHC 2820 (Admin) and *R* v *Barton* [2020] EWCA Crim 575.

EXTRACT

In *R* v *Ghosh* Lord Lane CJ said that Robin Hood and anti-vivisectionists would be found to be dishonest using the *R* v *Ghosh* test. In the following extract, does Lord Hughes agree? Why/why not?

Lord Hughes also cites *R* v *Gilks*, a case in which a man was given £100 too much by a bookmaker. He realised the mistake but kept the money anyway, saying that it would be wrong to keep an overpayment from a grocery store but bookmakers are 'fair game'. Lord Hughes states that a person like Gilks would not have been found to have been dishonest using the *R* v *Ghosh* test. Why? And why does Lord Hughes describe such an outcome as problematic?

What does Lord Hughes say is the correct test for dishonesty? According to Lord Hughes, will this test result in the man who travels or a bus without realising that he is meant to pay (because he is from a country where public transport is free) being held to be dishonest? Why/why not?

Ivey v *Genting Casinos* [2017] UKSC 67

Lord Hughes

53. [D]ishonesty is itself primarily a jury concept, characterised by recognition rather than by definition. Most of the Theft Act 1968 offences required dishonesty without any elaboration of its meaning: section 15 (dishonestly obtaining property by deception) was a prime example and the Fraud Act 2006, which replaces this and other Theft Act offences, adopts the same form. There are in section 2 of the Theft Act 1968 limited rules relating to when appropriation is *not* to be regarded as dishonest (claim of right, belief in consent of owner, belief that owner cannot be found) and a specific provision that it may be dishonest despite a willingness to pay for the goods, but these were designed to reflect existing rules of law, they apply only to appropriation, and they do not alter the underlying principle that dishonesty is not defined. This reflects the view of the Criminal Law Revision Committee that dishonesty was a matter to be left to a jury; it said at para 39 that 'Dishonesty is something which laymen can easily recognise when they see it'. That is not to suggest that there is not room for debate at the fringes whether particular conduct is dishonest or not, but the perils of advance definition would no doubt have been greater than those associated with leaving the matter to the jury. Over the succeeding half century, whilst there have undoubtedly (and inevitably) been examples of uncertainty or debate in identifying whether some conduct is dishonest or not, juries appear generally to have coped well with applying an uncomplicated lay objective standard of honesty to activities as disparate as sophisticated banking practices (for example *R* v *Hayes* [2015] EWCA Crim 1944) and the removal of golf balls at night from the bottom of a lake on a private golf course (*R* v *Rostron* [2003] EWCA Crim 2206).

54. A significant refinement to the test for dishonesty was introduced by *R* v *Ghosh* [1982] QB 1053. Since then, in criminal cases, the judge has been required to direct the jury, if the point arises, to apply a two-stage test. Firstly, it must ask whether in its judgment the conduct complained of was dishonest by the lay objective standards of ordinary reasonable and honest people. If the answer is no, that disposes of the case in favour of the defendant. But if the answer is yes, it must ask, secondly, whether the defendant must have realised that ordinary honest people would so regard his behaviour, and he is to be convicted only if the answer to that second question is yes.

[...]

57. Thirty years on, however, it can be seen that there are a number of serious problems about the second leg of the rule adopted in *Ghosh*.

1. It has the unintended effect that the more warped the defendant's standards of honesty are, the less likely it is that he will be convicted of dishonest behaviour.
2. It was based on the premise that it was necessary in order to give proper effect to the principle that dishonesty, and especially criminal responsibility for it, must depend on the actual state of mind of the defendant, whereas the rule is not necessary to preserve this principle.
3. It sets a test which jurors and others often find puzzling and difficult to apply.
4. It has led to an unprincipled divergence between the test for dishonesty in criminal proceedings and the test of the same concept when it arises in the context of a civil action.
5. It represented a significant departure from the pre-Theft Act 1968 law, when there is no indication that such a change had been intended.
6. Moreover, it was not compelled by authority. Although the pre-*Ghosh* cases were in a state of some entanglement, the better view is that the preponderance of authority favoured the simpler rule that, once the defendant's state of knowledge and belief has been established, whether that state of mind was dishonest or not is to be determined by the application of the standards of the ordinary honest person, represented in a criminal case by the collective judgment of jurors or magistrates.

58. The principal objection to the second leg of the *Ghosh* test is that the less the defendant's standards conform to what society in general expects, the less likely he is to be held criminally responsible for his behaviour. It is true that *Ghosh* attempted to reconcile what it regarded as the dichotomy between a 'subjective' and an 'objective' approach by a mixed test. The court addressed the present objection in this way, at p 1064:

> 'There remains the objection that to adopt a subjective test is to abandon all standards but that of the accused himself, and to bring about a state of affairs in which "Robin Hood would be no robber": *R* v *Greenstein* [1975] 1 WLR 1353. This objection misunderstands the nature of the subjective test. It is no defence for a man to say "I knew that what I was doing is generally regarded as dishonest; but I do not regard it as dishonest myself. Therefore I am not guilty". What he is however entitled to say is "I did not know that anybody would regard what I was doing as dishonest". He may not be believed; just as he may not be believed if he sets up "a claim of right" under section 2(1) of the Theft Act 1968, or asserts that he believed in the truth of a misrepresentation under section 15 of the Act of 1968. But if he is believed, or raises a real doubt about the matter, the jury cannot be sure that he was dishonest.'

And a little later the court added that upon the test which it was setting:

> 'In most cases, where the actions are obviously dishonest by ordinary standards, there will be no doubt about it. It will be obvious that the defendant himself knew that he was acting dishonestly. It is dishonest for a defendant to act in a way which he knows ordinary people consider to be dishonest, even if he asserts or genuinely believes that he is morally justified in acting as he did. For example, Robin Hood or those ardent anti-vivisectionists who remove animals from vivisection laboratories are acting dishonestly, even though they may consider themselves to be morally justified in doing what they do, because they know that ordinary people would consider these actions to be dishonest.'

59. Even if this were correct, it would still mean that the defendant who thinks that stealing from a bookmaker is not dishonest (as in *R* v *Gilks* [1972] 1 WLR 1341 – see para 73 below) is entitled to be acquitted. It is no answer to say that he will be convicted if he realised that ordinary honest people would think that stealing from a bookmaker is dishonest, for by definition he does not realise this. Moreover, the court's proposition was not correct, because it is not in the

least unusual for the accused not to share the standards which ordinary honest people set for society as a whole. The acquisitive offender may, it is true, be the cheerful character who frankly acknowledges that he is a crook, but very often he is not, but, rather, justifies his behaviour to himself. Just as convincing himself is frequently the stock in trade of the confidence trickster, so the capacity of all of us to persuade ourselves that what we do is excusable knows few bounds. It cannot by any means be assumed that the appropriators of animals from laboratories, to whom the court referred in *Ghosh*, know that ordinary people would consider their actions to be dishonest; it is just as likely that they are so convinced, however perversely, of the justification for what they do that they persuade themselves that no one could call it dishonest. There is no reason why the law should excuse those who make a mistake about what contemporary standards of honesty are, whether in the context of insurance claims, high finance, market manipulation or tax evasion. The law does not, in principle, excuse those whose standards are criminal by the benchmarks set by society, nor ought it to do so. On the contrary, it is an important, even crucial, function of the criminal law to determine what is criminal and what is not; its purpose is to set the standards of behaviour which are acceptable. As it was put in *Smith's Law of Theft* 9th ed (2007), para 2.296: '... the second limb allows the accused to escape liability where he has made a mistake of fact as to the contemporary standards of honesty. But why should that be an excuse?'

60. It is plain that in *Ghosh* the court concluded that its compromise second leg test was necessary in order to preserve the principle that criminal responsibility for dishonesty must depend on the actual state of mind of the defendant. It asked the question whether 'dishonestly', where that word appears in the Theft Act, was intended to characterise a course of conduct or to describe a state of mind. The court gave the following example, at p 1063, which was clearly central to its reasoning:

> 'Take for example a man who comes from a country where public transport is free. On his first day here he travels on a bus. He gets off without paying. He never had any intention of paying. His mind is clearly honest; but his conduct, judged objecttively by what he has done, is dishonest. It seems to us that in using the word 'dishonestly' in the Theft Act 1968, Parliament cannot have intended to catch dishonest conduct in that sense, that is to say conduct to which no moral obloquy could possibly attach.'

But the man in this example would inevitably escape conviction by the application of the (objective) first leg of the *Ghosh* test. That is because, in order to determine the honesty or otherwise of a person's conduct, one must ask what he knew or believed about the facts affecting the area of activity in which he was engaging. In order to decide whether this visitor was dishonest by the standards of ordinary people, it would be necessary to establish his own actual state of knowledge of how public transport works. Because he genuinely believes that public transport is free, there is nothing objectively dishonest about his not paying on the bus. The same would be true of a child who did not know the rules, or of a person who had innocently misread the bus pass sent to him and did not realise that it did not operate until after 10.00 in the morning. The answer to the court's question is that 'dishonestly', where it appears, is indeed intended to characterise what the defendant did, but in characterising it one must first ascertain his actual state of mind as to the facts in which he did it. It was not correct to postulate that the conventional objective test of dishonesty involves judging only the actions and not the state of knowledge or belief as to the facts in which they were performed. What is objectively judged is the standard of behaviour, given any known actual state of mind of the actor as to the facts.

[...]

74. These several considerations provide convincing grounds for holding that the second leg of the test propounded in *Ghosh* does not correctly represent the law and that directions based upon it ought no longer to be given. The test of dishonesty is as set out by Lord Nicholls in *Royal Brunei Airlines Sdn Bhd* v *Tan* and by Lord Hoffmann in *Barlow Clowes* [...]

When dishonesty is in question the fact-finding tribunal must first ascertain (subjectively) the actual state of the individual's knowledge or belief as to the facts. The reasonableness or otherwise of his belief is a matter of evidence (often in practice determinative) going to whether he held the belief, but it is not an additional requirement that his belief must be reasonable; the question is whether it is genuinely held. When once his actual state of mind as to knowledge or belief as to facts is established, the question whether his conduct was honest or dishonest is to be determined by the fact-finder by applying the (objective) standards of ordinary decent people. There is no requirement that the defendant must appreciate that what he has done is, by those standards, dishonest.

75. Therefore in the present case, if, contrary to the conclusions arrived at above, there were in cheating at gambling an additional legal element of dishonesty, it would be satisfied by the application of the test as set out above. The judge did not get to the question of dishonesty and did not need to do so. But it is a fallacy to suggest that his finding that Mr Ivey was truthful when he said that he did not regard what he did as cheating amounted to a finding that his behaviour was honest. It was not. It was a finding that he was, in that respect, truthful. Truthfulness is indeed one characteristic of honesty, and untruthfulness is often a powerful indicator of dishonesty, but a dishonest person may sometimes be truthful about his dishonest opinions, as indeed was the defendant in *Gilks*. For the same reasons which show that Mr Ivey's conduct was, contrary to his own opinion, cheating, the better view would be, if the question arose, that his conduct was, contrary to his own opinion, also dishonest.

Think about these questions.

- In [57] Lord Hughes lists a number of problems with the *R* v *Ghosh* test. Explain each of these criticisms in your own words (using your answers to the previous questions where relevant).
- According to Lord Hughes, which of these criticisms is the 'principal objection' to the second limb of the *R* v *Ghosh* test?

So the test for dishonesty is now as follows. First, the jury must determine the defendant's state of mind, including his knowledge or belief of relevant facts. Here, all genuinely held beliefs must be considered. Second, bearing in mind the defendant's state of mind, the jury must decide whether his conduct was dishonest according to the standards of ordinary, decent people.[36] Unlike the *R* v *Ghosh* test, there is no requirement that the defendant realised that his conduct was dishonest by those standards.

The judgment in *Ivey* v *Genting Casinos* addresses the problems with the *R* v *Ghosh* test outlined above. The same test is now used in both the civil and the criminal law, the test is less convoluted than the *R* v *Ghosh* test, and a defendant may no longer rely on his own passionately held beliefs to claim that he was unaware that his conduct was dishonest according to the standards of ordinary people. However, other concerns

[36] In *R* v *Hayes* [2015] EWCA Crim 1944 the Court of Appeal held that, in cases in which the defendant works in a particular industry, the test is still whether the defendant was dishonest according to the standards of reasonable and honest people. It is not whether he was dishonest according to the standards of that industry. As the Court remarked, 'Not only is there is no authority for the proposition that objective standards of honesty are to be set by a market, but such a principle would gravely affect the proper conduct of business. The history of the markets have shown that, from time to time, markets adopt patterns of behaviour which are dishonest by the standards of honest and reasonable people; in such cases, the market has simply abandoned ordinary standards of honesty' ([32]).

remain. First, Dyson and Jarvis have suggested that, in overruling *R* v *Ghosh*, the Supreme Court may have 'overstepped the mark'. As we will see later in the chapter, dishonesty is also a requirement of the offence of fraud. As the Fraud Act 2006 passed through Parliament, it was stated explicitly in both explanatory notes and Parliamentary debates that the *R* v *Ghosh* test for dishonesty would apply. Dyson and Jarvis accordingly state:

> Therefore, it could be said that when Parliament voted to enact the Fraud Bill it intended both that dishonesty should be an element of the new offences in what became ss. 2, 3 and 4 of the Fraud Act 2006, and that the test for dishonesty should be the two-stage *Ghosh* test. If Parliament had wished to depart from *Ghosh* then it had the perfect opportunity to do so … [W]here Parliament has approved of a test devised by the courts and it has introduced legislation with that test in mind then there is a very strong argument for saying that only Parliament should be able to alter that test and that the [Supreme Court] overstepped the mark when it did so.[37]

Second, in its judgment the Supreme Court stated that 'it is an important, even crucial, function of the criminal law to determine what is criminal and what is not; its purpose is to set the standards of behaviour which are acceptable' ([59]). At the same time, the Court said that dishonesty is 'characterised by recognition rather than by definition … Dishonesty is something which laymen can easily recognise when they see it' ([53]). This know-it-when-you-see-it approach seems to assume a shared, objective standard of honesty in society. Although Lord Hughes acknowledged that there may be 'room for debate at the fringes whether particular conduct is dishonest or not' ([53]), research by Stefan Fafinski and Emily Finch suggests that in fact values vary widely from person to person and across different socio-economic groups, cultures and locations. Titled 'The Honesty Lab', Fafinski and Finch's study presented more than 15,000 people with 50 potentially dishonest scenarios.[38] For many of the scenarios there was little consensus.[39] For example:

1. 43 per cent believed it was dishonest for a carer to try to persuade an elderly person to leave them something after their death;
2. 37 per cent said it was dishonest not to tell a shop assistant they had undercharged them;
3. 49 per cent of people thought it dishonest to knowingly watch a pirate DVD;
4. 58 per cent thought it dishonest to download music for free on the Internet.

In cases like these a test based on the standards of ordinary, decent people generates uncertainty, since ordinary, decent people may hold different views of what honesty requires.

Uncertainty can then create further problems. Richard Glover's discussion of the grounding of the *MSC Napoli* in January 2007 provides a useful example.[40] The *MSC Napoli* was a container ship which suffered a serious structural failure when it was on

[37] Dyson, M. and Jarvis, P. (2018) 'Poison Ivey or Herbal Tea Leaf?' 134 *Law Quarterly Review* 198.

[38] www.dishonestylab.com (accessed 11 July 2013).

[39] 'How 80% think it's OK to steal from work as study reveals our wavering moral compass', *Daily Mail*, 7 September 2009.

[40] Glover, R. (2010) 'Can Dishonesty Be Salvaged? Theft and the Grounding of the *MSC Napoli*' 74 *Journal of Criminal Law* 53.

its way from Antwerp to South Africa. The ship was deliberately grounded off Branscombe Bay in south Devon. The ship had a cargo of 2,318 containers; 105 of these were washed overboard, and 37 of these were washed up onto the beach. In the days that followed large crowds of up to 1,000 people at a time went to the beach and took items that had been washed up. Although unambiguous statements were made that unauthorised removal of items from the beach would be theft, no one was arrested or charged with the offence. In the following extract Glover discusses whether the uncertainty surrounding the meaning of dishonesty may have contributed to this.

EXTRACT

Glover argues that it is possible that the people who took items from the beach would not be found by a jury to have acted dishonestly. What reasons does he give for this?

What does Glover argue were the consequences of the uncertainty surrounding the meaning of dishonesty in the Branscombe Bay incident?

Glover, R. (2010) 'Can Dishonesty Be Salvaged? Theft and the Grounding of the *MSC Napoli*' 74 *Journal of Criminal Law* 53

It seems probable that a court [...] would have found that the conduct of the 'salvors' was dishonest by the standards of reasonable and honest people. However, it is also possible, to envisage a local court not coming to this conclusion [...] It was evident from the mixed views on the *Napoli* incident represented in the media, and notably in some of the 'blogs' attached to newspaper stories on the web, that there was not a common understanding as to the honesty or dishonesty of the 'looting' on Branscombe beach.

[...]

[T]he 'salvors' could conceivably argue that it was regarded as 'normal practice' in that area to 'loot and plunder' wrecks and, accordingly, whether it was private or commercial property their actions were not dishonest according to the 'standards of reasonable and honest people'. Indeed, one person suggested as much:

> There is a decent wreck every 25 years ... I don't regard it as stealing. We're cleaning up the beach as far as I am concerned.

Another commented:

> If we hadn't rescued them, they would have ended up in the sea and useless. I feel we are not stealing them, we are helping the authorities clear them up.

It is evident that the police were confronted with an uncertain legal position in relation to the concept of dishonesty. On the beach they faced 'the hordes of modern Robin Hoods' and because of the uncertain state of the law it was unclear whether they could, as a matter of law, be properly described as dishonest. The behaviour of the 'salvors' may have appeared *prima facie* dishonest, but a jury or court, particularly a local one, was entitled not to regard it as such, just as they were entitled to find Robin Hood not dishonest. Griew believed that one of the consequences of uncertainty was that there were longer trials because defendants had little to lose 'trying their luck' by pleading not guilty and hoping that the dishonesty element of theft would not be proved. However, the converse is what appears to have happened in relation to the *Napoli* incident. The police opted not to 'try their luck' in arresting or charging 'salvors' because, in the absence of a clear definition of dishonesty, they could not be confident that a court would regard the 'salvors' as dishonest. When this lack of certainty about theft is coupled with confusion about the application of salvage law it is, perhaps, not surprising that the police were hesitant to act.

This same uncertainty may also explain, at least in part, why so many people descended on Branscombe beach, despite warnings that removing items from the beach would be theft. It was genuinely unclear whether people would be regarded as dishonest and so commit the offence of theft. That is, as the law was vague, people lacked sufficient *ex ante* direction as to what amounted to dishonest behaviour. It seems likely that that this was exacerbated by police inaction. Consequently, the 'salvors' continued with their activities and caused serious disruption to the local community. For example, roads were blocked and the local school was forced to close for two days because buses could not get through. Some 'salvors' travelled considerable distances (from Bradford, Liverpool, Manchester and further afield) to participate in the 'salvage' and had it been clear that their activities were dishonest it seems at least possible that they would not have done so.

By failing to give individuals a clear indication of what conduct does and does not constitute the offence of theft, it might be argued that the uncertainty surrounding the meaning of dishonesty also violates the principle of maximum certainty (see Chapter 1). Plus, there is a real possibility that different juries considering cases with similar facts will arrive at different verdicts. Such inconsistency undermines the rule of law.

What makes these objections all the more important is the central role that the concept of dishonesty plays in the offence of theft. As we have seen, the *actus reus* of theft has been defined very broadly. In practice, the vast majority of cases will therefore hinge on whether or not the defendant acted dishonestly. This has led Graham Virgo to question the assumption in *Ivey* that dishonesty should have the same meaning in both the civil and criminal law.

EXTRACT

Virgo, G. (2018) 'Cheating and Dishonesty', 77 *Cambridge Law Journal* 18

There are many examples of situations where the criminal and civil law use the same concepts which are defined differently, and such divergence may be justified by virtue of the different functions of the criminal and civil law. Different tests of dishonesty could be justified because in the civil law dishonesty determines unacceptable conduct in order to impose liability, whereas dishonesty in the criminal law is concerned with identifying culpability, which requires consideration of the defendant's mental state. The effect of *Ivey* is to treat dishonesty in the criminal law as a mechanism for assessing conduct rather than culpability, albeit that the defendant's knowledge or belief about the facts is relevant to this objective assessment.

[...]

Ivey will impact other offences, notably theft for which it is dishonesty alone which renders conduct criminal, since, following *Hinks* [2001] 2 A.C. 241, appropriation does not require adverse interference with property rights contrary to the owner's wishes. When the *Ghosh* test of dishonesty applied, the defendant's belief that reasonable people would consider their conduct to be honest provided some protection against criminalising an otherwise legitimate interference with property rights. That safeguard has now gone, meaning that conviction for interference with property rights even though the owner of the property consents depends only on whether reasonable people would consider the conduct to be dishonest. Theft is now a crime which requires neither proof of harm nor subjective fault.

Virgo's argument that the Ivey test assesses conduct, not culpability, finds some support in data from mock trials conducted by Emily Finch.[41] The mock jury that was given the Ivey test to apply was unable to reach a verdict, because 'there was an instinctive preference for some element of subjectivity' and some jurors felt 'it was not fair to convict the defendant when she did not think that she had done anything wrong'.[42] In contrast, the mock jury that was asked to apply a purely subjective test 'demonstrated a strong desire for some element of objectivity to counterbalance the defendant's subjective viewpoint'.[43] Finch concludes, 'If it is true that juries know dishonesty when they see it, there is plentiful evidence here that they see it as a combination of subjectivity and objectivity'.[44]

Finally, it is important to note that – although the discussion of the *R* v *Ghosh* test in Ivey was technically obiter – in *R* v *Barton* [2020] EWCA Crim 575 a five-member Court of Appeal confirmed that the Ivey test should be followed. The Court of Appeal stated that it was bound to follow Ivey, since the Supreme Court had clearly intended for its decision to be binding. It also said, 'We would not wish it to be thought that we are following Ivey reluctantly. The concerns about Ghosh have resonated through academic debate for decades. Lord Hughes's reasoning is compelling' ([106]). Yet, as Laird has observed:

> the academic criticisms of Ghosh centred on the objective limb of the test and the fact that it assumes the existence of a community norm. Ironically, as a result of Ivey and the present case, the aspect of the Ghosh test that was most criticised by academics has become the defining feature of the test for dishonesty. The problems identified by academics have therefore been exacerbated.[45]

Now, think about these questions.

- According to Virgo, why might it be appropriate for the civil law and criminal law to define dishonesty differently?
- Look back over our discussion of dishonesty and make a list of arguments for and against the Supreme Court's decision in Ivey. In your opinion, was the Supreme Court right to overrule the *R* v *Ghosh* test?

[41] Finch, E. (2021) 'The elephant in the (jury) room: exploring mock jurors' understanding of different approaches to dishonesty' *Criminal Law Review* 513.

[42] ibid, 520.

[43] ibid, 526-527.

[44] ibid, 531.

[45] Laird, K. (2020) 'Commentary on R v Barton' Criminal Law Review 1065, 1068.

Quiz 8.4

1. For the purposes of theft, to determine whether a defendant acted dishonestly the court must consider ...
   - **a.** sections 2 and 6 of the Theft Act 1968.
   - **b.** section 2 of the Theft Act 1968 only.
   - **c.** section 2 of the Theft Act 1968 and the test laid down in *Ivey* v *Genting Casinos*.
   - **d.** the test laid down in *Ivey* v *Genting Casinos* only.
2. Which of the following summarises the test set out in *Ivey* v *Genting Casinos* accurately?
   - **a.** Was dishonesty a virtually certain consequence and did D realise this?
   - **b.** Dishonesty is a plain English word, so juries should simply apply their common sense.
   - **c.** Having regard to D's conduct and his state of mind, was he dishonest according to the standards of ordinary and honest people?
   - **d.** Was D dishonest according to the standards of ordinary and honest people and, if so, did D realise that what he was doing was by those standards dishonest?
3. Which of the following would you say was **not** a criticism of the *Ghosh* test for dishonesty?
   - **a.** The test did not give fair warning of what conduct does and does not constitute the offence of theft.
   - **b.** A defendant could be found to have acted dishonestly even though he had no idea others would consider his actions to be dishonest.
   - **c.** The test was too complicated and convoluted.
   - **d.** The test wrongly assumed that there is a single, shared standard of honesty in society.

Robbery

8.5 Define the requirements for establishing criminal liability for robbery.

The offence of robbery is defined by section 8 of the Theft Act 1968:

> **EXTRACT**
>
> Section 8 of the Theft Act 1968
>
> **8 Robbery**
>
> (1) A person is guilty of robbery if he steals, and immediately before or at the time of doing so, and in order to do so, he uses force on any person or puts or seeks to put any person in fear of being then and there subjected to force.

This tells us that the offence has four requirements:

1. The defendant committed theft
2. The defendant used force on any person or put or sought to put any person in fear of being then and there subjected to force
3. The defendant used force, or put or sought to put someone in fear of being subjected to force, immediately before committing theft or at the time of doing so
4. The defendant used force, or put or sought to put someone in fear of being subjected to force, in order to commit theft.

Number 1 requires proof of the *actus reus* and *mens rea* of theft. If the offence of theft is established you can then move on to the second, third and fourth requirements.

Numbers 2 and 3 are *actus reus* requirements. Number 4 is a *mens rea* requirement. We will work through them in turn.

1. The defendant committed theft

Robbery is an aggravated form of theft. So in order to establish robbery you must first prove that the defendant committed theft. If any of the *actus reus* or *mens rea* requirements for theft are absent then the defendant cannot be convicted of robbery.

An example is *R v Skivington* [1968] 1 QB 166. The defendant, Jim Skivington, had his wife's authority to go to her employer and collect her wages. Skivington went to his wife's employer's offices. He produced a knife and said, 'I want the money, I want the money'. When asked what money, he replied, 'My wife's wages'. The assistant manager handed some money over and Skivington left. The Court of Appeal held that Skivington had not committed robbery since there had been no theft. Skivington genuinely believed he had a legal right to the money and so was not dishonest under section 2(1)(a) of the Theft Act 1968. (In effect, Skivington had been charged with the wrong offence. He should have been charged with an offence against the person (see Chapter 6), not robbery.)

The broad meaning given to appropriation in the law of theft means that robbery also has a broad scope. In *Corcoran v Anderton* (1980) 71 Cr App R 104 the two defendants, Christopher Corcoran and Peter Partington, tried to snatch the victim's handbag. They crept up behind her, hit her in the back and tugged at her handbag. She screamed, fell over and let go of the bag. When she screamed the defendants panicked and ran away without the handbag. The Divisional Court upheld their robbery convictions. It did not matter that they had not escaped with the handbag. When they grabbed hold of the bag and tugged it they appropriated it. So this was not an attempted robbery. The offence of theft was complete and so the defendants were guilty of the full offence of robbery.

2. The defendant used force on any person or put or sought to put any person in fear of being then and there subjected to force

To satisfy this actus reus requirement the defendant must either: (i) have actually used force on another person; or (ii) have put someone in fear of being then and there subjected to force or sought to do so. Notice that the force or threat need not be used against the victim of the theft. A bank robber who threatens to shoot a customer commits robbery even though the person he threatens to use force against is not the person he is stealing from.

i. The defendant used force on any person

Two questions arise here. Must the force have been applied directly to the other person's body? And, how much force is necessary?

The first of these questions was addressed in *R v Clouden* [1987] Crim LR 56. The defendant came up behind the victim, pulled her shopping basket out of her hand and ran off with it. The Court of Appeal upheld his conviction for robbery. Although the prosecution must show that the defendant used force on the victim, it is not necessary to show that the force was applied directly to the victim's body. It was sufficient that Clouden had used force on the shopping basket, which in turn had caused force to be applied to the victim's body.

The other question – how much force is necessary? – was considered in *R v Dawson & James* (1976) 64 Cr App R 170. The two defendants, Anthony Dawson and Anthony James, and a third man (who was never caught), approached the victim. Two of them began to push the victim from side to side. While he was off balance the third man took the victim's wallet from his pocket. At trial Dawson and James were convicted of robbery. On appeal, the defendants argued that they had not used a sufficient amount of force for the offence of robbery. The Court of Appeal rejected this. Lawton LJ stated that they jury had been entitled to conclude that force had been used.

When we studied non-fatal offences against the person in Chapter 6 we saw that any contact, however slight, qualifies as force for the purposes of battery. But for the purposes of robbery the word 'force' has a slightly narrower meaning. Applications of force which are trivial or insignificant will not suffice. Suppose that Derek is a pickpocket. He takes Rodney's wallet from Rodney's trouser pocket. On these facts Derek probably makes some physical contact with Rodney (perhaps indirectly, via Rodney's clothing). But this will not amount to a use of force for the purposes of robbery. This was confirmed by the High Court in *P* v *DPP* [2012] EWHC 1657 (Admin). The defendant in this case snatched the victim's cigarette. The defendant was convicted of robbery and appealed, arguing that she had not used force on the victim. The High Court allowed the appeal and replaced the robbery conviction with a conviction for theft. Mitting J explained:

> [15] [...] This case falls squarely on the side of pickpocketing and such like, in which there is no direct physical contact between thief and victim. It cannot be said that the minimal use of force required to remove a cigarette from between the fingers of a person suffices to amount to the use of force on that person. It cannot cause any pain unless, perhaps, the person resists strongly, in which case one would expect inevitably that there would be direct physical contact between the thief and victim as well. The unexpected removal of a cigarette from between the fingers of a person is no more the use of force on that person than would be the removal of an item from her pocket. This offence is properly categorised as simple theft

So there must have been more than an insignificant amount of force used. Even so, robbery still encompasses a wide range of defendants – from defendants who use weapons and serious violence to those who push a person in order to take their handbag or wallet.

ii. The defendant put or sought to put any person in fear of being then and there subjected to force

Even if the defendant did not use force on another person, he may still be guilty of robbery if he put or sought to put any person in fear of being then and there subjected to force. The wording of the statute makes it clear that it is not necessary to show that the other person was actually scared or intimidated by the threat. It is enough that the defendant sought to put the person in fear of being subjected to force. Note also the importance of the words 'then and there'. The threat must be an immediate one.

Now, think about this question.

Does Derek satisfy this part of the *actus reus* of robbery in the following four scenarios?

1. Derek says to Rodney, 'I'm going to beat you up unless you give me £10 right away'.
2. Derek says to Rodney, 'If you don't give me £10 I'll be back next week to beat you up'.

3. Rodney and Cassandra are sitting together on a park bench when Derek walks up to them and says to Cassandra, 'I'm going to beat Rodney up unless you give me £10 right away'.
4. Cassandra is sitting on a park bench when Derek walks up to her and says, 'Give me £10 or I'm going to go and find Rodney and beat him up'. (Rodney is at home watching TV.)

3. The defendant used force, or put or sought to put someone in fear of being subjected to force, immediately before committing theft or at the time of doing so

This *actus reus* requirement focuses on when the force or threat of force occurred. The force or threat must have occurred 'immediately before' or 'at the time of' the theft. If the force or threat occurred after the theft was already complete there is no robbery. So if Derek steals something from a market stall and is then chased by a policeman, he does not commit robbery if he pushes people out of his way as he tries to escape (though he would be guilty of battery: see Chapter 6).

In *R v Hale* (1978) 68 Cr App R 415 the Court of Appeal considered the words 'at the time of' the theft. The defendant, Robert Hale, and his accomplice McGuire knocked on the door of the victim Mrs Carrett. When she opened the door they forced their way in. Hale put his hand over Mrs Carrett's mouth while McGuire went upstairs to search. McGuire then came downstairs with a jewellery box and asked where the rest was. All three then went upstairs and Mrs Carrett was asked where her money was. Hale and McGuire then each went to use the toilet and, before leaving, tied up Mrs Carrett and put socks in her mouth. At trial Hale was convicted of robbery. On appeal Hale argued that the theft was complete as soon as the jewellery box had been seized. The force that was used (tying up Mrs Carrett) therefore occurred, he said, after the theft was already complete.

EXTRACT

In the following extract, Eveleigh LJ applies the continuing acts doctrine (see Chapter 2).

Was the theft complete as soon as the jewellery box was seized? If not, when was the theft complete?

Was Mrs Carrett tied up at the time of the theft or after the theft was complete?

R v *Hale* (1978) 68 Cr App R 415

Eveleigh LJ

To say that [an appropriation] is over and done with as soon as [the thief] lays hands upon the property, or when he first manifests an intention to deal with it as his, is contrary to common-sense and to the natural meaning of words. A thief who steals a motor car first opens the door. Is it to be said that the act of starting up the motor is no more a part of the theft?

In the present case there can be little doubt that if the appellant had been interrupted after the seizure of the jewellery box the jury would have been entitled to find that the appellant and his accomplice were assuming the rights of an owner at the time when the jewellery box was seized. However, the act of appropriation does not suddenly cease. It is a continuous act and it is a matter for the jury to decide whether or not the act of appropriation has finished. Moreover, it is quite clear that the intention to deprive the owner permanently, which accompanied the assumption of the owner's rights was a continuing one at all material times. This Court therefore rejects the contention that the theft had ceased by the time the lady was tied up. As a matter of common-sense the appellant was in the course of committing theft; he was stealing.

There remains the question whether there was robbery. Quite clearly the jury were at liberty to find the appellant guilty of robbery relying upon the force used when he put his hand over Mrs. Carrett's mouth to restrain her from calling for help. We also think that they were also entitled to rely upon the act of tying her up provided they were satisfied (and it is difficult to see how they could not be satisfied) that the force so used was to enable them to steal. If they were still engaged in the act of stealing the force was clearly used to enable them to continue to assume the rights of the owner and permanently to deprive Mrs. Carrett of her box, which is what they began to do when they first seized it.

4. The defendant used force, or put or sought to put someone in fear of being subjected to force, in order to commit theft

This is a *mens rea* requirement. The force or threat of force must have been used in order to steal. So suppose that Derek gets into a fight with Roy. Derek punches Roy and knocks him to the ground. Derek then notices that Roy's wallet has fallen out of his pocket, so he picks it up and walks off with it. Whilst Derek has committed theft and an offence against the person, he is not guilty of robbery because he did not punch Roy in order to steal from him.

Quiz 8.5

1. In addition to proving the *actus reus* and *mens rea* of theft, the offence of robbery contrary to section 8 of the Theft Act 1968 requires proof of ...
   - **a.** application or threat of force with the intention to commit theft.
   - **b.** application of force before the theft.
   - **c.** application or threat of force before or during the theft in order to steal.
   - **d.** application or threat of force after the theft.
2. Which of the following statements is **incorrect**?
   - **a.** In *R* v *Clouden*, the defendant was guilty of robbery since an indirect application of force was sufficient.
   - **b.** In *R* v *Hale*, Hale was not guilty of robbery because force was only used after the theft was complete.
   - **c.** In *R* v *Skivington*, Skivington was not guilty of robbery because he had not acted dishonestly.
   - **d.** In *P* v *DPP*, P was guilty of theft, but not robbery, because the amount of force used was insignificant.
3. Which of the following is **not** one of the requirements of robbery?
   - **a.** D used force, or put or sought to put someone in fear of being subjected to force, immediately before committing theft or at the time of doing so.
   - **b.** D committed theft.
   - **c.** The force that D used or threatened was directed at the person whose property he appropriated.
   - **d.** D used force on any person or put or sought to put any person in fear of being then and there subjected to force.

Burglary

8.6 Define the requirements for establishing criminal liability for burglary.

The offence of burglary is defined by section 9 of the Theft Act 1968. As you'll see from the following extract, there are in fact two different types of burglary – section 9(1)(a) burglary and section 9(1)(b) burglary:

EXTRACT

Section 9 of the Theft Act 1968

9 Burglary

(1) A person is guilty of burglary if–

(a) he enters any building or part of a building as a trespasser and with intent to commit any such offence as is mentioned in subsection (2) below; or

(b) having entered any building or part of a building as a trespasser he steals or attempts to steal anything in the building or that part of it or inflicts or attempts to inflict on any person therein any grievous bodily harm.

(2) The offences referred to in subsection (1)(a) above are offences of stealing anything in the building or part of a building in question, of inflicting on any person therein any grievous bodily harm, and of doing unlawful damage to the building or anything therein.

(3) A person guilty of burglary shall on conviction on indictment be liable to imprisonment for a term not exceeding–

(a) where the offence was committed in respect of a building or part of a building which is a dwelling, fourteen years;

(b) in any other case, ten years.

This tells us that each type of burglary has five requirements:

1. The defendant entered a place
2. The place the defendant entered was a building or a part of a building
3. The defendant entered the building or part of a building as a trespasser
4. The defendant was knowingly or recklessly trespassing
5. Either: (a) the defendant intended to commit one of the specified offences at the time of entry (s.9(1)(a) burglary); or (b) after entering the building the defendant committed one of the specified offences or attempted to do so (s.9(1)(b) burglary).

In a problem question, it is best to begin by working through the first four requirements since these are the same for both types of burglary. Numbers 1, 2 and 3 are *actus reus* requirements. Number 4 is a *mens rea* requirement. If these are satisfied you can then move on to the final requirement, which is where you distinguish between section 9(1)(a) burglary and section 9(1)(b) burglary.

1. The defendant entered a place

The first *actus reus* requirement is that the defendant entered a building or a part of a building. The key issue here is what constitutes an entry.

It is generally accepted that a defendant may use an instrument to enter. So, for example, if Aubrey leaves his office window open and Derek uses a pole with a hook on the end to reach inside and pick up Aubrey's key ring and keys, Derek may be held to have entered Aubrey's office. Arguably, a defendant may also enter using an innocent agent. So if Derek tells his young son Damien to enter a sweet shop, pick up a chocolate bar and run straight out of the shop with it, Derek may be held to have entered the building through the innocent agency of his son.

Prior to the Theft Act 1968 the law stated that a defendant had entered a building if any part of his body, however small, had gone inside. So merely inserting a fingertip was enough for an entry.[46] In *R* v *Collins* [1973] QB 100 the Court of Appeal had to consider whether the same rule applied under the 1968 Act. Edmund Davies LJ set out the facts of this quite exceptional case.

(As you read the facts, bear in mind that at the time of *R* v *Collins* section 9(1)(a) burglary included entry of a building as a trespasser with intent to commit rape.[47])

EXTRACT

R v *Collins* [1973] QB 100

Edmund Davies LJ

This is about as extraordinary a case as my brethren and I have ever heard either on the bench or while at the bar [...] Let me relate the facts. Were they put into a novel or portrayed on the stage, they would be regarded as being so improbable as to be unworthy of serious consideration and as verging at times on farce. At about 2 o'clock in the early morning of Saturday, July 24, 1971, a young lady of 18 went to bed at her mother's home in Colchester. She had spent the evening with her boyfriend. She had taken a certain amount of drink, and it may be that this fact affords some explanation of her inability to answer satisfactorily certain crucial questions put to her at the trial. She has the habit of sleeping without wearing night apparel in a bed which is very near the lattice-type window of her room. At one stage in her evidence she seemed to be saying that the bed was close up against the window which, in accordance with her practice, was wide open. In the photographs which we have before us, however, there appears to be a gap of some sort between the two, but the bed was clearly quite near the window.

At about 3.30 or 4 o'clock she awoke and she then saw in the moonlight a vague form crouched in the open window. She was unable to remember, and this is important, whether the form was on the outside of the window sill or on that part of the sill which was inside the room, and for reasons which will later become clear, that seemingly narrow point is of crucial importance.

The young lady then realised several things: first of all that the form in the window was that of a male; secondly that he was a naked male; and thirdly that he was a naked male with an erect penis. She also saw in the moonlight that his hair was blond. She thereupon leapt to the

[46] *R* v *Davis* (1823) Russ & Ry 499.

[47] This strand of section 9(1)(a) burglary was removed by the Sexual Offences Act 2003 and replaced with a new offence of trespass with intent to commit a sexual offence (section 63 of the 2003 Act).

conclusion that her boyfriend, with whom for some time she had been on terms of regular and frequent sexual intimacy, was paying her an ardent nocturnal visit. She promptly sat up in bed, and the man descended from the sill and joined her in bed and they had full sexual intercourse. But there was something about him which made her think that things were not as they usually were between her and her boyfriend. The length of his hair, his voice as they had exchanged what was described as "love talk," and other features led her to the conclusion that somehow there was something different. So she turned on the bed-side light, saw that her companion was not her boyfriend and slapped the face of the intruder, who was none other than the defendant. He said to her, "Give me a good time tonight," and got hold of her arm, but she bit him and told him to go. She then went into the bathroom and he promptly vanished.

The complainant said that she would not have agreed to intercourse if she had known that the person entering her room was not her boyfriend. But there was no suggestion of any force having been used upon her, and the intercourse which took place was undoubtedly effected with no resistance on her part.

The defendant was seen by the police at about 10.30 later that same morning. According to the police, the conversation which took place then elicited these points. He was very lustful the previous night. He had taken a lot of drink, and we may here note that drink (which to him is a very real problem) had brought this young man into trouble several times before, but never for an offence of this kind. He went on to say that he knew the complainant because he had worked around her house. On this occasion, desiring sexual intercourse – and according to the police evidence he added that he was determined to have a girl, by force if necessary, although that part of the police evidence he challenged – he went on to say that he walked around the house, saw a light in an upstairs bedroom, and he knew that this was the girl's bedroom. He found a step ladder, leaned it against the wall and climbed up and looked into the bedroom. He could see through the wide-open window a girl who was naked and asleep. So he descended the ladder and stripped off all his clothes, with the exception of his socks, because apparently he took the view that if the girl's mother entered the bedroom it would be easier to effect a rapid escape if he had his socks on than if he was in his bare feet. That is a matter about which we are not called upon to express any view, and would in any event find ourselves unable to express one.

Having undressed, he then climbed the ladder and pulled himself up on to the window sill. His version of the matter is that he was pulling himself in when she awoke. She then got up and knelt on the bed, she put her arms around his neck and body, and she seemed to pull him into the bed. He went on:

> "I was rather dazed because I didn't think she would want to know me. We kissed and cuddled for about 10 or 15 minutes and then I had it away with her but found it hard because I had had so much to drink."

At trial Collins was convicted of section 9(1)(a) burglary. He appealed, arguing that he had not entered the building as a trespasser. The case reached the Court of Appeal.

The facts of *R* v *Collins* need to be considered in two stages: had he committed burglary before the girl invited him into the room and did he commit burglary when he accepted her invitation to enter the room. We will look at the second of these soon. For now, we are concerned with whether Collins had committed burglary before the girl invited him into the room. In his judgment Edmund Davies LJ said that a defendant can only be convicted of burglary if there has been an 'effective and substantial entry'. Since it was uncertain whether any part of Collins' body had entered the building whilst he was kneeling on the window sill (and, even if some part had, it was uncertain whether the jury would have regarded this as 'effective and substantial'), it had not been established that he had entered the building prior to being invited in.

In subsequent cases, however, the Court of Appeal has diluted the 'effective and substantial entry' test that it set out in *R* v *Collins*. In *R* v *Brown* [1985] Crim LR 212 the defendant, Vincent Brown, was standing outside a shop window. He lent through the window to rummage around for goods, so that the top half of his body was inside the shop. Commenting on the 'effective and substantial entry' test, the Court of Appeal said that the word substantial does not assist. The test should simply be whether the entry was effective, which in the case of Brown it was. However, following *R* v *Brown* came the case *R* v *Ryan* [1996] Crim LR 320, which casts doubt upon the requirement that the entry must have been effective. The defendant, Lee Ryan, put his head and arm inside the window of a house and became stuck. He had to be removed by the fire brigade. The Court of Appeal rejected Ryan's appeal against his burglary conviction, saying that the jury had been entitled to conclude that Ryan had entered the house. It did not matter that he had become stuck and unable to steal anything. It is hard to see how Ryan's entry could be described as effective!

So the current position is uncertain. Commentators have suggested that the 'effective entry' test should be interpreted broadly and understood as a de minimis rule, so that it only excludes insignificant or negligible entries (such as a fingertip),[48] or that we should simply discard the 'effective entry' test and return to the pre-1968 rule that a defendant enters a building if any part of his body, however small, has gone inside.[49]

2. The place the defendant entered was a building or a part of a building

The word 'building' includes garden sheds, greenhouses and farm outbuildings (such as stables or barns). Section 9(4) states that it also includes inhabited vehicles and vessels:

EXTRACT

Section 9(4) of the Theft Act 1968

(4) References in subsections (1) and (2) above to a building, and the reference in subsection (3) above to a building which is a dwelling, shall apply also to an inhabited vehicle or vessel, and shall apply to any such vehicle or vessel at times when the person having a habitation in it is not there as well as at times when he is.

So a caravan or a houseboat would qualify as a building while someone is living there (even if that person is away at the time).[50] However, a caravan or houseboat that is only used for holidays will only qualify as a building during the holidays and not at other times.

[48] Simester, A.P., Spencer, J.R., Stark, F., Sullivan, G.R. and Virgo, G.J. (2016) *Simester and Sullivan's Criminal Law: Theory and Doctrine* (6th edn). Hart Publishing: Oxford, p. 597.

[49] Ormerod, D. and Laird, K. (2015) *Smith and Hogan's Criminal Law* (14th edn). OUP: Oxford, p.1080.

[50] For example, in *R* v *Coleman* [2013] EWCA Crim 544 the defendant was convicted of burglary from a narrow boat on the Grand Union Canal that was used as a dwelling.

To constitute a building, a structure must have some degree of permanence. This can be illustrated by contrasting the following two cases:

Case 1: *B and S* v *Leathley* [1979] Crim LR 314

Dilara Mammadova/Shutterstock

- B and S stole goods from a freezer container in a farmyard. The container was sitting on railway sleepers and had not been moved for more than two years. It had lockable doors, was connected to an independent electricity supply and was intended to remain in place for the foreseeable future. The Crown Court at Carlisle held that the container was a building, commenting that it was 'a structure of considerable size and intended to be permanent or at least to endure for a considerable time'.

Case 2: *Norfolk Constabulary* v *Seekings and Gould* [1986] Crim LR 167

Kirsty Pargeter/123RF

- This case concerned two articulated lorry trailers that were being used as temporary storage space during building redevelopment by a supermarket. The trailers had been left on their wheels. An electric cable supplied power to each trailer. Steps were used for access and entry was made by unlocking the trailer shutters. The trailers had been in use for a year. The Crown Court at Norwich held that the trailers were not buildings. The distinction with B and *S v Leathley* seems to have been that, since the trailers still rested on their own wheels, they were vehicles, not buildings.

Sometimes a defendant might have had permission to be in some parts of a building but not others. An example is a hotel. Hotel guests have permission to be in communal areas and in their own rooms, but not the rooms of other guests. So if Derek sneaks into another guest's room he enters a separate part of the building as a trespasser.

In *R v Walkington* [1979] 1 WLR 1169 the defendant, Terence Walkington, entered a Debenhams store shortly before it was due to close. A store detective was monitoring him and followed him to an unattended till area.

Ken Schulze/Shutterstock

The till area was in the middle of a three-sided counter. Walkington moved into the till area, looked in the till (which he found was empty) and turned around to leave when he was stopped by the store detective. At trial, Walkington was convicted of section 9(1)(a) burglary. He appealed, arguing that he had not entered a separate part of the building.

EXTRACT

Read the following extract from the judgment of Geoffrey Lane LJ.

Was there sufficient evidence for the jury to conclude that the till area was a separate part of the building. Why/why not?

R v *Walkington* [1979] 1 WLR 1169

Geoffrey Lane LJ

One really gets two extremes, as it seems to us. First of all you have the part of the building which is shut off by a door so far as the general public is concerned, with a notice saying "Staff Only" or "No admittance to customers." At the other end of the scale you have for example a single table in the middle of the store, which it would be difficult for any jury to find properly was a part of the building into which the licensor prohibited customers from moving.

Here, it seems to us, there was a physical demarcation. Whether it was sufficient to amount to an area from which the public were plainly excluded was a matter for the jury. It seems to us that there was ample evidence on which they could come to the conclusion (a) that the management had impliedly prohibited customers entering that area and (b) that this particular defendant knew of that prohibition. Whether the jury came to the conclusion that the prosecution made out their case was a matter for them, but there is no dispute that the judge, in those two careful passages which I have read, left the matter fairly and correctly to the jury.

3. The defendant entered the building or part of a building as a trespasser

Whether or not the defendant was trespassing is a question of civil law. A trespasser is someone who enters without legal authorisation. The most common form of legal authorisation is the permission of the owner (or other occupiers such as the owner's family). Legal authorisation can also take other forms (such as a police search warrant).

If the defendant enters the building with the owner's permission but the owner later revokes this permission, the defendant must leave within a reasonable length of time. Should the defendant fail to leave within a reasonable length of time, he will be trespassing. Note, however, that to be guilty of burglary section 9(1) states that the defendant must have *entered* the building or part of a building as a trespasser. Suppose that Aubrey invites Derek into his house, but ten minutes later demands that Derek leave immediately. Derek procrastinates and leaves the house as slowly as he can. On his way out he steals a hat from the hat rack in the hallway. On these facts Derek may be trespassing at the moment he steals the hat, but he will not be guilty of burglary as he did not *enter* the building as a trespasser.[51]

The concept of trespass has raised two issues: mistaken authorisation and exceeding permission.

i. Mistaken authorisation

If the defendant received permission to enter, but the permission was based on some fundamental mistake, the defendant is trespassing. Think back to *R* v *Collins*. Earlier we saw that Collins had not committed burglary before the girl invited him into her bedroom. Now we need to ask whether he committed burglary when he accepted her invitation to enter the room. The girl's invitation to enter the room was based on her mistake as to Collins' identity: she thought Collins was her boyfriend. Mistakes as to a person's identity are regarded as fundamental and so Collins' permission to enter the room was void.

---

[51] Unless it can be established that the hallway is a separate part of the building, so that after being told to leave Derek entered a separate part of the building as a trespasser.

He therefore entered as a trespasser. (As we'll see in a moment, however, he was not guilty of burglary as he lacked the necessary *mens rea*.)

A defendant's permission to enter may also be invalidated by fraud or deception. So if Derek pretends to be an employee of the electricity board, and Aubrey invites him into his house to read the electricity meter, Derek's permission to enter Aubrey's house is invalidated by his deception.

ii. Exceeding permission

If a defendant has permission to enter, but exceeds this permission, he is a trespasser. A simple example is where Aubrey invites Derek, an electrician, to enter his house in order to gain access to the garage where the electricity meter is housed – but when Aubrey is not looking Derek sneaks upstairs and goes to sleep in one of the bedrooms. In this example, Derek was invited into Aubrey's house for a specified purpose. Derek exceeded this purpose and thus exceeded his permission to enter.

What about where the defendant's permission to enter was a general permission, not a permission that was limited to a specified purpose? Is it possible to exceed a general permission to enter? In *R* v *Jones & Smith* [1976] 1 WLR 672 the defendants, John Jones and Christopher Smith, went to the house of Smith's father Arthur and took two TVs. At trial, they were convicted of section 9(1)(b) burglary. On appeal, they argued that they had not entered the building as trespassers because Arthur Smith had given his son a general permission to enter the house at any time. The Court of Appeal rejected this argument and upheld the convictions. Commenting that 'When you invite a person into your house to use the staircase you do not invite him to slide down the banisters',[52] James LJ explained that it is possible to exceed a general permission to enter.

The decision in *R* v *Jones & Smith* means that the emphasis in the offence of burglary is very much on the defendant's guilty mind rather than manifest illegality. This gives the offence a very broad scope. Following *R* v *Jones & Smith* a shoplifter who enters a supermarket in order to steal an expensive bottle of champagne enters in excess of his permission to enter. He is therefore a trespasser and is guilty of burglary. Moreover, as we'll see in a moment, the shoplifter is guilty of section 9(1)(a) burglary as soon as he enters the supermarket with the intention to steal. So he is guilty of the full offence of burglary even if, having entered, he has a change of heart before he gets to the alcohol aisle, turns around and walks out empty-handed.

4. The defendant was knowingly or recklessly trespassing

Think back to *R* v *Collins* once again. We have seen that the girl's permission to Collins to enter the room was void because she had made a mistake as to his identity. Collins therefore entered the room as a trespasser. However, Edmund Davies LJ stated that a defendant can only be convicted of burglary if he knew he was trespassing or was reckless as to whether he was trespassing. Arguably, Collins believed he had permission to be in the bedroom, yet the judge at his trial failed to direct the jury to consider whether Collins satisfied this *mens rea* requirement. As a result the Court of Appeal allowed Collins' appeal and quashed his conviction.

So a defendant can only be convicted of burglary if he was knowingly or recklessly trespassing. We studied the meaning of these *mens rea* concepts in Chapter 4.

---

[52] *per* Scrutton LJ in *The Carlgarth* [1927] p.93.

5. Either: (a) the defendant intended to commit one of the specified offences at the time of entry (s.9(1)(a) burglary); or (b) after entering the building the defendant committed one of the specified offences or attempted to do so (s.9(1)(b) burglary)

The first four requirements are the same for both types of burglary. Once you have established that all four are satisfied, the final part of the offence requires you to distinguish between section 9(1)(a) and section 9(1)(b) burglary. When answering a problem question, it is sensible to begin with section 9(1)(a).

i. Section 9(1)(a) burglary

To prove section 9(1)(a) burglary you must establish that, at the moment he entered the building or part of the building as a trespasser, the defendant intended to commit one of the following three offences:

- Theft
- Infliction of GBH (this means the offence found in section 18 of the Offences Against the Person Act 1861)
- Criminal damage.

So, burglary is actually a broader offence than most people realise. It not only encompasses the person who enters a building or part of a building as a trespasser intending to steal, but also the person who enters with an intention to cause someone inside GBH and the person who enters with an intention to cause unlawful damage to property that is inside.

Note also that the key moment in time is the moment the defendant enters the building. It is at this moment that the defendant must have intended to commit theft, GBH or criminal damage. As long as the defendant entered with the necessary intention, he is guilty of section 9(1)(a) burglary – even if he changed his mind once inside and did not carry out the offence. Conversely, if the defendant only formed the intention after he had already entered, he is not guilty of section 9(1)(a) burglary. In this situation you need to consider section 9(1)(b) burglary instead.

ii. Section 9(1)(b) burglary

A defendant commits section 9(1)(b) burglary if, having entered a building or part of a building as a trespasser, he commits one of the following offences whilst inside:

- Theft
- Attempted theft
- Infliction of GBH (here this means either the offence found in section 18 of the Offences Against the Person Act 1861 or the offence found in section 20)
- Attempted infliction of GBH.

(Notice that, although criminal damage is one of the offences listed for section 9(1)(a) burglary, it is not on the list for section 9(1)(b) burglary.)

Unlike section 9(1)(a) burglary, the moment at which section 9(1)(b) burglary is committed is not the moment of entry. It is the moment at which the defendant commits (attempted) theft or (attempted) infliction of GBH. So for section 9(1)(b) burglary it is not necessary to show that the defendant intended to commit one of these offences when he entered the building. It is enough to show that he committed one of them once he was inside.

Quiz 8.6

1. For a charge of burglary contrary to section 9(1)(a) of the Theft Act 1968, based on an ulterior intention to commit theft, at what point in time must the defendant have possessed the necessary intention?
   - **a.** At the moment of entry.
   - **b.** After the appropriation.
   - **c.** After the entry, but before the time of appropriation.
   - **d.** At the time of the appropriation.
2. Which of the following is not an ulterior offence for the purposes of section 9(1)(b) burglary?
   - **a.** Infliction of grievous bodily harm.
   - **b.** Attempted theft.
   - **c.** Theft.
   - **d.** Criminal damage.
3. Which of the following would not be a building for the purposes of section 9 burglary?
   - **a.** A freezer container.
   - **b.** An inhabited caravan.
   - **c.** A bus.
   - **d.** A houseboat that is used as a dwelling.

Fraud

8.7 Define the requirements for establishing criminal liability for fraud.

Before the introduction of the Fraud Act 2006 this area of the criminal law was governed by a total of eight different deception offences:

- Obtaining property by deception (s.15 Theft Act 1968)
- Obtaining a money transfer by deception (s.15A Theft Act 1968)
- Obtaining a pecuniary advantage by deception (s.16 Theft Act 1968)
- Obtaining services by deception (s.1 Theft Act 1978)
- Procuring the execution of a valuable security by deception (s.20(2) Theft Act 1968)
- Securing the remission of a liability by deception (s.2(1)(a) Theft Act 1978)
- Inducing a creditor to wait for or forgo payment by deception (s.2(1)(b) Theft Act 1978)
- Obtaining an exemption from or abatement of liability by deception (s.2(1)(c) Theft Act 1978).

In 2002 the Law Commission published a report which criticised the complexity of this range of deception offences. The following extract is taken from this report:

EXTRACT

The Law Commission states that the overly particular list of 'overlapping but distinct' deception offences had 'undesirable consequences'. What were these undesirable consequences?

Law Commission (2002) *Fraud* (Law Commission Report No 276) Cm 5560

The need for simplification and rationalisation

3.10 At present, there is a multitude of overlapping but distinct statutory offences which can be employed in fraud trials. As Griew noted:

> No one wanting to construct a rational, efficient law of criminal fraud would choose to start from the present position. The law ... is in a very untidy and unsatisfactory condition. The various offences are not so framed and related to each other as to cover, in a clearly organised way and without doubt or strained interpretation, the range of conduct with which the law should be able to deal.

3.11 Arguably, the law of fraud is suffering from an "undue particularisation of closely allied crimes". Over-particularisation or "untidiness" is undesirable in itself, but it also has undesirable consequences.

3.12 First, it allows technical arguments to prosper. When the original Theft Act deception offences were first proposed by the CLRC in their Eighth Report, this problem was foreseen by a minority of the committee members:

> To list and define the different objects which persons who practise deception aim at achieving is unsatisfactory and dangerous, because it is impossible to be certain that any list would be complete. Technical distinctions would also inevitably be drawn – as they have been drawn under [the Larceny Act] 1916 s 32 – between conduct which did and which did not fall within the list.

3.13 The minority who took this view were in favour of a single deception offence, which would not define the offence by reference to the nature of the victim's loss or the relationship between that loss and the defendant's corresponding gain:

> The essence of the offence would be dishonestly using deception for the purpose of gain ... What particular type of gain the offender may aim at getting for himself or somebody else at the expense of his victim should be of no account except for the purpose of sentence.

3.14 They were echoing the sentiments of Lord Hardwicke:

> Fraud is infinite, and were a court once to ... define strictly the species of evidences of it, the jurisdiction would be cramped, and perpetually eluded by new schemes which the fertility of man's invention would contrive.

3.15 However, the majority of the committee took the view that it would be wrong to introduce a general offence. This disagreement was resolved by a compromise. The CLRC recommended two specific offences and a general offence which would carry a limited sentence of two years. This compromise did not find favour with Parliament, and a somewhat complex legislative history ensued. The proposed general offence was not adopted, and the present array of specific offences developed over subsequent years.

3.16 Nonetheless, the views of the minority who had advocated the general offence were found by Lord Goff in *Preddy* to have been "prescient". This was a mortgage fraud case. The defendants made false representations when applying for loans to buy property, and they were charged with obtaining property by deception. Although this is one of the most general deception offences, Lord Goff came to the reluctant conclusion that their actions fell outside it. The rest of the House agreed.

3.17 The difficulty lay in the nature of the property which the defendants obtained. The mortgage lenders provided the defendants with loans by making transfers from their accounts to the defendants' accounts. As Lord Goff explained, the resulting credit balances in the defendants' accounts were choses in action which had never belonged to anyone but the respective defendants. While the lenders had corresponding decreases in their respective accounts, at no time had they had any form of proprietary interest in the defendants' credit balances. Therefore these balances had never been property "belonging to another", for the purposes of section 15 of the Theft Act 1968.

3.18 In reaching this conclusion, Lord Goff considered the CLRC Eighth Report, and the subsequent legislative history. He made it clear that, in his view, the CLRC minority had been right to advocate a single deception offence. It is, perhaps, unsurprising that he reached this view. The defence argument in *Preddy* exploited the very elements of section 15 which the CLRC minority saw as irrelevant to the definition of fraud: the nature of the loss, and the relationship between the loss and the illegitimate gain.

3.19 *Preddy* was not the only case of its kind. It was only the most significant of a long string of highly technical cases involving deception offences: *Duru*, *Halai*, *King*, *Mitchell*, *Manjdadria*, and *Mensah Lartey* and *Relevy*. Each of these defendants argued that the particular consequences which he had brought about by deception fell outside the definition of the offence with which he was charged. By relying on a range of specific fraud offences, defined with reference to different types of consequence, the law is left vulnerable to technical assaults.

3.20 The second difficulty that arises from over-particularisation is that a defendant may face the wrong charge, or too many charges. Some of the cases cited in the previous paragraph would have been less problematic had the defendant been charged with a different offence. In *Mensah Lartey* and *Relevy* the defendants were charged with conspiring and attempting to procure the execution of a valuable security. The prosecution accepted in the Court of Appeal that they should have been charged with conspiring or attempting to obtain property by deception (although, since *Preddy*, section 15 would not have helped either). In *Duru* and *Mitchell*, the deceptions resulted in banks making out cheques in the defendants' favour. They were charged with obtaining property by deception, when the correct charge was procuring the execution of a valuable security.

3.21 This problem is not confined to cases which are wrongly prosecuted under one *deception* offence rather than another. In *Gomez* the defendant was the assistant manager of a shop. He deceived the manager into giving a customer goods in exchange for cheques which the defendant knew to be stolen. He was charged with theft. The case went to the House of Lords, because of an ambiguity in the concept of "appropriation" in theft. Four of their Lordships upheld the conviction, but Lord Lowry gave a powerful dissenting speech, and the issue has continued to cause difficulty. In fact, the argument need not have arisen in that case: the defendant would not have been able to raise it if he had been charged with obtaining property by deception, and he would have been squarely convicted on the agreed facts. It is not clear why the prosecutors chose to persist with bringing a theft charge. Perhaps they were aware of potential legal or factual problems that might arise if the wrong deception offence were charged. They may simply have been insufficiently familiar with the deception offences. In either event, a clear general deception offence might have enabled them to charge an offence which more comfortably reflected the conduct alleged, even though it also fell within the legal definition of theft.

3.22 A similar situation arose recently in *Vincent*. The defendant was charged with the offence of making off without payment. He had stayed in two hotels and left without paying the full bill. He argued that he had made arrangements to pay the bills "when he could", so that by the time he left there was no expectation that he would pay for the services at that point, and therefore payment "on the spot" was not required or expected. The trial judge directed the jury that this was only a defence if the agreement to defer payment was made in good faith by both parties, so it was no defence if the agreement had been brought about by fraud or deception. The Court of Appeal quashed the resultant convictions, stating that this direction was incorrect: even if the agreement was brought about by fraud, it still meant that the defendant was not expected to pay when he left, so he could not be guilty of making off without payment. The court stated that to catch this fraud a different offence would need to be charged, such as obtaining services by deception. Again, had the right charge been selected, much legal argument could have been avoided.

3.23 We do not argue that all the Theft Act offences could or should be combined into one. The fewer there are, however, the easier it is for prosecutors to choose the right one, thus decreasing the likelihood of mistakes. At present, in order to avoid mistakes, prosecutors may take the "belt and braces" approach. In Law Com No 228 we recognised that this practice brings its own problems:

> We are ...very conscious that there has been much criticism of the length and complexity of fraud trials ... [A]lthough much of the criticism was directed to the procedure in criminal trials, there was legitimate criticism of the substantive law in substantial fraud cases, which led to trials of excessive length and to perceptions of injustice. We are concerned to discover if it is possible to reduce the length and complexity of trials by simplifying the law, while always ensuring that the defendant is fully protected.

3.24 The over-particularisation of fraud offences can result in indictments made complex by the charging of alternative offences. A clearer, simpler law of fraud would make it easier for prosecutors to pursue one correct charge, which in turn would give fraud trials greater focus and structure.

Following the Law Commission's report the deception offences were replaced with a single offence of fraud, created by the Fraud Act 2006. Section 1 of the Act explains that the offence of fraud can be committed in three different ways:[53]

EXTRACT

Section 1 of the Fraud Act 2006

1 Fraud

(1) A person is guilty of fraud if he is in breach of any of the sections listed in subsection (2) (which provide for different ways of committing the offence).

(2) The sections are–

(a) section 2 (fraud by false representation),

(b) section 3 (fraud by failing to disclose information), and

(c) section 4 (fraud by abuse of position).

(3) A person who is guilty of fraud is liable–

(a) on summary conviction, to imprisonment for a term not exceeding 12 months or to a fine not exceeding the statutory maximum (or to both);

(b) on conviction on indictment, to imprisonment for a term not exceeding 10 years or to a fine (or to both).

We will look at each type of fraud in turn.

[53] Since all three are types of a single offence, there is no need for the prosecution to prove which one the defendant committed as long as the jury is sure that he did commit one of them. This means that it will not matter if the evidence establishes that fraud was committed in a different way to the one alleged by the prosecution.

Fraud by false representation

Fraud by false representation is defined by section 2 of the Fraud Act 2006:

EXTRACT

Section 2 of the Fraud Act 2006

2 Fraud by false representation

(1) A person is in breach of this section if he–

(a) dishonestly makes a false representation, and

(b) intends, by making the representation–

(i) to make a gain for himself or another, or

(ii) to cause loss to another or to expose another to a risk of loss.

This tells us that fraud by false representation has four requirements:

1. The defendant made a false representation
2. The defendant knew that the representation was, or might be, untrue or misleading
3. The defendant intended, by making the false representation, to make a gain for himself or another or to cause loss to another or to expose another to a risk of loss
4. The defendant acted dishonestly.

Number 1 is an *actus reus* requirement. Numbers 2, 3 and 4 are *mens rea* requirements. We will work through them in turn.

1. The defendant made a false representation

The sole *actus reus* requirement is that the defendant made a false representation. Subsections 2(2)–(5) provide further guidance on what constitutes a false representation. We will look at each subsection in turn.

The definition of false that is found in section 2(2)(a) is wider than you might have expected:

EXTRACT

Section 2(2)(a) of the Fraud Act 2006

(2) A representation is false if–

(a) it is untrue or misleading [...]

So representations are not only false when they are factually untrue. They are also false if they are factually true but nonetheless misleading. Suppose that Derek is a salesman in an electrical goods shop. Mike is interested in buying an LCD TV. When Mike asks Derek, 'Is this model a good one?' Derek replies, 'We haven't had a single bad review or dissatisfied customer'. Although factually true, this statement could be regarded as misleading if the shop has not received any customer feedback (good or bad) on that model, or if the shop has not yet sold any of that particular model.

Section 2(3) explains that a representation may be of fact, law or a person's state of mind:

EXTRACT

Section 2(3) of the Fraud Act 2006

(3) "Representation" means any representation as to fact or law, including a representation as to the state of mind of–

(a) the person making the representation, or

(b) any other person,

ACTIVITY

Which of the following representations is an example of: (a) a representation of fact; (b) a representation of law; (c) a representation of the state of mind of the person making the representation and (d) a representation of the state of mind of another person?

- Rodney says to Cassandra, 'I really want to marry you'
- Rodney tells Derek, 'Cassandra wants to marry me!'
- Dereks says to Rodney, 'It is unlawful to be married to two people at the same time'.
- Rodney says to Derek, 'I am not married'.

Section 2(4) states:

EXTRACT

Section 2(4) of the Fraud Act 2006

(4) A representation may be express or implied.

There are several examples of implied representations in the case law:

Someone who pays with a cheque accompanied by a cheque guarantee card impliedly represents that he has the bank's authority to do so:
***MPC* v *Charles* [1977] AC 177**

Since the bank had withdrawn Charles' authority to use his chequebook and cheque guarantee card his implied representation was false.

Shutterstock

Similarly, some who pays by credit card impliedly represents that he has the bank's authority to do so:
***R* v *Lambie* [1982] AC 449**

The bank had told the defendant to return her credit card because she had exceeded her credit limit. So her implied representation that she had authority to use the credit card was false.

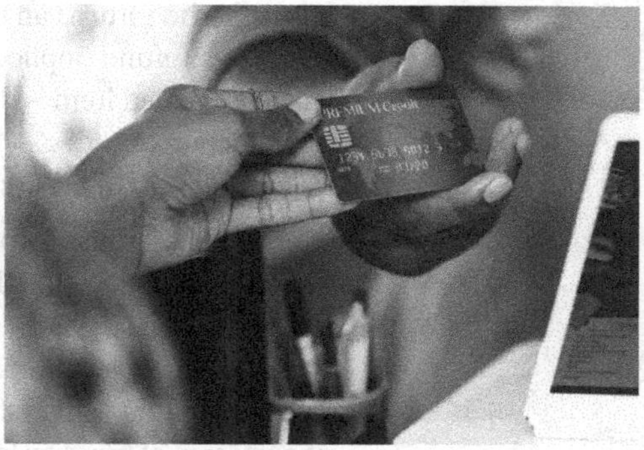

Shutterstock

Someone who orders food in a restaurant impliedly represents that they intend to pay for the food at the end of their meal:
***DPP* v *Ray* [1974] AC 370**

Shutterstock

Someone who takes a taxi impliedly represents that they have the money to pay the fare at the end of the journey:
***R* v *Waterfall* [1970] 1 QB 148**

Shutterstock

Someone who books his driving theory test impliedly represents that he will turn up to sit the test himself:
***DPP* v *Idrees* [2011] EWHC 624 (Admin)**

In this case the defendant had failed his driving theory test 15 times, so on the 16th attempt he arranged for someone else to sit the test in his place. He was convicted of fraud by false representation and his appeal against conviction was dismissed by the High Court.

Shutterstock

Someone who returns an item to a shop asking for a refund impliedly represents that the returned item is the one that was originally purchased:
R v *Hoxhalli* **[2016] EWCA Crim 724**

In this case the defendant purchased a shirt online from Topshop. She then took the dispatch note and a similar shirt, from a different retailer, into a local Topshop store and asked for a refund, which she received. She was convicted of fraud by false representation, and her appeal against conviction was rejected by the Court of Appeal.

Shutterstock

Although most of these cases were decided before the Fraud Act 2006, they will still be followed today.

Another case involving an implied representation was *R* v *Silverman* (1988) 86 Cr App R 213.[54] The defendant, Michael Silverman, was the manager of a plumbing and central heating firm. The victims – two sisters aged in their 60s who lived together in a maisonette – had employed Silverman's company to do work for them for 15 years. They had come to trust him. He told them that the boiler in the maisonette needed to be replaced and that the whole property needed to be rewired. He quoted them a figure of £2,875 for the new boiler and £20,000 plus VAT to rewire the property. These figures were grossly excessive, but because the sisters trusted him they employed him to do the work and paid him. At trial Silverman was convicted of a deception offence. He appealed, arguing that there had not been a false representation: he said how much he would charge to do the work and he was paid the amount he quoted.

EXTRACT

Read the following extract from the judgment of Watkins LJ.

Had Silverman made a false representation? If so, what was it?

Suppose that Aubrey needs a plumber. He looks online and finds the details of a local plumber, Derek. Derek gives Aubrey a ridiculously expensive quote, but because Aubrey is gullible he employs Derek to do the work. When Derek is finished he charges Aubrey the amount he quoted. In the light of *R* v *Silverman*, did Derek make a false representation?

R v *Silverman* (1988) 86 Cr App R 213

Watkins LJ

Mr. Hopmeier, who appeared below and appears here for the appellant, has argued, first, that the appellant made no representations to the complainants. He has not shrunk from conceding that the appellant was dishonest. He has submitted that the appellant quoted the sisters for the work to be done but that it was open to them either to accept or reject the quotation upon such advice as they might seek and perhaps in the light of tenders by others, and that the appellant was in much the same position as anyone else who is asked to quote for work to be done.

[54] See also *R* v *Wenman* [2013] EWCA Crim 340.

> He has argued that it is a dangerous concept to introduce into the criminal law that an excessively high quotation amounts to a false representation [...]. In certain circumstances that submission may we think be well founded. But whether a quotation amounts to false representation must depend upon the circumstances.
>
> It seems clear to us that the complainants, far from being worldly wise, were unquestionably gullible. Having left their former home, they relied implicitly upon the word of the appellant about their requirements in their maisonette. In such circumstances of mutual trust, one party depending upon the other for fair and reasonable conduct, the criminal law may apply if one party takes dishonest advantage of the other by representing as a fair charge that which he but not the other knows is dishonestly excessive.
>
> [...]
>
> There was material for a finding that there had been a false representation although it is true that the appellant had said nothing at the time he made his representations to encourage the sisters to accept the quotations. He applied no pressure upon them, and apart from mentioning the actual prices to be charged was silent as to other matters that may have arisen for question in their minds.
>
> [...]
>
> Here the situation had been built up over a long period of time. It was a situation of mutual trust and the appellant's silence on any matter other than the sums to be charged were, we think, as eloquent as if he had said: "What is more, I can say to you that we are going to get no more than a modest profit out of this."

It is also possible to make a representation via an innocent agent.[55] And to make a representation by omission, if the defendant is under a duty to pass on the relevant information.[56] In *R* v *Rai* [2000] 1 Cr App R 242 the defendant, Thomas Rai, had applied to the council for a grant to install a downstairs bathroom in the home of his elderly mother. The application was successful and he was awarded a grant of nearly £10,000. But before the building work started his mother died. Rai did not inform the council of his mother's death, and so the council went ahead and installed the downstairs bathroom. At trial Rai was convicted of a deception offence and this was upheld by the Court of Appeal. Another example of a representation by omission would be if Derek is filling in a car insurance application online and leaves blank the box which asks for details of previous speeding offences even though he has received two speeding tickets in the past year.

Finally, section 2(5) plugs a gap that existed in the previous law. Under the old deception offences, only people could be deceived. Machines could not be. The offences therefore did not apply in cases where a defendant entered false information into a machine and there was no other human involvement. An example would be where Derek gains access to Aubrey's online banking account and transfers money from Aubrey's account to his own. Section 2(5) of the Fraud Act 2006 now states:

EXTRACT

Section 2(5) of the Fraud Act 2006

(5) For the purposes of this section a representation may be regarded as made if it (or anything implying it) is submitted in any form to any system or device designed to receive, convey or respond to communications (with or without human intervention).

[55] *R* v *Varley* [2019] EWCA Crim 1074.

[56] *Government of UAE* v *Allen* [2012] EWHC 1712 (Admin).

So when Derek transfers the money from Aubrey's account to his own he impliedly represents that he is the account holder (or has the account holder's authority). Since this representation is false there is the *actus reus* of fraud.

Before moving on, it is worth emphasising that the only *actus reus* requirement of this type of fraud is that the defendant made a false representation. In particular, it is not necessary to show that the defendant actually gained anything as a result of the false representation, nor that the victim lost anything. As David Ormerod explains in the following extract, this is quite different to the old deception offences.

EXTRACT

In the following extract Ormerod explains that, whilst the old deception offences were 'result crimes', fraud is a 'conduct crime'. What questions does Ormerod say this raises? How would you answer these questions?

What are the practical difficulties that Ormerod says result from fraud being a conduct crime?

Ormerod, D. (2007) 'The Fraud Act 2006 – Criminalising Lying?' *Criminal Law Review* 193

Section 2 of the Act is the broadest form of the fraud offence and hence likely to be the most frequently charged. The *actus reus* requires only that a person made a false representation, and the *mens rea* is satisfied by proof that he knew the representation was or might be false, and that he acted dishonestly, with intent to gain or cause loss. Classic examples of conduct caught will be false representations on mortgage application forms, life insurance forms, etc. The offence is also designed to criminalise dishonest "phishing" on the internet.

Before scrutinising individual elements, it is worth emphasising how dramatic is the shift from a result-based deception to a conduct-based representation offence. Under the old law D's conduct had to deceive V thereby causing V to do whatever act was appropriate to the charge-transferring property, executing a valuable security, etc. Under section 2, there is no need to prove a result of any kind or that an alleged victim or indeed any person believed any representation or acted on it; or, crucially, that the accused succeeded in making a gain or causing a loss by his representation. The effect is that D may be liable even though V knows that D's statement is false or V would have acted in the same way even if he had known of the falsity. The new offence has no requirement that V's property interests are damaged (temporarily or permanently), nor even that V's property interests are imperilled; it is sufficient that D intends to cause loss or make a gain. It is wider than conspiracy to defraud since a lone actor can be guilty without even prejudicing anyone's economic interests. This wholly inchoate offence appears to criminalise lying.

Should lying be a sufficient basis for criminal liability? What is the wrong which D performs which warrants the criminal sanction? It is not one derived from intentionally harming V's interests directly – there need be no such harm. Similarly, it is not one of potentially damaging V's interests. The wrong seems to be the act of lying or misleading with intent to gain or cause loss; the harm might be construed as one of destabilising society's processes of property and financial transfers. Even if this is sufficient to warrant criminalisation, is it properly called fraud? Classic definitions such as that from Stephen J. include, even at their widest, an element of intent to deceive which is much narrower than an intention to gain.

The absence of any loss direct or potential to V's interests may make the evaluation of the degree of blameworthiness and appropriate punishment very difficult. If D has typed an impressive high yield investment prospectus into his computer and emailed it, he seems to have breached section 2. What sentence is appropriate? The representation might have made millions of pounds from gullible investors, or been universally treated as irritating spam and deleted.

This shift has other serious practical implications. Obviously, the offence is complete earlier – on the making of the representation. In some instances section 2 might also catch conduct committed later in time-if, after D, a motorist, has with honest mind filled his fuel tank and the entire proprietary interest in the petrol has passed to him, he then falsely represents to V, the cashier, that it will be paid for by D's company, he breaches section 2. Although the "start" date of offending may be more difficult to specify when drafting particulars, this is unlikely to be material in most cases. A further effect is that V, formerly cast in a leading role in proving the causal effect of D's deception, now becomes an optional extra. With liability complete on D's representation being made, no specific victim(s) need to be identified. No doubt prosecutors will still commonly prefer to call a victim to testify about the circumstances of the representation, but technically, all that matters is that D acted with the intention to gain or cause loss; the potential effect of the false representation need not be proved. As with the deception offences it replaced, there will be overlap with theft in cases in which the false representation enables D to 'appropriate' V's property, even if with V's consent, as in *Gomez*. Of course, section 2 goes further by criminalising, D who lies with the intent that V lend him property which D intends to return unaltered.

2. The defendant knew that the representation was, or might be, untrue or misleading

The first *mens rea* requirement is found in section 2(2)(b):

EXTRACT

Section 2(2)(b) of the Fraud Act 2006

(2) A representation is false if–

[...]

(b) the person making it knows that it is, or might be, untrue or misleading.

Notice that this requirement is not limited to knowledge that the representation was untrue or misleading. It is enough to show that the defendant knew that the representation *might be* untrue or misleading.

At the same time, remember that only knowledge will suffice. Less stringent *mens rea* concepts such as belief or suspicion are not enough. When determining what a defendant knew, any genuinely held religious beliefs should be considered.[57] It is also not enough that the reasonable man would have known that the representation was or might be untrue or misleading. As McCombe LJ explained in *R v Augunas* [2013] EWCA Crim 2046:

> What is required is that the accused person knows that the representation is, or might be, misleading. It is not enough that a reasonable person might have known this; what matters is the accused person's actual knowledge. In our judgment, it not good enough for the prosecutor to satisfy the jury that the accused ought to have appreciated that the representation made by him was or might be untrue or misleading, nor is it enough that the circumstances must have given rise to a reasonable suspicion that the representation was, or might be, untrue or misleading.

[57] *R v Wiseman [2023]* EWCA Crim 1363.

3. The defendant intended, by making the false representation, to make a gain for himself or another or to cause loss to another or to expose another to a risk of loss

As we saw earlier, the *actus reus* of fraud does not contain any requirement that the defendant actually made a gain or caused a loss. However, for this part of the *mens rea* it must be shown that the defendant *intended*, by making the false representation, to make a gain, cause a loss or expose another to a risk of loss. The two limbs here are alternatives: the prosecution must prove *either* that the defendant intended to make a gain for himself or *another or* that he intended to cause loss to another (or expose another to a risk of loss). It is not necessary to prove both.[58]

The meaning of the words 'gain' and 'loss' is explained in section 5:

EXTRACT

Section 5 of the Fraud Act 2006

5 "Gain" and "loss"

(1) The references to gain and loss in sections 2 to 4 are to be read in accordance with this section.

(2) "Gain" and "loss"–

(a) extend only to gain or loss in money or other property;

(b) include any such gain or loss whether temporary or permanent; and "property" means any property whether real or personal (including things in action and other intangible property).

(3) "Gain" includes a gain by keeping what one has, as well as a gain by getting what one does not have.

(4) "Loss" includes a loss by not getting what one might get, as well as a loss by parting with what one has.

Three important points emerge from section 5:

- Section 5(2)(a) states that the intended gain or loss must have been in money or other property. This is a point which students sometimes forget in the pressure of an exam, particularly when answering problem questions which involve a defendant who lies in order to trick someone into having sexual intercourse with him. Suppose that Derek says to his girlfriend Raquel, 'I love you and I want to marry you'. He only says this so that she will have sex with him. He does not mean it and intends to break up with her the next day. On these facts Derek has knowingly made a false representation, but he is not guilty of fraud because what he intended to gain (sexual intercourse) is not property. (To decide whether Derek has committed a sexual offence, read Chapter 7.)
- Section 5(2)(b) states that the intended gain or loss can be either temporary or permanent. This means that lying to someone in order to get them to lend you property can constitute fraud. Suppose that Derek asks to borrow Aubrey's sports car. Derek tells Aubrey that his own car has broken down and he is running late for an urgent meeting but, in fact, Derek's car has not broken down and he does not have a meeting to attend. He just fancies going for a drive in a sports car. On these facts Derek intends to make a temporary gain of property (Aubrey's sports car).

---

[58] *R* v *(David) Ames* [2023] EWCA Crim 1463.

- The meaning of the word 'gain' is wider than just acquiring something and the meaning of the word 'loss' is wider than just parting with something. Section 5(3) says that gain also includes keeping what one already has, and section 5(4) says that loss also includes not getting what one might get. So suppose that Derek has recently graduated from university. He uses his out-of-date NUS card to get a student discount at the cinema. Here he intends to make a gain (keeping some money that he would otherwise have had to part with) and he intends to cause the cinema a loss (since they don't receive money they might have got).

Lastly, notice one other important point. The defendant must intend to make the gain or cause the loss by making the false representation. In other words, the defendant must expect that his false representation will *cause* the anticipated gain or loss. Whether this causal link exists is a question of fact for the jury.[59]

Think about these scenarios.

1. Think back to *R* v *Linekar* (this was the case we studied in Chapter 7 on sexual offences, in which the defendant falsely stated that he intended to pay a prostitute for sexual intercourse). Suppose that Linekar was charged with fraud.
   - Could the prosecution argue that Linekar intended to make a gain for himself?
   - Could the prosecution argue that Linekar intended to cause a loss to the prostitute?
2. Derek has an interview for a job in a supermarket. He is in desperate need of income, so during the interview he lies about his A level grades and past experience. He figures that he will work so hard when he starts the job that his lies won't matter. Does Derek satisfy this part of the *mens rea* of fraud?[60]
   - Does Derek satisfy this part of the *mens rea* of fraud?

4. The defendant acted dishonestly

Note that the partial definition of dishonesty found in section 2(1) of the Theft Act 1968 does not apply here. So in all cases the standards of ordinary and decent people will be used to decide whether the defendant acted dishonestly. We studied this test above, in our examination of the offence of theft.

Fraud by failing to disclose information

Fraud by failing to disclose information is defined by section 3 of the Fraud Act 2006:

EXTRACT

Section 3 of the Fraud Act 2006

3 Fraud by failing to disclose information

A person is in breach of this section if he–

(a) dishonestly fails to disclose to another person information which he is under a legal duty to disclose, and

[59] *R* v *Gilbert* [2012] EWCA Crim 2392.

[60] In *R* v *Andrewes* [2022] UKSC 24, the defendant pleaded guilty to fraud by false representation after committing 'CV fraud'. He successfully applied for a job as a Chief Executive Officer, having lied on his CV about his previous education and experience. He was required to pay back the difference between the salary he received and the lower salary that he would have received had he not lied.

(b) intends, by failing to disclose the information–

(i) to make a gain for himself or another, or
(ii) to cause loss to another or to expose another to a risk of loss

This tells us that fraud by failing to disclose information has three requirements:

1. The defendant failed to disclose to another person information which he was under a legal duty to disclose
2. The defendant intended, by failing to disclose the information, to make a gain for himself or another or to cause loss to another or to expose another to a risk of loss
3. The defendant acted dishonestly.

Number 1 is an *actus reus* requirement. Numbers 2 and 3 are *mens rea* requirements. We will work through them in turn.

1. The defendant failed to disclose to another person information which he was under a legal duty to disclose

The *actus reus* of fraud by failing to disclose information is that the defendant was under a legal duty to disclose information to another person but failed to do so. The offence is thus targeted at deception by silence.

Whether or not there is a legal duty to disclose information is determined by the civil law.[61] Examples of when a duty exists include:

i. The duty of solicitors and estate agents to disclose information to their clients.
ii. The life insurance applicant's duty to tell the insurance company about his heart condition.
iii. The duty of a tenant to disclose that he has sub-let part of the premises, as required by his tenancy agreement.[62]
iv. The duty of a resident to disclose that he is no longer eligible for the single person discount on council tax.[63]

2. The defendant intended, by failing to disclose the information, to make a gain for himself or another or to cause loss to another or to expose another to a risk of loss

The offence of fraud by false representation had this same *mens rea* requirement. Everything we said about this requirement previously also applies here.

3. The defendant acted dishonestly

This is also the same as for fraud by false representation, which we studied above.

[61] *R v Razoq* [2012] EWCA Crim 674.

[62] *R v Zeroual* [2022] EWCA Crim 288.

[63] *R v Zeroual* [2022] EWCA Crim 288. The question in R v D [2019] EWCA Crim 209 was whether, for the purposes of council tax, there is a legal duty to disclose to the relevant local authority one's residence at a particular address. The Court of Appeal held that, whilst there is a legal obligation to pay council tax, the statutory scheme does not impose a legal obligation to notify the council of one's residence. The Court pointed out that this does not leave the council without remedy. Action may be taken in the civil courts, and in some instances the offence of fraud by false representation may apply.

Fraud by abuse of position

Fraud by abuse of position is defined by section 4 of the Fraud Act 2006:

EXTRACT

Section 4 of the Fraud Act 2006

4 Fraud by abuse of position

(1) A person is in breach of this section if he–

(a) occupies a position in which he is expected to safeguard, or not to act against, the financial interests of another person,

(b) dishonestly abuses that position, and

(c) intends, by means of the abuse of that position–

(i) to make a gain for himself or another, or

(ii) to cause loss to another or to expose another to a risk of loss.

This tells us that fraud by abuse of position has four requirements:

1. The defendant occupied a position in which he was expected to safeguard, or not act against, the financial interests of another person
2. The defendant abused that position
3. The defendant intended, by abusing that position, to make a gain for himself or another or to cause loss to another or to expose another to a risk of loss
4. The defendant acted dishonestly.

Numbers 1 and 2 are *actus reus* requirements. Numbers 3 and 4 are *mens rea* requirements. We will work through them in turn.

1. The defendant occupied a position in which he was expected to safeguard, or not act against, the financial interests of another person

The first *actus reus* requirement is that the defendant occupied a position in which he was expected to safeguard, or not act against, the financial interests of another person. A deliberate decision was made that the statute should not contain any further guidance on the types of positions that are covered by the offence, in order to maximise flexibility. As the following extract from the Law Commission makes clear, relationships where one party owes the other a fiduciary duty are covered. But it is not limited to fiduciary relationships. The offence could potentially also apply where the defendant has a moral, but not a legal, obligation to safeguard another person's financial interests.

EXTRACT

Read the following extract from the Law Commission's 2002 report on fraud.

What examples does it give of: (i) relationships that will be covered by the offence; and (ii) relationships that might be?

In a trial, whose responsibility is it to decide whether this *actus reus* requirement is satisfied?

Law Commission (2002) *Fraud* (Law Commission Report No 276) Cm 5560

7.38 The necessary relationship will be present between trustee and beneficiary, director and company, professional person and client, agent and principal, employee and employer, or between partners. It may arise otherwise, for example within a family, or in the context of voluntary work, or in any context where the parties are not at arm's length. In nearly all cases where it arises, it will be recognised by the civil law as importing fiduciary duties, and any relationship that is so recognised will suffice. We see no reason, however, why the existence of such duties should be essential. This does not of course mean that it would be entirely a matter for the fact-finders whether the necessary relationship exists. The question whether the particular facts alleged can properly be described as giving rise to that relationship will be an issue capable of being ruled upon by the judge and, if the case goes to the jury, of being the subject of directions.

The types of position that fall within fraud by abuse of position were considered by the Court of Appeal in *R* v *Valujevs* [2014] EWCA Crim 2888. The defendants in this case were unlicensed gangmasters. They supplied agricultural work, transport and accommodation to individuals who had come to the UK from Latvia and Lithuania. The defendants' strategy was to create 'debt bondage'. To this end, they required the workers to take up their offer of accommodation as a condition of finding work for them. They then charged grossly excessive rent, causing the workers to default on their payments. The defendants then imposed fines, which they deducted from the workers' wages. They were charged with several offences, including fraud by abuse of position. The trial judge held that there was no case to answer on the charge of fraud by abuse of position, on the basis of respect for commercial freedom. The prosecution appealed against this ruling.

EXTRACT

Read the following extract from the judgment of Fulford LJ. Section 4(1)(a) refers to a position in which a person is expected to safeguard, or not to act against, the financial interests of another person.

According to Fulford LJ, does the word 'expected' refer to: (a) the expectation of the potential victim; (b) the expectation of the defendant; or, (c) the expectation of the reasonable person?

The Court of Appeal held that there was evidence that the defendants occupied a position in which they were expected to safeguard, or not to act against, the financial interests of the victims. What facts did Fulford LJ point to in reaching this conclusion?

Fulford LJ also outlined some situations in which the section 4 offence would not apply. What were these? According to Fulford LJ, why should the section 4 offence not apply in these situations?

R v *Valujevs* [2014] EWCA Crim 2888

Fulford LJ

37 In this case, the relevant acts of the gangmasters that are relied on by the prosecution have been set out in the draft amended count, namely that the defendants allegedly "withheld earnings, charged inflated rental payments and imposed unwarranted financial penalties".

As described above, it is prohibited in the licensing standards to withhold or to threaten to withhold the whole or part of any payment due to a worker for any work they have done on account of "any matter within the control of the licence holder". In our view, at the very least, it is open to the jury on the evidence to decide that these defendants had gone beyond merely supplying workers and instead they had assumed control of and/or responsibility for collecting the wages of the workers or they controlled the amounts that the workers would be allowed to retain at the moment the wages were handed over. On either basis, the prosecution are able to contend that the defendants had taken on the obligation of paying the wages of the workers, and it is inherent in that commitment that the wages received by the workers will not be reduced by unwarranted financial penalties or deductions, unlawful demands for the repayment of suggested fines, or artificially inflated rental payments. (The prosecution does not rely on any other statutory/regulatory provision or any contractual term to establish an obligation by these defendants to pay the workers' wages without reductions.)

38 The duty not to withhold payment due to a worker has been imposed as part of an enforceable scheme to regulate the activities of gangmasters who provide labour, and in our judgment the prosecution is entitled to suggest that on this basis the relevant defendant "occupies a position in which he is expected to safeguard, or not to act against, the financial interests of another person" for the purposes of section 4. Put otherwise, having assumed responsibility for collecting the wages for a worker, or by exercising control over the wages that would be received by a worker at the point they are received, there is a clear expectation that the worker will receive them without a reduction in the form of (i) unwarranted financial penalties or deductions, (ii) unlawful demands for the repayment of suggested fines, or (iii) artificially inflated rental payments.

39 ... [These] three alternatives ought to be listed as separate particulars within the count as examples of how the defendants breached the obligation not to withhold wages. The jury will need to be directed that they can only convict if they all agree on at least one of the particulars.

40 We stress, we have focused on the regulatory scheme that applies to gangmasters and whether or not the approach taken on this appeal will apply in future cases as regards others who, in different roles, take on the responsibility for collecting the wages of a worker, employed or self-employed, is not for this court to determine.

41 Although the statute does not provide any assistance on the issue, in our view the "expectation" in section 4 of the 2006 Act is an objective one. It is for the judge to assess whether the position held by the individual is capable of being one "in which he is expected to safeguard, or not to act against, the financial interests of another person". If it is so capable, it will be for the jury thereafter to determine whether or not they are sure that was the case. It would be untenable to suggest that the expectation should be that of either the potential victim (the test would, in all likelihood, be too low) or the defendant (the test is likely to be set too high). Therefore, this is an objective test based on the position of the reasonable person.

[...]

43 The prosecution has relied on other forms of questionable financial behaviour on the part of the defendants as part of its reliance on section 4 of the 2006 Act, such as the general device of charging excessive sums for rent withholding work in order to ensure that the worker in question was indebted to the gangmaster, or lending money to workers for which claims are later made for repayment (as opposed to deducting sums from wages). In our judgment, potentially reprehensible behaviour of this kind falls outside the financial interests of a person the gangmaster could properly be expected to safeguard or not to act against. Individuals do not commit a criminal offence under section 4 of the 2006 Act if they seek rental payments in excess of the market rate and gangmasters are not under an obligation to provide employment for those seeking work. Gangmasters are entitled to ask for repayment of moneys that they have lent to workers. Although we recognise that these can be difficult situations, the individual is

able to look for accommodation or employment elsewhere and we are unpersuaded that this suggested behaviour on the part of the defendants arguably provides the basis for inclusion as particulars of a section 4 of the 2006 Act offence. In this critical sense we agree with the judge in the court below that to establish an abuse of position for the purposes of section 4 of the 2006 Act it is necessary for the prosecution to demonstrate a breach of a fiduciary duty, or a breach of an obligation that is akin to a fiduciary duty. This can conveniently be described, for instance, as a breach of trust or a breach of a privileged position in relation to the financial interests of another person. Section 4 does not apply to those who simply supply accommodation, goods, services or labour, whether on favourable or unfavourable terms and whether or not they have a stronger bargaining position. Therefore, the fact that an individual is a gangmaster who offers work or accommodation on particular terms, or lawfully requests the repayments of debts incurred by workers, does not ipso facto involve the abuse of a relevant position as regards the financial interests of another person.

44 We therefore concur with the conclusion of the judge that section 4 should not apply in "the general commercial area where individuals and businesses compete in markets of one kind or another, including labour markets, and are entitled to and expected to look after their own interests". We repeat, the critical factor in this case is that there is evidence that the defendants arguably assumed control of, and responsibility for, collecting the wages of the workers, or they controlled the wages at the moment that they were paid over, and the fact that they were acting as gangmasters merely provided the vital context relied on by the prosecution in which that role was assumed.

So fraud by abuse of position does not apply to those who supply accommodation, goods, services or labour on unfavourable terms simply by virtue of their stronger bargaining position. According to the Court of Appeal, what was crucial in *R* v *Valujevs* was that there was evidence that the defendants had either assumed responsibility for collecting the workers' wages or exercised control over the wages that they would receive. In the following extract, Jennifer Collins criticises this 'restrictive reading' of the fraud by abuse of position offence.

EXTRACT

Collins, J. (2016) 'Fraud by Abuse of Position and Unlicensed Gangmasters' 79 *Modern Law Review* 354

If identification of control or responsibility over monies is an attempt to identify the strongest basis for a relevant position of trust, the point arises that there are other strong reasons for leaving fraud by abuse of position to a jury in cases involving vulnerable migrant workers. Workers who are charged exorbitant rent or who are in debt bondage to intermediaries in the labour market are highly dependent upon those intermediaries. Their status in the labour market is nothing short of precarious. It is implausible that such individuals 'are entitled to and expected to look after their own interests', as Fulford LJ suggests. From this position of precariousness, ought there not to be an expectation that the source of this status must safeguard, or not act against, the vulnerable party's financial interests? Notably the workers in *Valujevs* were migrant workers, and thus part of a group of individuals who labour lawyers have noted 'are made particularly vulnerable by law' itself. Virginia Mantouvalou has identified 'exclusion from labour inspections, minimum wage and maximum working hours' legislation' as examples of ways in which the law creates vulnerability. Ought the criminal law to afford special protection using fraud by abuse of position to persons who are vulnerable to exploitation because of the rules of a legal system? The concern is that the potential for the section 4 offence to be read in this way is significantly impeded by the reasoning in *Valujevs*.

In the subsequent case *COL* v *DPP* [2022] EWHC 601 (Admin), the Divisional Court considered the judgment in *R* v *Valujevs*. In *COL* v *DPP*, the claimant (from the Philippines) worked for Mr and Mrs Aljaberi in Abu Dhabi. She worked from 7am to 10pm each day, providing childcare and completing domestic work, for $400 per month. In 2012, Mr Aljaberi obtained a diplomatic posting to the UAE Embassy in London. He and his family moved to London and asked the claimant to move with them, saying she would receive £1000 per month for a 40-hour working week. She agreed and a Tier 5 visa was obtained, according to which the claimant would lose her right to remain in the UK if she left her employment with Mr and Mrs Aljaberi. The claimant contended that, after moving to London, she was required to work 14–15 hours each day and was only paid £100–£200 each month. Her passport was taken from her, sometimes she was locked in the family home when Mr and Mrs Aljaberi were out, and she did not have access to medical care when she was sick. After she escaped, the matter was referred to the Crown Prosecution Service (CPS). The CPS decided against a prosecution for fraud by abuse of position, on the basis that this offence could not apply to the employer – employee relationship. This decision was challenged by judicial review. The Divisional Court quashed the decision of the CPS, holding that it had been based on a misdirection of law.

EXTRACT

Read the following extract from the judgment of Dove J.

According to the Divisional Court, can fraud by abuse of position apply in cases involving an employer – employee relationship?

Which features of the claimant's relationship with Mr and Mrs Aljaberi did the Divisional Court identify as important to its conclusion?

In your opinion, does the reasoning in *COL* v *DPP* address the concerns that Collins highlighted in the previous extract?

COL v *DPP* [2022] EWHC 601 (Admin)

Dove J

40. ... The relationship of employer and employee is not, when applying the principles set out in *Valujevs*, dispositive of the question of whether or not a relationship upon which section 4(1)(a) bites arises. It will, of course, be relevant but it may not in every case be the end of the determination of the matter. It is necessary to examine whether there are any particular features of the case beyond that relationship which might take that relationship out of the general commercial arena, and give rise to an expectation, objectively assessed, that the suspect should safeguard, or not act against, the financial interests of the complainant.

As the claimant in the present case submits, there were, on the basis of the material before the [CPS], clear features of the case which would entitle the conclusion that section 4(1)(a) of the 2006 Act was engaged. These features bear particularly upon the vulnerable nature of the claimant both generally, and also in the context of her relationship with Mr and Mrs Aljaberi. The evidence of the employment agreement in relation to her engagement by the employment agency in the UAE provides confirmation of her vulnerable position as a foreign worker in that country, in that it included various undertakings relating to the risks of financial abuse both by the employment agency and also by the persons for whom she was working. These vulnerabilities were compounded by her relocation to the UK on the basis of the Tier 5 visa application. As a consequence of the system of immigration regulation to which she was subject under the Tier 5 visa she was particularly beholden to Mr and Mrs Aljaberi since it was a condition of the visa that she should remain in their employment. Her status in the UK was heavily dependent upon Mr Aljaberi as her sponsor, a position which is of particular significance within the Tier 5 system of immigration regulation which applied at the time of these events.

Further potential vulnerability to exploitation arose in the circumstances of this case from the fact that Mr Aljaberi, by virtue of his position, had the potential to invoke diplomatic immunity in relation to any allegations against him of mistreatment or financial abuse. All of these features were quite absent from the [CPS's] consideration of the question of whether the relationship between the claimant and Mr and Mrs Aljaberi engaged section 4(1)(a) of the 2006 Act. This material appears not to have been assessed because the conclusion had been reached that since their relationship was one of employer and employee that put an end to the matter. In fact these features clearly supported the contention that in the particular relationship with which this case is concerned Mr and Mrs Aljaberi did occupy a position in which they would be expected to safeguard, and certainly not act against, the financial interests of the claimant bearing in mind the evidence which they provided of her potential vulnerability. In short, this was not simply a relationship of employer and employee: it was a particular relationship in which not only the question of employment, but also the provision of accommodation, and most pertinently the dependency of her immigration status in the UK on her sponsor and continued employment were integral elements of their relationship. The potential for exploitation in these circumstances was clear and these were features well beyond the simple relationship of employer and employee clearly capable of giving rise to an expectation of the kind envisaged in section 4 of the 2006 Act.

43. I am satisfied that the approach taken by the [CPS] to this issue was a clear misdirection and involved a failure to apply the relevant legal principles from the case of *Valujevs* to the particular circumstances of the claimant. This was a misdirection of law and, like the failure in the earlier decision in this case, a fatal flaw in the decision-making process. It led the [CPS] to finish the consideration of the case without completing an assessment of the evidence in relation to the other issues pertinent to the offence under section 4 of the 2006 Act. This conclusion is sufficient to lead to the decision in this case being quashed.

2. The defendant abused that position

The second *actus reus* requirement is that the defendant abused that position. We have just seen that, in *R* v *Valujevs*, there were three ways in which the defendants might have abused their position: imposing unwarranted financial penalties; making unlawful demands for the repayment of suggested fines; and, requiring artificially inflated rental payments. We also know that an employee who takes confidential trade secrets from his employer may be found to have abused a position in which he was expected to safeguard, or not act against, the financial interests of another.[64] Beyond this, however, there is relatively little guidance since (as with the word 'position') a deliberate choice was made to maximise flexibility by not defining the word 'abuse'. All that the statute does tell us – in section 4(2) – is that a defendant can abuse his position by inaction:

[64] The case *R (on the application of Corbiere Ltd)* v *Secretary of State for Justice* [2017] EWHC 3364 (Admin) focused on whether the claimant's ex-employee should be deported. The ex-employee had pleaded guilty to fraud by abuse of position after resigning from his job and taking his employer's trade secrets with him (highly confidential algorithmic trading strategies worth an estimated £30m).

EXTRACT

Section 4(2) of the Fraud Act 2006

(2) A person may be regarded as having abused his position even though his conduct consisted of an omission rather than an act.

3. The defendant intended, by abusing that position, to make a gain for himself or another or to cause loss to another or to expose another to a risk of loss

The offence of fraud by false representation had this same *mens rea* requirement. Everything we said about this requirement previously also applies here.

4. The defendant acted dishonestly

This is also the same as for fraud by false representation, which we studied above.

Quiz 8.7

1. How many different ways can the general offence of fraud be committed, contrary to section 1 of the Fraud Act 2006?
   - **a.** Three.
   - **b.** One.
   - **c.** Four.
   - **d.** Two.
2. What is the *actus reus* of fraud by false representation, as defined by section 2 of the Fraud Act 2006?
   - **a.** Dishonestly making a representation.
   - **b.** Intentionally making a false representation.
   - **c.** Making a false representation.
   - **d.** Making a representation to make a gain for himself or loss to another.
3. What are the *mens rea* requirements for fraud by false representation contrary to section 2 of the Fraud Act 2006?
   - **a.** Intention to make a gain/cause a loss, and dishonesty.
   - **b.** Knowledge that the representation is (or might be) true or misleading, with dishonesty.
   - **c.** Knowledge that the representation is (or might be) true or misleading, intention to make a gain/cause a loss.
   - **d.** Knowledge that the representation is (or might be) untrue or misleading, intention to make a gain/cause a loss, and dishonesty.
4. The *actus reus* of fraud by failing to disclose information contrary to section 3 Fraud Act 2006 would occur when ...
   - **a.** the defendant decides not to disclose information to another.
   - **b.** the defendant fails to disclose information that may be of benefit to another.
   - **c.** the defendant fails to disclose information that he or she is under a legal obligation to disclose.
   - **d.** the defendant gathers information.
5. Which of the following could lead to a prosecution for fraud by abuse of position contrary to section 4 of the Fraud Act 2006?
   - **a.** An employee of a betting shop alters a horse race betting slip placed by a customer so as to extend the employer's liability in the event that the horse wins. It does win, and the employee pays the extra stake money to the employer, pays out the original bet to the customer and keeps the rest of the money.
   - **b.** A finds a wallet in the street. He picks it up intending to hand it in at the local police station. He later decides to keep the wallet.
   - **c.** A has failed the driving theory test several times. B sat the test for A using A's driving licence.
   - **d.** D meets V in a bar. D pretends that he is a well-paid surgeon in order to impress V. Later that evening D and V have sexual intercourse. V says she would not have had sex with D if she had known that he lied to her.

Criminal damage

8.8 Define the requirements for establishing criminal liability for criminal damage.

The offence of criminal damage is defined by section 1(1) of the Criminal Damage Act 1971:

EXTRACT

Section 1(1) of the Criminal Damage Act 1971

1 Destroying or damaging property.

(1) A person who without lawful excuse destroys or damages any property belonging to another intending to destroy or damage any such property or being reckless as to whether any such property would be destroyed or damaged shall be guilty of an offence.

This tells us that criminal damage has six requirements:

1. The defendant destroyed or damaged an item
2. The item was property
3. The property belonged to another person
4. The defendant intentionally or recklessly destroyed or damaged the property
5. The defendant knew that the property belonged to another person or was reckless as to whether it did
6. The defendant lacked a lawful excuse.

Numbers 1, 2 and 3 are *actus reus* requirements. Numbers 4 and 5 are *mens rea* requirements. Number 6 is a defence which is peculiar to criminal damage offences. We will work through them in turn.

1. The defendant destroyed or damaged an item

The first *actus reus* requirement is that the defendant destroyed or damaged an item. The word 'destroyed' is relatively straightforward. Something that has been destroyed has ceased to exist. The case law has therefore focused on the word 'damage'.

Whether or not an item has been damaged is a question of fact for the jury. Although the trial judge may withdraw a case from the jury if there is no evidence that the item was damaged, the courts have interpreted the word 'damage' broadly. This means that, in practice, in most cases there will be sufficient evidence to leave the question whether an item has been damaged to the jury.

The case law shows that the courts have tended to apply two considerations when determining whether or not there is evidence that an item has been damaged. The first is whether the usefulness of the item was impaired (either permanently or temporarily). In *R v Fiak* [2005] EWCA Crim 2381 the defendant, Engin Fiak, had been arrested for drink-driving and for assaulting a police officer. At the police station he was placed in a cell and given a new, unused mattress, a clean, dry blanket and a pillow. While in his cell Fiak placed the blanket in the toilet and then flushed it repeatedly. As a result his own cell, as well as two others and the adjoining passage, were flooded. The water which caused the flooding was clean and the cell floor was waterproof. However, the blanket was rendered unusable until it was cleaned and dry and the cells had to be cleaned before they could be used again. At trial, Fiak was convicted of criminal damage of the blanket and his cell. He appealed, arguing that there was no evidence that either item had been damaged.

EXTRACT

Read the following extract from the judgment of Sir Igor Judge. He refers to two authorities.

What is the test that these two authorities set out?

Applying this test to the facts of Fiak's case, in the opinion of the Court had the blanket and cell been damaged?

R v *Fiak* [2005] EWCA Crim 2381

Sir Igor Judge

The issue in relation to criminal damage can be summarised very simply. Mr Belger [defence counsel] argued that there was no evidence that either the blanket or the cells were damaged. He suggested that clean water had flooded onto a waterproof floor, and that in the process the blanket was made wet by clean water. The blanket would have been reusable when dry. Cleaning up a wet cell floor does not constitute damage to the cell itself. However widely interpreted "damage" may be for the purposes of the Criminal Damage Act 1971, a wet blanket and a wet cell floor fall outside any sensible definition. The argument of course assumes that the absence of any possible contamination or infection from the lavatory itself, and the confident expectation that there would be none. In the 1971 Act, hardly surprisingly, the word "damage" itself is not further defined. The Concise Oxford Dictionary explains damage as "harm or injury impairing the value or usefulness of something ...". We need refer to only two authorities. The first is *Morphitis* v *Salmon* [1990] Crim LR 48, where the transcript of Auld J's judgment reads:

> "The authorities show that the term "damage" for the purpose of this provision, should be widely interpreted so as to conclude not only permanent or temporary physical harm, but also permanent or temporary impairment of value or usefulness."

This analysis was approved in *R* v *Whiteley* [1991] 93 CAR 25 where, after a comprehensive examination of the authorities, Lord Lane CJ summarised their effect.

> "Any alteration to the physical nature of the property concerned may amount to damage within the meaning of the section. Whether it does so or not will depend on the effect that the alteration has had upon the legitimate operator (who for convenience may be referred to as the owner) ... where ... the interference ... amounts to an impairment of the value or usefulness of the [property] to the owner, then the necessary damage is established."

Applying these principles to the present case, while it is true that the effect of the appellant's actions in relation to the blanket and the cell were both remediable, the simple reality is that the blanket could not be used as a blanket by any other prisoner until it had been dried out (and, we believe, also cleaned) and the flooded cells remained out of action until the water was cleared. In our judgment it is clear that both sustained damage for the purposes of the 1971 Act. There plainly was a case to answer.

Another case in which an item's usefulness was found to have been impaired is *Cox* v *Riley* (1986) 83 Cr App R 54. In this case, the defendant deliberately deleted the program from a printed circuit card that operated a computerised saw. On appeal, the Divisional Court upheld the defendant's conviction for criminal damage. His actions had rendered the saw inoperable and meant that time and money would need to be expended to reprogram the card. This case may be contrasted with the decision of the Divisional Court in *Drake* v *DPP* [1994] RTR 411.[65] The issue in this case was whether wheel clamping damages a car by rendering it unusable. The Court held that wheel clamping does not constitute damage. Laws J drew a distinction between adding something to an object and interfering with an object's integrity:

> [T]here must be some intrusion into what, in the course of argument, Mann LJ described as the "integrity of the object in question". There was no such intrusion here. There was nothing which, as a matter of ordinary language, could sensibly be regarded as damage to the car. Certainly the wheel clamp was applied to it. I do not, for my part, believe that a court could properly have held that this application amounted to "damage"

Think about this scenario.

Derek removes a part from the engine of Aubrey's sports car. Without this part the engine will not start.

- Has Derek damaged the car?

The second consideration the courts have applied is whether time and money will be required to remedy the defendant's actions. We have just seen that this was one of the reasons why the circuit card was held to have been damaged in *Cox* v *Riley*. Other examples include:

***Hardman* v *Chief Constable of Avon and Somerset* [1986] Crim LR 330**

The defendants were campaigners for nuclear disarmament. On the 40th anniversary of the Hiroshima bombing they painted paintings on a pavement. They used water-soluble paint so that, in time, the paintings would wash away. Their criminal damage convictions were upheld by the Crown Court at Bristol. In order to remove the paintings immediately the local authority had to use high-pressure water jets, which caused expense and inconvenience.

Shutterstock

[65] See also *Lloyd* v *DPP* [1992] RTR 215.

***Roe* v *Kingerlee* [1986] Crim LR 735**

The defendant smeared mud and graffiti on the walls of a police cell. The Divisional Court held that this was capable of constituting criminal damage. The Court emphasised that the damage need not be permanent and added that it had cost £7 to clean the cell.

Shutterstock

***Seray-Wurie* v *DPP* [2012] EWHC 208 (Admin)**

The defendant lived in a private residential estate. The management company for the estate put up two parking notices. The defendant wrote on these notices using a black marker pen. The High Court upheld his criminal damage conviction, saying that it would cost £90 to remove the writing from the signs.

Shutterstock

In some of these cases, such as *Hardman* v *Chief Constable of Avon and Somerset*, the damage was quite minor. The Court of Appeal has held that, where no more than trivial damage was caused during a peaceful protest, a conviction for criminal damage may be a disproportionate interference with the rights to freedom of thought, conscience and religion (Article 9), freedom of expression (Article 10) and freedom of assembly and association (Article 11) under the European Convention on Human Rights. According to the Court, a possible example would be where someone writes a message on a pavement using water soluble paint as part of a political protest.[66] However, if the damage was significant, or if it was violent or non-peaceful, then a conviction for criminal damage will always amount to a proportionate interference with these rights.[67]

If the nature of the item in question is such that the defendant's actions do not need to be remedied, there will be no damage. So, in *Morphitis* v *Salmon* [1990] Crim LR 48 the Divisional Court held that a scratch on a scaffolding bar was incapable of amounting to damage. The scratch did not impair the item's usefulness, and scaffolding bars are frequently scratched during ordinary use. Similarly, if the defendant's actions can be remedied with little effort and at no expense there will be no damage. In *A (A Juvenile)* v *R*

[66] *Attorney-General's Reference* (No 1 of 2022) [2022] EWCA Crim 1259, [116].

[67] It has been argued that the terminology and distinctions drawn in *Attorney-General's Reference (No 1 of 2022)* require further elaboration: Benn, A. (2023) 'Criminal Damage: The "Colston Four", Proportionality and the Concerns that Linger: *Attorney-General's Reference (No 1 of 2022)* [2022] EWCA Crim 1259' 87 *Journal of Criminal Law* 61.

[1978] Crim LR 689 the defendant spat on a police officer's raincoat. Streeter J in Kent Crown Court explained that this was incapable of constituting damage:

> [Spitting at a garment] could be an act capable of causing damage. However, one must consider the specific garment which has been allegedly damaged. If someone spat upon a satin wedding dress, for example, any attempt to remove the spittle might in itself leave a mark or stain [...] An article might also have been rendered "inoperative" if, as a result of what happened, it had been taken to dry cleaners. However, in the present case, no attempt had been made, even with soap and water, to clean the raincoat, which was a service raincoat designed to resist the elements

2. The item was property

At the start of this chapter we saw how section 4 of the Theft Act 1968 defines property for the purposes of the offence of theft. Section 10(1) of the Criminal Damage Act 1971 contains a similar, but not identical, definition for the offence of criminal damage:

EXTRACT

Section 10(1) of the Criminal Damage Act 1971

10 Interpretation

(1) In this Act "property" means of a tangible nature, whether real or personal, including money and–

(a) including 4(3)4(3) creatures which have been tamed or are ordinarily kept in captivity, and any other wild creatures or their carcasses if, but only if, they have been reduced into possession which has not been lost or abandoned or are in the course of being reduced into possession; but

(b) not including mushrooms growing wild on any land or flowers, fruit or foliage of a plant growing wild on any land.

For the purposes of this subsection "mushroom" includes any fungus and "plant" includes any shrub or tree.

The most important difference between this definition and the one found in the Theft Act 1968 is that, while the Theft Act's definition encompassed tangible and intangible property, section 10(1) is limited to tangible property. So a defendant cannot be guilty of criminally damaging something intangible like a copyright.

Two other differences between this definition and the one found in the Theft Act 1968 are:

- Section 10(1) encompasses land. So a defendant can be guilty of criminally damaging land, whereas section 4(2) of the Theft Act 1968 states that land can only be stolen in certain circumstances.
- According to section 10(1), a defendant cannot be guilty of criminally damaging wild mushrooms, flowers, fruit or foliage. By contrast, section 4(3) of the Theft Act 1968 states that these can be stolen if they are picked for sale or another commercial purpose.

Given the similarities between the two definitions, it may sometimes be possible to apply by analogy the case law on the meaning of property for the purposes of theft to the offence of criminal damage.

3. The property belonged to another person

To be guilty of the basic criminal damage offence the property must have belonged to another person. (As we'll see shortly, things are different for aggravated criminal damage. For the aggravated offence there is no requirement that the property belonged to someone else.)

The word 'belong' is defined in section 10(2), with further specific situations dealt with in sections 10(3) and 10(4):

EXTRACT

Sections 10(2)–10(4) of the Criminal Damage Act 1971

(2) Property shall be treated for the purposes of this Act as belonging to any person–

(a) having the custody or control of it;

(b) having in it any proprietary right or interest (not being an equitable interest arising only from an agreement to transfer or grant an interest); or

(c) having a charge on it.

(3) Where property is subject to a trust, the persons to whom it belongs shall be so treated as including any person having a right to enforce the trust.

(4) Property of a corporation sole shall be so treated as belonging to the corporation not with standing a vacancy in the corporation.

This is very similar to the definition of 'belong' in section 5(1) of the Theft Act 1968. As with the offence of theft, section 10(2) makes it clear that in criminal damage cases belonging is a broader concept than ownership. Property belongs to anyone who has 'custody or control' of the item, anyone with 'any proprietary right or interest' in the item and anyone who has a 'charge' over the item. It follows that, for the offence of criminal damage, property can belong to more than one person at a time. Moreover, it is possible for the owner of an item to be guilty of criminal damaging it if someone else has a proprietary right (such as a lien) over the item.

4. The defendant intentionally or recklessly destroyed or damaged the property

The first *mens rea* requirement is that the defendant destroyed or damaged the property either intentionally or recklessly. We studied these *mens rea* concepts in Chapter 4. It is worth emphasising that, following the House of Lords' decision in *R* v *G & another* [2003] UKHL 50, it is the *R* v *Cunningham* test for recklessness that applies.

5. The defendant knew that the property belonged to another person or was reckless as to whether it did

The second *mens rea* requirement is that the defendant knew that the property belonged to another person or was reckless as to whether it did. It follows that if the defendant genuinely believed that the property that he was damaging was his own, he is not guilty of criminal damage. This is illustrated by *R* v *Smith* [1974] QB 354. The defendant, David Smith, began renting a flat in 1970. With the landlord's permission, he installed some electric wiring for stereo equipment and put up roofing material, wall panels and laid floorboards. Unbeknown to Smith, when he installed the roofing, wall panels and floorboards they became part of the house and so became the landlord's property. Two years later Smith moved out of the flat. Before leaving, he damaged the roofing, wall panels and floorboards in order to recover the electric wiring he had installed. He was subsequently arrested for criminal damage. When interviewed by police Smith said, 'Look, how can I be done for smashing my own property. I put the flooring and that in, so if I want to pull it down it's a matter for me.' At trial the judge told the jury that Smith's belief that the property he damaged belonged to him was no defence. He was subsequently convicted, and appealed. The Court of Appeal allowed his appeal and quashed his conviction. James LJ explained:

> Construing the language of section 1(1) we have no doubt that the actus reus is "destroying or damaging any property belonging to another." It is not possible to exclude the words "belonging to another" which describes the "property." Applying the ordinary principles of mens rea, the intention and recklessness and the absence of lawful excuse required to constitute the offence have reference to property belonging to another. It follows that in our judgment no offence is committed under this section if a person destroys or causes damage to property belonging to another if he does so in the honest though mistaken belief that the property is his own, and provided that the belief is honestly held it is irrelevant to consider whether or not it is a justifiable belief.

Think about this scenario.

Derek has been charged with the criminal damage of property belonging to Aubrey. Derek genuinely believed that the property belonged to him, but this belief was an utterly unreasonable one to have held.

- Does Derek satisfy this part of the *mens rea*?

6. The defendant lacked a lawful excuse

A defendant who is charged with criminal damage can rely on any of the substantive defences that we will study in Chapter 11. In addition, section 5 of the Criminal Damage Act 1971 sets out two 'lawful excuses':

EXTRACT

Section 5 of the Criminal Damage Act 1971

5 "Without lawful excuse"

[...]

(2) A person charged with an offence to which this section applies, shall, whether or not he would be treated for the purposes of this Act as having a lawful excuse apart from this subsection, be treated for those purposes as having a lawful excuse–

(a) if at the time of the act or acts alleged to constitute the offence he believed that the person or persons whom he believed to be entitled to consent to the destruction of or damage to the property in question had so consented, or would have so consented to it if he or they had known of the destruction or damage and its circumstances; or

(b) if he destroyed or damaged or threatened to destroy or damage the property in question or, in the case of a charge of an offence under section 3 above, intended to use or cause or permit the use of something to destroy or damage it, in order to protect property belonging to himself or another or a right or interest in property which was or which he believed to be vested in himself or another, and at the time of the act or acts alleged to constitute the offence he believed–

that the property, right or interest was in immediate need of protection; and that the means of protection adopted or proposed to be adopted were or would be reasonable having regard to all the circumstances.

(3) For the purposes of this section it is immaterial whether a belief is justified or not if it is honestly held.

(4) For the purposes of subsection (2) above a right or interest in property includes any right or privilege in or over land, whether created by grant, licence or otherwise.

These lawful excuses are not available as a defence to other crimes such as assault or battery. They are unique to criminal damage.

The first lawful excuse, found in section 5(2)(a), applies where the defendant honestly believed that the owner of the property was consenting to the property damage or would have consented had they known about it. An example is *Jaggard* v *Dickinson* [1981] 2 WLR 118. Beverley Jaggard had been out drinking for the evening. At 10:45 pm she took a taxi to her friend's house. Her friend, who lived at number 67, had given her permission to treat the house as her own. Jaggard got out of the taxi and went to what she thought was her friend's house, but in fact was number 35. Finding that she was locked out she attempted to gain entry by smashing a window in the hallway, and then went to the back door and managed to get inside by smashing another window. It was found as fact that Jaggard had genuinely believed that she was breaking into her friend's house (which was identical in outward appearance to number 35), and that Jaggard's mistake was the result of voluntary intoxication.

At trial, Jaggard was convicted of criminal damage. On appeal, the Divisional Court quashed her conviction. Mustill J explained that, according to section 5(3), the lawful excuses are concerned with what the defendant genuinely believed – even if the belief was mistaken, was unreasonable and was the result of voluntary intoxication:

> It seems to us that the court is required by section 5(3) to focus on the existence of the belief, not its intellectual soundness; and a belief can be just as much honestly held if it is induced by intoxication, as if it stems from stupidity, forgetfulness or inattention

Given that Jaggard genuinely believed that the house belonged to her friend, and that her friend would have consented to her breaking in, she was entitled to rely on the lawful excuse contained in section 5(2)(a).

But there are limits to the scope of section 5(2)(a). In *Attorney-General's Reference (No 1 of 2023)* [2024] EWCA Crim 243 the defendant was a member of a group of protestors. The group asserted that climate change is an emergency and that anything short of immediate and substantial change will lead to terrible consequences for the planet and the human race. Along with other group members, the defendant targeted the offices of various organisations, political parties and trade unions, causing thousands of pounds worth of damage. She claimed that the occupiers would have consented to the damage had they been aware that it was carried out to alert those responsible for the premises to the nature and extent of man-made climate change. The damage, she said, was designed to 'shock' them, so that they 'wake up' ([14]). At trial the defendant was acquitted. The Attorney-General subsequently referred to the Court of Appeal the question of the correct interpretation of the section 5(2)(a) lawful excuse.

EXTRACT

Read the following extract from the judgment of Lady Carr CJ. She sets out four principles regarding the application of the section 5(2)(a) lawful excuse. What are these?

According to Lady Carr CJ, what is the correct interpretation of the words 'its circumstances'?

Attorney-General's Reference (No 1 of 2023) [2024] EWCA Crim 243 Lady Carr CJ

40 First, it is clear from the words "at the time of the act or acts alleged to constitute the offence" that the belief on which a defendant relies to establish the defence must be one held by the defendant at the time of the commission of the offence. It cannot be one formed to explain the conduct after the event. Nor can it be a belief founded on the actual or potential effect of efforts that might be deployed after the event to persuade the owner to consent. As the Judge directed the jury in this case, the damage cannot be an instrument of persuasion.

41 Secondly, the belief required must be a genuine belief, otherwise it is not a belief at all. Section 5(3) provides that the belief does not need to be justified but it must be honestly held. It follows that this element of the defence involves a subjective test.

42 Thirdly, the defendant's belief must be as to the consent of the person whom the defendant believed to be entitled to consent to the damage to the property in question (for convenience, described as the owner). The defendant must believe that the owner either had consented (as in Jaggard) or would have consented to the damage if they had known of the damage "and its circumstances". The inclusion of the phrase "would have" involves a certainty in the belief in the owner's consent, not merely that the owner might (or should) have consented. There is therefore a requirement that the defendant's honest belief must be that she was sure that that the owner would have consented.

43 Fourthly, in any case where the defence under section 5(2)(a) is raised there must be evidence that the defendant believed that the owner would have consented to the damage had they known of the damage and its circumstances.

44 The possessive pronoun "its" is central. It delimits the "circumstances". It is only the circumstances of the damage which are relevant. The circumstances must relate to the destruction of, or damage to, the property. Thus, the relevant circumstances may include matters such as the time, place and the extent of the damage caused. These factors would be linked to the damage and directly relevant to the owner's hypothetical decision as to consent. They do not include the political or philosophical beliefs of the person causing the damage.

45 One commonly postulated circumstance where the defence in section 5(2)(a) is likely to arise is the case of the stranger discovering a child locked alone in a car on a hot day. The child is at risk of harm unless freed. If the stranger damages the car window in order to free the child, the defence of lawful excuse under section 5(2)(a) may be available to them: they believed at the time that the owner of the car would have consented to the damaging of the window because the circumstances of the damage included the need for speedy action, the importance of rescuing the child, and the relative unimportance of the damage to the vehicle. There would be a direct connection between the damage (the broken window) and the circumstances (the freeing of the child).

46 The need for a direct nexus between the circumstances of the damage and the anticipated giving of consent is implicit in the statutory language. The circumstances must belong to the damage, not to the defendant. To this extent there is an objective element to the defence ...

> [T]he circumstances cannot be so remote from the damage as no longer to be part of the damage. There must be a sufficient connection between the damage and its circumstances.
>
> 47 Both the AG and the Advocate to the Court accept that the reason for the damage as advanced by C, namely that it was an act of protest against climate change, was a "circumstance" of the damage. Just as the stranger who broke the car window did so to rescue the child, so C agreed to damage the relevant premises as a protest against climate change. The issue of climate change was the immediate prompt for the causing of the damage but also it was the foundation of the alleged belief in the putative consent.
>
> 48 We agree with those submissions. We also agree that further explanation of C's views on climate change – the extent, reasoning or her wider motivations (including the need to draw attention to the subject matter of the protest) – lacked the necessary proximity to the damage. The issue is whether C honestly believed that the owner would have consented had they known of the damage and its circumstances. On the facts of this case what C had to say about the facts of or effects of climate change could not amount to the circumstances of the damage. Such evidence would be inadmissible in relation to the defence under section 5(2)(a).
>
> 49 The limits on the scope of the defence are defined by the words of section 5(2)(a). Parliament required a direct link between the damage and its circumstances ...[I]t was not Parliament's intention in enacting section 5(2)(a) to give protesters free rein to publicise their cause through the criminal courts. Section 5(2)(a) was not intended to afford a defence to protestors based on the merits, urgency or importance of their cause (nor the perceived need to draw attention to a cause or situation).
>
> 50 This is not to place artificial restrictions on the availability of the defence in a particular category of cases nor to adjudicate on any matter touching on the validity of political, moral or religious beliefs. Rather, that by applying the normal principles of statutory construction, the merits, urgency or importance of any matter about which the defendant may be protesting do not constitute the circumstances of the damage for the purpose of section 5(2)(a).

The second lawful excuse, found in section 5(2)(b), applies where the defendant damaged property in order to protect his own or someone else's property. For this lawful excuse to be available, the defendant must have: (i) damaged the property 'in order to' protect his or someone else's property; (ii) genuinely believed that the property was 'in immediate need of protection'; and (iii) genuinely believed that the steps he took to protect the property were 'reasonable having regard to all the circumstances'. The test for numbers (ii) and (iii) is entirely subjective. In *Unsworth* v *DPP* [2010] EWHC 3037 (Admin) the defendant Jacqueline Unsworth was caught cutting down her neighbour's conifer trees (which were 10–12 feet tall). She explained that she cut them down to protect her right to light in her kitchen and that the lack of light had caused her to become depressed. The Divisional Court confirmed that the test for numbers (ii) and (iii) is 'exclusively a test of the defendant's belief' ([7]). They do not require any objective assessment of the defendant's belief.

However, things are different for number (i). In spite of the apparently subjective wording of sections 5(2) and 5(3), the courts have injected some objectivity. This is illustrated by *R* v *Hill & Hall* (1989) 89 Cr App R 74. The defendants in this case, Valerie Hill and Jennifer Hall, lived near a US naval base in west Wales. One day they were found in possession of a hacksaw blade, which they said they intended to use to cut part of the perimeter fence of the base. The reason they gave was because they believed the naval base was used to monitor the movements of Russian submarines and so was a prime target for a retaliatory, or even pre-emptive, Russian nuclear strike. Any such attack would devastate the area, including the defendants' homes. So the defendants said that they wanted to compromise the security of the naval base by cutting the perimeter fence, in the hope that this might force the US to relocate the naval base elsewhere.

At trial Hill and Hall were convicted of possessing a hacksaw blade with intent to commit criminal damage.[68] On appeal, the Court of Appeal held that the defendants could not rely on the section 5(2)(b) lawful excuse.

EXTRACT

In the following extract Lord Lane CJ outlines a two-stage approach to deciding whether the section 5(2)(b) lawful excuse is available. What are these two stages?

Having distinguished the two stages, why was Hill unable to rely on the lawful excuse?

R v Hill & Hall (1989) 89 Cr App R 74

Lord Lane CJ

There are two aspects to this type of question. The first aspect is to decide what it was that the applicant, in this case Valerie Hill, in her own mind thought. The learned judge assumed, and so do we, for the purposes of this decision, that everything she said about her reasoning was true. I have already perhaps given a sufficient outline of what it was she believed to demonstrate what is meant by that. Up to that point the test was subjective. In other words one is examining what is going on in the applicant's mind. Having done that, the judges in the present cases - and the judge particularly in the case of Valerie Hill - turned to the second aspect of the case, and that is this. He had to decide as a matter of law which means objectively, whether it could be said that on those facts as believed by the applicant, snipping the strand of the wire, which she intended to do, could amount to something done to protect either the applicant's own home or the homes of her adjacent friends in Pembrokeshire.

He decided, again quite rightly in our view, that that proposed act on her part was far too remote from the eventual aim at which she was targeting her actions to satisfy the test. It follows therefore, in our view, that the judges in the present two cases were absolutely right to come to the conclusion that they did so far as this aspect of the case is concerned, and to come to that conclusion as a matter of law, having decided the subjective test as the applicants wished them to be decided.

The second half of the question was that of the immediacy of the danger. Here the wording of the Act, one reminds oneself, is as follows: She believed that "the property ... was in immediate need of protection."

Once again the judge had to determine whether, on the facts as stated by the applicant, there was any evidence on which it could be said that she believed there was a need of protection from immediate danger. In our view that must mean evidence that she believed that immediate

[68] Criminal Damage Act 1971, s.3.

> action had to be taken to do something which would otherwise be a crime in order to prevent the immediate risk of something worse happening. The answers which I have read in the evidence given by this woman (and the evidence given by the other applicant was very similar) drives this Court to the conclusion, as they drove the respective judges to the conclusion, that there was no evidence on which it could be said that there was that belief.

So unlike numbers (ii) and (iii) which are entirely subjective, the test for number (i) 'has both a subjective and an objective aspect'.[69] Not only must the defendant's reason for destroying or damaging the property have been to protect his own (or someone else's) property (subjective), the destruction or damage must also have been capable of protecting the property in question (objective). The court decided that this objective requirement was not satisfied in *R* v *Hill & Hall*. Note also that Lord Lane CJ emphasised that, even though number (ii) is subjective, the defendant must still produce some supporting evidence to demonstrate that he did in fact believe the property was in immediate need of protection. Hill and Hall had failed to produce any evidence that they did indeed believe that this was the case.

Think about this question.

The decision in *R* v *Hill & Hall* is controversial, for it seems hard to reconcile with the subjective wording of the statute. Can you think of any policy reasons for the decision?

Aggravated criminal damage

The offence of aggravated criminal damage is defined by section 1(2) of the Criminal Damage Act 1971:

EXTRACT

Section 1(2) of the Criminal Damage Act 1971

1 Destroying or damaging property.

[...]

(2) A person who without lawful excuse destroys or damages any property, whether belonging to himself or another–

- (a) intending to destroy or damage any property or being reckless as to whether any property would be destroyed or damaged; and
- (b) intending by the destruction or damage to endanger the life of another or being reckless as to whether the life of another would be thereby endangered.

shall be guilty of an offence.

[69] *Unsworth* v *DPP* [2010] EWHC 3037 (Admin), [11].

This tells us that aggravated criminal damage has five requirements:

1. The defendant destroyed or damaged an item
2. The item was property
3. The defendant intentionally or recklessly destroyed or damaged the property
4. The defendant intended, by the destruction or damage, to endanger the life of another or was reckless as to whether the life of another would be thereby endangered
5. The defendant lacked a lawful excuse.

Numbers 1 and 2 are *actus reus* requirements. Numbers 3 and 4 are *mens rea* requirements. Number 5 is a defence which is peculiar to criminal damage offences. We will work through them in turn.

1. The defendant destroyed or damaged an item

This is the same as for the basic criminal damage offence, which we studied above.

2. The item was property

The word 'property' has the same meaning as for the basic criminal damage offence, which we studied above. Notice that for aggravated criminal damage there is no requirement that the property belonged to another person; the defendant may commit the aggravated offence by damaging his own property.

3. The defendant intentionally or recklessly destroyed or damaged the property

This is the same as for the basic criminal damage offence, which we studied above.

4. The defendant intended, by the destruction or damage, to endanger the life of another or was reckless as to whether the life of another would be thereby endangered

This mens rea requirement is the aggravating factor which makes this such a serious offence (punishable by up to life imprisonment[70]). Notice that there is no corresponding *actus reus* requirement; there is no need to show that anyone's life was in fact endangered. What must be shown is that the defendant intended, by the destruction or damage, to endanger the life of another or that he was reckless as to whether the life of another would be thereby endangered. Intention and recklessness have the meanings that we studied in Chapter 4. Note in particular that recklessness here means *R* v *Cunningham* recklessness.[71]

In *R* v *Steer* [1987] 3 WLR 205 the defendant, Dennis Steer, armed himself with an automatic rifle and went to the home of his former business partner, David Gregory, against whom he bore a grudge. When Gregory and his wife looked out of their bedroom window, Steer fired a shot at the window and then another one at the front door. No one was hurt. The prosecution accepted that Steer had not intended to hurt Gregory or his wife, but contended that Steer had been reckless as to whether their lives would be endangered. At trial Steer was convicted of aggravated criminal damage. He appealed, emphasising that section 1(2)(b) of the Criminal Damage Act 1971 states 'intending *by the destruction or damage* to endanger the life of another or being reckless as to whether the life of another would be *thereby* endangered'. In other words, the property damage must be the means

---

[70] Criminal Damage Act 1971, s.4.

[71] *R* v *G & another* [2003] UKHL 50.

by which the defendant intends to endanger life or foresees life being endangered. Steer argued that in his case this requirement was not satisfied since it was not the damage he caused (a broken window) that endangered life, rather it was the bullet from the rifle shot. The case reached the House of Lords. The House of Lords accepted Steer's argument and quashed his conviction for aggravated criminal damage. Lord Bridge explained:

> Under both limbs of section 1 of the Act of 1971 it is the essence of the offence which the section creates that the defendant has destroyed or damaged property. For the purpose of analysis it may be convenient to omit reference to destruction and to concentrate on the references to damage, which was all that was here involved. To be guilty under subsection (1) the defendant must have intended or been reckless as to the damage to property which he caused. To be guilty under subsection (2) he must additionally have intended to endanger life or been reckless as to whether life would be endangered "by the damage" to property which he caused. This is the context in which the words must be construed and it seems to me impossible to read the words "by the damage" as meaning "by the damage or by the act which caused the damage." Moreover, if the language of the statute has the meaning for which the Crown contends, the words "by the destruction or damage" and "thereby" in subsection (2)(b) are mere surplusage. If the Crown's submission is right, the only additional element necessary to convert a subsection (1) offence into a subsection (2) offence is an intent to endanger life or recklessness as to whether life would be endangered simpliciter.
>
> It would suffice as a ground for dismissing this appeal if the statute were ambiguous, since any such ambiguity in a criminal statute should be resolved in favour of the defence. But I can find no ambiguity. It seems to me that the meaning for which the respondent contends is the only meaning which the language can bear.

5. The defendant lacked a lawful excuse

The lawful excuses contained in section 5(2) are not available on a charge of aggravated criminal damage. So for this offence, the term 'lawful excuse' simply means any of the substantive defences that we will study in Chapter 11.

Quiz 8.8

1. Which of the following is not an *actus reus* requirement of criminal damage according to section 1(1) of the Criminal Damage Act 1971?
   - **a.** D knew that the item belonged to another person.
   - **b.** The item in question was property.
   - **c.** The item in question belonged to another person.
   - **d.** D destroyed or damaged an item.
2. According to section 1(1) of the Criminal Damage Act 1971, what is the *mens rea* of criminal damage?
   - **a.** Being reckless or negligent as to whether any such property would be destroyed.
   - **b.** Intending to destroy or damage any such property or being negligent as to whether any such property would be destroyed.
   - **c.** Intending to destroy or damage any such property.
   - **d.** Intending to destroy or damage any such property or being reckless as to whether any such property would be destroyed or damaged.
3. The current case authority for recklessness in regards to criminal damage is ...
   - **a.** *Woollin.*
   - **b.** *R v G & another.*
   - **c.** *Smith.*
   - **d.** *Caldwell.*
4. When, according to section 5(2)(b) of the Criminal Damage Act 1971, might damage to another's property not be considered criminal damage?
   - **a.** If the defendant was protecting his own property.

  b. If the defendant was mistaken as to the ownership of the property.
  c. If ownership was shared.
  d. If the defendant had a right in law to the property.

5. Which of the following circumstances will translate ordinary criminal damage into aggravated criminal damage?
  a. The fact that the damage was caused by fire.
  b. The fact that life was endangered by shooting at the victim.
  c. The fact that the defendant has previous convictions for causing criminal damage.
  d. The fact that the defendant intended, by the destruction or damage, to endanger the life of another or was reckless as to whether the life of another would be thereby endangered.

Conclusion

Well done for making it to the end of the chapter! Much of the material we have worked through is quite detailed and technical. This technicality means that it is very important, when answering problem questions, to take extra care to be precise. For every possible offence that you consider, always take care to begin by clearly stating the following particulars:

Who the defendant is

Which crime or crimes the defendant may have committed

Which of the defendant's actions you are focusing on

What the item of property is

Who the victim of the offence was

1. Who the defendant is

Whether or not an item of property belongs to someone can depend on who is alleged to have stolen it.

For example, the car did not belong to the police in *R* v *Meredith* because Meredith was the defendant. If anyone else had been accused of stealing the car it would have belonged to the police!

2. Which crime or crimes the defendant may have committed

Several of the property offences overlap, so it is important to clearly state which offence you are focusing on.

For example, there are subtle differences between section 9(1)(a) and section 9(1)(b) burglary, so it is important to say which one you are discussing.

3. Which of the defendant's actions you are focusing on

The moment at which the offence was committed can be critical, so it is important to identify which of the defendant's actions constituted the offence.

For example, to establish robbery it is necessary to show that the defendant used force immediately before or at the time of the theft. This means that you need to identify exactly when the theft occurred.

4. What the item of property is

When there is more than one possible way of describing the item in question you need to select the most appropriate description.

For example, we saw how in *R* v *Easom* the wording of the charge was vital, and resulted in an acquittal instead of a conviction. We also saw in *Oxford* v *Moss* that the defendant was charged with theft of confidential information, which is not property. Arguably things might have been different had he been charged with theft of the exam paper.

5. Who the victim of the offence was

Where the property might have belonged to several people at once, it is important to state which person the defendant is accused of stealing from.

For example, we saw in *Ricketts* v *Basildon Magistrates' Court* that the defendant could not be convicted of theft from the British Heart Foundation shop but could be convicted of theft from the donor of the items.

Often it is possible to give all of this information in one short, concise sentence, such as: 'Derek would be charged with robbery of the handbag from Cassandra by wrenching it from her grasp'. Clarifying the particulars of the offence in this way at the outset can help ensure that you avoid errors later on.

Something else that students sometimes find confusing when studying this topic is the overlap between different offences. A common question is: 'Should I discuss every offence that might apply or just select one?' To answer this it is helpful to distinguish two types of situation:

- Sometimes a defendant can only be guilty of one offence if it can first be shown that he committed another (ulterior) offence. For example, a defendant can only be convicted of robbery if he committed theft. And a defendant can only be convicted of section 9(1)(b) burglary if he committed theft (or attempted theft) or infliction of GBH (or attempted infliction of GBH). In these instances, it is sensible to establish liability for the ulterior offence first, then move on to discuss the other offence.

- Sometimes two offences simply overlap. Of the offences we have studied in this chapter, this is most likely to occur with theft and fraud. When this happens, begin with the offence that you think is the most appropriate (bearing in mind not only the principle of fair labelling, but also the fact that a prosecutor is likely to charge the offence that he thinks is most likely to result in a conviction). If liability for this offence is established, it is still worth mentioning the alternative offence but you can deal with it more briefly.

Applying the law

8.9 Apply the law on property offences to hypothetical sets of facts.

The following events take place at Golfers' Paradise (a private golf club).

Jeong and Callum

Jeong (a club member) arranges to play a round of golf with his friend Callum (a former member who decided not to renew his membership). The club charges non-members a fee of £30 to play a round, so when they arrive Callum shows the club caretaker, Gary, his old membership card hoping that Gary will not notice that it has expired. Gary does not notice, and so does not charge Callum the £30 fee.

Before teeing off they go to the club shop and look at the golfing magazines. Even though there is a sign saying 'Please do not read the magazines until they have been paid for', Jeong picks up one of the magazines and reads three articles from it before returning it to the shelf without paying for it. Meanwhile Callum notices a voucher for free trolley hire in one of the other magazines. He rips it out, places the magazine back on the shelf without paying for it and then takes the voucher to the counter and says,'I have a voucher for free trolley hire'. Club assistant Tony had not seen Callum rip the voucher out of the magazine, and so accepts it. While Tony is outside getting a trolley, Callum sees some bottles of water behind the counter. He realises he has not brought anything to drink during his round, so leans over the counter and helps himself to a bottle of water. While he is leaning over the counter he notices a box of chocolate bars under the till. He takes one of those too, and then quickly hides the bottle of water and chocolate bar in his golf bag. Tony then returns with a trolley. Callum takes it, and he and Jeong embark on their round of golf.

Discuss the criminal liability of Callum and Jeong.

This scenario involves a number of potential offences. We will consider them in the order in which they occurred.

First, Callum shows Gary, the club caretaker, his old membership card. The charge here would be fraud by false representation (Fraud Act 2006, section 2).

Quiz 8.9

1. Which of the following statements about the offence of fraud by false representation is correct?
   - **a.** The representation must have been express, but may have been a representation of either fact or law.
   - **b.** The representation must have been an express representation of fact.
   - **c.** The representation may have been express or implied, and may have been a representation of either fact or law.
   - **d.** The representation may have been express or implied, but must have been a representation of fact.

2. When Callum showed Gary his old membership card, hoping that Gary would not notice that it had expired, he was impliedly representing by his conduct that he was a current member. Since this was untrue, it amounted to a false representation. The *actus reus* of fraud by false representation is thus established.

   Of the following four items, which one is not a *mens rea* requirement for fraud by false representation?
   - **a.** The defendant intended, by making the false representation, to make a gain for himself or another or to cause loss to another or to expose another to a risk of loss.
   - **b.** The defendant knew that the representation was, or might be, untrue or misleading.
   - **c.** The defendant acted dishonestly.
   - **d.** The defendant recklessly exposed another person to a risk of financial loss.

3. Applying these three *mens rea* requirements to Callum, the facts indicate that: (1) Callum knew that his membership card had expired, and so he knew his representation was untrue; and (2) Callum showed the expired card in order to avoid paying the £30 fee, and so his intention was to make a gain for himself (by keeping money he already had: section 5(3)). That just leaves the requirement that Callum acted dishonestly. Here the test from *Ivey* v *Genting Casinos* must be applied.

   Which of the following correctly summarises the *Ivey* test?
   - **a.** The defendant believed that what he was doing was immoral.
   - **b.** The defendant's thoughts and actions would be regarded as dishonest by the ordinary, honest person.
   - **c.** The defendant displayed an attitude of indifference as to whether his actions were honest or not.
   - **d.** The defendant's conduct and state of mind were dishonest according to the standards of reasonable and honest people, and the defendant realised this.

4. The next potential offence is Jeong reading three articles from the magazine in spite of the sign prohibiting this. The charge here would be theft of the magazine (Theft Act 1968, section 1).

   The magazine is obviously property, which belongs to another (the club shop). Whether or not there is the *actus reus* of theft therefore depends on whether Jeong appropriated the magazine.

   In the light of the decisions in *Lawrence* v *MPC*, *R* v *Morris* and *DPP* v *Gomez*, which of the following statements correctly summarises the legal test for appropriation?
   - **a.** Did D assume any of the rights of an owner without consent?
   - **b.** Did D assume any of the rights of an owner (regardless of consent)?
   - **c.** Did D assume all of the rights of an owner without consent?
   - **d.** Did D assume all of the rights of an owner (regardless of consent)?

5. If we apply the legal test for an appropriation to our scenario, Jeong assumed some rights of an owner by picking the magazine up and reading it. It is not necessary to show that he assumed all of the rights of an owner (*R* v *Morris*, *DPP* v *Gomez*). It is also irrelevant whether or not the shop consented to his actions (*Lawrence* v *MPC*, *DPP* v *Gomez*), although in this case the sign made it clear that his actions were unauthorised.

   Having established the *actus reus* of theft, the next question is whether Jeong satisfies the *mens rea*.

   The offence of theft has two *mens rea* requirements. One is that the defendant acted dishonestly. What is the other one?
   - **a.** The defendant intended to make a personal gain for himself.
   - **b.** The defendant caused the other person permanent deprivation.
   - **c.** The defendant had an intention to cause the other person permanent deprivation.
   - **d.** The defendant had an intention to permanently deprive the other person of the property.

6. If we consider dishonesty first, it seems unlikely that any of the mind-sets listed in section 2(1) of the Theft Act 1968 would apply. In particular, the sign made it clear that the club shop did not consent to customers reading the magazines before purchasing them (paragraph (b)). So whether or not Jeong acted dishonestly would be determined by applying the test from *Ivey* v *Genting Casinos*.

   If Jeong were found to have acted dishonestly, his liability would hinge on whether he intended to permanently deprive the club shop of the magazine. Although Jeong lacked such an intention – as the facts indicate he always planned to put the magazine back on the shelf – section 6(1) of the Theft Act 1968 states that there are two situations in which a defendant will be deemed to satisfy this mens rea requirement even though he lacked the necessary intention. The first of these situations is where the defendant intended to treat the thing as his own to dispose of regardless of the other's rights.

   What was the conclusion of the Court of Appeal in *R* v *Mitchell?*

   a. D lacked the *mens* rea of theft because, whilst he had intended to treat the BMW as his own, the circumstances showed he had not intended to treat it as his own to dispose of.

   b. When D took the BMW and used it as a getaway car, he intended to treat the car as his own to dispose of regardless of V's rights.

   c. D had intended to permanently deprive the victim of the car, and so there was no need to refer to the two situations listed in section 6(1).

   d. D lacked the mens rea of theft because he only ever planned to borrow the car and so had not intended to treat it as his own.

7. The second of the situations listed in section 6(1) is where the defendant intended to borrow the item and the borrowing was equivalent to an outright taking or disposal. According to *R* v *Lloyd*, what test should be applied to decide whether a borrowing was equivalent to an outright taking or disposal?

   a. Whether the defendant knew that the owner of the property would not have lent it to him if he had asked to borrow it.

   b. Whether the defendant could have bought a similar item for himself instead of borrowing it from the other person.

   c. Whether the intention is to return the item in such a changed state that it can truly be said that all its goodness or virtue has gone.

   d. Whether the intention is to keep the property for such a long time that it can be said that the defendant effectively regards the item as his own.

8. The next potential offence is Callum ripping the voucher out of the magazine. The charge here would be criminal damage of the magazine (Criminal Damage Act 1971, section 1(1)). The magazine was property that belonged to another (the club shop), so whether or not there is the *actus reus* depends on whether Callum damaged the magazine.

   Which of the following statements accurately summarises the approach of the Court of Appeal to the word 'damage' in *R* v *Fiak?*

   a. An item is damaged if it has been irreversibly altered without the prior permission of the owner.

   b. An item is damaged if its usefulness has been (permanently or temporarily) impaired.

   c. An item is damaged if it has been stripped of all its goodness or virtue.

   d. An item is damaged if its value has been substantially diminished.

   The prosecution would argue that the usefulness of the magazine has been impaired, since customers are less likely to buy it now that Callum has ripped the voucher out. By contrast, the defence would argue that many customers would still be happy to buy the magazine even without the voucher, and so the impact of Callum removing it is minimal and insignificant. Ultimately, whether or not the magazine has been damaged is a question of fact for the jury to decide. What would your opinion be if you were a juror?

   If the *actus reus* of criminal damage is established, the remainder of the offence will be straightforward. Callum damaged the property intentionally, he knew that the magazine belonged to the club shop, and he has no plausible claim that he had a lawful excuse.

9. Callum might also be charged with theft for ripping the voucher out of the magazine. However, notice the importance of framing this charge correctly. It would not be theft of the magazine – since Callum lacked an intention to permanently deprive the club shop of the magazine (for the same reasons Jeong lacked the *mens rea* of theft above). To be guilty of theft, Callum would have to be charged with theft of the voucher.

   The next potential offence is Callum using the voucher. Here the relevant offence would again be fraud by false representation (Fraud Act 2006, section 2).

   Which of the following statements is inaccurate?

   a. A person who orders food in a restaurant impliedly represents that he intends to pay for the food at the end of the meal.

   b. A person who pays by credit card impliedly represents that he has the bank's authority to do so.

c. A person who takes a taxi impliedly represents that he has the money to pay the fare at the end of the journey.

d. A tradesman who gives a potential customer a quotation impliedly represents that the quoted price is a fair one.

10. Lastly, Callum would be charged with burglary of the bottle of water and the chocolate bar (Theft Act 1968, section 9). Before considering whether the charge would be section 9(1)(a) or section 9(1)(b) burglary in respect of each item, it is best to begin with the four requirements which are common to both types.

Of the following four items, which one is not common to both section 9(1)(a) and section 9(1)(b) burglary?

a. The defendant was knowingly or recklessly trespassing.

b. The defendant entered the building or part of a building as a trespasser.

c. The place the defendant entered was a building or a part of a building.

d. The defendant intended to commit theft, infliction of GBH or criminal damage at the time of entry.

11. In Callum's case, it makes sense to begin by asking whether the area behind the counter was a separate part of the building. The facts of Callum's case are similar to those of *R* v *Walkington*.

In *R* v *Walkington* the Court of Appeal held that the jury's finding that the till area was a separate part of the building had been justified. What reason did the Court of Appeal give for this decision?

a. People generally know that they are not allowed to enter till areas in shops.

b. Walkington had stepped over a barrier in order to enter the till area.

c. There was a prominently displayed 'Staff only' sign.

d. The layout of the till area created a physical demarcation.

12. If the area behind the counter was a separate part of the building, the other three requirements which are common to both types of burglary appear straightforward: (1) Callum entered the counter area by leaning over and taking the water and chocolate bar – it is not necessary to show that his whole body entered (e.g. *R* v *Brown*); (2) Callum did not have legal authorisation to enter the counter area, and so was trespassing; and (3) Callum knew that he was trespassing (as evidenced by the fact that he waited until Tony went outside).

The remaining issue is therefore to decide which type of burglary applies in respect of each item.

Which one of the following four statements is inaccurate?

a. For section 9(1)(b) burglary, the defendant must have entered the building or part of a building as a trespasser and committed one of the ulterior offences whilst inside.

b. Criminal damage is listed as one of the relevant ulterior offences for section 9(1)(a) burglary, but not for section 9(1)(b) burglary.

c. For section 9(1)(a) burglary, the defendant must have intended to commit the ulterior offence at the moment of entry.

d. For section 9(1)(a) burglary, the defendant must have entered with an intention to commit one of the ulterior offences and subsequently attempted to commit the offence.

So let's apply this distinction between section 9(1)(a) and section 9(1)(b) burglary to the facts of Callum's case. First, Callum saw the bottles of water before leaning over the counter and lent over in order to take one. He therefore entered the counter area with an intention to steal the bottle of water (he intended to appropriate the water – which was property belonging to another – with a dishonest intention to permanently deprive the club shop of the property). So section 9(1)(a) burglary would apply in respect of the bottle of water.

Second, Callum only noticed the chocolate bars after he had lent over the counter. Section 9(1)(a) burglary therefore cannot apply, since he lacked any intention to steal the chocolate bar at the moment of entry. However, section 9(1)(b) burglary would apply because, having entered as a trespasser, Callum stole the chocolate bar whilst inside (he appropriated the chocolate – which was property belonging to another – with a dishonest intention to permanently deprive the club shop of the property).

Kristjan and Greg

Kristjan and Greg are halfway through their round of golf. Kristjan suggests, 'How about we make it more interesting? Whoever loses the next hole pays the winner £10.' Greg agrees. Kristjan hits his tee shot into a bunker. He is so frustrated that he strikes his golf trolley (which he has hired from the golf club for the day) with his golf club. This scratches the trolley and causes a small dent.

As he walks up the fairway Kristjan notices two lost golf balls in the long grass. When he picks them up he looks at them and sees the words 'Property of Golfers' Paradise Golf Club'. Kristjan looks around, sees that no one is watching and then quickly puts the balls in his golf bag.

When they have both finished the hole Kristjan asks Greg, 'How many shots did you take?' Greg replies, 'Six'. Kristjan says, 'In that case, I win. I only took five'. In fact, unbeknown to Greg, Kristjan had taken seven shots. Greg takes a £10 note from his wallet and gives it to Kristjan.

Discuss the criminal liability of Kristjan. How (if at all) would your answer be different if there had been nothing written on the two lost golf balls?

1. Here we only have to discuss the criminal liability of one person, Kristjan. We will work through the potential offences in the order in which they occurred.

First, Kristjan would be charged with criminal damage of the golf trolley (Criminal Damage Act 1971, section 1(1)). This is property which belonged to another (the golf club), so whether or not the *actus reus* of criminal damage is established depends on whether Kristjan damaged the trolley. When discussing the previous scenario, we saw that one of the considerations the courts apply when determining whether or not there is evidence of damage is whether the value or usefulness of the item has been (permanently or temporarily) impaired (e.g. *R* v *Fiak*). The other consideration the courts have applied is whether time and money will be required to remedy the defendant's actions.

One of the following four statements is incorrect, which one?

a. In *Seray-Wurie* v *DPP* writing on a parking notice with a black marker pen was held to be capable of amounting to damage.

b. In *Morphitis* v *Salmon* scratching a scaffolding bar was held to be capable of amounting to damage.

c. In *Hardman* v *Chief Constable of Avon and Somerset* painting on a pavement with water-soluble paint was held to be capable of amounting to damage.

d. In *Roe* v *Kingerlee* smearing mud and graffiti on the walls of a police cell was held to be capable of amounting to damage.

2. If the jury decided that the trolley had been damaged, there would be three remaining requirements for liability. Kristjan obviously knew that the trolley belonged to another person (the golf club), since he hired it from them. He also has no plausible claim of a lawful excuse. So liability would hinge on whether Kristjan damaged the property either intentionally or recklessly. Damaging the trolley does not appear to have been his direct intention (he was merely venting his frustration, so presumably would not have regarded himself as having failed if the trolley had not been scratched or dented). Whether or not it was his oblique intention would depend on how hard he struck the trolley (he would need to have struck it so hard that he foresaw damage as virtually certain: *R* v *Woollin*). If the prosecution instead alleged recklessness, Kristjan might argue that he was not reckless under the test from *R* v *Cunningham* because he was so angry that the risk of damaging the trolley never crossed his mind. Here the reasoning in *R* v *Parker* would be relevant.

In *R* v *Parker* (which we studied in Chapter 4) the defendant claimed that he was so angry that he acted without thinking and that as a result the risk of damaging the telephone never crossed his mind. Which of the following statements accurately describes the Court of Appeal's reasoning in this case?

a. Parker's actions demonstrated a 'couldn't care less' attitude. A defendant who displays such an attitude acts recklessly.

b. Parker had not foreseen the risk of damaging the phone. In the heat of the moment he acted without thinking and as a result the risk of damaging the phone never crossed his mind.

c. Parker had foreseen the risk of damaging the phone. He had deliberately closed his mind to this obvious risk and deliberately closing your mind to an obvious risk is equivalent to having foreseen it.

d. Parker's failure to consider the risk of damaging the phone was the result of his attitude of indifference. A defendant who displays such indifference acts recklessly.

3. The next possible offence is theft of the golf balls (Theft Act 1968, section 1). These were obviously property, and Kristjan appropriated them because by picking them up and putting them in his golf bag he assumed the rights of an owner (Theft Act 1968, section 3(1)). Whether or not there is the *actus reus* of theft therefore depends on whether the balls belonged to another person.

When is an item of property regarded as abandoned and ownerless?

a. When the owner puts the property up for sale.

b. When the owner intentionally relinquishes all of his rights over the property.

c. When the owner loses the property and gives up trying to find it.

d. When the owner has no idea that the property exists.

Moving on to the *mens rea* of theft, it is clear that Kristjan intended to permanently deprive the golf club of the balls. Liability therefore hinges on whether or not he acted dishonestly. Since the mind-sets listed in section 2(1) of the Theft Act 1968 do not appear to apply, the test from *Ivey* v *Genting Casinos* would need to be applied. So, having regard to Kristjan's conduct and his state of mind, was he dishonest according to the standards of ordinary and honest people? Here it is possible to construct competing arguments for the prosecution and defence. The defence might argue that it is common for golfers to keep lost balls they find, and that many other people in Kristjan's situation would have done the same thing. By contrast, the prosecution would argue that Kristjan ignored the clear wording written on the balls and that the fact he looked around before putting the balls in his golf bag shows that he knew he was acting dishonestly. If you were a juror, what would you decide?

4. Next, Kristjan lies about how many shots he took in order to win his bet with Greg. Here he could be charged with fraud by false representation (Fraud Act 2006, section 2). This appears straightforward. The *actus reus* is present since his statement that he only took five shots was untrue. And the *mens rea* appears to be present too, since he knew the statement was untrue, he intended to make a gain of £10 for himself, and his actions were dishonest (applying the *Ivey* v *Genting Casinos* test). But when Kristjan takes the £10 note from Greg, does he also commit theft? There is the *actus reus* of theft, since the £10 note was property belonging to another and Kristjan appropriated it (as we saw in the previous scenario, the test for appropriation is whether the defendant assumed any of the rights of an owner regardless of consent). There is also the *mens rea* of theft, since Kristjan intended to permanently deprive Greg of the £10 note and his actions will be deemed to have been dishonest under *Ivey* v *Genting Casinos*. The fact that Kristjan could be guilty of both fraud and theft for swindling Greg raises questions about the relationship between the two offences, which we will turn to in the Explore activity later.

Lastly, would your answer be any different if nothing had been written on the golf balls? The significance of this depends on who Kristjan is alleged to have stolen the balls from. Suppose, first, that he is charged with stealing the balls from the person who lost them. Although (as we saw above) the balls would be regarded as lost rather than abandoned, and so would still belong to the person who lost them for the purposes of theft, Kristjan might be able to argue that he did not act dishonestly.

Section 2(1) lists three mind-sets which are not dishonest. Which of the following mind-sets is not found in section 2(1)?

a. The defendant believed that the person the property belonged to could not be discovered by taking reasonable steps.

b. The defendant believed he had a legal right to appropriate the property.

c. The defendant believed that his actions were morally justified.

d. The defendant believed he would have had the consent of the owner if the owner had known about the appropriation.

Suppose instead that Kristjan was charged with theft of the golf balls from the golf club. Applying *R* v *Woodman* it is arguable that the balls belonged to the golf club, since the club had control of the site on which the balls were found. Once again, therefore, liability would hinge on the question of dishonesty. Kristjan may no longer be able to rely on section 2(1)(c), since it was straightforward to find out who owned the site on which the balls were found. The case would therefore hinge on the *Ivey* v *Genting Casinos* test. If you were a juror, would you decide that Kristjan acted dishonestly according to *Ivey*?

Harper and Darren

Harper has just finished his round of golf. A week earlier he had left one of his golf clubs – his driver – at the clubhouse by mistake. He decides to go to the clubhouse to ask whether anyone has found it and handed it in. On his way he walks past Phil, and notices a driver in Phil's golf bag that looks just like his own. Convinced that it belongs to him, Harper says to Phil, 'Where did you get that driver?' Phil answers, 'I bought it last year on holiday in the US.' Harper replies, 'Rubbish, that's mine and you know it'. He pushes Phil to the floor, takes the driver out of Phil's bag and walks off with it. In fact, Phil was telling the truth; the driver was not the one Harper had lost.

Harper goes to the clubhouse bar and decides to play on the quiz machine. However, instead of inserting a £1 coin he inserts a foreign coin that he has left over from his summer holiday which is the same size and shape as a £1 coin. When Harper gets an answer wrong he is so annoyed that he kicks the machine, causing a dent.

Harper then orders some food from the club restaurant. When he places his order he intends to eat his meal and then sneak out without paying. However, once he has finished eating he changes his mind, pays for his meal and goes home.

Meanwhile two other golfers – Anik and Dilshaad – go to the clubhouse bar where they are served by barman Darren, who is good friends with both of them. Darren hands them their drinks and says, 'These drinks are free of charge. Enjoy!' even though the bar manager Colin had earlier warned him to stop giving out free drinks.

Discuss the criminal liability of Harper and Darren.

1. Here it is logical to discuss Harper's liability first, since his alleged offences all occurred before Darren's. First, Harper would be charged with robbery of the driver (Theft Act 1968, section 8).

The offence of robbery has four requirements. The first is that the defendant committed theft. Of the four statements listed below, which one is **not** one of the other three requirements?

- **a.** The defendant used force on any person or put or sought to put any person in fear of being then and there subjected to force.
- **b.** The defendant used force, or put or sought to put someone in fear of being subjected to force, either immediately before committing theft or at the time of doing so, in order to escape the scene.
- **c.** The defendant used force, or put or sought to put someone in fear of being subjected to force, in order to commit theft.
- **d.** The defendant used force, or put or sought to put someone in fear of being subjected to force, immediately before committing theft or at the time of doing so.

2. Of the four requirements for robbery, three are straightforward in Harper's case: he used force on Phil; he used the force immediately before taking the driver out of Phil's golf bag; and he used the force in order to take the driver out of Phil's golf bag. Harper's liability for robbery therefore hinges on whether or not taking the driver from Phil amounted to theft. There was certainly the *actus reus* of theft: the driver was property, which belonged to Phil, and Harper appropriated it (by taking the driver and walking off with it he assumed the rights of an owner (Theft Act 1968, section 3(1)). Moreover, Harper thought the driver was his and so he intended to permanently deprive Phil of it. Liability therefore all hinges on whether or not Harper acted dishonestly.

In *R* v *Skivington*, why did the Court of Appeal conclude that Skivington had not committed robbery?

a. Skivington genuinely believed that ordinary, honest people would not have regarded his conduct as dishonest.

b. Skivington genuinely believed that, had his wife's employer known of all the circumstances, he would have consented to Skivington's actions, and so section 2(1)(b) of the Theft Act 1968 applied.

c. Skivington genuinely believed he had a legal right to the money he took, and so was not dishonest under section 2(1)(a) of the Theft Act 1968.

d. Ordinary, honest people would not have regarded Skivington's conduct as dishonest, and so he was not dishonest under the *Ivey* v *Genting Casinos test*.

3. Next, Harper would be charged with fraud by false representation for using a foreign coin on the quiz machine (Fraud Act 2006, section 2). The key provision here is section 2(5).

Which of the following statements summarises section 2(5) accurately?

a. Any form of communication with an electronic system or device can constitute a representation.

b. There can be no conviction for fraud unless a human mind was deceived.

c. There can only be a conviction for fraud if the defendant entered another person's password to gain access to a secure site.

d. A defendant makes a representation when he uses an electronic system or device only if there is some subsequent involvement from another human being.

4. Next, Harper would be charged with criminal damage for kicking the quiz machine and causing a dent (Criminal Damage Act, section 1(1)). Here the issues would be similar to those we looked at in the previous scenario in respect of Kristjan scratching and denting the golf trolley. First, was the quiz machine damaged? The defence would argue that, as long as the machine still worked, its usefulness had not been impaired. The prosecution, on the other hand, would argue that the value of the machine may have been reduced and that it might be necessary for the golf club to expend money to repair the damage. Second, if the quiz machine was damaged, the prosecution would be able to cite *R* v *Parker* in order to establish that Harper caused the damage recklessly.

The final charge against Harper would be fraud by false representation for ordering food in the club restaurant with no intention to pay for it (Fraud Act 2006, section 2). The key issue here is the moment at which the offence is complete, since Harper subsequently changed his mind and paid for the meal.

When is the offence of fraud by false representation complete?

a. Once the victim realises that the representation is false.

b. Once the defendant actually makes a gain or the victim suffers some loss.

c. As soon as the defendant makes the false representation.

Lastly, Darren gives free drinks to Anik and Dilshaad in spite of the manager Colin's express instruction not to. Darren would be charged with theft of the drinks (Theft Act 1968, section 1). The *actus reus* of theft is present, since the drinks are property belonging to another (the clubhouse bar) and by giving them away Darren assumes the rights of an owner (Theft Act 1968, section 3(1)). The first *mens rea* requirement is also satisfied: Darren intended to permanently deprive the clubhouse bar of the drinks. His liability therefore hinges on whether or not he acted dishonestly. Section 2(1)(b) would not apply, since the manager had made it clear that Darren was to stop giving away free drinks. So the test from *Ivey* v *Genting Casinos* would need to be applied. The defence might argue that Darren was attempting to cultivate goodwill and customer loyalty, and so his conduct should not be regarded as dishonest by the standards of ordinary and honest people. The prosecution, on the other hand, would emphasise that the manager Colin had told him to stop giving away free drinks. If you were a juror applying the Ivey test, what would you decide?

Applying the law II

Now, read this scenario involving Harper and Darren.

Suppose that a group of climate change protestors entered the golf club car park and damaged every parked car that was not electric. The protestors stated that they wanted to shock members of the golf club, so that they would switch to electric cars to help save the planet. The protestors claim that they are not guilty of criminal damage because the section 5(2)(a) lawful excuse applies: they believed that the members of the golf club would have consented to the damage had they been aware that it was carried out to raise public awareness of an environmental crisis.

Now, think about this question. Which option would be the most suitable answer to this question?

Which of the following statements best summarises the decision of the Court of Appeal in *Attorney-General's Reference (No 1 of 2023)*?

a. Section 5(2)(a) may apply where a defendant concocts a justification for his actions after the event.

b. The lawful excuse does not apply in such a case because, when asking whether the owner would have consented had they known of the damage and its circumstances, the defendant's views on climate change do not form part of the circumstances of the damage.

c. Even if the defendant knew that the owner of the property would not have consented to the damage, section 5(2)(a) may still apply if the defendant genuinely believed that the owner should have been willing to consent.

d. A defendant cannot have genuinely believed that the owner would consent to the damage unless the belief was a justifiable one.

Evaluating the law

8.10 Evaluate the case law on appropriation and dishonesty.

Think about this question

'The decisions of the House of Lords in *R* v *Gomez* [1993] AC 442 and *R* v *Hinks* [2001] 2 AC 241 were unsatisfactory and problematic, for a number of reasons. By contrast, the decision of the Supreme Court in *Ivey* v *Genting Casinos* [2017] UKSC 67 to overrule *R* v *Ghosh* [1982] QB 1053 is to be applauded.'

Discuss the extent to which you agree with this statement.

Step 1: Deconstruct the essay title

To prepare an essay plan for this question, you should begin by **deconstructing the essay title** and **identifying the key points** you need to address. Here, the statement in the essay title makes two key claims:

1. that the decisions in *DPP* v *Gomez* and *R* v *Hinks* on the meaning of appropriation are unsatisfactory and problematic for a number of reasons; and
2. that the Supreme Court's decision, in *Ivey* v *Genting Casinos*, to overrule *R* v *Ghosh* should be applauded.

Step 2: Work through each claim, form an opinion and construct a set of arguments in support of your views

To discuss the first of these claims, you need to outline the various criticisms of the decisions in *DPP* v *Gomez* and *R* v *Hinks* and explain the extent to which you agree with each criticism. In the chapter we examined four criticisms of these decisions:

- The breadth of the definition of an appropriation
- The distinction between the offence of theft and the offence of fraud
- The distinction between theft and criminal attempts
- The relationship between the criminal law and the civil law.

To prepare this part of your essay, you should begin by writing a short summary of each of these criticisms in your own words. Having done this, you then need to consider the extent to which you agree with each criticism. To help with this, look back at the notes you prepared in response to the following questions:

On the distinction between the offence of theft and the offence of fraud:

- Read the extract from Clarkson's comment. Think back to the principles we studied in Chapter 1. Which of these principles is Clarkson's argument based on? What reasons does Clarkson give for the importance of this principle?
- According to Clarkson, what are the key differences between theft and deception/fraud offences? Why does fair labelling require this distinction?
- What reasons does Glazebrook give for rejecting the argument that a distinction should be drawn between theft and the deception/fraud offences?
- Whose argument do you find most compelling: Clarkson's or Glazebrook's? Was the House of Lords in *DPP* v *Gomez* right to say that cases involving consensual appropriations can be prosecuted as theft?

On the relationship between the criminal law and the civil law:

- In the following extract from Lord Steyn's judgment he responds to some of the arguments Hinks' counsel gave for saying that she had not appropriated the property. What were these arguments?
- What reasons did Lord Steyn give for rejecting these arguments?
- According to Shute, what is the flaw in Beatson and Simester's argument?

- Why, in Shute's opinion, does *R* v *Hinks* not result in an 'unacceptable' conflict between the civil and criminal laws?
- Make a list of Simester and Sullivan's criticisms of the decision in *R* v *Hinks*.
- What reasons do Simester and Sullivan give for rejecting the arguments of those who (like Shute) have defended the decision in *R* v *Hinks*?

You may also find it helpful to read the relevant items in the further reading list.

Once you have formed an opinion on the relative weight of each of the criticisms of *DPP* v *Gomez* and *R* v *Hinks*, construct a set of arguments in support of your point of view.

To discuss the second of the claims contained in the essay title, you should begin by making a list of the various criticisms of the decision in ***R* v *Ghosh***. Write a short summary of each criticism in your own words, and decide how far (if at all) you agree with each one. To help with this, look back at the discussion of *R* v *Ghosh* earlier in the chapter and your answers to the following questions:

- Spencer drew a distinction between two types of question. What was this distinction? Why did Spencer argue that it was inappropriate to answer the second type of question by reference to what the defendant believed?
- In *R* v *Ghosh* Lord Lane CJ said that Robin Hood and anti-vivisectionists would be found to be dishonest using the *R* v *Ghosh* test. In the following extract, does Lord Hughes agree? Why/why not?
- Lord Hughes also cites *R* v *Gilks*, a case in which a man was given £100 too much by a bookmaker. He realised the mistake but kept the money anyway, saying that it would be wrong to keep an overpayment from a grocery store but bookmakers are fair game. Lord Hughes states that a person like Gilks would not have been found to have been dishonest using the *R* v *Ghosh* test. Why? And why does Lord Hughes describe such an outcome as problematic?
- What does Lord Hughes say is the correct test for dishonesty? According to Lord Hughes, will this test result in the man who travels on a bus without realising that he is meant to pay (because he is from a country where public transport is free) being held to be dishonest? Why/why not?
- In [57] Lord Hughes lists a number of problems with the *R* v *Ghosh* test. Explain each of these criticisms in your own words (using your answers to the previous questions where relevant). According to Lord Hughes, which of these criticisms is the 'principal objection' to the second limb of the *R* v *Ghosh* test?

Now you need to consider the extent to which the decision of the Supreme Court in *Ivey* v *Genting Casinos* addresses each of the criticisms of the *R* v *Ghosh* test. Are there are concerns about the common law test for dishonesty that were not addressed by the judgment in *Ivey* v *Genting Casinos*? To help you think about this, look back at the discussion earlier in the chapter, including your answers to the following questions:

- Glover argues that it is possible that the people who took items from the beach would not be found by a jury to have acted dishonestly. What reasons does he give for this?
- What does Glover argue were the consequences of the uncertainty surrounding the meaning of dishonesty in the Branscombe Bay incident?
- According to Virgo, why might it be appropriate for the civil law and criminal law to define dishonesty differently?

- Look back over our discussion of dishonesty and make a list of arguments for and against the Supreme Court's decision in Ivey. In your opinion, was the Supreme Court right to overrule the *R* v *Ghosh* test?

You may also find it helpful to read the relevant items in the further reading list.

Once you have formed an opinion on whether the decision in *Ivey* v *Genting Casinos* is to be applauded, construct a set of arguments in support of your point of view.

Step 3: Planning your introduction and conclusion

You now have all the material you need for the main body of your essay. The last task is to decide what to include in your introduction and conclusion. The introduction should contextualise your discussion by briefly outlining the principles from *DPP* v *Gomez*, *R* v *Hinks* and *Ivey* v *Genting Casinos*, and give an indication of the argument you will present in your essay. The conclusion should round off your essay with a succinct statement of your argument and a summary of your supporting reasons.

Property offences checklist

Having worked through this chapter, you should now have:

- An understanding of the offence of theft
- An ability to critically discuss the case law on appropriation
- An ability to critically discuss the test for dishonesty
- An understanding of the offence of robbery
- An understanding of the offence of burglary and the difference between section 9(1)(a) and section 9(1)(b) burglary
- An understanding of the offence of fraud and the difference between fraud by false representation, fraud by failing to disclose information and fraud by abuse of position
- An understanding of the offences of criminal damage and aggravated criminal damage.

Further reading

Ashworth, A. (2002) 'Robbery Re-assessed' *Criminal Law Review* 851.

Betts, G. (2019) 'Robbery and the Principle of Fair Labelling' 83 *Journal of Criminal Law* 205.

Clarkson, C. (1993) 'Theft and Fair Labelling' 56 *Modern Law Review* 554.

Edwards, I. (2009) 'Banksy's Graffiti: A Not-so-simple Case of Criminal Damage?' 73 *Journal of Criminal Law* 345.

Gardner, J. (1998) 'Property and Theft' *Criminal Law Review* 35.

Griew, E. (1985) 'Dishonesty: The Objections to *Feely* and *Ghosh*' *Criminal Law Review* 341.

Glazebrook, P. (1991) 'Thief or Swindler: Who Cares?' 50 *Cambridge Law Journal* 389.

Glover, R. (2010) 'Can Dishonesty Be Salvaged? Theft and the Grounding of the *MSC Napoli*' 74 *Journal of Criminal Law* 53.

Halpin, A. (1996) 'The Test for Dishonesty' *Criminal Law Review* 283.

Ormerod, D. (2007) 'The Fraud Act 2006 – Criminalising Lying?' *Criminal Law Review* 193.

Pace, P.J. (1985) 'Burglarious Trespass' *Criminal Law Review* 716.

Shute, S. (2002) 'Appropriation and the Law of Theft' *Criminal Law Review* 445.

Simester, A.P. and Sullivan, G.R. (2005) 'On the Nature and Rationale of Property Offences' in R.A. Duff and S.P. Green (eds) *Defining Crimes: Essays on the Special Part of the Criminal Law*. OUP: Oxford.

Ormerod, D. and Laird, K. (2019) 'Ivey v Genting Casinos – Much Ado About Nothing?' in D. Clarry (ed) *The UK Supreme Court Yearbook Volume 9: 2017-2018 Legal Year*. Appellate Press: London.

Tamblyn, N. (2020) 'Reforming Theft: Taking Without Consent' *Criminal Law Review* 597.

Answers on the Companion Website

Please visit the companion website for the answers to Key Questions, Quizzes, Applying the Law scenarios as well as student support including glossaries. Please visit www.pearsoned.co.uk/Macdonald

9

Intoxication

Learning Objectives

9.1 Recall the case law that applies to defendants who claim that they were so intoxicated that they were unable to form the necessary mens rea at the time of their alleged offence.

9.2 Recall the arguments for and against a substantive defence of involuntary intoxication.

9.3 Recall the case law that applies to defendants who claim that their intoxication caused in them a mistaken belief which should form the basis of a substantive defence.

9.4 Apply the law on intoxicated defendants to hypothetical sets of facts.

9.5 Evaluate whether involuntary intoxication should be available as a substantive defence.

Introduction

Imagine the following scenario.

It is Dave's birthday party. During the party he drinks a lot of alcohol (more than he would normally drink when socialising). By the end of the party Dave is very drunk. When one of his friends jokes him, saying 'You old man', Dave angrily punches his friend in the face, breaking his nose.

Dave has no history of violent behaviour and would not have punched his friend had he been sober. Should the law treat Dave **more leniently**, or **more strictly**, as a result of his voluntary intoxication?

If you think: **More leniently**

The law does not take a more lenient approach to intoxicated defendants, even if they would not have committed the offence had they been sober. As we will see in the chapter, this is summed up by the principle 'A drunken intent is nevertheless an intent'.

If you think: **More strictly**

The law takes a stricter approach to defendants who were intoxicated at the time of the alleged offence. As we saw in Chapter 2, normally a defendant cannot be convicted of a crime unless he formed the necessary *mens rea*. But in this chapter, we will see that there are three situations in which an intoxicated defendant may be convicted of a crime even though he did not have the necessary mens rea at the time of the offence.

A large proportion of violent crime is committed by intoxicated defendants. Research has consistently found that in roughly 40 per cent of all violent incidents the victim believed the offender was under the influence of alcohol.

In 2017–18, for example, there were 561,000 violent incidents in which the victim believed the offender was under the influence of alcohol. This constituted 39 per cent of all the violent incidents that year.

The same year, there were also 305,000 violent incidents in which the victim believed the offender was under the influence of drugs (21 per cent of all the violent incidents that year).[1] The law that we study in this chapter is therefore of great practical importance.

If you are answering a problem question which involves an intoxicated defendant, the first question to ask yourself is:

Why is the defendant adducing evidence of his intoxication? There are two possible reasons.

First, he might be using the fact he was intoxicated in order to argue that he lacked the *mens rea* of the offence he has been charged with. The defendant might say something like, 'I was so drunk that I had no awareness of what I was doing' or, 'I was so drunk that I was incapable of forming any intention to injure him'. A couple of real-life examples can be given to illustrate this:

1. A nurse is so drunk that she mistakes a baby for a log of wood, and puts the baby on the fire. The nurse could claim that she lacked the *mens rea* of murder since she never formed an intention to kill or seriously injure the baby.

[1] Office for National Statistics (2019) *The Nature of Violent Crime in England and Wales: Year Ending March 2018*.

2. The victim is lying in the defendant's bed, but the defendant is so drunk that he mistakenly thinks the man is a theatrical dummy and stabs the victim to death. The defendant could claim that he lacked the *mens rea* of murder since he did not know he was stabbing a person and so never formed an intention to kill or cause serious injury.[2]

There is a second reason why a defendant might adduce evidence of his intoxication. He might claim that his intoxication caused in him a mistaken belief which should form the basis of a substantive defence. For example, he might say something like, 'I was so drunk that I thought the victim was going to attack me, so I pushed him over to defend myself'.

In this chapter we will look at each of these two reasons in turn. The majority of the chapter will focus on the first reason, since this is more common in practice and has generated the most case law.

Denial of *mens rea*

9.1 Recall the case law that applies to defendants who claim that they were so intoxicated that they were unable to form the necessary mens rea at the time of their alleged offence.

The first reason a defendant may adduce evidence that he was intoxicated is in order to deny that he possessed the necessary *mens rea* at the time of the offence[3]. It is important to begin by noting that if the defendant *did* possess the *mens rea* of the offence, he may not seek to escape liability by arguing that he only formed the *mens rea* because he was intoxicated. In *R* v *Sheehan* [1975] 1 WLR 739 Geoffrey Lane LJ stated:

> Indeed, in cases where drunkenness and its possible effect upon the defendant's *mens rea* is an issue, we think that the proper direction to a jury is, first, to warn them that the mere fact that the defendant's mind was affected by drink so that he acted in a way in which he would not have done had he been sober does not assist him at all, provided that the necessary intention was there. A drunken intent is nevertheless an intent.

So if an intoxicated defendant satisfies both the *actus reus* and *mens rea* of an offence it is never a defence for him to say, 'I wouldn't have done it if I'd been sober'. He will be convicted, unless he can plead one of the mental condition or substantive defences we study in the next two chapters.[4]

1. The distinction between voluntary and involuntary consumption

If a defendant claims that he did not possess the necessary *mens rea* as a result of intoxication, you first need to determine whether he consumed the intoxicating substance voluntarily or not. Two examples of involuntary consumption would be where: Ashish is deceived and does not realise he is consuming the substance (e.g. James spiked Ashish's

---

[2] Both examples are mentioned by Lord Denning in his judgment in *Attorney-General of Northern Ireland* v *Gallagher* [1963] AC 349.

[3] In *R* v *Aidid* [2021] EWCA Crim 581 the Court of Appeal held that a jury should normally be directed that a drunken intent is nevertheless an intent whenever there is evidence of intoxication that might call into question whether the defendant was capable of forming the necessary intention, even if it was not part of the defendant's case that he was incapable of forming such an intent.

[4] Or loss of control (in a homicide case) or a lawful excuse (in a criminal damage case).

drink); and Ashish is compelled to consume the substance (e.g. because James points a gun at him and threatens to shoot him if he does not).

A strict view is taken of what constitutes involuntary consumption. In *R* v *Allen* [1988] Crim LR 698 the defendant drank his friend's home-made wine. The defendant believed the wine only contained low levels of alcohol. In fact, it contained high levels. The Court of Appeal held that the defendant had consumed the alcohol voluntarily. His mistake as to the level of alcohol the wine contained did not render his consumption involuntary.

Think about this scenario.

Ashish goes to a party. At the bar he asks for a glass of non-alcoholic fruit punch. Due to a mix-up he is actually given a glass of alcoholic fruit punch. Ashish drinks the punch.

Does he consume the alcohol voluntarily?

We will look at cases involving voluntary consumption first.

2. Drinking with intent

If the defendant consumed the substance voluntarily, the next question to ask is whether the defendant was consuming the intoxicating substance in order to give himself the courage to carry out a crime he was planning to commit.

In other words, was the defendant drinking with intent?

This was the issue in *Attorney-General of Northern Ireland* v *Gallagher* [1963] AC 349.

Attorney-General of Northern Ireland v *Gallagher*. The defendant, Patrick Gallagher, decided to kill his wife.

Shutterstock

He bought a knife and a bottle of whisky.

Shutterstock

He drank most of the bottle and then attacked his wife with the knife.

Shutterstock

At trial he was convicted of murder.

He appealed, arguing that he was so drunk at the time of the killing that he had been incapable of forming the *mens rea* of murder. The appeal reached the House of Lords.

EXTRACT

Read the following extract from the judgment of Lord Denning.

Could Gallagher use the fact he was intoxicated to argue that he lacked the mens rea of murder? Why/why not?

Attorney-General of Northern Ireland v *Gallagher* [1963] AC 349

Lord Denning

My Lords, I think the law on this point should take a clear stand. If a man, whilst sane and sober, forms an intention to kill and makes preparation for it, knowing it is a wrong thing to do, and then gets himself drunk so as to give himself Dutch courage to do the killing, and whilst drunk carries out his intention, he cannot rely on this self-induced drunkenness as a defence to a charge of murder, nor even as reducing it to manslaughter. He cannot say that he got himself into such a stupid state that he was incapable of an intent to kill [...] The wickedness of his mind before he got drunk is enough to condemn him, coupled with the act which he intended to do and did do.

So, in cases of drinking with intent, the defendant may not use evidence of his intoxication to claim he lacked the necessary *mens rea* at the time of the offence.

3. Consumption for medicinal purposes

If the defendant consumed the substance voluntarily, but was not drinking with intent, the next question to ask is whether the consumption was for medicinal purposes. If the consumption was for medicinal purposes, you must decide whether the defendant foresaw a risk that the drug would render him aggressive and dangerous and chose to take it.

In other words, you must decide whether consumption of the drug was reckless (using the *R* v *Cunningham* test that we studied in Chapter 4).

If the consumption *was* reckless, the case will be treated no differently to one involving voluntary consumption of alcohol or recreational drugs. But if the consumption was *not* reckless, the defendant will be deemed to have been involuntarily intoxicated.

An example is *R* v *Bailey* [1983] 1 WLR 760.

***R* v *Bailey* [1983] 1 WLR 760**
John Bailey's girlfriend left him for another man, Mike Harrison.

Shutterstock

Armed with an iron bar, Bailey went to Harrison's house.

Shutterstock

The two men sat down and discussed the matter over a cup of tea. When Bailey got up to leave he said he had lost his glove down the side of the chair he was sitting on.

Shutterstock

Harrison bent over to search for it. While Harrison's back was turned, Bailey struck him on the head with the iron bar.

Shutterstock

Harrison's head wound required ten stitches. At trial, Bailey was convicted of wounding with intent.[5] He appealed against his conviction. Bailey was a diabetic. There was evidence that earlier in the evening he had failed to take sufficient food after taking his normal dose of insulin. He claimed that, as a result, he had suffered an episode of hypoglycaemia at the time of the attack and was completely unaware of what he was doing. Since Bailey had taken the insulin for medicinal purposes, the Court of Appeal had to decide whether or not Bailey's consumption of the insulin was reckless. Griffiths LJ stated:

> It is common knowledge that those who take alcohol to excess or certain sorts of drugs may become aggressive or do dangerous or unpredictable things, they may be able to foresee the risks of causing harm to others but nevertheless persist in their conduct. But the same cannot be said without more of a man who fails to take food after an insulin injection. If he does appreciate the risk that such a failure may lead to aggressive, unpredictable and uncontrollable conduct and he nevertheless deliberately runs the risk or otherwise disregards it, this will amount to recklessness. But we certainly do not think that it is common knowledge, even among diabetics, that such is a consequence of a failure to take food and there is no evidence that it was known to this appellant. Doubtless he knew that if he failed to take his insulin or proper food after it he might lose consciousness, but as such he would only be a danger to himself unless he put himself in charge of some machine such as a motor car, which required his continued conscious control.

Since Bailey's consumption of the insulin was not reckless, he was deemed to have been involuntarily intoxicated. As we will see below, in cases involving involuntary intoxication you simply ask whether or not the defendant possessed the necessary *mens rea* at the time of the offence. Looking at the facts of Bailey's case – particularly the fact that he armed himself with the iron bar beforehand – the Court of Appeal held that he possessed the necessary *mens rea* at the moment he attacked Harrison. His appeal was therefore dismissed.

A second example is *R* v *Hardie* [1985] 1 WLR 64. Paul Hardie lived with his partner, Jeanette, and his daughter, Tonia. His relationship with Jeanette had broken down and she insisted that he move out. Hardie did not want to leave, but on the day of the

[5] Offences Against the Person Act 1861, s.18.

offence he packed a suitcase. In a distressed state, Hardie found an eight-year-old bottle of Valium™ (which was out-of-date) in the bathroom cabinet. He had never taken Valium before. He took one pill to calm his nerves. It did not have much effect, so later he took two more. Jeanette said to him, 'Take as many as you like, they are old stock and will do you no harm', so he took another two. Shortly afterwards he fell into a deep sleep. That evening Hardie (who was showing signs of intoxication) set fire to a wardrobe in a bedroom in the flat. At trial he was convicted of arson. He appealed against his conviction, arguing that he could not remember starting the fire and had been intoxicated at the time. The Court of Appeal held that Hardie's consumption of the Valium was not reckless. Parker LJ explained:

> In the present instance the defence was that the Valium was taken for the purpose of calming the nerves only, that it was old stock and that the appellant was told it would do him no harm. There was no evidence that it was known to the appellant or even generally known that the taking of Valium in the quantity taken would be liable to render a person aggressive or incapable of appreciating risks to others or have other side effects such that its self-administration would itself have an element of recklessness.

Like Bailey, Hardie was therefore deemed to have been involuntarily intoxicated. Unlike Bailey, however, the Court of Appeal held that it had not been proved beyond reasonable doubt that Hardie had the necessary *mens rea* when he started the fire. His conviction was therefore quashed.

4. The distinction between basic intent crimes and specific intent crimes

So far we have looked at cases involving drinking with intent and non-reckless consumption of a drug for medicinal purposes. Next we look at cases involving: reckless consumption of a medicinal drug; and, by far the most common type of scenario, voluntary consumption of alcohol or recreational drugs. The same rules apply to both these types of cases because, as we saw earlier, reckless consumption of a medicinal drug is treated no differently to voluntary consumption of alcohol or recreational drugs.

The leading case here is *DPP* v *Majewski* [1977] AC 443. The defendant, Robert Majewski, was involved in a pub fight. At trial he was convicted on three counts of assault occasioning ABH and three counts of assaulting a police officer in the execution of his duty. Majewski said that he had taken a mixture of drugs and alcohol that evening and as a result had 'completely blanked out'. He therefore claimed that he had not formed the necessary *mens rea*. His appeal against conviction reached the House of Lords.

The House of Lords' decision in *DPP* v *Majewski* sought to strike a balance between two competing sets of concerns. On the one hand, there is the concern based on the principle of individual autonomy (see Chapter 1) that people should not be convicted of a crime if they did not possess the necessary *mens rea*. On the other hand, there is the concern based on social welfare (see Chapter 1) that defendants should not be able to escape criminal liability on the basis that their own self-induced intoxication rendered them unable to form *mens rea*. Social welfare requires that people are deterred from voluntarily consuming intoxicating substances which render them aggressive and dangerous.

The House of Lords' decision was effectively an uneasy compromise between these two sets of concerns. The House of Lords drew a distinction between crimes of basic intent and crimes of specific intent. For specific intent crimes (which tend to be the more serious offences), a defendant can only be convicted if he possessed the necessary *mens rea* at the time of the offence. So for specific intent crimes the defendant may argue that he was unable to form *mens rea* as a result of his own voluntary intoxication.

For basic intent crimes, however, things are different. A defendant who is charged with a basic intent crime may not use the fact he was voluntarily intoxicated to claim that he lacked *mens rea*. Lord Elwyn-Jones LC explained:

> If a man of his own volition takes a substance which causes him to cast off the restraints of reason and conscience, no wrong is done to him by holding him answerable criminally for any injury he may do while in that condition. His course of conduct in reducing himself by drugs and drink to that condition in my view supplies the evidence of *mens rea*, of guilty mind certainly sufficient for crimes of basic intent.

The crimes Majewski had been charged with were crimes of basic intent. He was therefore unable to argue that his intoxication left him unable to form *mens rea*, and his convictions were upheld.

How to distinguish between crimes of specific intent and crimes of basic intent

The decision in *DPP* v *Majewski* means that the distinction between crimes of specific intent and crimes of basic intent is crucial. Unfortunately, however, the House of Lords did not clearly explain the difference between the two categories. In his judgment, Lord Elwyn-Jones LC explained the difference by citing the following extract from Lord Simon's judgment in *R* v *Morgan* [1976] AC 182:

> By 'crimes of basic intent' I mean those crimes whose definition expresses (or, more often, implies) a *mens rea* which does not go beyond the *actus reus*. The *actus reus* generally consists of an act and some consequence. The consequence may be very closely connected with the act or more remotely connected with it: but with a crime of basic intent the *mens rea* does not extend beyond the act and its consequence, however remote, as defined in the *actus reus*. I take assault as an example of a crime of basic intent where the consequence is very closely connected with the act. The *actus reus* of assault is an act which causes another person to apprehend immediate and unlawful violence. The *mens rea* corresponds exactly. The prosecution must prove that the accused foresaw that his act would probably cause another person to have apprehension of immediate and unlawful violence, or would possibly have that consequence, such being the purpose of the act, or that he was reckless as to whether or not his act caused such apprehension.

So, on this view, basic intent crimes are ones in which the *mens rea* 'does not go beyond the *actus reus*'. Specific intent crimes, by contrast, are ones in which the *mens rea* does go beyond the *actus reus*. An example is burglary under section 9(1)(a) Theft Act 1968. As we saw in the previous chapter, the *actus reus* of burglary is simply entry of a building (or part of a building) as a trespasser. The *mens rea* of section 9(1)(a) burglary goes beyond this, since it requires proof of an ulterior intention to commit theft, inflict GBH or damage property.

This explanation works for some offences. As Lord Simon explains in the extract above, it works for assault (a basic intent crime). It also works for burglary (a specific intent crime).[6] But it doesn't work for some other offences. For example, in *DPP* v *Majewski* Lord Elwyn-Jones confirmed that murder is a crime of specific intent.[7] Yet the *mens rea* of murder does not extend beyond the *actus reus*. In fact, as we saw in Chapter 5, the

[6] *R* v *Durante* [1972] 1 WLR 1612.

[7] See also *Attorney-General of Northern Ireland* v *Gallagher* [1963] AC 349.

mens rea does not even extend as far as the *actus reus*! It is sufficient for the *mens rea* of murder to show that the defendant had an intention to cause serious injury.

An alternative explanation of the distinction between basic intent crimes and specific intent crimes was offered by Lord Simon in his judgment in *DPP* v *Majewski*:

> [A] crime of specific intent requires something more than contemplation of the prohibited act and foresight of its probable consequences. The *mens rea* in a crime of specific intent requires proof of a purposive element.

This 'purposive element' explanation was also used by the Court of Appeal in *R* v *Heard* [2007] EWCA Crim 125. But it too is problematic. It also fails to explain why murder is a crime of specific intent. We saw in Chapter 5 that a defendant satisfies the *mens rea* of murder if he had a direct or oblique intention to kill or cause serious injury. Foresight of death or GBH as virtually certain is sufficient; it need not have been the defendant's purpose to cause death or GBH. The same also applies to GBH/wounding with intent.[8] This is a crime of specific intent,[9] yet it is sufficient to show that the defendant obliquely intended to cause GBH. In the absence of a satisfactory explanation of the difference between specific intent and basic intent crimes, the safest course of action is to follow existing precedents and produce a list of which crimes have been held to fall in which category. The following table accordingly categorises all of the offences that we study in this text:

Basic intent crimes	Specific intent crimes
Involuntary manslaughter[10]	Causing a person to engage in sexual activity without consent[18]
Wounding or infliction of GBH[11]	Murder[19]
Assault occasioning ABH[12]	Wounding or causing GBH with intent[20]
Battery[13]	Theft[21]
Assault[14]	Robbery[22]
Rape[15]	Burglary[23]
Assault by penetration[16]	
Sexual assault[17]	

(Not listed in this table are: (1) fraud: this, it is suggested, is a crime of specific intent since it requires proof of an ulterior intention; and (2) criminal damage: it has been

[8] Offences Against the Person Act 1861, s.18.

[9] *Bratty* v *Attorney-General of Northern Ireland* [1963] AC 386.

[10] *Attorney-General of Northern Ireland* v *Gallagher* [1963] AC 349.

[11] *DPP* v *Majewski* [1977] AC 443.

[12] *DPP* v *Majewski* [1977] AC 443.

[13] *DPP* v *Majewski* [1977] AC 443.

[14] *DPP* v *Majewski* [1977] AC 443.

[15] Based on the logic of the decision in *R* v *Heard* [2007] EWCA Crim 125.

[16] Based on the logic of the decision in *R* v *Heard* [2007] EWCA Crim 125.

[17] *R* v *Heard* [2007] EWCA Crim 125.

[18] Based on the logic of the decision in *R* v *Heard* [2007] EWCA Crim 125.

[19] *Attorney-General of Northern Ireland* v *Gallagher* [1963] AC 349; *DPP* v *Majewski*.

[20] *Bratty* v *Attorney-General of Northern Ireland* [1963] AC 386.

[21] *Ruse* v *Read* [1949] 1 KB 377.

[22] Based on the fact it is an aggravated form of theft.

[23] *R* v *Durante* [1972] 1 WLR 1612.

suggested that whether criminal damage (and aggravated criminal damage) is a crime of basic or specific intent depends on whether the prosecutor in the particular case alleges intentional or reckless damage.[24]

So the distinction between basic intent crimes and specific intent crimes was developed by the House of Lords in *DPP* v *Majewski* to reconcile the competing demands of the principle of autonomy and the principle of social welfare. For specific intent crimes – which tend to be the more serious – a defendant can only be convicted if it is shown that he possessed the necessary *mens rea* at the time of the offence. For basic intent crimes, by contrast, the defendant may not use the fact that he was voluntarily intoxicated to argue that he lacked *mens rea*.

Lastly, notice that a defendant who cannot be convicted of a specific intent crime because he lacked *mens rea* may be convicted of a basic intent crime instead. So if Ashish attacks Ryder and kills him, but was too drunk to have formed the *mens rea* of murder, Ashish may be convicted of the basic intent crime of involuntary manslaughter instead.

Think about this scenario.

Ashish has been at the pub for several hours, drinking heavily. He begins to argue with his friend Ryder. The argument gets heated and Ashish hits Ryder on the head with his beer bottle. Ryder suffers a deep wound which requires stitches. Medical evidence later shows that, at the moment he struck Ryder, Ashish was so drunk that he was incapable of forming *mens rea*.

Use the table of basic and specific intent offences above to decide which crime Ashish would be convicted of.

5. The immediate and proximate consequences of voluntary intoxication

Until recently, it was assumed that the rules from *DPP* v *Majewski* only applied to defendants who were voluntarily intoxicated at the time of the alleged offence. For example, in one of the appeals considered in *R* v *Coley* [2013] EWCA Crim 223 the defendant, Darren Harris, had been abusing alcohol for roughly six years. He would have spells where he would drink heavily and would then stop drinking abruptly. This had resulted in episodes of alcohol-induced psychosis, which involved hearing voices and having hallucinations. A few days before the alleged offence he had stopped drinking. So at the time of the offence he was not intoxicated, but was suffering psychotic symptoms. Although the defendant's mental condition was the result of voluntary intoxication, the Court of Appeal held that the case law on intoxication did not apply since the defendant was not intoxicated at the time of the offence. Hughes LJ stated, '*Majewski* applies to offences committed by persons who are then voluntarily intoxicated but not to those who are suffering mental illness' ([59]).

However, in *R* v *Taj* [2018] EWCA Crim 1743 a five-member Court of Appeal held that the rules from *DPP* v *Majewski* should apply not only to defendants who were voluntarily intoxicated at the time of the offence, but also to those who were no longer intoxicated but were suffering the 'immediate and proximate consequences' of voluntary alcohol/drug consumption.

[24] See Ormerod, D. and Laird, K. (2015) *Smith and Hogan's Criminal Law* (14th edn). OUP: Oxford, p.363. Cf *R* v *Coley* [2013] EWCA Crim 223.

On Sunday 31 January 2016, the defendant, Simon Taj, was driving his van when he came across the victim, Mohammed Awain, who had broken down.

Taj pulled over and asked if he could do anything to help. Awain asked Taj if he had any jump leads.

xiao yu/Shutterstock

Taj then started to become suspicious. He began questioning Awain, then walked off, called 999 and reported a possible bomb threat.

Simon Vayro/Shutterstock

Taj returned to Awain's car and asked him to open the boot. Awain did so. In the boot was electrical equipment and wires (Awain was an electrician by trade).

Having seen these items, Taj concluded that Awain was a terrorist. Shortly afterwards the police arrived, inspected the scene and reassured Taj that Awain was not a terrorist.

Rob Byron/Shutterstock

Taj then drove off. But, he said, he continued to think that Awain had a bomb and felt compelled to do something about it. So shortly afterwards he returned to the scene, armed himself with a tyre lever, approached Awain and struck him repeatedly on the head.

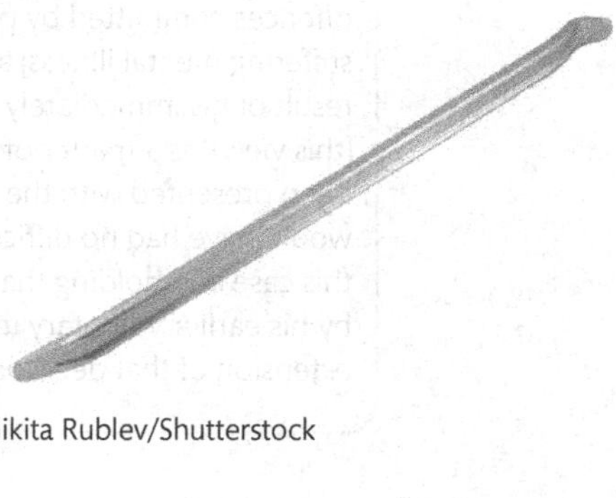

Nikita Rublev/Shutterstock

At trial, it was accepted that Taj had genuinely believed that Awain was a terrorist who needed to be stopped.

The psychiatric evidence showed that Taj was suffering from drug or alcohol induced psychosis at the time of the offence. Taj admitted that he had abused alcohol and drugs from a young age. He also admitted that: he knew that alcohol and cocaine could cause him to experience feelings of paranoia; in the weeks leading up to the offence he had been drinking heavily and using cocaine regularly; and, he had been out drinking heavily on Friday 29 January, well into the morning of Saturday 30 January. It was agreed that the requirements for the defence of insanity were not satisfied. The trial judge also held that the defence of self-defence was not available (for reasons we will examine in Chapter 11). Taj was accordingly convicted of attempted murder. Taj appealed against his conviction and, on appeal, the Court of Appeal took the opportunity to consider the ambit of the *DPP* v *Majewski* rules.

EXTRACT

Read the following extract from the judgment of Sir Brian Leveson P. In it, he discusses the view that a distinction should be drawn between those who are voluntarily intoxicated and those who are suffering from mental illness.

According to Sir Brian Leveson P, how (if at all) did this distinction apply in Taj's case?

R v *Taj* [2018] EWCA Crim 1743

Sir Brian Leveson P

56 *DPP v. Majewski* focused on crime committed while specifically under the influence of drugs or alcohol. Having said that, however, it is difficult to see why the language (and the policy identified) is not equally apposite to the immediate and proximate consequences of such misuse. That is not to say that long standing mental illness which might at some stage have been triggered by misuse of drugs or alcohol would be covered. The point is that a defendant who is suffering the immediate effects of alcohol or drugs in the system is, in truth, not in a different position to a defendant who has triggered or precipitated an immediate psychotic illness as a consequence of proximate ingestion of or drugs in the system whether or not they remain present at the time of the offence.

57 The fact is that medical science has advanced such that, in the modern age, the longer term *sequelae* of abusing alcohol or drugs are better known and understood; and, as in the present case, it was agreed that Taj's episode of paranoia which led him to mistake the innocent Mr Awain as a terrorist was a direct result of his earlier drink and drug-taking in the previous days and weeks. In the circumstances, we are not persuaded that the view [that *Majewski* applies to offences committed by persons who are then voluntarily intoxicated but not to those who are suffering mental illness] applies to Taj, given that his paranoia was the direct and proximate result of his immediately prior drink and drug-taking. Alternatively and if need be contrary to [this view], as a matter of common law, we have no doubt that, had the House in *Majewski* … been presented with the same medical evidence and facts as in the present case, the House would have had no difficulty in applying the general common law principle with equal force to this case and holding that Taj had no defence because his state of mind had been brought about by his earlier voluntary intoxication. We see that as an application of *Majewski*, rather than an extension of that decision or, at the highest, a most incremental extension.

So the *DPP* v *Majewski* rules apply not only to those who were voluntarily intoxicated at the time of the offence, but also to those who are no longer intoxicated but are suffering the 'immediate and proximate consequences' of alcohol or drugs in the system. How broadly the terms 'immediate' and 'proximate' will be interpreted remains to be seen.

Think about this question.

Think back to the facts of Darren Harris' case in *R* v *Coley*.

- Were his psychotic symptoms the 'immediate and proximate' consequence of voluntary intoxication?

The judgment in *R* v *Taj* also raises questions about the relationship between the *DPP* v *Majewski* rules and the defence of insanity. We will return to this issue in Chapter 10.

6. Involuntary intoxication

In the vast majority of cases the defendant will have voluntarily consumed alcohol or recreational drugs and the *DPP* v *Majewski* rules will apply. But what about those cases where the defendant consumed the intoxicating substance involuntarily? Or where the defendant became intoxicated inadvertently after consuming drugs for medicinal purposes?

In such cases, you do not need to apply the *DPP* v *Majewski* rules on basic and specific intent crimes. Instead, you simply ask whether or not the defendant possessed the necessary *mens rea* at the time of the offence in question. An example is *R* v *Kingston* [1995] 2 AC 355. The defendant, Barry Kingston, was involved in a dispute with his business partners. They employed a man named Kevin Penn to obtain information which could be used to discredit Kingston. Penn knew that Kingston had paedophilic tendencies. Penn invited a 15-year-old boy to his flat and gave him a drink containing sedatives. The boy later said that he remembered nothing in between sitting on the bed in Penn's flat and waking up the next morning. When Kingston arrived at Penn's flat Penn gave him a cup of coffee. Unbeknown to Kingston, the coffee was drugged. Later, Penn showed Kingston the boy naked on his bed. Kingston engaged in sexual acts with the boy, which Penn photographed and recorded.

At trial Kingston was convicted of a sexual offence and sentenced to five years' imprisonment. His appeal against conviction reached the House of Lords. Kingston did not deny that he had the necessary *mens rea* at the time he assaulted the victim. Rather, he argued that he only formed the *mens rea* because he had involuntarily consumed drugs which caused him to become disinhibited. He therefore argued that the courts should create a new substantive defence titled 'involuntary intoxication'. The Court of Appeal accepted this argument and quashed Kingston's conviction. But this decision was overturned by the House of Lords, who unanimously rejected the proposed new defence.

EXTRACT

Read the following extract from the judgment of Lord Mustill.

What (a) theoretical and (b)practical reasons does he give for rejecting a substantive defence of involuntary intoxication?

What specific concern does Lord Mustill express about the lack of a defence of involuntary intoxication?

R v *Kingston* [1995] 2 AC 355

Lord Mustill

To recognise a new defence of this type would be a bold step [...] I suspect that the recognition of a new general defence at common law has not happened in modern times. Nevertheless, the criminal law must not stand still, and if it is both practical and just to take this step, and if judicial decision rather than legislation is the proper medium, then the courts should not be deterred simply by the novelty of it. So one must turn to consider just what defence is now to be created. The judgment under appeal implies five characteristics.

1. The defence applies to all offences, except perhaps to absolute offences. It therefore differs from other defences such as [loss of control] and diminished responsibility.
2. The defence is a complete answer to a criminal charge. If not rebutted it leads to an outright acquittal, and unlike [loss of control] and diminished responsibility leaves no room for conviction and punishment for a lesser offence. The underlying assumption must be that the defendant is entirely free from culpability.
3. It may be that the defence applies only where the intoxication is due to the wrongful act of another and therefore affords no excuse when, in circumstances of no greater culpability, the defendant has intoxicated himself by mistake (such as by shortsightedly taking the wrong drug) [...]
4. The burden of disproving the defence is on the prosecution.

My Lords, since the existence or otherwise of the defence has been treated in argument at all stages as a matter of existing law the Court of Appeal had no occasion to consider the practical and theoretical implications of recognising this new defence at common law, and we do not have the benefit of its views. In their absence, I can only say that the defence appears to run into difficulties at every turn. In point of theory, it would be necessary to reconcile a defence of irresistible impulse derived from a combination of innate drives and external disinhibition with the rule that irresistible impulse of a solely internal origin (not necessarily any more the fault of the offender) does not in itself excuse although it may be a symptom of a disease of the mind: *Attorney-General for South Australia v. Brown* [1960] A.C. 432. Equally, the state of mind which founds the defence superficially resembles a state of diminished responsibility, whereas the effect in law is quite different. It may well be that the resemblance is misleading, but these and similar problems must be solved before the bounds of a new defence can be set.

On the practical side there are serious problems. Before the jury could form an opinion on whether the drug might have turned the scale witnesses would have to give a picture of the defendant's personality and susceptibilities, for without it the crucial effect of the drug could not be assessed; pharmacologists would be required to describe the potentially disinhibiting effect of a range of drugs whose identity would, if the present case is anything to go by, be unknown; psychologists and psychiatrists would express opinions, not on the matters of psychopathology familiar to those working within the framework of the Mental Health Acts but on altogether more elusive concepts. No doubt as time passed those concerned could work out techniques to deal with these questions. Much more significant would be the opportunities for a spurious defence. Even in the field of road traffic the "spiked" drink as a special reason for not disqualifying from driving is a regular feature. Transferring this to the entire range of criminal offences is a disturbing prospect. The defendant would only have to assert, and support by the evidence of well-wishers, that he was not the sort of person to have done this kind of thing, and to suggest an occasion when by some means a drug might have been administered to him for the jury to be sent straight to the question of a possible disinhibition. The judge would direct the jurors that if they felt any legitimate doubt on the matter – and by its nature the defence would be one which the prosecution would often have no means to rebut – they must acquit outright, all questions of intent, mental capacity and the like being at this stage irrelevant.

My Lords, the fact that a new doctrine may require adjustment of existing principles to accommodate it, and may require those involved in criminal trials to learn new techniques, is not of course a ground for refusing to adopt it, if that is what the interests of justice require. Here, however, justice makes no such demands, for the interplay between the wrong done to the victim, the individual characteristics and frailties of the defendant, and the pharmacological effects of whatever drug may be potentially involved can be far better recognised by a tailored choice from the continuum of sentences available to the judge than by the application of a single yea-or-nay jury decision. To this, there is one exception. The mandatory life sentence for murder, at least as present administered, leaves no room for the trial judge to put into practice an informed and sympathetic assessment of the kind just described. It is for this reason alone that I have felt any hesitation about rejecting the argument for the respondent. In the end however I have concluded that this is not a sufficient reason to force on the theory and practice of the criminal law an exception which would otherwise be unjustified. For many years mandatory sentences have impelled juries to return merciful but false verdicts, and have stimulated the creation of partial defences such as [loss of control] and diminished responsibility whose lack of a proper foundation has made them hard to apply in practice. I do not think it right that the law should be further distorted simply because of this anomalous relic of the history of the criminal law.

All this being said, I suggest to your Lordships that the existing work of the Law Commission in the field of intoxication could usefully be enlarged to comprise questions of the type raised by this appeal, and to see whether by statute a merciful, realistic and intellectually sustainable solution could be newly created. For the present, however, I consider that no such regime now exists, and that the common law is not a suitable vehicle for creating one.

So if a defendant was involuntarily intoxicated, the sole question is did he possess the necessary *mens rea* or not. If he did, the fact that he would not have committed the crime had he been sober is no defence.

7. Summary

The flow chart in Figure 9.1 presents an overview of the case law we have studied on defendants who adduce evidence of their intoxication in order to claim that they lacked the *mens rea* of an offence.

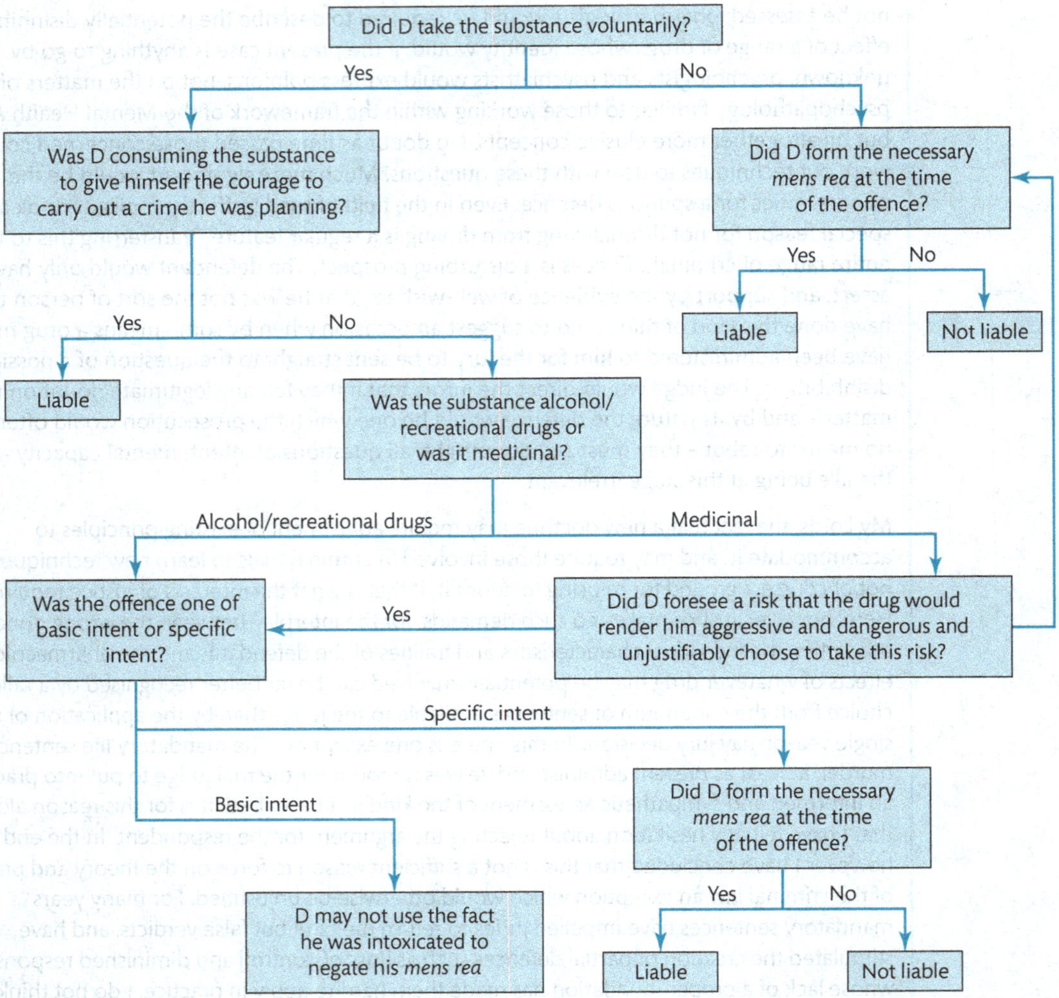

Figure 9.1 Adducing evidence of intoxication in order to deny *mens rea*: an overview

Quiz 9.1

1. If a person is intoxicated and commits an offence which they would not have committed had they been sober they are …
   a. Entitled to an acquittal.
   b. Able to argue the defence of drunken disinhibition.
   c. Liable to be convicted if they committed the *actus reus* of the offence with the necessary *mens rea*.
   d. Liable to be convicted of dangerous intoxication.
2. Does a mistake over the strength of alcohol knowingly consumed …
   a. convert what would otherwise be regarded as voluntary intoxication into involuntary intoxication?
   b. entitle the defendant to a complete acquittal?
   c. make no difference to the defendant's potential liability?
   d. convert what would otherwise be regarded as involuntary intoxication into voluntary intoxication?
3. Suppose a defendant forms the necessary *mens rea* for an offence, then consumes a large quantity of alcohol to give himself the courage to commit the offence and, as a result, did not necessarily possess the necessary *mens rea* at the time of committing the *actus reus*. Will he …

a. always be entitled to be acquitted of that offence?
b. be liable to be convicted only of a lesser offence?
c. be liable to be convicted of the offence as a matter of public policy?
d. only be liable to be convicted of the offence if it is proved that he possessed the necessary *mens rea* at the time he committed the *actus reus*?

4. Where D, who was voluntarily intoxicated, is charged with a basic intent crime then which of the following is true?
a. D will have a defence if he can show that the reasonable person would also have been voluntarily intoxicated in similar circumstances.
b. D may not use the fact that he was voluntarily intoxicated to argue that he lacked *mens rea*.
c. D will not be convicted if he was so intoxicated that he was incapable of forming the *mens rea* of the offence with which he is charged.
d. The prosecution must still prove that D had *mens rea* for the offence with which he is charged.

5. Which of the following statements is correct?
a. Rape is a crime of specific intent.
b. Theft is a crime of basic intent.
c. In all cases involving medicinal drugs, if D becomes intoxicated following consumption of the drug it will be treated as involuntary intoxication.
d. A defendant can only be convicted of a crime of specific intent if he possessed the necessary *mens rea* at the time of the offence.

6. Which of the following is not an example of involuntary intoxication?
a. D is forced at gun-point to drink a number of shots of vodka in quick succession.
b. D consumes two small glasses of wine without realising that his drink has been spiked by T with an intoxicating substance.
c. D consumes several glasses of wine. He asked for low-alcohol wine, but owing to a mistake (of which he was unaware) he was served wine with a high alcohol content.
d. D takes a normal dose of a painkiller drug, unaware that the drug can sometimes have an intoxicating effect and renders some individuals aggressive.

7. What was the reason for the rejection of the defence claimed in *R v Kingston*?
a. Kingston was voluntarily intoxicated and in possession of the necessary *mens rea* and so was guilty as charged.
b. It was not sufficient to acknowledge the special circumstances by mitigating the penalty which would otherwise be appropriate.
c. Mere disinhibition is insufficient to found a defence, so a drunken intent was still an intent whether produced through voluntary or involuntary intoxication.
d. Penal consequences should not attach to acts which are the ultimate consequence of involuntary intoxication.

Should there be a defence of involuntary intoxication?

9.2 Recall the arguments for and against a substantive defence of involuntary intoxication.

Since the decision in *R v Kingston* there has been much discussion of whether or not the law should recognise a substantive defence of involuntary intoxication. In the following extract Sullivan argues that, in certain limited circumstances, involuntary intoxication should constitute a defence.

EXTRACT

According to Sullivan, when should involuntary intoxication be available as a substantive defence? What reasons does Sullivan advance in support of this?

Sullivan, G. R. (1996) 'Making Excuses' in A. Smith and G. Sullivan (eds) *Harm and Culpability*. OUP: Oxford, pp.131–152

Nonetheless, there may have been principled reasons sufficient for the House of Lords to have upheld, rather than reversed, the Court of Appeal. An opportunity may have been missed for creative yet appropriate judicial law-making. Whether a defence should have been provided in *Kingston* depends, it will be argued, on conditions which may, or may not, have been present on the facts of that case. As stated already, disinhibition falling short of automatism cannot of *itself* excuse. But if such a condition arose blamelessly and induced conduct which would not otherwise have occurred, this will attenuate to some extent the culpability of the agent. That culpability would be further attenuated, it will be claimed, if, until the incident in question, the defendant had abstained from practising his paedophilia.

All we know of the defendant in *Kingston* is that he was a homosexual with paedophiliac predilections. The formative influences of sexual preference are obscure. In terms of orientation, our sexuality is something that we have rather than something we have made. If we are dealt a card marked for paedophilia, the most that can be asked of us is that we do not put it into play. The card cannot be surrendered and it would be a barbarity to punish for mere possession. Requiring forbearance in a matter so pervasive and unpredictable as sexual expression is to require a great deal, notwithstanding that the protection of a vulnerable class must always be the overriding concern. If a person of paedophiliac inclinations does not practise his paedophilia, he is entitled to that full dignity and respect which is due to all law-abiding citizens. Indeed, he may claim particular credit for sustaining a non-criminal status. If on a particular occasion he becomes blamelessly disinhibited by drugs and loses self-control when confronted with that temptation he otherwise avoids and resists, it is not obvious that the public interest requires him to suffer the total forfeit of credit which a conviction for a stigmatic offence entails.

The particularity of facts such as those related above renders the consequentialist claims of individual and general deterrence uncompelling. Retributivist claims are less clearly settled. It has already been suggested that his blameless state of disequilibrium must count in his favour, even if only as mitigation. It will be argued more fully below that mitigation may be upgraded to excuse if, until this particular occasion, the defendant had refrained from paedophiliac practices. However, were he a practising paedophile his conduct would not constitute an arguably condonable lapse from a standard he was able otherwise to sustain. Then, at most, he would be a candidate for mitigation. If he is, on the basis outlined above, a candidate for an acquittal, he may yet deservedly be convicted if the conduct for which he claims excuse was very grave, for example a killing. We are dealing with uncompelled conduct perpetrated with *mens rea*. In such cases previous good conduct and a blameless state of disequilibrium may be insufficient to outweigh the culpability evinced by a heinous wrong. We are not dealing with excusatory claims which, if made out, invariably sustain a plea for acquittal. It may depend on what it is the defendant has done.

In essence, this paper attempts to found the claim, adumbrated above, that involuntarily intoxicated persons of previous good character and others in similar cases can, if particular conditions be met, be excused for certain crimes. First, however, we should note the view taken by the House of Lords in *Kingston* that such cases are adequately treated by way of mitigation. This standpoint coheres with the unequivocal opinion of Lord Mustill that a conviction for a serious offence need not entail descriptively or prescriptively that the defendant was in any sense at fault. He endorsed a decision of the Privy Council to the effect that an undercover policeman acting with the knowledge and consent of his superiors and without recourse to entrapment or conduct to the prejudice of third parties would be guilty of trafficking in drugs notwithstanding that the 'trafficking' (carrying drugs out of the jurisdiction) was done solely in the interests of law enforcement. It follows that an involuntarily intoxicated person could at most hope for some degree of mitigation – the policeman's conduct seemed justified whereas the cases we are concerned with fall at most, to be excused.

By contrast with the House of Lords, the view taken here is that a conviction for a stigmatic offence is a sanction in its own right and that sanctions should be confined to the blameworthy. The non-conviction of the blameless should be a pervasive principle of substantive criminal law limited only by the need to theorize and practise criminal law as a system of rules and by the exigencies of forensic practicability. Those limitations entail that many 'normal' life narratives cannot afford grounds of excuse, however exculpatory the force of the narrative may be. But other accounts, not currently represented in standard defences, can be brought within the framework of substantive criminal law. If it can be done it should be done in order to diminish the incidence of unnecessary criminal convictions.

In its 2009 report *Intoxication and Criminal Liability* the Law Commission examined this issue. The following extract details the Law Commission's conclusions.

EXTRACT

According to the Law Commission, should there be a defence of involuntary intoxication?

What reasons did the Commission give for its recommendation?

In your opinion, should there be a defence of involuntary intoxication?

Law Commission (2009) *Intoxication and Criminal Liability* (Law Commission Report No 314) Cm 7526

4.1 It is trite law that, if D commits the external element of an offence with the required fault, then, subject to any defence he or she might have, D is liable for that offence.

4.2 In this Part we address the question whether D should be *excused* from liability, if his or her commission of an offence's external element with the required fault has been proved or admitted, on the basis that:

(1) D's state of involuntary intoxication reduced D's inhibitions to such an extent that, although D was acting voluntarily and with the required fault, he or she could not resist the temptation to commit the offence charged; or

(2) D's state of involuntary intoxication blurred D's moral vision to the extent that, although D acted with the required fault, appreciated what he or she was doing and could have acted otherwise, D did not appreciate the true moral gravity of his or her behaviour.

4.3 As the law stands, involuntary intoxication is not an excuse. Intoxication induced by the surreptitious act of a third party, for example, is irrelevant to the question of D's criminal liability if D acts with the fault required for liability, even if he or she would not have acted in that way if sober.

[…]

4.9 If created, a defence of reduced inhibitions or blurred moral vision would be relied on by D only in cases where it has been proved to the criminal standard that D committed the external element of the offence charged with the required fault. In our view, however, reduced inhibitions or blurred moral vision should have the effect, to a greater or lesser extent, of simply reducing the degree of blame that can be attached to D. In other words, evidence of involuntary intoxication in such cases should operate in the same way as do many (other) mitigating factors which were beyond D's power to control, such as a violent upbringing giving rise to an inability to control angry outbursts. With any like factor, D's involuntary intoxication may well justify a reduced sentence should he or she be convicted of an offence.

4.10 The justification given for the contrary position adopted by the Court of Appeal in *Kingston* was its view that "the purposes of the criminal law are not served" by holding D liable when "the inhibition which the law requires has been removed by the clandestine act of a third party". This approach accords with Professor Sullivan's (subsequently expressed) view that the law should take cognisance of D's lack of blameworthiness in such cases when attributing criminal liability. However, we are unable to perceive any sufficient reason for elevating the mitigating factor of reduced inhibitions or blurred perception of morality caused by involuntary intoxication to the status of a new defence that would entirely negative D's criminal liability.

4.11 Another argument which might be raised in support of a complete defence of involuntary intoxication is that, as some other extraneous mitigating acts - duress by threats and duress of circumstances - already have the effect of completely excusing D's otherwise proven liability (albeit with some exceptions), so involuntary intoxication should similarly entitle D to an absolute acquittal.

4.12 Such an argument is sustainable only insofar as reduced inhibitions or blurred perceptions of morality may properly be regarded as analogous to the existing excusatory defences. There are, however, stark differences between the mere fact of reduced inhibitions or blurred perceptions of morality induced by involuntary intoxication and the duress defences. To rely on duress by threats, D must reasonably have believed, as a result of a threat, that death or serious injury would result if the offence was not committed; and it must be the case that a reasonable person (with D's relevant characteristics) would have committed the offence in those circumstances. Acting with fault but in a disinhibited or less morally aware state caused by surreptitiously administered drugs is far removed from the negation of culpability implicit in the defence(s) of duress.

4.13 There are, moreover, other extraneous circumstances which mitigate the culpability of the offender without affecting his or her criminal liability. For example, the fact that D was provoked into committing an offence is irrelevant to D's liability, regardless of how grievous the provocation was, unless D is charged with murder. Provocative acts do not as a general rule affect D's liability, but are taken into consideration by the court only when passing sentence. It would be extremely difficult to justify a general excusatory defence of reduced inhibitions, obviating all liability, when it is accepted that the most grotesque acts of provocation cannot excuse liability for even relatively minor crimes.

4.14 The closest analogy with an existing complete defence is perhaps with insanity (of a temporary kind). However, the law does not permit the simple fact of blurred moral vision or moral disinhibition to amount to insanity in law.

4.15 There are also sound public policy reasons for rejecting a complete defence of reduced inhibitions or blurred moral vision founded on involuntary intoxication.

4.16 First, we agree that a defence of this sort would be too easy for the accused to manufacture. This would give rise to the very "disturbing prospect" that the defence would be spuriously raised in any case where there was evidence that the accused was intoxicated at the time the offence was committed, particularly when it is remembered that so many offences of violence are committed under the influence of alcohol.

4.17 After all, D would need to do no more than call witnesses to say that he or she acted out of character, and give evidence, perhaps bolstered by similar evidence from his associates, that alcohol or some other drug must have been added to his (alcoholic or non-alcoholic) drink, causing his inhibitions to be reduced to the level at which he could no longer resist engaging in the offence. As Lord Mustill noted, the defence would be one which the Crown would often have no means of rebutting, and D would be entitled to an acquittal if it was reasonably possible that the defence was true.

4.18 Reversing the burden of proof, that is, placing a legal obligation on D to prove the defence on the balance of probabilities, would make it more difficult for the defence to succeed. However, given the ease with which D would be able to fabricate evidence, the low standard of proof D would have to meet, and the problems the Crown would face in rebutting that evidence, there would still be considerable scope for successful reliance on an unmeritorious defence that allows culpable individuals to avoid all liability.

4.19 Secondly, the defence would be entirely subjective. The question would be whether D's personal inhibitions or moral compass, which ordinarily discourage D from committing the type of offence charged, were undermined as a result of involuntary intoxication to the extent that D should not be liable for that offence, even though D acted with the fault required for liability. There could be no "reasonable person" limb to the test because reasonable people do not have a latent disposition to commit crimes. For example, if the facts of *Kingston* were to recur, the jury would have to determine the inherent strength of D's particular sexual disposition towards adolescent boys and whether the degree to which he was affected by the intoxicant (the nature of which may be unknown) caused him, through his irresistible impulse or blurred awareness of morality, to commit an offence he would not otherwise have committed. It is questionable whether these are matters which expert witnesses would be able to throw much light on and, in the absence of relevant expert testimony, it is difficult to see how the jury could be expected to determine the question.

4.20 Thirdly, the stronger the accused's underlying but latent antisocial disposition, the easier it would be to rely successfully on the defence. If D has strong antisocial tendencies which can be kept under control when sober, but not when intoxicated, it would be relatively easy for D to demonstrate that the reduction in his or her inhibitions from the consumption of alcohol or some other drug is what caused the antisocial conduct on the occasion in question. The sole remaining issue would be whether or not the consumption was voluntary. Public safety requires that the strength of D's disposition to engage in antisocial conduct should not make it easier for D to claim a complete excuse for any crime committed in consequence.

4.21 Fourthly, if an excusatory defence were to be created for the situation where D's inhibitions are removed by an act for which he or she is not responsible, there would be little reason why the law should not recognise a general character based excusatory defence for any inherent condition or "irresistible impulse" for which D is equally not responsible. For example, if D's urge to commit sexual offences against children is so great that he cannot withstand it, then logic would require that he too should be able to rely on the excuse of "insufficient inhibition" in relation to any sexual offence he commits against a child. Indeed, if D has a disposition to behave in an antisocial way on account of the way he or she was raised during his or her formative years, again a matter beyond D's control, arguably there should also be an excuse from liability for that reason.

4.22 There may well be an argument for introducing a general defence of diminished responsibility or provocation, or a broader defence of insanity, but these are matters beyond our present remit. In the absence of any such radical reform of the criminal law it would be illogical and anomalous to create a specific defence for persons whose inhibitions were affected by involuntary intoxication.

4.23 In summary, the fact that the accused was involuntarily intoxicated at the time he or she committed the offence should normally be regarded as a mitigating factor, but it should not be elevated to the level of an excuse which would prevent any liability from attaching.

4.24 We agree with the view of Lord Mustill that: the interplay between the wrong done to the victim, the individual characteristics and frailties of the defendant, and the pharmacological effects of whatever drug may be potentially involved can be far better recognised by a tailored choice from the continuum of sentences available to the judge.

4.25 The law is clear in the light of the House of Lords' judgment in *Kingston* and, given our agreement with their Lordships' reasoning and approach, we make no recommendation for reform in this respect.

Quiz 9.2

1. According to Sullivan, when should involuntary intoxication be available as a substantive defence?

- **a.** Never.
- **b.** Whenever a defendant is disinhibited as a result of involuntary intoxication.
- **c.** When a defendant of previously good character and a blameless state of disequilibrium is disinhibited as a result of involuntary intoxication.
- **d.** When a defendant of previously good character is disinhibited as a result of involuntary intoxication.

2. In its report *Intoxication and Criminal Liability*, what was the Law Commission's conclusion on whether there should be a substantive defence of involuntary intoxication?

- **a.** There should instead be a broader defence of diminished responsibility that involuntarily intoxicated defendants could plead.
- **b.** There should not be a defence of involuntary intoxication.
- **c.** Involuntary intoxication should be available as a defence, but with a reversed burden of proof.
- **d.** Involuntary intoxication is analogous to duress and so it should constitute a substantive defence.

3. Which of the following was **not** a reason put forward by the Law Commission for rejecting the proposed new defence of involuntary intoxication?

- **a.** The defence would be entirely subjective.
- **b.** Convicting a blameless defendant such as Kingston of a serious offence does not serve the purposes of the criminal law.
- **c.** That there was insufficient reason for elevating the mitigating factor of reduced inhibitions or blurred perception of morality caused by involuntary intoxication to the status of a new defence that would entirely negate D's criminal liability.
- **d.** A defence of this sort would be too easy for the accused to manufacture.

Basis of a defence

9.3 Recall the case law that applies to defendants who claim that their intoxication caused in them a mistaken belief which should form the basis of a substantive defence.

The introduction to this chapter explained that there are two reasons why a defendant might adduce evidence that he was intoxicated. We can now turn to the second of these reasons: the defendant may claim that his intoxication caused in him a mistaken belief which should form the basis of a substantive defence.

For example, earlier in the chapter we looked at *R* v *Taj*, in which the defendant sought to plead self-defence after his consumption of alcohol and drugs resulted in psychosis and a mistaken belief that the victim was a terrorist. Another example is *R* v *O'Grady* [1987] QB 995. The defendant, Patrick O'Grady, had spent the day drinking with his friend Eddie McCloskey. O'Grady had consumed a large quantity of cider. McCloskey stayed the night at O'Grady's flat. O'Grady said that he was woken up the next morning by a bang on the head. He said he felt blood running down, and saw McCloskey standing next to him holding a piece of glass. The two men fought, and McCloskey was killed. A post mortem revealed that McCloskey had suffered serious wounds to the face as well as injuries to his hands, a fractured rib, severe bruising to the head, brain, neck and chest and a fractured spine. O'Grady claimed that he had acted in self-defence. He told police: 'I did not want to kill him. I wanted him alive, not dead. I had no enmity to him. If I had not hit him I would be dead myself.'

O'Grady was charged with murder. At trial, the jury acquitted him of murder but convicted him of manslaughter. He appealed against his conviction. The case reached the Court of Appeal. The issue on appeal was whether a mistaken belief caused by voluntary intoxication may be taken into account when applying the test for self-defence.[25] Lord Lane CJ stated:

> We have come to the conclusion that where the jury are satisfied that the defendant was mistaken in his belief that any force or the force which he in fact used was necessary to defend himself and are further satisfied that the mistake was caused by voluntarily induced intoxication, the defence must fail [...] There are two competing interests. On the one hand the interest of the defendant who has only acted according to what he believed to be necessary to protect himself, and on the other hand that of the public in general and the victim in particular who, probably through no fault of his own, has been injured or perhaps killed because of the defendant's drunken mistake. Reason recoils from the conclusion that in such circumstances a defendant is entitled to leave the Court without a stain on his character.

So where a defendant mistakenly believes he needs to use force to defend himself, and this mistake was the result of voluntary intoxication, he will be unable to plead self-defence. If the belief was *not* mistaken, or if the belief was *not* the result of voluntary intoxication, the defendant may still plead self-defence and the legal test (which we study in Chapter 11) must be applied in the normal way.

It is important to note that the principle from *R* v *O'Grady* applies whether the defendant has been charged with a crime of basic intent or a crime of specific intent. Lord Lane CJ said:

> We do not consider that any distinction should be drawn on this aspect of the matter between offences involving what is called specific intent, such as murder, and offences of so called basic intent, such as manslaughter.

This has been criticised, with commentators arguing that the *R* v *O'Grady* principle should only apply to basic intent crimes. The reason for this is best explained by contrasting the following two cases:

[25] We study this test in Chapter 11.

***R* v *Hatton* [2005] EWCA Crim 2951**
The defendant, Jonathan Hatton, met the victim, Richard Pashley, in a nightclub.

Shutterstock

During the evening Hatton consumed over 20 pints of beer and Pashley told people (falsely) that he was an officer in the SAS.

Shutterstock

The two men went back to Hatton's flat.

Shutterstock

The next morning Pashley was found dead, having been battered to death with a sledgehammer.

Shutterstock

Hatton's counsel wished to argue that Hatton's intoxicated state had led him to mistakenly believe that Pashley was an SAS soldier attacking him with a sword. The Court of Appeal followed *R* v *O'Grady* and held that Hatton could not found a defence of self-defence on a mistaken belief caused by voluntary intoxication. His murder conviction was accordingly upheld.

***R* v *Lipman* [1970] 1 QB 152**
The defendant, Robert Lipman, and the victim, Claudie Delbarre, both took LSD.

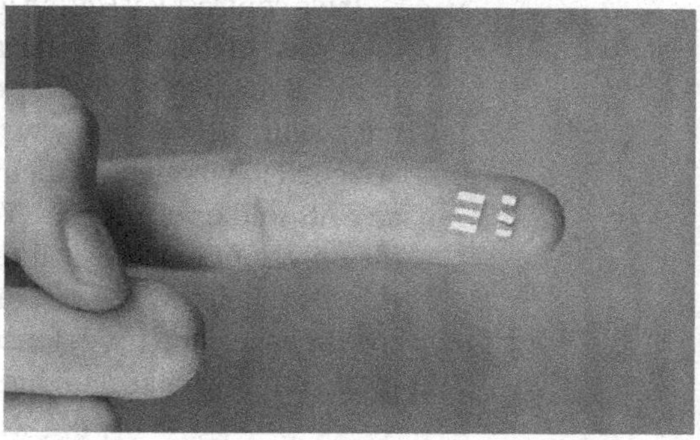

Shutterstock

Lipman said that in his LSD 'trip' he descended to the centre of the earth and was attacked by snakes, which he fought.

Shutterstock

In fact, during the LSD trip Lipman killed Delbarre by asphyxiating her (cramming eight inches of bed sheet into her mouth).

Shutterstock

As we saw earlier in the chapter, since murder is a specific intent crime it must be proved that the defendant acted with the necessary *mens rea*. At trial Lipman argued that he had not formed an intention to kill or seriously injure a human being since he believed he was attacking a snake. The jury accepted this, and so he was convicted of the basic intent crime of manslaughter instead. The Court of Appeal subsequently held that this was correct.

If we contrast *R* v *Hatton* and *R* v *Lipman*, Hatton was convicted of murder whereas Lipman was convicted of manslaughter. This seems to place too much weight on the content of the defendant's intoxication-induced belief. Both men killed their victim because they mistakenly believed they were under attack. It is strange that such importance should be attached to whether, in their intoxicated state, they believed they were being attacked by an SAS soldier or a snake. This could be rectified by saying that the *R* v *O'Grady* principle only applies to basic intent crimes. Hatton would then have been able to rely on his mistaken belief when responding to the murder charge. This would have meant that, if the jury accepted his defence of self-defence, he would have been convicted of the basic intent crime of manslaughter instead – achieving parity with *R* v *Lipman*.

Quiz 9.3

1. In *R* v *O'Grady*, why was the defendant's mistaken belief **not** taken into account?
   a. The criminal law never takes into account mistakes as to the need for, or extent of, force used.
   b. The question of mistake ought not to be considered separately from the question of intent.
   c. D's mistaken belief that any force, or the force which he in fact used was necessary to defend himself, was caused by voluntarily induced intoxication.
   d. D's interest in having his drunkenly induced mistake taken into account outweighed the public interest in penalising drunken acts of violence.

2. How can the decision in *R* v *Hatton* be distinguished from that in *R* v *Lipman*?
   a. *Hatton* was argued on the basis that there might have been a drunken mistake as to the need to use self-defence which would only arise if the necessary *mens rea* for murder was present, whereas in *Lipman* there was no such *mens rea*.
   b. Distinguishing between the two cases is impossible.
   c. There was credible evidence of self-defence in *Hatton* but none in *Lipman*.
   d. Both men killed their victim because they mistakenly believed they were under attack.

Conclusion

Intoxication is commonly referred to as a defence. This is actually misleading.[26] For a start, the law on intoxication does not provide an escape route to defendants who acted with the necessary *mens rea*. As we saw at the start of the chapter, the courts have applied the principle that 'A drunken intent is nevertheless an intent'. In fact, the courts have held that in three situations a defendant may be convicted of a crime even though he did not have the necessary *mens rea* at the time of the offence:

- D is charged with a basic intent crime and had voluntarily consumed alcohol or recreational drugs.
- D is charged with a basic intent crime and had recklessly consumed medicinal drugs.
- D had been drinking with intent.

[26] Simester, A.P. (2009) 'Intoxication is Never a Defence' *Criminal Law Review* 3.

In this chapter we have also seen that: there is no substantive defence for involuntarily intoxicated defendants; and defendants who mistakenly use force to defend themselves as a result of voluntary intoxication may not plead self-defence.

Instead of thinking of intoxication as a defence, when you answer an exam problem question you should begin by asking why the defendant wishes to adduce evidence of his intoxication. If it is in order to deny that he possessed the necessary *mens rea*, you should consider the effect of his intoxication as part of your discussion of the *mens rea* of the offence. On the other hand, if he wishes to claim that his intoxication caused in him a mistaken belief which should form the basis of a substantive defence, you should consider the effect of his intoxication as part of your discussion of the relevant substantive defence. Try to avoid referring to intoxication as a defence in its own right because it is not!

Applying the law

9.4 Apply the law on intoxicated defendants to hypothetical sets of facts.

The following scenario takes place at a professional networking event. Read the problem scenario carefully, then answer the multiple-choice questions below to apply your learning to the scenario.

Ashish and James

Law students Ashish, James and Priya attend a networking event for aspiring solicitors. The event is sponsored by a leading law firm and has a free bar. Even though Ashish is currently taking prescription medication for a chest infection, and was warned by his doctor not to mix the drugs with alcohol, he drinks several glasses of wine in quick succession. He becomes irritable. When he sees trainee solicitor Ryder flirting with Priya he picks up an empty wine bottle and hits Ryder on the head with it. Ryder suffers a deep gash which requires stitches. In the resulting mêlée James – who had been drowning his sorrows after receiving his latest coursework mark – pushes over Abdul. Abdul lands awkwardly and suffers a broken arm.

Ashish and James both claim that at the time of the brawl they were so intoxicated that they were completely unaware of what they were doing.

Discuss the criminal liability of Ashish and James.

Quiz 9.4

1. The question asks us to discuss the liability of two defendants, Ashish and James. We will consider Ashish first.

   When discussing Ashish's liability, the starting point is to determine what level of injury Wasim suffered in order to identify the relevant offence(s).

   Which of the following statements is incorrect?

   a. According to *DPP* v *Smith*, GBH simply means really serious harm.

   b. According to *Collins* v *Wilcock*, any contact, however slight, is sufficient for the *actus reus* of battery.

   c. According to *C* v *Eisenhower*, any injury which damages the outer layers of the skin (such as a scratch) qualifies as a 'wound'.

   d. According to *R* v *Chan-Fook*, to constitute ABH an injury need not be permanent but should not be so trivial as to be wholly insignificant.

2. Applying C v *Eisenhower*, we can conclude that Wasim suffered a wound. The continuity of Wasim's skin was obviously broken, since the question describes it as a 'deep gash' that required stitches. The relevant offences would therefore be the ones found in section 18 (wounding/GBH with intent) and section 20 (malicious wounding/infliction of GBH) of the Offences Against the Person Act 1861 (OAPA). As we saw in Chapter 6, it is logical to begin with the section 20 offence.

   The section 20 offence has three requirements. First, the defendant either wounded the victim or inflicted GBH. We have already established that Ashish wounded Wasim. Second, the wounding must have been unlawful. This too is satisfied – there is no suggestion that Ashish was acting in self-defence or that Wasim consented. Third, the defendant must have acted maliciously.

   According to the Court of Appeal in *R* v *Cunningham* what test should be used to establish malice?

   a. Did the defendant display a couldn't-care-less attitude as to whether the victim would suffer injury?

   b. Did the defendant either intend to do the type of harm that was in fact done or was he reckless as to whether such harm would occur or not?

   c. Did the defendant manifest ill-will or hatred towards the victim?

   d. Did the defendant fail to give any thought to an obvious and serious risk that the victim would suffer the harm?

3. So Ashish's liability for the section 20 offence hinges on whether or not he acted maliciously. However, it is important to note that Ashish claims that at the time of the brawl he was so intoxicated that he was completely unaware of what he was doing. Ashish's defence counsel will therefore claim that he lacked the necessary *mens rea*. They will argue that, if Ashish was completely unaware of what he was doing, he could not have formed an intention to cause the type of harm Wasim suffered nor would he have foreseen the risk that Wasim might suffer this harm. So we need to turn to the case law that applies when a defendant adduces evidence that he was intoxicated in order to deny that he possessed the necessary *mens rea* at the time of the offence.

   It is clear from the facts of the question that Ashish consumed the intoxicating substances (prescription medication coupled with several glasses of wine) voluntarily, and that he was not drinking with intent. So, given that Ashish took the prescription medication for medicinal purposes, we should apply the decisions in *R* v *Bailey* and *R* v *Hardie*.

   The following four statements each summarise one of the principles from *R* v *Bailey* and *R* v *Hardie* Which one is incorrect?

   a. If the defendant committed the *actus reus* of the offence, and did so with the necessary *mens rea*, then it is no defence for him to say that he would not have committed the crime had he been sober.

   b. If the defendant's consumption of the substance was not reckless, the defendant should be regarded as having been involuntarily intoxicated.

   c. Even if the defendant possessed the necessary *mens rea* at the time of the offence, he should not be found guilty if he consumed the substance non-recklessly, for medicinal purposes and would not have acted in the same way had he been sober.

   d. If the defendant's consumption of the substance was reckless, the case should be treated no differently to one involving voluntary consumption of alcohol or recreational drugs.

4. It seems clear that Ashish's consumption of the prescription medication, coupled with the glasses of wine, was reckless. He had been made aware of the risks of mixing the two by his doc and unjustifiably chose to do so anyway. Since his consumption was reckless, we should treat the case in the same way as one involving consumption of just alcohol or recreational drugs. The leading case here is *DPP*v *Majewski*. As we saw in the chapter, in this case the House of Lords drew a distinction between basic intent crimes and specific intent crimes.

   The following four statements each summarise one of the principles from *DPP* v *Majewski*. Which one is incorrect?

   a. A defendant can only be convicted of a specific intent crime if he possessed the necessary *mens rea* at the time of the offence.

   b. A defendant who is charged with a basic intent crime may not use the fact he was voluntarily intoxicated to claim that he lacked *mens rea*.

   c. For specific intent crimes the defendant may argue that he was unable to form *mens rea* as a result of his own voluntary intoxication.

   d. For basic intent crimes a defendant may only be convicted if he possessed the necessary *mens rea* at the time of the offence.

5. In order to decide whether Ashish is guilty of the section 20 (malicious wounding/infliction of GBH) and/ or the section 18 (wounding/GBH with intent) offences,

we therefore need to know whether these offences are crimes of basic or specific intent.

Which of the following statements categorises the two offences correctly?

a. Both the section 18 and the section 20 offences are crimes of basic intent.

b. The section 18 offence is a crime of basic intent; the section 20 offence is a crime of specific intent.

c. The section 18 offence is a crime of specific intent; the section 20 offence is a crime of basic intent.

d. Both the section 18 and the section 20 offences are crimes of specific intent.

Having discussed Ashish's liability we can now move on to consider James. Again, the starting point is to determine what level of injury the victim, Abdul, suffered in order to identify the relevant offence(s). Abdul suffered a broken arm. As we saw in Chapter 6, whether an injury amounts to ABH or GBH is a question of fact for the jury in the particular case. But generally the seriousness of a broken arm means it is likely to be regarded as GBH. So the relevant offences in James's case are the same ones as in Ashish's: section 18 (wounding/GBH with intent) and section 20 (malicious wounding/infliction of GBH) OAPA.

Looking back at our analysis of Ashish's liability, in your opinion would James be guilty of the section 18 and/or section 20 offences? Can you explain your reasoning? You may use the flow chart in Figure 9.1 to help you if you wish.

Maya, Suresh and Anton

During happy hour at your local pub the following events take place:

1. Lucas offers to buy teetotaller Maya a drink. Although Maya has always detested Lucas and considered him extremely sleazy, she accepts and asks him for an orange juice. Unbeknown to Maya, Lucas asks the barman to add a double shot of vodka. Maya drinks the juice without realising it contains alcohol. She becomes disinhibited. A short time later Lucas tells a dirty joke. Maya is so disgusted that she picks up her empty glass and throws it at him. Lucas suffers a scratch and a painful bruise. Maya later says she would not have thrown the glass had her drink not been spiked.
2. Suresh drinks several double shots of whisky. Earlier in the day his work colleague Vikram embarrassed him in a meeting in front of their boss. Having resolved to get revenge, Suresh drank the whisky in order to build up the courage to go and beat Vikram up. After leaving the pub Suresh returns to the office, finds Vikram and punches him in the face. Vikram suffers a black eye. Suresh later claims that he has no recollection of that evening.
3. Over the course of several drinking games Anton drinks a large quantity of alcohol. Before arriving at the pub he had also taken recreational drugs. When he leaves the pub he is so intoxicated that when he sees Rasheed walking towards him he mistakenly believes that Rasheed is a Roman gladiator about to attack him. Anton pushes Rasheed over, kicks him repeatedly and then runs away. Rasheed later dies from his injuries. Anton says that, in his intoxicated state, he genuinely believed Rasheed would have killed him if he hadn't defended himself.

Now, consider these questions.

1. Discuss the criminal liability of:
   - Maya
   - Suresh
   - Anton
2. How (if at all) would your answer be different if Anton had believed that Rasheed was a fire-breathing dragon, not a Roman gladiator?

Evaluating the law

9.5 Evaluate whether involuntary intoxication should be available as a substantive defence.

Think about this question.

'The lack of a substantive defence for involuntarily intoxicated defendants results in unjust convictions. This is demonstrated by *R* v *Kingston* [1995] 2 AC 355. Parliament should create such a defence as a matter of urgency.'

Discuss the extent to which you agree with this statement.

Step 1: Deconstruct the essay title

This question asks you to discuss whether Parliament should create a new substantive defence of involuntary intoxication. The statement asserts that the absence of such a defence results in unjust convictions. So your essay should consider whether the absence of such a defence does indeed result in injustice and – if so – whether the creation of a new substantive defence is an appropriate way of remedying this situation.

Step 2: Work through each argument, form an opinion and construct a set of arguments in support of your views

To help you with this, look back at the notes you prepared in response to the following questions.

On *R* v *Kingston*:

- Read the following extract from the judgment of Lord Mustill. What (a) theoretical and (b) practical reasons does he give for rejecting a substantive defence of involuntary intoxication?
- What specific concern does Lord Mustill express about the lack of a defence of involuntary intoxication?

On Sullivan's chapter 'Making Excuses':

- According to Sullivan, when should involuntary intoxication be available as a substantive defence? What reasons does Sullivan advance in support of this?

On the Law Commission's report *Intoxication and Criminal Liability*:

- According to the Law Commission, should there be a defence of involuntary intoxication?
- What reasons did the Commission give for its recommendation?
- In your opinion, should there be a defence of involuntary intoxication?

Look back at the various arguments for and against the creation of an involuntary intoxication defence. Once you have formed your own opinion on: (a) whether the absence of such a defence results in injustice; and (b) whether the creation of such a defence would be an appropriate way of remedying the situation, construct a set of arguments in support of your views and work out how you would respond to potential counter-arguments. You may find some of the items on the further reading list useful here.

Step 3: Planning your introduction and conclusion

You now have compiled all you need for the main body of your essay. The last task is to decide what to include in your introduction and conclusion.

The introduction should contextualise your discussion by briefly outlining the decision in *R* v *Kingston*, and give an indication of the argument you will present in your essay.

The conclusion should round off your essay with a succinct statement of your argument and a summary of your supporting reasons.

Intoxication checklist

Having worked through this chapter, you should now have:

- An understanding of the case law that applies when a defendant uses the fact he was intoxicated to claim he lacked *mens rea*
- A knowledge of which crimes are basic intent crimes and which are specific intent crimes
- An ability to critically discuss whether or not involuntary intoxication should be a substantive defence
- An understanding of the case law that applies to defendants whose intoxication causes them to mistakenly act in self-defence.

Further reading

Crosby, C. (2010) 'Culpability, *Kingston* and the Law Commission' 74 *Journal of Criminal Law* 434.

Law Commission (2009) *Intoxication and Criminal Liability* (Law Commission Report No 314) Cm 7526.

Simester, A. P. (2009) 'Intoxication is Never a Defence' *Criminal Law Review* 3.

Smith, R. and Clements, L. (1995) 'Involuntary Intoxication, the Threshold of Inhibition and the Instigation of Crime' 46 *Northern Ireland Legal Quarterly* 210.

Sullivan, G. R. (1994) 'Involuntary Intoxication and Beyond' *Criminal Law Review* 272.

Sullivan, G. R. (1996) 'Making Excuses' in A. Smith and G. Sullivan (eds) *Harm and Culpability*. OUP: Oxford.

Williams, R. (2013) 'Voluntary Intoxication – a Lost Cause?' 129 *Law Quarterly Review* 264.

Answers on the Companion Website

Please visit the companion website for the answers to Key Questions, Quizzes, Applying the Law scenarios as well as student support including glossaries. Please visit www.pearsoned.co.uk/Macdonald

10

Mental condition defences

Learning Objectives

10.1 Define the requirements for establishing the defence of sane automatism.

10.2 Define the requirements for establishing the defence of insanity.

10.3 Define the requirements for establishing the defence of diminished responsibility.

10.4 Apply the law on mental condition defences to hypothetical sets of facts.

10.5 Evaluate the changes made to the diminished responsibility defence by the Coroners and Justice Act 2009.

Introduction

In this chapter we study three defences which we have already encountered briefly earlier in the text. What the three have in common is that they all concern the mental condition of the defendant. The first two – which were mentioned briefly in Chapter 3 – are sane automatism and insanity. Although we refer to them as defences, they are different in nature from the substantive defences that we study in the next chapter. Substantive defences apply when the *actus reus* and *mens rea* of a crime have been established. By contrast, sane automatism and insanity are both best understood as a denial of the *actus reus.*[1] Defendants who plead one of these defences are denying that they acted voluntarily – which, as we saw in Chapter 3, is one of the core *actus reus* concepts. In other words, they are denying that they had the necessary mental capacity for criminal responsibility.

The third defence that we study in this chapter is diminished responsibility, which was mentioned briefly in the chapter on homicide.

The importance of these three concepts is illustrated by the following three examples:[2]

1. Sane automatism

REM guitarist cleared of air rage

The band's singer Michael Stipe and Buck's wife Stephanie burst into tears as the jury cleared him of a charge of being drunk on an aircraft last April, two counts of common assault, and one charge of damaging BA crockery.

After the verdict, Buck shook hands with junior prosecuting counsel Edward Lewis and told him: "I'm sorry about this whole situation."

Buck did not deny his behaviour but claimed a Zolpiden sleeping pill reacted violently with alcohol, turning him into a "non-insane automaton".

He told the trial at Isleworth crown court that he remembered nothing between shutting his eyes in his first class seat and waking up at Heathrow police station believing he must have suffered a heart attack.

2. Insane automatism

Sleepwalker cleared of murdering father

Jules Lowe was made the subject of a hospital order yesterday after a jury found him not guilty of murder by reason of insanity.

His father Edward Lowe, 83, was killed in a prolonged attack at the family home in Walkden, Greater Manchester in October 2003 after a drinking session. The victim had 90 injuries to his body and had been punched, kicked and stamped on.

Richard Marks QC, prosecuting, said Mr Lowe's defence of sleepwalking was "far fetched in the extreme".

---

[1] In *Loake v Crown Prosecution Service* [2017] EWHC 2855 (Admin) the High Court rejected the suggestion that the insanity defence constitutes a denial of *mens rea* and so is only available as a defence to crimes that require proof of *mens rea*. It held that the insanity defence 'rests on a broader base' ([54]) and so is available as a defence to crimes that contain an objective form of *mens rea* (such as the sexual offences we studied in Chapter 7) and to crimes of strict liability.

[2] Sources: 1. Sane automatism: https://www.theguardian.com/uk/2002/apr/06/world.jeevanvasagar; 2. Insane automatism: Sleepwalker cleared of murdering father; 3. Diminished responsibility: Sally Challen walks free as court rules out retrial for killing abusive husband.

But after hearing expert evidence, the jury at Manchester crown court decided the attack took place while Mr Lowe was sleepwalking in an "automaton" state and completely unaware of his own actions.

The judge, Mr Justice Richard Henriques, ordered under the Criminal Procedure Act that Mr Lowe, 32, be detained under a hospital order. He explained that the verdict of not guilty by way of insanity did not mean the defendant was insane in the normal sense of the word, but that Mr Lowe was subject to "automatism" due to his sleepwalking.

3. Diminished responsibility

Sally Challen walks free as court rules out retrial for killing abusive husband

Sally Challen, who was jailed for life for killing her husband in a hammer attack following decades of emotional abuse, has walked free from court after a judge announced she would not face a retrial.

Challen, 65, was sentenced at the Old Bailey in London on Friday to nine years and four months – time already served – for the manslaughter of her husband, Richard.

Speaking at a press conference afterwards, she said: "My family have served my sentence with me. They have kept me going for a long and terrible nine years. I want also to thank my friends in and out of prison who have stood by me."

Challen said she suffered years of controlling and humiliating abuse before she killed her 61-year-old husband in August 2010.

She was jailed for life for murder after a trial at Guildford crown court in 2011. In February this year the court of appeal quashed her conviction and ordered a fresh trial in light of new evidence about her mental state at the time of the killing.

Challen, of Claygate, Surrey, admitted manslaughter but pleaded not guilty to murder. She was due to face a new trial on 1 July, but at a hearing before Mr Justice Edis at the Old Bailey on Friday the prosecution said the crown accepted her plea to the lesser charge.

"Allowing full credit of one-third because it has always been your case that you killed him by reasons of diminished responsibility, that means you have already served an equivalent sentence and are therefore entitled by law to be released at once," Edis said.

To some extent, diminished responsibility overlaps with the defence of insanity. The chapter will set out the requirements for a **defence of diminished responsibility** and explain the **differences** between this **defence** and **insanity**. We will also look in detail at the changes that were made to the diminished responsibility defence by the Coroners and Justice Act 2009 and evaluate them.

Sane automatism

10.1 Explain the requirements for establishing the defence of sane automatism.

If a defendant successfully pleads the defence of sane automatism he is found not guilty. The defence has three requirements:

1. The defendant suffered a total destruction of voluntary control
2. The defendant's condition was caused by an external factor
3. The defendant's condition was not induced by voluntary intoxication.

We will work through these requirements in turn. We will also look at the situation where the defendant's condition was caused by a combination of sane automatism and voluntary intoxication.

1. The defendant suffered a total destruction of voluntary control

We studied the meaning of automatism in Chapter 3. We saw there that the Court of Appeal has held that it means a total destruction of voluntary control.[3]

2. The defendant's condition was caused by an external factor

Chapter 3 explained that, if the defendant suffered a total destruction of voluntary control, the next question to ask is whether this was caused by an external or an internal factor. The defence of sane automatism is only available if the defendant's condition was caused by an external factor. If the cause was an internal factor, you should instead consider the defence of insanity (and, in murder cases, the defence of diminished responsibility).

For example, in *R* v *Coley* [2013] EWCA Crim 223 the defendant, 17-year-old Scott Coley, entered his neighbour's house (with whom he was previously on good terms) clad in a balaclava and carrying a Rambo knife.

Brian A Jackson/Shutterstock

He attacked the victim, stabbing him repeatedly and causing life-threatening injuries.

Max Sky/Shutterstock

[3] *Attorney-General's Reference (No 2 of 1992)* [1994] QB 91; *R* v *Coley* [2013] EWCA Crim 223.

Coley was a regular user of strong cannabis. He played violent video games and on the evening of the offence had watched the action movie XXX and smoked cannabis.

Kemedo/Shutterstock

Three psychiatrists stated that Coley had probably suffered a brief psychotic episode induced by the cannabis.

They also said that it was possible that he was acting out the role of a character in a video game. At trial he was convicted of attempted murder. On appeal the Court of Appeal held that the defence of insanity was unavailable to Coley because his condition had been caused by an external, not an internal, factor (smoking cannabis).

The distinction between external and internal factors is a difficult one, as the following cases illustrate. First is a pair of cases involving diabetics. In *R* v *Quick* [1973] QB 910 the defendant, a diabetic named William Quick, was a nurse. He was charged with assaulting a patient. On the day of the offence he had taken insulin as normal but ate little food thereafter. As a result he suffered hypoglycaemia (i.e. low blood sugar levels). At trial the trial judge ruled that this evidence supported a defence of insanity, not a defence of sane automatism. Following this Quick changed his plea to guilty[4] and appealed, arguing that the trial judge's ruling was incorrect. The Court of Appeal agreed, holding that the cause of Quick's condition was the injection of insulin, which amounted to an external factor. The appropriate defence was therefore sane automatism. Lawton LJ stated:

> In this case Quick's alleged mental condition, if it ever existed, was not caused by his diabetes but by his use of the insulin prescribed by his doctor. Such malfunctioning of his mind as there was, was caused by an external factor and not by a bodily disorder in the nature of a disease which disturbed the working of his mind. It follows in our judgment that Quick was entitled to have his defence of automatism left to the jury and that Bridge J.'s ruling as to the effect of the medical evidence called by him was wrong.

Quick's conviction was therefore quashed. But compare *R* v *Quick* to *R* v *Hennessy* [1989] 1 WLR 287. The defendant, Andrew Hennessy, was also a diabetic. He was charged with motoring offences. He claimed that at the time of the offences he was in a hyperglycaemic state (i.e. too much blood sugar). He explained that this was because – as a result of stress, anxiety and depression – he had failed to take his proper dose of insulin. The trial judge ruled that this amounted to a claim of insanity, not sane automatism.

[4] At the time of the case a finding of not guilty by reason of insanity resulted in compulsory detention in a special hospital.

Following this Hennessy changed his plea to guilty and appealed, arguing that the trial judge's ruling was incorrect. The Court of Appeal rejected the appeal and held that the appropriate defence in Hennessy's case was insanity.

EXTRACT

Read the following extract from the judgment of Lord Lane CJ.

How does he distinguish the decision in *R v Quick*?

According to Lord Lane CJ, can stress, anxiety and depression amount to external factors? Why/ why not?

R v Hennessy [1989] 1 WLR 287

Lord Lane CJ

Thus in Quick's case the fact that his condition was, or may have been due to the injections of insulin, meant that the malfunction was due to an external factor and not to the disease. The drug it was that caused the hypoglycaemia, the low blood sugar. As suggested in another passage of the judgment of Lawton L.J. (at p. 922G–H), hyperglycaemia, high blood sugar, caused by an inherent defect, and not corrected by insulin is a disease, and if, as the defendant was asserting here, it does cause a malfunction of the mind, then the case may fall within [the insanity defence].

[...]

In our judgment, stress, anxiety and depression can no doubt be the result of the operation of external factors, but they are not, it seems to us, in themselves separately or together external factors of the kind capable in law of causing or contributing to a state of automatism. They constitute a state of mind which is prone to recur. They lack the feature of novelty or accident [...] It does not, in our judgment, come within the scope of the exception of some external physical factor such as a blow on the head or the administration of an anaesthetic.

Hennessy's conviction – and his two-year suspended prison sentence – were therefore upheld.

So in *R v Quick* the cause of the defendant's condition was the injection of insulin: an external factor. In *R v Hennessy*, by contrast, the defendant had not injected himself with anything. The diabetes simply ran its course. The diabetes was therefore the cause, and diabetes is an internal factor. This is a fine distinction! Both Quick and Hennessy were responsible for mismanaging their diabetes. Whilst their mismanagement took a different form in each case, it seems strange that this difference should result in such radically different legal outcomes.

Also important in cases involving diabetics is the principle that the defence of sane automatism is unavailable if there was prior fault on the defendant's part.

In *R v Clarke* [2009] EWCA Crim 921 the defendant, 49-year-old Trevor Clarke, had suffered from diabetes for 30 years. One day when he was driving he began to experience warning signs (sweating, tremor, anxiety) that he was about to suffer a hypoglycaemic episode. He ignored them and continued driving. When the hypoglycaemic episode began Clarke started driving erratically, eventually veering off the road. The car hit two children. The younger one, a four-year-old, was killed. The defence of sane automatism was unavailable to him because he had an awareness of his deteriorating condition and yet continued driving.

The three remaining cases are *R* v *Burgess* [1991] 2 QB 92, *R* v *T* [1990] Crim LR 256 and *R* v *Gower* [2025] Crim LR 220. In *R* v *Burgess* the defendant, Barry Burgess, was in love with his neighbour Katrina Curtis – but she just wanted to be friends. One evening they were watching videos together. Katrina fell asleep. While she was sleeping Burgess hit her on the head with a bottle and then grabbed her by the throat. She cried out. He appeared to come to his senses and showed great remorse over what had happened. Medical evidence suggested that Burgess had been sleepwalking. At trial, the trial judge ruled that Burgess' condition was caused by an internal factor and so the appropriate defence was insanity, not sane automatism. Burgess was found not guilty by reason of insanity. He appealed, arguing that the trial judge's ruling was incorrect. The Court of Appeal rejected his appeal. Lord Lane CJ held that Katrina rejecting Burgess' advances did not amount to an external factor. The cause of his condition was internal:

> One can perhaps narrow the field of inquiry still further by eliminating what are sometimes called the "external factors" such as concussion caused by a blow on the head. There were no such factors here. Whatever the cause may have been, it was an "internal" cause. The possible disappointment or frustration caused by unrequited love is not to be equated with something such as concussion.

So in both *R* v *Hennessy* and *R* v *Burgess*, the Court of Appeal insisted that the ordinary stresses and disappointments of life cannot amount to an external factor. But what about events that are exceptionally traumatic. In *R* v *T* the defendant took part in a robbery three days after having been raped. At the time of the offence she was suffering from PTSD and in a dissociative state as a result of the rape. At trial, the Crown Court judge held that the rape constituted an external factor, and she was able to plead a defence of sane automatism.

Although *R* v *T* was subsequently cited without disapproval by the Court of Appeal in *Attorney-General's Reference (No 2 of 1992)* (which we studied in Chapter 3), it was criticized by the Crown Court judge in *R* v *Gower*. David Gower (aged 81) killed his 78 year-old wife, who suffered from dementia. They had been married for 48 years. Expert evidence stated that Gower had been suffering from acute stress, leading to a dissociative response and a loss of voluntary control. At the pre-trial hearing, the Crown Court judge stated that the decision in *R* v *T* was 'impossible to reconcile' with cases such as *R v Hennessy* and *R* v *Burgess* ([90]). PTSD is an internal factor, he said, and so too are the causes of PTSD (such as Gower's caring responsibilities for his wife). No distinction can be drawn based on how acute the stress was that the defendant faced. As Mackay observes, the decision in *R* v *Gower* 'may not be at appellate level, but it deserves close scrutiny. If it were to be followed, it would exclude all forms of "psychological blow" automatism from the category of sane automatism, irrespective of the nature of the cause or trigger'.[5]

3. The defendant's condition was not induced by voluntary intoxication

The defence of sane automatism is unavailable if the defendant's condition was induced by voluntary intoxication. For example, we saw a few pages ago that in *R* v *Coley* the defendant was unable to plead insanity because his condition was caused by an external

[5] Mackay, R. (2025) 'Commentary on *R* v *Gower' Criminal Law Review* 220.

factor. The Court of Appeal held that Coley was also unable to plead sane automatism because his condition was induced by his voluntary consumption of cannabis.

If the defendant was voluntarily intoxicated, you should instead apply the law that we studied in the previous chapter on intoxication. So suppose the defendant voluntarily consumes two bottles of wine and ends up so drunk that he falls over and smashes a valuable ornament. He cannot plead sane automatism, even if he was so drunk that he was completely unable to control his bodily movements when he smashed the ornament, because his condition was the result of his own voluntary intoxication. The case would instead be governed by the principles set out in *DPP* v *Majewski* [1977] AC 443.

4. Sane automatism and voluntary intoxication

What is the position if the defendant's condition was the result of a combination of: (i) voluntary intoxication; and (ii) another external factor that was not self-induced? This issue arose in *R* v *Stripp* (1978) 69 Cr App R 318.

The defendant, David Stripp, had been out drinking with his fiancée. At the end of the evening Stripp caught the last bus home.

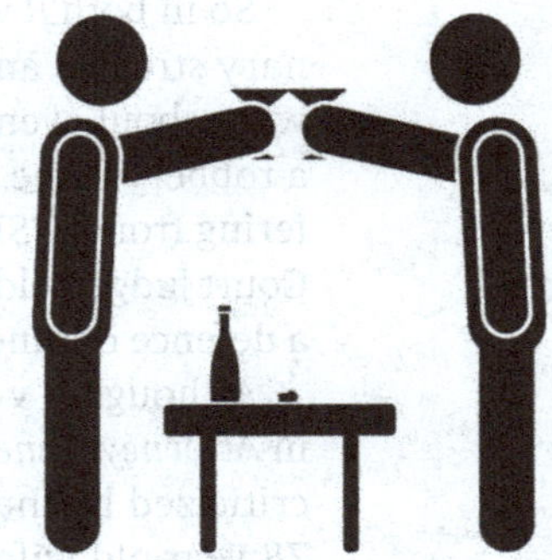

Mr. Rashad/Shutterstock

The next anyone saw of him was in the bus station, where he was found fast asleep on the lower floor of a double-decker bus.

Steve Mann/Shutterstock

Stripp got off the bus and said he wanted to go home. He then climbed into a single-decker bus and drove off in it.

Fejas/Shutterstock

Stripp drove the bus for half a mile. He failed to control it properly and left a trail of destruction behind him.

solarus/ShutterstockS

At trial Stripp was convicted of a number of driving offences. He appealed, arguing that he had acted in a state of automatism.

Leremy/Shutterstock

He claimed that on the original bus journey the bus had swerved causing him to bang his head. This bang, he said, left him concussed.

RNko/Shutterstock

The Court of Appeal held that, in a case where the defendant was both concussed and voluntarily intoxicated, the jury must determine whether the concussion or the intoxication was the dominant cause of the defendant's condition.

If it was concussion, he may plead sane automatism. If it was voluntary intoxication, the law that we studied in the previous chapter should be applied.

The Court of Appeal in *R* v *Stripp* also commented *obiter* on another, similar situation. Suppose Dale is so drunk that he falls over and bangs his head. As a result of concussion he is left completely unaware of what he is doing. Whilst in this state he runs into Mildred and knocks her over. Mildred suffers a broken arm. Medical evidence shows that the dominant cause of Dale's unawareness was his concussion. Could Dale plead sane automatism? Or would the defence be unavailable on the basis that his concussion was caused by his voluntary intoxication? The Court of Appeal in *R* v *Stripp* suggested that, in a case like this, sane automatism is available as a defence. Whilst defendants may not plead the defence when their condition was induced by voluntary intoxication (as in *R* v *Coley*), in a case like Dale's the link between his unawareness and his intoxication was too remote for this principle to apply.

Quiz 10.1

1. Sane automatism is a defence to which of the following offences?
   - **a.** All offences that require a *mens rea* to be proved by the prosecution.
   - **b.** All offences, including those of strict liability.
   - **c.** Only those offences that are fatal or non-fatal offences against the person.
   - **d.** Any offence which has a mandatory sentence of life imprisonment.
2. Which of the following states is most likely to give rise to a defence of sane automatism?
   - **a.** Epileptic seizure.
   - **b.** Hyperglycaemia (i.e. high blood sugar levels).
   - **c.** Hypoglycaemia (i.e. low blood sugar levels).
   - **d.** Sleepwalking.
3. Why was the defendant in *R* v *Clarke* not permitted to rely on the defence of sane automatism?
   - **a.** The cause of his condition was an internal factor.
   - **b.** A drunken intent is nevertheless an intent.
   - **c.** His driving was exceptionally dangerous.
   - **d.** He had an awareness of his deteriorating condition and yet continued driving.

Insanity

10.2 Explain the requirements for establishing the defence of insanity.

In a criminal trial, a person's sanity might be relevant for one of two reasons. First, the defendant may claim that he was insane at the time he committed the offence in question. Second, the defendant may claim that he is insane at the time of the trial and as a result is unfit to be tried. We do not examine the second of these in this text, since it is more a matter of procedure than of substantive criminal law. Instead, we focus on the first situation: where the defendant seeks to establish a defence on the grounds that he was insane at the time of the offence.

As we saw in Chapter 3, a defendant who successfully pleads the defence of insanity is found not guilty by reason of insanity. If the defendant is found not guilty by reason of insanity the trial judge can order hospitalisation, a supervision order or an absolute discharge.[6] The requirements for the defence of insanity were set out by the House of Lords in *M'Naghten's case* (1843) 10 C & F 200:

[6] Criminal Procedure (Insanity) Act 1964, s.5.

> [W]e have to submit our opinion to be, that the jurors ought to be told in all cases that every man is to be presumed to be sane, and to possess a sufficient degree of reason to be responsible for his crimes, until the contrary be proved to their satisfaction; and that to establish a defence on the ground of insanity, it must be clearly proved that, at the time of the committing of the act, the party accused was labouring under such a defect of reason, from disease of the mind, as not to know the nature and quality of the act he was doing; or, if he did know it, that he did not know he was doing what was wrong.

As this extract suggests, the defence of insanity has a reversed burden of proof. This was confirmed by the House of Lords in *Woolmington* v *DPP* [1935] AC 462. So a defendant who pleads insanity must prove, on the balance of probabilities, that the requirements for the defence are established.

M'Naghten's case tells us that the defence has three requirements:

1. The defendant was suffering from a disease of the mind
2. The defendant's disease of the mind caused a defect of reason
3. As a result of the defect of reason, the defendant either: (i) did not know the nature and quality of the act he was doing; or (ii) did not know that what he was doing was wrong.

These requirements are known as the *M'Naghten* rules. We will work through them in turn. We will then look briefly at two specific types of case: those where the defendant was both voluntarily intoxicated and suffering from a disease of the mind; and those where the defendant was suffering from an alcohol-induced disease of the mind.

1. The defendant was suffering from a disease of the mind

The first requirement is that the defendant was suffering from a disease of the mind. 'Disease of the mind' is a legal concept, not a medical one.[7] So whilst medical evidence is necessary,[8] whether or not the defendant was suffering from a disease of the mind is a question of law. It is important to remember this, because as we shall see a doctor would regard some of the courts' rulings on insanity as very strange indeed!

The principal restriction on what constitutes a disease of the mind is that it must arise from a factor that is internal to the defendant.

So, as we saw earlier in the chapter, if a defendant receives a bang on the head and suffers concussion the appropriate defence is sane automatism, not insanity, because his condition was caused by an external factor. Similarly, if the defendant's condition arose from the administration of an anaesthetic or from the injection of insulin (as in *R* v *Quick*) the appropriate defence is sane automatism, not insanity.

Aside from this restriction, the concept disease of the mind is very wide indeed. The leading case is *R* v *Sullivan* [1984] AC 156. The defendant, Patrick Sullivan, was an epileptic. He would suffer one or two seizures a week. One day he suffered a seizure whilst he was visiting an elderly neighbour, Mrs Killick. During the seizure he attacked Mr Payne, an elderly man who was also visiting. Sullivan was charged with maliciously inflicting GBH.[9] At trial, Sullivan initially pleaded not guilty. His counsel led evidence

---

[7] *R* v *Sullivan* [1984] AC 156.

[8] Section 1 of the Criminal Procedure (Insanity and Unfitness to Plead) Act 1991 states that the evidence of at least two medical practitioners is required for a verdict of not guilty by reason of insanity.

[9] Offences Against the Person Act 1861, s.20.

that the attack occurred during an epileptic seizure. However, the trial judge ruled that the relevant defence was insanity, not sane automatism. Following this ruling Sullivan chose to plead guilty to assault occasioning ABH (in order to avoid being found not guilty by reason of insanity[10]). He then appealed against the trial judge's ruling. On appeal, the key issue was whether the appropriate defence was sane automatism or insanity. The case reached the House of Lords.

EXTRACT

Read the following extract from the judgment of Lord Diplock.

How does he define a 'disease of the mind'?

To qualify as a disease of the mind, must the condition be a form of brain disease? Must the condition be permanent?

What is the rationale underlying Lord Diplock's definition of disease of the mind?

R v *Sullivan* [1984] AC 156

Lord Diplock

I agree [...] that "mind" in the *M'Naghten Rules* is used in the ordinary sense of the mental faculties of reason, memory and understanding. If the effect of a disease is to impair these faculties so severely as to have either of the consequences referred to in the latter part of the rules, it matters not whether the aetiology, of the impairment is organic, as in epilepsy, or functional, or whether the impairment itself is permanent or is transient and intermittent, provided that it subsisted at the time of commission of the act. The purpose of the legislation relating to the defence of insanity, ever since its origin in 1800, has been to protect society against recurrence of the dangerous conduct. The duration of a temporary suspension of the mental faculties of reason, memory and understanding, particularly if, as in Mr. Sullivan's case, it is recurrent, cannot on any rational ground be relevant to the application by the courts of the *M'Naghten* Rules, though it may be relevant to the course adopted by the Secretary of State, to whom the responsibility for how the defendant is to be dealt with passes after the return of the special verdict of "not guilty by reason of insanity."

[...]

My Lords, it is natural to feel reluctant to attach the label of insanity to a sufferer from psychomotor epilepsy of the kind to which Mr. Sullivan was subject, even though the expression in the context of a special verdict of "not guilty by reason of insanity" is a technical one which includes a purely temporary and intermittent suspension of the mental faculties of reason, memory and understanding resulting from the occurrence of an epileptic fit. But the label is contained in the current statute, it has appeared in this statute's predecessors ever since 1800. It does not lie within the power of the courts to alter it. Only Parliament can do that. It has done so twice; it could do so once again. Sympathise though I do with Mr. Sullivan, I see no other course open to your Lordships than to dismiss this appeal.

[10] At the time of the case a finding of not guilty by reason of insanity resulted in compulsory detention in a special hospital.

So the term 'disease of the mind' is not restricted to diseases of the brain. It encompasses any condition which impairs the defendant's faculties of reason, memory or understanding, regardless of whether the impairment is permanent or temporary. As a result, the House of Lords held that the relevant defence in *R* v *Sullivan* was indeed insanity. Sullivan's conviction – and his sentence of three years' probation with a medical supervision order – were therefore upheld.

In practice, then, the legal meaning attached to the term 'disease of the mind' can lead to peculiar outcomes. Epileptics may be regarded as insane. As we saw earlier in the chapter, other examples include: a diabetic who fails to take his proper dose of insulin and consequently suffers hyperglycaemia (*R* v *Hennessy*); and, a person who commits an offence whilst sleepwalking (*R* v *Burgess*). A further example is *R* v *Kemp* [1957] 1 QB 399. The defendant, Albert Kemp, attacked his wife during the night with a hammer. Kemp was a man of good character and he and his wife were a devoted couple. Kemp said that he had no memory of the attack. Medical evidence showed that he was suffering from arteriosclerosis (hardening of the arteries). The medical experts believed that this disease led to a congestion of blood in his brain, which caused a complete or partial loss of consciousness when he attacked his wife. Devlin J ruled that the relevant defence was insanity. He explained that the term 'disease of the mind' is not limited to diseases of the brain. It encompasses any condition which causes a malfunctioning of the mind:

> The law is not concerned with the brain but with the mind, in the sense that "mind" is ordinarily used, the mental faculties of reason, memory and understanding. If one read for "disease of the mind" "disease of the brain," it would follow that in many cases pleas of insanity would not be established because it could not be proved that the brain had been affected in any way, either by degeneration of the cells or in any other way. In my judgment the condition of the brain is irrelevant and so is the question of whether the condition of the mind is curable or incurable, transitory or permanent. There is no warranty for introducing those considerations into the definition in the *McNaghten Rules*. Temporary insanity is sufficient to satisfy them. It does not matter whether it is incurable and permanent or not.

As a result Kemp was found not guilty by reason of insanity.

2. The defendant's disease of the mind caused a defect of reason

The second requirement is that the defendant's disease of the mind caused a defect of reason. To establish a defect of reason, it must be shown that the defendant's powers of reasoning were impaired.

In *R* v *Clarke* [1972] 1 All ER 219 the defendant, May Clarke, went to a supermarket. She placed the items she wished to buy in her shopping basket but, at some point before she reached the checkout, she took three items (butter, coffee and mincemeat) out of her basket and put them into her handbag. She was charged with theft. She explained that she had been experiencing various domestic problems and was also feeling unwell. She said that things had been getting on top of her, which had left her feeling depressed and had been causing her to act absent-mindedly. At trial a psychiatrist testified that depression can cause absent-mindedness. The trial judge ruled that Clarke was raising a defence of insanity. As a result she chose to plead guilty. On appeal the Court of Appeal held that the trial judge's ruling was incorrect. Ackner J explained that Clarke was not claiming that she had suffered a defect of reason, and so was not raising a plea of insanity. She was simply denying that she had formed the *mens rea* of theft. The Court accordingly quashed the conviction.

EXTRACT

According to the following extract from Ackner J's judgment, why was Clarke not claiming that she had suffered a defect of reason?

R v Clarke [1972] 1 All ER 219

Ackner J

The *M'Naghten Rules* relate to accused persons who by reason of a disease of the mind are deprived of the power of reasoning. They do not apply and never have applied to a momentary failure by someone to concentrate. The picture painted by the evidence was wholly consistent with the appellant being a woman who retained her ordinary powers of reason, but who was momentarily absentminded or confused and acted as she did by failing to concentrate properly on what she was doing and by failing adequately to use her mental powers.

3. As a result of the defect of reason, the defendant either: (i) did not know the nature and quality of the act he was doing; or (ii) did not know that what he was doing was wrong

The third requirement for the defence is that the defendant *either*: (i) did not know the nature and quality of the act he was doing; *or* (ii) did not know that what he was doing was wrong. Proof of either of these will suffice.

i. The defendant did not know the nature and quality of the act he was doing

To establish that he did not know the nature and quality of the act he was doing, the defendant must prove that he had no appreciation of the physical aspects of his conduct. Here are three examples:

EXAMPLE

- The defendant who was in a state of automatism. An example would be *R v Sullivan*, where the defendant suffered an epileptic seizure and had no awareness of what was happening.
- The defendant who, as a result of a delusion, believed he was performing an act that was fundamentally different to the reality. For example, he thought he was slaying a dragon when in fact he was killing a human being.
- The defendant who had no understanding of the consequences of his act. The jurist Stephen gave the example of a person who cut off the head of a man who is asleep because he thought 'it would be great fun to see him looking for it when he woke up'.[11]

[11] Stephen, J.F. (1883) *A History of the Criminal Law of England* (vol II), p.166.

Requiring the defendant to prove that he had no appreciation of the physical aspects of his conduct means that the term 'nature and quality of the act' has a limited scope. Suppose that Dale is schizophrenic. As a result of a schizophrenic delusion, he believes he has been ordered to kill Mildred. He carries out these orders. Dale will be unable to prove that he did not know the nature and quality of his act because he was aware that he was killing a human being.

ii. The defendant did not know that what he was doing was wrong

If the defendant did know the nature and quality of his act, he may still have a defence of insanity if he can prove that he did not know that what he was doing was wrong. The question which has arisen here is what wrong means in this context.

This question was considered in *R* v *Keal* [2022] EWCA Crim 341. The defendant, Jonathan Keal, attacked his mother, father and grandmother with a knife, scissors, dumbbells and a cricket bat. He was charged with three counts of attempted murder. Keal had a long history of severe mental illness. When he attacked his family, he had a delusional belief that he was possessed by the devil. During the attacks he repeatedly apologised. His mother said that Keal was shouting 'I'm sorry, this isn't me, it's the devil'. Psychiatric experts agreed that he was in a psychotic state at the time of the offence and that the first two requirements of the *M'Naghten* rules were satisfied. They also agreed that, at the time of the attacks, Keal understood the nature and quality of his acts. Keal's defence of insanity therefore depended on whether he knew that what he was doing was wrong. The jury rejected the defence of insanity and found Keal guilty of attempted murder.

EXTRACT

According to the following extract from Lord Burnett CJ's judgment, what must a defendant prove in order to satisfy this part of the *M'Naghten* rules?

R v *Keal* [2022] EWCA Crim 341

Lord Burnett CJ

41. We endorse this analysis of the authorities. In order to establish the defence of insanity within the M'Naghten Rules on the ground of not knowing the act was "wrong", the defendant must establish both that (a) he did *not* know that his act was unlawful (i.e. contrary to law) and (b) he did *not* know that his act was "morally" wrong (also expressed as wrong "by the standards of ordinary people"). In our judgment, "wrong" means both against the law and wrong by the standards of ordinary reasonable people. Strictly a jury must be satisfied that the defendant did not know that what he was doing was against the law nor wrong by the standards of reasonable ordinary people. In practice how the jury is directed on this issue will depend on the facts and issues in the particular case.

So, to satisfy this part of the *M'Naghten* rules, the defendant must prove that he did not know that his act was unlawful *and* that he did not know that his act was immoral.

The decision in *R* v *Keal* has been criticised. First, Wortley points out that a defendant's ability to plead the insanity defence may be dependent on the content of their delusion.[12]

---

[12] Wortley, N. (2022) 'Commentary on *R* v *Keal*' *Criminal Law Review* 773.

A defendant who uses force in the delusional belief that he is being attacked by the devil could plead insanity because he is not aware that he is attacking a human being.[13] Whereas a defendant like Keal, who believes his actions are being controlled by the devil, cannot plead the defence.[14] Second, Grainger argues that the Court of Appeal's decision in *R* v *Keal*

> meant that Keal became stigmatised not as somebody unwell but as a convicted criminal, with implications for his employment, moral standing and ability to seek civil redress for any mismanagement of his case by mental health providers ... Were there clear policy reasons for this, such as the need to symbolise the defendant's wrongdoing through conviction, that might be a valuable outcome. Yet the trial judge's decision to issue a hospital order in lieu of a prison sentence is tantamount to admitting that criminal justice has no place here, whether in exacting retribution or protecting public safety. Counsel was right to question whether the case can fit with notions of culpability. Keal was seriously ill, not criminally culpable.[15]

Notwithstanding such criticisms, the Court of Appeal in *R* v *Keal* insisted that any reform of the *M'Naghten* rules is a matter for Parliament, not the courts. This was reiterated in the subsequent case *R* v *Usman* [2023] EWCA Crim 313.[16]

4. Insanity and voluntary intoxication

If at the time of the offence the defendant was both voluntarily intoxicated and suffering from a disease of the mind it is likely that the courts will adopt a similar approach to *R* v *Stripp*, that is the question will be whether the predominant cause of the defendant's condition was his voluntary intoxication or his disease of the mind. If it was his voluntary intoxication, the law on intoxication that we studied in the previous chapter will apply.[17] If it was his disease of the mind, the defendant may plead insanity and the M'Naghten rules will apply.[18]

5. Alcohol-induced insanity

Here we are dealing with a slightly different scenario to the previous one. The defendant is not voluntarily intoxicated at the time of the offence but is suffering from a condition which was caused by the consumption of alcohol (e.g. the defendant is a heavy drinker; after deciding to stop drinking he suffers withdrawal symptoms including hallucinations). Here it is open to the defendant to plead insanity.[19] So, in such a case:

[13] See *R* v *Oye* [2013] EWCA Crim 1725 (which we will study in Chapter 11).

[14] One way to have avoided this would have been to say that, in command delusion cases like Keal's, the defendant does not believe that his acts are his own. Therefore, he does not know that he is doing anything wrong.

[15] Grainger, M. (2022) 'Insanity and Command Delusions' 81 *Cambridge Law Journal* 467, 469.

[16] For comment, see Mackay, R. (2023) 'Commentary on *R* v *Usman*' *Criminal Law Review 600*.

[17] For an example, see *R* v *Lipman* [1970] 1 QB 152 (which we studied in Chapter 9).

[18] *R* v *Burns* (1973) 58 Cr App R 364.

[19] *R* v *Davis* (1881) 14 Cox CC 563. The judgment in *R* v *Taj* was not intended to cast doubt on this. At [56] of his judgment in *R* v *Taj*, Sir Brian Leveson P stated that the judgment was not intended to apply to 'long standing mental illness which might at some stage have been triggered by misuse of drugs or alcohol'.

1. You should begin by applying the *M'Naghten* rules. If these are satisfied, then the defence of insanity will apply.
2. If the *M'Naghten Rules* are not satisfied then, according to *R* v *Taj*, you should ask whether the defendant's condition was the immediate and proximate consequence of the consumption of drugs or alcohol. If so, then (as we saw in Chapter 9) the *DPP* v *Majewski* rules will apply.
3. If neither the *M'Naghten Rules* nor the *DPP* v *Majewski* rules apply, then you simply apply the *actus reus* and *mens rea* of the relevant offence in the normal way.

Before moving on, it is worth noting how difficult a jury's task may be in such a case. Following the judgment in *R* v *Taj*, a distinction must be drawn between, on the one hand, the defendant who is suffering from a disease of the mind triggered by voluntary consumption of drink or drugs and, on the other hand, the defendant whose mental state falls short of a disease of the mind but who is nevertheless suffering the effects of immediate and proximate substance misuse (i.e. numbers 1 and 2 on the list above). This task may be made even harder if the jury need to decide based on conflicting expert evidence.

Quiz 10.2

1. Which of the following statements about the defence of insanity is incorrect?
   - **a.** A defendant may only plead insanity if he was suffering from a disease of the mind.
   - **b.** A defendant may only plead insanity if his powers of reasoning were impaired.
   - **c.** If the defendant produces some evidence of insanity, the prosecution is required to prove beyond reasonable doubt that the defendant was in fact sane.
   - **d.** The requirements for the defence of insanity are set out in the *M'Naghten* rules.
2. Which of the following conditions is least likely to give rise to a defence of insanity?
   - **a.** Hyperglycaemia (i.e. too much blood sugar).
   - **b.** Epilepsy.
   - **c.** Concussion.
   - **d.** Sleepwalking.
3. If a defence of insanity succeeds, the defendant is found ...
   - **a.** not guilty by reason of insanity.
   - **b.** guilty by reason of insanity.
   - **c.** not guilty.
   - **d.** certifiably insane.
4. A defendant may have a defence of insanity if he does not know that what he or she is doing is wrong. By wrong the courts mean ...
   - **a.** either legally or morally wrong.
   - **b.** morally wrong.
   - **c.** legally wrong.
   - **d.** both legally and morally wrong.

Diminished responsibility

10.3 Explain the requirements for establishing the defence of diminished responsibility.

In Chapter 5 we studied the law of homicide. We saw that there are three special partial defences to murder. We studied one of these – loss of control – in Chapter 5. We now turn to one of the others: diminished responsibility.[20] Studying diminished responsibility here (instead of in the homicide chapter) allows us to compare and contrast it to the defence of insanity.

---

[20] The third partial defence – suicide pact – is not covered in this text.

There are a number of important differences between insanity and diminished responsibility. Two of these are:

- Insanity is a general defence, whereas diminished responsibility is a special defence. Diminished responsibility is only available as a defence on a charge of murder.
- A defendant who establishes a defence of insanity is found not guilty by reason of insanity. A defendant who establishes a defence of diminished responsibility, by contrast, is not guilty of murder but is guilty of (voluntary) manslaughter.

There is also a difference in the scope of the defences, as we will see shortly.

The defence of diminished responsibility is defined by section 2 of the Homicide Act 1957. This section was amended significantly by the Coroners and Justice Act 2009.[21] As we work through the test for the defence we will examine the changes introduced by the 2009 Act and evaluate their impact.

As amended, section 2 states:

EXTRACT

Section 2 of the Homicide Act 1957

2 Persons suffering from diminished responsibility

(1) A person ("D") who kills or is a party to the killing of another is not to be convicted of murder if D was suffering from an abnormality of mental functioning which –

(a) arose from a recognised medical condition,

(b) substantially impaired D's ability to do one or more of the things mentioned in subsection (1A), and

(c) provides an explanation for D's acts and omissions in doing or being a party to the killing

(1A) Those things are –

(a) to understand the nature of D's conduct;

(b) to form a rational judgment;

(c) to exercise self-control.

(1B) For the purposes of subsection (1)(c), an abnormality of mental functioning provides an explanation for D's conduct if it causes, or is a significant contributory factor in causing, D to carry out that conduct.

(2) On a charge of murder, it shall be for the defence to prove that the person charged is by virtue of this section not liable to be convicted of murder.

(3) A person who but for this section would be liable, whether as principal or as accessory, to be convicted of murder shall be liable instead to be convicted of manslaughter.

(4) The fact that one party to a killing is by virtue of this section not liable to be convicted of murder shall not affect the question whether the killing amounted to murder in the case of any other party to it.

[21] Section 52.

From this section we learn that: the defence of diminished responsibility is available to both the actual killer and accessories (s.2(1); s.2(3)); and the defence of diminished responsibility has a reversed burden of proof. The defendant must prove, on the balance of probabilities, that the defence is established (s.2(2)).[22]

Section 2(1) also tells us that the defence has four requirements:

1. The defendant was suffering from an abnormality of mental functioning
2. The defendant's abnormality of mental functioning arose from a recognised medical condition
3. The defendant's abnormality of mental functioning substantially impaired his ability to do one of the things listed in subsection (1A)
4. The defendant's abnormality of mental functioning provides an explanation for the defendant's participation in the killing.

All four of these requirements must be satisfied for the defence to apply. We will work through them in turn. We will then look at two specific types of difficult case: ones where the defendant wishes to plead diminished responsibility on the grounds of alcoholism; and ones where the defendant was suffering from an abnormality of mental functioning caused by a recognised medical condition but was also voluntarily intoxicated.

1. The defendant was suffering from an abnormality of mental functioning

The first requirement is that the defendant was suffering from an abnormality of mental functioning. In *R* v *Byrne* [1960] 2 QB 396 Lord Parker CJ explained that 'abnormal' means:

> a state of mind so different from that of ordinary human beings that the reasonable man would term it abnormal.

Although *R* v *Byrne* was a case decided under the old law, the guidance offered by Lord Parker CJ can still be used today (though you might wonder how much assistance it actually provides!).

The old law used the term 'abnormality of mind'. The Law Commission reported that psychiatrists had criticised this because 'abnormality of mind' was not a psychiatric term:[23]

> 5.111 [T]he definition has not been drafted with the needs and practices of medical experts in mind, even though their evidence is crucial to the legal viability of any claim of diminished responsibility. 'Abnormality of mind' is not a psychiatric term, so its meaning has had to be developed by the courts from case to case.

[22] The Court of Appeal has rejected the claim that the reverse burden of proof violates the presumption of innocence and Article 6(2) ECHR: *R* v *Lambert*; *R* v *Ali*; *R* v *Jordan* [2002] QB 1112; *R* v *Foye* [2013] EWCA Crim 475. In the latter case the Court explained that: (1) whilst the defence must prove the requirements for diminished responsibility, the prosecution still bears the burden of proving the *actus reus* and *mens rea* of murder; and (2) the defence concerns the inner workings of the defendant's mind, and in many cases it may be practically impossible for the prosecution to disprove beyond reasonable doubt an assertion that the defendant was suffering from diminished responsibility. In particular, the defendant might refuse to submit to, or cooperate with, a medical examination. *R* v *Foye* was followed by the Court of Appeal in *R* v *Wilcocks* [2016] EWCA Crim 2043.

[23] Law Commission (2006) *Murder, Manslaughter and Infanticide* (Report No 304) HC 30.

The Law Commission stated that the term 'abnormality of mental functioning' is 'preferred by psychiatrists' and so recommended that this be used instead.[24]

In order to plead diminished responsibility, the defendant must produce some medical evidence that he was suffering from an abnormality of mental functioning. If he fails to produce at least some relevant medical evidence the trial judge will not leave the defence to the jury. For example, in *R* v *Bunch* [2013] EWCA Crim 2498 the defendant, Martin Bunch, was convicted of murder. At trial he wished to argue diminished responsibility on the grounds of alcoholism, but called no medical evidence as to whether he was an alcoholic. The only evidence on this matter came from an expert prosecution witness, who stated that in her opinion there was no evidence of alcohol dependency. The trial judge accordingly refused to leave the defence of diminished responsibility to the jury. The defendant subsequently appealed. The issue for the Court of Appeal was whether the trial judge had been right to refuse to leave the defence to the jury.

EXTRACT

Read the following extract from the judgment of Holroyde J.

May a defendant plead diminished responsibility if he produces no medical evidence that he was suffering from an abnormality of mental functioning?

If the defendant produces medical evidence that he was suffering from an abnormality of mental functioning, must the jury accept this evidence?

R v *Bunch* [2013] EWCA Crim 2498

Holroyde J

11 The judge held, in our view correctly, that the amendment of section 2 by the 2009 Act did not diminish the authority of cases such as *Byrne* [1960] 2 QB 396 and Dix 74 Cr App R 306, in which it was held that medical evidence, though not in terms required by section 2 of the Act, was "a practical necessity" if the defence was to succeed, because the onus was on the defendant. The judge quoted from a passage at paragraph 19–83 of the current edition of Archbold in which the learned editors say, in our view correctly:

"... it will be for the jury to decide whether the accused was suffering from an abnormality of mental functioning, whether this arose from a medical condition, whether it substantially impaired his ability to do one of the three things mentioned in subsection (1A) and whether it caused, or was a significant contributory factor in causing the defendant to carry out the killing. Medical evidence will, however, be relevant to all these issues, particularly the first three (as to the second, it will be critical). As before ... it is submitted that the jury will not be bound to accept the medical evidence if there is other material before them which, in their good judgment, conflicts with it and outweighs it."

As this extract emphasises, whether or not a defendant was suffering from an abnormality of mental functioning is for the jury to decide. But whilst the jury is not bound to accept the medical evidence, it may only choose to depart from it if there is some material which conflicts with it and outweighs it. This is illustrated by *R* v *Brennan* [2014]

[24] Law Commission (2006) *Murder, Manslaughter and Infanticide* (Report No 304) HC 30, para 5.114

EWCA Crim 2387. In this case the defendant, who had a history of personality and mental health issues, stabbed the victim to death. At trial he raised the defence of diminished responsibility. The expert witness called by the defence gave evidence that, in her opinion, the defendant satisfied all the requirements for diminished responsibility. The expert called by the prosecution did not disagree with this assessment. Yet the jury rejected the defendant's plea of diminished responsibility and convicted him of murder. On appeal, the Court of Appeal quashed the murder conviction and substituted a conviction for manslaughter. Emphasising that juries must base their conclusions on the evidence, Davis LJ stated: 'Where there simply is no rational or proper basis for departing from uncontradicted and unchallenged expert evidence then juries may not do so.'

> But whilst the jury is not bound to accept the medical evidence, it may only choose to depart from it if there is some material which conflicts with it and outweighs it.

It is also important to point out that juries will often be faced with conflicting expert evidence. In *R* v *Brown* [2011] EWCA Crim 2796, for example, the defence's expert witness stated that the defendant was suffering from an adjustment disorder which caused an abnormality of mental functioning, whilst the prosecution's expert witness rejected the diagnosis of an adjustment disorder and stated that there was no abnormality of mental functioning. As Nicola Wake remarks:[25]

> The jury are therefore left with the unenviable task of deciding between the competing views of reputable medical experts.

One of the principal objectives of the changes to diminished responsibility was to improve the clarity of the law.[26] In the following extract Louise Kennefick discusses whether the new law achieves this objective, in the light of the roles of expert evidence and jury decision-making:

EXTRACT

In Kennefick's opinion, does the new law achieve its objective of greater clarity? Why/why not?

Kennefick, L. (2011) 'Introducing a New Diminished Responsibility Defence for England and Wales' 74 *Modern Law Review* 750

There is another line of argument which suggests that, as ideal as a trial by jury may seem, in more difficult cases, particularly involving expert evidence, the jury is simply unable to deal with the questions put before it. So rather than usurping the role of the jury, the expert is assisting the jury in coming to a decision; bringing its own complications. It is impossible to get inside the mind of the individual at the time of the offence, even for psychiatrists, therefore juries are being asked to base their decision on opinion, which usually involves choosing between two differing views.

---

[25] Wake, N. (2012) 'Psychiatry and the New Diminished Responsibility Plea: Uneasy Bedfellows?' 76 *Journal of Criminal Law* 122.

[26] The Law Commission, for example, stated: 'The definition of "diminished responsibility" should be modernised, so that it is both clearer and better able to accommodate developments in expert diagnostic practice' (Law Commission (2006) *Murder, Manslaughter and Infanticide* (Report No 304) HC 30, para 5.107).

In *R v Cannings*, Judge LJ goes so far as to warn that '... if the outcome of the trial depends exclusively or almost exclusively on a serious disagreement between distinguished and reputable experts, it will often be unwise, and therefore unsafe, to proceed.' This is largely due to the fact that as psychiatrists give opinion evidence, it is likely that one expert's opinion of the facts will differ from the other. However, place this argument in the hands of the jury, and further difficulties arise. Juries will be quite unfamiliar with the technical language used by forensic psychiatrists, and as Blom-Cooper and Morris point out, this can be bewildering, not least when it is presented for many hours, and over many days.

It appears, therefore, that the question as to who decides what in terms of the mental condition and criminal responsibility of the accused remains unclear, despite the goal of clarification underpinning the new law. What is clear, however, is that the system in place, which sees psychiatrists testifying in relation to responsibility, and juries attempting to decipher complicated psychiatric terminology, results in ambiguity, inconsistency and thus arguably unfair treatment of the mentally disordered offender.

2. The defendant's abnormality of mental functioning arose from a recognised medical condition

The second requirement for a defence of diminished responsibility is that the defendant's abnormality of mental functioning arose from a 'recognised medical condition'. This is another important change from the previous law. The old law stated:

> Where a person kills or is a party to the killing of another, he shall not be convicted of murder if he was suffering from such abnormality of mind (whether arising from a condition of arrested or retarded development of mind or any inherent causes or induced by disease or injury) as substantially impaired his mental responsibility for his acts and omissions in doing or being a party to the killing.

In other words, under the old law the defendant's abnormality of mind must have arisen 'from a condition of arrested or retarded development of mind or any inherent causes or induced by disease or injury'. This requirement was criticised for being both outdated and lacking any grounding in a medical diagnosis. In its 2006 report on the old law the Law Commission stated:[27]

> 5.111 [...] [D]iagnostic practice in diminished responsibility cases has long since developed beyond identification of the narrow range of permissible 'causes' of an abnormality of mind stipulated in the bracketed part of the definition. In any event, the stipulated permissible causes have never had an agreed psychiatric meaning. The outmoded stipulation of permissible causes has become as much a hindrance as a help. As Dr Madelyn Hicks put it to us:
>
> > [A]ttempting to specify the cause of mental disorders ... is irrelevant [and] misleading, and in fact there are almost always multiple causes stemming from the interaction between genetic vulnerability and life events.

For this reason, the new law uses the term 'recognised medical condition' instead of stipulating a list of permissible causes. The requirement of a recognised medical condition ensures that any successful plea of diminished responsibility is grounded in a

[27] Law Commission (2006) *Murder, Manslaughter and Infanticide* (Report No 304) HC 30.

medical diagnosis. It also enables the law to keep pace with changes in medicine and accommodate developments in diagnostic practice.

It is important to note, however, that the requirement of a recognised medical condition is potentially very broad. For a start, it is not limited to psychiatric illnesses. It could also encompass physical and psychological conditions. So, for example, diabetics and epileptics have recognised medical conditions. Other examples of medical conditions listed in the World Health Organization (WHO)'s International Statistical Classification of Diseases include: unhappiness; irritability and anger; suspiciousness and marked evasiveness; pyromania; paedophilia; sado-masochism; and kleptomania.[28]

The WHO's International Statistical Classification of Diseases also lists acute intoxication. Based on this, the defendant in *R* v *Dowds* [2012] EWCA Crim 281 argued that voluntary acute intoxication is a recognised medical condition which may form the basis of a successful plea of diminished responsibility. The defendant in this case, Stephen Dowds, was not an alcoholic and did not have an alcohol dependency. He was a binge drinker, who drank heavily but only drank when he chose to do so. One weekend, he stabbed his partner to death whilst heavily intoxicated. The trial judge ruled that the defence of diminished responsibility was unavailable to him, since he was voluntarily intoxicated. He was therefore convicted of murder. On appeal, he argued that the trial judge's ruling was incorrect. Pointing to the fact that acute intoxication appears in the WHO's list of medical conditions, Dowds' counsel argued that defendants should be allowed to plead diminished responsibility on the basis of voluntary acute intoxication. The Court of Appeal rejected this argument. Hughes LJ stated:

> 40 [...] It is enough to say that it is quite clear that the reformulation of the statutory conditions for diminished responsibility was not intended to reverse the well established rule that voluntary acute intoxication is not capable of being relied upon to found diminished responsibility. That remains the law. The presence of a "recognised medical condition" is a necessary, but not always a sufficient, condition to raise the issue of diminished responsibility.

So, for example, if a defendant suffered a psychotic episode as a result of the voluntary consumption of alcohol and drugs, diminished responsibility would not be available as a defence. The abnormality of mental functioning (the psychotic episode) arose from voluntary intoxication, not a from a recognised medical condition.[29] This reaffirms the stance taken under the old law that voluntary intoxication may not form the basis of a successful plea of diminished responsibility.[30]

It follows from Hughes LJ's statement in R v Dowds that a recognised medical condition 'is a necessary, but not always a sufficient' condition that 'whether any medical condition is "recognised" as falling within section 2 is a question of law rather than one of medicine'.[31] This raises the question whether there are other conditions that the courts may rule cannot provide a basis for a defence of diminished responsibility. Nicola Wake has accordingly commented:[32]

---

[28] See *R* v *Dowds* [2012] EWCA Crim 281, [31].

[29] *R* v *Foy* [2020] EWCA Crim 270.

[30] See, for example, *R* v *Fenton* (1975) 61 Cr App R 261.

[31] Mackay, R. (2021) 'What's happening with the reformed diminished responsibility plea?' 72 *Northern Ireland Legal Quarterly* 224, 229.

[32] Wake, N. (2012) 'Diminished Responsibility and Acute Intoxication: Raising the Bar?' 76 *Journal of Criminal Law* 197.

[T]he rationale for including the "recognised medical condition" requirement was "to ensure a greater equilibrium between the law and medical science" (*R* v *Brown (Robert)* [2011] EWCA Crim 2796 at [23]; Law Commission, *Murder, Manslaughter and Infanticide*, Law Com. Report No. 304 (2006) para. 5.114). The idea that the courts will be required to determine which recognised medical conditions are valid for the purposes of the partial defence is inimical to this aim.

Now, think about these questions.

Look back at the examples of medical conditions listed in the WHO's International Statistical Classification of Diseases.

- Do you think the courts might rule that any of these cannot form the basis of a plea of diminished responsibility?
- Which ones?
- Why?

Whilst the term 'recognised medical condition' is potentially very broad, it is also important to note that it could exclude some defendants who might have been able to plead diminished responsibility under the old law. As Louise Kennefick explains in the following extract, one possible example is the mercy killer who – whilst not suffering from a recognised medical condition – kills his terminally ill partner under great stress.

EXTRACT

In the following extract Kennefick refers to the 'benign conspiracy' that sometimes occurred under the old law. What was the benign conspiracy? Will it still be possible under the new law?

In your opinion, should the law be flexible enough to allow for benign conspiracies?

Kennefick, L. (2011) 'Introducing a New Diminished Responsibility Defence for England and Wales' 74 *Modern Law Review* 750

Thus, in practice, it is likely that psychiatric classificatory systems will play a more central role in establishing the existence of a recognised medical condition resulting in an abnormality of mental functioning. Of course, most diagnoses by experts under the original definition would have had some recognised medical basis. The new wording, however, makes this requirement essential, so in that respect, it clarifies the law. But this change in definition may have more far-reaching consequences than initially anticipated. Accepting that it has not yet been interpreted by the courts, the term 'recognised medical condition', as it stands, has the effect of narrowing the defence of diminished responsibility by excluding those disorders which may no longer or may not yet be accepted internationally as 'medical conditions'.

The original definition had progressed to the point where it was interpreted by the courts to show leniency to a 'highly stressed killer', in the sense that a defendant could receive a manslaughter verdict if the particular form of stress in question was pathologised as diminished responsibility. This trend is also reflected in prominent domestic violence cases of the early 1990s featuring the controversial 'Battered Woman's Syndrome'. Such forms of interpretation have been described as a 'benign conspiracy' which stretched the notion of 'abnormality of mind', to enable a verdict to meet the perceived justice of the case. The restriction of the law to internationally medically recognised and documented conditions brings the possibility of a defendant (for example a 'mercy-killer') being convicted of murder and given a mandatory life sentence, despite his or her responsibility for the killing being far removed from 'the gangland executioner and the serial killer who likes to torture his victims first'.

So although the introduction of 'recognised medical condition' may promote the principle of clarity, conversely, it draws into question the fairness of the situation for the offender pleading diminished responsibility. Should both the court and the expert utilise a strict interpretation of the phrase, the likelihood of a 'mercy killer' being brandished a 'murderer' and sentenced to life imprisonment increases. Thus, the new law of diminished responsibility has a potentially damaging impact on a particular group of offenders who could have availed of the partial defence under the original definition.

Time will tell how the system responds to this particular circumstance in practice. It may well be the case that the courts will likewise stretch their interpretation of the term 'recognised medical condition', or the experts their diagnoses, in order to enable the 'benign conspiracy' to continue, albeit in a slightly different guise. Should this be the case, whether or not the clarity of the law relating to diminished responsibility has been improved [...] would be brought into question.

Gibson argues that the benign conspiracy will continue under the new version of the diminished responsibility defence.[33] A combination of expert generosity and jury benevolence will, he suggests, allow mercy killers to link a stressful or emotional state with a recognised medical condition, such as reactive depression. However, the continuation of the benevolent conspiracy presents a fundamental challenge to the integrity of the reformed defence:

> Any manipulation of these requirements therefore risks diluting, if not *subverting*, the medical emphasis of the revamped defence. This is ironic given that greater medical precision was a distinct goal of diminished responsibility reform. A further irony materialises when it is recalled that such accuracy was intended to aid medical experts in presenting their evidence. The continuation of the benevolent conspiracy requires them to expand the borders of the defence *more* artificially than under the former plea. If one aim of the 2009 Act was to bring the legal and medical professions closer together, then this is a perverse prospect. Such an aim will be frustrated.

A study by Mackay and Mitchell examined a total of 90 cases decided under the new version of the diminished responsibility defence. They contrasted their findings with those of an older study, which examined a total of 157 cases decided under the old version of the defence. The following extract outlines their principal findings and offers some indication of the practical impact that the changes to the defence have had.

[33] Gibson, M. (2017) 'Pragmatism Preserved? The Challenges of Accommodating Mercy Killers in the Reformed Diminished Responsibility Plea' 81 *Journal of Criminal Law* 177.

EXTRACT

Read the following extract, which contrasts data from cases decided under the new version of the defence (the 'CPS cases') with data from cases decided under the old version (the 'Law Commission cases').

According to the study, have the changes to the defence led to an increase or a decrease in the proportion of cases with a contested plea? And, have the changes resulted in an increase or decrease in the proportion of cases resulting in a murder conviction?

Mackay, R. and Mitchell, B. (2017) 'The New Diminished Responsibility Plea in Operation: Some Initial Findings' *Criminal Law Review* 18

The "official" view has been that the old s.2 was in need of clarification and modernisation and that the reformulation contained in the revised section was designed to achieve that and nothing more. However, this study could be regarded as casting some doubt on this "official" view of the new s.2, the operation of which may be giving rise to unintended consequences. In particular, what is of note is that 43.3% of the CPS cases under the new plea were contested compared to 22.9% under the old plea. In addition, in 65.6% (n559) the finding was one of diminished responsibility, of which 13.5% (n58) were contested. In the Law Commission study in 80.3% of the cases (n5126) the finding was one of diminished responsibility, of which 6.3% (n58) were contested. In short, the new plea seems to have resulted in more contested pleas with convictions for murder being returned in 34.4% of these cases compared to a murder conviction rate of 14% under the old plea. While an increase in the number of convictions for murder was one of the clear reasons for abolishing provocation and introducing a new "loss of control" plea this was not true for diminished responsibility in that no such increase in murder convictions was ever suggested as a reason for reformulating s.2.

3. The defendant's abnormality of mental functioning substantially impaired his ability to do one of the things listed in subsection (1A)

The old law required that the defendant's 'mental responsibility' must have been 'substantially impaired'. But it provided no further guidance on what this meant. This was criticised by the Law Commission:[34]

> 5.110 [T]he definition says nothing about what is involved in a "substantial impairment [of] mental responsibility". The implication is that the effects of an abnormality of mind must significantly reduce the offender's culpability. The Act neither makes this clear, nor says in what way the effects of an abnormality of mind can reduce culpability for an intentional killing, such that a manslaughter verdict is the right result.

The new law seeks to remedy this ambiguity by stating that the defendant's abnormality of mental functioning must have substantially impaired his ability to do one of three things. These three things are listed in subsection (1A) of section 2. We will work through them in turn.

---

[34] Law Commission (2006) *Murder, Manslaughter and Infanticide* (Report No 304) HC 30.

i. The defendant's ability to understand the nature of his conduct

The first possibility is that the defendant's abnormality of mental functioning substantially impaired his ability to understand the nature of his conduct. This is similar to one of the limbs of the *M'Naghten* rules, which, as we saw earlier in the chapter, applies when the defendant did not know the nature and quality of his actions. But there is an important difference. The *M'Naghten* rules apply where the defendant lacked any understanding of the nature and quality of his actions. By contrast, for diminished responsibility the defendant must show that his ability to understand the nature of his conduct was *substantially* impaired. So a defendant who had only a partial understanding of the nature of his conduct will not be able to plead insanity, but may be able to plead diminished responsibility.

Of the three types of impairment listed in subsection (1A), research suggests that in practice this one is the least used and is not easily satisfied.[35] The Law Commission offered the following example of when it might apply:[36]

> [A] boy aged 10 who has been left to play very violent video games for hours on end for much of his life, loses his temper and kills another child when the child attempts to take a game from him. When interviewed, he shows no real understanding that, when a person is killed they cannot simply be later revived, as happens in the games he has been continually playing.

ii. The defendant's ability to form a rational judgement

The second possibility is that the defendant's abnormality of mental functioning substantially impaired his ability to form a rational judgement. One of the examples given by the Law Commission to illustrate when this would apply was:[37]

> [A] woman suffering from post traumatic stress disorder, consequent upon violent abuse suffered at her husband's hands, comes to believe that only burning her husband to death will rid the world of his sins.

The Court of Appeal considered the meaning of the term 'ability to form a rational judgment' in *R* v *Conroy* [2017] EWCA Crim 81. Jason Conroy had autism spectrum disorder, learning difficulties, and attention deficit hyperactivity disorder. He lived in a special residential home. He developed an obsessive interest in one of the other residents, Melissa Mathieson. One evening he waited until Melissa was asleep and went to her room. His plan was to strangle her, take her to his room and then have sex with her. When he tried to take Melissa to his room he dropped her. A member of staff heard the bang, went to investigate, and found Melissa's unconscious body. She died four days later. Conroy was charged with murder and sought to rely on diminished responsibility. Four medical experts gave evidence at his trial. They all agreed that Conroy suffered from an abnormality of mental functioning which arose from a recognised medical condition (autism). The key issue, on which the experts disagreed, was whether this abnormality substantially impaired his ability to form a rational judgement. In his direction to the jury the trial judge drew a distinction between a defendant's thought processes and

[35] Mackay, R. (2018) 'The Impairment Factors in the New Diminished Responsibility Plea' *Criminal Law Review* 462.

[36] Law Commission (2006) *Murder, Manslaughter and Infanticide* (Report No 304) HC 30, Para. 5.121. Whether it would apply when a defendant lacks understanding of the wrongfulness of his conduct is unclear. For an argument that it should apply in such cases, see Mackay, R. (2018) 'The Impairment Factors in the New Diminished Responsibility Plea' *Criminal Law Review* 462.

[37] Law Commission (2006) *Murder, Manslaughter and Infanticide* (Report No 304) HC 30, para 5.121.

the outcome of those processes. He told the jury that they should concentrate on the thought processes, not the outcome, and consider whether the thought processes were irrational. The jury subsequently rejected the diminished responsibility defence and convicted Conroy of murder. He appealed, arguing that the trial judge misdirected the jury.

EXTRACT

Read the following extract from the judgment of Davis LJ.

Should the jury in a case like this consider the defendant's thought processes, the outcome of those processes, or both? What reasons does Davis LJ give for this decision?

R v *Conroy* [2017] EWCA Crim 81

Davis LJ

30 In truth, as it seems to us, one cannot always neatly separate the "decision-making process" [...] from the actual ultimate decision: although of course it can be accepted that a jury may need, as part of its overall consideration, to consider how it was that in the particular defendant's mind the decision was arrived at. There may be cases where an entirely "irrational" decision may be taken: for example, to kill one's neighbour because of a fixed belief that he is an alien from Mars intent on blowing up innocent people in the village. But that decision and the motivation for it may then be accompanied, in terms of giving effect to the decision, by ostensibly logical and rational decisions with a view to carrying out the intended killing: for example by buying a knife, by waiting for the neighbour to be at home alone and so on.

[...]

35 [W]e revert to the judge's summing-up in this particular case. By his instruction to the jury he had in effect told them that the "outcome" need not be part of their deliberations. It has to be said that there is imprecision here in the judge's use of the word "outcome". On one view the outcome is simply the death of M. Another way perhaps of putting it is that the outcome is the act of killing M: which is not to be equated simply with her death. But the judge in fact added a yet further element, to the effect that the outcome was the killing of M "so that he could have sex with her": which is hardly just an outcome but also an additional statement of what the appellant's motivation and intention was. But be that as it may, the judge having so stated, he then went on to say that "on any view" this was an irrational "outcome": and the jury were therefore to focus on the appellant's thought processes that had led to that outcome.

36 It is that aspect which Mr Smith challenges on behalf of the appellant. He says that the judge had wrongly separated out the decision-making process from the outcome whereas the jury should have been invited to look at the position as a whole [...]

37 [...] As it seems to us, while of course any jury will need in the light of the available psychiatric evidence to assess a defendant's thinking processes in the context of assessing his ability to form a rational judgment, it is likely to be over-refined to divorce that consideration relating to a defendant's thinking processes from the actual outcome. Indeed, in some cases it may actually be extremely difficult to separate out the thought processes on the one hand from the "outcome" on the other hand. In some cases it may well be that the two may be entirely enmeshed. In our view, there is a potential danger in a direction such as this straying beyond what is actually stated in section 2 itself. The elements of section 2 should so far as possible not be glossed in a summing-up to the jury.

So any attempt to distinguish between thought processes and outcome is mistaken. The jury should consider the position as a whole when deciding whether the defendant's ability to form a rational judgement was substantially impaired. Note also that Davis LJ stressed that when directing juries trial judges should, so far as possible, stick to the statutory wording and avoid undue elaboration. As far as Conroy was concerned, however, the Court of Appeal concluded that the trial judge's misdirection did not impact the safety of the murder conviction, and so dismissed Conroy's appeal.

An example of a case in which the defendant's ability to form a rational judgement was found to have been substantially impaired is *R* v *Blackman* [2017] EWCA Crim 190. The defendant, Alexander Blackman, was an Acting Colour Sergeant in the Royal Marines. He was in command of a group of Marines in Helmand Province, Afghanistan. In September 2011, insurgents attacked a neighbouring command post. A helicopter was called in. It located one of the insurgents in a field and opened fire. Thinking the insurgent had been killed, a foot patrol led by Blackman embarked on a battle damage assessment. They found the insurgent badly wounded, but still alive. Blackman disarmed him, waited for the helicopter to move away, and then shot the insurgent at point blank range, saying, 'There you are, shuffle off this mortal coil, you cunt'. He then said to the other Marines, 'Obviously this doesn't go anywhere, fellas. I've just broke the Geneva Convention'. In 2013 Blackman was convicted of murder. In the light of fresh psychiatric evidence, the case was subsequently referred to the Court Martial Appeal Court. This evidence showed that Blackman had been suffering from an adjustment disorder. This had been caused by a number of factors, including the death of his father, the loss of other members of his unit, and his perception that he was receiving insufficient support from senior officers. The Court Martial Appeal Court held that the adjustment disorder had substantially impaired Blackman's ability to form a rational judgement. Although some of his actions were calculated, such as waiting for the helicopter to move away before shooting the insurgent, the Court stated:

> that type of planning is quite distinct from the effect of an adjustment disorder which can affect the ability to form a rational judgement about (1) the need to adhere to standards and the moral compass set by HM Armed Forces and (2) putting together the consequences to himself and others of the individual actions he is about to take. In our view, the adjustment disorder had put the appellant in the state of mind to kill, but the fact that he acted with apparent careful thought as to how to set about the killing had to be seen within the overarching framework of the disorder which had substantially impaired his ability to form a rational judgement ([111]).

iii. The defendant's ability to exercise self-control

Here we see another difference between insanity and diminished responsibility. A defendant who is unable to exercise self-control falls outside the *M'Naghten* rules and so cannot plead insanity. But an inability to exercise self-control may form the basis of a defence of diminished responsibility. This is illustrated by *R* v *Byrne* [1960] 2 QB 396. The defendant, Patrick Byrne, strangled a young woman and mutilated her dead body. The unanimous medical evidence was that Byrne was a sexual psychopath who suffered from violent perverted sexual desires which he found difficult or impossible to control. It was agreed that Byrne fell outside the scope of the *M'Naghten* rules, since he knew the nature and quality of his actions and he knew that they were wrong. But at his trial the judge ruled that he could not plead diminished responsibility either. Byrne was therefore convicted of murder. He appealed. The Court of Appeal held that the trial judge's ruling was wrong. Lord Parker CJ explained that diminished responsibility is broader than insanity, and is available to defendants whose ability to exercise self-control is substantially impaired. Byrne's murder conviction was therefore quashed and replaced with a manslaughter conviction (though he was still sentenced to life imprisonment).

The new law confirms the decision in *R* v *Byrne*. It expressly states that diminished responsibility is available to a defendant whose abnormality of mental functioning substantially impaired his ability to exercise self-control. The Law Commission offered the following example of when this would apply:[38]

> [A] man says that sometimes the devil takes control of him and implants in him a desire to kill, a desire that must be acted on before the devil will go away.

A further example is *R* v *Blackman,* which we looked at a moment ago. The Court Martial Appeal Court held that Blackman's adjustment disorder had also substantially impaired his ability to exercise self-control. The Court pointed out that, on previous deployments, Blackman had managed to control his anger and hatred for the insurgents, and his decision to kill on this occasion 'was probably impulsive' ([112]). Commenting on this decision, Gibson suggests that it '[dilutes] the ability to exercise self-control limb to vanishing point [by] ruling that self-control may be sufficiently impaired even where no loss of self-control is externally discernible'.[39]

iv. The meaning of 'substantially impaired'

So to establish diminished responsibility a defendant must show that his ability to do one of the three things listed in subsection (1A) was substantially impaired. We have looked at each of these three abilities. But what does the term 'substantially impaired' mean? This was discussed by the Supreme Court in *R* v *Golds* [2016] UKSC 61. In this case the Court considered two possible meanings of the word 'substantial'.

EXTRACT

Read the following extract from the judgment of Lord Hughes.

What does he say are the two possible meanings of 'substantial'? Which meaning applies to the diminished responsibility defence? What reasons does he give for saying that this is the correct meaning?

According to Lord Hughes, why was it necessary for the Supreme Court to explain the meaning of the word 'substantially'? Should trial judges always give this explanation to juries?

R v *Golds* [2016] UKSC 61

Lord Hughes

27 The admirably concise submissions of Mr Etherington QC for the appellant correctly point out that as a matter simply of dictionary definition, "substantial" is capable of meaning either (1) "present rather than illusory or fanciful, thus having some substance" or (2) "important or

---

[38] Law Commission (2006) *Murder, Manslaughter and Infanticide* (Report No 304) HC 30, para 5.121.

[39] Gibson, M. (2017) 'Diminished Responsibility in *Golds* and Beyond: Insights and Implications' *Criminal Law Review* 543.

weighty", as in "a substantial meal" or "a substantial salary". The first meaning could fairly be paraphrased as "having any effect more than the merely trivial", whereas the second meaning cannot. It is also clear that either sense may be used in law making. In the context of disability discrimination, the Equality Act 2010 defines disability in section 6 as an impairment which has a substantial and long-term effect on day to day activities, and by the interpretation section, section 212, provides that "'Substantial' means more than minor or trivial." It thus uses the word in the first sense. Conversely, the expression "significant and substantial" when used to identify which breaches by the police of the Codes of Practice under the Police and Criminal Evidence Act 1984 will lead to the exclusion of evidence (see for example *R* v *Absolam* (1988) 88 Cr App R 332 and *R* v *Keenan* [1990] 2 QB 54) is undoubtedly used in the second sense. It is to be accepted that the word may take its meaning from its context. It is not surprising that in the context of triggering a duty to make reasonable adjustments to assist the disabled, the first sense should be used by the Equality Act; the extent of adjustments required varies with the level of disability and a wide spectrum of both is to be expected. Mr Etherington additionally submits that this usage shows that the first sense does not entirely strip the word "substantially" of meaning.

[...]

36 [The use of the expression in the second of the senses identified above] accords with principle. Diminished responsibility effects a radical alteration in the offence of which a defendant is convicted. The context is a homicide. By definition, before any question of diminished responsibility can arise, the homicide must have been done with murderous intent, to kill or to do grievous bodily harm, and without either provocation or self-defence. Whilst it is true that at one end of the scale of responsibility the sentence in a case of diminished responsibility may be severe, or indeed an indefinite life sentence owing to the risk which the defendant presents to the public, the difference between a conviction for murder and a conviction for manslaughter is of considerable importance both for the public and for those connected with the deceased. It is just that where a substantial impairment is demonstrated, the defendant is convicted of the lesser offence and not of murder. But it is appropriate, as it always has been, for the reduction to the lesser offence to be occasioned where there is a weighty reason for it and not merely a reason which just passes the trivial.

Directing juries: good practice

37 As Mr Perry QC for the Crown rightly submitted, there are many examples of ordinary English words incorporating questions of degree, which are left to juries to apply without attempts at further definition. No-one attempts to define "reasonable" in the many contexts in which it appears. Nor should there be any further sophistication applied to the standard of proof required, that the jury be "sure", at least beyond the comparable expression "leaving no reasonable doubt". The same principle of leaving an ordinary word alone was applied by the House of Lords in *Brutus* v *Cozens* [1973] AC 854 to the expression "insulting", and would apply equally, no doubt, to its sister expressions "abusive" and "threatening". In all these cases the understandable itch of the lawyer to re-define needs to be resisted. Any attempt to find synonyms for such ordinary English expressions, although they involve questions of degree, simply complicates the jury's exercise, and leads to further semantic debate about the boundaries of meaning of the synonym.

38 Where, however, as here, there are two identifiable and different senses in which the expression in question may be used, the potential for inconsistent usage may need to be reduced. The existence of the two senses of the word "substantially" identified above means that the law should, in relation to diminished responsibility, be clear which sense is being employed. If it is not, there is, first, a risk of trials being distracted into semantic arguments between the two. Secondly, there is a risk that different juries may apply different senses. Thirdly, medical evidence (nearly always forensic psychiatric evidence) has always been a practical necessity

where the issue is diminished responsibility. If anything, the 2009 changes to the law have emphasised this necessity by tying the partial defence more clearly to a recognised medical condition, although in practice this was always required. Although it is for the jury, and not for the doctors, to determine whether the partial defence is made out, and this important difference of function is well recognised by responsible forensic psychiatrists, it is inevitable that they may express an opinion as to whether the impairment was or was not substantial, and if they do not do so in their reports, as commonly many do, they may be asked about it in oral evidence. It is therefore important that if they use the expression, they do so in the sense in which it is used by the courts. If there is doubt about the sense in which they have used it, their reports may be misunderstood and decisions made upon them falsified, and much time at trials is likely to be taken up unnecessarily by cross examination on the semantic question

[...]

40 It does not follow that it is either necessary or wise to attempt a re-definition of "substantially" for the jury. First, in many cases the debate here addressed will simply not arise. There will be many cases where the suggested condition is such that, *if* the defendant was affected by it at the time, the impairment could only be substantial, and the issue is whether he was or was not so affected. Second, if the occasion for elucidation does arise, the judge's first task is to convey to the jury, by whatever form of words suits the case before it, that the statute uses an ordinary English word and that they must avoid substituting a different one for it. Third, however, various phrases have been used in the cases to convey the sense in which "substantially" is understood in this context. The words used by the Court of Appeal in the second certified question in the present case ("significant and appreciable") are one way of putting it, providing that the word "appreciable" is treated not as being synonymous with merely recognisable but rather with the connotation of being considerable. Other phrases used have been "a serious degree of impairment" (*Seers*), "not total impairment but substantial" (*Ramchurn*) or "something far wrong" (*Galbraith*). These are acceptable ways of elucidating the sense of the statutory requirement but it is neither necessary nor appropriate for this court to mandate a particular form of words in substitution for the language used by Parliament. The jury must understand that "substantially" involves a matter of degree, and that it is for it to use the collective good sense of its members to say whether the condition in the case it is trying reaches that level or not.

So, for the purposes of diminished responsibility, 'substantial' means important or weighty,[40] and whether the impairment of the defendant's ability to do one of the things listed in subsection (1A) was substantial or not is a question for the jury (though, as noted above in *R* v *Brennan,* if there is uncontradicted and unchallenged expert evidence juries may not depart from this unless there is a rational basis for doing so). The Supreme Court in *R* v *Golds* also stated that in some cases the trial judge should explain the meaning of 'substantially' to the jury – such as where an expert witness or counsel may have caused confusion by mentioning the expression 'more than merely trivial' – but added that it is not always 'either necessary or wise' to define the word for the jury. In the following extract, Karl Laird criticises this position.

[40] In *R* v *Squelch* [2017] EWCA Crim 204 the Court of Appeal approved the trial judge's direction to the jury that substantially is 'an ordinary English word' which 'means less than total and more than trivial' ([37]). As Mackay notes, this appears to be 'a dilution of the strict approach in *Golds*', notwithstanding Davis LJ's statement that the direction 'amply complies' ([38]) with the judgment of Lord Hughes (Mackay, R. (2018) 'The Impairment Factors in the New Diminished Responsibility Plea' *Criminal Law Review* 462).

EXTRACT

Read the following extract from Laird's commentary.

According to Laird, how did the Supreme Court's judgment undermine its stated aim of ensuring the term 'substantially' is applied consistently?

Laird, K. (2017) 'Case Comment, Homicide: *R* v *Golds* (Mark Richard)' *Criminal Law Review* 316

The Supreme Court expressed concern about the possibility that different juries may attribute different meanings to "substantially". The court took the view that it was imperative to reduce the potential for inconsistent usage of this term. The court's judgment does little to bring consistency, however. The court concluded that ordinarily, judges should not define the meaning of "substantially" for the jury. The possibility of inconsistent interpretations of the term therefore remains, which not only undermines the court's aim, but also has the potential to be deeply unfair. If, to adopt the expression used by the Supreme Court, the trial judge feels that a risk has arisen that the jury has misunderstood the import of the expression "substantial", he will have to direct the jury that a more than merely trivial impairment is insufficient to make out the defence. If, however, no such risk has arisen, the jury may assume that a more than merely trivial impairment suffices. All things being equal, it will be easier for the defendant in the latter scenario to plead the defence than the defendant in the former. To achieve consistency in application and parity between defendants, the Supreme Court should have held that a direction must be given in every case. The court's failure to do so is especially surprising, given that it held that the inclusion of the term "substantially" fulfils an important function by ensuring that defendants are not found guilty of manslaughter rather than murder in the absence of sufficiently weighty reasons.

As we saw above, the old law simply said that the defendant's 'mental responsibility' must have been 'substantially impaired'. This was criticised for being imprecise and vague. The new law was designed to provide greater clarity. But some have expressed doubts. As we saw above, the requirement that the defendant's abnormality of mental functioning arose from a recognized medical condition was intended to ground the defence in a medical diagnosis. But the term 'substantially' is not a medical or psychiatric concept, nor are the three abilities specified in subsection (1A). Rather, they are evaluative, medico-legal concepts whose meaning needs further interpretation.[41]

Concern has also been expressed about the specificity of the new law, as the following extract illustrates.

EXTRACT

Read the following extract from Mackay's article 'The Coroners and Justice Act 2009 – Partial Defences to Murder: (2) The New Diminished Responsibility Plea'.

What concerns does he express about the changes introduced by the new law?

[41] Mackay, R. (2018) 'The Impairment Factors in the New Diminished Responsibility Plea' *Criminal Law Review* 462.

Mackay, R.D. (2010) 'The Coroners and Justice Act 2009 - Partial Defences to Murder: (2) The New Diminished Responsibility Plea' *Criminal Law Review* 290

However, the new plea's approach of spelling out what abilities need to be impaired inevitably means that "abnormality of mental functioning" is now narrower than "abnormality of mind" in that the only activities of the mind which are included are the three specified things in subs.(1A) of the 1957 Act as amended. In addition, there is a legitimate concern that these three specified things will, taken together, prove to be more limited in scope than those which fell within the original plea. This was certainly the view of Baroness Murphy who, during debate on the Bill in the House of Lords, put forward an amendment to allow for,

> "distortion of thinking or perception as a basis for a successful plea of diminished responsibility where the defendant was able to exercise self-control".

This would have more readily accommodated those whose mental disorder substantially impairs his or her perception of reality. It might also have included those with personality disorders, a condition which is now unlikely to fall within the new plea unless the defendant's ability to exercise self-control can be proved to have been substantially impaired. In any event, this amendment was roundly rejected by the Attorney General who said:

> "In the unlikely event of cases arising where a defendant's perception of reality is substantially impaired but his ability to understand the nature of his conduct, form a rational judgment and exercise self-control are not, we do not consider that he should benefit from the partial defence as these issues go right to the heart of the case for reduced responsibility in homicide cases where there is an abnormality of mental function."

However, what this remark fails to acknowledge is that under the original s.2 of the 1957 Act there was nothing in principle to prevent a substantial impairment of perception of reality from falling within its scope owing to the flexibility/obscurity of the plea's drafting.

4. The defendant's abnormality of mental functioning provides an explanation for the defendant's participation in the killing

The fourth and final requirement is found in section 2(1)(c). It is that the abnormality of mental functioning provides an explanation for the defendant's participation in the killing. Subsection (1B) provides further guidance, stating that the abnormality provides an explanation if 'it causes or is a significant contributory factor in causing' the defendant to participate in the killing. In other words, there must be a causal link between the defendant's mental abnormality and his participation in the killing.[42]

This is a new requirement. There was no equivalent provision under the old law. The rationale for this addition was to ensure that the defence would not be used where the killing had nothing to do with the defendant's mental abnormality. The Law Commission explained:[43]

---

[42] Whilst some have suggested that subsection (1B) is only illustrative, so that the explanation requirement may be satisfied absent a causal link, the stronger argument is that subsection (1B) defines the explanation requirement, meaning that a causal requirement must always be established. It appears that this is the interpretation that is being adopted by the courts. See Mackay, R. and Hughes, D. (2021) 'Explaining the "explanation" requirement in the new diminished responsibility plea' *Criminal Law Review* 461.

[43] Law Commission (2006) *Murder, Manslaughter and Infanticide* (Report No 304) HC 30.

5.124 The final choice of particular words is a matter for those drafting the legislation. However, we have framed the issue in these terms: the abnormality of mind [...] must be shown to be 'an explanation' for D's conduct. This ensures that there is an appropriate connection (that is, one that grounds a case for mitigation of the offence) between the abnormality of mental functioning [...] and the killing. It leaves open the possibility, however, that other causes or explanations (like provocation) may be admitted to have been at work, without prejudicing the case for mitigation.

This new requirement has, however, been criticised.

First, now that the Supreme Court in *R* v *Golds* has clarified that a 'substantial' impairment of the defendant's relevant abilities is one that is important or weighty, it is arguable that there is no need for an explanation requirement to ensure an appropriate connection between the defendant's abnormality of mental functioning and the killing. As Mackay and Hughes observe:

> An abnormality of mental functioning which in the Golds sense "substantially" impairs one or more of the relevant capacities, remembering that those capacities must impact on the specific event of D killing V, will "provide an explanation" for D's conduct because, given the level of impairment required, there will inevitably be an "appropriate connection" between D's abnormality of mental functioning and D's conduct in killing V[44] (at 465)

Mackay has pointed out that there is now a disparity between the defences of diminished responsibility and insanity:[45]

> The *M'Naghten Rules* do not contain any such similar causal requirement. All the Rules require is "a defect of reason, from disease of the mind". What is necessary is that a "disease of the mind" cause "a defect of reason". There is no additional need to prove that the "disease of the mind" *caused or was a significant contributory factor in causing, D to carry out his conduct*. As a result one is compelled to ask whether it will not now be easier for a defendant whose mental state at the time of the offence satisfies all the elements of both pleas (with the exception of this causal requirement) to prove insanity within the *M'Naghten Rules* rather than the new diminished responsibility plea.

It has also been suggested that the new causal requirement is too strict.[46] Imagine a defendant – who has a long history of schizophrenia – kills someone. Under the old law the defendant could plead diminished responsibility if his schizophrenia substantially impaired his mental responsibility. But under the new law the defendant may only plead diminished responsibility if he can also show that there was a causal link between his schizophrenia and the killing. So the fact that the defendant had a history of schizophrenia which substantially impaired his mental responsibility is no longer in *itself* regarded as a sufficient reason to reduce his responsibility from murder to manslaughter.[47] Simester and Sullivan accordingly state:[48]

---

[44] Mackay, R. & Hughes, D. (2021) 'Explaining the "explanation" requirement in the new diminished responsibility plea' *Criminal Law Review* 461, 465.

[45] Mackay, R.D. (2010) 'The Coroners and Justice Act 2009 – Partial Defences to Murder: (2) The New Diminished Responsibility Plea' *Criminal Law Review* 290.

[46] Simester, A.P., Spencer, J.R., Stark, F., Sullivan, G.R. and Virgo, G.J. (2016) *Simester and Sullivan's Criminal Law: Theory and Doctrine* (6th edn). Hart Publishing: Oxford, pp.751–754.

[47] See, for example, *R* v *Madaweni* [2025] EWCA Crim 1427.

[48] Simester, A.P., Spencer, J.R., Stark, F., Sullivan, G.R. and Virgo, G.J. (2016) *Simester and Sullivan's Criminal Law: Theory and Doctrine* (6th edn). Hart Publishing: Oxford, pp.753–754.

The new section 2 is undoubtedly a more clearly worded, more schematic provision than the earlier version. There is now a much clearer divide between the loss of control partial defence (as a partial condonation for persons in stressful circumstances) and diminished responsibility which looks to D's abnormal functioning. Yet if that new tidiness comes at the price of murder convictions and mandatory life sentences for schizophrenics and others in like case, who may never receive adequate treatment for their symptoms in a prison setting, it is hardly an exercise in liberal and humane law reform.

Now, think about these questions.

- Looking back over our study of diminished responsibility, what were the objectives of the changes introduced by the Coroners and Justice Act 2009? In your opinion, do the changes achieve these objectives?
- What are the drawbacks of the changes introduced by the Coroners and Justice Act 2009? In your opinion, do the benefits of these changes outweigh the costs?

5. Diminished responsibility and voluntary intoxication

Now that we have studied the four requirements for diminished responsibility, we need to look at two particular types of difficult case. The first type of difficult case is where the defendant: (1) suffers an abnormality of mental functioning that arose from a recognised medical condition (e.g. a paranoid schizophrenic experiences a psychotic episode), but (2) was also voluntarily intoxicated at the time of the killing.

The leading case here is *R v Dietschmann* [2003] UKHL 10.

In 1998 the defendant, Anthony Dietschmann, began a relationship with his aunt Sarah. They lived together until he was remanded in custody in November 1998.

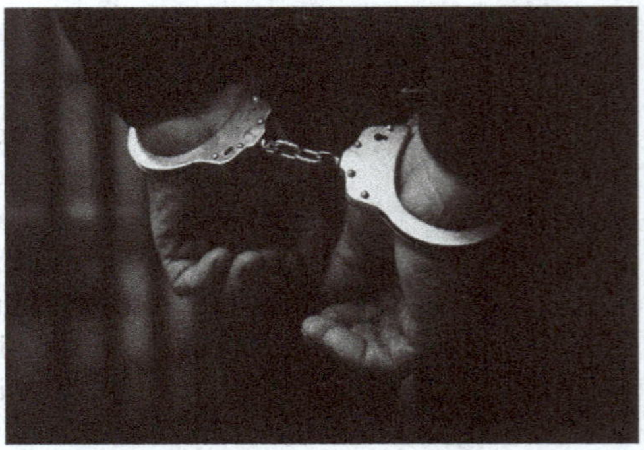

ronstik/Shutterstock

Whilst Dietschmann was in prison Sarah died. After his release, he began to drink heavily.

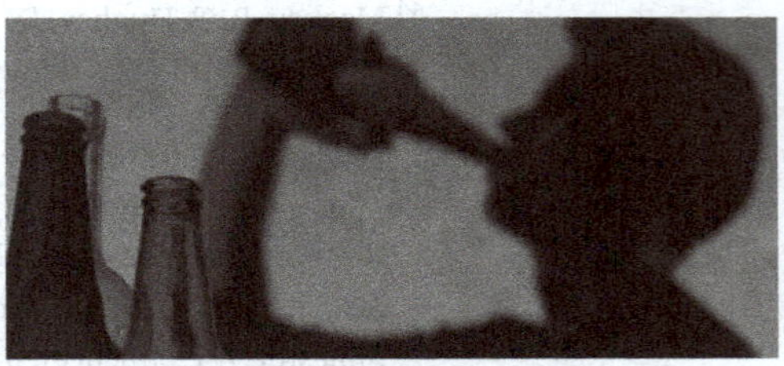

Photographee.eu/Shutterstock

One evening he was at a party with three other men, including the victim, Nicholas Davies.

Jacob Lund/Shutterstock

The men were dancing when Dietschmann's watch (which had been a gift from Sarah) fell off his wrist. He accused Davies of breaking the watch.

Fery setiawan/Shutterstock

A fight ensued. Dietschmann punched Davies and, when Davies fell over, Dietschmann stamped on his head several times and kicked him repeatedly. Davies died.

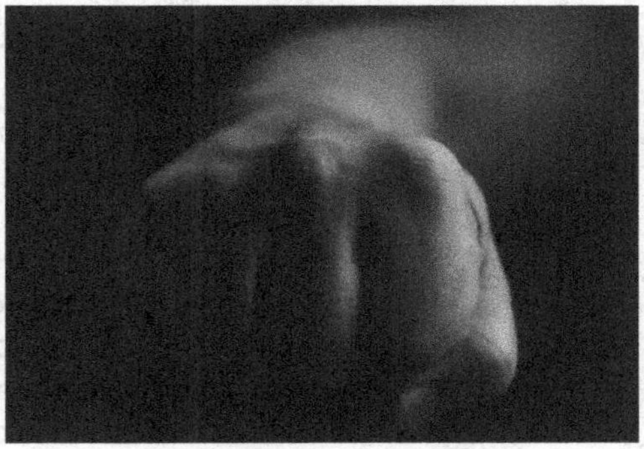

roundex/Shutterstock

At the time of the killing Dietschmann was not only drunk. Psychiatrists said that he was also suffering from a mental abnormality: an adjustment disorder which was a depressed grief reaction to Sarah's death.

At trial the judge told the jury that Dietschmann could only plead diminished responsibility if they were satisfied that he would still have killed Davies even if he had not been drunk. He was convicted of murder and his appeal reached the House of Lords. The House of Lords held that the trial judge had misdirected the jury, and set out the correct test to apply in cases like this one.

EXTRACT

Read the following extract from the judgment of Lord Hutton (with which the rest of the House of Lords agreed).

What test does he set out for juries to apply in cases where the defendant was both voluntarily intoxicated and had a mental abnormality?

R v *Dietschmann* [2003] UKHL 10

Lord Hutton

41 [...] [W]ithout attempting to lay down a precise form of words as the judge's directions are bound to depend to some extent on the facts of the case before him, I consider that the jury should be directed along the following lines:

> "Assuming that the defence have established that the defendant was suffering from mental abnormality as described in section 2, the important question is: did that abnormality substantially impair his mental responsibility for his acts in doing the killing? You know that before he carried out the killing the defendant had had a lot to drink. Drink cannot be taken into account as something which contributed to his mental abnormality and to any impairment of mental responsibility arising from that abnormality. But you may take the view that both the defendant's mental abnormality and drink played a part in impairing his mental responsibility for the killing and that he might not have killed if he had not taken drink. If you take that view, then the question for you to decide is this: has the defendant satisfied you that, despite the drink, his mental abnormality substantially impaired his mental responsibility for his fatal acts, or has he failed to satisfy you of that? If he has satisfied you of that, you will find him not guilty of murder but you may find him guilty of manslaughter. If he has not satisfied you of that, the defence of diminished responsibility is not available to him."

Although *R* v *Dietschmann* was decided under the old law, the same approach still applies today. So when considering a possible defence of diminished responsibility in a case like this the first step is to decide whether the defendant was suffering from an abnormality of mental functioning which arose from a recognised medical condition (the first two requirements we looked at earlier). If so, then when you get to the third requirement you should apply *R* v *Dietschmann*. So the test for the third requirement is not: has the defendant proved that he would still have killed the victim even if he had not been intoxicated? The correct test is: disregarding the effect of the defendant's voluntary intoxication, did the mental abnormality alone substantially impair the defendant's ability to do one of the things listed in subsection (1A)? If so, the final step is to apply the fourth requirement – was there a causal link between the mental abnormality and the killing? – in order to decide whether the defence is established.

6. Diminished responsibility and alcoholism

There is a second type of difficult case. Earlier we studied *R* v *Dowds* and saw that voluntary acute intoxication is not a recognised medical condition for the purposes of diminished responsibility. So a defendant who suffers an abnormality of mental functioning as a result of the *voluntary* consumption of alcohol or drugs cannot plead diminished responsibility. But what if the defendant was an addict, so that his consumption of alcohol/drugs was involuntary? In other words, may a defendant plead diminished responsibility if his mental abnormality was the result of alcoholism or drug addiction?

The Court of Appeal considered this in *R* v *Wood (Clive)* [2008] EWCA Crim 1305. The defendant, Clive Wood, killed the victim, Francis Ryan, with a meat cleaver and hammer after Ryan had made sexual advances towards him. On the day of the offence Wood had been drinking from the moment he woke up, and had consumed two to three litres of cider, several cans of lager, brandy and vodka. He was extremely drunk. Medical evidence also showed that he suffered from alcohol dependency syndrome. At trial Wood was convicted of murder. On appeal, the Court of Appeal explained the test that juries should apply in cases like this one.

EXTRACT

Read the following extract from the judgment of Sir Igor Judge P.

What approach does he set out for deciding whether the mental responsibility of an intoxicated alcoholic was substantially impaired?

R v *Wood* (*Clive*) [2008] EWCA Crim 1305

Sir Igor Judge P

41 [...] In deciding that question the jury should focus exclusively on the effect of alcohol consumed by the defendant as a direct result of his illness or disease and ignore the effect of any alcohol consumed voluntarily. Assuming that the jury has decided that the syndrome constitutes an abnormality of mind induced by disease or illness, its possible impact and significance in the individual case must be addressed. The resolution of this issue embraces questions such as whether the defendant's craving for alcohol was or was not irresistible, and whether his consumption of alcohol in the period leading up to the killing was voluntary (and if so, to what extent) or was not voluntary, and leads to the ultimate decision, which is whether the defendant's mental responsibility for his actions when killing the deceased was substantially impaired as a result of the alcohol consumed under the baneful influence of the syndrome.

This approach takes the logic of the judgment in *R* v *Dietschmann* and applies it in this specific context. So you begin by asking whether the first two requirements for diminished responsibility are satisfied: was the defendant suffering from a recognised medical condition (alcoholism) and did this condition cause an abnormality of mental functioning?[49] If so you should then apply the reasoning from *R* v *Wood (Clive)* when considering the third requirement: did the defendant's mental abnormality substantially impair his ability to do one of the three things listed in subsection (1A)? As Ashworth has commented, this is a 'fearsomely difficult question' in this context.[50] The Court of Appeal in *R* v *Wood (Clive)* stated that the jury should focus exclusively on the effect of the alcohol that was consumed as a direct result of the defendant's condition and disregard the effect of any alcohol that was consumed voluntarily. So the jury must first of all look back over the defendant's alcohol consumption and try to determine which drinks were consumed

[49] The Court of Appeal in *R* v *Wood (Clive)* ruled that in order to establish an abnormality of mental functioning it is not necessary to prove observable brain damage.

[50] Ashworth, A. (2008) 'Commentary on *R* v *Wood*' *Criminal Law Review* 977.

voluntarily and which were consumed as a result of alcoholism. Having done this, the jury must then focus exclusively on the alcohol that was consumed as a result of alcoholism and ask whether that alone substantially impaired the defendant's ability to do one of the three things listed in subsection (1A). If so, the jury must then apply the final requirement: was there a causal link between the defendant's alcoholism and the killing?

In the subsequent case *R* v *Stewart* [2009] EWCA Crim 593 the Court of Appeal elaborated on the test set out in *R* v *Wood (Clive)*. In the following extract Lord Judge CJ suggests guidance that could be given to juries who are applying the substantially impaired test to defendants with alcoholism.

EXTRACT

Make a list of the factors Lord Judge CJ suggests juries should consider when distinguishing alcohol that was consumed voluntarily from alcohol that was consumed as a result of the defendant's condition. To what extent do you think this reduces the difficulty of the jury's task?

R v *Stewart* [2009] EWCA Crim 593

Lord Judge CJ

33 Finally, and assuming that the particular defendant's alcohol dependency syndrome did indeed constitute an abnormality of [mental functioning] due to disease or illness, which was present at the time of the killing, directions about whether the defendant's mental responsibility for what he did was substantially impaired should be addressed in conventional terms. The jury should be assisted with the concept of substantial impairment, and may properly be invited to reflect on the difference between a failure by the defendant to resist his impulses to behave as he actually did, and an inability consequent on it to resist them.

34 In answering their questions, the jury should be directed to consider all the evidence, including the opinions of the medical experts. The issues likely to arise in this kind of case and on which they should be invited to form their own judgment will include (a) the extent and seriousness of the defendant's dependency, if any, on alcohol, (b) the extent to which his ability to control his drinking or to choose whether to drink or not, was reduced, (c) whether he was capable of abstinence from alcohol, and if so, (d) for how long, and (e) whether he was choosing for some particular reason, such as a birthday celebration, to decide to get drunk, or to drink even more than usual. Without seeking to be prescriptive about considerations relevant to an individual case, the appellant's pattern of drinking in the days leading to the day of the killing, and on the day of the killing itself, and notwithstanding his consumption of alcohol, his ability, if any, to make apparently sensible and rational decisions about ordinary day-to-day matters at the relevant time, may all bear on the jury's decision whether diminished responsibility is established in the context of this individual defendant's alcohol dependency syndrome.

35 We acknowledge that this decision will rarely be easy. Indeed it is fair to say that diminished responsibility has always raised complex and difficult issues for the jury, not least because the defence usually involves conflicting medical evidence addressing legal, not medical concepts, for a jury of lay persons to decide. The jury is often called upon to confront problems relating to the operation of the mind with which they will be unfamiliar. Nevertheless the resolution of these problems continues to be the responsibility of the jury, and when addressing their responsibility they are inevitably required to make the necessary judgments not just on the basis of expert medical opinion but also by using their collective common sense and insight into the practical realities which underpin the individual case.

So whether or not the defendant's mental abilities were substantially impaired is ultimately a question for the jury to answer. As well as using the medical evidence, they should use 'their collective common sense and insight into the practical realities which underpin the individual case'.

In *R* v *Stewart* the defendant, Patrick Stewart, had an alcohol dependency that was at the extreme end of the spectrum. At the time of the killing his blood-alcohol level was four times the legal limit for driving. The medical experts agreed that he was a chronic alcoholic. The defence's expert witness stated that Stewart had lost the ability to voluntarily control his drinking. By contrast the prosecution's expert witness stated that Stewart could choose whether or not to drink, pointing to periods in the past where Stewart had been alcohol-free. When determining what alcohol (if any) Stewart consumed voluntarily the jury were therefore faced with conflicting expert opinion. The possibility of conflicting medical evidence compounds the difficulty that juries face in cases involving alcoholics. Commenting on the judgment in R v Stewart, Ashworth has stated:[51]

> Lord Judge recognises that the jury's decision will not be easy in cases of this kind, particularly where (as in this case) the two expert witnesses disagree on the issue of substantial impairment. In effect, this judgment still requires the same kind of decision as did *Wood*, and is afflicted with the same problem of determining whether D's apparent choices of when and what to drink were real choices, or actions stemming chiefly from his alcohol dependency. It is telling that Lord Judge refers to "apparently sensible and rational decisions about ordinary day to day matters", the word "apparently" begging the key question. Some of the things said and done by D in this case after he gave himself up to the police might appear to be "sensible and rational", but a sample taken at the time showed that the level of alcohol in his blood was about four times the drink/driving limit. With people who are accustomed to consuming large amounts of alcohol, appearances may not always be a good guide.

However difficult the jury's task in cases like this, the approach set out in *R* v *Stewart* was endorsed by the Court of Appeal in the conjoined appeals *R* v *Joyce*; *R* v *Kay* [2017] EWCA Crim 647. The second of these cases involved both a psychiatric illness (as in *R* v *Dietschmann*) and alcohol/drug dependency (as in *R* v *Wood (Clive)* and *R* v *Stewart*). The defendant, Kay, was a paranoid schizophrenic. He had a long history of alcohol and drug abuse, even though drug use triggered and exacerbated his schizophrenia. In June 2015 he went on a three day 'bender', drinking large amounts of alcohol and taking multiple unlawful drugs including cocaine, heroin and amphetamines. In the grip of a psychotic episode, he stabbed the victim to death. At trial, Kay sought to rely on the defence of diminished responsibility. He argued that it was his schizophrenia that was primarily responsible for his psychotic state at the time of the killing. He also claimed that he had an alcohol and drug dependency syndrome and so his intoxication was involuntary. His defence was unsuccessful and he was convicted of murder. On appeal against his conviction, defence counsel claimed that *R* v *Stewart* left the jury 'with a stark binary choice: schizophrenia and dependency syndrome equals guilty of manslaughter, schizophrenia and voluntary intoxication equals guilty of murder' ([14]). Rejecting this argument, the Court of Appeal explained that, in Kay's case, there were three possibilities. First, that his schizophrenia was so severe that it alone substantially impaired his ability to do one of the things listed in subsection (1A). The

[51] Ashworth, A. (2009) 'Commentary on *R* v *Stewart*' *Criminal Law Review* 808.

difficulty with this in Kay's case was that there was no medical evidence that suggested that, absent alcohol or drug abuse, his schizophrenia impaired these abilities substantially. The second possibility was that a combination of schizophrenia and alcohol and drug dependency substantially impaired Kay's ability to do one of the things listed in subsection (1A). The difficulty with this was that the jury at Kay's trial had rejected this possibility. That left the final possibility, which was that his psychotic episode arose not from a recognised medical condition, but from voluntary intoxication. It followed that the defence of diminished responsibility was unavailable. Hallett VP summarised the Court's conclusion as follows:

> 20. [W]e see no reason to depart from the approach in *Stewart*. Coupled with the provisions of section 2(1) of the Homicide Act (as amended), it provides a clear and sensible approach for directing the jury. The approach is neither binary nor simplistic but is flexible enough to encompass a wide variety of factual circumstances in a manner that is fair to all. It takes full account of the kind of mental health issues under consideration and our increased understanding of them. In our view, it rightly does not necessarily provide even a partial defence to everyone diagnosed with schizophrenia, who, well aware of the possible consequences, chooses to abuse drink and drugs to excess and then kills.

Quiz 10.3

1. The defence of diminished responsibility is available to which of the following offences?

a. All serious offences.

b. Murder.

c. All offences.

d. Murder and all non-fatal offences against the person.

2. Which of the following statements summarises the decision in *R v Dowds* accurately?

a. That whilst acute intoxication appears in the World Health Organization's classification of diseases, it is not capable of being relied upon to found a defence of diminished responsibility.

b. That evidence of alcohol dependency syndrome is sufficient to establish the defence of diminished responsibility provided the offence in question is one of specific intent.

c. That evidence of voluntary intoxication is sufficient to establish the defence of diminished responsibility provided the offence in question is one of basic intent.

d. That evidence of voluntary intoxication is sufficient to establish the defence of diminished responsibility provided the offence in question is one of specific intent.

3. The defence of diminished responsibility has four requirements. The first is that the defendant was suffering from an abnormality of mental functioning. Which of the following is not one of the other three requirements?

a. That the abnormality of mental functioning explains the defendant's role in the killing.

b. That the abnormality of mental functioning substantially impaired the defendant's ability to understand, rationalise or control his actions.

c. That the abnormality of mental functioning arose from a recognised medical condition.

d. That the abnormality of mental functioning arose from an abnormality of mind.

4. Which of the following statements is incorrect?

a. Although medical evidence is not expressly required by section 2 of the Homicide Act 1957 (as amended), it is a practical necessity for the defence to succeed.

b. A jury is not bound to accept medical evidence of an abnormality of mental functioning if there is other material which, in their opinion, outweighs it.

c. If there is uncontradicted and unchallenged expert evidence of an abnormality of mental functioning the jury must accept it.

d. Whether or not D was suffering from an abnormality of mental functioning is a question of fact for the jury to decide, and so the jury is not bound to accept even unanimous expert evidence.

5. According to the Supreme Court in *R* v *Golds*, what is the meaning of the word 'substantially' in the term 'substantially impaired'?

a. Important or weighty.

b. More than merely trivial.

c. The meaning of the term is for the jury to decide on the facts of the particular case before it.

d. The meaning of the word is clear and there is no need for any further explanation.

Conclusion

Figure 10.1 presents an overview of the relationship between the three defences we have studied in this chapter.

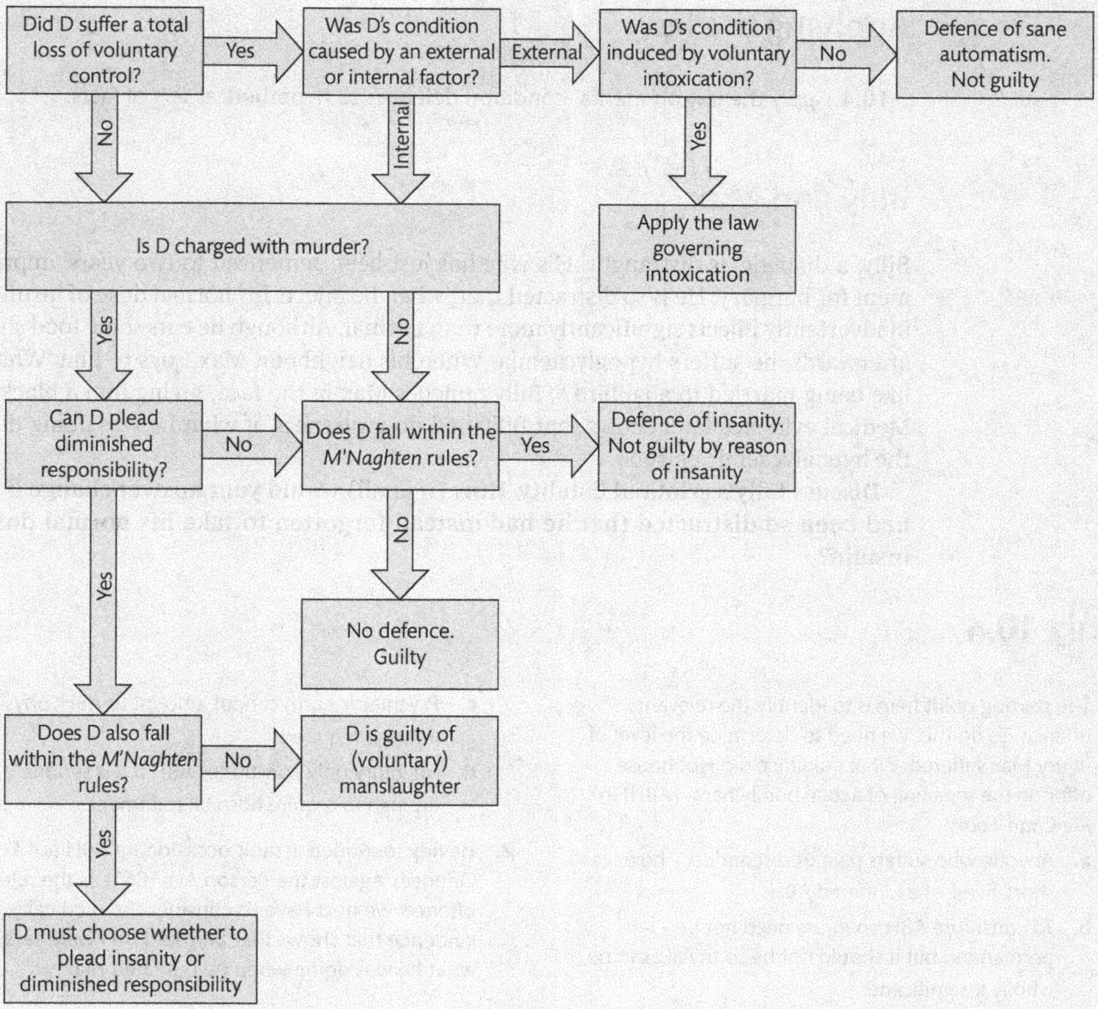

Figure 10.1 Mental condition defences: an overview

As you can see from this diagram, in a murder case it is possible that a defendant may satisfy the requirements for both insanity and diminished responsibility. The defendant must then choose which of the two to plead. Experience has shown that most defendants would prefer to be convicted of manslaughter on the grounds of diminished responsibility rather than be found not guilty by reason of insanity. Note, however, that if the defendant chooses to plead diminished responsibility it is open to the prosecution to argue that the defendant should instead be found not guilty by reason of insanity (and vice versa).[52]

Similarly, as we have seen in a number of cases in this chapter such as *R* v *Sullivan* and *R* v *Hennessy*, a defendant may sometimes have to choose between a defence of insanity and entering a guilty plea. Many defendants would prefer to plead guilty, especially if the crime they have been charged with is a minor one, in order to avoid possible hospitalisation.

Lastly, remember that even if the defendant cannot rely on any of the three defences we have studied in this chapter, it may still be possible for the defendant to argue that he lacked *mens rea*. We saw an example of this in *R* v *Clarke*. So remember to consider this possibility when answering an exam problem question!

Applying the law

10.4 Apply the law on mental condition defences to hypothetical sets of facts.

Billy and Max

Billy, a diabetic, is distraught. His wife has just been sentenced to two years' imprisonment for burglary. He is so distracted that, when he injects his normal dose of insulin, he inadvertently injects significantly more than normal. Although he eats some food shortly afterwards, he suffers hypoglycaemia. When his neighbour, Max, says to him 'What's it like being married to a jailbird?', Billy punches Max in the face, giving him a black eye. Medical evidence later shows that Billy had no awareness of what he was doing during the hypoglycaemic episode.

Discuss Billy's criminal liability. How (if at all) would your answer change if Billy had been so distracted that he had instead forgotten to take his normal dose of insulin?

Quiz 10.4

1. The starting point here is to identify the relevant offence. To do this, we need to determine the level of injury Max suffered. What guidance did Hobhouse LJ offer on the meaning of actual bodily harm (ABH) in *R* v *Chan-Fook*?
   - **a.** Anyone who suffers pain or discomfort – however short-lived – has suffered ABH.
   - **b.** To constitute ABH an injury need not be permanent, but it should not be so trivial as to be wholly insignificant.
   - **c.** Psychiatric harm cannot amount to ABH; physical injury is required.
   - **d.** An injury only constitutes ABH if it is serious enough to require hospital treatment.
2. Having identified assault occasioning ABH (s.47 of the Offences Against the Person Act 1861) as the relevant offence, we next have to consider the medical evidence that shows that Billy had no awareness of what he was doing when he punched Max.

[52] Criminal Procedure (Insanity) Act 1964, s.6.

How did the Court of Appeal define automatism in *R v Coley*?

a. A complete destruction of voluntary control.

b. An impaired understanding of reality.

c. An impaired ability to think rationally.

d. A substantial destruction of voluntary control.

3. So, when Billy punched Max he was in a state of automatism and acting involuntarily. The key question, however, is whether Billy acted in a state of sane automatism (in which case he will be found not guilty) or a state of insane automatism (in which case he will be found not guilty by reason of insanity). This depends on whether his unawareness was caused by an internal or an external factor.

Which of the following statements summarises *R v Quick*?

a. The cause of Quick's hypoglycaemia was his diabetes. Diabetes is a medical condition and so is an internal factor.

b. The cause of Quick's hypoglycaemia was him forgetting to eat after injecting insulin. Absent-mindedness is an internal factor.

c. The cause of Quick's hypoglycaemia was the injection of insulin, which amounted to an external factor.

d. The cause of Quick's hypoglycaemia was his stressful job, which caused him to forget to eat after injecting insulin. A stressful job is an external factor.

4. The alternative scenario asks whether things would be different if Billy had been so distracted that he had instead forgotten to take his normal dose of insulin. Which of the following statements summarises R v *Hennessy* accurately?

a. The cause of Hennessy's hyperglycaemia was him forgetting to self-inject his insulin. Absent-mindedness is an internal factor.

b. The cause of Hennessy's hyperglycaemia was his diabetes. Diabetes is a medical condition and so is an internal factor.

c. The cause of Hennessy's hyperglycaemia was the injection of insulin, which amounted to an external factor.

d. The cause of Hennessy's hyperglycaemia was stress, anxiety and depression, which caused him to forget to inject his insulin. Stress, anxiety and depression are external factors.

So, in R v *Hennessy* the cause of Hennessy's condition was held to be his diabetes. The Court of Appeal rejected the argument that stress, anxiety and depression amounted to external factors. Lord Lane CJ explained that "They lack the feature of novelty or accident" and they are "prone to recur". But something that is exceptionally traumatic can amount to an external factor, as in R v T where the defendant took part in a robbery three days after being raped. In Billy's case his wife has just been sentenced to two years' imprisonment and Max taunted him about this. Based on R v *Hennessy* and R v T, in your opinion would this be sufficiently traumatic to constitute an external factor?

If Billy's circumstances were sufficiently traumatic to constitute an external factor, he would be able to plead sane automatism. But if they do not, the cause of his condition would be his diabetes and he would have to plead insane automatism. For the defence of insanity to apply, the three requirements set out in *M'Naghten's case* would have to be satisfied. The first of these is that the defendant was suffering from a disease of the mind.

5. Which of the following statements is incorrect?

a. The term disease of the mind is not limited to brain disease.

b. Whether or not a defendant was suffering from a disease of the mind is determined solely by expert medical vidence.

c. Any disease that impairs a defendant's reasoning, memory or understanding is a disease of the mind.

d. A condition may amount to a disease of the mind even if it is not permanent.

6. In Billy's case his hypoglycaemia resulted in him having no awareness of what he was doing. This falls within the definition of disease of the mind set out in R v *Sullivan*: his reasoning, memory and understanding were impaired, albeit only temporarily.

The next requirement for the defence of insanity is that the disease of the mind caused a defect of reason. This will be satisfied in Billy's case. His powers of reasoning were impaired. The final requirement is that the defendant either did not know the nature and quality of the act he was doing or did not know that what he was doing was wrong. It is the first of these two possibilities that is relevant to Billy's case.

Which of the following defendants will be unable to prove that he did not know the nature and quality of his act?

a. A suffers from an epileptic seizure and has no awareness of what is happening.

b. B, suffering from a delusion, believes he is fighting a Tyrannosaurus Rex, when in fact he is attacking Billy.

c. C pushes Billy off a skyscraper, because he wants to watch Billy sprout wings and fly to safety.

d. D is a schizophrenic. As a result of a schizophrenic delusion he believes he has been ordered to kill Billy. He carries out these orders.

Charlie and Jim

Charlie is a big sports fan and is on his way to watch a match between his favourite team, the Wizards, and their biggest rivals, the Dragons.

Think about these questions.

1. Consider these scenarios and discuss Charlie's criminal liability in each.
   a. Charlie is a schizophrenic. As a result of a schizophrenic delusion, when Jim (a Dragons fan) walks towards him he mistakenly believes that Jim is a dragon about to attack him. Charlie attacks Jim, striking and kicking him repeatedly. Jim dies.
   b. Charlie is a schizophrenic. As a result of a schizophrenic delusion, Charlie believes he has been ordered to kill all Dragons supporters. When he sees Jim (who is wearing a Dragons scarf) he attacks him and kills him.
   c. Charlie has a mental condition which makes it very difficult for him to control feelings of anger and aggression. When he hears Jim (a Dragons fan) singing derogatory songs about the Wizards he erupts with anger, attacks Jim and kills him.
2. How (if at all) would your answers to each of these scenarios be different if Jim had suffered serious injuries but not died?

Mildred and Dale

Mildred is celebrating her 40th birthday in her local pub. One of her guests is Dale, an alcoholic who drinks at least a bottle of wine every day. After several glasses of wine Dale's urge to drink begins to subside, but Mildred orders another two bottles and encourages him to keep drinking by saying, 'C'mon mate, it's my birthday!' A little later (by which time Dale has drunk three more glasses and is beginning to slur his speech) Mildred's brother, Patrick, says to Dale, 'It's time for you to head home you old drunk'. Angered by this, Dale replies, 'What did you call me?' 'An old drunk', Patrick retorts. At this Dale picks up one of the empty wine bottles and hits Patrick on the head with it as hard as he can, causing a deep gash. A fight breaks out, in the course of which Mildred (who was already very drunk) falls over and bangs her head. When she gets up she punches Dale in the face, giving him a black eye.

Patrick is taken to hospital where, as a result of the carelessness of a junior doctor, he is given a drug to which he is allergic. He suffers a severe reaction and dies. Dale later states that, although he was aware of what he was doing when he struck Patrick, his consumption of alcohol had affected his powers of self-control. Meanwhile Mildred states that she was completely unaware of what she was doing for some time after falling and banging her head. Medical evidence subsequently shows that Mildred was both drunk and concussed when she struck Dale.

Now, consider this question.

Discuss the criminal liability of Dale and Mildred.

Evaluating the law

10.5 Evaluate the changes made to the diminished responsibility defence by the Coroners and Justice Act 2009.

Think about this question.

'The law governing diminished responsibility has been vastly improved by the changes introduced by the Coroners and Justice Act 2009. Before these changes the law in this area was ambiguous and insufficiently grounded in a medical diagnosis. This has now been rectified. As a result the law is now easier for juries to apply and arbitrary, inconsistent verdicts are unlikely.'

Discuss the extent to which you agree with this statement.

Step 1: Deconstruct the essay title

This question asks you to evaluate the changes made to the diminished responsibility defence by the Coroners and Justice Act 2009. The statement makes three assertions:

1. that the previous law was ambiguous and insufficiently grounded in a medical diagnosis;
2. that the new law is easier for juries to apply and less likely to result in arbitrary, inconsistent verdicts; and
3. that the new law is a vast improvement.

Step 2: Work through each assertion, form an opinion and construct a set of arguments in support of your views

To help you decide the extent to which you agree with each of these three assertions, look back at the notes you prepared in response to the following questions.

On Kennefick's article 'Introducing a New Diminished Responsibility Defence for England and Wales':

- In Kennefick's opinion, does the new law achieve its objective of greater clarity? Why/why not?
- In the following extract Kennefick refers to the 'benign conspiracy' that sometimes occurred under the old law. What was the benign conspiracy? Will it still be possible under the new law?
- In your opinion, should the law be flexible enough to allow for benign conspiracies?

On Mackay and Mitchell's article, 'The New Diminished Responsibility Plea in Operation: Some Initial Findings':

- Read the following extract, which contrasts data from cases decided under the new version of the defence [the 'CPS cases'] with data from cases decided under the old version [the 'Law Commission cases']. According to the study, have the changes to the defence led to an increase or a decrease in the proportion of cases with a contested plea? And, have the changes resulted in an increase or decrease in the proportion of cases resulting in a murder conviction?

On Laird's 'Case Comment, Homicide: R v *Golds (Mark Richard)*':

- Read the following extract from Laird's commentary. According to Laird, how did the Supreme Court's judgment undermine its stated aim of ensuring the term 'substantially' is applied consistently?

On Mackay's article 'The Coroners and Justice Act 2009 – Partial Defences to Murder: (2) The New Diminished Responsibility Plea':

- Read the following extract from Mackay's article 'The Coroners and Justice Act 2009 – Partial Defences to Murder: (2) The New Diminished Responsibility Plea'. What concerns does he express about the changes introduced by the new law?

On the changes introduced by the 2009 Act:

- Looking back over our study of diminished responsibility, what were the objectives of the changes introduced by the Coroners and Justice Act 2009? In your opinion, do the changes achieve these objectives?
- What are the drawbacks of the changes introduced by the Coroners and Justice Act 2009? In your opinion, do the benefits of these changes outweigh the costs?

Once you have looked back at your notes, decide whether you agree with each of the three assertions contained in the essay title. Then, for each assertion, construct a set of arguments in support of your opinion and work out how you would respond to potential counter-arguments. Try to use case law to support and illustrate the points you wish to make, and use items on the further reading list to supplement your notes.

Step 3: Planning your introduction and conclusion

You now have compiled all you need for the main body of your essay. The last task is to decide what to include in your introduction and conclusion.

The introduction should contextualise your discussion by: (1) briefly outlining the diminished responsibility defence and the changes made by the 2009 Act; and (2) giving an indication of the argument you will present in your essay.

The conclusion should round off your essay with a succinct statement of your argument and a summary of your supporting reasons.

Mental condition defences checklist

Having worked through this chapter, you should now have:

- An understanding of the meaning of automatism
- An understanding of the distinction between sane and insane automatism
- An understanding of the requirements for the defence of sane automatism
- An understanding of the requirements for the defence of insanity
- An understanding of the requirements for the defence of diminished responsibility
- A knowledge of the changes made to the diminished responsibility defence by the Coroners and Justice Act 2009
- An ability to critically discuss the changes made to the diminished responsibility defence by the Coroners and Justice Act 2009.

Further reading

Child, J.J., Crombag, H.S. and Sullivan, G.R. (2020) 'Defending the Delusional, the Irrational and the Dangerous' *Criminal Law Review* 306.

Gibson, M. (2017) 'Pragmatism Preserved? The Challenges of Accommodating Mercy Killers in the Reformed Diminished Responsibility Plea' 81 *Journal of Criminal Law* 177.

Kennefick, L. (2011) 'Introducing a New Diminished Responsibility Defence for England and Wales' 74 *Modern Law Review* 750.

Law Commission (2006) *Murder, Manslaughter and Infanticide* (Report No 304) HC 30.

Mackay, R.D. (2000) 'Diminished Responsibility and Mentally Disordered Killers' in A. Ashworth and B. Mitchell (eds) *Rethinking English Homicide Law*. OUP: Oxford.

Mackay, R. (2018) 'The Impairment Factors in the New Diminished Responsibility Plea' *Criminal Law Review* 462.

Mackay, R. (2021) 'What's happening with the reformed diminished responsibility plea?' 72 *Northern Ireland Legal Quarterly* 224.

Mackay, R. and Hughes, D. (2021) 'Explaining the "explanation" requirement in the new diminished responsibility plea' *Criminal Law Review* 461.

Mackay, R. and Mitchell, B. (2017) 'The New Diminished Responsibility Plea in Operation: Some Initial Findings' *Criminal Law Review* 18.

Manwaring, J. (2018) 'Windle Revisited' *Criminal Law Review* 987.

Simpson, B. (2021) 'R v Foy (Nicholas): voluntary intoxication, mental health and the case for diminished responsibility' 72 *Northern Ireland Legal Quarterly* 397.

Wake, N. (2012) 'Recognising Acute Intoxication as Diminished Responsibility? A Comparative Analysis' 76 *Journal of Criminal Law* 71.

Answers on the Companion Website

Please visit the companion website for the answers to Key Questions, Quizzes, Applying the Law scenarios as well as student support including glossaries. Please visit www.pearsoned.co.uk/Macdonald

11

Substantive defences

Learning Objectives

11.1 Define the requirements for establishing the substantive defence of necessity.

11.2 Define the requirements for establishing the substantive defences of duress by threats and duress of circumstances.

11.3 Identify arguments for and against allowing duress as a defence to murder.

11.4 Outline the relationship between duress of circumstances and necessity.

11.5 Define the requirements for establishing the substantive defences of prevention of crime and private defence.

11.6 Apply the law on substantive defences to hypothetical sets of facts.

11.7 Evaluate whether duress should be available as a defence to murder.

Introduction

Consider the following three scenarios. All three are based on cases and examples that we will encounter during the chapter.

The castaway

Dudarev Mikhail/Shutterstock

D is cast away in a small lifeboat with three other men. After more than two weeks lost at sea (including eight days without food and six days without water), D decides to try and save his own life by killing one of the other men on board and feeding on the man's blood and flesh. Four days later D is saved by a passing vessel.

The abused child

SpeedKingz/Shutterstock

D is 11 years old. His father is a violent man. One day, D's father forces D to help him kill V. D's contribution is to hold his father's gun whilst his father forces open the door to V's home.

The burgled man

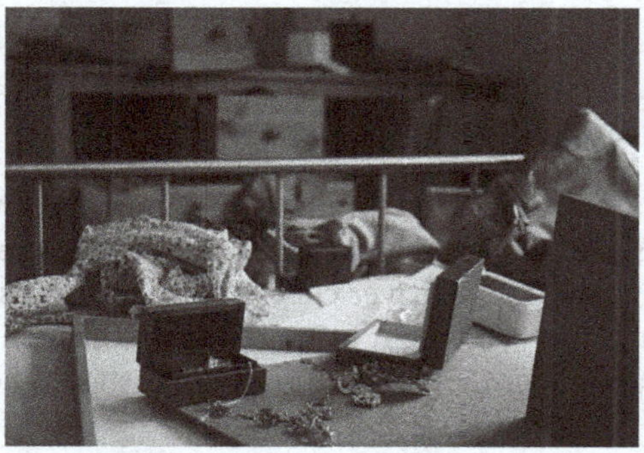

SpeedKingz/Shutterstock

D's home has been burgled many times. One night, D arms himself with an unlicensed shotgun. Two men break into his house. D shoots at them. One of the men is killed.

Should any of these three defendants have a defence to murder? If so, which?

Imagine you are discussing a defendant's criminal liability. You began by identifying the relevant criminal offence. You then worked through the *actus reus* and *mens rea* requirements of the offence and have concluded that they are all established. At this point it might seem that the defendant is liable for the crime. But this is not the end of the matter. There is a further stage, which is to consider whether the defendant can rely on a substantive defence. As we saw in Chapter 2, the anatomy of a crime is as shown in Figure 11.1.

Actus reus **+** ***Mens rea*** **−** **Substantive defence** **=** **Criminal offence**

Figure 11.1

When a defendant successfully relies on a substantive defence, we are effectively saying: 'Yes, you perpetrated the *actus reus* of the crime with the necessary *mens rea*, but we are nonetheless prepared to find you not guilty.' In other words, a substantive defence justifies or excuses commission of the crime.

In this chapter we examine five substantive defences: **necessity**; **duress by threats**; **duress of circumstances**; **prevention of crime**; and **private defence**. We begin with necessity.

Necessity

11.1 Define the requirements for establishing the substantive defence of necessity.

Suppose someone commits a crime in order to prevent something even worse from happening. In other words, the commission of the crime was the lesser of two evils. Should he be found guilty of the crime he committed? Or should he be able to argue that committing the crime was *necessary*?

In this section we begin by examining whether or not the criminal law recognises a defence of necessity. We then look at the difficult issue of whether necessity should be available as a defence to murder, before finally asking what test is used to determine whether the defence is available.

1. Is there a general defence of necessity?

A house is on fire. A man is trapped at an upstairs window. A fire engine has been called. The fire engine is just 200 metres away from the house when it reaches a set of traffic lights. The lights are red. The driver checks both directions, sees that the road is clear and so drives through the red light in order to save the man. If the driver of the fire engine was later charged with jumping the red light, should he be able to plead a defence of necessity?

This example was discussed by Lord Denning in *Buckoke* v *GLC* [1971] Ch 655. You may be surprised to learn that, although Lord Denning said the driver should be 'congratulated', he stated that the driver would not have a defence of necessity in law.

Lord Denning made these comments more than 40 years ago, and things have changed since then.[1] This example is nonetheless a powerful illustration of the courts' reluctance, for much of the twentieth century, to recognise the existence of a general defence of necessity.

Why were the courts so wary of a defence of necessity? To help us answer this question we can look at another of Lord Denning's judgments, this time in Southwark *LBC* v *Williams* [1971] Ch 734.

EXTRACT

Read the following paragraph from Lord Denning's judgment and then explain, in your own words, his reasons for not recognising the existence of a defence of necessity.

Southwark LBC v *Williams* [1971] Ch 734

Lord Denning

The reason is because, if hunger were once allowed to be an excuse for stealing, it would open a way through which all kinds of disorder and lawlessness would pass. So here. If homelessness were once admitted as a defence to trespass, no one's house could be safe. Necessity would open a door which no man could shut. It would not only be those in extreme need who would enter. There would be others who would imagine that they were in need, or would invent a need, so as to gain entry. Each man would say his need was greater than the next man's. The plea would be an excuse for all sorts of wrongdoing. So the courts must, for the sake of law and order, take a firm stand. They must refuse to admit the plea of necessity to the hungry and the homeless: and trust that their distress will be relieved by the charitable and the good.

Although Lord Denning insisted that the courts should 'refuse to admit the plea of necessity', there were others who seemed prepared to allow necessity as a defence in some, limited, circumstances. For example, in the same case (*Southwark LBC* v *Williams*) Edmund Davies LJ stated:

> [... O]ne thing emerges with clarity from the decisions, and that is that the law regards with the deepest suspicion any remedies of self-help, and permits those remedies to be resorted to only in very special circumstances. The reason for such circumspection is clear: necessity can very easily become simply a mask for anarchy. As far as my reading goes, it appears that all the cases where a plea of necessity has succeeded are cases which deal with an urgent situation of imminent peril.

Think about this question.

In this paragraph Edmund Davies LJ envisages an exception to the general rule that necessity should not be a defence. What title would you give to this exception?

There were other cases in which the courts seemed prepared to recognise a defence of necessity. In *Johnson* v *Phillips* [1976] 1 WLR 65 a driver stopped his car behind a parked

[1] In the years since *Buckoke* v *GLC* specific provisions have been enacted for situations like these. In emergencies drivers of fire engines, police cars and ambulances may regard red traffic lights as warnings to give way and may exceed speed limits: Traffic Signs Regulations 2002 (SI 2002/3113), reg. 36; Road Traffic Regulation Act 1984, s.87.

ambulance in a narrow one-way street. There had been an incident in a nearby pub, and other ambulances were expected to help remove people that had been injured. Since the driver's car was getting in the way a policeman asked the driver to reverse back along the street to clear the way for the other ambulances. The driver refused. He said that driving the wrong way down a one-way street is a criminal offence, and he was worried he might be prosecuted. He was subsequently convicted of wilfully obstructing the policeman in the execution of his duty. At his appeal against conviction the principal issue was whether the policeman was acting in the execution of his duty, which in turn depended on whether the policeman could lawfully tell the driver to disobey traffic regulations.

The driver's appeal was unsuccessful. On behalf of the Court Wien J stated:

> The law protects the liberty of the subject, but it must recognise that in certain circumstances which have to be carefully considered by the courts a constable may oblige persons to disobey a traffic regulation and not only in those cases that are explicitly dealt with by Parliament. In the judgment of this court a constable would be entitled, and indeed under a duty, to give such instruction if it were reasonably necessary for the protection of life or property.

So here we again see a willingness to recognise a defence of necessity.

These three cases give us a brief insight into the uncertainty that prevailed for much of the twentieth century as to whether a general defence of necessity existed. A key development came in 1989, when the House of Lords issued its judgment in *Re F (Mental Patient: Sterilisation)* [1990] 2 AC 1. This case involved a 36-year-old mentally handicapped woman who had the mental age of a small child. She was a patient in a mental hospital and had formed a sexual relationship with a male patient. The hospital staff did not want to restrict her (already limited) freedom by preventing sexual activity, but were anxious about the potentially disastrous effects pregnancy might have on her. As there were difficulties with all other methods of contraception the hospital concluded that she should be sterilised. As F was incapable of granting her consent to a sterilisation operation, F's mother applied to the courts for a declaration that F could be sterilised without her consent.

The House of Lords held that the doctors performing the sterilisation operation would not be acting unlawfully.

EXTRACT

The following extract is from the judgment of Lord Brandon. He said that there are two situations in which adult patients may be given medical treatment, even though they have not consented, provided that the treatment is in their best interests. What are these situations?

Lord Brandon then goes on to consider the underlying principle which justifies this position. What is this principle?

Re F (Mental Patient: Sterilisation) [1990] 2 AC 1

Lord Brandon

At common law a doctor cannot lawfully operate on adult patients of sound mind, or give them any other treatment involving the application of physical force however small ("other treatment"), without their consent. If a doctor were to operate on such patients, or give them other treatment, without their consent, he would commit the actionable tort of trespass to the person. There are, however, cases where adult patients cannot give or refuse their consent to an operation or other treatment. One case is where, as a result of an accident or otherwise, an adult patient is unconscious and an operation or other treatment cannot be safely delayed until he or she recovers consciousness. Another case is where a patient, though adult, cannot by reason of mental disability understand the nature or purpose of an operation or other treatment. The common law would be seriously defective if it failed to provide a solution to the problem created by such inability to consent. In my opinion, however, the common law does not so fail. In my opinion, the solution to the problem which the common law provides is that a doctor can lawfully operate on, or give other treatment to, adult patients who are incapable, for one reason or another, of consenting to his doing so, provided that the operation or other treatment concerned is in the best interests of such patients. The operation or other treatment will be in their best interests if, but only if, it is carried out in order either to save their lives, or to ensure improvement or prevent deterioration in their physical or mental health.

Different views have been put forward with regard to the principle which makes it lawful for a doctor to operate on or give other treatment to adult patients without their consent in the two cases to which I have referred above. The Court of Appeal in the present case regarded the matter as depending on the public interest. I would not disagree with that as a broad proposition, but I think that it is helpful to consider the principle in accordance with which the public interest leads to this result. In my opinion, the principle is that, when persons lack the capacity, for whatever reason, to take decisions about the performance of operations on them, or the giving of other medical treatment to them, it is necessary that some other person or persons, with the appropriate qualifications, should take such decisions for them. Otherwise they would be deprived of medical care which they need and to which they are entitled.

Lord Brandon's judgment focuses on medical treatment. His comments may therefore be understood as relating specifically to *medical necessity*. This may be contrasted with the judgment of Lord Goff, who advanced a broader conception of necessity that was not restricted to the context of medical treatment.

EXTRACT

Lord Goff explains that necessity might apply in three types of situation. What are these? Which one was relevant to the female patient in *Re F*?

Is Lord Goff's third type of situation limited to emergencies? If not, what are the requirements which Lord Goff says must be satisfied for a case to fall in the third of his categories?

Re F (*Mental Patient: Sterilisation)* [1990] 2 AC 1

Lord Goff

That there exists in the common law a principle of necessity which may justify action which would otherwise be unlawful is not in doubt. But historically the principle has been seen to be restricted to two groups of cases, which have been called cases of public necessity and cases of private necessity. The former occurred when a man interfered with another man's property in the public interest – for example (in the days before we could dial 999 for the fire brigade) the destruction of another man's house to prevent the spread of a catastrophic fire, as indeed occurred in the Great

> Fire of London in 1666. The latter cases occurred when a man interfered with another's property to save his own person or property from imminent danger – for example, when he entered upon his neighbour's land without his consent, in order to prevent the spread of fire onto his own land.
>
> There is, however, a third group of cases, which is also properly described as founded upon the principle of necessity and which is more pertinent to the resolution of the problem in the present case. These cases are concerned with action taken as a matter of necessity to assist another person without his consent. To give a simple example, a man who seizes another and forcibly drags him from the path of an oncoming vehicle, thereby saving him from injury or even death, commits no wrong. But there are many emanations of this principle, to be found scattered through the books. These are concerned not only with the preservation of the life or health of the assisted person, but also with the preservation of his property (sometimes an animal, sometimes an ordinary chattel) and even to certain conduct on his behalf in the administration of his affairs.
>
> [...]
>
> [W]hen a person is rendered incapable of communication either permanently or over a considerable period of time (through illness or accident or mental disorder), it would be an unusual use of language to describe the case as one of "permanent emergency" – if indeed such a state of affairs can properly be said to exist. In truth, the relevance of an emergency is that it may give rise to a necessity to act in the interests of the assisted person, without first obtaining his consent. Emergency is however not the criterion or even a pre-requisite; it is simply a frequent origin of the necessity which impels intervention. The principle is one of necessity, not of emergency.
>
> [...]
>
> [T]he basic requirements, applicable in these cases of necessity, [are] that, to fall within the principle, not only (1) must there be a necessity to act when it is not practicable to communicate with the assisted person, but also (2) the action taken must be such as a reasonable person would in all the circumstances take, acting in the best interests of the assisted person.

Having recognised a defence of necessity in *Re F*, nine years later the House of Lords confirmed the existence of the defence in *R* v *Bournewood Community and Mental Health NHS Trust* [1999] 1 AC 458. In this case a mentally incompetent patient, L, was informally admitted, detained and treated without invoking the procedure set out in the Mental Health Act 1983. The House of Lords unanimously agreed that this was justified by necessity. Lord Goff stated that 'all the steps in fact taken [...] were in fact taken in the best interests of L and, in so far as they might otherwise have constituted an invasion of his civil rights, were justified on the basis of the common law doctrine of necessity'. This made it clear that a defence of necessity does exist.

2. Is necessity available as a defence to murder?

Our starting point here is the famous case *R* v *Dudley and Stephens* (1884–85) LR 14 QBD 273.[2] The two defendants, the 17-year-old victim and a fourth man were cast away in an open boat 1,600 miles from land after their yacht, the *Mignonette*, sank. The only food they had was two tins of turnips. On their sixteenth day adrift (having had no food for

[2] For more information on the case, see Simpson, A.W.B. (1984) *Cannibalism and the Common Law*. University of Chicago Press: Chicago.

eight days and no water for six days) the two defendants killed the victim. They fed upon his body and blood for the following four days until (on their twentieth day adrift) they were picked up by a passing vessel. The boy was weak and unable to resist, but did not agree to being killed.

The jury found that the following were fact:

- If the men had not fed upon the boy they probably would not have survived the four days.
- The boy was likely to die first.
- At the time of the killing there was no reasonable prospect of relief.
- It appeared to the defendants that they would die of starvation unless one of the castaways was killed.
- There was no appreciable chance of saving life except by killing.

The sole issue in the case was whether the defendants could rely on a defence of necessity. The Court held that they could not.

EXTRACT

Read the following extract from the judgment of Lord Coleridge CJ.

List the reasons he gives for not allowing Dudley and Stephens to plead necessity.

R v *Dudley and Stephens* (1884–85) LR 14 QBD 273

Lord Coleridge CJ

Now it is admitted that the deliberate killing of this unoffending and unresisting boy was clearly murder, unless the killing can be justified by some well-recognised excuse admitted by the law. It is further admitted that there was in this case no such excuse, unless the killing was justified by what has been called "necessity." But the temptation to the act which existed here was not what the law has ever called necessity. Nor is this to be regretted. Though law and morality are not the same, and many things may be immoral which are not necessarily illegal, yet the absolute divorce of law from morality would be of fatal consequence; and such divorce would follow if the temptation to murder in this case were to be held by law an absolute defence of it. It is not so.

[...]

It is not needful to point out the awful danger of admitting the principle which has been contended for. Who is to be the judge of this sort of necessity? By what measure is the comparative value of lives to be measured? Is it to be strength, or intellect, or what? It is plain that the principle leaves to him who is to profit by it to determine the necessity which will justify him in deliberately taking another's life to save his own. In this case the weakest, the youngest, the most unresisting, was chosen. Was it more necessary to kill him than one of the grown men? The answer must be "No"

(Being guilty of murder, the defendants were initially sentenced to death. However, their sentences were later commuted to six months' imprisonment.)

There has been some debate as to the *ratio decidendi* of *Dudley and Stephens*. Some have argued that the correct interpretation of the case is that necessity is *never* available as a defence to murder. As we'll see later in the chapter, this was how the House of Lords appeared to interpret *Dudley and Stephens* in their decision in *R* v *Howe* [1987] AC 417. The issue in *R* v *Howe* was whether duress should be available as a defence to murder. Their Lordships held that it should not be. One of the reasons they gave was that, since the court in *Dudley and Stephens* had held that necessity is never a defence to murder, duress should not be a defence to murder either. For example, Lord Mackay in *R* v *Howe* stated:

> [F]or this House now to allow the defence of duress generally in response to a charge of murder would be to effect an important and substantial change in the law. In my opinion too, it would involve a departure from the decision in the famous case of *Reg.* v. *Dudley and Stephens*.

But Lord Mackay's statement rests upon a particular interpretation of *Dudley and Stephens*. There are others who have argued that *Dudley and Stephens* should be interpreted more narrowly. They argue that, whilst necessity will not normally be available as a defence to murder, there are some, limited, circumstances in which it may still apply.

One possible example can be found in Joe Simpson's book *Touching the Void* (which has also been made into a film). This book tells the story of Simpson's attempt to climb the 6344-metre Siula Grande in the Peruvian Andes with his friend Simon Yates.

On the descent Simpson slipped down an ice cliff, landed awkwardly, and broke his right leg. With bad weather closing in they needed to descend quickly to the glacier below. They tied themselves together, and Yates then began to lower Simpson down the mountain a bit at a time. As the storm conditions worsened and the daylight faded, Yates inadvertently lowered Simpson off a cliff. The pair were stuck. Simpson could not climb back up the rope, and Yates could not pull him up. They remained in this position for some time, until it became obvious that they were both going to be pulled to their deaths. Yates had no choice but to cut the rope.

Miraculously, Simpson survived. (He fell 50 metres into a deep crevasse. After regaining consciousness he managed to climb out, and over the next three days hopped and crawled the eight kilometres back to base camp.) But suppose Simpson had not been so fortunate. Suppose after Yates had cut the rope Simpson had fallen to his death. Would Yates have been guilty of murder?

Now, think about this scenario.

Suppose Yates has been charged with murder, and you are his defence lawyer. Yates was a factual and legal cause of Simpson's death (see the discussion of causation in Chapter 3), but you wish to argue that he lacked the *mens rea* of murder.

- Produce a brief skeleton argument which explains why Yates should be found not to have intended to kill, or cause serious harm to, Simpson.

Your alternative submission is that Yates has a defence of necessity. For this argument to succeed, you need to be able to distinguish *Dudley and Stephens*.

- Produce a brief skeleton argument which explains why Yates' situation is distinguishable from *Dudley and Stephens*.

In *Re A (Children) (Conjoined Twins: Surgical Separation)* [2001] Fam 147 Brooke LJ discussed a similar example. This was also a true story. On the night of 6 March 1987, shortly after leaving the Belgian port of Zeebrugge, the car and passenger ferry the *Herald of Free Enterprise* capsized. In total 193 people died.

EXTRACT

Read the following extract from Brooke LJ's judgment, which describes the incident which occurred during the Zeebrugge disaster.

Look at the reasons you gave for distinguishing Simon Yates' case from *Dudley and Stephens*, and then compare these to Brooke LJ's reasons (taken from a lecture given by Sir John Smith) for distinguishing the army corporal's actions from *Dudley and Stephens*. Did you manage to come up with the same arguments?

Re A (Children) (Conjoined Twins: Surgical Separation) [2001] Fam 147

Brooke LJ

At the coroner's inquest conducted in October 1987 into the Zeebrugge disaster, an army corporal gave evidence that he and dozens of other people were near the foot of a rope ladder. They were all in the water and in danger of drowning. Their route to safety, however, was blocked for at least ten minutes by a young man who was petrified by cold or fear (or both) and was unable to move up or down. Eventually the corporal gave instructions that the man should be pushed off the ladder, and he was never seen again. The corporal and many others were then able to climb up the ladder to safety.

In his third lecture, "Necessity and Duress" [part of the 1989 Hamlyn Lecture series, published under the title "Justification and Excuse in the Criminal Law"], Professor Smith evinced the belief, at pp 77–78, that if such a case ever did come to court it would not be too difficult for a judge to distinguish *R* v *Dudley and Stephens* 14 QBD 273. He gave two reasons for this belief. The first was that there was no question of choosing who had to die, the problem which Lord Coleridge CJ had found unanswerable in *R* v *Dudley and Stephens*, at p 287, because the unfortunate young man on the ladder had chosen himself by his immobility there. The second was that, unlike the ship's boy on the *Mignonette*, the young man, although in no way at fault, was preventing others from going where they had a right, and a most urgent need, to go, and was thereby unwittingly imperiling their lives.

I would add that the same considerations would apply if a pilotless aircraft, out of control and running out of fuel, was heading for a densely populated town. Those inside the aircraft were in any event "destined to die". There would be no question of human choice in selecting the candidates for death, and if their inevitable deaths were accelerated by the plane being brought down on waste ground the lives of countless other innocent people in the town they were approaching would be saved.

So, according to Brooke LJ, the *ratio decidendi of Dudley and Stephens* is not that necessity is never a defence to murder. In *Dudley and Stephens* any one of the four onboard the lifeboat could have been sacrificed in order to give the others a better chance of survival. Dudley and Stephens exercised some degree of selection. They decided that the victim should die in order to improve their own chances. To allow necessity as a defence in situations like this would open the door to all sorts of difficult questions. As Lord Coleridge CJ asked, 'Who is to be the judge of this sort of necessity? By what measure is the comparative value of lives to be measured?'

By contrast, neither of our two examples involved an element of selection. Yates did not choose between Simpson and himself. Simpson was self-selecting by virtue of the fact that he was hanging off the cliff. Similarly, the young man on the rope ladder was self-selecting by virtue of the fact that he was blocking the only escape route. In situations like these, where the defendant does not exercise any element of selection, there is a strong argument for saying that necessity should be available as a defence to murder.

It was on this basis that Brooke LJ held that the doctors separating the conjoined twins Jodie and Mary would not be committing murder.[3]

EXTRACT

Re A (Children) (Conjoined Twins: Surgical Separation) [2001] Fam 147

Brooke LJ

I have considered very carefully the policy reasons for the decision in *R* v *Dudley and Stephens* 14 QBD 273 supported as it was by the House of Lords in *R* v *Howe* [1987] AC 417. These are, in short, that there were two insuperable objections to the proposition that necessity might be available as a defence for the *Mignonette* sailors. The first objection was evident in the court's questions: who is to be the judge of this sort of necessity? By what measure is the comparative value of lives to be measured? The second objection was that to permit such a defence would mark an absolute divorce of law from morality. In my judgment, neither of these objections are dispositive of the present case. Mary is, sadly, self-designated for a very early death. Nobody can extend her life beyond a very short span. Because her heart, brain and lungs are for all practical purposes useless, nobody would have even tried to extend her life artificially if she had not, fortuitously, been deriving oxygenated blood from her sister's bloodstream.

It is true that there are those who believe most sincerely – and the Archbishop of Westminster is among them – that it would be an immoral act to save Jodie, if by saving Jodie one must end Mary's life before its brief allotted span is complete [...] But there are also those who believe with equal sincerity that it would be immoral not to assist Jodie if there is a good prospect that she might live a happy and fulfilled life if this operation is performed. The court is not equipped to choose between these competing philosophies. All that a court can say is that it is not at all obvious that this is the sort of clear-cut case, marking an absolute divorce from law and morality, which was of such concern to Lord Coleridge CJ and his fellow judges.

In the case of the conjoined twins, there was no element of selection. The doctors were not selecting whether to save Jodie or Mary. Sadly, Mary was 'self-designated' for death. The choice was whether both twins should die, or whether Jodie should be given a chance of survival.

[3] We examined the facts of this case in Chapter 4.

The principle from this case was summarised succinctly by Sir John Smith ([2001] Crim LR 400, 405):

> Where A is, as the defendant knows, doomed to die in the near future but even the short continuation of his life will inevitably kill B as well, it is lawful to kill A, however free of fault he may be.

Whilst it is possible to distinguish the *Conjoined Twins* case from *Dudley and Stephens*, Brooke LJ's judgment has been criticised. Whilst Mary may have been 'self-designated' for death, if the twins had not been separated Mary still had up to a few months of life left. The upshot of Brooke LJ's reasoning, therefore, was that denying Mary of these months of life was a lesser evil than denying Jodie a chance of survival. It has been suggested that such an approach opens the door to utilitarian assessments of the relative value of lives.[4]

Think about this scenario.

Jodie is desperately ill. Unless she receives a heart transplant within a week she will die. Meanwhile, another patient in the same hospital, Mary, is terminally ill with only three weeks left to live. However, Mary's heart is healthy. Suppose that a doctor killed Mary, so that Jodie could receive Mary's heart and be saved.

- Applying Brooke LJ's approach, would the doc be able to plead necessity as a defence to murder?
- How (if at all) is this case distinguishable from the *Conjoined Twins* case?

Critics of Brooke LJ's judgment argue that the approach of Ward LJ, which we study later in the chapter, is a better way to justify separating the conjoining twins.

Finally, before moving on, it is worth noting the decision of the Supreme Court in *R (on the application of Nicklinson)* v *Ministry of Justice* [2014] UKSC 38. Tony Nicklinson suffered from locked-in syndrome. He was left paralysed after suffering a stroke in June 2005. He wanted to die but was unable to end his own life without assistance. He sought a declaration that necessity would be available as a defence to anyone who assisted him to commit suicide or committed euthanasia. In its judgment the Court of Appeal held that the defence of necessity would not apply, stating that there is an important difference between killing a person in order to save the life of another (as in *Re A (Children) (Conjoined Twins: Surgical Separation)*) and killing a person because that person wishes their life to end. Only Parliament could extend the defence of necessity to cases of assisted suicide and euthanasia.[5] Although the issue was not pursued before the Supreme Court, Lord Neuberger indicated his agreement with the Court of Appeal's decision ([130]).

3. The test for the defence of necessity

Whilst the *Re F* and *Bournewood Trust* cases clarified that a defence of necessity does exist, neither case told us very much about the conditions which must be present for the defence to apply. So, what test should be used to determine whether a defendant may plead necessity?

---

[4] Michalowski, S. (2002) 'Sanctity of Life – Are Some Lives More Sacred Than Others?' 22 *Legal Studies* 377.

[5] *R (on the application of Nicklinson)* v *Ministry of Justice* [2013] EWCA Civ 961.

In the *Conjoined Twins* case Brooke LJ employed the following three-part test, which had originally been set out by the jurist Sir James Stephen in the late nineteenth century:

> According to Sir James Stephen there are three necessary requirements for the application of the doctrine of necessity: (i) the act is needed to avoid inevitable and irreparable evil; (ii) no more should be done than is reasonably necessary for the purpose to be achieved; (iii) the evil inflicted must not be disproportionate to the evil avoided.

However, this test is problematic, for it is too broad in scope.

Think about this scenario.

Trevor grabs hold of Derek and says, 'Go and kill Victor. Otherwise I'll kill you.' Petrified, Derek kills Victor.

- Does Derek satisfy the three parts of the test approved by Brooke LJ?

At the very beginning of our examination of necessity, we saw that the defence is designed for situations in which the commission of the crime is the lesser of two evils. In this example it is difficult to argue that Victor's death is a lesser evil than Derek's death, because this would seem to involve comparing the value of two people's lives. In other words, it should not be possible for Derek to argue that it was necessary to kill Victor in order to save himself, just as it was not possible for Dudley and Stephens to argue that it was necessary to kill their victim in order to save themselves. Yet both Derek and Dudley and Stephens seem to satisfy Brooke LJ's three-part test. This demonstrates that the test is over-inclusive

So where does this leave us? Given the historic uncertainty over the defence of necessity, and the lack of any agreed-upon test, the only way forward seems to be to allow the defence to develop on a case-by-case basis.

Quiz 11.1

1. Which one of the following is an accurate description of the defence of necessity?

- **a.** Necessity is only available as a partial defence in homicide cases.
- **b.** D is compelled to perform an act that would otherwise be a crime and is excused because his actions were not freely chosen.
- **c.** D chooses to commit a crime in order to prevent something even worse from happening.
- **d.** D had no control over his actions and so was not responsible for what occurred.

2. Which of the following statements is the most accurate?

- **a.** The existence of a general defence of necessity has been clear since the mid-nineteenth century.
- **b.** There is no defence of necessity in English law.
- **c.** Necessity is available as a defence in cases of euthanasia.
- **d.** The courts have recognised a general defence of necessity in certain circumstances.

3. The judgment in the case of *R* v *Dudley and Stephens* has sometimes been interpreted as saying…

- **a.** necessity can only arise in emergency type situations.
- **b.** necessity is not a defence to any crime.
- **c.** necessity is not available as a defence to murder in some circumstances.
- **d.** necessity is a defence only to manslaughter.

4. Which of the following did not form part of Brooke LJ's reasoning in the case of *Re A (Children) (Conjoined Twins: Surgical Separation)* [2001] Fam 147?
   a. The defendants in *R v Dudley and Stephens* had exercised an element in selection in deciding who should die to give the others a chance of survival.
   b. Jodie's chance of survival and living a normal life should be given greater weight than Mary's remaining few months of life.
   c. Allowing the twins to be separated did not mark an absolute divorce of law from morality.
   d. It was impossible to save Mary; she was self-designated for death.
5. What was Lord Neuberger's view on extending the *Re A (Children) (Conjoined Twins: Surgical Separation)* case to assisting suicide in *R (on the application of Nicklinson) v Ministry of Justice*?
   a. He agreed with the Court of Appeal, who had distinguished between assisting a person unable to assist themselves to commit suicide and killing a person destined to die in order to save the life of another and refused to extend the defence to cover the former.
   b. He agreed with the Court of Appeal, who had distinguished between assisting a person unable to assist themselves to commit suicide and killing a person destined to die in order to save the life of another and refused to extend the defence to cover the latter.
   c. He expressed the view that *Re A (Children) (Conjoined Twins: Surgical Separation)* had been wrongly decided and so the question of extending the defence did not arise.
   d. He thought that this was something the judges could do without reference to Parliament.
6. In which one of the following situations is D most likely to have a defence of necessity?
   a. D loses his way during an outdoor hike in a remote place and does not have any means of communication. Night draws in and it becomes cold. D breaks into an empty house that he happens upon, causing damage to it in the process, and spends the night there.
   b. D's wife falls pregnant with what would be their eighth child. D is already having a very hard time providing financially for his wife and existing children and knows that all of them will suffer if his resources have to be stretched to provide for yet another individual. Neither D nor his wife wants the extra child, so D repeatedly punches his wife in her stomach until she miscarries.
   c. D is a speluncean (cave) explorer and is in company with eleven other explorers. A sudden rock collapse separates two members of the group from the rest and prevents all of them from being able to progress further into the caves or retreat from them. All are stuck. D, one of the ten, realises that by setting explosives in one part of the cave a new path of escape can be made for the ten, but in doing so the two trapped explorers will be killed. D causes the explosion and the predicted outcomes occur.
   d. D is carefully driving along a country road when he rounds a corner and sees a herd of stampeding bulls coming his way and entirely blocking the width of the road. D reverses his car at great speed along the carriageway in which he had been travelling. A speed camera captures an image of his reckless and excessive speed.

Duress

11.2 Define the requirements for establishing the substantive defences of duress by threats and duress of circumstances.

Armed with a baseball bat Trevor walks up to Derek and says, 'I'm going to beat you up unless you go and beat up Victor'. As we've seen, if Derek beats up Victor he will not be able to plead necessity because it is not possible to say that Victor suffering serious harm is a lesser evil than Derek suffering serious harm. But all is not lost for Derek. He may instead be able to plead duress.

The defence of duress applies where a defendant commits a crime in order to avoid an immediate threat of death or serious harm. The following extract, taken from the judgment of Lord Widgery CJ in *R v Hudson* and *Taylor* [1971] 2 QB 202, explains the rationale for the defence:

EXTRACT

Using this extract, explain the reasons for allowing Derek (in our example above) a defence of duress.

R v Hudson and Taylor [1971] 2 QB 202

Lord Widgery CJ

[D]uress provides a defence [...] if the will of the accused has been overborne by threats of death or serious personal injury so that the commission of the alleged offence was no longer the voluntary act of the accused [...] It is essential to the defence of duress that the threat shall be effective at the moment when the crime is committed. The threat must be a 'present' threat in the sense that it is effective to neutralise the will of the accused at that time

However, the defence of duress also raises important policy considerations. As Lord Bingham explains in the following extract from *R* v *Hasan* [2005] UKHL 22, these policy considerations require that the courts take a strict approach towards the test for the defence:

> [T]he defence of duress is peculiarly difficult for the prosecution to investigate and disprove beyond reasonable doubt [...] The prosecution's difficulty is of course the greater when, as is all too often the case, little detail of the alleged compulsion is vouchsafed by the defence until the trial is under way [...] I must acknowledge that [these features of duress] incline me, where policy choices are to be made, towards tightening rather than relaxing the conditions to be met before duress may be successfully relied on.

As we work our way through the defence we will see examples of this tension between, on the one hand, the principle that a defendant should not be held responsible for behaviour that was not freely chosen and, on the other hand, the concern that the defence should be carefully circumscribed.

We begin by distinguishing two types of duress – duress by threats and duress of circumstances. We will then work through the two-limbed test that is used for the defence, before examining the position where a defendant voluntarily exposed himself to the threat, why the courts have held that duress is not available as a defence to murder and, finally, the relationship between duress of circumstances and necessity.

1. The distinction between duress by threats and duress of circumstances

So for duress to apply there must be an immediate threat of death or serious harm. When there is an express threat – such as when Trevor says 'I'm going to beat you up unless you go and beat up Victor' – the relevant type of duress is duress by threats. When there has been no expressly made threat, and the threat emanates instead from the situation the defendant finds himself in, the relevant type of duress is duress of circumstances. An example would be Lord Denning's hypothetical fireman, mentioned earlier. He jumped the red light because there was an immediate threat of death to the man trapped in the burning building.

Sometimes it can be difficult to distinguish between duress by threats and duress of circumstances.[6] In practice, however, the distinction between these defences does not matter since the same rules govern both. This was made clear by Woolf LJ in *R* v *Conway* [1989] QB 290 (the case which first recognised the existence of duress of circumstances).[7] So whether the threat of death or serious harm emanates from an expressly made threat or the situation the defendant finds himself in, the same test applies.

2. The test for duress

The test for duress was set out by the Court of Appeal in *R* v *Graham* [1982] 1 WLR 294 and was subsequently confirmed by the House of Lords in *R* v *Howe* [1987] AC 417. The test is as follows:

> (1) Was the defendant, or may he have been, impelled to act as he did because, as a result of what he reasonably believed [T] had said or done, he had good cause to fear that if he did not so act [T] would kill him or [...] cause him serious physical injury?
> (2) If so, have the prosecution made the jury sure that a sober person of reasonable firmness, sharing the characteristics of the defendant, would not have responded to whatever he reasonably believed [T] said or did by taking part in the killing?

(For cases involving duress of circumstances the test is simply amended to refer to the 'situation' instead of what 'T had said or done': see *R* v *Martin* [1989] 1 All ER 652.)

For convenience, we'll label the first part of this test the subjective limb and the second part the objective limb.

i. The subjective limb

So the subjective limb asks whether D may have been impelled to act as he did because, as a result of what he reasonably believed T had said or done, he had good cause to fear that if he did not so act T would kill him or cause him serious physical injury.

The subjective limb ... but with an objective streak

I've labelled this part of the test the 'subjective' limb because it focuses on whether the defendant reasonably *believed* he faced an immediate threat of death or serious physical injury. What someone believed is obviously subjective. But don't be fooled by the label. Although it's the subjective limb, this part of the test does still require some objective assessment. First, the defendant's belief must have been 'reasonable'. And second, as a result of what he reasonably believed, the defendant must have had 'good cause' to fear death or serious harm.

In the early 2000s some Court of Appeal decisions questioned the requirement that the defendant's belief must have been reasonable.[8] But in *R* v *Hasan* Lord Bingham rejected these suggestions. In keeping with his insistence that the defence of duress should be carefully circumscribed, he stated:

[6] To illustrate how fine the distinction can be, compare the following two scenarios: (1) D, who is banned from driving, is told by a menacing gang, 'Drive this car or we'll kill you' (duress by threats); and (2) D sees the gang running towards him with shouts of 'kill him', and the only way he can escape is by driving the car (duress of circumstances) (Ormerod, D. and Laird, K. (2014) *Smith and Hogan's Text, Cases, and Materials on Criminal Law* (11th edn). OUP: Oxford, p.358).

[7] He stated: 'What is important is that, whatever it is called, [duress of circumstances] is subject to the same limitations as the "do this or else" species of duress.'

[8] *R* v *David Paul Martin* [2000] 2 Cr App R 42; *R* v *Safi* [2003] EWCA Crim 1809.

It is of course essential that the defendant should genuinely, i.e. actually, believe in the efficacy of the threat by which he claims to have been compelled. But there is no warrant for relaxing the requirement that the belief must be reasonable as well as genuine.

ACTIVITY

Which one of the following three defendants could satisfy the subjective limb of the test for duress?

- T tells D3 that he will kill him unless he smashes up V's greenhouse. An ordinary, reasonable person in D3's situation would have had good cause to fear T's threat, but D3 dismisses it as nonsense.
- As a result of a misunderstanding, D1 believes T has threatened to kill him unless he smashes V's car windows. In fact, T did not threaten D1, and D1's mistake was unreasonable.
- D2 has made a mistake. He believes T is going to kill him unless he smashes up V's laptop. An ordinary, reasonable person in D2's situation would have made the same mistake.

A threat of death or serious physical injury

This is another example of the courts' strict approach to the defence of duress. The threat must have been of death or serious physical injury. Nothing else will suffice. So, whilst the Court of Appeal has stated, obiter, that a threat of rape amounts to a threat of serious physical injury,[9] it has rejected the argument that duress should be available where the defendant feared serious psychological harm,[10] and it has stated that a threat of false imprisonment will not suffice.[11]

In *R* v *Quayle* [2005] EWCA Crim 1415 the three defendants had been charged with offences under the Misuse of Drugs Act 1971. They had each been growing cannabis. It was for their own personal use, in order to alleviate serious levels of pain. One of the issues the Court of Appeal had to consider was whether the subjective limb of the test for duress should be broadened to encompass not just serious physical injury, but also serious levels of pain.

EXTRACT

In the following extract, what reasons does Mance LJ give for refusing to broaden the subjective limb?

R v *Quayle* [2005] EWCA Crim 1415

Mance LJ

There is, on any view, a large element of subjectivity in the assessment of pain not directly associated with some current physical injury. The legal defences of duress by threats and [duress] by circumstances should in our view be confined to cases where there is an imminent danger of physical injury. In reaching these conclusions, we recognise that hard cases can be postulated, but these, as Lord Bingham said, can and should commonly be capable of being dealt with in other ways. The nature of the sentences passed in the cases before us is consistent with this.

---

9 *R* v *A* [2012] EWCA Crim 434.

10 *R* v *Baker* [1997] Crim LR 497.

11 *R* v *Joseph* [2017] EWCA Crim 36.

Now, think about these questions.

Think back to Lord Denning's hypothetical fireman.

- If the burning building had been empty, but the fireman had jumped the red light in order to stop the fire from spreading to neighbouring buildings, would the fireman be able to plead duress of circumstances?
- In your opinion, should he be able to?

A threat of death or serious physical injury to anyone

In many cases – like our original example ('I'm going to beat you up unless you go and beat up Victor') – the threat will be made against the defendant. But the defence may still apply where the threat is made against someone else. This is entirely appropriate. A threat to kill or seriously injure the defendant's spouse or children may be just as (if not even more) compelling.

What if the threat is made against someone the defendant has never met before? May the defence still apply? In *R* v *Hasan* Lord Bingham addressed this question, and stated:

> the threat must be directed, if not to the defendant or a member of his immediate family, to a person for whose safety the defendant would reasonably regard himself as responsible.

It is important to point out that the defendant's sense of responsibility for the other person may stem from the threat itself. This was confirmed by Lord Woolf CJ in *R* v *Shayler* [2001] EWCA Crim 1977:

> the evil must be directed towards the defendant or a person or persons for whom he has responsibility or, we would add, persons for whom the situation makes him responsible [... For example] the situation where the threat is made to set off a bomb unless the defendant performs the unlawful act. The defendant may have not have had any previous connection with those who would be injured by the bomb but the threat itself creates the defendant's responsibility for those who will be at risk if he does not give way to the threat.

Now, think about this scenario.

An armed robber walks into a bank, points a gun at a customer, and says to the cashier, 'Hand over the money or I'll shoot this customer'. The cashier hands over the money.

- Suppose the cashier was charged with assisting the robbery. Could she plead duress, even though the customer the robber threatened to kill was a man she had never met before?

The threat must have been unavoidable and immediate (or almost immediate)

We began our study of duress by noting the tension between, on the one hand, the principle that a defendant should be excused from criminal liability if he was compelled to act by a threat of death or serious physical injury, and, on the other hand, the concern that the defence should be carefully circumscribed. Nowhere is this tension more apparent than the case law on the unavoidability and immediacy of the threat.

Our starting point is the Court of Appeal's decision in *R* v *Hudson and Taylor* [1971] 2 QB 202. A man called Wright was on trial for wounding. Hudson, aged 17, and Taylor, aged 19, were the principal witnesses for the prosecution. In the build-up to Wright's trial Hudson was approached by a group of men which included a man called Farrell, who had a reputation for violence. Farrell warned Hudson that if she 'told on Wright in court' they would 'cut her up'. Hudson passed this warning on to Taylor. Afraid of what might happen to them if they testified against Wright, they both decided to lie. This decision was confirmed when they arrived at court to give evidence and saw Farrell sitting in the public gallery. When giving evidence both Hudson and Taylor denied knowing Wright and, as a result, he was acquitted. In due course Hudson and Taylor were charged with perjury. At their trial the judge told the jury that Hudson and Taylor could not plead duress because the threat made by Farrell was not a 'present immediate threat capable of being then and there carried out'. They appealed, arguing that this was a misdirection.

EXTRACT

Read the following extract from the judgment of Lord Widgery CJ.

According to Lord Widgery CJ,was the trial judge's ruling that Farrell's threat was insufficiently immediate correct? How did Lord Widgery CJ suggest we should test whether a threat is sufficiently imminent for the defence of duress?

It was also suggested that Hudson and Taylor should not be permitted to plead duress because the threat they faced was avoidable. Outline this argument. Why did Lord Widgery CJ reject it?

R v *Hudson and Taylor* [1971] 2 QB 202

Lord Widgery CJ

This appeal raises two main questions; first, as to the nature of the necessary threat and, in particular, whether it must be "present and immediate"; secondly, as to the extent to which a right to plead duress may be lost if the accused has failed to take steps to remove the threat as, for example, by seeking police protection.

It is essential to the defence of duress that the threat shall be effective at the moment when the crime is committed. The threat must be a "present" threat in the sense that it is effective to neutralise the will of the accused at that time. Hence an accused who joins a rebellion under the compulsion of threats cannot plead duress if he remains with the rebels after the threats have lost their effect and his own will has had a chance to re-assert itself: *Rex* v. *M'Growther* (1746) Fost. 13; *Attorney-General* v. *Whelan* [1934] I.R. 518. Similarly a threat of future violence may be so remote as to be insufficient to overpower the will at that moment when the offence was committed, or the accused may have elected to commit the offence in order to rid himself of a threat hanging over him and not because he was driven to act by immediate and unavoidable pressure. In none of these cases is the defence of duress available because a person cannot justify the commission of a crime merely to secure his own peace of mind.

When, however, there is no opportunity for delaying tactics, and the person threatened must make up his mind whether he is to commit the criminal act or not, the existence at that moment of threats sufficient to destroy his will ought to provide him with a defence even though the threatened injury may not follow instantly, but after an interval [...] In the present case the threats of Farrell were likely to be no less compelling, because their execution could not be effected in the court room, if they could be carried out in the streets of Salford the same night. In so far, therefore, as the recorder ruled as a matter of law that the threats were not sufficiently present and immediate to support the defence of duress we think that he was in error. He should have left the jury to decide whether the threats had overborne the will of the appellants at the time when they gave the false evidence.

Mr. Franks, however contends that the recorder's ruling can be supported on another ground, namely, that the appellants should have taken steps to neutralise the threats by seeking police protection either when they came to court to give evidence, or beforehand. He submits on grounds of public policy that an accused should not be able to plead duress if he had the opportunity to ask for protection from the police before committing the offence and failed to do so. The argument does not distinguish cases in which the police would be able to provide effective protection, from those when they would not, and it would, in effect, restrict the defence of duress to cases where the person threatened had been kept in custody by the maker of the threats, or where the time interval between the making of the threats and the commission of the offence had made recourse to the police impossible. We recognise the need to keep the defence of duress within reasonable bounds but cannot accept so severe a restriction upon it. The duty, of the person threatened, to take steps to remove the threat does not seem to have arisen in an English case but, in a full review of the defence of duress in the Supreme Court of Victoria (*Reg.* v. *Harley and Murray* [1967] V.R. 526), a condition of raising the defence was said to be that the accused "had no means, with safety to himself, of preventing the execution of the threat."

In the opinion of this court it is always open to the Crown to prove that the accused failed to avail himself of some opportunity which was reasonably open to him to render the threat ineffective, and that upon this being established the threat in question can no longer be relied upon by the defence. In deciding whether such an opportunity was reasonably open to the accused the jury should have regard to his age and circumstances, and to any risks to him which may be involved in the course of action relied upon.

In our judgment the defence of duress should have been left to the jury in the present case, as should any issue raised by the Crown and arising out of the appellants' failure to seek police protection. The appeals will, therefore, be allowed and the convictions quashed.

The immediacy of the threat was also the principal issue in *R* v *Abdul-Hussain* [1999] Crim LR 570. The defendants in this case were Shiite Muslims from southern Iraq. They had fled Iraq to live in Sudan. Fearing that the Sudanese authorities would deport them back to Iraq, where they faced being tortured and killed, they hijacked a plane bound for Jordan and forced it to fly to England. At their subsequent trial for hijacking they pleaded duress.

In this case the threat was less immediate than in *R* v *Hudson and Taylor*. The trial judge pointed out that the threat depended on a number of 'contingent and consequential steps'. First, the defendants would have had to have been detected in Sudan. Second, the Sudanese authorities would have had to decide to arrest them. Third, having arrested them, the Sudanese authorities would have had to decide to deport them. And fourth, they would have had to have actually been deported. The trial judge said that the defence of duress requires the presence of a threat 'so close and immediate as will give rise to what is virtually a spontaneous reaction to the physical risk arising'. He accordingly withdrew the defence of duress from the jury. The defendants appealed against this ruling. The Court of Appeal held that the trial judge had been wrong to withdraw the defence of duress from the jury's consideration. The Court said that for duress to be available the threat must have been 'imminent', but need not have been 'immediate'. In this case the threat was an imminent one because it was hanging over the defendants when they hijacked the aircraft. The Court gave the following illustration in support of its reasoning:

> If Anne Frank had stolen a car to escape from Amsterdam and been charged with theft, the tenets of English law would not, in our judgment, have denied her a defence of duress of circumstances, on the ground that she should have waited for the Gestapo's knock on the door.

The reasoning in *R* v *Hudson* and Taylor and *R* v *Abdul Hussain* was criticised by Lord Bingham in *R* v *Hasan*. Stressing the policy concern that there should be strict limits on the defence of duress, Lord Bingham opined that in both cases there had been an unacceptable relaxation of the requirements that the threat must have been both immediate and unavoidable.

EXTRACT

According to Lord Bingham, was the threat the defendants faced in *R* v *Hudson* and *Taylor* unavoidable? Why/why not?

Notice that Lord Bingham's restatement of the immediacy requirement does qualify it slightly – he says the threat must have been immediate or 'almost' immediate. Is this of much practical significance?

R v *Hasan* [2005] UKHL 22

Lord Bingham

26. The recent English authorities have tended to lay stress on the requirement that a defendant should not have been able, without reasonably fearing execution of the threat, to avoid compliance. Thus Lord Morris of Borth-y-Gest in *Director of Public Prosecutions for Northern Ireland* v *Lynch* [1975] AC 653, 670, emphasised that duress

> "must never be allowed to be the easy answer of those who can devise no other explanation of their conduct nor of those who readily could have avoided the dominance of threats nor of those who allow themselves to be at the disposal and under the sway of some gangster-tyrant."

Lord Simon of Glaisdale, at p 687, gave as his first example of a situation in which a defence of duress should be available: "A person, honestly and reasonably believing that a loaded pistol is at his back which will in all probability be used if he disobeys ... " In the view of Lord Edmund-Davies, at p 708, there had been "for some years an unquestionable tendency towards progressive latitude in relation to the plea of duress".

> 27. In making that observation Lord Edmund-Davies did not directly criticise the reasoning of the Court of Appeal in its then recent judgment in *R* v *Hudson* [1971] 2 QB 202, but that was described by Professor Glanville Williams, *Textbook of Criminal Law*, 2nd ed (1983), p 636, as "an indulgent decision", and it has in my opinion had the unfortunate effect of weakening the requirement that execution of a threat must be reasonably believed to be imminent and immediate if it is to support a plea of duress [...] I can understand that the Court of Appeal in *R* v *Hudson* had sympathy with the predicament of the young appellants but I cannot, consistently with principle, accept that a witness testifying in the Crown Court at Manchester has no opportunity to avoid complying with a threat incapable of execution then or there. When considering necessity in *R* v *Cole* [1994] Crim LR 582, 583, Simon Brown LJ, giving the judgment of the court, held that the peril relied on to support the plea of necessity lacked imminence and the degree of directness and immediacy required of the link between the suggested peril and the offence charged, but in *R* v *Abdul-Hussain* [1999] Crim LR 570 the Court of Appeal declined to follow these observations to the extent that they were inconsistent with *R* v *Hudson*, by which the court regarded itself as bound.
>
> 28 [...] It should [...] be made clear to juries that if the retribution threatened against the defendant or his family or a person for whom he reasonably feels responsible is not such as he reasonably expects to follow immediately or almost immediately on his failure to comply with the threat, there may be little if any room for doubt that he could have taken evasive action, whether by going to the police or in some other way, to avoid committing the crime with which he is charged.

Since three of the other four Law Lords in *R* v *Hasan* expressly agreed with Lord Bingham's judgment, it seems clear that the approach taken in *R* v *Hudson* and *Taylor* and *R* v *Abdul-Hussain* should no longer be followed. The threat must have been both unavoidable and immediate (or almost immediate).

Indirectly conveyed threats

Suppose a defendant only learns of a threat secondhand. For example, Derek says to Denise, 'Trevor said he will beat us up unless we go and beat up Victor'. If Denise helps Derek attack Victor, should the defence of duress be unavailable to Denise because the threat from Trevor was communicated to her indirectly?

This issue was considered by the Court of Appeal in *R* v *Brandford* [2016] EWCA Crim 1794. The case concerned a drugs line run between London and Portsmouth. The co-defendants, Olivia Brandford and her partner Dean Alford, were in Alford's car when they were stopped by police in Portsmouth. Brandford was found to have concealed cocaine and heroin with a street value of between £1,500 and £2,300 in her vagina. They were charged with conspiring to supply controlled drugs. Brandford sought to rely on the defence of duress. She said that, the day before they were arrested, in London, Alford had told her that he needed to go to Portsmouth to sell drugs. He explained that he had inherited a debt from a friend of his who had been murdered. Alford asked Brandford to help him, saying that his life would be at risk if he lost any of the drugs. At trial, the trial judge ruled that the defence of duress was unavailable because Brandford had no firsthand knowledge of the threat made against Alford. Brandford appealed against her conviction, arguing that the trial judge's ruling was wrong.

EXTRACT

Read the following extract from the judgment of Gross LJ.

Was the trial judge correct to rule that the defence of duress is unavailable in cases where the threat is communicated to the defendant indirectly? Why/why not?

The Court of Appeal nonetheless concluded that 'the circumstances fell well short of the exacting requirements of the defence of duress' ([45]). Why?

R v *Brandford* [2016] EWCA Crim 1794

Gross LJ

39 [...] It is striking that amongst the limits on duress canvassed in the authorities to which we have referred, the indirect relaying of a threat is nowhere mentioned. For our part, we can envisage a situation where a threat is indeed very real, regardless of the fact that it is indirectly relayed. Take a threat made to a hypothetical D and her family by a messenger from an organised crime group, conveying a threat from a "crime boss" or the equivalent passing on of a threat from an emissary of a terrorist group. In our judgment, the question is not whether the threat was directly or indirectly relayed which is of significance, so much as its immediacy, imminence, the possibility of taking evasive action, the question of whether D reasonably believed the threat, his/her response to that threat and questions as to the response of a sober person of reasonable firmness sharing D's characteristics. It is very likely that the more directly a threat is conveyed, the more it will be capable of founding a defence of duress: e.g., the telling example of the loaded pistol in the back, given by Lord Simon of Glaisdale in *Director of Public Prosecutions for Northern Ireland* v *Lynch* [1975] AC 653, at p. 687. Conversely, the more indirectly the threat is relayed the more, all other things being equal, a defendant will struggle to satisfy the requirements of the defence, or (put in burden of proof terms) the more readily the prosecution will disprove it. However, the mere fact that the threat was conveyed indirectly does not seem to us to constitute a fatal bar to the defence. All must depend on the circumstances, of which the manner in which the threat is conveyed is but one, however important it may be ...

46 [...] Even on Brandford's account, there was vagueness in the threat – she was never given the names of those making them. The threats were only ever conveyed indirectly, via Alford. He himself did not threaten her and no one whom she believed was threatening him ever directly threatened her. There was plainly no *immediate* threat on the drive or in London that evening. In London, she was able to go out – on her own – to purchase the latex gloves and other items. Over that night, she watched Alford prepare the drugs. She suggested going to the police but neither she nor Alford acted on this suggestion. She contemplated her father paying off those threatening Alford – thus necessarily accepting that there was an opportunity to contact him. The next day, the 27th August, she and Alford were not under any immediate threat on the drive from London to Portsmouth. They were further able to stop, to enable Alford to dispose of the drugs he was carrying. Still, Brandford persisted in carrying the drugs. Taking Brandford's evidence at its highest but having regard to the tenor of Lord Bingham's speech in Hasan (*supra*) at [28], together with his disapproval of Hudson and Taylor (Hasan, at [27]), these threats simply lacked the immediacy to preclude Brandford taking evasive action, most obviously by going to the police. The inescapable inference is that she persisted out of love, infatuation or under pressure from Alford – but without the foundation of immediate threat essential for the defence of duress. Again, as observed in Hasan (at [26]), duress must never be allowed to be an "easy answer".

So, whilst the reasoning of the trial judge had been mistaken, it was correct that the jury had not been asked to consider the defence of duress. A jury would have been bound to find the defence disproved, because the immediacy requirement set out by the House of Lords in *R v Hasan* was clearly not satisfied. Moreover, as we will see shortly, there was also a second reason why the defence would have been bound to fail.

Mixed motives

Sometimes people have more than one reason for committing a crime. Suppose Trevor points a gun at Derek and says, 'If you help me commit this robbery I'll give you £100,000. If you don't I'll kill you'. Derek is terrified of being killed but also really wants to buy a new sports car, so he helps Trevor commit the robbery. Should Derek be able to plead duress even though he was in part motivated by the desire to buy a new car?

This issue of mixed motives was considered by the Court of Appeal in *R* v *Valderrama-Vega* [1985] Crim LR 220. The defendant had been charged with importing cocaine. He gave three reasons for committing the offence: (1) a mafia-type organisation had threatened him and his family with death or serious injury; (2) he was heavily in debt and under severe financial pressure; and (3) he had been threatened with disclosure of his homosexual inclinations. Of these three reasons, only the first could form the basis of a defence of duress. The Court held that the threat of physical violence need not have been the defendant's sole motivation for committing the offence. The correct approach is to apply a 'but for' test. But for the threat of physical violence would the defendant have committed the offence? If not, then he is entitled to plead duress.

Think about this question.

If you were the judge in Derek's case above, how would you direct the jury on the mixed motives issue?

Desisting once the threat has ceased

Someone who is compelled into committing a crime by an immediate threat of death or serious physical injury must stop committing the crime as soon as the threat has ceased. Once the threat has ceased the defence of duress will no longer be available. This is illustrated by *DPP* v *Mullally* [2006] EWHC 3448 (Admin).

Late one night Anne Mullally had reason to believe that her sister's partner was going to attack her sister. So she got in her car and drove to her sister's house. When Mullally arrived her sister's partner assaulted her and threatened to throw her down an external stairway. Mullally went back into the street outside and phoned the police. Her sister's partner had followed her, so she walked 100 metres up THE road to her parked car. She got in, drove back past her sister's house and, having seen that the police had arrived, headed home. On her way home she was stopped by police and asked to take a breath test. She was found to be over the legal limit and so was charged with drink-driving. She argued that she had been acting under duress. The Court said that when Mullally left her sister's house, got into her car and drove off there was an immediate threat of serious physical injury. However, 'from the moment she was aware that the police had attended at the premises, it ceased being necessary for her to continue to drive whilst over the limit in order to avoid a serious assault'. The Court accordingly directed that Mullally should be convicted of drink-driving.

ii. The objective limb

The second part of the test for duress is the objective limb. In this part of the test the jury must decide whether they are sure that a sober person of reasonable firmness, sharing the characteristics of the defendant, would not have responded to whatever he reasonably believed T said or did by taking part in the killing.

In *R* v *Graham* Lord Lane CJ explained the rationale underlying this part of the test. He said, 'As a matter of public policy, it seems to us essential to limit the defence of duress by means of an objective criterion formulated in terms of reasonableness'. The law should, he said, 'require [the defendant] to have the steadfastness reasonably to be expected of the ordinary citizen in his situation'.

'... sharing the characteristics of the defendant ...'

I have labelled this part of the test for duress the 'objective' limb because the jury have to assess the defendant's actions against the standard of the reasonable person. But, again, don't be fooled by the label. Although it is the objective limb, the jury may still take into account some of the characteristics of the defendant. But which ones? The leading case on this question is *R* v *Bowen* [1997] 1 WLR 372.

Cecil Bowen had been charged with a deception offence. He claimed that he had been acting under duress. He said that two men had accosted him in a pub and threatened to petrol bomb him and his family if he did not commit the offence. A psychologist gave evidence that Bowen had an IQ of 68 (which would have placed him in the lowest two per cent of the population) and that he was abnormally suggestible and vulnerable. The issue for the Court of Appeal was whether these characteristics could be taken into account when applying the objective limb of the test for duress. Stuart-Smith LJ reviewed the case law and then summarised the relevant principles as follows:

EXTRACT

R v *Bowen* [1997] 1 WLR 372

Stuart-Smith LJ

What principles are to be derived from these authorities? We think they are as follows.

(1) The mere fact that the defendant is more pliable, vulnerable, timid or susceptible to threats than a normal person is not a characteristic with which it is legitimate to invest the reasonable/ordinary person for the purpose of considering the objective test.

(2) The defendant may be in a category of persons whom the jury may think less able to resist pressure than people not within that category. Obvious examples are age, where a young person may well not be so robust as a mature one; possibly sex, though many women would doubtless consider they had as much moral courage to resist pressure as men; pregnancy, where there is added fear for the unborn child; serious physical disability, which may inhibit self protection; recognised mental illness or psychiatric condition, such as post-traumatic stress disorder leading to learnt helplessness.

(3) Characteristics which may be relevant in considering provocation, because they relate to the nature of the provocation itself, will not necessarily be relevant in cases of duress. Thus homosexuality may be relevant to provocation if the provocative words or conduct are related to this characteristic; it cannot be relevant in duress, since there is no reason to think that homosexuals are less robust in resisting threats of the kind that are relevant in duress cases.

(4) Characteristics due to self-induced abuse, such as alcohol, drugs or glue-sniffing, cannot be relevant.

(5) Psychiatric evidence may be admissible to show that the defendant is suffering from some mental illness, mental impairment or recognised psychiatric condition provided persons generally suffering from such condition may be more susceptible to pressure and threats and thus to assist the jury in deciding whether a reasonable person suffering from such a condition might have been impelled to act as the defendant did. It is not admissible simply to show that in the doctor's opinion a defendant, who is not suffering from such illness or condition, is especially timid, suggestible or vulnerable to pressure and threats. Nor is medical opinion admissible to bolster or support the credibility of the accused.

(6) Where counsel wishes to submit that the defendant has some characteristic which falls within (2) above, this must be made plain to the judge. The question may arise in relation to the admissibility of medical evidence of the nature set out in (5). If so, the judge will have to rule at that stage. There may, however, be no medical evidence, or, as in this case, medical evidence may have been introduced for some other purpose, e.g. to challenge the admissibility or weight of a confession. In such a case counsel must raise the question before speeches in the absence of the jury, so that the judge can rule whether the alleged characteristic is capable of being relevant. If he rules that it is, then he must leave it to the jury.

(7) In the absence of some direction from the judge as to what characteristics are capable of being regarded as relevant, we think that the direction approved in Reg. v. Graham (Paul) [1982] 1 W.L.R. 294 without more will not be as helpful as it might be, since the jury may be tempted, especially if there is evidence, as there was in this case, relating to suggestibility and vulnerability, to think that these are relevant. In most cases it is probably only the age and sex of the accused that is capable of being relevant. If so, the judge should, as he did in this case, confine the characteristics in question to these.

The Court then applied these principles to Cecil Bowen. Applying the first principle, it held that the evidence that Bowen was abnormally suggestible and vulnerable could not be taken into account. Applying the fifth principle, it held that Bowen's low IQ could not be taken into account either: 'We do not see how low IQ, short of mental impairment or mental defectiveness, can be said to be a characteristic that makes those who have it less courageous and less able to withstand threats and pressure.'

Now, think about this question.

Looking at the principles set out in *R* v *Bowen*, decide whether the characteristics of the following three defendants would be taken into account in the objective limb:

a. Psychiatric evidence shows that the defendant is unusually pliant and susceptible to pressure (based on *R* v *Horne* [1994] Crim LR 584).

b. A 28-year-old male forces the defendant, an elderly lady, to shoplift.

c. As a result of years of drug abuse, the defendant is a particularly paranoid and timid individual.

Voluntary intoxication may not be considered

In *R* v *Graham* Lord Lane CJ stated clearly that:

> The fact that a defendant's will to resist has been eroded by the voluntary consumption of drink or drugs or both is not relevant to this test.

3. Voluntary exposure to the threats

Derek is keen to join a local gang of anti-capitalism protestors, even though he has heard stories of some gang members being forced to commit minor acts of criminal damage against major financial institutions. A couple of weeks after joining the gang's leader, Trevor, says to Derek, 'Go and graffiti the bank in the High Street or I'm going to kill you'. Terrified, Derek sprays graffiti all over the bank. When he is subsequently arrested and charged with criminal damage Derek pleads duress.

In a situation like this should someone like Derek be allowed to plead duress? Or should the defence be unavailable because Derek voluntarily chose to associate with the people that subsequently threatened him, knowing that they might force him to commit criminal damage? In *R* v *Hasan* the House of Lords held that 'the defendant may not rely on duress to which he has voluntarily laid himself open'. So in our example, the defence of duress would not be available to Derek.

Now imagine a slightly different example. Suppose Trevor had instead said to Derek: 'I'm planning an armed robbery of the bank in the High Street tonight and I want you to help me. If you don't I'll kill you.' Terrified, Derek takes part in the armed robbery. Does the principle from *R* v *Hasan* still apply? When Derek joined he was aware that there was a chance he might be forced to commit minor acts of criminal damage. But he did not foresee that he might be forced to take part in an offence as serious as armed robbery.

The House of Lords also considered this issue in *R* v *Hasan*. Hasan worked as a driver and minder for a woman called Claire Taeger, who ran an escort agency and was involved in prostitution. A man called Frank Sullivan, who had a reputation for violence and being a drug dealer, became Taeger's boyfriend. Shortly after this Hasan stopped working for Taeger but he remained in contact with Sullivan. A couple of months later Sullivan forced Hasan to commit a burglary, saying that if he didn't he and his family would be harmed. Hasan was subsequently charged with aggravated burglary and pleaded duress.

In its judgment the House of Lords considered whether a defendant like Derek in our example should be able to plead duress if: (1) he voluntarily exposed himself to the risk of some pressure to commit crimes; but (2) was not aware that the pressure would be to commit an offence of the type he was forced to commit. Pointing to the policy reasons for carefully circumscribing the defence, and the fact that a defendant who pleads duress is 'seeking to be wholly exonerated from the consequences of a crime deliberately committed', Lord Bingham held that the defence should be unavailable. Since a defendant like Derek has 'voluntarily surrendered his will to the domination of another', he said that 'Nothing should turn on foresight of the manner in which, in the event, the dominant party chooses to exploit the defendant's subservience'. Lord Bingham then stated the following general principle:

> The policy of the law must be to discourage association with known criminals, and it should be slow to excuse the criminal conduct of those who do so. If a person voluntarily becomes or remains associated with others engaged in criminal activity in a situation where he knows or ought reasonably to know that he may be the subject of compulsion by them or their associates, he cannot rely on the defence of duress to excuse any act which he is thereafter compelled to do by them.

Two conditions must be satisfied for this principle to apply. The first is that the defendant 'voluntarily becomes or remains associated with others engaged in criminal activity'. The second is that the defendant 'knows or ought reasonably to know that he may be the subject of compulsion by them or their associates'.

The House of Lords held that this principle applied to Hasan. The defence of duress was therefore unavailable and Hasan's conviction for aggravated burglary was upheld. The principle was also applied in *R* v *Brandford*. As we saw before, in this case the Court of Appeal stated that there were two reasons why Brandford's defence of duress would inevitably have failed. The first was that the threat lacked immediacy. The second reason was that Brandford had voluntarily associated with Dean Alford, even though she was aware of Alford's previous conviction for dealing in Class A drugs, knew that Alford's friend had been murdered six months earlier, and knew that Alford himself had been attacked twice in the previous eight months. Gross LJ stated that 'Brandford must have appreciated that with serious violence as the norm or a regular feature, the risk of coercion was self-evident. Nevertheless, Brandford remained the partner of Alford …' ([46]).

ACTIVITY

Derek chooses to spend most evenings in his local pub. Other regulars at the pub include a local gangster, Trevor, who has a reputation for violence. If Derek sees Trevor he says 'Hello', but generally does his best to keep his distance. One day, at closing time, Trevor points a gun at Derek and forces him to take part in an armed robbery.

Which of the following three sentences correctly states the second of the two conditions for the principle from *R* v *Hasan* to apply?

- The defendant knew – or ought to have known – that he might be compelled to do something he didn't want to do (criminal or non-criminal).
- The defendant knew – or ought to have known – that he might be compelled to commit a crime of the type he foresaw.
- The defendant knew – or ought to have known – that he might be compelled to commit a crime (of any type).

Which of the following three sentences correctly states the second of the two conditions for the principle from *R* v *Hasan* to apply?

- The defendant knew – or ought to have known – that he might be compelled to commit a crime (of any type).
- The defendant knew – or ought to have known – that he might be compelled to commit a crime of the type he foresaw.
- The defendant knew – or ought to have known – that he might be compelled to do something he didn't want to do (criminal or non-criminal).

Suppose it never occurred to the defendant that the people he chose to associate with might subject him to compulsion, but if he had thought about it properly this possibility would have been obvious to him. Does the principle still apply?

- Yes
- No

Quiz 11.2

1. Which of the following kinds of threat is sufficient to give rise to a defence of duress?

a. Death or serious injury to D or to someone for whom he reasonably regards himself as responsible.

b. Death or serious injury to D, or to someone or some animal for whom he reasonably regards himself as responsible.

c. Death or injury to anyone.

d. Injury to D, or to someone for whom he reasonably regards himself as responsible, or to D's reputation.

2. For a defence of duress of circumstances to be successful, which one of the following is accurate?

a. D has acted in committing what would otherwise be a crime because he submitted to an irresistible urge, to which a reasonable person would also have submitted.

b. D has acted in committing what would otherwise be a crime because he did not resist the pressure put on him by the circumstances in which he found himself, and a reasonable person would also have not resisted.

c. D is faced with circumstances where he is under a moral obligation to commit an act that would otherwise be a crime.

d. D has acted in committing what would otherwise be a crime, because he did not resist the pressure put on him by the circumstances in which he found himself.

3. For duress to be available as a defence, what must be the relationship between the defendant and the threatened person?

a. The threatened person could be anyone, if the defendant reasonably regarded himself as responsible for them.

b. The threatened person must be the defendant himself.

c. There must have been a pre-existing special relationship between the defendant and the threatened person.

d. The threatened person must have been a member of the defendant's family.

4. How does the defence of duress operate so as to balance the interests of the imperilled defendant or someone for whom s/he is responsible and the public interest in deterring criminal behaviour?

a. It requires evidence that D genuinely believed in the existence of an unavoidable and immediate (or almost immediate) threat of death or serious physical injury AND that the reasonable person sharing all of D's characteristics would have responded to such threat as D had done.

b. It requires proof that D reasonably believed in the existence of an unavoidable and immediate (or almost immediate) threat of death or serious physical injury AND that the reasonable person in D's situation would have responded to such threat as D had done.

c. It requires evidence that D reasonably believed in the existence of an unavoidable and immediate (or almost immediate) threat of death or serious physical injury AND that the reasonable person in D's situation would have responded to such threat as D had done.

d. It requires evidence that D reasonably believed in the existence of an unavoidable and immediate threat of death or physical injury AND that the reasonable person in D's situation would have responded to such threat as D had done.

5. Which of the following statements about the defence of duress is true?

a. Duress is not available for any crime of violence.

b. Duress is available to all crimes except murder and being an accessory to murder.

c. Duress is available to all crimes except murder, being an accessory to murder and attempted murder.

d. Duress is available as a defence to any crime.

6. In which of the following would duress be allowed as a defence?

a. The defendant carries out the crime even if the threat has passed.

b. The defendant carries out the crime for a number of reasons, one of which was a threat of serious injury. Even without the threat of serious injury, the defendant would still have committed the crime.

c. The retribution threatened against the defendant or a person for whom he reasonably feels responsible is such as he reasonably expects to follow soon after his failure to comply with the threat, albeit not immediately or almost immediately after.

d. The retribution threatened against the defendant or a person for whom he reasonably feels responsible is such as he reasonably expects to follow immediately or almost immediately on his failure to comply with the threat.

4. To which crimes is duress available as a defence?

11.3 Identify arguments for and against allowing duress as a defence to murder.

Duress is a general defence, so in principle it is available as a defence to any crime. However, there are some exceptions. In *R* v *Howe* the House of Lords held that duress is not available as a defence to murder or being an accessory to murder. And in *R* v *Gotts* [1992] 2 AC 412 the House of Lords held, by a majority of three to two, that duress is also not available as a defence to attempted murder.[12]

[12] In *Caryn Moss* v *The King (Bahamas) [2023]* UKPC 28, the Privy Council left open the question whether duress is available as a defence to conspiracy to murder. For discussion, see Jasinski, D. (2025) 'An Opportunity Missed. Clarifying the Availability of the Common Law Defence of Duress to Conspiracy to Commit Murder' 89 *Journal of Criminal Law* 46.

There are some strong arguments in favour of allowing duress as a defence to murder. In fact, in *R* v *Hasan* Lord Bingham said that the 'logic of this argument is irresistible'. In the following extract, taken from the Law Commission's consultation paper *A New Homicide Act for England and Wales?*, the Law Commission argue that the refusal to allow duress as at least a partial defence to murder risks causing injustice.

(NB: The wording of para 7.7 in the extract has been amended in the light of the Supreme Court's judgment in *R* v *Jogee*, which we study in Chapter 13.)

EXTRACT

Law Commission (2005) *A New Homicide Act for England and Wales? A Consultation Paper* (Consultation Paper No 177)

7.5 [...] The following hypothetical examples, however, demonstrate the potential for injustice which can result from the present position.

EXAMPLE 1: D sees her violent husband speeding towards her, waving a gun, as she is waiting in her car at the lights. She speeds off even though she realises she will crash into a pedestrian who is crossing in front of her. She realises that she will cause him serious injury. The pedestrian dies as a result of his injuries.

EXAMPLE 2: D1, a psychopathic father, compels his eleven year old son, D2, through threat of death to participate in the murder of one of D1's rivals. D2 does no more than hold his father's gun whilst his father forces open the door to the rival's house prior to the killing.

7.6 In Example 1 D is liable for murder and accordingly she faces the mandatory life sentence. The absence of a defence of duress of circumstances means that the law cannot take into account the fact that she was acting under threat of death or serious harm and that at the time of acting she had no realistic alternative but to speed ahead.

7.7 In Example 2 D1 may be convicted of manslaughter on the basis of diminished responsibility but D2 must be convicted of murder if he [knew] what his father [would] do with the gun.

7.8 A blanket rule that duress can never apply as a defence to murder can cause injustice for particular groups of defendants. There is a very strong case that juveniles and young persons, who are much less mature than adults, and hence less able to withstand a threat of death, should be able to rely on the defence.

7.9 Under the present rule, by which the defendant incurs liability for murder notwithstanding that he did not intend to kill but only intended really serious harm, he has no defence of duress. This is potentially unjust where the defendant has acted under threat of death to himself.

Think about this question.

- Do you agree with the Law Commission that in their two examples it would be unjust for D and D2 to be convicted of murder and receive the mandatory life sentence?

If there are strong reasons for allowing duress as a (full or partial) defence to murder, why did the House of Lords in *R* v *Howe* hold that it is unavailable?

EXTRACT

Milgate has identified the following seven reasons for the House of Lords' decision (Milgate, H.P. (1988) 'Duress and the Criminal Law: Another About Turn by the House of Lords' 47 *Cambridge Law Journal* 61). Read the following extracts from the judgments of Lords Hailsham, Bridge, Griffiths and Mackay in *R* v *Howe* and then write a short description of each argument:

- The heroic argument
- The comparison with necessity
- The legislative argument
- The prosecution argument
- The executive action argument
- The charter for terrorists
- The uncertainty argument.

R v *Howe* [1987] AC 417

Lord Hailsham

In general, I must say that I do not at all accept in relation to the defence of murder it is either good morals, good policy or good law to suggest, as did the majority in *Lynch* and the minority in *Abbott* that the ordinary man of reasonable fortitude is not to be supposed to be capable of heroism if he is asked to take an innocent life rather than sacrifice his own. Doubtless in actual practice many will succumb to temptation, as they did in *Dudley* and *Stephens*. But many will not, and I do not believe that as a "concession to human frailty" the former should be exempt from liability to criminal sanctions if they do. I have known in my own lifetime of too many acts of heroism by ordinary human beings of no more than ordinary fortitude to regard a law as either "just or humane" which withdraws the protection of the criminal law from the innocent victim and casts the cloak of its protection upon the coward and the poltroon in the name of a "concession to human frailty."

[...]

I am not so shocked as some of the judicial opinions have been at the need, if this be the conclusion, to invoke the availability of administrative as distinct from purely judicial remedies for the hardships which might otherwise occur in the most agonising cases. Even in *Dudley* and *Stephens* in 1884 when the death penalty was mandatory and frequently inflicted, the prerogative was used to reduce a sentence of death by hanging to one of six months in prison. In murder cases the available mechanisms are today both more flexible and more sophisticated [...] The Parole Board will always consider a case of this kind with a High Court judge brought into consultation. In the background is always the prerogative and, it may not unreasonably be suggested, that is exactly what the prerogative is for. If the law seems to bear harshly in its operation in the case of a mandatory sentence on any particular offender there has never been a period of time when there were more effective means of mitigating its effect than at the present day. It may well be thought that the loss of a clear right to a defence justifying or excusing the deliberate taking of an innocent life in order to emphasise to all the sanctity of a human life is not an excessive price to pay in the light of these mechanisms.

[...]

Unlike the doctrine of provocation, which is based on emotional loss of control, the defence of duress, as I have already shown, is put forward as a "concession to human frailty" whereby a conscious decision, it may be coolly undertaken, to sacrifice an innocent human life is made as an evil lesser than a wrong which might otherwise be suffered by the accused or his loved ones at the hands of a wrong doer.

Lord Bridge of Harwich

[... My conviction that duress should be unavailable as a defence to murder] is now immensely strengthened by the knowledge that Parliament, even against the background of the plainly unsatisfactory present state of the law, has in ten years taken no action on the Report of the Law Commission, No. 83. If duress is now to be made available generally as a defence to murder, it seems to me incontrovertible that the proper means to effect such a reform is by legislation such as that proposed by the Law Commission. Not only is it for Parliament to decide whether the proposed reform of the law is socially appropriate, but it is also by legislation alone, as opposed to judicial development, that the scope of the defence of duress can be defined with the degree of precision which, if it is to be available in murder at all, must surely be of critical importance.

Lord Griffiths

But what, I think, is significant is the fact that although the [Law Commission's] report clearly recognised that English law did not extend the defence of duress to the actual killer and recommended that the law should be changed, Parliament never acted upon this advice. The report was laid before Parliament by Lord Elwyn-Jones L.C. in July 1977 but no steps have been taken to introduce a Bill upon the lines they recommended. This must at least be some indication that the community at large are not pressing for a change in the law to remedy a perceived injustice.

Against this background are there any present circumstances that should impel your Lordships to alter the law that has stood for so long and to extend the defence of duress to the actual killer? My Lords, I can think of none. It appears to me that all present indications point in the opposite direction. We face a rising tide of violence and terrorism against which the law must stand firm recognising that its highest duty is to protect the freedom and lives of those that live under it. The sanctity of human life lies at the root of this ideal and I would do nothing to undermine it, be it ever so slight.

[...]

I am not troubled by some of the extreme examples cited in favour of allowing the defence to those who are not the killer such as a woman motorist being hijacked and forced to act as getaway driver, or a pedestrian being forced to give misleading information to the police to protect robbery and murder in a shop. The short, practical answer is that it is inconceivable that such persons would be prosecuted; they would be called as the principal witnesses for the prosecution.

[...]

But the sentence for murder although mandatory and expressed as imprisonment for life, is in fact an indefinite sentence, which is kept constantly under review by the parole board and the Home Secretary with the assistance of the Lord Chief Justice and the trial judge. I have confidence that through this machinery the respective culpability of those involved in a murder case can be fairly weighed and reflected in the time they are required to serve in custody.

Lord Mackay of Clashfern

To change the law in the manner suggested by counsel for the appellants in the present case would, in my opinion, introduce uncertainty over a field of considerable importance. So far I have referred to the defence of duress as if it were a precisely defined concept but it is apparent from the decisions that it is not so [...] To say that a defence in respect of which so many questions remain unsettled should be introduced in respect of the whole field of murder is not to promote certainty in the law.

[...]

Since the decision in *Lynch* the Law Commission have published in their Report No. 83, to which I have referred, the result of an extensive survey of the law relating to duress and have made recommendations upon it which have been laid before Parliament. In my opinion, the problems which have been evident in relation to the law of murder and the availability of particular defences is not susceptible of what Lord Reid described as a solution by a policy of make do and mend. While I appreciate fully the gradual development that has taken place in the law relating to the defence of duress I question whether the law has reached a sufficiently precise definition of that defence to make it right for us sitting in our judicial capacity to introduce it as a defence for an actual killer for the first time in the law of England. Parliament, in its legislative capacity, although recommended to do so by the report of the Law Commission, has not taken any steps to make the defence of duress available generally to a charge of murder even where it has the power to define with precision the circumstances in which such a defence would be available.

In his article Milgate argues that none of the seven reasons advanced by the House of Lords in *R* v *Howe* is convincing.

EXTRACT

Read the following extract from Milgate's article and summarise why he rejects each of the House of Lords' reasons.

Milgate, H.P. (1988) 'Duress and the Criminal Law: Another About Turn by the House of Lords' 47 *Cambridge Law Journal* 61

(1) The heroic argument

This argument can be expressed quite simply. The "ordinary man," if asked to take innocent life to save his own, will not necessarily yield to temptation and comply with the demand. The law should encourage this high standard of human behaviour by exposing to criminal sanctions those who fail to live up to it [...]

Emotion aside, there are a number of problems with this argument. In the first place, it is out of step with general principle. Apart from a few exceptional cases, there is no duty in the criminal law to be a hero. Unless a special relationship exists, we can watch a child drown without fear of prosecution for murder; unless asked by the police to assist, we have no duty to wade in and tackle an armed robber. Moreover, even where the charge against the defendant arises from his own positive act of conduct, he will almost invariably be judged by the standard of the reasonable man and not the hero. So, for example, where a defendant has killed in self-defence he will avoid conviction if he used only such force as was reasonable under the circumstances.

Secondly, as the self-defence example shows, the criminal law does recognise that the reasonable man may justifiably take the life of an aggressor [...] Heroism is of course to be encouraged, but by religious or moral law, not by the criminal law.

[...] Furthermore, the House ignored the fact that the path of heroism may not always be clear. The case in which D's life is threatened unless he shoots V, an innocent third party, is, in an analytical sense, an easy one. But what if D's child is threatened? What if all three of his children are threatened? In this terrorist age these examples are not far-fetched. Are we really to deny D the defence of duress if he pulls the trigger and kills V? If so, are we genuinely giving supreme importance to the value of human life? Regrettably, not one of their Lordships discussed these difficult questions.

(2) The comparison with necessity

In 1884, in *Dudley and Stephens*, the House of Lords decided that necessity could not be a defence to murder, whatever the degree of participation. Since then it has been argued strongly that necessity and duress are analogous and that duress cannot be available on a murder charge whilst *Dudley and Stephens* remains part of the common law.

[... W]hilst parallels undoubtedly do exist between duress and necessity, these parallels are arguably no stronger than those that exist between duress and provocation. As Lord Lane pointed out in *Graham*: "Provocation and duress are analogous. In provocation the words or actions of one person break the self-control of another. In duress the words or actions of one person break the will of another." Why then was the analogy with necessity so persuasive in *Howe*? The high standard of conduct imposed by *Dudley and Stephens* is, as we have seen, exceptional, and it therefore seems strange that the House should be so heavily influenced by the case. Regrettably, Lord Mackay was vague on this point. He felt that even if there was merit in the analogy with provocation their Lordships "would not be justified in the present state of the law in introducing for the first time into our law the concept of duress acting to reduce the charge to one of manslaughter ..." Lord Hailsham offered rather more explanation. Although in his view both defences involved a "concession to human frailty," they were not analogous. The essence of provocation was that the killer had acted without self control. Duress, on the other hand, involved "a conscious decision" to do the relevant act. This distinction was vital and justified a divergent approach to the two defences. With respect to Lord Hailsham, this distinction seems too fine. Theoretically the man who kills under duress may make "a conscious decision" to kill, but in practice his will may be subject to enormous pressure. It is not obvious why his "human frailty" in succumbing to that pressure should be ignored, whilst the "human frailty" of the man who is provoked to kill may reduce murder to manslaughter.

(3) The legislative argument

Ten years ago the Law Commission recommended that duress should be available in all cases of murder. However, since then, Parliament has taken no action to implement that recommendation. Lords Bridge and Griffiths therefore argue that there is neither the legislative will nor the public pressure to extend the defence to the actual killer. This argument can easily be turned on its head. *Lynch* [which allowed duress as a defence to someone charged as an accessory to murder before it was overruled in *R* v *Howe*] was decided over twelve years ago and in all that time Parliament has done nothing to interfere with that decision. If Parliament was really so anxious that duress should not be available to a participant in murder, would it not have acted? In any event, is it part of the judicial function to second-guess Parliament in this way? In truth, the legislative argument gets us nowhere.

(4) The prosecution argument

The rule that duress can never be a defence to murder is clearly capable of operating harshly, particularly where the defendant who has acted under threat has played a very minor part in the killing. The House in Howe gave two reasons why in practice the law would not operate unjustly. I shall label these "the prosecution argument" and "the executive action argument" respectively [...]

Unfortunately, experience shows [the prosecution argument] to be over-optimistic. For example, the prosecution the subject of the appeal in *Anderton* v. *Ryan* was exactly the kind of prosecution which the Law Commission had predicted would never be brought. It is a complete evasion of the responsibilities of the House of Lords to avoid dealing with difficult cases on the basis that they will never get to court. They do. In fact, until a case is heard and the evidence tested, it may not be possible for the prosecutor to accept the truth of the defendant's exculpatory story; indeed, until then, he may not even be aware of it!

(5) The executive action argument

The executive action argument arises because a life sentence must, by law, be imposed if a defendant is found guilty of murder. Unlike manslaughter, there is no discretion: human frailty is ignored not only in reaching a verdict but also at the sentencing stage. However, Lord Griffiths again argues that the harshness of this position is more theoretical than real:

> ... the sentence for murder although mandatory and expressed as imprisonment for life, is in fact an indefinite sentence, which is kept constantly under review by the parole board and the Home Secretary with the assistance of the Lord Chief Justice and the trial judge. I have confidence that through this machinery the respective culpability of those involved in a murder case can be fairly weighed and reflected in the time they are required to serve in custody.

Others have not shared this confidence, for example Lord Wilberforce in Lynch:

> A law, which requires innocent victims of terrorist threats to be tried for murder and convicted as murderers, is an unjust law even if the executive, resisting political pressures, may decide, after it all, and within the permissible limits of the prerogative to release them. Moreover, if the defence is excluded in law, much of the evidence which would prove the duress would be inadmissible at the trial, not brought out in court, and not tested by cross-examination. The validity of the defence is far better judged by a jury, after proper direction and a fair trial, than by executive officials; and if it is said that to allow the defence will be to encourage fictitious claims of pressure I have enough confidence in our legal system to believe that the process of law is a better safeguard against this than inquiry by a government department.

Such argument is compelling, but was not even considered in Howe. One has to be concerned that a decision of this magnitude is based on such a superficial discussion of an important issue.

(6) The charter for terrorists

This argument is not a new one. It was raised by Lord Simon in his dissenting judgment in Lynch when he sounded a warning about the dangers of allowing a general defence of duress:

> Would it not enable a gang leader of notorious violence to confer on his organisation by terrorism immunity from the criminal law? ... your Lordships should hesitate long lest you may be inscribing a charter for terrorists, gang-leaders and kidnappers.

It is notable that this argument has not prevented duress being available as a defence to crimes other than murder. Nonetheless, it resurfaces in the speeches of Lords Hailsham and Griffiths in *Howe*, to support the view that duress should not be available to the murderer. Whilst no-one would deny the problems posed by terrorism in the nineteen-eighties, the "charter for terrorism" argument is now considerably weaker than it was in Lord Simon's day.

First, implicit in Lord Simon's argument is the assumption that, once raised, the defence of duress will almost invariably succeed. However, as Lord Hailsham admits in *Howe*, "juries have been commendably robust" in rejecting duress where appropriate, as the verdicts in the trials of Howe, Bannister and Burke clearly demonstrate. Moreover, the House of Lords in *Howe* itself has made the "automatic acquittal" even less likely by confirming that there is an objective element in the duress defence. The House held that where the defence of duress applies the accused is to be judged by the standard of the reasonable man, or more accurately by the "sober person of reasonable firmness sharing the defendant's characteristics." If duress were allowed as a defence to murder this objective element would provide a safeguard against the unmeritorious defendant.

Secondly, the charter for terrorism argument has lost much of its force as a result of recent Court of Appeal decisions which, in fairness, were reported after the House handed down its decision in *Howe*. It is now clear that where the defendant voluntarily joins a terrorist group or criminal gang, and is forced by pressure of violence to commit an offence for that group or gang, he cannot raise the defence of duress if, when he joined the gang, he knew that it took part in violent crime or that violence might be used against him to compel him to take part in the gang's activities. To that extent duress is not a charter for terrorists whatever the crime charged.

(7) The uncertainty argument

Finally, it is argued that duress should not be available on a charge of murder because it is too uncertain [...]

This is the weakest argument of all, given that it undermines the very basis on which common law operates. Common-law principles are not born fully developed from a single judicial statement; instead they evolve on a case by case basis as new factual situations arise. Recent case law on self-defence, and indeed on duress itself, shows this phenomenon operating in the context of the criminal law. The answer to uncertainty is to cure it-either by further case law or, if necessary, by legislation. Lord Mackay's comments can also be criticised on a narrower ground. Most of the uncertainties associated with duress apply whatever the crime charged [...] If duress is available on a rape charge, despite these uncertainties, it is difficult to see why it should be denied just because the charge is murder. In short, the uncertainty argument best exposes the decision in Howe for what it is – a major piece of judicial legislation, based on an apparently cursory examination of principle and policy.

The following three developments have all occurred in the years since Milgate wrote his article. All three strengthen his critique of the reasoning in *R* v *Howe*:

1. The comparison with necessity

As we saw earlier in the chapter, it now appears to be accepted that necessity may sometimes be a defence to murder. So the *ratio decidendi* of *R* v *Dudley and Stephens* is narrower than the House of Lords in *R* v *Howe* envisaged.

2. The executive action argument

The minimum period that must be spent in custody by those convicted of murder is now governed by the Criminal Justice Act 2003. This was designed to reduce the discretion of sentencing judges. For the least heinous category of murders, the presumption is that a minimum of 15 years should be served before consideration for parole. This framework reduces the extent to which concessions can be made when sentencing those who kill under duress.

3. The charter for terrorists

The strict principle expounded by the House of Lords in *R* v *Hasan* addresses the concern that members of terrorist groups or criminal gangs might effectively be able to confer immunity on one another.

In addition, Elkington has argued that, from a historical perspective, the decision in R v Howe was unfounded. Examining case law from 1266 until the end of the 19th Century, she concludes that "Duress was originally used for the most heinous of all crimes, treason, and during this time provided a defence to those who had killed in the course of conducting the treason. Therefore, the availability of the duress defence to treason (including killing), suggests that denying the defence to murder alone would be illogical".[13]

Quiz 11.3

1. In which one of the following situations will D have a defence of duress?
   a. D is the manager of a bank. He is accosted on his way to work one morning and told that there is a bomb in the shopping centre where the bank is located and that unless he assists his accosters in stealing the contents of the bank's safe then the bomb will be detonated at the peak shopping hour. He does as instructed.
   b. D is a member of a violent gang but has not himself committed any offences. The gang leader orders D to take part in a battery of a member of a rival gang. D refuses but is told that he will be killed for his disloyalty unless he obeys. D has no opportunity to escape and knows that the threat will be carried out if he does not do as ordered because he has seen the gang leader do the same to other disobedient members. D does as ordered.
   c. D, a prisoner serving a term of imprisonment, becomes suicidal when informed that his tariff, the minimum term that his imprisonment must last, has been significantly increased. He escapes from prison in order to avoid the certainty that he will kill himself.
   d. One night D is threatened with being seriously injured by some money lenders to whom he owes money. He knows that they are people who have carried out acts of extreme violence in the past to those who have failed to settle debts with them. D has no reasonable opportunity to escape from those making the threats. He takes a knife and robs the local petrol station in order to pay his debt.
2. Which of the following was one of the reasons offered by the House of Lords in *R v Howe* [1987] AC 417 in support of the view that duress should not be available as a defence to murder?
   a. Case law had made it clear that terrorists would not be able to use duress to confer immunity on one another.
   b. Case law has clarified the rules that govern the defence of duress.
   c. The culpability of a defendant can be reflected in the severity of the sentence imposed.
   d. The criminal law should not expect exceptional courage and self-sacrifice from ordinary people.
3. Which of the following was one of the reasons offered by Milgate in support of his view that duress should be available as a defence to murder?
   a. Parliament had not enacted the Law Commission's recommendation that duress should be a defence to murder.
   b. In practice, the discretion of prosecutors and sentencers would ensure injustice was avoided.
   c. Allowing duress as a defence to murder would enable terrorists to confer immunity on one another.
   d. There is no general duty in the criminal law to be a hero.

5. The relationship between duress of circumstances and necessity.

11.4 Outline the relationship between duress of circumstances and necessity.

Earlier on we examined the relationship between duress by threats and duress of circumstances. Before we conclude our study of duress, it is also important to consider the relationship between duress of circumstances and necessity.

[13] Elkington, A. (2023) 'The Historical Development of Duress and the Unfounded Result of Denying Duress as a Defence to Murder' 87 *Journal of Criminal Law* 207.

As we've worked through the defence of duress you may have noticed some similarities between the defences of duress of circumstances and necessity. Indeed, to some extent the two defences do overlap. In fact, the reluctance to recognise a defence of necessity for individuals like Lord Denning's fireman is probably one of the reasons why the courts created duress of circumstances in the first place. There are, however, the following important differences between the two defences:

- As we saw above, it appears that necessity may be a defence to murder in some, limited circumstances. By contrast, duress of circumstances is never available as a defence to murder.
- Unlike duress of circumstances, necessity is not limited to threats of death or serious physical injury. It might also apply, for example, in cases involving property damage.
- Duress of circumstances is only available if the threat was an immediate one. Necessity is not limited in this way.
- A defendant who mistakenly believed he faced an immediate threat of death or serious physical injury may still plead duress of circumstances, as long as his belief was a reasonable one. Necessity is not available in cases involving a mistaken belief.
- Necessity is only available if commission of the crime was the lesser of two evils. Duress of circumstances is not limited in this way.

Secnario 1. Which defence might potentially apply in Lord Denning's hypothetical fireman (from *Buckoke* v *GLC* [1971] Ch 655)? Necessity, duress of circumstances, or both?

Scenario 2. Which defence might potentially apply in the following scenario: Necessity, duress of circumstances, or both?

Dorothy, who is elderly and very frail, sees a group of young men walking towards her car shouting loudly. Believing they are going to attack her she drives off, well above the speed limit. In fact, the group were not going to attack her, but her mistake is found to have been a reasonable one.

Scenario 3. Which defence might potentially apply in *Re A (Children) (Conjoined Twins: Surgical Separation)* [2001] Fam 147? Necessity, duress of circumstances, or both?

Scenario 4. Which defence might potentially apply in *Re F (Mental Patient: Sterilisation)* [1990] 2 AC 1? Necessity, duress of circumstances, or both?

Scenario 5. Which defence might potentially apply in the following scenario: Necessity, duress of circumstances, or both?The only way for Dave to avoid serious physical injury is if he causes Victor serious physical injury instead. Dave seriously injures Victor and escapes unharmed.

Quiz 11.4

1. Which of the following statements is accurate?

a. The duress of circumstances and necessity defences overlap to an extent.

b. A defendant may plead duress of circumstances but necessity remains unavailable as a general defence.

c. The duress of circumstances and necessity defences do not overlap at all.

d. Duress of circumstances and necessity are two different names for the same defence.

2. Which of the following statements is accurate?
   a. Both necessity and duress of circumstances are unavailable as a defence to murder.
   b. Duress of circumstances is limited to threats of death or serious physical injury; necessity is not limited in this way.
   c. Mistaken beliefs may be taken into account in both necessity and duress, but only if the mistake was a reasonable one.
   d. Duress of circumstances and necessity are only available as a defence in cases involving an immediate threat.

3. Which of the following statements is inaccurate?
   a. Duress of circumstances is not available as a defence to murder; necessity may be in some limited circumstances.
   b. Necessity and duress of circumstances both require proof that the commission of the crime was the lesser of two evils.
   c. Necessity is available in a case involving property damage, but duress of circumstances is not.
   d. Necessity is available as a defence in cases involving non-immediate threats, whereas duress of circumstances requires that the threat was an immediate one.

Prevention of crime and private defence

11.5 Define the requirements for establishing the substantive defences of prevention of crime and private defence.

These defences are often referred to as self-defence, but in fact this is slightly misleading. The defences apply not only when the defendant was defending himself against an act of violence, but also when the defendant was protecting another person from violence, when the defendant was protecting his own or someone else's property and when the defendant was preventing the commission of a crime. So, for example, the defences may apply where a taxi driver uses force to stop a passenger from running away without paying.[14]

Prevention of crime and private defence are both complete defences. Successfully pleading either defence will result in the defendant being found not guilty. They are also general defences. They are available as a defence to any charge that involves the use of force against people or property, including murder. Note two further points here. First, even if the offence is one that does not inherently involve the use of force (such as dangerous driving), the defences are still available as long as on the facts of the case the defendant used force in response to an actual or perceived threat.[15] Second, the defence is only available in cases involving the direct application of force. In *R (on the application of the DPP)* v *Stratford Magistrates' Court* [2017] EWHC 1794 (Admin) the defendants blocked the passage of vehicles making their way to the Defence and Security Equipment International exhibition in London. Their intention was to prevent illegal arms sales in order to stop the commission of war crimes. They were charged with obstruction of the highway,[16] and

[14] *R* v *Morris* [2013] EWCA Crim 436.

[15] See *R* v *Riddell* [2017] EWCA Crim 413, in which the defendant was charged with dangerous driving (Road Traffic Act 1988, s.2). The same approach was applied in *Oraki* v *DPP* [2018] EWHC 115 (Admin), in which it was held that the defences are available on a charge of obstruction of a police officer in the execution of his duty.

[16] Highways Act 1980, s.139.

sought to rely on the prevention of crime defence. In its judgment the High Court stated that the defence is only available in cases involving the direct application of force. Simon LJ explained:

> 50 ... I have concluded that the defence applies to the direct application of force, although the force would not necessarily have to be applied directly against a person. It would apply for example to a defendant who attached him or herself to a lorry which was believed to be carrying chemical weapons ... In contrast, the defence would not be available to those who lie down in the road in front of lorries making their way to a place where crimes are believed to be taking place or who block access by chaining themselves to gates.

Our study of these defences begins by looking at the differences between prevention of crime and private defence and the relationship between them. We then move on to examine the test that is used for both of them.

1. The relationship between prevention of crime and private defence

Prevention of crime is a statutory defence.[17] It is found in section 3 of the Criminal Law Act 1967:

EXTRACT

Section 3 of the Criminal Law Act 1967

3. Use of force in making arrest, etc.

(1) A person may use such force as is reasonable in the circumstances in the prevention of crime, or in effecting or assisting in the lawful arrest of offenders or suspected offenders or of persons unlawfully at large.

(2) Subsection (1) above shall replace the rules of the common law on the question when force used for a purpose mentioned in the subsection is justified by that purpose.

Private defence, on the other hand, is a common law defence. There is a long- established common law right to use force in private defence.

You're probably already thinking, don't these defences often overlap? Suppose Trevor is armed with a gun and is about to kill your best friend. Heroically, you grab hold of Trevor, wrestle the gun from him, and your friend escapes unharmed. This looks like both prevention of crime (you prevented Trevor from committing murder) and private defence (you came to the defence of your friend).

Where the two defences overlap like this, which one applies? The answer is found in section 3(2) of the Criminal Law Act 1967 (above). The statutory prevention of crime defence supersedes the common law right of private defence, so when the two defences overlap you should apply the prevention of crime defence.

This does not render private defence redundant, for there may be some situations in which the prevention of crime defence would not be available because the threatened attack is not unlawful. Suppose that Trevor in our example was insane (and so would not be guilty of any crime by reason of insanity). You would then have to rely on the common

[17] In *R v Jones (Margaret) & others* [2006] UKHL 16 the House of Lords held that the word 'crime' in section 3 is limited to crimes under English law. It does not cover crimes under international law.

law right of private defence. The same would apply if Trevor was below the age of criminal responsibility (i.e. if he was nine years old or younger). So whilst you should apply the prevention of crime defence if possible, there may sometimes be occasions where it is necessary to invoke the common law right of private defence.

Earlier in the chapter we saw how Brooke LJ applied the defence of necessity in *Re A (Children) (Conjoined Twins: Surgical Separation)*. Ward LJ employed different reasoning. He held that the doctors separating the twins would not be guilty of murdering Mary because they could invoke the common law right of private defence:

EXTRACT

Re A (Children) (Conjoined Twins: Surgical Separation) [2001] Fam 147

Ward LJ

The reality here – harsh as it is to state it, and unnatural as it is that it should be happening – is that Mary is killing Jodie. That is the effect of the incontrovertible medical evidence and it is common ground in the case. Mary uses Jodie's heart and lungs to receive and use Jodie's oxygenated blood. This will cause Jodie's heart to fail and cause Jodie's death as surely as a slow drip of poison. How can it be just that Jodie should be required to tolerate that state of affairs? One does not need to label Mary with the American terminology which would paint her to be "an unjust aggressor", which I feel is wholly inappropriate language for the sad and helpless position in which Mary finds herself. I have no difficulty in agreeing that this unique happening cannot be said to be unlawful. But it does not have to be unlawful. The six-year-old boy indiscriminately shooting all and sundry in the school playground is not acting unlawfully for he is too young for his acts to be so classified [... *I*]*n law* killing that six-year-old boy in self-defence of others would be fully justified and the killing would not be unlawful. I can see no difference in essence between that resort to legitimate self-defence and the doctors coming to Jodie's defence and removing the threat of fatal harm to her presented by Mary's draining her lifeblood. The availability of such a plea of quasi-self-defence, modified to meet the quite exceptional circumstances nature has inflicted on the twins, makes intervention by the doctors lawful.

2. The test for the defences

So there is a slight difference in the scope of the two defences. But there is no difference in the test that is used to decide whether the defences are available.[18] As for duress, the test for prevention of crime and private defence has two limbs: the subjective limb and the objective limb.

i. The subjective limb

The subjective limb asks whether the defendant genuinely believed the use of force was required in order to prevent crime (or in private defence). Since this limb of the test focuses on the defendant's belief I have labelled it the subjective limb.

18 As David Ormerod observes: 'If D goes to the defence of E whom V is trying to murder, he is exercising the right of private defence but he is also seeking to prevent the commission of a crime. It would be absurd to ask D whether he was acting in defence of E or to prevent murder being committed and preposterous that the law should differ according to this answer' (Ormerod, D. and Laird, K. (2015) *Smith and Hogan's Criminal Law* (14th edn). OUP: Oxford, p.443).

Mistaken beliefs

First of all, note that we are concerned here with mistakes of fact, not mistakes of law. A defendant cannot rely on a mistake of law to plead these defences. For example, suppose that Derek genuinely believes that adultery is a crime. He uses force to prevent Victor from committing adultery. Derek cannot rely on the prevention of crime defence because the act that he prevented would not have been a crime.[19]

So our focus here is mistaken beliefs as to the facts. In *R* v *Williams (Gladstone)* [1987] 3 All ER 411 a man called Mason saw a youth snatch a woman's handbag. He chased the youth and got hold of him, intending to take him to a police station. But the youth managed to break free and ran off. Mason chased and managed to get hold of him once again. This time he knocked the youth to the ground and held him in an arm-lock. The defendant, Williams, only saw the latter stages of the incident and so to him it looked like Mason was attacking the youth. When Williams asked Mason what he was doing, Mason replied that he was a police officer and he was arresting the youth. This was untrue. When Mason was unable to produce identification Williams punched Mason in the face. Williams was charged with assault occasioning actual bodily harm.

This was obviously a case involving a mistaken belief. Williams believed that Mason was attacking the youth, but in fact Mason was trying to stop the youth from escaping. At Williams' trial the judge told the jury that Williams' mistake could only be taken into account if it was a genuine and reasonable belief. Williams was convicted and appealed, arguing that this was a misdirection. So the issue for the Court of Appeal was whether a mistaken belief must have been both genuine and reasonable in order to be taken into account.

EXTRACT

According to the following extract from the Court of Appeal's judgment, may the jury take into account: (a) only genuinely held beliefs which were reasonable; or (b) all genuinely held beliefs, whether they were reasonable or not?

If the answer is (b), how (if at all) is the reasonableness of the mistaken belief relevant?

R v *Williams (Gladstone)* [1987] 3 All ER 411

Lord Lane CJ

What then is the situation if the defendant is labouring under a mistake of fact as to the circumstances? What if he believes, but believes mistakenly, that the victim is consenting, or that it is necessary to defend himself, or that a crime is being committed which he intends to prevent? He must then be judged against the mistaken facts as he believes them to be. If judged against those facts or circumstances the prosecution fail to establish his guilt, then he is entitled to be acquitted.

[19] In *R* v *Jones (Margaret) & others* [2006] UKHL 16, Lord Hoffman stated: 'It is accepted that the reasonableness of the force used must be judged objectively in the circumstances which the defendant believed to exist, but this belief can extend only to facts and not to the legal consequences or implications of those facts' ([24]).

The next question is, does it make any difference if the mistake of the defendant was one which, viewed objectively by a reasonable onlooker, was an unreasonable mistake? In other words should the jury be directed as follows: "Even if the defendant may have genuinely believed that what he was doing to the victim was either with the victim's consent or in reasonable self-defence or to prevent the commission of crime, as the case may be, nevertheless if you, the jury, come to the conclusion that the mistaken belief was unreasonable, that is to say that the defendant as a reasonable man should have realised his mistake, then you should convict him."

[...]

The reasonableness or unreasonableness of the defendant's belief is material to the question of whether the belief was held by the defendant at all. If the belief was in fact held, its unreasonableness, so far as guilt or innocence is concerned, is neither here nor there. It is irrelevant. Were it otherwise, the defendant would be convicted because he was negligent in failing to recognise that the victim was not consenting or that a crime was not being committed and so on. In other words the jury should be directed first of all that the prosecution have the burden or duty of proving the unlawfulness of the defendant's actions; secondly, if the defendant may have been labouring under a mistake as to the facts, he must be judged according to his mistaken view of the facts; thirdly, that is so whether the mistake was, on an objective view, a reasonable mistake or not

The decision of the Court of Appeal in *R v Williams* (Gladstone) has been placed on a statutory footing by section 76 of the Criminal Justice and Immigration Act 2008. The relevant subsections are (3)–(5).

EXTRACT

These subsections identify one situation where the principle from *R v Williams* (*Gladstone*) does not apply. What is this situation?

Section 76 of the Criminal Justice and Immigration Act 2008

76 Reasonable force for purposes of self-defence etc.

(1) This section applies where in proceedings for an offence–

(a) an issue arises as to whether a person charged with the offence ("D") is entitled to rely on a defence within subsection (2), and

(b) the question arises whether the degree of force used by D against a person ("V") was reasonable in the circumstances.

(2) The defences are–

(a) the common law defence of self-defence;

(aa) the common law defence of defence of property; and

(b) the defences provided by section 3(1) of the Criminal Law Act 1967 (c. 58) or section 3(1) of the Criminal Law Act (Northern Ireland) 1967 (c. 18 (N.I.)) (use of force in prevention of crime or making arrest).

(3) The question whether the degree of force used by D was reasonable in the circumstances is to be decided by reference to the circumstances as D believed them to be, and subsections (4) to (8) also apply in connection with deciding that question.

(4) If D claims to have held a particular belief as regards the existence of any circumstances–

(a) the reasonableness or otherwise of that belief is relevant to the question whether D genuinely held it; but

(b) if it is determined that D did genuinely hold it, D is entitled to rely on it for the purposes of subsection (3), whether or not–

(i) it was mistaken, or

(ii) (if it was mistaken) the mistake was a reasonable one to have made.

(5) But subsection (4)(b) does not enable D to rely on any mistaken belief attributable to intoxication that was voluntarily induced.

An example of the type of situation in which subsection (5) might apply is *R* v *O'Grady* [1987] QB 995. O'Grady had spent the day drinking with his friends McCloskey and Brennan. They fell asleep at O'Grady's flat. When Brennan woke up the next morning O'Grady was covered in blood and McCloskey was dead. McCloskey had severe bruising, a fractured rib and more than 20 wounds on his face. He had bled to death from these wounds. O'Grady had a number of cuts to his head, hands and legs. O'Grady stated: 'I was awakened by a bang on the head and I jumped up and put my hand to my head and the blood was running down. I am not sure if it was one bang I got or more. I saw Eddie [McCloskey] standing up … he had a piece of glass in one hand … I made for him to stop him hitting me again. I picked up a piece of glass and I hit him. We were both standing up facing each other … We struggled … He was getting the better of me, trying to knock me over. I hit him to stop him hitting me again … I did not want to kill him. I wanted him alive, not dead. I had no enmity to him. If I had not hit him I would be dead myself.' At trial O'Grady was convicted of manslaughter.

One of the questions of fact the jury had to consider was whether O'Grady's belief that McCloskey was attacking him was mistaken. At his appeal against conviction the Court of Appeal held that if O'Grady had formed a mistaken belief, and this mistake was due to voluntary intoxication, the mistaken belief must be disregarded:

> We have come to the conclusion that where the jury are satisfied that the defendant was mistaken in his belief that any force or the force which he in fact used was necessary to defend himself and are further satisfied that the mistake was caused by voluntarily induced intoxication, the defence must fail [… A] defendant is not entitled to rely, so far as self-defence is concerned, upon a mistake of fact which has been induced by voluntary intoxication

The scope of subsection (5) was considered by the Court of Appeal in *R* v *Taj* (which we studied in Chapter 9). The Court held that subsection (5) applies not only to mistaken beliefs which are the result of being voluntarily intoxicated at the time, but also mistaken beliefs which are 'immediately and proximately consequent upon earlier drink or drug-taking, so that even though the person concerned is not drunk or intoxicated at the time, the short-term effects can be shown to have triggered subsequent episodes of e.g. paranoia' ([60]). On the other hand, the Court in *R* v *Taj* stated that subsection (5) does not apply to mistaken beliefs that are the result of long-term mental illness (whether or not the illness was caused by alcohol or drug misuse). So, for example, suppose a defendant being held in a police station suffers a psychotic delusion. As a result he believes that the police officers are evil spirits intent on harming him, and so punches them in order to escape. At this stage of the test, his mistaken beliefs must be taken into account.[20]

[20] *R* v *Oye* [2013] EWCA Crim 1725

ii. The objective limb

With the exception of 'householder cases' (where, as we'll see below, special rules apply[21]), the objective limb of the test asks whether the amount of force the defendant used was reasonable in the circumstances as he believed them to be. It is important to be clear that the test is not whether the defendant thought the amount of force used was reasonable. It is whether the amount of force used was objectively reasonable.

Subsections (6), (7) and (8) of section 76 of the Criminal Justice and Immigration Act 2008 provide some guidance on the application of the objective limb.

EXTRACT

Section 76 of the Criminal Justice and Immigration Act 2008

(6) In a case other than a householder case, the degree of force used by D is not to be regarded as having been reasonable in the circumstances as D believed them to be if it was disproportionate in those circumstances.

[...]

(7) In deciding the question mentioned in subsection (3) the following considerations are to be taken into account (so far as relevant in the circumstances of the case)—

(a) that a person acting for a legitimate purpose may not be able to weigh to a nicety the exact measure of any necessary action; and

(b) that evidence of a person's having only done what the person honestly and instinctively thought was necessary for a legitimate purpose constitutes strong evidence that only reasonable action was taken by that person for that purpose.

(8) Subsections (6A) and (7) are not to be read as preventing other matters from being taken into account where they are relevant to deciding the question mentioned in subsection (3).

Subsection (6) makes it clear that (in non-householder cases) it will always be deemed unreasonable to use a disproportionate amount of force. However, it is important to remember that in many cases involving prevention of crime or private defence the defendant will have to act in the heat of the moment. He will have to act instinctively, and will not have time to stop and ponder the amount of force that it would be reasonable to use. Subsection (7) makes some concession for this. It requires a jury to take into account the fact that the defendant may not have had the chance to 'weigh to a nicety the exact measure of any necessary action'. And it states that the fact that the defendant only did what they 'honestly and instinctively thought was necessary' to prevent crime or for private defence is 'strong evidence' that the amount of force used was reasonable.

Householder cases

Subsection (5A) explains that the application of the objective limb differs in householder cases:

> (5A) In a householder case, the degree of force used by D is not to be regarded as having been reasonable in the circumstances as D believed them to be if it was grossly disproportionate in those circumstances.

So whilst subsection (6) tells us that in non-householder cases it will always have been unreasonable to have used a disproportionate amount of force, subsection (5A) raises this threshold for householder cases. It tells us that in such cases it will always have been

[21] These were inserted by section 43 of the Crime and Courts Act 2013.

unreasonable to have used a grossly disproportionate amount of force. The Ministry of Justice explained the rationale of subsection (5A) as follows:[22]

> The provision is designed to give householders greater latitude in terrifying or extreme situations where they may not be thinking clearly about the precise level of force that is necessary to deal with the threat faced.

The interpretation of subsection (5A) was considered in R (*on the application of Collins*) v *Secretary of State for Justice* [2016] EWHC 33 (Admin).

EXTRACT

Read the following extract from the judgment of Sir Brian Leveson P.

According to this, if a defendant in a householder case used a disproportionate (but not grossly disproportionate) amount of force, does it automatically follow that the force used was reasonable?

In a householder case, how should the trial judge direct the jury on the objective limb?

R (on the application of Collins) v *Secretary of State for Justice* [2016] EWHC 33 (Admin)

Sir Brian Leveson P

18 [...] It is clear from the section that s. 76(3) adopts and preserves the second limb of self-defence at common law. As it has been for many years, the central question (and the standard) remains whether the degree of force that a defendant used was "reasonable in the circumstances as the defendant believed them to be". The standard remains that which is reasonable: the other provisions (and, in particular, s. 76(5A) and (6) of the 2008 Act) provide the context in which the question of what is reasonable must be approached. The test in the statute is not whether the force used was proportionate, disproportionate or grossly disproportionate.

19 The operation of s. 76(5A) automatically excludes a degree of force which is grossly disproportionate from being reasonable in householder cases. If the degree of force was not grossly disproportionate, s. 76(5A) does not prevent that degree of force from being considered reasonable within the meaning of the second self-defence limb. On the other hand, it does not direct that any degree of force less than grossly disproportionate is reasonable. Whether it was or was not reasonable will depend on the particular facts and circumstances of the case.

20 Thus, s. 76(5A), read together with s. 76(3) and the common law on self-defence, requires two separate questions to be put to the jury in a householder case. Presuming that the defendant genuinely believed that it was necessary to use force to defend himself, these are:

(i) Was the degree of force the defendant used grossly disproportionate in the circumstances as he believed them to be? If the answer is "yes", he cannot avail himself of self-defence. If "no", then;

(ii) Was the degree of force the defendant used nevertheless reasonable in the circumstances he believed them to be? If it was reasonable, he has a defence. If it was unreasonable, he does not

The Court went on to state that, understood in this way, subsection (5A) does not violate Article 2 of the European Convention on Human Rights (the right to life).

[22] Ministry of Justice (2013) *Use of Force in Self Defence at Place of Residence* (Circular no 2013/02 26 April 2013).

The decision in R (*on the application of Collins*) v *Secretary of State for Justice* was endorsed by a five-member Court of Appeal in *R v Ray* [2017] EWCA Crim 1391. In its judgment, the Court gave some further guidance on how trial judges should direct juries in householder cases.

EXTRACT

Read the following extract from the judgment of Lord Thomas CJ.

According to Lord Thomas CJ, why is a householder 'entitled to some latitude as to the degree of force used'?

R v *Ray* [2017] EWCA Crim 1391

Lord Thomas CJ

35 It nevertheless may not always be easy for a jury readily to appreciate the task that faces them in a householder case. It is therefore important that when summing up in cases where the householder's defence is raised the judge gives some colour to the issue of self defence which arises. It may be helpful to explain to the jury in general terms that Parliament has conferred a greater latitude in cases of a householder in his own home, for reasons they will doubtless readily understand. It can be pointed out that what might be an unreasonable degree of force used when confronting an aggressive individual in a club might not be so when used by a householder confronting an intruder in his own home. That is why it is particularly important that the jury assess the defendant's actions by reference to the circumstances in which he found himself and as he believed them to be – a point that can then be illustrated and expanded in the summing up with the detail appropriate to the case. However, it must of course be made clear to the jury that the use of force that is grossly disproportionate (completely over the top, in ordinary language) can never be reasonable.

36 It would, in our view, generally be helpful also to explain to the jury in such a case in everyday language the dilemma that would confront any householder when an intruder enters his or her house. The householder is entitled to some latitude as to the degree of force used; if the jury do not regard the degree of force as being completely over the top they need carefully to examine all the circumstances in determining whether the prosecution have proved that the degree of force used was unreasonable. It is this context that differentiates the householder case.

37 It would often be helpful, for that purpose, to spell out the kind of circumstances which the jury should consider in determining whether the degree of force used by a householder was reasonable. These might, for example, include the shock of coming upon an intruder, the time of day, the presence of other help, the desire to protect the home and its occupants, the vulnerability of the occupants, particularly children, or the picking up of an object (such as a knife or stick that would lawfully be to hand in the home), the conduct of the intruder at the time (or on any relevant previous occasion if known to the defendant). Each of these might lead to the view that what was done, such as using a knife, which otherwise in a different context might be unreasonable, in the circumstances of a householder coming on an intruder might, in all the circumstances of such a case, be reasonable.

38 Another useful illustration may be the question of retreat. S. 76(6A) makes clear that there is no duty to retreat; the possibility of retreat is but a factor in determining whether the degree of force used was reasonable. If there is a threat of confrontation in the street, then the option to retreat may be important in determining whether the use of any force was reasonable. In the case of an intruder in the home, however, the option of retreat is unlikely to arise in many cases and therefore the degree of force used, although otherwise appearing to be disproportionate, might nonetheless be assessed as reasonable.

Having considered the law that applies in householder cases, the next question is, what constitutes a 'householder case'? This is explained in subsections (8A)–(8F):

EXTRACT

Section 76 of the Criminal Justice and Immigration Act 2008

(8A) For the purposes of this section "a householder case" is a case where–

(a) the defence concerned is the common law defence of self defence,

(b) the force concerned is force used by D while in or partly in a building, or part of a building, that is a dwelling or is forces accommodation (or is both),

(c) D is not a trespasser at the time the force is used, and

(d) at that time D believed V to be in, or entering, the building or part as a trespasser.

(8B) Where–

(a) a part of a building is a dwelling where D dwells,

(b) another part of the building is a place of work for D or another person who dwells in the first part, and

(c) that other part is internally accessible from the first part, that other part, and any internal means of access between the two parts, are each treated for the purposes of subsection (8A) as a part of a building that is a dwelling.

(8C) Where–

(a) a part of a building is forces accommodation that is living or sleeping accommodation for D,

(b) another part of the building is a place of work for D or another person for whom the first part is living or sleeping accommodation, and

(c) that other part is internally accessible from the first part, that other part, and any internal means of access between the two parts, are each treated for the purposes of subsection (8A) as a part of a building that is forces accommodation.

(8D) Subsections (4) and (5) apply for the purposes of subsection (8A)(d) as they apply for the purposes of subsection (3).

(8E) The fact that a person derives title from a trespasser, or has the permission of a trespasser, does not prevent the person from being a trespasser for the purposes of subsection (8A).

(8F) In subsections (8A) to (8C)–

"building" includes a vehicle or vessel, and

"forces accommodation" means service living accommodation for the purposes of Part 3 of the Armed Forces Act 2006 by virtue of section 96(1)(a) or (b) of that Act.

The key points to note are as follows:

- The defendant must have been defending himself or another person (subsection (8A)(a)).[23] So if the defendant was protecting property or preventing crime, but not defending himself or another, the case is a non-householder one.

---

[23] During the Parliamentary passage of the Domestic Abuse Act 2021, the Government rejected a proposal to extend the householder provisions to also include victims of domestic abuse. For criticism of this, see Bettinson, V. & Wake, N. (2024) 'A New Self-Defence Framework for Domestic Abuse Survivors Who Use Violent Resistance in Response' 87 *Modern Law Review* 141.

- Householder cases include those where the defendant lives and works in the same building (subsection (8B)) and those where the defendant was a member of the armed forces and was in forces accommodation (subsection (8C)).
- The defendant must have been in, or partly in, the relevant building when the force was used (subsection (8A)(b)). So if the defendant was defending himself against an attack on the street, the case is a non-householder one.
- The defendant must not have been a trespasser at the time that force was used (subsection (8A)(c)).
- The defendant must have believed that the other person was in, or was entering, the building (or part of the building) as a trespasser (subsection (8A)(d)). Note that the question here is not whether the other person was *in fact* a trespasser. The question is whether the defendant genuinely *believed* (rightly or wrongly) that the other person was a trespasser.[24] Note also that the defendant need not believe that the other person entered the building as a trespasser, as long as he believes the other person is trespassing at the time the force is used.[25] Householder cases could therefore include a situation in which the defendant invites the other person into his home, but later asks the person to leave and they refuse to do so.
- The householder provisions still apply, even if the defendant is using the household to commit crime. In *R v Gill* [2023] EWCA Crim 259 the defendant was involved in drug dealing. The police obtained a search warrant for the defendant's home. Eight police officers arrived to execute the search warrant at 6am. They broke in through the front door using a battering ram and a hooligan bar. It took 24 seconds to get the door open, during which time they did not identify themselves as police. The victim, PC Long, entered the house first and shouted 'Police'. As he did so, the defendant stabbed him in the arm. The defendant was charged with wounding with intent (Offences Against the Person Act 1861, section 18). He said that he genuinely believed that other drug dealers were breaking into his house, and that he was acting to defend himself and his mother from the risk of death or serious injury. At trial, the judge held that the defendant could not rely on the householder provisions because his fear stemmed from his own criminal conduct (the drug dealing). The defendant was subsequently convicted. On appeal, the Court of Appeal held that the trial judge had misdirected the jury. Nowhere in section 76 does it say that someone who has admitted criminal acts should lose the protection of the householder provisions. The conviction was quashed and a retrial ordered.

Use of excessive force

If the defendant passes both the subjective and objective limbs the defence succeeds and the defendant is not guilty. But if the amount of force used by the defendant was not reasonable, then the defence fails. It is all or nothing.

This is particularly important in homicide cases. An example is *R v Clegg* [1995] 1 AC 482. Clegg was a soldier in Northern Ireland. Whilst on patrol a stolen car approached his patrol at speed. He fired three shots at the windscreen, and a fourth after the car had passed. The last shot, which was fired when the car was 15 metres down the road, killed a rear-seat passenger. Clegg argued that he had fired in defence of himself and a fellow soldier.

The case reached the House of Lords. It was argued that if the defendant genuinely believed the use of force was necessary, but the amount of force used was excessive (i.e. the defendant passed the subjective limb of the test, but failed the objective limb), he should be convicted of manslaughter, not murder. In other words, it was suggested that there should be a partial defence to murder of excessive force. The House of Lords rejected this suggestion.

---

[24] *R v Cheeseman* [2019] EWCA Crim 149. In *R v Magson* [2022] EWCA Crim 1064 the Court of Appeal emphasised that there must be some evidence that the defendant believed the other person was a trespasser in order for the case to be regarded as a householder case.

[25] *R v Cheeseman* [2019] EWCA Crim 149.

EXTRACT

Read the following extract from Lord Lloyd's judgment.

Why did he refuse to recognise a partial defence of excessive force?

R v *Clegg* [1995] 1 AC 482

Lord Lloyd

In other words, there is no half-way house. There is no rule that a defendant who has used a greater degree of force than was necessary in the circumstances should be found guilty of manslaughter rather than murder [... I]t is all or nothing. The defence either succeeds or it fails. If it succeeds, the defendant is acquitted. If it fails, he is guilty of murder.

[...]

I am not averse to judges developing law, or indeed making new law, when they can see their way clearly, even where questions of social policy are involved. A good recent example would be the affirmation by this House of the decision of the Court of Appeal (Criminal Division) that a man can be guilty of raping his wife (*Reg.* v. *R.* [1992] 1 A.C. 599). But in the present case I am in no doubt that your Lordships should abstain from law-making. The reduction of what would otherwise be murder to manslaughter in a particular class of case seems to me essentially a matter for decision by the legislature, and not by this House in its judicial capacity. For the point in issue is, in truth, part of the wider issue whether the mandatory life sentence for murder should still be maintained. That wider issue can only be decided by Parliament. I would say the same for the point at issue in this case. Accordingly I would answer the certified question of law as follows. On the facts stated, and assuming no other defence is available, the soldier or police officer will be guilty of murder, and not manslaughter. It follows that the appeal must be dismissed.

Think about this question.

If a similar case occurred today, would the defendant be able to plead the partial defence of loss of control?

Characteristics of the defendant

In 1999 a case involving Norfolk farmer Tony Martin hit the headlines and sparked a national debate. Martin's farmhouse, Bleak House, was extremely remote and had been burgled many times in the past. On 20 August 1999 two men, 16-year-old Freddie Barras and 30-year-old Brendan Fearon, broke into Bleak House. Armed with an unlicensed pump action shotgun, Martin shot at the intruders at least three times. Fearon was shot in the legs, and Barras was shot in the legs and in the back. Barras died from his injuries. Martin was charged with murder. At trial Martin argued that he acted in self-defence, but the jury rejected this and convicted him of murder.[26]

At Martin's subsequent appeal fresh psychiatric evidence was produced. According to this evidence, Martin had a long-standing paranoid personality disorder. As a result of this

[26] Morris, S. (2001). 'The killer who won a nation's sympathy', *The Guardian*, 30 October. Available at: www.theguardian.com/uk/2001/oct/30/tonymartin.ukcrime2#maincontent

disorder, Martin's perception of the threat the two intruders posed to his physical safety would have been much greater than the perception of the average person. One of the principal issues for the Court of Appeal in *R* v *Martin (Tony)* [2003] QB 1 was whether psychiatric conditions like this can be taken into account when applying the objective limb of the test for prevention of crime and private defence.

EXTRACT

According to the following extract from the judgment of Lord Woolf CJ, which of the defendant's characteristics can be taken into account when applying the objective limb and which cannot?

R v *Martin (Tony)* [2003] QB 1

Lord Woolf CJ

67. We would accept that the jury are entitled to take into account in relation to self-defence the physical characteristics of the defendant. However, we would not agree that it is appropriate, except in exceptional circumstances which would make the evidence especially probative, in deciding whether excessive force has been used to take into account whether the defendant is suffering from some psychiatric condition

So Martin's condition could be taken into account when applying the subjective limb, but not the objective limb. In other words, a defendant's psychiatric condition may be considered when deciding whether the defendant genuinely believed that the use of force was necessary to respond to a threat, but may not be considered when assessing whether the amount of force used in response to the threat was reasonable. This fine distinction has been criticised by commentators.[27]

It is worth noting three further points about the judgment in *R* v *Martin (Tony)*:

- First, you will have noticed in the extract from Lord Woolf CJ's judgment above that he stated that psychiatric conditions may be considered in 'exceptional circumstances'. The Court of Appeal commented on this in *R* v *Oye* [2013] EWCA Crim 1725. In this case the defendant, Seun Oye, was being held in a police station custody suite when he suffered a psychotic delusion. As a result of the delusion he believed that the police officers in the station were evil spirits intent on harming him, and so he punched them in order to escape. Referring to Lord Woolf's judgment, defence counsel argued that there were exceptional circumstances which meant that Oye's delusion should be taken into account when applying the objective limb. The Court of Appeal rejected this. Davis LJ stated:

  53. [...] Quite what Lord Woolf had in mind in his reference to "exceptional circumstances" is unexplained. But at all events if Martin was not considered an exceptional case then we do not see how or why the present case should be.

  Similarly, in *R* v *Taj* the Court of Appeal held that the defendant's psychosis should not be considered when applying the objective limb. It seems clear from these cases that Lord Woolf's reference to 'exceptional circumstances' will rarely be applied in practice.

[27] The authors of *Simester and Sullivan's Criminal Law*, for example, describe it as 'spurious' (Simester, A.P., Spencer, J.R., Stark, F., Sullivan, G.R. and Virgo, G.J. (2016) *Simester and Sullivan's Criminal Law: Theory and Doctrine* (6th edn). Hart Publishing: Oxford, p.701).

- Second, Martin's case predated the new rules regarding householder cases. So if a similar case occurred today, the jury would have to apply the rules set out in subsection (5A) of section 76 of the Criminal Justice and Immigration Act 2008.

Now, think about this question.

Imagine a jury was applying the new rules regarding householder cases to the facts of Tony Martin's case.

In your opinion, would Martin still be convicted? Or would Martin's claim of self-defence now succeed?

- Third, although the Court of Appeal rejected Martin's plea of self-defence it did hold that the paranoid personality disorder was an abnormality of the mind for the purposes of diminished responsibility. The Court therefore quashed Martin's murder conviction and substituted a manslaughter conviction on the grounds of diminished responsibility. Martin was sentenced to five years' imprisonment for manslaughter, and was released from custody in July 2003. In 2009, on the tenth anniversary of the offence, an unrepentant Martin said in an interview, 'I don't have any regrets at all, I don't see why I should'.[28]

Pre-emptive strikes

A defendant may be able to plead prevention of crime or private defence where he has acted pre-emptively. As Lord Griffiths stated in the Privy Council case *Beckford* v *The Queen* [1988] AC 130, 'A man about to be attacked does not have to wait for his assailant to strike the first blow or fire the first shot; circumstances may justify a pre-emptive strike'.

In *Attorney-General's Reference* (*No 2 of 1983*) [1984] QB 456 the defendant owned a shop in an area where there had been two nights of rioting. The defendant's shop had been damaged and goods had been looted. Fearing further attacks, the defendant made ten petrol bombs. He explained, 'I had no intention to injure anyone but to use purely as a last resort to keep them away from my shop'. At trial the defendant was acquitted of an offence under the Explosive Substances Act 1883. The Attorney-General referred to the Court of Appeal the question whether someone in a situation like the defendant's could plead self-defence. Whilst parts of the Court's reasoning are problematic,[29] the Court made it clear that a defendant may act pre-emptively where there is a threat of an imminent attack. Lord Lane CJ stated:

> It may be a reasonable excuse that the carrier is in anticipation of imminent attack and is carrying the weapon for his own personal defence [...] In our judgment a defendant is not left in the paradoxical position of being able to justify acts carried out in self-defence but not acts immediately preparatory to it.

The requirement that the anticipated crime must be imminent was reiterated by the High Court in *R (on the application of the DPP)* v *Stratford Magistrates' Court* [2017] EWHC 1794 (Admin), which we looked at earlier. Although the protestors in this case said that

[28] '"I don't regret killing that teenage burglar", says vigilante farmer Tony *Martin*', *Daily Mail*, 21 August 2009.

[29] In particular, Lord Lane CJ's statement that, 'He may still arm himself for his own protection, if the exigency arises, although in so doing he may commit other offences'. As Ormerod and Laird argue, it appears to be inconsistent to say 'He may do it – but he will commit an offence if he does' (Ormerod, D. and Laird, K. (2015) *Smith and Hogan's Criminal Law* (14th edn). OUP: Oxford, p.450).

they obstructed the highway in order to prevent illegal arms sales, there was insufficient evidence that they were acting to prevent an 'imminent and immediate' crime ([41]). Even if illegal arms sales were taking place at the exhibition, there was nothing to link the defendants' actions to the prevention of these sales since the vehicles they obstructed were not carrying prohibited weapons.

A duty to retreat?

In *R* v *Bird* [1985] 1 WLR 816 the defendant, Debbie Bird, was celebrating her 17th birthday at a house party. Bird's ex-boyfriend, Darren Marder, showed up at the party with his new girlfriend. A little later an argument broke out between Bird and Marder. She claimed that Marder grabbed hold of her and held her against a wall. To defend herself, she struck him with her hand. In the heat of the moment, she said it did not occur to her that the hand she struck him with was holding a glass. The glass smashed in Marder's face, and as a result he lost an eye. Bird was charged with malicious wounding under section 20 of the Offences Against the Person Act 1861.

At Bird's trial the judge told the jury that 'it is necessary that a person claiming to exercise a right of self-defence should demonstrate by her action that she does not want to fight'. In other words, there is a duty to retreat before using force in order to prevent crime or for private defence. Failure to try and retreat will result in these defences being unavailable. The issue for the Court of Appeal at Bird's appeal against conviction was whether this was a misdirection.

EXTRACT

According to the following extract from the judgment of Lord Lane CJ, is there a duty to retreat before using force in order to prevent crime or for private defence? If not, then how (if at all) is a defendant's attempt or failure to retreat relevant to the objective limb of the test?

R v *Bird* [1985] 1 WLR 816

Lord Lane CJ

The matter is dealt with accurately and helpfully in Smith and Hogan Criminal Law, 5th ed. (1983), p. 327:

> "There were formerly technical rules about the duty to retreat before using force, or at least fatal force. This is now simply a factor to be taken into account in deciding whether it was necessary to use force, and whether the force was reasonable. If the only reasonable course is to retreat, then it would appear that to stand and fight must be to use unreasonable force. There is, however, no rule of law that a person attacked is bound to run away if he can; but it has been said that– '... what is necessary is that he should demonstrate by his actions that he does not want to fight. He must demonstrate that he is prepared to temporise and disengage and perhaps to make some physical withdrawal' [Reg. v. Julien [1969] 1 W.L.R. 839, 842]. It is submitted that it goes too far to say that action of this kind is necessary. It is scarcely consistent with the rule that it is permissible to use force, not merely to counter an actual attack, but to ward off an attack honestly and reasonably believed to be imminent. A demonstration by [the defendant] at the time that he did not want to fight is, no doubt, the best evidence that he was acting reasonably and in good faith in self-defence; but it is no more than that. A person may in some circumstances so act without temporising, disengaging or withdrawing; and he should have a good defence."

> We respectfully agree with that passage. If the defendant is proved to have been attacking or retaliating or revenging himself, then he was not truly acting in self-defence. Evidence that the defendant tried to retreat or tried to call off the fight may be a cast-iron method of casting doubt on the suggestion that he was the attacker or retaliator or the person trying to revenge himself. But it is not by any means the only method of doing that

As a result of the misdirection, the conviction was quashed.

The decision in *R* v *Bird* has now been placed on a statutory footing, in subsection (6A) of section 76 of the Criminal Justice and Immigration Act 2008:[30]

> (6A) In deciding the question mentioned in subsection (3), a possibility that D could have retreated is to be considered (so far as relevant) as a factor to be taken into account, rather than as giving rise to a duty to retreat.

The defendant was the initial aggressor

The issue in *R* v *Bird* was whether there is a duty to retreat. *R* v *Rashford* [2005] EWCA Crim 3377 concerned a slightly different scenario. Imagine that Derek has just discovered that his wife has been having an affair with Victor. Furious, he sets off to Victor's house to confront him. When he arrives he grabs Victor by the scruff of the neck and yells angrily at him. Victor retaliates violently. He knocks Derek to the floor and kicks him several times. To escape, Derek trips Victor over and punches him in the face. Suppose that Derek is charged with an offence for punching Victor in the face. Should he be able to plead self-defence? Or should the defence be unavailable to him because he sought Victor out in the first place? In other words, should the defence be available to a defendant who was the initial aggressor?

EXTRACT

The following extract is taken from the judgment of Dyson LJ in *R* v *Rashford*.

If the defendant was the initial aggressor, is the defence automatically unavailable? If not, then in what circumstances may the initial aggressor plead self-defence?

R v *Rashford* [2005] EWCA Crim 3377

Dyson LJ

19 [... T]he mere fact that a defendant goes somewhere in order to exact revenge from the victim does not of itself rule out the possibility that in any violence that ensues self-defence is necessarily not available as a defence. It must depend on the circumstances [...] There may be a temptation whenever it is open to a jury to conclude that the defendant went to an incident out of revenge or was the aggressor to direct the jury that if they reach that conclusion then self-defence cannot avail the defendant. But if the judge wishes to give a direction along these lines the facts will usually require something rather more sophisticated where the possibility exists that the initial aggression may have resulted in a response by the victim which is so out of proportion to that aggression as to give rise to an honest belief in the aggressor that it was necessary for him to defend himself and the amount of force that he used was reasonable

[30] For detailed discussion of the duty to retreat, see Mark Dsouza, 'Retreat, Submission, and the Private Use of Force' (2015) 35 *Oxford Journal of Legal Studies* 727.

So the fact that the defendant was the initial aggressor does not necessarily bar him from relying on the defence.

The Court of Appeal revisited this issue in *R* v *Keane* [2010] EWCA Crim 2514, and provided further guidance. The defendant, Daniel Keane, had been on a night out at the pub. The victim was giving Keane and two women a lift home. On the way they stopped at a petrol station. Whilst the victim was inside paying for the petrol Keane got into an argument with one of the women, during which he pushed her over. When the victim got back he asked Keane what was going on. There was a conversation, which ended with the victim saying 'Just don't do it again'. As the victim turned to walk away Keane said, 'What are you going to do about it?' The victim stopped and turned back, and as he did so he began to take his hand out of his pocket. Thinking that the victim was going to hit him, Keane punched him in the face. The victim fell back and suffered a serious blow to the back of his head. At trial Keane was convicted of maliciously inflicting grievous bodily harm (section 20 Offences Against the Person Act 1861).

At Keane's appeal against conviction the Court of Appeal had to consider whether Keane could claim he was acting in self-defence. The Court reiterated the approach set out in *R* v *Rashford*.

EXTRACT

In the following extract, what test does the Court set out for deciding whether the initial aggressor may claim self-defence?

R v *Keane* [2010] EWCA Crim 2514

Lord Justice Hughes

17 [... S]elf-defence may arise in the case of an original aggressor but only where the violence offered by the victim was so out of proportion to what the original aggressor did that in effect the roles were reversed.

[...]

18 [... I]t is not enough to bring self-defence into issue that a defendant who started the fight is at some point during the fight for the time being getting the worst of it, merely because the victim is defending himself reasonably. In that event there has been no disproportionate act by the victim [...] The victim has not been turned into the aggressor. The tables have not been turned in that particular sense. The roles have not been reversed

Dismissing Keane's appeal, the Court emphasised a further principle, which was particularly relevant to Keane saying 'What are you going to do about it?'

EXTRACT

Read the following extract. What was the further principle the Court set out? Why was it relevant to Keane saying 'What are you going to do about it?'

R v *Keane* [2010] EWCA Crim 2514

Lord Justice Hughes

19 [...] We need to say as clearly as we may that it is not the law that if a defendant sets out to provoke another to punch him and succeeds, the defendant is then entitled to punch the other person. What that would do would be to legalise the common coin of the bully who confronts his victim with taunts which are deliberately designed to provide an excuse to hit him.

The use of force on an innocent third party

Can a defendant inflict force on an innocent third party in order to prevent someone else from committing a crime? This was considered by the Court of Appeal in *R* v *Hichens* [2011] EWCA Crim 1626.

When Hichens lost his hostel placement Kathleen Brown allowed him to stay in her flat. Brown had previously had an on-off relationship with a man called John Oliver. One day Oliver turned up at the flat acting abusively, threatening to beat Hichens up. The next morning he returned, again acting abusively. The police warned Oliver to stay away, and advised Brown not to let Oliver in if he showed up again. Later that evening Oliver turned up at the flat. Brown wanted to let him in, but Hichens stopped her from doing so. He grabbed Brown's arm, threw her on to the sofa, and then put his hand around her throat causing her to lose consciousness. He also threatened to break her jaw.

Hichens argued that he could rely on the prevention of crime defence. He argued that he assaulted Brown in order to prevent Oliver from entering the flat and beating him up. At Hichens' trial the judge withdrew the prevention of crime defence from the jury's consideration, and Hichens was convicted of battery. He appealed, arguing that the judge had been wrong to withdraw the defence from the jury.

EXTRACT

Read the following extract from the judgment of Gross LJ.

Is it correct to say that a defendant who used force on an innocent third party in order to prevent someone else from committing a crime may never plead the prevention of crime defence?

The Court of Appeal concluded that the trial judge was wrong to withdraw the prevention of crime defence from the jury's consideration, but nonetheless upheld Hichens' conviction. How did the Court justify this?

R v *Hichens* [2011] EWCA Crim 1626

Gross LJ

30. It is next convenient to focus on two separate strands. The first is whether self-defence at common law and the use of force in the prevention of crime under s.3 of the Criminal Law Act 1967 are capable of extending to the use of force, against an innocent third party, to prevent a crime being committed by someone else. If and in so far as the judge thought that these defences were not capable of extending to the use of force against an innocent third party, we respectfully disagree, and indeed Mr Wicks did not seek to contend otherwise. Although we suspect that the facts capable realistically of giving rise to such a defence will only rarely be encountered, examples can be adduced and two will suffice:

1. a police constable bundles a passerby out of the way to get at a man he believes about to shoot with a firearm or detonate an explosive device;
2. Y seeks to give Z car keys with Z about to drive. X, believing Z to be unfit to drive through drink, knocks the keys out of Y's hands and retains them.

As ever the fact that the defence is capable of being advanced is of course a very different question from whether it would succeed

[...]

33 [... W]e are wholly unable to contemplate a reasonable jury, properly directed, with a suitable and forceful emphasis on the question of remoteness, acquitting the appellant. Even on the most favourable view of the evidence for the appellant, we underline: (i) Miss Brown was doing what she was perfectly entitled to do, whether wisely or not; (ii) there was no risk to the appellant from Miss Brown, the victim of the slapping; (iii) there was, at the most, a possibility of a crime being committed by Oliver should he be admitted to the flat; (iv) at the time of the slapping no crime was being committed and Oliver was not in the flat; (v) the appellant had known that Oliver might be coming to the flat for some time before the incident; (vi) the appellant had obvious options including calling the police or leaving the flat and, in our judgment, ample time to exercise them. It follows that the appeal against conviction must be dismissed. We have no doubt that the conviction was safe.

Quiz 11.5

1. Which of the following defences is a complete defence to a charge of murder?

- **a.** Self-defence.
- **b.** Loss of control.
- **c.** Duress.
- **d.** Diminished responsibility.

2. What does section 3 of the Criminal Law Act 1967 do to the common law relating to the lawful use of force?

- **a.** It adds the prevention of crime and the arrest/detention of suspected offenders, actual offenders and escapees to the coverage of the common law, groups who were previously not covered.
- **b.** It replaces all of the common law regarding the legitimate use of force.
- **c.** It adds nothing, because it is merely declaratory of the common law.
- **d.** It replaces the common law rules on the use of force in the prevention of crime, in effecting or assisting in the lawful arrest of offenders or suspected offenders or of persons unlawfully at large, leaving the common law to deal with scenarios where someone defends themselves against behaviour which is not criminal.

3. Which of the following statements is correct?

- **a.** The defence of private defence can be used as a defence to all offences, but prevention of crime can only be used as a defence to offences involving physical violence.
- **b.** The defence of prevention of crime can be used as a defence to all offences, but private defence can only be used as a defence to offences involving physical violence.
- **c.** Successfully pleading private defence or prevention of crime will result in the defendant being found not guilty and both can be used to defend any charge involving the use of force against people or property, except murder.
- **d.** Successfully pleading private defence or prevention of crime will result in the defendant being found not guilty and both can be used to defend any charge involving the use of force against people or property, including murder.

4. The statutory prevention of crime defence supersedes the common law right of private defence, so when attempting to solve a problem involving the use of force by D you should...

- **a.** ask whether section 3 of the Criminal Law Act 1967 covers the situation and, if it does, use that to solve the problem.
- **b.** prioritise the statutory defence because, as it is a statutory defence, it is one that the defendant has to prove.
- **c.** prioritise the application of the common law defence if the facts of the problem disclose that D is defending himself from a criminal act.
- **d.** write about both defences, allowing equal space to explain both of them. According to the case of R v O'Grady [1987] QB 995...

5. According to the case of *R* v *O'Grady* [1987] QB 995...
   a. an intoxicated mistake will not give rise to the defence of self-defence if the crime charged is one of basic intent.
   b. a mistake can never be a defence to murder.
   c. an intoxicated mistake will not give rise to the defence of self-defence.
   d. an intoxicated mistake can never be a defence to murder.

6. Which of the following statements about the objective limb of the test for prevention of crime/private defence is incorrect?
   a. A defendant who acts pre-emptively is still able to seek to rely on the defences.
   b. A defendant who uses force on an innocent third party is still able to seek to rely on the defences.
   c. D's physical characteristics may be taken into account, but psychiatric ones will only be considered in exceptional circumstances.
   d. The defences are unavailable if D fails to demonstrate by his actions that he does not want to fight.

Conclusion

Think about these questions.

a. Now that you have read the chapter, in which (if any) of the three cases (*R* v *Dudley and Stephens*; *R* v *Bowen*; *R* v *Martin (Tony)*) would D be able to plead a substantive defence?

b. Is this what you expected?

In this chapter we have studied a total of five defences: necessity; duress by threats; duress of circumstances; prevention of crime; and private defence. As we have seen during the chapter, sometimes the different defences may overlap. For example:

- It may sometimes be difficult to distinguish between duress by threats and duress of circumstances, because it may be plausible to describe the facts of some cases in either way.
- There is a considerable overlap between prevention of crime and private defence.
- The defences of necessity and duress of circumstances may sometimes overlap. For example, Lord Denning's hypothetical fireman could potentially plead either necessity or duress of circumstances.
- The defences of necessity and private defence may sometimes overlap. For example, we saw that in the *Conjoined Twins* case Brooke LJ applied the defence of necessity, whilst Ward LJ applied the common law right of private defence.

One question that students often ask when answering exam problem questions is, in a case where the defences overlap, which one(s) should I discuss? So to conclude the chapter, here is some guidance:

- As we have seen, the test for the defence of duress is the same whether the case involves duress by threats or duress of circumstances. So if the facts could be presented in either way, you should simply explain this point and then apply the test for duress.
- We also saw earlier that if prevention of crime and private defence overlap, you should apply prevention of crime. This is a statutory defence and supersedes the common law right of private defence (Criminal Law Act 1967, section 3(2)).
- There remains uncertainty over the defence of necessity, particularly regarding the test that should be used for the defence. As we saw above, it seems that the courts will leave the defence to develop on a case-by-case basis. So if the problem question you are answering has similar facts to one of the existing cases on necessity, it would be

sensible to begin with this defence and argue that it should apply by analogy. But if the facts are not closely analogous, and there are other defences that could be used, it would be sensible to begin with these other defences instead. This is not to say that you shouldn't mention necessity at all. Rather, you should mention it as an alternative, more speculative, possibility.

Applying the law

11.6 Apply the law on substantive defences to hypothetical sets of facts.

Kai, Zheng, Theresa

Kai, Zheng and Theresa are at a nightclub. Shortly after midnight a fire breaks out, and Kai, Zheng and Theresa find themselves trapped in the chill-out room. The only escape route is through a small window. Kai begins to climb through the window, but becomes stuck. As the smoke and heat become more and more intense, Zheng realises that he and Theresa will die if they do not get out quickly – but the only way for them to escape is to cut off Kai's arm and push him through the window. Despite Kai's loud protestations, Zheng cuts off Kai's arm. As a result, all three of them manage to escape.

Now, think about these questions.

a. Discuss Zheng's criminal liability.

b. How (if at all) would your answer be different in each of the following three situations?

i. The fire brigade had arrived at the nightclub and begun to tackle the blaze. When Zheng said that he would have to cut off Kai's arm, Theresa had replied, 'We don't need to cut off his arm. The fire brigade are here. They will rescue us.' Zheng ignored Theresa's remarks, saying, 'We can't wait any longer', and cut off Kai's arm, enabling the three of them to escape through the window. Evidence subsequently shows that at the time Zheng cut off Kai's arm, the fire brigade had the fire under control and would have been able to rescue Zheng and Theresa from the chill-out room.

ii. Kai suffered a substantial loss of blood and as a result died shortly afterwards.

iii. Kai had insisted that he should climb through the window first, and pushed Zheng and Theresa out of the way. After Kai got stuck the room quickly filled with smoke. Zheng and Theresa died from smoke inhalation, but Kai was successfully rescued. (NB: In this scenario you should discuss the criminal liability of Kai, not Zheng.)

Tom

Teenager Tom lives with his parents. One day he is on his way home from college when Vito, a member of a local gang, walks up to him, points a knife at him, and says, 'Do as I say and you won't get hurt. I want you to break into Carlo's flat, find his wallet, and bring it to me'. Tom is too stunned to say anything. Vito continues, 'I'll wait here. Off you go. And don't think you can run away because I know where you live'. Terrified, Tom runs all the way to Carlo's flat – which is a quarter of a mile away – breaks in, finds Carlo's wallet, runs back to Vito and hands over the wallet.

Now, think about these questions.

a. Discuss Tom's criminal liability.

b. How (if at all) would your answer be different in each of the following four situations?

   i. Vito had gone to Carlo's flat with Tom, and stood by the front door keeping watch while Tom searched for Carlo's wallet.

   ii. When Vito pointed the knife at Tom he had said, 'Do it or I'll slash the tyres on your dad's car'.

   iii. Carlo happened to be one of Tom's neighbours, and Tom intensely disliked him. Tom felt no remorse about breaking into Carlo's flat, and in fact helped himself to a few of Carlo's DVDs while he was there.

   iv. Even though Vito's reputation for violence was well-known, a week earlier Tom had seen Vito at the local pub and had a drink with him.

Doug

Doug has just discovered that his wife Tessa has been having an affair with Vinnie. Furious, he storms round to Vinnie's house to confront him. When Vinnie opens his front door Doug begins to shout insults at him. Vinnie responds by pushing Doug over, and then jumps on top of him and begins to punch him. To get him to stop, Doug manages to pick up a stone from Vinnie's front garden and strikes Vinnie on the head with it, as hard as he can. Vinnie suffers a fractured skull, and has to spend several weeks in hospital.

Think about these questions.

1. Discuss Doug's criminal liability. How (if at all) would your answer be different in each of the following three situations?

   a. Doug had a personality disorder. As a result of this personality disorder, when Vinnie was on top of Doug punching him Doug was certain that Vinnie was going to kill him.

   b. Instead of picking up a stone, Doug had managed to get to his feet and started to run away. Seeing that Vinnie was chasing him, Doug pushed a passing pedestrian called Alice out of his way. Alice fell over and landed awkwardly, breaking her wrist.

   c. Doug had taken a knife with him. He didn't intend to use it, he just wanted to get his own back on Vinnie by scaring him. As Doug shouted insults at Vinnie, Vinnie had picked up a toy gun and pointed it at Doug. Although most people would have realised it was a toy, in the heat of the moment Doug thought Vinnie was going to shoot him, so he pulled out the knife and fatally stabbed Vinnie.

2. If you were the prosecutor in Doug's case, how would you argue that the amount of force he used was not reasonable (in the circumstances as Doug believed them to be)?
3. If you were Doug's defence counsel, how would you argue that the amount of force used was reasonable?

NB: Bear in mind also that Doug's defence counsel would have a plan B. They would argue that, if the prevention of crime defence is unavailable, Doug should be able to plead the partial defence of loss of control instead. In your opinion, does Doug satisfy the requirements for loss of control?

Quiz 11.6

1. The question asks us to discuss Doug's criminal liability. The starting point is to identify the relevant offence. Vinnie suffered very serious injuries, which would undoubtedly amount to GBH (*DPP* v *Smith*). The section 18 of the Offences Against the Person Act 1861 offence would apply since Doug did not only intend to cause Vinnie some harm (so satisfies the definition of malicious – *R* v *Cunningham*), but intended to cause Vinnie GBH (the additional *mens rea* requirement for the section 18 offence). Causing Vinnie GBH may not have been his direct intention – his purpose appears to have been to stop Vinnie from punching him, and so if Vinnie had suffered less serious injuries Doug would not have regarded this as a failure – but it was his oblique intention (*R* v *Woollin*). If you hit someone on the head with a stone as hard as you can it is virtually certain they will suffer serious harm. Doug cannot claim that in the heat of the moment he did not realise this, since deliberately closing your mind to something is equivalent to having foreseen it (*R* v *Parker*).

   We must therefore consider possible substantive defences. Since Doug used force to defend himself, the most relevant defences are prevention of crime (s.3 Criminal Law Act 1967) and private defence. Doug was preventing Vinnie from committing the offence of battery and, potentially, assault occasioning ABH. We must therefore focus on the prevention of crime defence, since where the two defences overlap prevention of crime supersedes private defence (s.3(2) Criminal Law Act 1967).

   Which of the following correctly states the first part of the test for the prevention of crime defence?

   a. Was it D's direct intention to prevent crime or was he acting for some other purpose?

   b. Did D reasonably believe the use of force was required in order to prevent crime?

   c. Would a reasonable person in D's position have regarded the use of force as necessary in order to prevent crime?

   d. Did D genuinely believe the use of force was required in order to prevent crime?

2. Turning to the objective part of the test, the first point to make here is that it does not appear to be a householder case. According to section 76(8A)(b) of the Criminal Justice and Immigration Act 2008, in householder cases the force must have been used by the defendant 'while in or partly in a building, or part of a building, that is a dwelling'. But in Doug's case it seems that the incident occurred outside (Doug picked up the stone from Vinnie's front garden). It is therefore a non-householder case.

   What is the objective limb of the test for prevention of crime?

   a. Did D genuinely believe that the amount of force used was reasonable?

   b. Was the amount of force used reasonable in the circumstances as D believed them to be?

   c. Was the amount of force used grossly disproportionate in the circumstances as D believed them to be?

   d. Did D genuinely believe that the amount of force used was not grossly disproportionate?

3. There are various points to consider when asking whether the amount of force Doug used was reasonable. On the one hand, Doug was being attacked and acted instinctively. Section 76(7) of the Criminal Justice and Immigration Act 2008 requires the jury in a case like Doug's to take into account: (a) that he may not have had the chance to 'weigh to a nicety the exact measure of any necessary action'; and (b) that if Doug only did what he 'honestly and instinctively thought was necessary' to prevent crime this is 'strong evidence' that the amount of force he used was reasonable.

   On the other hand, however, Doug struck Vinnie on the head – a particularly vulnerable part of the body – as opposed to somewhere else, such as his torso. Plus, the incident arose after Doug had stormed to Vinnie's house to confront him.

   Which of the following summarises the decision in R v Rashford correctly?

   a. If D was the initial aggressor, the defence of prevention of crime is unavailable to him.

   b. The fact that D was the initial aggressor does not necessarily bar him from relying on the prevention of crime defence.

   c. It is irrelevant whether D was the initial aggressor or not.

   d. In situations like these it is inappropriate to describe anyone as the initial aggressor.

4. So following *R* v *Rashford*, the fact that Doug went to Vinnie's house and confronted him does not necessarily mean he cannot rely on the prevention of crime defence. Further guidance on when an initial aggressor can rely on the defence was offered by the Court of Appeal in *R* v *Keane*.

   Which of the following was not one of the principles advanced by the Court of Appeal in *R* v *Keane*?

   a. If the roles had effectively been reversed, so that V had become the aggressor, then D may say that he was acting in self-defence.

b. If D starts a fight with V and ends up losing the fight, then D may say that he was using reasonable force to defend himself.

c. D may claim self-defence even if he was the initial aggressor if V's reaction was out of proportion to what D had done.

d. If D sets out to provoke V to attack him and succeeds, then D is not entitled to use force in response to V's attack.

5. Applying the principles from *R* v *Keane* to Doug's case, the first question to consider is whether Doug had deliberately set out to provoke Vinnie to attack him. If so, Doug may not rely on the prevention of crime defence. If not, the next question is whether Vinnie's reaction to Doug confronting and insulting him was so out of proportion that the roles had effectively been reversed. In other words, had Vinnie become the aggressor? If not, then the prevention of crime defence is unavailable to Doug. If so, then the final question to ask is whether the amount of force Doug used was reasonable.

Taking all of this into account, in your opinion would Doug pass the objective limb of the test for the defence?

If Doug fails the objective limb of the test for the prevention of crime defence, it seems unlikely that he would be able to plead another defence instead. Necessity only applies where the commission of the offence in question was the lesser of two evils. It would not apply in Doug's case, as it is not possible to say that Vinnie suffering serious harm was a lesser evil than Doug suffering serious harm. As for duress (of circumstances), there are three reasons why this defence is unlikely to be available.

First, duress is only available where the defendant had good cause to fear death or serious physical injury. It is arguable whether Vinnie punching Doug constituted a threat of serious physical injury. Second, if Doug were to fail the objective limb of the test for the prevention of crime defence because he used an unreasonable amount of force he would presumably also fail the objective limb of the test for duress (whether a sober person of reasonable firmness would have responded in the way that Doug did). And third, the prosecution could argue that by storming to Vinnie's house Doug voluntarily exposed himself to the threat of serious violence from Vinnie and so, in the light of the judgments in *R* v *Rashford*, *R* v *Keane* and *R* v *Hasan*, the defence of duress should be unavailable.

Turning to the first alternative scenario, the key question here is whether Doug's personality disorder could be taken into account when applying the objective limb of the test for the prevention of crime defence.

Which of the following summarises the principle from *R* v *Martin (Tony)* correctly?

a. The jury may take into account both D's physical characteristics and any psychiatric conditions.

b. The jury may take into account any psychiatric conditions but can only take D's physical characteristics into account in exceptional circumstances.

c. The jury may not take into account D's physical characteristics nor any psychiatric conditions.

d. The jury may take into account D's physical characteristics but can only take psychiatric conditions into account in exceptional circumstances.

6. In the light of *R* v *Martin (Tony)* and *R* v *Oye* it seems clear that Doug's personality disorder would not be taken into account. So, as far as the prevention of crime defence is concerned, Doug's personality disorder would make no difference to our original answer. It would also make little difference to our analysis of the defence of duress. Although the first limb of the test for duress is called the subjective limb, the House of Lords in *R* v *Hasan* [2005] UKHL 22 stated that only mistaken beliefs that are objectively reasonable should be considered. It is difficult to describe Doug's mistaken belief that Vinnie was going to kill him as objectively reasonable. And Doug will also be unable to plead insanity, because he retained an understanding of the nature and quality of his actions and that what he was doing was wrong (*M'Naghten's case*).

In the second alternative scenario the victim is Alice. She suffered a broken wrist, which would amount to GBH. The relevant offence is therefore malicious infliction of GBH (s.20 Offences Against the Person Act 1861). Doug acted maliciously – when he pushed Alice out of the way he either foresaw or deliberately closed his mind to the risk that Alice would suffer some harm (*R* v *Savage & Parmenter*) – but he did not intend to cause Alice GBH. His direct intention was to escape Vinnie, and had Alice not suffered serious harm Doug would not have regarded this as a failure. Nor was it his oblique intention to cause Alice serious harm since it is not virtually certain that shoving someone out of the way will cause them serious physical injury (*R* v *Woollin*). Therefore Doug did not form the additional mens rea required for the section 18 offence.

In terms of the prevention of crime defence, the key point here is that Doug was trying to prevent Vinnie from committing a crime, not Alice.

Which of the following was not one of the principles advanced by the Court of Appeal in *R v Hichens*?

a. A defendant who uses force on an innocent third party in order to prevent someone else from committing a crime may in principle plead the prevention of crime defence.

b. A defendant who uses force on an innocent third party in order to prevent someone else from committing a crime may never plead the prevention of crime defence.

c. Only rarely will a defendant who used force on an innocent third party be able to show that the force he used was reasonable.

d. To be able to rely on the prevention of crime defence, the defendant must show that the force used on the innocent third party was reasonable.

7. In the third alternative scenario Doug would be charged with murder. Although prevention of crime is available as a defence to murder, the defence of duress is not (*R v Howe*). In terms of prevention of crime, the first question to consider is whether Doug's mistaken belief that Vinnie was going to shoot him may be considered.

Which of the following statements about the prevention of crime defence is correct?

a. Mistaken beliefs that were genuinely held may be taken into account whether they were reasonable or not, as long as they were not caused by voluntary intoxication.

b. Any mistaken beliefs that were genuinely held may be taken into account, whatever the cause of the mistake.

c. Defendants must always be judged on the basis of the facts as they actually were, so mistaken beliefs may never be taken into account.

d. Mistaken beliefs that were genuinely held may be taken into account, as long as the mistake was a reasonable one to have made.

8. Moving on to the objective limb of the test, the question is whether the amount of force Doug used was reasonable in the circumstances as he believed them to be. (Again, this is subject to the principles from *R v Keane*, which we examined above.)

Which of the following statements summarises the decision in *R v Clegg correctly*?

a. If a defendant genuinely believed that it was necessary to use force to prevent a crime, but in the heat of the moment used more force than was reasonable, he should be convicted of manslaughter not murder.

b. In a case involving the prevention of crime defence, the jury has the discretion to convict the defendant of manslaughter instead of murder if it believes this is the most just outcome.

c. The prevention of crime defence is all or nothing. There is no rule that a defendant who used a greater degree of force than was necessary in the circumstances should be found guilty of manslaughter rather than murder.

d. Prevention of crime is never available as a defence to murder.

Evaluating the law

11.7 Evaluate whether duress should be available as a defence to murder.

Think about this question.

'It is impossible to justify the House of Lords' decision, in R v Howe [1987] AC 417, that duress should not be available as a defence to murder.'

How far (if at all) do you agree with this statement?

Step 1: Deconstruct the essay title

This question asks you to discuss whether **duress** should be available as a defence to murder. The statement asserts that it is impossible to justify the House of Lords' decision that duress should be unavailable as a defence to murder. Evaluation of this statement will therefore require discussion of the reasons the House of Lords offered for its decision in ***R* v *Howe***, and consideration of the reasons others have offered for making duress available as a defence to murder.

Step 2: Work through each assertions, form an opinion and construct a set of arguments in support of your views

To help you with this, look back at the notes you prepared in response to the following questions.

On the Law Commission's consultation paper *A New Homicide Act for England and Wales? A Consultation Paper*:

- Do you agree with the Law Commission that in their two examples it would be unjust for D and D2 to be convicted of murder and receive the mandatory life sentence?

On the House of Lords' decision in *R* v *Howe*:

- H.P. Milgate has identified the following seven reasons for the House of Lords' decision ('Duress and the Criminal Law: Another About Turn by the House of Lords' (1988) 47 *Cambridge Law Journal* 61). Read the following extracts from the judgments of Lords Hailsham, Bridge, Griffiths and Mackay in *R* v *Howe* and then write a short description of each argument:

1. The heroic argument
2. The comparison with necessity
3. The legislative argument
4. The prosecution argument
5. The executive action argument
6. The charter for terrorists
7. The uncertainty argument

On Milgate's article 'Duress and the Criminal Law: Another About Turn by the House of Lords':

- Read the following extract from Milgate's article and summarise why he rejects each of the House of Lords' reasons.

Look back at the various arguments for and against making duress available as a defence to murder. Once you have formed your own opinion on whether it should be available as a defence, construct a set of arguments in support of your opinion and work out how you would respond to potential counter-arguments. You may find some of the items on the further reading list useful here.

Step 3: Planning your introduction and conclusion

You have now compiled all you need for the main body of your essay. The last task is to decide what to include in your introduction and conclusion.

The introduction should contextualise your discussion by briefly explaining when duress is and isn't available as a defence and give an indication of the argument you will present in your essay.

The conclusion should round off your essay with a succinct statement of your argument and a summary of your supporting reasons.

Substantive defences checklist

Having worked through this chapter, you should now have:

- ✔ An understanding of the Courts' historical reluctance to recognise a defence of necessity, and an awareness of the types of situation in which such a defence has been recognised
- ✔ An ability to critically discuss *R* v *Dudley* and Stephens and whether necessity is ever available as a defence to murder
- ✔ An understanding of the two-limbed test for duress
- ✔ An understanding of the principle stated in *R* v *Hasan* for cases in which the defendant has voluntarily exposed himself to duress
- ✔ An ability to critically discuss the House of Lords' reasons in *R* v *Howe* for holding that duress is not available as a defence to murder
- ✔ An understanding of the differences between necessity and duress of circumstances and when to apply which defence
- ✔ An understanding of the relationship between prevention of crime and private defence and when to apply which defence
- ✔ An understanding of the two-limbed test for prevention of crime and private defence.

Further reading

Arenson, K.J. (2014) 'The Paradox of Disallowing Duress as a Defence to Murder' 78 *Journal of Criminal Law* 65.

Clarkson, C.M.V. (2004) 'Necessary Action: A New Defence' *Criminal Law Review* 81.

Gardner, S. (2005) 'Direct Action and the Defence of Necessity' *Criminal Law Review* 371.

Leverick, F. (2006) *Killing in Self-Defence*. OUP: Oxford.

Michalowski, S. (2002) 'Sanctity of Life – Are Some Lives More Sacred Than Others?' 22 *Legal Studies* 377.

Milgate, H.P. (1988) 'Duress and the Criminal Law: Another About Turn by the House of Lords 47 *Cambridge Law Journal* 61.

Rogers, J. (2001) 'Necessity, Private Defence and the Killing of Mary' *Criminal Law Review* 515.

Thomas, M.P. (2016) 'Defenceless Castles: The Use of Grossly Disproportionate Force by Householders in Light of *R (Collins)* v *Secretary of State for Justice* [2016] EWHC 33 (Admin)' 80 *Journal of Criminal Law* 407.

Answers on the Companion Website

Please visit the companion website for the answers to Key Questions, Quizzes, Applying the Law scenarios as well as student support including glossaries. Please visit www.pearsoned.co.uk/Macdonald

12

Inchoate offences

Learning Objectives

12.1 Define the requirements for establishing criminal liability for encouraging or assisting crime.

12.2 Define the requirements for establishing criminal liability for conspiracy.

12.3 Define the *actus reus* requirements for establishing criminal liability for criminal attempts.

12.4 Outline the arguments for and against the 'more than merely preparatory' test for the *actus reus* of attempts.

12.5 Define the *mens rea* requirements for establishing criminal liability for criminal attempts.

12.6 Apply the law on inchoate offences to hypothetical sets of facts.

12.7 Evaluate the 'more than merely preparatory' test for the *actus reus* of attempts, including the courts' application of this test.

Introduction

In Chapter 2, I explained that the criminal law would be seriously defective if it only contained offences like murder, rape, assault and theft. It needs a broader scope, in two respects. First, since the criminal law aims to prevent crimes as well as to punish those who commit them, it should also apply to preparatory actions. Second, the criminal law should encompass those who assist and encourage others to commit crimes, as well as those who actually commit them. This chapter and the next one look at each of these in turn. The next chapter focuses on accessories. This chapter focuses on inchoate offences.

The word 'inchoate' means: at an early stage, just begun, undeveloped. So inchoate offences are ones which apply where the defendant has embarked on a plan to commit a crime, but has not yet actually committed it. The rationale of inchoate offences is prevention. By penalising defendants at the preparatory stage, inchoate offences seek to prevent the harm that the offence would cause from happening.

The preventative function of inchoate offences is extremely important. Take the following three cases as examples:

Abu Hamza

An extremist preacher, Abu Hamza was convicted in 2006 of soliciting murder. Today, he could be convicted of the offence of encouraging or assisting murder under the Serious Crime Act 2007. Encouraging or assisting crime is the first offence we study in this chapter.[1]

Alex Bonney/Shutterstock

The airline liquid bomb plot

This was a terrorist plot to smuggle liquid explosives onto planes in soft drinks bottles. (It was this plot that led to liquids being prohibited in hand luggage on planes.) The seven plotters (including the four would-be suicide bombers) were convicted of conspiracy to murder. Conspiracy is the second offence we study in this chapter.[2]

Gwoeii/Shutterstock

[1] 'Hamza guilty of inciting murder', *BBC*, 7 February 2006.

[2] 'Liquid bomb plot: What happened', *BBC*, 7 September 2009.

Salih Khater

Khater drove his car at members of the public outside the Houses of Parliament, trying to kill as many people as possible. Fortunately, no-one was killed. Khater was convicted of attempted murder. The final offence we study in this chapter is criminal attempts.[3]

skyearth/Shutterstock

As these examples illustrate, the inchoate offences can encompass very serious instances of wrongdoing and so their preventative function is extremely important.

The inchoate offences that we study in this chapter are set out on the timeline in Figure 12.1. The first two offences we study are **encouraging or assisting crime** and **conspiracy**. These target the early stages of plans to commit crime, such as words of persuasion, offers of help and verbal agreements. The third offence we study is **criminal attempts**. This applies where the defendant has gone beyond mere preparation, but has not yet committed the planned offence.

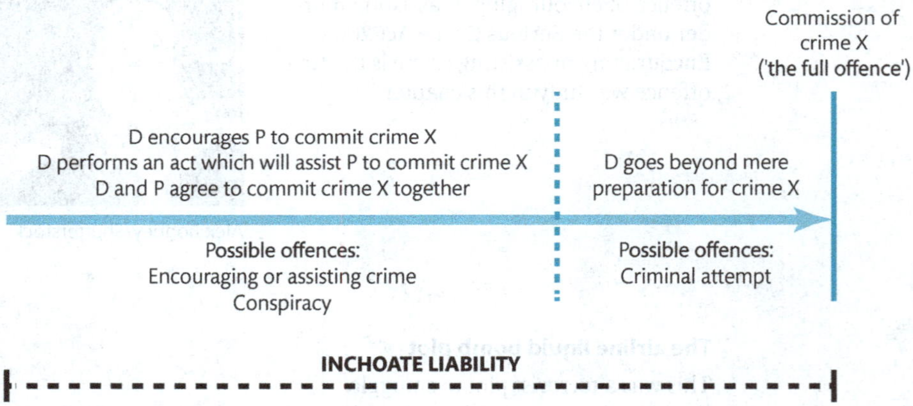

Figure 12.1

Inchoate crimes have a preventative rationale. They enable the authorities to arrest, prosecute and punish would-be offenders without having to wait for them to carry out the crime they had planned. One difficult issue that this raises is how early we should intervene. On the one hand there are some strong arguments in favour of having broad inchoate offences in order to enable early intervention, but on the other hand there are also good reasons for ensuring inchoate liability is tightly confined. Later in the chapter we will examine these competing principles and policy concerns when we evaluate the *actus reus* of criminal attempts.

---

[3] 'Westminster car crash driver Salih Khater jailed for life', *BBC*, 14 October 2019.

Before turning to the offences themselves, it is helpful to clarify the meaning of one term that will appear throughout the chapter: 'full offence'.

When we use this term we are referring to the crime that the defendant had planned to commit (or encourage or assist someone else to commit). So if two defendants agree to rob a post office together they are guilty of conspiracy to rob. The relevant inchoate offence is conspiracy and the relevant full offence is robbery. Or if a defendant tries unsuccessfully to have non-consensual sexual intercourse with someone else, he is guilty of attempted rape. The relevant inchoate offence is attempt and the relevant full offence is rape. Hopefully this will save any confusion later in the chapter!

Encouraging and assisting crime

12.1 Define the requirements for establishing criminal liability for encouraging or assisting crime.

Part 2 of the Serious Crime Act 2007 abolished the old common law offence of incitement and replaced it with three new offences which involve encouraging and assisting crime. These new offences were designed to be slightly broader than the offence of incitement. Like incitement, they apply to those who encourage others to commit a crime. But they also cover the defendant who assists someone else to commit a crime without actually encouraging them to do so (e.g. the defendant who provides vital equipment in exchange for payment).

The three offences are set out in sections 44, 45 and 46 of the Act.

EXTRACT

Sections 44, 45 and 46 of the Serious Crime Act 2007

44 Intentionally encouraging or assisting an offence

(1) A person commits an offence if –

(a) he does an act capable of encouraging or assisting the commission of an offence; and

(b) he intends to encourage or assist its commission.

(2) But he is not to be taken to have intended to encourage or assist the commission of an offence merely because such encouragement or assistance was a foreseeable consequence of his act.

45 Encouraging or assisting an offence believing it will be committed

(1) A person commits an offence if –

(a) he does an act capable of encouraging or assisting the commission of an offence; and

(b) he believes –

(i) that the offence will be committed; and

(ii) that his act will encourage or assist its commission.

46 Encouraging or assisting offences believing one or more will be committed

(1) A person commits an offence if –

(a) he does an act capable of encouraging or assisting the commission of one or more of a number of offences; and

(b) he believes –

(i) that one or more of those offences will be committed (but has no belief as to which); and

(ii) that his act will encourage or assist the commission of one or more of them.

(2) It is immaterial for the purposes of subsection (1)(b)(ii) whether the person has any belief as to which offence will be encouraged or assisted.

(3) If a person is charged with an offence under subsection (1) –

(a) the indictment must specify the offences alleged to be the "number of offences" mentioned in paragraph (a) of that subsection; but

(b) nothing in paragraph (a) requires all the offences potentially comprised in that number to be specified.

(4) In relation to an offence under this section, reference in this Part to the offences specified in the indictment is to the offences specified by virtue of subsection (3)(a).

These offences have been described by David Ormerod and Rudi Fortson as 'some of the most convoluted offences in decades'.[4] So if you find some of the next few pages hard, don't worry. Be reassured by the fact that even leading commentators have found these offences difficult!

There are five requirements which must be satisfied to establish liability for one of these offences. The first key point is that the *actus reus* of all three offences is identical. To establish the *actus reus*, the following requirement must be satisfied:

1. The defendant did an act that was capable of encouraging or assisting the commission of an offence.

The *mens rea* consists of three requirements. The first *mens rea* requirement is what distinguishes the three offences from each other, and is what makes section 44 the most serious of the three:

2. The defendant had *mens rea* in relation to the behaviour part of the full offence.

The next two *mens rea* requirements are the same for all three offences:

3. The defendant had *mens rea* in relation to the consequence and circumstance parts of the full offence.

4. The defendant had *mens rea* in relation to the *mens rea* part of the full offence.

The final requirement is found in section 50 of the Act (set out below). This section creates a reasonableness defence:

5. No offence is committed if it was reasonable for the defendant to act as he did.

[4] Ormerod, D. and Fortson, R. (2009) 'Serious Crime Act 2007: The Part 2 Offences' *Criminal Law Review* 389.

When answering an exam problem question, it is advisable to work through the requirements in this order. Begin with the *actus reus*, then identify which of the three offences applies in the particular case by applying the first *mens rea* requirement, then work through the other two *mens rea* requirements and finally, if both *actus reus* and *mens rea* are established, consider the reasonableness defence. We will accordingly work through the five requirements in this order.

1. The defendant did an act that was capable of encouraging or assisting the commission of an offence

To examine this *actus reus* requirement we need to look at the meaning of five key words: act; capable; encouraging; assisting and offence.

i. An act ...

Sections 44 to 46 each use the word 'act'. But in this context the word has a broader meaning than its ordinary dictionary meaning, in three respects. First, section 65(2)(b) states:

EXTRACT

Section 65(2)(b) of the Serious Crime Act

(2) A reference in this Part to a person's doing an act that is capable of encouraging or assisting the commission of an offence includes a reference to his doing so by –

[...]

(b) failing to take reasonable steps to discharge a duty.

So a defendant may commit these three offences by omission, if he had a legal duty to act and failed to take reasonable steps to discharge this duty. An example is a security guard who deliberately fails to turn on a burglar alarm at his employer's premises in order to help burglars steal from the premises.

Second, section 67 states:

EXTRACT

Section 67 of the Serious Crime Act 2007

67 Course of conduct

A reference in this Part to an act includes a reference to a course of conduct, and a reference to doing an act is to be read accordingly.

So although the word 'act' suggests that the prosecution must point to some specific single action, in fact the prosecution may point to a series of actions which amount to a course of conduct.

In *R* v *Russo* [2025] EWCA Crim 169, the Court of Appeal said that a 'course of conduct' has its 'ordinary English meaning' of 'a series of acts demonstrating a continuity of purpose' ([22]).

And third, section 66 states:

EXTRACT

Section 66 of the Serious Crime Act 2007

66 Indirectly encouraging or assisting

If a person (D1) arranges for a person (D2) to do an act that is capable of encouraging or assisting the commission of an offence, and D2 does the act, D1 is also to be treated for the purposes of this Part as having done it.

This section was drafted with criminal gangs in mind. Suppose that a gang leader, Vito, tells one of the gang members, Michael, to persuade Sonny to commit a murder. Michael does so. Section 66 states that, since Vito arranged for Michael to persuade Sonny, Vito may be treated as if he had performed the acts of encouragement himself. So Vito would be guilty of intentionally encouraging Sonny to commit murder.

ii. … that was capable …

There are four important points to note here.

First, since these three offences are inchoate crimes it is not necessary to show that the encouragement or assistance actually led to the full offence being committed. This is confirmed by section 49(1):

EXTRACT

Section 49 of the Serious Crime Act 2007

49 Supplemental provisions

(1) A person may commit an offence under this Part whether or not any offence capable of being encouraged or assisted by his act is committed.

So if Vito encourages Michael to murder Philip, there is no need to show that Michael actually committed the murder.

Second, it is also not necessary to show that the defendant's act did in fact provide encouragement or assistance. All that needs to be shown is that the act *was capable* of providing encouragement or assistance. Suppose that Vito posts a letter to Michael which encourages him to murder Philip. The letter gets lost in the post and never arrives. Although Michael did not receive the encouragement, Vito may still be convicted of intentionally encouraging murder since posting the letter was an act that was capable of providing encouragement.

Third, when framing the charge there is no need to specify the particulars of the full offence that the defendant encouraged or assisted. So the defendant would be charged with 'encouraging or assisting murder', not with 'encouraging or assisting the murder of Philip'. This was explained by the Law Commission as follows:

EXTRACT

Law Commission (2006) *Inchoate Liability for Assisting and Encouraging Crime* (Law Commission Report No 300) Cm 6878

D's liability is for encouraging or assisting an abstract and not a particular principal offence

5.13 D may not know the details of the prospective principal offence. Thus, D may provide P with a baseball bat believing that P will use it to rob V1. Instead, P uses it to rob V2. Alternatively, D may provide the baseball bat believing that P will use it to commit robbery but have no belief as to the identity of the victim. It matters not that D lacks knowledge or belief as to the details of the prospective principal offence. D is guilty of encouraging or assisting P to commit robbery rather than encouraging or assisting P to rob V.

This would be relevant in cases where the planned offence turns out to be impossible. Suppose that, unbeknown to Vito, Philip is already dead. Vito would simply be charged with intentionally encouraging murder, not with intentionally encouraging the murder of Philip. The fact that Philip is already dead would therefore be irrelevant.

Fourth, the offence may apply where the defendant encourages or assists the continuation of a crime that has already begun.[5] So, for example, if Michael is already in possession of an unlawful weapon, and Vito assists him to retain possession of it, then Vito may be liable for assisting the unlawful possession of a weapon.

Think about this question.

In the following three examples, does Vito do an act that is capable of encouraging or assisting murder?

- **a.** Vito says to Michael, 'If you kill Philip I'll pay you £1,000'. Michael rejects the offer.
- **b.** Vito writes a letter that encourages Michael to murder Philip. But on his way to the post box Vito changes his mind and, instead of posting the letter, he rips it up.
- **c.** Michael has decided to kill Philip. He asks Vito for Philip's address. Vito gives him an address in New York, which he thinks is where Philip lives. But, unbeknown to Vito, Philip has recently moved house and gone to live in Sicily.

iii. ... of encouraging ...

In this context the word 'encouraging' has a broader meaning than its ordinary sense of instigating or persuading. Section 65(1) states:

[5] *Scott v DPP* [2022] EWHC 91 (Admin).

EXTRACT

Section 65 of the Serious Crime Act 2007

65 Being capable of encouraging or assisting

(1) A reference in this Part to a person's doing an act that is capable of encouraging the commission of an offence includes a reference to his doing so by threatening another person or otherwise putting pressure on another person to commit the offence.

The case law on the old common law offence of incitement is also helpful in understanding the meaning of encouragement. The following two cases illustrate that: (1) the encouragement may be by words or by conduct, and may be express or implied; and (2) the encouragement need not be addressed to a particular person, and could be addressed to the world at large.

EXAMPLE

Invicta Plastics v *Clare* [1976] RTR 251

The defendant company produced a device called Radatec, which let out a high-pitched whine when within 800 yards of wireless telegraphy transmissions including those used for police radar speed traps. At the time of the case a licence was needed to use such devices. The company advertised Radatec in a motoring magazine.

The advert had a picture of a car with the Radatec device fitted to its windscreen and a speed limit sign in the background. The advert read, 'You ought to know more about Radatec. Ask at your accessory shop or write for name of nearest stockist'. The Divisional Court held that, looking at the advert as a whole, it impliedly encouraged unlicensed readers to use Radatec.

R v *Marlow* [1997] Crim LR 897

Michael Marlow produced a book which gave advice on how to grow and produce cannabis. The book was advertised and about 500 copies were sold. Some of those who bought the book were subsequently found to have attempted to produce cannabis using the methods described in the book.

The Court of Appeal held that the book 'amounted to an active and widespread encouragement of others to engage in the production and use of cannabis'.

The courts have also considered a further issue. Suppose that Michael goes to Vito and says, 'I've decided to kill Philip'. Vito congratulates him and encourages him to go through with it. Can Vito be convicted of encouraging murder even though Michael had already made his mind up to commit the crime? This was considered by the Court of Appeal in *R* v *Goldman* [2001] EWCA Crim 1684.[6] In this case a company called ESV placed an advert on the Internet advertising pornographic materials for sale, including

[6] See also *O'Shea* v *Coventry* Magistrates' Court [2004] Crim LR 948: in this case D had accessed websites featuring child pornography. The Divisional Court upheld his conviction for inciting the company maintaining the website to distribute indecent photographs of children. By accessing the website D had encouraged the company to maintain it.

paedophilic ones. The defendant, Terence Goldman, wrote to ESV and asked for photographs of girls aged 7 to 13. At trial he was convicted of inciting ESV to distribute indecent photographs of children under 16. He appealed against his conviction, arguing that he could not be guilty of inciting ESV to distribute the materials because ESV had already offered them for sale.

EXTRACT

Read the following extract from the judgment of Clarke LJ.

Had Goldman encouraged ESV to distribute indecent photographs? Explain Clarke LJ's reasoning.

R v *Goldman* [2001] EWCA Crim 1684

Clarke LJ

23. In the instant case, the appellant offered to buy indecent photographs for £75. As we have indicated, the provision of the photographs would have been a criminal offence. In our judgment that offer was a suggestion or proposal or persuasion or inducement to commit that offence. It is true that ESV had advertised its wares and that it was thought to be willing to provide the photographs. However in our judgment that is nothing to the point. ESV would not have sent the photographs except in response to an offer, and probably only in response to an offer which included a cheque. In ordinary language it required an element of persuasion or encouragement in the form of an offer before it would distribute the video tapes. It follows, in our judgment, that the letter of 9th June was an inducement to commit the offence. It was a suggestion or proposal or inducement to commit the offence and at the very least an attempt to incite it

So in our example Vito would be guilty of intentionally encouraging murder, notwithstanding the fact that Michael had already resolved to kill Philip before speaking to Vito.

Finally, note that it does not matter if no one else is aware of the defendant's acts of encouragement or assistance. So in our earlier example in which Vito posts a letter of encouragement to Michael which never arrives there is the *actus reus* of this offence even though no one else knew that Vito had posted the letter.[7]

iv. ... or assisting ...

The Serious Crime Act 2007 does not contain any definition of the word 'assist'. The ordinary meaning of the word should therefore be applied. The case law on 'aiding' can also be used (we study this in the next chapter). Note also that it does not matter if the defendant's acts of assistance were very minor. The Act does not contain any requirement that the defendant provided substantial assistance.[8]

The Act does deal with one particular type of situation.

[7] Cf. *State* v *Tally* 15 So 722 [1894], discussed in Chapter 13.

[8] In its report Law Commission (2006) *Inchoate Liability for Assisting and Encouraging Crime* (Law Commission Report No 300) Cm 6878, the Law Commission stated: 'D should be liable if his or her act is capable of assisting (or encouraging) another person to any extent. The marginal nature of any assistance or encouragement can be reflected in the sentence' (para 5.51).

EXTRACT

Section 65 of the Serious Crime Act

(2) A reference in this Part to a person's doing an act that is capable of encouraging or assisting the commission of an offence includes a reference to his doing so by –

(a) taking steps to reduce the possibility of criminal proceedings being brought in respect of that offence;

[...]

(3) But a person is not to be regarded as doing an act that is capable of encouraging or assisting the commission of an offence merely because he fails to respond to a constable's request for assistance in preventing a breach of the peace.

Two examples of when section 65(2)(a) might apply are: providing advice to someone on how to avoid detection and providing a gun for the perpetrators to use against any eye-witnesses.[9] But note that section 65(2)(a) will only apply if the act of assistance occurs before the offence is complete. Suppose that Michael kills Philip, and then tells Vito what he has done. Vito helps Michael flee the country. Vito cannot be guilty of assisting murder because he only assisted Michael after Philip was already dead. In such circumstances other offences would be used, such as perverting the course of justice.

v. ... the commission of an offence

A defendant may be guilty of encouraging or assisting any of the offences we have studied in Chapters 5, 6, 7 and 8 of this text.

Assessment advice

When answering an exam problem question, it is important to specify which offence the defendant encouraged or assisted. So don't just write 'D is guilty of intentionally encouraging crime'. You must write 'D is guilty of intentionally encouraging theft' or 'D is guilty of intentionally assisting rape'.

A defendant may also be guilty of encouraging or assisting someone to be an accessory to a crime. Suppose Vito encourages Michael to help Sonny kill Philip. Vito could be charged with intentionally encouraging Michael to be an accessory to murder.[10]

A defendant may also be charged with encouraging or assisting an inchoate offence. This is known as double inchoate liability. Note, however, that section 49 states that

[9] Law Commission (2006) *Inchoate Liability for Assisting and Encouraging Crime* (Law Commission Report No 300) Cm 6878, para A.91.

[10] This example is similar to the earlier one involving section 66. The key difference is that section 66 states that it only applies 'If a person (D1) arranges for a person (D2) to do an act that is capable of encouraging or assisting the commission of an offence, and *D2 does the act* [...].' So, in our example, if Michael ignored Vito section 66 would not apply. The prosecution would then have to charge Vito with intentionally encouraging Michael to be an accessory to murder.

double inchoate liability is only possible if the defendant is charged with the section 44 offence. This means that the potential forms of double inchoate liability are:

- Intentionally encouraging or assisting a person to encourage or assist someone else to commit a crime[11]
- Intentionally encouraging or assisting a person to conspire to commit a crime
- Intentionally encouraging or assisting a person to attempt to commit a crime.

Finally, a person cannot be charged with encouraging or assisting an offence if the offence in question exists for their protection. This is set out in section 51 of the Act:

EXTRACT

Section 51 of the Serious Crime Act 2007

51 Protective offences: victims not liable

(1) In the case of protective offences, a person does not commit an offence under this Part by reference to such an offence if –

(a) he falls within the protected category; and

(b) he is the person in respect of whom the protective offence was committed or would have been if it had been committed.

(2) "Protective offence" means an offence that exists (wholly or in part) for the protection of a particular category of persons ("the protected category").

Suppose that a 14-year-old girl encourages her 26-year-old boyfriend (who knows her age) to have sexual intercourse with her. Her boyfriend is charged with the offence of sexual activity with a child.[12] The girl cannot be charged with intentionally encouraging her boyfriend to commit sexual activity with a child, because she was the victim of the sexual offence and the offence exists for her protection.

2. The defendant had *mens rea* in relation to the behavior part of the full offence

The *actus reus* requirement is the same for each of the section 44, 45 and 46 offences. It is this first *mens rea* requirement that invites you to identify which one of the three offences applies to the facts of a particular case.

In Chapter 2, we saw that the *actus reus* of criminal offences can be divided into three separate parts: behaviour; consequences and circumstances. This distinction is important here. You need to begin by looking at the *actus reus* of the full offence and identify the behaviour part. The defendant must then be shown to have had *mens rea* in relation to this. The specific requirements are set out in the first four subsections of the 'tortuous'[13] section 47:

[11] Note that the charge would need to specify whether the defendant was intentionally encouraging/assisting the person to commit the section 44, 45 or 46 offence.

[12] Sexual Offences Act 2003, s.9.

[13] Ormerod, D. and Fortson, R. (2009) 'Serious Crime Act 2007: The Part 2 Offences' *Criminal Law Review* 389, 407.

EXTRACT

Section 47 of the Serious Crime Act 2007

47 Proving an offence under this Part

(1) Sections 44, 45 and 46 are to be read in accordance with this section.

(2) If it is alleged under section 44(1)(b) that a person (D) intended to encourage or assist the commission of an offence, it is sufficient to prove that he intended to encourage or assist the doing of an act which would amount to the commission of that offence.

(3) If it is alleged under section 45(b) that a person (D) believed that an offence would be committed and that his act would encourage or assist its commission, it is sufficient to prove that he believed –

(a) that an act would be done which would amount to the commission of that offence; and

(b) that his act would encourage or assist the doing of that act.

(4) If it is alleged under section 46(1)(b) that a person (D) believed that one or more of a number of offences would be committed and that his act would encourage or assist the commission of one or more of them, it is sufficient to prove that he believed –

(a) that one or more of a number of acts would be done which would amount to the commission of one or more of those offences; and

(b) that his act would encourage or assist the doing of one or more of those acts.

[...]

(7) In the case of an offence under section 44 –

[...]

(b) D is not to be taken to have intended that an act would be done in particular circumstances or with particular consequences merely because its being done in those circumstances or with those consequences was a foreseeable consequence of his act of encouragement or assistance.

So suppose Vito has encouraged Michael to commit rape. The behavioural element of the *actus reus* of rape is that the defendant penetrated the vagina/anus/mouth of the victim with his penis. To identify whether the section 44, 45 or 46 offence is the most appropriate, you should work through subsections (2) to (4) of section 47.

Begin with the section 44 offence since this is the most serious of the three. Section 47(2) states that for the section 44 offence the prosecution must prove that the defendant intended to encourage or assist the behaviour part of the full offence. Importantly, sections 44(2) and 47(7)(b) explain that in this context the meaning of intention is limited to direct intention.[14] In other words, it must have been the defendant's purpose to encourage or assist the behaviour part of the full offence. So in our example, for the section 44 offence to apply the prosecution must show that Vito's purpose was to encourage or assist Michael's act of penile penetration.

If the section 44 offence does not apply you should consider the section 45 and 46 offences instead. Both offences use the *mens rea* concept of belief. The difference

[14] We examined the different types of intention in Chapter 4.

between them is that section 45 applies where the defendant believes a specific full offence will be committed, whereas section 46 applies where the defendant believes that one of several full offences will be committed but is unsure which one.[15] So if Vito gives Michael a baseball bat believing Michael will use it to beat Philip up, rob Philip or smash the windows on Philip's Ferrari, but is not sure which, the relevant offence is section 46. However, if Vito simply believes Michael will use the baseball bat to beat Philip up the relevant offence is section 45.

Once you have determined whether section 45 or section 46 applies, the defendant must be shown to have had the following two beliefs:

1. For the section 45 offence the defendant must have believed that the behaviour part of the full offence would be committed (s.47(3)). For the section 46 offence the defendant must have believed that the behaviour part of one of the anticipated full offences would be committed (s.47(4)). As we saw in Chapter 4, to believe something is to have mentally accepted it as true.[16] So a belief is more than merely a suspicion. If the defendant only suspected that the behaviour part of the full offence would be committed he is not guilty of either offence. In our initial example this means that, if Vito thought Michael might commit the act of penile penetration, but concluded that he probably would not, Vito would not satisfy this *mens rea* requirement.
2. The defendant must have believed that his actions would encourage or assist commission of the behaviour part of the full offence. Note that it is not enough to show that the defendant believed his actions might provide encouragement or assistance. He must have believed that they *would* do so.

Figure 12.2 summarises how to approach this *mens rea* requirement.

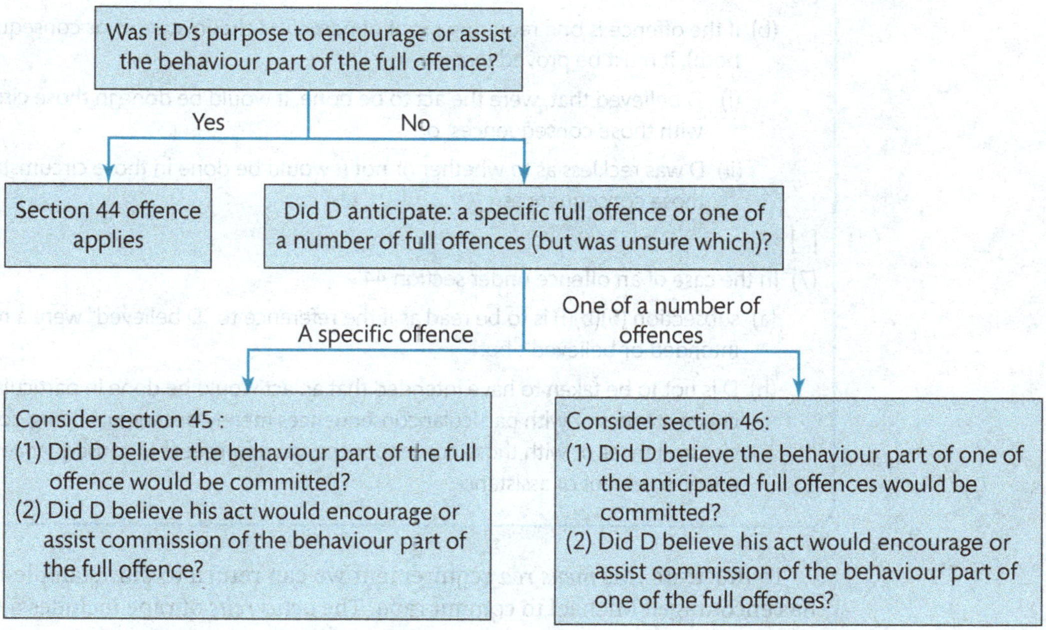

Figure 12.2 An overview of the section 47 *mens rea* requirement

[15] This interpretation of section 46 was adopted by the Court of Appeal in *R* v *Sadique* [2013] EWCA Crim 1150, effectively overruling the different interpretation adopted in *R* v *Sadique and another* [2011] EWCA Crim 2872.

[16] *R* v *Forsyth* [1997] 2 Cr App R 299.

Use Figure 12.2 to consider the following question.

One day Michael comes to Vito's home. Extremely agitated, he says 'This time I've had enough' and angrily demands to borrow Vito's handgun. Vito's knows that Michael has long held a grudge against Philip and is worried about what Michael might use the gun for. In spite of this he lends Michael the weapon.

How would you advise a prosecutor deciding whether to charge Vito for the section 44, 45 or 46 offence?

3. The defendant had *mens rea* in relation to the consequence and circumstance parts of the full offence

Here we move on to subsection 5(b) of section 47:

EXTRACT

Section 47(5)(b) of the Serious Crime Act 2007

47 Proving an offence under this Part

[...]

(5) In proving for the purposes of this section whether an act is one which, if done, would amount to the commission of an offence –

[...]

(b) if the offence is one requiring proof of particular circumstances or consequences (or both), it must be proved that –

(i) D believed that, were the act to be done, it would be done in those circumstances or with those consequences; or

(ii) D was reckless as to whether or not it would be done in those circumstances or with those consequences.

[...]

(7) In the case of an offence under section 44 –

(a) subsection (5)(b)(i) is to be read as if the reference to "D believed" were a reference to "D intended or believed"; but

(b) D is not to be taken to have intended that an act would be done in particular circumstances or with particular consequences merely because its being done in those circumstances or with those consequences was a foreseeable consequence of his act of encouragement or assistance.

To illustrate this *mens rea* requirement we can return to our example in which Vito has encouraged Michael to commit rape. The *actus reus* of rape includes a circumstance element: the penile penetration must have been non-consensual. According to section 47(5)(b), the prosecution must therefore show either:

- That Vito believed that, when Michael penetrated the victim's vagina/anus/mouth with his penis, he would do so without the consent of the victim (s.47(5)(b)(i)); in the case of the section 44 offence, it will also suffice for the prosecution to show that Vito directly intended that the penetration would be non-consensual (s47(7)); or

- That Vito was reckless as to whether or not Michael would penetrate the victim's vagina/anus/mouth with his penis without the consent of the victim (s.47(5)(b)(ii)).

The same applies where the *actus reus* of the full offence has a consequence element. Suppose Vito encourages Michael to kill Philip. The actus reus of murder includes a consequence element: death of the victim. So according to section 47(5)(b), the prosecution must show either:

- That Vito believed that, when Michael committed the act, it would cause Philip's death (s.47(5)(b)(i)); again, in the case of the section 44 offence direct intention will also suffice (s47(7)); or
- That Vito was reckless as to whether or not Michael's act would cause Philip's death (s.47(5)(b)(ii)).

So when applying this *mens rea* requirement to an exam problem question, you first need to identify the circumstance and consequence elements of the *actus reus* of the full offence. Remember that not all crimes have a circumstance and/or consequence element. Once you have identified the relevant circumstances and consequences you should then apply section 47(5)(b) to these.

4. The defendant had *mens rea* in relation to the *mens rea* part of the full offence

The final *mens rea* requirement is that the defendant had *mens rea* in relation to the *mens rea* part of the full offence. This is governed by subsection (5)(a) of section 47.

EXTRACT

Section 47(5)(a) of the Serious Crime Act

(5) In proving for the purposes of this section whether an act is one which, if done, would amount to the commission of an offence –

(a) if the offence is one requiring proof of fault, it must be proved that –

(i) D believed that, were the act to be done, it would be done with that fault;

(ii) D was reckless as to whether or not it would be done with that fault; or

(iii) D's state of mind was such that, were he to do it, it would be done with that fault; and

[...]

(6) For the purposes of subsection (5)(a)(iii), D is to be assumed to be able to do the act in question.

To illustrate this *mens rea* requirement we can once again use our example in which Vito encourages Michael to commit rape. Rape has two *mens rea* requirements: (1) that the defendant intentionally penetrated the victim's vagina/anus/mouth with his penis; and (2) that the defendant lacked a reasonable belief in consent. According to section 47(5)(a), the prosecution must therefore show:

- That Vito believed that Michael would intentionally penetrate the victim's vagina/anus/mouth with his penis, and that Michael would do so without a reasonable belief that the victim was consenting (s.47(5)(a)(i));

- That Vito was reckless as to whether Michael would intentionally penetrate the victim's vagina/anus/mouth with his penis, and as to whether Michael would do so without a reasonable belief that the victim was consenting (s.47(5)(a)(ii)); or
- That if Vito had committed the act of sexual intercourse himself, he would have intentionally penetrated the victim's vagina/anus/mouth with his penis and would have lacked a reasonable belief that the victim was consenting (s.47(5)(a)(iii)).

Section 47(6) deals with a very specific type of scenario. Suppose that Carmela encourages Michael to commit rape. As we saw in Chapter 7, women cannot commit the offence of rape as principals. At first it would therefore seem that section 47(5)(a)(iii) cannot apply. However, section 47(6) states that, in this context, the defendant 'is to be assumed to be able to do the act in question'. It follows that if Carmela intended penile penetration of the victim's vagina/anus/mouth and lacked a reasonable belief that the victim would consent she would satisfy this *mens rea* requirement by virtue of section 47(5)(a)(iii).

5. No offence is committed if it was reasonable for the defendant to act as he did

Finally, the defendant cannot be convicted of the section 44, 45 or 46 offences if it was reasonable for him to act as he did. The reasonableness defence is set out in section 50:

EXTRACT

Section 50 of the Serious Crime Act 2007

50 Defence of acting reasonably

(1) A person is not guilty of an offence under this Part if he proves –
  (a) that he knew certain circumstances existed; and
  (b) that it was reasonable for him to act as he did in those circumstances.

(2) A person is not guilty of an offence under this Part if he proves –
  (a) that he believed certain circumstances to exist;
  (b) that his belief was reasonable; and
  (c) that it was reasonable for him to act as he did in the circumstances as he believed them to be.

(3) Factors to be considered in determining whether it was reasonable for a person to act as he did include –
  (a) the seriousness of the anticipated offence (or, in the case of an offence under section 46, the offences specified in the indictment);
  (b) any purpose for which he claims to have been acting;
  (c) any authority by which he claims to have been acting.

Note the following two points:

- The test is whether the defendant's actions were objectively reasonable. It is not whether the defendant thought his conduct was reasonable.

- The burden of proof for this defence rests on the defendant. He must prove on the balance of probabilities that: (1) he knew the relevant circumstances existed; and (2) it was reasonable for him to act as he did in those circumstances (s.50(1)). Or, if he had made a mistake, he must prove that: (1) the mistaken belief was genuine; (2) the mistake was an objectively reasonable one; and (3) it was reasonable for him to act as he did in the circumstances as he believed them to be (s.50(2)).

Commentators have criticised the reasonableness defence for being vague and ill-defined.[17]

Think about these questions.

Do you think the reasonableness defence would be available in the following two situations? Should it be?

a. The defendant works in a hardware store. A customer asks to buy some rope, tape and a knife. The defendant believes that the customer will use the items to kidnap someone, but his boss tells him to stop being stupid and so he completes the sale.

b. The defendant is driving in the right-hand lane on the motorway. In his rear view mirror he notices a speeding car approaching fast. The defendant moves into the middle lane in order to let the speeding car continue unobstructed.

Quiz 12.1

1. Which of the following statements summarises the section 44 Serious Crime Act 2007 offence accurately?

a. The intentional performing by D of an act that is capable of encouraging or assisting the commission of an offence.

b. The intentional performing by D of an act that in fact encouraged or assisted another person to commit an offence.

c. The intentional or reckless performing by D of an act that is capable of encouraging or assisting the commission of an offence.

d. The intentional, reckless or negligent performing by D of an act that is capable of encouraging or assisting the commission of an offence.

2. How does the Serious Crime Act 2007 address the problem identified in *The Godfather films*, whereby the chain of command kept the original instigator of encouragement of or assistance to the commission of a crime (the gang leader) too far away from the final act of encouragement or assistance to be liable for it?

a. Section 67 of the Serious Crime Act 2007 ('Course of conduct') brings the gang leader within the scope of the offence.

b. Section 65(1) of the Serious Crime Act 2007 ('Being capable of encouraging or assisting') brings the gang leader within the scope of the offence.

c. Section 65(2)(b) of the Serious Crime Act 2007 ('failing to take reasonable steps to discharge a duty') brings the gang leader within the scope of the offence.

d. Section 66 of the Serious Crime Act 2007 ('Indirectly encouraging or assisting') brings the gang leader within the scope of the offence.

3. What important piece of clarity did the Law Commission insist upon in constructing the 'encouraging and assisting' offences?

a. They insisted that the crime encouraged or assisted be capable of actually being committed.

b. They insisted that it be necessary to prove that the person being encouraged or assisted knew that the

[17] Ormerod, D. and Fortson, R. (2009) 'Serious Crime Act 2007: The Part 2 Offences' *Criminal Law Review* 389.

actions they were being encouraged/assisted to carry out were offences.

c. They insisted that D's liability depends on encouraging and assisting an offence, for example, robbery, and not encouraging and assisting a particular offence, that is, the robbery of a particular person.

d. They insisted that 'encouraging' be restricted to positive acts of support or approval.

4. What is the *mens rea* requirement for section 44 of the Serious Crime Act 2007 considered to be?

a. Recklessness.

b. Direct or oblique intention.

c. Direct intention.

d. Negligence.

Conspiracy

12.2 Define the requirements for establishing criminal liability for conspiracy.

There are three different types of conspiracy offence: statutory conspiracy; conspiracy to defraud and conspiracy to corrupt public morals or outrage public decency. In this chapter we study just the first of these: statutory conspiracy. The simple reason for this is that the vast majority of conspiracies are statutory conspiracies.

Statutory conspiracy is governed by section 1 of the Criminal Law Act 1977:

EXTRACT

Section 1 of the Criminal Law Act 1977

1 The offence of conspiracy

(1) Subject to the following provisions of this Part of this Act, if a person agrees with any other person or persons that a course of conduct shall be pursued which, if the agreement is carried out in accordance with their intentions, either–

(a) will necessarily amount to or involve the commission of any offence or offences by one or more of the parties to the agreement, or

(b) would do so but for the existence of facts which render the commission of the offence or any of the offences impossible,

he is guilty of conspiracy to commit the offence or offences in question.

This tells us that the offence has three requirements:

1. An agreement …
2. … that a course of conduct shall be pursued which will necessarily amount to or involve the commission of an offence by one or more parties to the agreement
3. An intention that the crime will be carried out as planned.

In some circumstances (which are explained below) there will also be a fourth requirement:

4. Intention or knowledge of essential facts or circumstances.

Numbers 1 and 2 are *actus reus* requirements. Numbers 3 and 4 are *mens rea* requirements. We will work through them in turn.

1. An agreement ...

Agreement is the essence of a conspiracy. To establish an agreement it is not enough to show that one defendant encouraged the other to commit a crime himself. It must be shown that the defendants had decided to commit the unlawful plan as a joint collaborative project. In *R* v *Mehta* [2012] EWCA Crim 2824, for example, Toulson LJ stated, 'A conspiracy requires that the parties to it have a common unlawful purpose or design' ([36]).

For there to have been an agreement the defendants must have gone beyond the stage of negotiation. But once an agreement has been reached the crime of conspiracy is complete. In *R* v *Saik* [2006] UKHL 18 Lord Nicholls said: 'The offence therefore lies in making an agreement [...] The offence is complete at that stage' ([3]).[18] This means that there is no need to prove that the planned full offence was carried out. In fact, there is no need to prove that the defendants even began to put their plan into operation. So if Vito and Michael agree to commit a murder, but later change their minds, they are nonetheless guilty of conspiracy to murder.

The agreement may be a continuing one. Suppose Vito and Michael agree to commit a robbery in two weeks' time. A few days before the planned robbery they recruit Sonny. Sonny becomes a party to the agreement, and all three are guilty of conspiracy to rob.

There can also be an agreement even if some of the details of the planned offence still need to be worked out. So if Vito and Michael agree to rob a petrol station in two weeks' time, they are guilty of conspiracy to rob even if they haven't yet agreed which petrol station to rob or whether to commit the offence during the day or at night.

Note also that it is not necessary for all parties to the conspiracy to have communicated with one another. As long as all the defendants share the same common unlawful purpose it is not necessary for them all to have met, or have communicated with, each other.

EXAMPLE

- **Wheel conspiracies:** In a wheel conspiracy one central figure, D1, communicates with all of the other parties to the agreement. D2, D3, D4, D5 and D6 never actually communicate with one another.
- **Chain conspiracies:** In a chain conspiracy D1 communicates with D2, D2 communicates with D3, D3 communicates with D4 and so on.

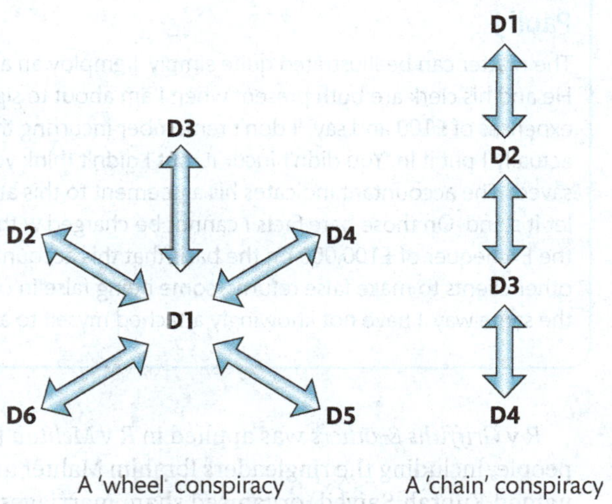

Figure 12.3

[18] See also *R* v *Oni* [2025] EWCA Crim 12.

It is possible for there to be one general conspiracy, with related sub-conspiracies. An example is *R* v *Ali (Ahmed) & others* [2011] EWCA Crim 1260. This case involved a terrorist plot to blow up transatlantic flights using explosives in plastic drinks bottles. All seven men were convicted of conspiracy to murder. However, although four of the men (the four would-be suicide bombers) knew that the plan was to use explosive devices to kill people, it was uncertain whether they knew that the intended target was transatlantic flights. For this reason, only the other three men – Ali (the ringleader), Tanvir Hussain (Ali's right-hand man) and Sarwar (the explosives expert) – were convicted of the more serious charge of conspiracy to murder by detonating explosive devices on transatlantic aircraft. The Court of Appeal held that these were distinct conspiracies. There was one general agreement between the seven men to commit murder, and a separate sub-agreement between three of them as to the method and scale of the murder to be carried out.

So there can be wheel conspiracies, chain conspiracies and sub-conspiracies. Whatever type of conspiracy is involved, however, it is essential to show that the parties shared a common unlawful purpose.

Without a shared common unlawful purpose there can be no conspiracy.

This is illustrated by R v Griffiths & others [1966] 1 QB 589. Griffiths and his co-defendants were all farmers who used the same accountant, a man named Booth. Booth showed each of the farmers various ways of dishonestly obtaining subsidies from the Ministry of Agriculture. Each farmer then made fraudulent claims to the Ministry. At trial, the farmers were convicted of all being parties to one large conspiracy to defraud the Ministry of Agriculture. They appealed, arguing that they had not all been parties to one conspiracy.

EXTRACT

Read the following extract from the judgment of Paull J.

Were the farmers all parties to one conspiracy? Why/why not?

R v *Griffiths & others* [1966] 1 QB 589

Paull J

The matter can be illustrated quite simply. I employ an accountant to make out my tax return. He and his clerk are both present when I am about to sign the return. I notice an item in my expenses of £100 and say: 'I don't remember incurring this expense.' The clerk says: 'Well, actually I put it in. You didn't incur it, but I didn't think you would object to a few pounds being saved.' The accountant indicates his agreement to this attitude. After some hesitation I agree to let it stand. On those bare facts I cannot be charged with 50 others in a conspiracy to defraud the Exchequer of £100,000 on the basis that this accountant and his clerk have persuaded 500 other clients to make false returns, some being false in one way, some in another, or even all in the same way. I have not knowingly attached myself to a general agreement to defraud.

R v *Griffiths & others* was applied in *R* v *Mehtab* [2015] EWCA Crim 1665. A group of people, including the ringleaders Ibrahim Mahter and Abdulgrani Makrani and a woman named Kubrah Saiyed, organised sham marriages to assist unlawful immigration into the UK. In 2011, the defendant, Syed Mehtab, married Saiyed.

There was some evidence that the marriage was a sham.

For example, they married within two months of meeting and the marriage certificate stated that they lived at different addresses. Crucially, Mehtab was charged with being a party to the wider conspiracy. His submission of no case to answer was rejected by the trial judge, and he was convicted. On appeal, the Court of Appeal held that the submission should have been accepted, and quashed the conviction. Whilst there was some evidence that Mehtab's marriage to Saiyed was a conspiracy to evade immigration laws, this was not the conspiracy with which he had been charged. He had been charged with being a party to the wider conspiracy led by Mahter and Makrani, but there was no evidence that Mehtab's marriage to Saiyed had been organised by Mahter and Makrani or even that Mehtab was aware of the wider conspiracy.

These decisions can be contrasted with *R* v *Bhatti & others* [2015] EWCA Crim 1305. The three defendants set up an organisation called Middlesex College, which offered various courses to overseas students. But in fact, the college provided no real education. Instead, it provided documents to non-EU foreign nationals that purported to show that they were studying at Middlesex College, in order to allow them to enter, or remain in, the UK as students. In other words, it offered bogus immigration status. A large number of people had used the service offered by the College. The defendants were convicted of conspiring to facilitate a breach of immigration law. They appealed, arguing that, as in *R* v *Griffiths & others*, the evidence did not reveal one single conspiracy, but rather a very large number of similar, but separate, conspiracies with individual students. The Court of Appeal rejected this argument, distinguishing *R* v *Griffiths & others*. Simon J explained that students who entered into an agreement with Middlesex College knew that others were doing the same thing in pursuance of the same criminal purpose. So, unlike Syed Mehtab and the farmers in *R* v *Griffiths & others*, the students had a shared purpose and knew that there was a wider scheme that went beyond the particular offence in which they were involved.

Lastly, there are some situations in which people might agree to commit a crime and yet not be guilty of conspiracy. These are set out in section 2(2) of the Criminal Law Act 1977:

EXTRACT

Section 2(2) of the Criminal Law Act 1977

2 Exemptions from liability for conspiracy.

[...]

(2) A person shall not by virtue of section 1 above be guilty of conspiracy to commit any offence or offences if the only other person or persons with whom he agrees are (both initially and at all times during the currency of the agreement) persons of any one or more of the following descriptions, that is to say–

(a) his spouse or civil partner;

(b) a person under the age of criminal responsibility; and

(c) an intended victim of that offence or of each of those offences.

Think about these scenarios.

Scenario 1

Vito and Michael want Philip to be sent to prison, so they agree that Vito should break Michael's arm and then frame Philip.

- Are Vito and Michael guilty of conspiring to cause GBH with intent?

Scenario 2.

Vito, Vito's wife Carmela and Vito's nine-year-old son Michael agree to beat up Philip.

- Are they guilty of conspiracy?
- Would your answer be any different if Michael is 11 years old?

The scope of section 2(2)(a) was considered in *R* v *Suski* [2016] EWCA Crim 24.[19] The defendant and his co-accused were unmarried, but they lived together and had children together. The defendant argued that section 2(2)(a) should be read down, to include couples in a relationship akin to a marriage. The Court of Appeal rejected this argument and applied the express terms of the statute. McCombe LJ commented, 'There are very good grounds why a court trying a charge of conspiracy should not have to inquire closely into the nature of personal relationships of alleged conspirators, infinitely variable as they are likely to be from case to case. Nor, in our judgment, should the criminal law turn upon such vagaries' ([23]).

2. . . . that a course of conduct shall be pursued which will necessarily amount to or involve the commission of an offence by one or more parties to the agreement

The first *actus reus* requirement focused on whether or not there was an agreement. The second *actus reus* requirement focuses on the content of the agreement. For this requirement to be satisfied, it must be shown that the defendants agreed on a course of conduct that necessarily involved at least one of them committing a crime.

A defendant may be charged with conspiracy to commit any of the offences we have studied in Chapters 5, 6, 7 and 8. A defendant may also be charged with conspiracy to commit an inchoate offence. This means the following charges are all theoretically possible:

- Conspiracy to commit one of the three encouraging or assisting offences we studied earlier in the chapter[20]
- Conspiracy to conspire to commit an offence
- Conspiracy to attempt to commit an offence.

In practice, however, it is hard to imagine circumstances in which it would be appropriate to charge a defendant with 'conspiring to conspire' or 'conspiring to attempt!' Very unusual facts would be needed!

Note also that there is no offence of conspiring to be an accessory to an offence.[21]

It is important to note that section 1(1)(a) states that the conspirators must be the ones who are going to commit the planned offence. Suppose that Vito and Michael agree that they will ask Sonny to murder Philip. On these facts, Vito and Michael are not guilty of conspiracy to murder. Their plan is for Sonny to commit the murder, and Sonny is not a party to the agreement. Instead, Vito and Michael would be guilty of conspiring to intentionally encourage Sonny to commit murder.

Section 1(1)(a) also uses the word 'necessarily'. It states that parties to an agreement are only guilty of conspiracy if their plan necessarily involves the commission of an offence. So what if the defendants' agreement was conditional, so that they will

[19] See also *R* v *Bala* [2016] EWCA Crim 560, in which the Court of Appeal held that section (2)(2)(a) does extend to a spouse under a polygamous marriage that is recognised as valid under English law.

[20] In *R* v *Russo* [2025] EWCA Crim 169, the Court of Appeal confirmed that a defendant may be charged with conspiring to do an act capable of encouraging or assisting an offence.

[21] *R* v *Kenning* [2008] EWCA Crim 1534.

only commit the full offence if certain circumstances exist at the time? Can they argue that their agreement did not necessarily involve the commission of a crime? This was the issue in *R* v *Jackson* [1985] Crim LR 442. A man named Whitlock was on trial for burglary. Whitlock agreed with three of his friends – Jackson, Golding and Jackson – that if he was convicted they should shoot him in the leg. The idea was that the sentencing court would show Whitlock some leniency if it believed he had been the victim of a shooting. Whitlock was subsequently convicted. His friends shot him. Whitlock was left permanently disabled and his friends were convicted at trial of conspiring to pervert the course of justice. On appeal against their convictions they argued that their plan had not necessarily involved the commission of a crime. Whitlock might have been acquitted of burglary, in which case they would not have shot him and attempted to pervert the course of justice. The Court of Appeal rejected their appeal. Purchas LJ stated:

> Planning was taking place for a contingency and if that contingency occurred the conspiracy would necessarily involve the commission of an offence. 'Necessarily' is not to be held to mean that there must inevitably be the carrying out of an offence. It means, if the agreement is carried out in accordance with the plan, there must be the commission of the offence referred to in the conspiracy count.

Similarly, in *R* v *Maxey* [2025] EWCA Crim 472 the Court of Appeal explained that a jury should first of all determine the intention of the defendant(s), then ask whether – if the agreement was carried out as intended – it would necessarily amount to or involve the commission of an offence. The wording used in the statute ('will necessarily amount to or involve the commission of any offence') relates to 'the legal quality of the intended outcome rather than the inevitability of the outcome resulting' ([24]).

There are two final points to note about the content of the agreement. First, section 2(1) states:

EXTRACT

Section 2(1) of the Criminal Law Act 1977

2 Exemptions from liability for conspiracy

(1) A person shall not by virtue of section 1 above be guilty of conspiracy to commit any offence if he is an intended victim of that offence.

This is similar to section 51 of the Serious Crime Act 2007, which we looked at for encouraging or assisting crime. Suppose that a 14-year-old girl and her 26-year-old boyfriend (who knows her age) agree to have sexual intercourse. According to section 2(1) of the Criminal Law Act 1977, the girl is not guilty of conspiracy to commit sexual activity with a child.[22] She was the intended victim of the conspiracy, and section 2(1) states that someone cannot be guilty of conspiring to commit an offence if they themselves were the intended victim.

Second, defendants may be guilty of conspiracy even if the planned full offence is, unbeknown to them, factually impossible. This is stated in section 1(1)(b). So if Vito and Michael agree to murder Philip, but unbeknown to them Philip had in fact been killed in a road accident earlier in the day, they are nonetheless guilty of conspiracy to murder. The fact that their planned crime was factually impossible is no defence.

[22] Sexual Offences Act 2003, s.9.

3. An intention that the crime will be carried out as planned

This *mens rea* requirement derives from the wording of section 1(1) of the Criminal Law Act 1977, which assumes that the conspirators must have intended that their agreement would be carried out. In spite of this, this *mens rea* requirement was thrown into doubt by the judgment of the House of Lords in *R* v *Anderson* [1986] AC 27.

The defendant, William Anderson, had been remanded in custody. So too had Ahmed Andaloussi. They spent one night in the same cell. Anderson told Andaloussi that he expected to be released on bail the next day. Andaloussi said that he was awaiting trial for serious drugs offences and that he wanted to try and escape from prison. The two men reached an agreement. Anderson would be paid £20,000. In return he would supply equipment, including diamond cutting wire, to Andaloussi's brother and friend who would smuggle the equipment into the prison and pass it on to Andaloussi.

The next day Anderson was released on bail as expected. He subsequently received a down payment of £2,000 before being injured in a road accident. The plan never got any further, but in evidence Anderson stated that he intended to supply the diamond wire once he received a further £10,000. He was then going to go and live in Spain and play no further part in Andaloussi's attempts to escape.

At trial Anderson was convicted. He appealed, claiming that he lacked the *mens rea* of conspiracy. He said that his sole interest was receiving the money for supplying the diamond wire. He did not want the plan to be put into action and in fact he was sure that the plan could not possibly succeed. The case reached the House of Lords.

EXTRACT

According to the following extract from the judgment of Lord Bridge, can a defendant be guilty of conspiracy if he lacked any intention that the agreement be carried out?

What does Lord Bridge say is the only *mens rea* requirement for the offence of conspiracy?

R v *Anderson* [1986] AC 27

Lord Bridge

I am clearly driven by consideration of the diversity of roles which parties may agree to play in criminal conspiracies to reject any construction of the statutory language which would require the prosecution to prove an intention on the part of each conspirator that the criminal offence or offences which will necessarily be committed by one or more of the conspirators if the agreed course of conduct is fully carried out should in fact be committed. A simple example will illustrate the absurdity to which this construction would lead. The proprietor of a car hire firm agrees for a substantial payment to make available a hire car to a gang for use in a robbery and to make false entries in his books relating to the hiring to which he can point if the number of the car is traced back to him in connection with the robbery. Being fully aware of the circumstances of the robbery in which the car is proposed to be used he is plainly a party to the conspiracy to rob. Making his car available for use in the robbery is as much a part of the relevant agreed course of conduct as the robbery itself. Yet, once he has been paid, it will be a matter of complete indifference to him whether the robbery is in fact committed or not. In these days of highly organised crime the most serious statutory conspiracies will frequently involve an elaborate and complex agreed course of conduct in which many will consent to play necessary but subordinate roles, not involving them in any direct participation in the commission of the offence or offences at the centre of the conspiracy. Parliament cannot have intended that such parties should escape conviction of conspiracy on the basis that it cannot be proved against them that they intended that the relevant offence or offences should be committed.

There remains the important question whether a person who has agreed that a course of conduct will be pursued which, if pursued as agreed, will necessarily amount to or involve the commission of an offence is guilty of statutory conspiracy irrespective of his intention, and, if not, what is the *mens rea* of the offence. I have no hesitation in answering the first part of the question in the negative. There may be many situations in which perfectly respectable citizens, more particularly those concerned with law enforcement, may enter into agreements that a course of conduct shall be pursued which will involve commission of a crime without the least intention of playing any part in furtherance of the ostensibly agreed criminal objective, but rather with the purpose of exposing and frustrating the criminal purpose of the other parties to the agreement. To say this is in no way to encourage schemes by which police act, directly or through the agency of informers, as agents provocateurs for the purpose of entrapment. That is conduct of which the courts have always strongly disapproved. But it may sometimes happen, as most of us with experience in criminal trials well know, that a criminal enterprise is well advanced in the course of preparation when it comes to the notice either of the police or of some honest citizen in such circumstances that the only prospect of exposing and frustrating the criminals is that some innocent person should play the part of an intending collaborator in the course of criminal conduct proposed to be pursued. The *mens rea* implicit in the offence of statutory conspiracy must clearly be such as to recognise the innocence of such a person, notwithstanding that he will, in literal terms, be obliged to agree that a course of conduct be pursued involving the commission of an offence.

I have said already, but I repeat to emphasise its importance, that an essential ingredient in the crime of conspiring to commit a specific offence or offences under section 1(1) of the Act of 1977 is that the accused should agree that a course of conduct be pursued which he knows must involve the commission by one or more of the parties to the agreement of that offence or those offences. But, beyond the mere fact of agreement, the necessary *mens rea* of the crime is, in my opinion, established if, and only if, it is shown that the accused, when he entered into the agreement, intended to play some part in the agreed course of conduct in furtherance of the criminal purpose which the agreed course of conduct was intended to achieve. Nothing less will suffice; nothing more is required.

Applying this test to the facts which, for the purposes of the appeal, we must assume, the appellant, in agreeing that a course of conduct be pursued that would, if successful, necessarily involve the offence of effecting Andaloussi's escape from lawful custody, clearly intended, by providing diamond wire to be smuggled into the prison, to play a part in the agreed course of conduct in furtherance of that criminal objective. Neither the fact that he intended to play no further part in attempting to effect the escape, nor that he believed the escape to be impossible, would, if the jury had supposed they might be true, have afforded him any defence.

Lord Bridge's answers to each of these two questions were both novel and controversial. We shall examine each in turn.

i. Can a defendant be guilty of conspiracy if he lacked any intention that the agreement be carried out?

Lord Bridge stated that it was not necessary to prove that Anderson intended that the agreement would be carried out. But if this is taken to its logical conclusion, the result is that there can be a conspiracy even if none of the conspirators intends to carry out the agreement! The point has been made forcefully by David Ormerod:

> If no intention needs to be proved on the part of conspirator A, then none needs to be proved on the part of another, B. But if A and B are the only parties, and neither has the intention that it should be carried out, how can there be a crime of conspiracy? A conspiracy which no one intends to carry out is an absurdity, if not an impossibility.[23]

As the extract from Lord Bridge's judgment showed (in particular the hire car example), he was concerned that defendants like Anderson might escape liability for the crime of conspiracy if the prosecution is required to show that each conspirator had an intention that the agreement would be carried out. However, there was a more satisfactory way of addressing this policy concern. Anderson's conviction could have been upheld on the basis that he was an accessory to the conspiracy to help Andaloussi escape. Anderson unquestionably had the *mens rea* of accessorial liability, and as we shall see in the next chapter an accessory can be tried, indicted and punished as a principal offender.

In the years since the House of Lords' judgment the Court of Appeal has not followed *R* v *Anderson* on this issue. An example is *R* v *McPhillips* [1990] 6 BNIL.[24] In this case the police stopped a car at about 11 pm. A man named Drumm was driving and the defendant, McPhillips, was in the passenger seat. Behind the driver's seat was a bomb. McPhillips admitted that they had agreed to place the bomb on the roof of a nearby hotel where there was a disco taking place, but he claimed that he had intended to give a telephone warning to the police so that the hotel could be evacuated before the bomb exploded. This was accepted as being true by the trial judge. The Court of Appeal of Northern Ireland therefore held that McPhillips could not be convicted of conspiracy to murder since he lacked any intention that the crime of murder be carried out. Lord Lowry CJ explained:

> [T]he accused must agree with another that murder will be committed and must intend that this will happen. The guilty act is the agreement that the crime contemplated will be committed; the guilty mind is the intention that that crime will be committed [... T]he agreed course of conduct was the planting of a 'no warning' bomb at the Seagoe Hotel and persons who had agreed to that course of conduct intending it to be carried out would be guilty of conspiracy to murder because, if the agreement had been carried out in accordance with their intentions it would (unless all the patrons of the disco had gone home or had a miraculous escape) necessarily involve the commission of murder. But, on the facts found here, this result would not have been in accordance with the intention of [McPhillips]. Therefore he was not guilty of conspiracy to murder.

(McPhillips was, however, convicted of conspiracy to cause an explosion and other explosives offences.)

Now, think about this question.

- If a case like *RvMcPhillips* happened today, could the defendant be convicted of one of the offences under the Serious Crime Act 2007 that we studied earlier in the chapter?

[23] Ormerod, D. and Laird, K. (2015) *Smith and Hogan's Criminal Law* (14th edn). OUP: Oxford, p.503.

[24] Another example is *R* v *Edwards* [1991] Crim LR 45.

Another example of the Court of Appeal not following *R* v *Anderson* on this issue is *R* v *Goddard & another* [2012] EWCA Crim 1756. The defendants, Daniel Goddard and Robin Fallick, were charged with conspiring to rape a child under 13. They exchanged text messages after meeting on a gay chat line (they had never met each other in person). The prosecution case focused on the following series of text messages which Fallick sent to Goddard (the messages which Goddard sent to Fallick were not available):

09:35 I need some help rapin a 6yo

09:37 Next friday night

09:39 Its rob in slough

09:41 tis ok. So your in?

10:46 He's about 4ft dark hair and eyes, slim, toned stomach tight round ass and perfect legs. Really soft smooth skin and ruby red lips.

11:02 He'll be with me, he's 6

11:09 Next friday. Yes we can do stuff but we need to make sure he doesn't drop us in it. i'm best friends with his mum, drug him is a poss?

At trial the two men were convicted. They appealed, arguing that the text message conversation was nothing more than a fantasy from which they both gained sexual pleasure and that they never had any intention of carrying out the plan. Quashing their convictions, the Court of Appeal concluded that there was insufficient evidence for any reasonable jury to be able to conclude beyond reasonable doubt that the two men had intended to carry out the agreement. Aikens LJ explained:

> 40 We have concluded that no reasonable jury, taking the prosecution evidence at its highest, could surely infer that the defendants intended to carry out the agreement. The evidence is all equivocal; it is as consistent with fantasy as with an intent to carry out the plan. It is particularly striking that these men never met at any stage, either before or after the text exchange nor did they even suggest meeting to discuss the plan further. Nor is there any evidence that they took any steps to advance the plan beyond suggesting "Friday night". No place or time or other practical details are identified. Nothing at all happened after the exchange of text messages. We appreciate that their silence in interviews and failure to mention that this was all a fantasy can be taken into account. But that is of very little weight given the other facts or rather lack of them.

So in spite of Lord Bridge's judgment in *R* v *Anderson*, it is now safe to say that a defendant can only be guilty of conspiracy if he had an intention that the agreement be carried out.[25]

ii. Must the defendant have intended to play some part in the agreed course of conduct?

According to Lord Bridge in *R* v *Anderson,* what must be shown to establish the *mens rea* of conspiracy is an intention to play some part in the agreed course of conduct. This was a radical suggestion which was strongly criticised by commentators. Suppose that Vito tells Michael and Sonny to go and murder Philip. Applying Lord Bridge's approach it would seem that Michael and Sonny are guilty of conspiracy to murder (since they intend to play an active part in the plan), but Vito is not (since he was not going to play any active part). This would be very difficult to justify. Not only is it at odds with the focus of the offence

[25] This conclusion is reinforced still further by Lord Nicholls' statement in *R* v *Saik* [2006] UKHL 18 that 'The conspirators must intend to do the act prohibited by the substantive offence' ([4]).

of conspiracy on the fact of an agreement. It would also 'place the godfathers of criminal conspiracies even further beyond the reach of the criminal justice system'.[26]

The Court of Appeal revisited this issue in *R* v *Siracusa & others* (1989) 90 Cr App R 340. This case involved a conspiracy to smuggle massive amounts of heroin (with a street value of more than £15m) from Kashmir to Canada via England, hidden in secret compartments in furniture. At trial the four defendants were all convicted of conspiracy to import heroin. They appealed against their convictions. In its judgment the Court of Appeal discussed Lord Bridge's judgment in *R* v *Anderson*.

EXTRACT

According to the following extract from the judgment of O'Connor LJ, what is required to establish 'an intention to play some part in the agreed course of conduct'?

Applying O'Connor LJ's approach to our example of Vito telling Michael and Sonny to go and murder Philip, does Vito have 'an intention to play some part in the agreed course of conduct'?

R v *Siracusa & others* (1989) 90 Cr App R 340

O'Connor LJ

We think it obvious that Lord Bridge cannot have been intending that the organiser of a crime who recruited others to carry it out would not himself be guilty of conspiracy unless it could be proved that he intended to play some active part himself thereafter. Lord Bridge had pointed out [...] that

> "in these days of highly organised crime the most serious statutory conspiracies will frequently involve an elaborate and complex agreed course of conduct in which many will consent to play necessary but subordinate roles, not involving them in any direct participation in the commission of the offence or offences at the centre of the conspiracy."

[...] Participation in a conspiracy is infinitely variable: it can be active or passive. If the majority shareholder and director of a company consents to the company being used for drug smuggling carried out in the company's name by a fellow director and minority shareholder, he is guilty of conspiracy. Consent, that is the agreement or adherence to the agreement, can be inferred if it is proved that he knew what was going on and the intention to participate in the furtherance of the criminal purpose is also established by his failure to stop the unlawful activity. Lord Bridge's *dictum* does not require anything more.

O'Connor LJ's reasoning pays only lip service to Lord Bridge's judgment in *R* v *Anderson*. Failing to stop an unlawful activity is hardly the same as playing an active part! But Lord Bridge's approach is so problematic that it is likely that *R* v *Siracusa* will be followed on this issue.

So we have effectively come full circle! We have looked at two key questions: (i) Can a defendant be guilty of conspiracy if he lacked any intention that the agreement be carried out? and (ii) Must the defendant have intended to play some part in the agreed course of conduct? We have seen that the House of Lords in *R* v *Anderson* answered 'Yes' to both questions, but subsequent case law has undermined the precedential status of this case such that today the answer to both questions seems to be 'No'!

[26] Fitzpatrick, D. (1993) 'Variations on Conspiracy' 143 *New Law Journal* 1180.

There is one final point to note. A person can only be convicted of conspiracy if at least one of the other parties to the agreement also had the *mens rea* of conspiracy.[27] Suppose that Vito and Michael agree that Michael should have sexual intercourse with Sandra. Vito knows that Sandra is only 15 years old, but Michael reasonably believes that she is 16. Michael lacks the *mens rea* of conspiracy to commit sexual activity with a child. This means that Vito cannot be guilty of conspiracy to commit this offence since he had not formed an agreement with another person who had the necessary *mens rea*.

4. Intention or knowledge of essential facts or circumstances

Section 1(2) specifies an additional *mens rea* requirement. However, this only applies if the following two conditions are satisfied:

1. The full offence which the defendants planned to commit has a circumstance element as part of its *actus reus*
2. The definition of the full offence specifies a *mens rea* requirement for this circumstance element which is less than knowledge or intention.

An example of when section 1(2) applies is conspiracy to commit rape. The definition of rape has a circumstance element as part of its *actus reus* (the victim was not consenting) and the definition of rape specifies a *mens rea* requirement for this circumstance element which is less than knowledge or intention (lack of a reasonable belief in consent).

EXTRACT

Section 1(2) of the Criminal Law Act 1977

(2) Where liability for any offence may be incurred without knowledge on the part of the person committing it of any particular fact or circumstance necessary for the commission of the offence, a person shall nevertheless not be guilty of conspiracy to commit that offence by virtue of subsection above unless he and at least one other party to the agreement intend or know that that fact or circumstance shall or will exist at the time when the conduct constituting the offence is to take place.

In other words, a defendant can only be convicted of conspiracy if he had intention or knowledge in relation to each circumstance element of the *actus reus* of the full offence he planned to commit.[28] So on a charge of conspiracy to rape, the defendant can only be convicted if he intended that the victim would not consent or knew that the victim would not consent. Lack of a reasonable belief that the victim would consent might suffice for the offence of rape, but not for the offence of conspiracy to rape.[29]

---

[27] Criminal Law Act 1977, s.1(2).

[28] This interpretation of section 1(2) was confirmed by the House of Lords in *R* v *Saik* [2006] UKHL 18. In this case the defendant was charged with conspiracy to launder money. He admitted that he suspected the money represented the proceeds of crime. However, the House of Lords held that suspicion as to this circumstance element of the full offence was insufficient. It had to be shown that he knew the money was the proceeds of crime. For critique, see Child, J. & Hunt, A. (2022) 'Beyond the Present-Fault Paradigm: Expanding *Mens Rea* Definitions in the General Part' 42 *Oxford Journal of Legal Studies* 438.

[29] In its 2009 report *Conspiracy and Attempts* (Report No 318) HC 41, the Law Commission proposed simplifying and relaxing the requirements contained in section 1(2). See further part 2 of its report.

It is worth noting that some agreements will concern future circumstances that are not yet known. For example, an agreement to sell goods even if they turn out to be counterfeit. In such cases, it is not possible to speak of knowledge – the defendants may not know whether the goods are counterfeit or not until they receive them – and so the focus should be on the defendants' intention.[30] At the time of the agreement, was it their intention to sell the goods even if they did turn out to be counterfeit?

Quiz 12.2

1. When does the statutory offence of conspiracy occur?
   - a. When one person encourages another to commit a crime.
   - b. When there is an agreement with at least two other people that someone should commit an offence.
   - c. When a person does an act that is more than merely preparatory to the commission of an offence.
   - d. When there is an agreement with at least one other person which will involve at least one of them committing an offence.
2. Which of the following best describes the *actus reus* of conspiracy?
   - a. The setting out between two or more persons to reach an agreement to do an act that will if done amount to a recognisable offence in law.
   - b. An agreement that is reached between two or more persons to do an act that will if done amount to a recognisable offence in law.
   - c. A resolve that is reached by a person to agree with others to do an act that will if done amount to a recognisable offence in law.
   - d. An agreement that is reached between any two or more persons to do an act that will if done amount to an unlawful act.
3. According to section 2(2) of the Criminal Law Act 1977, who could be a co-conspirator with A to a statutory conspiracy?
   - a. Another who has a valid defence.
   - b. An intended victim of the offence.
   - c. Anyone under the age of criminal liability.
   - d. A's spouse.
4. Which of the following statements is incorrect?
   - a. There can be an agreement even if some of the details of the planned offence have yet to be worked out.
   - b. To prove a conspiracy it is necessary to show that all parties to the agreement had met and communicated with one another.
   - c. To prove a conspiracy it is necessary to show that the parties to the alleged agreement shared a common unlawful purpose.
   - d. It is possible for there to be one general conspiracy, with related sub-conspiracies.
5. Which one of the following accurately describes the *mens rea* that is required for statutory conspiracy?
   - a. D must intend that the crime will be carried out as planned and (where the *actus reus* of the planned full offence specifies a circumstance requirement) have intention or knowledge in respect of the circumstance elements of the planned full offence.
   - b. D must intend that the crime will be carried out as planned and (where the *actus reus* of the planned full offence specifies a circumstance requirement) have the *mens rea* specified in the definition of the full offence in respect of those circumstances.
   - c. D must intend to play some part in the agreed course of conduct and (where the *actus reus* of the planned full offence specifies a circumstance requirement) have intention or knowledge in respect of the circumstance elements of the planned full offence.
   - d. D must intend that the crime will be carried out as planned, and intend to play some part in the agreed course of conduct, and (where the *actus reus* of the planned full offence specifies a circumstance requirement) have intention or knowledge in respect of the circumstance elements of the planned full offence.

[30] *Iqbal v City of Wolverhampton Council* [2025] EWCA Crim 498.

Attempts

12.3 Define the *actus reus* requirements for establishing criminal liability for criminal attempts.

The law of criminal attempts is governed by section 1(1) of the Criminal Attempts Act 1981:

EXTRACT

Section 1(1) of the Criminal Attempts Act 1981

1 Attempting to commit an offence.

(1) If, with intent to commit an offence to which this section applies, a person does an act which is more than merely preparatory to the commission of the offence, he is guilty of attempting to commit the offence.

This tells us that the offence has two requirements:

1. The defendant did an act that was more than mere preparation for the commission of the full offence
2. The defendant intended to commit the full offence.

Number 1 is an *actus reus* requirement. Number 2 is a *mens rea* requirement. We will work through them in turn.

1. The defendant did an act that was more than mere preparation for the commission of the full offence

Our examination of this *actus reus* requirement is broken down into three parts. First we examine the 'more than merely preparatory' test, before briefly looking at which offences it is a crime to attempt and impossible attempts.

i. The 'more than merely preparatory' test

Section 1(1) of the Criminal Attempts Act 1981 states that a defendant only satisfies the *actus reus* of an attempt if he has gone beyond mere preparation. As the timeline in Figure 12.4 illustrates, this means that there is an all-important distinction to be drawn between 'mere preparation' and 'more than mere preparation'.

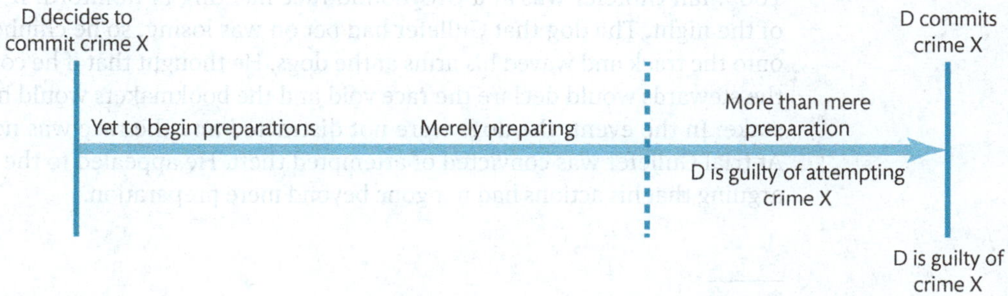

Figure 12.4

Whether a defendant has gone beyond mere preparation in a particular case is a question of fact for the jury to decide. However, the trial judge may only leave this issue to the jury if there is sufficient evidence for a reasonable jury to be able to convict. If there is no evidence that the defendant has gone beyond mere preparation he must be found not guilty.

We are going to look at six cases in which the Court of Appeal has had to decide whether there was any evidence that the defendant had gone beyond mere preparation.[31] Examining these cases will help you: (1) understand the distinction between mere preparation (= no liability for a criminal attempt) and more than mere preparation (= liable for a criminal attempt); and (2) evaluate whether the criminal law has drawn this dividing line appropriately. First, though, consider the following scenario.

Now, think about this question.

Vito has decided to kill Philip.

- At which of the following six stages do you believe the criminal law should impose liability for attempted murder?
- Why?

a. The day before the planned killing, Vito goes out and buys a gun on the black market.

b. Before leaving his house to go and kill Philip, Vito puts some bullets in his pocket and tucks his gun in his belt.

c. Vito follows Philip home from the pub.

d. While Philip (who is in a drunken stupor) fumbles around trying to find his front door key, Vito loads his gun.

e. Philip finally finds his front door key and puts it in the lock. Vito crooks his finger round the trigger of the gun and takes aim.

f. Vito fires the gun but misses.

Remember your answer to this question. You will shortly be able to use this to decide whether the law is as you believe it should be.

The first case for us to examine to see how the courts have applied the distinction between mere preparation and more than mere preparation is *R* v *Gullefer* [1990] 1 WLR 1063. Ian Gullefer was at a Greyhound race meeting in Romford. It was the last race of the night. The dog that Gullefer had bet on was losing, so he climbed over the fence onto the track and waved his arms at the dogs. He thought that if he could distract them the stewards would declare the race void and the bookmakers would have to refund his stake. In the event, the dogs were not distracted and the race was not declared void. At trial Gullefer was convicted of attempted theft. He appealed to the Court of Appeal, arguing that his actions had not gone beyond mere preparation.

[31] Oher cases include: *R* v *Bowlesand Bowles* [2004] EWCA Crim 1608; *Mason* v *DPP* [2009] EWHC 2198 (Admin); and *R* v *K* [2009] EWCA Crim 1931.

EXTRACT

In the following extract from Lord Lane CJ's judgment he explains that before the 1981 Act there were two different sets of cases which applied different tests for the *actus reus* of an attempt.

What tests did these lines of authority use? How is the 'more than merely preparatory test' different to these other two tests? How did Lord Lane CJ paraphrase the 'more than merely preparatory' test?

According to the Court of Appeal, had Gullefer gone beyond mere preparation?

R v *Gullefer* [1990] 1 WLR 1063

Lord Lane CJ

Was the appellant still in the stage of preparation to commit the substantive offence, or was there a basis of fact which would entitle the jury to say that he had embarked on the theft itself? Might it properly be said that when he jumped on to the track he was trying to steal £18 from the bookmaker?

Our view is that it could not properly be said that at that stage he was in the process of committing theft. What he was doing was jumping on to the track in an effort to distract the dogs, which in its turn, he hoped, would have the effect of forcing the stewards to declare "no race," which would in its turn give him the opportunity to go back to the bookmaker and demand the £18 he had staked. In our view there was insufficient evidence for it to be said that he had, when he jumped on to the track, gone beyond mere preparation

[...]

Since the passing of the Act of 1981, a division of this court in *Reg.* v. *Ilyas* (1983) 78 Cr.App.R.17, has helpfully collated the authorities [which preceded the Act]. As appears from the judgment in that case, there seem to have been two lines of authority. The first was exemplified by the decision in *Reg.* v. *Eagleton* (1854) 5 Dears C.C. 515. That was a case where the defendant was alleged to have attempted to obtain money from the guardians of a parish by falsely pretending to the relieving officer that he had delivered loaves of bread of the proper weight to the outdoor poor, when in fact the loaves were deficient in weight.

Park B., delivering the judgment of the court of nine judges, said, at p. 538:

> "Acts remotely leading towards the commission of the offence are not to be considered as attempts to commit it, but acts immediately connected with it are; and if, in this case, after the credit with the relieving officer for the fraudulent overcharge, any *further step* on the part of the defendant had been necessary to obtain payment, as the making out a further account or producing the vouchers to the Board, we should have thought that the obtaining credit in account with the relieving officer would not have been sufficiently proximate to the obtaining the money. But, on the statement in this case, no other act on the part of the defendant would have been required. It was the last act, *depending on himself*, towards the payment of the money, and therefore it ought to be considered as an attempt."

Lord Diplock in *Director of Public Prosecutions* v. *Stonehouse* [1978] A.C. 55, 68, having cited part of that passage from *Reg.* v. *Eagleton*, added: "In other words the offender must have crossed the Rubicon and burnt his boats."

The other line of authority is based on a passage in *Stephen's Digest of the Criminal Law*, 5th ed. (1894), art. 50: "An attempt to commit a crime is an act done with intent to commit that crime, and forming part of a series of acts which would constitute its actual commission if it were not interrupted." As Lord Edmund-Davies points out in *Director of Public Prosecution* v. *Stonehouse*, at p. 85, that definition has been repeatedly cited with judicial approval: see Byrne J. in *Hope* v. *Brown* [1954] 1 W.L.R. 250, 253 and Lord Parker C.J. in *Davey* v. *Lee* [1968] 1 Q.B. 366. However, as Lord Parker C.J. in the latter case points out, at p. 370G, *Stephen's* definition falls short of defining the exact point of time at which the series of acts can be said to begin.

It seems to us that the words of the Act of 1981 seek to steer a midway course. They do not provide, as they might have done, that the *Reg.* v. *Eagleton* test is to be followed, or that, as Lord Diplock suggested, the defendant must have reached a point from which it was impossible for him to retreat before the *actus reus* of an attempt is proved. On the other hand the words give perhaps as clear a guidance as is possible in the circumstances on the point of time at which *Stephen's* "series of acts" begin. It begins when the merely preparatory acts come to an end and the defendant embarks upon the crime proper. When that is will depend of course upon the facts in any particular case.

The judgment of Lord Lane CJ in *R* v *Gullefer* was followed by the Court of Appeal in *R* v *Jones* (Kenneth) [1990] 1 WLR 1057.

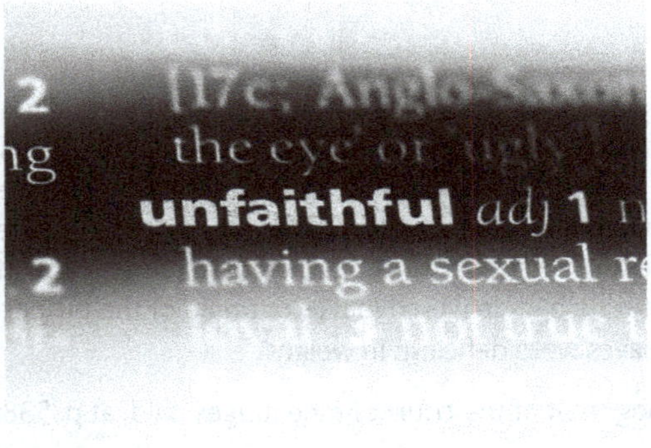

Casimiro PT/Shutterstock

Kenneth Jones had been having an affair with a woman named Lynn Gresley. She began a relationship with another man, Michael Foreman, and two months later broke off her relationship with Jones. As a result, Jones decided to kill Foreman.

Photographee.eu/Shutterstock

On the day of the offence Foreman took his daughter to school as normal. After she had got out of the car Jones jumped into the rear seat. He introduced himself and said he wanted to sort things out.

derek oldfield/Shutterstock

Foreman drove off, and subsequently pulled over on a grass verge. Jones then handed Foreman a letter he had received from Lynn.

Fred Mastison/Shutterstock

While Foreman was reading it Jones pulled a sawn-off shotgun out of the bag he was carrying. It was loaded. He pointed it at Foreman and said, 'You're not going to like this'. Foreman quickly grabbed the end of the gun and pointed it sideways. A struggle ensued, and Foreman managed to escape.

At trial Jones was convicted of attempted murder.

He appealed to the Court of Appeal. He argued that a defendant has only gone beyond mere preparation if he has performed the 'last act' within his power towards commission of the full offence. Since he still had to perform at least three more acts before he could have committed murder (remove the safety catch, put his finger on the trigger and pull the trigger) he claimed that he had not performed the last act and so had not gone beyond mere preparation.

EXTRACT

Read the following extract from the judgment of Taylor LJ.

Did the Court of Appeal accept Jones' arguments? Why/why not?

R v *Jones* (Kenneth) [1990] 1 WLR 1057

Taylor CJ

The words "an act which is more than merely preparatory to the commission of the offence" would be inapt if they were intended to mean "the last act which lay in his power towards the commission of the offence."

> Looking at the plain natural meaning of section 1(1) in the way indicated by the Lord Chief Justice [in *R* v *Gullefer*], the question for the judge in the present case was whether there was evidence from which a reasonable jury, properly directed, could conclude that the appellant had done acts which were more than merely preparatory. Clearly his actions in obtaining the gun, in shortening it, in loading it, in putting on his disguise, and in going to the school could only be regarded as preparatory acts. But, in our judgment, once he had got into the car, taken out the loaded gun and pointed it at the victim with the intention of killing him, there was sufficient evidence for the consideration of the jury on the charge of attempted murder. It was a matter for them to decide whether they were sure those acts were more than merely preparatory. In our judgment, therefore, the judge was right to allow the case to go to the jury, and the appeal against conviction must be dismissed.

Next are three cases which have generated controversy. The first is *R* v *Geddes* [1996] Crim LR 894. The defendant, Gary Geddes, was found in the boys' toilets in a school in Brighton. He had no right to be there, and had with him a large knife, some rope and a roll of masking tape. The prosecution alleged that Geddes had intended to kidnap a pupil. At trial, he was convicted of attempted false imprisonment. He appealed, arguing that his conviction should be quashed on the basis that he had not gone beyond mere preparation. His case reached the Court of Appeal.

EXTRACT

Read the following extract from the judgment of Lord Bingham CJ.

How did he paraphrase the 'more than merely preparatory' test?

According to the Court of Appeal, had Geddes gone beyond mere preparation? Why/why not?

What is your reaction to the outcome of this case?

R v *Geddes* [1996] Crim LR 894

Lord Bingham CJ

This appeal is concerned not with the correctness of the jury's decision of fact, but the correctness of the judge's ruling of law. Was the evidence summarised in the admissions sufficient in law to support a finding that the appellant did an act which was more than merely preparatory to the commission of the offence charged? The cases show that the line of demarcation between acts which are merely preparatory and acts which may amount to an attempt is not always clear or easy to recognise. There is no rule of thumb test. There must always be an exercise of judgment based on the particular facts of the case. It is, we think, an accurate paraphrase of the statutory test and not an illegitimate gloss upon it to ask whether the available evidence, if accepted, could show that a defendant has done an act which shows that he has actually tried to commit the offence in question, or whether he has only got ready or put himself in a position or equipped himself to do so.

> In the present case, as already indicated, there is not much room for doubt about the appellant's intention. Furthermore, the evidence is clearly capable of showing that he made preparations, that he equipped himself, that he got ready, that he put himself in a position to commit the offence charged [...] But was the evidence sufficient in law to support a finding that the appellant had actually tried or attempted to commit the offence of imprisoning someone? Had he moved from the realm of intention, preparation and planning into the area of execution or implementation? [...] Here it is true that the appellant had entered the school; but he had never had any contact or communication with any pupil; he had never confronted any pupil at the school in any way. That may well be no credit to him, and may indeed reflect great credit on the vigilance of the school staff. The whole story is one which fills the court with the gravest unease. Nonetheless, we cannot escape giving an answer to the fundamental legal question [...] So, for this purpose, must the contents of the rucksack, which give a clear indication as to what the appellant may have had in mind, but do not throw light on whether he had begun to carry out the commission of the offence. On the facts of this case we feel bound to conclude that the evidence was not sufficient in law to support a finding that the appellant did an act which was more than merely preparatory to wrongfully imprisoning a person unknown. In those circumstances we conclude that the appeal must be allowed and the conviction quashed.

The next case is *R* v *Campbell* (1990) 93 Cr App R 350. The police had received a tip-off that a post office in London was going to be robbed. After keeping watch of the post office for several days they saw the defendant, Tony Campbell, arrive on a motorbike. He was dressed in a motorcycle suit, crash helmet and gloves, and hung around in front of the post office for a while. Then he walked off. Half an hour later he reappeared. He walked towards the post office and, when he was a yard from the front door, the police stopped and searched him. He was found to be in possession of an imitation firearm, sunglasses and a threatening note. Campbell admitted that he had originally intended to rob the post office but claimed that by the time he was arrested he had changed his mind. He said he had decided that the dangers of committing the robbery were too great and simply not worth it.

At trial Campbell was convicted of attempted robbery. He appealed, arguing that he had not gone beyond mere preparation. The case reached the Court of Appeal.

EXTRACT

According to the following extract from the judgment of Watkins LJ, had Campbell gone beyond mere preparation? Why/why not? What is your reaction to the outcome of this case?

R v *Campbell* (1990) 93 Cr App R 350

Watkins LJ

> Looking at the circumstances here it was beyond dispute that the appellant, at the material time, was carrying an imitation firearm which he made no attempt to remove from his clothing. He was not, as he had done previously that day, wearing, as a form of disguise, sunglasses. It was

> not suggested that he had, in the course of making his way down the road past the post-box, turned and, so to speak, moved towards the door of the post office so as to indicate that he intended to enter that place.
>
> In order to effect the robbery it is equally beyond dispute it would have been quite impossible unless obviously he had entered the post office, gone to the counter and made some kind of hostile act – directed, of course, at whoever was behind the counter and in a position to hand him money. A number of acts remained undone and the series of acts which he had already performed – namely, making his way from his home or other place where he commenced to ride his motor cycle on a journey to a place near a post office, dismounting from the cycle and walking towards the post office door – were clearly acts which were, in the judgment of this court, indicative of mere preparation, even if he was still of a mind to rob the post office, of the commission that is of the offence of robbery. If a person, in circumstances such as this, has not even gained the place where he could be in a position to carry out the offence, it is extremely unlikely that it could ever be said that he had performed an act which could be properly said to be an attempt.

The outcome in *R* v *Campbell* may be contrasted with the decisions in *R* v *Tosti & White* [1997] Crim LR 746 and *R* v *MS* [2021] EWCA Crim 600. The defendants were seen walking to the door of a barn and examining the padlock. They realised they were being watched and ran off. Some oxygen-cutting equipment was found hidden nearby. The defendants were convicted of attempted burglary. They appealed, arguing that they had not gone beyond mere preparation. Their convictions were upheld by the Court of Appeal. Beldam LJ explained:

> [The defendants] had committed acts which were preparatory, but not merely so – so that it could be said the acts of preparation amounted to acts done in the commission of the offence.

On the face of it the conduct of Tosti and White seems very similar to Campbell's. Like Campbell, they were loitering outside a building that they planned to steal from. Yet Campbell's conviction for attempted robbery was quashed whilst Tosti's and White's were upheld. The key to reconciling the two cases is the different offences the men were charged with. Campbell was charged with attempted robbery. As we saw in Chapter 8, the essence of robbery is theft with violence. He had not embarked on this offence because he was never in a position where he could carry it out. By contrast, Tosti and White were charged with attempted burglary. The essence of burglary is entry as a trespasser with intent to steal. By examining the padlock on the barn door Tosti and White had embarked on gaining entry and so had begun to carry out the burglary. So it is possible to reconcile the two cases. However, the distinction between them is a fine one. In fact, Simester and Sullivan suggest that it 'may be considered so faint as to be invisible'.[32]

Our sixth case is *R* v *MS* [2021] EWCA Crim 600. The victim in this case was twelve-year-old SS. The defendant, MS, was SS's mother. She was separated from SS's father.

---

[32] Simester, A.P., Spencer, J.R., Stark, F., Sullivan, G.R. and Virgo, G. J. (2016) *Simester and Sullivan's Criminal Law: Theory and Doctrine* (6th edn). Hart Publishing: Oxford, p.343.

MS planned to go and live abroad with SS and her new boyfriend, but SS's father refused her permission to take SS out of the UK. In spite of this, MS and her boyfriend packed up all their belongings and booked a ferry from Dover to Calais. They were stopped at a service station on the M25 on their way to Dover. They had with them their passports and details of hotel bookings in France. MS was charged with attempted child abduction. At trial, the trial judge ruled that there was no case to answer. He said that, since MS had been stopped 85 miles away from Dover, her acts were no more than merely preparatory. The prosecution appealed against this ruling.

EXTRACT

According to the following extract from the judgment of Lord Justice Fulford VP, had MS gone beyond mere preparation? Why/why not?

What did Lord Justice Fulford VP say is the relevance (if any) of "geographical proximity"? How did he distinguish *R* v *Campbell*?

R v *MS* [2021] EWCA Crim 600

Lord Justice Fulford VP

34. It is important in our judgment not to lose sight of the considerable differences that exist between the various offences which may be attempted ... along with multiple different ways in which even similar or identical offences are attempted ... This results in highly fact-specific decisions as to whether the steps taken by the accused were no more than merely preparatory. [Counsel for MS], in support of his submissions that there needed to be "geographical proximity", raised the analogy of the offence of attempted murder, and suggested that it would be inconceivable that an individual could properly be said to have attempted murder at a distance of 85 miles from the intended victim. Depending always on the facts, the proximity of the accused to an intended murder victim may be critical in determining whether the steps taken by the accused were more than preparatory. In many cases when a sole offender contemplates murder (or an assault) by way of a direct physical attack, an attempt to commit the crime will only occur when the perpetrator and victim are in close proximity, when the action necessary (the *actus reus*) for attempting to kill or harm takes place (although we stress there will be undoubted exceptions to this sweeping generalisation). Similarly, in an attempted armed robbery of the kind contemplated in Campbell, proximity to the target premises, along with an evinced intention to enter, may be critical. Distance, or rather proximity, therefore, may be an important factor for attempted crimes of that kind. But no single factor, including proximity, constitutes a uniform test that applies to all species of offences. Child abduction by a person connected with the child is an entirely different offence to murder, assault and robbery. The action necessary for an attempted parental abduction, as in the instant case, may have been "embarked upon" at a considerable distance from the port or airport. For child abduction, geographical proximity does not have the same relevance as with other alleged crimes. Whether, prima facie, steps had been taken as part of the execution of the plan which were sufficiently close to the final act will always depend, therefore, on the ingredients of the offence and the facts of the case.

35. In the present trial, there was evidence that the respondent had left Stoke with the intention of leaving the country with her family and new boyfriend. She had the five relevant passports and the one-way tickets for the trip from Dover to Calais in her possession. She had booked accommodation for the journey through France en route to the port in Italy. The family had

packed their bags, loaded the car and had left their home. The respondent had expressed her clear intention to leave the country and she had forged the necessary permission document for this purpose. The car in which they were travelling was headed towards Dover (albeit they had 85 miles yet to travel), the time of the sailing had been changed at the last moment, and the respondent had checked the ferry times during the journey.

36. We are entirely confident that these various steps, viewed together, were ... part of the execution of [the] plan to abduct SS. They were steps immediately preceding the final act that were necessary to complete her plan and to bring about the commission of the intended offence (viz. by travelling on the ferry to France). Put otherwise, when arrested, she was in the position of attempting to commit the offence in question, rather than simply getting ready or putting herself in a position to do so, and we have no doubt she had embarked "upon the crime proper". The distance they had yet to travel to Dover on the motorway, which was a critical factor for the judge, was essentially unimportant given the multiple steps that, by the time they were intercepted, had been taken and the overall stage in the venture that had been reached. It was open to the jury, in our judgment, to conclude that the respondent was attempting to abduct SS.

Since the trial judge's ruling had been incorrect, the Court of Appeal ordered a new trial. The Court emphasised that, given the wide variety of offences that may be attempted, decisions as to whether a particular defendant has gone beyond mere preparation are 'highly fact-specific'. Whilst geographical proximity may be an important consideration in cases involving attempted murder, assault or robbery (such as *R* v *Campbell*), the fact that MS still had 85 miles to go to get to Dover was 'unimportant' when viewed in the wider context of her overall plan and the steps she had already taken.

Now, think about these questions.

Look back over the six cases we have studied on the 'more than merely preparatory' test and list the key principles expounded by the Court of Appeal.

Think back to our earlier example involving Vito and Philip.

1. Applying the principles set out by the Court of Appeal, at which of the following six stages does Vito go beyond mere preparation and commit a criminal attempt?
   a. The day before the planned killing, Vito goes out and buys a gun on the black market.
   b. Before leaving his house to go and kill Philip, Vito puts some bullets in his pocket and tucks his gun in his belt.
   c. Vito follows Philip home from the pub.
   d. While Philip (who is in a drunken stupor) fumbles around trying to find his front door key, Vito loads his gun.
   e. Philip finally finds his front door key and puts it in the lock. Vito crooks his finger round the trigger of the gun and takes aim.
   f. Vito fires the gun but misses.
2. How does your answer compare to your earlier answer (at which stage should Vito be liable for attempted murder)?

ii. Which offences can be attempted?

Section 1(4) of the Criminal Attempts Act 1981 states:

> (4) This section applies to any offence which, if it were completed, would be triable in England and Wales as an indictable offence, other than —
>
> (a) conspiracy (at common law or under section 1 of the Criminal Law Act 1977 or any other enactment);
>
> (b) aiding, abetting, counselling, procuring or suborning the commission of an offence;

This means that:

- A defendant can be convicted of attempting any of the crimes we have studied in Chapters 5, 6, 7 and 8 of this text, except for assault and battery (since these are summary offences).
- There is no offence of attempting to conspire. Nor is there an offence of attempting to be an accessory. But a defendant can be convicted of attempting to commit one of the three encouraging or assisting offences we studied earlier in the chapter.

It is also important to note that section 1(1) says 'If, with intent to commit an offence to which this section applies, *a person does an act* [...]'. This means that a defendant cannot be held liable for an attempt in respect of an omission.

Note also that a defendant can be convicted of an attempt even if the attempt was in fact successful and the defendant committed the full offence.[33] So if for some reason Vito is on trial for the attempted murder of Philip even though Philip has died (perhaps because Philip died from his injuries whilst the trial was in progress), it is no defence for Vito to say that he murdered Philip. The policy reasons for this are obvious!

iii. Impossibility

There are two basic types of impossibility: legal impossibility and factual impossibility.

Legal impossibility is where the defendant believes he is attempting a crime, but he is not. Suppose that Vito commits adultery, believing that adultery is a crime. He is not guilty of a criminal attempt. There is no offence of attempted adultery because adultery is not a crime!

Factual impossibility is different. There are two types of factual impossibility:

- **Inadequate means:** this is where the crime could potentially have been committed, but the means used by the defendant were simply incapable of success. Examples would be if Vito decides to kill someone, but mistakenly administers a harmless substance to the victim instead of deadly poison, or if Vito fires his gun at the victim without realising that the victim is just too far away and out of the range of his gun.
- **Physical impossibility:** this is where the situation was such that commission of the crime was simply not possible. Examples would be if Vito decides to steal the contents of a safe, but when he opens the safe discovers that it is empty, or if Vito stabs someone that he thinks is asleep but is in fact already dead.

---

[33] Criminal Attempts Act 1981, s.6(4).

Cases involving factual impossibility are governed by sections 1(2) and 1(3) of the Criminal Attempts Act 1981.

EXTRACT

Section 1 of the Criminal Attempts Act 1981

(2) A person may be guilty of attempting to commit an offence to which this section applies even though the facts are such that the commission of the offence is impossible.

(3) In any case where –

(a) apart from this subsection a person's intention would not be regarded as having amounted to an intent to commit an offence; but

(b) if the facts of the case had been as he believed them to be, his intention would be so regarded,

then, for the purposes of subsection (1) above, he shall be regarded as having had an intent to commit that offence.

These sections mean that factual impossibility is no defence to a charge of attempt. So in our four examples above, Vito would be guilty of three counts of attempted murder and one count of attempted theft.

The leading case on factual impossibility is *R* v *Shivpuri* [1987] AC 1. The defendant, Pyare Shivpuri, was arrested and found to be in possession of a powdered substance. When he was interviewed he said that the substance was either heroin or cannabis. However, when it was analysed the substance was found to be snuff. Shivpuri was charged with attempting to deal with illegal drugs. Drawing on sections 1(2) and 1(3) of the Criminal Attempts Act 1981, the House of Lords said that Shivpuri had to be judged on the basis of the facts as he believed them to be. His conviction was therefore upheld.

Quiz 12.3

1. The *actus reus* of a criminal attempt is committed where...

a. the defendant has carried out all the preparation for the offence and has started to embark upon the crime proper.

b. the defendants have started planning the offence and got some of the tools that they would need in order to commit the offence.

c. the defendant has failed to enter the premises on which it is intended that the full offence be committed.

d. the defendant has just spoken to the victim.

2. Why was Campbell not guilty of attempted robbery?

a. The post office had closed before he got there.

b. His plan had been to kill someone, not to steal anything.

c. He had decided not to commit the robbery before he arrived at the post office.

d. He never entered the post office, so never put himself in a position where he could commit the crime.

3. Impossibility is a defence to a charge of attempt in which one of the following circumstances?

a. The result D intends cannot be achieved because D has used an inadequate means to achieve it, or D is inadequately skilled to make the result occur.

b. D cannot complete the offence he is trying to complete because some aspect of the *actus reus* is absent.

c. The result D intends is not a crime at all, although he believes that it is.

d. The result D intends is physically impossible to accomplish.

The 'more than merely preparatory' test

12.4 Outline the arguments for and against the 'more than merely preparatory' test for the *actus reus* of attempts.

A number of commentators have criticised the outcome in *R* v *Geddes* and *R* v *Campbell*. In his article 'Attempt: The Conduct Requirement', Christopher Clarkson argues that – whilst the outcomes of these cases are 'highly unsatisfactory' – the 'more than merely preparatory' test should be retained, not replaced. What is needed, he says, is a reformulation of the test backed up with a set of illustrative examples.

EXTRACT

- What approach does Clarkson say explains most of the existing decisions on attempts?
- What problems does Clarkson identify with this approach?

Clarkson, C. (2009) 'Attempt: The Conduct Requirement' 29 *Oxford Journal of Legal Studies* 25

The leading decision on what constitutes acts which are 'more than merely preparatory' is *Gullefer* where it was ruled that the defendant had to have 'embarked on the crime proper'. An examination of many of the subsequent decisions suggests that the courts (in most cases) have tended to the view that there can only be an attempt where there has been a 'confrontation' with the victim (in cases of attempted rape, injury/death, kidnapping, false imprisonment, etc.) or with the property (in cases of attempted burglary, criminal damage, etc.). One can hardly have embarked on the crime proper without at least confronting the victim or property. For example, the defendant in *Jones*, intending to kill, had jumped into his victim's car armed with a loaded gun; he had confronted the victim when he got in the car and was liable for attempted murder. Similarly, in the attempted rape cases of *Attorney-General's Reference (No 1 of 1992)*, *Dagnall* and *Patnaik* the defendants were liable; in each of these cases there had been a confrontation with the person the defendant was planning to rape. The same approach has been adopted in a series of attempted burglary cases where the 'crime proper' involves an entry. In *Boyle and Boyle*, the defendants were liable for attempted burglary when they had broken down a door in their effort to gain entry to a building. Similarly, the defendant in *Tosti*, in examining the padlock with a view to gaining entry, had 'confronted' the building and embarked on the process of entry. Again, in *Toothill* the defendant who knocked at the proposed victim's door was liable for attempted burglary.

On the other hand, in cases where there has been no confrontation the defendants have tended to escape liability. In *Geddes*, the defendant trespassed on to school premises and was waiting in a boy's lavatory equipped with a knife, rope and masking tape with a view to capturing and restraining a boy when one entered the lavatory. It was held that he could not be liable for attempted false imprisonment as he had not 'actually tried' to commit the offence. The defendant could not have embarked on the crime of false imprisonment without at least confronting a boy. In *Campbell*, the defendant, wearing a partial disguise and carrying an imitation gun and threatening note, was arrested one yard from the door of a post office which he planned to rob. It was held that he had not progressed sufficiently far to be liable for attempted robbery. Robbery involves theft with force or threatened force. Without confronting the cashier he could not be said to have embarked on the crime proper. The defendant in *Gullefer*, who had disrupted a dog race in an effort to have the race declared void so that his stake would be refunded, had not confronted the bookmaker from whom it was alleged he had attempted to steal and so was not liable.

This approach, while it might explain most of the decisions, is nevertheless highly unsatisfactory in that too many offenders (such as those in *Geddes* and *Campbell*) who are on the point of committing the crime have escaped liability. The strictness of this approach is underlined when one recalls that in these cases the Court of Appeal has ruled that the actions of the defendants *could not* be 'sufficient in law' to amount to an attempt. Even if it had been ruled that these actions could amount to an attempt, there would still be a second hurdle to be overcome in that the jury would then have to consider 'as a question of fact' whether the acts were sufficient for an attempt.

In his discussion, Clarkson contrasts objectivist and subjectivist rationales of the law of attempts. Objectivist rationales suggest that the defendant must come close to committing the crime, so that he displays a degree of moral culpability similar to that involved in the commission of the full offence. On this view, by committing acts closely connected with the full offence, the defendant has crossed a moral threshold and displayed a 'vivid danger' and 'a clear threat of harm'. In contrast, subjectivist rationales support imposing liability at an earlier stage. Subjectivist rationales emphasise the mental element of the defendant. On this view, someone who intends to commit a crime is dangerous and all that should be required for liability is some conduct corroborative of the defendant's intention.

Clarkson argues that 'There are strong reasons why the crime of attempt should continue to be regarded as being of (almost) comparable gravity to the complete offence'. First, he points out that labels such as attempted murder and attempted rape are understood by the public to be very serious offences in which 'The defendant has broadly the same *mens rea* (or greater) than that required for the full offence'. Second, requiring that the defendant comes close to the actual commission of the full offence means that the would-be offender is given every possible opportunity to abandon the criminal enterprise. This treats would-be offenders as responsible agents who are susceptible to rational persuasion. Third, Clarkson states that respect for freedom, civil liberties and privacy requires that the criminal law only be extended if necessary. This assessment of necessity is easier when considering a specific context and a clearly defined harm that is being targeted. It is more difficult to demonstrate that a wider law of attempts is necessary, so drawing the line at an earlier point in time would risk an unwarranted extension of the criminal law.

In the following extract, Clarkson outlines his proposed reformulation of the law of attempts.

EXTRACT

- What is Clarkson's proposed reformulation of the law of attempts? How does it differ from the current law?
- On Clarkson's approach, would Geddes and Campbell have been guilty of an attempt?

Clarkson, C. (2009) 'Attempt: The Conduct Requirement' 29 *Oxford Journal of Legal Studies* 25

Accordingly, it is suggested that the primary rationale of a reformulated offence of attempt should be, as at present, that of punishing a person whose moral culpability can be regarded as broadly comparable to that of the completer. This is similar to Duff's proposal that the conduct required for an attempt should be 'constitutive of the agent's criminality'. Culpability being broadly comparable or constitutive of criminality is not the same as requiring it to be equal to that of the completer.

Such equality would only exist when the defendant has done all she needs to do to commit the crime. To be broadly comparable or constitutive of criminality, the defendant must have crossed a (relevant) threshold and have commenced, *or be about to commence*, on the execution of the crime. What is needed is a test that captures this crossing of a threshold and conduct displaying a 'vivid danger' that the full offence will be committed. The defendant in *Jones*, by entering the car and pointing a loaded gun at the victim had crossed this psychological threshold and displayed sufficient moral culpability and vivid danger to be liable for attempted murder.

Such a reformulated test needs to free itself from the present effective requirement that there must be a confrontation with, or 'attack' on, the victim or object of the crime. From the moment the defendant in *Geddes* trespassed on to school property, armed with his tools for capturing a boy, he had crossed the threshold towards the crime of false imprisonment; his actions displayed a vivid danger and he should be liable for an offence of attempted false imprisonment.

More controversial is whether a test reformulated along such lines should catch the [defendant in *Campbell*]. The key here involves fleshing out what is meant by 'crossing a threshold' and displaying 'vivid danger'. Crossing what threshold and a vivid danger of what? The answer lies in the charge the defendant is facing which will have been framed with reference to the defendant's established or alleged *mens rea*. The defendant's actions can only be understood and interpreted in the light of this *mens rea*. Given his *mens rea* (he was intending to commit robbery), did the defendant in *Campbell* cross a moral threshold towards *robbery* and did his actions display a vivid danger of *robbery* being committed? Views on this might differ but there is a strong argument that the test is satisfied once he, with his disguise, note and imitation firearm, approached the building in which the robbery was planned to take place.

[...]

Of course, a major problem will be how to capture this new degree of proximity. Legislation cannot be framed in terms of vague concepts, such as crossing thresholds or displaying a vivid danger. This is where the use of examples becomes important. What is needed is a general reformulation of the *actus reus* of attempt backed up by a series of examples. It has been suggested that such a test should require the defendant to have 'embarked on the commission of the offence' or be 'in the process of executing his or her plan to commit an intended offence'. However, such tests are capable of being construed too narrowly as requiring a need for confrontation with the victim or object. On a literal view, the defendant in *Geddes* had not embarked on the commission of the offence. Equally, they could be construed too broadly. At what point does one 'embark on the commission of the crime'. Did the defendant in *Jones* not commence on the execution of the crime when he left home in disguise with a loaded gun – or even when he simply bought the gun? This should not be enough for attempted murder. At this stage no relevant threshold had been crossed and no vivid danger displayed.

A possible reformulation could run along the lines of imposing liability for attempt when a person: 'does an act which is more than merely preparatory to, and is closely connected to, the commission of the offence in terms of time, location and acts under the control of the accused remaining to be accomplished'. Such a test is necessarily broad and open to the accusation of vagueness and being capable of generating uncertainty. However, this test has the advantage of stressing that mere preparatory acts will not suffice. The actions of the defendant in *Jones* in buying and shortening his gun and in setting forth armed with his gun are all merely preparatory acts. Further, unlike the present law, it emphasizes that the defendant must have come close to committing the offence but not so close as to have embarked on the crime. In terms of time and location and remaining acts to be done, the actions of the defendant in *Campbell* were closely connected to the full offence. With the aid of examples it would ensure that defendants in the controversial cases discussed above (such as *Geddes)* would be brought within its ambit. It is beyond the scope of this article to suggest a full list of examples. The important point is that, once one has established the rationale of the reformulated offence and its level of seriousness, the flavour of the examples becomes apparent.

Others have also warned of the dangers of an overly broad definition of the *actus reus* of attempts. Simester and Sullivan warn that it would 'carry an undue risk of oppressive policing and unsafe convictions based on dubious confessions'.[34] They point out that Campbell was convicted for possession of an imitation firearm (for which he received a sentence of three years' imprisonment), and that following *R* v *Geddes* Parliament introduced the offence of trespass with intent to commit a sexual offence.[35] 'It is better', they argue, 'to proceed in this piecemeal way than to resort to a broad and vague law of attempt susceptible to uncertainties of interpretation and oppressive modes of enforcement'.[36]

This area of the criminal law was reviewed by the Law Commission in its 2009 report *Conspiracy and Attempts* (Report No 318) HC 41. The following extract sets out the Commission's conclusions.

EXTRACT

What did the Law Commission recommend? What reasons did it give for these recommendations? Do you agree with them?

Law Commission (2009) *Conspiracy and Attempts* (Report No 318) HC 41

8.78 In the light of the mixed response we have received from consultation, and the absence of any consensus amongst our consultees, we have reached the conclusion that it would be inappropriate for us to recommend that the present offence of attempt should be redefined and supported by a list of examples for guidance.

8.79 Section 1(1) of the 1981 Act should therefore be retained without amendment. As explained above, we are mindful of the fact that there have been many cases [such as *R* v *Tosti*] in which the Court of Appeal has accepted that the present offence of attempt should be interpreted broadly, contrary to the narrow approach exemplified by *Geddes*. Bearing in mind the absence of any broad support from our consultees, and given that Parliament may intervene to rectify any future problems by creating new context-specific offences of preparation, we have concluded that the problem with the present law is insufficiently serious to warrant reform in the way we originally proposed.

8.80 It is worth adding, in closing, that the flexibility inherent in the present definition of the offence of attempt means that the courts currently have the power to draw the line separating mere preparation (incurring no liability) from attempt differently depending on the nature of the harm intended.

8.81 Where the line separating attempt from non-criminal preparation is drawn under the current law may depend on how serious, damaging and anti-social the intended offence is. In other words, it may be that the line will be drawn further back from the commission of the intended offence in proportion to the seriousness and/or anti-social nature of that offence. We accept that, if this is the approach which the courts adopt, consciously or otherwise, there is no compelling need for guiding examples. The inherent flexibility of the present inchoate offence, whatever label it bears, means that, by and large, the right decision will be reached for the type of offence intended.

8.82 On this view, cases such as *Geddes* should be seen as aberrations or deviations from the proper approach, and dealt with, as we suggest, by the creation of new context-specific offences where necessary.

[34] Simester, A.P., Spencer, J.R., Stark, F., Sullivan, G.R. and Virgo, G.J. (2016) *Simester and Sullivan's Criminal Law: Theory and Doctrine* (6th edn). Hart Publishing: Oxford, p.360.

[35] Sexual Offences Act 2003, s.63.

[36] Simester, A.P., Spencer, J.R., Stark, F., Sullivan, G.R. and Virgo, G.J. (2016) *Simester and Sullivan's Criminal Law: Theory and Doctrine* (6th edn). Hart Publishing: Oxford, p.360.

Quiz 12.4

1. Clarkson states that the law of attempts must balance two competing sets of principles and policy concerns. What are these?

a. Only convicting of an attempt those that are as culpable as those who commit the full offence versus only convicting those who have displayed a clear threat of harm.

b. The objectivist view that D's actions must have displayed a vivid danger versus the subjectivist view that all that should be required is some conduct corroborative of an intention to commit the full offence.

c. The subjectivist view that D's actions must have displayed a vivid danger versus the objectivist view that all that should be required is some conduct corroborative of an intention to commit the full offence.

d. Imposing liability on anyone that engages in conduct in furtherance of a criminal intention versus giving the police the powers to intervene at the earliest possible point in time.

2. Which of the following is **not** an argument advanced by Clarkson?

a. The law should not effectively require that there was a confrontation with the victim or object of the crime.

b. The rationale of the law of attempts should be to punish a person whose moral culpability is comparable to that of the person who commits the full offence.

c. All that should be required for liability for an attempt is some conduct that is corroborative of an intention to commit the full offence.

d. Offenders on the point of committing the crime have escaped liability.

3. Which of the following was **not** a reason given by the Law Commission for its decision to recommend that the current law on attempts should not be redefined?

a. The statutory definition of attempts is sufficiently flexible for the courts to reinterpret how the line between mere preparation and an attempt is drawn.

b. There was no broad consensus amongst consultees.

c. A widely drawn law of attempts ensures that no culpable defendants escape liability.

d. Parliament may intervene to create context-specific offences if and when necessary.

Mens rea requirements for establishing criminal liability for criminal attempts

12.5 Define the *mens rea* requirements for establishing criminal liability for criminal attempts.

2. The defendant intended to commit the full offence

In many cases of attempted crime all that distinguishes the defendant's criminal actions from wholly innocent ones is his guilty intention. Suppose that Dave kicks a football and it hits his neighbour's greenhouse. The ball bounces off the glass panes without breaking them. Did Dave attempt to cause criminal damage? Or did he have a lucky escape from an unfortunate accident? It all depends on whether or not Dave intended to smash the glass. As Lord Goddard CJ stated in *R v Whybrow* (1951) 35 Cr App R 141, in an attempt 'the intent becomes the principal ingredient of the crime'.

The central importance of intention is reflected in the Criminal Attempts Act 1981. Section 1(1) states that in order to be guilty of an attempt the defendant must have intended to commit the full offence. So, according to the statute, nothing less than an intention to commit the full offence will suffice. This means that sometimes the *mens rea* of the full offence is different to the *mens rea* of an attempt.

EXAMPLE

- In Chapter 5, we saw that the *mens rea* of murder is an intention to kill or cause GBH. By contrast, the *mens rea* of attempted murder is an intention to kill. For attempted murder an intention to cause GBH will not suffice.
- In Chapter 8, we saw that the *mens rea* of criminal damage is an intention to damage the property or recklessness whether the property is damaged. By contrast, the *mens rea* of attempted criminal damage is an intention to damage the property. Recklessness will not suffice.

Intention here means either direct intention or oblique intention.[37] We studied these two types of intention in Chapter 4.

Think about these questions.

In Chapter 6, we studied the crime of malicious infliction of GBH (section 20 of the Offences Against the Person Act 1861).

- What is the *mens rea* of attempted infliction of GBH?
- How is this different to the full offence?

So the general rule is that only intention suffices for the *mens rea* of an attempt. However, for some of the crimes we have studied in this text things are not quite this straightforward! For some crimes the courts have been willing to accept something less than intention in relation to circumstance and consequence elements of the full offence.

The first example is the Court of Appeal's decision in *R* v *Khan* [1990] 1 WLR 813 on attempted rape. The victim in this case met one of the defendants at a disco. Afterwards she accompanied him to a nearby house. At the house three men had non-consensual sexual intercourse with her. They were subsequently convicted of rape. The four defendants also tried to have sexual intercourse with her but failed. They were convicted at trial of attempted rape. They appealed to the Court of Appeal. The case focused on the *mens rea* of attempted rape.

EXTRACT

Read the following extract from the judgment of Russell LJ.

How (if at all) is the mens rea for attempted rape different to the mens rea for rape? What reasons did Russell LJ give for this conclusion?

R v *Khan* [1990] 1 WLR 813

Russell LJ

The only difference between the two offences is that in rape sexual intercourse takes place whereas in attempted rape it does not, although there has to be some act which is more than preparatory to sexual intercourse. Considered in that way, the intent of the defendant is precisely the same in rape and in attempted rape and the *mens rea* is identical

[37] *R* v *Mohan* [1976] QB 1. See also *R* v *Pearman* (1984) 80 Cr App R 259 and *R* v *Walker and Hayles* (1989) 90 Cr App R 226.

[...]

If this is the true analysis, as we believe it is, the attempt does not require any different intention on the part of the accused from that for the full offence of rape. We believe this to be a desirable result which in the instant case did not require the jury to be burdened with different directions as to the accused's state of mind, dependent upon whether the individual achieved or failed to achieve sexual intercourse.

This judgment was delivered several years before the introduction of the Sexual Offences Act 2003. The combined effect of *R* v *Khan* and the 2003 Act is that a defendant has the *mens rea* of attempted rape if he intended to penetrate the victim's vagina, anus or mouth with his penis and lacked a reasonable belief in consent. In other words, it is identical to the *mens rea* of rape (which we studied in Chapter 7).

The second example is the Court of Appeal's judgment in *A-G's Reference (No 3 of 1992)* [1994] 1 WLR 409. This case focused on attempted aggravated criminal damage. Four people were sitting in a parked car talking to two others who were standing on the pavement, when the four defendants drove past and threw a petrol bomb at them. The petrol bomb missed the parked car and hit a neighbouring wall. No one was injured and no property was damaged. The defendants were charged with attempted aggravated criminal damage.

In Chapter 8, we saw that the crime of aggravated criminal damage has two *mens rea* requirements. One relates to property damage (intention to damage property or recklessness whether property is damaged). The other relates to endangering life (intention to endanger life or recklessness whether life is endangered). At the defendants' trial the trial judge stated that for attempted aggravated criminal damage only intention will suffice in respect of both of these. Since the prosecution had produced no evidence that the defendants had an intention to endanger life she directed that the charges be dismissed.

The Attorney-General subsequently referred the issue to the Court of Appeal for clarification.

EXTRACT

Read the following extract from the judgment of Schiemann J.

What mens rea does he say must be shown in relation to: (a) property damage; and (b) endangering life?

Was the trial judge right to dismiss the charges against the defendants?

A-G's Reference (No 3 of 1992) [1994] 1 WLR 409

Schiemann J

[...] In the present case, what was missing to prevent a conviction for the completed offence was damage to the property [...] Such damage is essential for the completed offence. If a defendant does not intend to cause such damage he cannot intend to commit the completed offence. At worst he is reckless as to whether the offence is committed. The law of attempt is concerned with those who are intending to commit crimes. If that intent cannot be shown, then there can be no conviction.

However, the crime here consisted of doing certain acts in a certain state of mind in circumstances where the first named property and the second named property were the same, in short where the

> danger to life arose from the damage to the property which the defendant intended to damage. The substantive crime is committed if the defendant damaged property in a state of mind where he was reckless as to whether the life of another would thereby be endangered. We see no reason why there should not be a conviction for attempt if the prosecution can show that he, in that state of mind, intended to damage the property by throwing a bomb at it. One analysis of this situation is to say that although the defendant was in an appropriate state of mind to render him guilty of the completed offence the prosecution had not proved the physical element of the completed offence, and therefore he is not guilty of the completed offence. If, on a charge of attempting to commit the offence, the prosecution can show not only the state of mind required for the completed offence but also that the defendant intended to supply the missing physical element of the completed offence, that suffices for a conviction. That cannot be done merely by the prosecution showing him to be reckless. The defendant must intend to damage property, but there is no need for a graver mental state than is required for the full offence.
>
> The trial judge in the present case, however, went further than this, and held that not merely must the defendant intend to supply all that was missing from the completed offence – namely, damage to the first named property – but also that recklessness as to the consequences of such damage for the lives of others was not enough to secure a conviction for attempt, although it was sufficient for the completed offence. She held that before a defendant could be convicted of attempting to commit the offence it had to be shown that he intended that the lives of others should be endangered by the damage which he intended.
>
> She gave no policy reasons for so holding, and there is no case which bound her so to hold. The most nearly relevant case is *Reg.* v. *Khan (Mohammed Iqbal)* [1990] 1 W.L.R. 813. [...]
>
> What was missing in *Reg.* v. *Khan (Mohammed Iqbal)* was the act of sexual intercourse, without which the offence was not complete. What was missing in the present case was damage to the first named property, without which the offence was not complete. The mental state of the defendant in each case contained everything which was required to render him guilty of the full offence. In order to succeed in a prosecution for attempt, it must be shown that the defendant intended to achieve that which was missing from the full offence. Unless that is shown, the prosecution have not proved that the defendant intended to commit the offence. Thus in *Reg.* v. *Khan (Mohammed Iqbal)* [1990] 1 W.L.R. 813 the prosecution had to show an intention to have sexual intercourse, and the remaining state of mind required for the offence of rape. In the present case, the prosecution had to show an intention to damage the first named property, and the remaining state of mind required for the offence of aggravated arson.

Schiemann J's reasoning has been labelled the 'missing element' test. It draws a distinction between those elements of the full offence which were missing and those which were present. The defendant must have intended to supply the missing elements of the full offence. But for those elements which were present the *mens rea* of an attempt is the same as for the full offence. So, applying this to the case:

- **Endangering life:** Intention or recklessness suffices for the full offence. Since this part of the offence was present, intention or recklessness was also sufficient for an attempt.
- **Property damage:** This part of the offence was missing, so an intention to damage property was required.

In *R* v *Pace & Rogers* [2014] EWCA Crim 186 the Court of Appeal cast some doubt on the reasoning employed in *R* v *Khan* and *A-G's Reference (No 3 of 1992)*. Davis LJ stated:

> 62 Turning, then, to [section 1(1) of the Criminal Attempts Act 1981] we consider that, as a matter of ordinary language and in accordance with principle, an "intent

to commit an offence" connotes an intent to commit all the elements of the offence. We can see no sufficient basis, whether linguistic or purposive, for construing it otherwise.

Importantly, Davis LJ emphasised that *R* v *Pace & Rogers* concerned an impossible attempt.[38] The defendants worked at a scrap metal yard. Undercover police officers offered to sell them scrap metal, telling them that it was stolen. The defendants accepted the metal and paid for it. They were charged with attempted conversion of criminal property. At trial the judge ruled that it was sufficient that the defendants had a suspicion that the metal was stolen, since suspicion is sufficient for the full offence. Of course, the scrap metal was not stolen since it was owned by the police. Moreover, the fact that the police owned the metal meant that commission of the full offence was impossible. The Court of Appeal allowed the defendants' appeals against conviction, ruling that suspicion that the metal was stolen was insufficient for a criminal attempt. Only an intention or knowledge that the metal was stolen would suffice.

So we now have competing approaches to the *mens rea* of criminal attempts. On the one hand we have *R* v *Pace & Rogers*, which insists that only intention or knowledge will suffice for all elements of the offence, whilst on the other hand we have *R* v *Khan* and *A-G's Reference (No 3 of 1992)*, both of which are prepared to accept something less than intention in relation to circumstance and consequence elements of the full offence.[39] One way of reconciling the cases is to say that *R* v *Khan* and *A-G's Reference (No 3 of 1992)* apply to possible attempts, whereas *R* v *Pace & Rogers* applies to impossible attempts.[40]

Quiz 12.5

1. What is the *mens rea* of a criminal attempt?
   a. An intention to commit the full offence of objective recklessness as to whether it will be committed.
   b. An intention to commit the full offence or subjective recklessness as to whether it will be committed.
   c. Intention to commit the full offence.
   d. An intention to commit the full offence, or recklessness or negligence as to whether it will be committed.

2. Which of the following statements about the 'missing element' test from *A-G's Reference (No 3 of 1992)* is incorrect?
   a. The judgment in *R* v *Pace & Rogers* cast doubt upon the 'missing element' test, since the Court held that only an intention or knowledge that the metal was stolen would suffice.
   b. For those elements of the full offence that were missing the *mens rea* of an attempt is the same as for the full offence, but for those elements that were present D must have caused them intentionally.
   c. D must have intended to supply the missing elements of the full offence, but for those elements that were present the *mens rea* of an attempt is the same as for the full offence.
   d. One way of reconciling *R* v *Pace & Rogers* with *A-G's Ref (No 3 of 1992)* is to say that the 'missing element' test applies to possible attempts but not to impossible ones.

3. How might the judgment in *R* v *Pace & Rogers* [2014] EWCA Crim 186 be reconciled with *Attorney-General's Reference (No 3 of 1992)* [1994] 1 WLR 409?
   a. The 'missing element' test does not apply to impossible attempts.
   b. The 'missing element' test does not apply to offences with a mandatory sentence.
   c. The 'missing element' test does not apply to property offences.
   d. The 'missing element' test has been overruled.

[38] At [54].

[39] For an argument in favour of the approach in *R* v *Pace & Rogers*, see Yang, D. (2023) 'Recklessness and Circumstances in Criminal Attempts' 17 Criminal Law and Philosophy 359.

[40] A distinction which has been criticised as incoherent: Child, J.J. and Hunt, A. (2014) '*Pace and Rogers* and the *Mens Rea* of Criminal Attempt: *Khan* on the Scrapheap?' 78 *Journal of Criminal Law* 220.

Conclusion

In this chapter we have studied three types of inchoate offence: encouraging or assisting crime; conspiracy; and attempts. To conclude, here are three pieces of advice for answering exam problem questions:

- When you state which offence the defendant would be charged with, be sure to include details of the full offence. It is not enough to write 'D would be charged with conspiracy' or 'D would be charged with a criminal attempt'. You need to state which offence the defendant encouraged, assisted, attempted or conspired to commit. So write, 'D would be charged with conspiracy to rob' or 'D would be charged with attempted rape'.
- Sometimes it might be possible to charge a defendant with more than one of the offences we have studied in this chapter. Some students find this confusing, and when answering problem questions are unsure which offence they should focus on. As a rule of thumb, it is preferable to charge the defendant with a criminal attempt since this conveys greater proximity to commission of the full offence. If the defendant did not go beyond mere preparation: you should charge conspiracy if the defendants agreed to commit the unlawful plan as a joint collaborative project, and encouraging or assisting crime if they did not.
- There is another potential source of confusion. There is a large overlap between: (a) the encouraging or assisting crimes and conspiracy; and (b) the law governing accessories (which we study in the next chapter). As a result students are sometimes unsure which of these offences to discuss. As a rule of thumb, if the principal never went beyond mere preparation you should charge the defendant with an inchoate offence. But if the principal committed the full offence, you should charge the defendant with being an accessory. This gives due recognition to the fact that the full offence did occur.

Applying the law

12.6 Apply the law on inchoate offences to hypothetical sets of facts.

Vito and Michael

The following scenario involves the characters Vito and Michael. Read the problem scenario carefully, then answer the multiple-choice questions below to apply your learning to the scenario.

Vito has just found out that Philip is having an affair with his wife. Furious, he says to Michael, 'I want revenge'.

Think about these questions.

1. Discuss the criminal liability of Vito and Michael in the following situations:

   a. Vito says to Michael, 'I'm going to beat Philip up'. Wanting to protect Philip, Michael replies, 'Don't do that'. He then hands Vito a brick and says, 'Smash the windows on his Ferrari instead'. Vito takes the brick and sets off to Philip's house. By the time he arrives there he has calmed down and decides not to retaliate.

b. Vito says to Michael, 'Will you drive me to Philip's house? I want to break his nose'. At first Michael replies, 'Leave me out of it. It's nothing to do with me'. But when Vito says, 'I'll give you £1,000 to drive me to Philip's', Michael changes his mind. He drives Vito to Philip's house and drops him off outside. Unbeknown to Vito and Michael, however, Philip is away on a business trip and does not return home that evening.

c. Michael and Vito agree to kill Philip. Unbeknown to them, Philip was killed in a road accident earlier that day. Would your answer be any different if Michael and Vito agreed to pay Trevor to kill Philip (but when they ask, Trevor refuses)?

d. Vito, armed with a gun, says to Michael, 'Will you drive me to Philip's house? I'm going to kill him'. Michael agrees to take Vito to Philip's house. On the way there they are stopped by the police, who confiscate Vito's gun and arrest him. Michael tells the police that, after dropping Vito off, he planned to telephone Philip to warn him not to go home and then telephone the police.

e. Vito and Michael agree to go and beat Philip up. They set off to his house. When they arrive, Vito looks through the living room window and sees Philip sitting watching TV. As he tries to open the window, which he discovers is locked, he is apprehended by a passing policeman.

f. Vito and Michael agree to try and frighten Philip in order to 'warn him off'. So they make a petrol bomb, drive to Philip's house and lie in wait. When Philip arrives home from work in his car Vito throws the petrol bomb into the road close to Philip's car. No one is harmed and no property is damaged.

2. In your opinion, does Vito satisfy these two *mens rea* requirements? (Remember to consider both direct and oblique intention.)

Having identified the relevant offence, we can now work through the *mens rea* requirements of the section 45 offence. There are three *mens rea* requirements in total:

- First, Michael must have had *mens rea* in relation to the behaviour part of the full offence. This involves two questions: (1) Did Michael believe that Vito would damage Philip's Ferrari? and (2) Did Michael believe that his actions would encourage or assist Vito?
- Second, Michael must have had *mens rea* in relation to the consequence and circumstance parts of the full offence. The *actus reus* of criminal damage contains a circumstance element: that the property belonged to another person. So, according to section 47(5)(b), the question that must be asked here is: Did Michael believe that the property belonged to another person or, if not, was he reckless as to whether the property belonged to another person?
- Third, Michael must have had *mens rea* in relation to the *mens rea* part of the full offence. So, according to section 47(5)(a), the prosecution must show that either (1) Michael believed that Vito would smash the windows on Philip's Ferrari either intentionally or recklessly; (2) Michael was reckless as to whether Vito would smash the windows either intentionally or recklessly; or, (3) that if Michael had smashed the windows himself, he would have done so either intentionally or recklessly. As long as at least one of these three applies, this part of the *mens rea* is established.

In your opinion, would Michael satisfy all three of these *mens rea* requirements?

Suppose that you are Michael's defence counsel. How would you argue that his actions were objectively reasonable? Suppose that you are the prosecutor. How would you argue that Michael's actions were not reasonable? In your opinion, which side of the argument is the strongest? Liability is likely to hinge on this issue.

So the House of Lords in *R* v *Anderson* held that the only mens rea requirement for conspiracy is that D intended to play some part in the agreed course of conduct. Michael would seem to satisfy this: he intended to play a part by driving Vito to Philip's house. But case law since *R* v *Anderson* has reversed this decision. It now seems clear that it must be shown that D intended that the agreement would be carried out (see, e.g., *R* v *McPhillips* and *R* v *Goddard & another*), and it does not have to be shown that D intended to play a part in the agreed course of conduct (see, e.g., *R* v *Siracusa & others*). If we apply this first to Vito, it is clear that Vito intended for the agreement to be carried out. It was his direct intention; if the agreement had not been carried out, he would have regarded this as a failure. But section 1(2) of the Criminal Law Act 1977 states that a defendant can only be convicted of conspiracy if at least one of the other parties to the agreement also had the mens rea of conspiracy. So the key question is whether Michael had the necessary mens rea. This will determine not only whether Michael is guilty of conspiring to cause GBH with intent, but also whether Vito is guilty.

In your opinion, did Michael have an intention that the agreement would be carried out? (Hint: remember to consider both direct intention and oblique intention).

Applying this to Michael, it seems that he did not believe that Vito would cause Philip's death. He had not mentally accepted that Vito would cause Philip's death as true. Indeed, he aimed to prevent this from happening. But it is possible to argue that Michael was reckless as to whether Vito would cause Philip's death. If you were the prosecutor in Michael's case, how would you argue this?

If Michael satisfies this *mens rea* requirement, the remaining *mens rea* requirement would be that he had *mens rea* in relation to the *mens rea* requirement of the full offence (murder). This would be straightforwardly established: Michael believed that, if Vito were to cause Philip's death, Vito would do so with the *mens rea* of murder (section 47(5)(a)(i)). Finally, there is no realistic possibility of Michael arguing that his actions were objectively reasonable. So, in conclusion, Michael's liability for assisting murder believing murder would be committed (section 45 of the Serious Crime Act 2007) will hinge on whether he was reckless as to whether Vito would cause Philip's death.

As for Vito, although he would not be guilty of conspiracy or a criminal attempt, in practice he would be guilty of other offences that are not on our syllabus, such as possession of a firearm.

Some doubt has been cast on the 'missing element' test by *R* v *Pace & Rogers*. One way of reconciling the cases is to say that *R* v *Pace & Rogers* applies only to impossible attempts whereas *A-G's Reference (No 3 of 1922)* applies to possible attempts. Since Vito could potentially have committed the offence of aggravated criminal damage (e.g. if Philip's car had been damaged by the petrol bomb), his was a possible attempt and so the 'missing element' test will apply. Applying this test to Vito's case, the endangering life part of the offence was present. Therefore the *mens rea* for this part of the attempt is the same as for the full offence, i.e. either an intention to endanger life or recklessness whether life would be endangered. However, the damage to property part of the offence was not present (no property was damaged). Since this part of the offence was missing, only an intention to damage property will suffice.

Quiz 12.6

1. Vito calms down before he arrives at Philip's house, and so does not commit the full offence of criminal damage. If we turn instead to inchoate offences, Vito does not commit the offence of attempted criminal damage, since he does not embark upon the full offence - he never gets so far as to put himself in a position where he can commit criminal damage (*R* v *Campbell*). Nor is he guilty of conspiracy to commit criminal damage. Conspiracy requires an agreement. To establish an agreement, it is not enough to show the one defendant encouraged another to commit a crime. It must be shown that the defendants decided to commit the unlawful plan as a joint collaborative project (*R* v *Mehta*). In our case, Michael encouraged Vito to smash Philip's car windows, but Vito and Michael did not agree to commit criminal damage as a joint collaborative project.

   Therefore, our focus in part (a) is the liability of Michael. The relevant offences are the ones found in sections 44–46 of the Serious Crime Act 2007. As we work through the requirements for these offences, we will identify whether the section 44, 45 or 46 offence is the most relevant.

   The *actus reus* is identical for the section 44, 45 and 46 offences. It is that the defendant did an act that was capable of encouraging or assisting the commission of an offence.

   Which of the following statements summarises section 49(1) of the Serious Crime Act 2007 correctly?

   a. There cannot be the *actus reus* if no-one was aware of the act of encouragement/assistance.

   b. There can be the *actus reus* even if the encouragement/assistance did not lead to the full offence being committed.

   c. There can be the *actus reus* even if the defendant encouraged/assisted the commission of an offence that exists for his or her protection.

   d. There cannot be the *actus reus* unless the defendant's act led to someone being encouraged or assisted in fact.

2. It is the first *mens rea* requirement that allows us to distinguish between the section 44, 45 and 46 offences. Section 47 explains that the first step here is to identify the behavioural element of the *actus reus* of the relevant full offence. In Michael's case, the behavioural element of criminal damage is damaging property. For the section 44 offence to apply, Michael's purpose must have been to encourage or assist Vito to smash the windows on Philip's Ferrari (sections 44(2) and 47(7)(b)).

   This seems unlikely. Michael's purpose was to protect Philip. Applying Duff's success/failure test, Michael would not have regarded it as a failure if Vito had not smashed the windows of Philip's Ferrari.

   We must therefore consider the section 45 and 46 offences instead.

   What is the difference between the section 45 and section 46 offences?

   a. The section 45 offence applies where D believes an offence against the person will be committed. The section 46 offence applies where D believes a property offence will be committed.

   b. The section 45 offence applies where D believes a specific full offence will be committed. The section 46 offence applies where D suspects a specific full offence will be committed.

   c. The section 45 offence applies where D believes a specific full offence will be committed. The section 46 offence applies where D believes that one of several full offences will be committed but is unsure which one.

   d. he section 45 offence applies where the offence that was encouraged or assisted was actually carried out. The section 46 offence applies where the offence that was encouraged or assisted was not carried out.

3. The final part of the section 45 offence is that it was not reasonable for Michael to act as he did.

   Which of the following statements about the reasonableness defence is incorrect?

   a. The burden of proof for the reasonableness defence rests on the defendant.

   b. The reasonableness defence applies to the section 44, 45 and 46 offences.

   c. The test is whether the defendant thought he was acting reasonably.

   d. If the defendant made a mistake, he must prove that the mistaken belief was both a genuine one and that it was a reasonable mistake to have made.

4. Turning to scenario (b), one possibility here is to discuss whether Michael is guilty of one of the sections 44, 45 or 46 offences again. The reasoning would be similar to the previous scenario. The *actus reus* of the offences would be established, since Michael provided assistance by driving Vito to Philip's house. It does not matter that the full offence was not carried out (section 49(1)). Turning to the *mens rea*, Michael's purpose was to earn £1,000, not to assist Vito in breaking Philip's

nose, so the section 45 offence would apply instead of the section 44 offence. Since there is no possibility of Michael proving that his actions were objectively reasonable, liability will hinge on whether the three *mens rea* requirements are satisfied or not.

Another possibility to consider in this scenario is whether Vito and Michael are guilty of conspiracy to cause GBH with intent (section 1 of the Criminal Law Act 1977; section 18 of the Offences Against the Person Act 1861). One potential advantage of this (from a prosecutor's perspective) would be that both Vito and Michael would face criminal liability.

Which of the following statements about the *actus reus* of conspiracy is incorrect?

a. To establish an agreement, it must be shown that the defendants decided to commit the unlawful plan as a joint collaborative project.

b. The *actus reus* can be established even if the planned full offence is, unbeknown to the defendants, factually impossible.

c. The *actus reus* will not be established in cases where the defendants' agreement to commit the full offence is conditional.

d. For the *actus reus* to be established, it must be shown that the planned offence was going to be committed by one of the parties to the agreement.

5. Michael might try to argue that he and Vito did not form an agreement to commit the unlawful plan as a joint collaborative project. Michael only planned to drop Vito off outside Philip's house, and had little interest in whether Vito broke Philip's nose or not. The difficulty with this, however, is that Michael did not merely encourage Vito to go and commit the offence by himself. Michael provided actual assistance. The two men drove to Philip's house together. This is indicative of a joint project.

If there is an agreement in the sense of a joint collaborative project, it is clear that the plan was for one of the parties to the agreement (Vito) to commit the planned offence (GBH with intent). It does not matter that the planned offence was in fact impossible because Philip was away on a business trip. Section 1(1)(b) of the Criminal Law Act 1977 makes it clear that factual impossibility is no defence to a charge of conspiracy. So, we turn next to the *mens rea* of conspiracy.

Which of the following statements summarises the House of Lords' judgment in *R v Anderson* correctly?

a. It does not have to be shown that D intended that the agreement would be carried out, but it is necessary to show that D intended to play some part in the agreed course of conduct.

b. It must be shown that D intended that the agreement would be carried out and that D intended to play some part in the agreed course of conduct.

c. It must be shown that D intended that the agreement would be carried out, but it is not necessary to show that D intended to play some part in the agreed course of conduct.

d. It does not have to be shown that D intended that the agreement would be carried out nor does it have to be shown that D intended to play some part in the agreed course of conduct.

6. Turning next to scenario (c) the relevant offence in this scenario is conspiracy to murder. Two of the three requirements for the offence of conspiracy are straightforwardly established: there was an agreement between Michael and Vito; and both men intended that the agreement would be carried out. The key issues therefore concern the second *actus reus* requirement: that Michael and Vito agreed on a course of conduct that necessarily involved at least one of them committing a crime.

Which of the following statements is correct?

a. It does not have to be shown that one of the conspirators was going to commit the planned offence, but it must be shown that the planned offence was in fact possible.

b. It must be shown that one of the conspirators was going to commit the planned offence, but it does not have to be shown that the planned offence was in fact possible.

c. It does not have to be shown that one of the conspirators was going to commit the planned offence nor does it have to be shown that the planned offence was in fact possible.

d. It must be shown that one of the conspirators was going to commit the planned offence and it must be shown that the planned offence was in fact possible.

7. Next is scenario (d). As in the previous scenarios, Vito and Michael could not be charged with a criminal attempt here because they did not embark upon the full offence – they never got so far as to put themselves in a position where they could commit the full offence (murder) (*R v Campbell*). So our starting point is to consider whether Vito and Michael are guilty of conspiracy to murder. The *actus reus* of conspiracy is satisfied: the men reached an agreement (in the sense of deciding to commit the murder of Philip as a joint collaborative project); and they agreed a course of conduct that necessarily involved one of them (Vito) committing the murder. The key question, therefore, is whether the *mens rea* of conspiracy is satisfied.

In *R* v *McPhillips* why did the Court of Appeal of Northern Ireland hold that McPhillips could not be convicted of conspiracy to murder?

a. McPhillips knew that the bomb was incapable of exploding, and so lacked any intention that the crime of murder would be carried out.

b. McPhillips intended to give a telephone warning to police, and so lacked any intention that the crime of murder would be carried out.

c. McPhillips knew that the bomb was incapable of exploding, and so the planned offence was factually impossible.

d. McPhillips intended to give a telephone warning to police, and so could plead the defence of prevention of crime.

8. It would seem that Michael did not intend for Vito to murder Philip. He planned to telephone Philip and warn him, and to then telephone the police. So, applying *R* v *McPhillips*, Michael would not be guilty of conspiracy to murder. And, since a person can only be convicted of conspiracy if at least one of the other parties to the agreement also had the *mens rea* of conspiracy (section 1(2) of the Criminal Law Act 1977), if Michael lacked the *mens rea* it follows that Vito would not be guilty of conspiracy to murder either.

An alternative possibility in Michael's case would be the offences in sections 44, 45 and 46 of the Serious Crime Act 2007. Michael provided assistance by driving Vito to Philip's house, so the *actus reus* of these offences is satisfied. Turning to the *mens rea*, the section 44 offence would not apply since killing Philip was not Michael's purpose (in fact, Michael planned to try and save Philip). Of the section 45 and 46 offences the relevant one would be the section 45 offence, since Michael anticipated a specific full offence (murder). In terms of the section 45 offence, the key issue would be whether Michael had *mens rea* in relation to the consequence element of the full offence (i.e. Philip's death). According to section 47(5)(b), it must be proved that Michael either believed that Vito would cause Philip's death, or that he was reckless as to whether Vito would do so.

Which of the following statements defines 'belief' and 'recklessness' correctly?

a. 'Belief' is thinking that something might be true. 'Recklessness' is foreseeing a risk and unjustifiably choosing to take it.

b. 'Belief' is the mental acceptance of a fact as true or existing. 'Recklessness' is failing to give any thought to a risk that would have been obvious to the reasonable man.

c. 'Belief' is the mental acceptance of a fact as true or existing. 'Recklessness' is foreseeing a risk and unjustifiably choosing to take it.

d. 'Belief' is thinking that something might be true. 'Recklessness' is failing to give any thought to a risk that would have been obvious to the reasonable man.

9. Next, scenario (e). On these facts Vito and Michael are guilty of conspiracy to cause GBH with intent (section 1 of the Criminal Law Act 1977; section 18 of the Offences Against the Person Act 1861). They form an agreement, according to which they will both commit the offence of GBH with intent, and they both intend that the agreement will be carried out. But we need to consider whether their plan progressed far enough for them to also be guilty of a criminal attempt.

It is important to begin by considering which offence they might be charged with having attempted.

Which of the following is a way of reconciling the decisions in *R* v *Campbell* and *R* v *Tosti & White?*

a. Campbell was charged with attempted robbery. He had not yet decided which items he wished to steal, so had not yet embarked on the offence. Tosti and White, by contrast, were charged with attempted burglary. They had identified the items they wished to steal and so had embarked on the offence.

b. Campbell was charged with attempted robbery. He had not yet acquired the equipment he needed to commit the robbery, and so had not yet embarked on the offence. Tosti and White, by contrast, were charged with attempted burglary. They had acquired the equipment they needed to commit the burglary, and so had embarked on the offence.

c. Campbell was charged with attempted robbery. Unbeknown to him, the robbery he had hoped to commit was in fact impossible, so he was not guilty of a criminal attempt. Tosti and White, by contrast, were charged with attempted burglary. The burglary they had planned to commit was factually possible, so they were guilty of a criminal attempt.

d. Campbell was charged with attempted robbery. He had not embarked on this offence because he was never in a position where he could carry it out. Tosti and White, by contrast, were charged with attempted burglary. They had embarked on gaining entry to the barn and so had begun to carry out the burglary.

10. Having identified the appropriate charge in Vito's case – attempted burglary – we must now consider whether the *actus reus* and *mens rea* of an attempt are satisfied. As we have already seen, Vito's actions were more than merely preparatory (section 1(1) of the Criminal Attempts Act 1981). By trying to open the window Vito had embarked on the offence of burglary. And he did so with an intention to commit burglary. Therefore, both *actus reus* and *mens rea* are satisfied.

Having discussed Vito, we must now consider Michael's liability. Michael provided encouragement to Vito by agreeing to go and beat Philip up with him. But it was Vito, not Michael, who tried to open Philip's window. So Michael does not satisfy the *actus reus* of a criminal attempt since he did not personally do an act that was more than merely preparatory.

We must therefore consider other possible offences.

Which of the following offences did Michael commit?

a. Attempting to be an accessory to burglary
b. Being an accessory to attempted burglary
c. Being an accessory to attempted GBH with intent
d. Attempting to conspire to cause GBH with intent

11. Finally, scenario (f). We will focus on Vito first, as he was the one who threw the petrol bomb. If Philip was caused to apprehend the infliction of immediate unlawful force, then Vito would be guilty of assault. If Philip did not apprehend the infliction of immediate, unlawful force then Vito would be guilty of attempted assault. Michael was an accessory to the assault (or attempted assault).

However, assault is a relatively minor offence. We should therefore consider whether Vito may also have committed a more serious crime. In particular, given the factual similarity to *A-G's Reference (No 3 of 1992)*, we should consider whether Vito is guilty of attempted aggravated criminal damage.

Which of the following did the Court of Appeal apply in *A-G's Reference (No 3 of 1992)*?

a. The 'last act' test: D may only be convicted of an attempt if he performed the last act necessary for commission of the full offence.
b. The 'impossibility' test: D may only be convicted of an attempt if the full offence was factually possible.
c. The 'missing element' test: D must have intended to supply those elements of the full offence that were missing.
d. The 'success or failure' test: D may only be convicted if he would have regarded his attempt as a failure.

Evaluating the law

12.7 Evaluate the 'more than merely preparatory' test for the *actus reus* of attempts, including the courts' application of this test.

Think about this question.

'The case law on the "more than merely preparatory" test contained in section 1(1) of the Criminal Attempts Act 1981 is confused and inconsistent. Moreover, the statutory test is too limited in its scope. This results in defendants who should be convicted of a criminal attempt escaping liability.'

Discuss the extent to which you agree with this statement.

Step 1: Deconstruct the essay title

The question asks you to discuss the 'more than merely preparatory' test for the *actus reus* of criminal attempts. The statement contains two key assertions: first, that the case law on this test is 'confused and inconsistent'; and, second, that the test is too narrow in its scope. To discuss the statement, you will therefore need to consider each of these two assertions in turn.

Step 2: Work through each assertion, form an opinion and construct a set of arguments in support of your views

To help you consider the first of these two assertions, look back at your notes on *R* v *Campbell* and *R* v *Tosti & White*. On the face of it, these cases involved similar facts, yet the outcomes were different. In your opinion, is there a satisfactory way of reconciling the two cases? Are there other cases that could also be cited as examples of inconsistency?

On Clarkson's article 'Attempt: The Conduct Requirement', consider your notes on the following questions:

- What approach does Clarkson say explains most of the existing decisions on attempts? What problems does Clarkson identify with this approach?
- What is Clarkson's proposed reformulation of the law of attempts? How does it differ from the current law?
- On Clarkson's approach, would Geddes and Campbell have been guilty of an attempt?

On the Law Commission's report *Conspiracy and Attempts*, consider your notes on the following question:

- What did the Law Commission recommend? What reasons did it give for these recommendations? Do you agree with them?

Look back at the arguments for and against a broader test for the *actus reus* of criminal attempts. Once you have formed an opinion on whether the existing 'more than merely preparatory' test is too narrow in scope, construct a set of arguments in support of your opinion and work out how you would respond to potential counter-arguments. You may find some of the items on the further reading list useful here.

Step 3: Planning your introduction and conclusion

You have now compiled all you need for the main body of your essay. The last task is to decide what to include in your introduction and conclusion.

The introduction should contextualise your discussion by briefly outlining the *actus reus* of criminal attempts and give an indication of the argument you will present in your essay.

The conclusion should round off your essay with a succinct statement of your argument and a summary of your supporting reasons.

Inchoate offences checklist

Having worked through this chapter, you should now have:

- An understanding of the requirements for the three encouraging or assisting crime offences
- An understanding of the requirements for the crime of statutory conspiracy
- An understanding of the requirements for a criminal attempt
- An ability to critically discuss the 'more than merely preparatory' test for the *actus reus* of criminal attempts and the courts' application of this test.

Further reading

Child, J.J. and Hunt, A. (2014) 'Pace and Rogers and the *Mens Rea* of Criminal Attempt: Khan on the Scrapheap?' 78 *Journal of Criminal Law* 220.

Child, J. & Hunt, A. (2022) 'Beyond the Present-Fault Paradigm: Expanding *Mens Rea* Definitions in the General Part' 42 *Oxford Journal of Legal Studies* 438.

Clarkson, C. (2009) 'Attempt: The Conduct Requirement' 29 *Oxford Journal of Legal Studies* 25.

Donnelly, B. (2010) 'Possibility, Impossibility and Extraordinariness in Attempts' 23 Canadian *Journal of Law and Jurisprudence* 47.

Duff, R.A. (1996) *Criminal Attempts*. OUP: Oxford.

Glazebrook, P. (1969) 'Should We Have a Law of Attempted Crime?' 85 *Law Quarterly Review* 28.

Law Commission (2006) *Inchoate Liability for Assisting and Encouraging Crime* (Law Commission Report No 300) Cm 6878.

Law Commission (2009) *Conspiracy and Attempts* (Law Commission Report No 318) HC 41.

Ormerod, D. and Fortson, R. (2009) 'Serious Crime Act 2007: The Part 2 Offences' *Criminal Law Review* 389.

Rogers, J. (2008) 'The Codification of Attempts and the Case for "Preparation"' *Criminal Law Review* 937.

Answers on the Companion Website

Please visit the companion website for the answers to Key Questions, Quizzes, Applying the Law scenarios as well as student support including glossaries. Please visit www.pearsoned.co.uk/Macdonald

13

Accessories

Learning Objectives

13.1 Define the requirements for establishing that an individual is criminally liable as an accessory.

13.2 Outline the arguments for and against the decision of the Supreme Court in *R* v *Jogee*.

13.3 State the offences to which a defendant can be an accessory.

13.4 Outline the derivative principle on which the law on accessories is based.

13.5 Define the circumstances in which an individual's attempt to withdraw his previous assistance or encouragement will be deemed effective.

13.6 Apply the law on accessories to hypothetical sets of facts.

13.7 Evaluate the decision of the Supreme Court in *R* v *Jogee*.

Introduction

Consider the following four scenarios:

A group of soldiers stand and watch as some of their fellow soldiers rape a young woman. They do not say or do anything: they don't encourage or assist the rapists, but neither do they stop them. Are they accessories to the rape?

Shutterstock

A thief is trying to break into a van when he is interrupted by a passer-by. The thief gets into his getaway vehicle, which is being driven by his brother. The passer-by tries to stop them escaping. The thief sits in the passenger seat as the getaway driver murders the passer-by by running him over. Is the thief an accessory to the murder?

Shutterstock

A man guides a group of terrorists to a pub. He knows that the terrorists plan to attack the pub, but is unsure what form the attack will take. Is the man an accessory to the subsequent bomb attack?

Shutterstock

A man is on a night out with his friends. At the end of the evening, he and his friends start a fight with another group. The man punches and kicks members of the other group. One member of the other group is knocked to the floor. While the member of the other group is on the floor, one of the man's friends stamps on his head, killing him. Is the man an accessory to the murder?

Shutterstock

These scenarios are all taken from cases that we will study in this chapter. They illustrate the challenging and diverse fact scenarios to which the law on accessories applies. By the end of the chapter you will be able to explain the outcomes in each of these cases and discuss whether or not the relevant law is satisfactory.

The chapter begins by explaining how and why we **distinguish accessories from principals.** It then sets out the *actus reus* and *mens rea* **requirements for being an accessory**. The next part of the chapter then focuses on an area of law that has generated a lot of attention in recent years: **joint enterprise.** The penultimate part of the chapter looks at the **derivative principle** – the notion that a defendant cannot be guilty as an accessory if the principal did not in fact commit the full offence – and outlines a couple of exceptions to this principle. Finally, the chapter examines what a defendant must do in order to **withdraw from a criminal enterprise** that he has previously encouraged or assisted.

Before turning to the law, there are two quick terminological points to clarify.

First, accessorial liability is often referred to as secondary liability. Some of the extracts in this chapter accordingly refer to accessories as secondary parties. Second, for reasons we will see in a moment, when a defendant is an accessory to an offence most case law and literature on this topic will simply refer to him as being guilty of the offence and not say that he is guilty of being an accessory to the offence. For example, instead of saying that the defendant is guilty of 'being an accessory to murder' most would simply say that the defendant is guilty of 'murder'. In order to try and prevent confusion, in this chapter I do not adopt this approach. Instead, I will always refer in full to 'being an accessory to …', but as you read the quoted extracts and other literature on this topic you should bear this point in mind.

The distinction between principals and accessories

13.1 Define the requirements for establishing that an individual is criminally liable as an accessory.

The principal is the person who perpetrated the *actus reus* of the offence, whereas an accessory is someone who provided the principal with assistance or encouragement. So, to give a simple example, if Freddie breaks into Roshan's house and steals all his valuables Freddie is guilty of burglary as a principal. If Ronnie stands outside Roshan's house and keeps watch for Freddie, then Ronnie is an accessory to the burglary.

In most cases distinguishing the accessories from the principal will be straightforward. However, there are some situations in which the distinction is more difficult. Before considering these it is useful to begin by looking at section 8 of the Accessories and Abettors Act 1861, which states:

> Whosoever shall aid, abet, counsel, or procure the commission of any indictable offence, whether the same be an offence at common law or by virtue of any Act passed or to be passed, shall be liable to be tried, indicted, and punished as a principal offender.

(Section 44 of the Magistrates' Court Act 1980 contains an equivalent provision for summary offences.)

So the law treats accessories and principals identically for the purposes of procedure and punishment. An accessory to murder, for example, will receive the mandatory life sentence just as the principal will. If an accessory is to be tried, indicted and punished as a principal offender, you may well ask: is it really necessary to distinguish accessories from principals? There are at least two reasons why the distinction is important:

- The *actus reus* and *mens rea* requirements that the prosecution must prove differ according to whether the defendant is charged as a principal or an accessory. To give a simple example, a defendant can be guilty of drink-driving as a principal without any proof of *mens rea*. It is a strict liability offence. But for a defendant to be guilty of being an accessory to drink-driving, the prosecution must prove that he had the *mens rea* of being an accessory.
- For some offences there are classes of person who cannot be held liable as a principal. For example, women cannot commit rape as principals. But a woman can be convicted of being an accessory to rape. Similarly, although it is not a criminal offence for a person to commit suicide, someone who assists or encourages another person to do so can be convicted of being an accessory to suicide.[1]

Having explained why we distinguish accessories from principals, we can now look at four situations in which the distinction is not so straightforward:

1. Innocent agents

Innocent agency is where the defendant uses someone, who is unaware of the significance of his actions, to perpetrate the *actus reus* of the offence.

Suppose Freddie invites Roshan for dinner. Freddie knows that Roshan has a serious peanut allergy, but nonetheless asks his wife to cook a dish containing peanuts. Roshan eats the meal, suffers a severe allergic reaction and dies. Freddie's wife was an innocent agent. In a case like this one, the actions of the innocent agent are treated as being the actions of the defendant. So Freddie would be liable for Roshan's death as a principal.

2. Joint principals

Suppose that Ronnie and Freddie attack Roshan and Roshan dies.

If one of the men inflicts a specific wound that can be identified as the cause of death, then he will be the principal and the other an accessory. So if Freddie pulls out a knife

[1] Suicide Act 1961.

and inflicts a fatal stab wound, then Freddie is the principal and Ronnie is the accessory. But if there is no specific wound that can be identified as the cause of death, and Roshan dies from the cumulative effect of all his injuries, then Ronnie and Freddie will be liable as joint principals. So if they each attacked Roshan with the *mens rea* of murder, they will each be guilty of murder as a principal.

3. The prosecution can prove that the defendant was either a principal or an accessory, but cannot prove which

This was the position in *R* v *Giannetto* [1997] 1 Cr App R 1.

The Court of Appeal held that the defendant could be convicted, notwithstanding the fact that there was uncertainty over whether he was a principal or an accessory. This was because the prosecution had proved that he was either one or the other. So suppose that the prosecution prove that Ronnie either killed Roshan himself or paid Freddie to do it for him, but cannot prove which. Ronnie would be convicted of murder.

4. The prosecution can prove that one of two people committed the offence, but cannot prove which one

In this situation neither person can be convicted of the offence.

Suppose Ronnie, Freddie and Roshan are housemates. One day Roshan is found dead. The prosecution can prove that the killer was either Ronnie or Freddie, but cannot prove which. On these facts, Ronnie cannot be convicted since the prosecution cannot show, beyond reasonable doubt, that he was the killer. Nor can Freddie be convicted since the prosecution cannot show, beyond reasonable doubt, that he was the killer either. (Things would be different if the prosecution could prove that both Ronnie and Freddie were at least accessories. Then the principle from *R* v *Giannetto* would apply to both men.)

The *actus reus* and *mens rea* of being an accessory

A combination of case law and section 8 of the Accessories and Abettors Act 1861 tells us that the offence of being an accessory has the following three requirements:

1. The defendant must have aided, abetted, counselled or procured the commission of the offence
2. The defendant must have intended to aid, abet, counsel or procure the commission of the offence
3. The defendant must know or intend the essential elements of the principal's offence.

Number 1 is an *actus reus* requirement. Numbers 2 and 3 are *mens rea* requirements. We will work through them in turn.

1. The defendant must have aided, abetted, counselled or procured the commission of the offence

To establish the *actus reus* of accessorial liability, it is necessary to show that the defendant participated in the offence committed by the principal. Section 8 of the Accessories and Abettors Act 1861 specifies four forms of participation: aiding; abetting; counselling; and procuring. We will look at the meaning of each of these in turn. First, though, it is worth noting the following observations, which were offered by Lord Widgery CJ in *Attorney-General's Reference (No 1 of 1975)* [1975] QB 773.

EXTRACT

Attorney-General's Reference (No 1 of 1975) [1975] QB 773

Lord Widgery CJ

We approach section 8 of the Act of 1861 on the basis that the words should be given their ordinary meaning, if possible. We approach the section on the basis also that if four words are employed here, "aid, abet, counsel or procure," the probability is that there is a difference between each of those four words and the other three, because, if there were no such difference, then Parliament would be wasting time in using four words where two or three would do. Thus, in deciding whether that which is assumed to be done under our reference was a criminal offence we approach the section on the footing that each word must be given its ordinary meaning.

Think about this question.

Lord Widgery CJ states that the words 'aid', 'abet', 'counsel' and 'procure' should be given their 'ordinary meaning'.

- What do you understand to be the ordinary meaning of these words?
  - **a.** aiding
  - **b.** abetting
  - **c.** counselling
  - **d.** procuring

According to Lord Widgery CJ, it may be assumed that the words 'aid', 'abet', 'counsel' and 'procure' each have their own distinctive meaning. At the same time, however, it is clear that there is a significant degree of overlap. It is important to point out, therefore, that a jury may convict a defendant as long as they agree that the defendant satisfies at least one of the four modes of participation. It is not necessary for the jury to agree on which mode of participation is the most apt to the case in hand. For example, suppose a defendant is charged with 'abetting and counselling murder'. Six jurors conclude that the defendant abetted the murder. The other six conclude that the defendant counselled the murder. The defendant may be convicted of being an accessory to the murder, since the jury unanimously agree that he participated in the offence. It does not matter that there was a difference of opinion as to the most relevant form of participation.

With these introductory points in mind we can turn to examine the four forms of participation.

i. Aid

Aiding means to help or to assist. A simple example would be where Ronnie lends Freddie a baseball bat to use to smash Roshan's car windows. Ronnie would be guilty of aiding the criminal damage offence committed by Freddie.

In *Attorney-General* v *Able* [1984] QB 795 the five defendants were members of the executive committee of the Voluntary Euthanasia Society. The Society published a booklet titled 'A Guide to Self-Deliverance'. The booklet was aimed at people considering suicide. It began with a section titled 'Why you should think again'. This advised readers to think carefully and for a long period of time about whether to commit suicide and encouraged them to consider whether their problems could be overcome in other ways, such as medical treatment or way-of-life changes. It then set out five methods of 'self-deliverance'. In less than 18 months the Society sold over 8,000 copies. The Attorney-General applied to the courts for a declaration that supplying the book constituted the offence of aiding, abetting, counselling or procuring the suicide of another. In the High Court Woolf J held that supplying the booklet would amount to this offence in certain circumstances.

Four important points emerge from Woolf J's judgment. First, to establish that a defendant aided an offence it is not necessary to show that the assistance was a factual cause of the principal's offence. In other words, it is not necessary to show that, but for the assistance, the principal would not have committed the crime. Woolf J stated:

> [I]t does not make any difference that the person would have tried to commit suicide anyway. Nor does it make any difference, as the respondents contend, that the information contained in the booklet is already in the public domain.

So if Freddie says to Ronnie, 'I'm going to smash Roshan's car windows' and Ronnie responds by lending Freddie his baseball bat, Ronnie is an accessory to the subsequent criminal damage offence even though Freddie would still have committed the crime without Ronnie's help.

This leads on to the second point from *Attorney-General* v *Able*. Whilst it is not necessary to prove factual causation, it is necessary to prove that the defendant provided some assistance. Woolf J stated:

> There will also be cases where, although the recipient commits or attempts to commit suicide, the booklet has nothing to do with the suicide or the attempted suicide; for example, a long period of time may have elapsed between the sending of the booklet and the attempt. In such a case, again, I would agree [...] that there would not be a sufficient connection between the attempted suicide and the supply of the booklet to make the supplier responsible.

Similarly, if Ronnie lends Freddie his baseball bat but Freddie leaves the bat at home and instead uses a brick to smash Roshan's car windows, then Ronnie's actions have not provided any actual assistance. In this case, a prosecutor should instead consider charging Ronnie with abetting or counselling the criminal damage offence, since lending Freddie the bat could be deemed to be an act of encouragement.

The third point to note from *Attorney-General* v *Able* is that a defendant can be guilty of being an accessory without being present at the scene of the crime. Woolf J confirmed that those who published the booklet could be guilty of being accessories to suicide even though they would not be present when the principal ended his life. By the same token, Ronnie could be guilty of being an accessory to criminal damage even if he was not present when Freddie smashed Roshan's car windows.

Finally, it is clear from *Attorney-General* v *Able* that the act of assistance need not have occurred at the time of the principal's offence. The booklet could have provided assistance even if the principal read it some weeks before choosing to end his life. This was confirmed by the Court of Appeal in *R* v *Stringer* [2011] EWCA Crim 1396, with Toulson LJ explaining:

> 46 [...] It is one thing to say that D cannot be liable as an aider or abettor unless P acted with D's assistance or encouragement when he committed the offence. It is quite another to suggest that the act or words providing the assistance or encouragement must be performed or said at the moment of the commission of the offence. Such a limitation would exclude, for example, a person who supplied a murder weapon in

advance of the crime knowing the purpose for which P wanted it. The law would be defective if an aider and abettor could escape liability by seeing that there was a gap in time between his conduct and the conduct of P.

Before moving on, it is worth noting one further point: that a defendant may aid an offence even if the principal is unaware of the assistance he has provided. This may be illustrated using the facts of the US case *State* v *Tally* 102 Ala 25, 15 So 722 (1894). Judge Tally knew that his brothers-in-law had set out to kill the victim. He also knew that someone had sent a telegram to warn the victim. So Judge Tally ordered the telegraph operator not to deliver the telegram. The telegraph operator complied, and the brothers-in-law committed the offence. The judge was convicted of aiding the murder, even though the brothers-in-law were unaware of the judge's assistance when they killed the victim.

ii. Abet

The word 'abet' means to incite, instigate or encourage. Whilst each of the four modes of participation listed in the 1861 Act overlaps, there is a particularly large degree of overlap between the words 'abet' and 'counsel'. One way of distinguishing between them is to use the word 'abet' to refer to encouragement given at the time of the principal's offence, and to use the word 'counsel' to refer to encouragement given at an earlier stage. But this is not a hard-and-fast rule and there is nothing to prevent the word 'abet' from being used to refer to encouragement given before the principal commits his offence.

One important issue which has arisen here is whether a defendant abets a crime simply by being present at the scene whilst the offence is being committed. The leading case is *R* v *Clarkson* [1971] 1 WLR 1402. The defendants, David Clarkson and Joseph Carroll, were members of the army. One evening there was a party at their barracks. The victim, an 18-year-old girl named Elke von Groen, went to the party. Sometime after midnight the two defendants heard screaming and moaning coming from one of the rooms in the barracks. They entered the room and found Elke being repeatedly raped by a group of their fellow soldiers. They remained in the room for some time. Whilst they were in the room, there was no evidence that Clarkson and Carroll did anything to participate in the rape or to encourage it. But neither did they do anything to try and stop it.

At trial they were convicted of being accessories to rape. They appealed against their convictions. The case reached the Court Martial Appeal Court. The key issue in the case was whether the defendants had encouraged the rape merely by their presence in the room. The Court Martial Appeal Court allowed the defendants' appeal. Megaw LJ explained that being present at the scene of a crime is not, in itself, sufficient for the *actus reus* of being an accessory. As we saw when we studied omissions in Chapter 3, there is no general duty to prevent crime. It is not a crime to simply stand by and watch someone else commit an offence. Megaw LJ said that to establish the *actus reus* of being an accessory, the prosecution must prove that there was in fact assistance or encouragement. In the present case, the prosecution had failed to produce any evidence that Clarkson and Carroll had encouraged the rapists:

> [T]here was no evidence on which the prosecution sought to rely that either of the defendants Clarkson or Carroll had done any physical act or uttered any word which involved direct physical participation or verbal encouragement. There was no evidence that they had touched the girl, helped to hold her down, done anything to her, done anything to prevent others from assisting her or to prevent her from escaping, or from trying to ward off her attackers, or that they had said anything which gave encouragement to the others to commit crime or to participate in committing crime.

Admittedly the defendants' presence might have provided encouragement.[2] But this had to be proved with evidence. In the absence of such evidence, the convictions had to be quashed.

This principle was also applied in *R* v *Willett* [2010] EWCA Crim 1620. The defendant, Tommy Willett, and his brother, Albert, went to a car park intending to steal items from the cars parked there. Tommy Willett was attempting to break into a Mercedes van when the owner, Balbir Matharu, saw him and began to shout. Willett got back into Albert's car and they attempted to drive off, but Matharu stood in the way of the exit to block their escape. A witness said that Albert's car edged forward. Matharu was banging on the bonnet, but then appeared to trip. Albert drove forward and Matharu went under the car. Albert continued to drive. Matharu was dragged along the road and killed. Albert was convicted of murder. Tommy Willett was charged with being an accessory to the murder. At trial the judge told the jury that, in order to convict, they had to be sure that Tommy had provided either 'actual or tacit encouragement'. Willett was subsequently convicted.[3] He appealed to the Court of Appeal, arguing that the trial judge had been wrong to tell the jury that tacit encouragement was sufficient. The Court of Appeal agreed. Moses LJ reiterated that mere presence is insufficient. There must be encouragement in fact:

EXTRACT

R v *Willett* [2010] EWCA Crim 1620

Moses LJ

18 It is difficult to see that merely continuing to sit in the passenger seat of the Mondeo amounted to any encouragement to the driver to run over Mr Matharu. Events happened fast. There was an opportunity, at the last minute, we suppose, for the appellant to get out of the vehicle and remonstrate with Mr Matharu. But his failure to do so cannot, we think, be said to be an encouragement to the driver to run him over. The speed and turn of events makes such a suggestion unrealistic.

[...]

24 The difficulty in the judge's ruling lies in his apparent acceptance that "tacit" encouragement would be enough. We do not agree. Indeed, we are not sure what he meant by "tacit encouragement" in the context of this case. The danger with that expression is that it suggests that this appellant's continued presence was sufficient. For the reasons we have given, it was not.

Neither Clarkson and Carroll, nor Tommy Willett, had made prior arrangements to be present at the scene of the offence. Clarkson and Carroll only entered the room where the rapes were occurring when they heard sounds coming from inside, and when Willett got into his brother's car he did not know that their escape route would be blocked or that Albert would kill the victim. This raises the question: does the principle from these cases apply when the defendant actually made prior arrangements to be present at the

[2] For critical comment, see Cowley's argument that the judgment in *R* v *Clarkson* does not take into account the fact that the humiliation of a rape victim may be compounded by the presence of observers (Cowley, C. (2019) 'Complicity and Rape' 83 *Journal of Criminal Law* 30).

[3] 'Daughter's plea after father run over by thieves', *The Guardian*, 19 January 2006.

scene of the crime? Or is the fact that the defendant purposely arranged to be present sufficient to establish the *actus reus* of being an accessory?

This was the issue in *R* v *Coney* (1882) 8 QBD 534. The defendant went to watch an illegal prize-fight. The fighters were each convicted of assault. Coney was charged with being an accessory to the assaults. At trial the judge stated that Coney's voluntary attendance to watch the prize-fight was conclusive evidence of encouragement. The jury therefore convicted Coney. Coney appealed against his conviction. By a majority of 8–3, the Divisional Court held that the trial judge had misdirected the jury. The majority explained that, whilst voluntary, non-accidental presence at the scene of a crime is evidence of encouragement, it is not conclusive evidence. In other words, the same approach applies here as in *R* v *Clarkson* and *R* v *Willett*: the prosecution must prove that there was assistance or encouragement in fact. The fact that a defendant arranged to go and watch an offence being committed is evidence that he provided encouragement – indeed, it may be powerful evidence as if there had been no spectators the prize-fight would presumably not have gone ahead – but voluntary attendance is not in itself conclusive. The jury must also look at any other relevant evidence and decide whether the defendant did in fact provide encouragement. Since the trial judge had misdirected the jury, Coney's conviction was quashed.

An example of a case in which a defendant was convicted of being an accessory after watching an illegal performance is *Wilcox* v *Jeffery* [1951] 1 All ER 464. This case involved the famous US saxophonist Coleman Hawkins.

AP/Shutterstock

Hawkins came to London to play a concert. The concert was in fact illegal: Hawkins was only given permission to enter the UK on condition that he undertook no employment, paid or unpaid. The defendant, William Wilcox, was the owner and editor of a jazz magazine, *Jazz Illustrated*. Wilcox attended the concert and was subsequently convicted of being an accessory to the illegal performance. The Divisional Court dismissed his appeal against conviction, stating that there was ample evidence that Wilcox's presence at the concert had encouraged the performance. Not only had he voluntarily arranged to attend. He paid for a ticket. He did not boo or protest during the performance. He had also been at the airport to welcome Hawkins, and he later wrote a glowing review of the concert in his magazine.

Wilcox v *Jeffery* illustrates one further point: as with aiding, abetting does not require proof of factual causation. So whilst it is necessary to establish actual encouragement, it is not necessary to show that but for the abetting the principal would not have committed the crime.[4] This is clear from *Wilcox* v *Jeffery*: even if Wilcox had not attended the concert, the illegal performance would still have gone ahead.

iii. Counsel

The meaning of counsel was considered by the Court of Appeal in *R* v *Calhaem* [1985] QB 808. Parker LJ stated:

> We must therefore approach the question raised on the basis that we should give to the word "counsel" its ordinary meaning, which is, as the judge said, "advise," "solicit," or something of that sort.

So if Ronnie says to Freddie, 'I really think you need to teach Roshan a lesson. You should beat him up' – and Freddie later acts on this and punches Roshan in the face, giving him a black eye – Ronnie would be guilty of counselling the offence of assault occasioning ABH committed by Freddie. Similarly, if Freddie tells Ronnie that he plans to break Roshan's leg, and Ronnie advises him, 'The best time to attack him would be when he leaves the pub tomorrow night', Ronnie would be guilty of counselling Freddie's subsequent offence.

In *R* v *Calhaem* Parker LJ went on to offer some further guidance on the meaning of counselling:

EXTRACT

R v *Calhaem* [1985] QB 808

Parker LJ

There is no implication in the word itself that there should be any causal connection between the counselling and the offence. It is true that [...] the actual offence must have been committed, and committed by the person counselled. To this extent there must clearly be, first, contact between the parties, and, secondly a connection between the counselling and the murder. Equally, the act done must, we think, be done within the scope of the authority or advice, and not, for example, accidentally when the mind of the final murderer did not go with his actions. For example, if the principal offencer happened to be involved in a football riot in the course of which he laid about him with a weapon of some sort and killed someone who, unknown to him, was the person whom he had been counselled to kill, he would not, in our view, have been acting within the scope of his authority; he would have been acting entirely outside it, albeit what he had done was what he had been counselled to do.

---

[4] Nor is it necessary to prove that the encouragement or assistance made a contribution to the principal's commission of the offence. In *R* v *Rowe & others* [2022] EWCA Crim 27 the Court of Appeal held that there is no requirement for the prosecution to prove that the encouragement in fact contributed to the commission of the offence (at [134]). Similarly, in *R* v *Hussain & others [2023]* EWCA Crim 697 the Court of Appeal rejected the argument that the prosecution should be required to prove that the accessory made a 'measurable contribution' to the commission of the crime by the principal ([84]). For comment, see Krebs, B. (2023) 'Does complicity require a measurable contribution?' 87 *Journal of Criminal Law* 294.

Three important points emerge from this extract. First, Parker LJ explained that there must be 'contact between the parties'. A defendant cannot be held to have counselled the principal if his words of encouragement were never received. The position here is different to the position with acts of assistance. As we saw above, a principal can receive assistance without being aware of it (as *State* v *Tally* illustrated). But a person cannot receive encouragement if he is unaware of the encouragement! So if Ronnie sends Freddie a text message urging him to kill Roshan, but unbeknown to Ronnie Freddie has recently changed his number and so never receives the message, there can be no counselling since Freddie never received the words of encouragement.

Second, whilst the words of encouragement must have been received, it is not necessary to show that they were a factual cause of the principal's offence. In other words, as with both aiding and abetting, there is no requirement to show that, but for the counselling, the principal would not have committed the offence. So if Ronnie encourages Freddie to kill Roshan, Ronnie can be guilty of counselling murder even if Freddie had already made up his mind to carry out the killing[5]. This is confirmed by the following example from the Court of Appeal's judgment in *R* v *Giannetto* [1997] 1 Cr App R 1:

> Supposing somebody came up to [the defendant] and said, 'I am going to kill your wife', if he played any part, either in encouragement, as little as patting him on the back, nodding, saying, 'Oh goody', that would be sufficient to involve him in the murder, to make him guilty, because he is encouraging the murder.

The third point from *R* v *Calhaem* is that there must be some 'connection' between the principal's offence and the counselling. The principal's offence must be 'within the scope of the authority or advice'. Parker LJ explained this point in the extract above using the example of the principal killing someone during a riot who just happened, by sheer coincidence, to be the person the defendant had counselled him to kill. On these facts there would not be any sufficient connection between the counselling and the principal's offence. In *R* v *Calhaem* itself, the defendant, Kathleen Calhaem, hired a man named Julian Zajac to murder Shirley Rendell (Rendell was having an affair with a man that Calhaem was infatuated with). Zajac testified that, on the day of the murder, he went to Rendell's house with no intention of killing her. He said that he intended to act out a charade, so that both Rendell and Calhaem would think that he had attempted to kill Rendell. However, when he forced his way into Rendell's house she began to scream. Zajac said that her screams caused him to go 'berserk'. He hit her several times with a hammer and stabbed her. The Court of Appeal upheld Calhaem's conviction for counselling murder, on the basis that Zajac had acted within the scope of Calhaem's authority and advice.

Now, think about this question.

In the light of the guidance from *R* v *Calhaem*, do you think that counselling can be established in the following two scenarios?

a. Freddie has a long-standing feud with Roshan. Ronnie is aware of this and sends Freddie an email urging him to kill Roshan. For some reason, the email goes straight to Freddie's spam folder. Even though he never sees the email, Freddie kills Roshan.

[5] *R* v *Calhaem* was followed in both *R* v *Rowe & others* [2022] EWCA Crim 27 and *R* v *Hussain & others* [2023] EWCA Crim 697.

b. Ronnie pays Freddie £10,000 to kill Roshan. Freddie takes the money, even though he does not plan to kill Roshan. Instead, he intends to beat Roshan up and then disappear with Ronnie's money. However, Freddie later discovers that Roshan has been having an affair with his girlfriend. Incensed, he confronts Roshan and kills him.

iv. Procure

The meaning of 'procure' was considered by the Court of Appeal in *Attorney-General's Reference (No 1 of 1975)* [1975] QB 773. In this case the defendant secretly spiked his friend's drinks with alcohol, even though he knew that his friend would shortly be driving home. His friend was subsequently convicted of drink-driving. The defendant was charged with procuring the drink-driving offence. At trial the trial judge ruled that there was no case to answer (on the basis that there was no shared intention between the two men). Believing this to have been mistaken, the Attorney-General referred the case to the Court of Appeal as raising a point of law of general importance.

EXTRACT

Read the following extract from the judgment of Lord Widgery CJ.

How does he define 'procure'?

According to Lord Widgery CJ, to establish procurement is it necessary to show: (a) that there was a shared intention between the principal and the accessory; and (b) that there was a causal link between the accessory's actions and the principal's offence?

Attorney-General's Reference (No 1 of 1975) [1975] QB 773

Lord Widgery CJ

To procure means to produce by endeavour. You procure a thing by setting out to see that it happens and taking the appropriate steps to produce that happening. We think that there are plenty of instances in which a person may be said to procure the commission of a crime by another even though there is no sort of conspiracy between the two, even though there is no attempt at agreement or discussion as to the form which the offence should take. In our judgment the offence described in this reference is such a case.

If one looks back at the facts of the reference: the accused surreptitiously laced his friend's drink. This is an important element and, although we are not going to decide today anything other than the problem posed to us, it may well be that, in similar cases where the lacing of the drink or the introduction of the extra alcohol is known to the driver, quite different considerations may apply. We say that because, where the driver has no knowledge of what is happening, in most instances he would have no means of preventing the offence from being committed. If the driver is unaware of what has happened, he will not be taking precautions. He will get into his car seat, switch on the ignition and drive home and, consequently, the conception of another procuring the commission of the offence by the driver is very much stronger where the driver is innocent of all knowledge of what is happening, as in the present case where the lacing of the drink was surreptitious.

The second thing which is important in the facts set out in our reference is that, following and in consequence of the introduction of the extra alcohol, the friend drove with an excess quantity of

> alcohol in his blood. Causation here is important. You cannot procure an offence unless there is a causal link between what you do and the commission of the offence, and here we are told that in consequence of the addition of this alcohol the driver, when he drove home, drove with an excess quantity of alcohol in his body.
>
> Giving the words their ordinary meaning in English, and asking oneself whether in those circumstances the offence has been procured, we are in no doubt that the answer is that it has. It has been procured because, unknown to the driver and without his collaboration, he has been put in a position in which in fact he has committed an offence which he never would have committed otherwise.

It is clear from the facts of this case that it is not necessary to prove there was a shared intention in order to establish procurement. The principal had no idea that his drinks had been spiked. However, to prove procurement it is necessary to establish factual causation. It must be shown that, but for the defendant's actions, the principal would not have committed the offence. This was readily apparent in *Attorney-General's Reference (No 1 of 1975)*; if the defendant had not spiked his friend's drinks, his friend would not have committed the drink-driving offence. In this respect, then, procurement is quite different to aiding, abetting and counselling – since none of these other forms of participation require proof of factual causation.

It is important to distinguish procurement from two other, similar scenarios:

1. Procurement must be distinguished from innocent agency.

As we saw above, in a case of innocent agency the actions of the innocent agent are treated as being the actions of the defendant. The defendant is therefore guilty of the offence in question as a principal, not as an accessory. In a case involving procurement, by contrast, there is no innocent agent and so the defendant is guilty as an accessory, not a principal. In *Attorney-General's Reference (No 1 of 1975)*, for example, the defendant's friend was not an innocent agent. He was guilty of drink-driving as a principal. The defendant was an accessory to this offence.

2. Procurement does not apply if there was a break in the chain of causation between the accessory's actions and the principal's offence.

Therefore, procurement does not apply if the principal made a voluntary choice to commit the offence.[6] So suppose Ronnie offers to buy Freddie a drink. Freddie asks for something non-alcoholic. In spite of this, Ronnie buys him an alcoholic drink. Freddie decides to drink it, even though he knows it is alcoholic and he knows he has to drive home later. Freddie is subsequently convicted of drink-driving. Ronnie could not be convicted of procuring the drink-driving offence, since Freddie's voluntary choice to drive home breaks the chain of causation between Ronnie buying the drink and Freddie drink-driving. However, this does not mean Ronnie escapes liability as an accessory! The prosecution could instead argue that Ronnie aided the drink-driving offence, since he provided assistance by buying Freddie the drink.

v. Participation by omission?

Whether or not it is possible to be an accessory to an offence simply by doing nothing is an important question, particularly in cases like *R* v *Clarkson* and *R* v *Willett* which involve presence but no positive acts of assistance or encouragement. There are two types of situation in which an omission may satisfy the *actus reus* of being an accessory.

The first is illustrated by *Rubie* v *Faulkner* [1940] 1 KB 571. The defendant, George Rubie, was teaching a man called Percy James to drive. As they approached a bend,

[6] As we saw in Chapter 3, a voluntary choice is one which was free, deliberate and informed (*R* v *Pagett*).

James attempted to overtake a horse and cart even though he could not see what was coming round the bend. He pulled out to the other side of the road, a lorry came around the bend and James stalled the car, resulting in a collision. Even though Rubie could see the manoeuvre James was going to perform, he did not intervene. James was convicted of driving without due care and attention. Rubie was convicted of being an accessory to this offence. Rubie appealed against his conviction, arguing that he had not done or said anything to encourage the dangerous manoeuvre. His appeal against conviction was dismissed. The Divisional Court explained that, since Rubie was supervising a learner driver, he had a legal duty to intervene. By failing to do so he had breached this duty, and so he was an accessory to James' offence.

So it is clear from *Rubie* v *Faulkner* that a person may be an accessory to an offence by omission, if he breaches a legal duty to intervene. A further example would be where a child's father stands and watches as the mother deliberately injures the child. As we saw in Chapter 3, the father has a legal duty to intervene. His failure to do so is a breach of this duty and so he satisfies the *actus reus* of being an accessory.

It seems that a defendant may also be guilty as an accessory, even though he had no legal duty to intervene, if he had a legal power or right to do so. In *Du Cros* v *Lambourne* [1907] 1 KB 40 the defendant, Du Cros, owned a Mercedes car. He allowed his friend, Victoria Goodwin, to drive the car whilst he sat in the passenger seat. Goodwin was convicted of a speeding offence. Du Cros was convicted of being an accessory to the speeding offence. He appealed, arguing that he had done nothing but sit passively in the passenger seat. His appeal was dismissed by the Divisional Court. The Court held that:

> [Du Cros was] in control of the car, and that he could, and ought to, have prevented her from driving at this excessive and dangerous speed, but that he allowed her to do so and did not interfere in any way.

So if a defendant has the power or right to control the principal's actions, and fails to do so, he satisfies the *actus reus* of being an accessory.

Consider this scenario.

Ronnie owns a flat. He has a lodger, Freddie. He knows that people visit Freddie at the flat in order to buy and sell drugs but turns a blind eye since Freddie always pays the rent on time. Freddie is convicted of drugs offences.

Is Ronnie an accessory to these offences?

vi. The timing of the participation

There is one final point to note about the *actus reus* of being an accessory, which concerns the timing of the defendant's participation. A person cannot be liable as an accessory to an offence if the assistance or encouragement he provides comes after the offence is already complete. Suppose that Ronnie, Freddie and Roshan are housemates. Ronnie arrives home one day, only to discover that Freddie has just murdered Roshan. Ronnie agrees to help Freddie dispose of the body. On these facts, Ronnie is not liable as an accessory to Roshan's murder because the assistance he provides comes after the murder was already complete. This is not to say that Ronnie has committed no crime at all – there are specific offences aimed at those who help to conceal crimes that have been committed[7] – the key point is that the assistance came too late for Ronnie to be an accessory to the murder that had already occurred.

[7] See, for example, sections 4 and 5 of the Criminal Law Act 1967.

2. The defendant must have intended to aid, abet, counsel or procure the commission of the offence

There are two *mens rea* requirements for being an accessory, which must both be satisfied at the time of the defendant's assistance/encouragement. The easiest way to understand the difference between them is to remember that one of them relates to the defendant's thoughts about his own actions, whilst the other relates to the defendant's thoughts about the actions of the principal. We will begin by looking at the first of these: the defendant must have intended, by his actions, to aid, abet, counsel or procure the commission of the crime.

There are two points to note about this *mens rea* requirement. First, it asks whether the defendant intended to assist or encourage the principal to commit the offence. It does not ask whether it was the defendant's intention that the principal would go ahead and commit the offence. This may seem like a fine distinction, so imagine the following example.[8] The defendant, a shopkeeper, sells a customer a gun knowing that the customer might use it to commit a murder. The shopkeeper does not care whether the customer commits the murder or not. All the shopkeeper cares about is the profit he will make from the sale. On these facts, the shopkeeper does intentionally provide assistance. This may not be his direct intention (i.e. his purpose). But it is his oblique intention, since he realises that assistance is the inevitable consequence of completing the sale (see the *R* v *Woollin* direction, which we studied in Chapter 4). So, if the customer goes ahead and commits the murder, whether or not the shopkeeper is guilty of being an accessory to the murder will depend on whether he satisfies the final *mens rea* requirement, which we will look at shortly.

The second point to note about this *mens rea* requirement is that only intention will suffice. Recklessness is insufficient. This is particularly important in cases involving questions of oblique intention, like the shopkeeper example we just discussed, since the jury will have to decide whether the defendant foresaw assistance/encouragement as virtually certain (oblique intention) or whether the defendant only foresaw assistance/encouragement as a risk (even a grave risk) (recklessness). As we saw in Chapter 4, the dividing line between a risk and a virtual certainty is a difficult one.

Consider this scenario.

Ronnie invites a number of friends to his house for dinner. Even though Ronnie knows that Freddie will be driving home later that evening, he gives Freddie a large glass of wine and refills it several times during the meal. Freddie later drives home. He is stopped by police and subsequently convicted of drink-driving. Ronnie is charged with being an accessory to the drink-driving offence.

In your opinion, does he satisfy this *mens rea* requirement?

3. The defendant must know or intend the essential elements of the principal's offence

Whilst the previous *mens rea* requirement focused on the defendant's thoughts about his own actions, this *mens rea* requirement focuses on the defendant's thoughts about the actions of the principal. In *Johnson* v *Youden* [1950] 1 KB 544, Lord Goddard CJ explained that 'Before a person can be convicted of aiding and abetting the commission of an offence he must at least know the essential matters which constitute that offence'. Whilst some previous decisions of the Court of Appeal suggested that something less

[8] Similar examples were discussed in *National Coal Board* v *Gamble* [1959] 1 QB 11 and *R* v *Jogee* [2016] UKSC 8.

than knowledge may be sufficient,[9] the Supreme Court in *R* v *Jogee* [2016] UKSC 8 reiterated that the defendant must have had 'knowledge of any existing facts necessary for [the principal's actions] to be criminal' ([9]).

There are three issues to address in respect of this *mens rea* requirement. The first concerns the word 'knowledge'.

In cases where the defendant provides assistance or encouragement at the time of the principal's offence, the word 'knowledge' will be unproblematic, such as where Ronnie sees Freddie attacking Roshan and shouts encouragement. On these facts, when Ronnie provides encouragement he knows the essential elements of Freddie's offence. But in many cases the defendant will offer assistance or encouragement in advance of the principal's offence, such as where Ronnie provides Freddie with detailed information on a building Freddie is planning to burgle. In these cases, using the word 'knowledge' is awkward since a person cannot have knowledge of something that is yet to occur. So in these cases it is better to use the language of intention.[10] You begin by asking whether the defendant's purpose (direct intention) was for the principal to go ahead and commit the offence. If it was, this *mens rea* requirement is satisfied. If it was not, then you should ask whether the defendant knew that it was virtually certain that the principal would commit the offence (oblique intention). If he did, then this *mens rea* requirement is satisfied. If he did not, then this *mens rea* requirement would seem not to be satisfied (there is some ambiguity here because, as we will see later in the chapter, in *R* v *Jogee* the Supreme Court did not clearly state whether or not the *R* v *Woollin* threshold of virtual certainty applies in this context).

The second point to note is that it is not enough to show that the defendant knew that some prohibited conduct or consequence would occur.

It must be established that the defendant knew that the principal was committing the relevant offence, or intended that he would do so. This is an important distinction. It means that the defendant must have known or intended *both* that the principal would perpetrate the conduct specified in the *actus reus* of the relevant offence *and* that the principal would act in this way possessing the relevant *mens rea*. The point can be illustrated using the following two examples.

EXAMPLE

- Freddie murders Roshan. Ronnie is charged with being an accessory to the murder. It would not be enough to show that Ronnie intended that Freddie would perform the actions that caused Roshan's death. Ronnie must also have intended that Freddie would commit these actions with the *mens rea* of murder. So the prosecution would have to show that Ronnie intended: (1) that Freddie would attack Roshan; and (2) that Freddie would carry out the attack with an intention to kill Roshan or cause him serious harm.

[9] For example, *R* v *Bryce* [2004] EWCA Crim 1231, in which the Court said that it was sufficient to show that the defendant realised there was a real or substantial risk that the principal would commit the offence.

[10] Ormerod, D. and Laird, K. (2016) '*Jogee*: Not the End of a Legal Saga but the Start of One?' *Criminal Law Review* 539.

- Ronnie is charged with being an accessory to Freddie raping Roshan. It would not be enough to show that Ronnie intended that Freddie would have sexual intercourse with Roshan. The prosecution would have to show that Ronnie intended: (1) that Freddie would have non-consensual sexual intercourse with Roshan; and (2) that Freddie would penetrate Roshan intentionally and lack a reasonable belief that Roshan was consenting.

Consider this scenario.

Ronnie and Freddie are playing football in the street, using their neighbour's wall as a goal. Freddie kicks the ball at the wall as hard as he can. The ball goes much higher than he intended and smashes an upstairs window. Freddie is charged with criminal damage of the window. Ronnie is charged with being an accessory to criminal damage.

- Make a list of everything the prosecution must prove in order for Ronnie to be convicted.

The third issue we need to address is: how much knowledge must the defendant have of the details of the principal's offence?

At one extreme, must the defendant know all the specific details, that is, when, where and how the offence will be committed? Or, at the other extreme, is it enough that the defendant merely knew that something unlawful would occur? The courts' answer is somewhere between these two positions.

The leading case is *R* v *Bainbridge* [1960] 1 QB 129. The defendant, Alan Bainbridge, purchased oxygen-cutting equipment. Six weeks later the equipment was used to break into a Midland bank in Stoke Newington. Bainbridge was charged with being an accessory to the break-in. In evidence, Bainbridge said that he had bought the equipment for a man named Shakeshaft. He admitted that he suspected Shakeshaft wanted it for something illegal, but he said he thought Shakeshaft would use the equipment to dispose of stolen goods, not to break into a bank. At trial Bainbridge was convicted. He appealed, and the case reached the Court of Appeal.

EXTRACT

Read the following extract from the judgment of Lord Parker CJ.

According to Lord Parker CJ, for this mens rea requirement to be satisfied what must the defendant have known?

R v *Bainbridge* [1960] 1 QB 129

Lord Parker CJ

The court fully appreciates that it is not enough that it should be shown that a man knows that some illegal venture is intended. To take this case, it would not be enough if he knew – he says he only suspected – that the equipment was going to be used to dispose of stolen property. That would not be enough. Equally, this court is quite satisfied that it is unnecessary that knowledge of the particular crime which was in fact committed should be shown to his knowledge to have been intended, and by "particular crime" I am using the words in the same way in which [counsel for the defence] used them, namely, on a particular date and particular premises.

> [...]
>
> [The trial judge] in this case, in the passage to which I have referred, makes it clear that there must be not merely suspicion but knowledge that a crime of the type in question was intended, and that the equipment was bought with that in view. In his reference to the felony of the type intended it was, as he stated, the felony of breaking and entering premises and the stealing of property from those premises. The court can see nothing wrong in that direction.

So, on the facts of *R* v *Bainbridge*, the prosecution would not have to show that the defendant knew that the principal planned to break into the Stoke Newington branch of the Midland bank. But equally it is not enough to show that the defendant merely knew that something illegal was planned. The prosecution have to show that the defendant knew or intended that the principal would commit a crime of that type, that is, breaking and entering and theft. The jury at Bainbridge's trial had concluded that Bainbridge knew this type of crime would be committed, and so his appeal against conviction was dismissed.

A similar case is *DPP for Northern Ireland* v *Maxwell* [1978] 1 WLR 1350. Here, the House of Lords dealt with a slightly different scenario: where the defendant knows that the principal will commit one of several different offences, but is unsure which. The defendant, James Maxwell, was a member of a terrorist organisation in Northern Ireland. Members of the organisation told him to guide a group of men, who were strangers to the area, to a particular pub. Having reached the pub, Maxwell left. He knew that a terrorist attack was planned, but was unsure what form the attack would take. In fact, the men attempted (unsuccessfully) to bomb the pub. Maxwell was convicted of being an accessory to the attack. His appeal against conviction reached the House of Lords. In his judgment Lord Scarman explained the relevant principle as follows:

> [A defendant] may have in contemplation only one offence, or several: and the several which he contemplates he may see as alternatives. An accessory who leaves it to his principal to choose is liable, provided always the choice is made from the range of offences from which the accessory contemplates the choice will be made.

Since the attack on the pub was within the range of offences Maxwell had contemplated, his conviction was upheld.

Quiz 13.1

1. Which of the following could be an accessory?

- **a.** A person who helps or encourages the police in the apprehension of the principal.
- **b.** A person who helps or encourages the principal.
- **c.** Any item of evidence which is capable of helping or assisting the principal at trial.
- **d.** An item which is capable of helping or assisting the principal in the commission of the offence.

2. If an offence is committed by two or more people, who is the principal offender?

- **a.** The person who instigates the plan.
- **b.** The person who performs the *actus reus* of the full offence with the appropriate *mens rea*.
- **c.** The person who devises how the *actus reus* should be carried out.
- **d.** The person who first develops *mens rea*.

3. Which of the following statements is false?

- **a.** The actions of an innocent agent are regarded as being the actions of the defendant.
- **b.** An innocent agent is someone who initially helps, then realises their mistake and withdraws from the plan.
- **c.** An innocent agent might perform the *actus reus* with no knowledge they are committing a crime.
- **d.** An innocent agent can be either a child or an adult.

4. Which of the following statements is incorrect?

a. Aiding means to provide help or assistance either before or at the time of the commission of the offence.

b. Counselling means to cause the commission of the offence by inciting the principal offender.

c. Procuring means striving to bring about the commission of the offence by the principal offender.

d. Abetting tends to denote encouragement given at the time of the commission of the offence.

5. Which of the following statements is correct?

a. In *R* v *Coney* the Court held that voluntary, non-accidental presence at the scene of a crime constitutes conclusive evidence of encouragement.

b. In R v *Clarkson* the Court of Appeal upheld the defendants' convictions for being accessories to rape because they had failed to try and stop the attackers.

c. In *R* v *Willett* the Court of Appeal upheld the defendant's conviction for being an accessory to murder because he had remained seated in the passenger seat whilst the victim was run over and killed.

d. In *Wilcox* v *Jeffery* the Court held that there was ample evidence that the defendant had encouraged the illegal performance and so dismissed his appeal against conviction.

6. In which one of the following examples is D procuring an offence?

a. D agrees to leave diagrams of the layout of the internals of a bank in which he works for D2 to collect. D makes it clear he wants no part in the robbery that D2 plans.

b. D, a doctor, instructs a nurse, B, to administer to V a particular medication. The nurse believes it to be a harmless pain killer. D knows that V is in fact highly allergic to it. V dies.

c. D arranges with V, a 14-year-old girl he has met on an internet chat site, to meet him at a hotel for sex. V agrees. On the way V changes her mind and doesn't show up.

d. D is at the pub with D2. Knowing that D2 will be driving home later that evening, D puts vodka in what D2 believes to be a non-alcoholic drink. He repeats this, hoping that D2 will not notice. D2 does not notice. He starts to drive home when he is stopped by the police and fails a breathalyser test.

7. Which of the following statements most accurately describes the *mens rea* requirements for accessories?

a. The *mens rea* requirements for accessories are the same as for principals.

b. The *mens rea* of being an accessory is intention to aid, abet, counsel or procure the commission of the offence whilst realising there is a real risk the principal will carry out the offence. requirements for accessories are the same as for principals.

c. The *mens rea* of being an accessory is intention to aid, abet, counsel or procure the commission of the offence knowing or intending the essential elements of the principal's offence.

d. The *mens rea* of an accessory is irrelevant to a conviction.

8. Which of the following statements is incorrect?

a. It is not enough to establish the *mens rea* of being an accessory to show that the defendant knew that the principal was planning something unlawful.

b. A defendant may have the *mens rea* of being an accessory if he knows that the principal will commit one of several different offences but is unsure which.

c. It is enough to establish the mens rea of being an accessory to show that the defendant knew or intended that the actus reus of the full offence would occur.

d. A defendant may have the *mens rea* of being an accessory even if he did not know all the specific details of where and when the offence would be committed.

Joint enterprise

13.2 Outline the arguments for and against the decision of the Supreme Court in *R* v *Jogee*.

Suppose that Ronnie and Freddie work together to burgle Roshan's house. Ronnie acts as lookout whilst Freddie enters Roshan's house and steals all his valuables. Freddie will be guilty of burglary. As for Ronnie, establishing the *actus reus* and *mens rea* of being an accessory to the burglary will be straightforward: (1) he abetted (encouraged) Freddie by embarking on the crime with him; (2) he did so with an intention to abet Freddie; and (3) he provided encouragement with the intention that Freddie would commit the burglary. Cases like this one – in which two or more people act together with the shared purpose of committing a particular crime (or crimes) – are often referred to as a joint enterprise (even though 'joint enterprise' is not in fact a legal term[11]).

The shared purpose may be expressly agreed, as in the case of Ronnie and Freddie, or it could be an unspoken understanding (such as where gang members spontaneously attack a rival gang member together).

In some cases, the courts have applied a wide interpretation of the term joint enterprise. In *R* v *Gnango* [2011] UKSC 59 the defendant, 17 year-old Armel Gnango, was in a car park outside a block of flats talking to some friends who were sitting in a parked car. Gnango told them that he had come to meet a man who owed him money. When the man appeared from the building he was wearing a red bandana and armed with a gun. He began firing at Gnango. Gnango pulled out his gun and started firing back. The victim, 26-year-old Magda Pniewska, was walking across the car park as this happened. She was hit in the head and killed. The man wearing the bandana was never captured, so the law reports refer to him simply as Bandana Man. Evidence showed that it was Bandana Man who fired the fatal shot. So Bandana Man had committed murder, applying the doctrine of transferred *mens rea*. The issue in the case was whether Gnango was liable as an accessory to the murder. At trial Gnango was convicted. The Court of Appeal quashed Gnango's conviction. The prosecution appealed and the case reached the Supreme Court. By a majority of 6-1, the Supreme Court allowed the prosecution's appeal and restored Gnango's conviction. While different justifications were offered for the decision,[12] a majority of the Supreme Court judges (Lords Phillips, Judge, Wilson and Dyson) held that Gnango and Bandana Man were engaged in a joint enterprise to commit murder. They had a shared intention to have a shoot-out. Since both had an intention to kill or cause serious injury, the crime that Bandana Man committed – murder – was within the scope of their joint enterprise. The *actus reus* and *mens rea* of being an accessory to murder were therefore established.

The reasoning in *R* v *Gnango* has been criticised, for two reasons. First, imagine that Gnango had been shot and killed as Bandana Man intended. The Supreme Court's reasoning would lead to the conclusion that Gnango was encouraging his own murder. This seems artificial. As Lord Kerr stated in his dissenting judgment 'One might be alive to the very real risk that firing, if the target was not hit, would prompt return fire, but that is a significantly different thing from saying that this was encouragement to fire back. Being prepared to run the risk does not equate with encouraging an opponent to fire at you' ([123]). Second, it is questionable whether there was in fact a shared intention to have a shoot-out. A shoot-out involves not only firing at others, but also being fired at. Yet there were good reasons to think that neither man intended to be shot at. As Lord Kerr explained, 'It is at least just as likely that neither agreed to be fired on and that both hoped that they would avoid that unpleasant eventuality by hitting the target with their own shot' ([122]).

In spite of these difficulties, and the fact that *R* v *Gnango* was decided before the landmark case of *R* v *Jogee* (in which, as we will see below, the Supreme Court stated that proof of an agreement is not necessary to establish accessorial liability[13]), it was applied by the

[11] In *R* v *Jogee* [2016] UKSC 8, *Ruddock* v *The Queen* [2016] UKPC 7, the Supreme Court confirmed that 'the expression "joint enterprise" is not a legal term of art' ([77]).

[12] Lords Brown and Clark suggested that Gnango had made a significant contribution to Magda's death by causing Bandana Man to fire at him, and so Gnango was not merely an accessory to murder. Rather, he and Bandana Man were both liable for murder as joint principals.

[13] See further Virgo, G. (2024) 'The Return of Joint Enterprise' 83 *Cambridge Law Journal* 405.

Court of Appeal in *R* v *Seed* [2024] EWCA Crim 650. This case involved two rival gangs: the reds and the blues. The reds drove to an estate where members of the blues lived. When they arrived, there was an exchange of gunfire. A member of the reds was killed by one of the blues. Three members of the reds were charged with being accessories to the murder. At trial, they were convicted. Their appeals against conviction were dismissed. The Court of Appeal held that there was an agreement 'to shoot and be shot at' ([71]). It was no defence for the defendants to say that the victim was a member of their own side, since they had participated in the shoot-out intending to kill or cause serious injury. It is important to point out, however, that the principle from *R* v *Gnango* and *R* v *Seed* only applies if those involved know that it is virtually certain that the others are armed *and* will either open or return fire, *and* that they each intend to kill or cause serious injury. In *R* v *ARU* [2024] EWCA Crim 1101 such situations were described as 'rare' and 'anything but commonplace' ([48]). More common are cases involving groups of young men, some of whom are carrying knives, in which violence breaks out 'for no consequential reason' ([49]). Attempts to apply *R* v *Gnango* in such cases should be resisted, the Court said, unless there is 'very clear evidence of an agreement to stab and be stabbed' ([49]).[14]

Having looked at what constitutes a joint enterprise, we can now move on to the main focus of this section: what is the situation where one party to a joint enterprise steps outside the common purpose and commits some other offence. For example, suppose that, whilst Ronnie and Freddie were burgling Roshan's house, Roshan arrived home and disturbed them. Freddie had told Ronnie that he was going to take a gun with him for situations like this. Ronnie had urged him not to, but when Freddie insisted Ronnie said, 'Ok, as long as you only use it for show and don't shoot anyone'. But, upon seeing Roshan, Freddie took out the gun and fatally shot him. On these facts, Freddie is straightforwardly guilty of murder. But is Ronnie guilty as an accessory to the murder? In a line of cases that began with the Privy Council's decision in *Chan Wing-Siu* v *The Queen* [1985] AC 168, and included the House of Lords' decision in *R* v *Powell & Daniels*; *R* v *English* [1999] 1 AC 1, the courts held that where two people have a shared purpose to commit crime A, and during the commission of this crime one of them commits crime B, the other person will be liable as an accessory to crime B if the following four conditions are satisfied:

1. The parties must have been embarked on a joint enterprise
2. The offence must have been an incident of the joint enterprise
3. The defendant must have foreseen that the principal might commit the offence
4. The offence must have been of a type that the defendant foresaw.

Applying this to our example, Ronnie and Freddie were embarked on a joint enterprise and the murder was an incident of this. The prosecution would point to Ronnie's statement '... don't shoot anyone' to argue that Ronnie foresaw that Freddie *might* commit murder if they were disturbed during the burglary, and the killing was of the type that Ronnie foresaw (a shooting). So, under the law set out in *Chan Wing-Siu* and *R* v *Powell & Daniels*; *R* v *English*, Ronnie could be found guilty of being an accessory to the murder committed by Freddie. This became known as 'parasitic accessory liability'.[15]

Parasitic accessory liability was very controversial, particularly in homicide cases. For a principal like Freddie to be guilty of murder he must have intended to kill or cause GBH. But in cases of parasitic accessory liability, a defendant could be guilty of being

[14] For comment, see Krebs, B. (2025) 'Knife Fights and *Gnango*-Style Complicity: *R* v *ARU* [2024] EWCA Crim 1101' 89 *Journal of Criminal Law* 354.

[15] A term first used by Sir John Smith QC ('Criminal Liability of Accessories: Law and Law Reform' 113 *Law Quarterly Review* 453, 455).

an accessory to murder as long as he *foresaw* that the principal *might* commit murder (requirement 3 on the list above). In other words, a defendant like Ronnie could be guilty of being an accessory to murder – and therefore receive the mandatory life sentence – notwithstanding the fact that he had no intention that the victim should be killed or suffer GBH, nor any intention to assist or encourage the principal to commit murder.

In *R* v *Jogee* [2016] UKSC 8, *Ruddock* v *The Queen* [2016] UKPC 7, the Supreme Court was asked to reconsider the law set out in *Chan Wing-Siu* and *R* v *Powell & Daniels*; *R* v *English*. The certified point of general public importance was whether this law 'over-criminalises secondary parties'. In a judgment described as being of 'seminal' importance,[16] the Supreme Court rejected the approach taken in *Chan Wing-Siu*. In this section we are going to examine and evaluate the Supreme Court's judgment.

1. The law before *R* v *Jogee*

Before looking at the decision in *R* v *Jogee* itself, it is first worth examining in greater detail why parasitic accessory liability was so controversial.

EXTRACT

In the following extract Wilson and Ormerod discuss Simester's attempt to justify parasitic accessory liability.

What justification did Simester offer? Why do Wilson and Ormerod disagree with Simester? Who do you agree with, and why?

Wilson, W. and Ormerod, D. (2015) 'Simply Harsh to Fairly Simple: Joint Enterprise Reform' *Criminal Law Review* 3

Particularly in the case of murder, there is a significant injustice arising from the present state of the law founded on the joint enterprise approach. A conviction for being party to a joint enterprise may mean that D suffers all the consequences of a murder conviction, including the offence label and the mandatory sentence (ratcheted up in real terms by the Sch.21 tariffs to the Criminal Justice Act 2003), without necessarily having demonstrated any of the culpability or wrongdoing of the principal offender. Given that the wrong in murder is to kill with malice aforethought, to convict a secondary party of that crime simply upon proof of his contemplation or foresight that this may be what his principal has in mind takes considerable justification.

Simester offers one justification: it is not, in principle, wrong to punish D for the actions of P. By joining with P in a common criminal enterprise which has death as a foreseen outcome D changes his normative position in relation to that outcome. Rough justice it may be, he implies, but justice nevertheless, no less than GBH murder is [GBH murder is where someone is convicted of murder on the basis of the GBH rule]. We cannot absolve ourselves from responsibility for the consequences of our actions by blaming an unruly fate. That is not how our moral universe is organised. The problem with this argument in the context of PAL [parasitic accessory liability], however, is, as has been explained, that it fails to pay full regard to a central and defining feature underpinning criminal doctrine: that we must take responsibility for our own choices and their

[16] *R* v *Anwar* [2016] EWCA Crim 551, [20].

outcomes, not the choices of others and their outcomes. Standard accessorial liability accommodates this problem to a degree by basing the liability of secondary parties on their lending (unconditional) support to the criminal projects of the principal. This is why contemplation alone sufficed in *DPP of Northern Ireland* v *Maxwell*. In *Maxwell* D did not know precisely the crime to be committed, but by assisting P in the knowledge that P might intentionally commit one of a number of crimes, D was deemed, quite fairly, to have lent his support to any of those crimes, if committed. The unknown crime constitutes their common purpose. But in PAL, having lent support to one *crime*, D is also deemed to lend support to another merely because, although it forms no part of their common purpose, he has foreseen, out of the corner of his eye, the possibility that P might commit this further crime. Unconditional support is lent only to crime A and only constructive support, in effect, to crime B, a crime indeed which D may even have counselled his principal *not* to commit or which was at the periphery of his thinking when lending his support to crime A. What moral principle demands that I take responsibility not simply for the consequences of my own choices and those choices of my co-adventurer which I happen to share but also those which I do not share but happen to contemplate that he may, with a following wind, make at some stage in the future? In the specific context of murder, of course, the problem is exacerbated. D is liable despite not having chosen to kill; and not even having chosen to cause serious injury. D's choice, and *pace* Simester admittedly he makes one, is simply not to back out of a criminal enterprise when he realises that P may have more on his mind than what has been agreed. A conviction for murder, rather than manslaughter, is, given the power of the label and the mandatory sentence, not rough justice. It is injustice.

The extract from Wilson and Ormerod focuses on whether the rules governing parasitic accessory liability meant that, in homicide cases, defendants could be convicted of being an accessory to murder even though they were not sufficiently culpable to deserve the label 'murderer' and the mandatory life sentence. The following extract, taken from a report published by the House of Commons Justice Committee, discusses this issue in a broader context.

EXTRACT

Read the following extract from the Justice Committee's report and make a list of the concerns expressed by the witnesses to their enquiry.

How did the Government respond to these concerns?

House of Commons Justice Committee (2014) *Joint Enterprise: Follow-Up*, Fourth Report of Session 2014–15, HC 310

Joint enterprise as a social policy tool and a deterrent

26 Several of our witnesses used the metaphor of a "dragnet" to describe the operation of joint enterprise, claiming that it was hoovering up young people from ethnic minority communities who have peripheral, minor or even in some cases non-existent involvement in serious criminal acts, along with the principal perpetrators of those acts, and imposing draconian penalties on them. Melanie McFadyean argued that the doctrine was:

> a blunt powerful instrument operated crucially and centrally for social policy reasons as stated repeatedly in appeal court judgments and elsewhere, its remit to be tough on crime and to be seen to be so.

In oral evidence she cited a number of judgments and other sources in support of her contention. Other witnesses made similar arguments. Dr Dyson claimed that "The reason for the core of joint enterprise was almost certainly not normative or moral, but simply evidential and driven by policy. In particular, how do you deal with crimes with multiple defendants". Simon Natas of Irvine Thanvi Natas Solicitors argued that "The use of punitive law and order policies to combat youth crime is a blunt instrument which runs the risk of making matters worse, not only because young people are much less likely to cooperate with the authorities if they perceive the legal system to be unjust, but also because custodial sentences have been shown to increase, not reduce, reoffending".

27 A claim made in support of the use of joint enterprise is that it has the desirable effect of deterring young people from becoming involved in criminal activities associated with gangs. In 2009 the Metropolitan Police produced a video which has been shown in many schools in London to warn young people of the possible consequences for them of joint enterprise if they engage in gang activities; there has also been considerable publicity about some joint enterprise cases in recent years. Nevertheless, some of our witnesses expressed scepticism about the existence of a deterrent effect. Dr Crewe, for example, argued that:

> For deterrence to work, at least two conditions need to be met. One is that people are aware of the sanction or the penalty. As others have said, our experience in undertaking the research is that very few of our interviewees said that they had any idea of what joint enterprise was, or they had heard of it but understood it only vaguely, which is not surprising as it is difficult to understand ...
>
> The second condition that needs to be met is that, even among those who are aware of the sanction, it would have to have some impact on their behaviour ... We know from the research literature on deterrence that thinking that you will be caught has more of a deterrent effect than the length of sentence or the severity of the sanction.

28 We put to the Minister claims that the application of joint enterprise was being driven by social policy considerations, including the aim of deterring young people from involvement in criminal gang activities because of the severity of the penalties they might face. He said:

> We would all want people to think very carefully before they were involved in any crime, and the consequence of being involved in crime is the whole principle, I hope, of what we are looking at today. If it has an effect on gang culture, so be it. At the end of the day, my view - a non-legalistic view - is around justice. Justice for the victim is the most important thing.

29 We consider that there is a danger in justifying the joint enterprise doctrine on the basis that it sends a signal or delivers a wider social message. The application of the doctrine should be such as to ensure that people are found guilty of offences in accordance with the law as it currently stands, which includes the threshold of foresight for secondary participants. It is self-evident that if people are aware of the risk of conviction under joint enterprise, they should also recognize that involvement in gang activities which could lead to criminal offences may result in them being charged and convicted.

Joint enterprise and murder

36 One of the main influences on opinions about the fairness of the joint enterprise doctrine is the fact that, when a jury finds a secondary participant guilty of murder, a life sentence has to be imposed. Although the sentencer has some discretion in determining the tariff (the minimum term which must be served before a person is eligible for parole), a life sentence is potentially what its name indicates and release on completion of tariff is far from certain. The requirement to impose a life sentence in murder cases makes it all the more important that prosecutors exercise discriminatory judgment in deciding which charges to bring against each individual in cases where groups of people are involved and a death occurs. Because life sentences must be imposed on all those convicted of joint enterprise murder in such cases, it compounds the sense

of injustice on the part of those who believe that a convicted person did not intend that murder or serious harm should take place. They and their families contrast their secondary participation not only with person who dealt the fatal blow but also with murderers in other cases, and do not see it as appropriate that they have the same sentence. The mandatory life sentence also magnifies concerns over the *mens rea* threshold of foresight, through the contrast between the lowness of that threshold with the severity of the sentence on conviction. This contrast has been accentuated by the rise in the average minimum term of imprisonment imposed for a mandatory life sentence, from 12 years in 2003 to 21 years in 2013.

37 We asked the Minister whether the lack of flexibility and discretion in sentencing murder cases meant that it would be sensible to consider whether the doctrine of joint enterprise should be employed in those cases. He replied:

> That has been looked at, not only after previous reports from the Committee, but also by previous Secretaries of State. It is a really difficult decision. When people go to prison for a very long time, it has a huge effect on them and their families, but we have to balance that against their involvement under the legislation (*sic*). I understand where you are coming from, but it is a balance that has to be made to protect the public and to protect the victims.

2. The judgment in *R* v *Jogee*

Having looked at the criticisms of the old law, we can now turn to the judgment in *R* v *Jogee* [2016] UKSC 8, *Ruddock* v *The Queen* [2016] UKPC 7. The facts of these two cases, which the Supreme Court heard together, were as follows:

- Ameen Jogee spent the evening of 9 June 2011 with his co-defendant, Mohammed Hirsi. Shortly before midnight Jogee and Hirsi went to the home of a woman named Naomi Reid. There was an argument. Reid told them to leave and warned that her partner, Paul Fyfe, would be home soon. Jogee and Hirsi left, but added that they would be back later. A little later Hirsi returned to Reid's house alone. Reid phoned Jogee and told him to come and take Hirsi away. Jogee arrived, and the two men left. But soon after they returned to Reid's home once again. By now, Fyfe had also arrived at Reid's house. Whilst Fyfe was upstairs Hirsi went to the kitchen and picked up a knife. Jogee was armed with a bottle. When Fyfe came downstairs there was an angry exchange, during which Hirsi fatally stabbed Fyfe with the knife. At trial, Hirsi was convicted of murder and Jogee was convicted of being an accessory to the murder.
- Shirley Ruddock was convicted of being an accessory to the murder of Pete Robinson. Ruddock and his co-defendant, a man named Hudson, had stolen Robinson's car. Robinson was later found with his hands and feet tied and his throat cut. Hudson pleaded guilty to the murder. The prosecution's case was that Ruddock had assisted the murder by tying Robinson's hands and feet.

The Supreme Court's judgment, handed down by Lord Hughes and Lord Toulson JJSC, began by recounting a line of cases, from *R* v *Collison* (1831) 4 Car & P 565 to *R* v *Reid (Barry)* (1975) 62 Cr App R 109. These cases had established an important point, they explained, that parties to a joint enterprise could only be guilty of being an accessory to murder if they intentionally encouraged or assisted the principal to commit murder. In *Chan Wing-Siu*, however, the Privy Council departed from these authorities. According to *Chan Wing-Siu*, if P and D agree to commit crime A, and in the course of it P commits crime B, D may be convicted of being an accessory to crime B even if he did not intend for crime B to be committed, as long as he foresaw it as a possibility. Lords Hughes and Toulson said that this fails to distinguish between foresight and intention:

> [T]he rule in *Chan Wing-Siu* makes guilty those who foresee crime B but never intended it or wanted it to happen. There can be no doubt that if D2 continues to participate in crime A with foresight that D1 may commit crime B, that is evidence, and sometimes powerful evidence, of an intent to assist D1 in crime B. But it is evidence of such intent (or, if one likes, of "authorisation"), not conclusive of it ([66])

Having concluded that in *Chan Wing-Siu* the 'law took a wrong turn' ([87]), the next question for the Supreme Court in *R* v *Jogee* was whether to reverse 'a statement of principle which has been made and followed by the Privy Council and the House of Lords on a number of occasions' ([79]). The Court offered five reasons for so doing:

EXTRACT

R v *Jogee* [2016] UKSC 8, *Ruddock* v *The Queen* [2016] UKPC 7

Lord Hughes and Lord Toulson JJSC

80 Firstly, we have had the benefit of a much fuller analysis than on previous occasions when the topic has been considered. In *Chan Wing-Siu* only two English cases were referred to in the judgment – *Anderson and Morris* and *Davies*. More were referred to in the judgments in *Powell and English*, but they did not include (among others) *Collison*, *Skeet*, *Spraggett* or notably *Reid*.

81 Secondly, it cannot be said that the law is now well established and working satisfactorily. It remains highly controversial and a continuing source of difficulty for trial judges. It has also led to large numbers of appeals.

82 Thirdly, secondary liability is an important part of the common law, and if a wrong turn has been taken, it should be corrected.

83 Fourthly, in the common law foresight of what might happen is ordinarily no more than evidence from which a jury can infer the presence of a requisite intention. It may be strong evidence, but its adoption as a test for the mental element for murder in the case of a secondary party is a serious and anomalous departure from the basic rule, which results in over-extension of the law of murder and reduction of the law of manslaughter. Murder already has a relatively low *mens rea* threshold, because it includes an intention to cause serious injury, without intent to kill or to cause risk to life. The *Chan Wing-Siu* principle extends liability for murder to a secondary party on the basis of a still lesser degree of culpability, namely foresight only of the possibility that the principal may commit murder but without there being any need for intention to assist him to do so. It savours, as Professor Smith suggested, of constructive crime.

84 Fifthly, the rule brings the striking anomaly of requiring a lower mental threshold for guilt in the case of the accessory than in the case of the principal.

85 As to the argument that even if the court is satisfied that the law took a wrong turn, any correction should now be left to Parliament, the doctrine of secondary liability is a common law doctrine (put into statutory form in section 8 of the 1861 Act) and, if it has been unduly widened by the courts, it is proper for the courts to correct the error.

The Supreme Court then set out the correct approach. It emphasised that 'joint enterprise' is not a legal term and there are no special rules that apply to so-called joint enterprise cases. In all cases, the 'ordinary principles of secondary liability' should be applied ([76]). In other words, even in a case which might be described as a joint enterprise you should apply the same *actus reus* and *mens rea* requirements as for any other case involving accessories. These are the three requirements that we worked through earlier in the chapter.

As well as clarifying the correct approach, the Supreme Court offered some guidance on the application of the *actus reus* and *mens rea* requirements of being an accessory in joint enterprise cases. Five points are worth noting. First, if the prosecution is able to prove the existence of a common purpose, this is likely to be sufficient to constitute proof of the *actus reus* and *mens rea* requirements of being an accessory:

> 78 As we have explained, secondary liability does not require the existence of an agreement between D1 and D2. Where, however, it exists, such agreement is by its nature a form of encouragement and in most cases will also involve acts of assistance. The long established principle that where parties agree to carry out a criminal venture, each is liable for acts to which they have expressly or impliedly given their assent is an example of the intention to assist which is inherent in the making of the agreement. Similarly, where people come together without agreement, often spontaneously, to commit an offence together, the giving of intentional support by words or deeds, including by supportive presence, is sufficient to attract secondary liability on ordinary principles. We repeat that secondary liability includes cases of agreement between principal and secondary party, but it is not limited to them.

As this extract illustrates, however, it is possible to establish the *actus reus* and *mens rea* requirements of being an accessory without proving that the parties shared a common purpose. Accordingly, in some cases – such as those involving a spontaneous outbreak of violence – it may be better to avoid the language of joint enterprise and common purpose:

> 95 In cases where there is a more or less spontaneous outbreak of multi-handed violence, the evidence may be too nebulous for the jury to find that there was some form of agreement, express or tacit. But, as we have said, liability as an aider or abettor does not necessarily depend on there being some form of agreement between the defendants; it depends on proof of intentional assistance or encouragement, conditional or otherwise. If D2 joins with a group which he realises is out to cause serious injury, the jury may well infer that he intended to encourage or assist the deliberate infliction of serious bodily injury and/or intended that that should happen if necessary. In that case, if D1 acts with intent to cause serious bodily injury and death results, D1 and D2 will each be guilty of murder.

Second, earlier in the chapter we considered the example of the shopkeeper who sells a customer a gun knowing that the customer might use it to commit a murder, not caring whether the customer commits the murder or not. The customer subsequently commits the murder. We saw that the shopkeeper satisfied the first *mens rea* requirement of being an accessory: he (obliquely) intended to assist the customer to commit the murder. His liability therefore hinges on the second *mens rea* requirement. It was not the shopkeeper's direct intention that the murder would be committed. His purpose was to make a profit on the sale, and he would not have considered it a failure if the victim had not been killed. Nor was it his oblique intention to assist the murder. He knew the customer might commit the offence, but he did not foresee it as virtually certain. The Supreme Court in *R* v *Jogee* seemed to confirm this analysis:

> [10] ... [T]here can be cases where D2 gives intentional assistance or encouragement to D1 to commit an offence and to act with the mental element required of him, but without D2 having a positive intent that the particular offence will be committed. That may be so, for example, where at the time that encouragement is given it remains uncertain what D1 might do; an arms supplier might be such a case.

Third, the Court noted that the defendant's intention may be conditional – indeed, in cases involving joint enterprises, it often will be:

> 92 In cases of secondary liability arising out of a prior joint criminal venture, it will also often be necessary to draw the jury's attention to the fact that the intention to assist, and indeed the intention that the crime should be committed, may be conditional. The bank robbers who attack the bank when one or more of them is armed no doubt hope that it will not be necessary to use the guns, but it may be a perfectly proper inference that all were intending that if they met resistance the weapons should be used with the intent to do grievous bodily harm at least. The group of young men which faces down a rival group may hope that the rivals will slink quietly away, but it may well be a perfectly proper inference that all were intending that if resistance were to be met, grievous bodily harm at least should be done.

Similarly, where a group of young men set out to attack a specific person, they may also have a conditional intention to attack anyone that should happen to get in their way.[17]

Fourth, we saw above that under the old law the final requirement of parasitic accessory liability was that the offence that the principal committed was of a type that the defendant foresaw. This often required juries to consider whether the attack that occurred was of a different type to the attack that the defendant foresaw, in particular, whether an attack with one weapon (such as a gun) was of a different type to an attack with a different weapon (such as a knife). In *R v Jogee* the Supreme Court stated that the emphasis should shift away from the weapon used and towards whether the defendant intended to assist or encourage the crime committed:

> 98 … The tendency which has developed in the application of the rule in *Chan Wing-Siu* to focus on what D2 knew of what weapon D1 was carrying can and should give way to an examination of whether D2 intended to assist in the crime charged. If that crime is murder, then the question is whether he intended to assist the intentional infliction of grievous bodily harm at least, which question will often, as set out above, be answered by asking simply whether he himself intended grievous bodily harm at least. Very often he may intend to assist in violence using whatever weapon may come to hand. In other cases he may think that D1 has an iron bar whereas he turns out to have a knife, but the difference may not at all affect his intention to assist, if necessary, in the causing of grievous bodily harm at least. Knowledge or ignorance that weapons generally, or a particular weapon, is carried by D1 will be evidence going to what the intention of D2 was, and may be irresistible evidence one way or the other, but it is evidence and no more.

Lastly, the Supreme Court discussed the position in a homicide case in which P and D violently attack the victim, P is guilty of murder, but D lacked the *mens rea* of being an accessory to murder. The Court stated that 'If a person is a party to a violent attack on another, without an intent to assist in the causing of death or really serious harm, but the violence escalates and results in death, he will be not guilty of murder but guilty of manslaughter' ([96]). This would normally be because D intended to assist or encourage the infliction of some harm falling short of GBH, but is not limited to such cases. It is sufficient that D knew or intended that P would commit an act that was unlawful and which the reasonable person would have realised involved a risk of some harm (see the dangerousness test for unlawful act manslaughter, detailed in Chapter 5). In fact, in such a case, the Court stated that D would only escape liability for being an accessory to manslaughter if the death was 'caused by some overwhelming supervening act by the perpetrator which nobody in the defendant's

[17] *R v BHV* [2022] EWCA Crim 1690. The application of this to the facts of *R v BHV* has been criticised for involving a speculative leap: see Wong, A. H. L. (2023) 'Speculative leap in inferring conditional intent' 82 *Cambridge Law Journal* 228. For a contrasting view, see Freer, E. (2024) 'Commentary on *R v BHV* [2022] EWCA Crim 1690' *Criminal Law Review* 181.

shoes could have contemplated might happen and is of such a character as to relegate his acts to history' ([97]). In other words, anything done or said by D must have 'faded to the point of mere background' ([12]). This is a high threshold.[18] It does not apply if the cause of death was simply the 'escalation of a fight' ([33]).[19] Nor would it apply because P uses a weapon of which D was unaware.[20] In fact, Krebs suggests that an act will only qualify as overwhelming and supervening if it was both wholly unexpected (from the perspective of general life experience) and so momentous as to consign the accessory's deeds to history.[21] The fact that knives are often produced in violent incidents means that P producing a knife of which D was unaware cannot be regarded as wholly unexpected.

So, in cases involving fights between rival gangs, if D did not form the *mens rea* necessary to be convicted of being an accessory to murder, he will almost inevitably be convicted of being an accessory to manslaughter instead. The Supreme Court said that this undermined one of the key policy reasons for the decision in *Chan Wing-Siu*. In that case, the Privy Council stated 'Where a man lends himself to a criminal enterprise knowing that potentially murderous weapons are to be carried, and in the event they in fact are used by his partner with an intent sufficient for murder, he should not escape the consequences'. The Court in *R v Jogee* stated that this wrongly implied that, were it not for the decision in *Chan Wing-Siu*, D 'would escape all criminal liability' ([74]). Moreover, the Court added, 'There was no consideration in *Chan Wing-Siu*, or in *Powell and English*, of the fundamental policy question whether and why it was necessary and appropriate to reclassify such conduct as murder rather than manslaughter. Such a discussion would have involved, among other things, questions about fair labelling and fair discrimination in sentencing' ([74]).[22] The Court continued:

> 75 In *Powell and English* Lord Hutton referred to the need to give effective protection to the public against criminals operating in gangs (at p 25), but the same comments apply. There does not appear to have been any objective evidence that the law prior to *Chan Wing-Siu*

[18] Simester and Stark also argue that, in practice, the language of overwhelming supervening acts has obscured the need for the prosecution to establish the *actus reus* and *mens rea* requirements of being an accessory, particularly the requirement to prove that the crime that the accessory intentionally encouraged or assisted was a cause of the victim's death. See Simester, A. P. and Stark, F. (2025) 'Overwhelming Supervening Acts – A Corrective' 84 *Cambridge Law Journal* 345.

[19] For example, in *R v Grant* [2021] EWCA Crim 1243 the defendants armed themselves with weapons and drove around until they found the victim. Instead of getting out of the car and confronting the victim face-to-face, as originally agreed, the driver drove into the victim, killing him. Grant, who had been in the front passenger seat, argued that the driver's departure from the agreed plan rendered the original plan obsolete and so was an overwhelming supervening act. This was rejected by the Court of Appeal. The Court explained that there was nothing to suggest that the driver's actions were so 'distanced in time, place or circumstances' from the conduct of the defendant that it would not be realistic to regard the driver's offence as encouraged or assisted by the defendant. The Court went on to state: 'Save perhaps for exceptional circumstances which are not readily easy to envisage, there will be no need to direct the jury on the concept of [an overwhelming supervening act] simply because the fatal injuries were inflicted using an entirely different kind of weapon or method of killing than that originally contemplated and/or the perpetrator intended to kill rather than to inflict really serious harm' ([38]). This was cited with approval and applied in *R v Ayre* [2025] EWCA Crim 255. For comment, see Krebs, B. (2022) 'Causation, Remoteness and the Concept of the "Overwhelming Supervening Act"' 86 *Journal of Criminal Law* 42.

[20] *R v Tas* [2018] EWCA Crim 2603, followed in *R v Harper* [2019] EWCA Crim 343, *R v Lanning* [2021] EWCA Crim 450 and *R v Smith* [2022] EWCA Crim 1808. For comment, see Krebs, B. (2021) 'Underwhelming supervening acts' 85 *Journal of Criminal Law* 403.

[21] Krebs, B. 'Overwhelming Supervening Acts, Fundamental Differences, and Back Again?' 86 *Journal of Criminal Law* 420. She argues that the overwhelming, supervening act test should be regarded as a remoteness principle that seeks to limit accessorial liability for murder and manslaughter on grounds of fair attribution.

[22] For an argument that, in such a case, a conviction for being an accessory to manslaughter is unsatisfactory – and that a new, lesser offence should be created titled 'Risking another's collateral offending' – see Wang, V.B. (2019) 'A Normative Case for Abolishing the Doctrine of Extended Joint Criminal Enterprise' 83 *Journal of Criminal Law* 144.

failed to provide the public with adequate protection. A further policy reason suggested by Lord Hutton for setting a lower *mens rea* requirement for the secondary party than for the principal was that the secondary party has time to think before taking part in a criminal enterprise like a bank robbery, whereas the principal may have to decide on the spur of the moment whether to use his weapon. But the principal has had an earlier choice whether to go armed or not. As for the secondary party, he may have leisure to think before going out to rob a bank, but the same is not true in many other cases (for example, of young people who become suddenly embroiled in a fight in a bar and may make a quick decision whether or not to help their friends).

Assessment advice

So, if you are answering a problem question that involves a joint, fatal, violent attack, when discussing the liability of the secondary parties you should begin by considering whether they are guilty of being an accessory to murder. Here you apply the normal *actus reus* and *mens rea* requirements of being an accessory, as follows:

---

1. Did D aid, abet, counsel or procure the commission of murder by P? (i.e. did D's actions in fact provide encouragement or assistance to P?)
2. Did D intend to aid, abet, counsel or procure the commission of murder by P? (i.e. did D intend to aid, abet, counsel or procure either the intentional killing of V by P, or the intentional causing of GBH to V by P?)
3. Did D know or intend the essential elements of P's offence? (i.e. was it D's direct intention that P should intentionally kill or cause GBH to V? If not, did D know that it was virtually certain that P would intentionally kill or cause GBH to V?)

Assessment advice

If the defendant lacks the necessary *mens rea* of being an accessory to murder, then you should instead consider whether he is guilty of being an accessory to manslaughter. The relevant type of manslaughter will be unlawful act manslaughter, and so the *actus reus* and *mens rea* requirements will be as follows:

---

1. Did D aid, abet, counsel or procure the commission of manslaughter by P? (i.e. did D's actions in fact provide encouragement or assistance to P?)
2. Did D intend to aid, abet, counsel or procure the commission of manslaughter by P? (i.e. did D intend to aid, abet, counsel or procure the intentional commission by P of an act, where that act was unlawful, dangerous and was the cause of V's death?)
3. Did D know or intend the essential elements of P's offence? (i.e. was it D's direct intention that P should intentionally commit the unlawful, dangerous act that caused V's death? If not, did D know that it was virtually certain that P would intentionally commit the unlawful, dangerous act that caused V's death?)

Having set out the correct approach, the Supreme Court then considered the position of the two defendants, Jogee and Ruddock. At the trials of both men, the trial judge had given a jury direction based on the *Chan Wing-Siu* principle. As such, their murder convictions could not stand. Jogee was subsequently retried. At his retrial, the jury acquitted him of being an accessory to murder but convicted him of being an accessory to manslaughter.[23] In Ruddock's case, the Jamaican Court of Appeal concluded that there should not be a retrial, and instead substituted a conviction of being an accessory to manslaughter.[24]

3. Evaluation of *R* v *Jogee*

In its judgment in *R* v *Jogee*, the Supreme Court addressed the concern that the effect of its decision would be 'to render invalid all convictions which were arrived at over many years by faithfully applying the law as laid down in *Chan Wing-Siu* and in *Powell and English*' ([100]). Rejecting this concern, the Court explained:

> 100 … The error identified, of equating foresight with intent to assist rather than treating the first as evidence of the second, is important as a matter of legal principle, but it does not follow that it will have been important on the facts to the outcome of the trial or to the safety of the conviction. Moreover, where a conviction has been arrived at by faithfully applying the law as it stood at the time, it can be set aside only by seeking exceptional leave to appeal to the Court of Appeal out of time. That court has power to grant such leave, and may do so if substantial injustice be demonstrated, but it will not do so simply because the law applied has now been declared to have been mistaken

So, whilst for appeals against conviction brought within time (i.e. within 28 days) the key criterion is whether the conviction is unsafe, for appeals brought out of time an extra hurdle applies. Leave to appeal will only be granted if 'substantial injustice' can be demonstrated. As the Supreme Court indicated, this is a high threshold.

The 'invidious task of determining how this concept [substantial injustice] ought to be applied in the context of an individual who has been convicted of a serious criminal offence, often murder, based upon what the Supreme Court has since characterised as being a legal wrong turn'[25] fell to the Court of Appeal in *R* v *Johnson* [2016] EWCA Crim 1613. In this case, the Court of Appeal considered the cases of 13 men. Between them, these 13 men had been involved in a total of six separate incidents of violence. Five of the six victims died; the other was stabbed. Twelve of the men were convicted of being accessories to murder, the other was convicted of wounding with intent to cause GBH.[26] All 13 were convicted prior to the Supreme Court's judgment in *R* v *Jogee* and sought leave to appeal against their convictions.

EXTRACT

Read the following extract from the Court of Appeal's judgment.

What are the policy reasons for the 'substantial injustice' requirement? What factors will the courts take into account when determining whether this requirement is met?

[23] 'Ameen Jogee jailed for manslaughter in joint enterprise test case', *The Guardian*, 12 September 2016.

[24] *Shirley Ruddock* v *R* [2017] JMCA Crim 6.

[25] Laird, K. (2017) 'Commentary on *R* v *Johnson*' *Criminal Law Review* 216, 218.

[26] Offences Against the Person Act 1861, s. 18. He was convicted on the basis that the prosecution had established that he was either a principal or an accessory.

R v *Johnson* [2016] EWCA Crim 1613

Lord Thomas CJ, Sir Brian Leveson P and Lady Hallett LJ, V-P

18 In our view, as was accepted, the fact that there has been a change in the law brought about by correcting the wrong turning in *Chan Wing-Siu* and *R* v *Powell*, *R* v *English* is plainly, in itself, insufficient. As the Supreme Court stated at paragraph 100, a long line of authority clearly establishes that if a person was properly convicted on the law as it then stood, the court will not grant leave without it being demonstrated that a substantial injustice would otherwise be done. The need to establish substantial injustice results from the wider public interest in legal certainty and the finality of decisions made in accordance with the then clearly established law. The requirement takes into account the requirement in a common law system for a court to be able to alter or correct the law upon which a large number of cases have been determined without the consequence that each of those cases can be re-opened. It also takes into account the interests of the victim (or the victim's family), particularly in cases where death has resulted and closure is particularly important.

[...]

21 In determining whether that high threshold has been met, the court will primarily and ordinarily have regard to the strength of the case advanced that the change in the law would, in fact, have made a difference. If crime A is a crime of violence which the jury concluded must have involved the use of a weapon so that the inference of participation with an intention to cause really serious harm is strong, that is likely to be very difficult. At the other end of the spectrum, if crime A is a different crime, not involving intended violence or use of force, it may well be easier to demonstrate substantial injustice. The court will also have regard to other matters including whether the applicant was guilty of other, though less serious, criminal conduct. It is not, however, in our view, material to consider the length of time that has elapsed. If there was a substantial injustice, it is irrelevant whether that injustice occurred a short time or a long time ago. It is and remains an injustice.

The guidance in *R* v *Johnson* makes it clear that the substantial injustice requirement will only be met in the 'rarest of cases'.[27] Indeed, the Court of Appeal refused all 13 men leave to appeal against their convictions.[28]

---

[27] Laird, K. (2017) 'Commentary on *R* v *Johnson*' *Criminal Law Review* 216, 220. Similarly, in *R* v *Anwar* [2016] EWCA Crim 551 the Court of Appeal emphasized that 'the same facts which would previously have been used to support the inference of *mens rea* before the decision in *Jogee* will equally be used now. What has changed is the articulation of the *mens rea* …' ([22]), and so it is 'difficult to foresee circumstances in which there might have been a case to answer under the law before *Jogee* but, because of the way in which the law is now articulated, there no longer is' ([20]).

[28] The first case in which a defendant succeeded in demonstrating substantial injustice was *R* v *Crilly* [2018] EWCA Crim 168. Crilly and two other men planned to burgle a flat that they believed was unoccupied. They were not armed and no violence was intended. Having entered the flat, they discovered that the owner, 71-year-old Mr Maduemezia, was in fact inside (he had not answered the front door because he was hard-of-hearing and had not heard the knock on the door). One of the other men, David Flynn, punched Mr Maduemezia, causing him to fall over. He died from the head injuries he suffered. At trial, Flynn was convicted of murder and Crilly was convicted of being an accessory to the murder. On appeal, the Court of Appeal stated that the prosecution's case against Crilly 'was to all intents and purposes a case about his foresight', adding that 'The evidence against him was not so strong that we can safely and fairly infer the jury would have found the requisite intent to cause really serious bodily harm had the issue been left to them by the judge' ([40]). There was thus a strong argument that a *R* v *Jogee* compliant direction would have made a difference and so the substantial injustice requirement was met. A retrial was ordered. Before the retrial, Crilly pleaded guilty to manslaughter.

The extract from *R* v *Johnson* above states that, when applying the substantial injustice requirement, the primary factor to consider is whether the outcome at the defendant's trial would have been any different had the jury been asked to apply the law as stated in *R* v *Jogee* instead of *Chan Wing-Siu*.[29] Here, the notion of conditional intention may play a significant role. One of the incidents considered in *R* v *Johnson* involved a man named Michael Hall. The violence in Hall's case occurred outside a pub late at night, and was between two groups. One group included Michael Hall, a woman named Laura Mitchell (who we will discuss later in the chapter), and the eventual killer, Carl Holmes. The other group included the victim, Andrew Ayres, and two brothers, Craig and Dean Powell. The incident began with an argument over a taxi. Hall, Mitchell and Holmes were all involved in the violence, punching and kicking members of the other group. There was then a lull in the violence. Some of Hall and Mitchell's group (but not Hall and Mitchell themselves) walked down the road to a friend's house, where they collected a knuckleduster, a CS spray canister and a medieval mace. When they returned, the members of the other group realised that they were about to be attacked again and tried to run away. Craig Powell escaped, but Hall caught Dean Powell, pulled him to the ground and punched and kicked him. Andrew Ayres was also caught and knocked over. Carl Holmes then stamped on Ayres' head with such force that he died from his injuries. At trial Hall and Mitchell were both convicted of being accessories to Ayres' murder.

In *R* v *Johnson* Hall argued that he would not have been convicted of being an accessory to Ayres' murder had the prosecution been required to prove that he intended to encourage or assist the infliction of serious injury on the victim (as required by *R* v *Jogee*), and so therefore his conviction was unsafe. The Court of Appeal rejected this, stating:

> The jury must by their verdict have concluded that [Hall] foresaw that Holmes would attack the third member of the group, the deceased, with intent to cause really serious bodily injury. In the circumstances it would have been open to them to infer that he had the necessary conditional intent now required ([189]).

Therefore, the Court said, there was not 'a sufficiently strong case that the defendant would not have been convicted of murder if the law had been explained to the jury as set out in *Jogee*', and so substantial injustice had not been established ([191]). In the following extract, Stark discusses the Court's reasoning, particularly its use of the notion of conditional intention.

EXTRACT

In this extract Stark suggests that the approach to conditional intention in *R* v *Johnson* means that few instances of substantial injustice will be found, and that *R* v *Jogee* may have changed little. Why?

[29] Similarly, in *R* v *McLeod & others* [2017] EWCA Crim 800 the Court of Appeal held that the substantial injustice threshold had not been met because the inference of the necessary intention was 'irresistible' and so a *R* v *Jogee* compliant direction 'would not have made a difference' ([48]). See also *R* v *Quinn* [2017] EWCA Crim 1071, *R* v *Grant-Murray*; *R* v *McGill* [2017] EWCA Crim 1228, *R (on the application of Davies)* v *Criminal Cases Review* Commission [2018] EWHC 3080 (Admin), *R* v *Towers* [2019] EWCA Crim 198, *R* v *Daley* (Kyrone) [2019] EWCA Crim 627 and *Cunliffe* v *Criminal Cases Review Commission* [2019] EWHC 926 (Admin).

Stark, F. (2017) 'The Taming of *Jogee*?' 76 *Cambridge Law Journal* 4

Those appeals heard in *Johnson* that engaged the two-crime analysis characteristic of PAL [parasitic accessory liability], and where the jury was directed in terms of foresight of crime B, were scuppered by the Court's willingness to use *D1's* foresight to find a conditional intention on his part to assist or encourage *D2* intentionally to cause (at least) GBH, if such violence proved necessary. *Jogee* is clear that such conditional intention will suffice for accessorial liability for murder. If such a conditional intention is found on the facts, then it will not be possible to argue that manslaughter was a more appropriate verdict.

A good example of the Court's broad approach to conditional intention is the appeal in *Hall*. That the defendant "foresaw that [*D2*] would attack [*V*] ... with intent to cause really serious bodily injury" was found to be consistent with a finding of conditional intention to assist or encourage the intentional causing of GBH (at [189]). Here (despite the Court's vague reference to "the circumstances" of the case), conditional intention looks suspiciously like foresight of crime B combined with a decision to continue with the original plan to commit crime A, namely PAL. If conditional intention to assist or encourage offending can easily be found in such cases, the impact of *Jogee* on past convictions will be limited: few will be unsafe, and few instances of "substantial injustice" will be found, because the jury will (having applied *Chan Wing-Siu*, etc.) have been sure that the defendant foresaw crime B's possible commission in the course of crime A's commission. *Johnson* may also suggest that, in the future, convictions for murder could legitimately be returned routinely – on the post-*Jogee* basis of conditional intention – in cases where the defendant foresaw the possibility of GBH being caused intentionally, and continued with an underlying criminal plan nonetheless. This will be particularly the case where the defendant knew that the principal was armed (e.g. at [21]). In short, *Jogee* may have changed little.

As well as looking suspiciously like the *Chan Wing-Siu* test of foresight,[30] there is a further, conceptual, problem with the courts' approach to conditional intention in *R* v *Jogee* and *R* v *Johnson*. As Simester has explained,[31] if D has a conditional intention, that intention must relate to a future action by D himself (such as where D opens the back door of a lorry intending to steal the contents, should they turn out to be valuable). D cannot have a conditional intention that relates to the future action of someone else. If D lends P a baseball bat for P to use to attack his business partner, V, should V continue to help himself to money from their business, then it is P whose intention is conditional. Importantly, once D has passed the baseball bat to P, the *actus reus* of accessorial liability has occurred. D has aided P. The question is whether D intended to assist P to attack V. D either had such an intention or he didn't.[32] He cannot have had a conditional intention to assist, because he had already provided assistance!

---

[30] See also *R* v *Agera* [2017] EWCA Crim 740 (in which the Court of Appeal concluded: 'Once the jury concluded that Lansana knew that Agera might use the knife to stab (i.e. he had that conditional intent), its size could only lead the jury to conclude that he intended that, if used, at least serious bodily injury would be caused' ([36])) and *R* v *Johnson Haynes* [2019] EWCA Crim 1217 (in which the Court of Appeal concluded: 'He knew before the group attack began that the one of the attackers had a knife with him and had the foresight that that man may use that knife to kill or cause grievous bodily harm. In our judgment, this provides a powerful case that he was a party to a joint enterprise in which he personally intended that grievous bodily harm would be inflicted' ([45])).

[31] Simester, A. (2017) 'Accessory Liability and Common Unlawful Purposes' 133 *Law Quarterly Review* 73.

[32] See also Child, J. (2017) 'Understanding Ulterior Mens Rea: Future Conduct Intention is Conditional Intention' 76 *Cambridge Law Journal* 311.

So, suppose that Roshan owes Freddie some money. Freddie wants to be paid, so asks Ronnie to come with him to 'rough Roshan up a bit'. Although Ronnie knows that Freddie is carrying a knife, he agrees to go with him because Freddie says he will only use the knife if 'Roshan pulls a knife on me first'. But, when they confront Roshan, Freddie immediately pulls out the knife and fatally stabs him. If Ronnie was charged with being an accessory to the murder, the first step would be to establish the *actus reus*. If Ronnie was found to have provided assistance or encouragement by agreeing to go with Freddie, the *actus reus* would be established. The next question would be whether, when he provided this assistance/encouragement, Ronnie had an intention to assist or encourage Freddie to kill or cause GBH to Roshan. Properly analysed, this is not an instance of conditional intention, for the reason explained above. The correct approach is to begin by asking whether, when he agreed to go with Freddie, it was Ronnie's direct intention to assist or encourage Freddie to intentionally kill or cause GBH to Roshan. If not, the next question is whether it was Ronnie's oblique intention.

This brings us to another criticism of the reasoning in *R* v *Jogee*. The Supreme Court stated clearly that foresight must be distinguished from intention. Foresight is evidence from which (oblique) intention may be inferred.[33] Yet it did not explicitly state the degree of foresight that is required for (oblique) intention to be inferred. In particular, it did not say whether the *R* v *Woollin* direction should be used in this context. This omission is discussed by Ormerod and Laird in the following extract.

EXTRACT

In the following extract, what is the omission to which Ormerod and Laird refer? What issues do they say arise as a result of this omission?

Ormerod, D. and Laird, K. (2016) '*Jogee*: Not the End of a Legal Saga but the Start of One?' *Criminal Law Review* 539

What the Supreme Court failed to mention is the fact that the common law, in the context of murder at least, imposes a high threshold on the types of foresight from which a jury will be entitled to infer intent. After over 25 years or so of incremental narrowing (i.e. from *Hyam* – *Woollin*), the House of Lords finally agreed in *Woollin* that: (1) the defendant can be guilty of murder as a principal offender where he intended to kill or cause really serious harm; (2) intention is not limited to purpose or desire; (3) a jury is not entitled to "find" that the defendant intended to kill or cause really serious harm unless they conclude that death or really serious harm was a virtually certain consequence, barring some unforeseen intervention, and the defendant appreciated that this was the case; (4) there is a threshold on foresight – anything less than foresight of virtual certainty will not be sufficient to entitle the jury to find intention; and (5) foresight is merely evidence and does not equal intention, given that the Court of Appeal subsequently confirmed in *Matthews and Alleyne* that the law has not yet reached a definition of intent in murder in terms of appreciation of a virtual certainty. Therefore the jury retains its "moral elbow room".

[33] Note that the Supreme Court in *R* v *Jogee* repeatedly used the word 'infer', notwithstanding the fact that the House of Lords preferred the word 'find' instead of 'infer' in the *R* v *Woollin* direction (see Chapter 4).

In *Jogee*, the Supreme Court concluded that: (1) the defendant can be guilty of murder as a secondary offender where he intended to assist or encourage the principal to kill or cause really serious harm with intent; (2) intention is not limited to purpose or desire; and (3) a jury may "infer" that the defendant possessed the requisite intent if they conclude that he foresaw the principal's intentional conduct. Crucially, however, there is no explicit statement as to what threshold of foresight the defendant must possess before the jury will be entitled to infer the requisite intent – will the defendant's foresight of even the slightest possibility of the principal intentionally acting in the proscribed way be sufficient for a jury to be entitled to infer that he possessed the requisite intention? Alternatively, does there have to be a high level of foresight before the jury will be entitled to infer from this foresight that he possessed the requisite intention? It is the failure to specify what intention means in this context that could lead to difficulty.

[...]

It is unclear whether it is safe to conclude from this omission that the Supreme Court did not intend for some version of the *Woollin* direction to apply. The House of Lords in *Woollin* did expressly state that its decision applied only to murder and did not state whether it extended to accessorial liability. Indeed, Lord Steyn prefaced his judgment in *Woollin* by remarking that intention does not necessarily have the same meaning in every context of the criminal law. To the extent that the restatement of the law in *Jogee* applies in non-murder cases, a different formulation may therefore be applicable anyway. There will, we suggest, be considerable reluctance to apply the virtual certainty test, because if applied rigorously that test will mean that it will be difficult to secure convictions for murder for any participant.

It is submitted that there are three issues arising as a result of this uncertainty around foresight and intention. First, it is unclear how judges are to direct juries on the law. Different judges may direct juries in different ways, which makes resolution of this issue a priority. Secondly, as a matter of principle, there is lack of clarity on whether there ought to be parity as to the level of foresight required of the principal and the accessory. Resolution of this issue is made more complicated by the fact that two different questions are being asked. In relation to the principal, the issue relates to a consequence, whereas for the accessory, the issue is partly about someone else's state of mind. Thirdly, without speedy resolution by the Court of Appeal there is the danger that the debate the House of Lords sought to put an end to in *Woollin* will be replayed which would be undesirable as the law would be thrown into a state of confusion.

Returning to the example involving Freddie and Ronnie, imagine that they were standing trial as co-defendants: Freddie charged with the murder of Roshan; and, Ronnie charged as an accessory to this murder. Now imagine that the trial judge deems it necessary to explain the meaning of 'oblique intention' to the jury. If you were a juror, you would probably find it confusing to be told that: (1) if Ronnie foresaw that Freddie might kill or cause GBH to Roshan, you may 'infer' from this that he (obliquely) intended to assist or encourage Freddie to kill or cause GBH; but, (2) you may only 'find' that Freddie (obliquely) intended to kill or cause GBH to Roshan if he foresaw death or GBH as a virtual certainty (as per *R* v *Woollin*). As Ormerod and Laird state, it is not clear why there should be this disparity between principals and accessories, and there is a danger that some – but not all – trial judges will direct juries in accordance with *R* v *Woollin* in respect of both principals and accessories, resulting in uncertainty and dissimilar treatment of similar cases. At the same time, however, Ormerod and Laird acknowledge that there will be 'considerable reluctance' to apply the *R* v *Woollin* direction to defendants like Ronnie because it will make it difficult for prosecutors to secure convictions of secondary parties in such cases. Ronnie, for example, would argue that he did not foresee death or GBH as virtually certain because he believed Freddie would only use the knife if Roshan pulled out a knife first.

There is a further question about the Supreme Court's decision in *R v Jogee* that should be considered: whether the Court was, in fact, merely correcting a 'wrong turn' taken in the earlier decision in *Chan Wing-Siu*. In a detailed examination of the case law, Stark offers an 'alternative history' according to which parasitic accessory liability was not an invention of the Privy Council in *Chan Wing-Siu*. In fact, he argues, parasitic accessory liability had existed in some form since at least the sixteenth century. As the following extract explains, the significance of *Chan Wing-Siu* was that it confirmed that, where P and D agree to commit crime A together, and during the commission of crime A P commits crime B, D must have *subjectively* foreseen the possibility of P committing crime B (as opposed to the previous approach of asking whether crime B was a probable outcome of pursuing crime A).

EXTRACT

According to Stark, how does the reaction at the time to the decision in *Chan Wing-Siu* support his claim that the Privy Council in that case did not misstate the law?

If the decision in *R v Jogee* was not correcting a 'wrong turn', how does Stark say the decision should be understood? Why is this significant, in his opinion? Do you agree?

Stark, F. (2016) 'The Demise of "Parasitic Accessorial Liability": Substantive Judicial Law Reform, Not Common Law Housekeeping' 75 *Cambridge Law Journal* 550

In light of the discussion above, the thesis that the Privy Council's decision in *Chan Wing-Siu* bucked a clear trend in endorsing intention as the fault element in *all* instances of secondary liability, and introduced a "new principle" that changed "the common law in a way which made it more severe ... widening the scope of secondary liability by the introduction of new doctrine", is highly suspect. Although it was claimed in *Jogee* that *Chan Wing-Siu* was "based on an incomplete, and in some respects erroneous, reading of the previous case law", the Supreme Court/Privy Council cannot escape a similar charge. The court cited selectively, giving the most sympathetic view of history that it could. On the alternative history argued for in this article, which it is submitted explains more of the decided cases, *Chan Wing-Siu* (despite the Privy Council citing few cases) simply confirmed what was already becoming clearer in the case law: there was a "wider principle" (i.e. PAL) beyond standard aiding and abetting, "whereby a secondary party is criminally liable for acts by the primary offender of a type which the former foresees but does not necessarily intend". Indeed, the appellants in *Chan Wing-Siu* do not seem to have argued otherwise, basing their case on the requirement of *foresight of a probability* of collateral offending, rather than suggesting intention was the relevant standard (although they maintained the intellectual muddle of claiming there to be "tacit agreement" regarding Crime B where in fact there was none).

[...]

Indeed, had the decision in *Chan Wing-Siu* been as revolutionary and flawed as the Supreme Court/Privy Council suggested, one might have expected this to be noticed. Yet, in 1984, J.C. Smith described the Privy Council's decision as "a valuable restatement and clarification of ... the law". This was not simply a case of the significance of the decision being missed in its immediate aftermath. In 1997, Smith stated that "It would be quite wrong to suppose that parasitic accessorial liability ... is a recent development in the law, an innovation by the Privy Council in *Chan Wing-Siu*". Similarly, Spencer, writing in 1985, thought that the Privy Council's decision was consistent with the contemporary English approach, not a new development. The 1985 edition of *Archbold* mentions *Chan Wing-Siu* only once, without adverse comment. Although the case was not initially applied universally, the Court of Appeal endorsed it fairly promptly.

[...]

The claim that *Chan Wing-Siu* was a "wrong turn", and departing from it was in large part a matter of precedent (and therefore constitutionally straightforward), is thus unconvincing. The more compelling reading of *Jogee* is that the Supreme Court/Privy Council engaged in substantive law reform. This could have been made explicit, and the decision sold as a continuation of the historical narrowing of PAL. Just as the law had moved from a focus on: (1) furthering the common purpose, to (2) probable collateral offending, to (3) contemplated/foreseen collateral offending, it was now moving to focus on (4) intentional encouragement/assistance of the collateral crime, thus rendering PAL conceptually identical to ordinary aiding and abetting (and redundant). Many would have viewed such a judicial change as desirable, regarding PAL – a judicial development – as the genesis of much injustice. Being explicit about the change would, however, have meant engaging more directly with the proper process of revisiting previous decisions, and raised more clearly constitutional concerns about judicial activism. Although the Supreme Court/Privy Council is no doubt right that *corrections* of clear common law "errors" are largely unproblematic constitutionally, there are clearer concerns raised by more substantive reform of even the common law (as the prosecution maintained in *Jogee*). The reasons the change in *Jogee* is problematic, once the alleged precedential "error" has been dismissed as a smokescreen, are as follows: (1) the law as stated (defensibly, as shown above) in *Chan Wing-Siu* had been relatively settled for over 30 years; (2) requiring intentional encouragement or assistance for all secondary liability was not a reform the Law Commission had proposed when it had considered accessorial liability; and (3) Parliament had not apparently contemplated reforming the law, despite recent encouragement to do so. Once that shield of precedent and history has been shattered, the question is whether the *other* reasons provided by the Supreme Court/Privy Council in *Jogee* justified such dramatic law reform being undertaken by the courts, not the legislature. It is unfortunate that this question was so easily avoided in *Jogee*, but this paper opens up the possibility for it to be addressed more straightforwardly in the future. *Jogee* should be seen for what it is: significant judicial law reform, not common law housekeeping.

Stark's argument raises the question whether the abolition of parasitic accessory liability in *R* v *Jogee* was, in fact, desirable. Interestingly, in *Miller* v *The Queen* [2016] HCA 30 the High Court of Australia chose not to follow *R* v *Jogee* and instead affirmed the existence of parasitic accessory liability.[34] In the following extract, Simester explains why, in his opinion, the High Court of Australia was right not to follow *R* v *Jogee*.

EXTRACT

Read the following extract. What is Simester's opinion on each of the following issues:

- Whether embarking on a joint criminal enterprise is a distinctive wrong;
- The lower *mens rea* that parasitic accessory liability requires of the defendant, compared to the principal;

[34] Krebs, B. (2017) 'Accessory Liability: Persisting in Error' 76 *Cambridge Law Journal* 7.

- Whether parasitic accessory liability is draconian; and,
- The difficulties in requiring proof of abiding/abetting/counselling/procuring in all cases involving accessories?

Do you agree with Simester's critique? Should English law recognise a distinctive form of liability for secondary parties involved in a joint enterprise?

Simester, A.P. (2017) 'Accessory Liability and Common Unlawful Purposes' 133 *Law Quarterly Review* 73

In order to understand the latest divide between our jurisdictions, we need to specify more precisely what the Supreme Court did in *Jogee*. Most prominently, the court abolished what in Australia is called the doctrine of *extended joint criminal enterprise*, sometimes known in England as "parasitic accessorial liability". According to that doctrine, where S, the secondary party, and P, the perpetrator, form a common unlawful purpose to commit a crime (crime A), and set out together to pursue it, then in addition to any liability S may have regarding crime A, S becomes liable as a party to any further crime (crime B) committed by P in the pursuance of crime A, provided S realises that a crime of that further type is a possible upshot of their carrying out the common purpose. Extended joint criminal enterprise liability therefore supplies a distinct channel of complicity liability, separate from aiding and abetting because it does not require the prosecution to prove specifically that S has assisted or encouraged crime B. Indeed, as the House of Lords recognised in *Powell*, it operates to sustain liability even where S has actively discouraged P from committing crime B, but proceeded nonetheless with the plan to commit crime A.

That boat has now sailed from English shores. No longer can S become guilty of foreseen ancillary crimes by pursuing a shared criminal purpose with P. S must be a party *directly* to any crime of which S is convicted. *Extended* joint criminal enterprise liability is thus interred, at least for now.

So much is well known. What may be less obvious is that the doctrine of *joint criminal enterprise* itself - of "plain vanilla" joint enterprises, as Lord Hoffman once called them - is also abolished. Suppose that S and P decide to attack V. They find and confront V, who is punched by P. Prior to *Jogee*, S could be convicted of battery just in virtue of the fact that S had a common purpose with P that the battery be committed. No more. From the perspective of complicity liability, a common unlawful purpose is no longer doctrinally significant (although it may still have evidential significance). What must now be shown, under English law, is that S *aided, abetted, counselled, or procured* P's crime. Of course, the practical effects of this second difference are small. Doubtless, S can still be convicted of battery, since it will usually be straightforward to prove that one who joins in a common purpose thereby encourages the perpetrator. (More on this below.) But this is now a matter to be proved in its own right. In terms of formal doctrine, it is the encouragement, not the shared purpose, that must now be shown

[...]

There are no simple solutions in the field of complicity law. The problems are complex and nuanced. Rational arguments can be made both for and against the merits of extended joint criminal enterprise liability. Those arguments are not knock-down ones, and it is not helpful to suggest otherwise. The High Court [of Australia], while embracing the grip of precedent, addressed those arguments somewhat indirectly. Endorsing the earlier discussion in *R.* v *Powell*; *English*, the court pointed to evidential difficulties associated with group wrongdoing, as well as to its inherent dangerousness and tendency to escalate. *Miller* v *The Queen* also acknowledges the distinctive normative character of the wrong involved in embarking on a joint criminal enterprise.

On the other hand, the Supreme Court [in *Jogee*] made virtually no effort to argue against joint enterprise liability at the level of principle. It merely pointed to the so-called "anomaly" of requiring a "lower" *mens rea* standard for S than for P. But the *mens rea* standard isn't lower. It is different. As the well-known case of *Callow* v *Tillstone* illustrates, sometimes S's *mens rea* can be far more stringent than is demanded of P. Given that *actus reus* requirements differ between accessories and principals, it is hardly surprising that the *mens rea* elements also differ. S needs to *intend* his or her own act of involvement, *and* have *mens rea* regarding P's acts as well as regarding P's *mens rea*. More generally, it is a mistake to think that S's culpability must equal P's. What matters is whether S is *sufficiently* culpable to be held guilty of P's crime.

Still, there is the broader worry that extended joint criminal enterprise law may be Draconian in practice. Curiously, the law in jurisdictions such as Australia, Canada, and New Zealand has not generated parallel controversy to that in England. The High Court in *Miller* v *The Queen* was not presented with evidence that it has become a state weapon of systematic injustice. Albeit without citing any such evidence, the Supreme Court saw things differently. The decision in *Jogee* is clearly informed by a sense that the application of extended joint criminal enterprise liability rules has in recent years produced significant injustice.

Given the lack of analysis of this problem, it is plausible that the difficulty may arise not from common purpose liability doctrine per se but from how it has been applied: from over-zealous findings of shared criminal purposes – with foresight – against those on the periphery of wrongdoing. Common purpose liability should be a form of guilt by *enterprise*, not by association; a point emphasised forcefully by the High Court in *Miller* v *The Queen*. If extended joint criminal enterprise doctrines have indeed been abused, or indeed are prone to abuse, that certainly supplies a reason to see them off. But one should always hesitate before casting out the baby with the bathwater. Extended joint criminal enterprise doctrines could instead have been tweaked to avoid overreach, for instance by tightening the definition of joint enterprises and, perhaps, by requiring that S foresaw P's further crime as *probable*; or by limiting convictions to cases where S was certain that the collateral offence would be committed by P in the event of particular, foreseen circumstances. Such revisions would, of course, depart from existing case law, but not to the radical extent that *Jogee* does.

Alas, once joint enterprise liability was castigated as an egregious error in law, it had to go. The Supreme Court backed itself into a corner. That is unfortunate because it meant that the court never took seriously the question whether common unlawful purpose *should* have legal significance. In principle, having two distinct channels of complicity liability affords the law greater flexibility and moral sensitivity when determining whether S is a participant in P's crime. Direct aiding/abetting doctrines are simply too blunt by themselves to capture, without substantial over- or under-inclusion, all forms of association with P's crime that warrant a finding of guilt alongside P.

Despite the attention lavished upon them, the key features of common unlawful purpose liability are not its *mens rea* elements. They are (i) a distinctive *actus reus*, i.e. joining in a common purpose, which cannot simply be reduced to assistance or encouragement; (ii) the unlawfulness of that *actus reus* in its own right; and (iii) S's presence in the pursuance of their common purpose. By collapsing common purpose liability into mere aiding/abetting, the law obviates – and so loses sight of – these crucial features, which are not shared by acts of aiding/abetting. Lending P a jemmy is not anti-social at all *until* we know that P's plans for its use are wrongful. Setting out with P on a criminal enterprise is entirely a different matter.

The High Court of Australia was right to point to the discussion of merits in *R.* v *Powell*; *English*. As Lord Steyn observed in that case, joint criminal enterprises are dynamic and often escalate. Unlike aiding/abetting scenarios, S signs up to that dynamic character on an ongoing basis. As such, common unlawful purpose doctrine responds to contingencies of scope, which is what really matters here, rather than contingencies of S's intention. It allows the common law to accommodate fast-moving developments, provided they occur in the pursuance and within the foreseen scope of the criminal enterprise (in which S has a non-contingent intention to engage), and in the presence of S. Moreover, as Lord Steyn also noted, the doctrine allows the courts to overcome at least some of the traditional evidential difficulties associated with group wrongdoing.

The Court in *Jogee* overestimates the capacity of aiding/abetting law to accommodate such difficulties. Joint criminal enterprises are a distinct moral phenomenon. Indeed, only by recognising that can we adequately protect the law of aiding and abetting. Absent legislative reform, the inadequacy of traditional aiding/abetting doctrine to deal with the complexity of multi-party wrongdoing will inevitably generate pressure, either to restore joint criminal enterprise liability or – disastrously – to water down the *mens rea* requirements of aiding and abetting itself. Let us hope that London opts for the former, and ultimately realigns itself with Canberra.

In contrast to Simester, there are other commentators who welcome the decision in *R* v *Jogee*.[35] In the following extract, Dennis Baker explains why he disagrees with Simester's criticism of *R* v *Jogee*.[36]

EXTRACT

In your opinion, in Baker's example should D1 be guilty of being an accessory to rape (as well as burglary)? Why/why not?

According to Baker, how would Simester seek to justify convicting D1 of being an accessory to rape? Why does Baker reject this? With whom do you agree?

Baker, D. J. (2017) 'Unlawfulness's Doctrinal and Normative Irrelevance to Complicity Liablity: A Reply to Simester' 81 *Journal of Criminal Law* 393

Why should joining an underlying joint enterprise result in a rape or murder conviction, if the secondary party does not assist or encourage such conduct and if she does not intend such conduct to be perpetrated?

Suppose D1 jointly perpetrates a burglary with D2 and knows for a fact that D2 is a sexual predator who in the past was convicted and jailed for two counts of rape. Suppose D1 also believes that there is a remote possibility that if there is a lone woman (V) in the house they intend to burgle, then there is a possibility that D2 might try to rape or sexually harass V during the course of the burglary. As it turns out, D2 finds a young woman showering on the third floor of the house and rapes her. D1 is on the first floor of the house packing their sacks with goods while unbeknown to her D2 is raping V. D1 discovers the rape only after they leave the house, because D2 boasts about it to D1. Also, suppose that D1 knowing about D2 sexual predilections

[35] In a series of interviews with prisoners convicted of joint enterprise murder, Hulley, Crewe and Wright found that prisoners at the early stage of their sentence explicitly rejected the legitimacy of their conviction. Over time, these individuals set aside their feelings of unfairness and accepted their conviction and sentence, not because they had come to accept the legitimacy of the conviction but as a way of coping with their situation psychologically. See Hulley, S., Crewe, B. and Wright, S. (2019) 'Making Sense of "Joint Enterprise" for Murder: Legal Legitimacy or Instrumental Acquiescence?' 59 *British Journal of Criminology* 1328.

[36] See also Dyson, M. (2018) 'Principals without distinction' *Criminal Law Review* 296.

made D2 agree in advance that he would not sexually harass any occupants should they stumble across someone, but that they should both leave immediately if an occupant is present.

Simester would make them both liable for burglary and also for rape. For Simester, the rape conviction is fair as it punishes D1 for jointly perpetrating the burglary rather than singly perpetrating the burglary and because she foresaw a rape or sexual offence as a possible collateral consequence of joining D2 to burglarise a house. Under *Jogee*, only D2 would be liable for the rape. Simester would argue that D1 changed her normative position by joining the underlying burglary and therefore it does not matter that she did not intend to encourage a rape to be perpetrated. For Simester, it does not matter that there was no assistance or encouragement apropos the rape, it is enough that D1 was participating in an underlying joint enterprise with foresight of rape as a remote possibility. The problem with Simester's argument is that he does not provide a positive (normative) justification for it. He gives no supporting arguments other than to apply the term 'change of normative position' ... What is meant by change of normative position is that D1's position has changed from one where she is acting rightly or at least is acting in a normatively neutral sense, to one where she is acting wrongly. But the wrong is the burglary *per se*: how does that wrong extend to cover the independent wrong involved in the collateral crime of rape? For D1's change of normative position to cover the collateral crime, she would have to be involved in it in a very substantial way and would have to have comparable fault. If D1 were to hold V down with the intention of helping D2 to rape V, D1's wrongdoing as an intentional assister of rape would not be too far behind that of the rapist. Even if there is not exact equivalence as far as culpability is concerned, at least in this sort of case where there is very substantial and direct assistance at the time when the crime is being perpetrated, it might be argued that D1's normative position extends to D2's rape.

Now, think about this question.

Look back over the extracts you have read in this section on joint enterprise and make a list of the arguments for and against the decision in *R* v *Jogee*.
In your opinion, which set of arguments is the strongest?

Quiz 13.2

1. Which of the following statements about joint enterprise cases is correct?
   - **a.** In joint enterprise cases, the *actus reus* and *mens rea* of accessorial liability differ from other cases involving accessories.
   - **b.** 'Joint enterprise' is not a legal term and no special rules apply in such cases.
   - **c.** In joint enterprise cases, special rules apply to determine the liability of accessories.
   - **d.** Joint enterprise is a technical, legal term with a special meaning.
2. Which of the following statements is incorrect?
   - **a.** To prove the *actus reus* and *mens rea* of being an accessory it is necessary to show that the parties shared a common purpose.
   - **b.** In so-called joint enterprise cases the same *actus reus* and *mens rea* requirements apply as for any other case involving accessories.
   - **c.** Proof of a common purpose will often be sufficient to establish the *actus reus* and *mens rea* of being an accessory.
   - **d.** In a joint enterprise case, the defendant's intention to assist the crime may be conditional.
3. Which of the following statements is correct?
   - **a.** In *R* v *Johnson* all 13 men were granted leave to appeal against their convictions.
   - **b.** The Supreme Court in *R* v *Jogee* rejected the concern that the effect of its judgment would be to render invalid a large number of convictions that were arrived at by applying the principle from *Chan Wing-Siu* v *The Queen*.

c. The Supreme Court in *R* v *Jogee* expressed concern that a large number of people convicted on the basis of the principle from *Chan Wing-Siu* v *The Queen* would successfully appeal against their convictions.

d. Anyone that was convicted on the basis of the principle from *Chan Wing-Siu* v *The Queen* may now bring an appeal against their conviction.

4. Which of the following is **not** one of the criticisms of the judgment in *R* v *Jogee* [2016] UKSC 8?

a. The Supreme Court did not state whether or not the *R* v *Woollin* direction applies in this context.

b. The Supreme Court's claim that the law took a wrong turn in *Chan Wing-Siu* v *The Queen* is a misrepresentation of the Privy Council's decision in that case.

c. The Supreme Court's use of the term 'conditional intention' was conceptually problematic.

d. The Supreme Court's judgment has unduly relaxed the requirements for liability in these types of case.

To which offences may a defendant be an accessory?

13.3 State the offences to which a defendant can be an accessory.

A defendant can be convicted of being an accessory to any of the offences we studied in Chapters 5, 6, 7 and 8 of this text. He may also be convicted of being an accessory to the offences we studied in Chapter 12. So, for example, a defendant could be convicted of being an accessory to a conspiracy,[37] or of being an accessory to a criminal attempt.[38]

There is, however, one restriction on when a defendant may be guilty as an accessory. If a statutory offence was designed to protect a specific class of persons, a member of that class cannot be liable as an accessory to the offence. For example, in *R* v *Tyrrell* [1894] 1 QB 710 the principal, Thomas Ford, had sexual intercourse with the defendant, Jane Tyrrell. Tyrrell was under the age of 16. She was convicted of being an accessory to Ford's offence of having sexual intercourse with a girl aged between 13 and 16. The conviction was quashed. Tyrrell could not be convicted as an accessory to this offence since she was a member of the class of persons that the offence existed to protect.

Quiz 13.3

1. Which of the following is not an offence known to law?

a. Attempting to be an accessory to murder.

b. Being an accessory to attempted murder.

c. Being an accessory to manslaughter.

d. Being an accessory to murder.

2. Which of the following is not an offence known to law?

a. Being an accessory to assault occasioning ABH.

b. Being an accessory to attempted criminal damage.

c. Being an accessory to attempted adultery.

d. Being an accessory to a conspiracy to commit theft.

3. What is the principle from *R* v *Tyrrell* [1894] 1 QB710?

a. That a person may be an accessory by omission, if he or she breaches a legal duty to intervene.

b. An accessory is liable to be punished as a principal offender.

c. A person cannot be an accessory to an offence if they are a member of the class of persons the offence was designed to protect.

d. An accessory's liability derives from the liability of the principal.

[37] *R* v *Anderson* (1984) 80 Cr App R 64. This was the Court of Appeal judgment in the House of Lords case *R* v *Anderson* [1986] AC 27. We saw in the previous chapter that it would arguably have been more appropriate to have charged William Anderson with being an accessory to the conspiracy to help Andaloussi escape from prison.

[38] *R* v *Hapgood and Wyatt* (1870) LR 1 CCR 221.

The derivative principle

13.4 Outline the derivative principle on which the law on accessories is based.

Freddie asks his friend Ronnie for some information on a property he intends to burgle. Ronnie gives Freddie all the information he needs. The day before the burglary, Freddie has a change of heart and decides not to go through with it. On these facts, Ronnie may be guilty of an inchoate offence such as intentionally encouraging and assisting burglary.[39] But Ronnie cannot be convicted of being an accessory to burglary, because the burglary never took place. You cannot be an accessory to an offence that did not occur!

This is a simple illustration of the derivative principle. According to the derivative principle, an accessory's liability derives from the liability of the principal. So if the principal is not guilty of any offence, the accessory cannot be either.

Whilst the law on accessories is based on the derivative principle, there are two exceptions in which a defendant may be liable as an accessory even though the principal is not guilty:

1. The first exception is where the reason the principal is not guilty of the relevant offence is because a substantive defence applies.

   This is illustrated by *R* v *Bourne* (1952) 36 Cr App R 125. The defendant twice forced his wife to have sexual intercourse with a dog. His wife was not guilty of any offence against the dog because she had a defence of duress. But the Court of Appeal upheld the defendant's conviction for being an accessory to a sexual offence against the dog.

2. The second exception is where the reason the principal is not guilty of the relevant offence is because he lacked the necessary *mens rea*.

   This is illustrated by *R* v *Cogan & Leak* [1976] QB 217. The defendant, Michael Leak, terrorised his wife into submitting to sexual intercourse with John Cogan. Leak then told Cogan that his wife would consent to sex with him. Cogan had sex with Mrs Leak believing that she was consenting. Cogan's conviction for rape was quashed on appeal on the basis that he lacked the *mens rea* of rape.[40] But Leak's conviction for being an accessory to rape was upheld.

Note that, although the principal had not committed any crime in either of these cases, the actus reus of the relevant offence did still occur. So in cases like *R* v *Bourne* and *R* v *Cogan & Leak* the liability of the accessory is best understood as deriving from the fact that the defendant procured the *actus reus* of the offence in question.[41]

---

[39] Serious Crime Act 2007, section 44 (see Chapter 12).

[40] At the time the *mens rea* of rape was lack of a genuine belief in consent. As we saw in Chapter 7, today the *mens rea* is lack of a reasonable belief in consent. Since the jury in the case found that Cogan had no reasonable grounds for his belief that Mrs Leak was consenting, if the case had occurred today Cogan would have been guilty of rape.

[41] See the judgment of the Court of Appeal in *R* v *Millward* [1994] Crim LR 527.

Quiz 13.4

1. For what reason was the defendant in *R* v *Bourne* found guilty as an accessory to a crime in respect of which the principal was not prosecuted?
   a. The *actus reus* of the offence had not occurred.
   b. The defendant in *R* v *Bourne* was not guilty of being an accessory, since he was able to rely on a substantive defence.
   c. The *actus reus* of the full offence had taken place; the reason the principal was not guilty of the offence was because she had a defence of duress.
   d. The court applied the derivative principle to the resolution of the case.
2. D1 and D2 are bus drivers. D1 is attempting to reverse his bus out of the garage, but he cannot see properly, so he asks D2 to indicate when it is safe to move the bus. D2 indicates to D1 that it is safe to reverse the bus, but D2 does not see a pedestrian who is knocked over, suffering minor injuries. D1 is acquitted of careless driving because the court accepts that he was not at fault in relying on directions from D2. Why is D2 not guilty of being an accessory to careless driving?
   a. Since D1 was found to have not driven carelessly.
   b. D2 would have a defence of necessity.
   c. D2's conduct constituted an omission, and you cannot be liable as an accessory in respect of an omission.
   d. D1 and D2 were joint principals, so if one is acquitted the other must be too.
3. According to the derivative principle, in which of the following could D **not** be guilty of being an accessory?
   a. D pays P, an assassin, a large sum of money to kill V. P takes the money, then disappears without killing V.
   b. P burgles V's house while D stands outside keeping watch.
   c. P commits a fraudulent transaction online because D is pointing a gun at her threatening to kill her.
   d. D encourages P to have sex with V. V is not consenting but, as a result of D's deception, P genuinely and reasonably believes that V is consenting.

Withdrawal

13.5 Define the circumstances in which an individual's attempt to withdraw his previous assistance or encouragement will be deemed effective.

Suppose that a defendant provides assistance or encouragement, but then has a change of heart. If the principal has not yet committed the relevant offence, it is possible for the defendant to withdraw and avoid accessorial liability. In this section we will look at some case law which identifies the factors to take into account when deciding whether a defendant's purported withdrawal was in fact effective. As we look at the cases, remember that whether or not a purported withdrawal is effective is a question of fact, to be determined by the jury having regard to the features of the particular case before it.[42]

The first case to consider is *R* v *Becerra & Cooper* (1975) 62 Cr App R 212.

[42] *R* v *O'Flaherty & others* [2004] EWCA Crim 526.

Antonio Becerra, John Cooper and a third man broke into the home of an elderly lady, Mrs Francis, in the early hours of the morning.

Akhenaton Images/Shutterstock

Becerra was carrying a knife. Cooper entered the building first, climbing in through Mrs Francis' bedroom window.

DZMITRY BYCHKOU/Shutterstock

Mrs Francis turned her bedside light on. Cooper went over to her, punched her, jumped on top of her and covered her head with a pillow.

Bacho/Shutterstock

Becerra and the other man then entered and Becerra cut the telephone wires. Cooper then said to Becerra, 'Give me the knife in case somebody jumps me'. Becerra handed the knife over.

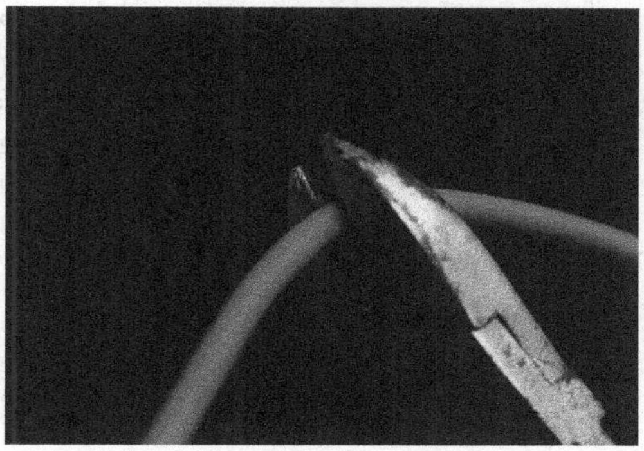

Albert Yarullin/Shutterstock

At this point Mr Lewis, who lived in a first floor flat in the house and had heard noises from below, came downstairs.

Serge Vo/Shutterstock

Becerra and the third man heard him, climbed out of the window and ran away. Before leaving, Becerra called to Cooper, 'Come on, let's go'.

Andrey_Popov/Shutterstock

Cooper tried to exit via the back door, but found it was locked. He was confronted by Mr Lewis.

Ricardo Reitmeyer/Shutterstock

There was a struggle. Cooper stabbed Mr Lewis four times. One of the wounds was fatal. Becerra and Cooper both pleaded guilty to burglary.

Max Sky/Shutterstock

At trial, Cooper was convicted of murder and Becerra was convicted of being an accessory to the murder.

Becerra appealed against his conviction, arguing that he had withdrawn before Cooper murdered Mr Lewis. The appeal reached the Court of Appeal.

EXTRACT

Read the following extract from the judgment of Roskill LJ. Is it sufficient for an effective withdrawal for a defendant to change his mind and leave the scene of the crime?

Roskill LJ cites with approval a passage from a Canadian case, *Whitehouse*. This passage identifies one 'essential element' for an effective withdrawal. What is this?

Roskill LJ then refers to an English case, *Croft*. The passage from this case identifies another requirement for an effective withdrawal. What is this?

Applying these requirements to the facts of *R* v *Becerra & Cooper*, does Roskill LJ conclude that Becerra's purported withdrawal was effective? Why/why not?

R v *Becerra & Cooper* (1975) 62 Cr App R 212

Roskill LJ

[Counsel for the defence] referred us to several Canadian cases, to only one of which is it necessary to refer in detail, a decision of the Court of Appeal of British Columbia in *Whitehouse* (alias *Savage*) (1941) 1 W.W.R. 112. I need not read the headnote. The Court of Appeal held that the trial judge concerned in that case, which was one of murder, had been guilty of misdirection in his direct on to the jury on this question of "withdrawal." The matter is, if I may most respectfully say so, so well put in the leading judgment of Sloan J. A., that I read the whole of the passage at pp. 115 and 116: "Can it be said on the facts of this case that a mere change of mental intention and a quitting of the scene of the crime just immediately prior to the striking of the fatal blow will absolve those who participate in the commission of the crime by overt acts up to that moment from all the consequences of its accomplishment by the one who strikes in ignorance of his companions' change of heart? I think not. After a crime has been committed and before a prior abandonment of the common enterprise may be found by a jury there must be, in my view, in the absence of exceptional circumstances, something more than a mere mental change of intention and physical change of place by those associates who wish to dissociate themselves from the consequences attendant upon their willing assistance up to the moment of the actual commission of that crime. I would not attempt to define too closely what must be done in criminal matters involving participation in a common unlawful purpose to break the chain of causation and responsibility. That must depend upon the circumstances of each case but it seems to me that one essential element ought to be established in a case of this kind: Where practicable and reasonable there must be timely communication of the intention to abandon the common purpose from those who wish to dissociate themselves from the contemplated crime to those who desire to continue in it. What is 'timely communication' must be determined by the facts of each case but where practicable and reasonable it ought to be such communication, verbal or otherwise, that will serve unequivocal notice upon the other party to the common unlawful cause that if he proceeds upon it he does so without the further aid and assistance of those who withdraw.

The unlawful purpose of him who continues alone is then his own and not one in common with those who are no longer parties to it nor liable to its full and final consequences." The learned judge then went on to cite a passage from 1 Hale's Pleas of the Crown 618 and the passage from Saunders and Archer (*supra*) to which I have already referred.

In the view of each member of this Court, that passage, if we may respectfully say so, could not be improved upon and we venture to adopt it in its entirety as a correct statement of the law which is to be applied in this case.

The last case, an English one, is *Croft* (1944) 29 Cr.App.R. 169; [1944] 1 K.B. 295, a well known case of a suicide pact where, under the old law, the survivor of a suicide pact was charged with and convicted of murder. It was sought to argue that he had withdrawn from the pact in time to avoid liability (as the law then was) for conviction for murder.

The Court of Criminal Appeal, comprising Lawrence J. (as he then was), Lewis and Wrottesley JJ. dismissed the appeal and upheld the direction given by Humphreys J. to the jury at the trial. Towards the end of the judgment Lawrence J. said, at p. 173 (pp. 297 and 298): "... counsel for the appellant complains – although I do not understand that the point had ever been taken in the court below – that the summing-up does not contain any reference to the possibility of the agreement to commit suicide having been determined or countermanded. It is true that the learned judge does not deal expressly with that matter except in a passage where he says: 'Even if you accept his statement in the witness-box that the vital and second shot was fired when he had gone through that window, he would still be guilty of murder if she was then committing suicide as the result of an agreement which they had mutually arrived at that that should be the fate of both of them, and it is no answer for him that he altered his mind after she was dead and did not commit suicide himself.' ... the authorities, such as they are, show in our opinion, that where a person has acted as an accessory before the fact, in order that he should not be held guilty as an accessory before the fact, he must give express and actual countermand or revocation of the advising, counselling, procuring, or abetting which he had given before."

It seems to us that those authorities make plain what the law is which has to be applied in the present case.

We therefore turn back to consider the direction which the learned judge gave in the present case to the jury and what was the suggested evidence that Becerra had withdrawn from the common agreement. The suggested evidence is the use by Becerra of the words "Come on let's go," coupled, as I said a few moments ago, with his act in going out through the window. The evidence, as the judge pointed out, was that Cooper never heard that nor did the third man. But let it be supposed that that was said and the jury took the view that it was said.

On the facts of this case, in the circumstances then prevailing, the knife having already been used and being contemplated for further use when it was handed over by Becerra to Cooper for the purpose of avoiding (if necessary) by violent means the hazards of identification, if Becerra wanted to withdraw at that stage, he would have to "countermand," to use the word that is used in some of the cases or "repent" to use another word so used, in some manner vastly different and vastly more effective than merely to say "Come on, let's go" and go out through the window.

So for Becerra's withdrawal to have been effective, he would have needed to unequivocally communicate notice of his withdrawal to Cooper and to have done something 'vastly more effective' to countermand his actions than simply saying 'Come on, let's go' and running off.

So generally, in order to withdraw effectively, a defendant must: (1) unequivocally communicate notice of his withdrawal; and (2) take steps to countermand (i.e. negate) his assistance/encouragement. Notice, though, that there is no requirement for the defendant to show that he took reasonable steps to prevent the principal from committing the offence.[43] This was significant in *R* v *Grundy* [1977] Crim LR 543, in which the courts said there was evidence of an effective withdrawal. The defendant in this case had provided information to two men about premises they planned to burgle. But two weeks before the planned burglary the defendant had a change of heart. During these two weeks he tried to persuade the men not to go ahead with the burglary. At trial the judge ruled there was insufficient evidence of an effective withdrawal for the issue to be left to the jury. The Court of Appeal said that this was wrong and quashed Grundy's conviction. There was evidence of an effective withdrawal, and so the jury should have been left to decide whether Grundy's purported withdrawal was effective or not.

It is also important to note that the requirements for an effective withdrawal may not be as strict in cases involving spontaneous, as opposed to preplanned, violence. In *R* v *O'Flaherty & others* [2004] EWCA Crim 526 the three defendants – Errol O'Flaherty, Phillip Ryan and Mitchell Toussaint – had been to a nightclub. After the club shut, violence broke out between two groups of young men: one which included the three defendants and another which included the victim, Marcus Hall. Importantly, the violence occurred in two locations. First, the three defendants and others exchanged blows with Marcus Hall in a road called Flowers Way outside the nightclub. O'Flaherty was armed with a cricket bat, Ryan was armed with a beer bottle and Toussaint was armed with a claw hammer. Hall then ran around the corner into Park Street West, chased by a number of the group including O'Flaherty but not Ryan or Toussaint. In Park Street West Hall was struck and stabbed. O'Flaherty stood within a few feet of the attack, holding the cricket bat. At trial, the three defendants were all convicted of being accessories to the murder. They appealed against their convictions. On appeal, one of the issues the Court of Appeal had to consider was whether the defendants had withdrawn from the course of violence before the fatal blow was struck.

EXTRACT

Read the following extract from the judgment of Mantell LJ.

What distinction does he draw between cases of spontaneous violence and cases of preplanned violence?

What reasons does Mantell LJ give for allowing the appeals of Ryan and Toussaint?

What reasons does Mantell LJ give for dismissing the appeal of O'Flaherty?

R v *O'Flaherty & others* [2004] EWCA Crim 526

Mantell LJ

61 [... T]he decision in *R* v *Mitchell and King* (1998) 163 JP 75, so far as we can see, an authority not brought to the attention of the judge, shows that in a case of spontaneous violence in principle it is possible to withdraw by ceasing to fight, throwing down one's weapons and walking away. In that case one of Mitchell's defences was that he had withdrawn before the fatal injuries had been

---

[43] *R* v *O'Flaherty & others* [2004] EWCA Crim 526.

inflicted. It was stated by the Court (p. 81) that in those circumstances the jury had to be directed (a) that they must be satisfied that the fatal injuries were sustained whilst the joint enterprise was continuing and that the defendant was still acting within that joint enterprise, and (b) that they must be satisfied that the acts which caused the death were within the scope of the joint enterprise.

62 In *R* v *Mitchell and King* this Court also considered Soan J.A.'s statement in *R* v *Whitefeld* that "where practicable and reasonable there must be timely communication of the intention to abandon the common purpose". It held that while communication of withdrawal is a necessary condition for disassociation from pre-planned violence it is not necessary when the violence is spontaneous.

[...]

65 It is not arguable that the learned judge should have withdrawn the case of O'Flaherty from the jury. The fact that he followed the group to Park Street West still armed with the cricket bat provided an evidential foundation for the jury to conclude, if properly directed, that he was "still in it". There are significant differences so far as Ryan and Toussaint are concerned. In a case of spontaneous violence such as this where there has been no prior agreement the jury will usually have to make inferences as to the scope of the joint enterprise from the knowledge and actions of the individual participants. Ryan and Toussaint were solely in the fray in Flowers Way, and in Ryan's case only for some 7 seconds. There was no evidence from which it could be inferred that pursuit was part of any joint enterprise by them. Since there was no evidence that any injury causative of death was inflicted in Flowers Way, there was no evidence concerning them on the charge of murder to go to the jury. Accordingly their cases should have been withdrawn.

66 We turn to the effect of the directions. We are clear that even had it been proper to leave Ryan and Toussaint's cases to the jury the effect of the failure to direct the jury that the fatal injuries had to have been sustained when the joint enterprise was continuing and that the particular defendant was still acting within that joint enterprise would have rendered their convictions unsafe. The position of O'Flaherty differs. He followed the group to Park Street West holding the cricket bat. He was present carrying the cricket bat as the group attacked Hall. Although it is right to say that the jury would have to be satisfied that he was present and at the very least providing encouragement or prepared to lend support it would seem to this court that no other conclusion would have been available to a reasonable jury than was arrived at by this jury.

A final case to consider here is *R* v *Mitchell* [2008] EWCA Crim 2552. We saw the facts of this case earlier in the chapter in our discussion of *R* v *Johnson*. The case involved an outbreak of violence late at night between two groups, one of which included Michael Hall (who we examined previously), Laura Mitchell, and the eventual killer, Carl Holmes. Mitchell was centrally involved in the initial outbreak of violence, kicking and punching several members of the other group. There was then a lull in the violence, during which time Mitchell stayed in the pub car park. She had lost both her shoes and was trying to find them. When the rest of Mitchell's group returned they attacked the members of the other group again, and the victim, Andrew Ayres, was killed. At trial Mitchell was convicted of being an accessory to the murder. She appealed against her conviction on two grounds, both of which were rejected by the Court of Appeal.[44]

- First, she argued that there were in fact two separate joint enterprises: the original attack, which she participated in and which had come to an end; and a second attack which she had not participated in. The Court rejected this, saying that the jury at her

[44] Here is a news story from the time of the unsuccessful appeal: https://www.thebureauinvestigates.com/stories/2014-03-31/case-study-laura-mitchell-convicted-of-murder-under-joint-enterprise

trial had been entitled to find that there had been one ongoing joint enterprise which had had a temporary lull whilst the group members collected weapons.

- Second, she argued that she had withdrawn from the joint enterprise. She only remained in the pub car park to find her shoes, and had not taken part in the further incidents of violence. The Court rejected this also, saying that the jury had been entitled to find that she had not withdrawn from the joint enterprise. She had played a leading role in starting the violence, and had remained present at the scene of the violence.[45]

Assessment advice

Finally, when answering an exam problem question remember the following two points:

- A defendant can only withdraw before the principal commits the relevant offence. It is not possible to withdraw once the principal has committed the crime.
- Even if the defendant did withdraw effectively, he may still be liable for some other offence, such as the inchoate offences of conspiracy or encouraging and assisting crime.

Quiz 13.5

1. A defendant may validly withdraw from the commission of a planned offence if he does which of the following?

a. He communicates clearly to the other participants that he has withdrawn, takes steps to countermand his assistance/encouragement, reports the planned offence to the police and does what he can to thwart any further criminal actions.

b. He communicates clearly to the other participants that he has withdrawn, takes steps to countermand his assistance/encouragement, and reports the planned offence to the police.

c. He communicates clearly to the other participants that he has withdrawn and takes steps to countermand his assistance/encouragement.

d. He ceases to participate any further in the planned offence.

2. What is the significance of the extent to which a joint attack was pre-planned or spontaneous when it comes to considering whether there has been an effective withdrawal?

a. Communication of withdrawal is not required if the violence was pre-planned, but is required if it was spontaneous.

b. In cases involving pre-planned violence (but not spontaneous violence) it is necessary to take reasonable steps to prevent the principal from continuing the attack in order to withdraw effectively.

c. Communication of withdrawal is not required if the violence was spontaneous, but is required if it was pre-planned.

[45] Following the judgment of the Supreme Court in *R v Jogee*, Mitchell launched a second appeal against conviction arguing that the change in the law in *R v Jogee* would have made a difference to the verdict in her case. This appeal was dismissed by the Court of Appeal (*R v Mitchell* [2018] EWCA Crim 2687). The Court explained that 'the evidence of her foresight was strong evidence of her conditional intent that grievous bodily harm would be caused' ([6]) and so a *R v Jogee* compliant direction would not have made a difference. NB: As noted here, she then tried to appeal again after the *Jogee* judgment, arguing that the outcome would have been different had *Jogee* been applied at her trial. This was also unsuccessful: https://www.theguardian.com/uk-news/2018/nov/14/woman-looked-for-shoes-during-car-park-court-hears

d. Whether a joint attack was pre-planned or spontaneous is of no significance when it comes to considering whether there has been an effective withdrawal.

3. In *R v Becerra and Cooper*, which two things did the CA say are needed for an effective withdrawal?
   a. An offer to pay the victim compensation and genuine remorse at the previous acts of assistance/encouragement.
   b. An offer to pay the victim compensation and steps to negate the previous acts of assistance/encouragement.
   c. Unequivocal communication of withdrawal and genuine remorse at the previous acts of assistance/encouragement.
   d. Unequivocal communication of withdrawal and steps to negate the previous acts of assistance/encouragement.

Conclusion

The topics we have covered in this chapter include some of the most difficult material in the whole text. So to conclude the chapter, here are three pieces of advice for answering exam problem questions:

1. Before considering the liability of any possible accessories, you should always begin by discussing the liability of the principal.

As we have seen, the liability of an accessory derives from the liability of the principal. So, unless one of the exceptions to the derivative principle applies, if the principal is not guilty of any offence there can be no accessorial liability!

2. Always remember to specify the offence that the defendant was an accessory to.

In exams it is quite common for students to write something like 'The defendant would be guilty of being an accessory'. This doesn't provide enough information. You need to write 'The defendant would be guilty of being an accessory to murder' or 'The defendant would be guilty of being an accessory to theft'.

3. There is a considerable overlap between the law on accessories and the inchoate offences.

This leaves some students unsure which offences they should discuss. As a rule of thumb, you should discuss accessorial liability before considering inchoate offences. This is because finding a defendant guilty as an accessory recognises that the full offence actually occurred.

Applying the law

13.6 Apply the law on accessories to hypothetical sets of facts.

Ronnie and Freddie

The following scenario involves the characters, Ronnie and Freddie. Read the problem scenario carefully, then answer the multiple-choice questions below to apply your learning to the scenario.

Ronnie and Freddie are members of a criminal gang. Roshan is the leader of a rival gang. Discuss the criminal liability of Ronnie and Freddie in the following situations.

Problem scenario 1

Freddie suggests to Roshan that they meet up at his local pub for a drink to resolve their differences. When Roshan arrives, Ronnie and Freddie are in the middle of a game of pool. Roshan walks over to them and Freddie immediately attacks him, striking him repeatedly with his pool cue. Ronnie stands and watches, not doing or saying anything. Roshan suffers serious injuries, including a broken arm. Ronnie later tells police that he had no idea that Freddie had invited Roshan to the pub.

Think about this question.

How (if at all) would your answer be different in each of the following two scenarios:

- **a.** Ronnie had known that Freddie had invited Roshan so that he could attack him and Ronnie had gone to the pub in order to watch; and
- **b.** Ronnie owned the pub in which the attack occurred?

In the second alternative scenario Ronnie owns the pub in which the attack occurred. The key question here is whether the principle from *Du Cros* v *Lambourne* would apply.

- If you were the prosecutor, how would you argue that *Du Cros* v *Lambourne* applies? If you were Ronnie's defence counsel, how would you try and distinguish *Du Cros* v *Lambourne*?
- Remember too that if the principle from *Du Cros* v *Lambourne* does apply, so that the *actus reus* of being an accessory is established, you would then need to go on to consider whether Ronnie possessed the *mens rea* of being an accessory. In your opinion, did Ronnie possess the necessary *mens rea*?

Problem scenario 2

Freddie asks Ronnie to find out where Roshan lives. Ronnie does so and gives Freddie the address. Ronnie expects some sort of violence, but is unsure what form this will take. That evening Freddie breaks into Roshan's house planning to kill him. Unbeknown to Freddie, Roshan had been killed in a road accident earlier that day.

Problem scenario 3

Ronnie and Freddie agree to go and beat Roshan up with wooden posts. They drive to Roshan's house in Ronnie's car. When they arrive, Ronnie says to Freddie, 'I'm not sure this is such a good idea. I'm going home'. Freddie replies, 'I'm going through with it'. Ronnie leaves. Freddie attacks Roshan. Roshan suffers serious injuries.

These cases give us some idea of what is required for a purported withdrawal to be effective. Where there is insufficient evidence of an effective withdrawal, the issue will not be left to the jury. But if there is evidence of an effective withdrawal, the decision whether the defendant did withdraw effectively or not is one for the jury.

Now, think about these questions.

- Looking at the existing case law, do you believe there is evidence of an effective withdrawal in Ronnie's case? Why/why not?
- Note also that, even if Ronnie did withdraw effectively, he may face liability for an inchoate offences instead. Which inchoate offences did he commit?

Problem scenario 4

Ronnie and Freddie agree to go and beat up Roshan with wooden posts. Ronnie says to Freddie, 'For goodness' sake don't kill him'. They attack Roshan. Freddie relentlessly hits Roshan on the head as hard as he can with a wooden post. Roshan dies.

How (if at all) would your answer be different in each of the following two scenarios: (i) medical evidence shows that Roshan died from the cumulative effect of all of the injuries the men inflicted; and (ii) unbeknown to Ronnie, Freddie had taken a knife with him. After striking Roshan with the wooden posts, Freddie pulls out the knife and fatally stabs him?

Quiz 13.6

1. Before discussing the liability of any possible accessories it is important to begin by considering the liability of the principal offender, in this case Freddie. In this scenario it seems clear that Freddie has committed the offence of GBH with intent (section 18 of the Offences Against the Person Act 1861). We studied this offence in Chapter 6. The victim, Roshan, has suffered 'serious injuries' which include a broken arm. This would be held to amount to GBH. The attack was unlawful (there are no issues around consent or self-defence) and Freddie acted maliciously and with an intention to cause GBH (his purpose was to cause Roshan serious injuries; had he not done so, he would have regarded this as a failure).
   We must therefore consider whether Ronnie is an accessory to Freddie's offence.

   Which of the following is not one of the requirements for establishing liability as an accessory?

   a. The defendant aided, abetted, counselled or procured the commission of the offence.

   b. The defendant agreed to aid, abet, counsel or procure the offence prior to its commission.

   c. The defendant intended to aid, abet, counsel or procure the commission of the offence.

   d. The defendant knew or intended the essential elements of the principal's offence.

2. To establish the *actus reus*, it must be shown that Ronnie aided, abetted, counselled or procured Freddie's offence. In Ronnie's case, the most relevant of these four words is 'abetted'. The key issue is whether Ronnie abetted Freddie's crime simply by being present at the scene whilst the offence was committed.

   Which of the following summarises the outcome of *R* v *Clarkson* [1971] 1 WLR 1402 accurately?

   a. The prosecution only needs to establish that the defendants were present at the scene of the offence. This had not been done, since it had been shown that Clarkson and Carroll only entered the room after the rape was complete.

   b. The prosecution only needs to establish that the defendants were present at the scene of the offence. This had been done, since it had been shown that Clarkson and Carroll had stood and watched whilst the rape was committed.

   c. The prosecution must prove that there was in fact assistance or encouragement. No evidence had been produced that Clarkson and Carroll had encouraged the rapists.

   d. The prosecution must prove that there was in fact assistance or encouragement. This had been done, since it had been shown that Clarkson and Carroll had spoken words of encouragement.

3. The principle from *R* v *Clarkson* was also applied in *R* v *Willett*. In our question, the facts tell us that 'Ronnie stands and watches, not doing or saying anything'. So, following *R* v *Clarkson*, this does not constitute encouragement or assistance. We should therefore

consider an alternative possibility: that Ronnie may have been an accessory by omission.

Which of the following statements is **incorrect**?

- **a.** In *Rubie* v *Faulkner* the defendant, George Rubie, had a legal duty to intervene and so could be liable as an accessory for breaching this duty.
- **b.** A child's father stands by and watches as the mother deliberately injures the child. The father had a legal duty to intervene, and so can be liable as an accessory for his failure to do so.
- **c.** In *R* v *Willett* the defendant, Tommy Willett, had the opportunity to get out of the car and walk away. He failed to do so, and so could be liable as an accessory.
- **d.** In *Du Cros* v *Lambourne* the defendant, Du Cros, had the power or right to control Victoria Goodwin's actions and failed to do so, and so could be liable as an accessory.

4. Having established that there is not the *actus reus* of being an accessory in the original scenario, we now need to consider the two alternative scenarios. First, would it make a difference if Ronnie had known that Freddie had invited Roshan so that he could attack him, and Ronnie had gone to the pub in order to watch? In other words, does the principle from *R* v *Clarkson* still apply if Ronnie had purposely arranged to be present at the scene of the crime?

Which of the following statements about the decision in *R* v *Coney* (1882) 8 QBD 534 is **inaccurate**?

- **a.** The Court stated that the fact the defendant arranged to be present at the scene of the crime provides evidence of encouragement.
- **b.** The Court stated that the fact the defendant arranged to be present at the scene of the crime is not conclusive evidence of encouragement.
- **c.** The Court stated that, even if presence at the scene of the crime was non-accidental, the prosecution must still prove assistance or encouragement in fact.
- **d.** The Court stated that if the defendant arranged to be present at the scene of the crime there is a presumption that there was encouragement in fact which can only be rebutted if evidence is produced that the defendant did not in fact offer any encouragement.

5. Once again, our starting point is to discuss the liability of the principal offender, Freddie. He did not commit murder, since he did not cause anyone's death. Roshan had already died earlier that day. Nor did he commit attempted murder, since his actions never went beyond the merely preparatory. Breaking into Roshan's house was not more than merely preparatory, because Freddie never got himself into a position where he could carry out the killing (see Chapter 12, and in particular *R* v *Campbell*). The most likely offence, therefore, is burglary, since Freddie entered Roshan's house as a trespasser with an intention to cause someone inside serious harm (section 9(1)(a) of the Theft Act 1968). For section 9(1)(a) burglary it does not matter that Freddie did not in fact injure anybody once inside.

Having established the liability of the principal offender, we can now ask whether Ronnie is liable as an accessory to burglary. The *actus reus* is straightforward: Ronnie aided Freddie by giving him Roshan's address. The first *mens rea* requirement is that Ronnie intended to aid the commission of the burglary.

Which of the following statements about this *mens rea* requirement is **inaccurate?**

- **a.** Only intention will suffice; recklessness is insufficient.
- **b.** All that is needed for this *mens rea* requirement is that there was an intention to assist or encourage; it does not matter that the defendant was indifferent as to whether the principal would go ahead and commit the offence.
- **c.** In cases involving procurement, this *mens rea* requirement has to be adjusted to an intention that the defendant intended to bring about commission of the offence.
- **d.** It is not enough for this *mens rea* requirement just to show that the defendant intended to aid, abet, counsel or procure; it must also be shown that it was the defendant's intention that the principal would go ahead and commit the offence.

6. It seems clear that Ronnie satisfies the first *mens rea* requirement. Even if it wasn't his direct intention to assist Freddie (which seems doubtful), it was certainly his oblique intention since he knew that assistance was the virtually certain consequence of giving Freddie the address.

So, we must turn to the second *mens rea* requirement: that Ronnie knew or intended the essential elements of Freddie's offence. The facts of the question tell us that Ronnie expected some sort of violence but was unsure what form this would take.

In *DPP for Northern Ireland* v *Maxwell* [1978] 1 WLR 1350, the House of Lords set out which of the following principles?

- **a.** D is not liable as an accessory unless he knew the principal would choose to commit the specific offence he did in fact commit.
- **b.** As long as D foresaw that the principal would commit the *actus reus* of the relevant offence, it is irrelevant whether or not D foresaw that the

principal would perpetrate the *actus reus* with the relevant *mens rea*.

c. As long as D knew that the principal was going to do something illegal, it does not matter whether or not D knew the precise offence the principal would commit.

d. If D contemplates several offences, and the principal chooses to commit one of the offences D contemplated, D may be liable.

7. In this case, Freddie attacks Roshan with a wooden post, causing him serious injuries. The injuries would constitute GBH, Freddie acted unlawfully (there are no issues regarding consent or self-defence), Freddie acted maliciously (he foresaw that Roshan would suffer some harm: *R* v *Cunningham; R* v *Savage & Parmenter*), and it was his direct intention to cause Roshan GBH (he would have regarded it as a failure had Roshan not suffered a serious injury). He is therefore guilty of GBH with intent (section 18 of the Offences Against the Person Act 1861). On the face of it, Ronnie appears to satisfy the *actus reus* and *mens rea* of being an accessory. He aided Freddie by giving him a lift in his car. This assistance was intentional: at the time he provided the assistance, it was Ronnie's direct intention to help Freddie to attack Roshan. And Ronnie knew that Freddie would commit the crime of GBH with intent. However, when they arrive Ronnie has second thoughts. He decides to go home and take no further part in the planned offence and informs Freddie of this fact. The question, therefore, is whether this purported withdrawal was effective or not.
Which of the following statements is **inaccurate?**

a. In *R* v *Mitchell* Mitchell's actions (staying in the pub car park to search for her shoes) were insufficient to constitute an effective withdrawal from the unlawful activity.

b. In *R* v *O'Flaherty & others* the Court of Appeal held that communication of withdrawal is a necessary condition for effective withdrawal from pre-planned violence.

c. In *R* v *Becerra & Cooper* Becerra's actions (saying 'Come on, let's go' and exiting through the window) were insufficient to constitute an effective withdrawal from the unlawful activity.

d. In *R* v *Grundy* Grundy's actions (trying to persuade the two principals not to go through with the burglary) were insufficient to constitute an effective withdrawal from the unlawful activity.

8. Freddie is guilty of murdering Roshan. His actions were a factual and legal cause of Roshan's death (but for Freddie's actions Roshan would not have died, and Freddie's actions made a significant contribution to Roshan's death (*Cheshire*)). And when Freddie committed the *actus reus* his direct intention was to at least cause serious harm to Roshan, so he acted with the *mens rea* of murder.

Is Ronnie guilty of being an accessory to the murder? The *actus reus* appears to be satisfied; Ronnie assisted Freddie by participating in the attack on Roshan. The key issue is thus whether Ronnie satisfies the two *mens rea* requirements. The fact that Ronnie said to Freddie 'For goodness' sake don't kill him' shows that he realised there was a real risk that Freddie might commit murder. But what is the significance of this? Here we must return to the judgment in *R* v *Jogee*.

Which of the following statements about *Chan Wing-Siu* v *The Queen and R* v *Jogee* is correct?

a. In *R* v *Jogee* the Supreme Court approved the following principle from *Chan Wing-Siu* v *The Queen:* if P and D embark on a joint enterprise to commit crime A, and in the course of this P commits crime B, D is guilty as an accessory to crime B if he foresaw it as a possibility, even if he did not intend it.

b. The Supreme Court in *R* v *Jogee* said that it disagreed with the principle the Privy Council applied in *Chan Wing-Siu* v *The Queen*, but held that it was too late to reverse a principle that had been applied for many years and in a large number of cases.

c. In *R* v *Jogee* the Supreme Court approved the following principle from *Chan Wing-Siu* v *The Queen:* in a joint enterprise, a secondary party may be criminally liable for a greater criminal offence committed by the primary offender of a type which the former foresaw but did not necessarily intend.

d. In *R* v *Jogee* the Supreme Court disagreed with the judgment in *Chan Wing-Siu* v *The Queen*, stating that participation in crime A with foresight of crime B is evidence of an intention to encourage/assist crime B, but not conclusive of it.

9. In the first alternative scenario medical evidence shows that Roshan died from the cumulative effect of all of the injuries the men inflicted.
If Roshan died from the cumulative effect of all the injuries the men inflicted, how (if at all) would this change your answer?

a. Ronnie would no longer be able to claim that the attack went beyond the scope of his agreement with Freddie, and so he would be guilty of being an accessory to murder.

b. Assuming Freddie and Ronnie both had an intention to cause Roshan at least serious harm, they would both be guilty of murder as joint principals.

c. Ronnie would no longer be able to claim that the attack was fundamentally different to what he had expected, and so would be guilty of being an accessory to murder.
d. It would make no difference.

10. In the second alternative scenario Freddie is again guilty of murder. Is Ronnie an accessory to the murder? This time, the fatal injury was a stab wound and Ronnie was unaware that Freddie had armed himself with a knife.

According to the judgment in *R* v *Jogee*, which of the following statements is correct?

a. Where P and D formed an agreement to commit a particular offence, this is evidence that may be considered when deciding whether the *actus reus* and *mens rea* of being an accessory are established. However, if P had a weapon that was fundamentally different to any weapons of which D was aware, then D cannot be found to have formed the necessary *mens rea*.
b. If P and D formed an agreement to commit a particular offence, but P committed a greater offence, D cannot be convicted of being an accessory to the greater offence. In determining the scope of the agreement, the fact that D knew – or didn't know – that P had a particular weapon may be considered but is not conclusive.
c. If P and D formed an agreement to commit a particular offence, but P committed a greater offence, D cannot be convicted of being an accessory to the greater offence. Similarly, if P had a weapon that was fundamentally different to any weapons of which D was aware, then D cannot be found to have formed the necessary *mens rea* of being an accessory.
d. Where P and D formed an agreement to commit a particular offence, this is evidence that may be considered when deciding whether the *actus reus* and *mens rea* of being an accessory are established. Similarly, the fact that D knew – or didn't know – that P had a particular weapon is evidence of what D's intention was, but not conclusive.

Evaluating the law

13.7 Evaluate the decision of the Supreme Court in *R* v *Jogee*.

Think about this question.

'The decision of the Supreme Court in *R* v *Jogee* [2016] UKSC 8, *Ruddock* v *The Queen* [2016] UKPC 7 should be applauded. Parasitic accessory liability produced harsh results that it was impossible to justify. The law that now applies to so-called joint enterprises is both fairer and more coherent.'

Discuss the extent to which you agree with this statement.

Step 1: Deconstruct the essay title

The statement in this question makes three assertions. First, it says that the decision in *R* v *Jogee* should be applauded. Second, it says that the law on parasitic accessory liability that existed prior to *R* v *Jogee* produced harsh results that it was impossible to justify. Third, it says that the law that applies now, following *R* v *Jogee*, is fairer and more coherent. It is sensible to begin by considering the second and third assertions. Once you have formed a view on these assertions you will be able to decide whether you agree with the first assertion.

Step 2: Work through each assertion, form an opinion and construct a set of arguments in support of your views

To consider the second assertion, look back at the notes you prepared in response to the following questions.

On Wilson and Ormerod's article 'Simply Harsh to Fairly Simple: Joint Enterprise Reform':

- In the following extract Wilson and Ormerod discuss Simester's attempt to justify parasitic accessory liability. What justification did Simester offer? Why do Wilson and Ormerod disagree with Simester? Who do you agree with, and why?

On the Justice Committee's report *Joint Enterprise: Follow-Up*:

- Read the following extract from the Justice Committee's report and make a list of the concerns expressed by the witnesses to their enquiry. How did the Government respond to these concerns?
- To consider the third assertion, look back at the notes you prepared in response to the following questions.

On Stark's article 'The Taming of Jogee?':

- In this extract Stark suggests that the approach to conditional intention in *R* v *Johnson* means that few instances of substantial injustice will be found, and that *R* v *Jogee* may have changed little. Why?

On Ormerod and Laird's article '*Jogee*: Not the End of a Legal Saga but the Start of One?:

- In the following extract, what is the omission to which Ormerod and Laird refer? What issues do they say arise as a result of this omission?

On Stark's article 'The Demise of "Parasitic Accessorial Liability": Substantive Judicial Law Reform, Not Common Law Housekeeping':

- According to Stark, how does the reaction at the time to the decision in *Chan Wing-Siu* v *The Queen* support his claim that the Privy Council in that case did not misstate the law?
- If the decision in *R* v *Jogee* was not correcting a 'wrong turn', how does Stark say the decision should be understood? Why is this significant, in his opinion? Do you agree?

On Simester's article 'Accessory Liability and Common Unlawful Purposes':

Read the following extract. What is Simester's opinion on each of the following issues:

- Whether embarking on a joint criminal enterprise is a distinctive wrong;
- The lower *mens rea* that parasitic accessory liability requires of the defendant, compared to the principal;
- Whether parasitic accessory liability is draconian; and,
- The difficulties in requiring proof of abiding/abetting/counselling/procuring in all cases involving accessories?

Do you agree with Simester's critique? Should English law recognise a distinctive form of liability for secondary parties involved in a joint enterprise?

On Baker's article 'Unlawfulness's Doctrinal and Normative Irrelevance to Complicity Liability':

- In your opinion, in Baker's example should D1 be guilty of being an accessory to rape (as well as burglary)? Why/why not?
- According to Baker, how would Simester seek to justify convicting D1 of being an accessory to rape? Why does Baker reject this? With whom do you agree?

Once you have formed an opinion on the second and third of the assertions made by the essay title, you will be able to decide whether you agree with the first assertion: that the decision in *R* v *Jogee* 'should be applauded'.

The next step is to use your notes to construct a set of arguments in support of your opinion on each of the three assertions, and to work out how to respond to potential counter-arguments. You may find some of the items on the further reading list helpful here too.

Step 3: Planning your introduction and conclusion

You now have compiled all you need for the main body of your essay. The last task is to decide what to include in your introduction and conclusion.

The introduction should contextualise your discussion by briefly outlining the judgment in *R* v *Jogee*, and give an indication of the argument you will present in your essay. The conclusion should round off your essay with a succinct statement of your argument and a summary of your supporting reasons.

Accessories checklist

Having worked through this chapter, you should now have:

- An understanding of how to distinguish accessories from principals
- An understanding of the requirements that must be satisfied for a defendant to be convicted of being an accessory to an offence
- A knowledge of the Supreme Court judgment in *R* v *Jogee* and an ability to critically discuss it
- An understanding of the derivative principle and the exceptions to it
- An understanding of the requirements for a defendant to withdraw effectively from a criminal enterprise.

Further reading

Baker, D. J. (2017) 'Unlawfulness's Doctrinal and Normative Irrelevance to Complicity Liablity: A Reply to Simester' 81 *Journal of Criminal Law* 393.

Dyson, M. (2018) 'Principals Without Distinction' *Criminal Law Review* 296.

Dyson, M. (2022) 'The Contribution of Complicity' 86 *Journal of Criminal Law* 389.

Grigg, E. (2019) 'Joint Enterprise Liability: Recent Developments and Judicial Responses' 83 *Journal of Criminal Law* 128.

House of Commons Justice Committee (2012) *Joint Enterprise* (11th Report of Session 2010–12) HC 1597.

House of Commons Justice Committee (2014) *Joint Enterprise: Follow-Up* (4th Report of Session 2014–15) HC 310.

Krebs, B. 'Overwhelming Supervening Acts, Fundamental Differences, and Back Again?' 86 *Journal of Criminal Law* 420.

Law Commission (2007) *Participating in Crime* (Law Commission Report No 305) Cm 7084.

Ormerod, D. and Laird, K. (2016) '*Jogee*: Not the End of a Legal Saga but the Start of One?' *Criminal Law Review* 539.

Simester, A.P. (2017) 'Accessory Liability and Common Unlawful Purposes' 133 *Law Quarterly Review* 73.

Simester, A. P. and Stark, F. (2025) 'Overwhelming Supervening Acts – A Corrective' 84 *Cambridge Law Journal* 345.

Stark, F. (2016) 'The Demise of "Parasitic Accessorial Liability": Substantive Judicial Law Reform, Not Common Law Housekeeping' 75 *Cambridge Law Journal* 550.

Stark, F. (2017) 'The Taming of Jogee?' 76 *Cambridge Law Journal* 4.

Sullivan, G.R. (2008) 'Participating in Crime: Law Com No 305 – Joint Criminal Ventures' *Criminal Law Review* 19.

Wilson, W. (2008) 'A Rational Scheme of Liability for Participating in Crime' *Criminal Law Review* 3.

Wilson, W. and Ormerod, D. (2015) 'Simply Harsh to Fairly Simple: Joint Enterprise Reform' *Criminal Law Review* 3.

Answers on the Companion Website

Please visit the companion website for the answers to Key Questions, Quizzes, Applying the Law scenarios as well as student support including glossaries. Please visit www.pearsoned.co.uk/Macdonald

Credits

Chapter 1

Shutterstock: Refluo/Shutterstock; baldyrgan/Shutterstock; Anna Chelnokova/Shutterstock; Visual Generation/Shutterstock; Miceking/Shutterstock.

Chapter 2

123RF: olegdudko/123rf.com; rvlsoft/123rf.com; **Shutterstock**: carballo/Shutterstock.

Chapter 3

Guardian News & Media Limited: Steven Morris, Devoted husband who strangled wife in his sleep walks free from court, The Guardian, 20 Nov 2009; Steven Morris, Berlinah Wallace jailed for life for 'sadistic' acid attack on Mark van Dongen, *The Guardian*, 23 May 2018; **Telegraph Media Group Limited**: Nicola Harley, Former grammar school boy who did not help drowning teenager whilst high on drink on drugs is jailed for manslaughter, *Telegraph*, 26 January 2017;-**Incorporated Council of Law Reporting:** R v Stone & Dobinson [1977] QB 354; R v Miller [1983] 2 AC 161; Airedale NHS Trust v Bland [1993] AC 789; R v Cheshire [1991] 1 WLR 844 Beldam LJ stated; Environment Agency v Empress Car Co (Abertillery) Ltd [1999] 2 AC 22; R v Smith [1959] 2 QB 35; R v Cheshire [1991] 1 WLR 844; R v Blaue [1975] 1 WLR 1411; **Thomson Reuters Corporation:** Ashworth, A. (1989) 'The Scope of Criminal Liability for Omissions' 105 Law Quarterly Review 424, Reprinted with permission from Andrew Ashworth.

Shutterstock: Zdenek Sasek/Shutterstock; zizi_mentos/Shutterstock; Zdenek Sasek/Shutterstock; Stepan Gusiev/Shutterstock; Zdenek Sasek/Shutterstock; Lemonade Serenade/Shutterstock; Yana_P/Shutterstock; Simakova Mariia/Shutterstock; Panda Vector/Shutterstock; Cherstva/Shutterstock; north100/Shutterstock.

Chapter 4

House of Lords: Recklessness following R v Caldwell [1982] AC 341.

Shutterstock: r.classen/Shutterstock; Stephen Barnes/Shutterstock; Tatiana Kasatkina/Shutterstock; oleksandr biliy/Shutterstock; Will Oliver/EPA/Shutterstock.

Chapter 5

Incorporated Council of Law Reporting: Attorney-General's Ref (No 3 of 1994) [1998] AC 245 Lord Mustill; Lord Steyn in R v Powell & English [1999] 1 AC 1; House of Lords in DPP v Newbury & Jones [1977] AC 500; R v Church [1966] 1 QB 59; R v Watson [1989] 1 WLR 684; Andrews v DPP [1937] AC 576 HL Lord Atkin; House of Lords in R v Adomako [1995] 1 AC 171; R v Adomako Lord Mackay; **Law Commission**: Law Commission (2006) Murder, Manslaughter and Infanticide (Report No 304) HC 30; Law Commission (2006) Murder, Manslaughter and Infanticide (Report No 304) HC 30, para 1.31; Law Commission (2005) A New Homicide Act for England and Wales? A Consultation Paper (Consultation Paper No 177); Law Commission (2006) Murder, Manslaughter and Infanticide (Report no. 304) HC 30, para 5.18; Law Commission (2006) Murder, Manslaughter and Infanticide (Law Commission Report No 304) HC 30; **Thomson Reuters (Professional) UK Limited**: Ashworth, A. (1990) 'Reforming the Law of Murder' *Criminal Law Review* 75. Reproduced with permission of the Licensor through PLSclear; Ashworth, A. (1990) 'Reforming the Law of Murder' Criminal Law Reproduced with permission of the Licensor through PLSclear; Withey, C. (2011) 'Loss of Control, Loss of Opportunity?' *Criminal Law Review* 263. Reproduced with permission of the Licensor through PLSclear; Ashworth, A. (2007) 'Principles, pragmatism and the Law Commission's recommendations on homicide law reform *Criminal Law Review* 333. Reproduced with permission of the Licensor through PLSclear; **England and Wales Court of Appeal**: R v Ahluwalia [1992] 4 All ER 889; **Sage Publications**: Edwards, S. (2010) 'Anger and Fear as Justifiable Preludes for Loss of Self-Control', *Journal of Criminal Law* 74(3), 223–241; **Court of Appeal**: R v JM & SM [2012] EWCA Crim 2293 Lord Judge CJ; R v Dawson (1985) 81 Cr App R 150 Watkins LJ; R v Wacker [2002] EWCA Crim 1944 Kay LJ; R v Misra [2004] EWCA Crim 2375 Judge LJ; R v Rudling [2016] EWCA Crim 741; R v Kuddus [2019] EWCA Crim 837; Laird, K. (2018) 'Commentary on R v Rose (Honey Maria) *Criminal Law Review* 78; R v Kuddus [2019] EWCA Crim 837 Sir Brian Leveson P; R v Winterton [2018] EWCA Crim 2435 Macur LJ.

123RF GB Limited: Helder Almeida/123RF; Aleksandrs Tihonovs/123RF; Joseph Belanger/123RF; ostill/123RF; **Shutterstock**: Curioso/Shutterstock; Dennis Steen/Shutterstock; Studio Romantic/Shutterstock; carl ballou/Shutterstock; Be Panya/Shutterstock.

Chapter 6

Incorporated Council of Law Reporting: Robert Goff LJ in Collins v Wilcock [1984] 1 WLR 1172; R v Venna [1976] QB 421 Court of Appeal; Collins v Wilcock [1984] 1 WLR

1172;Fagan v Metropolitan Police Commissioner [1969] 1 QB 439; R v Ireland & Burstow [1998] AC 147; R v Donovan [1934] 2 KB 498; The House of Lords in DPP v Smith [1961] AC 290;R v Cunningham [1957] 2 Q.B. 396; R v Richardson [1999] QB 444; R v Brown [1994] 1 AC 212; R v Wilson [1997] QB 47; **Sage Publications**: Pegg, S. and Thomas, M. (2019) 'Deception and Qualifications: Revisiting the Ruling in R v Richardson?' 83 *Journal of Criminal Law* 298; Demetriou, S. (2016) 'Not Giving Up the Fight: A Review of the Law Commission's Scoping Report on Non-fatal Offences Against the Person' 80 *Journal of Criminal Law* 188; **Thomson Reuters Corporation**: Ryan, S. (2019) '"Active deception" v non-disclosure: HIV transmission, non-fatal offences and criminal responsibility' *Criminal Law Review* 4; Laird, K. (2018) 'Commentary on R v BM' *Criminal Law Review* 848 Reproduced with permission of the Licensor through PLSclear; Pegg, S. (2019) 'Not so clear cut: the lawfulness of body modifications' *Criminal Law Review* 579, Reproduced with permission of the Licensor through PLSclear; Gibson, M. [2016] 'Getting Their "Act" Together? Implementing Statutory Reform of Offences Against the Person' *Criminal Law Review* 597, Reproduced with permission of the Licensor through PLSclear; **Her Majesty's Stationery Office**: Adapted from table at pp. 200–4 of Law Commission (2015) Reform of Offences Against the Person (no. 361) HC 555.

Chapter 7

Incorporated Council of Law Reporting: King v Williams [1923] KB 340: 341; R v Williams is [1923] 1 KB 340; R v Olugboja [1982] QB 320; **Sage Publications**: Gunby, C., Carline, A. and Beynon, C. (2010) 'Alcohol-related Rape Cases: Barristers' Perspectives on the Sexual Offences Act 2003 and Its Impact on Practice' 74 *Journal of Criminal Law* 579; Sharpe, A. (2016) 'Expanding Liability for Sexual Fraud Through the Concept of "Active Deception": A Flawed Approach' 80 *Journal of Criminal Law* 28; Larcombe, W., Fileborn, B., Powell, A., Hanley, N. and Henry, N. (2016) '"I Think it's Rape and I Think He Would be Found Not Guilty": Focus Group Perceptions of (un)Reasonable Belief in Consent in Rape Law' 25 Social & Legal Studies 611; **Thomson Reuters Corporation**: Ormerod, D. (2020) 'Rape and Deception (Again)' *Criminal Law Review* 877; Herring, J. (2005) 'Mistaken Sex' *Criminal Law Review* 511, reproduced with permission of the Licensor through PLSclear"; Temkin, J. and Ashworth, A. *(2004)* 'The Sexual Offences Act 2003 – (1) Rape, Sexual Assaults and the Problems of Consent' *Criminal Law Review* 328; **Cambridge University Press**: Finch, E. and Munro, V. (2006) 'Breaking Boundaries? Sexual Consent in the Jury Room' 26 Legal Studies 303; **The Home Office**: Home Office (2002) Protecting the Public: Strengthening Protection Against Sex Offenders and Reforming the Law on Sexual Offences (Cm 5668).

Shutterstock: Kheng Guan Toh/Shutterstock; Rob Hyrons/Shutterstock; SurfsUp/Shutterstock; Stoatphoto/Shutterstock; Inspiring/Shutterstock.

Chapter 8

Guardian News & Media Limited: Tom Roberts, Couple who found winning lottery ticket ordered to pay back money, 24 July 2009, Guardian News & Media Limited; Steven Morris, If you go down to the beach today... you're bound to find something to steal, 23 January 2007, Guardian News & Media Limited; Stop the sale of 'West Bank' produce, 14 December 2009, Guardian News & Media Limited; **Southwark News Limited**: Josh Salisbury, Warrant for Bermondsey man's arrest after stealing free newspapers at London Bridge, 15 February, 2019, Southwark News Limited; **Church Times**: Ed Beavan, Protester goes out for a date, 28 January 2009; **Incorporated Council of Law Reporting**: R v Kelly [1999] QB 621; R v Woodman [1974] QB 754; R v Morris [1984] AC 320; DPP v Gomez [1993] AC 442; Lawrence v MPC [1972] AC 626; R v Hinks [2001] 2 AC 241; R v Lloyd [1985] QB 829; R v Ghosh [1982] QB 1053; R v Collins [1973] QB 100; R v Walkington [1979] 1 WLR 1169; Steer [1988] AC 111; **John Wiley & Sons, Inc**: Clarkson, C. (1993) 'Theft and Fair Labelling' 56 *Modern Law Review* 554; **Cambridge University Press**: Glazebrook, P. (1991) 'Thief or Swindler: Who Cares?' 50 *Cambridge Law Journal* 389; Spencer, J. 'Dishonesty: What the Jury Thinks the Defendant Thought the Jury Would Have Thought' (1982) 41 *Cambridge Law Journal* 222; Virgo, G.(2018) 'Cheating and Dishonesty', 77 *Cambridge Law Journal* 18; Thomson Reuters: Shute, S. (2002) 'Appropriation and the Law of Theft' *Criminal Law Review* 445; Ormerod, D. (2007) 'The Fraud Act 2006 – Criminalising Lying?' *Criminal Law Review* 193; **Oxford University Press**: Simester, A.P. and Sullivan, G.R. (2005) 'On the Nature and Rationale of Property Offences' in R.A. Duff and Stuart P. Green (eds) *Defining Crimes: Essays on the Special Part of the Criminal Law*. Oxford: OUP, 168–195; **Sage Publications**: Glover, R. (2010) 'Can Dishonesty Be Salvaged? Theft and the Grounding of the MSC Napoli' 74 *Journal of Criminal Law* 53; **University of Bristol**: Collins, J. (2016) 'Fraud by Abuse of Position and Unlicensed Gangmasters' 79 *Modern Law Review* 354.

123RF: Kirsty Pargeter/123RF; **Shutterstock**: Dilara Mammadova/Shutterstock; Ken Schulze/Shutterstock; Andrey_Popov/Shutterstock; Rawpixel.com/Shutterstock; Vichie81/Shutterstock; Mikecphoto/Shutterstock; Mind Pro Studio/Shutterstock; Sorbis/Shutterstock; Jon Rehg/Shutterstock; Inked Pixels/Shutterstock; Alena Veasey/Shut terstock; Michael D Brown/Shutterstock; Zdenek Sasek/Shutterstock;Trueffelpix/Shutterstock; Karolina Madej/Shutterstock.

Chapter 9

Incorporated Council of Law Reporting: Lord Denning in his judgment in Attorney-General of Northern Ireland v Gallagher [1963] AC 349; R v Sheehan [1975] 1 WLR 739 Geoffrey Lane LJ; Attorney-General of Northern Ireland v Gallagher [1963] AC 349 Lord Denning; DPP v Majewski | [1977] AC 443; R v Morgan [1976] AC 182; R v Kingston [1995] 2 AC 355 Lord Mustill; **Oxford University Press**: Sullivan, G. R. (1996) 'Making Excuses' in A. Smith and G. Sullivan (eds) *Harm and Culpability*. Oxford: OUP, 131–52.

Shutterstock: Mark1987/Shutterstock; Siberian Photographer/Shutterstock; rock-the-stock/Shutterstock; Motortion Films/Shutterstock; Andranik Hakobyan/Shutterstock; gpointstudio/Shutterstock; Rainer Fuhrmann/Shutterstock; xiao yu/Shutterstock; Simon Vayro/Shutterstock; Rob Byron/Shutterstock; Nikita Rublev/Shutterstock; Aniczkania/Shutterstock; Dmitry_Tsvetkov/Shutterstock; Karen Grigoryan/Shutterstock;lmkelly/Shutterstock; Microgen/Shutterstock; likovec/Shutterstock; Maliwan Prangpan/Shutterstock.

Chapter 10

Guardian News & Media Limited: Jeevan Vasagar, REM guitarist cleared of air rage, Sat 6 Apr 2002, Guardian News & Media Limited; Jane Perrone, Sleepwalker cleared of murdering father, 19 Mar 2005, Guardian News & Media Limited; Amelia Hill and Matthew Weaver, Sally Challen walks free as court rules out retrial for killing abusive husband, 7 June 2019; **Incorporated Council of Law Reporting**: R v Hennessy[1989]1WLR287; R v Burgess[1991]2QB 92and RvT; R v Sullivan[1984]AC156; R v Kemp [1957] 1 QB 399; R v Byrne[1960]2QB396; R v Dietschmann [2003] 1 AC 1209; **John Wiley & Sons, Inc**: Kennefick, L. (2011) 'Introducing a New Diminished Responsibility Defence for England and Wales '74 *Modern Law Review* 750; **Thomson Publishing Services**: Mackay, R. and Mitchell, B. (2017) 'The New Diminished Responsibility Plea in Operation : Some Initial Findings' *Criminal Law Review* 18; Laird, K. (2017) 'Case Comment, Homicide: R v Golds (MarkRichard)' *Criminal Law Review* 316.

Shutterstock: Brian A. Jackson/Shutterstock; Max Sky/Shutterstock; Kemedo/Shutterstock; Mr. Rashad/Shutterstock; Steve Mann/Shutterstock; Fejas/Shutterstock; solarus/Shutterstock; Leremy/Shutterstock; RNko/Shutterstock;ronstik/Shutterstock; Photographee.eu/Shutterstock; Jacob Lund/Shutterstock; Fery setiawan/Shutterstock; roundex/Shutterstock.

Chapter 11

Incorporated Council of Law Reporting: Southwark LBC v Williams [1971] Ch 734; Re F (Mental Patient: Sterilisation) [1990] 2 AC 1; R v Dudley and Stephens (1884–85) LR 14 QBD 273; R v Howe | [1987] 2 WLR 568; R v Hudson and Taylor [1971] 2 QB 202; R v Hasan [2005] UKHL 22; R v Graham [1982] 1 WLR 294; R v Bowen [1997] 1 WLR 372; R v Hasan [2005] 2 WLR 709 House of Lords; R v Howe [1987] AC 417; Re A (Children) (Conjoined Twins: Surgical Separation) [2001];Fam 147; R v Clegg [1995] 1 AC 482; R v Martin (Tony) [2003] QB 1; Beckford v The Queen [1988] AC 130. **Cambridge University Press**: Milgate, H.P. (1988) 'Duress and the Criminal Law: Another About Turn by the House of Lords' 47 *Cambridge Law Journal* 61.

Shutterstock: Dudarev Mikhail/Shutterstock; SpeedKingz/Shutterstock; SpeedKingz/Shutterstock; Film Four/Pathe/Kobal/Shutterstock.

Chapter 12

Incorporated Council of Law Reporting: R v Saik [2007] 1 AC 18; R v Griffiths & others [1966] 1 QB 589; R v Anderson [1986] AC 27; R v Gullefer [1990] 1 WLR 1063; R v Jones (Kenneth) [1990] 1 WLR 1057; R v Khan [1990] 1 WLR 813; A-G's Reference (No 3 of 1992) [1994] 1 WLR 409. Oxford University Press: Clarkson, C. (2009) 'Attempt: The Conduct Requirement', *Oxford Journal of Legal Studies*, vol. 29, issue 1, pp. 25–41. Used with permission from Oxford University Press.

Shutterstock: Alex Bonney/Shutterstock; Gwoeii/Shutterstock; skyearth/Shutterstock;Casimiro PT/Shutterstock; Photographee.eu/Shutterstock; Derek Oldfield/Shutterstock; Fred Mastison/Shutterstock.

Chapter 13

Incorporated Council of Law Reporting: Attorney-General's Reference (No 1 of 1975) [1975] QB 773; Attorney-General v Able [1984] QB 795; R v Calhaem [1985] QB 808; Du Cros v Lambourne [1907] 1 KB 40; Johnson v Youden [1950] 1 KB 544; R v Bainbridge [1960] 1 QB 129; R v Jogee [2017] AC 387 / Ruddock v the Queen [2017] AC 387; **Thomson Reuters (Professional) UK Limited**: Wilson, W. and Ormerod, D. (2015) 'Simply Harsh to Fairly Simple: Joint Enterprise Reform', *Criminal Law Review*; Ormerod, D. and Laird, K. (2016) 'Jogee: Not the End of a Legal Saga but the Start of One?', *Criminal Law Review*; Simester, A.P. (2017) 'Accessory Liability and Common Unlawful Purposes' 133, *Law Quarterly Review*; **Dr Findlay Stark**: Stark, F. (2017) 'The Taming of Jogee? 76 *Cambridge Law Journal*; **Cambridge University Press**: Stark, F. (2016) 'The Demise of "Parasitic Accessorial Liability": Substantive Judicial Law Reform, Not Common Law Housekeeping', 75 *Cambridge Law Journal* ; **Sage Publications**: Baker, D. J. (2017) 'Unlawfulness's Doctrinal and Normative Irrelevance to Complicity Liablity: A Reply to Simester' 81 *Journal of Criminal Law*.

Shutterstock: Seita/Shutterstock; Ideyweb/Shutterstock; Vectorpocket/Shutterstock;B Sanja/Shutterstock; AP/Shutterstock; Akhenaton Images/Shutterstock; Dzmitry Bychkou/Shutterstock; Bacho/Shutterstock; Albert Yarullin/Shutterstock; Serge Vo/Shutterstock; Andrey_Popov/Shutterstock; Ricardo Reitmeyer/Shutterstock; Max Sky/Shutterstock.

Index

Note: Page numbers followed by n represent foot notes.